# Encyclopedia of
# *Islam*
## and the
# Muslim World

# Editorial Board

# Encyclopedia of

# *Islam*

# and the

# Muslim World

Editor in Chief
Richard C. Martin

Volume 1
A-L

**MACMILLAN
REFERENCE
USA™**

**THOMSON**
**GALE**

New York • Detroit • San Diego • San Francisco • Cleveland • New Haven, Conn. • Waterville, Maine • London • Munich

**Encyclopedia of Islam**
Richard C. Martin, Editor in Chief

**Library of Congress Cataloging-in-Publication Data**

Encyclopedia of Islam and the Muslim world / edited by Richard C.
Martin.
      p. cm.
Includes bibliographical references and index.
   ISBN 0-02-865603-2 (set) — ISBN 0-02-865604-0 (v. 1) — ISBN
0-02-865605-9 (v. 2)
   1. Islam—Encyclopedias. I. Martin, Richard C.
BP40.E525 2003
909'.097671—dc21

2003009964

This title is also available as an e-book.
ISBN 0-02-865912-0
Contact your Gale sales representative for ordering information.

Printed in the United States of America
10 9 8 7 6 5 4 3 2

# Contents

**ENCYCLOPEDIA OF ISLAM AND THE MUSLIM WORLD**

# Editorial and Production Staff

Kate Millson and Corrina Moss
*Project Editors*

Joann Cerrito, Melissa Hill, and Mark Mikula
*Editorial Support*

Jonathan Aretakis
*Copy Chief*

Nancy Gratton
*Copy Editor*

Ann McGlothlin Weller
*Proofreader*

Barbara Cohen
*Indexer*

Barbara Yarrow
*Manager, Imaging and Multimedia Content*

Dean Dauphinais
*Senior Editor, Imaging and Multimedia Content*

Lezlie Light
*Imaging Coordinator*

Deanna Raso
*Photo Researcher*

Shalice Shah-Caldwell
*Research Associate*

Cynthia Baldwin and Jennifer Wahi
*Art Directors*

Autobookcomp
*Typesetter*

Mary Beth Trimper
*Manager, Composition*

Evi Seoud
*Assistant Manager, Composition*

Rhonda Williams
*Print Buyer*

**MACMILLAN REFERENCE USA**

Frank Menchaca
*Vice President*

Hélène Potter
*Director, New Product Development*

# Introduction

A growing number of scholars and pundits have declared that the twenty-first century will be the era of Islam. Such predictions, whether intended in a positive or negative light, err in failing to appreciate the spread and influence of Islam during the past millennium and a half, especially on the continents of Asia and Africa. Nonetheless, events during the first decade of the new millennium have underscored the importance of knowing about Islamic history and understanding the great diversity and richness of Muslim social, cultural, and religious practices. Suicide bomber attacks on the World Trade Center in New York and the Pentagon in Washington, D.C., on September 11, 2001, killed over three thousand persons. These tragic events and the media coverage of the aftermath as well as of the two wars subsequently fought in the Muslim countries of Afghanistan and Iraq have dramatically shown how little is known in the West about Islam and the Muslim world. Islam is, and has been for nearly fifteen centuries, a global religious and political phenomenon. Muslim networks of communication, from the annual pilgrimage to Mecca to the vast new power of the World Wide Web, have enabled Muslims to establish postmodern identities in a rapidly changing world, while at the same time preserving and reinvigorating a variety of time-honored traditions and practices. The *Encyclopedia of Islam and the Muslim World* is a sourcebook of information about Islam, its past and present, addressed to students and general readers as the twenty-first century begins its first decade.

The *Encyclopedia of Islam and the Muslim World* presents in two volumes some 504 articles, alphabetically arranged, in incremental lengths generally of 200, 500, 1,000, 3,000, and 5,000 words. The work of some 500 scholars appears in these pages, carefully reviewed and edited in a common style for easy access by readers who may presently have limited or no knowledge of Islam. It has also been prepared as a teaching and learning resource for teachers and students, from the high school grades through university. The alphabetical ordering of articles that follow, in the List of Articles, will enable readers to locate topics of interest quickly. A synoptic outline of the contents of the *Encyclopedia*, found within the frontmatter on pages xxxi–xxxiv, provides readers with an overview by topic and subtopic of the range and kinds of information presented in the main body of the *Encyclopedia*. Approximately 170 photographs, drawings, maps, and charts appear throughout the two volumes. A glossary in the back matter of volume two, which lists commonly used Arabic and other Islamic terms, such as *shari'a*, or "Islamic law," will enable general readers to determine quickly the meaning of essential but perhaps less familiar terms in Islamic studies.

The *Encyclopedia* is truly an international work that reflects the diversity of ideas and practices that have characterize the Islamic world throughout its history. This diversity is reflected among the editors who organized and compiled this work and the scores of scholars who wrote the articles contained in it. The associate editors' national origins are Canada, Iran, and South Africa; their religious affiliations or backgrounds include Sunni and Shi'ite Islam; and their scholarly training has been in sociology, the history of religions, and Islamic studies. An even greater diversity exists among the contributing scholars who live and teach in North America, Europe, Africa, and Asia, including the Middle East. They represent the fields of history, philosophy, religious studies, anthropology, sociology, political science, and the fine arts, among others. In its totality, then, this work represents a broad expanse of scholarly knowledge about Islam, accessible in two volumes.

Islam increasingly is recognized as a vital force in the contemporary world, a source of collective social identity, and religious expression for over one billion people around the world, who comprise a fifth of the global population. Public interest in learning about Islam is a very recent phenomenon, however. Events of the past few decades have generated a demand for information about Islam on an unprecedented scale in the history of Islamic studies in the West. In negative terms, these events include violence: the colonial and postcolonial encounters between Europeans and Muslims in Asia and Africa, the Israeli-Palestinian conflict, Hindu-Muslim clashes in South Asia, Serbian ethnic cleansing of Muslim populations in the Balkans, and the heavily televised American-led wars in the Gulf, Afghanistan, and Iraq. In positive terms, the recent years have seen productive Muslim diaspora communities emerge in Europe and the Americas, Islamic patterns of democracy and civil society develop in some countries in Africa and Asia, and venues of dialogue arise among Muslims, Jews, and Christians about their common moral and social concerns as well as their differences. That non-Muslims are learning more about Islam and their Muslim neighbors through tools like this encyclopedia must also be counted as a positive turn, and a much-needed one.

Scholars, journalists, and writers of all sorts have responded robustly to this newly recognized importance of Islam and the Muslim world, thus creating a wealth of information about Islam now available in bookstores, libraries, and newsstands around the world. More significant for readers of this work, the Internet hosts an expanding plethora of Web sites on Islamic teachings, practices, sectarian groups, and organizations. Many Web sites are sponsored by Muslim scholars, organizations, and institutions and provide authentic, and sometimes competing, information about Islamic beliefs and practices. Unfortunately, others offer hostile interpretations of Islam. The *Encyclopedia of Islam and the Muslim World* is designed to help students and general readers cope with this growing demand and almost overwhelming supply of information.

The decision to call this work the *Encyclopedia of Islam and the Muslim World* was made after considering other, less felicitous alternatives. The editors wanted to produce a work that was about Islamic cultures, religion, history, politics, and the like as well as the people who have identified with Islam over the past fourteen centuries. For the scope of the social and cultural aspects of the subject matter of the *Encyclopedia*, the editors chose the phrase "Muslim World." The label "Muslim World" is not meant to suggest that diversity and variety are lacking in what Muslims think, believe, and do as Muslims. Nor is the Muslim World as represented in this work to be thought of as separate from the rest of the world. Indeed, it will be clear to readers of articles on virtually all topics included below that Islamic history and Muslim people have been deeply and richly engaged in and interacting with world history and are perhaps even more so in the modern world, as the late Marshall G. S. Hodgson so persuasively argued in his monumental three-volume work, *The Venture of Islam: Conscience and History in a World Civilization* (1974).

The growing demand for accessible knowledge about Islam in recent decades has produced a number of histories, encyclopedias, and dictionaries that serve different purposes. In addition to Hodgson's comprehensive historical essay on Islamic civilization, *The Cambridge History of Islam* (1970) brought together substantial treatments of historical periods and geographical regions of Islamic societies. Another important and even older work that is widely used by scholars is the ongoing project known as the *Encyclopaedia of Islam*. The first edition was published in four volumes in Leiden (1908–1938); the second and much larger edition recently reached its completion in twice as many volumes with a significantly expanded list of contributing scholars; and the third edition is now being planned. The *Encyclopedia of Islam and the Muslim World* brings to general readers in accessible form the rich tradition of serious scholarship on Islam and Muslim peoples found in the *Cambridge History* and the *Encyclopaedia of Islam*, and it addresses information about Islam in the twenty-first century that is not discussed in the older sources. More recently, *the Oxford Encyclopedia of the Modern Islamic World* (1995) appeared in four volumes. The focus of this latter work is, as the title suggests, on Islam in the modern world, generally dated from the beginning the eighteenth century through the last decade of the twentieth. The *Encyclopedia of Islam and the Muslim World* by contrast seeks to contextualize contemporary Islam within the longer history of Islam, and it includes discussion of significant world events involving the Islamic world over the past decade.

In preparing this new resource on Islam, the editors sought to frame some of the traditional as well as the more recent aspects of Islam in newer categories. Thus, for example, readers will find articles covering "Material Culture," "Vernacular Islam," "Identity, Muslim," "Secularism," "Disputation," and "Expansion of Islam." A major feature of the *Encyclopedia* is the large number of brief biographical sketches (nearly two hundred) of major figures in Islamic history, men and women, past and present. The editors also included articles on several important and sometimes contested ethical and social issues, including "Ethnicity," "Gender," "Homosexuality," "Human Rights," and "Masculinities," along with the more traditional entries on gender (usually concentrating on the feminine roles) and marriage. The events of September 11, 2001, occurred after the Table of Contents was prepared and authors were commissioned to write the articles. Nonetheless, new articles on "Terrorism," "Usama bin Ladin," and "al-Qaʿida," among others, were added.

History, of course, will continue to unfold for humankind worldwide, including Muslims. The *Encyclopedia* includes a number of interpretive articles, such as "Ethics and Social Issues," which provide frameworks for understanding ongoing events in Islamic history.

Editorial style is a matter of great importance in a work such as the *Encyclopedia*. Readers can easily get lost in technical terms and diacritical marks on words borrowed from Arabic and Persian. Integrating work from a great number of scholars from around the world, each with differing practices in academic expression and in transliterating Islamic languages into Latin letters, presented some challenges to the academic editors and the editorial staff at Macmillan. To make things easier on readers, especially for those not initiated into the argots of Islamic technical terms, the editors decided to minimize the diacritical marks on loanwords from Arabic, Persian, Urdu, Turkish, and other Islamic languages. We encouraged authors and copy editors to romanize those Islamic terms that have made it into the English language, such as jihad, hajj, and Ramadan, as evidenced by their inclusion in modern dictionaries such as *Webster's Third New International Dictionary*. Where it seemed helpful, editors supplied brief parenthetical definitions and identifications, both in the text and in the Glossary.

The people who made this project possible brought great ideas to it, are extremely talented and competent, and were wonderful to work with. Hélène Potter, Macmillan's Director of New Product Development, designed the project and brought to it a considerable knowledge about Islam. More than an industry leader, Hélène became first and foremost a friend and colleague. She is an accomplished professional with an uncanny understanding of the knowledge industry she serves. Corrina Moss, an Assistant Editor with Macmillan, worked on the project throughout and kept in touch daily on editorial matters large and small. To Corrina went the unpleasant task, pleasantly administered, of keeping the associate editors and especially me on task. Elly Dickason, who was the publisher in 2000 when this project was approved, and Jonathan Aretakis, chief copy editor, also deserve expressions of praise and gratitude—Elly for supporting the project from the moment she reviewed it, and Jonathan for making sure the articles are factually and stylistically appropriate.

My colleagues Saïd Arjomand, Marcia Hermansen, and Abdulkader Tayob served as Associate Editors. The associate editors brought broad vision and detailed knowledge to their tasks of helping to organize the contents of the *Encyclopedia*, and I am indebted to them for making my own knowledge limitations less problematic in producing it. Rochelle Davis, a specialist in Arabic and Islamic studies, served as Assistant Editor, responsible for reading page proofs and preparing the Glossary. However, she contributed much more to the *Encyclopedia*, with an eye for grammatical and content errors that greatly improved the penultimate draft. My friend and colleague of many years, John Voll, Editorial Consultant, kindly advised Hélène Potter and me of matters we should consider in the formative stages of planning the *Encyclopedia*, and he contributed several important articles to it.

On behalf of Saïd, Marcia, Abdulkader, Rochelle, and John, I would like to dedicate this project to our many Muslim and non-Muslim colleagues around the world, with whom we share the task of teaching and writing about Islam in a high-tech, troubled world that needs to know more about itself. To that end we hope this work will help disseminate useful knowledge about one of the world's great civilizations to those who have a desire and need to know.

*Richard C. Martin*
*Creston, North Carolina*
*August 15, 2003*

# List of Entries

# List of Contributors

Rula Jurdi Abisaab
University at Akron, OH
*Karaki, Shaykh ʿAli*
*Majlisi, Muhammad Baqir*

Khaled Abou El-Fadl
University of California, Los Angeles, Law School
*ʿAbd al-Razzaq al-Sanhuri*
*Qanun*

Asma Afsaruddin
University of Notre Dame, South Bend, IN
*Bukhari, al-*
*Ibn Maja*
*Muslim ibn al-Hajjaj*
*Nasaʾi, al-*

Kamran Aghaie
University of Texas, Austin
*Molla*
*Rawza-Khani*
*Taʿziya (Taʿziye)*

Ahrar Ahmad
Black Hills State University, SD
*Reform: South Asia*

Ali Abdullatif Ahmida
University of New England
*Qadhdhafi, Muʿammar al-*

Iqtidar Alam Khan
Aligarh Historians Society, Aligarh India
*Empires: Mogul*
*Sultanates: Delhi*

Kristian Alexander
University of Utah
*Revolution: Islamic Revolution in Iran*

Richard T. Antoun
State University of New York, Binghamton
*Minbar (Mimbar)*

Ghazala Anwar
University of Canterbury, New Zealand
*Feminism*
*Veiling*

Etin Anwar
Hamilton College, NY
*Harem*
*Women, Public Roles of*

Saïd Amir Arjomand
State University of New York, Stony Brook
*Globalization*
*Majlis*
*Monarchy*
*Revolution: Classical Islam*
*Revolution: Modern*
*Sultanates: Seljuk*

Jacqueline M. Armijo
Stanford University
*East Asia, Islam in*
*East Asian Culture and Islam*

Touraj Atabaki
University of Utrecht, The Netherlands
*Khiva, Khanate of*
*Pan-Turanism*

Khalil Athamina
Birzeit Univeristy, Palestine
*Kunti, Mukhtar al-*

Fakhreddin Azimi
University of Connecticut
*Fedaʾiyan-e Islam*
*Mosaddeq, Mohammad*
*Nationalism: Iranian*

Ihsan Bagby
University of Kentucky
*American Culture and Islam*

Henning L. Bauer
University of California, Los Angeles, NELC
*Empires: Sassanian*

Munir Beken
University of Washington
*Music*

Jonathan Berkey
Davidson College
*Education*

Carel Bertram
University of Texas, Austin
*Buraq*

Anne H. Betteridge
University of Arizona
*Imamzadah*
*Nawruz*

Anna Bigelow
Loyola Marymount University
*Hinduism and Islam*

Sheila S. Blair
  Boston College
  *Art*
  *Calligraphy*
  *Dome of the Rock*
  *Manar, Manara*
  *Mihrab*

Khalid Yahya Blankinship
  Temple University, PA
  *Hospitality and Islam*
  *'Umar*

Jonathan Bloom
  Boston College
  *Art*
  *Calligraphy*
  *Dome of the Rock*
  *Manar, Manara*
  *Mihrab*

Gert Borg
  University of Nijmegen, The
    Netherlands
  *Arabic Literature*

Thyge C. Bro
  Stilliitsvej
  *Ibn Battuta*
  *Kano*
  *Travel and Travelers*

Jonathan E. Brockopp
  Bard College, Annandale, NY
  *Malik, Ibn Anas*
  *Shari'a*

Patrice C. Brodeur
  Connecticut College
  *Christianity and Islam*
  *Islam and Other Religions*

Daniel W. Brown
  Mount Holyoke College, MA
  *Martyrdom*
  *Sunna*

Arthur F. Buehler
  Louisiana State Univeristy, Baton
    Rouge
  *Saint*
  *Silsila*
  *Sirhindi, Shaykh Ahmad*

Paul D. Buell
  Western Washington University
  *Empires: Timurid*

Richard C. Campany, Jr.
  Senior Analyst, Harris Corporation
  *Communism*

Sandra S. Campbell
  Santa Barbara, CA
  *Fitna*

Juan Eduardo Campo
  University of California, Santa
    Barbara
  *Ahl al-Bayt*
  *Arab League*
  *Death*
  *Hinduism and Islam*
  *Jahannam*
  *Janna*
  *Mojahedin-e Khalq*
  *Nar*
  *Terrorism*

Abdin Chande
  Sidwell Friends School, Washing-
    ton, D.C.
  *African Culture and Islam*
  *Haj 'Umar al-Tal, al-*
  *Saleh bin Allawi (Jamal al Layl)*
  *Zanzibar, Sa'idi Sultanate of*

William C. Chittick
  State University of New York,
    Stony Brook
  *Ibn 'Arabi*
  *Wahdat al-Wujud*

Peter B. Clarke
  King's College, University of
    London
  *Conversion*
  *Moravids*

Frederick Colby
  Duke University
  *Mi'raj*

Nora Ann Colton
  Drew University
  *Economy and Economic Institutions*

Miriam Cooke
  Duke University
  *Internet*

Rkia E. Cornell
  University of Arkansas
  *Basri, Hasan al-*
  *Muhasibi, al-*
  *Rabi'a of Basra*

Stephen Cory
  University of California, Santa
    Barbara
  *Ahl al-Kitab*

Lucy Creevey
  University of Connecticut,
    Torrington
  *Bamba, Ahmad*
  *Touba*

Stephanie Cronin
  University College, Northampton,
    England
  *Muhammad Reza Shah Pahlevi*
  *Reza Shah*

Edward E. Curtis IV
  University of North Carolina,
    Chapel Hill
  *Jamil al-Amin, Imam*
  *Malcolm X*
  *Muhammad, Elijah*
  *Muhammad, Warith Deen*
  *United States, Islam in the*

Farhad Daftary
  Institute of Ismaili Studies, London
  *Assassins*
  *Shi'a: Isma'ili*

Ahmad S. Dallal
  Stanford University
  *Astrology*
  *Astronomy*
  *Hijri Calendar*

Suleman Dangor
  University of Durban, South Africa
  *Mu'awiya*

Elton L. Daniel
  University of Hawaii
  *Manicheanism*

Virginia Danielson
  Harvard University
  *Umm Kulthum*

Linda T. Darling
  University of Arizona
  *Erbakan, Necmeddin*
  *Jevdet Pasha*
  *Kemal, Namek*
  *Political Organization*
  *Refah Partisi*
  *Tanzimat*

Rochelle Davis
  Stanford University
  *Bedouin*

Devin DeWeese
  Indiana University
  *Central Asia, Islam in*
  *Central Asian Culture and Islam*

Sylviane Anna Diouf
  New York University
  *Americas, Islam in the*

Fred M. Donner
  University of Chicago
  *Expansion*

Nadia Maria El Cheikh
  American University of Beirut,
    Lebanon
  *Empires: Byzantine*

Caleb Elfebein
  University of California, Santa
    Barbara
  *Terrorism*

Farid el Khazen
  American University of Beirut,
    Lebanon
  *Lebanon*

Abdullahi Osman El-Tom
  National University of Ireland
  *Healing*

Haggai Erlich
  Tel Aviv University, Israel
  *Ethiopia*

Carl W. Ernst
  University of North Carolina,
    Chapel Hill
  *Tariqa*
  *Tasawwuf*

Farid Esack
  Union Theological Seminary, NY
  *Qur'an*

Mohammad H. Faghfoory
  Mary Washington College,
    Fredricksburg, VA
  *Abu 'l-Qasem Kashani*
  *Na'ini, Mohammad Hosayn*
  *Nuri, Fazlallah*

Rizwi Faizer
  Independent Scholar, Canada
  *Abu Bakr*
  *Hijra*
  *Jahiliyya*
  *Marwan*
  *Military Raid*
  *Muhammad*
  *Sukayna*
  *Uthman ibn 'Affan*

Muneer Goolam Fareed
  Wayne State University, MI
  *Adhan*
  *Dietary Laws*
  *Du'a*
  *Ijtihad*
  *Jami'*
  *Mufti*

Aslam Farouk-Alli
  University of Cape Town, South
    Africa
  *Cairo*
  *Holy Cities*
  *Modernization, Political: Administra-*
    *tive, Military, and Judicial Reform*

R. Michael Feener
  University of California, Riverside
  *Makassar, Shaykh Yusuf*

Leonor Fernandes
  American University in Cairo,
    Egypt
  *Khanqa (Khanaqa, Khanga)*

Michael M. J. Fischer
  Massachusetts Institute of
    Technology
  *Hasan*
  *Husayn*

Joyce Burkhalter Flueckiger
  Emory University
  *Vernacular Islam*

Allen J. Frank
  Independent Scholar
  *Reform: Muslim Communities of the*
    *Russian Empire*

Anne-Sophie Froehlich
  Der Spiegel, Germany
  *Modernization, Political: Authoritari-*
    *anism and Democratization*

Osman M. Galal
  University of California, Los Ange-
    les, School of Public Health
  *Medicine*

Patrick Franke
  Martin-Luther-Universität,
    Germany
  *Minorities: Dhimmis*

Patrick D. Gaffney
  University of Notre Dame
  *Khutba*
  *Masjid*

Gene Garthwaite
  Dartmouth College
  *Khan*

F. Gregory Gause III
  University of Vermont, Burlington
  *Ba'th Party*
  *Saudi Dynasty*
  *Socialism*

Claudia Gazzini
  Princeton University
  *'Abd al-Hamid Ibn Badis*
  *Fez*
  *Madani, 'Abbasi*
  *Zaytuna*

Najib Ghadbian
  University of Arkansas
  *Islamic Jihad*

Behrooz Ghamari-Tabrizi
  Georgia State University
  *'Abd al-Karim Sorush*
  *Mojtahed-Shabestari, Mohammad*
  *Motahhari, Mortaza*
  *Shari'ati, 'Ali*

Robert Gleave
  University of Bristol, England
  *Akhbariyya*
  *Ayatollah (Ar. Ayatullah)*
  *Ghayba(t)*
  *Hilli, 'Allama al-*
  *Hilli, Muhaqqiq al-*
  *Hisba*
  *Hojjat al-Islam*
  *Imamate*
  *Marja' al-Taqlid*
  *Minorities: Offshoots of Islam*
  *Muhtasib*

*Niyabat-e 'amma*
*Sayyid*
*Sharif*
*Shaykh al-Islam*
*Shi'a: Zaydi (Fiver)*
*Taqiyya*
*Taqlid*
*Tusi, Muhammad Ibn al-Hasan*
   *(Shaykh al-Ta'ifa)*
*Ulema*
*Velayat-e Faqih*

Matthew Gordon
  Miami University, Ohio
  *Empires: Abbasid*

Joel Gordon
  University of Arkansas
  *'Abd al-Hamid Kishk (Shaykh)*
  *'Abd al-Nasser, Jamal*
  *Muhammad 'Ali, Dynasty of*
  *Sadat, Anwar al-*

Sebastian Günther
  University of Toronto, Canada
  *Rashid, Harun al-*

Ursula Günther
  University of Hamburg, Germany
  *Fatima*
  *Ghazali, Zaynab al-*
  *Human Rights*

Hugh Talat Halman
  University of Arkansas
  *Khidr, al-*

Gail G. Harrison
  University of California, Los Ange-
    les, School of Public Health
  *Medicine*

Perween Hasan
  Dhaka University, Bangladesh
  *South Asian Culture and Islam*

Sohail H. Hashmi
  Mount Holyoke College, MA
  *'Abd al-Rahman Kawakibi*
  *'Abd al-Wahhab, Muhammad Ibn*
  *'Abduh, Muhammad*
  *Afghani, Jamal al-Din*
  *Banna, Hasan al-*
  *Dawla*
  *Fundamentalism*
  *Husayn, Taha*
  *Jihad*

*Modernization, Political:*
  *Constitutionalism*
*Pan-Arabism*
*Pan-Islam*
*Reform: Arab Middle East and North*
  *Africa*
*Rida, Rashid*
*Shaltut, Mahmud*
*Qutb, Sayyid*
*Wahhabiyya*

Mona Hassan
  Princeton University
  *Baghdad*

Jane Hathaway
  Ohio State University
  *Eunuchs*

Christer Hedin
  Stockholm University, Sweden
  *Da'wa*

Robert W. Hefner
  Boston University
  *Muhammadiyya (Muhammadiyah)*

Marcia Hermansen
  Loyola University, Chicago
  *Biography and Hagiography*
  *Biruni, al-*
  *Genealogy*
  *Mahdi*
  *Masculinities*
  *Miracles*
  *Rahman, Fazlur*
  *Wali Allah, Shah*

Annie C. Higgins
  University of Chicago
  *Kharijites, Khawarij*

Carole Hillenbrand
  University of Edinburgh, Scotland
  *Sultanates: Ayyubid*

Konrad Hirschler
  University of London, England
  *Historical Writing*

Qamar-ul Huda
  Boston College
  *Ghazali, Muhammad al-*
  *Organization of the Islamic*
    *Conference*
  *Orientalism*

Aaron Hughes
  University of Calgary, Canada
  *Andalus, al-*
  *'Asabiyya*
  *Heresiography*
  *Science, Islam and*

Amir Hussain
  California State University,
    Northridge
  *Rushdie, Salman*

Shams C. Inati
  Villanova University, Pennsylvania
  *Ibn Sina*
  *Wajib al-Wujud*

Torsten Janson
  Lund University, Sweden
  *Da'wa*

Rasool Ja'fariyan
  Independent Scholar
  *Hosayniyya*
  *Mashhad*
  *Qom*

R. Kevin Jaques
  Indiana University, Bloomington
  *Ahl al-Hadith*
  *Ibn Khaldun*
  *Islamicate Society*
  *Islamic Society of North America*
  *Religious Beliefs*
  *Shirk*
  *Traditionalism*

Shamil Jeppie
  University of Cape Town, South
    Africa
  *Haron, Abdullah*
  *Mahdist State, Mahdiyya*

Charlotte Jirousek
  Cornell University, Ithaca, NY
  *Clothing*

David L. Johnston
  Yale University
  *Fasi, Muhammad 'Allal al-*
  *Ikhwan al-Muslimin*
  *Islamic Salvation Front*

Shalahudin Kafrawi
  Binghamton University, NY
  *Murji'ites, Murji'a*
  *Mu'tazilites, Mu'tazila*

Hossein Kamaly
  Columbia University
  *Reform: Iran*

Ousmane Kane
  Columbia University
  *Askiya Muhammad*
  *Mansa Musa*
  *Timbuktu*

Nico J. G. Kaptein
  Leiden University, The
    Netherlands
  *Bid'a*

Zayn R. Kassam
  Pomona College, CA
  *Gender*
  *Tusi, Nasir al-Din*

Santhi Kavuri-Bauer
  San Francisco State University
  *Architecture*

Ahmad Kazemi Moussavi
  International Institute of Islamic
    Thought and Civilization,
    Malaysia
  *Usuliyya*

John Kelsay
  Florida State University,
    Tallahassee
  *Dar al-Harb*
  *Dar al-Islam*

Gregory C. Kozlowski
  DePaul University, Chicago
  *Akbar*
  *Waqf*

Gudrun Krämer
  Free University of Berlin, Germany
  *Ghannoushi, Rashid al-*
  *Hukuma al-Islamiyya, al- (Islamic*
    *Government)*
  *Pluralism: Political*
  *Political Islam*

Kathryn Kueny
  Lawrence University, KY
  *Circumcision*
  *Tafsir*
  *Pilgrimage: Hajj*

Scott A. Kugle
  Swarthmore College, PA
  *South Asia, Islam in*

Timur Kuran
  University of Southern California,
    Los Angeles
  *Capitalism*
  *Property*
  *Riba*

Charles Kurzman
  University of North Carolina,
    Chapel Hill
  *Liberalism*
  *Modernism*
  *Modern Thought*
  *Secularism, Islamic*

John C. Lamoreaux
  Southern Methodist University,
    Dallas
  *Dreams*

Bruce B. Lawrence
  Duke University
  *Internet*
  *Networks, Muslim*

Oliver Leaman
  University of Kentucky
  *Greek Civilization*
  *Ibn Rushd*

David Lelyveld
  William Paterson University,
    Wayne, NJ
  *Ahmad Khan, (Sir) Sayyid*
  *Aligarh*
  *Iqbal, Muhammad*

Franklin D. Lewis
  Emory University
  *Persian Language and Literature*
  *Rumi, Jalaluddin*

Roman Loimeier
  University of Bayreuth, Germany
  *Abu Bakr Gumi*
  *Ahmad Ibn Ibrahim al-Ghazi*
  *'Uthman Dan Fodio*

Mazyar Lotfalian
  Berkeley
  *Abu 'l-Hasan Bani-Sadr*
  *Bazargan, Mehdi*
  *Fadlallah, Muhammad Husayn*
  *Najaf*

F. Ghislaine Lydon
  University of California, Los
    Angeles
  *Sahara*

Akbar Mahdi
  Ohio Wesleyan University
  *Youth Movements*

Mohamed Mahmoud
  Tufts University, MA
  *Muhammad 'Ahmad Ibn Abdullah*

Javed Majeed
  English Scholar
  *Modernity*

Margaret Malamud
  New Mexico State University, Las
    Cruces
  *Khirqa*

Jamal Malik
  University of Erfurt, Germany
  *Colonialism*
  *Jama'at-e Islami*
  *Jam'iyat-e 'Ulama-e Hind*
  *Jam'iyat-e 'Ulama-e Islam*
  *Jam'iyat-e 'Ulama-e Pakistan*
  *Maududi, Abu l-A'la'*

Louise Marlow
  Wellesley College, MA
  *Political Thought*

Richard C. Martin
  Emory University
  *bin Ladin, Usama*
  *Disputation*
  *Maslaha*
  *Pilgrimage: Ziyara*
  *Qa'ida, al-*
  *Wazir*

Herbert W. Mason
  Boston University
  *Hallaj, al-*

Adeline Masquelier
  Tulane University, LA
  *Zar*

Philip Mattar
  U.S. Institute of Peace, Washing-
    ton D.C.
  *Husayni, Hajj Amin al-*
  *Intifada*

Rudi Matthee
  University of Delaware
  *'Abbas I, Shah*
  *Empires: Safavid and Qajar*

William McCants
  Princeton University
  *'Abd al-Baha'*
  *Babiyya*
  *Bab, Sayyed 'Ali Muhammad*

Aminah Beverly McCloud
  DePaul University, Chicago
  *Farrakhan, Louis*
  *Muslim Student Association of North America*
  *Nation of Islam*

Kimberly McCloud
  Monterey Institute for International Studies, CA
  *Taliban*

Jon McGinnis
  University of Missouri, St. Louis
  *Kindi, al-*

Liz McKay
  University of Canterbury, New Zealand
  *Veiling*

Christopher Melchert
  University of Oxford, England
  *Shafi'i, al-*
  *Tabari, al-*
  *Thaqafi, Mukhtar al-*

Charles Melville
  Pembroke College, Cambridge University, England
  *Empires: Mongol and Il-Khanid*

Murat C. Mengüç
  McGill University, Canada
  *Young Ottomans*
  *Young Turks*

Barbara D. Metcalf
  University of California, Davis
  *Adab*
  *Ahl-e Hadis / Ahl al-Hadith*
  *Deoband*
  *Khan, Reza of Bareilly*
  *Tablighi Jama'at*

Gail Minault
  University of Texas, Austin
  *Khilafat Movement*
  *Purdah*

Ziba Mir-Hosseini
  School of Oriental and African Studies, University of London, England
  *Divorce*
  *Mahr*
  *Marriage*
  *Nikah*
  *Polygamy*

Majid Mohammadi
  State University of New York, Stony Brook
  *Hashemi-Rafsanjani, 'Ali-Akbar*
  *Hojjatiyya Society*
  *Khamane'i, Sayyed 'Ali*
  *Kho'i, Abo 'l Qasem*
  *Komiteh*
  *Pasdaran*
  *Sadr, Muhammad Baqir al-*
  *Sadr, Musa al-*

Mahmood Monshipouri
  Quinnipiac University, CN
  *Secularization*

Ebrahim Moosa
  Duke University
  *Ethics and Social Issues*
  *Ghazali, al-*
  *Qadi (Kadi, Kazi)*

Parviz Morewedge
  Rutgers University, New Brunswick, NJ
  *Falsafa*
  *Kalam*
  *Knowledge*

Harald Motzki
  University of Nijmegen, The Netherlands
  *Hadith*

Hassan Mwakimako
  University of Nairobi, Kenya
  *Material Culture*
  *Sultanates: Modern*
  *Yahya bin 'Abdallah Ramiya (Shaykh)*

Azim Nanji
  Institute of Ismaili Studies, London, U.K.
  *Aga Khan*
  *Akhlaq*
  *Ikhwan al-Safa*
  *Khojas*
  *Nizari*

Seyyed Hossein Nasr
  George Washington University
  *Ishraqi School*
  *Mulla Sadra*

Gordon D. Newby
  Emory University
  *Arabia, Pre-Islam*
  *Judaism and Islam*

Andrew J. Newman
  University of Edinburgh, Scotland
  *Sadr*

Jorgen S. Nielsen
  University of Birmingham, England
  *Europe, Islam in*
  *European Culture and Islam*

A. Rashied Omar
  Notre Dame, IN
  *Conflict and Violence*

Irfan A. Omar
  Marquette University, Milwaukee, WI
  *Humor*

M. Sait Özervarli
  Center for Islamic Studies, Istanbul, Turkey
  *'Abd al-Jabbar*
  *Abu 'l-Hudhayl al-'Allaf*
  *Ash'arites, Ash'aira*
  *Baqillani, al-*
  *Maturidi, al-*
  *Nazzam, al-*

James Pavlin
  Rutgers University, New Brunswick, NJ
  *Ibn Taymiyya*

John R. Perry
  University of Chicago
  *Nader Shah Afshar*
  *Zand, Karim Khan*

Daniel C. Peterson
  Brigham Young University, UT
  *Allah*
  *Fatwa*
  *Identity, Muslim*

David Pinault
  Santa Clara University, CA
  *Muharram*
  *Shi'a: Imami (Twelver)*

Karen C. Pinto
  University of Alberta, Canada
  *Cartography and Geography*

Randall L. Pouwels
  University of Arkansas
  *Mazru'i*

Avril A. Powell
  School of Oriental and African
    Studies, University of London,
    England
  *Ahmadiyya*
  *Ahmad, Mirza Ghulam*

Donald Quataert
  Binghamton University, NY
  *Empires: Ottoman*

Sholeh A. Quinn
  Ohio University
  *Isma'il I, Shah*
  *Tahmasp I, Shah*

Rasul Bakhsh Rais
  Quaid-i Azam University, Pakistan
  *Jinnah, Muhammad 'Ali*
  *Pakistan, Islamic Republic of*

Amal Rassam
  Queens College, City University of
    New York
  *Ethnicity*
  *Tribe*

David Robinson
  Michigan State University
  *Africa, Islam in*

Everett K. Rowson
  New York University
  *Homosexuality*

Uri Rubin
  Tel Aviv University, Israel
  *Asnam*

John Ruedy
  Georgetown University
  *Bourghiba, Habib*

Abdullah Saeed
  University of Melbourne, Australia
  *Coinage*
  *Umma*

Walid A. Saleh
  University of Toronto, Canada
  *Sultanates: Ghaznavid*

Lamin Sanneh
  Yale University Divinity School
  *Translation*

E. M. Sartain
  American University in Cairo,
    Egypt
  *Suyuti, al-*

Irene Schneider
  University of Halle, Germany
  *Pluralism: Legal and Ethno-Religious*

Warren C. Schultz
  DePaul University, Chicago
  *Crusades*
  *Nizam al-Mulk*
  *Saladin*
  *Sultanates: Mamluk*

Florian Schwarz
  Ruhr University Bochum, Germany
  *Bukhara, Khanate and Emirate of*

Michael Sells
  Haverford College, PA
  *Mi'raj*

Mansur Sefatgol
  University of Tehran, Iran
  *Mollabashi*
  *Wazifa*

Christopher Shackle
  School of Oriental and African
    Studies, University of London,
    England
  *Urdu Language, Literature, and
    Poetry*

Sa'diyya Shaikh
  Temple University, PA
  *'A'isha*

William Shepard
  University of Canterbury,
    Christchurch, New Zealand
  *Khalid, Khalid Muhammad*

Reeva Spector Simon
  Columbia University
  *Futuwwa*

Tahir Fuzile Sitoto
  University of Natal, South Africa
  *'Ada*

Tamara Sonn
  The College of William and Mary,
    Williamsburg, VA
  *HAMAS*
  *Hizb Allah*

Susan A. Spectorsky
  City University of New York
  *Ibn Hanbal*

Diana Steigerwald
  California State University, Long
    Beach
  *'Ali*
  *Azhar, al-*
  *Karbala*

Devin J. Stewart
  Emory University
  *Shi'a: Early*

Paula Stiles
  University of St. Andrews, Scotland
  *Marwa, Muhammad*
  *Shar'it Shangalaji, Reza-Qoli*
  *Shaykhiyya*
  *Siba'i, Mustafa al-*

Nancy L. Stockdale
  University of Central Florida
  *Iran, Islamic Republic of*
  *Khomeini, Ruhollah*
  *Nationalism: Arab*

Claudia Stodte
  Der Spiegel, Germany
  *Liberation Movement of Iran*
  *Modernization, Political: Authoritari-
    anism and Democratization*

Liyakatali Takim
  Independent Scholar
  *Ja'far al-Sadiq*
  *Muhammad al-Nafs al-Zakiyya*

Amin Tarzi
  Monterey Institute of International
    Studies, CA
  *Mujahidin*
  *Taliban*

Osman Tastan
  Ankara University, Turkey
  *Law*
  *Mazalim*

Abdulkader Tayob
  University of Nijmenen, The
    Netherlands
  *Hajj Salim Suwari, al-*
  *Religious Institutions*
  *Yusuf Ali, Abdullah*

Alfons H. Teipen
  Furman University, SC
  *Empires: Umayyad*

Frances Trix
  University of Michigan, Ann Arbor
  *Balkans, Islam in the*

Berna Turam
  McGill University, Canada
  *Nur Movement*

A. Uner Turgay
  McGill University, Canada
  *Ataturk, Mustafa Kemal*
  *Gasprinskii, Isma'il Bay*
  *Nationalism: Turkish*
  *Nursi, Said*

Sufia Uddin
  University of Vermont, Burlington
  *Awami League*

Nelly van Doorn-Harder
  Valparaiso University, IN
  *Nahdlatul Ulama (NU)*
  *Southeast Asia, Islam in*
  *Southeast Asian Culture and Islam*

Kees Versteegh
  University of Nijmegen, The
    Netherlands
  *Arabic Language*
  *Grammar and Lexicography*

Knut S. Vikør
  University at Bergen, Norway
  *Ahmad Ibn Idris*

John O. Voll
  Georgetown University
  *Islam and Islamic*
  *Mahdi, Sadiq al-*
  *Republican Brothers*
  *Salafiyya*
  *Tajdid*
  *Turabi, Hasan al-*
  *West, Concept of in Islam*

Peter von Sivers
  University of Utah
  *'Abd al-Qadir, Amir*

John Walbridge
  Indiana University, Bloomington
  *Baha'allah*
  *Baha'i Faith*
  *Libraries*
  *Madrasa*
  *Suhrawardi, al-*

Elizabeth Warnock Fernea
  University of Texas, Austin
  *Childhood*

Earle Waugh
  University of Alberta, Canada
  *Dhikr*

Mark Wegner
  Tulane University, LA
  *Succession*

David Westerlund
  Uppsala University, Sweden
  *Da'wa*

Brannon M. Wheeler
  University of Washington
  *Abu Hanifa*
  *Body, Significance of*
  *Madhhab*
  *Prophets*

Gerard Wiegers
  Leiden University, The
    Netherlands
  *Devotional Life*
  *'Ibadat*
  *Qibla*
  *Ritual*

Quintan Wiktorowicz
  Rhodes College, TN
  *Modernization, Political:*
    *Participation, Political Movements,*
    *and Parties*

Peter Lamborn Wilson
  Independent Scholar
  *Angels*

Mark R. Woodward
  University of Arizona
  *Reform: Southeast Asia*

Neguin Yavari
  Columbia University
  *'Atabat*

Muhammad Qasim Zaman
  Brown University
  *Caliphate*
  *Imam*
  *Ma'mun, al-*
  *Mihna*
  *Rashidun*

# Synoptic Outline of Entries

*This outline provides a general overview of the conceptual structure of the* Encyclopedia of Islam
and the Muslim World. *The outline is organized under nine major categories, which are further
split into twenty-five subcategories. The entries are listed alphabetically within each category or
subcategory. For ease of reference, the same entry may be listed under several categories.*

**Biographies: Political and other
Public Figures**
'Abbas I, Shah
'Abd al-Qadir, Amir
'Abd al-Rahman Kawakibi
'Abd al-Hamid Kishk (Shaykh)
'Abd al-Karim Sorush
'Abd al-Nasser, Jamal
'Abd al-Razzaq al-Sanhuri
Abu l-Qasem Kashani
Ahmad Ibn Ibrahim al-Ghazi
Ahmad Khan, (Sir) Sayyid
Akbar
Askiya Muhammad
Ataturk, Mustafa Kemal
Bourghiba, Habib
Erbakan, Necmeddin
Fasi, Muhammad 'Allal al-
Gasprinskii, Isma'il Bay
Isma'il I, Shah
Jevdet Pasha
Kemal, Namik
Khalid, Khalid Muhammad
Mahdi, Sadiq al-
Mansa Musa
Marwan
Mosaddeq, Mohammad
Muhammad Reza Shah Pahlevi
Muslim ibn al-Hajjaj
Nader Shah Afshar
Nizam al-Mulk
Nuri, Fazlallah
Nursi, Said
Qadhdhafi, Mu'ammar al-
Reza Shah
Rushdie, Salman
Sadat, Anwar al-

Saladin
Saleh bin Allawi
Shar'it Shangalaji, Reza-Qoli
Sirhindi, Shaykh Ahmad
Tahmasp I, Shah
Uthman dan Fodio
Wali Allah, Shah
Yahya bin 'Abdallah Ramiya
Zand, Karim Khan

**Biographies: Religious and Cultural
Figures**
'Abd al-Baha'
'Abd al-Hamid Ibn Badis
'Abd al-Jabbar
'Abd al-Wahhab, Muhammad Ibn
'Abduh, Muhammad
Abu Bakr
Abu Bakr Gumi
Abu Hanifa
Abu 'l-Hasan Bani-Sadr
Abu 'l-Hudhayl al-'Allaf
Afghani, Jamal al-Din
Aga Khan
Ahmad, Mirza Ghulam
Ahmad Gran
Ahmad ibn Idris
'A'isha
'Ali
Bab, Sayyed 'Ali Muhammad
Baha'allah
Bamba, Ahmad
Banna, Hasan al-
Baqillani, al-
Basri, Hasan al-
Bazargan, Mehdi

Biruni, al-
Bukhari, al-
Fadlallah, Muhammad Husayn
Farrakhan, Louis
Fatima
Ghannoushi, Rashid al-
Ghazali, al-
Ghazali, Muhammad al-
Ghazali, Zaynab al-
Hajj Salim Suwari, al-
Haj 'Umar al-Tal, al-
Hallaj, al-
Haron, Abdullah
Hasan
Hashemi-Rafsanjani, 'Ali-Akbar
Husayn
Husayn, Taha
Husayni, Hajj Amin al-
Khidr, al-
Karaki, Shaykh 'Ali
Hilli, 'Allama al-
Hilli, Muhaqqiq al-
Ibn 'Arabi
Ibn Battuta
Ibn Hanbal
Ibn Khaldun
Ibn Maja
Ibn Rushd
Ibn Sina
Ibn Taymiyya
Iqbal, Muhammad
Ja'far al-Sadiq
Jamil al-Amin, Imam
Jinnah, Muhammad 'Ali
Khamane'i, Sayyed 'Ali
Khan, Reza of Bareilly
Kho'i, Abol Qasem

Intifada
Khojas
Komiteh
Nahdatul Ulama (NU)
Organization of the Islamic
  Conference
Refah Partisi
Taliban
Young Ottomans
Young Turks

### Groups, Organizations, Schools, and Movements: Religious
Aligarh
Ash'arites, Asha'ira
Assassins
Ahmadiyya
Deoband
Feda'iyan-c Islam
HAMAS
Hizb Allah
Ikhwan al-Muslimin
Ikhwan al-Safa
Islamic Jihad
Islamic Society of North America
Majlis
Muslim Student Association of
  North America
Salafiyya
Shaykhiyya
Tablighi Jama'at
Ulema
Umma
Usuliyya
Wahhabiyya
Youth Movements

### History: Concepts
'Asabiyya
Dawla
Genealogy
Historical Writing
Hukuma al-Islamiyya, al- (Islamic
  Government)
Modernity
Orientalism
Secularism
Socialism
Traditionalism

### History: Events
Religious and Political
Intifada
Mihna
Modernization
Muharram

### History: Institutions
Caliphate
Capitalism

Coinage and Exchange
Economy and Economic Institu-
  tions
Education
Libraries
Religious Institutions
Waqf

### History: Periods, Dynasties, Governments
Arabia, Pre-Islam
Ayyubids
Bukhara, Khanate and Emirate of
Colonialism
Empires: Abbasid
Empires: Byzantine
Empires: Mongol and Il-Khanid
Empires: Mogul
Empires: Ottoman
Empires: Safavid and Qajar
Empires: Sassanian
Empires: Timurid
Empires: Umayyad
Expansion
Hijra
Hijri Calendar
Khiva, Khanate of
Mahdist State, Mahdiyya
Modernity
Monarchy
Moravids
Muhammad 'Ali, Dynasty of
Rashidun
Sultanates: Delhi
Sultanates: Ghaznavid
Sultanates: Mamluk
Sultanates: Modern
Sultanates: Seljuk
Tribe

### History: Catalysts of Change
Globalization
Greek Civilization
Internet
Liberation Movement of Iran
Terrorism
Mihna
Networks, Muslim
Succession
Tajdid
Travel and Travelers

### Law
'Ada
Law
Mazalim
Mufti
Muhtasib
Property
Qanun

Riba
Shari'a
Taqlid

### Politics and Society
Military Raid
Minorities: Dhimmis
Minorities: Offshoots of Islam
Modernization
Monarchy
Nationalism
Pan-Arabism
Pan-Islam
Pan-Turanism
Pasdaran
Pluralism: Legal and Ethno-
  Religious
Pluralism: Political
Political Islam
Political Organization
Political Thought
Polygamy
Reform: Arab Middle East and
  North Africa
Reform: Iran
Reform: Muslim Communities of
  the Russian Empire
Reform: South Asia
Reform: Southeast Asia
Republican Brothers
Revolution: Classical Islam
Revolution: Islamic Revolution in
  Iran
Revolution: Modern
Saudi Dynasty
Secularization
Succession
Tanzimat
Velayat-e Faqih

### Religion: Groups, Movements, and Sects
Ahl al-Bayt
Ahl al-Hadith
Ahl al-Kitab
Ahl-e Hadis / Ahl al-Hadith
Akhbariyya
Babiyya
Baha'i Faith
Bedouin
Fundamentalism
Futuwwa
Hojjatiyya Society
Ishraqi School
Islamic Salvation Front
Jam'iyat-e 'Ulama-e Hind
Jam'iyat-e 'Ulama-e Islam
Jam'iyat-c 'Ulama-e Pakistan
Jama'at-e Islami
Kharijites, Khawarij

Khilafat Movement
Liberalism
Madhhab
Modernism
Mojahedin-e Khalq
Mujahidin
Muhammadiyya (Muhammadiyah)
Murji'ites, Murji'a
Mu'tazilites, Mu'tazila
Nation of Islam
Nizari
Nur Movement
Qa'ida, al-
Religious Beliefs
Religious Institutions
Shi'a: Early
Shi'a: Imami (Twelver)
Shi'a: Isma'ili
Shi'a: Zaydi (Fiver)
Tariqa
Traditionalism
Umma

### Religion: Ideas, Beliefs, Concepts, and Doctrines
Allah
Angels
Asnam
Bid'a
Body, Significance of
Buraq
Dar al-Harb
Dar al-Islam
Death
Ghayba(t)
Hadith
Harem
Heresy
Imamate
Jahiliyya
Janna
Jahannam
Jihad
Kalam
Khirqah
Mahdi
Miracles

Mi'raj
Modern Thought
Nar
Niyabat-e'amma
Prophets
Qibla
Qur'an
Riba
Shirk
Silsila
Sunna
Tafsir
Taqiyya
Taqlid
Tasawwuf
Ta'ziya (Ta'ziye)
Wahdat al-Wujud
Wajib al-Wujud
Wazifa
Zar

### Religion: Institutions
Azhar, al-
Caliphate
Deoband
Hisba
Khanqa (Khanaqa, Khanga)
Madrasa
Masjid

### Religion: Places and Sites
'Atabat
Dome of the Rock
Hojjatiyya Society
Holy Cities
Hosayniyya
Imamzadah
Jami'
Karbala
Mashhad
Mihrab
Minbar
Najaf

### Religion: Practices and Rituals
Adhan
Bid'a

Circumcision
Da'wa
Devotional Life
Dhikr
Dietary Laws
Disputation
Du'a
Fatwa
Fitna
'Ibadat
Ijtihad
Khutba
Martyrdom
Muharram
Nawruz
Pilgrimage: Hajj
Pilgrimage: Ziyara
Ritual

### Religion: Relations with Non-Muslims
Christianity and Islam
Conversion
Crusades
Globalization
Hinduism and Islam
Islam and Other Religions
Judaism and Islam
Manicheanism

### Religion: Titles and Offices
Ayatollah (Ar. Ayatullah)
Hojjat al-Islam
Imam
Islam and Islamic
Islamicate Society
Khan
Mahdi
Marja' al-Taqlid
Molla
Mollabashi
Qadi (Kadi, Kazi)
Saint
Sayyid
Sharif
Shaykh al-Islam
Wazir

# List of Maps

*Maps accompany the following entries, and are located on the provided pages.*

# A

## 'ABBAS I, SHAH (1571–1629)

Shah 'Abbas I, the fifth ruler of the Safavid dynasty, ruled Iran from 1587 until 1629, the year of his death. Shah 'Abbas came to power at a time when tribal unrest and foreign invasion had greatly reduced Iran's territory. Once on the throne he set out to regain the lands and authority that had been lost by his immediate successors. His defeat of the Uzbeks in the northeast and the peace he made with the Ottoman Empire, Iran's archenemy, enabled Shah 'Abbas to reform Iran's military and financial system. He diminished the military power of the tribes by creating a standing army composed of slave soldiers who were loyal only to him. These so-called *ghulam*s (military slaves) were mostly Armenians and Georgians captured during raids in the Caucasus. In order to increase the revenue needed for these reforms the shah centralized state control, which included the appointment of *ghulam*s to high administrative positions.

With the same intent he fostered trade by reestablishing road security and by building many caravan series throughout the country. Under Shah 'Abbas, Isfahan became Iran's capital and most important city, endowed with a new commercial and administrative center grouped around a splendid square that survives today. His genius further manifested itself in his military skills and his astute foreign policy. He halted the eastward expansion of the Ottomans, defeating them and taking Baghdad in 1623. To encourage trade and thus gain treasure, he welcomed European merchants to the Persian Gulf. He also allowed Christian missionaries to settle in his country, hopeful that this might win him allies among European powers in his anti-Ottoman struggle. Famously down to earth, Shah 'Abbas was a pragmatic ruler who could be cruel as well as generous. Rare among Iranian kings, he is today remembered as a ruler who was concerned about his own people.

*A detail from a miniature painting of 'Abbas I (1571–1629) appears in the volume one color plates.*

*See also* **Empires: Safavid and Qajar.**

### BIBLIOGRAPHY

Matthee, Rudolph P. *The Politics of Trade in Safavid Iran: Silk for Silver, 1600–1730.* Cambridge, U.K.: Cambridge University Press, 1999.

Savory, Roger. *Iran under the Safavids.* Cambridge, U.K.: Cambridge University Press, 1980.

*Rudi Matthee*

## 'ABD AL-BAHA' (1844–1921)

'Abd al-Baha' 'Abbas, also known as 'Abbas Effendi, was the son of Baha'allah (Mirza Husayn 'Ali, 1817–1892), the founder of the Baha'i religion. In his final will and testament, Baha'allah designated him as his successor and authoritative expounder of his teachings. Born in Tehran on 23 May 1844, he grew up in the household of a father committed to the teachings of the Babi movement and consequently shared his father's fate of exile and intermittent imprisonment until the Young Turk revolution of 1909.

As a result, 'Abd al-Baha' received little formal education and had to manage the affairs of his father's household at a very early age. Despite these setbacks, he demonstrated a natural capacity for leadership and a prodigious knowledge of human history and thought.

'Abd al-Baha' corresponded with and enjoyed the respect of a number of the luminaries of his day, including the Russian author Leo Tolstoy and the Muslim reformer Muhammad 'Abduh. He left behind a small portion of what is a large corpus of still-unexplored writings that include social commentaries, interpretations, and elaborations of his father's works, mystical treatises, and Qur'anic and biblical exegeses.

Upon his release from house imprisonment in 1909, 'Abd al-Baha' traveled to North Africa, Europe, and North America advocating a number of reforms for all countries, including the adoption of a universal auxiliary language, global collective security, mandatory education, and full legal and social equality for women and minorities. He also warned of a coming war in Europe and called for a just system of global government and international courts where disputes between nations could be resolved peacefully.

'Abd al-Baha' died on 28 November 1921. According to his will and testament, his eldest grandson, Shoghi Effendi Rabbani, became the head of the Baha'i community and the sole authorized interpreter of his grandfather and great-grandfather's teachings.

*See also* **Baha'allah; Baha'i Faith.**

*William McCants*

# 'ABD AL-HAMID IBN BADIS (1889–1940)

'Abd al-Hamid Ibn Badis was the leader of the Islamic reformist movement in Algeria and founder of the *Association des Uléma Musulmanes Algériens* (AUMA). He was born in 1889 in Constantine, where he also died in 1940. After receiving a traditional education in his hometown, Ibn Badis (locally referred to as Ben Badis) studied at the Islamic University of Zaytuna, in Tunis, from 1908 to 1912. In the following years he journeyed through the Middle East, particularly in Egypt and Saudi Arabia, where he came into contact with modernist and reformist currents of thought spreading within orthodox Sunni Islam.

Ibn Badis became the most prominent promoter of the Islamic reformist movement in Algeria, first through his preaching at the mosque of Sidi Lahdar in his hometown, and, after 1925, through his intensive journalistic activity. He founded a newspaper, *Al-Muntaqid* (The critic), which closed after a few months. Immediately afterwards, however, he began a new and successful newspaper, *Al-Shihab* (The meteor), which soon became the platform of the reformist thinking in Algeria, until its closure in 1939. Through the pages of *Al-Shihab*, Ibn Badis spread the Salafiyya movement in Algeria, presented his Qur'anic exegesis, and argued the need for Islamic reform and a rebirth of religion and religious values within a society that, in his view, had been too influenced by French colonial rule. He further argued that the Algerian nation had to be founded on its Muslim culture and its Arab identity, and for this reason he is also considered a precursor of Algerian nationalism. He promoted the free teaching of Arabic language, which had been marginalized during the years of French rule, and the establishment of free schools for adults, where traditional Qur'anic studies could be taught.

In May 1931 he founded the AUMA (also Association of Algerian Muslim Ulema), which gathered the country's leading Muslim thinkers, initially both reformist and conservative, and subsequently only reformist, and served as its president until his death. Whereas the reformist programs promoted through *Al-Shihab* had managed to reach an audience limited to the elite educated class of the country, the AUMA became the tool for a nationwide campaign to revive Islam, Arabic, and religious studies, as well as a center for direct social and political action. Throughout the country he founded a network of Islamic cultural centers that provided the means for the educational initiatives he advocated and the establishment of Islamic youth groups. He also spearheaded a campaign against Sufi brotherhoods, accusing them of introducing blameworthy innovations to religious practice, and also of cooperating with the colonial administration. He played an important political role in the formation of the Algerian Muslim Congress in 1936, which arose in reaction to the victory of the Popular Front in France, and was active politically in the country until his premature death in 1940. Thanks to his activities as leader of the AUMA and to his writing in *Al-Shihab*, Ibn Badis is considered by some to be the most important figure of the Arab-Islamic cultural revival in Algeria during the 1930s.

*See also* **Reform: Arab Middle East and North Africa; Salafiyya.**

## BIBLIOGRAPHY

Merad, Ali. *Le Réformisme Musulman en Algérie de 1925 a 1940.* Paris: Mouton, 1967.

Safi, Hammadi. "Abdel Hamid Ben Badis entre les exigencies du dogme et la contrainte de la modernité." In *Penseurs Maghrébins Contemporains.* Casablanca: Editions EDDIF, 1993.

*Claudia Gazzini*

# 'ABD AL-HAMID KISHK (SHAYKH) (1933–1996)

A pioneering "cassette preacher" of the 1970s, 'Abd al-Hamid Kishk was born in the Egyptian Delta village of Shubrakhut, the son of a small merchant. Early on he experienced vision impairment, and lost his sight entirely as a young teen. He memorized the Qur'an by age twelve, attended religious schools in Alexandria and Cairo, then enrolled at al-Azhar University. He graduated in 1962, first in his class, but rather than an expected nomination to the teaching faculty, he was appointed imam at a Cairo mosque.

Kishk ran afoul of the Nasser regime in 1965. He claimed he was instructed to denounce Sayyid Qutb, refused, and subsequently was arrested and tortured in prison. In the early 1970s, cassette recordings of his sermons and lessons began to proliferate throughout Egypt; by the late 1970s he was arguably the most popular preacher in the Arab world. Attendance at his mosque skyrocketed, reaching 100,000 for Friday sermons by the early 1980s. In September 1981 he was arrested as part of Anwar al-Sadat's crackdown on political opponents, and was in prison when Sadat was assassinated. Upon his release he regained his following. He published his autobiography, *The Story of My Days*, in 1986. He died a decade later, in 1996.

## BIBLIOGRAPHY

Jansen, Johannes J. G. *The Neglected Duty: The Creed of Sadat's Assassins and Islamic Resurgence in the Middle East.* New York and London: Macmillan, 1986.

Kepel, Gilles. *Muslim Extremism in Egypt: The Prophet and Pharaoh.* Berkeley and Los Angeles: University of California Press, 1993.

*Joel Gordon*

# 'ABD AL-JABBAR (935–1025)

'Abd al-Jabbar was a Mu'tazilite theologian and Shafi'ite jurist, known as Qadi 'Abd al-Jabbar b. Ahmad al-Hamadani. He was born in Asadabad in Iran about 935, studied *kalam* with Abu Ishaq al-'Ayyash in Basra, and associated with the prominent Mu'tazilite scholar Abu 'Abdullah al-Basri in Baghdad. 'Abd al-Jabbar was appointed as chief judge of Rayy with a great authority over other regions in northern Iran by the Buyid wazir Sahib b. 'Abbad in 977. Following his dismissal from the post after the death of Ibn 'Abbad, he devoted his life to teaching. In 999 he made a pilgrimage to Mecca through Baghdad, where he spent some time. He taught briefly in Kazvin (1018–1019) and died in 1025 in Ray.

As the teacher of the well-known Mu'tazilites of the eleventh century, such as Abu Rashid al-Nisaburi, Ibn Mattawayh, Abu 'l-Husayn al-Basri, and as the master of Mu'tazilism in its late period, 'Abd al-Jabbar elaborated and expanded the teachings of Bahshamiyya, the subgroup named after Abu Hashim al-Jubba'i. He synthesized some of the Mu'tazilite views with Sunni doctrine on the relation of reason and revelation, and came close to the Shi'ite position on the question of leadership (*imama*). He is also a significant source of information on ancient Iranian and other monotheistic religions.

'Abd al-Jabbar wrote many works on kalam, especially on the defense of the Qur'an, and on the Prophet of Islam. Some of his books, including most of his twenty-volume work *al-Mughni*, have been published. Commentaries on two of his lost books, *Sharh al-usul al-khamsa* by Qiwam al-Din Mankdim and *al-Muhit bi'l-taklif* by Ibn Mattawayh, are also available.

*See also* **Kalam; Mu'tazilites, Mu'tazila.**

## BIBLIOGRAPHY

Frank, Richard M. "The Autonomy of the Human Agent in the Teaching of 'Abd al-Gabbar." *Le Museon* 95 (1982): 323–355.

Heemskerk, M. T. *Suffering in the Mu'tazilite Theology: Abd al-Jabbar's Teaching on Pain and Divine Justice.* Leiden: Brill, 2000.

Hourani, George F. *Islamic Rationalism: The Ethics of Abd al-Jabbar.* Oxford, U.K.: Clarendon Press, 1971.

Peters, J. R. T. M. *God's Created Speech: A Study in the Speculative Theology of the Mu'tazili Qadi l-Qudat Abul-Hasan 'Abd al-Jabbar bn Ahmad al-Hamadani.* Leiden: Brill, 1976.

*M. Sait Özervarli*

# 'ABD AL-KARIM SORUSH (1945– )

'Abd al-Karim Sorush is the pen-name of Hassan Haj-Faraj Dabbagh. Born in 1945 in Tehran, Sorush attended Alavi High School, an alternative school that offered a rigorous curriculum of Islamic studies in addition to the state-mandated, standardized education in math and sciences. He studied Islamic law and exegesis with Reza Ruzbeh, one of the founders of the school. He attended Tehran University, and in 1969 graduated with a degree in pharmacology. He continued his postgraduate education in history and philosophy of science at Chelsea College in London. In 1979 he returned to Iran after the revolution, and soon thereafter was appointed by Ayatollah Khomeini to the Cultural Revolution Council. He resigned from this controversial post in 1983.

In his most celebrated book, *Qabz va Bast-i Teorik-i Shari'at* (The theoretical constriction and expansion of the *shari'a*), Sorush developed a general critique of dogmatic interpretations of religion. He argued that, when turned into a dogma, religion becomes ideological and loses its universality. He held that religious knowledge is inevitably historical and culturally contingent, and that it is distinct from religion, the truth of which is solely possessed by God. He posited that culture, language, history, and human subjectivity mediate the comprehension of the revealed text. Therefore, human understandings of the physical world, through science, for instance, and the changing nature of the shared values of human societies (such as citizenship and social and political rights) inform and condition religious knowledge.

There was a contradiction between Sorush's understanding of epistemological problems of human knowledge, which he saw as logical and methodical, and his emphasis on the historical contingencies of the hermeneutics of the divine text. This contradiction was resolved in his later writing in favor of a more hermeneutical approach. In his early work, he was influenced by analytical philosophy and skepticism of a post-positivist logic, whereas in his later writings he adopted a more hermeneutical approach to the meaning of the sacred text. In his earlier work he put forward epistemological questions about the limits and truthfulness of claims regarding knowledge, but in two important later books, *Siratha-yi mustaqim* (1998, Straight paths) and *Bast-e tajrubih-e Nabavi* (1999, The expansion of the prophetic experience), he emphasized the reflexivity and plurality of human understanding. In his plural usage of the Qur'anic phrase "straight paths," Sorush offered a radical break with both modernist and orthodox traditions in Islamic theology.

In the 1990s, Sorush emerged as one the most influential Muslim thinkers in Iran. His theology contributed to the emergence of a generation of Muslim reformers who challenged the legitimization of the Islamic Republic's rule based on divine sources rather than on democratic principles and popular consent.

*See also* **Iran, Islamic Republic of; Khomeini, Ruhollah.**

## BIBLIOGRAPHY

Sadri, Mahmoud, and Sadri, Ahmad, eds. *Reason, Freedom, & Democracy in Islam: Essential Writings of 'Abdolkarim Soroush.* Oxford and New York: Oxford University Press, 2000.

*Behrooz Ghamari-Tabrizi*

# 'ABD AL-NASSER, JAMAL (1918–1970)

The Egyptian leader who dominated two decades of Arab history, Jamal 'Abd al-Nasser was born 15 January 1918, the son of a postal official. Raised in Alexandria and Cairo, he entered the military academy and was commissioned in 1938. Thereafter, he joined a secret Muslim Brotherhood cell, where he met fellow dissidents with whom he later founded the Free Officers. On 23 July 1952 the Free Officers seized power; within a year they outlawed political parties and established a republic. In 1954, they dismissed the figurehead president Muhammad Najib (Naguib) and repressed all opposition. Elected president in June 1956, Nasser ruled until his death. Under his leadership Egypt remained a one-party state. The ruling party changed names several times; the Arab Socialist Union, formed in 1962, survived until 1978 when Nasser's successor, Anwar al-Sadat, abolished it.

A charismatic leader, Nasser drew regional acclaim and international notoriety for his championship of pan-Arabism and his leadership role in the Non-Aligned Movement. His popularity soared during the 1956 Suez Crisis, sparked by Egypt's nationalization of the Suez Canal Company. The tripartite British-French-Israeli invasion failed to topple his regime and solidified his reputation. Frustrated with the pace of social and economic reform, in the early 1960s Nasser promoted a series of socialist decrees nationalizing key sectors of industry, agriculture, finance, and the arts. Egypt's relations with the Soviet bloc improved, but Nasser never turned entirely away from the West. In regional affairs the years after Suez were marked by a series of setbacks. The United Arab Republic (1958–1961) ended with Syria's cessation, and the Yemeni civil war (1962–1967) entangled Egyptian troops in a quagmire.

Many contend that Nasser never recovered from the disastrous defeat by Israel in June 1967. Yet he changed the face of Egypt, erasing class privileges, narrowing social gaps, and ushering in an era of optimism. If Egyptians fault his failure to democratize and debate the wisdom of Arab socialism or the state's secular orientation, many still recall his populist intentions. When he died suddenly of a heart attack on 28 September 1970, millions accompanied his coffin to the grave.

*See also* **Nationalism: Arab; Pan-Arabism.**

## BIBLIOGRAPHY

Gordon, Joel. *Nasser's Blessed Movement: Egypt's Free Officers and the July Revolution.* 2d ed. Cairo: American University in Cairo Press, 1996.

Jankowski, James. *Nasser's Egypt, Arab Nationalism, and the United Arab Republic.* Boulder, Colo.: Lynne Rienner, 2002.

*Joel Gordon*

# 'ABD AL-QADIR, AMIR (1807–1883)

During the early nineteenth century, 'Abd al-Qadir governed a state in Algeria. His family, claiming descent from Muhammad, led a Qadiriyya brotherhood center (*zawiya*) in western Algeria. In 1831 the French conquered the port of Oran from the Ottomans. Fighting broke out in the Oranais among those tribes formerly subjected to Turkish taxes and those privileged to collect them. The Moroccan sultan, failing to pacify the tribes on his border, designated 'Abd al-Qadir's influential but aging father as his deputy. He, in turn, had tribal leaders proclaim his son commander of the faithful (*amir al-mu'minin*) in 1832.

The highly educated and well-traveled new amir negotiated two treaties with France (1834–1837). Happy to cede the job of tribal pacification to an indigenous leader, the French acknowledged him as the sovereign of western Algeria. 'Abd al-Qadir received French money and arms with which he organized an administration, diplomatic service, and supply services, including storage facilities, a foundry, and textile workshops, for a standing army of six thousand men. Unfortunately, frequent disputes, and even occasional battles, punctured the treaties. The final rupture came when 'Abd al-Qadir began expanding into eastern Algeria. In response, the French decided on a complete conquest of Algeria and destroyed 'Abd al-Qadir's state (1839–1847), exiling him to Damascus. During his exile, the amir immersed himself in religious studies. He reemerged briefly into the public eye when riots shook Damascus in July 1860. It was then that Muslim resentment against perceived advantages enjoyed by Christians under the Ottoman reform edict of 1839 exploded into widespread killings and lootings. Virtually alone among the notables of Damascus, 'Abd al-Qadir shielded Christians from Muslim attackers.

*See also* **Tasawwuf.**

## BIBLIOGRAPHY

Aouli, Smaï; Redjala, Ramdane; and Zoummeroff, Philippe. *Abd el-Kader*. Paris: Fayard, 1994.

Danziger, Raphael. *Abd al-Qadir and the Algerians: Resistance to the French and Internal Consolidation* New York: Homes & Meier, 1977.

*Peter von Sivers*

## 'ABD AL-RAHMAN KAWAKIBI (1849?–1902)

An Arab nationalist and reformer, 'Abd al-Rahman Kawakibi was born in Aleppo, Syria, where he was educated and worked as an official and journalist until being forced by Ottoman opposition to relocate to Cairo in 1898. He joined the circle of Arab intellectuals surrounding Muhammad 'Abduh and Rashid Rida. Kawakibi's ideas are elaborated in two books, *Taba'i' al-istibdad* (Characteristics of tyranny) and *Umm al-qura* (Mother of cities). In the first, he argues that the Muslims's political decline is the result of their straying from original Islamic principles and the advent of mystical and fatalist interpretations. Such passivity, he argues, plays into the hands of despotic rulers, who historically have benefited from false interpretations of Islam. The book was a condemnation of the rule of the Ottoman Turks, and particularly of the sultan 'Abd al-Hamid II. A revival of Islamic civilization could come only after fresh interpretation of law (*ijtihad*), educational reforms, and sweeping political change, beginning with the institution of an Arab caliphate in the place of the Ottoman Turks. The theme of renewed Arab leadership in the Muslim *umma* is developed in the second book. The title is taken from a Qur'anic reference to Mecca, where Kawakibi places a fictional conference of representatives from various Muslim countries aimed at charting the reform of Muslim peoples.

*See also* **Modernization, Political: Administrative, Military, and Judicial Reform; Modernization, Political: Authoritarianism and Democratization; Modernization, Political: Constitutionalism; Modernization, Political: Participation, Political Movements, and Parties.**

## BIBLIOGRAPHY

Husry, Khaldun S. *Three Reformers: A Study in Modern Arab Political Thought*. Beirut: Khayats, 1966.

Kramer, Martin. *Islam Assembled: The Advent of the Muslim Congresses*. New York: Columbia University Press, 1986.

*Sohail H. Hashmi*

## 'ABD AL-RAZZAQ AL-SANHURI (1895–1971)

'Abd al-Razzaq al-Sanhuri was one of the most distinguished jurists and principal architects of modern Arab civil laws. Al-Sanhuri, a native of Alexandria, Egypt, obtained his law degree from what was then known as the Khedival School of Law of Cairo in 1917. He held different public posts including that of assistant prosecutor at the Mixed Courts of Mansura and as a lecturer at the Shari'a School for Judges. In 1921, he was awarded a scholarship to study law at the University of Lyon in France. In France, he wrote two doctoral dissertations, one on English law and the other on the subject of the caliphate in the modern age. In 1926, al-Sanhuri returned to Egypt where he became a law professor at the National University (now the Cairo University), and eventually became the dean of the law faculty. Because of his involvement in politics, and defense of the Egyptian Constitution, he was fired from his post in 1936, and left Egypt to become the dean of the Law College in Baghdad.

After one year, he returned to Egypt where he held several high-level cabinet posts before becoming the president of the Council of State in 1949. Initially, al-Sanhuri supported the movement of the Free Officers who overthrew the Egyptian monarch in 1952, but because of al-Sanhuri's insistence on a return to civilian democratic rule and his defense of civil rights, he was ousted from his position and persecuted. After 1954, al-Sanhuri withdrew from politics and focused his efforts on scholarship and modernizing the civil codes of several Arab countries. Al-Sanhuri heavily influenced the drafting of the civil codes of Egypt, Iraq, Syria, Libya, and Kuwait. One year before his death in Egypt, al-Sanhuri completed a huge multivolume commentary on civil law, called *al-Wasit fi sharh al-qanun al-madani*, which is still considered authoritative in many parts of the Arab world. He also wrote several highly influential works on Islamic contractual law, the most famous of which are *Masadir al-haqq fi al-fiqh al-Islami* and *Nazariyyat al-aqd fi al-fiqh al-Islami*. One of al-Sanhuri's most notable accomplishments was that he integrated and reconciled the civil law codes, which were French based, with classical Islamic legal doctrines. For instance, he is credited with making Egyptian civil law more consistent with Islamic law.

*See also* **Law; Modernization, Political: Constitutionalism.**

## BIBLIOGRAPHY

Hill, Enid. *Al-Sanhuri and Islamic Law*. Cairo: American University of Cairo Press, 1987.

*Khaled Abou El-Fadl*

# 'ABD AL-WAHHAB, MUHAMMAD IBN (1703–1792)

Muhammad Ibn 'Abd al-Wahhab was a religious scholar and conservative reformer whose teachings were elaborated by his followers into the doctrines of Wahhabism. Ibn 'Abd al-Wahhab was born in the small town of 'Uyayna located in the Najd territory of north central Arabia. He came from a family of Hanbali scholars and received his early education from his father, who served as judge (*qadi*) and taught hadith and law at the local mosque schools. Ibn 'Abd al-Wahhab left 'Uyayna at an early age, and probably journeyed first to Mecca for the pilgrimage and then continued to Medina, where he remained for a longer period. Here he was influenced by the lectures of Shaykh 'Abdallah b. Ibrahim al-Najdi on the neo-Hanbali doctrines of Ibn Taymiyya.

From Medina, Ibn 'Abd al-Wahhab traveled to Basra, where he apparently remained for some time, and then to Isfahan. In Basra he was introduced directly to an array of mystical (Sufi) practices and to Shi'ite beliefs and rituals. This encounter undoubtedly reinforced his earlier beliefs that Islam had been corrupted by the infusion of extraneous and heretical influences. The beginning of his reformist activism may be traced to the time when he left Basra around 1739 to return to the Najd.

Ibn 'Abd al-Wahhab rejoined his family in Huraymila, where his father had recently relocated. Here he composed the small treatise entitled *Kitab al-tawhid* (Book of unity), in which he most clearly outlines his religio-political mission. He castigates not only the doctrines and practices of Sufism and Shi'ism, but also more widespread popular customs common to Sunnis as well, such as performing pilgrimages to the graves of pious personages and beseeching the deceased

for intercession with God. More generally, following a line of argument developed much earlier by Ibn Taymiyya, Ibn 'Abd al-Wahhab challenged the authority of the religious scholars (ulema), not only of his own time, but also the majority of those in preceding generations. These scholars had injected unlawful innovations (*bid'a*) into Islam, he argued. In order to restore the strict monotheism (*tawhid*) of true Islam, it was necessary to strip the pristine Islam of human additions and speculations and implement the laws contained in the Qur'an as interpreted by the Prophet and his immediate companions. Thus, Ibn 'Abd al-Wahhab called for the reopening of *ijtihad* (independent legal judgment) by qualified persons to reform Islam, but the end to which his *ijtihad* led was a conservative, literal reading of certain parts of the Qur'an.

Aspects of Ibn 'Abd al-Wahhab's teachings, including asceticism, simplicity of faith, and emphasis on an egalitarian community, quickly drew followers to his cause. But his condemnation of the alleged moral laxity of society, his challenge to the ulema, and to the political authority that supported them estranged him from his townspeople and, some claim, even from his own family. In 1740, he returned to his native village of 'Uyayna, where the local ruler (amir) 'Uthman b. Bishr adopted his teachings and began to act on some of them, such as destroying tombs in the area. When this activity caused a popular backlash, Ibn 'Abd al-Wahhab moved on to Dir'iyya, a small town in the Najd near present-day Riyadh. Here he forged an alliance with the amir Muhammad b. Sa'ud (d. 1765), who pledged military support on behalf of Ibn 'Abd al-Wahhab's religious vocation. Ibn 'Abd al-Wahhab spent the remainder of his life in Dir'iyya, teaching in the local mosque, counseling first Muhammad b. Sa'ud and then his son 'Abd al-'Aziz (d. 1801), and spreading his teachings through followers in the Najd and Iraq.

*See also* **Wahhabiyya.**

## BIBLIOGRAPHY

Philby, Harry St. John Bridger. *Arabia*. New York: Scribners, 1930.

Smith, Wilfred Cantwell. *Islam in Modern History*. Princeton, N.J.: Princeton University Press, 1957.

*Sohail H. Hashmi*

# 'ABDUH, MUHAMMAD (1849–1905)

Muhammad 'Abduh was one of the most influential Muslim reformers and jurists of the nineteenth century. 'Abduh was born in the Nile River delta in northern Egypt and received a traditional Islamic education in Tanta. He graduated from al-Azhar University in Cairo in 1877, where he taught for the next two years. It was during this period that he met Jamal al-Din Afghani, whose influence upon ʿAbduh's thought over the next decade would be profound. When Afghani was expelled from Egypt in 1879, ʿAbduh was also briefly exiled from Cairo to his native village. He returned to Cairo the following year to become editor of the official government gazette, al-Waqaʾiʿ al-Misriyya (Egyptian events), and began publishing articles on the need for reform in the country. When the British occupied Egypt following the ʿUrabi revolt of 1882, ʿAbduh was sentenced to three years's exile for assisting the nationalists. He lived briefly in Beirut before joining Afghani in Paris, where the two would publish the short-lived but highly influential journal al-ʿUrwa al-wuthqa ("The firmest grip," based on the Qurʾanic references 2:256 and 31:22). ʿAbduh returned to Beirut following the journal's demise in 1884, and it was during this sojourn that he first met Rashid Rida, who would become his chief biographer and most distinguished disciple.

In 1888, following his increasing estrangement from Afghani and a consequent rethinking of his earlier revolutionary ideas, ʿAbduh was allowed to return to Cairo. He soon began a rapid ascent in Egyptian judicial and political circles. Beginning as a judge in the new "native courts" created by the Egyptian government, ʿAbduh became a member of the newly created administrative board for al-Azhar University in 1895. In 1899, he was appointed a member of the Legislative Council, an advisory body serving at the behest of the khedive, the ruler of Egypt, and more importantly became in the same year the grand mufti, or the chief Islamic jurist, of Egypt. As the head of Egypt's religious law courts, ʿAbduh championed reforms that he saw as necessary to make shariʿa relevant to modern problems. He argued that the early generations of Muslims (the salaf al-salihin, hence the name Salafiyya, which is given to ʿAbduh and his disciples) had produced a vibrant civilization because they had creatively interpreted the Qurʾan and hadith to answer the needs of their times. Such creative jurisprudence (ijtihad) was needed in the present, ʿAbduh urged. In particular, modern jurists must consider public welfare (maslaha) over dogma when rendering judgments. The legal opinions (fatwas) he wrote for the government and private individuals on such issues as polygamy, divorce, and the status of non-Muslims bore the imprint of his reformist attitudes.

During the last years of his life, ʿAbduh collaborated with Rashid Rida in publishing the journal al-Manar, founded by Rida in 1898. The journal became a forum for not only ʿAbduh's legal rulings and reformist essays, but also a Qurʾanic commentary that had reached the middle of the fourth sura (chapter) when ʿAbduh died in 1905. Rida would continue publishing the journal until his death in 1935.

The most systematic presentation of ʿAbduh's approach to Islamic reform is found in his essay Risalat al-tawhid (The theology of unity). In opposition to European positivist philosophers, he argues that reason and revelation are separate but inextricably linked sources for ethics: "The ground of moral character is in beliefs and traditions and these can be built only on religion. The religious factor is, therefore, the most powerful of all, in respect both of public and of private ethics. It exercises an authority over men's souls superior to that of reason, despite man's uniquely rational powers" (p. 106).

See also **Afghani, Jamal al-Din; Reform: Arab Middle East and North Africa; Rida, Rashid; Salafiyya.**

## BIBLIOGRAPHY

ʿAbduh, Muhammad. The Theology of Unity. Translated by Ishaq Musaʿad and Kenneth Cragg. London: George Allen & Unwin, 1966.

Hourani, Albert. Arabic Thought in the Liberal Age: 1798–1939. Cambridge, U.K.: Cambridge University Press, 1983.

Kerr, Malcolm H. Islamic Reform: The Political and Legal Theories of Muhammad ʿAbduh and Rashid Rida. Berkeley: University of California Press, 1966.

Sohail H. Hashmi

# ABU BAKR (573–634)

Abu Bakr b. Abi Quhafa, the first caliph (r. 632–634), and a member of the clan of Taym of the tribe of the Quraysh, was the first adult male convert to Islam, and the Prophet's close companion. A merchant and an expert on the genealogies of the Arab tribes, Abu Bakr came to be known as al-Siddiq, the truthful, or the one who trusts, a reference to the fact that he alone immediately believed the Prophet's story of his night journey to Jerusalem. Recognized even in Mecca as the foremost member of the Muslim community after Muhammad, he is credited with the purchase and release of several slaves, including Bilal, renowned for proclaiming the first Muslim call to prayer. Abu Bakr was chosen by Muhammad to accompany him on his "flight" or hijra to Medina in 622 C.E. He became Muhammad's father-in-law when his young daughter, ʿAʾisha, married the Prophet.

Taking the title Khalifat rasul Allah, meaning Successor to the Messenger of God, Abu Bakr became the first caliph of Islam upon Muhammad's death in 632 C.E. Just before his death, Abu Bakr refused to recall the expedition sent to Syria. At the same time, he was forced to battle the wars of Apostasy, or Ridda, against the Yemen, Yamama, and the tribes of Asad, Ghatafan, and Tamim, who refused to pay the tithe or zakat, which was considered an integral part of accepting Islam. It was because of the death of many leaders during these battles that Abu Bakr, on the advice of ʿUmar, ordered Zayd b. Thabit to compile a collection of the Qurʾanic verses.

See also **Caliphate; Succession.**

## BIBLIOGRAPHY

Kennedy, Hugh. *The Prophet and the Age of the Caliphate.* London: Longman Group Ltd., 1986.

Motzki, Harald. "The Collection of the Qur'an: A Reconsideration of Western Views in Light of Recent Methodological Developments." *Der Islam* 78 (2001): 1–34.

Watt, Montgomery W. "Abu Bakr." In *Encyclopedia of Islam.* 2d ed. Leiden: E. J. Brill, 1960.

*Rizwi Faizer*

*See also* **Modern Thought; Political Islam; Wahhabiyya.**

## BIBLIOGRAPHY

Loimeier, Roman. *Islamic Reform and Political Change in Northern Nigeria.* Evanston, Ill.: Northwestern University Press, 1997.

Tsiga, Ismaila A. *Sheikh Abubakar Gumi: Where I Stand.* Ibadan, Nigeria: Spectrum Books Ltd., 1992.

*Roman Loimeier*

## ABU BAKR GUMI (1922–1992)

Abu Bakr Gumi, born in Gumi/Sokoto province, northern Nigeria, was a leading personality in the development of the Nigerian Islamic reform movement and author of a number of influential works, such as *Al-ʿaqida as-sahiha bi-muwafaqat ash-shariʿa* (The sound faith according to the prescriptions of the shariʿa) and *Radd al-adhhan fi maʿani al-qurʾan* (Reconsidering the meaning of the holy Qurʾan).

Gumi was one of the first northern Nigerians to experience a dual education in the Islamic sciences as well as in the British colonial education system. After completing his Qurʾanic as well as primary school education, Gumi attended the Sokoto Middle School from where he went to the Kano Law School to be trained as a qadi (Muslim judge) from 1942 to 1947. After graduation he worked briefly as scribe to Alkali Attahiru in Sokoto. In 1947 he became a teacher at the Kano Law School and was transferred to Maru, Sokoto Province, in 1949, where he had a confrontation with a local imam as well as the sultan of Sokoto over the question of *tayammum*, the ritual ablution with sand. In the context of this confrontation with the established authorities Gumi was supported by Ahmadu Bello, the future prime minister of northern Nigeria, who in 1955 called upon Gumi to act as his advisor in religious affairs and in 1956 appointed him deputy grand kadi of northern Nigeria. In this position, and later (from 1962) as grand kadi, Gumi was able to carry out a number of reforms in the judicial system of northern Nigeria and to fight effectively against the influence of the Sufi brotherhoods, especially the Qadiriyya and the Tijaniyya. After Bello's assassination in 1966, Gumi lost his institutional backing and started to develop a network of followers that became, in the 1970s, northern Nigeria's first reformist Muslim organization, the Jamaʿat izalat al-bidʿa wa-iqamat as-sunna (Association for the removal of innovation and for the establishment of the sunna, 1978). Gumi remained influential in Nigerian religious politics in the 1980s when he acted as advisor to presidents Shehu Shagari (1979–1983) and Ibrahim Babangida (1985–1993). From 1962, Gumi was also a member of the Rabitat al-ʿalam al-Islami (Muslim World League), where he sat in the Legal Committee, and a member of the World Supreme Council for the Affairs of Mosques.

## ABU HANIFA (699–767)

Abu Hanifa al-Nuʿman b. Thabit b. Zurti was the eponymous founder of the Hanafi school (*madhhab*) of Islamic law. His birth dates are given variously but the year 699 is considered the most sound based on many biographical dictionaries. Abu Hanifa died and was buried in Baghdad, though sources differ concerning the month of his death. A shrine was built in 1066 over the site of his tomb, and the quarter of the city is called the al-Aʿzamiyyah after Abu Hanifa's epithet *al-Imam al-Aʿzam*, the "Great Imam."

In his *Jawahir al-mudiyya*, Ibn Abi al-Wafaʾ provides a genealogy, on the authority of Abu Ishaq Ibrahim b. Muhammad al-Sarifini (d. 1243), which links Abu Hanifa's family with the Sassanian kings, the Kayyanid kings, and Judah, the eldest son of the prophet Jacob. Many sources mention that Abu Hanifa was of Persian descent, that his family were sellers of silk. Shams al-Din al-Dhahabi (d. 1374) reports that Abu Hanifa's grandfather Zurti (also given as Zuta) is said to have been a slave brought from Kabul to Kufa where the family was attached to the Arab tribe of Taym-Allah b. Thaʿlaba. Other sources claim that Abu Hanifa's family was from Babylon, or the city of Anbar (on the Euphrates about forty miles from Baghdad).

Most Muslim biographical dictionaries focus on the relative authority of Abu Hanifa as a transmitter of hadith reports. It is said that a number of the younger ahaba (Companions) were still alive during the lifetime of Abu Hanifa but he only transmitted hadith from one of these, the well-known Anas b. Malik (d. 709 or 711). Among the tabiʿun (Followers) from whom he transmitted hadith reports are ʿAta' b. Abi Rabah (d. 732 or 733), al-Shaʿbi (d. 724) and Nafiʿ, the client of Ibn ʿUmar. Many authorities regard Abu Hanifa as a trustworthy transmitter but others question the authority of his sources. In his *Mizan al-iʿ tidal*, al-Dhahabi cites opinions that Abu Hanifa should be considered weak as a transmitter of hadith, and that his legal opinions rely upon personal opinion (*raʾy*). Abu Ishaq al-Shirazi (d. 1083) criticizes Abu Hanifa for having received most of his knowledge of hadith reports from Ibrahim al-Nakhaʾi rather than from the sahabah who were still reliable transmitters during his lifetime.

In terms of his reputation as a jurist, Abu Hanifa is credited with founding the Hanafi school of law, and is given the epithet "imam" because of this role. In his *Tadhkirat al-huffaz*, al-Dhahabi repeats a conversation in which Yazid b. Harun says that Sufyan al-Thawri (d. 778) was more knowledgeable in hadith but Abu Hanifa was more knowledgeable in jurisprudence and law. Even Muhammad b. Idris al-Shafi'i (d. 820), whose legal opinions often rival those of the Hanafis, is reported to have attributed great learning in jurisprudence to Abu Hanifa. Many sources refer to Hammad b. Abi Sulayman (d. 738) as Abu Hanifa's primary teacher in jurisprudence, and Joseph Schacht considers Abu Hanifa to have adapted the bulk of his legal opinions from him. Yazid b. Harun also states that he did not know anyone more pious and rational than Abu Hanifa. Bishr b. al-Walid reports that Abu Hanifa used to pray all night, and that he never learned or transmitted a hadith that he did not himself practice.

After Abu Hanifa's death his legal opinions and the hadith reports that he transmitted were compiled into texts. There are no extant collections of works composed by Abu Hanifa himself. His legal opinions can be found in the *Ikhtilaf Abi Hanifa wa Ibn Abi Layla* and the *al-Radd 'ala siyar al-Awza'i*, both attributed to Abu Yusuf (d. 798), one of Abu Hanifa's closest disciples. To another of Abu Hanifa's disciples, Muhammad al-Shaybani (d. 805), is attributed the *al-Hujjah fi ikhtilaf ahl Kufah wa ahl al-Madinah* and the *Kitab al-asl fi al-furu'*, both containing the legal opinions of Abu Hanifa which later became the basis for Hanafi legal scholarship. Some of the hadith reports transmitted by Abu Hanifa can be found collected in the *Sharh ma'ani al-athar* and *Bayan mushkil al-hadith* of Ahmad b. Muhammad al-Tahawi (d. 933), and in the later *Jami' masanid Abi Hanifa* compiled by Abu al-Mu'ayyad Muhammad b. Mahmud al-Khwarizmi (d. 1257).

Classical Hanafi jurisprudence developed primarily as compendia and commentaries on the legal opinions of Abu Hanifa and their interpretation by his main students, Abu Yusuf and Muhammad al-Shaybani. The *Mukhtasar fi al-fiqh Abi Hanifa al-Nu'man* by Ahmad b. Muhammad al-Quduri (d. 1037) contains a collection of the opinions of these three Hanafi authorities, as does the *Kitab al-mabsut* of Muhammad b. Ahmad al-Sarakhsi (d. 1090). The works of later Hanafi scholars such as Abu Bakr b. Mas'ud al-Kasani (d. 1191), 'Ali b. Abi Bakr al-Marghinani (d. 1197), 'Abdallah b. Ahmad al-Nasafi (d. 1310), 'Uthman b. 'Ali al-Zayla'i (d. 1342), Ibn Nujaym (d. 1562), and 'Abd al-Hakim al-Afghani (d. 1907) are largely based upon these earlier compilations of opinions going back to Abu Hanifa and his immediate disciples. These works, building upon the opinions of Abu Hanifa and his main students, show the influence of Abu Hanifa upon the development of Islamic legal theory and case law.

Abu Hanifa is also credited with a number of creedal and theological works, though some scholars assign the reaction of these to followers of Abu Hanifa. Two such works are the *al-'Alim wa al-muta'allim* and the *Fiqh al-absat*, which contain a series of questions and answers between Abu Hanifa and his disciple Abu Muti' al-Balkhi (d. 799). Extant is a letter written by Abu Hanifa to 'Uthman al-Batti, which resembles the perspective found in these other works. Also attributed to Abu Hanifa is the *Fiqh al-akbar*, the so-called *Fiqh al-akbar II*, and the *Wasiyyat Abi Hanifa*. The ten creedal articles of the *Fiqh al-akbar* closely parallel the views found in the *Fiqh al-absat*, but scholars such as Arent Jan Wensinck have assigned later dates to the *Fiqh al-akbar II* and the *Wasiyyat Abi Hanifa*, though they may have been influenced by the earlier works. The creedal works of later Hanafis such as Tahawi and Abu al-Layth al-Samarqandi (d. 993) may also show the influence of Abu Hanifa's theology. Because of Abu Hanifa's close association to these creedal statements, later scholars have emphasized the influence of Abu Hanifa on the development of widespread and officially sanctioned definitions of Muslim belief.

*See also* **Law; Madhhab.**

## BIBLIOGRAPHY

Abu Zahra, Muhammad. *Abu Hanifa*. 2d ed. Cairo: 1947.

Dhahabi, Shams al-Din Muhammad b. Ahmad. *Mizan al-i 'tidal fi naqd al-rijal*. Beirut: Dar al-Ma'arif, n.d.

Dhahabi, Shams al-Din Muhammad b. Ahmed. *Kitab tadhkirat al-huffaz*. Beirut: Dar al-Kutub al-'Ilmiyya, n.d.

Dhahabi, Shams al-Din Muhammad b. Ahmed. *Siyyar a'lam al-nubala'*. Beirut: Mu'assasat al-Risala, 1993.

Ibn Abi al-Wafa', 'Abd-Qadir b. Muhammad. *Al-Jawahir al-mudiyya fi tabaqat al-Hanafiyya*. Beirut: Mu'assasat al-Risala, 1993.

Ibn Hajar, Ahmad b. 'Ali. *Tahdhib al-tahdhib*. Beirut: Dar al-Kutub al-'Ilmiyya, 1994.

Ibn al-'Imad, Abd al-Hayy. *Shadharat al-dhahab fi akhbar min dhahab*. Beirut: Dar al-Afaq al-Jadida, n.d.

Schacht, Joseph. *Origins of Muhammadan Jurisprudence*. 2d ed. Oxford, U.K.: Oxford University Press, 1953.

Wensinck, Arent Jan. *The Muslim Creed: Its Genesis and Historical Development*. Cambridge, U.K.: Cambridge University Press, 1932.

*Brannon M. Wheeler*

## ABU 'L-HASAN BANI-SADR (1933– )

Abu 'l-Hasan Bani-Sadr, born in 1933 to a clerical family from the city of Hamadan, became the first president-elect of the Islamic Republic of Iran after the 1979 revolution. He studied Islamic law and economics at the University of Tehran, then continued his studies at the Sorbonne, in Paris, where his focus was on economics and the role of Islam in social change. Like many of his contemporaries, who combined western European training with an Islamic education, he developed a focus on interpreting Islam as a "unitarian" ideology (*towhidi*) for economic and cultural independence from the West, based on the notion of divine unity.

Bani-Sadr lived in exile in Europe from 1963 until 1979, as a result of his political activities at Tehran University. In Europe he became one of the most important activists of the National Front in Iran and abroad and a key organizer of Iranian students outside Iran. He came in contact with Ayatollah Khomeini first in 1972, in Najaf, and later in France where Khomeini spent his last days in exile. In 1980, Bani-Sadr became the first president-elect of the Islamic Republic of Iran with 75 percent of the vote. He did not represent any organization or political party. In contrast, his opponents in the Islamic Republic Party (IRP) were well-organized and made advances in the parliamentary election, and in the spring of 1980 they dominated the parliament. In 1980 and 1981 effective power shifted to the IRP parliamentary majority who named Prime Minister Raja' I ignoring Bani-Sadr's candidates for the cabinet. He later lost his presidency to conservative rivals in the IRP, as a result of a parliamentary vote of incompetence and impeachment. Later he fled the country and once again joined the exiled opposition in Paris.

*See also* **Iran, Islamic Republic of; Revolution: Islamic Revolution in Iran.**

## BIBLIOGRAPHY

Keddie, Nikki R. *Roots of Revolution: An Interpretive History of Modern Iran.* New Haven, Conn.: Yale University Press, 1981.

*Mazyar Lotfalian*

# ABU 'L-HUDHAYL AL-ʿALLAF (750–C. 850)

Muhammad b. al-Hudhayl b. ʿUbaydallah al-ʾAbdi was the first philosophically minded theologian of the Muʿtazilite school. Born in Basra around 750 C.E., he lived in the neighborhood of foragers (*ʿallafun*), where he spent the early part of his life. He was a student of ʿUthman al-Tawil, who was one of the disciples of Wasil b. ʿAta, the founder of al-Muʿtazila. He moved to Baghdad in 818 and lived a long life, as various dates between 840 and 850 are given for his death. Abu 'l-Hudhayl opposed some views of his contemporary theologians, such as the skeptic dualism of Salih b. ʿAbd al-Quddus, the determinism of Dirar b. Amr, the physics of Abu Bakr al-Asamm, and the ethical theory of Bishr b. Ghiyas al-Marisi. He also engaged in polemical discussions with the followers of other religions, especially those of the ancient Iranian

beliefs. His nephew and critic Abu Ishaq al-Nazzam as well as Yahya b. Bishr and Abu Yaʿqub al-Shahham were among his closest students.

Abu 'l-Hudhayl's numerous works are not extant, though some of his views are quoted in early *kalam* sources. His metaphysics of created beings, indivisible atoms, motion, and the cause-effect process of generation (*tawallud*) provoked intellectual discussions and controversies among Muʿtazilites. In order to protect the unity (*tawhid*) of God as the main principle, he denied the essential nature of things as well as the potentiality of being prior to its existence. He also rejected a division between the essence and attributes of God. Abu 'l-Hudhayl found no contradiction between the authority of God and His doing good actions with wisdom, since it is unthinkable that God does evil or injustice with a total absence of deficiency in Him. Therefore, He would only create the best and the most convenient (*aslah*) circumstances for His creatures.

Abu 'l-Hudhayl's atomistic ontology and highly philosophical terminology shaped the mind of later Muʿtazilites, and his systematic reflections on theological topics make him one of the most influential thinkers of Muʿtazilite thought at the beginning of its classical age.

*See also* **Muʿtazilites, Muʿtazila.**

## BIBLIOGRAPHY

Dhanani, Alnoor. *The Physical Theory of Kalam: Atoms, Space, and Void in Basrian Muʿtazili Theology.* Leiden: Brill, 1994.

Ess, Josef van. "Abu'l-Hudhayl in Contact: The Genesis of an Anecdote." In *Islamic Theology and Philosophy: Studies in Honor of George F. Hourani.* Edited by Micheal Marmura. Albany: State University of New York Press, 1984.

Frank, Richard M. *The Metaphysics of Created Being According to Abu'l-Hudhayl al-Allaf: A Philosophical Study of the Earliest Kalam.* Istanbul: Nederlands Historisch-Archaeologisch Instituut, 1966.

Frank, Richard M. "The Divine Attributes According to the Teaching of Abu'l-Hudhayl al-Allaf." *Le Museon* 82 (1969): 451–506.

Frank, Richard M. *Being and their Attributes: The Teachings of Basrian School of the Muʿtazila in the Classical Period.* Albany: State University of New York Press, 1978.

*M. Sait Özervarli*

# ABU 'L-QASEM KASHANI (1882–1962)

Born in Tehran, Abu 'l-Qasem Kashani studied in Najaf and became a *mujtahid* (religious scholar) at the age of twenty-five. He began his political activities in Najaf against the British domination of Iraq. In 1916, Kashani's father was killed in an uprising and British authorities condemned Kashani to death in absentia. He fled to Iran in 1921 and began teaching and preaching in Tehran.

Kashani was imprisoned in the 1930s because of his pro-German activities. In 1949, after an attempt on the Shah's life, he was exiled to Lebanon. In June 1950, he returned to Iran, was elected to the Majlis, and became its Speaker.

During the crisis over the nationalization of Iran's oil industry and the ensuing conflict with the British (1950–1953), Kashani made and broke alliances with the *Feda'iyan-e Islam* and the National Front of Dr. Mohammad Mosaddeq. He was instrumental in the assassination of the prime ministers 'Abd al-Husayn Hazhir and Husayn 'Ali Razmara.

Kashani was an anti-British, anticolonialist, anticommunist, constitutionalist, nationalist, and pan-Islamist religious-political leader. Although Kashani's opinions about Iranian nationalism, the role and function of the *shari'a*, and attitude toward the West differed from his clerical predecessors and successors, political activities of the Shi'ite ulema after World War II were greatly inspired and influenced by his views and activities. Indeed, many of his ideas were elaborated by leaders of the revolution of 1978 and 1979, including Ayatollah Khomeini, and formed the foundation of the Islamic government.

*See also* **Feda'iyan-e Islam; Iran, Islamic Republic of; Majlis; Mosaddeq, Mohammad.**

## BIBLIOGRAPHY

Akhavi, Shahrough. "The Role of Clergy in Iranian Politics, 1949–1954." In *Mosaddiq, Iranian Nationalism, and Oil.* Edited by James Bill and Roger Louis. Austin: University of Texas Press, 1988.

Faghfoory, Mohammad H. "The Role of the Ulama in Twentieth Century Iran with Particular Reference to Ayatullah Hajj Sayyid Abulqasim Kashani." Ph.D. diss., University of Wisconsin-Madison, 1978.

*Mohammad H. Faghfoory*

# 'ADA

Like all legal systems and theories, Islamic law and its legal theory are not free from ambiguity and tensions. Nowhere is such ambiguity more pronounced than in the treatment of *'ada* or custom (alternatively called *'urf*) in Islamic legal theory.

Generally, the term *'ada* is derived from Arabic, and means local customs, recurring habits, and social mores of the people. In the context of the epistemology of Islamic law, especially as it relates to what constitutes formal sources of law, classical Islamic jurisprudence does not recognize custom as a formal source. In the normative structure of Islamic

law, it is the Qur'an as God's revealed word that is rated as the first primary source. Prophet Muhammad's sunna, that is, his conduct, authentic sayings, acts, and behavior that he approved is rated as the second primary source. In addition to these two sources there other sources (or legal principles) such as the consensus (*ijma'*) of Muslim jurists or scholars and analogical reasoning (*qiyas*)—these combined then constitute what have become the normative formal sources of Islamic law.

However, notwithstanding the accepted normative hierarchy of what constitutes formal sources, Islam's encounter with other host cultures has compelled Islamic legal theory to evaluate the status of custom. For example, through such encounters, *'ada*, that is, the hitherto ambiguous source, has throughout the history of Islamic legal theory served as a flexible legal principle that helps Islamic law to evolve and thus meet the challenge of changing circumstances and times. This assertion finds ample support in Muslim juristic thinking. For example, a reflection on the founding jurists of the two main Sunni schools of Islamic law, namely, the Maliki and Hanafi schools, shows how various legal rules that were passed by the founders of these schools were based on the strength of communal practice and norms. A good example here is the ruling passed by Imam Malik b. Anas (d. 795 C.E.) that a woman cannot contract herself in marriage. On the same question, the Hanafi jurist, Imam Abu Hanifa (d. 767 C.E.) gave a different ruling that allowed a mature woman to contract herself. What is crucial to note here, though, is not so much the question of which of the two opinions is better, but rather the fact that the basis of the two legal rulings is primarily informed by social reality and what is popular communal practice. Noel James Coulson in his seminal article titled "Muslim Case Law" has presented a cogent argument in which he demonstrates that the opinion of Malik reflects the dominant view of marriage and the position of women within a predominantly patriarchal tribal society of Medina. And by contrast, Abu Hanifa's judgment mirrors the cosmopolitan nature of Kufa where women enjoyed a slightly more accommodating environment than in Medina.

Although often denied, the impact of *'ada* in Muslim legal theory is also evident in Muhammad b. Idris al-Shafi'i (d. 819 C.E.), founder of the Shafi'i school. For instance, the force of communal praxis and the ethos of Egypt obliged al-Shafi'i to change a range of legal rulings that he sanctioned while in Baghdad before his migration to Egypt.

In addition to the aforementioned early jurists, the efficacy of *'ada* is also stressed by Abu Ishaq al-Shatibi (d. 1388) whom Wael Hallaq in his *A History of Islamic Legal Theories* regards as representing the "culmination" of maturity in Islamic legal theory. A critical reading of Shatibi's legal philosophy illustrates that *'ada*, though often measured under the concept of *maslaha* (public good), does occupy a central position in his legal thought. For Shatibi, Islamic law in its early phase, that is, in the prophetic era of Muhammad, simply confirmed most of the pre-Islamic Arabian customs practiced by the people before their acceptance of Islam. For example, Islamic laws like *diya* (blood money), rituals of hajj (pilgrimage), and interestingly even the *Jum'a* (Muslim Friday congregational prayers), though taking a strict Islamic identity, were initially practices that were predominant in pre-Islamic Arabia. As habitual and popular customs these were rehabilitated by Islamic law and confirmed as Islamic practice.

Moving away from the formative classical period into the modern period, especially from the eighteenth to the twentieth century, examples gleaned from Africa and Asia also show that the predominance of custom not only shaped and influenced *shari'a*, but custom became a law operating on its own right independent of *shari'a*. What is discernible here is that custom in the modern context ceases to be merely a creative legal tool whose utility is only limited to make Islamic law adaptable to changing circumstances, but as "customary law" it becomes part of a dual legal system that is on par with *shari'a*. Again, Coulson provides a good example when he points out how in both Africa and Asia local practices, especially as they pertain to land tenure, were mostly "regulated by customary rules" (p. 261). These either complemented *shari'a* or simply subsumed it. For instance, in the Indian subcontinent this is illustrated in the popular "*shari'a* act of 1937" that was initially designed to cater to all Muslims in the region. However, as it turned out, a majority of Muslims preferred to be exempted from *shari'a* thus giving primacy to customary laws over the former.

Finally, it can be concluded that social exigencies, especially in the sociocommercial spheres, have compelled a majority of Muslim jurists, albeit reluctantly, to recognize *'ada* as a reliable legal tool. This recognition has come largely through what these jurists normally refer to as "creative legal devices." In particular, it is through these creative legal tools, of which custom is one of the central principles, that popular religious practices that would otherwise be rejected by *shari'a* find acceptance. Thus maxims such as: "What is known through custom is legally binding" and "what is evident through custom is as authentic as the text or *shari'a*" became acceptable principles in Islamic legal theory.

*See also* **Africa, Islam in; American Culture and Islam; Law; South Asia, Islam in; Southeast Asian Culture and Islam.**

## BIBLIOGRAPHY

Coulson, Noel James. "Muslim Custom and Case Law." In *Islamic Law and Legal Theory*. Edited by Ian Edge. New York: New York University Press, 1996.

Hallaq, Wael. *A History of Islamic Legal Theories: An Introduction to Sunni Usul al-Fiqh*. Cambridge, U.K.: Cambridge University Press, 1993.

Kamali, Mohammad Hashim. *Principles of Islamic Jurisprudence*. Selangor, Malaysia: Pelanduk Publications, 1989.

Libson, Gideon. "On the Development of Custom as a Source of Law in Islamic Law." *Islamic Law and Society* 4, no. 2 (1997): 131–155.

Masud, Khalid M. *Islamic Legal Philosophy: A Study of Abu Ishaq al-Shatibi's Life and Thought*. Delhi: International Publishers, 1989.

Ziadeh, Farhat. "'*Urf* and Law in Islam." In *The World of Islam: Studies in Honor of Philip K. Hitti*. Edited by J. Kritzek and R. Winder. London: Macmillan, 1959.

*Tahir Fuzile Sitoto*

# ADAB

The term *adab* fundamentally denotes a custom or norm of conduct. In the early centuries of Islam, the term came to convey either an ethical implication of proper personal qualities or the suggestion of the cultivation and knowledge of a range of sensibilities and skills. In its plural form, *adab* acquired the meaning of rules of conduct, often specified for a particular social or occupational group, like the *aadaab* (pl.) of the legist or the prince. In addition, *adab* specified the accomplishments that made one polished and urbane, an expert in the arts not subsumed under the category of religious learning. Often, in recent times, *adab* has meant simply literature in the narrow sense.

Underlying the concept of *adab* is a notion of discipline and training, indicating as well the good breeding and refinement that results from such self-control and training. In all its uses, *adab* reflects a high value placed on the employment of the will in proper discrimination of correct order, behavior, and taste. The term implicitly or explicitly distinguishes cultivated behavior from that deemed vulgar, for example, from pre-Islamic custom. The term's root sense of proper conduct and discrimination, of discipline, and moral formation, especially fostered in the Sufi tradition, has been brought to the fore in many modern reform movements. In that sense, *adab* is often coupled with *akhlaq* ("manners," "ethics") and is now understood to be within the reach of ordinary people and not only educated or holy specialists.

*See also* **Arabic Literature; Ethics and Social Issues.**

## BIBLIOGRAPHY

Gabrieli, F. "Adab." In Vol. 1, *Encyclopedia of Islam*. 2d ed. Leiden: Brill, 1960.

Metcalf, Barbara D., ed. *Moral Conduct and Authority: The Place of Adab in South Asian Islam*. Berkeley: University of California Press, 1984.

*Barbara D. Metcalf*

# ADHAN

The *adhan* along with its abridged accompaniment, the *iqama*, is an oral rite linked to mosques, daily prayer, sacred identity, and birth rites. The *adhan* and the *iqamah* are usually called outside and inside mosques, respectively: The former signals prayer times, and the latter the beginning of congregational prayer. The *adhan* given in public signals the presence of Islam, and gives members of a largely decentralized faith a sense of belonging. The *adhan* functions as a disjuncture between the sacred and the profane, between the Friday prayer, for instance, and the world of trade. It also distinguishes Islam from other religions: When Muslims needed some means to announce the prayer, they asked for a horn, a Christian symbol, but were providentially directed to the *adhan*, instead. Finally, the *adhan* is chanted into the right ear of a newborn and the *iqama* into the left ear.

The *adhan* consists of invocations and attestations: Four glorify God, two attest to His Oneness, two attest to Muhammad being Messenger, two call to prayer, two call to success, two glorify God, and one declares His Oneness. The Shi'ites add: 'Ali is the friend of God, and prayer is the best of deeds. For a while some mosques in Europe replaced the *muezzin* who called the *adhan* with a tape recorder, while in Turkey, in 1948, the government decreed that the *adhan* be given in Turkish. Both these efforts ultimately failed.

*See also* **Devotional Life; 'Ibadat; Masjid.**

### BIBLIOGRAPHY

Parkin, David, and Headley, Stephen C., eds. *Islamic Prayer across the Indian Ocean: Inside and Outside the Mosque.* Surrey, U.K.: Curzon, 2000.

*Muneer Goolam Fareed*

# AFGHANI, JAMAL AL-DIN (1839–1897)

Jamal al-Din Afghani, one of the most influential Muslim reformers of the nineteenth century, was most likely born in Asadabad, Iran, into a Shi'ite family. Throughout his life, however, he emphasized his Afghan ancestry, perhaps to broaden his appeal to Sunni Muslims. Little concrete information is available about his early life, but he probably received a traditional Islamic education in Iran and Iraq. During a visit to India around 1855, he was exposed to Western scientific and political thought for the first time. His stay in India coincided with the Sepoy Mutiny of 1857 (the Indian revolt against the East India Company), and his attitudes toward European and particularly British imperialism may have begun to form then. Around 1866, Afghani began his peripatetic career as a Muslim intellectual and political activist by accepting a post in the government of Afghanistan. Over the next thirty years he traveled to or resided in Istanbul, Cairo, Paris, London, Tehran, and St. Petersburg, frequently being forced to relocate because of his reformist views and political activities. Afghani is commonly viewed as the nineteenth century's chief ideologue of pan-Islamism. But his ideas, many of them expressed through the journal *al-'Urwa al-wuthqa* (The firmest grip; a reference to Qur'an 2:256, 31:22), which he copublished with Muhammad 'Abduh, never amounted to a coherent ideology. More than anything else, Afghani was driven by opposition to European imperialism in Muslim countries, which he argued could be fought only by a rejuvenation of Islamic culture.

*See also* **Reform: Arab Middle East and North Africa; Pan-Islam.**

### BIBLIOGRAPHY

Hourani, Albert. *Arabic Thought in the Liberal Age: 1798–1939.* Cambridge, U.K.: Cambridge University Press, 1983.

Keddie, Nikki R. *An Islamic Response to Imperialism: Political and Religious Writings of Sayyid Jamal ad-Din "al-Afghani."* Berkeley: University of California Press, 1983.

*Sohail H. Hashmi*

# AFRICA, ISLAM IN

Islam has an important past and present within Africa. It has been present in Africa since the very early days of the faith, and it constitutes the practice of roughly half the population of the continent, or some 250 million people. While most of the Muslims live in the northern half, important communities can be found in South Africa, Malawi, and other parts of southern Africa. This history and this importance are often misunderstood in the West and in the Mediterranean centers of the Islamic world. Scholars and the intelligent lay public do not naturally identify Africa with Islam.

Indeed, Africa is usually equated with sub-Saharan or "black" Africa in most definitions. Egypt and the Maghreb are lumped with the Middle East in the language of the World Bank, U.S. State Department, and most ministries of foreign affairs, as well as in this encyclopedia. The defining characteristic of Islam is often the Arabic language, as the first language of communication in the home, business, government, and the media, as well as identification with the Arab world and thus the origins of Islam. This is not a clear definition, however, since Berber languages are still widely spoken in the Maghrib and the Sahara, while Arabic is spoken by much of the Sudan and important minorities across sub-Saharan Africa.

This article focuses on sub-Saharan Africa and deals with Muslim societies rather than "Islam" in one area or another.

These societies, throughout history and to the present, demonstrate all of the varieties of the faith that one might expect: orthodox practice, radicalism, Sufism, and many creative combinations with local, non-Islamic practices. Muslims in Africa have practiced the jihad of the sword from time to time, but they have also demonstrated a great deal of tolerance of other practices—"pagan," Christian, and other. The Maliki school of law has traditionally been dominant in north and west Africa, while the Shafi'ite pattern has prevailed along the Red Sea and the Swahili coast.

## Northeast Africa

The earliest Muslim presence in Africa actually antedates the event known as the *hijra*, when Muhammad left Mecca for Medina in 622 C.E. At a time when the Prophet was already beginning to feel the hostility of his Meccan compatriots, he sent a large portion of his followers—about one hundred according to the principal hadith—to the Christian emperor of Aksum (ancient Abyssinia), an important state in northeast Africa, for safekeeping in 615 and 616 C.E. This is sometimes called the first *hijra*. Muhammad called for this community to return after he established himself in Medina, and there is little evidence of any ongoing Muslim group in Aksum or any other part of Ethiopia at this time. But the brief exile demonstrates the presence at that time of Ethiopians, including Ethiopian Orthodox Christians, in Mecca and other areas around the Red Sea, as well as the good relations between the early Arab Muslims and people in northeast Africa.

Reasonably good ties continued after Muslim communities emerged in northeast Africa close to the Red Sea. Most of these communities lived in the lowland and eastern areas, but some spread into the mountainous region called Abyssinia, which was dominated by Aksum and then a series of other states that privileged Christianity and the Orthodox Church. Relations between the two faith communities worsened when these states, with their Christian and Solomonic ideology, expanded to the east in the fourteenth and fifteenth centuries; they executed many Muslims and forced the conversion of others. Muslims responded to this in the movement led by Ahmad ibn Gran, a cleric and warrior from the coastal region in the sixteenth century. This conflict, often characterized by the terms "crusade" and "jihad" in the registers of the two faiths, has often been taken as characteristic of Ethiopia and the Horn of Africa. Hostile confrontations have certainly occurred: for example, cases of forced conversion of Muslims by expansive Christian emperors in the late nineteenth century, or the conflict over the brief tenure of Lij Iyasu as Menilik's successor as emperor of Ethiopia between 1913 and 1916. Lij Iyasu came from a family that included both Muslims and Christians, and he sought to bring some Muslims into positions in his brief government. He failed because of his own inexperience, the strong Christian and church predilections of the court, and the conflict between the Axis and Allies during World War I. But Ethiopia's population today is close to 50 percent Muslim, and Muslims have been able to coexist with Christians and other non-Muslim communities most of the time.

## Gateways of Islam in Africa

*The History of Islam in Africa* (2000) identifies two main "gateways" of Islamization in the continent. One is the East African coast, which became accessible to sailors and merchants coming down the Red Sea and the Persian Gulf, just as it had been for previous centuries for Southeast Asians. The other is Egypt, and by extension the Maghreb and the Sahara.

The first Muslims on the East African coast followed in the wake of a lot of other maritime travelers from the Near East, South, and Southeast Asia. They used an old, well-tested technology of sailing close to the coast, down the Red Sea or the Persian Gulf, and then along the Indian Ocean. Primarily Arab, they were interested in acquiring ivory, gold, other metals, leather goods, and some slaves. They interacted with the fishing and agricultural peoples along the coast who spoke the language that today is called Swahili, which takes its name from the plural of *sahil*, and literally means "people of the coast." Over time, roughly the last one thousand years, the Swahili language evolved to include a considerable Arabic vocabulary, in addition to some Malay and other infusions, within a basic Bantu lexicon and language structure.

The language was the basis for a culture, and both were built around small towns along the ocean, running about two thousand miles from Mogadishu in the north (today's Somalia) to Sofala in the south (today's Mozambique). Most of the towns were autonomous city-states, confined essentially to islands or the coast, with very small hinterlands devoted to farming. The inhabitants of these city-states were committed to the vocations of agriculture, fishing, shipbuilding, and trade. They lived in the cosmopolitan world built around the Indian Ocean and practiced Islam, but acknowledged local gods and customs. The more wealthy Swahili often claimed paternal origins among the Arabs or Persians. They used Islamic forms in the architecture of their homes, as well as for mosques and other public buildings. Many of them fulfilled the pilgrimage obligation, which was easier to perform than from other parts of the African continent.

The most prosperous period for the Swahili city-states ran roughly from 1250 to 1500 C.E. Lamu, located in an archipelago along the northern coast of modern Kenya, Mombasa, a larger city on the southern coast, and Zanzibar, the island which forms part of Tanzania, were among the best-known and most active cities. The most prosperous was probably Kilwa, an island off the southern coast of Tanzania. It was tied in to the interior trade, including the commerce in gold that tapped into the old Zimbabwe states.

The main location of the Swahili language, culture, and people, and of the practice of Islam, was concentrated on this East African littoral until very recent times. Most of the

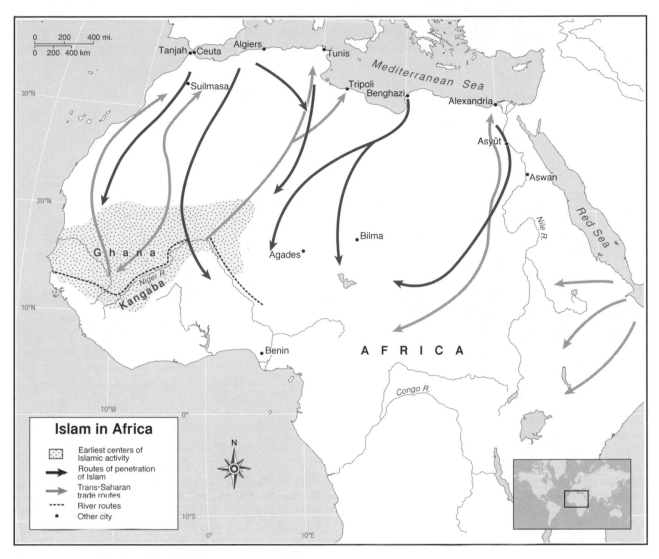

**Islam in Africa**

- (dotted) Earliest centers of Islamic activity
- (arrow) Routes of penetration of Islam
- (gray arrow) Trans-Saharan trade routes
- (dashed) River routes
- • Other city

Islam penetration routes into Africa. XNR PRODUCTIONS, INC./GALE

Muslims were Sunni, but some belonged to the Kharijite persuasion through their connections with Oman, a small state at the southeastern end of the Arabian peninsula. The literate elite, and especially the "professional" Muslims, understood and wrote Arabic, but Islam was typically taught orally through Swahili explanations. The recourse to explanation in the local language was common practice throughout Africa and many parts of the Islamic world. Beginning about three hundred years ago some scholars and writers began to adapt the Arabic alphabet to the language, and thereby create a written or 'ajami literature alongside the older oral one. The written corpus contained the same stories, chronicles, and poetry as the one that had been transmitted orally down the generations.

The Swahili Muslims did not emphasize the spread of Islam into the interior, by preaching, colonization, or the military jihad. They were generally content to practice their faith, ply their trades, and interact with the people of the interior who were largely non-Muslim. The spread of Islam into the interior, and of the Swahili language and culture, did not begin until the late eighteenth century, under the impetus of Omani Arabs, who made Zanzibar their base. The Omani sultans controlled a significant portion of the Swahili region in what we could today call Tanzania and Kenya, primarily for commercial reasons. They continued to trade in ivory and gold, but now added a significant commerce in slaves. Some were sent to the Middle East and South Asia, while others were used at the coast to produce cloves and grain for export. The Zanzibari system resulted in more active contact between coast and hinterland, and the spread of Islam and the Swahili culture to the entrepôts and towns of the interior.

These networks laid the basis for the widespread practice of Islam in East Africa in the nineteenth and twentieth centuries. The main agents of islamization were merchants and teachers, not the reform-minded scholars who became so prominent in West Africa. The Omanis themselves were

A mud brick mosque in Timbuktu, Mali, built in the European medieval period. Timbuktu was founded by a nomadic tribe called the Tuareg, who only kept loose control of it. Eventually, it became a part of the Muslim empire of Sudan, and functioned as a major trading post that connected North Africa with West Africa and thereby facilitated the spread of Islam. © WOLFGANG KAEHLER/CORBIS

Kharijites, but most of the older Swahili communities as well as many of the slaves were Sunni. Relations across these doctrinal lines were not difficult. The jihadic tradition remained a minor theme, except when it came to resistance to European domination.

The "Egyptian" or North African gateway is usually emphasized in treatments of islamization in Africa. The Saharan region obviously marked the "entrance" to sub-Saharan Africa. It was not an obstacle to trading caravans, but it was to armies. Indeed, there is only one example—the Moroccan expedition of 1591—of a military force successfully crossing the desert and winning victories on the southern side. Arabs used the expression *sahil* or "coast" to apply to the two edges of the desert. The Arab and Berber Muslims of North Africa established networks of trade on both sides of the desert and rhythms of caravan trade that resembled the movement of ships along the Indian Ocean coast of East Africa. By 1000 it is possible to identify indigenous as well as North African Muslim communities in the towns of West Africa connected to the trans-saharan trading networks. In contrast to the pattern in East Africa, merchant capital

became very important in the Saharan and sub-Saharan interior of West Africa from an early time, and for many centuries was the motor force of Islamic practice.

North Africans often called sub-Saharan Africa the *Bilad al-Sudan*, the "land of the blacks." Geographers and historians have used this term and divided it into western, central and eastern portions. The eastern or Nile section corresponds to the modern nation of Sudan, while the western portion corresponds to most of the West African Sahel.

The greatest amount of literature about Islamic practice, generated by internal and external observers, deals with the West African region. Scholars have used this material to create a threefold pattern of islamization. Islam was first a minority religion, practiced essentially by traders; it then became the practice of Muslim courts; and finally, either by processes of military jihad or Sufi orders, or both, it became the practice of those living in the rural areas, farmers and pastoralists. It was at this point that it became the dominant religion, in the last two to three centuries. This formula can be useful, if it is applied selectively and discretely to the different parts of the Sahel and to areas further south in the continent.

The eastern Sudan or Sahel, what is called the Sudan today, is something of an exception to this rule. Adjacent to the Nile River, it lay along a natural axis of advance from Egypt to the south. Egyptian travelers and armies, whether in ancient or Islamic times, had often advanced up the Nile, and communities in the region sometimes returned the favor. Once the Muslims had established control of Egypt, they confronted the Nubian kingdoms that had adopted Monophysite or Orthodox forms of Christianity as the state religion in earlier centuries. Muslims and Christians then worked out a pact, called *baqt*, by which the weaker Christian states paid a small tribute and allowed trade through their areas in exchange for noninterference in their affairs. This arrangement endured for several centuries. It was endangered by the limited participation of some Nubian armies in the European-led Crusades of the twelfth century, and finally ended by the Mamluks in the fifteenth century. After this period Arabic became the dominant language of the northern Nile valley and the lingua franca of the wider region.

## West African Patterns
In the western and central Sudan the process was different. The early Muslim communities were merchants who lived in good relations with and on the sufferance of non-Muslim courts. These early Muslims were Arab and Berber but they were soon joined by Soninke, Mandinka, and other communities of local origin. By the time of the empire of Mali (fl. 1200–1400), some ruling classes had adopted Islam, although not necessarily to the exclusion of local or "ethnic" religious practices. Mali in particular is remembered for the pilgrimage of Mansa Musa in 1324 and for the visit that Ibn Battuta paid to the court of his brother and successor, Mansa Sulayman, in 1352 and 1353. The court of the Songhay Empire (fl. c. 1450–1591) is also remembered for adherence to Islam. Indeed, Askiya Muhammad (1493–1528) is remembered not just for his pilgrimage but also for his discussions with the famous jurisconsult al-Maghili and for some serious efforts to spread the faith in the Niger Buckle (the area around Timbuktu and Gao) in the early years of his reign. The state of Bornu, in the area of Lake Chad in the central Sudan, is remembered for an early adoption of Islam at the court as well as for its longevity (about one thousand years, into the nineteenth century).

In the last 250 years Islam has spread much more widely throughout northern Africa thanks to Sufi orders and reform movements. The oldest order was the Qadiriyya, but its network for some time consisted principally of an elite group of scholars across the Sudan, the Sahara, and North Africa. A Qadiriyya revival and spread in the late eighteenth century was followed by rivalry with the Tijaniyya and other orders with strong bases in North Africa and the Holy Cities. The competition increased in the nineteenth century, all across

this belt, along the Swahili coast, and in the East African interior. Sufi practice was not challenged by reform movements, akin to the Salafiyya or the Wahhabiyya, until the mid-twentieth century.

Indeed, Sufism was the principal vehicle by which Islamic practice spread from city to countryside in the Sudan or Sahel. In the eighteenth and nineteenth centuries it was accompanied by reform movements, led by scholars who increasingly complained of the lax, mixed, or corrupt practice of the faith in the cities, courts, and countryside. Increasingly these scholars, usually with Sufi affiliations of their own, resorted to the jihad of the sword and led military movements to replace the regimes that they criticized. The most successful of these movements, in terms of its breadth, depth, and literary heritage, was the one led by ʿUthman dan Fodio in Hausaland in the early nineteenth century. It resulted in the Sokoto Caliphate, a regime that dominated most of the northern part of Nigeria as well as the southern fringe of today's Niger. Many Muslims of northern Nigeria today see the caliphate as a kind of social charter for the present day and have pushed for the establishment of *shariʿa* (Islamic law).

The strongest fusion of Sufi identity and militant reform came in the mid-nineteenth century with the mobilization led by Umar Tal, a scholar and pilgrim whose origins were in Senegal. Umar made the pilgrimage to Mecca, was initiated into the highest ranks of the Tijaniyya order by a Moroccan in Medina, and returned to West Africa in the 1830s to pursue a career of teaching and writing. In 1852, however, after some campaigns of recruitment, he launched a jihad of the sword against the non-Muslim states of the Upper and Middle Niger and the Upper Senegal Rivers. He particularly targeted the Bambara Kingdom of Segu, which he defeated in 1860 and 1861. He also had some encounters with the French and an expansive governor named Faidherbe in Senegal, and this has given him and his Tijaniyya affiliation an aura of resistance to European conquest. At the end of his life Umar attacked the Muslim state of Masina or Hamdullahi, principally because of their aid for the "pagan" Bambara of Segu. This conflict between two Muslim armies and communities, both of Pulaar or Fulbe culture, caused great consternation in the West African Islamic world. It also led to Umar's death in 1864 and to the premature limitation of the ambitious movement that he launched.

The greatest expansion of Islam in sub-Saharan Africa took place in the colonial period, particularly under the overrule of the British in Nigeria and the Sudan and the French through most of the old western and central Sudan. In these instances Islam provided an alternative tradition to the secular or Christian identities of the rulers and the missionaries who typically accompanied them. It has often meant closer approximation to the styles of dress, architecture, and roles of women characteristic of the Middle East. Europeans rulers, on the other hand, sought to develop institutions and practices for dealing with their Muslim subjects. They co-opted portions of the Islamic legal and educational systems, tried to control the pilgrimage, and sought to create "colonial" forms of Islam. The best-known creation was *Islam noir*, the "black Islam," which was supposed to characterize French West Africa. The European colonial authorities often styled themselves as "Muslim powers" and made comparisons with practices in India, Indonesia, and other areas.

By the time of independence in most sub-Saharan countries in the 1960s, Muslim communities had established closer ties with the faithful in the Middle East, and particularly in Egypt and Saudi Arabia. The centrality of these areas, combined with the pilgrimage and institutions such as Al-Azhar University, encouraged this process. At the same time the Arab Muslim communities made significant human and material investments in sub-Saharan Africa. This investment stimulated some criticism of Sufi and other African Muslim practices, particularly in the Sudan, Nigeria, and adjacent areas. In other regions the "Arab" and Saudi influence was not as pronounced, and patterns such as the "maraboutic" (a synonym for a cleric, derived from the term "almoravid") domination of Islam characteristic of Senegal were maintained.

## The Suwarian Pattern

One of the most intriguing and original creations of Muslims in Africa is the Suwarian tradition. This term, coined by the historian Ivor Wilks, goes back to a certain Al-Hajj Salim Suwari, a learned cleric from the Middle Niger region who lived around 1500. The Suwarian tradition expresses the rationale used by Muslims who lived as minorities in "pagan" regions, particularly the communities of merchants who originally left the western Sudan for regions of woodland and forest to the south, in search of gold and other items of trade. This began in the thirteenth and fourteenth centuries, when the Empire of Mali was at its height and sent out colonies of traders, *juula*, who retained their ties with the state, the Mandinka language, and their Muslim identity. It continued into the twentieth century.

*Juula* came to be an ethnic, linguistic, and religious designation for these people, who typically lived in demarcated neighborhoods within the main commercial towns and organized trade between the forest areas of the south and the Sahel to the north. They left the realm of "politics" to their local hosts. They constituted a Muslim minority within a non-Muslim majority, corresponding to the first "phase" of islamization mentioned above. They worshiped, educated their children, distributed their property, and in almost every respect conducted their lives as would Muslims anywhere in Africa or the rest of the world. They were no less learned nor pious than believers elsewhere, and they did not compromise their faith. But they could not afford to, and generally did not want to, change the religious identities of their hosts, who welcomed their presence and accorded them favors because

of the prosperity they brought through trade. They were not about to try transforming the *Dar al-kufr* in which they lived into a *Dar al-Islam*.

Over time the *juula* colonies developed a theological rationale for their relations with non-Muslim ruling classes and subjects on the basis of the teachings of Suwari. He made the pilgrimage to Mecca several times and devoted his intellectual career to reflection upon the situation of Muslim minorities. Drawing upon Middle Eastern jurists and theologians, he reformulated the obligations of the faithful. Muslims must nurture their own learning and piety, and thereby furnish good examples to the non-Muslims who lived around them. They could accept the jurisdiction of non-Muslim authorities, as long as they had the necessary protection and conditions to practice the faith. In this position Suwari followed a strong predilection in Islamic thought for any government, albeit non-Muslim or tyrannical, as opposed to none. The military jihad was a resort only if the faithful were threatened. In essence, Suwari esteemed that God would bring non-Muslims to convert in His own time, and it was not the responsibility of the Muslim minorities to decide when ignorance or unbelief would give way to faith.

In practice, of course, the Muslims and non-Muslims did not function in isolation. Across the many times and places of the woodlands and forest, they were in constant contact with each other, and conceived of the relationship as two estates: the merchant estate, which was Muslim, and the ruling classes, which were "pagan" or at least "ignorant" from the standpoint of Islam. But the ruling classes typically esteemed the merchants and their religion, and sought the *baraka* or blessing that Muslims might bring to the political realm. This esteem was reflected in a number of ways, for example, in the demand for amulets produced by clerics for their "pagan" hosts. A British traveler in the early nineteenth century, Joseph Dupuis, gives an account of this demand in the Kingdom of Asante (today's Ghana) in his *Journal of a Residence in Ashantee*:

> The talismanic charms fabricated by the Muslims, it is well known, are esteemed efficacious according to the various powers they are supposed to possess, and here is a source of great emolument, as the article is in public demand from the palace to the slave's hut; for every man (not by any means exempting the Muslims) wears them strung around the neck. . . . Some are accounted efficacious for the cure of gunshot wounds, others for the thrust or laceration of steel weapons, and the poisoned barbs of javelins, or arrows. Some, on the other hand, are esteemed to possess the virtue of rendering the wearer invulnerable in the field of battle, and hence are worn as a preservative against the casualties of war.

> Besides this class of charms, they have other cabalistic scraps for averting the evil of natural life: These may

also be subdivided into separate classes; some, for instance, are specific nostrums in certain diseases of the human frame, some for their prevention, and some are calculated either to ward off any impending stroke of fortune, or to raise the proprietor to wealth, happiness and distinction. (London, 1824, 1966, appendix, page xi)

The relationship between leading merchants and rulers is captured well in another passage from the same author, in the same kingdom. Merchants, clerics, and rulers were all residents of the same city, Kumasi, the capital of Asante. The speaker here is the head of the local Muslim community, and he talks of his role with the Muslim estate, mainly through education, and his ties to the power structure:

"When I was a young man," said the Bashaw (Pasha), "I worked for the good of my body. I traded on the face of God's earth, and traveled much. As my beard grew strong [I became older] I settled at Salgha [a trading center] and lastly removed to this city. I was still but an indifferent student [of Islam] when, God be praised, a certain teacher from the north was sent to me by a special direction, and that learned saint taught me the truth. So that now my beard is white, and I cannot travel as before, [but] I am content to seek the good of my soul in a state of future reward. My avocations at Kumasi are several, but my chief employment is a school which I have endowed, and which I preside over myself. God has compassioned my labors [i.e., made them prosper], and I have about 70 pupils and converts at this time.

Besides this, the king's heart is turned towards me, and I am a favored servant. Over the Muslims I rule as *qadi*, conformably to our law. I am also a member of the king's council in affairs relating to the believers of Sarem and Dagomba [areas to the north with significant Muslim populations]." (Dupuis, p. 97)

The Suwarian tradition was a realistic rationale for Muslims living in the woodland and forest regions of West Africa in the last five or six centuries. It suggests the kinds of positions which many Muslims throughout the world have taken when they found themselves in situations of inferior numbers and force, took advantage of their networks for trade, and enjoyed generally good relations with the local authorities because of the goods and prosperity that they could attract.

Some Muslims have searched for wisdom and inspiration within African societies. They have established links with indigenous healing practices, divination systems, and cosmologies. They have created worlds of mediating spirits and possession cults, such as the *bori* of Hausaland or the *gnawa* of Morocco. These fused religious worlds have come under increasing criticism in the last two centuries from movements of reform and the closer integration of sub-Saharan Africa with the Middle East.

*See also* **Ahmad Ibn Ibrahim al-Ghazi; Ahmad Ibn Idris; Hajj Salim Suwari, al-; Suyut, al-; Tariqa; Zar.**

## BIBLIOGRAPHY

Abun-Nasr, Jamil. *The Tijaniyya. A Sufi Order in the Modern World.* Oxford, U.K.: Oxford University Press, 1965.

Brenner, Louis. *West African Sufi. The Religious Heritage and Spiritual Search of Cerno Bokar Saalif Tall.* London: Hurst, 1984.

Brenner, Louis. *Controlling Knowledge. Religion, Power and Schooling in a West African Muslim Society.* London: Hurst, 2001.

Clarke, Peter. *West Africa and Islam.* London: Edward Arnold, 1982.

Cooper, Barbara. *Marriage in Maradi: Gender and Culture in a Hausa Society in Niger, 1900–1989.* London: Heinemann and Currey, 1997.

Cruise O'Brien, Donal. *The Mourides of Senegal.* Oxford, U.K.: Oxford University Press, 1971.

Dupuis, Joseph. *Journal of a Residence in Ashantee (1824).* London: Frank Cass, 1966.

Hiskett, Mervyn. *The Development of Islam in West Africa.* London: Longman, 1984.

Last, D. Murray. *The Sokoto Caliphate.* London: Humanities Press, 1967.

Levtzion, Nehemia, and Hopkins, J. F. P. *Corpus of Early Arabic Sources for West African History.* Cambridge, U.K.: Cambridge University Press, 1981.

Levtzion, Nehemia, and Pouwels, Randall, eds. *The History of Islam in Africa.* Athens: Ohio University Press, 2000.

Mazrui, Ali, and Shariff, Ibrahim. *The Swahili: Idiom of an African People.* Trenton, N.J.: Africa World History, 1994.

Robinson, David. *The Holy War of Umar Tal. The Western Sudan in the Mid-Nineteenth Century.* Oxford, U.K.: Oxford University Press, 1985.

Robinson, David. *Paths of Accommodation. Muslim Societies and French Colonial Authorities in Senegal and Mauritania, 1880 to 1920.* Athens: Ohio University Press, 2000.

*David Robinson*

## AFRICAN CULTURE AND ISLAM

Islam, an Afro-Asiatic faith, has long been known to be a religion of great synthesis that has interacted with local cultures, enriching them and being enriched by them. It has impacted on African society in various ways for almost a millennium, if not longer, adding to the fabric of these cultures.

## Spread of Islam in Africa

Islam made its presence felt in much of Africa (the East coast and Horn of Africa as well as West Africa) mainly through trade and migration. In West Africa, for instance, Islam was introduced from North Africa by the Berbers through the trans-Saharan trade as early as the ninth century. Later, trading networks developed among local African groups such as the Mande (Dyula/Wangara) whose area of operation spanned a wide area extending from as far west as Senegal to northern Nigeria in the east. This trade network, or diaspora, was closely associated with the diffusion of Islamic studies, including mysticism in the later centuries, and enabled Islam to penetrate peacefully beyond the Sahel—the semiarid region of African between the Sahara and the savannahs—into the savannah area. In the coastal trading communities of East Africa the process of interaction between the Middle Eastern immigrants, mainly south Arabians, and the dominant African groups created a new urban ethos in which Islam blended with the indigenous local culture to produce Swahili Islam. The cross-cultural trade in many parts of Africa, apart from reinforcing cultural self-identity and nurturing religious commitment, fostered a pluralist structure in which commerce, Islam, and the indigenous system supported the urban network. In this way a balance was established between local ritual prescriptions and those of universal Islam.

Islam in Africa therefore was primarily an urban religion (with an urban ethos) that fostered commitment to its religious system ranging from ethnic self-identity to Islamic self-identity, universal and transethnic in scope. Islamic penetration in the rural areas, on the other hand, made piecemeal infiltration over a long period of time with significant gains awaiting a much later period. The religion therefore entered much of Africa peacefully through the agency of trade and later gained status after the migrant community (purveyors of the written word and the visual symbols of Islam) was integrated into the political setup before finally the ruling elite embraced the faith and appropriated its symbols for political purposes.

The intensity of Islam varied from one region of Africa to another and was influenced by a number of factors, including the length of interaction between Islam and the traditional religion, the compatibility or incompatibility of the worldviews of the two religious systems, and the level of resilience of the indigenous integrative symbols to sustain traditional structures of the local religion. Islam has its written scripture, a prescribed ritual, a historical and systematized myth, and a supra-ethnic religious identity. Its interaction with African traditional religions is therefore governed by the tension between its supra-ethnic universality of its *umma* and the ethnocentrism of African traditional religion. As Dean Gilland

put it, for the African, the ethnic group is the matrix in which his religion takes shape, the meaning of myth communicated, and a person's sacramental relation to nature experienced. This means that when the symbols of the ethnic group are challenged by a new system, recombination of old and new forms may appear to reorganize the group and to compensate for any loss. More specifically, becoming a Muslim and joining this universal *umma* involves offering prayers in a mosque frequented by members of other ethnic groups, adoption of Muslim behavior patterns and dress code in some cases, and using a certain language (e.g., for quite a long time Kiswahili in the case of East Africa). The *Kano Chronicle*, a record of Hausa kings of sixteenth or seventeenth century inspiration first written down in the nineteenth century whose sources were largely oral, brings out clearly the struggle between the two religious systems, the Islamic and the traditional one, after the symbolic tree is cut down and a mosque built in its place.

## Indigenous Culture and Islam

The old forms and symbols of the indigenous system are often not discarded but retrieved and reinforced and recast in a new form. In the artistic and architectural domains, for instance, there has been a unique blending of Islamic structure and African representation. Once a balance had been reached between the local religious practices and the universal ritual prescriptions of Islam the next step was to cast the imagery and iconography of African ancestral pillars, shrines, and so on into Islamized form. Where Islam was introduced such items as charms, amulets, certain types of clothing, and prestige goods were incorporated into local societies. More importantly, the local altar-shrine was transformed into the mosque in such a way that the physical configuration represented a qualitative leap into verticality. Thus, as Labelle Prussin notes, the single, towering pyramidal earthen cone became the *mihrab* (it also served as a minaret) with its system of projecting wooden pickets extending out of this massive structure. The ends of these wooden pickets served as a scaffold for workers to climb and repair the walls. The ancestral conical structure pillar (the Voltaic tradition) was now redirected to a new focal center, that of Mecca. In certain cases, as Prussin and Rene Bravmann have observed, some of the mosques that were built in Mali had *mihrab*s that evoked the image of an African mask (which traditionally represents powerful forces). This is how the mosques were constructed by the Mande of West Africa with Islam clearly inspiring the use of certain architectural features in the spatial configuration. The Islamic architectural tradition (mediated through the Maghrebian heritage) in turn inspired the architectural imagery or style represented by the thatched domes of the Senegal-Guinea area for mosques and maraboutic (referring to a Muslim scholar or saint in North Africa or parts of West Africa) shrines following the example of the domed cities of Tripoli and Cairo. Islamic-type designs were also emulated and led to the adoption of arabesque wall patterning instead

A mud brick mosque in Mopti, Mali, in Northwest Africa. Africa is home to more than one billion Muslims. © CHARLES AND JOSETTE LENARS/CORBIS

of the attached African charms. This calligraphy allowed for a new system of spatial organization. More than this, Islamic script was used in decorative ways even in non-Muslim areas such as modern-day Ghana, where in the nineteenth century the Asantehene, head of the Asante confederacy, wore clothes with Arabic writing in various colors. Islam had clearly filtered through Asante politicoreligious structure such that both in terms of ideas and in the realm of the arts it provided a medium through which the ideology of the Asante was communicated.

Islam, which for many centuries coexisted well with traditional African religion, gradually over time attempted to replace it as the dominant faith of some regions without major clashes. What made this possible was the fact that the Islamic faith was much more adaptable in Africa with very minimal requirements for new members who at the very least were expected to change their names after reciting the testimony of faith. The observance of Islamic duties along with the understanding of the faith were supposed to follow later. For the first generation of Muslims, introduction to Islamic cultural values was what came first whereas Islamization itself could take generations to realize. At this level there was accommodation to social and political structures of authority.

This was the period when the learned Muslims, as in West African kingdoms, played a key role in administration and diplomacy. Eventually, however, a number of these African rulers adopted Islam and in doing so may partly have undermined the basis of their legitimacy as guardians of African ancestral religious traditions. Nevertheless, they did not completely renounce ties with the African traditional religion, which continued to be the religion of many of their subjects. This arrangement assisted in maintaining order although it did not please some West African Sufi leaders of the eighteenth and nineteenth centuries who launched their jihads (reform movements) of Islamic revivalism (some of which had mahdist/messianic overtones) to establish Islamic states. The theme of Islamic revivalism will be discussed later.

## Colonialism

Colonialism facilitated the growth of Islam in areas of Africa as far apart as Tanzania (Tanganyika) in East Africa and Senegal in West Africa through the activities of Muslim brotherhoods (Sufi orders), traders, and others. For some African groups the loss of power with the onset of colonial rule made them gravitate toward Islam, which was seen as an alternative to the prevailing colonial order. The difficulties of a new life under the colonial system, which uprooted the African from his traditional universe, presented Islam with an opportunity to provide a new framework as meaningful and all-embracing as the old African one. This, for instance, happened with Amadou Bamba's Murid brotherhood in Senegal, which converted thousands of people whose earthly kingdoms had been destroyed by colonialism. In 1888 Bamba established Touba/Tubaa as a great holy city (some say) to rival Mecca, and he was buried there in 1927. Every year hundreds of thousands of his followers visit his tomb on the anniversary of his death. For the uprooted African who joined the faith, the Muslim supra-ethnic *umma* provided a solidarity and a sense of belonging not very different from that of the African village/ethnic one. Moreover, while the Islamic prescriptions replaced the indigenous ones, in matters of worship, however, the Muslim ritual prayer did not completely dislodge the traditional rituals of seeking to appease the ancestors. In fact, the Muslim religious leaders and teachers came to perform the same kind of role as the African healers and medicine men in curving out the domain of popular religion.

## Indigenization of Islam

Yet, despite Muslim efforts to purge African elements from their faith, their religion continued to display a level of "Africanness" that revealed the indigenization of Islam in these regions of West Africa. How else would one explain the continued presence of, for instance, the *bori* cult in northern Nigeria? There, women tend to follow the traditional cults even with the sustained impact of Islam in Hausaland for centuries, including producing such well-known major religious Fulani reformers of the nineteenth century such as

Shaykh 'Uthman dan Fodio? There must be a level of affinity between the two religious systems that allows this to happen. For instance, the belief in mystical powers (*jinn*/invisible supernatural creatures) allows Islam to be accommodated to the African spirit world that is so important to understanding the African religious universe. In fact, the ancestral beliefs have been recombined with Muslim practice to form a new "folk" religion with emphasis on, say, saint veneration (which popular Islam and Sufism reinforce) that approximates local ancestor veneration.

The practice of curing illnesses attributed to occult forces provided an opportunity for the Muslim healing system to flourish and allowed for the services of Muslim healers/holy men (who provided additional healing choices to local practitioners) to be in high demand. The appearance of new epidemic diseases such as smallpox and cholera, which arose in the nineteenth and twentieth centuries in hinterland East Africa (and which the local people could not adequately deal with), led the people to turn increasingly to the Muslim healing system. Muslim prayers and amulets were more popular than Muslim secular remedies in this atmosphere of suspicion (which took the form of sorcery and witchcraft accusations). Apart from the fact that Muslim amulets were believed to embody the words of the Supreme Being and not that of the intermediary powers (making them therefore more potent, as the Asante believed), Muslim literacy played a role as a potential source of healing. Furthermore, Sufi masters who had attained a closeness to God through following the path of spiritual enlightenment were believed to have special powers that made their prayers efficacious. This *baraka* (blessing power that heals) was passed on in families and explains why the scholarly Sufi lineages of the Sahara have played a pivotal role in mediating Islam between North and West Africa.

While the influence of the *tariqa* (Sufi orders) has been undermined to some extent in some parts of Africa such as Tanzania, the commitment to Sufistic engagement with faith nevertheless continues to be strong in West Africa and especially in Senegal, although even there it is facing the challenge of the Salafi reformers. Sufism, far from being a predominantly rural phenomenon that would fade away as Muslim societies became increasingly modernized, has continued to thrive and to engage African Muslims of the urban centers as well. Yet for some educated young African Muslims who are discomfited by magical practices, saint veneration, hierarchy, and the authoritarianism of some Sufi orders, the Salafi message has seemed attractive.

The Salafi reform is itself at some level quite conservative and traditional; to the extent that this is true, Salafi reform and Sufi traditionalism are constantly engaged in an overlapping movement of interaction. Will they creatively synthesize from the values of their common Islamic heritage while acknowledging the entanglements and creative encounters between and within cultures? It remains to be seen what the outcome of this clash will be. It is clear though that underlying the conflict between them are struggles for power and control of the Muslim community by these competing groups.

## Gender and Islam in Africa

What type of cultural interface has taken place between Islam and Africa in the area of gender relations? More specifically, what has been the role of Islam with respect to the status of women in the regions of Africa where Islam has been introduced? Did Islam introduce patriarchy in Africa? Many African societies were patriarchal (polygamous as well) even before their encounter with Islam. Nevertheless, where Islam was introduced and its values incorporated in the socioeconomic and political structures of these societies (especially those with a propensity for state/empire building) a hierarchical social organization resulted in which there were clear demarcations of male and female spheres of activity. This, of course, did vary from society to society. For instance, the Yoruba women of southwestern Nigeria continued to be market women even after the coming of Islam whereas their Hausa counterparts in northern Nigeria tended to lead more secluded lives. It is significant to note that the Mahdiyya movement, which was established in 1941 in Ijebul-Ode in southern Nigeria by the southern Muslim scholar, Muhammad Jumat Imam, emphasized the education of women, their attendance of mosques together with men, and their inclusion in public affairs (hence no Qur'anic basis for the practice of *purdah*, or female seclusion. By way of comparison, among the Tuareg-Berbers of the Sahara (who tend to be matriarchal) their unveiled women continued to enjoy far more freedom of movement than their Arab counterparts in North Africa.

The Sufi *dhikr* (chant) practices and the spirit possession cults (*bori* among Hausas in West Africa and *zar* in Ethiopia and Sudan) have offered women possibilities for autonomous spiritual expression and for creation of networks of mutual support. Mysticism in particular has opened the room for the acceptance of female authority (for instance, Sokna Magat Diop of the Murids) or religious leadership located within the female realm. Moreover, the Qadiriyya order accepted the female leadership of Shaykha Binti Mtumwa (a former slave or person of low status) who founded a branch of the order in Malawi and was successful in attracting many women. Therefore, both possession cults and Sufi brotherhoods have allowed women to establish a sphere of action in hierarchical societies where control of the state is a male domain. These orders have incorporated women in both East and West Africa, especially in the area of education, fund raising, and the like, although women have a much larger scope in Senegal than in Nigeria in leadership of brotherhoods.

During the period of economic hardships in the last several decades, issues of cultural authenticity have become rooted in Islamic identity in opposition to what has been perceived as Western cultural domination. These women reject Western feminism, which they see as an extension of Western cultural domination worldwide, a domination that makes Western values and ideas be the normative values that everyone else should strive for. The role of these women has expanded as liberalization of the political process and the emergence of multiparty politics have led them to establish organizations and to embrace a particular agenda, including the Muslim dress code, and involvement in cultural politics. The Islamists and radical reformist activists are engaged in contesting existing gender relations and social justice. They use the text (scripture) as their framework whereas the secular activists' frame of reference is based on certain abstract concepts such as egalitarianism, humanism, human rights, and pluralism, concepts that have emerged from Western discourses on the subject.

The roles of men and women are constantly changing due to urbanization, education, and cross-cultural contacts. For some women these changes have generated new freedom and opportunities for self-improvement.

## Islamic Law and Politics

As a political force, Islam united much of Africa in the past and was willing to accommodate local (including legal) practices. Nevertheless, as the level of Islamization deepened the learned Muslim scholars began to call for a strict interpretation of the *shari'a* (Islamic law), which they saw as different from the African legal or customary practices. Some obvious areas of difference included, for instance, Islamic emphasis on individual ownership of land (and property inheritance through the male side of the family) whereas in various African societies land belonged to the community. Also, the way Islamic law was interpreted (some have suggested) tended to give men considerably more power over property matters than perhaps was the case in some African societies. Scholars, however, need comparative data across a number of African societies to make a meaningful comparison.

Unlike African customary law, which is unwritten, Islamic law (which covers both public and private life) is written and provides an extensive framework within which Muslim *qadi*s (judges) analyze legal issues and deduce new laws to handle new situations in the *umma*. Islamic law emphasizes the rights or obligations of individuals whereas African customary law (in which economic and social relations, especially in "stateless" societies, were regulated by customs maintained by social pressure and the authority of elders) is based on kinship ties in matters of marriage and property. It extends to commercial and criminal law and also has rules regarding the conduct of political leaders or those entrusted with authority. In their encounter with other legal systems European colonial powers left these systems functioning in some societies (for instance, Sudan and Nigeria as part of the Britain's self-serving policy of indirect rule) while in others they allowed

Muslim judges to apply Islamic civil and family law except in criminal matters, which were tried by European courts. In the postcolonial period the scope of Islamic law, where it is applied, is limited to religious issues and civil cases; the modern trend, with its emphasis on equal rights of citizens, is to have laws that apply across the board without recognizing any distinctions based on religion or gender.

Recognition of Islamic laws in many African states after independence has created tensions and political controversy especially when the secular elites have sought to forge a uniform system of law or at least have attempted to modify Muslim personal law (in aspects such as marriage for girls) to bring it in line with the inherited Western law and African customary practices. There has been a wide variety of responses to the dilemma of how much scope to give to religious laws. Mozambique, for instance, has made attempts to recognize traditional and religious marriages (thus doing the basic minimum) whereas Sudan has made *shari'a* the law of the land. The call by Muslim groups in northern Nigeria for nationalization of Islamic law (to apply beyond northern Nigeria) has unleashed the *shari'a* debate, a source of tension in national politics in a country where at the very least only half or slightly more than half the population is Muslim. In African Muslim societies in general, however, it has been noted that there is often an antistate discourse underlying the call for Islamic law by Muslim groups, which seek to foster their religious and cultural autonomy in societies (with failed political institutions and secular ideologies such as socialism) in which state and secular institutions have failed to respond to their needs.

## Coexistence of Islam and African Religion

The coexistence of Islam and African traditional religion has cultural and linguistic implications as well. The Arabic language has provided abstract concepts, particularly religious ones, that reveal Islamic modes of thought and expression. Islamic influence is, in fact, revealed both at the explicit and suggestive levels in languages as different as the Berber dialects, Hausa, Swahili, and Somali to name just a few. These languages have absorbed the Islamic worldview (though at some level languages such as Swahili have been progressively secularized over time during and after the colonial period, making them more neutral).

Islamic culture has generally held the written word in such high esteem that wherever Islam has reached in Africa versions of its script have been adopted in those regions of sustained contact. Moreover, Islamic penetration of Africa introduced Arabic as the language of religious discourse among scholars, official correspondence between Islamized states, and historical writing during the period of the Muslim kingdoms. Good examples of important records that were produced by Timbuktu scholars were the monumental *Tarikh al-Fatash* and *Tarikh al-Sudan*. Both East and West Africa have also produced Afro-Islamic literature (from the panegyrics of the Prophet to poetry) based on the local languages, which have absorbed a lot of Arabic loanwords in the spheres of religion, politics, and commerce. In some of these areas, however, the written word has competed with the oral literature especially among such clan-based people as the Somali.

In the linguistic dimension it is often assumed that when Arabic and an African language such as Swahili, Berber, Hausa, Fulani, Harari, Somali, and others come into contact the latter will invariably be influenced by the former. It is, of course, undeniable that as a result of contact with Arabic these languages (which are related in their ethos to Arabic) have absorbed many Arabic loanwords. In fact, some had in the past a written tradition in Arabic script. Nevertheless, there is an unstated assumption that these languages have borrowed from Arabic rather passively without contributing anything back. This may explain the fact that while there are a number of studies that trace Arabic loanwords in various African languages, fewer comparable studies, if any, have been undertaken to study, say, the influence of Swahili on the Arabic dialects spoken in Oman or south Yemen (Hadhramaut). This influence should be expected given that the Red Sea separates the Arabian peninsula from Africa and this proximity resulted in a profound interaction in a number of spheres. The Arabs, by their own tradition, recognize African ancestry through Ishmael's mother Haggar, who was Egyptian. Also, Arabs recognize the active presence of Africans in the evolution of pre-Islamic Arabic culture and the important role that Ethiopia and Ethiopians played in the early history of Islam.

How will both Islam and African indigenous traditions fare in the twenty–first century in the era of globalization? Can both systems penetrate Western secular culture, whose secular institutions and ideologies have not functioned well in Africa? Are African religious traditions destined to die out as socioeconomic changes (not to mention the colonial experience) have disrupted the cultural nexus in which these traditions have thrived? This is rather unlikely as African indigenous cultures have demonstrated much resilience even as their followers enter the fold of either Islam or Christianity (Ali Mazrui's triple heritage) and the African ancestors are poised to raise their heads once again in the synthetic and syncretic religious universe. With one quarter of the world's 1.2 billion Muslims living in Africa (making Muslims, half the continent's population, the most numerous followers of any religion) the final chapter of the unfolding global resurgent Islam is yet to be written.

*See also* **Africa, Islam in; Bamba, Ahmad; Timbuktu; Touba; Zar.**

## BIBLIOGRAPHY

Bravmann, Rene A. *African Islam*. Washington, D.C.: The Smithsonian Institution, 1983.

Chande, Abdin. "Radicalism and Reform in East Africa." In *The History of Islam in Africa*. Edited by Randall Pouwels and Nehemia Levitzion. Athens: Ohio University Press, 2000.

Clark, Peter. *West Africa and Islam*. London: Edward Arnold Ltd., 1982.

Dunbar, Roberta Ann. "Muslim Women in African History." In *The History of Islam in Africa*. Edited by Randall Pouwels and Nehemia Levitzion. Athens: Ohio University Press, 2000.

Gilland, Dean S. *African Religion Meets Islam: Religious Change in Northern Nigeria*. Lanham, Md.: University Press of America, 1986.

Harrow, Kenneth, ed. *Faces of Islam in African Literature*. Portsmouth, N.H.: Heinemann, 1991.

Owusu-Ansah, David. *Islamic Talismanic Tradition in Nineteenth Century Asante*. Lewiston, N.Y.: Mellen, 1991.

Pouwels, Randall, and Levitzion, Nehemia, eds. *The History of Islam in Africa*. Athens: Ohio University Press, 2000.

Pouwels, Randall. *Horn and Crescent*. Cambridge, U.K.: Cambridge University Press, 1987.

Prussin, Labelle. *Hatumere: Islamic Design in West Africa*. Berkeley and Los Angeles: University of California Press, 1986.

Sanneh, Lamin. *Piety and Power*. Maryknoll, N.Y.: Orbis Books, 1996.

Westerlund, David, and Rosander, Eva Evers, eds. *African Islam and Islam in Africa: Encounters between Sufis and Islamists*. Athens: Ohio University Press, 1997.

*Abdin Chande*

# AGA KHAN

Aga Khan is the title inherited by the modern imams of the Shi'a Nizari Isma'ili Muslims. The title was first granted by the Iranian ruler Fath 'Ali Shah to Imam Hasan 'Ali Shah (1804–1881), who also served as governor of Qum, Mahallat, and Kirman. Forced to leave Iran, he settled eventually in British-ruled India. His son, Shah Ali Shah, Aga Khan II (1830–1835), was imam for four years and was succeeded after his death by his eight-year-old son who became well known internationally as Sir Sultan Muhammad Shah, Aga Khan III (1877–1957). He guided the community into the twentieth century by locating social welfare, educational, economic, and religious institutions within the framework of a structured community constitution to promote better organization and governance. His leadership played a crucial role in enabling the community, some of whose members had migrated from India to Africa, to adapt successfully to historical change and modernity.

In addition to his responsibilities as imam and spiritual leader for the welfare of his followers, Aga Khan III played an

Sir Sultan Muhammed Shah Aga Khan, known as Aga Khan III, became the leader of the Shi'a Nizari Isma'ili Muslims of India in the late nineteenth century at the age of eight. As the Indian subcontinent evolved politically in the beginning of the twentieth century, Aga Khan spoke out for education, social change, and women's rights. LIBRARY OF CONGRESS, THE

important role as a statesman in international and Muslim affairs. He was president of the League of Nations from 1937 to 1938 and also played an important role in the political evolution of the Indian subcontinent. Deeply committed to social reform and education among Muslims of Africa and Asia he assisted in the creation of several institutions such as schools, hospitals, and the East African Muslim Welfare Society. He was also an eloquent advocate for the education of women and the advancement of their social and public role. In addition to other writings and speeches, he wrote two books, *India in Transition* (1918) and his *Memoirs* (1954). He died in 1957 and is buried in Aswan, Egypt.

Aga Khan IV, Shah Karim al-Husayni, was born in 1936 and was educated in Europe and at Harvard University. During his leadership, a worldwide community emerged successfully through complex and turbulent changes. The Ismailis, who live in some thirty countries and represent cultural and geographical diversity, acknowledge the spiritual authority of the imam and have responded actively to his guidance. This has enabled them to build further on inherited institutions and to create common purpose in their endeavors through well-coordinated local, national, and international institutions.

Aga Khan IV also created the Aga Khan Development Network, to promote a humanitarian, intellectual, and social vision of Islam and tradition of service to society. Its international activities have earned an enviable reputation for their commitment to the development of societies, without bias to national or religious affiliation, and to the promotion of culture as a key resource and enabling factor in human and social development. The Award for Architecture and the Trust for Culture promote concern and awareness of the built environment, and cultural and historical preservation. Various institutions of higher education, such as the Aga Khan University, Central Asian University, and the Institute of Ismaili Studies promote scholarship and training in a wide variety of fields.

The Aga Khan's leadership and vision continue to be reflected in the increasingly significant global impact that these community institutions and the network are having in the fields of social, educational, economic, and cultural development.

*See also* **Khojas; Nizari.**

## BIBLIOGRAPHY

Aziz, K. K., ed. *Aga Khan III: Selected Speeches and Writings.* London: Kegan Paul International, 1998.

Daftary, Farhad. *The Ismailis: Their History and Doctrines.* Cambridge, U.K: Cambridge University Press, 1990.

*Azim Nanji*

## AHL AL-BAYT

*Ahl al-bayt*, or "people of the house," is a phrase used with reference to the family of the prophet Muhammad, particularly by the Shi'a. In early Arabian tribal society, it was a designation for a noble clan. It occurs only twice in the Qur'an, once in regard to Ibrahim's family (11:73), but more significantly in a verse that states, "God only wishes to keep uncleaness away from you, O people of the house, and to purify you completely" (33:33). The context suggests that this statement pertains to women in Muhammad's household, a view held by Sunni commentators. Some authorities have applied it more widely to descendants of Muhammad's clan (Banu Hashim), the Abbasids, and even the whole community of Muslims. Since the eighth century C.E., however, the Shi'a and many Sunnis have maintained that Qur'an 33:33 refers specifically to five people: Muhammad, 'Ali b. Abi Talib (Muhammad's cousin), 'Ali's wife Fatima (Muhammad's daughter), and their two children, Hasan and Husayn. Ulema invoke hadiths in support of this view, as seen in Tabari's *Jami' al-bayan* (c. tenth century C.E.). Thus, in South Asia, they are called "the five pure ones" (*panjatan pak*). They are also known as "people of the mantle" (*kisa'*) in remembrance of the occasion when the Prophet enveloped them with his mantle and recited this verse.

Belief in the supermundane qualities of the *ahl al-bayt* and the imams descended from them form the core of Shi'ite devotion. They are the ideal locus of authority and salvation in all things, both worldly and spiritual. As pure, sinless, and embodiments of divine wisdom, they are held to be the perfect leaders for the Muslim community, as well as models for moral action. Many believe that they possess a divine light through which God created the universe, and that it is only through their living presence that the world exists. Twelver Shi'ite doctrine has emphasized that the pain and martyrdom endured by *ahl al-bayt*, particularly by Husayn, hold redemptive power for those who have faith in them and empathize with their suffering. Moreover, they anticipate the messianic return of the Twelfth Imam at the end of time, and the intercession of the holy family on the day of judgment. During the middle ages, Nizari Isama'ili *da'i*s in northern India even identified the *ahl al-bayt* with Hindu gods (Brahma, Vishnu, Kalki, Shiva, and the goddess Shakti) and the Pandavas, the five heroes of the *Mahabharata* epic. The Shi'ite ritual calendar is distinguished by holidays commemorating events in the lives of the holy family, and it is common for the "hand of Fatima," inscribed with their five names, to be displayed in processions and to be used as a talisman.

Sunnis also revere the *ahl al-bayt*, attributing to them many of the sacred qualities that the Shi'a do. This is especially so in Sufi *tariqa*s (brotherhoods), most of which trace their spiritual lineage to Muhammad through 'Ali. Several *tariqa*s hold special veneration for the holy five and the imams, such as the Khalwatiyya, the Bektashiyya, and the Safawiyya, which established the Safavid dynasty in Iran (1502–1722). In many Muslim communities, high social status is attributed to those claiming to be *sayyid*s and *sharif*s, blood-descendants of the *ahl al-bayt*. Indeed, many Muslim scholars and saints are members of these two groups, and their tombs often become pilgrimage centers.

Although the Saudi-Wahhabi conquest of Arabia (nineteenth to early twentieth centuries) led to the destruction of many *ahl al-bayt* shrines (including Fatima's tomb in Medina), elsewhere their shrines have attracted large numbers of pilgrims in modern times. These include those of 'Ali (Najaf, Iraq), Husayn (Karbala, Iraq and Cairo, Egypt), 'Ali al-Rida (the eighth imam; Mashhad, Iran), and also of women saints such as Sayyida Zaynab ('Ali's daughter; Cairo) and Fatima al-Ma'suma (daughter of the seventh imam; Qom, Iran). Nizari Isma'ilis (Khojas) make pilgrimages to their living imam, the Aga Khan, also a direct descendent of the Prophet's household.

Contemporary heads of state in several Muslim countries have claimed blood-descent from the family of the Prophet to obtain religious legitimacy for their rule: the 'Alawid dynasty of Morocco (1631–present), Hashimite dynasty of Iraq (1921–1958) and of Jordan (1923–present), and many of the ruling mullahs in Iran, including the Ayatollah Khomeini (r. 1979–1989), whose tomb has become a popular Iranian Shi'ite shrine. Even former President Saddam Husayn of Iraq (r. 1979–2003) has claimed descent from *ahl al-bayt*.

*See also* **Hadith; Imam; Imamate; Karbala; Mahdi; Sayyid; Sharif; Shi'a: Imami (Twelver); Shi'a: Isma'ili.**

## BIBLIOGRAPHY

Ayoub, Mahmoud. *Redemptive Suffering in Islam: A Study of the Devotional Aspects of 'Ashura in Twelver Shi'ism*. The Hague: Mouton Publishers, 1978.

Hoffman-Ladd, Valerie J. "Devotion to the Prophet and His Family in Egyptian Sufism." *International Journal of Middle East Studies* 24 (1992): 615–637.

Schubel, Vernon James. *Religious Performance in Contemporary Islam: Shi'i Devotional Rituals in South Asia*. Columbia: University of South Carolina Press, 1993.

*Juan Eduardo Campo*

# AHL-E HADIS/AHL-AL HADITH

The Ahl-e Hadis emerged as a distinctive orientation among Indian ulema in the late-nineteenth-century milieu of reformist thought, publication, debate, and internal proselytizing. Like other reformers, they fostered devotion to the prophet Muhammad and fidelity to *shari'a*. Unlike them, they opposed jurisprudential *taqlid* (imitation) of the classic law schools in favor of direct use of hadith. They also opposed the entire institution of Sufism, a stance that further marginalized them. Like the Deobandis, they claimed to be heirs of Shah Wali Allah (d. 1763), and they encouraged simplification of ceremony and the practice of widow remarriage. Their practices in the canonical prayer (including uttering "amen" aloud and lifting their hands at the time of bowing) led to conflicts ultimately settled in British courts.

Core supporters of the Ahl-e Hadis came from educated and often well-born backgrounds. Cosmopolitan in orientation, they identified themselves with similar groups in Afghanistan and Arabia. Within India, they turned to princes for support, most famously with the marriage of Maulana Siddiq Hasan Khan (1832–1890) to the ruling Begum of Bhopal. Siddiq Hasan supported the classic interpretations of jihad, without the apologetic glosses of the day. Despite his writing to the contrary, he was suspected of disloyalty, as was another major figure in the movement, Sayyid Nazir Husain (d. 1902), who was briefly arrested as a "Wahhabi," as supporters of the Arab Muhammad Abd al Wahhab (1703–1792) were called. Suspicion of the Ahl-e Hadis abated by 1889, marked by the success of a campaign to drop the word "Wahhabi" in official British colonial correspondence.

The armed Lashkar-e Tayyiba, affiliated with the Ahl-e Hadis in Pakistan, is alleged to have been active both within Pakistan and Kashmir since the 1990s.

*See also* **Deoband; Fundamentalism.**

### BIBLIOGRAPHY

Metcalf, Barbara Daly. *Islamic Revival in British India: Deoband 1860–1900.* Princeton, N.J.: Princeton University Press, 1982.

Saeedullah. *The Life and Works of Muhammad Siddiq Hasan Khan, Nawwab of Bhopal.* Lahore, Pakistan: Sh. Muhammad Ashraf, 1973.

*Barbara D. Metcalf*

# AHL AL-HADITH

The Ahl al-Hadith (people of the traditions) appear to have developed out of a pious reaction to the assassination of Caliph Yazid b. Walid (d. 744). Prior to Yazid's assassination, scholars who emphasized hadith (traditions of the prophet Muhammad) as the primary source for interpreting the Will of God were disorganized and fairly removed from the widespread emphasis on applying varying levels of reason to the Qur'an. Yazid's assassination was interpreted by more conservative groups as a revolution against the predestined plan of God. Whether or not the early Ahl al-Hadith were aligned with the Umayyad caliphate, as were many of the Jabriyya (advocates of predestination), it is clear that many understood Yazid's assassination as a sign of the general decay of the Muslim community, the blame for which they assigned to the uncontrolled use of personal opinion by the Ahl al-Ra'y (people of considered opinion). After the Abbasid revolution (c. 720–750), the Ahl al-Hadith developed into the main group opposed to the dominance of the rationalist theology of the Mu'tazilites. During the religious inquisition or Mihna (833–850) many of the Ahl al-Hadith were imprisoned for refusing to agree to the doctrine of the Created Qur'an. Members of the Ahl al-Hadith, such as Ahmad Ibn Hanbal (d. 855), became important religious and social leaders due to

their refusal to recant their beliefs in the eternal nature of the Qur'an. After the Mihna, the Ahl al-Hadith led an anti-rationalist movement that forced advocates of rationalist thought underground. In the centuries following the initial triumph of the Ahl al-Hadith, a middle ground emerged that placed greater emphasis on a combination of reason and tradition. The Ahl al-Hadith formed a school of legal thought named after Ahmad Ibn Hanbal that continued to pursue legal methods that focused less on uses of reason and more on tradition. The Hanbali fixation on tradition led to a series of reform movements that have sought to "revive" the moral and ethical standards of the first generations of Muslims. The contemporary influence of Ahl al-Hadith ideology continues to be important for a number of diverse groups. Organizations such as the Indonesian Muhammadiyah and the Islamic Society of North America, as well as the violent al-Qaʿida and Islamic Jihad, each bases its ideologies on ideas that emerged out of the Ahl al-Hadith and Hanbali movement over the last eight centuries.

*See also* **Ibn Hanbal; Kalam; Muʿtazilites, Muʿtazila; Traditionalism.**

### BIBLIOGRAPHY

Hallaq, Wael. *A History of Islamic Law and Legal Theories.* Cambridge, U.K.: Cambridge University Press, 1997.

Schacht, Joseph. *The Origins of Muhammadan Jurisprudence.* Oxford, U.K.: Clarendon Press, 1950.

*R. Kevin Jaques*

# AHL AL-KITAB

The term *ahl al-kitab*, or people of the book, refers to followers of scripture-possessing religions that predate the Qur'an, most often Jews and Christians. In some situations other religious groups, such as Zoroastrians and Hindus, have been considered to be people of the book. Some Qur'anic verses also reference the Sabeans, who are usually understood to be one of several gnostic Judeo-Christian sects such as the Mandeans, the Elchasaites, or Archontics. Muslims recognize the holy books possessed by the Jews (*al-Tawrah:* Torah; *al-Zabur:* Psalms) and Christians (*al-Injil:* Gospel) as legitimate revelations. However, they believe that some portions of these scriptures were abrogated and superceded by the Qur'an and the Christians and Jews corrupted others.

The Qur'an provides an ambivalent picture of the people of the book, sometimes praising and sometimes condemning them. Muslims are said to worship the same God as the people of the book, who were likewise honored with divine revelations (Q 2:62). However, the people of the book are also criticized for certain faults and sometimes referred to as unbelievers (Q 5:18, 9:29–35). These differences in tone seem to be connected with the circumstances in which Qur'anic revelations were delivered. In Mecca the Prophet's message was directed against the idolaters who opposed him, and Muhammad believed that the Jews and Christians, as fellow monotheists, would recognize him as a prophet. After his arrival in Medina, however, it became apparent that most Jews and Christians were not going to submit to Islam. As a result, the Meccan suras generally express more favorable opinions of the people of the book, and the Medinan suras more negative images.

Despite recognizing the privileged place of the Jews as having received multiple prophets, the Qur'an criticizes them for resisting God and corrupting or hiding his Scriptures (Q 2:75, 3:78, 4:46f, 5:13, 5:41). They are also charged with teaching falsehoods (Q 2:78, 3:79), and with immoral practices such as greed, theft, idolatry, persecuting the prophets, charging interest, and failing to honor the Sabbath (Q 2:49–61, 65, 3:75, 4:153–156, 160–161, 5:56–64, 7:163–166). Because of their sins, the Qur'an asserts that God cursed the Jews (Q 5:13). Those Jews who did not submit to Islam faced the same eternal punishment as polytheists and other unbelievers (Q 2:80f).

Christians are generally portrayed sympathetically in the early suras. They are described as being the closest friends to Muslims, while Jews and idolaters are said to be hostile to Islam (Q 5:82). However, the Qur'an disagrees with Christians over several doctrinal issues. Although the Muslim holy book recognizes Jesus' prophethood (Q 3:45–53), it denies that he was divine or was crucified (Q 4:157–158, 5:116–117). It also rejects the Christians' doctrine of the Trinity and their teaching that Jesus was the Son of God (Q 4:171–172, 19:35), accusing proponents of these doctrines of being unbelievers, in danger of hellfire (Q 5:76f). As with the Jews, Christians are also charged with distorting the Scriptures.

Muslim representations of ahl al-kitab in hadith and early juristic literature demonstrate an increased familiarity with Jewish and Christian beliefs and practices, because the people of the book initially represented the majority population in the expanded Muslim empire. On the whole, this literature presents ahl al-kitab in a negative light. Many hadiths seem concerned about their undue influence and warn Muslims not to imitate them. Hadith literature also lays the groundwork for the practice of assigning protected status (known as dhimmi status) to people of the book who submitted to Muslim political authority. This arrangement made it possible for Jews and Christians to practice their faiths while living in Muslim societies. Although treated as second-class citizens, non-Muslim communities were largely able to coexist peacefully with Muslims for centuries, without experiencing the active persecution that minority religious groups often encountered in Europe.

Islamic literature from the eleventh through eighteenth centuries generally deals with ahl al-kitab within the context of their dhimmi status. Although dhimmis were understood to be inferior to Muslims, some Jews and Christians managed to attain high positions in Islamic states. A few, such as John of Damascus (d. c. 748), even engaged in theological discussions with Muslims. Islamic polemical literature associated with scholars such as Ibn Hazm of Córdoba (d. 1064), Ibn al-'Arabi (d. 1148), and al-Ghazali (d. 1111) repeated earlier criticisms of Jews and Christians, posited different theories to explain the corruption of their scriptures, and assigned blame for this calamity to well-known figures such as the Old Testament prophet Ezra, the Christian apostle Paul, and the Byzantine emperor Constantine. The people of the book were also accused of concealing biblical prophecies foretelling the coming of Muhammad and the triumph of Islam. Sufi works, such as the poetry of Jalal al-Din Rumi, look to Jesus and other biblical saints as models but contain similar criticisms of Jews and Christians. All these texts reflect a belief in Muhammad as the bearer of God's crowning revelation, supplanting the partial revelations of the biblical Scriptures.

During modern times, substantial changes in the relationship between the Islamic world and the West led to shifts in Muslim attitudes toward the people of the book. From the early 1800s, Islamic modernists acknowledged that Muslims could learn some things from the "Christian" West, but they continued to assert Islam's superiority as a religious system. Colonizing European states attempted to impose Western values upon Islamic populations, but westernizing Muslim governments failed to achieve the promised prosperity. With the breakdown of the dhimmi system and the rise of nationalism, ethnic and religious violence has erupted throughout the Muslim world. This is most noticeable in the region of Palestine, where many Muslims see the establishment of Israel as a Western colonial project. During the late twentieth century, Islamic revivalists (or "Islamists") increased their influence and largely rejected the "compromises" of the modernists. The Islamists advocate a return to the glorious Islamic civilization of the past, with its division of the world into dar al-islam and dar al-harb ("house of war"; i.e., that part of the world not ruled by Islamic government) and returning non-Muslim minorities to their former dhimmi status.

*See also* **Christianity and Islam; Islam and Other Religions; Judaism and Islam; Minorities: Dhimmis.**

## BIBLIOGRAPHY

Busse, Heribert. *Islam, Judaism, and Christianity: Theological and Historical Affiliations.* Translated by Allison Brown. Princeton, N.J.: Markus Weiner Publishers, 1998.

Goddard, Hugh. *Muslim Perceptions of Christianity.* London: Grey Seal, 1996.

Lazarus-Yafeh, Hava. *Intertwined Worlds: Medieval Islam and Bible Criticism.* Princeton, N.J.: Princeton University Press, 1992.

Lewis, Bernard. *The Jews of Islam*. Princeton, N.J.: Princeton University Press, 1984.

Ridgeon, Lloyd, ed. *Islamic Interpretations of Christianity*. New York: St. Martin's Press, 2001.

Watt, William Montgomery. *Muslim-Christian Encounters: Perceptions and Misperceptions*. London: Routledge, 1991.

*Stephen Cory*

# AHMAD IBN IBRAHIM AL-GHAZI (1506–1543)

Ahmad b. Ibrahim al-Ghazi is known in Ethiopian Christian literature as Ahmad Gran, "the left-handed," political leader of an Islamic jihad movement in sixteenth-century Ethiopia. He rose to power in the context of a century-old struggle for domination in Ethiopia between the Christian emperors who reigned in Ethiopia's central and northern highlands and the rulers of a number of Muslim emirates in that region's eastern high- and lowlands. In the 1510s and 1520s, the emperor Libna Dingil (r. 1508–1540) had managed to overcome the resistance of the Amir of Adal, Garad Abun, as well as of Iman Mahfuz, the Amir of Zaila.

Ahmad b. Ibrahim al-Ghazi grew up in the province of Hubat south of Adal's capital city of Harar and had married Bati Del Wanbara, a daughter of Imam Mahfuz. In the desperate situation of 1527, he was able to unite, under his leadership a number of Somali war bands as well as the forces of the Muslim emirates to defeat an Ethiopian army. With the support of Ottoman artillery, al-Ghazi's army was subsequently able, in 1529, to inflict a crushing defeat upon Ethiopia's united army. Thereupon, he decided to embark on a jihad with the aim to conquer Ethiopia as a whole.

Al-Ghazi led a number of campaigns, recorded by his companion, the Yemenite scholar Shihab al-Din Ahmad b. 'Abd al-Qadir, under the title *Kitab Futuhat al-Habasha al-Musamma Bahjat az-Zaman*. Al-Ghazi's Muslim armies were able to conquer, between 1529 and 1535, almost all the Ethiopian Christian territories, from Showa in the south to Tigray in the north. Ethiopia's transformation into a Muslim imamate was, however, preempted by the intervention of the Portuguese in 1541. Also, Ethiopia's new emperor, Galawdewos (r. 1540–1559), managed to reorganize the Christian forces and to stop al-Ghazi's advance.

In a battle near Woyna Dega, in Dembya province, al-Ghazi was killed by a Portuguese fusilier. The Muslim empire of Ethiopia subsequently disintegrated as quickly as it had been conquered, and most Christians who had converted to Islam after 1529 converted back to Ethiopian Christianity. In the aftermath of al-Ghazi's death, Emperor Galawdewos was able to advance as far as Harar, where he was stopped in 1559 by Imam Nur b. al-Mujahid, al-Ghazi's nephew and successor. Al-Mujahid ruled Adal-Harar until his death in 1568.

*See also* **Africa, Islam in; Ethiopia; Jihad.**

## BIBLIOGRAPHY

Abir, Mordechai. *Ethiopia and the Red Sea: The Rise and Decline of the Solomonic Dynasty and Muslim-European Rivalry in the Region*. London: Frank Cass, 1980.

*Roman Loimeier*

# AHMAD IBN IDRIS (1750–1837)

Ahmad b. Idris was a Sufi teacher who influenced the formation of many reforming Sufi brotherhoods in the nineteenth century.

Although he never formed *tariqa* (brotherhood) of his own, Ibn Idris was a key figure in the development of Sufi thought in the nineteenth century. Being firmly based in traditional Sufism, in the line from Ibn 'Arabi, Ibn Idris promoted the idea of *tariqa* Muhammadiyya—focusing the Sufi experience on following the example of and having mystical encounters with the Prophet—while vehemently rejecting blind imitation (*taqlid*) of earlier scholars. According to his teaching, it is the responsibility of each generation of Muslim scholars to discover the Muslim path by relying directly on the sources of divine revelation and not be restricted to what earlier and fallible human authorities have decreed.

Ibn Idris was born in Maysur, a village near Larache in Morocco, and received his basic training in the reformist scholarly milieu in Fez of the late eighteenth century, before moving through Egypt to Mecca in 1799. He stayed in Mecca during the Wahhabi occupation, unlike many colleagues, and had an ambivalent relationship to the Wahhabis; he shared some of their reformist views but rejected their recourse to anathema and violence against other Muslims. After a later disturbance in Mecca, he left in 1828 and settled in Sabya, the capital of 'Asir, then a part of Yemen, where he stayed for the remainder of his life. Several of his students formed important Sufi brotherhoods to disseminate his ideas, among them the Sanusiyya of the Sahara, the Khatmiyya and Rashidiyya/Dandarawiyya of Sudan, Egypt, and the Indian Ocean regions, and the Salihiyya of Somalia.

*See also* **Africa, Islam in; Tariqa; Tasawwuf; Wahhabiyya.**

## BIBLIOGRAPHY

O'Fahey, Rex S. *Enigmatic Saint: Ahmad Ibn Idris and the Idrisi Tradition*. Evanston, Ill.: Northwestern University Press, 1990.

Radtke, Bernd; O'Kane, John; Vikør, Knut S.; and O'Fahey, Rex S. *The Exoteric Ahmad Ibn Idris: A Sufi's Critique of the Madhahib and Wahhabis.* Leiden: Brill, 2000.

Thomassen, Einar, and Radtke, Bernd, eds. *The Letters of Ahmad Ibn Idris.* London: Hurst, 1993.

*Knut S.Vikør*

## AHMAD GRAN *See* **Ahmad Ibn Ibrahim al-Ghazi**

## AHMADIYYA

The Ahmadiyya movement was founded by Mirza Ghulam Ahmad in the Punjab province of British India in 1889, at a time of competition for converts among new Muslim, Hindu, Sikh, and Christian reform and missionary movements. Divisions among Sunni Muslims on appropriate responses following the failure in 1857 of a widespread rebellion against the British were reflected in the growth of new religious movements in the north west, particularly at Deoband and Aligarh. Ghulam Ahmad's claims to be the recipient of esoteric spiritual knowledge, transmitted to him through visions, attracted attention in such a setting. Doctrinally, he aroused hostility among Sunnis mainly because of his own claim to prophethood. His definition of jihad as concerned with "cleansing of souls," rather than with military struggle, was less controversial at a stage when most Muslims had accepted the practical necessity of acquiesence to British rule. Some have viewed the insights that drew disciples to him as sufistic in essence, though his denunciation of rivals caused detractors to question the spirituality of the movement.

In 1889, shortly after publishing his first book *Al-Barahin al-Ahmadiyya* (Ahmadiyya proofs; 4 vols, 1880–1884), Ghulam Ahmad began to initiate disciples. His claims two years later that he was both *masih* (messiah) and *mahdi* (rightly guided one), and subsequent claims to powers of prophethood, caused outrage among Muslims, which was expressed in tracts and newspapers and in *fatawa* condemning him for denying the doctrine of *khatm al-nabuwwa* (finality of Muhammad's prophethood). Public controversies also marked relations with his non-Muslim rivals, notably the Arya Samaj Hindu revivalist leaders with whom he clashed frequently, especially after he claimed to be an avatar of Krisna, and with Protestant Christian missionaries in the Punjab. Christians objected to his view that Jesus had died naturally in Kashmir, and that Ghulam Ahmad was the promised "second messiah." He cultivated good relations, however, with the British colonial authorities who appreciated his advocacy of loyalty to the Raj. Although his personal dynamism, including the fear he inspired through the issuing of death prophecies, was responsible for his notoriety among his Punjab enemies, it also drew many initiates, mainly from Sunni Islam. On his death, a disciple, Maulvi Nur al-Din, became his *khalifa* (successor; 1908–1914).

The movement took stronger institutional form on 27 December 1891, when Ghulam Ahmad called the first annual gathering at Qadiyan, subsequently the center for all Ahmadi activities. Newspapers were soon established, including *Al-Hakam* (1897) and *The Review of Religions* (1902). Directed by Ghulam Ahmad that Ahmadis should demand separate categorization from Sunnis in the 1901 census, and that non-Ahmadi Muslims were *kafir*s (unbelievers), that intensified Sunni hostility. The community nevertheless prospered. Although scorned for their allegedly low social origins, many Ahmadis were of middle-class professional status (landowners, entrepreneurs, doctors, and lawyers). Those of lower origins took advantage of opportunities offered within the community to raise their educational level and hence status. Many Ahmadi women were well educated. Numbers rose to approximately nineteen thousand in Punjab by 1911, rising to about twenty-nine thousand by 1921. Careful marriage arrangements, as well as missionary activity, helped increase the membership, which then spread outside India, particularly in Africa and Southeast Asia, through well-organized overseas missionary programs.

A split in 1914 divided the movement in the Punjab but did not obstruct progress, for those who remained at Qadiyan, and the new, Lahore-based, secessionary branch, continued to use similar missionary and disciplinary methods to consolidate their communities. Differing mainly on understandings of Ghulam Ahmad's status, the Qadiyanis retained the caliphal leadership, whose incumbents (since 1914 the sons and grandsons of Ghulam Ahmad) have reinforced belief in the founder's prophetic claims. The Lahoris, organized as the Ahmadiyya Anjuman-e Isha 'at-e Islam, regarded Ghulam Ahmad as the "*mujaddid* [reformer] of the fourteenth century," and are less easily distinguishable from Sunni Muslims, except in holding Ghulam Ahmad to have been the "promised messiah." The crucial difference over prophethood has maintained the separate identities of the branches wherever Ahmadiyya has since spread, although missionary work among non-Muslims, especially overseas, tends to stress common ground in Islam. While Ghulam Ahmad's direct successors, notably his son, the second caliph, Bashir al-Din Mahmud Ahmad, together with Sir Muhammad Zafrullah Khan, have contributed the most influential publications to Qadiyani proselytism, the Lahoris received notable intellectual and missionary leadership from Maulana Muhammad 'Ali in the Punjab, and Khwaja Kamal al-Din in London.

During the period of overt nationalist struggle in India in the 1920s and 1930s some Lahoris began to support wider

Members of the Muslim Ahmadiyya group, including their leader, Hazrat Mirza Tahir Ahmad Khalifatul Masih IV, left, begin the Initiation ceremony at an international Ahmadiyya convention in Germany in 2001. In the late nineteenth century, Ahmadiyya's founder, Mirza Ghulam Ahmad, started this branch of Islam after claiming to be a prophet who received spiritual visions. AP/WIDE WORLD PHOTOS

Indian-Muslim agendas. Even though Zafrullah Khan was made president of the Muslim League conference in 1931, most Qadiyanis maintained their strong pro-British stance while clashing verbally and violently with some militant Sunni movements, notably the Ahrars. Yet both groups' generally loyal stance ensured them considerable practical protection against possible recriminations from Muslims while colonial rule lasted.

Independence and Partition brought new problems for both groups. When the Gurdaspur district was allotted to India many Qadiyanis migrated to Pakistan, where they established a new headquarters at Rabwa. Pakistan has not proved congenial to the interests of either branch, although Zafrullah Khan was made Pakistan foreign minister and others initially gained important posts in the civil service, army, and air force. Latent antagonism escalated during the constitution-making controversies of the late 1940s, coming to a head in 1953 when anti-Ahmadiyya riots, encouraged by ulema seeking the constitutional declaration of Ahmadis as non-Muslims, resulted in many deaths. Although the government fell and a judicial inquiry condemned the attacks,

continual pressure on the community culminated in the National Assembly's declaration of the Ahmadis as non-Muslim in 1974. The military rule of Zia ul-Haq, which favored Islamization policies on a narrowly Sunni basis, proved disadvantageous to all minorities: His Ordinance XX of April 1984 prohibited Ahmadis from calling themselves Muslim. Subsequent prohibitions, notably on publishing, and on calling their places of worship mosques, have severely restricted Ahmadi religious life in Pakistan. The head of the Rabwa community, the fourth *khalifa*, Mirza Tahir Ahmad, migrated to London in the mid-1980s, after which many South Asian Ahmadis have settled outside the subcontinent, thereby strengthening the generally economically prosperous Ahmadi missionary communities, belonging to both branches, which were already established in many parts of Africa, in Fiji, and in Southeast Asia, as well as in North America and Europe. Although both branches report growth, there are no reliable statistics on numbers and distribution. Both branches continue to publish prolifically, but there has been little scholarly evaluation of academic and institutional developments, most accounts using the general term *Ahmadi* to describe both branches.

*See also* **Ahmad, Mirza Ghulam; Pakistan, Islamic Republic of; South Asia, Islam in.**

BIBLIOGRAPHY

Ahmad, Hazrat Mirza Ghulam. *Islami usul ki filasafi*, (1896). Translated by Muhammad Zafrulla Khan as *The Philosophy of the Teachings of Islam*. Tilford, Surrey, U.K.: Islam International Publications Ltd., 1996.

Friedmann, Yohanan. *Prophecy Continuous: Aspects of Ahmadi Religious Thought and its Medieval Background*. Berkeley, Los Angeles, and London: University of California Press, 1989.

Jones, Kenneth W. *Socio-Religious Reform Movements in British India*. Cambridge, U.K.: Cambridge University Press, 1989.

Khan, Sir Muhammad Zafrullah. *Ahmadiyyat: The Renaissance of Islam*. London: Tabshir Publications, 1978.

Lavan, Spencer. *The Ahmadiyah Movement: A History and Perspective*. Delhi: Manohar Book Service, 1974.

*Avril A. Powell*

# AHMAD KHAN, (SIR) SAYYID (1817–1898)

Sayyid Ahmad Khan was an educational and political leader of Muslims who were living under British rule in India. He developed concepts of religious modernism and community identity that mark the transition from Mogul India to the rise of representative government and the quest for self-determination. Born and educated in Delhi in the surviving remnant of the Mogul regime, Sayyid Ahmad embarked on a career in the British subordinate judicial service, the lower-level law courts where Indian judges presided and cases were conducted in Indian languages, and was posted in a series of north Indian towns and cities. During these years he published historical and religious texts and was one of the pioneers of the printing of Urdu prose. He remained loyal to the British during the 1857 revolt, and worked to reconcile Indian, Muslim, and British institutions and ideologies. In 1864, he founded the Scientific Society in Ghazipur (shifted the following year to Aligarh), which was devoted to translating practical and scientific works into Urdu. In 1869, he traveled to England to write a defense of the life of the Prophet and to examine British educational institutions. While in England, he conceived the idea of founding a residential college primarily for Muslims and devoted the rest of his life to the cause of the Muhammadan Anglo-Oriental College, Aligarh, which was founded in 1875. During this period, he became a prolific writer on religious, social, and political issues. In 1887, he announced his opposition to the Indian National Congress on the grounds that representative government was not in the best interests of Muslims. Knighted by the British in 1888, he left a legacy of political separatism

that future generations transformed into a movement for the creation of Pakistan as a separate state for South Asian Muslims.

*See also* **Aligarh; Education; Liberalism, Islamic; Modernism; Modern Thought; Pakistan, Islamic Republic of; South Asia, Islam in; Urdu Language, Literature, and Poetry.**

BIBLIOGRAPHY

Lelyveld, David. *Aligarh's First Generation: Muslim Solidarity in British India*. 2d ed. New Delhi: Oxford University Press, 1996.

Troll, Christian W. *Sayyid Ahmad Khan: A Reinterpretation of Muslim Theology*. New Delhi: Vikas Publishing House, 1978.

*David Lelyveld*

# AHMAD, MIRZA GHULAM (LATE 1830s–1908)

Mirza Ghulam Ahmad was born into a landowning Sunni family at Qadiyan in Gurdaspur district, Punjab, northwest India. He initiated disciples into his Ahmadiyya movement in 1889, after announcing that messages received in visions designated him the *mujaddid* (renewer of Islam) for the age. He also claimed to be the *masih-i maw'ud* (promised Messiah), and the *mahdi* (rightly guided one), and to have powers of miracle and prophecy. Most Sunni Muslims deemed such a denial of *khatm al-nubuwwa* (finality of Muhammad's prophethood) heretical, but his movement grew to nearly twenty thousand adherents in his lifetime. He was succeeded in 1908 by the first *khalifa* of the Ahmadiyya movement, Maulawi Nur al-Din.

*See also* **Ahmadiyya.**

BIBLIOGRAPHY

Ahmad, Hazrat Mirza Ghulam. *Islami usul ki filasafi*. (1896). Translated by Muhammad Zafrulla Khan as *The Philosophy of the Teachings of Islam*. Tilford, Surrey, U.K.: Islam International Publications Ltd., 1996.

Friedmann, Yohanan. *Prophecy Continuous: Aspects of Ahmadi Religious Thought and its Medieval Background*. Berkeley, Los Angeles, and London: University of California Press, 1989.

*Avril A. Powell*

# 'A'ISHA (614–678 C.E.)

'A'isha bint Abi Bakr was the favorite wife of the prophet Muhammad and a significant religious and political figure in early Islam. The daughter of Umm Ruman and one of the Prophet's companions, Abu Bakr (the first caliph of Islam after the death of the Prophet), she married Muhammad at a young age. Her intelligence, beauty, and spirited personality are well recorded in historical sources.

The hadith tradition records a unique level of intimacy shared by the Prophet and 'A'isha. They bathed in the same water, he prayed while she lay stretched out in front of him, he received revelation when they were under the same blanket, and he expressed a desire to be moved to 'A'isha's chambers when he knew his death was approaching. Affection and playfulness also characterized their relationship. They raced with each other and enjoyed listening to the singing of Ethiopian musicians together. The Prophet related that when 'A'isha was pleased with him, she would swear "By the God of Muhammad" and when she was annoyed with him she would swear "By the God of Abraham." She regularly engaged the Prophet on issues of revelation and religion. Recognizing her intelligence and perceptiveness, he told the Muslims "Take two-thirds of your religion from al-Humayra," the term of affection referring to the rosy-cheeked 'A'isha.

A scandal once surrounded 'A'isha, who was mistakenly left behind during a caravan rest stop on an expedition with the Prophet. She returned to Medina escorted by a young man who had found her waiting alone. Amid the ensuing gossip and speculation about 'A'isha's fidelity, one of the Prophet's companions, 'Ali, advised Muhammad to divorce her. This caused her to bear deep resentment against 'Ali, which manifested itself in her later opposition to him as Muhammad's successor. Finally a Qur'anic revelation exonerated her of all suspected wrongdoing, proclaiming her innocence. This same revelation established the punishment for false accusations of adultery.

In the lifetime of the Prophet she, together with Muhammad's other wives, was referred to as "Mother of the Believers." She is known to have transmitted approximately 1,210 traditions (hadiths), only 300 of which are included in the canonical hadith collections of Bukhari and Muslim. She is said to have transmitted hadith to at least eighty-five Muslims, as well as to have corrected inaccuracies in the hadiths reported by some of the Prophet's male companions.

After the death of the Prophet, she was critical of the third caliph, 'Uthman, but also called his killers to accountability during the caliphate of 'Ali. Together with the Companions Zubair and Talha, she mobilized opposition to 'Ali, culminating in the Battle of the Camel (656 C.E.). The name of the battle reflects the centrality of 'A'isha's role in the conflict, seated on her camel in the middle of the battlefield. This struggle over succession marked the development of a major civil war (called *fitna*) in Islam, which ultimately contributed to one of the most significant religious and political divisions in the Muslim world. The representations of 'A'isha in subsequent Shi'ite and Sunni polemics reflected some of the

historical antagonisms between the two. Many Shi'ite Muslims reviled 'A'isha, whereas Sunni Muslims embraced her as a revered wife of the Prophet. Tradition holds that she was consulted on theological, legal, and other religious issues, and was also known for her poetic skills. She is buried at al-Baqi in Medina.

*See also* **'Ali; Bukhari, al-; Fitna; Muhammad; Shi'a: Early; Sunna.**

## BIBLIOGRAPHY

Abbott, Nabia. *'A'ishah: The Beloved of Muhammad.* Chicago: University of Chicago Press, 1942.

Mernissi, Fatima. *The Veil and the Male Elite: A Feminist Interpretation of Women's Rights in Islam.* Reading, Mass: Addison Wesley, 1992.

Spellberg, Denise A. *Politics Gender and the Islamic Past: The Legacy of 'A'isha Bint Abi Bakr.* New York: Columbia University Press, 1994.

*Sa'diyya Shaikh*

# AKBAR (1542–1605)

Jalal al-Din Akbar was born in 1542 as his father Humayun fled India before the forces of the Afghan warlord Sher Shah Sur. After thirteen years of exile, his father returned to rule India, but died in a fall in a matter of months. Akbar came to the throne at the age thirteen in 1555. He ruled until his own death in 1605.

Akbar's reputation as the true founder of the Mogul empire rests partly on his own reign of fifty years and partly on the writings of Abu 'l-Fazl, a loyal companion who was Akbar's ardent supporter. Abu 'l-Fazl's *A'in-i Akbari* and *Akbarnamah* presented the image of Akbar as a political genius. Abu 'l-Fazl saw Akbar as the "perfect man" (*insan-i kamil*) of Sufi lore: a master of both the temporal and spiritual realms. He, therefore, inflated Akbar's reputation whenever possible.

In practical terms, Akbar adopted some of the administrative practices of the defeated Sher Shah. As the influence of his grandfather and father's aging courtiers declined, Akbar was free to recruit a new corps of advisors, like Abu 'l-Fazl. These advisors depended on his patronage for their own status. During Akbar's reign, India saw an influx of silver bullion as European traders began massive purchases of Indian cloth. Because of the cash nexus created by increased commerce, Akbar was able to manage a system in which officials received salaries either directly from the imperial treasury or through assignments of the government's revenue allotment from the capitol of the province for specific districts. The central authority gained an unprecedented degree of control over state officials. Akbar's reputation was further enhanced as the British came to rule India. They saw him as a model for their own style of rule: religiously neutral, but strict in his assertion of central power.

*See also* **Empires: Mogul; South Asia, Islam in.**

## BIBLIOGRAPHY

Alam, Muzaffar, and Subrahmanyam, Sanjay, eds. *The Mughal State 1526–1750*. New Delhi: Oxford University Press, 1998.

*Gregory C. Kozlowski*

# AKHBARIYYA

Akhbariyya was a movement in Twelver Shi'ism that emphasized a return to the sources of the law (Qur'an and hadith). Hadith in Twelver Shi'ism include accounts of the sayings and actions of the imams (normally termed *akhbar*). The Akhbariyya styled themselves as followers of the imams (through the *akhbar*) that record their rulings, rather than the interpretations of these texts by later scholars. The origins of the Akhbari movement are a debated point both within the Twelver tradition, and among Western commentators. The Akhbaris themselves, however, see their movement as the original Shi'ism, which was later corrupted by scholars who had imitated Sunni methods of jurisprudence. Their opponents, termed Usulis (or in some texts, *mujtahids*), considered the Akhbaris an innovative movement (*bid'a*), arising in the sixteenth century with the work of Muhammad Amin al-Astarabadi (d. 1626). There is evidence to support both interpretations of the movement's origins. Early Muslim heresiographical works, such as Shahrastani's *Kitab al-milal wa al-nihal* (c. 1127), talk of the division of the *imamiyya* into *mu'taziliyya* and *akhbariyya*. Whether these early Akhbaris can be linked to the later, better-defined, movement is unclear.

In biographical works, Astarabadi is normally described as the founder of the movement, though Astarabadi viewed himself as its "reviver." He was followed by a number of scholars who explicitly identified themselves with the Akhbariyya. What united these scholars was a call for the return to the sources in a belief that the meaning of the imams' words and actions was readily available, but had been lost by centuries of excessive interpretation. They identified this excessive interpretation with the introduction of the doctrine of *ijtihad* into Shi'ite legal thinking by al-'Allama al-Hilli (d.1325). Akhbaris also criticized other juristic practices linked with the theory of *ijtihad*. In particular, they viewed the "canonical four books" of Twelver Shi'ite hadith as containing only "sound" (*sahih*) traditions. They believed that the

hadith in these books should not be examined by the traditional means of establishing historical accuracy. Furthermore, the Akhbariyya maintained that these traditions were never ambiguous in meaning, and were in no need of interpretation. In this sense, the Akhbariyya can be viewed as literalist, or even fundamentalist.

The Akhbariyya drew on the diverse areas of Safavid Twelver intellectual life. There were Akhbaris who were influenced by mysticism and philosophy, such as Muhammad Taqi al-Majlisi (d. 1659/1660) and Muhsin Fayd al-Kashani (d. 1680), as well as the stricter, more legalistic manifestations of Shi'ism, such as Mulla Muhammad Tahir Qummi (d. 1686) and al-Hurr al-Amili (d. 1693). What they shared was a common attitude toward the manner in which the *shari'a* might be known. They were, then, in the main a movement of law, and often referred to themselves as a *madhhab* (school of law). As an intellectual force, the Akhbariyya died out in Iran and Iraq in the early nineteenth century, though they continued for a short time thereafter to be influential in India. Even today, there continue to be scholars who follow a methodology similar to Akhbarism in the Shi'ite world, particularly in the Persian Gulf area and southern Iran.

*See also* **Law; Mu'tazilites, Mu'tazila; Shi'a: Imami (Twelver).**

## BIBLIOGRAPHY

Gleave, Robert. *Inevitable Doubt: Two Theories of Shi'i Jurisprudence*. Leiden: E. J. Brill, 2000.

Tabataba'i, H. Modarresssi. "Rationalism and Traditionalism in Shi'i Jurisprudence." *Studia Islamica* 59 (1984): 141–158.

*Robert Gleave*

# AKHLAQ

*Akhlaq*, the plural form of *khuluq*, refers to innate disposition or character and, by extension in Muslim thought, to ethics. In the Qur'an the term is used to refer to the prophet Muhammad's exemplary ethical character (68:4). The Qur'an also emphasizes the significance of ethically guided action as the underpinning for a committed Muslim life. Qur'anic ethics emphasize in particular the dignity of the human being, accountability, justice, care and compassion, stewardship of society and the environment, and the obligation to family life and values. Faith and ethics are thus intertwined in the Qur'an and linked further to the Prophet as a moral exemplar.

In elaborating and further developing ethical thought, Muslims, throughout history, developed a diverse set of expressions: philosophical, theological, legal, and literary.

These expressions were framed within a context of vigorous intellectual debate and in interaction with the legacies of many ancient traditions, including the works attributed to Aristotle and Plato, and Iranian, Indian, Jewish, and Christian thought.

The Muslim philosophical tradition of ethics developed an intellectual framework for rationally grounded moral action. Some of the key thinkers who contributed to this were al-Farabi (d. 950), Ibn Miskawayh (d. 1030), Ibn Sina (d. 1037), and Nasir al-Din Tusi (d. 1273/74). Their works in turn influenced other major figures, including the Sunni scholar al-Ghazali (d. 1111), who did not always agree with them. The philosophical tradition, in common with other early groups such as the Mu'tazila and the Shi'a, emphasized reason and logic in arguing for a universal ethical framework. Ethical action in their view did not oppose religiously grounded ethics, rather it sought to enhance their meaning and appreciation by philosophical reasoning and took account of personal and social, as well as political, virtues. Al-Farabi's classic al-Madinah al-Fadilah (The excellent city) explores the ideals of a political community that produces the greatest good for all its citizens.

Muslim legal tradition also developed a framework for guiding individual and social behavior. In Muslim law (shari'a) jurists classified acts according to their moral value, ranging from obligatory, meritorious, indifferent, disapproved, and the forbidden. All actions thus fell within these normatively and juristically defined categories and provided religiously defined prescriptions that could be enacted at a personal as well as a social level to followers by scholars trained in jurisprudence and religious sciences.

Mystically grounded ethics as developed in the Sufi tradition emphasized the necessity of an inner orientation and awareness for guiding human action, leading to greater intimacy, knowledge, and personal experience of the divine. Ethical acts were linked to spiritual development, and Sufi teachers wrote manuals, guides, and literary works to illustrate the way—tariqa—which represented, in their view, the inner dimension of outward acts.

In the modern period, as Muslims have come into greater contact with each other and with the rest of the world, their ethical legacy, while still continuing to be influential in its traditional forms, is also being challenged to address emerging issues, changing needs, and social transition. Muslim scholars are debating and formulating responses to a variety of issues, prominent among which are the ethical bases of political, social, and legal governance; the ethics of a just economic order; family life; war and peace; biomedical ethics; human rights and freedoms; the ethics of life; and the broader question raised by globalization, degradation of the environment, and the uses and abuses of technology.

*See also* **Adab; Ethics and Social Issues; Falsafa.**

## BIBLIOGRAPHY

Cook, Michael. *Commanding Right and Forbidding Wrong in Islamic Thought.* New York: Cambridge University Press, 2000.

Izutsu, Toshihiko. *Ethno-Religious Concepts in the Quran.* Montreal: McGill University Press, 1966

*Azim Nanji*

## AKHUND *See* Molla

## 'ALI (600–661)

'Ali ibn Talib, born in Mecca about 600 C.E., was the cousin and son-in-law of the prophet Muhammad, father of the Prophet's grandsons Hasan and Husayn, and fourth caliph (656–661) of the Muslim *umma* (community of believers).

At a very young age, 'Ali was adopted by Muhammad, who brought him up like his own son. When Muhammad received the divine revelation, 'Ali was still a very young boy. He was the first male to accept Islam, and to dedicate all his life to the cause of Islam. 'Ali's courage became legendary because he led several important missions.

At the Prophet's death, the community split into two major groups contending for political succession. During a gathering of the *ansar* (helpers), Abu Bakr was elected first caliph. A group led by 'Ali and his supporters (Zubayr, Talha, Miqdad, Salman al-Farsi, and Abu Dharr Ghifari, among others) held that 'Ali was the legitimate heir of the Prophet. To preserve the unity of the Muslim *umma*, 'Ali is said to have kept a low profile and concentrated his efforts on religious matters. The first version of the Qur'an was attributed to him by some of his contemporaries. In the period preceding his caliphate, 'Ali, known for his learning in Qur'an and sunna, had given advice on secular and spiritual matters. On several occasions, he disagreed with Uthman (the third caliph) and criticized him on the application of certain Islamic principles.

Following Uthman's murder, the *ansar* invited 'Ali to accept the caliphate and he agreed only after a long hesitation. All through his brief governing period, 'Ali faced strong opposition. First he was opposed by 'A'isha, Muhammad's wife, but the strongest opposition came from Mu'awiya, who had his stronghold in Syria. Two companions of the Prophet, Talha and Zubayr, already frustrated in their political ambitions, were further disappointed by 'Ali, in their efforts to secure for themselves the governorships of Basra and Kufa. Thus they broke with him and asked to bring Uthman's murderers to trial. 'Ali appointed 'Abd Allah b. 'Abbas governor of Basra, and went to Kufa in order to gain support against Mu'awiya. He formed a diverse coalition, comprised of men like 'Ammar b. Yasir, Qays b. Sa'd b. 'Ubada, Malik Ashtar, and Ash'at b. Qays Kindi.

'Ali opened negotiations with Mu'awiya, hoping to gain his allegiance. Mu'awiya insisted on Syrian autonomy under his own leadership. Thus he mobilized his Syrian supporters and refused to pay homage to 'Ali, on the pretext that his people had not participated in his election. After a few months of confrontation, 'Amr b. 'As advised Mu'awiya to have his soldiers raise parchments inscribed with verses of the Qur'an on their spearheads; the goal was to bring about the cessation of hostilities between the people of Iraq, who formed the bulk of 'Ali's army, and the people of Syria. 'Ali saw through the stratagem, but only a minority wanted to pursue the fight. Hence he ended the fight and sent Ash'at b. Qays to find out Mu'awiya's intentions. Mu'awiya suggested that each side should choose an arbiter; together, the two men would reach a decision based on the Qur'an. This decision would then be binding on both parties. 'Amr b. 'As, the Syrian representative, and Abu Musa Ash'ari, the Iraqi representative, met to draft an agreement, but in the meantime 'Ali's coalition began to collapse. The arbiters and other eminent persons met at Adruh in January 659 to discuss the selection of the new caliph. Both parties agreed to the choice of 'Ali and Mu'awiya and were willing to submit the selection of the new caliph to an electorate body (shura). In the public declaration that followed, Abu Musa kept his part of the agreement, but 'Amr b. 'As deposed 'Ali and declared Mu'awiya caliph.

Meanwhile, Mu'awiya had followed an aggressive course of action by making incursions into the heart of Iraq and Arabia. By the end of 660 'Ali, who was regarded as caliph only by a diminishing number of partisans, lost control of Egypt and Hijaz. He was struck with a poisoned sword by a Kharijite named 'Abd-al-Rahman b. Muljam while praying in a mosque at Kufa. 'Ali died at the age of sixty-three and was buried near Kufa in late January 661. 'Ali's death brought to an end the era of Rashidun, the four "rightly-guided" caliphs. The Sunnis believe that the order of merit corresponds to the chronological historical order of succession of the four first caliphs (Abu Bakr, 'Umar, 'Uthman, and 'Ali). The Shi'ites preferred 'Ali over the first three caliphs; they never accepted Mu'awiya or any later caliphs, and took the name shi'at 'Ali, or 'Ali's Party.

Several places are mentioned as 'Ali's shrine. But most Shi'ite scholars are in agreement that 'Ali was buried in Ghari, west of Kufa, at the site of present-day Najaf. These scholars explained the discrepancies among the various reports by maintaining that 'Ali himself requested to be buried in a secret place so as to prevent his enemies from desecrating

Although many Muslims forbid representing the Prophet and his family in images, this fresco depicts 'Ali ibn Abi Talib, fourth caliph of Islam, and the cousin and brother-in-law of Muhammad. Muhammad raised 'Ali like a son, and 'Ali became the first male to accept Islam. Here, 'Ali holds the body of an imam killed during political power struggles after Muhammad's death. © SEF/Art Resource, NY

his grave. Under the Safavid Empire, his grave became the focus of much devoted attention, exemplified in the pilgrimage made by Shah Isma'il I (d. 1524) to Najaf and Karbala. Today a gold-plated dome rises above 'Ali's tomb. The interior is decorated with polished silver, mirror work, and ornamental tiles. A silver tomb rises over the grave itself, and the courtyard has two minarets. The recitation of special prayers over 'Ali's grave is considered particularly beneficial in view of 'Ali's role as intercessor on the Day of Judgment. Sunni polemicists have often accused the Shi'ites of preferring pilgrimages to the tombs of 'Ali and other imams over the pilgrimage to Mecca.

It is important to note that 'Ali's position became important to different groups of Muslims starting from the early period. For the Shi'a, he is said to have participated in the Prophet's ascension (mi'raj) to heaven and acquired several honorific titles. The 'Alya'iyya believed in the divinity of Muhammad and 'Ali, and gave preference in divine matters to 'Ali. Among Sufis he is renowned as a great Sufi saint for his piety and poverty as well as the possessor of esoteric knowledge. The early Shi'ite traditions regarded 'Ali as the most judicious of the Companions and the Prophet nicknamed him

Abu Turab (Father of Dust) because he saw him sleeping in the courtyard of the mosque. Some sources agree that 'Ali was a profoundly religious man, devoted to the cause of Islam and the rule of justice in accordance with the Qur'an and the sunna.

One of the basic differences between Shi'ism and Sunnism concerns the question of the respective roles of 'Ali (and the other imams) on the one hand, and Muhammad on the other. Shi'ism shares with Sunnism the belief that Muhammad, as seal of the prophets, was the last to have received revelation (*wahy*). Classical Shi'ite doctrine holds that 'Ali and the other imams were the recipients of inspiration (*ilham*). But it is only the legislative prophecy that has come to an end, that is, the previous prophets such as Abraham, Moses, Jesus, and Muhammad, the last of the legislative prophets, introduced a new religious law while abrogating the previous one; the guidance of humanity must continue under the *walaya* (Institution of the Friends of God) of an esoteric prophecy (*Nubuwa batiniyya*). Thus 'Ali, the first imam, is designated as the foundation (*asas*) of the imamate. He is the possessor of a divine light (*nur*) passed on from Muhammad to him, and later from him on to the other imams. The Sunnis believe that the Prophet did not explicitly name his successor after his death; the Shi'ites, on the contrary, hold that he explicitly named his successor 'Ali at Ghadir Khumm, an oasis between Mecca and Medina.

According to the Shi'a, a passage in the Qur'an (2:118) shows that the imamate is a divine institution; the possessor thereof must be from the seed of Ibrahim: "And when his Lord tested Abraham with certain words, and he fulfilled them. He said, 'Behold, I make you a leader [imam] for the people.' Said he, 'And of my seed?'" Even the Sunnis hold that the true caliph can only be one of the Quraysh tribe, but based on this verse the Shi'a maintain that the divinely appointed leader must himself be impeccable (*ma'sum*). The primeval creation of 'Ali is therefore a principle of the Shi'ite faith. According to them, as expressed by Muhammad Baqir Majlisi (d. 1698), Muhammad explicitly designated (*nass jali*) 'Ali as his successor by God's command:

> When the ceremonies of the pilgrimage were completed, the Prophet, attended by 'Ali and the Muslims, left Mecca for Medina. On reaching Ghadir Khumm, he [the Prophet] halted, although that place had never before been a halting place for caravans. The reason for the halt was that verses of the Qur'an had come upon him, commanding him to establish 'Ali in the Caliphate. Before this he had received similar messages, but had not been instructed explicitly as to the time for 'Ali's appointment. He had delayed because of opposition that might occur. But if the crowd of pilgrims had gone beyond Ghadir Khumm they would have separated and the different tribes would have gone in various directions. This is why Muhammad ordered them to assemble here, for he had things to say to 'Ali which he wanted all to hear. The message that came from the

Most High was this: "O Apostle, declare all that has been sent down to thee from thy Lord. No part of it is to be withheld. God will protect you against men, for he does not guide the unbelievers" (5:71). Because of this positive command to appoint 'Ali as his successor, and perceiving that God would not countenance further delay, he and his company dismounted in this unusual stopping place. The day was hot and he told them to stand under shelter of some thorn trees . . . when the crowd had all gathered, Muhammad walked up on to the platform of saddles and called 'Ali to stand at his right. After a prayer of thanks he spoke to the people, informing them that he had been forewarned of his death, and saying, "I have been summoned to the Gate of God, and I shall soon depart to God, to be concealed from you, and bidding farewell to this world. I am leaving you the Book of God [Qur'an], and if you follow this you will not go astray. And I am leaving you also the members of houschold [*ahl al-bayt*], who are not to be separated from the Book of God until they meet me at the drinking fountain of Kawthar." He then called out, "Am I not, more precious to you than your own lives?" They said "Yes." Then it was that he took 'Ali's hands and raised them so high that he showed the whites of his armpits, and said, "Whoever has me as his master (*mawla*) has 'Ali as his master. Be friend to his friend, O Lord, and be an enemy to his enemies. Help those who assist him and frustrate those who oppose him." (Donaldson, p. 5)

This *sura* concluded the revelation: "This day I have perfected your religion for you, and have filled up the measure of my favors upon you, and it is my pleasure that Islam be your religion" (5:5). The event of Ghadir Khumm is not denied by Sunnis but interpreted differently by them. For the Sunnis, Muhammad wanted only to honor 'Ali. They understood the term *mawla* in the sense of friend, whereas the Shi'a recognized 'Ali as their master; the spiritual authority of 'Ali was passed afterward to his direct descendants, the rightful guides (*imams*). The successor of the Prophet, for the Sunnis, is his *khalifa* (caliph), the guardian of religious law (*shari'a*), while for the Shi'ites, the successor is the inheritor (*wasi*) of his esoteric knowledge and the interpreter, par excellence, of the Qur'an. Since Muhammad was the last Prophet who closed the prophetic cycle, the Shi'a believe that humanity still needs spiritual guidance: the cycle of imamate must succeed the cycle of prophecy. Another tradition gives us some insight into the key role of 'Ali, based on the status of Aaron: "O people, know that what Aaron was to Moses, 'Ali is to me, except that there shall be no prophet after me." (Poonawala and Kohlberg, p. 842). The imamate is a cardinal principle of Shi'ite faith. It is only through the imam that true knowledge can be obtained. 'Ali, as the *Wasi*, assisted Muhammad in his task. The Prophet received the revelation (*tanzil*) and established the religious law (*shari'a*), while 'Ali, the repository of the Prophet's knowledge, provided its spiritual exegesis (*ta'wil*). Thus the imamate, the heart of Shi'ism, is closely tied to 'Ali's spiritual mission. For Sunnis, the imamate is necessary because of the revelation and is considered a law among the laws of religion. For them, the imamate is not part of the principles of religion and belief, whereas for Shi'ites, the imamate is a rational necessity and an obliged grace (*lutf wajib*).

From the beginning, Shi'ite Islam has emphasized the importance of human intellect placed in the service of faith. The origins of the encouragement given to intellect goes back to 'Ali the commander of the faithful (*amir al-mu'minin*). According to a saying attributed to him, there is an intimate bond between intellect and faith: "Intellect [*'aql*] in the heart is like a lamp in the center of the house" (Amir-Moezzi, p. 48). The heart's eye of the faithful can see the divine light (*nur*) when there is no longer anyone between God and him; it is when God showed Himself to him, since *'aql* is the interior guide (*imam*) of the believer.

In early Sufi circles, 'Ali was especially renowned for his piety and poverty. He is said to have dressed simply. His biographies abound in statements about his austerity, rigorous observance of religious duties, and detachment from worldly goods. He is also described as the most knowledgeable of the Companions, in terms of both theological questions and matters of positive law. Abu al-Qasim al-Junayd (d. 910) considered 'Ali as his "master in the roots and branches [of religious knowledge] and in perseverance in the face of hardship" (Poonawala and Kohlberg, p. 846). With the growth of Sufi doctrine in the tenth and eleventh centuries, increasing emphasis was placed on 'Ali's possession of a knowledge imparted directly by God (*'ilm laduni*). Most of the Sufis believe that each shaykh or *pir* (sage) inherited his knowledge directly from 'Ali. The investment of the cloak as a symbol of the transmission of spiritual powers is closely associated to 'Ali: the two precious things shown to Muhammad during the mystical ascent (*mi'raj*) were spiritual poverty and a cloak that he had placed on 'Ali and his family (Fatima, Hasan, and Husayn).

Sufi orders flourished particularly in Central Asia and Persia; Muslim scholars became imbued with Shi'ite speculative theology and Sufism. One of the earliest representatives of this trend was 'Ali b. Mitham Bahrani (d. 1281), who saw in 'Ali the original shaykh and founder of the mystical tradition. For them 'Ali's mission is seen as the hidden and secret aspect of prophecy. This underlying idea is based on the *Khutbat al-bayan*: "I am the Sign of the All-Powerful. I am the Gnosis of mysteries. I am the companion of the radiance of the divine Majesty. I am the First and the Last, the Manifest and the Hidden. I am the Face of God. I am the mirror of God, the supreme Pen, the Tabula secreta. I am he who in the Gospel is called Elijah. I am he who is in possession of the secret of God's Messenger" (Corbin, p. 49). Or this next one: "I

carried Noah in the ark, I am Jonah's companion in the belly of the fish. I am Khadir, who taught Moses, I am the Teacher of David and Solomon, I am Dhu al-Qarnayn" (Poonawala and Kohlberg, p. 847). According to another tradition (Amir-Moezzi, p. 30), Muhammad and 'Ali were created from the same divine light (*nur*) and remained united in the world of the spirits; only in this world did they separate into individual entities so that mankind might be shown the difference between Prophet and *Wali*. It is only through him that God may be known.

*See also* **Caliphate; Imamate; Shi'a: Early; Succession.**

## BIBLIOGRAPHY

Amir-Moezzi, Mohammad Ali. *The Divine Guide in Early Shi'ism.* Translated by David Streight. Albany, N.Y.: State University of New York, 1994.

Corbin, Henry. *History of Islamic Philosophy.* Translated by Liadain Sherrard and Philip Sherrard. London: Kegan Paul International, 1993.

Donaldson, Dwight M. *The Shi'ite Religion.* London: Luzac, 1933.

Hollister, John. *The Shi'a of India.* London: Luzac, 1955.

Jafri, S. H. M. *The Origins and Early Development of Shi'a Islam.* London and New York: Longman, 1979.

Momen, Moojan. *An Introduction to Shi'i Islam: The History and Doctrines of Twelver Shi'ism.* New Haven, Conn.: Yale University Press, 1985.

Mufid, Shaykh al-. *Kitâb al-Irshâd.* Translated by I. K. A. Howard. New York: Muhammadi Trust, 1981.

Poonawala, Ismail K., and Kohlberg, Etan. "'Ali b. Abi Taleb." In Vol. 1, *Encyclopaedia Iranica.* London and Boston: Routledge & Kegan Paul, 1982.

*Diana Steigerwald*

# ALIGARH

The north Indian city of Aligarh, site of Aligarh Muslim University, has played a leading role in the political life and intellectual history of South Asian Muslims since the middle of the nineteenth century. The importance of Aligarh arose initially under the leadership of Sayyid Ahmad Khan (1817–1898). Through a series of organizations and institutions, the "Aligarh movement" (the social, cultural, and political movement founded by Sayyid Ahmad Khan) sought to prepare Muslims for changes in technology, social life, and politics associated with British rule, the rise of nationalism, and the conditions of modernity. In 1865, Aligarh became the headquarters of the Aligarh Scientific Society, and, in 1875, the Mahomedan Anglo-Oriental College, the forerunner of the university established there in 1920. Aligarh was the first headquarters of the Muslim League, a party established in 1906 to secure recognition of Muslims as a separate political community within India, a concept that ultimately led in 1947 to the partition of India and the creation of Pakistan as a separate nation-state for South Asian Muslims. After partition, the Aligarh Muslim University remained one of a small group of national universities in India.

In its early years, the Aligarh College attracted patronage and recruited students from Muslim communities throughout India, both Sunni and Shiʿa, as well as significant numbers of Hindus. Aside from some short-lived efforts to include Arabic studies and Urdu as a language of instruction, the college followed the standard British imperial curriculum. Official British patronage became more significant after 1887, when Sayyid Ahmad Khan called for Muslim opposition to the newly founded Indian National Congress. In the twentieth century, Aligarh became an arena for opposing political tendencies among Muslims, including supporters of Indian nationalism and international socialism, as well as of Muslim separatism. Aligarh graduates achieved prominence as writers, jurists, and political leaders. At the same time, Aligarh was the target of much opposition, particularly for its association with social reform and religious modernism. In 1906 the Aligarh Zenana Madrasa provided separate education for girls, and became the Aligarh Women's College in 1925.

When Sir Sayyid Ahmad Khan died in 1898, his successors initiated a campaign to establish an autonomous, all-India educational system for Muslims under the auspices of an affiliating university. The university established in 1920, however, was confined to Aligarh and remained under British control. In response, Mohandas K. Gandhi and two Aligarh graduates, the brothers Shaukat ʿAli and Muhammad ʿAli, led a noncooperation campaign that established an alternative nationalist institution, the Jamiʿa Milliʿa Islamiya, outside the campus gates and subsequently relocated to Delhi. In the final years before independence and partition, Aligarh students toured India on behalf of the Pakistan cause, though others devoted themselves to the ideal of a united and secular India.

Zakir Hussain, the first postindependence vice chancellor of Aligarh Muslim University, and later president of India, succeeded in preserving the university's Muslim identity as a way of preparing Muslims for full participation in national life. A center for Urdu writers and historians of Mughal India, many of them Marxists, the university has so far been able to fend off efforts to undermine its role as an national center for Indian Muslims.

*See also* **Ahmad Khan, (Sir) Sayyid; Education; Modernism; Pakistan, Islamic Republic of; South Asia, Islam in; Urdu Language, Literature, and Poetry.**

**BIBLIOGRAPHY**

Graff, Violette. "Aligarh's Long Quest for 'Minority' Status: AMU (Amendment) Act. 1981." *Economic and Political Weekly* 25, no. 32 (1980): 1771–1781.

Hasan, Mushirul. "Nationalist and Separatist Trends in Aligarh, 1915–47." *The Indian Economic and Social History Review* 22, no. 1 (1985): 1–34.

Lelyveld, David. *Aligarh's First Generation: Muslim Solidarity in British India.* 2d ed. New Delhi: Oxford University Press, 1996.

*David Lelyveld*

# ALLAH

*Allah* is the Arabic equivalent of the English word *God*, and is the term employed not only among Arabic-speaking Muslims but by Christians and Jews and in Arabic translations of the Bible. A contraction of *al-ilah*, meaning "the god," Allah is cognate with the generic pan-Semitic designation for "God" or "deity" (Israelite/Canaanite *El*, Akkadian *ilu*) and is particularly close to the common Hebrew term *Elohim* and the less frequent *Eloah*. It is thus, strictly speaking, not a proper name but a title.

In the Islamic context, as in Jewish and Christian usage, Allah refers to the one true God of monotheism. This is how the term occurs in the *shahada* or "profession of faith," the simplest, earliest, and most basic of Islamic creeds, in the first part of which the believer affirms that there is no "god" (*ilah*) but "God" or "the god" (Allah). However, the *shahada* itself seems to imply that Allah was already known to the first audience of the Islamic revelation, and that they were called upon to repudiate other deities. And this is precisely the picture given in the Qurʾan. "If you ask them who created them," the Qurʾan informs the prophet Muhammad regarding his pagan critics, "they will certainly say 'Allah.'" (43:87; compare 10:31; 39:38). Pagan Arabs swore oaths by Allah (as witnessed at 6:109; 16:38; 35:42).

Pre-Islamic Arabs believed in supernatural intercessors with God (10:18; 34:22), for whom they appeared to claim warrant from Allah. (See, for example, 6:148.) Indeed, Allah seems (in their view) to have headed a pantheon of pre-Islamic deities or supernatural beings, not altogether unlike El's rule over the Canaanite pantheon, and, like El, he seems to have been rather distant and aloof. While the data are fragmentary and open to some question, pre-Islamic Arabs seem to have paid more attention to Allah's daughters and to the *jinn* (or genies) than to him. Even the Qurʾan seems to concede genuine existence to a divine retinue (as at 7:191–195; 10:28–29; 25:3). However, just as the Canaanite gods are

This tilework at the tomb of Baba Qasim in Isfahan, Iran, spells Allahu Akbar, or "God is Great." Allah, the Arabic name for God, appears frequently in Islamic art and architecture in calligraphic script. © ROGER WOOD/CORBIS

replaced by an angelic court in Israelite faith, Islam rejects the independent deities of pagan Arabia in favor of a very much subordinated "exalted assembly" (see 37:8; 38:69) that exists to carry out the decrees of the one true God, who is, says the Qur'an, nearer to the individual human than that person's jugular vein (50:16). In this, as in other respects, Islam regards itself as a restoration of the religion taught by earlier prophets but marred by successive human apostasies (see 42:13).

The Qur'an identifies Allah as the creator, sustainer, and sovereign of the heavens and the earth. (See, for example, 13:16; 29:61, 63; 31:25; 39:38; 43:9, 87.) Following the scriptural text, Muslims characterize him by the ninety-nine "most beautiful names" (7:180; 17:110; 20:8), which serve to identify his attributes. (Eventually, repetition of and meditation upon these names became an important practice in the tradition of Sufi mysticism.) They portray a being who is self-sufficient, omnipotent, omniscient, eternal, merciful yet just, benevolent but terrible in his wrath. The picture of Allah in the Qur'an employs distinctly anthropomorphic language (referring, for example, to the divine eyes, hands, and face), which, virtually all commentators have long agreed, are to be taken figuratively.

Allah has revealed himself throughout history via messages to various prophets by means of both the seemingly routine processes of nature and the periodic judgments and catastrophes directed against the rebellious. He will reveal himself even more spectacularly at the end of time when, as judge of humankind, he pronounces doom or blessing upon every individual who has ever lived. The faith of Muhammad

and the Qur'an is centered on absolute "submission" (*islam*) to his will.

The Qur'an describes God as "Allah, one; Allah, the eternal refuge. He does not beget nor is He begotten, and there is none equal to Him" (112:1–4). In subsequent Islamic thought, such straightforward denial of divine family life (probably aimed at both the pre-Islamic pantheon and Christian concepts of God the Father and God the Son) was expanded into a much broader doctrine of the divine unity, denoted by the non-Qur'anic word *tawhid* ("unification" or "making one"). Philosophers and theologians debated such questions as whether God's attributes were identical to God's essence, or whether, being multiple, they must be additional and in a sense external in order not to compromise the utter and absolute simplicity of the divine essence. They debated how the undeniably manifold cosmos had emerged out of the pure oneness of God. The issue of whether God's speech (i.e., the Qur'an) was coeternal with him, or subsidiary and created, rising to political prominence in the second and third centuries after Muhammad. The overwhelming personality depicted in the revelations of Muhammad became the Necessary Existent (*wajib al-wujud*), and the obvious dependence of life on his will (particularly apparent in the harsh desert environment of Arabia) was taken to point to the utter contingency of all creation upon a God who brought it into being out of nothing. Perhaps not unrelated was the rise to dominance in Islam of a doctrine of predestination or determinism, which had obvious roots in the Qur'an itself (as, for example, at 13:27; 16:93; 74:31). In the meantime, though, while the philosophers were elaborating a view of Allah tending to extreme transcendence, Sufi theoreticians were emphasizing his immanence and experiential accessibility and, in practice, often breaking down the barrier between Creator and creatures—and occasionally shocking their fellow Muslims.

The famous "Throne Verse" (2:255) offers a fine summary of basic Islamic teaching regarding God: "Allah! There is no god but he, the Living, the Everlasting. Neither slumber nor sleep seizes him. His are all things in the heavens and the earth. Who is there who can intercede with him, except by his leave? He knows what is before them and what is behind them, while they comprehend nothing of his knowledge except as he wills. His throne extends over the heavens and the earth. Sustaining them does not burden him, for he is the Most High, the Supreme." The depth of Muslim devotion to Allah is apparent virtually everywhere in Islamic life, including even the use of elaborate calligraphic renditions of the word as architectural and artistic ornamentation.

*See also* **Asnam; Qurʾan; Shirk.**

## BIBLIOGRAPHY

Ghazali, al-. *The Incoherence of the Philosophers.* Translated by Michael E. Marmura. Provo, Utah: Brigham Young University Press, 2000.

Rahbar, Daud. *God of Justice: A Study in the Ethical Doctrine of the Qurʾan.* Leiden: E. J. Brill, 1960.

Watt, W. Montgomery. *Islamic Philosophy and Theology: An Extended Survey.* 2d ed. Edinburgh: Edinburgh University Press, 1985.

Williams, Wesley. "Aspects of the Creed of Imam Ahmad ibn Hanbal: A Study of Anthropomorphism in Early Islamic Discourse." *International Journal of Middle East Studies* 34, no. 3 (2002): 441–463.

*Daniel C. Peterson*

## ALMORAVIDS *See* **Moravids**

## AMERICAN CULTURE AND ISLAM

The interface between American culture and Islamic culture in the American Muslim community is a multifaceted issue. Understanding this interface entails exploring the influence of American culture on the Muslim community and how American Muslims view American culture. Another aspect of this interface is the influence of Muslims and Islamic culture on American culture and the American public's perception of Muslims and Islam.

The Muslim community itself is multilayered. A sizable portion of the Muslim community consists of those who do not attend a mosque, associate with other Muslim organizations, and do not practice Islam. This group has little interest in maintaining Islamic culture and, therefore, they are the most willing to assimilate into American culture. For many of them, their identity as American is paramount. This article does not focus on this group, but instead focuses on those Muslims who identify and associate with Muslim groups.

The Muslims who do associate with mosques and Muslim organizations are composed of immigrants (the majority being first generation), the children of immigrants (largely second generation) and converts (largely African American with significant numbers of Caucasian and Hispanic Americans). The dynamics of the interface of American and Islamic culture in these groups differ. First-generation immigrants bring to America a set of customs shaped by the Muslim world, and these customs are affected by the American environment. Converts, already acculturated when they adopt Islam, modify their American culture to fit into the new environment of Islam. The children of immigrants, raised in America, are acculturated to two cultures and they must decide how each one fits.

### American Culture's Impact on Muslims

In the early decades of the Muslim presence in America (1920–1970), Muslim immigrant groups, possibly pressured by the dominant paradigm of the melting pot, allowed for the inclusion of many American cultural practices (e.g. dancing the twist in the youth associations and Saturday night bingo in the mosque). Also, converts to the major heterodoxical Islamic groups, such as the Nation of Islam and the Moorish Science Temple, mixed freely Islamic and American practices (e.g. chairs in the mosque, hymns, and fasting during Christmas).

All of that changed beginning in the 1970s when large waves of newly-arrived, Islamically self-confident immigrants opposed the earlier immigrants's "Americanized" mosques, and convert groups began trying to incorporate "authentic" Islam into their practice. The new paradigm of ethnic pride and multiculturalism gave greater acceptance and legitimacy to the "foreignness" of Muslim practice, and the new powerful trend of Islamic revivalism gave motivation to Muslims to retain their Islamic practice. The overtly American cultural practices disappeared in mosques and Muslim organizations.

Thirty years later, the Muslim community has aged and mellowed, and a new consensus is emerging that American Muslims should adhere to those aspects of Islam that are truly Islamic as opposed to old-world cultural practices, and then allow the adaptation of those aspects of American culture that

Muslim men leave a mosque in Washington, D.C. Muslims who associate with mosques are composed of immigrants, second-generation Americans, and converts to Islam. © CATHERINE KARNO/CORBIS

while in America the mosque is a center of activities with community dinners and festivals with games and gifts for children. American marriages are often events for the entire mosque community, as opposed to the extended family.

The role of the imam in America has likewise changed dramatically. In the Muslim world the imam is simply the prayer leader, but the imam in America serves more as a pastor—much of his time spent in counseling, administering the mosque, and serving as spokesman for the mosque to the wider community.

**Marriage.** Muslim marriage customs in America have changed but not significantly. One major shift is that the signing of the marriage contract is sometimes a public event and not a private family affair as in the Muslim world. The public signing event resembles an American wedding ceremony with some differences—the bride and groom sit and often face the congregation. Signing the contract and the traditional wedding banquet (*walima*) in America often occur on the same occasion, which is not always the case in the Muslim world. Marriage gifts are often brought to the wedding banquet, which is the American custom, as opposed to the Muslim world where gifts are more often brought before the banquet.

Arranged marriages among Muslim immigrants are still common but in many cases the marriage is only half arranged: the son/daughter picks a mate and then informs the parents who begin the process of arranging the marriage. Muslim youth in America are certainly more involved in choosing a mate than their counterparts in the Muslim countries. One of the results is that interethnic marriages are slowly increasing. One of the persistent legal questions in the immigrant community occurs when the son or daughter desires to marry a good Muslim of another ethnic group, and the parents prohibit the marriage. More and more imams are taking the side of the youth and pressuring the parents to relent. The traditional dowry (*mahr*) in America is usually a very reasonable amount whereas in the Muslim world the dowry is often high because of its role in reinforcing status and class. For many individuals, especially those who do not have a family in America, Muslim matchmaking services are very popular. The matrimonial sections in Muslim magazines are widely used and Internet services, such as MuslimMatch.com and Zawaj.com, offer an array of services.

**Gender.** The issue of gender equity has become one of the most controversial issues in the Muslim community. About one-quarter of regular mosque participants in America are women, and in African American mosques over one-third of participants are women. These percentages are extremely low for Christian churches but in comparison to the Muslim world, where women have no role in the mosque, this is a significant difference. Women are most active in administering the weekend school and other social events. Two-thirds of mosques allow women to sit on their governing board, but

are not contradictory to Islam. This is a new paradigm that guards against changes in core religious practices while welcoming the assimilation of certain American cultural practices. The idea is to be fully Muslim and American. Overall, the impact of American culture on the Muslim community has been significant but it has not touched basic Islamic practice. In other words, Saturday night bingo has not returned to the mosque, but pizza is the favorite food at mosque dinners.

**The mosque.** The greatest impact of the American environment on the Muslim community has been the transformation of the role of the mosque and the imam. Muslims have adopted a congregational model for the mosque as a self-governed community center, which is unlike the Muslim world where the mosque is simply a place of prayer, and the family and other institutions perform key cultural tasks. In America the mosque is a center for educating children, socialization, and major cultural events like marriages and funerals. For example, celebrating the major Muslim holidays in the Muslim world is largely tied to the extended family

Mosques in the United States have developed as self-governed community centers, providing sites for educating children, socialization, and major cultural events. This is unlike the mosque's role in the Muslim world it is simply a place for prayer. © G. JOHN RENARD/CORBIS

only one-half have had women sit on their board in the last five years. Many Muslim women, who are unhappy with the progress of American mosques, have moved outside the mosque to organize. On the local level, women have established numerous study groups. On the national level Muslim women's groups have been established, such as Muslim Women's League, North American Council for Muslim Women, and Muslim Women Lawyer's Committee for Human Rights (KARAMA). Some Muslim organizations have become more inclusive of women: In 2000 the Islamic Society of North America elected for the first time a female vice president, and there are a significant number of Muslim student associations, dominated by second-generation immigrants, that have female presidents. The clear trend is that women's involvement is growing.

**Youth.** Youth bear the greatest pressure to assimilate American culture, and as a result many immigrants and African Americans have ceased to practice Islam. The issue of the assimilation of Muslim youth is, therefore, a major problem in the eyes of most Muslims. The Muslim youth who have maintained their association with the Muslim community evince outward aspects of American culture such as dress, sports, food, and entertainment—Muslim youth groups have their own "Islamic" rap music, and comedy shows—but they have fit it all within the boundaries of Islam. Dancing is still

not present in Muslim youth groups, except that Imam Warith Deen Muhammad's organization provides limited occasions where dancing is permitted. Imam Muhammad is the son and successor to Elijah Muhammad, founder of the Nation of Islam. In 1975, when Imam Muhammad took the reins of the Nation of Islam, he transformed the organization into a "mainstream" Islamic group. The organization has gone through many name changes, and the present name since 2002 is American Society of Muslims. It is the largest African American Muslim group.

The loser in all this is not so much Muslim religious practice but ethnic cultural practice. Many youth are shedding their ethnic identity but maintaining a Muslim identity that supercedes all other identities. Muslim youth are, therefore, less interested in how Islam is practiced back in their parents's home countries and more interested in identifying a legitimate Islamic tradition that is scripturally based and relevant to life in America. Muslim youth best exemplify the new paradigm of retaining core Islamic practices while adopting American culture.

**Holidays and patriotism.** The Muslim community in America does not practice any of the American holidays as a group. Thanksgiving probably receives the most recognition from Muslims as a holiday. Christmas and Easter are tied closely to

Christianity and therefore unacceptable. The national holidays such as the Fourth of July and Memorial Day have not had any official recognition except in the American Society of Muslims under the leadership of Imam Muhammad. Patriotic symbols such as the flag and patriotic rhetoric are largely absent from mosques and Muslim gatherings, except again for Imam Muhammad's organization. However, this is slowly changing, especially after the terrorism attacks of 11 September 2001. Many national Muslim advocacy groups have extended Fourth of July greetings, and the Islamic Society of North America displayed American flags on their platform during their annual conference. Individual Muslims do observe some of these holidays: Some have family dinners with turkey on Thanksgiving and even fewer have Christmas trees and let their children trick-or-treat on Halloween.

**Muslim perception of American culture.** The vast majority of Muslims recognize the good of American culture—political and religious freedom, self-reliance, and business practices—but they are critical of aspects of American culture, especially the moral laxity in sexual mores, and alcohol and drug consumption. In one study over one-third (37%) of Muslims agreed that America is immoral, while over half (54%) disagreed. Mosque leaders are even more disturbed: 67 percent agree that America is immoral compared to 33 percent who disagree (Bagby).

The Muslim community is virtually unanimous in believing that Muslims should be involved in the civic and political life of America—93 percent of Muslims (Zogby) and 89 percent of mosque leaders (Bagby) agree that Muslims should be involved in politics. Isolation from American society is firmly rejected. Yet a large portion of American Muslims feel that Muslims are unwelcome in the public sphere: 57 percent of Muslims believe that the attitude of America toward Muslims is unfavorable since 11 September 2001 (Zogby); 56 percent of mosque leaders feel that American society is hostile to Islam (Bagby).

## Influences of Islam on American Culture

Muslims and Islam are no longer invisible in America—they have been given recognition and, in some respects, acceptance by major shapers of culture.

**Presence of Islam.** President Ronald Reagan was one of the first U.S. presidents to mention mosques alongside churches and synagogues as part of the religious fabric of America. Mention of Muslims with the other religions is commonplace now, especially after President George W. Bush visited a mosque and pronounced Islam a religion of peace soon after the terrorism attacks of 11 September. *Iftar* (meal at the end of the fasting day) dinners at the White House during Ramadan have become regular occasions since the mid-1990s.

**Perception of Muslims in the media.** Movies have been less kind to Muslims and Islam. Ugly stereotyping of Muslims and Arabs in particular has a long history in Hollywood. Jack

Shaheen has estimated that only 5 percent of movies that include Muslims or Arabs show a human image of them. Since the late 1970s the image has been that of terrorists—from *Black Sunday* (1977) to *Iron Eagles* (1986) to *The Siege* (1998). Nevertheless signs of change have appeared as some of the more positive images of Muslims and Islam in movies have appeared in the 1990s—*Robin Hood Prince of Thieves* (1991), *13th Warrior* (1999), and *Three Kings* (1999).

Negative stereotyping is reflected in the poor approval rating for Muslims in the American public, although significant changes have occurred since 11 September 2001. Before 11 September 2001 the public's approval of Muslims hovered around 25 percent, but ironically with President George W. Bush's strong endorsement of mainstream Islam, approval ratings shot up to a high of 47 percent in October 2001 but have since begun to dip (Waldman and Caldwell).

**Sufism.** The most popular Muslim poet in America is Rumi and with this popularity has come some appreciation for Sufism. Sufi groups starting with Hazrat Inayat Khan's Sufi Order in the West in the early 1900s and more recently a group led by Shaykh Nazim al-Haqqani has had moderate success in attracting Americans, largely white. Although Sufi groups are a small percentage of the total Muslim population in America, their more positive image has translated into greater acceptance in certain circles of intellectuals and New Agers.

**African American community.** While Islam might have been invisible in Caucasian America, the impact of Islam on African American peoples has been substantial. The Nation of Islam (1930–1975), although a heterodoxical movement within Islam, still brought the idea of Islam to millions of African Americans. Malcolm X, who left the Nation of Islam to embrace a more mainstream understanding of Islam, is an icon in African-American history. The minister Louis Farrakhan, who resurrected the Nation of Islam in 1979, has maintained great popularity in the African-American community, especially among its youth. Imam W. Deen Muhammad has garnered much respect due to his interfaith efforts. In light of this history, Islam has signified black pride and militancy for African Americans.

Muslims have also played a key role in the 1990s effort to bring about a gang truce throughout the nation. Louis Farrakhan and Imam Jamil Al-Amin (former H. Rap Brown) were active in the gang summits that started in 1992 to broker a cease-fire between the rival gangs known as the Bloods and the Crips. The decline in gang violence through the 1990s can be linked to these gang truces.

**African American culture.** Islam has also impacted African American culture. One obvious manifestation is the adoption of Muslim names, undoubtedly an influence of the celebrities and sports figures who are Muslim or have Muslim parents—Muhammad Ali, Kareem Abdul Jabbar, Ahmad Rashad, Tupoc

Shakur, and others. From the 1970s to the present, the names Jamal, Kareem, Ali, and Rashad have become popular African American names. One of the top African American female names is now Aaliyah, obviously the result of the popularity of the singer by the same name.

Other cultural manifestations occur in the hats and garb of African Americans, especially when they want to express their black consciousness. Through the influence of the large number of Muslims in prisons, the impact of Islam might also be detected in popular African American culture in the baggy pants look and even in hugging among men, which is now a common form of greeting. The fact that major gangs call themselves "nations" can also be seen as an influence by the black nationalism of the Nation of Islam.

**Hip-Hop.** In entertainment Islam has had a tremendous impact on hip-hop culture. The ideology of the Nation of Islam and the Five Percenters, both heterodoxies within Islam, have had the greatest influence, but some rappers have been influenced by mainstream Muslim leaders such as Imam Muhammad and Imam Jamil Al-Amin. Public Enemy and Chuck D, Ice Cube, Queen Latifah, Big Daddy Kane, and Sister Souljah are just a few names that mention in their lyrics Minister Farrakhan or the ideas of the Nation of Islam and the Five Percenters. Other rappers such as Mos Def, Q-Tip, Everlast, Styles of Beyond, Devine Styler, and Jurassic 5 have roots in the mainstream Muslim community. A few rap groups such as Native Deen market themselves exclusively to the Muslim community.

**Communication.** Muslim youth and certain Muslim groups have enthusiastically embraced the Internet. Major Web sites exist for news, information, books, and Islamic resources, such as IslamiCity.com, IslamOnline.com, Ummah.com, and SoundVision.com. Web sites of Muslim Student Associations are also numerous and full of useful information and resources. Muslims who are on the fringes of mosques and Muslim organizations are the most active in the use of the Web. Muslim women in particular have benefited immensely from the presence of a cyber-sisters community. Ideological groups are also quite active on the web. Many Muslims sometimes bemoan the proliferation of these sites and the emergence of the cyber mufti who have few links to the Muslim community. Many mosques, however, are far behind the curve—many do not have computers and others do not use them for communication.

*See also* **Americas, Islam in the; Farrakhan, Louis; Malcolm X; Muhammad, Warith Deen; Nation of Islam.**

## BIBLIOGRAPHY

Bagby, Ihsan; Perl, Paul M.; and Froehle, Bryan T. *The Mosque in America: A National Portrait.* Washington, D.C.: Council of American-Islamic Relations, 2001.

Curtis IV, Edward E. *Islam in Black America: Identity, Liberation, and Difference in African-American Islamic Thought.* Albany: State University of New York Press, 2002.

Eck, Diana L. *A New Religious America: How a "Christian Country" Has Become the World's Most Religiously Diverse Nation.* New York: Harper San Francisco, 2001.

Haddad, Yvonne Yazbeck, and Esposito, John L. *Muslims on the Americanization Path?* New York: Oxford University Press, 2000.

McAlister, Melani. *Epic Encounters: Culture, Media, and U.S. Interests in the Middle East, 1945–2000.* Berkeley: University of California Press, 2000.

McCloud, Aminah Beverly. *African American Islam.* New York: Routledge, 1995.

Shaheen, Jack G. *Reel Bad Arabs: How Hollywood Vilifies a People.* New York: Olive Branch Press, 2001.

Smith, Jane I. *Islam in America.* New York: Columbia University Press, 1999.

Waldman, Steven, and Caldwell, Deborah. "Americans' Surprising Take on Islam: A New Poll Shows That Americans Have Not Turned Anti-Islam." *Beliefnet.* 9 January 2002. http://www.beliefnet.com/story/97/story_9732.html (2 Februrary 2003).

Zogby International and Project Maps. "American Muslim Poll (Nov/Dec 2001)." *Project Maps.* 19 December 2001. http:// www.projectmaps.com/pmreport.pdf (2 February 2003).

*Ihsan Bagby*

## AMERICAS, ISLAM IN THE

The Islamic presence in pre-Columbian times is a point of contention, with some writers asserting that Arab and West African Muslims settled in the Americas between the eleventh and the fourteenth centuries; others dispute these assertions, citing a lack of archaeological and other historical evidence.

The undisputed spread of Islam in the Americas started in the early sixteenth century with the arrival of a small number of Moriscos (Muslims forced to adopt Christianity who may have maintained their faith in secret) from Spain, and millions of enslaved West Africans. It is estimated that 15 to 20 percent of the twelve to fifteen million Africans deported through the Atlantic slave trade were Muslim. Their prayers, fasts, refusal of pork and alcohol, circumcision, collecting of *zakat*, mosques, Qur'anic schools, and importation of Qur'ans from Africa and Europe have been documented for countries as diverse as Peru, Brazil, the United States, Jamaica, Trinidad, Guyana, and Cuba. Manuscripts written in Arabic have been recovered in several countries, most notably in Bahia, Brazil, where Muslims from Nigeria led a series of revolts between 1807 and 1835. There is evidence that the African Muslims succeeded in converting both enslaved and free people to Islam, and accusations of Islamic proselytism among Native Americans surfaced in the sixteenth century. West Africans maintained Islam in America during four centuries of slavery, but could not transmit the religion to the generations who were born in the Americas. With the end of the international slave trade in the late 1860s, Islam disappeared as an overtly practiced religion among people of African descent. However, cultural and linguistic traces remain today.

In the nineteenth century, Islam emerged again in the Americas with the arrival of Asian and Arab Muslims. After the abolition of slavery in the British colonies in 1834, Muslim indentured laborers from India were introduced to Trinidad and Guyana, along with the much larger numbers of Hindus. Between 1890 and 1939 the Dutch brought indentured Muslim workers to Dutch Guiana (Surinam) from their colony in Indonesia. They now represent 75 percent of the Muslim population of Suriname, the country with the highest percentage of Muslims (about 25%) in the Americas.

By the end of the nineteenth century, religious and political unrest, along with economic transformations in the Ottoman Empire, led to the emigration of Syrians and Lebanese, who established themselves throughout North and South America. Among them was a minority of Muslim Lebanese and Syrians who migrated, concentrating their settlements in Brazil—which counts the largest Muslim population in Latin America—Argentina, Venezuela, Mexico, and Canada. In South and Central America most were traders, while in Canada, the majority were farmers.

In the twentieth century new Muslim populations settled in the Americas. After World War I, a small number of followers of the Indian-founded Ahmadiyya sect settled in South America and the Caribbean; and Albanians and Yugoslavs migrated to the Canadian prairies. Palestinians started to arrive after 1948 and again, in successive waves, following the Middle Eastern wars of 1967 and 1973.

Today, Islam continues to spread throughout the Americas through the natural growth of the existing Muslim population, conversions, and continued immigration from Muslim nations. Statistics are unreliable, but there are an estimated 1.4 million Muslims living in Latin America and the Caribbean, 253,000 in Canada, and about 6 million in the United States.

*See also* **American Culture and Islam; United States, Islam in the.**

## BIBLIOGRAPHY

Diouf, Sylviane A. *Servants of Allah: African Muslims Enslaved in the Americas.* New York: New York University Press, 1998.

Kettani, M. Ali. *Muslim Minorities in the World Today.* London: Mansell Publishing Limited, 1986.

*Sylviane Anna Diouf*

# ANDALUS, AL-

Al-Andalus is the geographic term used to denote those areas of modern Spain that came under Muslim control in the Middle Ages. Today, the term (Spanish, *Andalucía*) refers to a particular territory located in southern Spain. Al-Andalus or Muslim Spain (both terms will be used interchangeably), with its famous mosques, irrigated gardens, developments in poetry, philosophy, and science, is often referred to as the cultural golden age of Islam. The actual Muslim presence there lasted 781 years (711–1492 C.E.) and its influence on everything from architecture to science is still palpable. For the sake of convenience, what follows is divided into three parts: history and main developments, cultural achievements, and the Jews of al-Andalus.

### History and Main Developments

Prior to the arrival of the Muslims, Spain was under the control of the Visigoths, who maintained firm control of the region with the help of a rigid church hierarchy. In 711, Arab and Berber forces, under the leadership of Tariq b. Ziyad, defeated the Visigothic King Rodrigo at the River Barbate. The Arab armies tried to move as far as France but were eventually repelled in 732 by Charles Martel. During the first decades after 711, al-Andalus functioned as a frontier outpost with the Umayyad caliph in Damascus appointing its governor. Around the year 750, however, a dynastic struggle in the East led to change in rule from the Umayyads to the Abbasids. Significantly, in 756, an Umayyad prince by the name of 'Abd al-Rahman I arrived in Spain. He was able to gain sufficient political support there, thereby creating an independent and sovereign state, referred to as the Marwanid dynasty, based in Cordoba.

The high point of the Marwanid dynasty occurred during the rule of Abd al-Rahman III, who reigned for fifty years (912–961). This coincided with a period of stability after he had subdued revolting factions and stopped the advances of the neighboring Christians—something his predecessors had been unable to accomplish. He was also responsible for the construction of the monumental royal city, Madinat al-Zahra', just outside of Cordoba. Under his rule, Cordoba became a true cosmopolitan center, rivaling the great cities of the Islamic East and far surpassing the capitals of Western Europe. After the death of Abd al-Rahman III, the central caliphate gradually fragmented into a number of smaller kingdoms (*tawa'if*, sing., *ta'ifa*), ruled by various "party kings" (*muluk al-tawa'if*).

The fourteenth-century Alhambra Palace and Fortress in al-Andalus in southern Spain shows the influence of the nearly eight hundred-year Muslim presence there which began early in the Middle Ages. © PATRICK WARD/CORBIS

The history of al-Andalus in the eleventh-century is one of gradual diminishment as various Christian monarchs attempted to encroach upon the area held by the Muslims, an area that they felt compromised the national and religious unity of Spain. This reconquering (Spanish, *Reconquista*) became so vigorous that the various Muslim kingdoms had no choice but to seek help from the Almoravids, a dynasty based in North Africa. The result was that al-Andalus, for all intents and purposes, lost its independence, becoming little more than an annex of a government situated in North Africa.

In 1147, the puritanical Almohades, another dynasty based in North Africa, invaded Spain. This dynasty was determined to put an end to the religious laxity that they witnessed among the Andalusian intellectual and courtier classes. They demanded, inter alia, the conversion of all Christians and Jews to Islam. It was during this period that many Jews left Spain: the majority went north to Christian territories. According to some modern commentators, the Almohade invasion signaled the end of one of the most fascinating and eclectic eras of world history.

By the thirteenth century, al-Andalus was essentially comprised of Granada and its immediate environs. Here the Nasrid dynasty, with its royal palace in the al-Hamra' (Alhambra), ruled as quasi-vassals of the Christian king. The

Alhambra, with its open courts, fountains, and irrigated gardens, is today one of the best preserved medieval castles in Europe. In 1492, under the leadership of King Ferdinand of Aragon and Queen Isabella of Castile, the Reconquista was completed. All those who were not Christian (i.e., Muslims and Jews) were expelled from Spain.

## Cultural Achievements

From a cultural and philosophical perspective, the achievements associated with the inhabitants of al-Andalus are unrivalled. The Marwanid capital, Cordoba, alone had over seventy libraries, which encouraged many great architects and scientists to settle there. The caliphs and rich patrons, in turn, established schools to translate classical philosophic and scientific texts into Arabic. Although the center at Cordoba gradually fragmented into a number of kingdoms, there nevertheless ensued a rich intellectual, cultural, and social landscape that was grounded on the notion of *adab*, the polite ideal of cultured living that developed in the courts of medieval Islam. The *adab* (pl., *udaba'*) was an individual defined by his social graces, literary tastes, and ingenuity in manipulating language.

One of the main developments within Andalusian literature was the *muwashshah*. The *muwashshah*, which seems to have originated in the ninth century, is a genre of stanzaic poetry whose main body is composed in classical Arabic with its ending written in vernacular, often in the form of a quotation (*kharja*). The main themes were devoted to love, wine, and panegyric; eventually, this genre proved popular among Sufis (e.g., ibn Arabi). The *muwashshah* was also a popular genre among non-Muslims, especially among Hebrew poets.

Al-Andalus is also associated with some of the most famous names of Islamic intellectual history. Unlike the great majority of philosophers in the Muslim East, the overarching concern of Andalusian Islamic thinkers was political science. Questions that they entertained were: What constitutes the perfect state? How can such a state be realized? What is the relationship between religion and the politics? And, what should the philosopher, who finds himself in an unjust state, do? Another important feature of Islamic philosophy in al-Andalus was an overwhelming interest in intellectual mysticism, which stressed that the true end of the individual was the contact (*ittisal*) between the human intellect and the Divine Intellect.

Philosophy in al-Andalus reached a high-point with Ibn Bajja (d. 1139). His *Tadbir al-mutawahhid* (Governance of the solitary) examines the fate of a lone individual who seeks truth in the midst of a city that is concerned primarily with financial gain and carnal pleasures. Such an individual must, according to Ibn Bajja, seek out other like-minded individuals and avoid discussing philosophy with non-philosophers. Ibn Tufayl (d. 1185) picks up this theme in his philosophical novel *Hayy ibn Yaqzan*. The goal of this work is to show that the unaided human intellect is capable of discovering Truth without the aid of divine revelation. Ibn Tufayl, according to tradition, was also responsible for encouraging the young Ibn Rushd (d. 1198) to write his commentaries on the works of Aristotle. Within this context, Ibn Rushd wrote not one but three commentaries to virtually the entire Aristotelian corpus. These commentaries, in their Latin translations, were the staple of the European curriculum until relatively recently.

Sufism, or Islamic mysticism, was also a prominent feature of the intellectual and cultural life of al-Andalus. In fact, one of the most important Sufis, Ibn Arabi (d. 1240), was born in Murcia in southeastern Spain. After a mystical conversion as a teenager, he set out on a life of asceticism and wanderings. Ibn Arabi essentially interpreted the entire Islamic tradition (jurisprudence, the Qur'an, hadith, philosophy) through a mystical prism.

### The Jews of al-Andalus

The culture of al-Andalus would also have a tremendous impact on non-Muslim communities living there. The *adab* ideal (mentioned in the previous section) proved to be very attractive to the local population (both Jewish and Christian), who adopted the cosmopolitan ideals of Islamicate culture, including the use of Arabic. Within the history of Jewish civilization, al-Andalus (Hebrew, *ha-Sefarad*) holds a special place. Legend has it that the Jews not only welcomed, but also physically helped, the Muslims conquer the oppressive Visigoth rulers. The cooperativeness of the Jews and their ability to integrate into Andalusian Arab society subsequently created an environment in which Jews flourished. Arabic gradually replaced Aramaic as the language of communication among Jews: By adopting Arabic (although they would write it in Hebrew characters, and today this is called Judeo-Arabic), Jews inherited a rich cultural and scientific vocabulary. It was during the tenth century, for example, that Jews first began to write secular poetry (although written in Hebrew, it employed Arabic prosody, form, and style).

The names of famous Jews who lived in al-Andalus reads like a "who's who" list of Jewish civilization. Shmuel ha-Nagid (993–1055), for example, became the prime minister (wazir) of Granada. His responsibilities included being in charge of the army (i.e., having control over Muslim soldiers), in effect becoming one of the most powerful Jews between Biblical times and the present day. His poetry recounting battles is among the most expressive of the tradition. The fact that a Jew could attain such a prominent position within Muslim society reveals much about Jewish-Muslim relations in Spain. Other famous Hebrew poets included Moshe ibn Ezra (d.1138) and Judah Halevi (d.1141), whose sacred poetry is still part of the Jewish liturgy. Al-Andalus was also the birthplace of the most famous Jewish philosopher: Moses Maimonides (d.1204), who attempted to show the compatibility between religion and philosophy by arguing that the former was based not on superstition, but rational principles.

In sum, al-Andalus was not only a region, but also represented a way of life that Muslims and Jews look back at with fondness. With its rich contributions to science, literature, architecture, and interfaith relations, al-Andalus played a prominent role in Islamic history.

*See also* **European Culture and Islam; Judaism and Islam.**

### BIBLIOGRAPHY

Ashtor, Eliayahu. *The Jews of Moslem Spain*. Philadelphia: Jewish Publication Society of America, 1973–1979.

Brann, Ross. *The Compunctious Poet: Cultural Ambiguity and Hebrew Poetry in Muslim Spain*. Baltimore, Md.: Johns Hopkins University Press, 1991.

Ibn Arabi. *Sufis of Andalusia: The Rûh al-quds and al-Durrat al-fâkhira of Ibn 'Arabî*. Translated by R. W. J. Austin. Berkeley: University of California Press, 1971.

Ibn Bâjja. *Tadbîr al-mutawahhid/El régimen del solitario*. Edited and translated by Miguel Asín Palacios. Madrid: n.p., 1946.

Ibn Tufayl. *Hayy ibn Yaqzân: A Philosophical Tale*. Translated by Lenn E. Goodman. Los Angeles: Gee Tee Bee, 1983.

Kennedy, Hugh. *Muslim Spain: A Political History of al-Andalus*. London: Longman, 1996.

Menocal, María Rosa; Scheindlin, Raymond P.; and Sells, Michael, eds. *The Literature of al-Andalus.* Cambridge, U.K.: Cambridge University Press, 2000.

Watt, W. Montgomery. *A History of Islamic Spain.* Edinburgh: Edinburgh University Press, 1965.

*Aaron Hughes*

# ANGELS

The word "angel" appears frequently in the Qur'an, having entered the Arabic language (in pre-Islamic times) as a loan from Aramaic or Hebrew, possibly via Ethiopic, and so indicating Christian as well as Jewish cultural influences. In any case the word has always been accepted as an exact equivalent of the Greek *angelos,* angel or messenger, used in pre-Christian times to define the functions of certain "messengers of the gods" such as Hermes or Iris (the rainbow). The remarkable homogeneity of "Abrahamic" Jewish/Christian/Islamic angelology cannot convincingly be traced to a "Mosaic" source, but derives very obviously from Zoroastrian influences on Judaism during the Babylonian Exile.

Despite the unanimity of the Qur'an, hadith, and sunna on the doctrine of belief in angels, a certain ambiguity arises when these beings are considered in both theology and metaphysics. How precisely does angelic nature situate itself between earth and heaven, between human and divine? It may be said that monotheism simply cannot do without a means of immanence, lest the gulf of God's transcendence end by severing all possible relations between the two levels of reality. Put simply, the angels provide a third term, a metaphorical bridge or ladder between earth and heaven. Thus the Prophet spoke of each raindrop having its angel, and of the angels as messengers bearing God's revelation to humans, and human prayers to God. The task of angelic theology consists in justifying this metaphysical "need" without detracting from God's ominipotence and unity.

The standard Islamic angelology is based on both Qur'anic and extra-Qur'anic tradition; for instance "the Spirit" (*al-ruh*) is mentioned in the Qur'an, but is identified by tradition with Metatron, the Jewish angel "nearest to the Throne." The angel of death is mentioned (Q. 32:11) but not named; tradition knows him as 'Izra'il. Jibril (Jibra'il) (Gabriel) is named three times, Mika'il (Mikal) (Michael) once. Israfil, who will blow the trumpet at Resurrection, appears neither in the Qur'an nor hadith, but became very popular—and symbolically necessary to form a quaternity of great archangels, under the Spirit and above the countless ranks of the heavenly host. Munkar and Nakir, the angels who weigh or question the souls of the dead in their graves, are likewise absent from canonical sources but much discussed by established authorities and universally accepted by believers. The following might represent a traditional Islamic angelography:

From the soles of his feet to this head, Israfil, angel of the Day of Judgment, has hairs and tongues over which are stretched veils. He glorifies Allah with each tongue in a thousand languages, and Allah creates from his breath a million angels who glorify Him. Israfil looks each day and each night toward Hell, approaches without being seen, and weeps; he grows thin as a bowstring and weeps bitter tears. His trumpet or horn has the form of a beast's horn and contains dwellings like the cells of a bee's honeycomb; in these the souls of the dead repose.

Mika'il was created by God five thousand years after Israfil. He has hairs of saffron from his head to his feet, and his wings are of green topaz. On each hair he has a million faces and in each face a million eyes and tongues. Each tongue speaks a million languages and from each eye falls seventy thousand tears. These become the Kerubim who lean down over the rain and the flowers, the trees and fruit.

Jibra'il was created five hundred years after Mika'il. He has sixteen hundred wings and hair of saffron. The sun is between his eyes and each hair has the brightness of the moon and stars. Each day he enters the Ocean of Light 360 times. When he comes forth, a million drops fall from each wing to become angels who glorify God. When he appeared to the Prophet to reveal the Qur'an, his wings stretched from the East to the West. His feet were yellow, his wings green, and he wore a necklace of rubies or coral. His brow was light, his face luminous; his teeth were of a radiant brightness. Between his two eyes were written the words: "There is no god but God, and Muhammad is the Prophet of God."

The angel of death, 'Izra'il, is veiled before the creatures of God with a million veils. His immensity is vaster than the heavens, and the East and West are between his hands like a dish on which all things have been set, or like a man who has been put between his hands that he might eat him, and he eats of him what he wishes; and thus the angel of death turns the world this way and that, just as men turn their money in their hands. He sits on a throne in the sixth heaven. He has four faces, one before him, one on his head, one behind him, and one beneath his feet. He has four wings, and his body is covered with innumerable eyes. When one of these eyes closes, a creature dies.

In part from Greek philosophy, especially neo-Platonism, Islamic tradition elaborated a cosmic angelology based on the celestial Spheres—as for instance in the many versions of the Prophet's *mir'aj* or Night Ascension into the Heavens, where he learns the ritual of prayer from the angels in their ranks. He is at first carried by the Buraq, a strange hybrid of mule, angel, woman, peacock, and then accompanied by Jibra'il. Even this greatest angel, however, cannot accompany Muhammad to "the Lote Tree of the Farthest Limit" (that is, the beatific vision of theophany). This symbolizes the theological premise that angels, although more perfectly spiritual than humans, are in fact ontologically less central. God orders the

This Persian miniature depicts Adam among the angels. According to the Qur'an, God demands that the angels worship Adam, even though they are closer to the divine than Adam is. When the angel Iblis refuses to bow to Adam, Iblis falls from God's grace and becomes Satan. © Réunion des Musées Nationaux/Art Resource, NY angels to bow and worship Adam (in a legend probably adapted from the heretical Christian "Adam and Eve Books") even though Adam is created of clay and the angels of light. The angel Iblis refuses to acknowledge the divine in the human, and thus falls from grace and becomes Satan. (The sufi al-Hallaj therefore praised Iblis as the only true monotheist!) As an angel Iblis should be "made of" light, but in some versions he is described as a great *jinni* and therefore of a fiery nature. The *jinni* constitute a different class of supernatural beings, also attested in the Qur'an; some of them were converted to true faith by Solomon or Muhammad himself.

'Abd al-Karim al-Jili (a Sufi influenced by Ibn 'Arabi) describes the angelic Spheres thus: The first heaven is that of the Moon. The Holy Spirit is here, "so that this heaven might have the same relation to earth as spirit to body." Adam dwells here in silvery-white light. The second heaven is that of Mercury (identified with the Egyptian Hermes and the prophets Idris and Enoch). Here the angels of the arts and crafts reside bathed in a gray luminousness. The third heaven, that of Venus, is created from the imagination and is the locale of the World of Similitudes, the subtle forms of all earthly things, the source of dreams and visions. The prophet Joseph lives here in yellow light. The heaven of the Sun is created from the light of the heart; Israfil presides over a host of prophets in a golden glow. The heaven of Mars, of the death-angel 'Izra'il, is blood-red with the light of judgment. That of Jupiter is blue with the light of spiritual power (*himma*) and is lorded over by Mika'il. Here reside the angels of mercy and blessing, shaped as animals, birds, and men; others appear, in Jili's words, "as substances and accidents which bring health to the sick, or as solids and liquids that supply created beings with food and drink. Some are made half of fire and half of ice. Here resides Moses, drunk on the wine of the revelation of lordship." The seventh heaven (first to be created from the substance of the First Intelligence) is that of Saturn, and consists of Black Light, symbolic of *fana'*, annihilation in the divine Oneness.

The grandeur of this cosmic vision is given a metaphysical dimension by the Persian philosopher Ibn Sina (Avicenna) who, speaking of the angels, says, "The soul must grasp the beauty of the object that it loves; the image of that beauty increases the ardor of love; this ardor makes the soul look upward. Thus imagination of beauty causes ardor of love, love causes desire, and desire causes motion" on the level both of the Spheres (which are drawn in love toward their Archangel-Intellects) and of human souls (who are drawn in love toward their guardians or personal angels).

On the fringes of Islamic orthodoxy such mystical angelology shaded into occultism. Elaborate concordances of angelic correspondences, names, powers, symbols, and the like evolved out of the late classical synthesis (e.g., those described in the Egyptian Magical Papyri). Amulets were constructed, evocations and seances performed. Like their medieval and Renaissance counterparts in Europe, Islamic hermeticists sought and practiced the "angelic conversation." At its highest level of sophistication this magical angelology aims at no benefit other than existential participation in the divine or angelic consciousness. "By philosophy man realizes the virtual characteristics of his race. He attains the form of humanity and progresses on the hierarchy of beings until in crossing the straight way (or 'bridge') and the correct path, he becomes an Angel" (Brethren of Purity [*Risalat al-jami'ah*]).

*An artistic representation of Muhammad's ascent to heaven appears in the volume one color plates.*

*See also* **Mi'raj; Religious Beliefs.**

## BIBLIOGRAPHY

Corbin, Henry. *Avicenna and the Visionary Recital*. Translated by Ralph Manheim. Princeton, N.J.: Princeton University Press, 1969.

Hallaj, Mansur. *The Tawasin*. Translated by A. A. at-Tarjumana. Berkeley, Calif.: Diwan Press, 1974.

Rumi, Maulana Jalaluddin. *The Mathnawi*. Translated by Reynold A. Nicholson. London: Luzac & Co., 1978.

Wilson, Peter Lamborn. *Angels*. London: Thames & Hudson, 1980.

*Peter Lamborn Wilson*

# ARABIA, PRE-ISLAM

The term "Arabia" has been variously applied in both modern and ancient times to refer to a vast territory stretching from the borders of the Fertile Crescent in northern Syria to the tip of the Arabian Peninsula and from the borders of the Euphrates to the fertile regions of the Transjordan. For the ancients, this vague term, "Arabia," referred to the dwelling places of the varieties of South Semitic speakers lumped together under the term "Arab." For speakers of Hebrew and Aramaic, the term Arab ('*arab*) carried the semantic notion of the desert or the wilderness ('*arabah*), since the Arabs they encountered were primarily the nomadic and seminomadic desert dwellers engaged in long-distance commerce, animal husbandry, or supplying cavalry troops to imperial armies. The result is that ancient textual references to Arabia and its inhabitants, the Arabs, are both inconsistent and imprecise in terms of geographic boundaries, ethnic identity, and language use. The meager textual evidence available to us shows us that many of the northern Arabs used Aramaic and Hebrew as well as varieties of Arabic in pre-Islamic times. After the rise of Islam, however, the Arabic of northwest Arabia, the region of the Hijaz, became the dominant language of the Arabs, and it, along with its cognate dialects, formed the Arabic known today.

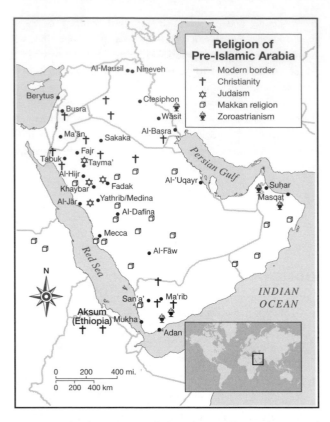

**Religion of Pre-Islamic Arabia**
— Modern border
† Christianity
✡ Judaism
▫ Makkan religion
⚱ Zoroastrianism

Location of Christianity, Judaism, the Makkan religion and Zoroastrianism in pre-Islamic Arabia. XNR PRODUCTIONS/GALE

The geography and natural ecology of the Arabian peninsula has affected both the culture and the history of Arabia. It is bounded in the north by a desert of soft sand, the Nafud, as well as a desert in the south, the Rubʿ al-Khali, the so-called Empty Quarter. Both the Red Sea on the west and the Gulf on the east are barriers to entry with few natural ports. There are no permanent water-courses in Arabia and only scattered oases in the interior. The ancient geographers used the term *natura maligna* for Arabia, and even when using *Arabia Felix*, "Happy Arabia," for the south, they intended some irony. Its average rainfall is less than three inches per year, and much of that falls within a period of just four or five days. Because of the forbidding landscape and the harsh climate, for much of Arabia's history, it resisted successful invasion. Such harsh conditions, however, have provided refuge for those fleeing persecution and those seeking the economic opportunities of long-distance trading. Trade was assisted because Arabia was the home of the domestication of the West Asiatic camel, the dromedary, and the invention, around the beginning of the first millennium C.E., of the North Arabian camel saddle, which enabled camels to be used for cavalry warfare as well as for transporting trade goods.

### History

Historical knowledge of Arabia goes back to the Greek historian Herodotus, to a few Akkadian texts, and to the Bible, but sound historical records only come from the period

of Roman domination of the eastern Mediterranean. Much legendary material has influenced the writings of the early history of Arabia, particularly the biblical legends, which hold that the Amelikites were the first "Arabs." This legend is adopted by Arabs themselves, who link themselves to the Israelite soldiers who annihilated the Amelikites and settled in the Hijaz in their stead. R. Dozy and D. S. Margoliouth elaborated a secularized version of the biblical legends to make Arabia the Semitic prototypical home and Arabic the prototypical Semitic language. Associated with this theory is the so-called desiccation theory of Arabia, which holds that Arabia was lush and verdant in prehistorical times, only becoming dry later, driving out the Semitic inhabitants into the Mediterranean basin. While modern geological exploration of Arabia has substantiated a shift in climate in the peninsula from more wet toward dry, there is no evidence to substantiate any of the theories that Arabia was the original home of the Semites or that all Semitic languages derive from Arabic.

According to a report that combines inscriptional evidence and legend, Arabia was the temporary capital of Nabonidus (556–539 B.C.E.), the last ruler of Babylon. In the third year of his reign, he invaded the Hijaz as far as Yathrib (Medina), and dominated the famous Arabian caravan cities in the northwest quadrant. Some scholars see his motives as economic, while others dismiss the historicity of the whole event as part of a Jewish midrashic invention.

### Inhabitants

Among the important pre-Islamic peoples of Northwest Arabia were the Nabataeans, who, by the time of the arrival of Roman imperial presence in the eastern Mediterranean, dominated the region's trade from around Damascus to the Hijaz. They had been pastoral nomads who had settled in their heartland around Petra. The Nabataeans plied their trade through the areas of Transjordan, across the Wadi ʿArabah to Gaza and al-ʿArish (Rhinocolura). There is also evidence that they used the interior route of the Wadi Sirhan to carry goods to Bostra for distribution to Damascus and beyond. Nabataean wealth and influence attracted the Romans into an unsuccessful invasion of Arabia in 26 B.C.E. under the leadership of Caesar Augustus's Egyptian prefect, Aelius Gallus. The Nabataeans were able to resist Roman domination until 106 C.E., when Arabia Nabataea became a Roman province. In later history, the name "Nabataean" became identified with irrigation and agriculture, because the Nabataeans are credited with the development of hydraulic technology in the region. In modern Arabic, "Nabataean" (*nabati*) refers to vernacular poetry in the ancient style.

Most modern historians regard the Nabataeans as Arabs, but the picture is more complex and illustrative of the problems of ethnic identification in the pre-Islamic period. The Nabataeans were philhellenes, using Greek art and culture, and Aretas III issued coins with Greek legends after 82 B.C.E. They used a form of Arabic as their language for trade within the Arabian peninsula, writing it down in a modified Aramaic script that influenced the development of the North Arabian alphabetic script. They acted as a culture-bridge between the Arabian interior and the Roman Hellenized Mediterranean, and, depending on who was reporting, they could present a different face to different peoples, Greek, Aramaic, or Arabic.

Jews had been inhabitants of Arabia from biblical times, but the destruction of the Temple in Jerusalem in 70 C.E. sent larger numbers into Arabia. Around this time the apostle Paul spent time in Arabia after his conversion to Christianity, possibly to recruit converts, as did another Pharisee, Rabbi Akiba, who went to Arabia to obtain support for Simon Bar Kochba in the Second Roman War in 132 C.E. Some Jews formed independent communities in Arabia, such as the small enclaves of priests, who kept themselves isolated to avoid ritual contamination so that they would be ready under Levitical strictures to resume their duties if the Temple should be rebuilt. Most, however, seem to have joined existing communities comprised of Jews and non-Jews along the trade routes stretching from the Hijaz to Yemen. The most prominent of these settlements was the city of Yathrib, known in both Aramaic and Arabic as Medina.

## Roman Arabia

By 106 C.E., the Romans dominated most of the former territories of the Nabataeans and the adjacent Syrian cities of Gerasa and Philadelphia (modern Jarash and Amman in Jordan), creating a province through the formal annexation of the Nabataean kingdom under the Roman emperor Trajan. This province, known as *Provincia Arabia*, was bounded by the western coast of the Sinai Peninsula, the present Syrian-Lebanese border to a line south of Damascus, and the eastern coast of the Red Sea as far as Egra (*Mada'in Salih* in the Hijaz). Gaza prospered as a major seaport and outlet for the province's commerce. This trade continued under Roman domination, and the borders were fortified by semipermeable lines of fortifications and client states. Under the Romans, Bostra (Bozrah; now Busra ash-Sham) in the north became the capital around a legionary camp. Petra remained a religious center until the penetration of Christianity in the area. The construction of a highway, the *Via Traiana Nova*, linking Damascus, via Bostra, Gerasa, Philadelphia, and Petra, to Aelana on the Gulf of Aqaba, set the border of Arabia (*Limes Arabicus*) along the lines of an ancient biblical route. Paved by Claudius Severus, the first governor of *Provincia Arabia* in about 114 C.E., it improved communication and established a modicum of control over the influx of pastoral nomads into settled territory. More importantly, the road insured the increase in prosperity of the cities along the route.

At the end of the third century, the Roman emperor Diocletian divided Arabia into a northern province, enlarged

Treasury, Petra, Jordan; built by the Nabataeans between the third century B.C.E. and the first century C.E. The Nabataeans were a wealthy, important tribe of the pre-Islamic era who had been nomadic and then settled around Petra. Their culture bridged Arabic and Hellenic cultures, incorporating elements of both. THE ART ARCHIVE

by the Palestinian regions of Auranitis and Trachonitis, with Bostra as the capital, and a southern province, with Petra as capital. The southern province, united to Palestine by the emperor Constantine I "the Great," became known as Palaestina Salutaris (or Tertia) when detached again in 357 and 358 C.E. The cities of both provinces enjoyed a marked revival of prosperity in the fifth and sixth centuries and fell into decay only after the Arab conquest after 632 C.E.

During the period in which the Judaean Desert finds were deposited in the caves, the area containing the discovery sites remained off the main conduits of trade and communication, and it is their remoteness that, for the most part, provided their value as retreats from the demands of the central settled world. The practice of using the Judaean Desert caves as *genizot*, religious treasuries, continued from the time of the Roman Wars through as late as the eleventh century C.E. The presence of Byzantine Greek and Arabic texts indicates that the local populations both knew of the existence of the caves and made use of them as depositories for important documents. This fact has had important implications in discussions about the presence of copies of the "Damascus Covenant" found in the Cairo Genizah. None of the texts found at the Judaean Desert discovery sites mentions *Provincia Arabia* or other geographic terms associated with Arabia. The texts, particularly the texts from the Byzantine and Islamic periods, indicate that the inhabitants of the region, who deposited the finds, were well connected not only with Palestine but also with Egypt and the larger world of the Mediterranean.

## Southern Arabia

The southern portion of Arabia, known generically as the Yemen, had ancient connections with Africa, India, and the Far East, as well as the Mediterranean. It was culturally and linguistically connected with the Horn of Africa. Among the theories of the Arabian origin of the Semites, some have cited the presence of speakers of a Semitic language unlike Arabic in Yemeni highlands. Additionally, the relationship between South Arabian and Ethiopic languages points to continuous contacts between the two areas. Attempts, however, to devise a comprehensive ethnographic categorization of the inhabitants of Arabia have so far failed. This is in part due to problems with categorization itself (what is a Semite, for example) and in part due to the paucity of evidence. Relying on Arabian histories and indigenous theories of ethnography are problematic, because all were written after the rise of Islam, which advances the religious notions of the family relationship among all Arabs and promotes the elaboration of the explanation of that relationship through genealogy. The so-called Table of Nations from Genesis 10 was invoked by early Islamic scholars, and the figures of Joktan, Hazarmaveth, and Sheba are identified with Qahtan, Hadramawt, and the Sabaeans.

An increasing amount of archaeological and inscriptional evidence support the meager and legendary historical material surrounding the histories and influence of at least four major kingdoms in southern Arabia, the Sabaeans, or kingdom of Sheba; the Minaeans; the kingdom of Qataban; and the kingdom of Hadramawt. These kingdoms were supported by a combination of trade and agriculture. Elaborate aqueducts, dams, and terracing helped sustain these kingdoms as well as giving evidence of their ability to marshal considerable resources for their construction and maintenance. We do not know the reasons for the demise of these kingdoms. The Qur'an (34:15–16) attributes the breaking of the dam at Ma'rib in the kingdom of the Sabaeans as divine retribution for their sins. Secular theories attribute the demise of organized agriculture in the southern region to the combined factors of the repeated breaking of dams and waterworks and the rise of the influence of Ethiopia in southern Arabia.

It is probably from the time of the breaking of the Ma'rib dam that some southern Arabian tribes migrated north, intermixing with the Arabs of the Hijaz in many places, including the city of Yathrib/Medina. This migration may also be linked with increasing economic opportunities in the northern part of Arabia resulting from the domestication of the camel, the invention of the North Arabian camel saddle, and the increasing use of camel cavalry forces in the armies of the Roman and Persian empires.

Premodern Arabia possessed little arable land, but southern Arabia was the habitat for frankincense and myrrh, the aromatic resins from conifers found in Arabia and the Horn of Africa. Because southern Arabia was the home of those much-sought-after aromatics and the trans-shipment point for Asian and African trade goods, including slaves, it was a much-desired location for colonies and extensions of empires. These products were sought as luxury trade-goods from as early as Old Kingdom Egypt, when this was known as the land of Punt. They were used for funerary and liturgical ceremonies, often in large quantities. The use of frankincense is attested in the biblical offerings mentioned in Leviticus 2:14–16 and 24:7, and also in the Talmud as a medicine and a painkiller. In Christian liturgy, incense was an important part of the celebration of the mass. Trade in aromatics, gold, and luxury items from Africa and India made the west coast of Arabia the conduit to the Mediterranean and linked southern Arabia with the settled areas of Syria.

Knowledge of Persian interest in Arabia begins with Darius I (r. 521–485 B.C.E.). He sent an exploratory expedition from India to the Red Sea, probably to increase trade. Greek interest was stimulated first by Alexander the Great and Nearchus of Crete, but Alexander died in 328 B.C.E., just before executing plans to conquer the peninsula. This interest prompted the Greek naturalist and philosopher Theophrastus (c. 372–287 B.C.E.) to describe South Arabia, providing one of the earliest historical accounts. The Ptolemies of Egypt, successors to Alexander's rule, pursued ambitions in the Red Sea. The Syrian Seleucids promoted the use of the northern routes to India, probably in an attempt to diminish Egyptian and Arab domination of eastern luxury goods. The establishment of the Parthian state in the mid-third century B.C.E. weakened the Seleucids, but Antiochus III was still strong enough to conduct an expedition in 204 and 205 against Gerrha on the Arabian shore of the Persian Gulf.

In the second and first centuries B.C.E., major changes took place in the economy and power of the southern kingdoms of Arabia. The Mediterranean world learned the secret of the use of the monsoon trade winds to navigate to India, and mountain tribes began invading the settled kingdoms. By the end of the first century B.C.E., the Sabaean kingdom was under the rule of the tribe of Hamdan, and the kingdoms of Ma'in and Qataban were destroyed. Roman attempts to conquer *Arabia Felix* failed, but Rome's influence was extended first through the Nabataeans and later through Egyptian and Ethiopic Christianity.

Sometime around 50 C.E., an anonymous author wrote the *Periplus of the Erythraean Sea*, an account in Greek of the ethnography and trade in the Red Sea. In the middle of the second century C.E., the geographer Claudius Ptolemy (fl. 127–151 C.E.) wrote a detailed description of Arabia from the perspective of Roman interests in the region. While some scholars identify some sites mentioned by Ptolemy with modern Arabian cities, like Macoraba as Mecca and Yathrippa as Yathrib/Medina, others discount this identification and claim that knowledge of ancient Arabia cannot be derived from from the Greco-Roman sources. In the case of the identification of Yathrippa as Yathrib, there is inscriptional support, however, from a Minaean inscription, where Ythrib is found. The general picture from these sources is that an active culture of trade and agriculture linked Arabia with Africa, South Asia, and the East Mediterranean world.

## Arabia Between Two Empires

By the middle of the third century c.e., religious and political competition between the Roman empire and the new Persian Sassanian empire had intensified with Arabia as one of the centers of the conflict. Both sides were intent on political and economic domination through conversion. For the Romans, that meant Christianity, and sometime around 213 c.e., Origen visited Arabia, probably at Petra, to bring that area into religious and political orthodoxy. In 244 c.e., M. Julius Philippus, known as Philip the Arab, acceded to the Roman imperial throne, and there is strong evidence that he was a Christian. His predecessor, Gordianus III, had defeated the second Sassanian emperor, Shapur I (r. 241–272 c.e.), and, although he concluded a peace with the Persians, continued attempts to control Arabia. The Persians, whose official religion was the nonproselytizing Zoroastrianism, used Nestorian Christian and Jewish missionaries as their agents in Arabia.

Knowledge of Arabian history from the fourth through the beginning of the sixth centuries is meager because of the lack of written sources. In part, this is due to the decline of the urban centers in Arabia. While Arabia was no less strategically important to the two empires during this period, the creation of the buffer-states of the Lakhmids on the Sassanian side and the Ghassanids on the Roman/Byzantine side provided both empires indirect means of controlling the flow of goods and traffic into the settled areas. Because the buffer states were a main source of camel cavalry, some scholars have noted a process of Bedouinization corresponding to the decline of urban areas in this period as it became more profitable to raise and sell camels. The Ghassanids and the Lakhmids mirrored their sponsor-states by engaging in warfare, even when Rome and Persia were ostensibly at peace.

In the sixth century c.e., conflicts again arose, this time through the agency of the Persian-sponsored Jewish state in the Yemen under Yusuf Dhu Nuwas and Byzantium's Monophysite ally, the kingdom of Aksum. When Dhu Nuwas attempted to return Najran to his control, he met resistance from armed Christian missionaries, whom he defeated. With Byzantine naval support, the Aksumites invaded Arabia, defeated Dhu Nuwas, and established an Abyssinian-ruled client state. Its ruler, Abraha, rebuilt the Ma'rib dam erected a cathedral in San'a', and attempted to conquer Mecca. His defeat, traditionally in 570 c.e. and recorded in Qur'an 105, coupled with an invasion of the Yemen by the Sassanian ruler Khusraw I Anushirwan (r. 531–579 c.e.), drove the Abyssinians

from Arabia. The southern portion of Arabia remained under Persian control until the rise of Islam.

## Religions

Shortly before the birth of Muhammad in 570 c.e., Mecca and its environs in the Hijaz rose to historical prominence. In part, this view is in retrospect from the vantage of knowing that Islam came from there, but it is also in part because the dominant Meccan tribe seems to have been able to amass some political and economic hold over the region. The tribe of Qureish, whose name possibly means "dugong," was likely a group of Arabs involved in the Red Sea trade and moved inland with the decline of Roman authority in that sea. Their rule was both economic and theocratic. Their major shrine was the Ka'ba at Mecca, one of several such Ka'ba in Arabia at the time. They managed to import the worship of many local Arabian deities to Mecca, so that polytheism under the Qureish became a kind of federal cult.

It is difficult to speak with any precision about the native polytheism of the Arabs, because almost all of what is known comes through hostile Islamic sources. Allah was worshipped as a creator deity and a "high god," but the everyday cult seems to have been dominated by several astral deities, ancestors, and chthonic spirits, such as the *jinn*. Animal sacrifices seem to have been used to propitiate the more than three hundred deities mentioned by early Muslim historians. Circumambulation of the Ka'ba and other cultic objects was also a usual practice, often during "sacred" months of pilgrimage to religious sites. Little is known of the theological or moral nature of pre-Islamic polytheism in Arabia, and the Muslim critique of the pre-Islamic period portrays it as devoid of all redeeming features. From the scanty evidence available, the cult promoted loyalty to family, clan, and tribe, a sentiment that Arabs carried over into the Islamic period as Islam was characterized as a "super-tribe" uniting all Arabs under one common genealogy.

While Christianity was present from an early period in Arabia, and there is evidence of the political connections and dimensions of Arabian Christians to their coreligionists in the surrounding countries, little is known of Arabian Christian beliefs and practices except through Islamic sources. Qur'anic evidence indicates that, while the full range of Gospel narratives is not represented, the Qur'an represents particularly the Gospel of Luke quite accurately and with close readings. Recent scholarship in this area is challenging the earlier notions that the Qur'an portrayed only a heterodox form of Christianity and is pointing to a more mainstream pre-Islamic Christianity, albeit divided among the various Christological heresies of the day.

As seen from the above survey of Arabian history, religion among the pre-Islamic Arabs was closely tied to the political ambitions of several foreign powers that wished to dominate Arabia. At the time of the rise of Islam, converting to one of

The ruins of the Marʾib Dam, created circa the sixth century B.C.E. in Marʾib, Yemen, by the Sabaens, one of four major kingdoms of southern Arabia to predate Islam. Aqueducts and dams were an important part of the Sabaeans's infrastructure and rise to power. Secular historians have postulated that the decline of pre-Islamic kingdoms may have had to do with the breakdown of their dams and aqueducts; the Quʾran attributes the destruction of the Marʾib Dam to divine punishment of the Sabaeans's sins. The Balaq mountains are in the background. © Archivo Iconografico, S.A./Corbis

the varieties of Judaism or Christianity in Arabia meant choosing not only a religion but also a political and social agenda dominated by a foreign power.

### Literary Legacy

One of the major legacies of pre-Islamic Arabian culture to later Arab and Islamic culture was the development of the poetic and formal language often termed "classical" Arabic. In the century or century and a half before the birth of Muhammad in 570 C.E., the Arab tribes in the Hijaz developed a literary form of Arabic that stood alongside the various dialects. This was a composite, formal language with a highly inflected grammatical system. It also had a flexible system for generating new vocabulary based on extensive use of the Arabic verbal root system that allowed for easy adoption of new terms and concepts within the language itself. It was also open to the adoption of terms from the surrounding languages of Hebrew, Aramaic, Latin, Ethiopic, among others. As a "meta-language" it undoubtedly reflected the growing political expansion of the Qureish and their economic unification of the Hijaz, but it also seems to have grown from the common experiences of local religious practices, Bedouin

travel songs, and the panegyrics of the courts of the Arab dynasties along the borders of the Roman and Persian empires.

There is also speculation that this language was used for formal prose in treaties, formal agreements, and in writing Jewish and Christian scripture, but, as mentioned above, there is little evidence of biblical translations into Arabic in the pre-Islamic period. Instead, there is more evidence that Jews and Christians had their own "dialects" of Arabic, with added vocabulary from the Jewish and Christian languages of the eastern Mediterranean. These dialects likely served as the conduits for much of the foreign religious vocabulary that found its way into Arabic.

The poetry that has survived from the pre-Islamic period was transmitted orally and only transcribed in the Islamic period. It was composed by a poet to be preserved and recited by a reciter, a *rawi*, who may also have been a poet or an apprentice. In this poetry, each poetic line had independent meaning, and the entire poem was comprised of thematic sections, which concentrated on travel, love, praise, and so on. The most famous of these "odes," termed *qasida*s, are known as the *Mu'allaqat*, or "suspended odes." Various stories are given to explain the name, but the writers of these poems became known as the masters of Arabic poetic composition, and their style of poetry so influential that later Islamic poetry in Persian and other Islamic languages as well as Arabic survived until modern times.

The style of poetry known as *saj'*, rhymed prose, was another influential poetic form, apparently used by seers and holy men for prognosticative pronouncements. This form of poetic language is found in many places in the Qur'an, giving rise to the accusation that Muhammad was a poet or mantic seer.

*A photo of an alabaster relief of a camel and its rider appears in the volume one color plates.*

*See also* **Arabic Language; Arabic Literature; Asabiyya; Empires: Sassanian; Muhammad.**

## BIBLIOGRAPHY

Arnold, W. T., et al. *Studies of Roman Imperialism.* Manchester, U.K.: Manchester University Press, 1906.

Bowersock, G. W. *Roman Arabia.* Cambridge, Mass.: Harvard University Press, 1983.

Breton, J.-F. *Arabia Felix from the Time of the Queen of Sheba: Eighth Century B.C. to First Century A.D.* Notre Dame, Ind.:University of Notre Dame Press, 1999.

Burton, R. F., et al. *Sir Richard Burton's Travels in Arabia and Africa: Four Lectures from a Huntington Library Manuscript.* San Marino, Calif.: Huntington Library, 1990.

Bury, G. W. *The Land of Uz.* London: Macmillan and Co. Ltd., 1911.

Cleveland, R. L. *An Ancient South Arabian Necropolis: Objects from the Second Campaign, 1951, in the Timnaí Cemetery.* Baltimore, Md.: Johns Hopkins Press, 1965.

Crone, P. *Meccan Trade and the Rise of Islam.* Princeton, N.J.: Princeton University Press, 1987.

Díabrowa, E., and Uniwersytet Jagielloiínski. Instytut Historii. *The Roman and Byzantine Army in the East: Proceedings of a Colloqium [sic] Held at the Jagiellonian University, Kraków in September 1992.* Kraków: Drukarnia Uniwersytetu Jagielloínskiego, 1994.

Doughty, C. M. *Travels in Arabia Deserta.* Cambridge, U.K.: Cambridge University Press, 1988.

Esin, E. *Mecca, the Blessed; Madinah, the Radiant.* New York: Crown Publishers, 1963.

Graf, D. F. *Rome and the Arabian Frontier: From the Nabataeans to the Saracens.* Aldershot, Hampshire, U.K., and Brookfield, Vt.: Ashgate, 1997.

Grohmann, Adolf. *Arabic Papyri from Khirbet el-Mird.* Louvain: Publications Universitaires, 1963.

Hoyland, R. G. *Arabia and the Arab: From the Bronze Age to the Coming of Islam.* New York, Routledge, 2001.

Kennedy, D. L., and Braund, D. *The Roman Army in the East.* Ann Arbor, Mich.: Journal of Roman Archaeology, 1996.

Korotaev, A. V. *Ancient Yemen: Some General Trends of Evolution of the Sabaic Language and Sabaean Culture.* Oxford, U.K. and New York: Oxford University Press, 1995.

MacAdam, H. I. *Studies in the History of the Roman Province of Arabia: The Northern Sector.* Oxford, U.K.: B.A.R., 1986.

Montgomery, J. A. *Arabia and the Bible.* Philadelphia: University of Pennsylvania Press, 1934.

Newby, G. D. *A History of the Jews of Arabia: From Ancient Times to Their Eclipse under Islam.* Columbia: University of South Carolina Press, 1988.

Peters, F. E. *Jerusalem and Mecca: The Typology of the Holy City in the Near East.* New York: New York University Press, 1987.

Peters, F. E. *The Arabs and Arabia on the Eve of Islam.* Aldershot, Hampshire, U.K., and Brookfield, Vt.: Ashgate, 1999.

Peters, F. E., and NetLibrary Inc. *Muhammad and the Origins of Islam.* Albany: State University of New York Press, 1994.

Philby, H. S. J .B. *The Land of Midian.* London: Benn, 1957.

Phillips, W. *Qataban and Sheba: Exploring the Ancient Kingdoms on the Biblical Spice Routes of Arabia.* New York: Harcourt Brace, 1955.

Playfair, R. L. *A History of Arabia Felix or Yemen, From the Commencement of the Christian Era to the Present Time: Including an Account of the British Settlement of Aden.* Salisbury, N.C.: Documentary Publications, 1978.

Ricks, S. D. *Western Language Literature on Pre-Islamic Central Arabia: An Annotated Bibliography.* Denver, Colo.: American Institute of Islamic Studies, 1991..

Salibi, K. S. *The Bible Came from Arabia.* London: Pan Books, 1987.

Sawyer, J. F. A., and Clines, D. J. A. *Midian, Moab and Edom: The History and Archaeology of Late Bronze and Iron Age Jordan and North-west Arabia.* Sheffield, U.K.: JSOT Press, 1983.

Schippmann, K. *Ancient South Arabia: From the Queen of Sheba to the Advent of Islam.* Translated by Allison Brown. Princeton, N.J.: Markus Wiener, 2001.

Schulz, E., et al. *Vegetation on the Northern Arabian Shield and Adjacent Sand Seas.* Reston, Va.: U.S. Dept. of the Interior Geological Survey, 1985.

Segal, Arthur. *Town Planning and Architecture in Provincia Arabia.* Oxford, U.K.: B. A. R., 1988.

Shahid, Irfan. *Rome and the Arabs: A Prolegomenon to the Study of Byzantium and the Arabs.* Washington, D.C.: Dumbarton Oaks, 1984.

Simon, R. *Meccan Trade and Islam: Problems of Origin and Structure.* Budapest: Akádemiai Kiadó, 1989.

Sowayan, Saad Abdullah. *Nabati Poetry.* Los Angeles: University of California Press, 1985.

Spijkerman, A., and Piccirillo, M. *The Coins of the Decapolis and Provincia Arabia.* Jerusalem: Franciscan Printing Press, 1978.

Van Beek, G. W. *Hajar Bin Humeid; Investigations at a Pre-Islamic Site in South Arabia.* Baltimore, Md.: Johns Hopkins Press, 1969.

Zwemer, S. M. *Arabia: The Cradle of Islam: Studies in the Geography, People and Politics of the Peninsula, with an Account of Islam and Mission-Work.* New York and Chicago: F. H. Revell Company, 1900.

*Gordon D. Newby*

# ARABIC LANGUAGE

A people with the name of *Aribi* is first mentioned in a cuneiform inscription from the eighth century B.C.E., where it denotes a nomadic tribe. In later centuries tribes named *ʿrb* are mentioned in several sources, for instance in the Torah (Jeremiah 25:24). It is not known what kind of language these people spoke but it is clear that they had some connection with the North Arabian desert, even though they did not dwell in the Arabian Peninsula itself. Probably their language belonged to the continuum of Semitic languages that was spoken all over the Middle East and that included Aramaic, Hebrew, Canaanite, and others.

The full penetration of the Arabian Peninsula dates from a later period. In the southern part of the peninsula the South Arabian kingdoms such as those of the Minaeans and the Sabaeans flourished from the thirteenth century B.C.E. onward. Their language was South Arabian, a language related to the Ethiopian languages. They had domesticated the camel, which was used for carrying loads but not yet as a riding animal. The South Arabians maintained frequent trade relations with the Middle East, usually by the sea route, and through these contacts the camel was introduced in the north as well. Around the beginning of the common era when a riding saddle was developed for the camel, it became possible to penetrate the desert and even live there permanently. Presumably, some of the tribes that wandered in the border area between sedentary land and the desert fringe eventually made the shift to a nomadic life in the desert and thus developed what may be called a Bedouin society.

In the northern part of the peninsula thousands of (usually short) inscriptions attest to the presence of a language that was very much akin to the Arabic language as it is known today. This language was characterized by the form of the article, *h-* or *hn-*, as distinct from the Arabic article *al-*, but related to the Hebrew form *ha-*. This language type is usually called Early North Arabic; it was divided into several varieties such as Thamudaean and Lihyanitic. The first inscription in a language that may be recognized as Arabic is the inscription from al-Namara in Syria (328 C.E.) erected by Imruʾ al-Qays who calls himself "King of the Arabs." The language shows some similarities with the South Arabian of the South Arabian kingdoms, while at the same time preserving the traces of its relatedness to the Northwest Semitic languages.

Around the fifth century Arabic-speaking tribes lived in large parts of the Arabian peninsula as well as in the areas to the north of the peninsula as far as the Syrian desert and the Sinai; some of them even settled in sedentary areas such as the city of Aleppo. These tribes were Christians. The Bedouin tribes in the peninsula were polytheists. They greatly increased their influence when they took over the caravan trade from the South Arabian kingdoms and settled themselves as middlemen in places like Mecca.

The al-Namara inscription is written in a language with a declensional system, similar to the language of the pre-Islamic poems. It was in this language that the Qurʾan was revealed. According to the indigenous tradition all tribes at the eve of Islam used this language as their vernacular language, although later grammarians document a number of differences between the varieties of the various tribes (*lughat*). Thus, for instance, the eastern tribes are said to have used a phoneme /ʾ/ (*hamza*), which was absent in the dialect of the western tribes, but present in the language of poetry and the Qurʾan. According to others the vernacular language of the tribes had already shifted to a different type of language, in which, for instance, case-endings had disappeared. In this view, the language of poetry and the Qurʾan was a literary language that was no longer used as a spoken language but served as a kind of supra-tribal variety, based on the language of the eastern tribes (sometimes called poetico-Qurʾanic koine).

## The Spread of the Arabic Language

After the death of the prophet Muhammad the Islamic conquests brought the religion and the language of the Arab tribes into a large area stretching from Islamic Spain to Central Asia. The languages originally spoken in this area (Coptic, Persian, Syriac, Berber) gave way to the linguistic onslaught of Arabic, and even though some of the speakers remained bilingual, the entire area was Arabized within a century. The Arabic as spoken by the inhabitants of this vast empire differed considerably from the language of the Qurʾan, especially in the sedentary centers that were established in the early years of the conquest, such as Basra, Kufa, Fustat, and Kairouan. There was a reduction of the phonemic inventory (loss of interdentals, merger of the phonemes *dad* and *zaʾ*), loss of case-endings and modal endings, reduction of grammatical categories, and emergence of a genitive exponent and aspectual particles. Syntactically speaking, the language had shifted from a synthetic to an analytic type, usually called New Arabic.

There are many theories about the reasons for this change, which affected all domains of grammar. Those who believe that even before Islam the vernacular language of the Bedouin already exhibited some New Arabic changes tend to minimize the role of the new learners of the language. They

This modern example of Arabic calligraphy by Aziz Muhammad Al Shabli reads: "Thanks be to God the Lord of the Universe," which is the first line of the Qur'an. Originating in the Near East, Arabic was brought by Islamic conquests in the century after Muhammad's death to a vast geographical area reaching from parts of Spain to Central Asia. AZIZ MOHAMMED AL SHABLI/ACCESS

believe the various vernaculars of the Bedouin were homogenized when members from different tribes were thrown together in the conquering armies. As a result, the vernacular varieties that emerged after the conquests became very different from the language of the Qur'an. Others look for the cause of the linguistic changes in the languages spoken by the inhabitants of the conquered territories. According to them, this substratal influence affected the structure of New Arabic by carrying over features of languages such as Coptic, Persian, Syriac, and Berber to the Arabic language, as spoken by its new speakers. Yet another factor to be taken into account is the process of language acquisition itself. In every language-learning process in an informal setting the native speakers tend to simplify their language and the new learners apply universal strategies of simplification to this input. The result is a drastic reduction of the phonemic inventory and of grammatical categories, a general disappearance of redundancy, and a restructuring of the language.

Whatever the causes of the linguistic changes, there can be no doubt that very early on in the conquests there was a marked difference between the language of the religious and literary heritage on one hand, and the colloquial speech of the Arab empire on the other. According to the classic description of this situation by Ibn Khaldun, the scholars of Arabic became concerned about this corruption of speech and started to codify the language in their grammar books lest the language of the holy scriptures become incomprehensible for later generations.

The original conquest was just the first stage in the Arabization process since it reached only the sedentary areas, in particular the new garrison towns established by the Arab armies. Later centuries brought successive waves of Bedouin migrants to the conquered territories. These were responsible for the Arabization of much larger areas. In some cases they re-Bedouinized the sedentary dialects of the cities. In Baghdad, for instance, the dialect of the Muslims became Bedouinized while the Christians and Jews retained the original sedentary dialect. In North Africa the second wave of migration is associated with the invasion of the Bedouin tribes of the Banu Hilal and the Banu Sulaym in the tenth and eleventh centuries C.E., which brought Arabic to large parts of the countryside.

There is no consensus about the language these Bedouin spoke. Those who maintain that the vernacular of the Bedouin tribes in the pre-Islamic period had already changed in the direction of New Arabic believe that there was not much difference between the dialects of the first and the second invasion. Others believe that the Bedouin tribes continued to speak a type of Arabic that was basically identical with the pre-Islamic Arabic of poetry and Qur'an. In this view, the Bedouin did not lose their speech until the fourth century of the Hijra (Islamic calendar). This is corroborated by the grammarians who explain that the Bedouin dialects became corrupted through exposure to the sedentary way of speaking.

## Arabic in Islamic Society

At the beginning of Islam, Arabic became the language of both private and public life in the Arab empire. During a transitional period the indigenous languages remained in use, for instance in Egypt where Greek and Coptic were used for administrative purposes along with Arabic. But at the end of the first century of the Hijra, Arabic was firmly established as the official language of the empire. The languages that used to be spoken in the conquered territories disappeared or remained in use in a restricted domain only, such as Coptic and Syriac. In the Arab West, Berber remained in use in the countryside and has indeed never been replaced completely by Arabic until the present day.

The codification of standard Arabic by the grammarians started during the second century of Islam, but even before that there must have existed some kind of norm in writing, possibly connected with the emergence of an epistolary style in the chancelleries. The earliest Arabic documents, the Egyptian papyri from the first century of the Hijra, already contain "mistakes" that show the existence of a standard as target in writing. Such mistakes are very common and with the growth of literacy they became even more frequent. In modern linguistic terminology texts containing deviations from the grammatical norms of the standard language are usually called "Middle Arabic." This term does not denote a well-defined variety of the language but is used as a general label for all nonstandard texts. Some of the mistakes reflect the vernacular language, for instance, when people write *la yaktubu* "they do not write" rather than the more formal *la yaktubuna*, but very often one encounters pseudo-corrections, when people in their attempt to write standard Arabic overstep their target, for instance when they write *lam yaktubuna* "they did not write" instead of *lam yaktubu*. The introduction of vernacular features in written language could also serve to create a humorous effect. This occurs particularly in literature aiming at a popular audience, such as the stories in the *Arabian Nights* or in dialect poetry.

The acceptance of deviations from the norms was particularly strong in non-Muslim circles. Jewish and Christian writers, who did not have the same attachment to the language of the Qur'an, felt free to use a more popular kind of language. Thus we find Jewish writers using certain vernacular constructions when writing to fellow Jews, but studiously avoiding these when writing for a more general Muslim audience. One might even say that this kind of Arabic became an in-group language with a special status. This Judaeo-Arabic was written in Hebrew characters and contained a large number of Hebrew loanwords.

Arabic remained the language par excellence of the Islamic empire for well over five centuries, until the Mongol conquest of Baghdad in 1258. Even in Mamluk Egypt, where the political and military elite consisted of Turkic-speaking people, Arabic continued to be regarded as a language of prestige. Mamluk intellectuals used it in writing, even though Qipcaq Turkic was their colloquial language. In the East the position of Arabic as a religious, cultural, and administrative language started to change from the tenth century onward. Middle Persian, the language of the Persian empire, had become marginalized after the conquests, but New Persian (Farsi) became popular as the language of poetry in the ninth century. The dynasty of the Samanids reintroduced it as the language of the court, and in the sixteenth century the Safavid dynasty started to use it as the new "national" language of Iran. As a result, the spreading of Islam in South and Southeast Asia took place in Persian, particularly when the Moguls began to use it as their literary language. In the Islamic East, Arabic was retained solely as the language of the Qur'an, Persian having become the language of preaching, literature, and administration.

With the advent of the Turkic peoples Arabic gradually lost its position in the Islamic West as well. In the Seljuk Empire and later in the Ottoman Empire the language of administration became Ottoman Turkish, while Persian was the language used by the intellectual elite for cultural purposes. Arabic was relegated to the domain of religion, although it continued to serve as a source for thousands of loanwords in both Persian and Turkish, ranging from learned words such as *mo'allem* "teacher" in Persian and *akide* "dogma" in Turkish to common words such as *ve-* 'and' in both languages. Yet, when the Arab world became integrated in the Ottoman Empire, spoken Arabic was treated as a minor provincial language and its written variety was only used for religious purposes. Even though most inhabitants of the Arab provinces did not know Turkish, official contacts with the empire had to take place in that language.

The nineteenth-century Arab renaissance (*Nahda*) brought a change in the self-awareness of the Arabs and the position of Arabic. In Egypt, Muhammad 'Ali initiated a movement to translate European writings into Arabic. In its wake a new idiom was created to convey the new ideas, and the language was modernized through the introduction of a host of new terms in the fields of the technical sciences, economics, and politics. Once again, Arabic became a language in which political and administrative issues were discussed.

The fall of the Ottoman Empire signified a new beginning for Arabic but the simultaneous invasion of the colonial powers introduced a new danger to the language. Because of the military and cultural dominance of the English and the French the attitude toward Arabic was often a negative one. After the Arab countries gained their independence Arabic became the official language of most of these countries and the symbol of Arab nationalism. In the Mashreq, it did not take long before English was replaced by Arabic, but in the formerly French-dominated countries it took decades before the French language had disappeared from the administrative, educational, and legal systems.

### Fusha and ʿAmmiyya

The contemporary linguistic situation in the Arab world is characterized by diglossia, in which two varieties of the language have strictly separate roles or functions in the speech community. The so-called High variety, called *fusha* or *al-ʿarabiyya*, is the language learned at school as the carrier of a rich religious and literary heritage; it is the language that is used in writing, both in the educational system and the media, and in formal speech. The Low variety, called *ʿammiyya* or in North Africa *darija*, is the colloquial language, which is the mother tongue of all speakers. It is the language of everyday communication, the language of friends and family, the language of informal speaking.

The coexistence of two varieties of the language is not without its problems. Since the standard language is learned at school, only those who are literate have access to the written production. For the vast majority of the population the formal language is not immediately comprehensible so that a large part of linguistic communication in the community is beyond their linguistic competence. The two varieties have quite different associations, the standard language being associated with education and therefore with social success and wealth, whereas the vernacular is associated with illiteracy and poverty. At the same time, its function as the language of informal talk makes it the symbol of in-group communication, whereas the standard language is seen as a stereotyped and distanced means of communication.

Language choice between standard and vernacular depends on a number of factors such as the person of the interlocutor, the topic being spoken about, and the setting of the speech act. By their language choice speakers express their attitude toward these factors, their evaluation of the situation and the interlocutor. Since language variation is not a matter of choice between two discrete varieties, but takes place on a continuum between the highest standard and the lowest vernacular, there are endless possibilities of language choice. Such linguistic behavior is often indicated with the term of code-mixing. Since the span of the continuum attainable for the individual speaker directly depends on the degree of literacy, most people may be said to have only a relatively small variation at their disposal. But even the best educated speakers are unable to extemporize in standard Arabic and inevitably mix vernacular elements in their speech.

Because of its symbolic value as a binding element for all Arabic-speaking peoples language choice is intimately connected with Arab nationalism. The *fusha* is the symbol of Arab unity, whereas the vernacular dialects stand for divisiveness and regionalism (*iqlimiyya*). It is widely believed in the Arab world that during the colonial period the European powers intentionally propagated the study and the use of the dialect in order to divide the Arab world. Even today, Western interest in dialectology is still regarded as a manifestation of neo-imperialism. This creates a problem for Arab politicians who wish to show their adherence to the ideals of Arab nationalism but at the same time their strong ties with the population. Politicians like Jamal ʿAbd al-Nasser made a skillful use of the language variation by mixing standard and vernacular in their political speeches. The connection with the standard language is especially strong in those countries that emphasize their role in the Arab nationalist movement. The different attitudes toward Arab nationalism correlate with the attitude toward the vernacular. In those countries where Arab nationalism is part of the dominant ideology the use of standard Arabic is emphasized and attempts to replace it with the vernacular are met with severe criticism.

The attitude toward the dialect is not wholly negative, however. In a country such as Egypt the *ʿammiyya* may be said to hold a special position. Because of the pride they take in their country Egyptians are also proud of the Egyptian dialect, and although they share with other Arab countries the mistrust toward the imperialists who used the dialect to further their own interests and although in Egypt, too, the *fusha* holds a special prestige position, the use of the dialect is widespread even in situations where in other countries it would be unthinkable to use dialect. Thus, Egyptian presidents are never averse to using partly Egyptian dialect in their political speeches—at least for internal use; in their contacts with other Arab countries they tend to switch to standard Arabic. Since the Egyptian film industry and more recently the television soaps have gained enormous popularity outside Egypt, knowledge of this dialect in other Arab countries is widespread and many speakers of other dialects are familiar with Egyptian.

In North Africa the linguistic policies of the French have left unmistakable traces. After independence there was a class of intellectuals who only knew French and could not communicate in Arabic. The first decades after gaining independence were therefore characterized by a movement toward Arabization, the replacement of French by Arabic in domains such as administration and education. Several school reforms were needed before at least primary and secondary schools adopted Arabic as the main medium of instruction. Even today French/Arabic bilingualism in North Africa is widespread and French has retained a special position of prestige. In particular among intellectuals the mixing of French and Arabic in *franco-arabe* has remained popular.

In the Levant, Syria, and Lebanon became independent from French colonial rule with a somewhat different outcome. In Syria, French never took hold the way it did in the

Maghreb. In Lebanon, however, bilingualism was connected with a widespread feeling, both among Muslims and Christians, that Lebanon was a bicultural country. The civil war has changed this situation in the sense that Arabic-French bilingualism has become associated more exclusively with the Christian community.

## Arabic as a World Language

After the Arab conquest of the Iberian Peninsula in 711 C.E., the influence of the Arabic language spread beyond the borders of the Islamic world. Due to its role as the language in which Greek philosophy and science were transmitted, European scholars came to regard Arabic as the language of culture and scholarship. A large amount of translations of Arabic texts circulated in Western Europe, and through the contact with Arab culture in al-Andalus many loanwords, such as *algebra, zero, algorithm, alchemy, sugar, artichoke, apricot,* and *admiral,* entered the European languages. This international role of Arabic ended with the Renaissance when Western Europe rediscovered the Greek sources and no longer needed Arabic as an intermediary.

Nowadays, Arabic is spoken as a mother tongue outside the Arab world in a number of linguistic enclaves, such as Anatolian Arabic in Turkey, and tiny pockets of speakers in Uzbekistan, Afghanistan, Iran, and Cyprus. Malta is a different case altogether. Here, the Maltese language, written in Latin characters, has become the only Arabic dialect with the status of a national language. The Maltese, who are Christians, tend to deny the connection of their language with the Arabic-speaking world and prefer to regard the language as a remnant of the Phoenician language.

Apart from these enclaves, large numbers of Arabs have migrated outside the Arab world (*mahjar*). In the Americas, early immigrants came mostly from Lebanon and Syria. Most of them were merchants, who assimilated without difficulty to their new countries, especially in Latin America. Most of them retained Arabic and in countries such as Brazil and Argentina they even managed to establish a thriving literary tradition.

The immigration of speakers of Arabic to western Europe has a different background. In the early 1960s the western European countries started to hire unskilled laborers from the Mediterranean countries on a large scale. The original plan was to hire these people for a restricted period of time and then remigrate them to the countries of origin. Soon it became apparent that they were there to stay. As a result the western European countries suddenly realized that they had a sizable Arabic-speaking minority. In most of these countries the official policy of the government consisted in providing education in the home language of the immigrants' children. Nonetheless, many children of the second and third generation are losing their language of origin and shifting to the dominant language. In most cases they go through a lengthy period of code-switching in which they mix their home language and the language of the country they are living in.

The main role of Arabic outside the Arab world is that of being the language of the Qur'an, even though in many regions it was not the language of the Islamic spreading of the faith (*da'wa*). This role was played in the East by Persian, and further east by Malay. In Africa, the language in which Islam was preached was Hausa or Swahili. Yet, for all Muslims Arabic has a special status as the language chosen by God for his last revelation. The reverence for this status does not lead, however, to intensive study of the language itself. Ordinary Muslims in countries such as Iran, Turkey, Indonesia, Pakistan, Nigeria, and Senegal do not know more Arabic than a few *ayah*s from the Qur'an, even though in some of these countries there is an extensive public or private network of Qur'an schools where the text of the Holy Book and the basic elements of Arabic are being taught.

Historically, Arabic functioned in Africa not only as a religious language but also as a language of trade. Even before West Africa was Islamicized, Arabic was used there as a lingua franca between the courts of different kingdoms. This is also clear from the loanwords in African languages, which are not restricted to the domain of religion but comprise also other semantic domains. In Hausa, for instance, such words as "book" (*littaafi*) and "news" (*laabaari*) derive from Arabic as do some conjunctions such as *saboo da* "because," from Arabic *sabab* "reason." In Swahili something like 30 percent of the lexicon is derived from Arabic. Most of these loans were introduced by a small class of so-called *mallam*s (Ar. *mu'allim* "teacher") who maintained the ties with Arabic even after the trade connections had been severed.

In Asia, Islam was spread by Persian-speaking traders and missionaries. Here the Arabic language was known exclusively from the text of the Qur'an. Even though the ordinary believers did not know Arabic, they became used to some of the religious terms through the recitation of the Qur'an. Other Arabic words entered the Asian languages through Persian, as evidenced by their phonological shape, for instance, in Urdu *hazirin* "audience," with Persian z for Arabic *dad*. A further source of borrowing was the written medium. A small class of scholars used their pilgrimage to Mecca in order to study the Islamic sciences and through their books they introduced hundreds or even thousands of loanwords from Arabic. It has been estimated that in Malay more than three thousand words were borrowed in this way, for instance, the word *hukum* "judgment," which gave rise to the derived verb *menghukumkan* "to pronounce judgment."

The relatively low level of knowledge of Arabic may be changing with the increasing influence of Arabic sites on the Internet. In some countries, such as Mali, learning Arabic has become quite fashionable among young people. In other countries, international Islamic contacts may lead to an increase in Arabic as the primary language of Islam.

*See also* **African Culture and Islam; Arabic Literature; Grammar and Lexicography; Identity, Muslim; Pan-Arabism; Persian Language and Literature; Qur'an; South Asian Culture and Islam; Urdu Language, Literature, and Poetry.**

## BIBLIOGRAPHY

Ayalon, Ami. *Language and Change in the Arab Middle East: The Evolution of Modern Political Discourse.* New York and Oxford, U.K.: Oxford University Press, 1987.

Bakalla, Muhammad Hasan. *Arabic Linguistics: An Introduction and Bibliography.* London: Mansell, 1983.

Blau, Joshua. *The Beginnings of the Arabic Diglossia: A Study of the Origins of Neo-Arabic.* Malibu, Calif.: Undena, 1977.

Bulliet, Richard W. *The Camel and the Wheel.* 2d ed. New York: Columbia University Press, 1990.

Diem, Werner. *Hochsprache und Dialekt: Untersuchungen zur heutigen arabischen Zweisprachigkeit.* Wiesbaden: F. Steiner, 1974.

Ferguson, Charles A. "The Arabic Koine." *Language* 25 (1959a): 616–630.

Ferguson, Charles A. "Diglossia." *Word* 15 (1959b): 325–340.

Fischer, Wolfdietrich. *Grundriss der arabischen Philologie,* Vol. 1: *Sprachwissenschaft.* Wiesbaden: L. Reichert, 1983.

Fischer, Wolfdietrich, and Jastrow, Otto. *Handbuch der arabischen Dialekte.* Wiesbaden: O. Harrassowitz, 1980.

Holes, Clive. *Modern Arabic: Structures, Functions and Varieties.* London and New York: Kegan Paul International, 1995.

Miller, Ann M. "The Origin of the Modern Arabic Sedentary Dialects: An Evaluation of Several Theories." *Al-'Arabiyya* 19 (1986): 47–74.

Rouchdy, Aleya. *The Arabic Language in America.* Detroit: Wayne State University Press, 1992.

Versteegh, Kees. *The Arabic Language.* 2d ed. Edinburgh: Edinburgh University Press, 2001.

*Kees Versteegh*

# ARABIC LITERATURE

Literature may be defined in numerous ways, but in Arabic literature some of the prominent phenomena that are associated with the modern concept of literature—individual creativity, authenticity of feeling, and fictionality—will not easily be detected by an unaware reader. Arabic literature as well as other non-Western literatures is firmly rooted in its own tradition and can hardly be appreciated otherwise.

## Arabic Literature: Notions and Concepts

The modern Arabic equivalent for literature is *adab*, but in its traditional context this concept also refers to notions like "education," "general knowledge," and "decency." It is derived from the pre-Islamic *da'b* (pl. *adab*) that denotes "good, accepted practice." In medieval Arab society *adab* can probably be best compared to the concept of "belles lettres." It does not, however, include the most esteemed form of Arabic literature of *shi'r*, or poetry, as a category.

To understand the status of *shi'r*, its early development within pre-Islamic society has to be discussed. This society was divided along lines of families, tribes, and clans. Within the clan the prominent social characters were the *sayyid* (chief), the *kahin* (the soothsayer, expert of the supernatural), and the *sha'ir*, the keeper of earthly knowledge memorized in a nonscriptural society. This *sha'ir*—or "poet"—knew by heart the clan's history, the affiliations with other clans, and the battle deeds of the clan in skirmishes with other clans. Battle cries, invectives of the enemy, and boasting of the hero were commonly uttered in poetical form and were memorized by the poet, in order to be handed down to the next generation.

In a development for which we have no record, another kind of poetry emerged in this pre-Islamic society called the *qasida* (or "ode"). These poems, too, were memorized by the poet. In the course of time he started to compose this kind of poetry himself. The practice of memorizing and composing poetry was a craft that was handed down from one generation to next, the poet's apprentice being called *rawi* or "transmitter" (pl. *ruwat*).

## Pre-Islamic Arabic Poetry

An Arabic poem was composed on the basis of two form principles: meter and rhyme. Each poem had a fixed meter that could be chosen from the sixteen metrical patterns that Arabic prosodical tradition defined, although it has to be said that classical poets were mainly using only six of these. Contrary to Western metrical tradition, the Arabic meters were based on the length of syllables rather then on stress. This does not mean that Arabic poetic language knew no stress, but it was not the principle for metric scansion. The poet is expected to retain the same meter throughout each poem he composes, which may run into dozens of verses.

Apart from this feature, called monometer, the poet uses the same rhyme throughout the poem, which is called monorhyme. The rhyme cluster is always based on one specific consonant accompanied with long or short vowels. In the correct rhyme a limited variation of vowels is allowed. Each line of poetry is divided into two hemistichs, which deceptively makes the poem in print seem like two columns.

This elaborated form requires a high degree of craftsmanship and it suggests a long evolution, but no sources are available for this. It may also seem that in its form Arabic poetry is extremely monotonous, but it is often the subtle play between the formal rules, the listeners expectation, and the poet's elegant solutions that makes this poetry a vibrant art.

Pre-Islamic (or pre-classical) Arabic poetry can be divided thematically into two groups: short, monothematic poems, often "situational" poetry, and long, polythematic poems called *qasida*s.

**Qasida.** The *qasida* is the most prestigious poetical creation throughout Arab history. Even nowadays it is deemed the ultimate work of artistic achievement of Arab culture. It is a tripartite composition that follows a thematic sequence: In the *nasib* the poet—often in a dialogue with his companions—recalls his memory of a love affair. To give in to his grief meant that the poet broke his self-control (*sabr*). The immediate occasion he uses to legitimize this is his coming across the remnants of the camp left by the tribe to which his beloved belongs. This description is usually vivid and realistic, although to our modern taste the beloved is hardly portrayed as an actual person.

In the second part of the *qasida* the poet distances himself from this emotional reminiscence by dwelling on his travels through the desert, describing his mount and the desert environment with its specific fauna (*rahil*). Sometimes this second part is very short, condensed to the words *daʿ dha*: "leave that (love affair) behind!"

The final part of the *qasida* offers the poet a relative freedom in the choice of his theme. He may address the chief of a tribe with a panegyric ode (*madih*), use his poem as a warning against an enemy, indulge in boasting on his own exploits, or simply offer a vivid description of a natural phenomenon like an all-refreshing shower.

The traditional *qasida*, its form, and its content, have remained influential not only for Arabic literature, but also for later developments in Turkish and Persian literature.

**Marthiya.** Apart from the *qasida* another genre adopted this prestigious form. From a traditional wailing exclamation, probably common to the universal rituals of death, Arab women developed a kind of poetic dirge that kept the middle between "situational" poetry and the *qasida*. The *marthiya* was composed in remembrance of a deceased brother, husband, or father, but it followed the formal (not the thematic) requirements of the *qasida*. The reason for this is that *marathi* were considered poetry of the public domain, inciting to blood vengeance in case of violent death and helping to reinvigorate social values and the ideal of knightly vigor on which women and children depended for their security. Contemporary to the early emergence of Islam the poetess al-Khansaʾ (d. c. 645) produced a considerable number of such dirges on her brothers in which one might read a stance of opposition toward the social changes that the new religion brought with it against such pre-Islamic virtues as bravery, hospitality, generosity, and tribal loyalty.

**Shifting themes and forms.** Shortly before the emergence of Islam, Arabic poetry underwent a few thematic innovations: Love poetry gradually became an independent genre, introducing the beloved as taking part in a—probably fictitious—dialogue. In this period one also finds religious poetry reflecting a set of (popular) Christian and Jewish monotheistic concepts among the urban class of traders, as opposed to pagan worship of natural objects or polytheism that were still widespread on the Arabian Peninsula.

In cases where prestigious poetry was not deemed suitable, other literary forms were in use: The meter *rajaz* served all kinds of "situational" poetry like working songs, invectives, obscene poetry, and exhortations. Later this meter was used for lengthy didactic poems.

Rhymed prose (*sajʿ*) was used for soothsayer predictions and enchantments, for folkloric sayings and proverbs, and, finally, for the text of the Qurʾan.

### Poetry in Early Islam and the Umayyad Era

The production of poetry subsided remarkably with the beginning of Islam. First, the prophet Muhammad's attitude toward poetry was ambiguous. He renounced poetry and poets when he was accused of being a "poet" himself. A quote from the Qurʾan runs, "And the poets—the perverse follow them; hast thou not seen how they wander in every valley and how they say that which they do not," a reference to their baseless boasting (Arberry, trans., 26:224–226). On the other hand he realized that his status, comparable with that of a pre-Islamic chief, demanded the presence of a "court poet" as well, in his case the famous Hassan b. Thabit (d. 670). Another reason for the declining popularity of poetry may well have been the general preoccupation of the new Muslims with the expansion and stabilization of the new state. This decline in poetic production, however, was only temporary. The Umayyad era quickly gave an impetus for new developments in Arabic poetry.

Although the polythematic *qasida* as the masterpiece par excellence never ceased to exist, its parts developed into separate kinds of poetry in the Umayyad era. The *nasib* developed into love poetry and the *rahil* with its descriptions of nature into forms of bucolic poetry like descriptions of hunting parties and gardens. Together with older poetic kinds like wine poetry (*khamriyya*) and the general topic of description (*wasf*), these parts constituted the plethora of themes that a poet from this era could address.

The dichotomy of early Islamic society, its division into a Bedouin and a trader class, becomes clear in love poetry. In the *nasib*-part of the *qasida*, the beloved is mainly a nonpresent entity. She has left with her tribe and all that the poet can do is regret her departure and remember their past affair. Following this tradition the *ʿudhri* type of love poetry (named after the tribe ʿUdhra) creates an even greater division between the poet and his beloved: She becomes the unreachable projection of the poet's love from which he can only suffer and then whither away from passion. This kind of poetry might best be called "idealistic" and it provided Arabic literature with some almost mythical love pairs like Majnun and his Layla.

With the emergence of Islam and the continued ritualistic pilgrimage to Mecca, the population in the Hijaz cities like Mecca and Medina became gradually more affluent. Once a year they provided an intertribal and international forum where all Muslims could gather. The huge crowds involved in the hajj consisted of both men and women, offering many opportunities for both sexes to meet and have affairs. These paved the way for the so-called *hijazi* love poetry, in which the poet vividly describes his adventures, and cites extensively from (fictitious) dialogues between his beloved's companions and her or between the protagonists themselves. As opposed to *'udhri* love poetry, this new development can be called "realistic" love poetry.

In many ways the poetic developments of the Umayyad era reflect the development from a tribal society with nonhereditary succession to an urban society with dynastic power and an affluent court life in which the poet serves to embellish the environment of his *maecenas*.

### Poetry in the Abbasid Era

The transition from the Umayyad to the Abbasid dynasty and the transfer of the seat of the caliphate from Damascus to Baghdad can be considered the revolution of the *mawali*, or second- and third-generation converted Muslims who were not of Arab origin, but descendants of Persian or Byzantine families. Often these families had held high positions in the Sassanid kingdom in Persia.

In the early Abbasid era Arabic poetry consolidated its courtly functions. Most poets were in one way or another attached to the court, the highest-ranking poets being companions of the caliphs themselves.

The bond of Arabic literature with its pre-Islamic, Bedouin basis became more and more symbolic, although one of the greatest poets of this era, Abu Nuwas (d. c. 814), had had his poetic training through living with Arab tribes. His allegiance to the urban lifestyle motivated his utter contempt for those primitive conditions that he expressed in ridiculing Bedouin life. His most famous poems are the *khamriyyat* (about drinking scenes) and the *mujun*, more or less obscene poems about (pederastic) love.

In this poetry by Abu Nuwas and by the later Abu Tammam (d. 845), the *hijazi* tradition of realistic love poetry, of the self-confident individual, lives its triumph. The idealistic *'udhri* love poetry comes to an end with the late-eighth-century poet al-'Abbas b. al-Ahnaf (b. c. 750). His courtly love poetry has often (but probably not rightly) been interpreted as the source of courtly love poetry in the "Toubadours et

Trouvères" tradition in southern France through Arab-ruled al-Andalus (southern Spain).

The poetry of the Abbasid era provided a huge, sparkling collection of love poems, obscene poetry, repentance poetry for unbecomely behavior, semi-religious poetry pondering mortality, and detailed descriptions of gardens and gadgets in everyday life. In short every possible theme that an affluent class of intellectuals can think of was represented. The same period witnessed the emergence of literary theory and literary criticism. Inspired by the "philological" culture that Islamic society was (the Qur'an being the verbatim reproduction of God's word), both poets and linguists set out to explore the possibilities of the Arabic language, a discipline that inevitably led to mannerism and far-fetched metaphors in poetry.

Abu Tammam and the ninth-century poet al-Buhturi (d. 897/898) opposed this tendency by presenting two collections of poetry (both called *Hamasa*: courage) for which they selected canonical poetry of the Umayyad and pre-Islamic periods.

During the tenth century the central authority in Baghdad started to lose its grip on some of the outer regions like Egypt and Syria. As a consequence local "kings" established their own courts and court cultures in which one or more poets were essential assets. By this time some poets had reached an independent status, so that they could allow themselves to be hired by the most bidding party, like the famous poet al-Mutanabbi (d. 965) who started his career with Sayf al-Dawla (d. 967), ruler of Aleppo, then moved to the court of Kafur in Cairo and finally joined the Buwayhid court of 'Adud al-Dawla (d. 983) in Iraq. This mobility shows how poets had gained a role as spokesmen for the rulers of the time, voicing the king's greatness and acting as the laureate poets on important occasions.

### Al-Andalus

The downfall of the Umayyad caliphate had caused one of the members of the Umayyad family, 'Abd al-Rahman I (d. 788), to flee westward to the Iberian Peninsula where he established the kingdom of Cordoba in 752. This marked the beginning of Andalusian history, an outstanding period in Islamic history. This period is still referred to by Arabs as the multicultural "state" par excellence because it meant the peaceful coexistence of Jews, Christians, and Muslims. Al-Andalus soon disintegrated into petty kingdoms like Toledo, Sevilla, and Granada, but this never impeded cultural and intellectual progress. Only periods of foreign rule by orthodox Muslim forces from North Africa could temporarily infringe on it, until finally Granada fell to the Spanish Reconquista in 1492, the formal end of Andalusian history.

At the various courts in the main cities of al-Andalus, literature reached a remarkable apogee. One of the contributions Andalusion poets made to Arabic literature was the innovative form of the *muwashshah*, a poem with a strophical structure. It is unclear what the origin of this poem was. Certain types of strophic poetry were known in the East by the eighth century, but they never reached the level of prestigious poetry. The origin of the *muwashshah*, with its rhyme structure divided into stanzas and choruses and its idiosyncratic meter, should probably be sought in local Romance poetic traditions, probably in songs. This is at least suggested by the use of vernacular Arabic, Hebrew, and even the local Romance dialect, for instance, in the last verse of some *muwashshah*s, as a kind of humorous clue.

## The Centuries of Decline: Amateur Poetry

In the classical period the poet was a respected craftsman, famous for composing his art in courtly circles. Meanwhile in urban society the high status of Arabic-Islamic education, with its emphasis on language and the ornate use of it, produced an even greater number of literati who were able to produce verse at any given occasion. A great number of these "occasional" poems concerning every possible aspect of life (but often, of course, on the theme of love) are still to be found scattered in many *'adab*-works on a wide range of subjects, often helping to embellish the context.

It was mainly this class of literati that composed poetry between the thirteenth and eigteenth centuries (the *qurun al-inhitat*, or the centuries of decline in Arab culture). It is hard to name any famous poets of this period, but recent research has shown that poetry probably never stopped to be of high quality and originality. This is, however, a period that needs more attentive study than it has hitherto received.

## Arabic Prose

The oldest fragments of Arabic prose are the accounts of intertribal skirmishes on the Arab peninsula. These accounts, interlaced with poetry, may not be very accurate as a reflection of reality, but on the other hand they cannot be regarded as fiction. A second prose collection was the Prophet's biography, the *sira*, which by its nature cannot be considered fiction. The structure of these stories—chain of spokesmen, followed by the story itself, with short poems in between—remains the same in later prose collections. However, the context often became more frivolous like in al-Isfahani's (d. 967) *Kitab al-Aghani* (Book of songs), a huge collection of stories about poets and singers. One should be careful to use these for historic purposes because they are of an anecdotal character, representing neither pure historical facts nor pure fiction.

Another development within Arabic prose is the abundant growth of *'adab* literature in the Abbasid era, probably best rendered as "belles lettres," the well-wrought discourse for which any subject could serve as a topic. Al-Jahiz (d. 868), the *homo universalis* of his time, was the unrivaled champion of the genre.

Apart from these *'adab*-works, Arabic popular culture knew a strong storytelling tradition, but what remained of it is scarce: outlines of heroic adventures and etiologies of personal names.

Bringing the sub-literary storytelling and the *'adab* genre together was an innovation introduced from outside the Arab world, generating "mirrors of princes," like *Kalila wa-Dimna*, an adaptation into Arabic by Ibn al-Muqaffa' (d. c. 760) of the original Indian Pancatantra.

Among the class of the cultural elite in the later Abbasid era a unique genre emerged that used rhymed prose as its form and was composed following a more or less fixed structure with a story of two characters meeting in an urban environment without recognizing each other. After a humorous description of chaos and confusion, recognition occurs and all ends in a kind of comical clue. This *maqama* remained popular well into the nineteenth century. With time it became less bound to its original structure and could be used for didactic purposes as well.

Fiction in the modern sense of the word entered Arabic culture with the *Arabian Nights*, in which the frame story and a number of sub-stories are from an Indian-Persian origin and enlarged with a number of Egyptian popular stories.

## Modern Arabic Literature

Normally the entering of the Arab world into modern times is identified with Napoleon Bonaparte's temporary occupation of Egypt (1789–1801). The obvious difference in culture, scientific knowledge, and social structure between the two worlds caused Muhammad 'Ali (1769–1849), an Albanian officer who freed Egypt from Ottoman rule, to direct his attention to the West, mainly France. He sent a mission of scholars to Paris to gather scientific knowledge that could be translated and applied in Egypt. The witness report of this mission, written by al-Tahtawi (d. 1873), is one of the earliest accounts of the new confrontation between East and West.

Another channel of communication between East and West had remained open for much longer: the contacts between the Maronite community in Syria and the Roman Catholic Church of Rome. This contact was parallelled by American-based Presbyterian missionary activities in Lebanon. This new phase in Middle Eastern history, known as the *Nahda* (sometimes translated as Renaissance), led to the establishment of printing presses and newspapers, to Western-style schooling, and to flourishing cultural activities. In the field of literature it proved to be less obvious to copy Western standards and genres. Arab authors initially tried to use old forms, like the *maqama*, as a substitute for the narrative genre. The theme of these regenerated *maqama*s often had something to do with the East-West opposition.

In poetry it was even more difficult to adopt Western standards, so that well in the twentieth century the old monorhyme/monometer standard of the *qasida* remained undisputed. These poets could, however, not escape from expressing modern themes. So-called neo-Classicist poets could well be expected to eulogize the introduction of radio in the 1920s in the most lofty of ways.

## The Mahjar

As a result of deteriorating economical, social, and political circumstances in the second half of the nineteenth century in the-then Ottoman province of Syria/Lebanon, a great number of Arabs from these regions migrated to the Americas. Literary aspirations emerged within these Arab communities, resulting in the establishment of Arabic newspapers, literary periodicals, and societies, the most prominent of which became al-Rabita al-Qalamiyya (The Pen Club) in the Boston/New York area (1920). Its most famous member (and its chairman) was Jibran Khalil Jibran (d. 1931).

Far from their homeland, confronted with an alien environment, and having lived through the aftermath of existential shocks like the First World War and the Titanic disaster, these young poets dared to experiment and address ideas, themes, and personal emotions that were hitherto unknown in Arabic literature. The thematical innovations of this Mahjar-generation only had their influence on literature in the homeland much later, if at all.

## The Romantic Poets and Apollo

In Egypt the important poets of the 1920s and 1930s were deeply influenced by English romantic poets such as William Blake (d. 1827), Samuel Coleridge (d. 1834), Lord Byron (d.1824), and Percy Shelley (d. 1822). Love, subjectivism, inward concentration, and dreamy nationalism were among the ingredients of this poetry.

At first the young poets in the Diwan group, named after a study in literary criticism, advocated traditional forms, but later another group of poets gathered around the periodical *Apollo* promoted experiments in the use of form, partly as a consequence of their romantic inspiration, which sometimes came close to escapism.

## Arabic Poetry after World War II

The Second World War hardly had a direct impact on the Arab world, but it was all the more influential in its consequences. The divide between capitalism and socialism split the Arab world as well as Europe, not to mention the beginning struggle in many countries for independence from the colonialist powers.

As a reaction to the Romanticism of the twenties and thirties post–World War II poetry became extremely political, the slogan being *iltizam*: political commitment. A number of these poets gathered around the periodical *al-Adab* that was published in Beirut. The members of this group became split by the choice between Marxism and Arab nationalism. *Iltizam* as a concept kept playing a significant role until the 1980s.

Another innovation came from Iraq: the Free Verse movement. It advocated the complete abolishment of all traditional forms like meter and rhyme, thereby producing blank verse or prose poetry.

Poetry that was so politically motivated could in the end only produce its counterpart, in this case the group of poets who were being identified with the periodical *Shi'r* in Beirut (1957–1969). Their poetry can be qualified as intellectual, highly sensitive, and open to the West. On the other hand symbols that refered to ancient times (Phoenician culture for the poets in Syria/Lebanon; Sumerian and Akkadian culture for those from Iraq) became popular as an expression of nationalist feelings. The most significant poet among this generation was the Syrian 'Ali Ahmad Said (also known as Adunis (b. 1930), together with Nizar Qabbani (d. 1998), one of the most popular poets until the present period.

Meanwhile in Iraq, but even more so in Egypt, under the influence of socialist ideology, *iltizam* poetry developed to social realistic poetry, which in its turn paved the way for Palestinian resistance poetry with its strong political bias.

## The Arabic Novel

Under the influence of Western fiction, especially by French romantic novelists, the first attempts to write novels can be considered emulations of Western models. The genre of the novel was almost entirely strange to Arabic tradition. Some early attempts were still shaped like the medieval Arabic *maqama*, but this rhymed prose structure was soon given up.

Just before the beginning of the twentieth century the historic novel emerged, inspired by the works of Sir Walter Scott (1771–1832) and Alexandre Dumas (1802–1870). With the rise of nationalism around 1910 in Egypt, the scope of early novels changed to realistic stories placed in the vivid environment of the contemporary Egyptian countryside (e.g., *Zaynab* by Muhammad Husayn Haykal [d. 1956], considered as the first serious novel in the Arab world, and *al-Ayyam* by Taha Husayn [d. 1973]).

In the 1920s the influence of French realism and of Russian prose made itself felt in short-story writing, but Arabic prose really went its own way from the 1930s onward, when it obtained the psychological dimension of realistic autobiography, humor, and social criticism. This opened the way to the main directions of post-World War II prose: existentialism (Lebanon), social realism (Egypt, Algeria, Morocco), social criticism (Egypt, Palestine), neo-realism (Egypt), and feminism (throughout the Arab world). A modern generation that started to publish in the 1960s added a lyrical, ironical, and plainly realistic flavor as a result of which modern Arabic prose nowadays complies to international standards, without losing the local color that Arab novelists as real storytellers will never neglect. Nagib Mahfuz (b. 1911) is rightly considered to be one of the great international novelists of the twentieth century.

Novelist Nagib Mahfuz, pictured here, won the Nobel Prize in literature in 1988. The novel was a completely new genre in Arabic when, early in the twentieth century, writers in the Arab world began their attempts at long prose. Though these early works were heavily dictated by the style of French and Russian novels, by the 1930s writers of prose in Arabic began developing in many different directions. NEW YORK TIMES PICTURES

The main reason for the rapid development of prose should be sought in the fact that—as opposed to poetry—it was a relatively new form in Arabic literature, not burdened by age-old tradition.

In the West, Arabic literature is best known for two creations: the *Arabian Nights* and the novels of Nagib Mahfuz that earned him the Nobel prize for literature in 1988, although it is paradoxical that neither can be considered as representative of the Arabic literary tradition.

*See also* **Arabic Language; Biography and Hagiography; Historical Writing; Persian Language and Literature; Qurʾan.**

## BIBLIOGRAPHY

Allen, Roger. *The Arabic Literary Heritage: The Development of Its Genres and Criticism.* Cambridge U.K.: Cambridge University Press, 1998.

Allen, Roger M. A. *An Introduction to Arabic Literature.* Cambridge, U.K.: Cambridge University Press, 2000

Allen, Roger; Kilpatrick, Hilary; and De Moor, Ed, eds. *Love and Sexuality in Modern Arabic Literature.* London: Saqi, 1995.

Badawi, M. M. *A Critical Introduction to Modern Arabic Poetry.* Cambridge, U.K.: Cambridge University Press, 1975.

Brugman, J. *An Introduction to the History of Modern Arabic Literature in Egypt.* Leiden: E. J. Brill, 1984.

Grunebaum, Gustave E. von. *Themes in Medieval Arabic Literature.* London: Variorum Reprints, 1981.

Jad, Ali B. *Form and Technique in the Egyptian Novel 1912–1971.* London: Ithaca Press, 1983.

Jayyusi, Salma Khadra. *Trends and Movements in Modern Arabic Poetry.* Leiden: E. J. Brill, 1977.

Jones, Alan. *Early Arabic Poetry*, Vol. 1: *Marathi and Suʿluk Poems (Edition, Translation and Commentary).* Oxford, U.K.: Ithaca Press, 1992.

Kilpatrick, Hilary. *The Modern Egyptian Novel: A Study in Social Criticism.* London: Ithaca Press, 1974.

Lichtenstadter, Ilse. *Introduction to Classical Arabic Literature.* New York: Schocken Books, 1976.

Meisami, Julie S., and Starkey, Paul, eds. *Encyclopedia of Arabic Literature.* London and New York: Routledge, 1998.

Moreh, Shmuel. *Modern Arabic Poetry 1800–1970.* Leiden: E. J. Brill, 1976.

Pinckney-Stetkevych, Suzanne. *The Mute Immortals Speak: Pre-Islamic Poetry and Poetics of Ritual.* Ithaca, N.Y.: Cornell University Press, 1993.

Somekh, Sasson. *The Changing Rhythm: A Study of Najib Mahfuz's Novels.* Leiden: E. J. Brill, 1973.

Stetkevych, Jaroslav. *Muhammad and the Golden Bough.* Bloomington: Indiana University Press, 1996.

*Gert Borg*

# ARAB LEAGUE

Also known as the League of Arab States (Jamiʿat al-Duwal al-ʿArabiyya), the Arab League was founded in 1945 as a grouping of Arab states. The Arab League's objectives are to solidify cooperation among its members in the areas of defense, politics, communications, society, and culture. It has its roots in pan-Arab nationalism and anticolonialism, but it recognizes in principle the independence and sovereignty of the diverse nation-states that constitute its membership. Its founding members are Egypt, Iraq, Jordan, Lebanon, Syria, Saudi Arabia, and Yemen. Permanently based in Cairo, the Arab League now has twenty-two members, the most recent to join being Djibouti (1977) and the Comoros Islands (1993). The Palestine Liberation Organization (now the Palestinian Authority) was launched and given observer status by the League in 1964; it won full member status in 1976.

The League houses a number of specialized agencies, including those dealing with communication, labor, Palestine, civil aviation, and cities. It also convenes the Arab Summit, a periodic gathering of Arab heads of state.

The Arab League has established ties of cooperation and mutual consultation with other international and regional organizations, including the United Nations and the Organization of African Unity. Islamic religion does not constitute either its core ideology, nor its primary purpose; Islam is notably absent from the League charter. Moreover, the overt secular influence that Jamal 'Abd al-Nasser's Egypt exercised over the League was a major factor in the creation of the Muslim World League in 1962. Nonetheless, the Arab League does maintain formal relations with the Organization of the Islamic Conference. Islam has also shaped its organizational style, as reflected in its flag, which has a crescent moon (*hilal*) on a green field.

The League's effectiveness has often been called into question. Its efforts to forge a common front against Israel have been unsuccessful, as evidenced by the expulsion of Egypt for signing the Camp David peace accords with Israel in 1979 (Egypt was reinstated in 1987). In March 2002, however, it unanimously supported a Saudi-sponsored peace initiative that offered recognition of Israel in return for that state's withdrawal from the West Bank and the Golan Heights. The League has also had mixed success in resolving conflicts among its own member states, as demonstrated by its failure to prevent Iraq's invasion of Kuwait in 1990, and its inability to force Iraq's withdrawal in the face of international intervention.

*See also* **'Abd al-Nasser, Jamal; Organization of the Islamic Conference.**

## BIBLIOGRAPHY

Hasou, Tawfiq Y. *The Struggle for the Arab World: Egypt's Nasser and the Arab League.* London, Boston: KPI, 1985.

*Juan Eduardo Campo*

# ARCHITECTURE

Islamic architecture is in part comprised of those buildings and built environments intended for use in Islamic worship, commemoration, and instruction. Among the architecture of this group are mosques, madrasas or schools, mausoleums, and shrines. Islamic architecture may also be considered as the creation of patrons and builders who profess Islam or those that live in a region ruled by Muslims. These buildings can generally be described as secular, and include *suqs* (marketplaces), *hammams* (public baths), *khans* (inns), caravanseries or roadside inns, palaces, and houses.

## Defining Islamic Architecture

Although Islamic architecture is infinitely varied in plan, elevation, building material, and decorative programs, there are several recurring forms found in all types of buildings, be they religious, secular, public, or private. These basic components are the dome, the arch, and the vault (Fig. 1 a–c). Before describing the different aspects of Islamic architecture it is important to pause and ask if such a categorization is viable.

This question stems from three considerations. First is the fact that the forms and decorative practices of these buildings are largely adaptations of pre-Islamic models. Thus it is not improper to ask if Islamic architecture should in fact be labeled Classical, Sassanian, or Hindu. If all that was being considered were forms emptied of meaning and function then the answer to this question would be a resounding yes. The second consideration derives from the fact that many of the architectural forms considered as Islamic architecture were built for secular purposes. How, then, can a religious category designate houses, inns, baths, or even cities? Are there essential qualities of these secular spaces that give them meaning as Islamic architecture? Finally, there is a question of fit. If Christians, Jews, and Hindus living within an Islamic region build similar forms then would not the designation be too narrow? And, conversely is the designation too broad? For how can a Malaysian congregational mosque built in the twenty-first century be placed under the same analytic category as an Umayyad congregational mosque of the eighth century, when they are not built of the same materials and do not display common decorative practices or forms?

While such considerations are beyond the scope of this article, it is important to realize that contemporary historians of Islamic architectural history weigh these questions critically. Some have responded by introducing more specified categories of Islamic architecture, such as those based on regional, dynastic, and chronological designations. Others have introduced new analytic models, for example, by studying the development of certain architectural forms, such as the minaret, or a practice, such as the use of public inscriptions. Taken together, recent scholarship of Islamic architecture presents a more historically contingent and culturally varied approach to the study of Islamic architecture. Many of the problems associated with the category of Islamic architecture arise from what is taken as the meaning of architecture. If Islamic architecture is simply a material entity, composed of classical forms, then the notion of Islamic architecture as being distinct from Byzantine or Sassanian becomes questionable. However, if by architecture we mean a dynamic space that produces relationships between people and helps individuals understand and articulate their identity through their engagement (or disengagement) with that space then the meaningfulness of Islamic architecture can be seen as a distinct construction.

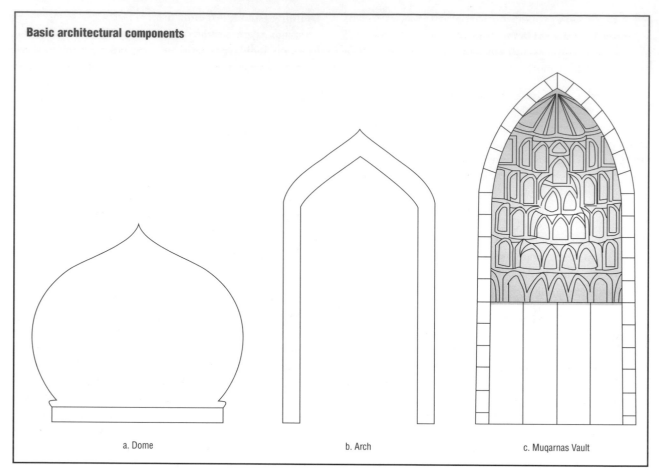

**Basic architectural components**

a. Dome     b. Arch     c. Muqarnas Vault

Figure 1.

## The Mosque

The mosque is the preeminent dynamic space that stands at the center of Islamic society and culture. It is both a spiritual site of worship and a social site of education, debate, and discussion of religion, politics, and current events. Arab caliphs and their governors were the first builders of architectural mosques. Emerging from a Bedouin culture that did not necessitate permanent architecture, these early Islamic rulers adopted and adapted the building traditions of the cultures they conquered to guide the formation and style of the new mosques. Two notable sources that contributed to the early mosques's forms and styles were the Byzantine and Sassanian Empires. In the conquered regions previously dominated by these cultures Arabs established garrison cities and ordered the founded mosques to provide the Islamic community with a space to meet and pray. The mosques that appeared in the first centuries of Islamic history were either renovated structures, for example, Christian churches converted into mosques, or they were new buildings constructed from recycled parts of abandoned buildings, particularly columns of Roman ruins. Some Islamic rulers, such as the Umayyad builders of the Dome of the Rock (completed in 692 C.E.) and the Great Mosque of Damascus (706–714 C.E.), employed Byzantine

artisans practiced in mosaic design to decorate their structures with dazzling images of vegetation, jewelry, and Qur'anic inscriptions. Over time, the practice of employing local building techniques, decorative practices, and architectural forms resulted in mosques of different regions and periods of the Islamic world appearing visually dissimilar. They are, however, all connected by their principal function: to provide a central space for the Islamic community to unite, pray, and exchange information.

The prophet Muhammad's house was the first constructed mosque (Fig. 2). Established soon after his community moved to Medina in 622 C.E., it was a simple, unremarkable enclosure. The principal consideration of Muhammad's mosque was to provide a large, open, and expandable courtyard so the ever-growing community could meet in one place. The walls of the courtyard were made of mud-brick and had three openings. The walls surrounded an open space of about 61 square yards (56 meters). On the east side of the courtyard were the modest living quarters of Muhammad and his family. Palm tree trunks were used for the columns and palm leaves for the roof of a covered area called the *zulla*, which was built to protect worshipers from the midday sun. The *zulla*

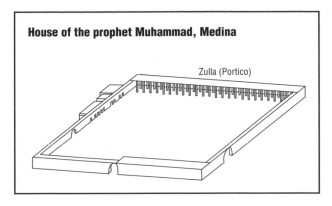

**House of the prophet Muhammad, Medina**

Zulla (Portico)

Figure 2.

marked the direction Muslim prayer was originally oriented—north, toward the holy and venerated city of the Jews, Jerusalem. Later, Muhammad, while in prayer, received divine enlightenment that caused him to change the direction of prayer south to the Kaʿba in Mecca. The *zulla* was therefore moved to concur with the new *qibla* (direction of prayer). Besides the *qibla*, another architectural form introduced at the first mosque was the *minbar* (stepped platform or pulpit) from which Muhammad addressed the growing Islamic community.

The Prophet's mosque, with its austere plan, large square enclosure, orientation toward the *qibla*, and *minbar*, provides the basic elements of subsequent mosque architecture. The first mosque type to emerge was the hypostyle plan (Fig. 3). Its basic unit, the bay (a covered area defined by four columns), could be expanded upon so the mosque could grow with the community. The hypostyle mosque typically has an inner courtyard, called the *sahn*, surrounded by colonnades or arcades (*riwaq*s) on three sides. Within the courtyard there is usually an ablutions fountain, where the *wudu* (minor ablution) is performed before the *salat* (prayer). There are three entrances into the *sahn*. The principal entrance can be a monumental portal as built in Cairo in the Fatimid Mosque of al-Hakim (1002 C.E.). Passing through the *sahn*, the worshiper walked into a covered sanctuary area or *haram*. The *haram* of the Great Mosque of Cordoba (786, 962–966 C.E.) is one of the most visually breathtaking. The arches of the double-arch arcades are composed of alternating red brick courses and pale stone voussoirs that when viewed from within the sanctuary produce a visually captivating labyrinthine configuration over one's head. Once inside the sanctuary of a mosque the focus is the *qibla*, a directional wall that indicated which way to pray. In the center of the wall was often a semicircular niche with an arched top, known as the *mihrab*. In large mosques a *minbar* located to the right of the *mihrab* was also included. It was from atop the minbar that on Fridays the *khutba* (sermon) was delivered by the imam or prayer-leader. The *minbar* is based on the stepped platform that was used by Muhammad. It ranges from a simple three-step elevation to a highly decorated monumental stairway of many steps. The

very top of the *minbar* is never occupied as it is symbolically reserved as the space of Muhammad, the original imam.

In large mosques another platform called the *dikka* is provided at the rear of the sanctuary, or in the courtyard, and along the same axis as the *mihrab*. A *qadi* repeats the sermon and prayer from the *dikka* for those standing too far from the minbar. Located outside of some mosques is a minaret that, along with the dome, has become the architectural symbol of Islam due to its ubiquitous presence and high visibility. Constructed as a tower, it either stands outside the mosque precinct or it is attached to the outer walls or portals of the mosque. The minaret varies in shape, ornamentation, and number depending on the region and building conventions of the patron. Besides visually broadcasting the presence of the mosque and Islam within a city or landscape the minaret also serves as an effective place for the *mu'adhdhin* or "caller" (also *muezzin*) to perform the *adhan* (call to prayer) and be heard for a great distance. The *maqsurah* is a later addition made to the hypostyle-plan mosque. It is a differentiated, protective space, adjacent to the *qibla* wall. The *maqsurah* is found in mosques where the imam or ruler wanted either to be protected or ceremonially separated from the congregation. It was originally built as a raised platform separated with a wooden screen that allowed total to partial concealment of its occupants.

**Types of Mosques.** There are two general types of mosques. The first is the congregational mosque, known as the *jamiʿ masjid*. The *jamiʿ* (from the Arabic word for "to gather") is built on a large scale to accommodate the entire Islamic community of a town or city. The second type is known simply as *masjid* (from the Arabic word meaning "to prostrate oneself"). *Masjid*s are small community mosques used daily by members of a quarter, or an ethnic group within a city. *Masjid*s were also constructed as subsidiary structures next to mausoleums, palaces, caravanseries, and madrasas. Early *masjid*s and *jamiʿ masjid*s, while different in size, shared the same architectural forms and style. However, as Islamic rulers grew in wealth and power starting in the late seventh century, they built monumental *jamiʿ masjid*s in their cities to reflect the preeminence of Islam and the permanence of their dynasty. Adapting the basic building elements of vaults, arches, and domes, these rulers built mosques that from the exterior appeared to span large areas and soar to great heights. To create a stunning visual experience in the interior the *jamiʿ masjid*s were ornamented with complex geometric and arabesque or vegetal decoration in mosaic and stucco. Quartered marble decorated the lower walls, or dados, and Qurʾanic and historical inscriptions in stucco and mosaic Arabic script engaged the intellect.

**Regional Variation of Mosques.** Although there is no one style to unify the mosques of the Islamic world, they can be divided into broad regional variants. The mosque style of

**Hypostyle Plan**

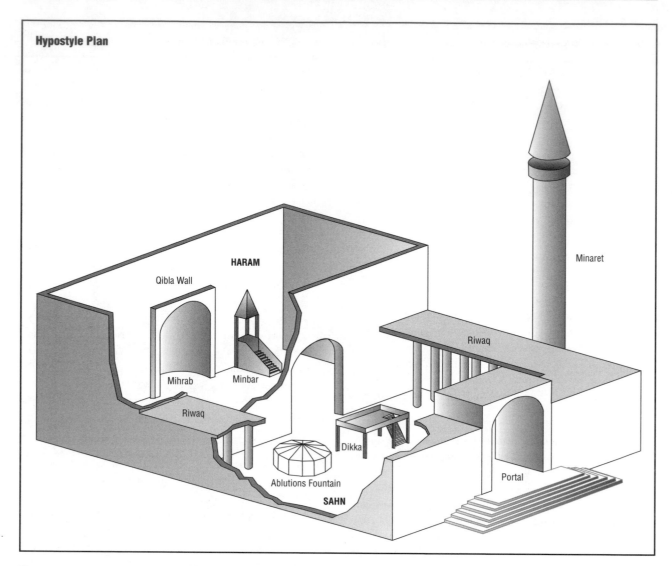

HARAM

Qibla Wall

Mihrab

Minbar

Riwaq

Ablutions Fountain

Dikka

SAHN

Minaret

Riwaq

Portal

Figure 3.

central Arabia was an early development influenced by church-building of the Syrian Byzantine Empire and palace-building of the Sassanian Persian Empire. In the east, the ground plans of the Great Mosques of Kufa (638 C.E.) and Basra (635 C.E.) were square like those of Zoroastrian temples. When the Great Mosque of Kufa was rebuilt in 670, its *haram* was based on the *apadana*s or throne rooms of Achaemenian kings: five rows of tall stone columns supporting a teak ceiling. Similarly, the Great Mosque of Damascus, built by the Umayyad caliph al-Walid between 706–714, was based on indigenous building conventions. Architects used the preexisting enclosure of the *temenos* and church, but since the mosque had to be oriented to the south, the *qibla* wall was on the longer side of the rectangular space. Also, due to the constraints of the preexisting quadrangle, the courtyard was transversal in orientation rather than longitudinal. The *haram* contained a short, wide central nave with a gabled roof and a wooden dome in its center. Three aisles of double-tiered arches,

parallel to the *qibla* wall, supported a gabled ceiling. Al-Walid, wanting to outdo the neighboring churches and temples, employed Syrian-Christian artisans to richly decorate the interior of the mosque with imported gold and colored mosaics and marble, and even used rock crystal for the *mihrab*.

The early Abbasid caliphate, ruling from Baghdad from 749 to 847, first built their mosques with square floor plans as the early Umayyads had done in the region. However, after the Abbasids moved their capital to Samarra, their mosques reflected the rectangular hypostyle form favored by the later Umayyads. The Great Mosque of Samarra, built by al-Mutawakkil from 848 to 852, was the largest hypostyle mosque of its time with nine rows of columns in the sanctuary that supported a thirty-five-foot-high ceiling. The mosque is most famous for Malwiyya, the colossal spiral minaret. Once faced with gold tiles, Malwiyya's great size and unusual shape made the Great Mosque of Samarra a highly visible presence in the surrounding landscape.

Sub-Saharan West African mosques are unique in their use of organic materials that are constantly replenished over time, such as tamped earth, timber, and vegetation. Due to seasonal deterioration during the wet and dry seasons, the mosques are constantly being repaired and resurfaced. The predominant quality of these structures is their rounded organic form, reinforced with projecting timber beams or torons, which also serve as supports for scaffolding when the mosque is being resurfaced. The Great Mosque of Djenné (thirteenth century) is the most representative of the West African mosques. Its tall rounded towers and engaged columns, which act as buttresses, easily flow into each other and give the structure its characteristic verticality and overwhelming majesty.

The central-planned, domed mosque of the Ottomans is yet another distinctive type. When the Ottomans conquered Constantinople in the fifteenth century they converted the Byzantine church of Hagia Sophia into a mosque by framing it with two pointed minarets. Later in the nineteenth century they added roundels inscribed with calligraphic writing of the names of Muhammad, Allah, and the early caliphs. Using the Hagia Sophia as their prototype, Ottoman rulers built mosques in the principal cities of their empire. The mosques were defined by large spherical domes, with smaller half-domes at the corners of the square, and four distinctively shaped minarets—tall, fluted, and needle-nosed—that were typically placed at the exterior corners of the mosque complex. The Selimiye Cami (Mosque of Selim) in Edirne, Turkey (1507–1574), best characterizes the central-plan Ottoman mosque.

Moving further east to Seljuk Iran, another type of mosque emerges known as the four-*iwan* mosque. The *iwan* is an open vaulted space with a rectangular portal or *pishtaq*. In a Seljuk mosque four of these *iwan*s would be oriented around a central courtyard. The Great Mosque of Isfahan, built in this style in the twelfth century, is a monumental four-*iwan* mosque. Of these, the principal or *qibla iwan* is the largest, with a large domed *maqsura* and *muqarnas* vaulting. To lend it further visual impact, two minarets were added at the corners of the portal. The *iwan* that stood opposite the *qibla iwan* followed in size, and it was both smaller and shallower. The lateral *iwan*s were the smallest. While the exterior of the mosque was unadorned, the inward-facing *iwan*s were decorated with architectural ceramic tiles of turquoise, cobalt blue, white, deep yellow, and green. The decorative designs contained geometric and arabesque patterns as well as Kufic inscriptions. The layout of the Great Mosque of Isfahan influenced countless other mosques in Iran, Central Asia, and South Asia.

From their start, the mosques of South Asia were syncretic structures. They were the by-products of hired Hindu masons, indigenous architectural material taken from destroyed or decaying Hindu buildings, and necessary elements of mosque architecture such as the *mihrab*. The mosques were trabeated at first and decorated with popular Hindu motifs such as vegetal scrolls and lotuses. The plans of South Asian mosques ranged from traditional hypostyle, to Persian four-*iwan* types, and to single-aisle domed plans. The earliest mosques of the Delhi sultanate (1192–1451) were hypostyle and built out of reused materials from Hindu and Jain temples such as the Quwwat al-Islam in Delhi of the late twelfth century. The greatest achievement of this mosque is the monumental minaret, the Qutb Minar. Standing at 238 feet it was a victory tower that announced the power of the new religion to the surrounding landscape.

The next significant mosque type of South Asia is the single-aisle plan with five bays that used stucco and colored stones as surface decoration and squinch and *muqarnas* vaulting. These mosques had monumental central portals and domes. The Bara Gumbad mosque in Delhi, built by Sultan Sikandar Lodi in 1494, and the Qal'a-e-Kuhna mosque of Sher Shah (1540–1545) exemplify this style. It was this basic form of mosque architecture that was later adopted by the great Mogul dynasty (1426–1848). Two exemplary Mogul-style mosques are Akbar's Great Mosque of Fatehpur Sikri (1571–1572) and Shah Jahan's Great Mosque at Delhi (1650–1656). These mosques have large courtyards and are built from the local red sandstone combined with white marble to create decorative geometric and vegetal patterns. The distinctive feature of Akbar's mosque at Fatehpur Sikri is the monumental portal on the south side called the Buland Darwaza. Its form is that of a colossal *pishtaq* (tall central portal), derived from Timurid origins. It is embellished with native Indian architectural elements as well such as small open pavilions called *chatris* and lotus-shaped medallions. Located on the west side of the great courtyard is the sanctuary, a three-domed prayer-hall with a central *pishtaq*. The Great Mosque of Delhi was based on the four-*iwan* plan. Three onion-shaped bulbous marble domes surmount the *qibla iwan*, the same shape used for the dome of the Taj Mahal. The minarets are divided into four parts and are capped with small pavilions. Smaller, private mosques built for the Mughal palaces of Lahore, Agra, and in Delhi reflect the fine marble carving skills of the Indian artisans. Faced with white marble, elegantly carved with vegetal patterns, these mosques were then topped with graceful onion-shaped domes with lotus molding and metallic finials. These private imperial mosques were the architectural counterparts of the elegant gems so highly prized by the Mughals.

### Shrines and Mausoleums

Shrines and mausoleums that commemorate important places and people of the Islamic world comprise another important component of sacred Islamic architecture. The first great shrine was al-Haram al-Sharif or Dome of the Rock in Jerusalem. Built between 687 and 691 by the Umayyad caliph 'Abd al-Malik, it covers a renowned irregular rock formation. Muslims believe that is was from this rock that Muhammad began his night journey, or *isra'*, to heaven. Located on the Temple Mount of Mount Moriah its golden dome is seen for miles reflecting in the landscape. The sanctuary of the Dome of the Rock is in the shape of an octagon and is surmounted by a tall drum and dome. The rock is surrounded by a screen and then a circular arcade of alternating columns and piers. Next is an octagonal arcade that is surrounded by the outer walls that together create a double ambulatory. A frieze of Kufic inscriptions in gold tile on blue background is found on the inside and outside of the octagonal arcade. It is the first occurrence of Qur'anic inscription in Islamic architecture. Adding to the sumptuous quality of the interior are other mosaics of turquoise, blue, and green tiles that could be depictions of the lush foliage of Paradise, and royal insignia of those vanquished by Muslim conquest.

The mausoleums of imams, rulers, the wealthy, and saints comprise the other part of Islamic commemorative architecture. Although the prophet Muhammad dictated that burials should be simple and without grave markers mausoleums are found throughout the Islamic world. Following the forms of the Dome of the Rock and the Byzantine martyrium, which the former was also inspired by, the Muslims founded their own funerary architecture. The basic form of the mausoleum was a square enclosure, derived from the shape of a house where the dead were traditionally buried, surmounted by a dome. In cities such as Mamluk Cairo (1250–1517), the domed square plan compelled builders to plan vertically instead of laterally due to spatial and structural constraints of preexisting streets. To deflect the admonitions of the Muslim orthodox that perceived tomb building as irreligious, Arab builders in North Africa, Egypt, the Arabian Peninsula, and the Levant made the mausoleum part of larger religious complexes. The mausoleum is thus often one part of a complex composed of a mosque, madrasa, or religious school, and sometimes a hospital or *khanqa* (residence of a Sufi leader). Although the buildings had unique functions, they shared the same architectural elements. The architects unified the complex with geometric and arabesque designs to decorate the buildings, marble revetment, *muqarnas* or stalactite vaults (also called honeycomb vault), and ceramic tiles, among countless other regional variants and conventions.

While the mausoleum met with periodic waves of disapproval in the Arabian world it was a fully acceptable form in the Persianate world of Iran, Anatolia, Iraq, Central Asia, Afghanistan, and South Asia. The two basic forms of Persianate mausoleum are the yurt-inspired tomb tower such as the northern Iranian Gunbad-e Qabus (1007) and the domed square and later octagonal tombs, like the Tomb of the Samanids in Bukhara (tenth century), the Ilkhanid Sultaniya mausoleum of Iljeytu (early fourteenth century), and the

famous Taj Mahal (1631–1643) of Shah Jahan in India. In eleventh-century Egypt another type of mausoleum emerged called the canopy mausoleum, because it was open to the elements. An example of this type is the Fatimid funerary complex of Sab'a Banat in Fustat. A later Fatimid development of the mausoleum form is the *mashhad*, a large square domed tomb connected to a three-room unit entered through a portal and organized around a courtyard that served pilgrims. The mashhad of Sayyida Ruqayya, an 'Alid saint, built in 1133, is an example of this type of mausoleum. The final type of mausoleum to be considered here makes skillful use of one of the most famous architectural forms: the *muqarnas*. A stalactite squinch usually found in the transitional zones between wall and dome, the *muquarnas* was used in all types of Islamic architecture. During the Ayyubid (1099–1250) and Mamluk (1250–1517) periods, the mausoleum was brought out of the cemetery and into the urban fabric. With their increased visibility these tombs became centers for transmitting political information and education of the Sunni religious schools of law. They were also gathering centers for the followers of Sufism. Building the mausoleum in the city of Cairo compelled a few changes in design. As there was little room to build laterally, the focus of the architecture was on the drum and dome of the building, built ever higher and with more richly textured transitional zones and domes.

## Secular Architecture

One of the secular types of Islamic architecture is the palace, which matches the mosque in reflecting the rich variety of forms, ornamentation, and the sophisticated skills of artisans. Built as large complexes rather than singular units, Islamic palaces were generally self-sustaining, and most contained bastion walls, towers, gates, baths, stables, private quarters, public meeting spaces, workshops, offices, hospitals, *harams* or *zenanas* (reserved for the women of the palace), libraries, pavilions, fountains, and gardens. These palaces were built as the architectural embodiment of the ruler, the spatial metaphor of his dominion, and, if built in idyllic settings with surrounding gardens, were considered earthly paradises. The first palaces were built by the Umayyads and were modeled after Roman villas. Serving as hunting lodges or rural residences these include the Qasr al-Hayr, Khirbat al-Mafjar, and Khirbat al-Minya of the eighth century. Other well-known palaces are the Fatimid Palace of al-Qahira (1087–1092), Umayyad Madinat al-Zahira of Cordoba (936–976), the Nasrid Alhambra in Granada, Spain (early fourteenth century), the Ottoman Topkapi complex, and Mogul Fatehpur Sikri and Red Fort, built in Delhi during the sixteenth century.

Islamic secular architecture is also public in nature. Among these buildings are the caravanseries and *hammams*. The caravanserai was a stopping place for travelers to rest and water and feed their animals. A typical caravanserai had a large open courtyard with a single large portal. Inside, along the walls, were covered arcades that contained identical stalls to accommodate a traveler, and his servants. Animals were usually kept in the courtyard or stables located in the corners. Caravansaries were usually fortified with bastions and turreted walls. As with mosques and palaces, caravansaries vary in ornamentation and form from region to region. Inside the city the *khan* housed the travelers and merchants. These structures were multistoried and overlooked a central courtyard. The animals and goods were kept on the ground floor and apartments were located above.

The public bath or *hammam* was another architectural form found in many Islamic cities. Along with the *khan* it was located in the *suq* or marketplace. Adopted from the Romans, the *hammam* was used for washing and purification before Friday prayer. It was composed of large rooms for steam baths as well as others for soaking in hot and cold water, all of which communicated through waiting halls. Utilizing marble covered floors and walls, arches, large ornamented domes that helped circulate hot air, *muqarnas* vaults, and stucco decoration, some public baths were highly luxurious environments. Men and women bathed separately either in their own *hammam*, if there were two in a town, or on different days or at designated times.

### Residential Architecture

The final type of Islamic architecture to be considered is the domestic. The typical house built in Islamic societies is oriented inward. A bent entrance that turns at a sharp angle marks the transition from the outside world to the home. The entrances of homes do not usually align with those across the street, so the privacy of the interior is maintained. On the inside the rooms are arranged around a central courtyard and range from the private spaces of the family to semiprivate spaces where male guests, who were not members of the family, could enter. The open courtyard ventilates the house. A central basin or fountain, part of most courtyards, also provides a cooling effect and the soothing sound of falling water. In more prosperous households delicately carved wooden screens called *mashraabiyyat* were used to create private space, filter air from the outside, and allow light to enter the home. The exterior of an Islamic house is often left unadorned. Only upon entering the home will the visitor know the class status of the owner.

*See also* **Adhan; Art; Dome of the Rock; Holy Cities; Jamiʿ; Manar, Manara; Mashhad; Masjid; Mihrab; Minbar (Mimbar); Religious Institutions.**

### BIBLIOGRAPHY

Abu-Lughod, Janet. "The Islamic City: Historical Myth, Islamic Essence, and Contemporary Relevance." *International Journal of Middle Eastern Studies* 19 (1987): 155–176.

Blair, Sheila S., and Bloom, Jonathan M. "The Mirage of Islamic Art: Reflections on the Study of an Unwieldy Field." *Art Bulletin* 85 (2003): 152–184.

Bloom, Jonathan. *Minaret: Symbol of Islam.* Oxford, U.K.: Oxford University Press, 1989.

Creswell, K. A. C. *A Short Account of Early Muslim Architecture.* 2d ed. Aldershot, U.K.: Scholar Press, 1989.

Frishman, Martin, and Hasan-Uddin, Khan, eds. *The Mosque: History, Architectural Development & Regional Diversity.* London: Thames and Hudson, 1994.

Grabar, Oleg. *The Formation of Islamic Art.* New Haven, Conn.: Yale University Press, 1987.

Hillenbrand, Robert. *Islamic Architecture: Form, Function and Meaning.* New York: Columbia University Press, 1999.

Hoag, John D. *Islamic Architecture.* New York: Abrams, 1977.

Michell, George, ed. *Architecture of the Islamic World: Its History and Social Meaning* (1978). New York: Thames and Hudson, 1984.

*Santhi Kavuri-Bauer*

## ART

Islamic art is generally reckoned to cover all of the visual arts produced in the lands where Muslims were an important, if not the most important, segment of society. Islamic art differs, therefore, from such other terms as Buddhist or Christian art, for it refers not only to the arts produced by or for the religion of Islam but to the arts of all Islamic cultures. Islamic art was not necessarily created by or for Muslims, for some Islamic art was made by Christian, Jewish, or even Hindu artists working for Muslim patrons, and some Islamic art was created for non-Muslim patrons. The term does not refer to a particular style or period, but covers a broad purview, encompassing the arts produced over one-fifth of the globe in the traditional heartland of Islam (from Spain to India) during the last fourteen hundred years.

At the beginning of the twenty-first century Islam is the world's fastest growing religion. It has spread beyond the traditional heartland of Islam in North Africa, the Near East, and west Asia to southeast Asia and sub-Saharan Africa. Muslims comprise nearly one-quarter of the world's population; the largest Muslim populations are in southeast Asia, and there are sizable Muslim communities in Europe and North America. The term *Islamic art* is therefore becoming increasingly unwieldy, and in current usage concerning modern art, the adjective "Islamic" is often restricted to purely religious expressions such as calligraphy.

The idea of an Islamic art is a distinctly modern notion, developed not by the culture itself but by art historians in Europe and America trying to understand a relatively unfamiliar world and to place the arts created there into the newly developing field of art history. In light of the nationalism that developed during the early twentieth century, some scholars, particularly those in the Islamic lands, questioned the use of the term, opting instead for nationalistic names, speaking of, say, Turkish or Persian art. But these terms are also misleading, for Islam has traditionally been a multiethnic and multicultural society, and it is impossible to distinguish the contribution of, for example, Persian-speaking artists in what is today Turkey. Other scholars, particularly in the late twentieth century, have questioned the term Islamic art as too general, since it refers neither to the art of a specific era nor to that of a particular place or people. Instead, they opt for regional or dynastic categories such as Maghribi (i.e., North African) or Mamluk (i.e., Egyptian and Syrian, thirteenth to sixteenth centuries) art. While these terms can be useful, they overlook the common features that run through much of the art created in the traditional lands of Islam and fragment the picture, particularly for those who are unfamiliar with this area and its rich cultural traditions. Without slighting the differences among the arts created in different regions in different periods, this entry focuses on the common features that run through many of the arts created within the broad rubric of Islamic art: the distinct hierarchy of forms and the themes of decoration.

## Forms

Apart from architecture, the arts produced in the Islamic lands follow a different formal hierarchy than that of Western art, where painting and sculpture are the two most important forms and are used to make religious images for worship. These forms play a relatively minor role in Islamic art, where instead the major forms of artistic expression are the arts of the book, textiles, ceramics, woodwork, metalwares, and glass. In Western art, these are often called the "minor," "decorative," or "portable" arts, but such labels are pejorative, implying that these forms are secondary, less meaningful and less permanent than the more important, stable, and therefore "noble" arts of painting and sculpture. To use such terms is to view the world of art from the vantage point of the West, and one of the significant features of Islamic art is that it introduces the viewer to different ways of looking at art.

**Bookmaking.** Of all the arts created in the Islamic lands, the most revered was the art of the book, probably because of the veneration accorded to writing the revealed word of God. Calligraphers were deemed the most important type of artist and paid the most for their work. They penned many fine manuscripts, but the fanciest were exquisite copies of the Qur'an. Those made for use in a congregational mosque were large, multivolume sets, often divided into either seven or thirty parts so that the entire text could be read over the course of a week or a month. Personal copies of the Qur'an were generally smaller, but they, too, often had fine penmanship. The great reverence for writing spilled over into the production of other texts, particularly in Iran, India, and Turkey, and it was one of the reasons that printing with movable type only began to be adopted in the Islamic lands in the eighteenth and nineteenth centuries.

Most fine manuscripts made in the Islamic lands also had fine decoration. In early times the calligrapher seems to have also been responsible for the illumination, which was usually added after the writing. For example, the famous scribe known as Ibn al-Bawwab (his nickname literally means "son of a doorman") did both the writing and the decoration in a fine but small copy of the Qur'an made at Baghdad between 1000 and 1001. In early times calligraphers may have prepared all their own materials, but from the fourteenth century onward, the crafts became increasingly specialized, and we know of distinct calligraphers, illuminators, and binders. In the sixteenth and seventeenth centuries, they were joined by a host of other specialists, ranging from draftsmen to gold beaters, gold sprinklers, rubricators (those who drew the lines), and the like. All worked together in a team to produce some of the most sublime books ever created in which all the elements were carefully harmonized in a unified and balanced whole.

**Textiles.** A second major art form popular in the traditional Islamic lands is textiles. They were the most important economically and have often been likened to the heavy industries of modern times. The four main fibers used were wool, cotton, linen, and silk, but the making of fine textiles lay not only in producing the fibers, but even more in the expense of procuring the dyes, the mordants to fix the colors, the materials for the looms, and the transport of both fibers and finished goods. It is often hard for modern viewers to appreciate these textiles, since few have survived from medieval times intact. Most were literally worn to shreds, and, unlike in other cultures, only a handful were preserved as grave goods since Muslims traditionally wrap the body in a plain white sheet for burial. Nevertheless in their own times, these textiles were immensely valuable not only in the Muslim lands but also across the globe: Medieval Europeans commonly used imported Islamic textiles to wrap the bones of their saints, and hence, paradoxically, most medieval Islamic textiles have been preserved in Christian contexts.

Textiles were also important for the history of art. Until large sheets of paper to make patterns and cartoons became readily available in the fourteenth century, motifs and designs were often disseminated through the medium of textiles. Textiles are readily portable—they can be folded and carried on an animal's back without fear of breaking—and were transported over vast distances between Spain and Central Asia. The mechanical nature of weaving on a loom also encouraged the production of multiples and the use of symmetrical, repeating, and geometric designs that are characteristic of much Islamic art.

Of all textiles, the one most identified with the traditional Islamic lands is the knotted carpet. Indeed the traditional heartland of Islam is often dubbed "the rug belt." Technically the knotted carpet consists of a textile in which additional

Bold geometric designs were typical patterns used by Muslim artists. This tile mosaic was created in Samarkand, Uzbekistan. © GERARD DEGEORGE/CORBIS

threads, usually wool or silk, are knotted into a woven substratum to form a furry surface. The origins of the technique are obscure and controversial, with different ethnic groups claiming precedence. Carpet weaving was already practiced for a millennium before the advent of Islam and may well have been developed by nomads to take advantage of the materials at hand, namely the wool produced by the sheep they herded. Nomads typically used portable looms, which could be dismantled and carried on horseback when the camp moved, to weave small carpets with a limited repertory of geometric designs that were generated from the technique of weaving itself.

In the fourteenth century this individual or family craft was transformed into a cottage or village industry. Carpets became larger and were made in multiples, with some groups available for export. They were expensive items used by the rich and powerful as status symbols. Depictions of enthroned rulers ranging from Mongol manuscripts of the Persian national epic to Italian panel paintings of the Madonna and Child prominently display Islamic knotted carpets beneath the throne, testifying to their international status.

Carpet-weaving was transformed again in the sixteenth century into a national industry. Rulers of the Safavid and Ottoman dynasties set up state workshops with room-sized looms that required teams of weavers to produce carpets measuring over twenty feet across. Unlike the carpet-weaving of nomads, which could be put down or picked up at will, these large-scale enterprises required vast amounts of materials prepared and purchased before work began to insure a uniform product. Designers prepared paper patterns with elaborate floral designs that could only be executed successfully with hundreds of knots per square inch. Some designs even emulated the design of traditional Persian gardens, with depictions of water channels filled with fish, ducks, and geese crossing and dividing rectangular parterres planted with cypresses, fruit trees, and flowers. When the carpet was spread on the floor, the person sitting on it would have been surrounded by a verdant refreshing garden.

**Metals, Ceramics, and Glasswares.** Other common art-forms created in the Muslim lands comprise metalwares, ceramics, and glasswares. These techniques have been dubbed the "arts of fire" as they are based on the use of fire to transform minerals extracted from the earth into works of art. The discovery of fire to transform humble materials into utensils was one of the hallmarks of the rise of civilization in West Asia, and the manufacture of shimmering metalwares, ceramics, and glass continued to be characteristic of the

Islamic lands until modern times. Iron and copper alloys were crafted into weapons, tools, and utensils, while silver and gold were made into jewelry and coins. Ceramics were used for storage, cooking, and serving food, and glass was used for lighting, keeping and serving foods, and storing perfumes and medicines. Unlike the Christian lands, where vessels of silver and gold were used in church liturgy, Islam required no such luxury objects in the mosque, and the finest bowls, plates, and pitchers are merely expensive versions of objects used in daily life.

Base metal, ceramic, and glass shapes were also made in such rare and costly materials as gold and silver, rock crystal, jade, and ivory. The pious disapproved of using gold vessels, and many items of precious metal were melted down for coin in times of need. A rare silver box made for the Spanish Umayyad heir-apparent Abu Walid Hisham in 976 is the same shape and dimensions as an ivory example made for the Spanish Umayyad chamberlain 'Abd al-Malik in Spain between 1004 and 1005. The metal box even copies the details of the ivory box, including the strap over the top, which is hammered from the same sheet of silver as the rest of the lid. The strap is useless on the silver box, but imitates the metal strap that would have held the lid in place on a wooden or ivory box.

Another case of similar vessels in different media is the series of small jugs made for the Timurid rulers of Central Asia in the fifteenth century. Some gold ones are illustrated in contemporary manuscripts, and examples survive in several materials, including jade, metal, and ceramic. The jugs, which measure about 6 inches (15 centimeters) high, have a globular body and short cylindrical neck with a handle shaped like a dragon. The shape derives from Chinese porcelains. The inscriptions on the Timurid examples make it clear that they were wine jugs, and the various materials correspond to the rank of the patron. Jade, technically a type of white nephrite, became available after the Timurids seized the jade mines in Khotan in Chinese Turkestan. The use of jade was reserved for rulers, as it was not only rare and expensive but also thought to counteract poison. Timurid rulers and their courtiers also commissioned similar jugs made of brass, sometimes inlaid with gold and silver, but some anonymous examples were probably made for sale on the open market as were the cheaper ceramic ones.

## Themes of Decoration

Unlike other artistic traditions, particularly the Chinese, where form alone can be considered sufficient to turn an object into a work of art, much Islamic art is highly decorated. Surfaces were elaborately adorned using a wide variety of techniques and motifs. While different styles of decoration were popular at different times and places, several themes of decoration occur everywhere. These include figural decoration, flowers, geometry, color, and writing.

Known for detailed ceramic work, this Islamic ceramic was found within the tomb of Muhammad in Mecca. © ARCHIVO ICONOGRAFICO, S.A./CORBIS

**Figural Imagery.** Many people believe that images of people are forbidden in Islam, but this assumption is wrong. The Qur'an forbids idolatry, but it has little to say on the subject of figural representation, which was apparently not a subject of great importance in Arabia during the late sixth and early seventh centuries. Furthermore, Muslims have little need to depict images in their religious art. For Muslims, God is unique, without associate; therefore He cannot be represented, except by His word, the Qur'an. Muslims worship God directly without intercessors, so they have no need for images of saints, as Christians do. The prophet Muhammad was human, not divine, so Muslims do not worship him as Christians worship Jesus. Furthermore, the Qur'an is not a continuous narrative. Thus, Muslims do not need religious images to proselytize in the way that Christians use depictions of Christ or stories from the Bible to teach their faith.

Over time this lack of images hardened into law, and the absence of figures, technically known as aniconism, became a characteristic feature of Islamic religious art. Thus, mosques, mosque furnishings such as *minbar*s (pulpits) and *mihrab*s (recesses in the wall facing Mecca), and other types of religious buildings such as madrasas do not usually contain pictures of people. But there is no reason that Muslims cannot depict people in other places and settings. Thus palaces could, and indeed often did, have images of people, particularly servants, guards, and other members of a ruler's retinue. Similarly, bathhouses were often decorated with bathers, sometimes nude, and other scenes of relaxation and pleasure.

These types of secular building were often more architecturally inventive than religious structures, which tended to follow traditional lines. But secular structures have not survived as well as mosques and religious structures, which were continuously venerated and maintained, and so the historical record is spotty, and many of the best-known secular buildings to survive in the Islamic lands are those that have long been abandoned. Archaeological excavation and restoration of such sites as the bathhouse at Qusayr Amra, built in the Jordanian desert by the Umayyads in the early eighth century, and Samarra in Iraq, the sprawling capital built by the Abbasids upstream from Baghdad in the mid-ninth century, show that already in early Islamic times bathhouses and palaces were decorated with pictures of people engaging in activities inappropriate in religious situations.

Similarly, copies of the Qur'an do not have pictures of people, but many nonreligious books made in the Islamic lands do. These range from scientific treatises to histories, chronicles, and literary works, both prose and poetry. Sometimes, illustrations were needed to explain the text, as in copies of al-Sufi's treatise on the fixed stars, *al-Kawakib al-thabita*. They show that the classical tradition of depicting the constellations as humans and animals was continued in Islamic times. Sometimes, however, illustrations were added even when the text did not demand them. One of the most frequently illustrated texts to survive from medieval Islamic times is al-Hariri's *Maqamat* (Seances or Sessions). Eleven illustrated copies produced before 1350 have survived, and the number suggests that there were once many more. This work recounts the picaresque adventures of the cunning merchant Abu Zayd as he travels throughout the Muslim world, hoodwinking his rivals. The success of the text, which became very popular among the educated bourgeoisie of the Arab lands, depended on its verbal pyrotechnics, with triple puns, subtle allusions, and complex rhymes. The illustrations emphasize a different aspect of the text—the protagonist's adventures in faraway lands—and provide rare glimpses of daily life in medieval times, including scenes of villages, markets, and libraries.

The tradition of figural imagery was particularly strong in the Persian world, which had a long history of figural representation stretching back to pre-Islamic times, and the illustrated books made there and in the nearby Persian-speaking lands such as India from the fourteenth century onward have some of the most stunning illustrations ever painted. Virtually all of them include people and animals, both real and imaginary. A few even include images of the prophet Muhammad, but these are not meant as religious icons but to illustrate historical or literary texts. The *mi'raj*, the Prophet's mystical journey from Jerusalem to heaven and back mentioned in the Qur'an (17:1), was elaborated, particularly by Sufis or mystics, and scenes illustrating it commonly show the Prophet on his mystical steed Buraq. In some cases the Prophet's face is visible, but by Ottoman times a conservative reaction had set in and artists often covered his face and even his body with a veil.

Since figural imagery was unnecessary in Islamic religious art, other themes of decoration became more important. Many of them had been subsidiary elements in the arts of pre-Islamic times. In Byzantine art, for example, depictions of people had been set off, framed, or linked by vegetal designs (that is, stylized fruits, flowers, and trees) and geometric elements (shapes and patterns). In Islamic times, these subsidiary elements were transformed into major artistic themes. At first artists used recognizable elements, such as trees or plants, as in the mosaics used in the Great Mosque of Damascus erected by the Umayyad caliph al-Walid in the early eighth century. With the growing reluctance to depict figures, such specific and realistic representations were replaced by more stylized, abstracted, and geometricized motifs.

**Geometry.** Such an abstract style was already popular by the ninth century and is found on carved plaster and woodwork made from North Africa to Central Asia. The extraordinary range of this style suggests a common origin in the Abbasid capitals of Iraq, and German excavations at the site of Samarra in the early twentieth century uncovered many examples in molded and carved stucco. The most distinct type uses a slanted, or beveled, cut, which allowed the plaster slab to be released quickly from the mold. In the beveled style, motifs are abstracted and geometricized and the distinction between foreground and background is blurred.

This type of design based on natural forms such as stems, tendrils, and leaves rearranged to form infinite geometric patterns became a hallmark of Islamic art produced between the tenth century and the fifteenth. To describe it, Europeans coined the word "arabesque," literally meaning "in the Arab style," in the fifteenth or sixteenth century when Renaissance artists incorporated Islamic designs in book ornament and decorative bookbindings. Over the centuries the word has been applied to a wide variety of winding, twining vegetal decoration in art and meandering themes in music.

The nineteenth-century Viennese art historian Alois Riegl laid out the principal features of the arabesque in Islamic art. In it, the tendrils of the vegetation do not branch off from a single continuous stem, as they do in nature, but rather grow unnaturally from one another to form a geometric pattern. He pointed out that the arabesque also has infinite correspondence, meaning that the design can be extended indefinitely in any direction. The structure of the arabesque gives the viewer sufficient information to extend the design in his or her imagination.

The popularity of the arabesque was due no doubt to its adaptability, for it was appropriate to virtually all situations and media, from paper to woodwork and ivory. It was used on the illuminated pages that were added to decorate the beginning and end of fine manuscripts, particularly copies of the Qur'an. These decorated pages became increasingly elaborate and are often called carpet pages. The largest and finest were produced in Egypt and Syria during the period of rule by the Mamluks (r. 1250–1517). The frontispieces in these grand manuscripts of the Qur'an (some measure a whopping 30 inches, or 75 cm, high) are decorated with elaborate geometric designs of polygons radiating from central star shapes.

From the fourteenth century the arabesque was gradually displaced by more naturalistic designs of chrysanthemum, peony, and lotus flowers, motifs adopted from Chinese art during the period of Mongol rule in Iran. This floral style was disseminated westward to the Ottomans, rulers of the eastern Mediterranean region after 1453 from their capital at Istanbul. Artists working at the court of the longest-reigning and most powerful of the Ottoman sultans, Suleyman (r. 1620–1666), developed a distinct floral style with composite flowers and slender, tapering leaves with serrated edges. Designers working in the court studio drew up patterns in this style, which craftsmen then executed in various media, ranging from ceramics to textiles.

The pervasiveness of geometric designs throughout Islamic art has been traced to the importance of textiles, and Golombek coined the phrase "the draped universe of Islam." The production of fibers and dyes formed the mainstay of the medieval Islamic economy. In addition to clothing, textiles were the main furnishings of dwellings and even, in the form of tents, the dwellings themselves. The central role of textiles is underscored by the Ka'aba in Mecca, which Muslims believe is the house that Ibrahim (Abraham) erected for God and which is the central shrine of Islam, a cubic stone building that has been veiled in cloth coverings since the dawn of the faith. The structure of weaving favors angular designs based on the intertwining of warp and weft, and interlaced designs, found even in writing, may be another example of the textile mentality that permeated Islamic society.

**Color.** Another theme that runs through much Islamic art is the exuberant use of color. Bright and vivid colors are found not only in illustrated manuscripts, but also in media where they might not be expected. For example, metalworkers in the Islamic lands developed the technique of inlay, in which a vessel made of one metal (typically bronze or brass) is inlaid with another (typically, silver, copper, or gold). Designs were further set off in a bituminous black that absorbs light, in contrast to the surrounding metallic surfaces that reflect it. In this way, metal workers could decorate their wares with elaborate scenes that resembled paintings or work out enormous inscriptions that seem to glow from the object and set off the patron's name or Qur'anic text in lights, as it were.

Woodworkers achieved similar effects by combining ivory or bone with ebony, teak, and other precious woods. The

"Prince on a Brown Horse," Mogul miniature painting, eighteenth century. Mogul emporers employed large numbers of painters who became known for their depictions of humans and animals in a naturalistic style. © THE BURSTEIN COLLECTION/CORBIS

most expensive pieces of woodwork were mosque furnishings such as *maqsura*s (screens to enclose an area in front of the mihrab), *minbar*s (pulpits), and Qur'an stands. The designs on these pieces were usually geometric, with elaborate interlacing and strapwork patterns. Perhaps the most stunning is the stupendous *minbar* made in 1137 at Cordoba for the Almoravid mosque in Marrakesh, which has thousands of individual panels meticulously carved in a variety of rare and exotic woods with arabesque designs. These panels were fitted flawlessly into a complex geometric scheme, so that the decoration can be equally appreciated from near and far away.

Islamic ceramics are also notable for their wonderful colors. Potters constantly invented new and different techniques of over- and underglaze painting. Their finest effort was the development of the luster technique, in which vessels and tiles were painted with metallic oxides and then fired in a reducing atmosphere so that the oxygen burned away, leaving the shimmering metal on the surface. The technique may have been invented by glassmakers in Egypt and Syria in the eighth century, but soon passed to potters, who developed its full potential, first in ninth-century Iraq, then in Fatimid (969–1171), Egypt, and finally in Iran. Luster potters working there in the city of Kashan in the late twelfth and early thirteenth centuries also developed the overglaze-painted technique known as *minai* or enameling, in which several colors and gold are painted on top of already-glazed wares, which are then fired a second time at a relatively low temperature. Luster and *minai* ceramics represent the most expensive kind of pottery made in medieval times, for they required costly materials, special kilns, and extra fuel for a second firing. The techniques may well have been kept secret, and, to judge from signed works and treatises, the craft tradition passed down through certain families.

The decorative combination of blue and white, so often identified with Chinese porcelains, derived from the Islamic lands where potters invented the technique of painting in cobalt under a transparent glaze. The technique, developed by the same Kashan potters working in Iran in the early thirteenth century, was then exported to China where it appears on blue-and-white porcelains made in the fourteenth century. Indeed, potters in the Islamic lands were constantly in competition with their colleagues in China, and ideas bounced back and forth from culture to culture. Thus, Kashan potters probably adopted an artificial or stone-paste body to imitate the hard body of porcelain, made by the Chinese with kaolin, an element not available in Iran and other Muslim lands.

Various explanations have been proposed for this lavish use of color throughout much of Islamic art. Some scholars trace it to the drab and dusty landscape that pervades the heartland of Islam. (The word khaki, for example, derives from the Persian word meaning dusty or dust-colored.) This explanation is insufficient, however, as people from other desert or steppe regions do not necessarily value color as highly as Muslims do. Other scholars see the extensive use of color as evoking Paradise, described in the Qur'an as a rich and verdant place where men recline on silken pillows. Muslims, particularly mystics, often elaborated the symbolic values of color, but these values were often contradictory and meaningful only in specific geographical or chronological contexts. Black, for example, was adopted by the Abbasids as their standard, and their rivals, the Fatimids, adopted white. The auspicious or heavenly associations may have been outweighed by practical considerations, since copper oxide, a ubiquitous coloring agent, produces a green color in a lead glaze and a turquoise blue color in an alkaline one.

**Writing.** Of all the themes that run through Islamic art, the most important is writing. Islam, perhaps more than any other religion, values writing, and inscriptions permeate Islamic art more than any other artistic tradition. The value of the word is due to the sanctity of the revelation, and from earliest Islamic times virtually all types of Islamic art were decorated with writing, even when the medium makes it difficult to add an inscription. Sometimes writing supplements an image, but often writing is the sole type of decoration.

The texts inscribed on works of Islamic art range in subject matter. Some contain verses from the Qur'an, Traditions of the Prophet (called hadith in Arabic), and other religious texts. Others are short pious phrases recalling God's power and omnipotence (the most common is *al-mulk lillah*, dominion belongs to God) or invoking the name of the Prophet, his family, and other significant religious figures such as the Four Orthodox caliphs who succeeded Muhammad as leaders of the Muslim community in the early seventh century. Probably the most common type of text inscribed on works of Islamic art comprises benedictions and good wishes, which can range from a single word (the most common is *baraka*, blessing) to long phrases with rhyming pairs of nouns and adjectives.

These inscriptions, particularly on expensive pieces, sometimes contain historical information, including the name of the patron, the date, the place the object was made, and even the name of the artist. Art historians always look for this type of information since it helps to localize a work of art, but it is important for other reasons as well. Historical information also implies that the work of art was a specific commission, made for a particular individual at a specific moment or to commemorate a specific event. The historical information also tells us in which direction to view a work of art, since this information is usually included at the end of the text. Signatures allow us to establish the biographies of artists, a type of person not generally recorded in histories and chronicles, and thereby fill out the artistic record.

Many different styles of script were used to decorate works of Islamic art. Historical information was often written in a more legible rounded hand, because the patron or artist wanted his name to be clear. In contrast, aphorisms and pious phrases were often written in a more stylized angular script. Some might have been intended as puzzles designed to amuse or even tease the user. For example, a group of slip-covered earthenware vessels made in northeastern Iran and Central Asia in the ninth and tenth centuries (when the area was under the domination of the Samanid dynasty) is inscribed with aphorisms in Arabic such as "Knowledge is bitter to the taste at first, but sweeter than honey in the end" or "He who is content with his own opinion runs into danger." These aphorisms are written in brown or black against the cream slip in an extremely complex script in which the letters are stretched out or distorted and the strokes braided and intertwined. The texts are very difficult to read, and somewhat like a modern cryptic puzzle; decipherment was part of the enjoyment they engendered.

In other cases the difficulty in deciphering the inscriptions on a work of Islamic art may have been due to the artist's illiteracy. The person who drew up the inscription was not necessarily the same person who executed it on the work of art, and some artists may not have been literate, particularly those of lower status who worked with cheaper materials in repetitive forms. A group of overglaze-painted earthenware vessels made in the Abbasid lands in the ninth century is often decorated in the center with a few lines of text containing blessings and the name of the potter. The texts are formulaic and often unreadable, with words cut off, and the inscriptions show that the pieces were not a specific commission but made for sale on the open market. Nevertheless, they are eloquent testimony for a world in which writing and written sentiments were appreciated at all levels of society.

*See also* **Architecture; Calligraphy; Mihrab.**

## BIBLIOGRAPHY

Baer, Eva. *Metalwork in Medieval Islamic Art.* Albany: State University of New York Press, 1983.

Baer, Eva. *Islamic Ornament.* Edinburgh: Edinburgh University Press, 1998.

Blair, Sheila S. *Islamic Inscriptions.* Edinburgh: Edinburgh University Press, 1998.

Blair, Sheila S., and Bloom, Jonathan M. *The Art and Architecture of Islam: 1250–1800.* New Haven, Conn. and London: Yale University Press, 1994.

Bloom, Jonathan M., and Blair, Sheila S. *Islamic Arts.* London: Phaidon, 1997.

Brend, Barbara. *Islamic Art.* London and Cambridge, Mass.: British Museum Press/Harvard University Press, 1991.

Ettinghausen, Richard, Grabar, Oleg, and Jenkins-Madina, Marilyn. *Islamic Art and Architecture: 650–1250.* New Haven, Conn. and London: Yale University Press, 2001.

Ferrier, R. W., ed. *The Arts of Persia.* New Haven, Conn. and London: Yale University Press, 1989.

Golombek, Lisa. "The Draped Universe of Islam." In *Content and Context of Visual Arts in the Islamic World.* Edited by P. P. Soucek. University Park, Pa., and London: Pennsylvania State University Press, 1988.

Grabar, Oleg. *The Formation of Islamic Art.* New Haven, Conn.: Yale University Press, 1973.

Grabar, Oleg. *The Mediation of Ornament.* Princeton, N.J.: Princeton University Press, 1992.

Hattstein, Markus, and Delius, Peter, eds. *Islam: Art and Architecture.* Cologne: Könemann, 2000.

Hillenbrand, Robert. *Islamic Art and Architecture.* London: Thames and Hudson, 1999.

Irwin, Robert. *Islamic Art in Context: Art, Architecture, and the Literary World.* New York: Abrams, 1997.

Pope, Arthur Upham, and Ackerman, Phyllis, eds. *A Survey of Persian Art from Prehistoric Times to the Present.* London and New York: Oxford University Press, 1938–1939.

Raby, Julian, ed. *Catalogue of the Nasser D. Khalili Collection of Islamic Art.* Oxford, U.K.: Oxford University Press, 1992.

*Sheila S. Blair*
*Jonathan M. Bloom*

# 'ASABIYYA

The English equivalent of the term *'asabiyya* is akin to "social solidarity" or "tribal loyalty." It is an abstract noun that derives from the Arabic root *'asab*, meaning "to bind." It refers to a special characteristic or set of characteristics that defines the rather vague essence of what constitutes a particular group. As a sociological principle, it would be especially significant within the political thought of Ibn Khaldun (1332–1406). *'Asabiyya*, according to him, is the social bond that is particularly evident among tribal groups and is based more on social, psychological, physical, and political factors than on those of genetics or consanguinity. It is not unique among the Arabs; rather, each group possesses its own distinct *'asabiyya*. In this way, Ibn Khaldun identified a Jewish *'asabiyya*, a Greek *'asabiyya*, and so on. He also perceived an intimate connection between *'asabiyya* and religion. For a religion to be effective it must evoke a feeling of solidarity among all the members of the group. In this way one could have diverse *'asabiyyat*; for example, an *'asabiyya* to one's tribe, one's guild, and ultimately to one's religion. Ibn Khaldun argues that Islam brought a strong sense of *'asabiyya* to the Arabs and was responsible for the benefits that Islamic civilization produced.

*See also* **Ibn Khaldun.**

## BIBLIOGRAPHY

Baali, Fuad. *Society, State, and Urbanism: Ibn Khaldun's Sociological Thought.* Albany: State University of New York Press, 1988.

*Aaron Hughes*

# ASH'ARITES, ASH'AIRA

The Ash'arites, who were also known as al-Ash'ariyya, were the largest Sunni theological school, and were named after the school's founder, Abu 'l-Hasan al-Ash'ari, who lived in the late ninth and early tenth centuries (873–935). Little is known of al-Ash'ari's personal and scholarly life. The most often repeated information in the sources is that at the age forty, after a series of visions, he changed his position in Islamic theology. He left his Mu'tazilite teacher Abu 'Ali al-Jubba'i over a theological dispute on divine grace and human responsibility (exemplified by the famous example of three brothers with different eschatological fates), and accepted the authority of Ahmad b. Hanbal. Al-Ash'ari thus adhered to the principles of the traditionalist Sunni majority (*Ahl al-sunna wal-jama'a*), although despite their opposition he defended the necessity of using rational argumentation, which was widely practiced by Mu'tazilites, in justifying these principles. Following his conversion he even wrote a short treatise in favor of the argumentative method in Islamic theology. In combining Sunni doctrines with Mu'tazilite methodology he was regarded as the founder of the first and later dominant theological school among Sunnis. There were some other independent scholars who tried partly to apply rational methodology to Sunni doctrines before Al-Ash'ari, such as Ibn Kullab, Harith al-Muhasibi, and Abul-'Abbas al-Qalanisi, but they were not recognized as the masters of a school by later Sunni theologians. With the exception of the followers of the Hanafite theologian Abu Mansur al-Maturidi in Central Asia, almost all Sunni theologians were regarded as Ash'arite, although they departed from al-Ash'ari in some points.

Al-Ash'ari's immediate students, Abu 'l-Hasan al-Bahili, Ibn Mujahid al-Ta'i, and others, were not influential in the history of Ash'arism. However the following generation, among them Abu Bakr al-Baqillani (d. 1013), Ibn Furak (d. 1015), Abu Ishaq al-Isfara'ini (d. 1027), and 'Abd al-Qahir al-Baghdadi (d. 1037), played a major role in the formation of the school. Al-Baqillani, for instance, was regarded as the second founder, due to his contributions in rationalizing the Ash'arite school through his doctrines of atomism, nonexistence, and so on.

Although Ash'arite scholars suffered for a while from the persecution of Buwayhid sultans and the Seljuk Wazir al-Kunduri in the eleventh century, their conditions rapidly changed shortly after gaining a wide support of the Seljuks during the time of the famous intellectual wazir Nizam al-Mulk. He established the Nizamiyya madrasa (school) in Nishapur, in which Ash'arite views were officially taught, and then spread to other parts of the Islamic world as far away as North Africa and Muslim Spain. At this time leading Ash'arite thinkers were Imam al-Haramayn al-Juwayni (d. 1085) and his student Abu Hamid al-Ghazali (d. 1111), both of whom taught at the Nizamiyya School. Al-Juwayni and al-Ghazali imported some philosophical terms and topics into Ash'arite *kalam* and legitimized the use of formal Aristotelian logic in both Islamic theological and legal theories.

In the twelfth century, a philosophical trend dominated among the so-called modern or later theologians (*al-muta'akhkhirun*). This trend gained in strength with the works of later independent-minded thinkers of the school, such as Fakhr al-Din al-Razi (d. 1209), Sayf al-Din al-Amidi (d. 1233), and Qadi al-Baydawi (d. 1286). Ash'arite thought came under the influence of Avicennan Neoplatonist cosmology and mostly absorbed the Islamic philosophical tradition in Sunni theology after a major but ineffective stand by the well-known philosopher Averroes. Thinkers of genius from Central Asia, especially 'Adud al-Din al-Iji (d. 1355) and his students Sa'd al-Din al-Taftazani (d. 1389) and Sayyid Sharif al-Jurjani (d. 1413), contributed to the interpretation and expansion of Ash'arite thought by producing large commentaries throughout the fourteenth century. Ottoman thinkers

of the fifteenth and sixteenth centuries, though officially Maturidite, also contributed to this philosophical production by their commentaries and marginal notes on the works of the above-named Central Asian Ash'arites.

The Ash'arite school continued to exist in the seventeenth century in the works of the Egyptian al-Lakani and the Indian al-Siyalkuti. After a continuous modernization process in the Muslim world that took place in the eighteenth and nineteenth centuries, the Sunnis from both the Ash'arite and Maturidite traditions, such as Muhammad 'Abduh of Egypt, Shibli Nu'mani of India, and Izmirli Ismail Hakki of Ottoman Turkey, attempted a methodological renovation within Islamic theological thought. During this period of modernity, sectarian concerns and identities weakened among Muslim intellectuals, since they took an eclectic and broader approach in order to satisfy the demands of their age. The contemporary Muslim modernists followed their predecessors in detaching themselves from a strict identification with a particular school of thought. However, Ash'arism still continues to maintain its existence in Sunni societies today.

Ash'arite thinkers, following al-Mu'tazila, dealt with the main theological issues of Islamic faith, including arguments for the existence of God, divine unity, revelation, prophecy, and eschatology. They aimed to refute the opposing views of other religions and philosophical schools in a rational dialectical method. But they also discussed the controversial theological issues first raised by the Mu'tazilites, such as the existence of attributes of God (*sifat Allah*), the nature of divine speech (*kalam Allah*), the possibility of seeing God in the future life (*ru'yat Allah*), the question of divine omnipotence and human free will (*irada*), and the fate of a believing sinner (*murtakib al-kabira*). In Ash'arite theology God has eternal attributes such as knowledge, speech, and sight, which are, in their system, essential for His knowing, speaking, or seeing. Since it belongs to his eternal attribute of speech, the Qur'an as God's word was uncreated. Unlike the traditionalist Sunni school and al-Ash'ari himself, later Ash'arites did not oppose the metaphorical interpretation of corporeal terms attributed to God in the Qur'an. As for the question of free will and predestination, Ash'arites took a middle position between the Mu'tazilites and Jabrites in emphasizing God's creation of human acts, which each person freely chooses.

There are some differences between the Ash'arites and Maturidites, the second Sunni theological school, but they are usually regarded as methodological and nonessential. Ash'arites, for instance, rejected *takwin* (which means "to bring into existence") as a divine attribute, the eternalness of God's actions, unlike his attributes, and the necessity of believing in the existence and unity of God through rational arguments in the absence of divine revelation, which are among the Maturidite theses.

*See also* **Kalam; Mu'tazilites, Mu'tazila.**

## BIBLIOGRAPHY

Frank, Richard M. "Bodies and Atoms: The Ash'arite Analysis." In *Islamic Theology and Philosophy*. Edited by Michael E. Marmura. Albany: State University of New York Press, 1984.

Frank, Richard M. "The Science of Kalam." *Arabic Science and Philosophy* 2 (1992): 7–37.

Frank, Richard M. *Al-Ghazali and the Ash'arite School*. Durham, N.C.: Duke University Press, 1994.

Gimaret, Daniel. *La doctrine d'al-Ash'ari*. Paris: Cerf., 1990

Gwynne, Rosalind W. "Al-Jubba'i, al-Ash'ari and the Three Brothers: The Uses of Fiction." *The Muslim World* 75, no. 3–4 (1985): 132–161.

Makdisi, George. "Ash'ari and the Ash'arites in Islamic Religious History." *Studia Islamica* 17 (1962): 37–80.

Makdisi, George. "Ash'ari and the Ash'arites in Islamic Religious History." *Studia Islamica* 18 (1963): 19–39.

Nakamura, Kojiro. "Was Ghazali an Ash'arite." In *Memoirs of the Research Department of the Toyo Bunko*. Tokyo: The Oriental Library, 1993.

Watt, W. Montgomery. *The Formative Period of Islamic Thought*. Oxford, U.K.: Oneworld Press, 1998.

Watt, W. Montgomery. "al-Ash'ariyya." In Vol. 1, *Encyclopedia of Islam*. 2d ed. Leiden: E. J. Brill, 1999.

*M. Sait Özervarli*

## ASKIYA MUHAMMAD (R. 1493–1529)

The ruler of the Songhai Empire between 1493 and 1529, Muhammad b. Abi Bakr Ture is also known as Askiya al-Hajj Muhammad, or Askiya Muhammad. His origins are debated. According to the two Tawarikh, or "histories" (*Tarikh al-Sudan* and *Tarikh al-Fattash*), he belonged either to the Ture or the Sylla clan of the Soninke. Because they were associated with trade, the Soninke were one of the earliest groups to convert to Islam south of the Sahara. Askiya al-Hajj Muhammad overthrew the dynasty of the Sunni in 1493, and established the dynasty known as the Askiya who ruled the Songhai Empire from 1493 until the Moroccan invasion of the Songhai in 1591. Unlike his predecessor, Sunni 'Ali, Askiya Muhammad was said to be a pious Muslim, and very supportive of Muslim scholars in Timbuctu, and other parts of Songhai. In 1496, Askiya Muhammad set off for the pilgrimage to Mecca. On his way to Mecca, he visited Egypt, and was appointed by the Abbassid caliph al-Mutwakkil as his deputy to rule Songhai in his name. Askiya al-Hajj Muhammad consulted two major Muslim scholars on how to rule Songhai according to the *shari'a*. One of them was 'Abd al-Karim al-Maghili (d. 1503 or 1504), and the other was Jalal al-din al-Suyuti (d. 1505). Askiya Muhammad extended the Songhai Empire to include tributary lands to the east, west, and north. No further expansion of the Songhai Empire occurred after his reign. He was deposed in 1528 by his son Musa.

*See also* **Africa, Islam in; African Culture and Islam.**

## BIBLIOGRAPHY

Hiskett, M. *The Development of Islam in West Africa*. London and New York: Longman, 1984.

Hunwick, John, ed. *Shari'a in Songhai: The Replies of Al-Maghili to the Questions of Askia al-Hajj Muhammad*. Oxford, U.K.: Oxford University Press, 1985.

*Ousmane Kane*

## ASNAM

*Asnam* is the Arabic word for "idols" (sing., *sanam*). The origin of the term is found in the Semitic root *S.L.M.* (by a shift of *l* into *n*), which denotes "image." Hence, the Arabic *sanam* is basically the corporeal image of the deity.

The term *asnam* occurs in the Qur'an, and in all instances but one it refers to the idols worshiped by Abraham's pagan adversaries (6:74; 21:57; 26:71). Twice the idols worshiped by the latter are called *awthan* (sing., *wathan*; see 29:17, 25). Abraham's contemporaries worship the *asnam/awthan* "apart from" (*min duni*) God, which means that belief in these idols represents what the Qur'an labels elsewhere as *shirk* ("association"), that is, worshiping deities that are considered God's associates. Three of God's "associates" are mentioned by name in another Qur'anic passage (53:19–23): Allat, Manat, and al-'Uzza. The Qur'an sets out to deny that they were God's daughters, a typical element of *shirk*, and denounces them as sheer names. In yet another Qur'anic passage (71:23), five "gods" (*aliha*) worshiped by Noah's contemporaries are mentioned by name.

In extra-Qur'anic sources, the dichotomy between the worship of the *asnam* and the monotheistic legacy of Ibrahim, the founder of the Ka'ba in Mecca, is retained. The traditions say that when Mecca became too small for the descendants of Abraham and Ishmael, they looked for dwellings outside Mecca, taking with them stones from the homeland, which they cherished and turned into idols. Nevertheless, according to these sources even far away from Mecca they preserved many of Abraham's values, such as the rites of the pilgrimage to Mecca, but they contaminated them with various elements of *shirk*. The shrines of some of these idols are said to have been built on the model of the Ka'ba, and sometimes were even called "Ka'ba."

Conversely, idolatry is said to have been imported into Arabia from outside by one 'Amr b. Luhayy of the tribe of Khuza'a, who ruled in Mecca before the advent of Quraysh. He is said to have imported idols mainly from Syria. Among them the five idols of Noah's time are mentioned. The establishment of the worship of Hubal at the Ka'ba is also attributed to this 'Amr. Names of numerous additional *asnam* are mentioned in the sources with details about the tribes who worshiped them.

Of the three "daughters" of God, Manat is said to have been the first to be introduced in Arabia, then Allat, then al-'Uzza. Manat's shrine was in Qudayd (near Mecca, on the Red Sea shore), Allat's in al-Ta'if, and al-'Uzza's in Nakhla. Pilgrims brought votive gifts to the shrines and sacrificial slaughter took place on special stones (*nusub*) there.

Apart from the collective idols, some traditions speak about domestic *asnam* whose carved wooden images were held in each family household (*dar*) in Mecca. There are also reports about similar tribal and domestic idols in pre-Islamic Medina. The shrines of the main idols as well as the domestic images were reportedly destroyed in Muhammad's days, following the spread of Islam in Arabia.

Modern scholars have doubted the historicity of the notion of Arabian idolatry being a deformed version of an initial Ibrahimic monotheism centered on the Ka'ba, and have rejected it as reflecting Qur'anic and Islamic concepts projected back into remote pre-Islamic phases of history. On the other hand, other Islamicists noted the possibility that Ibrahim's image as a monotheistic prototype could have been known already in pre-Islamic Arabia.

*See also* **Allah; Shirk.**

## BIBLIOGRAPHY

Hawting, G. R. *The Idea of Idolatry and the Emergence of Islam: From Polemic to History.* Cambridge, U.K.: Cambridge University Press, 1999.

Lecker, Michael. "Idol Worship in Pre-Islamic Medina (Yathrib)." *Le Muséon* 106 (1993): 331–346.

Rubin, Uri. "The Ka'ba—Aspects of Its Ritual Functions." *Jerusalem Studies in Arabic and Islam* 8: 97–131.

*Uri Rubin*

## ASSASSINS

Assassins was a name originally applied by the Crusaders and other medieval Europeans, starting in the twelfth century, to the Nizari Isma'ilis of Syria. Under the initial leadership of Hasan Sabbah (d. 1124), the Nizaris founded a state centered at the stronghold of Alamut, in northern Iran, with a subsidiary in Syria. The Nizari state in Iran was destroyed by the Mongols in 1256. In Syria the Nizaris reached the peak of their power and glory under Rashid al-Din Sinan (d. 1193), the original "Old Man of the Mountain" of the Crusaders, who had extended dealings with the Crusaders and their

Frankish ruling circles in the Near East. The Syrian Nizaris permanently lost their political prominence when they were subdued by the Mamluks in the early 1270s.

The Nizaris and the Crusaders had numerous military encounters in Syria from the opening decade of the twelfth century. But it was in Sinan's time (1163–1193) that the Crusaders and their occidental observers became particularly impressed by the highly exaggerated reports and widespread rumours about the Nizari assassinations and the daring behavior of their *fida'is*, or devotees, who carried out suicide missions against their community's enemies in public places. The Nizari Isma'ilis became infamous in Europe as "the Assassins." This term, which appears in medieval European literature in a variety of forms (Assassini, Assissini, and Heyssisini), was evidently based on variants of the Arabic word *hashishi* (plural, *hashishiyya* or *hashishin*), which was applied pejoratively to the Nizaris of Syria and Iran by other Muslims. The term was used in the sense of "low-class rabble" or "people of lax morality" without claiming any special connection between the Nizaris and hashish, a product of hemp. This term of abuse was picked up locally in Syria by the Crusaders as well as by other European travelers and emissaries and was adopted to designate the Nizari Isma'ilis.

Medieval Europeans, and especially the Crusaders, who remained generally ignorant of Islam and its divisions, were also responsible for fabricating and disseminating, in the Latin Orient as well as in Europe, a number of interconnected legends about the secret practices of the Nizaris, including the "hashish legend." It held that as part of their training this intoxicating drug was systematically administered to the *fida'is* by their beguiling chief, the "Old Man of the Mountain." The so-called Assassin legends revolved around the recruitment and training of the Nizari *fida'is*, who had attracted the Europeans' attention. These legends developed in stages and culminated in a synthesized version popularized by Marco Polo, who applied the legends to the Iranian Nizaris and created the "secret garden of paradise," where the *fida'is* supposedly received part of their indoctrination. Henceforth, the Nizari Isma'ilis were portrayed in European sources as a sinister order of drugged assassins bent on senseless murder and mischief.

Subsequently, Westerners retained the name Assassin in general reference to the Nizari Isma'ilis, even though the term had now become in European languages a new common noun meaning a professional murderer, although its etymology had been forgotten. Silvestre de Sacy (1758–1838) finally succeeded in solving the mystery of the name Assassin and its etymology, but he and other orientalists subscribed variously to the Assassin legends. Modern scholarship in Isma'ili studies, based on genuine Isma'ili sources, has now deconstructed the Assassin legends revealing their fanciful nature and also showing that the name Assassin is a misnomer rooted in a doubly pejorative appellation without basis in any communal or organized use of hashish by the Nizari Isma'ilis or their *fida'is*, Shi'ite Muslims who were deeply devoted to their community.

*See also* **Crusades; Shi'a: Isma'ili.**

## BIBLIOGRAPHY

Daftary, Farhad. *The Assassin Legends: Myths of the Isma'ilis.* London: I. B. Tauris and Co., 1994.

Lewis, Bernard. *The Assassins: A Radical Sect in Islam.* London: Weidenfeld and Nicolson, 1967.

*Farhad Daftary*

## ASTROLOGY

Despite consistent critiques of astrology by Muslim scientists and religious scholars, astrological prognostications required a fair amount of exact scientific knowledge, and thus gave partial incentive for the study and development of astronomy. In the early Arabic sources, the term *'ilm al-nujum* was used to refer to both astronomy and astrology. Soon after, however, astronomy was unambiguously differentiated from astrology, and a clear terminological and conceptual distinction was made between the two sciences. The titles *'ilm al-falak* (the science of the celestial orb) and *ilm al-hay'a* (the science of the configuration of heavens) were used to refer to the exact science of astronomy, while *'ilm ahkam al-nujum* (judicial astrology), or simply *'ilm al-nujum* (the science of the stars), referred exclusively to astrology. Both fields were rooted in the Greek, Persian, and Indian traditions, and were cultivated for many centuries in Muslim societies. In all of these earlier traditions, interest in the science of astronomy has been closely connected to astrology.

The connection between astronomy and astrology in the inherited scientific legacies was founded on the idea of a correlation between stellar configurations and events in the sub-lunar world. Thus, for example, the same cosmology underlying Ptolemy's *Almagest*—the most influential Greek astronomical work—provided the theoretical foundations of the *Tetrabiblos*, an influential astrological work by the same author. In Muslim societies, astrology continued to be practiced and to draw on and encourage astronomical knowledge, and a good portion of the funding for astronomical research was motivated by the desire to make astrological predictions. A number of observatories were funded and founded for the professed objective of conducting observations that could be used in astrological computation. Astrology was also commonly practiced in courts. In particular, one such form of court astrology was *iktiyarat*—a branch of astrology that aimed at determining the optimal astrological conditions for initiating large undertakings, such as the building of cities or the launching of military campaigns. Another popular form of astrological prediction was *mawalid* (nativities), which involves charting the horoscopes of the beginnings of both personal and collective occurrences, including the birth of individuals, as well as the birth of prophets, historical leaders, religions, and nations. The classic work of Arabic astrology is Abu Ma'shar al-Balkhi's (d. 886) *Kitab al-madkhal al-kabir* (The great introduction).

Yet, although astrology continued to have appeal within the elite political culture and in popular practice, the larger, socially based religious culture vehemently opposed it. Moreover, while many astronomers served as court astrologers, many more condemned astrology and distanced themselves from it. Most of these astronomers did not treat astrology as a valid scientific discipline, and went out of their way to distance their exact science from it. Despite its continued practice, a clear line was drawn between astrology and astronomy. Thus, of the hundreds of Arabic works dealing with the sciences of the stars, the vast majority are on astronomy, while only a small portion of this legacy relates to astrological subjects.

*See also* **Astronomy; Science, Islam and.**

## BIBLIOGRAPHY

Kennedy, E. S., and Pingree, David. *The Astrological History of Masha'allah.* Cambridge, Mass.: Harvard University Press, 1971.

Pingree, David. *The Thousands of Abu Ma'shar.* London: The Warburg Institute, 1968.

Saliba, George. "Astronomy, Astrology, Islamic." In Vol. 1, *Dictionary of the Middle Ages.* Edited by J. R. Strayer. New York: Scribners, 1978.

*Ahmad S. Dallal*

## ASTRONOMY

Before Islam, Arab knowledge of the stars was limited to the division of the year into precise periods on the basis of star risings and settings. This area of astronomical knowledge was known as *anwa'*, and it was largely overshadowed by the traditions of Arabic mathematical astronomy that emerged in the Islamic period. From its beginnings in the ninth and through the sixteenth centuries, astronomical activity in the Muslim world was widespread and intensive. The first astronomical texts that were translated into Arabic in the eighth century were of Indian and Persian origin. The earliest extant Arabic astronomical texts date to the second half of the eighth century and were influenced by the Indian and Persian traditions. However, the greatest formative influence on Arabic astronomy is undoubtedly Greek, on account of the use in Greek astronomy of effective geometrical representations. The *Almagest* of Ptolemy (second century C.E.), in particular, exerted a disproportionate influence on all of medieval astronomy through the whole of the Arabic period and until the eventual demise of the geocentric astronomical system. However, at the same time the first Arabic translation of this text were prepared, original work of Arabic astronomy was also produced. Thus, original astronomical research went hand in hand with translation and, from its very beginnings in the ninth century, Arabic astronomy attempted to revise, refine, and complement Ptolemaic astronomy, rather than simply reproduce it.

In its earlier stages, Arabic astronomy reworked and critically examined the observations and the computational methods of Greek astronomy and, in a limited way, was able to explore problems outside its set frame. Arabic astronomy witnessed further developments in the tenth and eleventh centuries as a result of systematic astronomical research as well as developments in other branches of the mathematical sciences. In this period, steps were also taken toward the establishment of large-scale observatories. Subsequently, several programs of astronomical observations involved the establishment of observatories in institutional setups where collective programs of astronomical research were executed. Advances in trigonometry resulting from the full integration of the Indian achievements in the field, as well as from new discoveries in the tenth and eleventh centuries, played a central role in the further development of Arabic astronomy. As a great synthesis of the Greek, Indian, and Arabic astronomical traditions, the *al-Qanun al-Mas'udi* of the illustrious astronomer al-Biruni (973–c. 1048) represents the culmination of this first stage in the development of Arabic astronomy.

Following its systematic mathematization, the rethinking of the theoretical framework of astronomy was further developed after the eleventh century, leading to a thorough evaluation of its physical and philosophical underpinnings. One of the main objectives of this reform tradition was to come up with models in which the motions of the planets could be generated as a result of combinations of uniform circular motions, while at the same time conforming to the accurate Ptolemaic observations. The Ptolemaic models were considered defective because they posited physically impossible models in which spheres rotate uniformly around axes that do not pass through their centers. The reform tradition continued well into the fifteenth and sixteenth centuries, and the list of astronomers working within it comprises some of the greatest and most original Muslim scientists. The work produced within this tradition had a formative influence on the work of Copernicus.

In addition to theoretical astronomy, practical astronomical problems occupied a great many astronomers who were responsible for significant advances in the field. Some of these problems had a specific Islamic character, whereas others had to do with the general practical needs of society. The general kind includes such problems as finding the

The Great Bear, from a seventeenth-century Persian manuscript of the constellations, after the tenth-century Book of Stars by al-Husayn. ART ARCHIVE/NATIONAL LIBRARY OF CAIRO/DAGLI ORTI

direction of one locality with respect to another, a problem that requires determining the longitudes and latitudes of these localities as well as other aspects of mathematical geography. The "Islamic" problems, on the other hand, were problems related to Islamic worship such as determining the times of prayer, the time of sunrise and sunset in relation to fasting, the direction of the *qibla* (the direction of the Ka'ba in Mecca, which Muslims have to face during prayer), crescent visibility in connection with the determination of the beginning of the lunar month, and calendar computations. The methods employed to solve these problems varied from simple approximative techniques to complex mathematical ones.

Problems like the determination of the direction of the *qibla* and the times of prayer also gave a great impetus to the science and art of instrument building. Astrolabes, quadrants, compass boxes, and cartographic grids of varying degrees of sophistication were designed and introduced to solve some of these problems. Many of these same instruments were also used for other astronomical observations and computations; the most important of these is the astrolabe, which was a versatile medieval observational instrument and calculator. Extensive tables were also compiled in connection with time keeping, finding the direction of the *qibla*, and other astronomical functions.

*See also* **Astrology; Biruni, al-; Hijri Calendar; Science, Islam and; Translation.**

## BIBLIOGRAPHY

King, David. *Astronomy in the Service of Islam.* Aldershot, Hampshire, U.K.: Variorum, 1993.

Rashed, Roshdi, ed., in collaboration with Morelon, Régis. *Encyclopedia of the History of Arabic Science,* Vol. 1: *Astronomy—Theoretical and Applied.* London and New York: Routledge, 1996.

Saliba, George. *A History of Arabic Astronomy: Planetary Theories During the Golden Age of Islam.* New York: New York University Press, 1994.

Samso, Julio. *Islamic Astronomy and Medieval Spain.* Aldershot, Hampshire, U.K.: Variorum Reprints, 1994.

*Ahmad S. Dallal*

## 'ATABAT

*'Atabat,* or exalted thresholds, are the Shi'ite shrine cities located in modern Iraq. The *'atabat* contain the tombs of six of the Shi'ite imams as well as other pilgrimage sites. The *'atabat* are located in Najaf, Karbala, Kazamayn, and Samarra. Najaf is the burial place of 'Ali b. Abi Talib, cousin and son-in-law of the prophet Muhammad, and first in the line of Shi'ite imams, who died in 661 C.E. Karbala is where Husayn, 'Ali's son and the third imam, was martyred in a battle against the Umayyads (r. 661–750 C.E.) in 680 C.E. It is a cornerstone of Shi'ite belief that Husayn, courageous and principled, went to battle against all odds, and his demise prefigures and embodies the fate of all those who take an active stand against oppression and injustice. The site of Husayn's martyrdom had emerged as a Muslim holy site by the middle of the seventh century. Kazamayn entered the sacred landscape of Shi'ism in the ninth century, as the burial site of the seventh and ninth imams, Musa al-Kazim (d. 802 C.E.) and Moham-mad al-Taqi (d. 834 C.E.). Kazamayn is also the burial site of many a medieval Shi'ite luminary. Samarra, which lies at a distance from the rest of the *'atabat,* contains the tombs of the tenth and eleventh imams, Ali al-Naqi (d. 868 C.E.) and Hasan al-'Askari (d. 873 C.E.). The twelfth imam entered occultation in Samarra in 941 C.E.

The *'atabat* are also significant as centers of Shi'ite learning. Najaf has housed, since the time of the Shaykh al-Ta'ifa Abu Ja'far Muhammad Tusi in the eleventh century, several educational institutions whose scholarly and financial networks have played an important role in determining intellectual and political trends in modern Shi'ism.

Under Ottoman and later under Iraqi control, the *'atabat* have served in recent history as havens against government persecution for those Iranian Shi'ite scholars of the Qajar and the early Pahlevi periods who have spoken out against the ruling establishment at home. Ayatollah Khomeini, the leader of the 1979 Islamic revolution in Iran, was exiled to the *'atabat* (Najaf) by Muhammad Reza Shah Pahlevi in 1963. In turn, after the success of the Islamic Revolution in Iran, those clerics opposed to the religious and political stance of the ruling hierarchy of the Islamic Republic have used the *'atabat* as relatively secure bases from which to continue their doctrinal warfare against the religious establishment in Iran. However, it must also be borne in mind that since the 1980s, the Shi'ite community and religious leaders resident in the *'atabat* were themselves targeted by the Ba'thist government of former President Saddam Husayn in Iraq. Minority leaders, the ulema of the *'atabat,* especially of Najaf and Karbala, have been subjected to numerous incarcerations and assassinations, intensified in the wake of the first Gulf War (1991).

Another important feature in the social fabric of the *'atabat,* directly related to their centrality in settling doctrinal orthodoxy and implementing political agendas, is the vast network of patronage and the nature of finances in the shrine cities. These networks are comprised mainly of donations and religious dues provided by the Shi'ite communities worldwide, with significant portions from the merchant classes of northern India, to the *maraji' al-taqlid* who reside there.

*See also* **Holy Cities; Mashhad.**

## BIBLIOGRAPHY

Cole, Juan R. I. "Indian Money and the Shii Shrine Cities of Iraq, 1186–1950." *Middle Eastern Studies* 22 (1986): 461–480.

Litvak, Meir. *Shi'i Scholars of Nineteenth-Century Iraq, The 'Ulama' of Najaf and Karbala.* Cambridge, U.K.: Cambridge University Press, 1986.

*Neguin Yavari*

## ATATURK, MUSTAFA KEMAL (1881–1938)

Mustafa Kemal (Ataturk) was born in 1881 into a family of modest means in Salonica, then an Ottoman port city in what is today a city in Greece. He died in Istanbul on 10 November 1938. His father, 'Ali Riza Bey, was a progressive person and worked at the customs house. His mother, Zubeyde Hanim, was a devout Muslim who instilled Islamic values in young Mustafa. Only seven years old at the death of his father, he was raised by his mother and completed his early education at local schools. In 1893 he began his studies at a military secondary school where his teacher gave him his second name, Kemal (perfection), owing to Mustafa's outstanding performance in mathematics. Two years later he attended the military academy in Manastir and later entered the War Academy. He graduated in 1905 with the rank of staff captain, and in 1906 was assigned to the Fifth Army in Damascus. In 1907 his duties took him to Macedonia where he established connections with the Young Turks. He participated in the defense of Tripolitania at Tobruk and Derna against the Italian invasion (1911–1912), was appointed as a military attaché to Sophia, and returned to Istanbul to distinguish himself at the Dardanelles in 1915. During World War I, he served on various fronts such as the Caucasus, Palestine, and Aleppo.

Rejecting the Mudros Armistice (30 October 1918), which the Allied powers had imposed on the Ottomans, Mustafa Kemal moved on to Anatolia in May 1919 to begin his nationalist struggle against the invasion and partition of the country. That same year, at the congresses of Erzurum (23 July) and Sivas (4 September), he defined the nationalist demands and goals for independence. It was during this period that he molded various regional paramilitary defense associations into a nationalist army. On 23 April 1920, he established the Great National Assembly in Ankara, claiming exclusive legitimacy in representing the Turkish interests. He was unanimously elected the first president of the assembly. During the War of Independence, Mustafa Kemal served as the commander in chief of the armed forces.

The Armistice of Mudanya (11 October 1922) sealed the victory of the Turkish forces. Within days, the assembly abolished the sultanate (1 November 1922), though leaving the caliphate in the Ottoman House. The Lausanne Conference (November 1922–July 1923) recognized Turkey's full independence and defined its borders. On 23 October 1923, the Second Grand National Assembly, controlled by Halk Firkasi (People's Party, later Cumhuriyet Halk Partisi—Republican People's Party) proclaimed the republic and elected Mustafa Kemal its first president. Thus a six hundred-year-old political tradition was brushed aside, and sovereignty placed directly in the hands of the people.

The early years of the republic witnessed fundamental political and social changes. Determined to modernize and secularize his country, and intent upon breaking away from the past, the assembly, under Mustafa Kemal's guidance, passed a number of laws that brought revolutionary changes. In 1924, the same year that the caliphate was abolished, the Ministry of Seriat (Islamic law) was dismantled and replaced by the Ministry of Justice. In 1925, the Gregorian Calendar replaced the Islamic one, and the fez, which had come to symbolize Islamic headgear, was banned. The wearing of the veil by women was strongly discouraged. The dervish (Sufi) orders were dissolved. The adoption of Swiss Civil Code in 1926 completely negated the Islamic laws of marriage, divorce, and inheritance that had been in practice for centuries. The replacement of the Arabic script with the Latin script in 1928 closed the door to the Ottoman past, and compelled the

Mustafa Kemal, known as Ataturk (1880–1930), was elected as Turkey's first president. He transformed Turkey from a traditional society into a modern one by secularizing previously Islamic institutions and laws. © HULTON-DEUTSCH COLLECTION/CORBIS

Turks to look to the future. The passage, in 1934, of a law requiring Turks to use family names further underscored this trend; indeed, Mustafa Kemal's own surname of Ataturk (Father of Turks) was bestowed upon him by the National Assembly. In the same year, women were given the right to vote. In foreign policy, Turkey followed Mustafa Kemal's dictum: "Peace at Home, Peace in the World."

Mustafa Kemal's reforms were revolutionary. The policies of his Republican People's Party were expressed in six principles: republicanism, nationalism, populism, etatism, secularism, and revolutionism. Within these principles Turkey was transformed from a traditional society into a modern nation state. Secularism received particular attention. The Kemalist regime relentlessly pursued secularist policies and dismantled the Islamic institutions. In view of the founder of the new Turkish Republic, centuries-old Islamic institutions and laws could not sufficiently serve the needs of a modern society. Mustafa Kemal believed that Islam would be best served if it were confined to belief and worship rather than brought into the affairs of the state. In his address to the nation on the tenth anniversary of the Turkish Republic in 1933, he promised further progress and asked Turks to "judge time not according to the lax mentality of past centuries, but in terms of the concepts of speed and movement of our century."

See also **Nationalism: Turkish; Revolution: Modern; Secularism, Islamic; Young Turks.**

## BIBLIOGRAPHY

Mango, Andrew. *Ataturk*. Woodstock, N.Y.: Overlook, 2000.

Walker, Barbara, et al. *To Set Them Free: The Early Years of Mustafa Kemal Ataturk*. Grantham, N.H.: Tompson and Rutter, 1981.

*A. Uner Turgay*

# AWAMI LEAGUE

The Awami (People's) League was founded by Husain Shaheed Suhrawardy in June 1949 in the East Bengal (renamed East Pakistan in 1955) province of Pakistan. H. S. Suhrawardy gathered senior members of the Muslim League whose power had diminished in their own party and young, ambitious politicians who were opposed to communalism in Pakistan. Both groups, however, were united in the belief that the Muslim League, which spearheaded Pakistan's independence movement, no longer represented the needs of the majority of the populace.

In 1949, though barely two years old, Pakistan was already plagued by economic, political, and social disparities between its two major regional wings. This strife was further complicated by the geographical complexity consisting of the four provinces in the west (Northwest Frontier Province, Baluchistan, Punjab, and Sindh) with East Bengal in the east, which was separated by approximately one thousand miles of India. Some of the first signs of hostilities between East and West Pakistan arose as early as 1948 when Muhammad 'Ali Jinnah, the central architect of the creation of Pakistan, visited the eastern province and proceeded to criticize Bengalis for not learning Urdu, the lingua franca of West Pakistan. Tensions in the regions continued to escalate and in 1952 student efforts to make Bengali a recognized national language led to violent clashes with the police resulting in the deaths of four Dhaka University students. This tragic event further intensified the cultural divide that haunted this young nation.

The people of West Pakistan generally associated the Bengali language with a Hindu India and, therefore, believed that Bengalis should be obligated to learn Urdu, a language clearly associated with Islam. Furthermore, West Pakistani officials deemed Bengali to be closely aligned with pro-Indian sentiment, which was highly unpopular in West Pakistan. This fear and suspicion of Bengali Muslims contributed to West Pakistan's refusal to cede many of the demands of Bengali Muslims. They therefore resisted efforts to recognize Bengali as a national language until 1954.

The desperate economic situation plaguing East Pakistan fostered the belief among its inhabitants that their province was being treated as a colony instead of as an equal partner in the burgeoning nation. Although East Pakistan experienced significant economic growth, the province reaped little of the pecuniary benefits with most of the national expenditures directed toward West Pakistan. Furthermore, few Bengalis held important positions in the administration with even fewer represented in the military. These escalating tensions precipitated the unprecedented move of a splinter group, consisting of East Pakistani politicians, to create a new political party to achieve the common goals of the Bengali population.

In 1949 Husain Shaheed Suhrawardy, Ataur Rahman, Maulana Bashani, Shamsul Huq, and Shaykh Mujibur Rahman co-founded the Awami Muslim league. It was the first party truly to provide alternate representation for the people of East Pakistan. In the late 1950s it changed its name to the Awami League, welcoming non-Muslims into its fold, thus marking a significant shift toward secularism. By 1956 the Awami League was the most popular party in East Pakistan and became the Muslim League's main contender for power.

From 1958 to 1971 Pakistan was reduced to an administrative state with four years of martial law and a diminished role for its fledgling political parties. In February of 1966 Shaykh Mujibur Rahman, the dominant figure in the Awami League, presented the "Six Point Demand" to the other political parties desiring to work collectively to oust the West Pakistani government of Muhammad Ayub Khan. The demands called for separate but equal federation of powers between East and West Pakistan, governed by a parliament elected on the basis of one person/one vote throughout both parts of Pakistan. Gaining the support of the Awami League was equivalent to gaining the support of East Pakistan, but Mujib was only willing to put the Awami League's support behind the coalition if the coalition from West Pakistan was willing to support his "Six Point Demand" (see Mujibur, Appendix 2, pp. 127–128).

For the Bengalis the "Six Point Demand" clearly and concisely reflected goals that would balance powers between the two regions and place Bengalis on an equal footing with their brethren in the western province. Consequently, this "Six Point Demand" consolidated Bengali support for the Awami League. However, it was simultaneously viewed by those in West Pakistan as a document that would work against the tenets laid out in the creation of a united Pakistan.

In Pakistan's first general election in December 1970 the Awami League won 167 of the 169 National Assembly seats allotted to East Pakistan. This landslide victory was due in part to other parties boycotting the elections. In West Pakistan, Zulfiqar Ali Khan Bhutto's Pakistan People's Party won 83 of the 131 seats allotted to that province. With this Awami League victory, the National Assembly should have been able

In Dhaka, Bangladesh, activists for the Awami League, one of the country's two dominant political parties, shout anti-government slogans, protesting the removal of portraits of Shaykh Mujibar Rahman, Bangladesh's independence hero and a founder of the Awami League. In addition to the Awami's rival party, the BNP, there are more than twenty smaller political parties in Bangladesh. AP/WIDE WORLD PHOTOS

to push through the "Six Point Demand" swiftly. Instead, General Yahya Khan (who served as martial law administrator from 25 March 1969 until 20 December 1971) postponed the convening of the National Assembly. This led to an outbreak of violence, the arrest of Shaykh Mujib on charges of treason, and the eventual war for independence resulting in Bangladesh's declaration of independence on 16 December 1971.

Shaykh Mujib, also known as Bangabandhu ("Friend of Bengal"), ruled Bangladesh as its first prime minister until his assassination on 15 August 1975. He is remembered as a great charismatic leader successful in creating the ideological base that united and defined a nation. The constitution of Bangladesh was framed upon Shaykh Mujib's four principles of democracy, socialism, secularism, and nationalism. Yet after independence he was unable to move the country forward economically or democratically. Less than a year after independence, Shaykh Mujib was accused of being ineffectual—a criticism which further contributed to his decision to limit the Bangladeshi multiparty system. Further leading to Mujib's downfall was the famine of 1974. In January 1975 the constitution was amended to make Mujib president for five years, giving him full executive authority. A few months later he created the Bangladesh Krishak Sramik Awami League (BAKSAL, Bangladesh Farmers, Workers, and People's League) while simultaneously outlawing all other political parties. He then created a paramilitary force called the Rakhi Bahini, which was known for its intimidation tactics.

Under Mujib's rule, the Awami League faltered in meeting its goals and consequently lost its popularity with the people. However, after Mujib's death, Bangladesh experienced a number of military coups and counter-coups, resulting in a resurgence of the Awami League's popularity in the 1980s. Consequently, in June 1996 the League won an overall majority in the Parliament with Shaykh Hasina Wajid, daughter of Shaykh Mujib, sworn in as prime minister. During her tenure in office, Wajid had sought to prosecute her father's killers and attempted to put forward a pro-democracy platform and pro-socialist economy that encouraged a private sector. Consequently, the League's rivals often accused it of being too pro-India and secular.

In 1977 Ziaur Rahman, one of Bangladesh's most-decorated major generals during the war for independence, became Chief Martial Law Administrator and president of Bangladesh from 1977 until his assassination in May 1981. He was also the founder of the Bangladesh National Party (BNP). In his first year in office Ziaur Rahman amended the constitution, created by the Awami League government in 1972, to make Islam, and not secularism, one of its guiding principles, a move that ushered in an era of warmer relations between Bangladesh and Pakistan. Today, there are currently more than twenty political parties in Bangladesh with varying platforms emphasizing communism, secularism, and Islamic interests. However, the Awami League, and its main rival, the BNP, continue to dominate national politics. The BNP, led by Khaleda Zia, widow of Ziaur Rahman, runs on a platform that favors democracy and is more oriented toward Islam. As this young nation strives to develop its political system, the question of whether the state should be secular or Islamic continues to dictate political discourse.

*See also* **Pakistan, Islamic Republic of; South Asia, Islam in.**

## BIBLIOGRAPHY

Ahamed, Emajuddin. *Bangladesh Politics.* Dhaka: Centre for Social Studies, 1980.

Baxter, Craig. *Bangladesh.* Boulder, Colo.: Westview Press, 1980.

Baxter, Craig. *Bangladesh: A New Nation in an Old Setting.* Boulder, Colo.: Westview Press, 1984.

Khan, Mohmmad Mohabbat, and Thorp, John P., eds. *Bangladesh: Society, Politics & Bureaucracy.* Dacca, Bangladesh: Center for Administrative Studies, 1984.

Maniruzzaman, Talukdar. "Bangladesh Politics: Secular and Islamic Trends." In *Islam in Bangladesh: Society, Culture and Politics.* Edited by Rafiuddin Ahmed. Dacca: Bangladesh Itihas Samiti, 1983.

Mascarenhas, Anthony. *Bangladesh: A Legacy of Blood.* London: Hodder and Stoughton, 1986.

Mujibur Rahman, Sheikh. *Bangladesh, My Bangladesh: Selected Speeches and Statements.* Edited by Ramendu Majumdar. New Delhi: Orient Longman, 1972.

Sisson, Richard, and Rose, Leo E. *War and Secession: Pakistan, India and the Creation of Bangladesh.* Berkeley: University of California Press, 1990.

Ziring, Lawrence. *Bangladesh: From Mujib to Ershad. An Interpretive Study.* New York: Oxford University Press, 1992.

*Sufia Uddin*

# AYATOLLAH (AR. AYATULLAH)

The term *ayatollah* (Ar. *ayatullah*), literally "Sign of God," refers to high-ranking scholars within the Twelver Shi'ite tradition. The term emerged in the early modern period (late 19th century) to describe the elite of the Shi'ite scholarly community. In modern works, many early Shi'ite scholars were anachronistically given the rank of ayatollah. Ayatollahs are nearly always experts in Islamic jurisprudence (*fiqh*), and are normally required to have written extensively in this area. The requirements for qualification as an ayatollah are not entirely clear in traditional descriptions of the Shi'ite hierarchy, though the rank of *ijtihad* and associated qualifications of learning are often mentioned. *Ijtihad* is a condition, though not everyone who has attained it will be called "ayatollah." The vagueness is due to absence of rigid ranks in the Shi'ite hierarchy. Before and since the Islamic Revolution in Iran (1979), the term "grand ayatollah" was used for the "sources of imitation." Since the revolution, there has been a tremendous increase in the use of the term for the Iranian clerical elite.

Ayatollahs are found at the apex of the scholarly structure, having studied in traditional seminaries (*madrasa*s) and having passed through a number of intermediate ranks (among which is *Hojjat al-Islam*). A scholar seems to be granted the rank of ayatollah through general agreement among the scholars. A person might be referred to as ayatollah by one writer and, when no one disputes the appellation, most scholars subsequently refer to him as ayatollah. An ayatollah, theoretically, holds this rank until he dies, though in recent times, ayatollahs (such as ayatollahs Shari'atmadari and

Muntazeri in Iran) have lost their status after serious disputes with supposedly higher-ranking Ayatollah Ruhollah Khomeini.

*See also* **Hojjat al-Islam; Khomeini, Ruhollah; Marja' al-Taqlid; Shi'a: Imami (Twelver).**

**BIBLIOGRAPHY**

Mottahedeh, Roy. *The Mantle of the Prophet: Religion and Politics in Iran.* London: Chatto and Windus, 1986.

*Robert Gleave*

# AZHAR, AL-

Al-Azhar is a mosque and a university founded in Cairo by the Fatimid Isma'ili imam and caliph al-Mu'izz li-Din Allah (d. 975). Today it is the most important religious university in the Muslim world, and it is one of the oldest universities ever founded for both religious and secular studies. After the conquest of Egypt (969), Jawhar al-Siqilli founded al-Qahira (Cairo), where he built the mosque that was first known as *jami' al-Qahira* (the mosque of Cairo). The mosque was completed in nearly two years and first opened its doors in 972. It had one minaret and occupied half the area of the present day al-Azhar mosque. Since then, it has become one of the most well known mosques in the Muslim world. Its name is an allusion to Zahra' (The Radiant), a title given to Fatima, the daughter of prophet Muhammad. Al-Azhar began to acquire its academic and scholastic nature in 975, during the reign of al-Mu'izz when the Qadi Abu 'l-Hasan 'Ali ibn al-Nu'man al-Qayrawani sat in the court of al-Azhar and read the *Kitab al-iqtisar* (a work of Shi'ite jurisprudence, or *fiqh)*, written by his father, Abu Hanifa al-Nu'man. Al-Nu'man's family formed the intellectual elite of the Fatimids and became the first teacher in al-Azhar.

In 998, al-Azhar moved a step further toward becoming an Islamic university. The Fatimid caliph al-'Aziz Billah approved a proposal by his trusted minister Ya'qub ibn Killis to establish an educational system. He assigned a number of regular teachers to carry out an educative mission. The teachers were trained by Ibn Killis and his system became the core of the academic education at al-Azhar. Furthermore, these teachers followed an organized curriculum and they received regular payments from the Fatimid government. The teaching was not limited to the religious sciences, but included discussions and free debates between scientists. Thus al-Azhar acquired the characteristics of an academic university. The diversified courses were a part of the teaching curriculum (the jurisprudence of four different schools of law, Arabic language, and literature). When the Ayyubid dynasty (1169–1252) took power, they wanted to erase every trace of the Fatimids. Al-Azhar's reputation did not cease growing and the Shi'ite view was eclipsed by the Sunni interpretation of faith. Later, al-Azhar became the most important Sunni center of knowledge.

Under the reign of the Mamluks, between 1250 and 1517, many scientists sought refuge in al-Azhar, and were received with open arms. The arrival of these scientists undoubtedly contributed to the enrichment of its teaching; al-Azhar had its golden age during the fourteenth and fifteenth centuries. Sciences such as medicine, mathematics, astronomy, geography, and history were studied there.

In 1822 the educational system was regulated and the highest diploma then delivered by al-Azhar was called *al-ʿalamiyya*, which was equivalent to a doctorate. In 1950, al-Azhar's educational system was divided into three faculties: Islamic law (*al-shariʿa*), principles of the religion (*usul al-din*), and Arabic language. In 1961, besides its teaching of Islamic sciences, al-Azhar opened technical and practical faculties to teach medicine, engineering, agriculture, and other subjects. This widening of teaching was intended to make al-Azhar radiate not only in religious sciences but also in scientific disciplines. However, the addition of a modern, non-traditional curriculum was controversial among more conservative Muslim intellectuals.

*See also* **Education; Madrasa; Zaytuna.**

## BIBLIOGRAPHY

Lapidus, Ira M. *Muslim Cities in the Later Middle Ages.* Cambridge, Mass.: Harvard University Press, 1967.

Tritton, A. S. *Materials on Muslim Education in the Middle Ages,* London: Luzac, 1957.

*Diana Steigerwald*

# B

## BABIYYA

The Babi movement began during a period of heightened chiliastic expectation for the return of the Twelfth Imam (or Hidden Imam), who Shi'ite Muslims believe will fill the world with justice. As such, the movement attracted not only students of religion, but members from all strata of society who probably sought change in the existing order.

The initial converts to the Babi movement were mid- to low-level clerics from the Shaykhi school of Twelver Shi'ite Islam. The school, founded upon the teachings of Shaykh Ahmad al-Ahsa'i, was mainstream with regard to Shi'ite law, Akhbari in its veneration for the utterances ascribed to the twelve imams, and theosophical in its approach to metaphysical matters. Shaykh Ahmad's successor, Sayyed Kazem, developed the eschatological teachings of his predecessor and taught that the advent of the "promised one" was imminent, although he did not specify if this figure was to be an intermediary of the hidden imam or the imam himself.

On 22 May 1844, 'Ali Mohammad, a young merchant who had briefly attended the classes of Sayyed Kazem in Karbala, told a fellow Shaykhi disciple, Mulla Hosayn Boshrui, that he was the "gate" (*bab*) of the Hidden Imam and wrote an extemporaneous commentary on the Qur'anic Sura of Joseph, the *Qayyum al-asma*, to substantiate his claim. So impressed was Molla Hosayn and other students of Sayyed Kazem with the eloquence and learning of 'Ali Mohammad and his ability to produce verses (*ayat*) at great speed and with no apparent forethought that they publicly endorsed his claims to be the gate of the Hidden Imam, while privately they believed that his station was much higher. The exact nature of the Bab's claims remained a matter of controversy during the first four years of his seven-year prophetic career. Although he initially made no explicit claim to prophethood, he implicitly claimed to receive revelation by emulating the style of the Qur'an in the *Qayyum al-asma*.

After the formation of the first core of believers, who, along with the Bab, were referred to as the first Vahed (Unity), the group dispersed at his instruction to proclaim the advent of the Bab, whose new theophany was to be initiated by his pilgrimage to Mecca, reaching a crescendo with his arrival in the holy cities of Iraq. The Bab instructed Molla Hosayn to disseminate his teachings in Iran and deliver the *Qayyum al-asma* to the shah and his chief minister. Another disciple was sent to Azerbaijan, while others were instructed to return to their homes to spread the new message. The majority of the Bab's first disciples departed for Iraq, including Molla 'Ali Bastami, who was sent as a representative to the holy cities. There, he preached the new message in public. As a result, both the messenger and the author of the message were condemned as heretics in a joint *fatwa* by prominent Sunni and Shi'ite ulema in Iraq.

Following this episode, the Bab decided not to meet with his followers in Karbala as he had planned so as not to further raise the ire of an already enraged clerical establishment. This led to the disaffection of some of his more militant followers, who were expecting the commencement of a holy war. It also emboldened the Bab's critics, particularly the rival claimants for leadership of the Shaykhi community.

Persecution of the Babis in Iran began in 1845 and the Bab himself was confined to his home in June 1845. During this period he was forced to publicly deny certain claims that had been attributed to him, which he was willing to comply with since his actual claim was much more challenging, as witnessed in his later epistles and public statements, particularly from 1848 onward. By asserting that he was the recipient of revelation and divine authority, whether explicitly or implicitly by emulating the style of the Qur'an, the Bab challenged the right of the ulema to collect alms on behalf of the Hidden Imam and interpret scripture in his absence. Further, his claim to be the *Qa'im* (the one who rises at the end of time), made explicit at his public trial in Tabriz, indirectly threatened the stability of the Qajar monarchy of Iran, which held power as the Shadow of God on earth and depended upon the quiescent Shiʿite clergy for legitimacy.

Despite the hostility of much of the high-ranking clergy, the Bab continued to win converts from among the ulema, including two very prominent personalities: Sayyed Yahya Darabi and Molla Mohammad ʿAli Hojjat al-Islam Zanjani. In 1846, he managed to leave Shiraz and make his way to the home of the governor of Isfahan, Manuchehr Khan Moʿtamad al-Dawla, a Georgian Christian convert to Islam who sympathized with the Bab's cause. There, he enjoyed increasing popularity, which further roused the ulema, who incited the shah against the Bab. Following the death of his patron, he was placed under arrest. From this point on, the charismatic persona of the Bab was removed from the public arena, as he was transferred from prison to prison until his final execution at the hands of government troops on 9 July 1850.

Although the Bab continued to influence the movement from prison through the dissemination of thousands of pages of writing, leadership of the community devolved upon his chief lieutenants, notably Molla Hosayn, Molla Mohammad ʿAli Barforushi (also known as the Qoddus, "the Most Holy"), Qorrat al-ʿAyn, the well-known poetess (also known as Tahereh, "the Pure One"), Darabi, Zanjani, and Mirza Hosayn ʿAli Nuri (later known as Bahaʾallah). The latter, together with Qoddus and Tahereh, presided over a decisive meeting of Babis at Badasht, where a formal break with Islamic law was initiated when Tahereh publicly removed her veil. She was later put to death in 1852 upon the orders of the government, ratified by leading doctors of law. Qoddus would also die at the instigation of some members of the ulema following his capture at the shrine of Shaykh Tabarsi, where he, Molla Hosayn, and an embattled group of Babis defended themselves against government troops in the province of Khurasan. Molla Hosayn and most of the fort's defenders lost their lives there. Similarly, Darabi and Zanjani led large groups of Babis in armed resistance to government troops at Nayriz and Zanjan, but ultimately met the same fate as their fellow believers. In 1852, as a result of an assassination attempt on the life of Naser al-Din Shah by some Babis, several hundred to a few thousand of the Bab's followers were brutally executed or imprisoned. Among them was Mirza Husayn ʿAli Nuri, the future Bahaʾallah, who suffered a four-month captivity in a darkened pit (*siyah chal*), followed by exile to Iraq.

Although the demographic makeup of the Babi movement cannot be determined with precision, it is safe to say that it was largely an urban movement with significant concentrations of converts in rural areas. While it initially drew upon Shaykhi ulema, it later attracted followers from a range of social classes, particularly merchants and craftsmen. Finally, preaching and conversion were confined to predominantly Shiʿite areas in Iraq and Iran.

As has been stressed by modern scholars, the Babi movement served as a vehicle of social protest, uniting a number of otherwise inimical heterodox and social classes in opposition to the established order. Despite this shared desire for social change (which still remains to be proven), the Bab's charismatic personality and forceful writing also played a central role in attracting converts and admirers, even in the West. Rather than being an unwitting product of messianic expectation, content to remain within the bounds of traditional Shiʿite notions of the function of the Hidden Imam as the Mahdi and reformer of Islam, the Bab enunciated a supra-Islamic message that included new laws and social teachings designed, by his own admission, to prepare the people for a second theophany: the coming of "Him Whom God will make manifest" (*man yuzhiruhuʾllah*).

Although there were a number of claimants to this theophany in the 1850s, most Babis followed the Bab's nominee, Bahaʾallah's half-brother Mirza Yahya (also known as Subh Azal). After Bahaʾallah claimed this station in 1863, however, the majority of Babis recognized him as the fulfillment of the Bab's prophecies concerning the second theophany and subsequently identified themselves as Bahaʾis. The Bab's followers, who continued to owe their allegiance to Subh Azal, became known as Azalis and played an important role in Iran's constitutional revolution in 1906.

*See also* **Bab, Sayyed ʿAli Muhammad; Bahaʾallah; Bahaʾi Faith.**

## BIBLIOGRAPHY

Amanat, Abbas. *Resurrection and Renewal: The Making of the Babi Movement in Iran, 1844–1850*. Ithaca, N.Y.: Cornell University Press, 1989.

MacEoin, Denis. *Rituals in Babism and Bahaʾism*. London: British Academic Press, 1994.

*William McCants*

# BAB, SAYYED ʿALI MUHAMMAD (1819–1850)

Sayyed ʿAli Muhammad, later known as "the Bab," was born on 20 October 1819 in Shiraz, the provincial capital of Fars. A descendent of the prophet Muhammad's family, the Bab traced his lineage from the tribe of Quraysh to his father, Sayyed Muhammad Reza, a merchant in the bazaar of Shiraz. In his early childhood, the Bab's father died and he came under the care of his maternal uncles. During his adolescence and young adulthood, the Bab's uncle Hajji Mirza Sayyed ʿAli was his most stalwart supporter, overseeing his limited education, guiding his early business ventures as a merchant, and later becoming one of the earliest adherents of his nephew's new creed.

The Bab's demure demeanor as a child matured into quiet, religious contemplation, as noted by his contemporaries. His personal piety led him to undertake a pilgrimage to the Shi'ite holy shrines in Iraq between 1840 and 1841. While there, the Bab, an adherent of the Shaykhi school of Twelver Shi'ite Islam, attended a few classes given by the Shaykhi leader Sayyed Kazem Rashti. On 22 May 1844, three years after his return to Shiraz, the Bab advanced his claim to divine authority from God to one of Kazem's students, Mulla Hosayn, and soon after gained a large following among seminarians who in turn made many converts among merchants and even upper-class landowners, including Mirza Husayn 'Ali Nuri, who later founded the Baha'i religion.

Although the Bab couched his claims in abstruse language early in his career, the implications were not lost upon the Shi'ite ulema. In particular, they viewed his assertion to reveal verses in the same manner as Muhammad as a violation of a cardinal tenet of Shi'ite and Sunni Islam—that Muhammad was the last of God's messengers. He was tried by religious judges and condemned to death for heresy. As a result of clerical agitation, he was soon arrested and suffered imprisonment until his execution on 9 July 1850, at the age of thirty.

During his prophetic career, the Bab composed numerous religious texts of varying genres. Some of the more notable titles include the *Qayyum al-asma'* (his earliest, post-declaration doctrinal work), the Persian and Arabic *Bayans* (two separate books detailing the laws of his new religion), and *Dala'il sab'a* (an apologetic work).

*See also* **Babiyya; Baha'allah; Baha'i Faith.**

## BIBLIOGRAPHY

Amanat, Abbas. *Resurrection and Renewal: The Making of the Babi Movement in Iran, 1844–1850.* Ithaca, N.Y.: Cornell University Press, 1989.

MacEoin, Denis. *The Sources for Early Babi Doctrine and History.* Leiden: E. J. Brill, 1992.

*William McCants*

# BAGHDAD

"Have you seen in all the length and breadth of the earth

A city such as Baghdad? Indeed it is paradise on earth."

(al-Khatib al-Baghdadi, in Lassner, *Topography*, p. 47)

Thus begins a poem attributed variously to 'Umara b. 'Aqil al-Khatafi and Mansur al-Namari in praise of Baghdad, the illustrious capital of the Abbasid caliphate in Iraq for close to

A bust of Muslim caliph Abu Ja'far al-Mansur, in Baghdad, which he founded. AP/WIDE WORLD PHOTOS

five centuries. The city was founded by the second Abbasid caliph, Abu Ja'far al-Mansur, on the banks of the Tigris River where it most closely approaches the Euphrates. While officially called Dar al-Salam, or the Abode of Peace, which recalls Qur'anic descriptions of Paradise (6:127; 10:25), the name Baghdad itself is reminiscent of a pre-Islamic settlement in the vicinity. However, this metropolis is not to be confused erroneously with the ancient towns of Babylon, Seleucia, and Ctesiphon.

Following the turbulence and social upheavals of the Abbasid assumption of power from the Umayyads, al-Mansur sought to move his capital to a more secure location in the East. The proclamation of Abu l-'Abbas as the first Abbasid caliph in 749 C.E. had irrevocably shifted the locus of imperial power away from Damascus, the Umayyad capital, to a series of successive sites in Iraq. Al-Mansur himself was initially based in al-Hashimiyyah, adjacent to Qasr Ibn Hubayra and close to Kufa. The Rawandiyya uprising of 758 C.E., however, soon exposed the location's vulnerability, and al-Mansur began a thorough investigation of sites from which he could consolidate his rule.

In accordance with the information gathered from scouts, local inhabitants, and personal observation, the minor village of Baghdad was selected as an ideal location for the future Abbasid capital. The area had much to recommend itself in terms of its central location, fertile lands, temperate climate, ease of receiving provisions via the Tigris and Euphrates Rivers, the convening of caravan routes nearby, and the natural defenses provided by the surrounding canals. Construction of the imperial capital began in the year 762 C.E., though work was halted temporarily that same year while al-Mansur suppressed further uprisings emanating from Medina and Basra. Over one hundred thousand architects, artisans, and laborers from across the empire were employed in the creation of this city, at tremendous financial expense, over a period of four years.

An alternative name for Baghdad, al-Madina al-Mudawwara, or the Round City, reflects the circular layout of al-Mansur's initial foundation. Baghdad was designed as a series of concentric rings, with the caliphal palace, known as Bab al-Dhahab, or the Golden Gate, and the attached grand congregational mosque located in the center, along with separate structures for the commander of the guard and the chief of police. The caliph was thereby equidistant from all points within the city, as well as surrounded by its considerable fortifications. Only the residences of his younger children, those of his servants and slaves, and various government offices shared access onto this inner circle. Four walkways radiated outward from the central courtyard in the directions of northeast, southeast, southwest, and northwest, passing through the inner circle of surrounding structures; then an enclosure wall followed by an interval of space; then a residential area followed by another interval; then a large wall of outer defense, a third interval, a second smaller wall; and finally a deep, wide moat surrounding the entire complex.

The Round City initially retained an austere administrative and military character. On the city's outskirts, large land grants at varying distances from the capital were given to members of the Abbasid family, the army, and chiefs of the government agencies. In addition to the initial settlers, comprised of those loyal to the caliph and his new regime, large numbers of laborers, artisans, and merchants migrated to Baghdad in pursuit of the largesse showered upon those necessary to sustain the new imperial capital. What quickly grew to be a thriving market within the walls of the Round City was ultimately perceived to be a security threat and, in 773 C.E., was transferred southwest of Baghdad, to al-Karkh. There, the commercial activities of the Abbasid capital flourished, and Baghdad rapidly developed into an economically vibrant metropolis.

The main markets of Baghdad were subdivided according to their various specialties which included food, fruit, flowers,

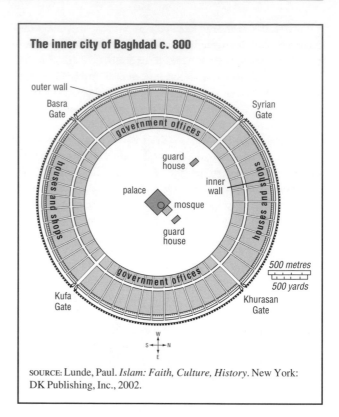

The inner city of Baghdad circa 800.

SOURCE: Lunde, Paul. *Islam: Faith, Culture, History*. New York: DK Publishing, Inc., 2002.

textiles, clothes, booksellers, goldsmiths, cobblers, reedweavers, soapmakers, and moneychangers that served the populace and government officials. Baghdad exported textiles and items made of cotton and silk, glazed-ware, oils, swords, leather, and paper, to mention only a few, through both local and international trade. The *muhtasib*, a government-appointed regulator, ensured the fair practices of the marketplace as well as supervised the public works of proliferating mosques and bathhouses. The opulence and luxury of court life in Baghdad were legendary, and reflected the vast political and economic power of the Abbasid Empire.

The magnanimity of the Abbasid caliphs and the well-placed inhabitants of Baghdad also extended into encouraging intellectual pursuits, thereby establishing the Abbasid capital as one of the world's most sophisticated and prestigious centers of learning. Renowned Islamic scholars of diverse geographical and ethnic origins held sessions in the mosques and colleges of cosmopolitan Baghdad, attracting innumerable seekers of legal, philological, and spiritual knowledge. Bookshops and the private homes of individual scholars and high government officials, such as the wazir, also served as venues for intellectual discussion and debate. Inns located near the mosques provided lodging to those who had devoted themselves to scholarly pursuits, and accommodations were later made available within the institutions of the *madrasa* (legal college) and *ribat* (Sufi establishment), both of which also offered stipends to affiliated students.

Scientific research in the fields of astronomy, mathematics, medicine, optics, engineering, botany, and pharmacology also prospered within the Abbasid capital. Alongside experimentation and exploration, translation of Hellenic, Indic, and Persian texts received patronage from dignitaries, physicians, and scientists in response to the professional and intellectual demands of an expanding Islamic society. Public libraries, both attached to mosques and as separate institutions, contributed further to the dissemination of knowledge among the populace, while the establishment of hospitals as charitable endowments throughout the city ensured the provision of free medical care to anyone who so required it. Mobile clinics were even dispatched to remote villages on a regular basis, with the aims of offering comprehensive health coverage.

The political fragmentation of the sprawling Abbasid Empire ultimately contributed to a decline in the revenues and hence in the general fortunes of the capital in Baghdad. Increasing civil disturbances in the face of weakened central authority, as well as rife Sunni-Shi'ite conflicts, resulted in the deterioration and destruction of vast segments of the waning metropolis. Nevertheless, Baghdad retained its prestige as the center of the Islamic caliphate and a symbol of Muslim cultural, material, and scholarly achievement. It was therefore with great consternation that news was received of the Mongols's savage invasion and ravaging of the city in 1258 C.E. Hundreds of thousands of Baghdad's inhabitants, including the caliph and his family, leading personalities, and scholars were mercilessly put to death, and the great scientific and literary treasures of Baghdad were burned or drowned in the waters of the Tigris.

Thereafter, Baghdad was transformed into a provincial center within the Mongol Empire, under the control of the Ilkhanids until 1339 C.E. and then the Jalayrids until 1410 C.E. The Karakoyunlu Turkomans and the Akkoyunlu Turkomans ruled Baghdad successively, until the city was conquered by Shah Ismail in 1508 C.E. and incorporated into the Safavid Empire. A subsequent Perso-Ottoman struggle for Baghdad and its symbolic sites resulted in Sultan Sulayman the Magnificent's conquest of the city in 1534 C.E., only to be lost again to the Safavids, and then regained by the Ottoman Sultan Murad IV in 1638 C.E. Baghdad remained the capital of the region's Ottoman province for nearly three centuries, and was occupied by the British in March 1917, during the course of World War I. In 1921, it became the seat of Faysal b. Husayn's kingdom under British Mandate and remained the capital of Iraq throughout its successive developments into an independent constitutional monarchy (1930), federated Hashimite monarchy (1958), and then republic (1958).

See also **Caliphate; Empires: Abbasid; Revolution: Classical Islam; Revolution: Islamic Revolution in Iran; Revolution: Modern.**

## BIBLIOGRAPHY

Jawad, Mustafa, and Susa, Ahmad. *Baghdad*. Baghdad: al-Majma' al-'Ilmi al-'Iraqi, 1958.

Lassner, Jacob. *The Topography of Baghdad in the Early Middle Ages: Text and Studies.* Detroit: Wayne State University Press, 1970.

Lunde, Paul. *Islam: Faith, Culture, History.* New York: DK Publishing, 2002.

Makdisi, George. *Religion, Law and Learning in Classical Islam.* Brookfield, Vt.: Gower, 1991.

Makdisi, George. "The Reception of the Model of Islamic Scholastic Culture in the Christian West." In *Science in Islamic Civilisation: Proceedings of the International Symposia.* Edited by Ekmeleddin Ihsanoglu. Istanbul: Research Centre for Islamic History and Culture, 2000.

Sayyad, Nezar, al-. *Cities and Caliphs: On the Genesis of Arab Muslim Urbanism.* New York: Greenwood Press, 1991.

Tabari, Muhammad al-. *Abbasid Authority Affirmed.* Translated by Jane Dammen McAuliffe. Albany: State University of New York Press, 1995.

Wheatley, Paul. *The Places Where Men Pray Together: Cities in Islamic Lands, Seventh through Tenth Centuries.* Chicago: University of Chicago Press, 2001.

*Mona Hassan*

# BAHA'ALLAH (1817–1892)

"Baha'allah," a title meaning "splendor of God," was the name given to Mirza Husayn 'Ali Nuri, prophet and founder of the Baha'i faith.

Born in Tehran into an elite bureaucratic family, he was converted in 1844 to the Babi religion, the messianic movement begun that year by the Iranian prophet Sayyed 'Ali Muhammad, commonly known as the Bab ("Gate"). He played a significant role in the early Babi community. Imprisoned as a Babi in 1852, he was exiled to Iraq, where he became the de facto leader of the Babis. He was summoned to Istanbul by the Ottoman government in April 1863 and then arrested and exiled again to Edirne in European Turkey. There he made an open claim to prophethood that was eventually accepted by most Babis, though opposed by his younger brother, Subh-e Azal. Alarmed by disputes among the Babi exiles, the Turkish government imprisoned Baha'allah in Acre, Palestine, in 1868, where he lived under gradually improving conditions until his death. His eldest son, 'Abd al-Baha', was recognized by most Baha'is as his successor. His tomb near Acre is now a Baha'i shrine.

Baha'allah wrote extensively, mostly letters to the believers. His works included commentary on scripture, Baha'i law, comments on current affairs, prayers, and theological discussions of all sorts. Though his writings were grounded in the esoteric Shiʿite thought of the Bab, he was politically sophisticated, and his own religious thought is often best seen in the context of the Westernizing reformers of the nineteenth century Middle East. The social liberalism of the modern Baha'i faith has its roots in Baha'allah's writings.

Baha'allah is considered a "manifestation of God" by Baha'is and is thus a prophet of the rank of Moses, Jesus, and Muhammad.

See also **'Abd al-Baha'; Bab, Sayyed 'Ali Muhammad; Baha'i Faith.**

## BIBLIOGRAPHY

Baha'u'llah. *Tablets of Baha'u'llah Revealed after the Kitab-i-Aqdas.* Translated by Habib Taherzadeh. Wilmette, Ill.: Baha'i Publishing Trust, 1988.

Balyuzi, Hasan. *Baha'u'llah: the King of Glory.* Oxford, U.K.: George Ronald, 1980.

Cole, Juan R. I. *Modernity and the Millenium: The Genesis of the Baha'i Faith in the Nineteenth-Century Middle East.* New York: Columbia University Press, 1998.

*John Walbridge*

# BAHA'I FAITH

The Baha'i faith was founded by Baha'allah as an outgrowth of the Babi religion, the messianic movement begun in 1844 by the Iranian prophet Sayyed 'Ali Muhammad, commonly known as the Bab ("Gate").

## History

After the execution of the Bab in 1850 and the pogrom following a Babi attempt to assassinate the shah, the Babi movement suffered a crisis of leadership. Its titular leader was Mirza Yahya, known as Subh-e Azal, but from the mid-1860s the effective leader was Azal's elder brother, Baha'allah. Both were exiles in Baghdad. Baha'allah later wrote that he had had mystical experiences while imprisoned in Tehran in 1852, and by the early 1860s he had begun hinting that he was "he whom God shall make manifest," the Babi messiah. On 21 April 1863 he announced this claim to several close associates, an event that Baha'is now consider the beginning of their religion. Baha'allah nonetheless continued to recognize the nominal leadership of Azal. The final break came in 1867 when he wrote to Azal formally claiming prophethood. The Babis then split into three main groups. By the end of the 1870s those who had accepted the claim of Baha'allah were the large majority and came to be known as Baha'is. A smaller number, the Azalis, stayed loyal to Subh-e Azal and vociferously opposed Baha'allah. A few accepted neither claim.

Through his extensive correspondence and meetings with pilgrims during his exile in Acre, Baha'allah organized the new community. He rejected the militancy and esoteric Shiʿite mysticism characteristic of the Babis, instead stressing political neutrality and progressive themes such as international peace, education, and the emancipation of women and slaves. By the time of the death of Baha'allah in 1892, the Iranian community had recovered from the disasters of the Babi period, and small but growing communities, mainly consisting of Iranian émigrés, had been established in many countries of the Middle East, the Russian Empire, and India.

After Baha'allah's death most Baha'is accepted the leadership of his eldest son, 'Abd al-Baha'. In the 1890s small but influential communities of Baha'i converts from Christianity were established in Europe and North America. Despite the turmoil caused by World War I and by revolutions in Iran, Turkey, and Russia, 'Abd al-Baha' was able to establish an institutional structure for most of the major Baha'i communities, increasingly in the form of elected governing committees known as spiritual assemblies. The most important event of his ministry, however, was a series of journeys to Europe and America from 1911 to 1913. These trips were the occasion for an increasing stress on the liberal social teachings of the Baha'i faith.

'Abd al-Baha' was succeeded in 1921 by his grandson, Shoghi Effendi Rabbani, whose English education and Western orientation marked a final break with the religion's Islamic roots. Shoghi Effendi was not a charismatic figure like his grandfather and preferred to focus on institution-building and consolidation. The most spectacular achievement of his ministry was a series of "teaching plans," in which Baha'i missionaries settled in scores of new countries and territories, notably in Latin America, Africa, and the Pacific. By the 1950s some of these communities were growing rapidly. Shoghi Effendi wrote extensively and systematically in Persian and English, standardizing Baha'i theological self-understanding and practice. His translations of several volumes of Baha'allah's writings became the standard Baha'i scriptures for Western Baha'is. He also wrote a history of the Babi and Baha'i Faiths and translated a history of the Babi religion. These works also became fundamental for the self-understanding of Western Baha'is. Finally, through his construction of Baha'i shrines and temples in Haifa, Acre, and several Western cities, he made the Baha'i faith more visible and created a Baha'i architectural idiom.

Shoghi Effendi died in 1957, leaving neither an heir nor a will. In 1963, after a six-year interregnum, the various Baha'i national spiritual assemblies elected an international governing body, the Universal House of Justice, which has since been elected every five years. The Universal House of Justice continued Shoghi Effendi's programs of teaching plans and construction. There are now several million Baha'is in the world, most in the developing world, leaving only a small minority in Iran or Islamic countries.

This garden leads to the $250 million Baha'i Shrine of the Bab in Haifa, Israel that was completed in 2001 after ten years of construction. Built by the great grandson of Baha'allah, founder of the Baha'i faith, it is one of many Baha'i shrines and temples throughout the Muslim world and the West. Baha'i is a religion that split from Islam. It emphasizes the unity among all religions, races, and nations. AP/WIDE WORLD PHOTOS

## Baha'i Theology, Beliefs, and Practices

The theological roots of the Baha'i faith are in the Babi religion, which was essentially an esoteric Shi'ite movement. The fundamental Baha'i theological conception is that of the logos figure of the manifestation of God: the prophet as the perfect mirror of God's attributes. Human beings and all other creatures are lesser mirrors of God's various attributes. The prophet is thus a model and a revealer of God's knowledge and will. God's full plan is revealed gradually by a series of prophets, who guide humanity's emergence into a worldwide spiritual civilization. Baha'allah is of particular significance, since his ministry marks the beginning of human maturity and world unity. Thus, for Baha'is all religions are fundamentally true, having been based on prophecy, though the Baha'i faith is destined to supercede them. The differences among religions are due either to the differing circumstances of the time and place of their revelation or to gradual corruption of the original message.

The characteristic feature of Baha'allah's revelation is its stress on unity, a theme expressed in Baha'i social teachings.

Thus, racism, nationalism, religious fanaticism, prejudice of any sort, and the degradation of women are condemned in Baha'i teachings. Likewise, there is no Baha'i clergy, and all believers are considered fundamentally equal. The theme of unity permeates Baha'i thought and practice, giving the community a decidedly egalitarian character.

The Baha'i faith is nominally a religion of law, but its religious law, though generally analogous to Islamic law and practice, is usually simpler and less demanding. There is a daily prayer, an annual nineteen-day fast, nine major holy days, and a "feast" every nineteen days on the first day of each month of the Baha'i calendar. Regulations governing marriage, divorce, and funerals are simple. Baha'is are monogamous, and marriage is conditioned on the consent both of the couple and of living parents. In practice, Baha'i communal life often is less concerned with worship than with community administration and particularly the goal of expanding the community.

Baha'i scripture consists of the authenticated writings of Baha'allah and 'Abd al-Baha'. Shoghi Effendi's works are authoritative as interpretation, and writings of the Universal House of Justice are authoritative in legislative and administrative matters. Writings of individuals are considered personal opinion and not binding on others. Because the authoritative writings are so voluminous, Baha'i writers have tended to focus on collection and collation. Most Baha'i theological writing has been polemical rather than speculative in character. There is no developed Baha'i legal tradition. Since the 1970s there has been increasingly vigorous academic and theological study of the Baha'i faith.

*See also* **'Abd al-Baha'; Babiyya; Baha'allah.**

## BIBLIOGRAPHY

Smith, Peter. *The Babi and Baha'i Religions: From Messianic Shi'ism to a World Religion.* Cambridge, U.K.: Cambridge University Press, 1987.

Stockman, Robert. *The Baha'i Faith in America.* Wilmette, Ill.: Baha'i Publishing Trust, 1985–1995.

Walbridge, John. *Sacred Acts, Sacred Space, Sacred Time.* Bahá'í Studies 1. Oxford: George Ronald, 1996.

*John Walbridge*

# BALKANS, ISLAM IN THE

Since the late fourteenth century there have been Muslim communities in southeast Europe. For most of their history they were an important and integral part of the Ottoman Empire. In the nineteenth and twentieth centuries when ethnic-based nation-states came to power in the Balkans, most of these Muslim communities lost prominence and some disappeared. Recent attempts by certain nationalist forces to erase the history of Muslims in the Balkans have led to new interest in these Muslim peoples of Europe.

## Expansion of Islam into Southeast Europe

Ottoman armies and Sufi missionaries brought Islam into southeast Europe in the late fourteenth and fifteenth centuries. Beginning with the conquest of eastern Thrace in the mid-1300s, the Ottomans soon took Macedonia. They fought Serbian prince Lazar and his Balkan army at Kosovo in 1389, and defeated Bulgaria soon after in 1393. Along with military conquest, the Ottomans brought Muslim settlers from Anatolia to occupy main march routes and river valleys. In 1456 Athens fell to the Ottomans, followed by Bosnian and Albanian lands, and finally Belgrade in 1521.

There was significant conversion of local people to Islam, principally among Bosnians and Albanians, but also across the Balkans. This conversion was gradual, continuing throughout the fifteenth, sixteenth, and seventeenth centuries, and even later among some Albanians. Except for the *devsirme*, the forced recruitment of Christian boys for special military and governmental service, this conversion to Islam was voluntary. The Balkans had been a region of contention between western, or Latin, and eastern, or Byzantine, forms of Christianity. In Bosnia and Albania neither form of Christianity had been well preached or well established. In contrast the Sufi missionaries brought a tolerant form of religion and the Ottoman state a system of order based broadly on religious affiliation. The advantages of being Muslim were economic and cultural and included exemption from the head tax, privileges in land owning, and opportunities in state administration and the military, as well as links with the vibrant culture and society of Istanbul.

## History and Main Developments

During the Ottoman period, lasting from the fourteenth century to the early twentieth century, the history of Muslims in the Balkans largely parallels the history of the empire itself. When the Ottoman Empire was at its height in the sixteenth century, the Balkan cities of Edirne, Sarajevo, and Salonika (the latter with a significant Jewish population) were rich cosmopolitan centers of trade and learning, with impressive mosques, *madrasa*s (schools), and bridges. Three of Sultan Suleyman the Magnificent's grand wazirs—Ibrahim the Greek, Rustem the Bulgarian, and Mehmet Sokullu, a Slav from Bosnia—were converted Muslims from the Balkans. At the end of the seventeenth century, Albanian Muslims from the Koprulu family (Mehmet, Ahmed, Mustafa, and Husein) served as grand wazirs and provided well-needed stability in a century of decline. For, as western European countries gained power in trade routes and military prowess, formerly the purview of the Ottomans, the Ottoman Empire weakened economically and the Austro-Hungarian Empire took territories from the Ottomans, including Hungary, part of present-day Croatia (1699), and later Bosnia (1878). The position of Muslim communities gradually declined as well until the

Expansion of the Ottoman Empire into southeast Europe. XNR PRODUCTIONS, INC./GALE

breakup of Ottoman power in the Balkans left many of them vulnerable.

The following period in the history of Muslims in the Balkans, the time of growth of nation-states, began variably in the nineteenth and twentieth centuries, with southern Greece becoming independent in 1821, followed by Serbia (whose northern part had been autonomous since 1815), Romania, and Bulgaria, all in 1878, and later by Albania in 1912. During these times there were forced migrations, massacres, and expulsions of Muslims, especially from the eastern Balkans, for the new nation-states were largely conceived as ethnic units tied to language and a form of Christianity. In contrast, many Balkan Muslims, who did not fit in the new nation-state design, were seen as allied with the Ottomans who had been increasingly ineffective and oppressive in the last century of their rule. Thousands of Muslims were forced to flee to Turkey. This would continue throughout the twentieth century with Balkan Muslims from Greece, Macedonia, Kosovo, and Bulgaria emigrating to the safety of Muslim Turkey. The exceptions to this were Muslims from the western Balkan lands of Albania and Bosnia. Most stayed in the Balkans throughout these times, although some Bosnian Muslims did emigrate in and after 1878. The large part of Bosnian Muslims, themselves Slavs, continued as landowners and free peasants under Austria-Hungary's rule, and remained later as part of Yugoslavia. As for the Albanian Muslims, some led the Albanian nationalist movement for independence; overall, Muslims made up 70 percent of the new independent state of Albania. There were also smaller communities of Slavic Muslims, Albanian Muslims, and Roma Muslims who stayed where they were and thus became minorities in different Balkan lands.

Nationalism also came to the Turks. It is interesting that an Albanian Muslim from Struga in present-day Macedonia, Ibrahim Temo, was one of the four founding members of what became known as the Young Turks. The founder of modern Turkey, Mustafa Kemal, later known as Ataturk, was a Balkan Muslim from Salonika.

Later in the twentieth century, the Muslims in Bosnia came to be seen as an ethnic group as well. Before World War II they were considered a religious community. But after the war, with the secularization of the Communist Party and growing importance of "nationalities," they officially became an ethnic group under the label "Muslim" in 1968. Just as "Jew" in the United States can have both ethnic and religious meaning, so "Muslim" had both meanings in Yugoslavia. With the warfare in the 1990s, this ambiguity became a problem so that today the ethnic term for Bosnian Muslim is "Bosnjak."

## Characteristics and Cultural Achievements

The Muslims of the Balkans are largely Sunni of the Hannafi school. There are also Sufi communities with more inclusive theologies, including the Sunni Naqshibandi, as well as the Halveti, Mevlevi, Qadiri, Rifaʿi, Saʾdi, Melami, and Bektashi orders. Of these, the Bektashi rose to special prominence in Albania in the twentieth century, only to become a target of Communist Enver Hoxha's regime (1944–1991). Also in Bulgaria there are communities of Aliʾids. As in other parts of the Ottoman world, religious poetry known as *merthiye*s and *nefes* stems from these orders, and *mevlud*s and *ghazel*s from the larger Muslim communities.

Better known to the broader world than religious poetry is the remarkable architecture of Muslims in the Balkans. This includes the older sections of cities with their bazaars, mosques, fountains, *hamams* (baths), *türbes* (mausolea), *madrasa*s (schools), and old Ottoman homes. One of the masterpieces of Ottoman architecture is the Selimiye Mosque in Edirne (1575) by Sinan. Also well known were other remarkable mosques like the Ferhat Pasha Mosque of Banja Luka (1579), the Aladza Mosque in Foca (1550), and the Gazi Husrevbegova Mosque of Sarajevo (1530), all in Bosnia, as well as the famous Ottoman bridge at Mostar in Herzegovina (1566).

## Contemporary Situation and Concerns

The war in Bosnia (1992–1995) between Serbian and Croatian nationalists and Muslim Bosnians led to the destruction of the famous mosques of Banja Luka and Foca and the severe

Composition of Bosnia-Herzegovina following the signing of the 1995 Dayton Peace Accords. XNR PRODUCTIONS, INC./GALE

damaging of the Gazi Husrevbegova Mosque in Sarajevo, as well as the destruction of many more Islamic sites throughout Bosnia. The famous bridge at Mostar, and the Oriental Institute in Sarajevo, where important historical documents of the Ottoman period were housed, were both deliberately targeted and destroyed. The war in Kosovo (1999) led to the destruction of many Islamic monuments and documents there as well. One of the purposes of these civil wars was to erase the Islamic heritage of these regions of the Balkans. This is not new. There were once many mosques in Belgrade that were destroyed in the late nineteenth century. Such destruction was in marked contrast to the usual Ottoman policy that had promoted tolerance for Christian and Jewish institutions.

Nevertheless there remain Muslim communities in the Balkans. The greatest number of Muslims are still in Bosnia, although many were killed in the war and many more became refugees. The next largest population of Muslims in the Balkans is in Albania, but many were secularized during the long communist rule. Albanians in Kosovo are also mainly Muslim. But of all the Albanian Muslims in the Balkans, those in western Macedonia are among the most observant. They form at least one-third of the population, but have been kept out of most state jobs and universities. Bulgaria has three different Muslim populations: Turks, who are the largest group; Pomaks, who are Slavs living in the southern mountains; and Roma, who are largely Muslim. During communist rule in Bulgaria, there were at times direct policies to "bulgarize" the Muslim peoples by forcing them to change their Muslim names to Slavic Bulgarian ones, and there were prohibitions against circumcision. In the 1980s over 300,000 Turks from Bulgaria went to Turkey rather than submit to these policies. Since then, some have returned and the policies in post-communist Bulgaria are not as restrictive. Romania has two small Muslim communities. In Greece, most Muslims left or were part of the population transfers in the early 1920s. There remain, however, the Turkish Muslims of western Thrace in northeast Greece.

An irony of the fighting in Bosnia at the end of the twentieth century is that the attempt of Serbian and Croatian nationalists to eradicate the Islamic history and the Muslim people of the region has resulted in a reinvigoration of Islamic practices there. The Bosnians, who were once among the most secularized of Muslims, now include those who are more observant. But the long tradition of tolerance and mutual respect of Balkan Islam, for which places like Sarajevo were justly famous, has been severely damaged.

*See also* **Empires: Ottoman; Europe, Islam in.**

## BIBLIOGRAPHY

Bringa, Tone. *Being Muslim the Bosnian Way: Identity and Community in a Central Bosnian Village*. Princeton, N.J.: Princeton University Press, 1995.

Donia, Robert J., and Fine, John V. A. *Bosnia and Hercegovina: A Tradition Betrayed*. New York: Columbia University Press, 1994.

Eminov, Ali. *Turkish and Other Muslim Minorities in Bulgaria*. London: Hurst & Company, 1997.

Hasluck, Frederick William. *Christianity and Islam under the Sultans*. Oxford, U.K.: The Clarendon Press, 1929.

Pasic, Amir. *Islamic Architecture in Bosnia and Hercegovina*. Translated by Midhat Ridjanovic. Istanbul: Research Centre for Islamic History, Art, and Culture, 1994.

Popovic, Alexandre. *L'Islam Balkanique: les musulmans du sudest europeen dans la periode post-ottomane*. Berlin: Otto Harrassowitz, 1986.

Poulton, Hugh, and Taji-Farouki, Suha. *Muslim Identity and the Balkan State*. London: Hurst & Company, 1997.

Trix, Frances. "The Resurfacing of Islam in Albania." *The East European Quarterly* 28, no. 4 (1995): 533–549.

*Frances Trix*

## BAMBA, AHMAD (1853–1927)

Ahmad Bamba was the founder of the Muridiyya (Mouride) Brotherhood. Born in the Baol region in Senegal, Ahmad was initiated into the Qadiriyya Brotherhood (*tariqa*) by Shaykh Sidia in Mauritania. He founded his own brotherhood in 1886 and established the town of Touba (Senegal) as the capital of his order in 1887. Shaykh Ahmad Bamba was highly respected for his learning and piety but he also attracted followers who were struggling against the French occupation.

The new brotherhood spread rapidly and was associated with rumors of a possible uprising. In 1895, Ahmad Bamba was exiled to Gabon and was not permitted to return to Senegal until 1902. His return attracted a wave of new followers and more rumors of rebellion. The French exiled him again in 1903, this time to Mauritania. Ahmad returned to Senegal in 1907. Again large numbers of followers flocked to him and the French were concerned. After 1910, however, the French began to trust the Muslim leader somewhat more, even turning to him for help on occasion. Most notably, he recruited troops and raised money for French efforts in World War I. For this he was made a Chevalier de la Légion d'Honneur in 1919. Ahmad Bamba, however, collaborated reluctantly. He was a religious man and a mystic, given to meditation and scholarship. His brotherhood was organized on a principle of total obedience, hard work, and self-denial and became the most powerful religious group in Senegal.

*See also* **Africa, Islam in; Colonialism; Tariqa; Touba.**

## BIBLIOGRAPHY

Behrman, Lucy C. *Muslim Brotherhoods and Politics in Senegal*. Cambridge, Mass.: Harvard University Press, 1970.

Coulon, Christian. *Le Marabout et le Prince: Islam et Pouvoir au Sénégal*. Paris: Pedone, 1981.

Creevey, Lucy. "Ahmad Bamba 1850–1927." In *Studies in West African Islamic History*, Vol. 1: *The Cultivators of Islam*. Edited by John Ralph Willis. London: Frank Cass, 1979.

O'Brien, Donal Cruise. *The Mourides of Senegal: The Political and Economic Organization of an Islamic Brotherhood*. Oxford, U.K.: Clarendon Press, 1971.

*Lucy Creevey*

## BANNA, HASAN AL- (1906–1949)

Hasan al-Banna was an Islamic reformer and the founder of Ikhwan al-Muslimin (Muslim Brotherhood). Banna was born in Mahmudiyya, a town near Alexandria, Egypt. In addition to receiving the traditional education in Qur'an, hadith, elementary principles of law, and Arabic language, Banna became a member of the Hasafiyya Sufi order during his teen years. Although members of the Brotherhood would later attack Sufism, Banna always acknowledged the strong influence of Sufism in his religious outlook and social activism.

In 1923, Banna enrolled in Dar al-'Ulum in Cairo, the national teachers' training college, whose eclectic curriculum of traditional Islamic and modern Western subjects had been shaped by Muhammad 'Abduh and Rashid Rida. In 1927, he was sent to his first teaching assignment in a primary school in Isma'iliyya. Located in the Suez Canal zone, Isma'iliyya was home to large numbers of European civilians as well as British military personnel. Banna was exposed daily to foreign imperialism in a direct manner that he had not experienced in Cairo. He began to question the reasons for Egypt's political subservience and the means for its revival. Only through a revival of Islamic consciousness among the masses, Banna concluded, could imperialism be combated.

In March 1928, Banna and six other men founded an organization attached to the Hasafiyya order to "command the right and forbid the wrong." By the following year, the organization was already referred to as Ikhwan al-Muslimin. The organization began as an educational society, meant to instill or revive Islamic convictions among ordinary Egyptians. Its primary goal was to create an Islamic society based on the model of the earliest Muslim generations. Banna traveled throughout the canal zone, lecturing, collecting donations, organizing chapters, and building offices and mosques. The Brotherhood's organization reflected Banna's Sufi background. Chapters consisted of groups of young men organized hierarchically according to the level of commitment and knowledge demonstrated. Tying the various chapters together was Banna, the *murshid* (guide) of the movement, and a *majlis al-shura* (advisory council) composed officially of twelve members, though sometimes more.

By 1932 Banna had moved the headquarters of the Brotherhood to Cairo, reflecting his intention to play a much more active role in Egypt's politics. The Brotherhood was also firmly entrenched in regional politics by the late 1940s through branches in Palestine, Syria, Iraq, and Sudan. Banna's ideological vision may be gleaned from his numerous writings, the two most important being his memoirs (*Mudhakkirat*) and a published collection of his letters (*Majmu'at al-rasa'il*). For him Islam was a holistic creed, providing Muslims guidelines for private piety, public morality, and social justice. The logical extension of this view was the establishment of an Islamic state. The leadership of such a state could only come from committed and informed Muslims, and the Brotherhood was to prepare itself for this role.

Banna could not quell dissension within the Brotherhood once it entered the turbulent Egyptian politics of the 1940s. His control over the "secret apparatus," the armed wing of the organization that planned and carried out attacks on government officials and institutions, was particularly tenuous. More militant members refused to follow his agreement with the Egyptian government to merge the Brotherhood militia into the Egyptian army during the first Arab-Israeli war (1948–1949). Following a military decree banning the organization, Prime Minister Mahmud Fahmi al-Nuqrashi was assassinated in December 1948 by a student associated with the Brotherhood. In retaliation, the secret police assassinated Banna on 12 February 1949.

*See also* **Ikhwan al-Muslimin.**

## BIBLIOGRAPHY

Abu Rabi', Ibrahim M. *Intellectual Origins of Islamic Resurgence in the Modern Arab World.* Albany: State University of New York Press, 1996.

Banna, Hasan al-. *Five Tracts of Hasan al-Banna (1906–1949): A Selection from the Majmuat Rasail al-Imam al-Shahid Hasan al-Banna.* Translated by Charles Wendell. Berkeley: University of California Press, 1978.

Commins, David. "Hasan al-Banna (1906–1949)." In *Pioneers of Islamic Revival.* Edited by Ali Rahnema. London: Zed Books, 1994.

Mitchell, Richard P. *The Society of the Muslim Brothers.* New York: Oxford University Press, 1969.

*Sohail H. Hashmi*

# BAQILLANI, AL- (?–1013)

Qadi Abu Bakr Muhammad b. al-Tayyib b. Muhammad, also known as Ibn al-Baqillani, was an Ash'arite theologian and Malikite jurisprudent. Al-Baqillani was regarded as the second founder of Ash'arism for his contribution to the systematization of the school.

Born in Basra he lived mostly in Baghdad, and studied theology under al-Ash'ari's students Ibn Mujahid al-Ta'i and Abu 'l-Hasan al-Bahili, and *fiqh* (jurisprudence) under Abu 'Abdallah al-Shirazi and Ibn Abu Zayd al-Qayrawani. He attended discussion meetings with representatives of other schools in Shiraz, was sent to Constantinople as a special envoy to Byzantine rulers, served as a judge (*qadi*) in Uqbera and Saghr towns, and taught in Baghdad until his death in 1013.

Well known for his disputational skills and polemical writings, al-Baqillani's books are mainly on theology. A large work, *Hidayat al-mustarshidin wa al-maqna' fi usul al-din*, is preserved at al-Azhar library (ms. no. 342) in Cairo. His works, which largely collected and classified Ash'arite views, played a major role in the establishment and spread of the school. He emphasized the existence of atoms in order to avoid the idea of pre-eternity of the universe and elaborated some concepts in Sunni kalam, such as empty space, the continuous creation of accidents due to their incapability of lasting more than one unit of time, and the rational possibility of miracles. However, he preserved the Salafi (Salafiyya) tendency of not interpreting Qur'anic expressions attributed to God suggesting anthropomorphism. Most of his books include lengthy polemics against other monotheistic religions. His skepticism toward the compatibility of ancient metaphysics with Islamic doctrines led him to oppose the use of formal logic in religious disciplines. In some issues of Islamic legal methodology, such as *ijtihad* and *ijma'*, he influenced later jurists.

*See also* **Ash'arites, Ash'aira; Kalam.**

## BIBLIOGRAPHY

Chaumont, E. "Baqillani, théologien ash'arite et juriste malikite, contre les legistes à propos de l'ijtihad et de l'accord unanime de la communauté." *Studia Islamica* 79 (1994): 79–102.

Grunebaum, Gustave E., von. *A Tenth-Century Document of Arabic Literary Theory and Criticism: The Sections on Poetry of al-Baqillani's I'jaz al-Qur'an.* Chicago: Chicago University Press, 1950.

Haddad, Wadi Z. "A Tenth-Century Speculative Theologian's Refutation of the Basic Doctrines of Christianity: al-Baqillani." In *Christian-Muslim Encounters.* Edited by Y. Yazbeck Haddad and Wadi Zaydan Haddad. Gainsville: University Press of Florida, 1995.

*M. Sait Özervarli*

## BASRI, HASAN AL- (642–728)

Hasan al-Basri was one of the most famous early Sunni theologians and ascetics. Born in Medina, he lived in Basra, where he was renowned for his piety, learning, and eloquence. He produced sermons, short commentaries on the Qur'an, aphorisms, and statements on ethics. In theology, he occupied a middle position on the subjects of free will and predestination. He believed that humans choose their actions, but that God determines the outlines of fate. He criticized Umayyad caliphs and officials, but did not oppose them politically. His spiritual practice stressed self-reflective contemplation. He is considered a father of Sufism and appears as the source of many Sufi lineages.

*See also* **Kalam; Tasawwuf.**

*Rkia E. Cornell*

## BA'TH PARTY

The Ba'th Party is the governing party in Iraq and Syria, and is theoretically committed to the cause of Arab nationalism and unity. The Ba'th (Arabic for resurrection or renewal) Party was founded by two French-educated Syrian school teachers, Michel 'Aflaq (Greek Orthodox Christian) and Salah al-Din al-Bitar (Sunni Muslim), in 1943. "Regional commands" of the Ba'th were founded in many Arab countries, all in principle subject to the "national command" of the founders. The party's slogan, "unity, freedom and socialism," rallied students, intellectuals, and army officers to its cause in many Arab states, and it played an important role in the tumultuous politics of Syria, Iraq, and Jordan in the 1950s. However, the party never achieved a strong mass following and had little electoral success anywhere. The Ba'th came to power in Syria in 1963 and in Iraq in 1968 through military coups. In power, the party in both countries effectively centralized control of the economy in government hands and instituted distributionist policies that originally benefited both the urban and rural middle and lower classes, though over time at the cost of economic growth and efficiency. Both the Syrian and Iraqi Ba'th came to rely on religious minorities to staff sensitive military and security positions—Alawis in Syria and Sunnis in Iraq—as the popularity of the governments waned. A bitter split developed within the party in 1966, reflected in the extremely hostile relations between Ba'thist Syria and Ba'thist Iraq. Like many ruling parties, the Ba'th lost much of its ideological élan once in power, and became the vehicle for increasingly personalized rule in Syria and Iraq.

*See also* **Nationalism: Arab.**

## BIBLIOGRAPHY

Devlin, John F. *The Ba'th Party: A History from Its Origins to 1966.* Stanford, Calif.: Hoover Institution Press, 1976.

Kienle, Eberhard. *Ba'th v. Ba'th: The Conflict Between Syria and Iraq, 1968–1989.* London: I. B. Tauris & Co., 1990.

*F. Gregory Gause III*

## BAZARGAN, MEHDI (1907–1995)

The son of a merchant from Tabriz, Mehdi Bazargan was born in Tehran, Iran. Educated both in traditional Islamic *madrasa* and modern schools, he completed his studies at *Ecole Polytéchnique* and *Ecole Normale* in France. Muhammad Mosaddeq (b. 1882) admired Bazargan's engineering approach to social organization, such as Tehran's fresh water project (c. 1952), and commissioned him to fill the gap resulting from the departure of British experts after the nationalization of Iran's oil industry. He became a founder of the Engineering Association of Iran in 1945 and of the National Liberation Movement in 1961.

Bazargan was one of a group of Islamic thinkers who convened to discuss current issues in the early 1960s, and was especially interested in adapting Shi'ite Islam to the technological world without importing its ideology. Most people in this group became prominent leaders of the Iranian Revolution. Bazargan was imprisoned along with other nationalist leaders in 1963. After the revolution of 1979, he became the prime minister of the provisional government. Bazargan was later ousted due to the occupation of the American embassy and hostage taking by students and his meeting with Brzezinski in Algiers.

*See also* **Iran, Islamic Republic of; Liberation Movement of Iran; Reform: Iran; Revolution: Islamic Revolution in Iran.**

## BIBLIOGRAPHY

Chehabi, H. E. *Iranian Politics and Religious Modernism: The Liberation Movement of Iran Under the Shah and Khomeini.* Ithaca, N.Y.: Cornell University Press, 1990.

*Mazyar Lotfalian*

# BEDOUIN

The Bedouin are nomadic peoples of Arabia known in Arabic as *bedu*, *'arab*, and *a'rab*. They are especially known for keeping camels, whose domestication in the third millenium made trade and raiding—their main occupations—easier. In addition, they keep flocks of sheep and goats, and more recently, engage in seasonal agriculture and work in state armed forces. Living in long, low-lying black tents made of camel and goat hair and wooden poles, the Bedouin migrate on a seasonal basis in search of pasture for their animals. The tent and its contents are individual property, but water, pasture, and land are the common property of the tribe.

Every tent represents a family, and an encampment of tents—*hayy*— constitutes a clan, or *qawm*. A group of kindred clans forms a tribe, or *qabila*, and *'asabiyya* is the unconditional loyalty of a clansmember to his or her tribe. A weaker tribe buys protection by paying the stronger tribe a price—*khuwa*.

Bedouin have been characterized historically by urban Arab writers as vengeful and destructive, finding the agriculture and craft of sedentary life distasteful. In his *al-Muqadimma*, Ibn Khaldun (1332–1406), the Tunisian philosopher-historian, hypothesized that civilizations have a predetermined life cycle; they fall prey to the nomads in the frontiers whose bonds of solidarity (*'asabiyya*) are strong. However, others have described Bedouins by their well-known values of generosity and hospitality and high standards of poetic compositions.

As state power has infringed on Bedouin areas of control, moves to settle the Bedouin, to provide schools for children, and to employ adults in wage-labor have met with mixed success in Egypt, Jordan, Israel/Palestine, and the Arabian Gulf states. Bedouin strive to maintain their culture, social mores and traditions, while at the same time enjoying the benefits of technology, education, and health standards.

*See also* **Arabia, Pre-Islam; 'Asabiyya; Ibn Khaldun.**

## BIBLIOGRAPHY

Abu Lughod, Lila. *Veiled Sentiments.* Berkeley: University of California Press, 1986.

Abu Lughod, Lila. *Writing Women's Worlds.* Berkeley: University of California Press, 1993.

Baily, Clinton. *Bedouin Poetry from Sinai and the Negev: Mirror of a Culture.* Oxford: Clarendon Press, 1991.

Lancaster, William. *The Rwala Bedouin Today.* Cambridge: Cambridge University Press, 1981.

Lewis, Norman. *Nomads and Settlers in Syria and Jordan, 1800–1980.* New York: Cambridge University Press, 1987.

Shryock, Andrew. *Nationalism and the Genealogical Imagination: Oral History and Textual Authority in Tribal Jordan.* Berkeley: University of California Press, 1997.

*Rochelle Davis*

# BID'A

A *bid'a* (pl. *bida'*) is an innovation in theology, ritual, or the customs of daily life, that did not exist in early Islam but came into existence in the course of history.

The term itself does not appear in the Qur'an, be it that the Holy Book includes other derivations of the root *bd'*. In the hadith literature *bid'a* is often used in contrast with the term *sunna*. In this sense sunna denotes the exemplary standard for Muslim life, as this was established by the prophet Muhammad and the pious Muslims of early Islam; for this reason, a *bid'a*, being a deviation from the normative sunna, was almost exclusively regarded as negative. This idea can be found in the canonical collections of hadith literature and, for example, was put into words in the Prophetic saying: "The worst of all things are novelties (*muhdathat*); every novelty is an innovation (*bid'a*), and every *bid'a* is an error (*dalala*), and every error "leads to hell."

Apart from this negative understanding of the concept of *bid'a*, a positive interpretation also could be given to the term. This was done by using another saying from the hadith literature. These words are attributed to the second caliph 'Umar who, after he had seen an innovation in the rite of the ritual prayer (*salat*), is reported to have said: "Truly, this is a good *bid'a*." On the basis of this saying the great jurisconsult al-Shafi'i (767–820) made a distinction between good and objectionable *bid'a*s. As a result of this, the possibility was created to introduce new ideas and practices into Islam for which there were no precedents in early Islam, but which could now be accepted as good innovations. Later scholars further manipulated the term *bid'a* by adding various other, most often legal, adjectives to it. For example, the prolific Egyptian author Jalal al-Din al-Suyuti (1445–1505) mentions the application of the five legal classifications (*al-ahkam al-khamsa*) to the term, thus making a distinction between "forbidden," "reprehensible," "indifferent," "recommended," and "obligatory" *bid'a*s.

Although this flexible interpretation of the concept of *bid'a* was thus known from an early period onward, various later scholars adhered to its negative interpretation exclusively. A well-known representative of this stream is the theologian and jurisconsult Taqi al-Din Ibn Taymiyya (1263–1328), who spent his entire life fighting *bidʿa*s, which had been added to the original doctrine and practice of Islam, for example, the cult of saints. Under the influence of his teachings, Muhammad ibn ʿAbd al-Wahhab (1703–1792) founded the rigid and intolerant reform movement known as Wahhabiyya, which, for example, regarded the use of tobacco and coffee as *bidʿa*. This Wahhabi ideology is also followed by the present-day Kingdom of Saudi Arabia, where consequently the concept of *bidʿa* in its negative sense plays a prominent part in religious and social discourse. An interesting example of this is the official view on the celebration of the birthday (*mawlid*) of the prophet Muhammad, an opinion that was voiced often by the Grand Mufti of the Kingdom, ʿAbd al-ʿAziz ibn Baz (1910–1999). This festival is strictly forbidden, because it is regarded as a *bidʿa*, "while every *bidʿa* is an error." Despite the enormous respect for the Prophet, Wahhabis reject celebrating his *mawlid* because it is rightly understood as a later innovation.

On the whole, however, in present-day Islam only a minority adhere to this limited, negative interpretation of the concept of *bidʿa*, while the majority of Muslims approves of a flexible interpretation, which is more compatible with modern beliefs and practices.

*See also* **Religious Institutions; Sunna.**

## BIBLIOGRAPHY

Fierro, Maribel. "The Treatises Against Innovations (*kutub al-bidaʿ*)." *Der Islam* 69 (1992): 204–246.

Goldziher, Ignaz, "Hadith and Sunna." In Vol. 2, *Muslim Studies (Muhammedanische Studien)*. Edited by S. M. Stern. Translated by C. R. Barber and S. M. Stern. London: Allen & Unwin, 1971.

Rispler, Vardit. "Toward a New Understanding of the Term *bidʿa*." *Der Islam* 68 (1991): 320–328.

*Nico J. G. Kaptein*

# BIN LADIN, USAMA (1957– )

Usama bin Ladin is a Saudi dissident and leader of the al-Qaʿida organization. He was born in 1957 in Saudi Arabia. His father, Muhammad bin Ladin, was a Yemeni commoner who became a successful building contractor. He moved his family to Saudi Arabia in the 1930s. Muhammad sired seventeen sons and established the Saudi Bin Ladin Group, a construction firm that eventually won large contracts from the Saudi royal family to renovate important icons of Saudi and Islamic religion and culture. These included several buildings in the cities of Mecca and Medina and many mosques, including the al-Aqsa Mosque in Jerusalem.

Usama's mother, one of four wives to Muhammad bin Ladin, was from Damascus, Syria. Usama has remained close to her throughout his life. He married one of his mother's Syrian relatives, with whom he had a son. Usama attended school in Saudi Arabia where he came under the influence of the thought of Muhammad Qutb, the brother of an influential Islamist ideologue named Sayyid Qutb and a Jordanian activist, ʿAbdallah ʿAzzam, who actively recruited Arab Muslim fighters to mount a jihad against the Soviet military occupation of Afghanistan in the early 1980s. That Usama bin Ladin visited and lived for a while in Europe has been reported by some writers, but it is unclear when that might have been, where he actually lived in Europe, or what he did while he was there.

After the Soviet army invaded Afghanistan in 1979, bin Ladin went to Pakistan. There he met several leaders of jihadi movements who were mounting resistance efforts against the Russians on behalf of the Afghani Muslims. He joined forces with ʿAbdallah ʿAzzam to recruit non-Afghani Muslims, mainly Arabs, and to raise money and purchase weapons for an armed resistance against the Soviet military. After al-Qaʿida's growth and success, the two men had a falling out that led to the assassination of ʿAzzam. Usama's considerable inherited wealth (estimated at between $270 and $500 million) from his father formed an important material contribution to this effort against the Soviets. According to several sources, another significant element in support of Arab militia resistance in Afghanistan (alleged and never denied) was money from the United States, channeled through the Central Intelligence Agency (C.I.A.)

Usama bin Ladin will not be remembered as a religious scholar or intellectual in the Muslim world. He nonetheless has attracted a considerable following, first of *mujahidin* (guerilla) fighters against real and perceived enemies of Islam, such as the Soviet military and the U.S. In addition he has gained passive approval and verbal support for his cause more widely among Muslims around the world—many of whom openly disavow the terrorism and violence that is attributed to his leadership even while providing such support. Bin Ladin's writings include poetry and coauthored treatises and statements that use code words and symbols (such as references to Crusaders and Jews) to express opposition to the State of Israel, European Christendom, and the United States, especially their respective control of and military encroachment on the Islamic holy sites in Jerusalem, Mecca, and Medina.

Bin Ladin's theological worldview follows the Salafi and Wahhabi puritanical interpretation and expression of Islam, as well as the trenchant articulation of this strain of Islam provided by the Egyptian dissident intellectual, Sayyid Qutb. Some observers have argued that although the fallen Soviet Union, the United States, and the globalization of capitalism were the spectacular targets of bin Ladin's active career, in fact it is accommodationist Muslim regimes (like his native Saudi Arabia) that rely on U.S. and Western support that have been the real targets of his criticism and activism.

See also **Fundamentalism; Jihad; Qaʿida, al-; Qutb, Sayyid; Terrorism; Wahhabiyya.**

### BIBLIOGRAPHY

Gunaratna, Rohan. *Inside Al Qaeda: Global Network of Terror.* New York: Columbia University Press, 2002.

*Richard C. Martin*

# BIOGRAPHY AND HAGIOGRAPHY

Islamic civilization from an early period gave importance to various biographical genres, for example, the life (*sira*) of the Prophet, works establishing priority in joining the Muslim community, and lives of saints, but rarely, until the modern period, autobiographies.

Particularly important is the relationship between early biography and the hadith collections. The *ʿilm al-rijal*, or "science of the men," was a branch of Islamic historiography verifying the reliability (*taʿdil*) of hadith transmitters according to criteria such as their direct acquaintance with the Prophet and their veracity and virtues. The qualities (*fadaʾil*) and special merits (*khasaʾis*) of important persons constitute a subsection of most hadith collections and reveal early Muslim concepts of charisma, character, or religious authority. Another hadith topic that blossomed into a genre of biographical literature is asceticism (*zuhd*). Compilations on this subject provide insights into the early development of Sufism and how ascetic behaviors established rankings of merit and authority.

Muslim religious biography and hagiography were composed in specific genres. One of the most important biographical forms is the *tabaqat* (ranks or classes). This name refers to the system for the arrangement of biographical notices according to notions of contiguity, rank, or virtue. The earliest extant example is the *Kitab al-tabaqat al-kabir* of Ibn Saʿd (d. 845), which contains some 4,250 biographical notices of men and women of the first Islamic generations. The inclusion of ordinary persons in the classical biographical dictionaries indicates how the history of the Islamic community was understood in this period as being constituted, to a large extent, by the contribution of individuals to building up and transmitting its specific worldview and culture.

The telling of lives in traditional Islamic biographical forms does not present a series of events or cumulative

reflections as contributing to character development. Rather, biographical notices serve to establish origins and display a person's type or example through presenting his or her discrete actions and sayings. The *tabaqat* genre, which is most popular in Arabic, might focus on certain religious professions such as the biographies of jurists, judges, Qurʾan reciters and memorizers, or Sufis. Other *tabaqat* works chronicle individuals from a particular city or region, and some represent "centennial" biographies that record all prominent Muslims who died in a particular Islamic century.

*Tadhkira* (memorial) works are collections of the lives of persons engaged in scholarly or religious activities. They are more common in later periods, especially in Iran, the Ottoman Empire, and South Asia.

*Malfuzat* are records of audiences of notable scholars or Sufis. This genre is indigenous to South Asian Islam where the early Indian Sufis are known largely through records preserved in this form. *Malfuzat* as a biographical genre often provides a more spontaneous, authentic flavor of the person and his circle in contrast to the more idealized portrayals of the *tadhkirat*. Individual biographies (*tarjama*, pl. *tarajim*) and autobiographies were less common in earlier periods although a small number may be found. Notable is al-Ghazali's *Deliverance from Error* (d. 1111) a narrative of his spiritual search for truth. One should not neglect to mention the biographical significance of other related genres, for example, letters and travel accounts, such as those of the famous Ibn Battuta (1304–1369).

In the medieval period bio- or autobiographical notices were sometimes prefaced or appended to a scholar's works and read like a curriculum vitae, that included the individual's teachers, places visited, and works studied, transmitted, or composed. Medieval Muslim autobiography and biography often featured accounts of dreams or visionary experiences indicating that the tradition considered such events as important and meaningful.

More recently, Western literature has influenced biographical and autobiographical writing in many Islamic societies. In South Asia innovations in the tradition of religious biography were related to the development of Urdu as a modern prose language in the late nineteenth century and to efforts to combine Islamic and "modern" learning embodied in the Aligarh movement. Most significant among this trend are the writings of Shibli Nuʿmani (1857–1914), who prepared a series of monographs on "Heroes of Islam" including studies of the caliph ʿUmar, the jurist Abu Hanifa, the poet Rumi, and the theologian al-Ghazali, as well as the Prophet. This new style of biography was marked by critical evaluation and a rationalist treatment of the subject.

As the forces of westernization have increasingly penetrated many Muslim societies, the canons of modern literature have tended to favor the novel, short story, and poetry written in free verse over traditional biographical forms. With the decline in the popularity of Sufism, the audience for collective memorials and devotional biographies has also decreased. In most regions the traditional Islamic biographical forms have declined in importance as secular, literary life stories take precedence and may provide inspiration for serialization as televised historical dramas.

Traditional genres of religious biography still persist in religious contexts and in more traditional segments of Muslim societies. In the modern period, however, a number of new developments have occurred. Among the most striking are: an increased use of religious biography for personal edification; its use in reinforcing symbols of national or regional identity; and its functioning to inspire or legitimate political action and Islamist identifications.

For example, in Iranian Shi'ism the lives of the imams have been a source of inspired poetry and performances of commemoration. A significant and instructive trend in their modern use is that during the prerevolutionary period in Iran, the focus of Husayn's biography shifted from his role as tragic martyr to portraying him as an activist challenging the unjust social order.

The role of females also receives increased attention. Traditional Muslim scholars now present early Muslim heroic women in ways that honor their contributions to Islamic history while reinforcing traditional patterns of female behavior. In contrast, the Moroccan feminist historian Fatima Mernissi has presented a revisionist look at the lives of a number of prominent early Muslim women that attempts to recover their independence of action and defiance of supposed cultural norms. Zaynab al-Ghazali, a contemporary Egyptian activist in the Muslim Brotherhood, offered her prison memories in *Hayati* (My life) in the form of a heroic narrative with hagiographic undertones. Islamist autobiographies and convert narratives of American and European Muslims open up further possibilities for hybridization in biographical accounts.

*See also* **Arabic Literature; Genealogy; Historical Writing.**

## BIBLIOGRAPHY

Hermansen, Marcia. "Interdisciplinary Approaches to Islamic Biographical Materials." *Religion* 18, no. 4 (1988): 163–182.

Lawrence, Bruce B. *Notes from a Distant Flute: The Extant Literature of Pre-Mughal Indian Sufism.* Tehran: Imperial Iranian Academy of Philosophy, 1978.

Malti-Douglas, Fedwa. *Medicines of the Soul: Female Bodies and Sacred Geographies in a Transnational Islam.* Berkeley: University of California, 2001.

Mojaddedi, Jawid. *Sufi Biographies from Al-Sulami to Jami: Reworking Time Past.* Richmond, Va.: Curzon, 2000.

Roded, Ruth. *Women in Islamic Biographical Collections: from Ibn Sa'd to Who's Who.* Boulder, Colo.: L. Rienner Publishers, 1994.

*Marcia Hermansen*

# BIRUNI, AL- (C. 973–1050)

Al-Biruni was a polymath of the Islamic eleventh century who wrote in multiple scientific fields. Included among his subjects were astronomy, mathematics, pharmacology, and mineralogy, and he also contributed important works of history and cultural studies.

Al-Biruni originated from the region of Khwarazm, and his name refers to the fact that he was born in a suburb of the capital. Although Persian, he preferred to write in Arabic. When Sultan Mahmud of Ghazna conquered Khwarazm in 1017, al-Biruni was taken as a prisoner to his capital. He became the court astrologer and then accompanied Mahmud on his expeditions to northwestern India. This led al-Biruni to study Sanskrit and Indian religions and customs, which he recorded in *Kitab ta'rikh al-Hind* (*Alberuni's India*). His writings include significant observations on the natural features, social structure, and religious practices of the non-Muslim Indians. He was a prolific author of some 180 works of varying lengths, including many important treatises on mathematical and astronomical topics.

*See also* **Astronomy; Historical Writing; Knowledge; Science, Islam and.**

## BIBLIOGRAPHY

Biruni, al-. *Alberuni's India.* Translated by Eduard Sachau. London: Keegan Paul, 1910.

*Marcia Hermansen*

# BODY, SIGNIFICANCE OF

The body is the locus of human existence and activity in Islam. Islamic law stipulates the regular purification of the body, requires the use of a body in performing rituals, and views the body as the site of both social continuity and punishment in the case of violating social norms.

Purification and renunciation of the body are required for both men and women in Islamic law. Ritual purification involves washing and wiping certain parts of the body, and is invalidated by natural bodily emissions (urine, feces, pus,

Though these Muslim women wear their veils in slightly different styles, all of the women are sufficiently covered. © PETER TURNLEY/CORBIS

blood, vomit), sleep, unconsciousness, insanity, and sexual contact. Most jurists also agree that touching one's genitals (penis, vagina, anus) also invalidates purification. The ritual fast during the month of Ramadan requires keeping substances from entering the body (food, drink, medicine) and abstinence from sex.

The body is also of symbolic importance for the rites of the pilgrimage to Mecca. While in the sanctuary at Mecca pilgrims are not allowed to eat the meat of wild animals or plants. Pilgrims are not allowed to have sex, and marriages performed during the pilgrimage are invalid. Nor are pilgrims allowed to wear sewn clothing or apply perfume to their bodies. The hair and fingernails of pilgrims cannot be cut during the pilgrimage but are cut upon exiting from the sanctuary at the end of the pilgrimage. Many classical sources report that the prophet Muhammad distributed his hair and fingernails, cut at the end of his last pilgrimage, to his followers as relics.

Islamic law recognizes the body as the legal sphere of the individual. The "private area" (ʿurwah), the area which must be covered in public, is defined differently for men and women. For men it is the area between the waist and the knees, for women it is the area from the neck to the ankles,

although some authorities also include in this the female voice. Crimes such as theft require the amputation of limbs (hands and feet), and other crimes such as fornication require death by stoning under certain circumstances.

*See also* **Circumcision; Gender; ʿIbadat.**

## BIBLIOGRAPHY

Katz, Marion Holmes. *Body of Text: The Emergence of the Sunni Law of Ritual Purity.* Albany: State University of New York Press, 2002.

Reinhart, Kevin A. "Impurity/No Danger." *History of Religions* 30 (1990–1991): 1–24.

Zannad, Traki. *Les lieux du corps en Islam.* Paris: Publisud, 1994.

*Brannon M. Wheeler*

## BOURGHIBA, HABIB (1901–2000)

Habib Bourghiba was the most prominent leader of Tunisia's Neo-Destour movement, which led that country to independence from France in 1956. Born into a middle-class family of limited resources at Monastir in 1901, Bourghiba was educated at the prestigious Sadiqi College and at the Lycée Carnot in Tunis; subsequently he earned a law degree at the University of Paris. After returning to Tunisia in the mid-1920s, he became increasingly involved in the Destour (constitutionalist) movement, which was seeking Tunisia's autonomy from France. By the 1930s he broke with its leadership, which he considered too socially and religiously conservative, and founded the Neo-Destour party, which tended toward secular and liberal nationalism.

Once independence came, however, he transformed the Neo-Destour party—later the Destourian Socialist Party—into a ruling single party. This action allowed him to gain and maintain a tight grip over the Tunisian political process for three decades. He was elected three times without opposition to the presidency, ultimately becoming president for life in 1974. In the meantime, the economy stagnated or declined and the gap between the ruling elites and the masses widened, not only materially, but also culturally. Various Islamist groups arose in a protest movement appealing to traditional religious values. In November 1987, with Bourghiba's physical and mental health clearly deteriorating, he was deposed by the sitting Prime Minister Zine el Abidine Ben Ali. Habib Bourghiba died in his native city of Monastir.

*See also* **Modernization, Political: Constitutionalism; Secularism, Islamic.**

## BIBLIOGRAPHY

Murphy, Emma C. *Economic and Political Change in Tunisia: from Bourguiba to Ben Ali.* New York: St. Martin's Press, 1999.

*John Ruedy*

# BUKHARA, KHANATE AND EMIRATE OF

Conventional terms for the political entities in Central Asia were ruled by the khans of the Shibani-Abulkhayrid (1500 to 1598), the Toqay-Timurid (1598 to the late 18th century) families, and the emirs of the Uzbek Manghit tribe (1785 to 1920). The core territories of the khanate and emirate were the string of oases along the course of the river Zarafshan with the cities Bukhara and Samarkand. During most of the sixteenth to mid-eighteenth centuries, Tashkent and Balkh also belonged to the Bukharan dominions.

In 1500, Muhammad Shibani drove the Timurids from Transoxania and conquered a territory reaching from Tashkent to Khwarazm and Khurasan. Shibani, a descendant of Genghis Khan through his grandson Shiban, had served Timurid

and Chaghatay rulers during the last decades of the fifteenth century. The principal source of Muhammad Shibani's authority was his claim of descent from Genghis Khan. He derived additional authority from the fact that his grandfather, Abu 'l-Khayr, had ruled a large confederation of Turco-Mongol tribes in Western Siberia known as the Uzbeks. But Muhammad Shibani also propagated Islamic legitimacy by adopting the title of caliph.

Sovereignty in the extended Shibanid-Abulkhayrid family was corporate, embodied in the sultans (agnatic princes who traced their descent from Abu 'l-Khayr through their father's lineage) under the overall khanship of Muhammad Shibani. The khan distributed the conquered territories as appanages (land grants) among the eligible Abulkhayrid princes. The crisis following the unexpected death of Muhammad Shibani Khan in battle against Safavid Qizilbash troops (1510) led to a major reorganization of rule. A short power struggle between the leaders of the major Abulkhayrid clans was resolved in a general meeting (*quriltai*) convened in 1512 in Samarkand. Supreme sovereignty as khan was from then on nominally assigned to the senior Abulkhayrid agnate.

The appanages became hereditary dominions. The principal appanages, each dominated by one of the Abulkhayrid cousin clans, were Bukhara, Samarkand, Tashkent, and Miyankal (the region between Samarkand and Bukhara). In 1526 Balkh and the lands between the Hindu Kush and the River Amu were regained and allotted to the Jani-Beg clan. This appanage system remained relatively stable until the mid-century, when unclear succession in Bukhara triggered open interclan conflict. Abdallah II, a member of the Jani-Beg clan, eventually established himself in Bukhara in 1557 and gradually expanded his domination over the other Abulkhayrid appanages. Abdallah took residence in Bukhara and initiated large-scale urban development projects.

The political process of electing a supreme khan on the basis of seniority and distributing the territory as appanages to the eligible junior members of the royal clan was continued by the Toqay Timurids, another clan that claimed descent from Genghis Khan and took over in the secession crisis that followed the death of Abdallah's son in 1598. The number of appanages was reduced to two: Bukhara, the residence of the supreme khan and capital of the northern and central territories of the khanate, and Balkh, the center of the areas south of the Amu.

The military backbone of Abulkhayrid and Toqay-Timurid rule were the Uzbek emirs, leaders of the Turco-Mongol nomadic tribal groups who had brought Muhammad Shibani to power. They gradually merged with the old ruling class of Timurid Central Asia. The hierarchy of the emirs symbolically followed a pattern of military-tribal organization that is thought to date back to the army of Genghis Khan. However,

The Kalyan Minaret, built circa 1127, in Bukhara, Uzbekistan. The emirate of Bukhara was abolished in 1920 when its last amir, 'Alim, went into exile during the occupation of the city by Russian revolutionary troops. © DIEGO LEZAMA OREZZOLI/CORBIS

this does not mean that the Uzbek emirs were a closed group, nor that they were restricted to military duty. The borderline between military and civil administration was to some extent fluid. Service in the civil administration appears to have been an integral part of an emir's career.

On the other hand, high civil officials of nontribal background could enter the ranks of the emirs. Until the mid-eighteenth century, the highest offices were the *ataliq*, the *divanbegi*, and the *hakim*. The *ataliq* (princely tutor) seems to have served as military-administrative counselor and a liaison between the khan and the sultans. *Hakim*s served as governors of territorial subunits of the appanages. The *divanbegi* was the head of the fiscal administration. However, to what extent this title (and others of lower rank) matched well-defined administrative duties or rather were nominal ranks is difficult to determine. The high ranks of religious offices were filled by members of a limited number of families of noble descent (*sayyid, khwaja*), the most noteworthy being the Juybari *khwaja*s.

The emirs were compensated for their services by assignments of pastureland and the revenues from villages. Originally given to an individual and frequently redistributed, these grants tended to become hereditary, and as a result certain emirid clans and their tribal followings became closely linked to defined territories. The Manghit tribal group thus came to dominate the oasis of Bukhara and the pasturelands around Qarshi.

The growing imbalance between the authority of the khan and the tribal leaders resulted in a radical change in the crisis that followed the temporary surrender of the khan of Bukhara to Nadir Shah in 1740. The *ataliq* Muhammad Rahim, an emir of the Manghit clan, was able to assume power in Bukhara and even to adopt the title khan in 1756. His cousin Shah Murad (1785–1800) abolished the khanate and ruled with the caliphal title *amir al-mu'minin* (Commander of the Faithful), thus lending his nonregal status additional Islamic legitimacy.

The transition from the neo-Chinggisid khanate to the Manghit emirate can be characterized by two major developments: The legitimation of rule was now Islamic rather than based on descent from Genghis Khan, and the power of the non-Manghit Uzbek emirs was systematically reduced. The Manghit emirs of Bukhara created a small standing army and so were able to become largely independent of tribal military support. The connection of military resources and access to regional revenues that had always made the Uzbek emirs a potential threat to the rulers's authority was gradually dissolved. In the second half of the nineteenth century, the emirate of Bukhara appears to have become a fairly centralized state. The emirate was governed through a complex military-civil bureaucracy headed by a chief minister called *qoshbegi*. The territory was divided into provinces (twenty-seven in 1915) which in turn consisted of fiscal-administrative units. The oasis of Bukhara was under direct administration, while the other provinces were governed by officials called *bek*s.

Already during the reign of the emir Nasrallah (1826–1860) the emirate felt the incipient impact of the conflicting imperialistic interests of Russia and Britain. In 1868, the emir Muzaffar al-Din (1860–1885) had to accept the annexation of the eastern part of his dominions, including Samarkand, by tsarist Russia. The so-called friendship treaty between the governor general of Russian Turkestan and the emir of Bukhara in 1873 sealed the emirate's loss of independence. Though nominally still a sovereign state, the emirate was gradually integrated into the sphere of influence of the Russian Empire. In 1920, Russian revolutionary troops occupied Bukhara. The last emir, 'Alim (r. 1910–1920), went into exile and the emirate was abolished.

*A photo of the arched entryway to the Miri-Arab Madrasa appears in the volume one color plates.*

*See also* **Central Asia, Islam in; Central Asian Culture and Islam.**

## BIBLIOGRAPHY

Becker, Seymour. *Russia's Protectorates in Central Asia: Bukhara and Khiva, 1865–1924.* Cambridge, Mass.: Harvard University Press, 1968.

McChesney, Robert D. *Central Asia: Foundations of Change.* Princeton, N.J.: Darwin Press, 1996.

*Florian Schwarz*

## BUKHARI, AL- (810–870)

Muhammad b. Isma'il al-Bukhari, who was born in Bukhara in central Asia, compiled the most important hadith collection in Sunni Islam, called *al-Jami' al-sahih* (The sound collection). Al-Bukhari is said to have started to learn hadiths ("the sayings" of the prophet Muhammad) at about ten years of age, having been blessed with a remarkably retentive memory and a sharp intellect. At the age of sixteen, he made the pilgrimage and traveled to Mecca and Medina to study with well-known hadith teachers there. He next went to Egypt, and spent the following sixteen years traveling through much of Asia in the pious pursuit of hadiths. On his return to Bukhara, he began to scrutinize the roughly 600,000 reports he had collected. He is said to have applied the most stringent standards in determining the reliability of these reports, which led him to record only about 7,397 of them. His painstaking efforts resulted in the *Sahih*, which by the tenth century had achieved near universal recognition among Muslims, who regarded al-Bukhari's collection as including the most reliable and sound hadiths attributed to the Prophet, based particularly on analysis of their chains of transmission. The *Sahih* continues to enjoy an almost "canonical" status today, second only to the Qur'an in importance as the source for moral and legal prescriptions. The standard edition in use today was prepared by 'Ali b. Muhammad al-Yunini (d. 1302). Numerous commentaries have been written on the *Sahih*; in recent times, partial and complete translations of this collection have been made in a number of languages. Al-Bukhari died in his hometown of Bukhara at age sixty.

*See also* **Hadith.**

## BIBLIOGRAPHY

Rauf, Muhammad Abdul. "Hadith Literature." In Vol. 1, *Arabic Literature to the End of the Umayyad Period.* Edited by A. F. L. Beeston, et al. Cambridge, U.K.: Cambridge University Press, 1983.

Robson, James. "al-Bukhari." In Vol. 1, *Encyclopaedia of Islam.* Edited by H. A. R. Gibb, et al. Leiden: E. J. Brill, 1960.

*Asma Afsaruddin*

## BURAQ

In sura 17:1 of the Qur'an, the prophet Muhammad, led by the angel Gabriel, journeys in one night (*israq'*) to "the Far Distant Place of Worship," interpreted as Jerusalem. In the hadith, Muhammad continues on to the heavens (*mi'raj*), describing his mount as a small white steed, called al-Buraq. Later literary and art-historical traditions give al-Buraq a human face, wings, and dappled coloration. This miraculous steed is depicted in the fourteenth-century world history of Rashiduddin, the fifteenth-century Timurid *Mi'rajname*, and sixteenth-century Safavid *Khamsas* of Nizami. Buraq's importance continues today, appearing in Sunni paintings commemorating a hajj to Mecca, or in Shi'ite popular art, which often shows al-Buraq alongside Husayn's horse at Karbala.

*See also* **Mi'raj; Tasawwuf.**

*Carel Bertram*

# C

## CAIRO

The foundations of present-day Cairo rest upon the ancient capital of Memphis, one of the oldest urban settlements in the world, which flourished between 5000 and 2500 B.C.E. Memphis was finally surpassed by the seaport of Alexandria when Egypt became a Mediterranean colony of the Greeks, but its strategic position ensured continuous settlement. As a result, the city was still thriving at the time of the Roman conquest around 24 B.C.E. Although the region was contested by the Romans and Persians at the opening of the seventh century C.E., it was finally the Arabs who prevailed, thereby setting into motion the genesis of Cairo or al-Qahira, The Victorious City, as it is still referred to in Arabic. Cairo would in time grow into one of the most important religious, cultural, and political centers of the Muslim world.

The urban centers that sprouted under Islamic civilization surfaced from either army camps, that eventually developed into permanent cities, or princely towns established to commemorate new dynasties and to affirm their authority. Cairo was conceived out of an amalgamation of such regions, in which an army camp settlement fused with the princely centers established at its periphery. As such, the successive stages of Cairo's genesis also capture the histories of her past masters.

In 640 C.E. the forces of the illustrious Arab general ʿAmr ibn al-ʿAs reached what is present-day Cairo. He set up camp there and established the first mosque in Africa, which still stands and is one of the most important religious icons of Cairo today. The settlement itself came to be known as Fustat, which simply means "entrenchment," and eventually developed into a burgeoning city. The first major dynastic shift in the Muslim empire left its mark upon the Egyptian landscape as well and the Abbasid victory over the Ummayads in 750 C.E. gave rise to the princely town of al-ʿAskar (the Cantonment). In the century that followed the communities of Fustat and al-ʿAskar fused to form a combined settlement

stretching along the axis of the Nile River. The atmosphere of growing provincial autonomy in the period that followed fueled the ambitions of Ahmad ibn Tulun, a man of Turkish extraction appointed as deputy for the governor of Egypt. He founded his own princely city slightly to the north of al-ʿAskar in 870 C.E., which was called al-Qataʾiʿ (the Wards), reflecting its feudal base. The awesome mosque of Ibn Tulun, built between 876 and 878, is one of the most prominent legacies inherited from that era and still stands, surrounded by the crowded metropolis of today.

The most significant event in the genesis of Cairo is undoubtedly the rise of the Shiʿite Fatimid dynasty in Tunisia at the beginning of the tenth century. The Fatimid caliphate reached its full expression on Egyptian soil and it was its fourth caliph, Muʿizz al-Din, who gained sovereignty over the area in 969. His brilliant general Jawhar led the campaign and almost immediately began staking out the walls of a new palace city after his arrival. The city was initially called al-Mansuriyya but was renamed al-Qahira al-Muʿizziyya four years later, to commemorate and celebrate the arrival of the caliph. With the coming of Muʿizz al-Din, Cairo or al-Qahirah was formally inducted into world history.

Al-Qahirah was developed into a city of lavish beauty and intellectual vitality under the Fatimids. But the city remained largely inaccessible to common people from areas like Fustat, who could only enter the royal enclosure by special permit. Ironically, the al-Azhar University, which is today recognized as one of the most important intellectual centers of Sunni Islam, was established by the Fatimids to promote their Shiʿite doctrine.

The closing of the eleventh century marked the beginning of the first Crusade and also the decline of the Fatimid dynasty. In the period between 1164 and 1169 Cairo became a pawn in the power struggle between the Seljuks of Syria and the Christian forces in Jerusalem. Although still nominally ruled by the Fatimids, true control of the city eventually fell

A 1996 aerial view of Cairo and the Nile River. Cairo evolved at the site of the ancient city of Memphis, one of the first urban settlements, dating from 5000 B.C.E. In the tenth century C.E., the Shi'ite Fatimid dynasty built a palace city called al-Qahira al-Mu'izziyya. Al-Qahira, or Cairo, was at that time a walled, beautiful city inaccessible to non-royals from outlying areas. Entry to the royal area was granted with special permission. © THOMAS HARTWELL/CORBIS SABA

into the hands of the young Sunni governor Saladin (Salah al-Din) al-Ayyubi, sent to defend Cairo against the Crusader campaigns. Saladin in time established the Ayyubid dynasty and even reconquered Jerusalem. His mercurial rise contributed once again to the further transformation of Cairo. Under him, the mosque of 'Amr was restored and al-Azhar University was purged of its Shi'ite bias. A madrasa (school) was founded at the tomb of Imam al-Shafi'i soon after the Ayyubid conquest of Egypt and a mausoleum commemorating the great imam is still in existence today. But Saladin's most important and long-lived addition to the city was the Citadel, built for him in 1176 as a place of refuge and continuously expanded upon by later generations.

By the fourteenth century Cairo was recognized as a world capital, reaching its zenith under the Mamluks. Cairo's greatest growth and development took place in this period. In spite of constant forays against the Crusaders and Mongols, the Mamluk rulers still devoted energies to the development of the city. For example, Sultan Qalawun erected his famous hospital in the heart of the city during this era. Although the Cairo of the fifteenth century still surpassed any European city in terms of urban development and population, this period also marks the beginning of its decline. Cairo's economic prosperity was reduced considerably due to Vasco da Gama's successful circumnavigation of Africa and his arrival in India in 1498. The East-West Oriental spice trade with Europe, which passed through Egypt, was thereby severed, stranding Cairo in a backwater of the rapidly changing global map. Not even the Ottomans, who finally ousted the Mamluks in 1517, were able to hamper the city's downward spiral.

The modernizing reforms instituted by Isma'il Pasha in the late nineteenth century ultimately breathed life back into Cairo. These reforms ironically were inspired by the urban developments of modern-day Europe. Cairo is today the largest metropolis in the Middle East and is now being stifled by overurbanization resulting from overcentralization. This is but the latest challenge facing the City Victorious. Having always been at the forefront of Arab and Islamic trends, it is a challenge to which Cairo will surely rise.

*See also* **Sultanates: Ayyubids; Sultanates: Ghaznavid; Sultanates: Mamluk; Sultanates: Seljuk.**

### BIBLIOGRAPHY

Abu-Lughod, Janet. *Cairo: 1001 Years of the City Victorious.* Princeton, N.J.: Princeton University Press, 1971.

Ibrahim, Saad Eddin; Sobhi, Hoda M; and El-Ahwal, Abdel K. "Problems of Over-Urbanization: The Case of Cairo." In *The Middle East City: Ancient Traditions Confront a Modern World.* Edited by Abdulaziz Y. Saqqaf. New York: Paragon House Publisher, 1987.

Mitchell, Timothy. *Colonising Egypt.* New York: Cambridge University Press, 1988.

Raymond, Andre. "Cairo." In *The Modern Middle East.* Edited by Albert Hourani; Philip S. Khoury; and Mary C. Wilson. London: I. B. Tauris & Co Ltd, 1993.

Rodenbeck, Max. *Cairo: The City Victorious.* London: Picador, 1998.

Rogers, J. M. "Al-Kahira." In *The Encyclopaedia of Islam.* Edited by E. Van Donzel; B. Lewis; and Ch. Pellat. Leiden: E. J. Brill, 1978.

*Aslam Farouk-Alli*

## CALIPHATE

In classical and medieval Islamic history and juristic theory, the Arabic term *khilafa*, of which "caliphate" is the anglicized form, denotes the political headship of the Muslim community. The term *khalifa*—which is used in the Qur'an with reference to Adam (2:30) and David (38:26), besides seven other occurrences in the plural—is understood in Sunni juristic theory as the successor of the prophet Muhammad. The position of the caliph is the most central of all political institutions in the history of classical Islam, and issues pertaining to the legitimacy of those occupying this office, the scope of its powers, and the theoretical and practical accommodations forced upon it during the course of its long career are central to the political and religious history of Islam.

## History of the Institution

Sunni Muslims believe that Muhammad did not appoint anyone to succeed him on his death. According to this view, which has also been generally adopted by modern scholars of early Islamic history, a number of the companions of Muhammad congregated in Medina immediately after his death to deliberate on the question of his succession. At this meeting, Abu Bakr, a member of Muhammad's tribe of Quraysh and one of the most influential of his companions, was elected as the first caliph. The succession was soon recognized by the other companions, including 'Ali, the initially recalcitrant cousin and son-in-law of Muhammad, who was later to become the focus of the legitimist claims of the Shi'a. The latter's view of Muhammad's succession is squarely at odds with that of the Sunnis. To them, Muhammad had, in fact, designated a successor in the person of 'Ali, and most of the companions of the Prophet were culpable for subverting this explicit testament, as indeed were the successors of the first-generation Muslims for their continued denial of the claims of 'Ali's descendants, the imams, to the political and religious headship of Islam.

As the rival Shi'ite and Sunni perspectives on early Islam—and especially on the locus of legitimate authority after Muhammad—suggest, there are competing, often irreconcilable, narratives that comprise the history and historiography of the early caliphate. In the form that these and other narratives have come down to the present day, they are also relatively late (with the earliest extant sources on the caliphate dating from the 9th century), and their content and structure often reveal considerable instability in how they were transmitted or variously rearranged by different hands before, and even after, being committed to writing. Early Islamic historiography may provide rich clues to the controversies on questions of religious and political authority during the first centuries of Islam, but it does not serve well as a reliable guide to the history of the caliphate. Yet, if sources do not lend themselves to a detailed reconstruction of the careers of individual caliphs during Islam's first two centuries or more, modern scholars generally agree that even the tendentiousness of the extant accounts does allow an overview of the caliphate's history along something like the following lines.

The caliphate of Abu Bakr (632–634), which signified the continuation of the polity that Muhammad had founded in Medina, was challenged by a number of tribes in the Arabian Peninsula. They had acknowledged Muhammad's authority by embracing Islam and sending tribute to Medina, but several of them now refused to continue their tributary status, and some renounced allegiance to the new faith as well. Abu Bakr's first challenge was to subdue these rebellious tribes to secure the future of the nascent caliphate. The armies he sent against them did not stop at reasserting Medina's authority, however, but embarked on an extraordinarily daring path of conquests outside the Arabian Peninsula. Muhammad had already led campaigns in the Syrian desert, and Muslim armies now began operations simultaneously in the Byzantine territories of Syria and Palestine and in the Sassanian territories. The degree to which the conquest of the Byzantine and Sassanian territories was the result of careful planning or coordination from Medina is uncertain; yet by the time Abu Bakr died (634), two years after the death of Muhammad, the early Islamic state was already on its way to becoming a major world empire.

The beginnings of the administrative organization of the caliphate are credited to Abu Bakr's immediate successor, 'Umar ibn al-Khattab (r. 634–644). He created a military register (*diwan*) for the payment of the troops and for the disbursement of pensions to other members of the Muslim community. It was in his reign that the first garrison towns were established in the conquered lands, a system of taxation was put in place, and efforts were made to minimize the social and economic disruptions inherent in this rapid conquest. Yet it was not just the conquered people but also the new conquerors who had to cope with the changes set in motion by the expansion of the Medinan state. Entire tribes came to settle in the newly acquired territories, and, quite apart from such rivalries as they may have brought with them from their earlier environs, new grievances and conflicts were provoked by the competing claims of those who had converted to Islam early or late (which determined the share of one's stipends), by the unfamiliar demands of the nascent state on its subjects, and by the conduct and policies of the caliph or his agents.

Such resentments came to the surface in the reign of 'Uthman ibn 'Affan (r. 644–656), the third successor of Muhammad, who was eventually murdered in Medina by disaffected Arab tribesmen from the garrisons of Kufa, Basra, and Egypt. The murder of 'Uthman inaugurated the series of bitter conflicts within the Muslim community that are collectively known as the *fitna*—a highly evocative term suggesting a time of temptation and trial, dissension, and chaos. This civil war, Islam's first, was to continue throughout the reign of 'Uthman's successor, 'Ali ibn Abi Talib (r. 656–661), and it ended only with the latter's assassination and the rise of the Umayyad dynasty (r. 661–750). The events of these years were debated by Muslims for centuries: It is to these events that later Muslims looked in explaining and arguing over their sectarian divisions, some of which were to prove permanent. Even in later centuries, it was never easy to explain how the first community of believers, formed by the Prophet's own guidance, had fallen into such turmoil so soon after his death.

**The Umayyads.** Like their predecessors, the Umayyads too were members of the Quraysh tribe. Unlike their predecessors, all four of whom came, after much controversy, to be set apart from subsequent rulers and to be revered by Sunni Muslims as the Rashidun, the "rightly guided" caliphs, the rise of the Umayyads marked the establishment of a caliphal dynasty. Mu'awiya (r. 661–680), the founder of this dynasty, based his rule on careful cultivation and manipulation of ties with tribal notables (*ashraf*), and it was through such ties that he was able not just to govern but also to have his son, Yazid I (r. 680–683), recognized as his heir. This system of rule through tribal intermediaries was short-lived, however. On Mu'awiya's death, several disparate revolts—often characterized as the second civil war—erupted in different parts of the empire. Among these was the revolt of Husayn, the son of 'Ali and the grandson of the Prophet, who was killed in Iraq in 680 along with a small band of his followers. Though hardly momentous at the time it occurred, this event was to acquire profound importance in the history of Shi'ite Islam as the symbolic focus of Shi'ite piety and religious identity. At the time, however, far more serious threats to the Umayyads were represented by the revolt of 'Abdallah ibn al-Zubayr in the Hijaz, in Arabia, and by factional warfare between Arab tribes in Syria and Mesopotamia. In 684, with the civil war still in progress, Marwan ibn al-Hakam (r. 684–685) was elected caliph in Syria, marking the transfer of ruling authority from Mu'awiya's descendants, the Sufyanid clan (of which 'Uthman had been a member), to another clan of the Umayyad family. This clan, the Marwanids, was to rule as caliphs until the overthrow of the Umayyad dynasty in 750.

The Marwanids governed their empire through powerful generals appointed from the capital, Damascus, and through increasingly elaborate administrative departments (*diwan*s). Late antique administrative structures and traditions continued under the Umayyads even as they underwent sometimes rapid changes that expressed the evolving Arab and Islamic identity of the new empire. Around the turn of the eighth century, the language of the administration was itself changed from ancient Persian and Greek to Arabic and a new system of coinage, clearly asserting the Islamic identity of the new rulers, was instituted. This identity was expressed even more strikingly in monumental architecture, of which the two most famous extant examples are the Dome of the Rock in Jerusalem, built during the reign of the caliph 'Abd al-Malik (r. 685–705), and the Umayyad Mosque in Damascus, built under his successor al-Walid I (r. 705–715).

Though the Umayyads are often portrayed as worldly "kings" in Arabic historiography (an unfavorable image that owes much to the fact that early Islamic historiography is largely the work of those who were unfavorably disposed toward this dynasty), it was under their rule that Islamic religious, cultural, and political institutions began to take their distinctive shape. The caliphs, though far removed from the austere lifestyle of the Rashidun, were hardly the ungodly rulers that medieval Arab chroniclers and many modern scholars have often represented them to be. As Crone and Hinds have shown, their coins, their official pronouncements, and their panegyrists often characterized them as the "deputies of God," a formulation frowned on by the religious scholars but one that suggests something of the scope and seriousness of Umayyad religious claims. The caliphs are known to have given decisions on matters involving Islamic law and ritual, and some of them are featured as authorities in early collections of hadith. Above all, the existence of a powerful centralized political authority provided the crucial context in which the early development of Islam and of Muslim communal and cultural identity took place.

Yet the growing community of Muslims also posed serious challenges to the Umayyads. Since the conquest of the Middle East, the economic well-being of the state was based on the principle that the non-Muslims paid the bulk of the taxes on the land, while the Muslims were responsible for only the religiously obligated taxes on their wealth. In theory, anyone who joined the ranks of the Muslims was entitled to the same concessions; in practice, a large influx of previously taxed non-Arabs threatened the revenues of the empire, with the result that the new Muslims (the *mawali* or "clients") often continued to be taxed as if they had not converted to Islam. The Umayyads never satisfactorily resolved the problem of how to integrate the new non-Arab Muslims into the Muslim community, and they thereby created considerable resentment against their dynasty. This was compounded by the grievances of those Arabs who had given up their military careers and settled down in the conquered lands, but felt discriminated against or unfairly treated by the military generals and their (sometimes non-Muslim) tax-collecting agents. There was, moreover, increasingly destructive tribal factionalism within the Umayyad army that severely weakened the caliphate both through faction-based military revolts and the systematic persecution of members of a faction each time a rival came to power.

Shi'ite groups led a number of revolts against the Umayyads, as did the Kharijites, erstwhile followers of 'Ali who had separated from him when he agreed to negotiate with what the Kharijites regarded as Mu'awiya's iniquitous party. The revolt that brought the Umayyad dynasty to an end in 750 also began as a Shi'ite movement that called, as had many others before it, for returning the rule back to the rightful descendants of the Prophet and for rule according to the "book of God and the sunna of His Prophet." It was not, however, the descendants of 'Ali but those of al-'Abbas, an uncle of the Prophet, that came to power with what is often characterized by modern scholars as the "Abbasid revolution."

**The Abbasids.** The new center of the empire was Iraq rather than Syria, and bureaucrats of Iranian origin were prominent in the Abbasid caliphate (750–1258) from its inception. The new empire was, like its predecessor, also an "Arab kingdom," and indeed there were important continuities between the

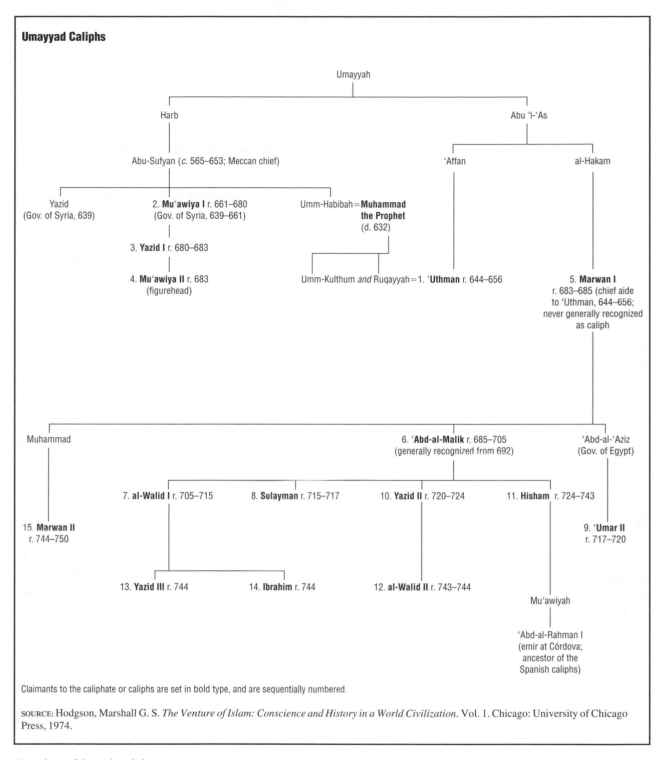

**Umayyad Caliphs**

Claimants to the caliphate or caliphs are set in bold type, and are sequentially numbered.

SOURCE: Hodgson, Marshall G. S. *The Venture of Islam: Conscience and History in a World Civilization.* Vol. 1. Chicago: University of Chicago Press, 1974.

Geneology of the early caliphs.

Umayyad and the early Abbasid caliphates. Yet, the latter was much more inclusive in terms of the ethnic origins of its soldiers and bureaucrats and much more successful in assimilating its non-Arab subjects into the Islamic empire. Its ideological emphases were also different from its predecessor's. Unlike the Umayyads but like the 'Alids, the Abbasids emphasized from the outset their kinship with the Prophet as the justification for their claims to the caliphate. This was to remain a major basis of their legitimist claims, though it was scarcely the only one. The early Abbasid caliphs also tried to invoke, especially in their regnal titles, the messianic expectations rife at the time; they sought, as had the Umayyads in their own ways, to bolster their authority with appeals to pre-Islamic royal traditions and symbolism, and they presided over elaborate circles of patronage that involved a broad spectrum of the cultural and religious elite of the time. Baghdad, founded by al-Mansur (r. 754–775) as his new capital, had evocative imperial symbolism inscribed in its very design, but it soon also became the center of culture and learning, and of interaction not only between various Muslim groups and emerging schools and sects but also between Muslims and non-Muslims.

The first century of Abbasid rule was a time of extraordinary cultural and religious efflorescence, not just in Baghdad but also in the major provincial towns. It was during this time that the eponymous founders of the major schools of Sunni and Shi'ite law flourished. The systematic collection of the traditions of the Prophet, the hadith, began to take place during this time; some of the first extant works of hadith date to this period, as does the earliest major biography of the Prophet, the *Sira* of Ibn Ishaq (d. 767). Under royal patronage, systematic efforts were made to translate ancient philosophical and scientific works into Arabic, and this was the age that saw formative developments in Islamic theology, notably the rise of the rationalist Mu'tazila, as well as the beginnings of what later emerged as Sunni and Shi'ite Islam.

But this formative age was also a time of considerable political turmoil. A number of Shi'ite revolts, of which the most serious took place in Medina and Basra in 762, threatened Abbasid rule. The existence of the descendants of 'Ali, the Shi'ite imams, and their followers in the midst of the community continued to challenge Abbasid legitimacy. Khurasan, where the Abbasid revolt had originated, saw many uprisings against the caliphal state in the early decades after the revolution. The empire was also shaken by a destructive civil war between two sons of Harun al-Rashid (r. 786–809), eventuating in the murder of the incumbent caliph, al-Amin (r. 809–813), and the succession of his brother and the governor of Khurasan, al-Ma'mun (r. 813–833). This murder, and the widespread uncertainty and disorder that accompanied and followed the civil war, considerably weakened the Abbasid state, necessitating extensive effort on the part of the caliph to reassert his authority. This effort took some unusual forms.

Unlike his Abbasid predecessors, al-Ma'mun made strong claims to religious authority, namely to an ability to lay down at least some of what his subjects must believe. Toward the end of his reign, he instituted the *mihna*, an inquisition to enforce conformity to the theological doctrine that the Qur'an ought to be regarded as the "created" word of God. Irrespective of the provenance of this idea or its theological merit, it allowed the caliph to assert his own authority as the arbiter of the community's religious life. The inquisition was apparently intended not only to extend the scope of caliphal authority but also to humble many of those scholars of hadith and law whose growing influence in society the caliph resented and who consequently were among the principle

victims of the *mihna*. But al-Ma'mun died shortly after the inquisition began, and though it continued in effect under two of his immediate successors, it did more, in the long run, to define the "uncreatedness" of the Qur'an as a Sunni creed and to solidify the ranks of the early Sunni scholars than it did to enhance the caliph's religious authority. Later caliphs were usually happier to align themselves with the Sunni religious scholars in asserting their own roles in the community's religious life than they were in confronting or challenging them.

Toward the end of the first century of Abbasid rule, the caliph was still in control of large parts of his realm, but his empire was not as extensive as it had been at the beginning of the dynasty, and it was rapidly shrinking. Some of the provinces were already becoming independent in all but name, and at the heart of the empire, the caliph had to cope with the increasing power of a new military force, Turkish "slave soldiers" drawn from the lands of the Central Asian steppe, a force that in later decades contributed substantially to the political and economic weakness of the Abbasid state. This pattern of a shrinking state and the caliph's increasing dependence on military generals was to continue for much of subsequent Abbasid history. From the middle of the tenth century, the caliphs came under the sway of ruling families that controlled the Abbasid realm, and often the person of the caliph himself, in all but name. The Buyids, a family of Shi'ite military adventurers from Iran, ruled what was left of the Abbasid caliphate from the middle of the tenth to the middle of the eleventh century. They were supplanted by the staunchly Sunni Turkish Seljuks, who then oversaw the Abbasid caliphs until toward the end of the twelfth century. Even as the caliphate declined in effective political power, and for all the humiliations that individual caliphs were meted out at the hands of the warlords, the symbolic significance of the caliphal institution grew during these centuries. The Shi'ite Buyids not only maintained the caliphate but sought also to legitimize their own rule by seeking formal recognition from the caliphs. The Seljuk sultans and their wazirs were often far more powerful than the caliph or his officials, but they too continued to be formally subservient to the caliph.

Not all caliphs during this period were equally helpless, however. At times of political transition, when the warlords were weak, and depending on the personal abilities and initiative of individual caliphs, the latter could exercise a prominent role in the political and religious life of the realm. Notable among such caliphs were al-Qadir (r. 991–1031) and al-Qa'im (r. 1031–1075) in the Buyid period, and al-Nasir (r. 1180–1225), who reigned at a time when the Seljuk power had waned and who utilized his ties with Sufi and chivalric (*futuwwa*) groups, which he reorganized with himself at their head, to reassert his authority during a remarkably ambitious reign. But such revivals were sporadic and they did not do very much to seriously stem the effects of the long decline the caliphate had already undergone. In the middle of the thirteenth century, the caliphate of Baghdad was terminated altogether at the hands of the Mongols, whose ravages included the destruction of large parts of the eastern Islamic world. The caliphate was revived—and the Mongol tide finally stemmed—by the Mamluks of Syria and Egypt, but the Abbasid caliphs of the Mamluk era never had the prestige or the symbolic capital possessed by many of their predecessors in Baghdad. The Mamluk era and, with it, the shadow Abbasid caliphate ended with the Ottoman conquest of Egypt in 1517.

## Ideological Challenges to the Caliphate

From the time of its inception, the caliphate faced challenges of varying degrees of gravity to its existence. Many of these challenges were political. Civil wars resulted in some of the major shifts in the caliphal office: the end of the Rashidun era and the emergence of the Umayyads; the transfer of the caliphate from the Sufyanids to the Marwanids; the Abbasid revolution; and the war between al-Amin and al-Ma'mun. There was secession of territories that had once been part of the caliphate, internal rebellions and warfare with external foes, and, eventually, the loss of effective caliphal control of the heartland of the empire itself and, indeed, even of the caliphs's own freedom of action. Some of the challenges to the caliphate were also ideological, in that they denied the legitimacy of those who occupied this office or contested the basic assumptions on which the Sunni institution of the caliphate was predicated. The Kharijites, for all the antagonism within their ranks, denied the legitimacy not only of 'Uthman's later years but also that of most of his successors. Their position that a ruler who was guilty of a grave sin ought to be deposed brought them into frequent and bloody conflict with the government. Indeed all but the most moderate of the Kharijites were eventually eliminated, but not before they had forcefully raised the question of what constituted a legitimate ruler, under what circumstances must an unjust and sinful ruler be deposed, and what were the terms of membership in the community of Muslims. As Crone has shown, some of the Kharijites as well as certain Mu'tazili theologians were not convinced that the position of a caliph was necessary at all, though this view did not attract much support from the Muslim community.

If the history of the caliphate is viewed from the perspective of the majoritarian Sunnis rather than from that of the Shi'a, then the latter must be seen as representing a more durable challenge to the legitimacy of the caliphate than had even the Kharijites. Divided into many different sects, the Shi'a agreed that the headship of the Muslim community belonged properly to a member of the "people of the house" (ahl al-bayt). What this phrase connoted was a matter of some uncertainty in early Islam, though the term came to be generally understood to refer to the family of the Prophet. As

such the Abbasids, too, could and did claim to be the ahl al-bayt, and indeed their revolutionary propaganda had demanded the installation as caliph of the "acceptable one (al-rida) from the family of Muhammad." The descendants of 'Ali, however, denied that any but their own number was properly entitled to the caliphate, though there were sharp disagreements among them on the precise qualifications of the person who was to be the political-religious head of the community—the imam. Since the time of their sixth imam, Ja'far al-Sadiq (d. 765), the Imami Shi'a had found it prudent to hold largely quietist political views: The imam did not have to show his entitlement to this position by actually taking up arms against the iniquitous order, as certain other Shi'as thought he must. This meant that, despite tensions, the Imamis could continue to live in peace under the caliphs. But the Isma'ili Shi'a, differing with the Imamis on the identity of those of Ja'far's descendants who were to be recognized as imams, thought and acted differently. A state established by the Qarmati Isma'ilis in northeastern Arabia gave much grief to the Abbasids during the tenth century. In the early tenth century, a stronger and more ambitious Isma'ili state, the caliphate of the Fatimids, was established in Ifriqiyya (modern-day Tunisia) from where it moved, in 969, to Egypt.

The Fatimids saw themselves as Isma'ili imams as well as caliphs, demanding absolute authority over their followers and challenging, with considerable might and a splendor to match, the legitimist claims of all other rival states and rulers. The pressure of these claims was felt widely, and not just by the Abbasids. Thus it was in response to them, and not primarily as an affront to the Abbasids, that the Umayyads who had been ruling Spain ever since the fall of the Umayyad caliphate in Damascus, began to also style themselves as caliphs in the tenth century. The Abbasids, however, outlived both of these claimants to the caliphate. And while the Fatimid caliphate was in existence, the Shi'ite Buyids of Iraq were happier to pay nominal allegiance to the Sunni Abbasids than they were to the Fatimids, and even the Qarmati Isma'ilis remained opposed to the latter. As for the population of Egypt, most people preferred to remain Sunnis, and it was to the Sunni Abbasid caliphate that the celebrated Saladin looked when he terminated Fatimid rule in 1171.

## The Caliphate in Constitutional Theory

Detailed formulations of Sunni public law are the product of times when the caliphate had largely ceased to be an effective political institution. The most influential of these, the *Ahkam al-sultaniyya* of the Shafi'i jurist al-Mawardi (d. 1058), was written in the later Buyid period, when the caliphs had for decades lived in often humiliating circumstances under the tutelage of their military overlords. Even so, the caliph occupies the center of al-Mawardi's exposition, with all powers of appointment and dismissal concentrated in his person, to be "delegated" to others as needed. The principal functions of the caliph, as al-Mawardi saw them, were: the preservation of religion according to its agreed-upon principles; implementation of the law, preservation of order, and the security of the realm against internal and external threats; undertaking jihad; the collection of the taxes as required by the sacred law, the *shari'a*, and the proper disbursement and use of the revenues; and the appointment of the appropriate officials for discharging the various functions of the state; and close personal supervision of public affairs. Al-Mawardi's formulations were plainly idealistic; indeed, some of them would have been so even when the Abbasids presided over a large and powerful empire. Yet, in a milieu of political decline, they served important functions. They were simultaneously a way of protesting against the existing circumstances, through a rearticulation of caliphal privileges and his centrality to the life of the community, and a means of bringing juristic theory into some accord with changing circumstances. As for the former, it is noteworthy that the caliph al-Qadir, under whom al-Mawardi wrote his treatise, had himself made efforts to reassert some of his authority against the later Buyids and, as Gibb has suggested ("Al-Mawardi's Theory"), this treatise may have been part of the same effort. But, the jurist also made important concessions to changing times: The person elevated to the caliphate ought to be the "best" of all those available, yet one who was not such could validly occupy the position; the caliph could hold his position even with his powers severely limited by a military usurper, provided the latter continued to abide by the *shari'a*; and independent rulers of outlying provinces could be recognized as legitimate and indeed integrated into the caliphal system if they formally submitted to the caliph and did not contravene the *shari'a*.

Jurists like al-Mawardi sought to tread a difficult path between trying to formalize and legitimize the status quo, to adapt the *shari'a* itself to the changing circumstances, and to encourage the existing authorities to conform in some manner to the *shari'a*. Later jurists went much beyond al-Mawardi in their concessions to realpolitik. For instance, al-Ghazali (d. 1111) argued that the interests of the community dictated that any military usurper be deemed legitimate, for the effort to remove him would inevitably result in political chaos and bloodshed; indeed, whoever was recognized as caliph by the military ruler was to be accepted as a legitimate caliph. Such juristic formulations meant the recognition of a reality the jurists (or the caliphs, for that matter) were powerless to change. They also signified efforts to safeguard the historical continuity of the Muslim community. To concede that the constituted political authority was (and for centuries past had been) illegitimate would have meant that the overall political framework in which the community lived was fundamentally illegitimate, and, unlike the Shi'a, the Sunni scholars were not willing to go so far. Yet, as Khaled Abou El Fadl has shown, if they acknowledged the legitimacy of the existing order and had a stake in its preservation, many Sunni jurists did not necessarily close all doors to the possibility of rebellion against unjust rule. Leaving such a possibility open may not

have had much practical efficacy, though it did serve as a pointed reminder of the jurists' view that a ruler was legitimate only insofar as he did not flagrantly contravene the basic norms of justice and of the *shari'a*— that is, as long as he allowed the continuance of a world in which the scholars could do their work of providing practical religious guidance to the community. For the most part, however, Sunni political thought had made its peace with the political realities long before the extinction of the Abbasid caliphate of Baghdad. The resurrected Abbasid caliphate of Cairo did not receive much attention from later scholars. Rather, jurists like Ibn Taymiyya (d. 1328) ignored the institution altogether, focusing instead on the implementation of the *shari'a* by the ruler—whoever he might be—in collaboration with the religious scholars.

### Historic and Symbolic Significance of the Caliphate

The fundamental importance of the caliphate, irrespective of the actual conduct of individual caliphs or the political fortunes of the institution, lies in what it symbolizes of the classical history of Islam and of the Muslim community. The early caliphate was not only the force behind the military expansion of the Arab Muslims immediately after the death of Muhammad, it was also the institution that kept the Muslims together as a religious and political entity. For all the adverse views that abound about the Umayyads in Arabic historiography, it was through their caliphate that the political survival of the Muslim community was assured. And it was in the framework of the caliphal state, under the Umayyads and then under the Abbasids, that the religious and cultural institutions of Islam evolved. The formation of Islam, its intellectual life, and culture in the first centuries, is, in short, not merely intertwined with but inconceivable without the caliphate.

Even as it declined, the caliphate continued to represent the historical continuity of the Muslim community. It also represented the ideal of the *shari'a*'s supremacy in the collective life of the community. The symbolic weight of the caliphal institution continued to be felt, as long as the caliphate lasted, in the investitures sought by many of the rulers who were independent of the caliphate in all but name. This symbolic power could be revived even long after the institution associated with it had become extinct. For much of their history, the Ottoman sultans had not claimed to be "caliphs," yet even they began to do so from the late eighteenth century. This was largely meant to assert Ottoman authority over those who lived in territories now lost to the sultan, and thereby also to bolster his weakening standing vis-à-vis the European powers of the time. Such claims on the part of the sultans had resonance in several Muslim societies, especially as the latter came under colonial rule and began more anxiously to look for a visible symbol of the worldwide Muslim community. This sentiment found its most powerful expression in India, where what was in fact the Indian subcontinent's very first mass-movement of the colonial period was launched in defense of the Ottoman caliphate at the end of the First World War—a movement that came to an end only with the formal termination of the Ottoman caliphate by Republican Turkey in 1924. That was not the end of the symbolic significance of the caliphate, however. For it was in the debates surrounding the dissolution of the Ottoman caliphate that some of the first modern discussions on the "Islamic state" were to find their point of departure in the twentieth century.

*See also* **Empires: Abbasid; Empires: Ottoman; Empires: Umayyad; Kharijites, Khawarij; Monarchy.**

## BIBLIOGRAPHY

Abou El Fadl, Khaled. *Rebellion and Violence in Islamic Law.* Cambridge, U.K.: Cambridge University Press, 2001.

Azmeh, Aziz al-. *Muslim Kingship: Power and the Sacred in Muslim, Christian, and Pagan Polities.* London: I. B. Tauris, 1997.

Crone, Patricia. "Ninth-century Muslim Anarchists." *Past and Present* 167 (2000): 3–28.

Crone, Patricia. *Slaves on Horses.* Cambridge, U.K.: Cambridge University Press, 1980.

Crone, Patricia, and Hinds, Martin. *God's Caliph: Religious Authority in the First Centuries of Islam.* Cambridge, U.K.: Cambridge University Press, 1986.

Gibb, H. A. R. "Al-Mawardi's Theory of the Caliphate." In his *Studies on the Civilization of Islam.* London: Routledge and Kegan Paul, 1962.

Gibb, H. A. R. "Some Considerations on the Sunni Theory of the Caliphate." In his *Studies on the Civilization of Islam.* London: Routledge and Kegan Paul, 1962.

Hawting, G. R. *The First Dynasty of Islam.* 2d ed. London: Routledge, 2000.

Hibri, Tayeb El-. *Reinterpreting Islamic Historiography: Harun al-Rashid and the Narrative of the ʿAbbasid Caliphate.* Cambridge, U.K.: Cambridge University Press, 1999.

Hodgson, Marshall G. S. *The Venture of Islam: Conscience and History in a World Civilization.* Chicago: University of Chicago Press, 1974.

Kennedy, Hugh. *The Prophet and the Age of the Caliphates.* London: Longman, 1986.

Lambton, A. K. S. *State and Government in Medieval Islam.* Oxford, U.K.: Oxford University Press, 1981.

Madelung, Wilferd. *The Succession to Muhammad: A Study of the Early Caliphate.* Cambridge, U.K.: Cambridge University Press, 1997.

Mawardi, Al-. *The Ordinances of Government.* Translated by W. H. Wahba. Reading, U.K.: Garnet Publishing, 1996.

Qadi, Wadad al-. "The Term 'Khalifa' in Early Exegetical Literature." *Die Welt des Islams* 28 (1988): 392–411.

Safran, Janina M. *The Second Umayyad Caliphate: The Articulation of Caliphal Legitimacy in al-Andalus.* Cambridge, Mass.: Center for Middle Eastern Studies, Harvard University, 2000.

Sanders, Paula. *Ritual, Politics, and the City in Fatimid Cairo.* Albany: State University of New York Press, 1994.

Tabari, Al-. *The History of Al-Tabari.* Albany: State University of New York Press, 1985–1999.

Tyan, Emile. *Institutions du droit public musulman,* Vol. 1: *Le califat.* Paris: R. Sirey, 1954.

Zaman, Muhammad Qasim. *Religion and Politics under the Early ʿAbbasids.* Leiden: Brill, 1997.

*Muhammad Qasim Zaman*

# CALLIGRAPHY

Muslims have always deemed calligraphy, the art of beautiful writing, the noblest of the arts. The first chapters of the Qurʾan revealed to the prophet Muhammad in the early seventh century (suras 96 and 68) mention the pen and writing. Writing in Arabic script soon became a hallmark of Islamic civilization, found on everything from buildings and coins to textiles and ceramics, and scribes and calligraphers became the most honored type of artist. We know the names, and even the biographies, of more calligraphers than any other type of artist. Probably because of the intrinsic link between writing and the revelation, Islamic calligraphy is meant to convey an aura of effortlessness and immutability, and the individual hand and personality are sublimated to the overall impression of stateliness and grandeur. In this way Islamic calligraphy differs markedly from other great calligraphic traditions, notably the Chinese, in which the written text is meant to impart the personality of the calligrapher and recall the moment of its creation. Islamic calligraphy, by contrast, is timeless.

The reed pen (*qalam*) was the writing implement par excellence in Islamic civilization. The brush, used for calligraphy in China and Japan, was reserved for painting in the Islamic lands. In earliest times Muslim calligraphers penned their works on parchment, generally made from the skins of sheep and goats, but from the eighth century parchment was gradually replaced by the cheaper and more flexible support of paper. From the fourteenth century virtually all calligraphy in the Muslim lands was written on paper. Papermakers developed elaborately decorated papers to complement the fine calligraphy, and the colored, marbled, and gold-sprinkled papers used by calligraphers in later periods are some of the finest ever made.

Almost all Islamic calligraphy is written in Arabic script. The Qurʾan was revealed in that language, and the sanctity of the revelation meant that the script was adopted for many other languages, such as new Persian, Ottoman Turkish, and Urdu. Unlike many other scripts that have at least two distinct forms of writing—a monumental or printed form in which the letters are written separately and a cursive or handwritten form in which they are connected—Arabic has

# Alphabet Arabe

| Valeur | Nom | Finales | Médiantes | Initiales | | II Mauritanique ou Occidental | I Cuphique ou Oriental |
|--------|------|---------|-----------|-----------|----|-------------------------------|------------------------|
| A | Alif | ا ا | ا | ا ا | A | لـلـا | لـلـا |
| B | Be | ـب ـب ب | ـبـ ـبـ | بـ بـ | B | ـدـ | ـلـ |
| T | Te | ـت ـت ت | ـتـ ـتـ | تـ تـ | G | حـ | حـ |
| TZ | Thse | ـث ـث ث | ـثـ ـثـ | ثـ ثـ | D | ـلـ | ـد |
| G | Gjim | ج جّ | جـ | جـ ج | H | ٦ d ها | ها |
| H | Hha | ح حّ | حـ | حـ ح | V | ٩ ٩ ٩ | ٩ ٩ |
| CH | Cha | خ خّ | خـ | خـ خ | Z | ر ر ر | ـد |
| D | Dal | د د | د | د د | Ch | حـ | حـ |
| DZ | Dhsal | ذ ذّ | ذ | ذ ذ | T | ظ ظ ظ | ط ط ط |
| R | Re | ـر ـر ر | ـر ـر | ر ر | I | ٥ـ ـدـ | S ـا |
| Z | Ze | ـز ـز ز | ـز ـز | ز ز | C | لـلـ | ـلـد |
| S | Sin | ـس ـس س | ـسـ | ـسـ سـ | L | ل ل ل | ل ل ل |
| S¡ | Sjin | ـش ـش ش | ـشـ | ـشـ ش | M | مـ مـ م | مـ مـ |
| S | Sad | ص ص ص | ـصـ | صـ صـ | N | د ـد ـد | ل ل ل |
| D | Dad | ض ض ض | ـضـ | ضـ ضـ | S | سـ سس س | للـ |
| T | Ta | ط ط | ط | ط ط | Hh | ٤ ٤ ٤ | حـ ـدـ |
| D | Da | ظ ظ | ظ | ظ ظ | Ph | ٩ ٩ ٩ | ٩ ٩ ٩ |
| y | Ain | ع ع | عـ | عـ ع | Ts | ـطـ | ـطـ |
| G | Gain | غ غ | غـ | غـ غ | K | ٩ ٩ ٩ | ٩ ٩ ٩ |
| PH | Phe | ـف ـف ف | فـ | فـ ف | R | ر ر ا | ـدـ |
| K | Kaf | ـق ـق ق | ـقـ | قـ ق | Sch | سس سس سس | للـ |
| C | Kef | ـك ـك ك | ـكـ | كـ ك | Tz | ـد ـد ـد | ـل ـل ـل |
| L | Lam | ل ل ل | لـ | لـ ل | Th | ـد ـد ـد | ـد ـد ـد |
| M | Mim | م م | مـ | مـ م | Ch | حـ | حـ |
| N | Nun | ن ن | نـ | نـ ن | Dhs | ـدـ | ـدـ |
| W | Vau | و و | و | و و | Dz | ـدـ | ط ط |
| H | He | ه ـه ه | ـهـ | هـ هـ | Thz | ٤ ٤ ٤ | ط ط |
| J | Je | ـي ـيّ ي | ـيـ | يـ ي | Gch | ٤ ٤ ٤ | ٤ ٤ ٤ |
| La | Lamalif | لا لا لا | لا | لا لا | La | لا | لا |

The Arabic alphabet. Arabic calligraphy is done with a *qalam*, a type of reed pen, rather than with a brush as in East Asia. Islam's reverence for the written word contributes to calligraphy's status as the religion's most honorable art form. © Historical Picture Archive/Corbis only the cursive form, in which some, but not all, letters are connected and assume different forms depending on their position in the word (initial, medial, final, and independent).

The cursive nature of Arabic script allowed calligraphers to develop many different styles of writing, which are usually grouped under two main headings: rectilinear and rounded. Since the eighteenth century, scholars have often called the rectilinear styles "Kufic," after the city of Kufa in southern Iraq, which was an intellectual center in early Islamic times. This name is something of a misnomer, for as yet we have no idea which particular rectilinear style this name denoted. Scholars have proposed various other names to replace *kufic*, including Old or Early Abbasid style, but these names are not universally accepted, in part because they carry implicit political meanings, and many scholars continue to use the term *kufic*.

Similarly, scholars often called the rounded styles *naskh*, from the verb *nasakha* (to copy). The *naskh* script is indeed the most common hand used for transcription and the one upon which modern styles of typography are based, but the name is also something of a misnomer, for it refers to only one of a group of six rounded hands that became prominent in later Islamic times. As with *kufic*, scholars have proposed several other names to replace *naskh*, such as new style (often abbreviated N.S.), or new Abbasid style, but these names, too, are not universally accepted.

Medieval sources mention the names of many other calligraphic hands, but so far it has been difficult, even impossible, to match many of these names with distinct styles of script. Very few sources describe the characteristics of a particular style or give illustrations of particular scripts. Furthermore, the same names may have been applied to different styles in different places and at different times. Hence it may never be possible to link the names of specific scripts given in the sources with the many, often fragmentary, manuscripts at hand, especially from the early period.

Both the rectilinear and the rounded styles were used for writing from early Islamic times, but in the early period the rounded style seems to have been a book hand used for ordinary correspondence, while the rectilinear style was reserved for calligraphy. Although no examples of early calligraphy on parchment can be definitively dated before the late ninth century, the importance of the rectilinear style in early Islamic times is clear from other media with inscriptions, such as coins, architecture, and monumental epigraphy. The *Fihrist* by Ibn al-Nadim (d. 995) records the names of calligraphers who worked in the Umayyad and Abbasid periods, and both coins and the inscriptions on the first example of Islamic architecture, the Dome of the Rock erected in Jerusalem by the Umayyad caliph 'Abd al-Malik in 692, show that from earliest times Umayyad calligraphers applied such aesthetic principles as balance, symmetry, elongation, and stylization to transform ordinary writing into calligraphy.

Calligraphers in early Islamic times regularly used the rectilinear styles to transcribe manuscripts of the Qur'an. Indeed, the rectilinear styles might be deemed Qur'anic hands, for we know only one other manuscript—an unidentified genealogical text in Berlin (Staatsbibliotheque no. 379)—written in a rectilinear script. None of these early manuscripts of the Qur'an is signed or dated, and most survive only in fragmentary form, and so scholars are still refining other methods, both paleographic and codicological, to group and localize the scripts used in these early parchment manuscripts of the Qur'an.

The major change in later Islamic times was the gradual adoption and adaptation of round hands for calligraphy. From the ninth century calligraphers transformed the round hands into artistic scripts suitable for transcribing the Qur'an and other prestigious texts. The earliest surviving copy of the Qur'an written in a rounded hand is a small manuscript, now dispersed but with the largest section preserved in the Chester Beatty Library in Dublin (ms. 1417). It bears a note in Persian saying that the manuscript was corrected by a certain Ahmad ibn 'Ali ibn Abu 'l-Qasm al-Khayqani in June 905, and it is tacitly accepted that the rounded hand was developed in Iran or nearby Iraq, heartland of the Abbasid caliphate. In the ensuing centuries calligraphers continued to develop and elaborate the rounded style, and from the fourteenth century virtually all manuscripts of the Qur'an were written in one of the six round scripts known as the Six Pens (Arabic, *al-aqlam al-sitta*; Persian, *shish qalam*). These comprise three pairs of majuscule-miniscule hands, *thuluth-naskh*, *muhaqqaq-rayhan*, and *tawqi'-riqa'*, and calligraphers delighted in juxtaposing the different scripts, particularly the larger and smaller variants of the same pair.

Various explanations have been proposed for this transformation of rounded book hands into proportioned scripts suitable for calligraphing fine manuscripts. These explanations range from the political (e.g., the spread of orthodox Sunni Islam) to the sociohistorical (e.g., the new role of the chancery scribe as copyist and calligrapher), but perhaps the most convincing are the practical. The change from rectilinear to rounded script coincided with the change from parchment to paper, and the new style of writing might well be connected with a new type of reed pen, a new method of sharpening the nib, or a new way that the pen was held, placed on the page, or moved across it. In the same way, the adoption of paper engendered the adoption of a new type of black soot ink (*midad*) that replaced the dark brown, tannin-based ink (*hibr*) used on parchment.

From the fourteenth century calligraphers, especially those in the eastern Islamic lands, developed more stylized forms of rounded script. The most distinctive is the hanging script known as *nasta'liq*, which was particularly suitable for transcribing Persian, in which many words end in letters with large bowls, such as *ya'* or *ta'*. Persian calligraphers commonly used *nasta'liq* to pen poetic texts, in which the rounded bowls at the end of each hemistich form a visual chain down the right side of the columns on a page. They also used *nasta'liq* to pen poetic specimens (*qit'a*). These elaborately planned calligraphic compositions typically contain a Persian quatrain written in colored and gold-dusted inks on fine, brightly colored and highly polished paper and set in elaborately decorated borders. The swooping strokes of the letters and bowls provide internal rhythm and give structure to the composition. In contrast to the anonymous works of the early period, these calligraphic specimens are frequently signed and dated, and connoisseurs vied to assemble fine collections, which were often mounted in splendid albums.

Calligraphy continues to be an important art form in modern times, despite the adoption of the Latin alphabet in some countries such as Turkey. Some calligraphers are trying to revive the traditional styles, notably the Six Pens, and investigate and rediscover traditional techniques and materials. Societies teaching calligraphy flourish. The Anjuman-e Khushnvisan-e Iran (Society of Iranian Calligraphers), for example, has branches in all the main cities of the country, with thousands of students. Other artists are extending the calligraphic tradition to new media, adopting calligraphy in new forms, ranging from three-dimensional sculpture to oil painting on canvas. More than any other civilization, Islam values the written word.

*See also* **Arabic Language; Arabic Literature; Art.**

## BIBLIOGRAPHY

Bloom, Jonathan M. *Paper Before Print: The History and Impact of Paper in the Islamic World.* New Haven, Conn., and London: Yale University Press, 2001.

Khatibi, Abdelkebir, and Sijelmassi, Mohammed. *The Splendour of Islamic Calligraphy.* London: Thames and Hudson, 1994.

Lings, Martin. *The Qur'anic Art of Calligraphy and Illumination.* London: World of Islam Festival Trust, 1976.

Safadi, Y. H. *Islamic Calligraphy.* Boulder, Colo.: Shambala, 1979.

Schimmel, Annemarie. *Islamic Calligraphy.* Leiden: E. J. Brill, 1970.

Schimmel, Annemarie. *Calligraphy and Islamic Culture.* New York: New York University Press, 1984.

*Sheila S. Blair*
*Jonathan M. Bloom*

# CAPITALISM

Among the claims of the contemporary literature known as "Islamic economics" is that Islamic law provides an economic system conducive to free exchange. Where this system allegedly differs from capitalism, which also promotes economic freedoms, is that it avoids sharp inequalities, chronic corruption, and mass exploitation. If Muslims restructure their economic relations according to Islamic stipulations, say the proponents of Islamic economics, they can obtain all the benefits of capitalism without incurring its costs. Specifically, they can achieve prosperity, steady innovation, and material security—all traits associated with today's advanced market economies—within a framework based on honesty and brotherly cooperation.

If this logic resonates with many Muslims, the reason is that the current economic performance of the Islamic world is generally disappointing. The predominantly Muslim countries included in the annual "Corruption Index" of Transparency International all rank as substantially "more corrupt" than the typical advanced economy. Except for the small oil-exporting countries of the Arabian peninsula, not a single Muslim-governed state is among the world's wealthiest countries, and many Muslim countries are impoverished. The Islamic world's participation in world trade is low in relation to its share of global population. Although the basic economic institutions of the Islamic world are formally similar to those of the successful market economies, there is a consensus that they do not perform as well.

Like many secular critics of capitalism, Islamists attribute this situation to Western imperialism. Starting in the eighteenth century, they argue, European traders and financiers, along with the states that supported them, destroyed local crafts, monopolized natural resources, secularized the judicial system, and gradually took over key aspects of economic governance. They also lowered the Islamic world's standards of honesty and weakened its ethic of brotherly cooperation.

## Institutional Sources of Underdevelopment

In fact, European imperialism was a result, rather than the leading cause, of the Islamic world's economic shortcomings. Prior to embarking on the global colonization drive whose results included the economic subjugation of the world's Muslim peoples, the West underwent a sustained institutional transformation that gave rise to modern capitalism. During this transformation, which began around the eleventh century, the institutions of the Islamic world also experienced changes, but these were relatively minor. As late as the nineteenth century, the contractual forms recognized by the Islamic court system were essentially those developed a millennium earlier. The concept of a juridical person had no place in Islamic law. Nor did Islamic law recognize joint-stock companies or corporations. Although money lending remained a flourishing profession among both Muslims and non-Muslims, there were no banks. For these reasons, among others, the Islamic world's economic system was now inefficient in relation to the emerging capitalist system of the

West. It is this handicap that subjected the Middle East and the rest of the Islamic world to Western economic domination.

As this domination was taking shape, the Islamic world experienced no general economic decline in the absolute sense. But it started showing clear signs of underdevelopment, as measured by the living standards, productivity levels, and institutional dynamism prevailing in the West.

In early stages of the West's economic ascent, the Islamic world's market institutions were at least as efficient as their Western counterparts, and in some respects more so. Its partnership laws, which were codified by jurists generally familiar with the needs of merchants and investors, gave traders a remarkable array of contractual options. Although interest was formally banned, financiers easily circumvented the prohibition, which, in any case, was often interpreted loosely, as disallowing only exploitative interest charges. Disputes between partners, and between buyers and sellers, were settled informally through arbitration or formally through the Islamic courts, whose jurisdiction covered all economic transactions. A wide range of social service organizations, including schools, charities, commercial centers, and rest stops for caravans, were established in a decentralized manner through *waqf*s, or Islamic trusts. The typical *waqf* also served as a wealth shelter, for its assets were relatively safe from confiscation and its founder could shower himself, his relatives, and even his descendants with material benefits. To a degree, the privileges enjoyed by *waqf* founders compensated for the chronic weakness of private property rights. For several centuries—estimates of the end point range from the fourteenth century to the eighteenth century—this system afforded the Islamic world a standard of living that was equal, if not superior, to that of Europe.

### The Rise of Modern Capitalism

Meanwhile, the West underwent the momentous structural transformation that resulted in capitalism. This transformation included the strengthening of individual property rights, the recognition of juridical persons in a growing number of sectors, and a sustained broadening of the menu of contractual forms available to investors, traders, workers, and consumers. By the eighteenth century, and unmistakably by the nineteenth, the relative sophistication of Europe's economic institutions allowed its financiers and merchants to dominate economies all across the globe. The main reason why the Islamic world fell into a state of underdevelopment is that changes taking place outside the Islamic world had the effect of reducing the efficiency of pre-capitalist economic institutions based on Islamic law.

Why Islamic law itself failed to generate the basic institutions of capitalism has long been a matter of controversy. One thing is certain. The explanation is not, as nineteenth- and early-twentieth-century thinkers were inclined to believe, that Islam is inherently hostile to commerce or prosperity. The classical sources of Islam are replete with provisions designed to facilitate exchange and production. Nor can the lag be attributed to policies aimed at retarding growth. The Islamic world's structural transformation was delayed because certain institutions well suited to the economic conditions of classical Islam produced unintended consequences.

### Unintended Consequences

One of these institutions was the Islamic inheritance system. Outlined in the Qur'an, the Islamic inheritance system requires two-thirds of a person's estate to be apportioned among members of his or her extended family according to criteria dependent on the composition of the possibly numerous heirs and their relationships to the deceased. Prior to the modern era, this system raised the cost of keeping productive enterprises intact across generations. Equally important, because the death of even one partner resulted in termination of the enterprise, and in the dissolution of its assets, the prevailing inheritance rules created incentives for keeping partnerships small and ephemeral. Consequently, the growing complexity that characterized the productive, financial, and commercial enterprises of Europeans was not observed in territories under Islamic law. By contrast, the relative flexibility of European inheritance regimes allowed practices designed to keep estates intact, such as primogeniture. These practices facilitated the establishment of larger and longer-lasting enterprises, which then stimulated the development of increasingly sophisticated accounting systems, specialized markets, and contractual forms in order to minimize operating costs.

Until the Western-inspired economic reforms of the nineteenth century, Islamic civilization offered no corporate structures capable of serving as prototypes for durable financial or mercantile organizations. The one major Islamic institution that some consider an exception is the *waqf*. Established to provide a service in perpetuity, a *waqf*, like a corporation, was meant to outlive its founder and employees. Nevertheless, it lacked most of the freedoms associated with corporate status. Most significant, it was supposed to refrain from remaking its internal rules and modifying its objectives. Still another unintended effect of the *waqf* system was that, by enhancing material security, it dampened incentives for seeking stronger property rights. Economic historians generally believe that in the West the strengthening of individual property rights played a critical role in the rise of modern capitalism.

By the nineteenth century, it was clear that the traditional economic institutions of the Islamic world had become a liability. The institutional borrowings that followed included new forms of organization, including complex partnerships, joint-stock companies, and corporations. Another historical break that occurred at this time was the establishment of various secular courts to adjudicate commercial and financial disputes involving contractual forms alien to traditional Islamic law.

In January, 1998, this Indonesian money changer was busy working the phones after a day of panic buying at supermarkets that left the Indonesian rupiah volatile and led the United States and the International Monetary Fund (IMF) to send top officials to the country in an attempt to salvage a bailout effort. With the exception of a few oil-rich countries in the Middle East, no Muslim country is among the world's wealthiest. The lingering effects of the transition from an older, Islamic economic order to Western capitalism has left many Muslim countries in poverty and has led some Islamists to blame the West for their countries' suffering and social turmoil. AP/WIDE WORLD PHOTOS

### Weberian Thesis

The foregoing institutional explanation for the underdevelopment of the Middle East calls into question its most celebrated alternative: the Weberian thesis, which traces the origins of capitalism to the ideological creativity of the Protestant Reformation. Weber's argument was challenged by R. H. Tawney, who showed that capitalist institutions preceded, even created, what Weber called the capitalist spirit. Tawney's observation suggests that where capitalist institutions failed to evolve through locally driven processes, as in the Islamic Middle East, vigorous and successful entrepreneurship would be limited.

At the time that Weber wrote, bilateral trade between the Islamic world and western Europe was almost entirely under the control of Europeans, who provided much of the requisite financing, know-how, and transportation. It thus seemed that the Middle East lacked the entrepreneurship essential to

modern capitalism. In fact, the infrastructure of capitalism was inadequate, and Middle Easterners, being latecomers to operating under modern economic institutions, lacked basic experiences and resources. Significantly, it was during the twilight of the traditional Islamic economic order and the transition to modern capitalism—the eighteenth century to the early twentieth century—that the Christians and Jews of the region by and large gained economic ground against its Muslims. Entitled since the early days of Islam to choice of law, which they had sometimes exercised in favor of indigenous non-Muslim contractual forms, the Christian and Jewish religious minorities began using modern contractual forms about a century before Muslims were able to do so. Equally important, many operated under the protection of European-operated courts, as opposed to local Islamic courts.

*See also* **Communism; Economy and Economic Institutions; Globalization.**

### BIBLIOGRAPHY

Çizakça, Murat. *A Comparative Evolution of Business Partnerships: The Islamic World and Europe, with Special Reference to the Ottoman Archives.* Leiden: E. J. Brill, 1996.

Ibrahim, Mahmood. *Merchant Capital and Islam.* Austin: University of Texas Press, 1990.

Issawi, Charles. "The Entrepreneurial Class." In *The Arab World's Legacy.* By Charles Issawi. Princeton, N.J.: Darwin Press, 1981.

Kuran, Timur. "Islam and Underdevelopment: An Old Puzzle Revisited." *Journal of Institutional and Theoretical Economics* 153 (1997): 41–71.

Kuran, Timur. "The Provision of Public Goods under Islamic Law: Origins, Impact, and Limitations of the Waqf System." *Law and Society Review* 35 (2001): 841–897.

Rodinson, Maxime. *Islam and Capitalism.* Translated by Brian Pearce (1966). Reprint, New York: Pantheon, 1973.

*Timur Kuran*

## CARTOGRAPHY AND GEOGRAPHY

There exist hundreds—if not thousands—of cartographic images of the world and various regions scattered throughout the medieval and early modern Arabic, Persian, and Turkish manuscript collections, worldwide. Yet most of these maps have lain virtually untouched and have often been deliberately ignored on the grounds that they were not accurate representations of the world. What many failed to see is that these schematic, geometric, and often perfectly symmetrical images of the world are iconographic representations of the way in which the medieval Muslims perceived it. Granted, these were stylized visions restricted to the literati—the readers, collectors, commissioners, writers, and copyists of the geographic texts within which these maps are found. However, the plethora of extant copies produced all over the Islamic world, including India, testifies to the enduring and widespread popularity of these medieval Islamic cartographic visions. For nothing less than six centuries (eight, if nineteenth-century South Asian examples are included), these cartographic visions were perpetuated primarily in one fossilized cartogeographic series: the *Kitab al-masalik wa al-mamalik* (Book of roads and kingdoms).

What all these extant maps say is that—at least from the thirteenth century onward, whence copies of these map-manuscripts begin to proliferate—the world was a very depicted place. It loomed large in the medieval Muslim imagination. It was pondered, discussed, and copied with minor and major variations again and again.

### Al-Idrisi and Piri Re'is

The better-known examples of this Islamic mapping tradition, in contemporary Eastern as well as Western scholarship, is the work of the twelfth century North African geographical scholar al-Sharif al-Idrisi (d. 1165). The Norman king, Roger II (1097–1154), commissioned al-Idrisi to produce an illustrated geography of the world. This yielded al-Idrisi's *Nuzhat al-mushtaq fi ikhtiraq al-afaq* (The book of pleasant journeys into faraway lands), also known as the *Book of Roger*. Al-Idrisi divided the world according to the Ptolemaic system of seven climes, with each clime broken down into ten sections. The most complete manuscript (1469) contains one world map and seventy detailed sectional maps.

The sixteenth-century Ottoman naval captain, Muhyiddin Piri Re'is (d. 1554), was another Muslim cartographer who has become famous worldwide. Renowned for the earliest extant map of the New World, Piri Re'is and his accurate early-sixteenth-century map of South America and Antarctica have been the subject of many a controversial study. Piri Re'is also produced detailed sectional maps but—like the Italian *isolarii*—he restricted himself to the coastal areas of the Mediterranean. The second version of his *Kitab-i Bahriyye* (Book of maritime matters) contains 210 unique topo-cartographic maps of important Mediterranean cities and islands.

The striking mimesis (geographical accuracy) of these two Muslim cartographic traditions has caused the work of al-Idrisi and Piri Re'is to be elevated above the rest of the Middle Eastern mapping corpus in contemporary scholarship. Aside from the problems of attribution that abound with these two cartographers (none of the extant al-Idrisi maps, for instance, date back to his time, while Piri Re'is's map is thought to be a copy of one by Christopher Columbus), scholarly focus on this more mimetic end of the Islamic mapping tradition has occluded an enormous body of maps that were much more popular in the medieval and early modern Islamic world than the work of al-Idrisi or Piri Re'is.

### The "Wondrous" Tradition

In actuality, maps occur in a wide variety of Islamic texts and contexts. A popular location for classical Islamic world and cosmographic maps is in the so-called *'Aja'ib* ("wondrous") literary tradition, which includes descriptions of flora, fauna, architecture, and other wonders of the world. Best known of this genre is the work of the thirteenth century Iranian writer, Zakariyya' ibn Muhammad al-Qazwini (d. 1283), whose work *'Aja'ib al-makhluqat wa ghara'ib al-mawjudat* (The wonders of creatures and the marvels of creation) focuses on the wonders of the world—real and fabulous. Copies from the late thirteenth century onward (during the lifetime of the author) began to incorporate illustrations of flora and fauna as well as world maps.

Copies of Siraj al-Din Abu Hafs 'Umar Ibn al-Wardi's (d. 1457) *Kharidat al-'aja'ib wa faridat al-ghara'ib* (The unbored pearl of wonders and the precious gem of marvels) offer a variation of the 'Aja'ib tradition that incorporates at least one world map along with other cartographics, such as a Qibla map (a way-finding diagram for locating Mecca), and inset maps of Qazwin and other cities. Judging by the plethora of pocket book–size copies that still abound in every Oriental manuscript collection, the *Kharidat al-'Aja'ib* must have been a bestseller in the late medieval and early modern Islamic world. Moreover, it is significant that this Arabic bestseller always incorporated, within the first four or five folios, a classical Islamic world map.

Eventually the classical Islamic world maps also crept into general geographical encyclopedias, such as Shihab al-Din Abu 'Abdallah Yaqut's (d. 1229) thirteenth century *Kitab Mu'jam al-Buldan* (Dictionary of countries). The earliest prototype of this type of map is found in a copy of Abu 'l-Rayhan Muhammad ibn Ahmad al-Biruni's (d. after 1250) *Kitab al-tafhim* (Book of instruction). World maps are also used to open some of the classic histories. Copies of such well-known works as Ibn Khaldun's (d. 1406) *Muqaddimah* (The prologue) often begin with an al-Idrisi map, while copies of the historian Abu Ja'far Muhammad ibn Jarir al-Tabari's (d. 923) *Ta'rikh al-rusul wa-al-muluk* (History of prophets and kings) sometimes included a Ptolemaic "clime-type" map of the world as a frontispiece. Similarly, classical Islamic maps of the world found their way into sixteenth-century Ottoman histories, such as the scroll containing Seyyid Lokman's *Zubdetu't-tevarih* (Cream of histories) produced in the reign of Suleyman I (1520–1566).

### New Maps for New Purposes

From the fifteenth century until the late nineteenth century, hajj (pilgrimage) manuals containing map-like pictures of the holy sites proliferated. An excellent example of this prototype is the *Futuh al-Haramayn* (The conquests of the holy sites) manuscript series. Around the same time, a tradition began in mosques of including a glazed tile containing a schematic representation of the Ka'ba adjacent to the *mihrab* (prayer niche). If the definition of precisely what constitutes a map can be stretched, then even the map-like images found in Islamic miniature paintings can be incorporated into the Islamic cartographic repertoire.

Some scholars believe that the source of this rich and widespread medieval Islamic propensity to make maps lies in the earliest Arabic textual references to maps. For instance, the silver globe (al-Sura al-Ma'muniya) that the Abbasid caliph al-Ma'mun (r. 813–833) is said to have commissioned from the scientists working in his Bayt al-Hikma (House of knowledge). The problem with the al-Ma'munid silver globe is that it is probably mythical. Other than an extremely vague passage cited in Abu 'l-Hasan 'Ali ibn al-Husayn al-Mas'udi's (d. 956) Kitab al-tanbih wa-al-ishraf (Book of instruction and revision), there are no descriptions of it. Al-Mas'udi's description is very confused. It suggests an impossibly complicated celestial map superimposed upon a globe, an extremely sophisticated armillary sphere of which there are no extant example until the fourteenth century. At least one scholar, David King, has interpreted this description to suggest an astrolabe with world-map markings superimposed on it.

There also are a few references to maps from the end of the first century of Islam (c. 702). Apparently, al-Hallaj ibn Yusuf, the Umayyad governor of the eastern part of the Muslim empire, commissioned maps, for military purposes, of the region of Daylam (south of the Caspian Sea), as well as a plan of the city of Bukhara. Requests for maps for military purposes are highly unusual in Islamic history. Not until the time of the Ottoman sultan Mehmet II (r. 1444–1446; 1451–1481) are there similar requests for maps for military purposes. Unfortunately, none of the al-Hallaj requests are extant, and there are no detailed descriptions of these maps themselves.

In Kitab al-buldan (Book of countries) Ahmad ibn Abi Ya'qub al-Ya'qubi (d. c. late ninth century) reports that a plan of the round city of Baghdad was drawn up in 758 for the Abbasid caliph, al-Mansur (r. 754–775). The Egyptian chronicler al-Maqrizi mentions that a "magnificent" map on "fine blue" silk with "gold lettering" upon which was pictured "parts of the earth with all the cities and mountains, seas and rivers" was prepared for the Fatimid caliph al-Mu'izz (r. 953–975) and even entombed with him in his mausoleum in Cairo.

The only extant source containing maps prior to the Kitab al-masalik wa al-mamalik series is a ninth-century copy of Abu Ja'far Muhammad ibn Musa al-Khwarazmi's (d. 847 C.E.) Kitab surat al-ard (Picture of the Earth). Composed primarily of a series of zij tables (tables containing longitudinal and latitudinal coordinates), it also includes four maps. Two are unidentifiable, one is a map of the Sea of Azov, and one is of the Nile. Of all the maps in this manuscript, only the map of the Nile appears to be directly related to maps of the Nile that one finds in later carto-geographic works.

## The Start of the Mapping Phenomenon

In order to understand the mapping traditions that flowered in the Islamic world in the later middle ages and early modern period, one has to go back to the tradition that sired them all. It can be argued that the fons origo of the Islamic mapping tradition is none other than the so-called "Islamic Atlas." This carto-geographical tradition is best known by the title of its most prolifically copied version: al-Istakhri's Kitab al-masalik wa al-mamalik (Book of roads and kingdoms). For convenience, this may be referred to as the KMMS mapping tradition. The "S" at the end of this acronym is used to specify those versions of this manuscript series that contain cartographic images (standing for Sura, pl. Suwar).

Most of the KMMS maps occur in the context of geographical treatises devoted to an explication of the world, in general, and the lands of the Muslim world, in particular. These "map-manuscripts" generally carry the title of Kitab al-masalik wa al-mamalik, although they are sometimes named Surat al-ard (Picture of the earth) or Suwar al-aqalim (Pictures of the climes/climates). These manuscripts emanated from an early tradition of creating lists of pilgrim and post stages that were compiled for administrative purposes. They read like armchair travelogs of the Muslim world, with one author copying prolifically from another.

Beginning with a brief description of the world and theories about it—such as the inhabited versus the uninhabited parts, the reasons why people are darker in the south than in the north, and the like—these geographies methodically discuss details about the Muslim world, its cities, its people, its roads, its topography, and other such features. Sometimes the descriptions are interspersed with anecdotal matter, including tales of personal adventures, discussions with local inhabitants, or debates with sailors as to the exact shape of the earth and the number of seas. They have a rigid format that rarely varies: first the whole world, then the Arabian Peninsula, then the Persian Gulf, then the Maghreb (North Africa and Andalusia), Egypt, Syria, the Mediterranean, upper and lower Iraq, as well as twelve maps devoted to the Iranian provinces, beginning with Khuzistan and ending in Khurasan, including maps of Sind and Transoxiana. The maps, which usually number precisely twenty-one, follow exactly the same format as the text and are thus an integral part of the work.

## The al-Balkhi Tradition and Controversy

Not all these geographical manuscripts contain maps, however. Rather, maps are found only in those referred to generally as part of the al-Balkhi/al-Istakhri tradition—the "Classical School" of geographers. This particular geographical genre is also referred to as the "Atlas of Islam." A great deal of mystery surrounds the origins and the architects of this manuscript-bound cartographic tradition. This is primarily because not a single manuscript survives in the hand of its original author. Furthermore, it is not clear who initiated the tradition of accompanying geographical texts with maps.

Scholars of the eighteenth and nineteenth centuries hold that Abu Zayd Ahmad ibn Sahl al-Balkhi (d. 934), who—as his *nisba* (patronym) suggests—came from Balkh in Central Asia, initiated the series, and that his work and maps were later elaborated upon by Abu Ishaq ibn Muhammad al-Farisi al-Istakhri (fl. early tenth century) from Istakhr in the province of Fars. Al-Istakhri's work was, in turn, elaborated upon by Abu al-Qasim Muhammad ibn Hawqal (fl. second half of tenth century), who came from upper Iraq (the region known as the *Jazira*). Abu ʿAbdallah Muhammad al-Muqaddasi (d. c. 1000), from Jerusalem (Quds), is considered the last innovator in this series.

The problem is that virtually no biographical information exists on the authors other than al-Balkhi. One is forced to rely on scraps of information in the geographical texts themselves for information about their authors. The difficulty is compounded by the fact that, in all the forty-three titles that Ibn al-Nadim credits to al-Balkhi, not one even vaguely resembles the title of a geographical treatise. According to the biographers, al-Balkhi was famous as a philosopher and for his *tafsir* (commentaries on the Qurʾan)—in particular one known as *Naʿm al-qurʾan*—which was praised by many judges. He is not, however, known in the biographical record for his geographical treatises. Yet stories of how al-Balkhi sired the Islamic mapping tradition endure. It is for this reason that the genre is generally referred to as the "Balkhi school of mapping." The attribution of a whole school of mapping to a shadowy, mythical father who was anything but a specialist on geography or cartography is unfounded.

The confusion is further compounded by the fact that many of the surviving copies contain either incomplete colophons (inscriptions containing attribution of authorship) or no colophons at all. Additionally, the texts are sometimes so mixed up in the surviving manuscripts that it is often difficult to disentangle them. The numerous incomplete and anonymous manuscripts, sometimes abridged, along with the versions translated into Persian, only cloud the matter further.

### Images of Other Worlds

Since none of the *KMMS* manuscripts date back to their original authors, the issue of authorship of the first carto-geographical manuscript and precisely what it looked like is immaterial. What is relevant is that these geographical manuscripts include some of the earliest pictographic images of the world in an Islamic context. Since all images are socially constructed, these iconic carto-ideographs contain valuable messages of the milieux in which they were produced. They are a rich source of new information that can be used as alternate gateways into the Islamic past. They can tell about the time period in which they were copied, and provide hints about the period in which they were originally conceived.

Since the extant examples stretch in time from the eleventh century to the nineteenth, and range from the heart of the Middle East to its peripheries, they provide us with insights from a broad range of time and space. The earliest extant set of Islamic maps comes from an Ibn Hawqal manuscript housed at the Topkapi Saray Museum Library firmly dated to the year 1086 by a clear colophon. Counterintuitively, this manuscript also contains the most mimetic maps of all the existing *KMMS* copies. This version of the *KMMS* even has an extraordinary triple folio fold-out map of the Mediterranean. Indeed, it is the world-map version of this manuscript that proliferates in a more embellished form via the Ibn al-Wardi manuscript copies from the fifteenth century. The striking mimesis of these maps stands in stark contrast to the maps of the later *KMMS* copies, which over the centuries abandon any pretense of mimesis entirely.

After the *KMMS* set, a series of more and more stylized maps emerges that move further into the realm of *objects d'art* and away from direct empirical inquiry. By the nineteenth century the *KMMS* maps become so stylized that, were it not for the earlier examples, it would be hard to recognize them as the maps at all. Between these two extremes there are a series of *KMMS* world maps that range from somber in form and color (some even contain grids) to outright gaudy and lacking in fine detail. In the crevices of these maps the real and the imaginary, the terrestrial and the cosmographical, and the empirical and the fictional dance confusingly in front of people of today.

*An ancient map appears in the volume one color insert.*

*See also* **Biruni, al-; Ibn Battuta; Ibn Khaldun; Persian Language and Literature.**

## BIBLIOGRAPHY

Cosgrove, Denis, ed. *Mappings.* London: Reaktion Books, 1999.

Goodrich, Thomas. *The Ottoman Turks and the New World: A Study of "Tarih-i Hind-i Garbi" and Sixteenth-Century Ottoman Americana.* Wiesbaden: Otto Harrassowitz, 1990.

Hapgood, Charles H. *Maps of the Ancient Sea Kings: Evidence of Advanced Civilization in the Ice Age.* New York: E. P. Dutton, 1979.

Harley, J. B., and Woodward, David, eds. *The History of Cartography: Cartography in the Traditional Islamic and South Asian Societies.* Chicago: University of Chicago Press, 1992.

King, David. *World-Maps for Finding the Direction and Distance to Mecca: Innovation and Tradition in Islamic Science.* Leiden: E. J. Brill, 1999.

Kramers, Johannes Hendrik. *Analecta Orientalia: Posthumous Writings and Selected Minor Works.* Leiden: E. J. Brill, 1954.

McIntosh, Greg. *The Piri Reis Map of 1513.* Athens: University of Georgia Press, 2000

Sezgin, Fuat. *Geschichte Des Arabischen Schrifttums: Mathematische Geographie und Kartographie im Islam und*

*Ihr Fortleben im Abendland. Historische Darstellung*. Frankfurt: Institut für Geschichte der Arabisch-Islamischen Wissenschaften an der Johann Wolfgang Goethe-Universität Frankfurt am Main, 2000.

Soucek, Svat. *Piri Reis and Turkish Mapmaking after Columbus*. London: The Nour Foundation, 1996.

*Karen C. Pinto*

# CENTRAL ASIA, ISLAM IN

Central Asia is a modern geographical designation covering an area of considerable political, ethnic, and linguistic diversity, but marked by a distinctive cultural synthesis rooted in the meeting of the civilization of Inner Asia with that of the Middle East and the Islamic world. In terms of contemporary political boundaries, it comprises the newly independent post-Soviet states of Kazakhstan, Uzbekistan, Kyrgyzstan, Tajikistan, and Turkmenistan, as well as adjacent parts of the Chinese province of Xinjiang, of northern Afghanistan, of northeastern Iran, and of the Russian Federation.

The chief historical regions comprising Central Asia include Mawarannahr, often called Transoxiana or Transoxania, the traditional heartland; the Farghana valley; the Tarim basin, often called Chinese or East Turkistan and now forming the major part of the province of Xinjiang in the People's Republic of China; the Syr Darya valley, with its commercial oasis towns; the steppe regions to the north known since the eleventh century as the Dasht-e Qipchaq; the region of the Amu Darya delta to the south of the Aral Sea, known historically as Khwarazm; and Khurasan, typically regarded as the northeasternmost province of Iran, but more often closely linked with Transoxiana in political, ethnic, and economic terms.

## From the Arab Conquest to the Mongol Invasion

The Arab conquest of Iran brought Muslim armies to Khurasan, and raids were conducted as far as Balkh and into Transoxania already during the 650s, as Arab governors based first in Basra in Iraq and later (from 667) in Marv began the dual policy of establishing garrison towns in some areas, with Arab families transplanted from Iraq, and elsewhere leaving local dynasts in power as tributary rulers. A new stage in the conquest of Central Asia began with the appointment, in 705, of Qutayba b. Muslim as the governor of Khurasan. Qutayba's ten-year career brought the military conquest of Bukhara and Samarkand as well as of Khwarazm, and the initiation of campaigns into Farghana and as far beyond the Syr Darya as Isfijab; it also saw important institutional developments, as Arab garrisons were established in Bukhara and Samarkand, troops were levied from the local population to serve with the Muslim armies, mosques were built in these cities, and measures were undertaken to induce conversion to Islam.

These patterns of Arab rule established under Qutayba proved more enduring than his conquests. Following his murder by mutinous troops in the Farghana valley in 715, Arab control in Transoxania was soon rolled back, and nearly a quarter-century passed before the Muslim armies were able to take the initiative again. Local rulers such as the Sogdian king Ghurak regained their independence and successfully fought the Arabs, but a new force from the steppe—the Turgesh confederation—posed a more serious threat to Arab control. The Turgesh were able to raid deep into Transoxania and eventually into Khurasan as well. The death of the Turgesh ruler in 737, however, led to the collapse of his confederation; Ghurak died the same year, and soon afterward a new Umayyad governor of Khurasan, Nasr b. Sayyar, was able, during the 740s, to reconquer central Transoxania, the Farghana valley, and parts of eastern Khurasan that had reverted to local rulers, and to lead successful campaigns as far as Tashkent.

Soon, however, the Abbasid revolution, a movement that took shape militarily in Khurasan, swept the Umayyads from power; Abbasid agitation there began even before the arrival of the famous Abu Muslim in 747, and both the Arab colonists in Khurasan and Transoxania and local converts to Islam played significant roles in the success of the Abbasid cause. Disaffection with Umayyad rule was particularly strong among the local converts, resentful of policies that relegated them to a subordinate status vis-à-vis the Arabs. Nevertheless, the series of religiously tinged revolts that broke out in Transoxania and Khurasan beginning in the late Umayyad era continued through the first decades of Abbasid rule. Abbasid control in Central Asia in fact remained tenuous until the revolt of Rafiʿ b. Layth beginning in 806. This revolt posed such a serious threat that the caliph himself, Harun al-Rashid, was compelled to set out to deal with it. Following his death in 809, his son al-Maʾmun, installed as governor in Marv, succeeded in suppressing it, and after his elevation as caliph in 813, al-Maʾmun—still based in Marv—conducted a series of decisive campaigns against independent local rulers that may be regarded as the culmination of the Arab conquest of Central Asia.

Almost as soon as it was solidified, Abbasid control in Central Asia devolved upon local governors loyal to the caliph and at least nominally dependent upon him. One of the participants in al-Maʾmun's suppression of the revolt of Rafiʿ b. Layth was one Tahir b. Husayn, whom the caliph appointed governor of Khurasan in 821. The Tahirid dynasty ruled Khurasan and Transoxania until its destruction in 873 by the Saffarids of Sistan. Members of the Samanid family also took part in al-Maʾmun's campaigns, and served the Tahirids as governors in Samarkand, Farghana, and Tashkent.

Samanid dynasts expanded their power through campaigns deep into the steppe, and with the collapse of the Tahirids received caliphal recognition as the rightful governors of Transoxania. The real foundations of the dynasty's power were laid by Isma'il Samani, who destroyed the Saffarids in 900 and established Bukhara as the center of his realm. The dramatic decline in the political importance of the Abbasid caliphs that preceded the Samanid era (900–999) left the Samanids the rulers of an essentially independent state based in Central Asia; their patronage of religious and cultural institutions made tenth-century Central Asia one of the most vibrant and influential parts of the Muslim world.

Well into the first half of the tenth century, the Samanids retained their ability to project their power into the steppe to the north and northeast of Transoxania, but the Samanid era also brought crucial developments in the political and cultural history of the Turks of Central Asia. The tenth century marks the beginning of the large-scale involvement of Turkic peoples in Islamic civilization. Before this time, Turks from Central Asia had already played an important role in Muslim history as military slaves active at the caliphal court in Baghdad as well as other, more westerly parts of the Muslim world. The institution of Turkic military slaves would remain an important avenue for the assimilation of Turkic (and other) peoples into Islamic civilization, and, beginning with the Ghaznavids, would yield a substantial number of ruling dynasties from India to Egypt. Ultimately more important for Central Asian history, however, was the large-scale conversion to Islam by Turkic peoples; this was happening along the frontiers of Samanid Central Asia, but the tenth century also saw the establishment of Islam in remoter regions of Turkic Inner Asia, far beyond the limits reached by Muslim armies. During the middle of the tenth century, a member of a Turkic dynasty based in East Turkistan, in the city of Kashghar, adopted Islam, evidently in the course of a power struggle with a rival member of the same dynasty. The narrative of his conversion, which was elaborated and celebrated from at least the eleventh century to the twentieth, identified him as Satuq Bughra Khan. The convert was successful, and the dynasty, which has come to be known as that of the Qarakhanids, soon expanded its territories to the west, moving against the Samanid frontiers in the Syr Darya basin and, with the conquest of Bukhara in 999, effectively putting an end to the Samanid state. In this case, however, religious frontiers had shifted substantially; the Turks from the steppe who conquered sedentary Central Asia were already Muslims, and the ulema of Bukhara are famously reported to have counseled the city's population that they were under no obligation to defend their Samanid rulers, insofar as the Qarakhanids were good Muslims.

The Qarakhanids are of tremendous importance as the initial custodians of the Turkic/Islamic cultural synthesis and sponsors of the first Islamic Turkic literature. Qarakhanid patronage yielded the Turkic *Qutadghu bilig*, a "mirror for princes" completed around 1070 by Yusuf of Balasaghun for a Qarakhanid ruler of Kashghar. The Qarakhanids are also important, however, simply as the holders of power in much of Central Asia, at the regional and local level, for over two centuries. Even as supreme power in Central Asia shifted to the Seljuks or the Qarakhitays or the Khwarazmshahs, local dynasties linked to the Qarakhanid tradition continued to rule in Samarkand, in parts of the Farghana valley, and in towns of the Syr Darya basin. The last known Qarakhanid dynast was removed by the Khwarazmshah Muhammad (target of the Mongol invasion) only in 1209.

Of even greater significance for the Islamic world at large was the third Muslim Turkic dynasty to appear in Central Asia during the Samanid era, that of the Seljuks. The Seljuk royal house emerged, in the latter tenth century, as tribal leaders among the Oghuz Turks who nomadized near the lower course of the Syr Darya, northeast of the Aral Sea. The narrative of Seljuk origins links their adoption of Islam to a power struggle, again with conversion signaling a break with their former overlord as well as an alliance against him with the Muslim people of the Syr Darya town of Jand. By the early eleventh century the Seljuks were involved in the military and political turmoil that accompanied the division of the Samanid realm between the Ghaznavids, in Khurasan, and the Qarakhanids, in Transoxania, and quickly dominated both regions, leaving the Qarakhanid dynasts as vassals but effectively crushing the Ghaznavid presence in Khurasan with their defeat of Mahmud's son and successor, Mas'ud, in 1040 at Dandanqan, near Marv. Thereafter the Seljuks began their phenomenal sweep through Iran and the Middle East, seizing Baghdad by 1055 and defeating the Byzantines in Anatolia in 1071.

Seljuk success in Central Asia itself was less overwhelming than further west. By the first half of the twelfth century, Seljuk dynasts were plagued by the devastating raids, deep into Khurasan, of other groups of Oghuz ("Ghuzz") nomads who did not accept their rule, and the final blow to Seljuk power in the east came in 1141, when the sultan, Sanjar, was defeated in the Qatvan steppe, northeast of Samarkand, by the Qarakhitays. The latter, remnants of the Qitan people who had dominated northern China (as the Liao dynasty) since the early tenth century, had fled westward after their ouster from China in the 1120s and dominated the steppe regions of Central Asia down to the Mongol conquest. The non-Muslim Qarakhitays were for the most part absentee overlords with regard to Transoxania, and most regions remained in the hands of local elites, whether Qarakhanid dynasts or, as in the case of Bukhara, a prominent family of Hanafi jurists known as the Al-e Burhan.

The Qarakhitay defeat of the Seljuks provided an opportunity for expansion by a dynasty of local rulers based in

Khwarazm, whose ancestors had assumed control there in the service of the Seljuks. These Khwarazmshahs, under nominal Qarakhitay suzerainty, extended their power into Khurasan and into the lower Syr Darya valley, and by the beginning of the thirteenth century had become the most powerful rulers in the eastern Islamic world. The ambitions of the Khwarazmshah Muhammad (r. 1200–1218) led him to clash with the Ghurid dynasty based south of the Hindu Kush, with the Abbasid caliph al-Nasir (who was intent on restoring the caliphate's political power), with his Qarakhitay overlords, and finally with the new Inner Asian power, the Mongols under Genghis Khan. Muhammad's disastrous rebuff of the khan's diplomatic and commercial overtures led to the Mongol invasion that, from 1216 to 1223, devastated much of Transoxania and Khurasan and destroyed the Khwarazmian state.

## The Mongol and Timurid Periods, 1220–1500

Mongol rule was established in Central Asia well before the subsequent Mongol campaign of 1256–1258, which destroyed the Abbasid caliphate and brought all of Iran and much of the Middle East under Mongol control. The impact of the Mongol conquest likewise endured much longer in Central Asia than elsewhere in the Muslim world, above all through the political principles established in the thirteenth century and maintained, in one form or another, down to the eighteenth. These principles made sovereignty a prerogative reserved solely for blood descendants of Genghis (Chinggis) Khan. They inaugurated a political tension—between Chinggisids with the theoretical right to rule, and powerful tribal chieftains with direct control over the nomadic military forces crucial to the Chinggisids's power—that would shape Central Asian political history down to the Russian conquest. The descendants of Genghis Khan alone could bear the sovereign title *khan*, and were known by the Turkic term *oghlan* (the "sons," par excellence). In the parts of the Mongol-ruled world that were Islamized, the princes of the blood who did not rise to supreme power (but always remained potential candidates for that role) were more often known by the Muslim term signaling sovereign authority, *sultan*. The tribal chieftains, by contrast, were known by the Turkic term *bek* or what came to be its Arabic equivalent, *emir* (with scions of the tribal elite referred to by the Arabo-Persian hybrid *emir-zada*, that is, "born of an *emir*," typically shortened to *mirza*).

As the Mongol empire split along regional lines in the middle of the thirteenth century, different parts of Central Asia fell to different ruling lineages stemming from the four sons of Genghis Khan. Khwarazm, parts of the lower Syr Darya basin, and much of the Dasht-e Qipchaq came to be regarded as part of the realm (*ulus*) of the descendants of Jochi (the "Golden Horde"), centered in the lower Volga valley, while much of Iran was in the hands of the Ilkhanid realm centered in Azerbaijan, that was ruled by descendants of Genghis Khan's grandson, Hulegu, who had led the campaign of 1256–1258. The heartland of Transoxania, as well as the Tarim basin, parts of Khurasan, and the eastern parts of the Dasht-i Qipchaq, were nominally part of the *ulus* of Genghis's son Chaghatay, though in fact, through much of the second half of the thirteenth century, this region was dominated by Qaydu, a descendant of Genghis's son and first successor Ogodey. Not until the early fourteenth century did the Chaghatayid lineage reassert itself, under the khans Esen Buqa and Kebek. In each of these western successor states of the Mongol empire, the process of Islamization was underway already in the thirteenth century, and by the second quarter of the fourteenth century khans from each of the Chinggisid dynasties ruling there—as well as members of the tribal aristocracy and ordinary nomads—had become Muslims.

By the 1330s, however, the Ilkhanid state was disintegrating, and real power in most of the Chaghatayid *ulus* had reverted to the tribal chieftains, who made and unmade khans to suit their own ends. It was in the western part of the Chaghatayid realm that Timur, an emir of the Barlas tribe based in southern Transoxania, rose to power during the 1360s; within a decade he had succeeded in consolidating his power over Transoxania and Khurasan and had begun the career of conquest that would make him master not only of Central Asia, but of Iran and much of the Middle East as well, culminating with campaigns as far east as Delhi and as far west as Ankara. Following Timur's death in 1405, his descendants were able to maintain control only over his Central Asian domains, in Transoxania, Iran, and Khurasan (where Herat soon emerged as a cosmopolitan center of cultural patronage). The Timurid state in Central Asia fractured soon after the death of Timur's son and successor Shahrukh in 1447, with separate branches of the Timurid lineage holding power in Khurasan and Transoxania.

## The Uzbek Era, 1500–1865

Timur, though not a Chinggisid, clearly sought to evoke the legacy of Genghis Khan's conquests during his lifetime, and his successors likewise cultivated their Inner Asian heritage alongside their patronage of Islamic institutions. Nevertheless, the Timurids were regarded as usurpers by real Chinggisids, and the principal challenges to his rule in Central Asia, and to that of his descendants, came from the nomads of the Dasht-e Qipchaq, ruled by Chinggisids from the lineage of Jochi. By the time of Timur, the Turkic nomads of the eastern half of the Dasht-e Qipchaq, who belonged to what remained of the Jochid *ulus* (i.e., the "Golden Horde"), had come to be known by the designation Uzbek (*ozbek*); the origin of this appellation is obscure, but is ascribed by indigenous tradition to the impact of the adoption of Islam by Ozbek Khan of the Golden Horde (r. 1313–1341).

Timur himself faced invasions into his domains by nomadic armies from the northern steppe led by various Jochid rulers and tribal chieftains. Timur's efforts to secure stability and peace on his northern frontier were continued by his successors; Shahrukh succeeded in securing Khwarazm by 1413, but his son Ulugh Beg's meddling in Jöchid affairs led to his serious defeat by one would-be *khan* near Sighnaq in 1427. Shortly after this event, a young prince from the lineage of Shiban (the fifth son of Jochi), named Abu 'l-Khayr Khan, succeeded, with the aid of the powerful chieftains of the Manghit tribe, in establishing his power over most of the Uzbek tribes of the Dasht-e Qipchaq, and established a confederation strong enough to challenge the Timurids and influence internal Timurid politics.

**The Qalmaqs.** This first Uzbek confederation was shaken by attacks from the Qalmaqs (i.e., the Kalmyks or Oyrats, western Mongols) in the mid-fifteenth century, and collapsed after Abu 'l-Khayr Khan's death (c. 1469), but the founder's grandson, known as Muhammad Shibani Khan, succeeded in reformulating a substantial part of the coalition by the end of the fifteenth century. As internal dissension weakened the Timurid state in Transoxania, Shibani Khan succeeded in conquering Samarkand and Bukhara in 1500, consolidated his hold on Transoxania and seized Khwarazm by 1505. He moved across the Amu Darya to attack the Timurids in Khurasan soon after the death of the last powerful Timurid, Sultan Husayn Bayqara, seizing the Timurid capital, Herat, in 1507. His ambitions were cut short late in 1510 when he was defeated and killed in battle with the Safavid ruler Shah Isma'il near Marv. The Safavid victory led to a virtually total withdrawal of Uzbek forces from Transoxania. Within two years, however, the Uzbeks, led by Muhammad Shibani Khan's nephew 'Ubaydullah and other descendants of Abu 'l-Khayr Khan, had expelled the Safavid forces and their Timurid supporters (including Babur, who would found the Mogul empire of India) from Transoxania. Khurasan became a battleground between the Safavids and the Uzbeks, with Herat changing hands several times during the sixteenth century.

**The Qazaqs.** The Qazaqs with whom Muhammad Shibani Khan fought were of precisely the same ethnic stock as his Uzbek followers; the name *qazaq* ("freebooter") had been applied pejoratively to the components of Abu 'l-Khayr Khan's Uzbek confederation who broke with Abu 'l-Khayr and followed other Chinggisids out of his coalition. The essentially political, rather than ethnic, distinction between Qazaq and Uzbek remained somewhat fluid through the sixteenth century. After their Uzbek kinsmen moved with the Shibanids or other Chinggisids into Transoxania, Khwarazm, and Khurasan, the Qazaqs occupied the Dasht-e Qipchaq, and continued their large-scale, seasonal pastoral nomadic migrations. The Qazaqs too were ruled by Chinggisid sultans, and came to be divided into three loosely affiliated units (*zhüz*) known in the West as "hordes." The middle Syr Darya valley became the focus of frequent wars between the Qazaq

Chinggisids and the Uzbek khans of Transoxania, with towns such as Tashkent, Sayram, and Turkistan held by the Qazaqs through much of the seventeenth century.

**The 'Arabshahids.** In Khwarazm, meanwhile, a separate Chinggisid dynasty supported by Uzbek nomads from the Dasht-e Qipchaq took power following the ouster of the Safavid forces that occupied the region after the defeat of Muhammad Shibani Khan. This dynasty, often referred to as the 'Arabshahids, extended its control to the south, into Khurasan, during the middle of the sixteenth century, and maintained power in Khwarazm to the early eighteenth century. One of its members, Abu 'l-Ghazi Khan (r. 1643–1663), is known for his harsh measures against the Turkmen nomads inhabiting the frontiers of the Khwarazmian oasis, for his reorganization of the Uzbek tribes of Khwarazm, and for the two historical works he wrote in Chaghatay Turkic.

The polity in Transoxania and, later, in parts of Khurasan that was reformulated by the kinsmen of Muhammad Shibani Khan following the defeat at Marv, was not a centralized state, much less an empire, but rather a collection of loosely linked appanages assigned to Chinggisid princes who took part in the conquest. There were thus separate and essentially co-equal Chinggisid sultans based in Samarkand, Bukhara, Tashkent, Balkh, and other appanages, with the senior member of the extended ruling clan recognized as khan. The equilibrium that maintained this decentralized system broke down in the 1550s, and gave way to bitter struggles among the princes that culminated in the gradual, and bloody, consolidation of power by 'Abdallah Khan. The latter's success in eliminating rivals meant that when his son was murdered shortly after 'Abdallah's own death in 1598, the tribal chieftains and urban elites of Transoxania were compelled to seek a Chinggisid khan from an altogether different Jochid lineage, one that had recently been dislodged from its hereditary realm along the lower Volga by the Russian conquest of the commercial emporium of Astrakhan. This dynasty, known variously as that of the Janids, the Ashtarkhanids, or the Toqay Timurids ruled Transoxania and Balkh until 1747.

Despite the stability seemingly implied by the long reigns of Ashtarkhanid rulers such as Imam Quli Khan (r. 1611–1642), 'Abd al-'Aziz Khan (r. 1645–1681), Subhan Quli Khan (r. 1681–1702), and Abu 'l-Fayz Khan (r. 1711–1747), this era saw the steady erosion of the khans's authority in favor of powerful tribal chieftains, and the steady diminution of the state itself. By the beginning of the eighteenth century, the power of the Chinggisid khans had been seriously weakened both in Khwarazm and in Transoxania, to the benefit of the tribal aristocracy, and political instability was exacerbated by economic dislocation and external military threats. In particular, the renewed success of the Mongol Junghars (Oyrats) in the Dasht-e Qipchaq sent waves of Qazaq refugees into Transoxania in the 1720s, devastating the region's agricultural base and prompting in turn the flight of much of the sedentary population there into the Farghana valley and other areas. The Junghar threat also induced some Qazaq Chinggisids to seek protection from the Russian empire, and the formal submission of these khans later served as a pretext for the extension of Russian control over the Qazaq steppes.

**The Afghan Turkmen.** The political and military weakness of Central Asia was further underscored by the invasion of Nader Shah, the warlord of the Afshar tribe of Turkmens who seized power in Iran in 1728, driving out the Afghans who had put an end to the Safavid dynasty six years earlier. His conquest of Bukhara and Khwarazm in 1740 helped launch the final stage in the transition to the new dynasties of Uzbek tribal origin that would rule much of Central Asia into the second half of the nineteenth century. In Bukhara, a chieftain of the Manghit tribe who had formerly served the weak Ashtarkhanid ruler Abu ʾl-Fayz Khan had the latter ruler deposed and killed soon after Nader Shah's assassination in 1747. In Khwarazm, Nader Shah's conquest led to an extended period of profound disorder, culminating in the occupation of the capital, Khiva, by the Yomut tribe of Turkmens in 1768. In this case it was a chieftain of the Qonghrat tribe, who likewise had filled important state positions under the Chinggisid khans there, who succeeded in driving out the Yomuts and restoring order. The Manghit and Qonghrat dynasties thus established ruled Bukhara and Khiva, respectively, even after the Russian conquest, surviving as protectorates of the Russian state until 1920.

Nader Shah's career also set the stage for the emergence of Ahmad Shah Durrani (r. 1747–1773), the Afghan warlord who was able to seize the regions of Balkh and Herat to add to his base in Qandahar and Kabul, and thereby forged the basis for modern Afghanistan; the Manghits of Bukhara continued to contest the loss of Balkh, however, and permanent Afghan control of the region that became known as "Afghan Turkistan" was not secured until the middle of the nineteenth century.

**The Khanate of Qoqand.** In the Farghana valley, finally, another Uzbek tribal dynasty took shape in the first half of the eighteenth century, as chieftains of the Ming tribe made the town of Qoqand (or Khuqand) their base and extended their control throughout the valley; this region proved to be the most economically dynamic area of Central Asia during the eighteenth and nineteenth centuries, and the Ming dynasty was able to exploit the valley's agricultural and commercial wealth to build a state that became the most powerful in Central Asia during the first half of the nineteenth century. Under ʿAlim Khan (r. 1798–1809) and his brother ʿUmar Khan (r. 1809–1822), the khanate of Qoqand expanded to the north, seizing Tashkent and the towns of the middle Syr Darya; further Qoqandian expansion into the Dasht-i Qipchaq brought both Qazaq and Qirghiz nomads under the khanate's control, and led inevitably to a confrontation with the Russian empire, which was expanding into the same regions from the north.

The khans of Qoqand were also closely involved in affairs of East Turkistan, where political structures had developed quite differently from those of western Central Asia in the Uzbek era. There, dynasts of the lineage of Chaghatay had withstood challenges from both the Timurids and the Uzbek Chinggisids to the west, and from the Mongol Junghars to the north, down to the late seventeenth century. Shifting political alignments involving rival branches of a family of Naqshbandi *khwaja*s (descendants and Sufi successors of a sixteenth-century shaykh of Transoxania known as Makhdum-e Aʿzam), which had been established in the region from the late sixteenth century, contributed to the conquest of the region by the Junghars in 1681, putting an end to the Chaghatayid dynasty. The Junghars installed Afaq Khwaja (d. 1694), leader of the Aqtaghliq ("White Mountain") *khwaja* faction, as their governor in Kashghar. Struggles between the *khwaja* factions continued after his death, leading the Junghars first to deport the leaders of both factions, and later to switch their support to the rival Qarataghliq ("Black Mountain") faction.

**The Manchus.** By the middle of the eighteenth century, however, *khwaja* contenders were seeking support against the Junghars through the growing power of the Manchu empire (the Qing dynasty of China). The climactic struggle between the Manchus and the Junghars for domination of the Inner Asian heartland culminated in the total destruction of the Junghar state in 1758. The *khwaja* state too was destroyed, as the Manchus incorporated both the Tarim basin and the Junghar homeland into their empire (it would become known as the "New Province," Xinjiang, of China), but the *khwaja* lineages continued to stir up rebellions among the Muslims of the region, with the active support, beginning in the 1820s, of the khans of Qoqand based in the Farghana valley. A major uprising of Chinese Muslims from 1862 to 1876 kept the Qing dynasty occupied as the Qoqandian adventurer Yaʿqub Bek carved out his own state, with the support of an Aqtaghliq *khwaja* based in Kashghar. The suppression of the revolt led to the Qing reconquest of the Tarim basin by 1878. The Turkic Muslim population of East Turkistan was able to reassert its independence sporadically following the collapse of the Manchu dynasty in 1911, with several attempts to create an East Turkistan Republic during the 1930s and 1940s. The Chinese communist victory in 1949 led to the region's incorporation into the People's Republic of China as the Xinjiang Uyghur Autonomous Region. The PRC's colonization policy brought a massive influx of Han Chinese that has reduced the Muslim component to approximately 60 percent of the region's population.

**The Russian Conquest and the Soviet Era, 1865–1991**
During the late eighteenth century and the first half of the nineteenth, the rulers of the Uzbek tribal dynasties in the three khanates of western Central Asia—Bukhara, Khiva, and Qoqand—were succeeding where the Chinggisid khans had long failed: They crushed the power of the tribal chieftains,

instituted military reforms that lessened their dependence on the tribal forces, created a more centralized bureaucratic apparatus for state administration, and concentrated far more power in their own hands than any Chinggisid khan had held for centuries. Despite this period of relative revitalization, however, the three Central Asian khanates were hopelessly outmatched militarily by the expanding Russian empire.

Russian commercial ties with Central Asia had developed extensively from the latter sixteenth century, as the conquest of the last successor states of the Golden Horde opened Siberia to Russian conquest. By the latter eighteenth century, Russian encroachment from the Volga-Ural valley and Siberia had reduced the Qazaqs to vassal status. The suppression of Qazaq revolts in the 1830s and 1840s brought Russian forces into the Syr Darya valley, where they attacked Qoqandian outposts already in the 1850s.

The outright military conquest of southern Central Asia followed the freeing of Russian military resources by the end of the Crimean War, and by the suppression of Muslim resistance in the North Caucasus. Russian troops moved against the towns of the middle Syr Darya valley in 1864, and seized Tashkent in 1865. Operations southwest of Tashkent brought confrontations with Bukharan troops, culminating in the Russian capture of Samarkand in 1868 and the establishment of a Russian protectorate over the khanate of Bukhara. A Russian force marched on Khiva in 1873 and forced a similar arrangement on the Qonghrat khan. Further defeats of Qoqandian forces brought the submission of that khanate as well, but repeated revolts and social unrest in the Farghana valley led Russian officials to dissolve the khanate of Qoqand in 1876 and bring its territories under direct Russian rule. The Turkmen nomads to the south of Khwarazm put up a stiffer resistance, surrendering to Russian control only after a massacre of Turkmen men, women, and children at Gok Tepe, near modern-day Ashgabat, in 1881. By 1895, negotiations between the Russian and British empires had defined the southern border of the Russian holdings in Central Asia, corresponding to the present-day borders of the Central Asian republics with Iran and Afghanistan.

Russian rule at first brought few changes to the daily lives of Central Asian Muslims, but growing contacts between Russians and Central Asians, as well as economic changes brought on by increased trade with Russia, led to the emergence of small native circles intent upon revitalizing local society through educational and cultural changes. Following the 1905 revolution in Russia, these groups—known as *jadidists*, a term applied to reformist Muslims throughout the Russian empire—became increasingly concerned with political issues, and it was from among them that the Russian Bolsheviks would find their first allies among the native population following the revolutions of 1917. These reformist circles were important for launching the reevaluation of communal

identities and mores that would create the modern Soviet nations of Central Asia. The Bolshevik victory in the Civil War was followed, in Central Asia, by an administrative reorganization that reflected both practical concerns and Lenin's rhetoric about national self-determination. This "national delimitation" drew borders for the new people's republics, in part on the basis of older administrative units, but in part on the basis of ethnographic and linguistic surveys conducted by scholars and officials using a somewhat arbitrarily chosen set of ethnic and national designations. The basic work was done by 1924; changes in the hierarchical status of the units thus created, within the system of union republics, autonomous republics, and autonomous regions that comprised the ethnically defined structures of the USSR, continued until 1936, leaving five union republics—the Kazakh, Uzbek, Kirgiz, Tadzhik, and Turkmen republics (using the Russianized names that were official through the Soviet period)—in western Central Asia.

Soviet policy demanded the strict subordination of national identities to the construction of socialist society. However, from the mid-1960s to the mid-1980s local elites were able to develop considerable autonomy in republican affairs, and, within limits, to give expression to Sovietized national cultures. In the 1980s Soviet reformers sought to rein in the entrenched national bureaucracies, citing corruption and abuses of power in the republics. Increasingly vocal nationalist movements demanded the assertion of cultural and political rights, culminating in declarations of sovereignty by all of the Central Asian republics. With the failed coup attempt of August 1991 and the dissolution of the USSR later that year, each of the republics declared independence. By that time, however, the local communist elites had co-opted the nationalist movements and ensured their hold on power, now as nationalists rather than communists. The 1990s saw, in all the Central Asian republics, a rollback of political rights asserted during the last years of the Soviet regime, the often brutal stifling of political dissent, and the total monopolization of power by the former republican communist parties, now appropriately renamed. At the same time, the republican elites appeared to be committed to the enterprise of nation-building, understanding their power to be rooted in existing political structures rather than in any revolutionary transformation of the prevailing conceptions of communal identity, which those structures served to reify.

*See also* **Central Asian Culture and Islam; Communism; Reform: Muslim Communities of the Russian Empire.**

## BIBLIOGRAPHY

Bacon, Elizabeth. *Central Asians under Russian Rule: A Study in Culture Change.* Ithaca, N.Y.: Cornell University Press, 1966.

Barthold, V. V. *Four Studies on the History of Central Asia.* Translated by V. Minorsky and T. Minorsky. Leiden: E. J. Brill, 1962.

Barthold, V. V. *Turkestan Down to the Mongol Invasion,* 4th ed. Translated by V. Minorsky and T. Minorsky. Edited by C. E. Bosworth. London: Luzac & Co., 1977.

Becker, Seymour. *Russia's Protectorates in Central Asia: Bukhara and Khiva, 1865–1924.* Cambridge, Mass.: Harvard University Press, 1968.

Beckwith, Christopher I. *The Tibetan Empire in Central Asia: A History of the Struggle for Great Power among Tibetans, Turks, Arabs, and Chinese during the Early Middle Ages.* Princeton, N.J.: Princeton University Press, 1987.

Biran, Michal. *Qaidu and the Rise of the Independent Mongol State in Central Asia.* Richmond, Surrey, U.K.: Curzon Press, 1997.

Bosworth, C. E. *The Ghaznavids: Their Empire in Afghanistan and Eastern Iran 994–1040.* Edinburgh: Edinburgh University Press, 1963.

Bregel, Yuri. "Tribal Tradition and Dynastic History: The Early Rulers of the Qongrats according to Munis." *Asian and African Studies* 16 (1982): 357–398.

Bregel, Yuri. *An Historical Atlas of Central Asia.* Leiden: Brill, 2003.

Burton, Audrey. *The Bukharans: A Dynastic, Diplomatic and Commercial History, 1550–1702.* New York: St. Martin's Press, 1997.

Daniel, Elton L. *The Political and Social History of Khurasan under Abbasid Rule 747–820.* Minneapolis and Chicago: Bibliotheca Islamica, 1979.

Fletcher, Joseph. "The Naqshbandiyya in Northwest China." In *Studies on Chinese and Islamic Inner Asia.* Edited by Beatrice Forbes Manz. Aldershot, Hampshire, U.K.: Variorum, 1995.

Forbes, Andrew D. W. *Warlords and Muslims in Chinese Central Asia: A Political History of Republican Sinkiang 1911–1949.* Cambridge, U.K.: Cambridge University Press, 1986.

Frye, Richard N. *Bukhara: The Medieval Achievement* (1965). Costa Mesa, Calif.: Mazda Publishers, 1997.

Golden, Peter B. "The Karakhanids and Early Islam." In *The Cambridge History of Early Inner Asia.* Edited by Denis Sinor. Cambridge, U.K.: Cambridge University Press, 1990.

Golden, Peter B. *An Introduction to the History of the Turkic Peoples: Ethnogenesis and State-Formation in Medieval and Early Modern Eurasia and the Middle East.* Wiesbaden: Otto Harrassowitz, 1992.

Holdsworth, M. *Turkestan in the Nineteenth Century: A Brief History of the Khanates of Bukhara, Kokand and Khiva.* London: Central Asian Research Centre, 1959.

Manz, Beatrice Forbes. *The Rise and Rule of Tamerlane.* Cambridge, U.K.: Cambridge University Press, 1989.

McChesney, Robert D. *Waqf in Central Asia: Four Hundred Years in the History of a Muslim Shrine, 1480–1889.* Princeton, N.J.: Princeton University Press, 1991.

McChesney, Robert D. *Central Asia: Foundations of Change.* Princeton, N.J.: Darwin Press, 1996.

Pierce, Richard A. *Russian Central Asia, 1867–1917: A Study in Colonial Rule.* Berkeley and Los Angeles: University of California Press, 1960.

Saray, Mehmet. "The Russian Conquest of Central Asia." *Central Asian Survey* 1 (1982): 1–30.

*Devin DeWeese*

# CENTRAL ASIAN CULTURE AND ISLAM

Central Asia played a pivotal role in the early debates about what it meant to be a Muslim, as the early practical experience of negotiating relations with the local population on the Central Asian frontiers left its mark in the developing consensus about the conditions for membership in the Muslim community, and for enjoyment of the privileges it entailed.

## Islamization in Central Asia

Already in the eighth century there were signs of the dominance of the inclusive approach toward membership in the Islamic community that would prevail throughout the history of Islamic Central Asia. Local resentment grew over the unequal treatment often accorded new converts by Umayyad governors who, in response to declining revenues, toughened requirements for conversion and even rescinded the remission of the *jizya*, the poll tax on non-Muslims, promised to prospective converts. This helped turn the region into the staging ground for the Abbasid revolution. In doctrinal terms it lent support to the view that formal affirmation of faith and of affiliation with the Muslim community was sufficient to be regarded as a member of the *umma* in good standing, even if the people thus brought into the fold were not proficient in practice or clear on details of doctrine. This principle, articulated in the movement of the Murji'a that gained wide support in Khurasan and Transoxania (Mawarannahr), was later enshrined in Hanafi juridical thought, which dominated Central Asian life from the ninth century to the twentieth century. It thereby shaped the process of Islamization in Central Asia, not only among the sedentary rural and urban population, but along the steppe frontiers as well, where the process of conversion appears to have begun in many cases with the establishment of social bonds between Muslim townspeople and nearby Turkic nomadic communities. This gave the latter a formal affiliation with the *umma*, with details of practice and belief to be worked out later.

There was considerable religious diversity in Central Asia at the time of the Arab conquest, and it persisted in later times. Manichean communities were active in Samarkand until the tenth century, Christian groups can be traced into the fourteenth century, and Buddhism was not supplanted from the northeastern part of the Tarim basin until the fifteenth century. Despite the frequent setbacks to Islamization in Central Asia, the region became quite early on a major center of Islamic learning, literature, and art.

## Cultural Patronage and Religious Scholarship

The full flowering of Islamic science and literature, in Persian and Arabic, came in the tenth century under Samanid patronage. The Samanid court at Bukhara sponsored the Persian poets Rudaki and Daqiqi, and the compilation of the *Shahname* (Book of kings) by Firdawsi (who later enjoyed Ghaznavid patronage as well); Arabic poetry was also cultivated, as were translations from Arabic and other languages into Persian. The Samanids also patronized scientific endeavors, building on traditions that had produced pivotal works instrumental in the development of astronomy and mathematics in the Islamic world at large, and later in western Europe as well. Whereas in the ninth century scholars of Central Asian origin, such as Muhammad b. Musa al-Khwarazmi, Abu Ma'shar al-Balkhi, and Abu 'Abbas Ahmad al-Farghani, were drawn west to Baghdad, Samanid patronage kept these figures' successors at home, so to speak, and made tenth-century Bukhara the scene of a remarkable intellectual synthesis marked especially by scholars of encyclopedic breadth. The compendium of all branches of scholarship known as the *Mafatih al-'ulum* was produced for the Bukharan court by Abu 'Abdallah Muhammad al-Khwarazmi, and an important tradition of geographical study was sponsored by Samanid officials. The encyclopedic tradition shaped the work of the remarkable Khwarazmian al-Biruni (d. 1048), who distinguished himself in the natural sciences as well as in history and geography, and who later served the Ghaznavid sultans Mahmud and Mas'ud as well. The illustrious polymath Ibn Sina (d. 1037), especially renowned in medicine and philosophy, spent his formative years in Samanid Bukhara.

Perhaps the most important contribution of pre-Mongol Central Asia to the religious culture of the larger Islamic world, however, lies in scholarship on hadith and in the juridical sciences and theology. Already in the ninth century, under the Tahirids, Central Asia produced several of the compilers of the major collections of hadiths regarded as authoritative throughout the Muslim world, above all the two pivotal traditionists, Muhammad b. Isma'il al-Bukhari (d. 870), who lived much of his life near Samarkand, and Muslim b. Hajjaj of Nishapur (Ar. Nisabur) (d. 875). The growth and development of the Hanafi school of jurisprudence, which came to dominate interpretation and application of the *shari'a* in much of the Ottoman-ruled world and in the Indian subcontinent, was largely the work of Central Asian scholars. Central Asia has been predominantly Hanafi in its juridical orientation throughout the Islamic period. There was a limited, but important, Shafi'i presence in some areas. The region of Tashkent became a bastion of the Shafi'i school (and produced the noted tenth-century jurist Abu Bakr Qaffal al-Shashi), as did the town of Taraz, while parts of Khwarazm were predominantly Shafi'i until well after the Mongol conquest. Already before the Samanid era, however, the supremacy of the Hanafi school in Bukhara, and in the rest of Transoxania, was credited to the imam Abu Hafs al-Bukhari (d. 877), and from the tenth century to the fourteenth, Transoxania was by far the most productive region of the Muslim world in terms of the scholars and books that would define the Hanafi tradition.

The Samanid era saw the formulation of the theological school associated with the name of Abu Mansur Muhammad al-Maturidi (d. c. 944) of Samarkand. His theological elaborations, on a Hanafi foundation, defined the lines of religious thought that dominated the eastern Islamic world for centuries and, with the active support of Seljuk patronage, became firmly established in the Middle East beginning in the twelfth and thirteenth centuries. It was the era of Seljuk patronage, indeed, that produced many of the great classics of Hanafi jurisprudence in Transoxania. The central works include the *Usul* of Fakhr al-Islam 'Ali b. Muhammad al-Pazdawi (d. 1089), the *Mabsut* and *Usul al-fiqh* of Muhammad b. Ahmad al-Sarakhsi (d. c. 1096), known as "Shams al-A'imma," and the *Hidaya* of Burhan al-Din 'Ali al-Marghinani (d. 1197). The activities of Hanafi jurists extended to juridical and civil administration as well, and hereditary transmission of the estates and power they were able to amass was common. The most famous case is the family known as the Al-e Burhan in Bukhara, whose members were recognized as the chief civil authorities in the city even by the non-Muslim Qarakhitays.

The Mongol conquest naturally meant a setback for the institutional foundations of Islamic religious culture, and for state involvement in the application and interpretation of the *shari'a*, but its impact on religious life was not as far-reaching as is often supposed. If the transmission of juridical traditions in Central Asia is considered there is little evidence of any substantial discontinuity coinciding with the establishment of Mongol rule. With the conversion of the Mongol elites to Islam, patronage of Islamic scholarship, literature, art, and architecture expanded. During the fourteenth century a number of important Turkic religious works were produced and dedicated to khans and tribal chieftains of the Jochid and Chaghatayid realms. Timur patronized religious scholars as well as artisans and poets, often bringing prominent figures from the regions he conquered back to his capital in Samarkand, and scholars such as Sa'd al-Din Taftazani (d. 1390) and 'Ali Jurjani (d. 1413) thus worked for a time in Transoxania; on the other hand, some jurists found the cultivation of the Mongol heritage under Timur and his successors abhorrent and quit the Timurid realm for the Ottoman state or other parts of the Muslim world. By the Timurid era, in any case, the Hanafi school's dominance in Central Asia had become a virtual monopoly. Hanafi juridical scholarship continued in Transoxania into the twentieth century, until the closure of all *madrasas* by the Soviets in the late 1920s. Early in the Uzbek period, patronage of the religious sciences took on a new political importance in light of the emergence of the Shi'ite state of Safavid Iran. The ulema of Transoxania supported the Uzbek rulers by declaring the Qizilbash to be the equivalent of infidels, thereby justifying the constant raiding and open warfare in Khurasan through the sixteenth and seventeenth centuries. The religious frontier thus established was rarely an insurmountable obstacle to commerce or intellectual exchange, but nevertheless set the further development of religious culture in Central Asia apart from its traditional connections to Iran.

## Sufism in Central Asia

The most important religious development of the post-Mongol era was the rise of Sufi communities organized according to the principle of the *silsila* or chain of spiritual transmission, and their emergence as important factors in political and economic history. The history of Sufism (*tasawwuf*) in Central Asia down to the Mongol conquest remains poorly studied, but it appears that by the tenth century a number of originally independent mystical currents, some with local roots and some imported from outside Central Asia, had coalesced under the designation of *tasawwuf*. In the eleventh and twelfth centuries major new patterns of Sufi activity and organization appear with the career of Abu Sa'id b. Abil-Khayr (d. 1049) of Mayhana, in present-day Turkmenistan, who cultivated a high public profile in Ghaznavid Nishapur, and with the hereditary Sufi tradition of Ahmad-e Jam (d. 1141), whose natural descendants remained prominent well into the Uzbek era.

The Mongol and Timurid periods saw the crystallization of Sufi traditions that would dominate religious life in Central Asia down to the nineteenth century, in the form of organized orders that emerged around *silsila*s traced back to the prophet Muhammad through prominent saints of the thirteenth century. One was the Kubravi tradition, whose eponym, Najm al-Din Kubra, died in 1221 during the Mongol attack on his native Khwarazm. Another was the Yasavi tradition, named for Khwaja Ahmad Yasavi, whose center of activity was the middle Syr Darya valley. The Khwajagani tradition emerged in the thirteenth century as well, among the disciples of Khwaja 'Abd al-Khaliq Ghijduvani, from a town near Bukhara. This tradition produced a lineage that became known as the Naqshbandiyya, after Baha' al-Din Naqshband of Bukhara (d. 1389). Representatives of these and other traditions were engaged in vigorous competition with one another, for court patronage and for popular support, in the context of the political and social turmoil of Transoxania and Khurasan in the fourteenth century. As part

of that competition, many groups appear to have experimented with different ways of legitimizing the authority and efficacy of their specific ritual and devotional practices and their claims of spiritual preeminence, appealing to visionary sanctions of various sorts, hereditary transmission, demonstrated spiritual results, and other signs in addition to the *silsila*, which would become the normative mode of legitimation by the latter fifteenth century. Some of these Sufi communities, moreover, were actively engaged in Islamization, not in the sense of changing the beliefs of the Turkic nomads who became based in southern Central Asia through the Mongol invasion (though this may have happened as well), but in the sense of forging social and economic bonds with nomadic communities that were undergoing the profound dislocations of the Mongol era (i.e., tribal reorganization and adaptation to the enclosed nomadism of Transoxania and Khurasan).

By the late fifteenth century, the Naqshbandiyya was emerging as the dominant Sufi tradition of Central Asia, largely through the efforts of Khwaja 'Ubaydullah Ahrar, a native of Tashkent who spent much of his life in Timurid Samarkand, and who exemplified the political engagement and the cultivation of economic power that became the hallmark of the Naqshbandi order. At the same time, the Naqshbandiyya was beginning its expansion beyond Central Asia, into the Ottoman Empire and the Indian subcontinent. The decentralized polity of the early Uzbek era favored intensified competition among representatives of the Naqshbandi, Yasavi, and Kubravi orders, but Naqshbandi dominance was assured by the second half of the sixteenth century. From then until the early eighteenth century, the Naqshbandiyya was a truly pervasive influence in all aspects of Central Asian political, economic, and cultural life.

The eighteenth century saw important changes in religious life, beginning with the introduction of the Mujaddidi (renewal) current of the Naqshbandi order, which had taken shape in seventeenth-century India, into Central Asia. The Mujaddidiyya offered an alternative source of legitimation for rulers seeking to counter the limitations on their power imposed by entrenched urban and tribal elites, and several Mujaddidi shaykhs were closely allied with khans of the Manghit and Ming dynasties in promoting religious "reform" in a way that undermined traditional Sufi groups and the popular practices associated with them. The late eighteenth and nineteenth centuries saw several reform efforts of this type, which entailed the condemnation of many long-established religious practices that had diffused from Sufi circles into the larger society as un-Islamic innovations. Local Sufi traditions survived, however, as did the local customs fought by the reformers, and the real blow to Central Asia's legacy of Sufism came only with the Soviet era.

## Pilgrimage and Shrine Culture

One of the most characteristic features of Islamic religious practice in Central Asia, and one that linked the lower classes with the religious and social elites, was the widespread phenomenon of pilgrimage (*ziyarat*) to saints's shrines (*mazars*). This phenomenon was closely linked, but never entirely coterminous, with the spread of Sufism. Shrine-centered religious practice is evidenced already in the tenth century, and by the twelfth century there is extensive information on the large numbers of shrines in Khurasan in the hagiographies focused on the life of Abu Sa'id b. Abu 'l-Khayr. From the same century dates the incident of the discovery of the reputed grave of 'Ali near Balkh, under the Seljuks, suggesting already the political ramifications of cultivating shrine traditions, as well as the compilation of the earliest guide to holy places in Central Asia, entitled *Lata'if al-azkar*, by a member of the Al-e Burhan of Bukhara. By the Mongol era, shrine culture was well entrenched, and appears to have played some role in the acculturation of the Mongol elites and ordinary nomads to the Muslim environment. Ibn Battuta reported that even pagan Mongols brought offerings to the shrine of Qutham b. 'Abbas, the famous martyred *Shah-e zinda* in Samarkand, and there is some evidence of shrines serving as portals, in effect, for passage from the world of Mongol administrative service to the devotional and contemplative life of Sufism. In the fifteenth century, a shrine guide for Bukhara included a defense of the practice of *ziyarat*, but the legitimacy and efficacy of pilgrimage to saints's shrines were taken for granted through most of Central Asian history. The reform efforts of the early nineteenth century targeted some practices associated with shrines, and the Soviets directed intense, and destructive, antireligious measures against them, but in neither case were there permanent inroads into the public consciousness of shrines and their many roles. The collapse of Soviet antireligious efforts in the late 1980s led to a remarkable revival of *ziyarat*, including the reconstruction of numerous shrines as well as the "rediscovery," by quite traditional methods (not unlike those that revealed 'Ali's burial place in the twelfth century), of long-forgotten sites.

The centrality of shrine-centered religious practice in the daily lives, and in connection with the most pressing human needs, of the majority of Central Asian Muslims is a major, and visible, part of the complex of normative religious customs that characterized traditional life in Islamic Central Asia. Other elements of this complex are more difficult to trace in literary sources from earlier centuries, but it seems clear that, during the Uzbek period at least, religious trends that were evident already in the Mongol and Timurid eras were solidified and became the standard features of traditional Islamic life down to the social and religious upheavals launched by the Soviet regime in Central Asia during the late 1920s. Some of these elements include the continuation of madrasa-based juridical education in such cities as Bukhara, which continued to attract students from among Muslim communities in the Russian empire as well as from India and

Afghanistan; the expansion of Muslim education and literacy into the nomadic regions, especially among the Qazaqs; the incorporation of shrines and sacred lineages into the religious practice, social structure, and epic traditions of the nomads; the prominence of hereditary religious and social prestige in families linked to eminent local jurists and, especially, Sufi saints of the past; the permeation of kinship structures and communal life by elements of Sufi practice and thought; and the expansion of religiously defined and regulated occupational organizations in urban and rural environments, integrating the basic elements of craft production into a spiritual worldview that infused labor and its fruits with sacrality and religious meaning.

*See also* **Central Asia, Islam in; Maturidi, al-; Pilgrimage: Ziyara; Tasawwuf.**

## BIBLIOGRAPHY

Basilov, V. N. "Honour Groups in Traditional Turkmenian Society." In *Islam in Tribal Societies: From the Atlas to the Indus*. Edited by Akbar S. Ahmed and David M. Hart. London: Routledge & Kegan Paul, 1984.

Bulliet, Richard W. *The Patricians of Nishapur: A Study in Medieval Islamic Social History*. Cambridge, Mass.: Harvard University Press, 1972.

Gross, J-Ann, and Urunbaev, Asom. *The Letters of Khwaja 'Ubayd Allāh Ahrar and His Associates*. Leiden: Brill, 2002.

Madelung, Wilferd. "The Spread of Maturidism and the Turks." In *Actas do IV Congresso des Estudos Arabes et Islâmicos, Coimbra-Lisboa*. Leiden: Brill, 1971.

Malamud, Margaret. "Sufi Organizations and Structures of Authority in Medieval Nishapur." *International Journal of Middle East Studies* 26 (1994): 427–442.

Sviri, Sara. "Hakim Tirmidhi and the Malmati Movement in Early Sufism." In *Classical Persian Sufism: From its Origins to Rumi*. Edited by Leonard Lewisohn. London and New York: Khaniqahi Nimatullahi Publications, 1993.

*Devin DeWeese*

## CHILDHOOD

Childhood in Islam, like childhood in any great religious tradition, is seen generally as a period of education and training, a time of socialization for the future adult. The child is seen as the crucial generational link in both the religious community and the family unit, the key to its continuation, the living person that ties the present to the past. The idea of childhood, the place of the child, the duties of the child are basic issues and have been since the beginning of Islam. Childhood ends in a formal sense at the age of puberty, when performance of the religious duties (Five Pillars) marks the ritual passage into the early stages of adulthood.

Socialization of the child takes place primarily within the family unit, the home, and the father and mother are ultimately responsible for their offspring. However, grandparents, aunts, uncles, and cousins are also expected to participate in a child's rearing and usually did so in the past. Religious socialization also takes place in the home (for boys and girls) and in the mosque (for boys) but also in the Qur'anic school or *kuttab* (for boys and girls). A knowledge of the Qur'an is deemed necessary for a child's religious development, and most parents, even the poorest, try to send their sons and daughters to the *kuttab*.

Socialization for values of the society begins even earlier, as soon as a child is conscious of others. These values vary somewhat according to geographical, historic, and economic differences within Muslim communities but in general they are designed to develop *'aql* or reason in the child and to make the child *mu'addab*, one who is polite and disciplined. In the Arab world, a child is taught respect for food, for religion, for the kin group, hospitality to guests, and, above all, respect for and obedience to the authority of the father.

Most Muslim societies might be classified as patrilineal (the exception being parts of Southeast Asia, in which a matrilineal descent is observed). In the reckoning of one's descent in patrilineal societies, one's kin-group membership passes through the male line on the father's side. This means that all children retain their father's name throughout their lives, but a daughter, unlike a son, cannot pass membership on to her children. Male and female descendants inherit from the father, according to the specifics of Islamic legal codes. This hierarchical organization means that the oldest male, father or son, holds authority over his descendants, but is also the primary economic provider for the group, and thus controller of the group's economic resources. In exchange, the male head of household is expected not only to provide for but to protect the group, including sons and daughters, throughout their lives.

The period of childhood socialization is marked by ritual events, both religious and secular: ceremonies surrounding birth and naming; circumcision, for all boys and some girls; graduation from Qur'anic school, particularly for boys; and finally marriage. Marriage is the crucial step in tying individual members to the group, and the birth of children confers on the newly united pair full membership in the family unit and in Islam. "When a man has children he has fulfilled half his religion, so let him fear God for the remaining half," states one of the hadiths of the prophet Muhammad.

Further, throughout childhood, there is strong socialization for future roles in the family and the Muslim community; from a very early age, children are given responsibilities. Girls are expected to help in the home and care for siblings; boys may be asked to help in family business or on their father's farm. This traditional picture, in practice, is changing, as people in the Muslim world become more mobile, and as the family group becomes more attenuated. The father is still seen as head of household, but the mother frequently shares economic responsibilities by working outside the home, and this places stress on family expectations for both sons and daughters. Free public education has supplemented, but not replaced, Qur'anic education for all children.

Still, the basic approach to childhood as a time of learning rather than as a carefree time for play remains. To become a full member of the Islamic community, a child is expected to learn the Qur'an, respect parents, and gradually assume responsibilities within the family and the religious community, so that the untutored child becomes the disciplined Muslim adult.

*See also* **Circumcision; Education; Gender; Marriage.**

## BIBLIOGRAPHY

Ghazzali, Muhammad ibn Muhammad Abi Hamid al-. *Ayyuha al-Walad*. Cairo: Dar al-I'tisam, 1983.

Warnock Fernea, Elizabeth, ed. *Children in the Muslim Middle East*. Austin: University of Texas Press, 1995.

*Elizabeth Warnock Fernea*

## CHINA *See* **East Asia, Islam in**

## CHRISTIANITY AND ISLAM

The history of Christian-Muslim or alternatively Muslim-Christian relations began at the inception of Islam in the first half of the sixth century of the Common Era. As Islam began to spread beyond the Arabian Peninsula soon after the death of the prophet Muhammad in 632 C.E., the encounter between Muslims and Christians entered a new phase of military, political, and social interactions. A century later, while these kinds of interaction continued along the already far-flung borders of the new Islamic empire spreading from Spain to the Indus river, new patterns emerged within both majority Christian and majority Muslim polities. They reflected the weight of different theological and political contexts on daily social life, leading to a variety of mostly polemical and apologetic stances that Christians and Muslims developed regarding each other. This religious and political mix came to a head during the period of the major Crusades (twelfth to thirteenth centuries C.E.), creating the subsequent dominant paradigm in Christian-Muslim relations, the repercussions of which are still felt to this day, and especially since the creation of the State of Israel in 1948. But not all historical periods or geographical locations were the same; pockets of mutually beneficial encounters existed here and there on both sides of the transient political borders. Moreover, the history of Christian-Muslim relations has not unfolded in isolation from other religious and, more recently, nonreligious worldviews.

### The Period of the Prophet Muhammad's Life: Circa 570–632 C.E.

The history of the prophet Muhammad's life is difficult to ascertain with precision. Through a careful examination of pre-Islamic poems, the Qur'an, early hadith, and biographies, all of which have entailed in the past century serious debates as to their validity as historical sources, it is nevertheless possible to suggest a likely course of events in this first period of Muslim-Christian encounters. Prior to 610 C.E., the year when the prophet Muhammad received the first Qur'anic revelation, his encounters with Christians probably took place during his caravan trips into greater Syria, as the tradition of his meeting with the Christian monk Bahira would indicate. There may also have been occasional encounters with Christians of unknown theological leanings passing through Mecca. The biography of the prophet Muhammad mentions other kinds of encounters, not all of which are historically verifiable. For instance, soon after 610 C.E., the Prophet met with Waraqa ibn Nawfal, who was a cousin of the Prophet's wife Khadija. Waraqa ibn Nawfal was a Christian scholar who confirmed the Prophet's mission. Another encounter is said to have occurred in 615 C.E., when early converts to Islam migrated for a short while to the Christian kingdom of Axum (Abyssinia). In 628 C.E., a delegation of Christians from the town of Najran in South Arabia came to visit the Prophet in Medina, and sometime before the Prophet died, in 632 C.E., he would have sent letters to existing rulers such as the Byzantine emperor Heraclius and the Negus of Axum, as well as the Sassanian emperor Chosroes. These five instances demonstrate a variety of possible or imagined encounters, all of which have been used for various goals in Muslim-Christian relations, both at the time of their production and in subsequent interpretations.

The varieties of Qur'anic passages addressing Christians directly or indirectly (as people of the book, together with Jews, for example) reflect the transforming nature of the prophet Muhammad's encounters with them as his own status changed over time. The same applies to the other two religious systems he interacted with in Arabia: Judaism and Meccan polytheism. In all three cases, the variation in tone, from tolerance to polemics, seems to reflect the extent to which his prophetic message was being accepted or rejected at each moment of his reception of Qur'anic revelations, a process that lasted about twenty-three years. In terms of Christianity in particular, there is at best a conditional acceptance of Christians, and at worst a judgment associating them to both *shirk* (polytheism/idolatry) and *kufr* (unbelief). The various Christian voices referred to in the Qur'an are, for the most part, not reflective of the major Christian theologies that Muslims would come to encounter soon after the death of the prophet Muhammad, in 632 C.E. These misperceptions of mainstream, seventh-century Christian theologies, by being preserved in the Qur'an, negatively predisposed subsequent generations of Muslim interpreters of Christianity. A contextual sociopolitical reading of these various passages, harking back in part to the old Islamic hermeneutical principle of abrogation (in which later Qur'anic revelations must take precedence over prior ones), is one way to make sense of their variety and, at times, contradictory nature. This is especially important when the passages are juxtaposed ahistorically, either within the period of the Prophet's life or for contemporary ideological purposes.

### The First Islamic Conquests: 632–750 C.E.

During the Islamic empire's first phase of rapid expansion, between 632 and 750 C.E., two numerically important religious systems become incorporated under Muslim political control: Eastern Christianity, both Chalcedonian (i.e., Byzantinian) and non-Chalcedonian (especially Monophysite and Nestorian), and Zoroastrianism. By then, Jews constituted only a small minority of the population scattered across the newly conquered areas, and did not represent any political threat. The first to try to make sense of Islam as the religion of their new Muslim rulers were Eastern Christians, since Western (that is, Roman) Christians were not affected directly by the Muslim conquests until the later part of this period, and mostly in the Iberian Peninsula lying at the Western fringe of the new Islamic empire. In all cases, however, Christians perceived Islam within their own respective theological worldviews. As early as around 660 C.E., the arrival of Arab Muslims is interpreted by the Monophysite Armenian bishop Sebeos as a judgment of God in light of Genesis 21:12–13, according to which Muslims are identified as Arab descendants of Hagar and her son Ishmael, who were promised by God to become a great nation. This theological interpretation was linked to a political situation wherein most Monophysite and Nestorian Christians welcomed the arrival of Arab Muslims, for it put an end to their political subordination to the Byzantine Christians. As the new rulers took control over the course of the eighth century, new interpretations developed. For both Monophysites and Nestorians, Islam came to represent a judgment on the part of God against those who accepted the Christological definitions of the Council of Chalcedon (451 C.E.). As for those Eastern Christians under Muslim control who continued to support

The Tomb of St. John the Baptist in the Umayyad Mosque in Damascus, which was built on an earlier church, is said to house the skull of John the Baptist, valued by both Muslims and Christians. Over the centuries, despite much polemical opposition and violence, Christianity and Islam maintain many important similarities and have shared many positive encounters. ART ARCHIVE/DAGLI ORTI

the Byzantine or Chalcedonian theology, such as the Melkite John of Damascus, they came to describe Islam as a Christian heresy.

The early Muslim conquerors followed the momentum built toward the end of the Prophet's life: The first phase of interaction with Christians (and Jews) was confrontational, and all Jews and Christians were expelled from the Arabian Peninsula. It was not until the later seventh and eighth centuries, when Muslim political conquests began to take root in majority Christian and Zoroastrian areas, that more lenient attitudes and practices developed, legitimized by a retrieval of the earlier and more tolerant Qurʾanic passages toward Christians in particular. These interpretations and legal elaborations were needed to formalize the relationship of Muslims to the Christians and Zoroastrians who formed a majority of the population in their respective western and eastern halves of the new (Islamic) Umayyad Empire (661–750 C.E.). This new political context also explains why, to the theological concept of the people of the book (*ahl al-kitab*), used by the prophet Muhammad to link the Jewish, Christian, and Islamic notions of divine revelation, was added a parallel and pragmatic concept of the people of the protective covenant (*ahl al-dhimma*), erroneously understood by some today as second-class citizenship. This concept was based on two Qurʾanic references (9:8, 10) initially referring to idolaters in general. This covenantal concept helped regulate Christians, Jews, and Zoroastrians as political minorities who received protection from ruling Muslims in exchange for poll taxes. Yet, the situation and opportunities for advancement varied tremendously from one individual Christian to another, and from one geographical area or historical period to another. For example, many educated Christians reached high positions of power during the Umayyad and subsequent Abbasid dynasties, especially in the fields of medicine, philosophy, and administration.

### The Stabilizing of Relations: 750–1085 C.E.

In the three centuries that followed the takeover of the central Islamic lands by the Abbasid dynasty in 750 C.E., the Islamic world rose to its apex of cultural, religious, and political efflorescence. This *pax islamica* resulted in much tolerance toward its internal religious minorities in general, albeit within an Islamic *dhimmi* paradigm of power. The translation of mostly Greek and Syriac philosophical and scientific works into Arabic during the middle of the ninth century culminated in the establishment of Caliph Al-Ma'mun's (786–833 C.E.) *bayt al-hikma* (house of wisdom). It was later directed by the Nestorian Christian translator Hunayn ibn Ishaq (809–873 C.E.). As a positive example of Christian-Muslim relations at the center of the Abbasid Empire, the *bayt al-hikma* internally promoted intellectual pursuits of truth and resulted in a striking degree of interreligious tolerance and mutual influence, especially among the educated elite. Externally, as the empire's borders continued to be disputed, a pronounced antagonism arose among both Western European and Byzantine Christians, who feared the power of the then-greatest empire on earth. Among Western Christians, the most obvious development was linked to the slow *Reconquista* efforts in Spain that culminated in the Christian takeover of Toledo in 1085. This movement was fueled by very negative anti-Islamic rhetoric. As for Byzantine Christians, the continuing warfare also helped sustain more polemical views of Islam, building on the earlier notion that Islam was a heresy with the difference that authors now had access to original Qur'anic and other Arabic writings (or translations of them) to sustain their polemical arguments. Yet, some Byzantine writers were more moderate, acknowledging some similarities between Christianity and Islam, such as the common basis in monotheism.

During the same period, an equally diverse spectrum of views on Christianity emerged among Muslims. While there was better access to mainline Christian theologies, greater knowledge did not always result in greater tolerance and understanding. Many factors explain the rise in Muslim polemical attitudes toward Christianity: changing demographic realities, wherein Christians were still the majority in many central areas of Islamdom, but the balance of numerical power was gradually shifting in favor of Islam; changing theological realities within the Muslim community, including the search for Islamic legitimization in Biblical roots; social competition, especially in times of economic difficulties; and the need to defend Islam against other major worldviews. But not all Muslim perceptions of Christianity were polemical, and not all Muslim authors lived in situations where the above factors were equally present. As different Christian theologies produced different perceptions of Islam, so did different Islamic theologies (Mu'tazili, Ash'ari, Maturidi, traditionalist, Sufi, and so on) produce different perceptions of Christianity.

### The Period of the Crusades: 1085–1300 C.E.

After the fall of Toledo in 1085, Western Christians became embolded by the successes of what they have called the *Reconquista*. Their success was in sharp contrast to the Eastern Byzantine Christians, who had suffered great territorial losses at the hands of the Muslim Seljuk Turks in the aftermath of the battle of Manzikert in 1071. A decade later, Byzantine emperor Alexius (r. 1081–1118) took power and later requested help from Western Christians to fight back the Muslims. Pope Urban II responded with the preaching of the first Crusades in Clermont, France, in 1095. By the fall of 1096, a people's expedition was galvanized by Peter the Hermit. Numbering about twenty thousand, it ended up disintegrating before leaving Europe. In its wake, however, it left a trail of suffering. Many lives were lost, and whole Jewish communities were exterminated.

At the same time, an amalgamation of five armies from different parts of Western Europe responded to the call: they numbered between fifty and sixty thousand. They crossed over into Asia Minor in 1097, captured Antioch in 1098, and conquered Jerusalem on 15 July 1099. The Christian population of Jerusalem had been expelled from that city in fear of treachery just prior to the Crusader conquest. The Muslim governor, together with some of his military garrison, was allowed safe-conduct at the moment of the conquest, but the remaining Muslim and small Jewish civilian populations were massacred: More than forty thousand lives were taken. In contrast, when Saladin re-conquered Jerusalem in 1187, no blood was spilled upon entering the city. By 1302, the Crusaders had gradually lost control of all their small principalities on the eastern shores of the Mediterranean.

In contrast to this military approach to Muslim-Christian relations, smaller but significant rapprochements were taking place from the eleventh century onwards. They allowed for the transmission of knowledge from the Islamic world into Christian Europe, with the translation of Arabic works into Latin. This began primarily in Spain and Sicily with the rediscovery of the ancient Greek heritage, now greatly enriched by centuries of Muslim commentaries. This movement took place in both older monasteries and newer educational establishments such as language schools, colleges, and universities, first in Bologna, Salerno, Montpellier, Paris, and Oxford prior to 1200 With this rapid increase in efforts to understand the Muslim world, with key figures such as the Italian Francis of Assisi (1182–1226 C.E.) and the Spaniard Raymond Lull (c. 1232–1316 C.E.), important seeds of the later fifteenth- and sixteenth-century European Renaissance were sown in the very midst of an internal Christian resistance to the Crusades.

### The New Balance of Power: 1300–1500 C.E.

The defeat of the first Crusades did not end the desires of European Christians for expansion, nor did it stop certain Muslims from continuing their own. The *Reconquista* gradually expanded to include the whole of the Iberian Peninsula, ending with the fall of the last Muslim kingdom in Grenada in 1492. At the other end of the Mediterranean, Ottoman expansion crossed over into southeastern Europe in 1354, eventually ending the Byzantine Empire with the capture of Constantinople in 1453. They won the battle of Kosovo in 1389 and Nicopolis in 1396, making them rulers of the Balkans. The expansion stopped at the gates of Vienna in 1529. A similar siege took place again in 1683, demonstrating the strong Ottoman pressures on Central and Eastern Europe for over a century and a half.

At the same time, by the end of the fifteenth century, the southwestern Europeans, especially the Spaniards and Portuguese, gained new strategic power through three combined discoveries: Christopher Columbus's "discovery" of the Americas in 1492; Vasco de Gama's navigation around Africa via the Cape of Good Hope in 1497, which opened up a new spice trading route to Southeast Asia that avoided central Muslim lands; and Magellan and Pigafetta's westward circumnavigation of the earth by 1522 C.E. These discoveries suddenly enlarged the predominantly Mediterranean geographical scope of the first eight centuries of Christian-Muslim interactions into the beginnings of a global one, adding new Christian missionary pressures, especially in West Africa as well as South and Southeast Asia, where Muslim rule had been gradually expanding for centuries.

## The New European Christian Rise in Power: 1500–1800 C.E.

In the sixteenth century, the rapid takeover of ocean routes worldwide ushered in a new age of European Christian power. It resulted in a gradual encroachment on increasingly vast areas of inhabited lands through a forceful combination of military, political, economic, and missionary activities. While these new, long-term processes were unfolding on the peripheries, the Ottoman Empire continued to be a threat to the central and eastern European Christian powers and the Mughal Empire slowed down European incursions into South Asia.

In between the Ottoman and Mughal empires, the Safavid Empire (based primarily in Iran) vied for control of central Islamic lands. Dynamic internal Muslim transformations continued to flower along traditional lines, both within those three centralized empires and on many peripheries of Islamic expansion, especially in sub-Saharan Africa, and in southeastern and northwestern Asia. However, few understood the significance of the new technologies that led to the magnitude of the European encroachment along many peripheries of the Islamic world and their disruption of traditional internal sources of economic revenues, such as the spice and silk roads, due to new ocean trade routes. These technological threats were also ideational and symbolic, as with the new missionary efforts to spread worldwide the already embattled forms of European Christianity, even when conducted with greater sensitivity to local customs, as exemplified in the efforts of the first Jesuits in the later half of the sixteenth century in India, China, and Japan. These combined processes would subsequently increase in speed and depth, leading to tension and confrontation between Muslims and Christians worldwide on a much wider scale.

## The Period of European Colonialism and Western Imperialism: 1800 onward

With Napoleon's brief conquest of Egypt in 1898, Europeans embarked on a political and military trajectory that would gradually make them colonial masters not only over majority Muslim countries, but over almost the entire planet. While this surge in European colonialism was particularly successful among the British, French, Dutch, and Russians, who divided up among themselves most of the Islamic world, it still remained strong among the older imperial powers of Spain and Portugal, while the newer national polities of Italy, Germany, and Belgium also vied for their share of the world. A few Muslim areas retained a degree of political independence, such as what later became Turkey, Saudi Arabia, and (to a lesser degree) Iran, which had to balance pressures from the British in the south and the Russians in the north, a prelude to the later pressures of the Cold War by their respective successors the United States and the Soviet Union. Thanks in part to large oil revenues, both Saudi Arabia and Iran would later become the launching pads for two distinct, transnational, and anti-Western Islamic political ideologies confronting Western imperialism: Khomeinism and Wahhabism. The first began with the Iranian Revolution of 1979 and the latter produced as one of its offshoots the extremist al-Qaʿida, with the resulting terrorist attacks on key symbols of American global hegemony on 11 September 2001.

Intertwined with the growing European colonialism of the nineteenth and early twentieth centuries, the Christian missionary movement continued unabated, although it was now linked to a civilizational project of modernity understood as democracy and the rule of law within new nation-state structures. This European colonial project legitimized in the eyes of most Europeans their own increased militarization at home and the interconnected colonial control of peoples worldwide. European colonialism eventually fragmented the world, including the Islamic parts of it, into unavoidable yet often unmanageable semblances of nation-states. This project had to do as much with older competing Catholic, Protestant, and Orthodox Christian identities as with newer, non-Christian philosophies (deism, atheism, utilitarianism, materialism, human rights, and the like), a point often misunderstood by many generations of Muslims who have reduced the modern West to Christianity. In turn, many Westerners, whether religious or not, have themselves simplistically essentialized the complexities of the Islamic world, wanting to believe that it is quintessentially unmodernizable. They have forgotten how many centuries it took Western Catholic and Protestant Christianities to come to terms with modernity, and fail to consider the ongoing struggles of parts of the Orthodox Christian world, not to mention vast numbers of Christians in economically disadvantaged areas around the world.

Orientalism is a long-standing, scientific tradition of interpretation of the Other developed in Western universities especially in the nineteenth and twentieth centuries to explain "Eastern" realities from Morocco to Japan. This tradition reinforced the stereotype of Islam as unmodernizable. Orientalists only too often contributed to the rationale for colonial domination of the world, especially in Muslim areas. This explains why, since the late nineteenth century, many Muslims have become suspicious of efforts on the part of non-Muslim Westerners to interpret Islam. However, with increased migrations of Muslims from majority Muslim countries to the West and the increase in conversions to Islam among both European and U.S. citizens, especially among African Americans, together with the increased Westernization of important segments of majority Muslim countries, new Islamized Western and secularized Islamic identities have emerged in the last half century challenging the existence of a West/Islam dichotomy as was promulgated by orientalist thinking.

In addition to colonialist and orientalist discourses, the already complex internal Western dynamic spawned new competing economic and political ideologies, such as liberalism, socialism, and communism, eventually spreading the Cold War (1950–1989) unto the rest of the non-Western world, into newly formed nations that were already struggling to define themselves in the new, postcolonial era. This resulted in various hybrid forms of political ideology, such as pan-Arabism, Indonesian pancasila ideology, and the creation of Pakistan along ethnic rather than religious lines (even though Pakistani identity was initially the effort to transform a South Asian Muslim identity into a national/ethnic one). For every national case, the Islamic heritage in majority Muslim countries was problematized differently, resulting in a variety of Muslim and Islamic nationalisms that rivals the variety of secular and Christo-secular Western nationalisms.

The greatest force underlying the modernization (often reduced to Westernization) process ensuing from Western colonialism and post-colonial economic imperialism, most recently known under the concept of globalization, has come in the name of science and has been linked to a philosophy of positivism. These combined claims to truth have reinforced the various new technologies with which they are associated. While most Muslims have adopted Western scientific education as part of various nationalist educational projects, this ever-rapid increase in scientific knowledge has continued to provide a secularizing West its military and political superiority, undermining traditional faith-claims both at the center of power in the West and on the Muslim and other peripheries.

A resistance to positivist science and liberal Christianity first developed in the United States in the second decade of the twentieth century, taking the form of Christian Protestant fundamentalism. Fundamentalism later spread around the world under different names and varying forms, resulting in the ideologization of anticolonial and, later, anti-imperialist religious discourses. Eventually it fueled a few religious revolutions and coup d'etats, the most memorable being that of Iran in 1979. During the late 1980s and 1990s, another form of accommodation has led to the creation of a network of scholars engaged in the Islamization of Knowledge project.

But by the end of the Cold War in 1989, Westerners and Muslims had lost a common enemy in communism; they could now turn more directly onto each other, in what is still often reduced to a simplistic West versus Islam dichotomy.

In contrast, mostly among educated and cosmopolitan elites, the late twentieth century witnessed the emergence of a genuine Christian-Muslim or Muslim-Christian dialogue. This new movement stressed the importance of listening to one another and learning from each other's tradition. This process, carefully attuned to ensuring a better power dynamic between its participants, has often led to common statements by Muslims and Christians on a variety of issues. Sponsored at times by international religious organizations, governments, or non-governmental organizations, these dialogues have opened up new avenues of understanding that aim to respect the differences and have built on the similarities that exist among Christians and Muslims. While participating in dialogue does not require a liberal theological point of view, it tends to attract religious people with such a perspective, often limiting the potential impact this approach could have on transforming the history of Christian-Muslims relations toward one of greater understanding and cooperation given the wealth of information now available on their shared history.

## Conclusion

The history of Muslim-Christian relations includes a wide spectrum of interactions encompassing all aspects of human life. Two extreme interpretations need to be avoided because they are wrong historically. The first is reductionism. It is dangerous to reduce this complex history to one of endless confrontations between essentialized conceptualizations of Islam and Christianity, treating them as mutually exclusive realities that turn every Christian and Muslim into unavoidable enemies. The examples of constructive interactions between Muslims and Christians in both times of peace and war are too numerous to justify oversimplifying this history into one of military confrontations. The second danger is to deny the complex power dynamics that have always existed among Christians, Muslims, and others within Christian and post-Christian as well as Muslim and other societies. These dynamics reveal both destructive and constructive behaviors and patterns, as well as a spectrum of beliefs that range from inclusive to exclusive and are held by both sides in what have become the two numerically largest religious identities today. Knowing this history requires a sensitive understanding at the dawn of a yet insecure future for the human race.

*See also* **Balkans, Islam in the; Crusades; European Culture and Islam; Islam and Other Religions; Judaism and Islam; Religious Beliefs.**

## BIBLIOGRAPHY

Bamyeh, Mohammed A. *The Social Origins of Islam: Mind, Economy, Discourse*. Minneapolis: University of Minnesota Press, 1999.

The minaret of a mosque and the belltowers of Christian churches cohabitate in Bethlehem on the West Bank. LEFTERIS PITARAKIS/AP/ WIDE WORLD PHOTOS

Borrmans, Maurice. *Guidelines for Dialogue between Christians and Muslims.* Translated by R. Marston Speight. Mahwah, N.J.: Paulist Press, 1990.

Brown, Stuart E., ed. *Meeting in Faith: Twenty Years of Christian-Muslim Conversations Sponsored by the World Council of Churches.* Geneva: W.C.C. Publications, 1989.

Daniel, Norman. *Islam and the West: The Making of an Image.* Oxford, U.K.: Oneworld, 1993.

Goddard, Hugh. *A History of Christian-Muslim Relations.* Chicago: New Amsterdam Books, 2000.

Goddard, Hugh. *Christians and Muslims: From Double Standards to Mutual Understanding.* Richmond, U.K.: Curzon, 1995.

Haddad, Juliette Nasri, ed. *Declarations Communes Islamo-Chretiennes: 1954–1995.* Beyrouth: Dar el-Machreq, 1997.

Haddad, Yvonne Yazbeck, and Haddad, Wadi Saidan, eds. *Christian-Muslim Encounters.* Gainesville: University Press of Florida, 1995.

Hillenbrand, C. *The Crusades: Islamic Perspectives.* Edinburgh: Edinburgh University Press, 1999.

Laiou, Angeliki E., and Mottahedeh, Roy Parviz, eds. *The Crusades from the Perspective of Byzantium and the Muslim World.* Washington, D.C.: Dumbarton Oaks Research Library and Collection, 2001.

Ridgeon, Lloyd, ed. *Islamic Interpretations of Christianity.* New York: St Martin's Press, 2001.

Runciman, S. *A History of the Crusades.* Cambridge, U.K.: Cambridge University Press, 1951.

Waardenburg, Jacques, ed. *Muslim-Christian Perceptions of Dialogue Today: Experiences and Expectations.* Leuven: Peeters, 2000.

Zebiri, Kate. *Muslims and Christians Face to Face.* Oxford, U.K.: Oneworld, 1997.

*Patrice C. Brodeur*

# CIRCUMCISION

The role of circumcision (*khitan*) in Islamic society has shifted dramatically due to issues of gender, custom, and law. Nowhere mentioned in the Qur'an, circumcision was a common practice in Arabia that was incorporated into the Islamic legal system to varying degrees and for a variety of reasons. Both Josephus and Philo of Alexandria note its presence in Egypt, Ethiopia, and Arabia prior to the coming of Islam. Philo observes that Egyptian males and females were circumcised after the fourteenth year before marriage, while Josephus claims the Arabs performed it just after the thirteenth year, at the time Ishmael was circumcised.

Legally, Islamic scholars debate whether the practice is obligatory or sunna (customary), or whether its obligations be extended solely to males, or to males and females. Al-Shafi'a considers the practice an equal duty for both sexes, while Malik and others consider it sunna for males. The disagreement over gender requirements continues in current cultural practice. Female circumcision is embraced in southern Egypt, Ethiopia, Somalia, the Sudan, and West Africa, and a minor form is practiced by Southeast Asian *Shafi'is* in Indonesia and Malaysia. It is condemned by many Muslims and non-Muslims who reside outside of these areas, mostly for humanitarian and health reasons. Many legal schools also deliberate the time a circumcision should be performed. Some recommend the seventh day following the birth of a male child, while others propose its performance after a child reaches his tenth birthday. Again, such legal variation is mirrored in contemporary practice. In the Middle East, circumcision occurs between the ages of two and seven, while in Europe and North Africa male Muslims are circumcised in hospitals immediately after birth. Suffice it to say that today there is no standard orthodox practice when it comes to circumcision. Not all Muslims practice circumcision (specifically, those in China), and many who do adhere to vastly different cultural norms.

The justifications for circumcision also vary dramatically in Islamic sources and practice. Many hadith link circumcision with purification (*tahara*). It often appears in lists that include other acts of general hygiene, including the clipping of nails, the use of the tooth-stick, the trimming of mustaches, and the depilation of both the armpits and the pubic region. Some hadith also link the practice back to Ibrahim, who circumcised himself at the age of eighty with a pickax. Unlike Judaism, Islam does not view circumcision as the sole signifier of the covenant between God and his people. Circumcision stands as just one of many tests Ibrahim performed to demonstrate his adherence to the true faith. Many Muslims bypass these exegetical intricacies and simply take the view that Muhammad mandated the practice. The legal and customary support for circumcising just prior to the onset of puberty also suggests the practice was performed as a rite of passage, one that would ready an individual for marriage. As a rite of passage, male circumcision ceremonies in places like Java and Morocco are accompanied with purificatory rites, sacrifices, and feasts. When conducted today, female circumcision is a much less celebratory act, rarely accompanied by such festivities. To interpret circumcision in Islam from a religious studies standpoint, the manipulation of the genitalia exemplifies ultimate divine control over one's human, procreative instincts. Thus one cut symbolizes a total submission to God.

*See also* 'Ada; Body, Significance of; Gender; Law.

## BIBLIOGRAPHY

Bloch, Maurice. *From Blessing to Violence: History and Ideology in the Circumcision Ritual of the Merina of Madagascar.* Cambridge, U.K.: Cambridge University Press, 1986.

Kister, M.J. *Concepts and Ideas at the Dawn of Islam.* Aldershot, Great Britain; Brookfield, Vt.: Ashgate/Varioram, 1997.

Robinson, Francis. *Atlas of the Islamic World Since 1500.* New York: Facts On File, 1982.

*Kathryn Kueny*

# CLOTHING

Islamic dress has for centuries been used to symbolize purity, mark status or formal roles, distinguish believer from nonbeliever, and identify gender. Traditionally Muslims were admonished to dress modestly in garments that did not reveal the body silhouette and extremities. Head coverings were also expected. However, dress forms vary in different periods and regions, as does interpretation of and adherence to Muslim dress codes. The most prominent forms of Near Eastern dress can be classified as Arab or Turkic/Iranian in form, with degrees of blending between the two modes occurring where interaction between these cultures has been greatest.

Arab dress can be seen from northern Syria to North Africa. The basic dress of both men and women is based on the simple tunic, an unfitted garment pulled on over the head,

common in the region since Roman times (*qamis* or *thawb*). The earlier form of Arab dress, unseamed wrapped garments (*izar* and *rida*), have survived as the consecrated garments (*ihram*) worn by pilgrims to Mecca. The *thawb* is well suited to desert heat, providing both protection from the sun and ventilation. A wide unfitted mantle (*jallaba* or *aba*; hooded *burnus*) may also be worn. Typical materials are cotton or fine wool, with dense silk embroidery applied to necklines and borders. To this might be added sashes and shawls. Men's head coverings might be a turban, or a simple shawl bound at the forehead, arranged on the head according to status, affiliation, local usage, or practical need. Turbans are the most well known of Muslim headgear, however. Hats or caps may also be worn either separately or under turbans. Women's clothing is based on the same basic garment forms but differs in color, embellishment, materials, and accessories. In public, women's garments were traditionally hidden by veils that covered all parts of the body to the ground or only head, shoulders, and face.

Turkic dress was widely influential throughout the Islamic world. The Seljuk Turks emerged from Central Asia, establishing dynasties in Iran and Asia Minor by the eleventh century. By the mid-sixteenth century the Ottoman Empire encompassed most of the lands surrounding the eastern Mediterranean.

The traditional Turkish ensemble for either men or women consisted of loose-fitting trousers (*salvar, don*) and a shirt (*gomlek*), topped by a variety of jackets (*cebken*), vests (*yelek*), and long coats (*entari, kaftan, uc etek*). The use of coats and trousers derived from their nomadic origins in Central Asia. Trousers protect a rider's legs from chafing, and coats or jackets can be more readily donned or doffed than tunics while on horseback, as required in a variable climate. Layering of garments was an important aesthetic element. Garments were arranged to display the patterns and quality of fabrics on all layers and add bulk to the body image. The more formal the occasion or the higher the status of the wearer, the more layers worn, with richer materials further indicating wealth. Colorful sashes that added mass to the body image also served as a repository for weapons and personal articles. Ottoman Turkish headgear typically consisted of a brimless hat or cap in a variety of sizes and forms indicating official status, gender, and regional identity. Scarves were usually wrapped into a turban over the hat. The form of the turban indicated status, occupation, religious affiliation, or regional origin. Women's scarves were wrapped and tied around the head, frequently in layers, with a larger veil worn over all in public.

Specific forms of dress were worn by Ottoman officials throughout the Ottoman Empire. The nearly five-hundred-year presence of Ottoman rule throughout much of the Arab world led to some blending of garment forms, particularly in northern Arab regions adjacent to Anatolia, and also in urban

Traditional male Arab dress is depicted in this 1936 postcard from the region. CORNELL COSTUME AND TEXTILE COLLECTION

Modesty in dress was enjoined in Islam for both men and women, although the particulars of pious modesty are not precisely defined in the Qur'an. The body of Islamic law and scholarship, however, has provided more specific directives that have nonetheless been applied differently in different times and places. Generally some sort of headcovering or veiling (*hijab*) is mandated for both men and women. In some countries such as Iran and Saudi Arabia all women are required to veil, although the forms of veiling vary. In some other societies veils may be a matter of choice.

Throughout the Islamic world, dress has been used to manage distinctions of rank, gender, and religion. Under Ottoman law, for example, dress of the various religious communities within the empire was regulated, with specific colors and forms of headgear, shoes, and garments defined. Garments, particularly coats, were an important aspect of court ceremonial throughout the Muslim world. The court reception of emissaries, celebration of religious holidays, installation of officials, or honoring of heroes always called for the presentation of ceremonial robes and other textile gifts, with the richness of the fabrics or fur linings a mark of the degree of honor conferred upon the recipient. The wearing of luxurious materials such as silk and gold thread was often restricted, however, although such restrictions were often ignored. The wearing of silk, particularly next to the skin, was widely held to be an impious luxury for good Muslims. A colorful satin cloth that had a cotton weft and silk warp, and therefore a cotton inner surface and a silk outer face, allowed the wearer to conform to this religious admonition while enjoying the luxurious outer appearance of a silk garment. This textile was widely used in the Islamic world, known as *kutnu* in the Near East, and *mashru* in northern India and Pakistan. However, the most pious avoided luxurious materials and colors, and wore clothing of simple wool, cotton, or linen.

Beginning in the nineteenth century, westernization of dress occurred together with modernization of political, military, and educational institutions, since initially modernization was officially perceived as consonant with westernization. Also the emergence of a modern textile industry in many regions led to the disappearance of the more costly handmade textiles once used in traditional dress. Since dress had long been closely regulated under Muslim law, departures from traditional dress became highly charged political and social issues. The banning of the turban and the introduction of the fez by the Ottoman sultan Mahmut II in 1829 (as well as a westernized military uniform) caused great controversy as did similar decrees in Iran in 1873. These reforms were intended to symbolize modernization of military and administrative institutions, yet a century later the fez had become a symbol of Ottoman traditionalism. Following the founding of the Turkish Republic, Mustafa Kemal (Ataturk) met resistance when he banned the fez in 1925, and even more so when he urged abandonment of the veil for women.

Arab centers of the eastern Mediterranean and North Africa. The adoption of buttoned vests or jackets of silk or wool decorated with embroidery, and the loose-fitting trousers called *salvar* in Turkish or *sirwal* in Arabic are evidence of such borrowings in Arab dress. The dress of Muslim sub-Saharan Africa is derived from that of the Arabs who brought Islam there in the eleventh century.

Traditional dress in Iran shares with that of Turkey forms indicative of nomadic origins, with layered coats and *salvar* as typical features of dress. These forms were also introduced into Muslim northern India from Central Asia by the Turkic Gaznevids in the eleventh and twelfth century, and by the Moguls in the sixteenth century. Such forms are reflected in Mogul court dress, where for men trousers (*paijama*) were typically combined with front-opening coats or jackets of varying length and cut (*angarkha* or *jama*). For women, the characteristic ensemble might include a bodice or tunic (*kurta* or *choli*) and skirt (*gaghra*), and/or trousers (*salwar*), as well as a veil. The exquisitely fine and complex silks and cottons of India are a distinctive characteristic of dress from this region.

Since mandated ideas of proper dress had for centuries been the means of distinguishing Muslim from non-Muslim, these issues continue to have great emotional force throughout the Muslim world. In the 1980s and 1990s dress reemerged as a symbolic flashpoint between religious conservative and secularist elements in Islamic societies.

*Examples of traditional clothing appear in the volume one color insert.*

*See also* **Art; Body, Significance of; Khirqa; Veiling.**

## BIBLIOGRAPHY

Jirousek, Charlotte. "The Transition to Mass Fashion System Dress in the Later Ottoman Empire." In *Consumption Studies and the History of the Ottoman Empire, 1550–1922: An Introduction.* Edited by Donald Quataert. Albany: State University of New York Press, 2000.

Koçu, Resat Ekrem. *Türk Giyim Kusam ve Süsleme Sözlügü* (Dictionary of Turkish: (Dress, Accessories, and Embellishment.) Ankara: Sümerbank, 1969.

Lindisfarne-Tapper, Nancy, and Ingham, Bruce, eds. *Languages of Dress in the Middle East.* Richmond, Surrey, U.K.: Curzon Press, 1997.

Mayer, L. A. *Mamluk Costume: A Survey.* Geneva: Albert Kundig, 1952.

Scarce, Jennifer. *Women's Costume of the Near and Middle East.* London: Unwin Hyman, 1987.

Stillman, Yedida Kalfon. *Arab Dress from the Dawn of Islam to Modern Times: A Short History.* Edited by Norman Stillman. Leiden, Boston, and Köln: Brill, 2000.

*Charlotte Jirousek*

# COINAGE

When Islam emerged in 610 c.e., Mecca did not have its own coinage. Instead, it relied entirely on the coins of neighboring regions, particularly the Byzantine and Sassanid empires. Being both a trading town and a pilgrimage center, Mecca attracted a wide range of the coins in circulation at the time. Neither the prophet Muhammad nor his immediate political successors sought to change this. When the Muslims conquered much of the Byzantine and Sassanid empires after the death of the Prophet in 632 c.e., they left the administrative structures of these regions, including their mints and coinages, largely intact.

As a result of the Muslim conquests of the seventh century c.e., rapid economic expansion and currency circulation occurred in the Near East, along with Muslim migration from Arabia to the newly conquered regions. Regular cash stipends began to flow out to Muslims from the Central Treasury (*bayt al-mal*) in Medina during the caliphate of 'Umar I (r. 634–644), and there was substantial inflow of taxes and tributes from the conquered lands to the treasury, first located in Medina, then in Damascus during the Umayyad period. The monetization of the economy that resulted from this expansion required not only large amounts of cash (coins) but also a standard monetary unit for transactions and account keeping. In response, the silver dirham, modeled on the Sassanid drachma, was adopted, with the coins being provided by the former Sassanid mints.

Economic expansion continued with the establishment of the Umayyad caliphate, but the silver dirham remained the unit of currency. As mints did not generally issue gold coins, the market had to rely largely on the Byzantine *solidi* to meet its gold currency needs. The *solidi* themselves suffered wear and tear, which led at times to a less than uniform weight. Similarly, the silver dirhams in circulation, or those minted by the Muslims, showed discrepancies. Strong pressure therefore existed for a standard currency, including a unit based on gold, the production of which could be controlled by the Muslims.

Following minor attempts at currency reform by caliphs such as 'Umar I, 'Ali b. Abi Talib and Mu'awiyah, which went only as far as adding an Islamic inscription or date to existing Byzantine or Sassanid coins, 'Abd al-Malik b. Marwan (r. 685–705), the Umayyad caliph, took the initiative. Between 696 and 698, he changed the form as well as the weight of the dinar and dirham and regulated minting. The coins emphasized the emerging power of Muslims and of Islam as a religion, with Islamic inscriptions such as "There is no God but Allah and Muhammad is the messenger of Allah." Unlike Byzantine and Sassanid coins, the reformed coins did not bear the Caliph's image.

The pre-reform dinar had weighed approximately 4.55 grams, but 'Abd al-Malik reduced it to 4.25 grams. The fineness of the dinar was set at a minimum 96 percent gold alloy. The weight of the pre-reform dirham had been approximately 3.98 grams, but 'Abd al-Malik standardized it to 2.97 grams. This weight remained largely unchanged until the mid-ninth century c.e. The fineness of the silver dirham was also maintained at near 96 percent. Though the capital, Damascus, minted some coins, particularly gold dinars, 'Abd al-Malik did not centralize minting in that city. This function was given to provincial mints, and here the caliph relied heavily on his governor in Iraq, al-Hajjaj b. Yusuf, to impose coinage reform on the eastern regions of the caliphate. Later, caliph Hisham b. Abd al-Malik (r. 724–743) also tightened control over the quality of both dinar and dirham.

'Abd al-Malik's reformed coinage set a standard that continued in some respects well into the following Abbasid period. In order to standardize further the coinage of the powerful Abbasid caliphate, the caliph al-Ma'mun (r. 813–833) introduced new coinage in 821 and 822. He abolished inclusion of the caliph's or the provincial governor's name on coins, ordered that both gold and silver coins should follow

An 1877 banknote for fifty Kurush from the Ottoman Empire. At the beginning of the Muslim empire after Muhammad's death, Muslim conquerers did not impose their own currency system on their subjects, because Mecca did not have its own coinage. Instead, it used the currency of nearby areas. Today, each Muslim nation has its own currency. THE ART ARCHIVE/DAGLI ORTI (A)

specific design guidelines and inscriptions, and appears to have centralized the production of coin dies. His successor, al-Mu'tasim, however, reintroduced the addition of the caliph's name. In the post-Mu'tasim period, some Abbasid caliphs even added the name of the heir-apparent or would-be successor. From the early ninth century to the middle of the tenth century C.E., the vast Abbasid caliphate thus acquired a significantly uniform coinage, which vastly aided internal and external, and Muslim and non-Muslim, commerce and trade. These dinars and dirhams were imitated in Europe and elsewhere.

With the decline in Abbasid power, the disintegration of the caliphate, and the emergence of independent provinces and dynasties, central control of the coinage as well as its uniformity were lost. Independent provinces began minting their own dinars and dirhams and determining the fineness of their coins. Although the fineness of gold dinars was at times maintained and even excelled, for instance under the Fatimid caliph al-'Amir (r. 1101–1130) and the Ayyubid sultan al-Kamil (r. 1218–1238), large variations did occur. For this reason, there is disagreement among scholars on the use of the terms "Islamic dinar" and "Islamic dirham" as a standard unit of currency in the Muslim world, particularly in respect of the post-tenth-century C.E. period, except insofar as it refers to the theoretical dinar and dirham of the Muslim jurists (fuqaha').

Despite the variation in the quality of the coinage under different dynasties, certain features introduced by reformers remained common. These included inscriptions symbolizing the religious basis of the coinage, an indication of the mint year, the mint name, and often the name of the caliph or ruler under whom the coin was issued. Coins from Islamic dynasties have therefore an important historical significance. Apart from their commercial role, they can tell us much about the political and economic condition and the artistic and aesthetic tendencies of the time.

In the modern period, each Muslim state has its own coinage and, like other countries, has abandoned the gold standard, even though Muslim jurists have not relinquished the concept of the gold dinar or the silver dirham in their legal texts. In many juristic discussions, money proper is still the dinar and the dirham of early Islam. However, as part of a wider Islamic revival, the idea of a specifically Islamic standard unit of currency, a dinar, has been revived, though not necessarily based on the earlier gold dinar. The most visible aspect of this was the adoption in 1975 of the Islamic Dinar as its unit of accounting by the Islamic Development Bank, an international Islamic financial institution whose shareholders are member states of the Organization of the Islamic Conference (OIC). The value of the Islamic Dinar is equivalent to one SDR—Special Drawing Right—of the International Monetary Fund.

*See also* **Economy and Economic Institutions; Law; Networks, Muslim.**

## BIBLIOGRAPHY

Ehrenkruetz, Andrew S. *Monetary Change and Economic History in the Medieval Muslim World.* Edited by Jere L. Bacharach. Hampshire, U.K.: Ashgate Publishing, 1992.

El-Hibri, Tayeb. "Coinage Reform Under the Abbasid Caliph al-Ma'mun." *Journal of the Economic and Social History of the Orient* 36 (1993): 58–83.

Grierson, Philip. "The Monetary Reform of 'Abd al-Malik." *Journal of the Economic and Social History of the Orient* 3 (1960): 241–264.

Miles, G. C. "Dinar." In *The Encyclopaedia of Islam.* Leiden: E. J. Brill, 1960.

Miles, G. C. "Dirham." In *The Encyclopaedia of Islam.* Leiden: E. J. Brill, 1960.

*Abdullah Saeed*

# COLONIALISM

Modern colonialism goes back to the era of European discovery in the fifteenth century, connecting exploitation of raw materials with missionary ideas. Since then colonialism has taken several and different forms, and various colonial powers (such as the Portuguese and French in Africa, French and British in the Middle East and South Asia, the Dutch in Southeast Asia, the Spanish in South America) tried to support their own hegemonies in Europe as well as competing and contesting materially and politically in order to control the new world economy.

The independence of the United States ushered in another phenomenon: White colonial regions became independent as they became semi-sovereign vis-à-vis their colonial motherlands. At the same time European industrial countries contested for the safeguarding of raw materials, markets, and possibilities of emigration in what they considered to be unexploited and virgin regions.

## Colonial Expanison

Modern colonial expansion and colonization (when few European settlers appeared in the Muslim world) started in the wake of the breakdown of Muslim empires, from within the boundaries of the territorial European states established in the eighteenth century into the borders of national markets. Hence, colonialism did not expand beyond traditional and primitive societies but into closed political entities, such as the territorial princely states or successor states, which had replaced the great empires. By the eighteenth century the world economy was already reorganized, and European expansion had gradually changed the terms of trade for Muslim countries. A tremendous societal upheaval occurred as parts of the traditional society were increasingly integrated into world market relations. This complex process came about primarily through technical innovation (e.g., perennial irrigation systems), investment of capital, and privatization of landed property (e.g., the 1793 permanent settlement in India). Next to the traditional urban and agrarian sectors, colonial urban and agrarian sectors were established, using a colonial infrastructure. The previously important nomadic sector was noticeably marginalized. A colonial administrative and military force was set up, visualized in new settlements, such as civil lines and cantonments. The education system was replaced or paralleled by a new European one suiting colonial interests.

In doing so two broad patterns were followed: direct rule, virtually excluding indigenous political structures, as favored by the Spanish and Portuguese in the Americas, and by the French in Africa (especially after the French Revolution); and indirect rule, which by contrast, incorporated traditional indigenous political structures and was favored by the British in South Asia, the Dutch in Southeast Asia, and by the Germans and Belgians in Africa. The reasons for these differences were pragmatic—the cost-effectiveness through the involvement of few Europeans—as well as ethnocentric, wherein non-whites and whites were considered fundamentally different, and therefore controllable only by their

own leaders and systems. Often corporate bodies of merchants initiated a system of indirect rule, such as the various East Indian Companies. In this way vast colonies could be ruled remotely through the "resident," the agent of indirect rule.

The colonial restructuring was accompanied by profound changes in the socio-psychological sphere of Muslim societies as well. Traditional systems of society, values, and relations were gradually replaced by abstract, anonymous state agents—whether through direct or indirect rule. This process ushered in new societal formations, especially in the political sphere, since with the increasing expansion of the colonial sector, traditional forces came to break down or looked for alternative structures. But not all sectors and areas were seized by the politically dominant colonial sector, as their integration was not always profitable, such as in parts of traditional and tribal areas. They were consequently ignored, and they still are socioeconomically neglected areas.

The colonialization of the Islamic world in the nineteenth century occurred over several decades. The process can be divided into three phases: from 1820, when colonial power was already firmly established, to 1856, when Muslim countries struggled for recognition in the changing geopolitical reality; and, from 1856 to 1880 nearly all Muslim countries lost their economic and financial independence and became dependent on the Europeans. During the period from 1880 to 1910 most of these countries—apart from those Muslim countries controlled by the Ottoman caliphate—were subject to direct colonial military and political control: economic colonialism had become political colonialism. In this situation of political subservience, the traditional urban divines, particularly theologians, were responsible for the traditional legitimization of the ruler. At the same time, in the colonial urban sector, Islamic repertory was gradually used as an ideology and a mobilizing force by those societal formations that had become partly integrated into this colonial sector. In contrast to this, in the traditional agrarian sector Islam prevailed in the form of egalitarian peasant culture, as can be seen from a number of Sufi and Mahdi movements.

The idea of universal caliphate, which had been used by the Ottomans since the middle of the eighteenth century, particularly for reasons of foreign policy, became a vehicle for pan-Islamic propaganda, notably by Sultan ʿAbd al-Hamid II. Though this propaganda was politically unsuccessful and led to the demise of the caliphate in 1924, the propaganda triggered a hefty discussion of the idea of a universal caliphate outside of Turkey: On the one hand the validity of the idea was questioned (ʿAbd al-Raziq); on the other, Indian Muslims staged a khilafat movement. A colonial crackdown, however, put this movement down.

The Second World War accelerated the process of decolonialization but left the former colonies with basic structural problems that were a result of colonialism, such as insufficient societal integration, artificial boundaries, and narrowly based economies.

Beside these socio-historical and political developments, one needs to consider the normative aspect underlying the colonial process: A colonial collective image of Islam was created, going as far back as the Crusades and revived at a time when Europeans had started to project their own imaginations onto Muslim societies—a phenomenon that historian Edward Said has called "Orientalism." In this view, the heterogeneous Islamic world was reduced to a monolithic, antimodern, and anti-intellectual world excluded from world history.

Nineteenth-century colonial politics was legitimized as evolutionary and modern, while the "Orient" was constructed as a cultural space, diametrically opposed to the values and norms of the West, which were considered to be inherently universal. This unidimensional social evolutionism proclaimed Europe as embodying hegemonic power. In doing so, various discourses about the Orient promulgated the societal decline, dogmatism, despotism, and irrationality of the region. Eventually this hegemonic claim produced new "Orientalist" sciences.

Against the backdrop of a postulated universal evolutionary history, the Orientalist sciences analyzed the object "Orient" in its historical development, making use of the Hegelian categories of alienation and reconciliation. In this way, colonial administrations were provided with a "scientifically proven" image about the stage of development attained by the Orient, which was seen to be alienated from its classical high culture. Cultural theories provided the colonial administration with this Orientalist image, which ran counter to the historical one of classical high culture. On the basis of this construction, colonial measures to "reconcile" the Orient with its alienated tradition were to be implemented as an export of progress. Thus terms like "modern" and "traditional" or "primitive" became scientific categories, establishing an epistemological supremacy of Europe that was firmly established politically.

In this way authority was created on the object "Orient" not only for the Europeans but also gradually, through reciprocal perceptions, for the "Orientals" themselves. Subsequently, authority was derived from the instrumentalization of the Weberian demand for "value-free" social sciences, that became "objective" insofar as they were considered to be not ideologically biased, but unquestionably "true."

While the power relations cannot be ignored, it is important to note the cultural hybridization of the colonial process, for example, the reciprocity of colonializer and colonialized. Indeed, the colonialized peoples had a function in the colonial process, for the establishment of European dominance was essentially based on the cooperation of local informants,

colonial traders, and rulers. Therefore, contemporary debates became the starting point for the colonial reception of Oriental society. Naturally, the oscillating processes between Europeans and non-Europeans openly and latently shaped both societies. If projection is considered to be a cultural technique for self-affirmation and demarcation, then assigning a collective (negative) identity to the (colonialized) "other" implied the colonialists' generating their own identity in a specific colonial context. Indeed, some European enlightenment figures even had gone as far as to use the "Orient" as a didactic background to criticize their own urban societies, thereby setting out the frame of reference for their own identities.

The intrinsic impact of reciprocity and mutuality of the colonial process may have found one political manifestation in indirect rule, which was, however, not implemented in its totality, because the British administration got involved in internal affairs of these societies very quickly, at times resembling the French system of direct colonial administration. In India one manifestation of British indirect rule was the establishment of an honors system and the issuing of titles. The residency system provided for the cultural success of imperialism, a success that found its climax in the "invention of tradition" as it represented colonial authority in Victorian India through different devices, such as highly ritualistic events to mark Queen Victoria's accession in 1876 to the title "Kaisar-e Hind" (Empress of India, combining the imperial titles of Roman "Caesar," German "Kaiser," and Russian "Czar.")

The nineteenth-century Orientalist image and action not only cemented the dominant image of the Orient in the West but also affected the self-statement of the Orient. Consequently this image changed non-Western practices concretely—from blind imitation of modernization to a total rejection of Western society, thereby forming a "strange alliance" between western Orientalism and Muslim fundamentalism, whence one side satisfied the essentializing fantasies of the other.

## Colonialism and the Emergence of Islamic Movements

The deep traces of colonialism that changed the whole landscape of the Muslim world brought about new social formations, and new Islamic movements:

- Reform Islam was prominent among pastoral and tribal societies, based on Wahhabiyyan and other ideas.

- Reform Sufism started off in urban, pastoral, and tribal areas, first against feudal rule and later opposing European intrusion. In doing so, the figure of prophet Muhammad became even more pivotal, hence the establishment of "Muhammadan Paths" (*turuq Muhammadiyya*) in the colonialized regions.

This kind of mystical approach found its climax in the movement of the Mahdi of Sudan.

- A third trend was Islamic modernism, represented primarily by intellectuals, bureaucrats, and the military, and manifested in creations of the colonial system, like the Aligarh Movement in India, the Young Ottomans, and the so-called pan-Islamic movement.

These movements adjusted to the new conditions and opted for the integration of the colonial system with Islamic theology. Jamal al-Din al-Afghani and Sayyid Ahmad Khan were two exponents of the modernizing trend, however different their motivations may have been. Precondition for the ideologization of Islam was a renewed call for the reintroduction of independent reasoning (*ijtihad*) at the cost of adherence to one's school of law (*taqlid*). Timeless categories developed in the course of Western civilization were now regarded as immanently Islamic. The use of media in exile—mostly in the metropolises of their colonial motherlands—was part of that strategy.

As a result of colonialism a three-layered structure emerged: secularized urban (post-colonial) state regimes, traditional urban nonpolitical Muslim religious associations, and urban middle-class opposition movements that stood for some kind of a reconstruction of a Muslim state.

Subsequently, after political independence following the Second World War, the new Muslim states were mostly centralized and secularized, based on military or bureaucratic elites with state capitalism or socialism favoring the ruling elites. Islamic modernism was replaced by secular nationalism, co-opting Muslim leaders who would legitimize this centralism. To be sure, the identity-giving Islamic symbolism was used for the mobilization of wider strata of society.

The nonpolitical Muslim religious associations mostly stayed quietistic, while new movements among parts of the ulema played on their Islamicity. Some of them referred to concepts tuned to colonial society, basically so as not to fall behind completely in terms of political influence. The opposition movements stood for the reconstruction of a Muslim state and reorganized Islam in different ways, for example, the theory of the caliphate providing an extended interpretation to legitimize power, rendering Islam into a comprehensive system that was to counter Western ideologies.

One branch of this Muslim cultural manifestation is of quite some importance. For example, religious fundamentalism, which has to be seen as a reaction to colonial encroachment as well as a demarcation against folk-religious traditions, reevaluating Islam in terms of political ideology, was elaborated upon only during the 1930s.

Its carriers were integrated into the post-colonial system, due to which they adopted and adapted its major terms, giving them an Islamic garb. This normative replacement enabled these Islamic classicists to transcend traditional boundaries and legitimize modern developments within the Islamic semiotics. In this process of reinvention of tradition, code- or identity-switching is most important, providing this political Islam with its particular dynamics.

The latest development in the wake of colonialism is the emigration of large Muslim communities to Europe and North America. The migration pattern follows colonial and historical traditions, that is, Maghrebian Muslims in France, Southeast Asian Muslims in the Netherlands, South Asian Muslims in Britain, and Turkish Muslims in Germany.

*See also* **Fundamentalism; Orientalism.**

## BIBLIOGRAPHY

Al-Azmeh, Aziz. *Islam and Modernities*. London: Verso, 1993.

Malik, Jamal, ed. *Perspectives of Mutual Encounters in South Asian History: 1760–1860*. Leiden: E. J. Brill, 2000.

Said, Edward. *Orientalism: Western Conceptions of the Orient*. London: Routledge & Kegan Paul, 1979.

Schulze, Reinhard. *Geschichte der islamischen Welt im 20. Jahrhundert*. Munich: Beck, 1994.

*Jamal Malik*

# COMMUNISM

Both communism and Islam pose solutions to social, moral, economic and political order. Their differences, however, are numerous and fundamental. Communist movements have developed throughout the Islamic world but they have been limited to a narrow social base, and have most often been composed of non-Muslims. Communist groups became deeply involved with debating the Marxist-Leninist theoretical reasons for this failure to obtain mass support. These debates further fragmented most communist movements in the Islamic world. Communism in the Middle East was never a serious contender for power, and the collapse of the Soviet Union further marginalized communism worldwide.

Islamic scholars critiqued communism in several areas. Foremost, communism denies the existence of God. In doing so, it is directly opposed to Islam and Islamic tenets of faith. Further, Islam views history in a different way than does communism. Rather than the communist dialectic, and the movement of history from capitalism to communism, Islam views history as a search for faith and truth. Historical development of society ends when Islam is accepted, not when capitalism is swept away by communism. Finally, in seeking social justice, Islam does not seek to make all persons equal; it accepts that some will have more than others. Islam achieves social justice through acceptance of the obligation of those with more to provide for those with less, through processes such as *zakat* (alms giving).

Before the Second World War, communist movements in the Middle East consisted of small groups of intellectuals, drawn to its anticolonial stance. The post-war environment, with Soviet expansionism and the collapse of the colonial powers, was initially considered by most communists as an opportunity to reach the masses. Soviet support to these groups was not automatic. The Cold War saw the Soviet Union faced with often-contradictory policies of supporting communist revolutionary movements and supporting governments aligned with Soviet interests. For instance, support to the Egyptian government under Jamal 'Abd al-Nasser was valuable to Soviet interests, but conflicted with addressing the needs of the Egyptian Communist Party. In other cases, such as Iran, the Soviets provided clandestine support to the communists. Meanwhile, under the Eisenhower Doctrine, the United States formalized its opposition to communist movements in the Middle East. Under this doctrine, the United States intervened militarily in Lebanon in 1958, and formed the Baghdad Pact against Soviet expansionism. Neither the United States nor the Soviet Union fully understood the driving forces of the area, as was demonstrated to each in Iran and Afghanistan in the late 1970s.

In Egypt, Palestine, and Lebanon in the 1920s, well-to-do intellectuals founded communist or socialist political groups. After the Second World War, the Syrian Communist Party, which had attracted support from Kurds and other minorities, grew to some importance in the 1950s, but never became a serious contender for power. The Lebanese Communist Party, outlawed until 1970, never gained more than a few thousand members. The Egyptian Communist Party shared the anticolonial views of Nasser, but he banned the party and imprisoned its leaders following his 1952 coup. Since then, communism in Egypt has been represented by a number of peripheral splinter groups.

In Iran, after the First World War, a major communist movement developed in Iran, where contact with Russian communists in Azerbaijan resulted in the formation of the Adalat Party, in 1917. In 1920 this became the Ferqeh-ye Komunist-e Iran. Outlawed in 1929, it was reestablished as the Tudeh Party in 1941. This was outlawed in 1949, but continued to develop underground. Party membership consisted mainly of intellectuals, military officers, and other elites, and its leadership was heavily factionalized. Following the overthrow of Mohammad Mosaddeq (1953), the Iranian government took firm action against the Tudeh, and decimated the Party. Splinter communist elements continued to be active in Iran through the late 1970s, playing a role in the

Islamic Revolution of 1979. These groups were eliminated or driven out of Iran as the clerics consolidated their power.

The Iraqi Communist Party (ICP, founded in 1934) has played a role out of proportion to its size in Iraqi politics, beginning with its participation in the independence movement against the British. The overthrow of the Hashemite kingdom in 1958 brought the party to national importance. The ICP mobilized a quarter-million demonstrators against a conservative coup attempt in 1959, and had its own armed militia. Its rival, the Ba'th Party, a secular, socialist movement espousing Arab unity and anticolonialism, immediately was plunged into conflict with the ICP after seizing power in 1963, and quickly outstripped it in influence. In 1974, all opposition parties, including the ICP, were consolidated into the Progressive National Front (PNF), which allowed the Ba'ath to firmly control the opposition movements. From 1978 to 1979, the government arrested and executed many ICP leaders, while others fled the country.

Only one Middle Eastern state, the People's Republic of Yemen, has had a Marxist government. While a British colony, a violent independence movement developed with Soviet support. Following independence in 1967, the Soviet-funded National Liberation Front, a Marxist group, took and held power. The Front was convulsed by factionalism, and quickly became more ideological and repressive. To divert popular dissent, the Front fought skirmishes with neighboring Oman, Saudi Arabia, and North Yemen. When the Soviet Union collapsed, South Yemen no longer received Soviet aid, and the long-standing attempt to merge North and South Yemen under a single, noncommunist government, officially succeeded in 1990, although outbreaks of unrest still occur.

The late 1960s saw a resurgence of splinter communist movements among students and intellectuals, as Maoism and Guevarism became popular. These movements had no significant mass appeal, but because of the violent tendencies of the groups, they had some political impact as governments attempted to control them. Some Palestinian groups absorbed these ideologies and their emphasis on violence and revolution. The Popular Front for the Liberation of Palestinian (PFLP), the Democratic Front for the Liberation of Palestine (DFLP), and the Popular Front for the Liberation of Palestine-General Command (PFLP-GC) all combined Marxist-Leninism with Palestinian nationalism. In most countries, there were no more than a few hundred adherents of these revolutionary communist ideologies, and these were often splintered into several groups with narrow ideological differences.

The model of communist revolt, involving mobilizing the proletariat, failed in the Middle East. Attempts by some communists to adapt their principles to local conditions failed due to the ideological rigidity of communist leadership.

Other factors included the suppression of communist movements by almost all regional governments, ideological infighting and factionalism among the communists, and the availability of alternative social and economic structures that satisfied most of the populations. The collapse of the Soviet Union left most communists further isolated from public opinion.

*See also* **'Abd al-Nasser, Jamal; Ba'th Party; Political Organization; Political Thought; Socialism.**

## BIBLIOGRAPHY

Batatu, Hana. *The Old Social Classes and the Revolutionary Movements in Iraq: A Study of Iraq's Old Landed and Commercial Classes and of its Communists, Ba'thists and Free Officers.* Princeton, N.J.: Princeton University Press, 1978.

Cottam, Richard W. *Nationalism in Iran.* Pittsburgh, Pa.: University of Pittsburgh Press, 1979.

Ismael, Tareq Y., and El-Sa'id, Rifa'at. *The Communist Movement in Egypt, 1920–1988.* Syracuse, N.Y.: Syracuse University Press, 1990.

*Richard C. Campany, Jr.*

## CONFLICT AND VIOLENCE

In the contemporary period, Islam is frequently depicted as predisposed to conflict and violence. The intractable Middle East conflict and recent events in which Muslim extremists have been implicated in acts of terror have only served to reinforce this widespread perception. To discern the veracity of the assertion that in some special way Islam is related to deadly conflict, it is important to situate the discussion within a concrete sociohistorical context. Islam, conflict, and violence do not occur in a social vacuum. Moreover, in order to correctly understand the ethical norms of Islam represented in the Muslim sacred scripture, the Qur'an, and in the exemplary conduct of the prophet Muhammad, it is necessary to analyze the historical milieu within which such norms were negotiated.

When the prophet Muhammad (570–632 C.E.) brought the Qur'an to the Arabs in the early seventh century, pre-Islamic Arabia was steeped in oppressive social relations and caught up in a vicious cycle of violence. Muhammad's egalitarian message quickly began to threaten the Meccan elite. They opposed his teachings with great vehemence. He was forced to send some of his early followers to seek refuge in Abyssinia and later, in 622 C.E., he himself fled to the nearby city of Medina. Throughout the Meccan period, the early Muslims responded to the mental anguishes, physical abuse, and persistent threats to their lives with passive resistance. It was only thirteen years into his prophetic mission that Muhammad and the early Muslims were permitted to engage in armed resistance, but only under certain stringent conditions, as specified in the Qur'an.

> Permission [to fight] is given to those against whom war is being wrongfully waged. God has indeed the power to succor them: those who have been driven from their homelands against all right for no other reason than their saying, "Our Lord and Sustainer is God! For, if God had not enabled people to defend themselves against one another, monasteries and churches and synagogues and mosques—in which God's name is abundantly extolled—would surely have been destroyed." (22:39–40)

It is interesting to note that the above verses give precedence to the protection of monasteries, churches, and synagogues over that of mosques in order to underline their inviolability and the duty of the Muslim to safeguard them against any desecration or abuse, and protect freedom of belief. The aim of fighting according to this critical verse is the defense of not only Islam, but also of religious freedom in general.

In the succeeding decade (622–632 C.E.) Muhammad and his growing band of followers engaged in a series of battles to defend Islam against the military aggression of their adversaries, including the critical battles of Badr, Uhud, and Khandaq. Warfare was a desperate affair in seventh-century Arabia. A chieftain was not expected to display weakness to his enemies in a battle, and some of the Qur'anic injunctions seem to share this spirit (4:90). Because the Qur'an was revealed in the context of deadly conflict, several passages deal with the ethics of warfare. (5:49; 8:61; 11:118–119; 49:9; 49:13). The most contentious of these is the so-called sword verse (*ayat al-sayf*).

> Once the sacred months have passed, you may kill the idolaters when you encounter them, and take them [captive], and besiege them, and prepare for them each ambush. But if they repent and establish worship and pay the poor-due, then leave their way free. Lo! God is Forgiving, Merciful. (9:5)

Some classical Muslim commentators have construed this verse to imply that Muslims are obligated to fight non-Muslims until they embrace Islam in the case of polytheists, or pay a special tax known as *jizya*, in the case of Jews and Christians who are referred to as the "people of the book."

Yet other verses include exhortations to peace: "Thus, if they let you be, and do not make war on you, and offer you peace, God does not allow you to harm them" (4:90). The Qur'an quotes the Torah, the Jewish scriptures, which permits people to retaliate eye for eye, tooth for tooth, but like the Gospels, the Qur'an suggests that it is meritorious to forgo revenge in a spirit of charity (5:45). Hostilities must be brought to an end as quickly as possible and must cease the minute the enemy sues for peace (2:192–193). The Qur'an, moreover, makes it emphatically clear that conflict can only be successfully ameliorated through the establishment of justice, which transcends sectarian self-interests. (4:135; 7:29)

> O Believers! Stand firmly for justice, as witnesses for God, even it is means testifying against yourselves, or your parents, or your kin, and whether it is against the rich or the poor, for God prevails upon all. Follow not the lusts of your hearts, lest you swerve, and if you distort justice or decline to do justice, verily God knows what you do. (4:135)

The just war is always evil, but sometimes one has to fight in order to avoid the kind of persecution that Mecca inflicted on the Muslims (2:191; 2:217), or to preserve decent values (4:75; 22:40). During his stay in Medina, Muhammad attempted to resolve the conflict with the Meccan leaders and their allies by entering into a peace treaty at a place called al-Hudaybiya. The treaty came to be known as *sulh al-Hudaybiya*. *Sulh* is an important term in Islamic law (*shari'a*). The purpose of *sulh* is to end conflict and hostility among adversaries so that they may conduct their relationships in peace and amity (49:9). The word itself has been used to refer both to the process of restorative justice and peacemaking and to the actual outcome of that process. Even though *sulh al-Hudaybiya* never actually achieved its aims because the Meccan tribesmen violated its conditions, it remains as an instructive conflict-intervention strategy.

In 630 C.E., the Muslims gained their most significant victory when they captured the city of Mecca, remarkably without bloodshed. This provided Muhammad with a second opportunity to institute a genuine *sulh* process. In a spirit of magnanimity, he forgave his enemies and enacted a process of reconciliation. A general amnesty was proclaimed in which all tribal claims to vengeance were abolished. Three years later Muhammad died in Medina at the age of sixty-three.

The Qur'anic term most often conflated with that of violence is jihad. The Arabic verb *jahada* from which the verbal noun jihad is derived literally means "to strive hard, to exert strenuous effort and to struggle." As a multivalent Islamic concept, it denotes any effort in pursuit of a commendable aim. Jihad is a comprehensive concept embracing peaceful persuasion (16:125) and passive resistance (13:22; 23:96; 41:34), as well as armed struggle against oppression and injustice (2:193; 4:75; 8:39). The Islamic concept of jihad should not be confused with the medieval concept of holy war since the actual word *al-harb al-muqaddasa* is never used in the Qur'an. In Islam, a war is never holy; it is either justified or not. Moreover, jihad is not directed at other faiths. In a statement in which the Arabic is extremely emphatic, the Qur'an insists, "There must be no coercion in matters of faith!" (2:256). More than this, the protection of freedom of belief and worship for followers of other religions has been made a sacred duty of Muslims. This duty was fixed at the same time when the permission for armed struggle (*jihad al-qital*) was ordained (22:39–40).

In mystical (Sufi) traditions of Islam the greatest form of jihad, personal jihad, is to purify the soul and refine the disposition. This is regarded as the far more urgent and momentous struggle and it is based on a prophetic tradition (hadith). Muhammad is reported to have advised his companions as they return after a battle, "We are returning from the lesser jihad [physical fighting] to the greater jihad [*jihad al-nafs*]." Sufis have traditionally understood this greater form of jihad to be the spiritual struggle to discipline the lower impulses and base instincts in human nature. The renowned thirteenth-century Sufi scholar, Jalal al-Din Rumi, articulated such an understanding of jihad when he wrote: "The prophets and saints do not avoid spiritual struggle. The first spiritual struggle they undertake is the killing of the ego and the abandonment of personal wishes and sensual desires. This is the greater jihad" (Chittick, trans., p. 151).

After the demise of the Prophet and the completion of the textual guidance of the Qur'an, Muslims were faced with the challenge of interpreting and applying the Islamic normative principles on conflict and violence to their own peculiar sociohistorical contexts. Subsequent generations of Muslims have interpreted these normative values in such a way as to give Islam a paradoxical role in human history. In the first three centuries of Islam the classical doctrine of jihad was forged by Muslim jurists primarily in response to the imperial politics of the Abbasid caliphate on the one hand and the Byzantine Empire on the other. Abrogating the Meccan experience and predicating itself on selected verses of the Qur'an, one finds the following: "And fight them on until there is no more oppression and tumult (*fitnah*) and religion should be for God" (2:193). Classical scholars developed a doctrine of jihad in which the world is simply divided into a dichotomy of abodes: the territory of Islam (*dar al-islam*) and the territory of war (*dar al-harb*). In accordance with this belligerent paradigm, a permanent state of war (jihad) characterized relations between the two abodes. The only way a non-Muslim territory could avert a jihad was either to convert to Islam or to pay an annual tribute or poll tax (*jizyah*). The classical belief erroneously perceived of jihad as the instrument of the Islamic caliphate to expand Muslim territories.

Though most Muslim artists refrain from creating representations of the prophet Muhammad and his family, this 1368 Turkish book painting depicts the Prophet, with his face covered by a white cloth, leading his disciples on horseback to Badr to confront the pagan Meccan army. THE ART ARCHIVE/TOPKAPI MUSEUM ISTANBUL/HARPER COLLINS PUBLISHERS

This controversial interpretation of jihad failed to capture the full range of the term's rich meaning. The reductionist interpretation of jihad, though not unanimous, came to dominate subsequent Muslim juristic thinking. One of the earliest scholars who represented an alternative perspective was Sufyan al-Thawri (b. 715). Al-Thawri believed that jihad was only justified in defense. The classical doctrine of jihad has and continues to be challenged by Muslim jurists. A number of modern Muslim reform movements have employed the classical doctrine of jihad to legitimate their struggles against colonial or postcolonial secular state rule. Other contemporary Muslim scholars, such as Muhammad Abu Zahra, Mahmud Shaltut, Muhammad al Ghunaimi, Louay M. Safi, and Ridwan al-Sayyid, have criticized the classical doctrine of jihad as being seriously flawed since it violates some of the essential Islamic principles on the ethics of war. Safi has written objecting to the classical doctrine: "Evidently, the classical doctrine of war and peace has not been predicated on a comprehensive theory. The doctrine describes the factual conditions that historically prevailed between the Islamic state, during the 'Abassid and Byzantium era, and thus, renders rules which respond to specific historical needs" (Safi, p. 44).

Safi and Al-Sayyid as well as a number of other contemporary scholars hold that the classical doctrine of hegemonic jihad is contingent on a historical context and thus has a limited application. They have argued for a recovery of the alternative interpretation of classical scholars, such as Malik ibn Anas, the founder of the Maliki school of Islamic jurisprudence, who identified a third option, the territory of peaceful covenant or coexistence or (dar-al-sulh or 'ahd). He had in mind the long-standing cordial relationship that had existed between the early Muslims and the Abyssinian Christian state. He recalled that the prophet Muhammad himself had sent the earliest group of his followers from Mecca to seek refuge from persecution in Abyssinia. They lived there peacefully for many years, and some of them did not return, even after Muslims were in power in Mecca. Moreover, the Prophet had advised peaceful coexistence with the Abyssinians, reportedly saying: "Leave the Abyssinians in peace as long as they leave you in peace." Safi contends that the fact that the early Muslims did not make any attempts to turn Abyssinia into an Islamic state is sufficient evidence that a third way, the "Abyssinian paradigm," was an Islamically sanctioned alternative.

The alternative paradigm represented by the Abyssinian model was marginalized and ignored by the partisan interpretations of the classical Muslim jurists. Contemporary Muslims are currently reclaiming this third paradigm of peaceful coexistence. Others called on contemporary Muslims to reclaim the rich Sufi tradition on conflict transformation by relinking the lesser jihad to that of the greater jihad (p. 108). Both have profound implications for expanding Muslim resources for conflict transformation and peace-building efforts.

*A candid photograph appears in the color insert.*

*See also* **Fitna; 'Ibadat; Jihad; Political Islam.**

## BIBLIOGRAPHY

Abou El Fadl, Khaled. *Rebellion and Violence in Islamic Law.* New York: Cambridge University Press, 2001.

Armstrong, Karen. *Muhammad: A Biography of the Prophet.* San Francisco, Calif.: Harper San Francisco, 1992.

Chittick, William, trans. *The Sufi Path of Love: The Spiritual Teachings of Rumi.* Albany: State University of New York Press, 1983.

Khadduri, Majid. *War and Peace in Islam.* New York: AMS Press, 1979.

Lings, Martin. *Muhammad: His Life According to the Earliest Sources.* New York: Inner Traditions International, 1983.

Peters, Rudolph. *Jihad in Classical and Modern Islam: A Reader.* Princeton, N.J.: Markus Wiener Publishers, 1996.

Safi, Louay M. *Peace and the Limits of War—Transcending Classical Conception of Jihad.* Herndon, Va.: International Institute of Islamic Thought, 2001.

Said, Abdul Aziz; Funk, Nathan C.; and Kadayifci, Ayse S., eds. *Peace and Conflict Resolution in Islam.* New York: University Press of America, 2001.

*A. Rashied Omar*

# CONVERSION

In Islam conversion consists of the recitation of the *shahada* or profession of faith which is composed of two affirmations from the Qur'an that have been integrated to form a single declaration of faith in the uniqueness and oneness of God and the finality of His revelation to the prophet Muhammad. It reads "There is no god but God [Allah, the Arabic proper name for God used by both Arabic-speaking Muslims and Christians], and Muhammad is the Messenger of God." The Qur'an uses the terms "The Messenger of God" and "The Prophet" synonymously to refer to Muhammad, who is implicitly declared to be the last of God's genuine prophets.

Some Muslim scholars, among them the renowned Persian mystic, philosopher, and theologian al-Ghazali (1058–1111 C.E.), are of the opinion that a declaration of intent (*niya*), made prior to the recitation of the *shahada*, is necessary for its validity and for the validity of such ritual acts as prayer, fasting, and almsgiving. On the other hand many Muslim lawyers are persuaded that *niya* is only necessary for the validity of prayer (*salat*).

In early Islam conversion was not a condition for membership of the *umma* or Muslim community. Prior to the surrender of Mecca in 629 C.E. the Jews of Medina had the same rights and obligations as other members of the *umma*. After the fall of Mecca to Muhammad the *zakat* (alms tax) was levied on converts to Islam, benevolence being one of the chief virtues of the true believer, and the *jizya* (a personal poll-tax to be paid, where possible, in money) was imposed on all non-Muslims (with the exception of certain categories of persons including women, the poor, the enslaved, and impoverished monks) who wanted to join the *umma*.

### Jihad and Conversion

While the spread of Islam is a religious duty, the Qur'an also instructs believers that there should be no compulsion in matters of religion (2:256), thus seemingly ruling out coercion as a means of conversion. There are many scholars of Islam, Muslim and non-Muslim, who are persuaded, largely on the basis of this text, that the obligation to perform jihad of the sword (*al-jihad bi-il-sayf*)—sometimes described as the lesser form of jihad, in contrast to *jihad bi-il-nafs* or moral and spiritual jihad, as the greater form—is only legitimate where the free practice of Islam is impeded.

Where jihad of the sword is contemplated there is the obligation of the summons, *da'wa*, which is based on Qur'an 17:15 and 16:25. The summons is meant to inform those to be attacked that Islam does not intend to pursue war for material gain such as property but for the purpose of defending or strengthening Islam. There are differences of opinion between the four principal Sunni schools of law (*madhahib*) on the necessity of *da'wa* for people who have previously been summoned to Islam. The Malikites believe it to be obligatory in this case also, the Hanafites recommend it, and the Shafites and Hanbalites say it is a matter of indifference.

Islam has rarely spread, in the sense of converting large numbers of non-Muslims of a territory, through jihad of the sword. The fundamentalist eighteenth-century reform movement in Arabia, the Wahhabiyya, as it is called by its opponents and by Europeans—the members referred to themselves as the Muwahiddun or Unitarians—was essentially a reform movement, not a drive to convert non-Muslims. Where and when jihad of the sword has been used its effect has usually been to establish a Muslim as the ruler of a territory, an outcome that was by no means always followed by large-scale attempts to convert the local population. A partial explanation for this can be found in Islamic political theory according to which the imposition of Muslim rule over a territory is sufficient to make that territory part of dar al-islam (the abode of Islam). The principal carriers of Islam have been holy men, jurists, traders, and, in the case of the spread of Islam to the Western world in modern times, economic migrants, refugees, and asylum seekers

In the time of the prophet Muhammad, conversion by conquest and political submission was basically limited to two societies, the Bedouins of Arabia and the Berbers of the Maghrib. After the prophet Muhammad's death in 632 C.E. the military conquest of the Fertile Crescent and Egypt was swift but did not account for the conversion of most of the population of these regions. This was to come about through a process of acculturation as the local people moved from the rural areas to the garrison towns (*amsar*) such as Qayrawan (Maghrib), Kufa (Iraq), and Basra (Iraq), as traders, craftsmen, laborers, and domestics who over time adopted the Arabic language and Islam.

### Trade, Commerce, Sufism/Mysticism, and Conversion

The image non-Muslims in many parts of the world have had and continue to have of Islam is that of a progressive, modern religion offering literacy, a widely spoken language, numeracy, and the opportunity to participate in a wider commercial, political, and trading network. Islam often spread very slowly and even laboriously, its own progress greatly affected by the changing local economic, political, and religious situation in which it found itself. Islam's development in the Malay-Indonesian archipelago is a case in point. Archaeology tells us that by the late eleventh century there was a Muslim presence in Indonesia, and it would not be surprising given the commercial attraction of the archipelago and its role as a natural staging post between the Middle East and India on one side and China, where there has been a Muslim presence in the South from the ninth century, if Islam did not in fact arrive even earlier. According to Marco Polo who visited North Sumatra in 1292 the kingdom of Ferlak (Perlak) in present-day Aceh was already Muslim. If the process of expansion was slow it was also peaceful. Only in the fourteenth century did Islam spread to Northeast Malaya and Brunei, to the court of east Java, and to the southern Philippines. And it was to take another two hundred years before it found its way in to other parts of the archipelago when Sufism or mysticism (*tasawwuf*), in institutionalized and noninstitutionalized forms, came to play a pivotal role in the widespread dissemination of Islam among the people of Java and elsewhere. According to tradition Islam was brought to Java by nine saints or *wali*s, and over a long period of four hundred years more gradually penetrated the society at all levels, never, however, displacing entirely other religious traditions.

The importance of Sufism in the conversion of large numbers to Islam elsewhere can hardly be exaggerated. The conversion of Bengal, like that of Java, is also attributed to Sufis. Institutionalized forms of Sufism and principally the Sufi *tariqa*s or brotherhoods, among them the *Qadiriyya*, Tijaniyya, and Sanusiyya orders, were crucial to the expansion of Islam in North Africa and Africa south of the Sahara, as were the Mevlevi and Bektashi Sufi brotherhoods in Anatolia.

The indispensable role performed by traders, scholars, and holy men in laying the foundations of Islam is evident almost everywhere from the medieval empires of Takrur,

Ghana, Mali, Kanem Bornu, and Songhay, to the Nile Valley, the Horn, and the East African coast, and across much of the Asian sub-continent, Central Asia, and as far as China. In all of these regions Islam first arrived with traders who were often clerics or were accompanied by clerics and/or holy men. We know from a variety of sources including the travel writings of the fourteenth-century Moroccan Ibn Battuta (1304–1368/77 c.e.) that the first Muslims in ancient Ghana, Mali, China, Indonesia, Somalia, and elsewhere lived separately and followed their own way of life, making little or no attempt to convert others. In places this period of seclusion was followed by one of engagement with the wider society that usually resulted in mixing or syncretism, a development that gave rise to conservative reaction, sometimes in the form of jihad of the sword.

### Exile, Slavery, Economic Migration, and Conversion

Political exiles, convicts, and slaves have also been important vehicles for the dissemination of Islam as in the case of South Africa, where such people began to arrive from Southeast Asia in the mid-seventeenth century and formed the Cape Malay Muslim community. From the mid-nineteenth century Muslims arrived from India to form another distinct Islamic community, some coming as British-indentured labor to work on the sugar plantations, others as merchants and traders, and others as hawkers.

Economic migration has been the main vehicle for the spread of Islam to the Western world in modern times. No more than an exotic appendage to western European religion in the mid-twentieth century, largely through migration, the Muslim faith has become increasingly familiar across the European Union, and comprises an estimated fifteen million members, including relatively large numbers of converts from Christianity and other faiths. While there are no reliable statistics, the number of Muslims in North America would appear to be over four million and the number of mosques to serve them about two thousand.

### The Political, Cultural, and Religious Consequences of Conversion

Thus, in the spread and development of Islam, military conquest has never been as important or effective as the creation of an Islamic environment, educational system, trading networks, and generally the building up of Muslim institutions. It was these initiatives that facilitated the development of Islam in Iran over several centuries from a small community of mainly Arab Muslims to one that included the majority of the population by the early years of the eleventh century. Sometimes conversion was an individual affair, sometimes it was collective in the sense that if the leader of a community or ethnic group converted the rest of the people would follow.

This notwithstanding, it is worth noting that the establishment of Muslim rule in a territory, whether by conquest or by peaceful means, did not necessarily constitute a challenge to the existing political order nor was it necessarily the prelude to a campaign by the new government to convert all of the inhabitants of that territory to Islam. Where jihad of the sword has been employed it needs to be remembered that the primary objective has not always been expansion but the reform of the Muslim community, as in the case of the Wahhabiyya movement and as was most likely the case with the Sokoto jihad in northern Nigeria in the late eighteenth and early nineteenth century.

Examples abound where Muslim rule led to little or no immediate change for the majority of the population under it. In Egypt, Coptic Christians were given governmental posts until the fourteenth century when pressure from the ulema (scholars) forced a change. While the Muslim conquest of India eliminated the dominant Hindu political-military class, the Chhatri, it confirmed the privileged status of the Brahmins who remained the guardians of a cultural vision that was non-Muslim. Even at the height of its power the Muslim community consisted of only a quarter of the population of Delhi and Agra. And the Muslim conquest of Iran and the surrounding regions initially favored the spread of other faiths, among them Nestorianism and Manichaeism, rather than Islam. In Java the introduction of Islam offered a new dimension to existing traditional, Buddhist, and Hindu religious beliefs and practices, bringing few significant changes to the political life of society.

Where Muslims conquer non-Muslim territory Muslim canon law (*shari'a*) guarantees to protect the life, liberty, and, in a modified way, the property of that section of the local population that has not been captured in arms. These people are known as *ahl-al-dhimma* (people of the covenant) or simply as *dhimmi*s. All free adults who enjoy *dhimmi* status must pay the above-mentioned *jizya* or poll-tax and pay a tax (*kharaj*) on their real estate, over which they no longer enjoy the right of disposal. Strictly speaking, the status of *dhimmi*s is open only to "people of scripture" (*alh-al-kitab*), that is, Jews, Christians, and Sabaeans, a category that is interpreted to cover Zoroastrians. In practice most Muslim countries will tolerate all peoples regardless of whether they are "people of scripture" or not.

Where *dhimmi* status was granted it carried with it the obligation to contribute toward the maintenance of Muslim armies, to dress differently from Muslims, and to renounce such rights as the right to bear arms and to ride on horseback. Legal restrictions were also imposed in relation to testimony in law courts, protection under criminal law, and marriage. Apart from such restrictions, what in practice happens is that a non-Muslim community in a Muslim state virtually governs itself under its own responsible leader who acts as its link with the Muslim government. And where conversion to or from Islam is concerned it is expected that the leadership of the community that has made the conversion will inform its counterpart of the event.

## Conclusions

This account of the dynamics of conversion to Islam confines itself for the most part to the Muslim world. It is not exhaustive nor could it be given the great complexity and cultural diversity of that world. Appearance to the contrary notwithstanding, it is not intentionally reductionist. If greater consideration has been given to what might be termed the human, material, observable aspects of the phenomenon of conversion, and little has been said of its intellectual, spiritual, and theological dimensions, this should not be taken to mean that these dimensions are not more important elements of the process of becoming a Muslim or being Muslim.

Conversion in Islam is a radical call to reject all that associates the human with the divine, and on this foundation engages the convert in the task of personal and social transformation. It is a dynamic and multifaceted process of transformation that in some cases is gradual and in others abrupt; in some cases total, in others partial.

The path to Islam is more varied than outlined above. As students of conversion to Islam are aware individuals and whole communities have come to Islam having been first influenced by the personal example of a practicing Muslim, or through a process of intellectual conversion in which scholarly literature has played an important part, or through guidance given in a dream or a vision in which a *wali* or holy person, and even the prophet Muhammad himself, have appeared as counselors and guides, through mystical experiences, as a result of a search for healing, protection, and security, and for order and discipline in one's life. Either all or a combination of these triggers, and others, have activated the interest of individuals and communities in Islam and led to conversion.

*See also* **Da'wa; Expansion; Minorities: Dhimmis; Tasawwuf.**

## BIBLIOGRAPHY

Clarke, Peter B, ed. *New Trends and Developments in The World of Islam*. London: Luzac Oriental, 1998.

Haddad, Yvonne Yazbeck, ed. *The Muslims of America*. New York and Oxford, U.K.: Oxford University Press, 1991.

Horton, Robin. "African Conversion." *Africa* 41 (1971): 85–108.

Katz, E. Ulrich. "Islam in Indonesia." In *Islam*. Edited by Peter B. Clarke. London: Routledge, 1990.

Shaban, M. "Conversion to Early Islam." In *Conversion to Islam*. Edited by Nehemia Levtzion. New York: Holmes and Maier, 1979.

*Peter B. Clarke*

# CRUSADES

Both the word "crusades" and its Arabic equivalent, *al-hurub al-salibiyyah*, are modern terms. What these words refer to, however, can be quite different depending on who is using them. The dominant trend in secular academic research on the Crusades since the 1970s has been one of expansion of the topic in terms of activities and military campaigns included, of time span, and of geographic expanse. Despite this revisionism, there is little doubt that in the popular parlance of nonspecialists, the Crusades refers to the almost two-century-long presence (1097–1291 C.E.) of Latin Christians from central and western Europe in the Holy Land of the eastern Mediterranean coastal strip. Thus, while events after 1291—such as the Christian reconquest of Spain, campaigns against heretics in or on the borders of Latin Christendom, or the European conflicts with the Ottoman Empire—are now within the domain of current scholarship on the Crusades (particularly in Europe), they do not figure large in the discourse of the Crusades ongoing in the contemporary population of the Holy Land.

## Overview of the Crusades

At the Council of Clermont in 1095, Pope Urban II delivered a sermon that set in motion the Crusades. Precisely what he said is unknown, nor is there agreement as to his motivations and goals, but in the aftermath of Clermont, clergy, nobles, and commoners mobilized for campaigns to reconquer Jerusalem, which had been in Muslim hands since 638 C.E. While what comes next follows the common shorthand of referring to major Crusade campaigns by numbers, it should be emphasized that this practice does not take into account the steady stream of armed pilgrims flowing into and out of the Holy Land nor the numerous smaller military campaigns that they undertook.

The First Crusade (1097–1101) resulted in the establishment of four Crusader states in lands of the eastern Mediterranean littoral: the County of Edessa, the Principality of Antioch, the County of Tripoli (although the city itself was not captured until 1109), and the Kingdom of Jerusalem. In light of the obstacles these first crusaders faced in their long journey east—shortages of supplies, uneasy relations with the Byzantine Empire, travel across rough and unfamiliar terrain inhabited by hostile populations, lack of organization, and internal rivalries, to name but a few—this initial success was remarkable. Indeed, the First Crusade almost ended at Antioch between 1097 and 1098, where the Crusaders first laid siege to the Muslims for several trying months, and upon victory were subsequently besieged themselves by numerically superior forces.

This Crusader victory is usually linked to the disunited opposition they faced. In the late eleventh century C.E., there was no single powerful Muslim state to oppose the invasion of the *ifranj* (Franks), as the Muslims called the invaders. In many cities of the Seljuk confederation, military authorities known as *atabeg*s were busy establishing their autonomy, and were often preoccupied by rivalries with other local Muslim rulers. The Sunni Abbasid caliphate in Baghdad was unable to directly influence military affairs. The Shi'ite Fatimid caliphate in Cairo, itself engaged in a struggle against the Seljuks for control of Jerusalem, did comparatively little to counter the Crusader incursion. In the words of the Muslim chronicler Ibn al-Athir: "When the Franks—may God curse them—extended their control over what they had conquered of the lands of Islam, and it turned out well for them that the troops and the kings of Islam were preoccupied with fighting each other, at that time opinions were divided among the Muslims, desires differed and wealth was squandered" (Hillenbrand, 31). Over the next four decades the Crusaders entrenched themselves in the landscape of Outremer (literally, "across-the-sea"), skirmished with the Muslims, and began the construction of numerous castles, made necessary by their constant shortage of manpower.

The first major success of the Muslim counter-Crusade was achieved by the Turkish military leader Zangi, the *atabeg* of Mosul and Aleppo. After consolidating his control over northern Syria and the Jazira (northwestern Iraq), he launched a series of campaigns against the Crusaders, culminating in his capture of Edessa in 1144. Zangi's elimination of this Crusader state gave added impetus to calls in Europe for another major Crusade. Forces of the Second Crusade subsequently arrived in Syria in 1147, and after heated discussion between the resident Crusaders and the new arrivals, decided to attack Damascus, ironically one of the Muslim cities whose ruler up to that point had coexisted with the Franks. This campaign ended in defeat for the Crusaders on the outskirts of Damascus in July 1148.

Zangi's career as a counter-Crusader was cut short by his assassination in 1146, but was continued by his son Nur al-Din. Nur al-Din expanded the area under his control, occupying Damascus in 1154, and, utilizing the vocabulary of jihad, he launched attacks against the Franks. In response to numerous Crusader sorties against Egypt in the 1160s, Nur al-Din sent a contingent of his forces to aid the Fatimid state. This force was led by the Kurdish general Shirkuh, who had in his service his nephew Salah al-Din Yusuf b. Ayyub, subsequently known as Saladin to the Crusaders. Upon his uncle's death, Saladin took command of this force, and by March 1169, took control of Egypt, subsequently bringing the Fatimid Caliphate to an end. Following the death of Nur al-Din in 1174, Saladin moved against his former overlord's heirs and brought Damascus and eventually most of Syria (Aleppo submitted in 1183) and the Jazira (Mosul submitted in 1186) under his control. He then mounted a major campaign against the Franks, defeating the bulk of their forces at the battle of the Horns of Hattin near Tiberius on 4 July 1187. Jerusalem fell to him by October of that year, and the Crusader holdings were reduced to a few castles and coastal cities.

These victories made Saladin a hero. A contemporary poet wrote of him,

You took possession of Paradises palace by palace,

When you conquered Syria fortress by fortress.

Indeed, the religion of Islam has spread its blessings over created beings,

But it is you who have glorified it. (Hillenbrand 1999, p. 179)

The defeat of the Latin forces also sparked the Third Crusade (1189–1192), in which three European monarchs were personally involved: the German emperor Frederick I, King Philip II of France, and King Richard I (the Lionheart) of England. Frederick drowned in Anatolia on his way to Outremer, and Philip and Richard quarreled from the moment of their arrival in the Latin East. Nevertheless, their combined forces helped recapture Acre, henceforth the capital of the truncated Kingdom of Jerusalem. After Philip's return to France, Richard led a series of campaigns against Saladin and, by his departure in 1192, had aided in the reestablishment of Latin control over most of the coastal cities and their immediate hinterlands.

Saladin's death in 1193 provided a temporary respite to the Crusaders, as his successors (collectively known as the Ayyubids, from the name of Saladin's father) engaged in struggles over preeminence in the lands that had been united by Saladin. In these struggles, some Ayyubid princes were not adverse to making temporary alliances with the Franks against their Ayyubid rivals. The diversion of the Fourth Crusade (1204) to Constantinople, which was sacked and subsequently occupied, did little to change this situation in Outremer. These divisions among the Ayyubids contributed to the complex narrative of the Fifth Crusade (1217–1229). Recognizing the strategic importance of Egypt, this crusade began with the Franks besieging and eventually occupying the Egyptian port city of Damietta. In the face of intra-Ayyubid rivalries, the Ayyubid ruler of Egypt, al-Malik al-Kamil, offered to give Jerusalem to the Franks if they would leave Egypt, but the Crusaders refused. By 1221, the Crusaders were forced out of Egypt. The Fifth Crusade came to an end in the bizarre events of 1228–1229, in which the emperor Frederick II, excommunicated for his delays in fulfilling his crusading vows, successfully negotiated a treaty with al-Malik al-Kamil allowing the Christians to take control of certain

Crusades 1096–1229. XNR Productions, Inc./Gale

sites in Jerusalem, yet was bombarded with offal by the residents of Acre as he left to return to Europe. The last Crusader presence in Jerusalem was eliminated in 1244, when the city was sacked by Kharazmian warriors, themselves displaced from their homelands by the Mongol invasions from Central Asia.

The final major crusade to the Latin East was that of King Louis IX of France (1248–1254). Louis and his forces succeeded in capturing Damietta in 1249, but were subsequently defeated at Mansura in 1250 by the forces of the late Ayyubid ruler of Egypt, al-Malik al-Salih. Upon surrender and payment of a large ransom, Louis went to Acre, where he spent four years strengthening fortifications before returning to France.

To understand the end of the Crusader presence in Outremer, one must return to events of 1249–1250. During the course of Louis's Crusade in late 1249, the Ayyubid al-Malik al-Salih died. When his son Turanshah arrived from Syria in early 1250 to succeed his father, he took steps to limit the influence of key groups among his father's supporters.

Saladin, an early Muslim hero, conquered Egypt, most of Syria, and finally even Jerusalem by 1187. His victories banished the Crusaders from most territories; they began another Crusade, however, by 1189. © CORBIS-BETTMANN

The main target of Turanshah's punitive actions was the corps of his father's mamluks, or military slaves. In his struggles against his Ayyubid rivals, al-Malik al-Salih had built up a sizable regiment of these military slaves, who while still youths had been purchased as slaves from regions outside the Islamic world and subsequently converted to Islam and trained in military techniques. His regiment was known as the Bahri mamluks, since their barracks were located on an island in the river (*bahr*) Nile. Faced with loss of influence and possibly life, these mamluks of al-Malik al-Salih turned against Turanshah, and murdered him shortly after the victory of Mansura.

After this regicide, the history of the subsequent decade of the history of Muslim Egypt and Syria is dominated by a complex struggle for power, further complicated by the Mongol invasions. The decade ended with the definitive establishment of the Mamluk Sultanate in 1260 by Baybars, one of those Bahri mamluks. After consolidating Mamluk control, Sultan Baybars launched his forces against the Crusaders, capturing Antioch (in 1268) and several major Crusader castles. After Baybars' death in 1277 there was a brief lull, but attacks against the Crusaders resumed later in the reign of the Sultan Qalawun, who conquered Tripoli shortly before his death in 1289. Upon the capture of Acre in 1291 by the forces of Qalawun's son, al-Ashraf Khalil, the few Crusaders left on the coastal strip abandoned their holdings and fled, thus bringing Frankish presence in Outremer to an end, although no one at the time realized it. In order to discourage Crusader attempts to reoccupy the Muslim coastal cities, the Mamluks razed their fortifications.

## The Crusades in the Muslim World Today

A survey of scholarly literature and public discourse in the modern Muslim world reveals that the Crusades have great relevance and resonance today. They are commonly seen as the forerunner of the European colonial efforts of the first half of the twentieth century, placed in the context of perceived centuries of Western antagonism to the Islamic world, and often explicitly linked to the establishment of the modern state of Israel. (Crusade references appeared, for example, in a series of post–1956 Suez crisis Egyptian postage stamps celebrating Egypt as "Tomb of the Invader." One stamp celebrates Saladin's victory at Hattin; a second shows Louis IX in chains after his defeat at Mansura.) It is not uncommon to find references to Saladin and his victory at Hattin in political speeches or celebrated in books. In 1992, a larger-than-life statue of Saladin was unveiled in Damascus. The Crusades also figure in some modern Islamist writing, in which the failures of current leaders to resist Western incursions are compared to the successes of the heroes of the counter-Crusades. And while Hillenbrand (and others) have pointed out the pitfalls of the anachronistic use of nationalistic labels in the study of medieval history, the symbols and perceived lessons of the Crusades have been incorporated into the rhetoric of Arab nationalist movements in particular. Thus in the words of one Arab intellectual, the Crusades when viewed through Arab eyes are seen as an act of rape (Maalouf, 266).

*See also* **Christianity and Islam; Saladin.**

## BIBLIOGRAPHY

Hillenbrand, Carole. *The Crusades: Islamic Perspectives.* Chicago and London: Fitzroy Dearborn, 1999.

Maalouf, Amin. *The Crusades Through Arab Eyes.* London: Al Saqi Books, 1984.

Mayer, Hans Eberhard. *The Crusades.* 2d ed. Translated by John Gillingham. Oxford, U.K.: Oxford University Press, 1986.

Riley-Smith, Jonathan. *The Crusades: A Short History.* New Haven, Conn., and London: Yale University Press, 1987.

Riley-Smith, Jonathan. *The Atlas of the Crusades.* London and New York: Facts on File, 1991.

Runciman, Steven. *A History of the Crusades.* 3 vols. Cambridge, U.K.: Cambridge University Press, 1951–1954.

*Warren C. Schultz*

**CUSTOM** *See* ʿAda

# D

## DAR AL-HARB

The term *dar al-harb*, which literally means "the house or abode of war," came to signify in classical jurisprudence a geopolitical reality; hence, it may also be rendered the "territory" of war.

In the most basic sense the term indicates territory not governed by Islam, in contrast to territory under Islamic rule, *dar al-islam*. More precisely, these territories are geopolitical units within which Islam is not the established religion, where the ruler is not a Muslim, and where there exists no mechanism by which political or military leaders may seek the counsel of Islamic religious specialists. Use of the phrase *dar al-harb* further indicates the threat of war from the Muslim community. Muslim jurists differed on the mechanisms by which this threat of war could become a reality. For the majority, the leader of the Muslims must fulfill the obligation of "calling" the people of a non-Islamic territory to Islam. Once a people, through its rulers, refused the opportunity (1) to establish Islam as the state religion, or (2) to enter into a tributary arrangement with the leader of the Muslims, it was understood that war could follow. In accord with normative traditions, this war should be understood as an aspect of jihad, or the struggle to "make God's cause succeed," specifically by spreading Islamic government throughout the earth. It is important to note that the purpose of the war to expand the territory of Islam was not to make converts, but rather to establish Islamic government.

In modern times, the notion of *dar al-harb* has been employed by some Muslims to speak about territories lost to the forces of colonialism or, more generally, secularism. In this connection, the ruling of the Shah ʿAbd al-ʿAziz (d. 1824) regarding the status of British India is of great interest. As he had it, given British dominance in the subcontinent, India should no longer be considered Islamic territory. It was rather part of *dar al-harb*. Mirroring subsequent discussions in Islamic political and juridical thought, ʿAbd al-ʿAziz's followers drew differing conclusions from his ruling, some believing that cooperation with the British, particularly in the field of education, was a necessary prelude to a renewal of Islam and its cultural influence. Others were more inclined toward direct action with the goal of British withdrawal.

*See also* **Dar al-Islam.**

### BIBLIOGRAPHY

Kelsay, John. *Islam and War: A Study in Comparative Ethics.* Louisville, Ky.: Westminster/John Knox Press, 1993.

Shaybani, Muhammad ibn Hasan al-. *The Islamic Law of Nations.* Translated by Majid Khadduri. Baltimore, Md.: Johns Hopkins University Press, 1966.

*John Kelsay*

## DAR AL-ISLAM

The term *dar al-islam*, which literally means "the house or abode of Islam," came to signify Islamic territory in juridical discussions. For the majority, it is thus suggestive of a geopolitical unit, in which Islam is established as the religion of the state, in contrast to *dar al-harb*, territory not governed by Islam. The signs of legitimacy by which one could speak of a geopolitical unit as *dar al-islam* would include a ruler or ruling class whose self-identity is Islamic, some institutional mechanisms by which consultation between the political and religious elite is possible, and a commitment to engage in political and military struggle to extend the borders of the *dar al-islam*.

For others, the relationship between *dar al-islam* and existing political arrangements was not so easily negotiated. Thus, in one tradition the proto-Shiʿa leader Jaʿfar al-Sadiq (d. 765) is presented as suggesting that the territory of Islam exists wherever people are free to practice Islam and to engage in calling others to faith—even if the leadership in such a place does not acknowledge or establish Islam as the state religion. Correlatively, a territory in which the ruler or ruling class identifies with Islam, but where the (true) interpretation of Islamic sources is suppressed, is not *dar al-islam*, but something else.

In the modern period, one of the most vexing questions for jurists, and indeed for Muslims generally, has to do with the ongoing power of the symbol of *dar al-islam*. The experience of colonialism, the demise of the historic caliphate, and the formation of modern states present serious challenges to those who would follow classical precedent and utilize this symbol. One line of thought, expressed most succinctly by Shah 'Abd al-'Aziz (d. 1824), held that the influx of British power meant that India was no longer *dar al-islam*. As such, the Muslim community was under an obligation to struggle and bring about the restoration of Islamic influence. Others, by contrast, understood the classical use of the term as connected with an outmoded and even non-Islamic emphasis on empire. For these, in ways analogous to the thinking of Ja'far al-Sadiq, Islam "abides" wherever Muslims practice their religion and call others to faith.

*See also* **Dar al-Harb.**

## BIBLIOGRAPHY

Kelsay, John. *Islam and War: A Study in Comparative Ethics.* Louisville, Ky.: Westminster/John Knox Press, 1993.

Shaybani, Muhammad ibn Hasan al-. *The Islamic Law of Nations.* Translated by Majid Khadduri. Baltimore, Md.: Johns Hopkins University Press, 1966.

*John Kelsay*

# DA'WA

Since the late nineteenth century, conceptions of *da'wa* have re-emerged as central in the formulation of Islam. *Da'wa* is increasingly associated with socially vital activities, such as edification, education, conversion, and charity. However, the term also alludes to the Qur'an and the normative Islamic history. Due to this combination, *da'wa* has become a functional tool in face of the challenges of modernity. *Da'wa* is sometimes equated with Christian ideas of mission and evangelization. Muslims themselves are, as a rule, wary of that comparison; and indeed, such translations tend to overlook the variations and socio-political specificity of *da'wa*. This term has been conceptualized, institutionalized, and applied for divergent purposes throughout the course of history. Furthermore, Muslim endeavors to convert non-Muslims to Islam have often been understood in terms other than *da'wa*. This is true, for instance, of the significant Sufi ventures of recruitment, which historically largely appear to have been disinterested in *da'wa* terminology. Thus, *da'wa* should be regarded as but one type of Islamic discourse of mobilization, sometimes in conflict with others.

This entry introduces the range of conceptions of *da'wa*, paying attention to scriptural occurrence, historical development, and, finally, modern understandings and organizations.

## Scriptural Occurrence

The word *da'wa* is derived from an Arabic consonant-root, *d-'-w*, with several meanings, such as call, invite, persuade, pray, invoke, bless, demand, and achieve. Consequently, the noun *da'wa* has a number of connotations too. In the Qur'an and the sunna, *da'wa* partly has a mundane meaning and refers to, for instance, the invitation to a wedding. Sometimes the mundane and spiritual meanings are interconnected. In one account of the sunna (Bukhari), the invitation to Islam is allegorically referred to as an invitation to a banquet. Spelled with a long final vowel, the word means lawsuit.

Theologically, *da'wa* refers to the call of God to Islam, conveyed by the prophets: "God summons to the Abode of Peace" (10:25). Like the previous prophets, Muhammad is referred to as "God's caller" or "God's invitor," *da'i Allah* (46:31). God's call has to be distinguished from the false *da'wa* of Satan (14:22). Conversely, *da'wa* refers to the human call directed to God in (mental) prayer or invocation. The One God answers the *da'wa* directed to Him, whereas the prayers of the unbelievers are futile. The human *da'wa* is the affirmative response to the *da'wa* of God. It is not to be confused with *salat*, ritual prayer. When referring to human prayer or invocation, the Qur'an makes no distinction between *da'wa* and *du'a*, a related form of the same consonant-root. During the course of theological history, however, the term *du'a* evolved into a particular, technical concept, described and regulated in philosophical and devotional works, not least in handbooks of prayer.

Apart from affirming God's call in prayer, however, humankind is invited to live in accordance with the will of God: "Let there be one nation (*umma*) of you, calling to the good, enjoining what is right, forbidding what is wrong" (3:104). Thus *da'wa* is intimately interconnected with *shari'a*, the sacred law. As illustrated by verse 3:104, cited above, *da'wa* also has a social dimension in the Qur'an. The community of believers, the *umma*, who have received the invitation, shall convey the message to others. A commonly cited verse reads: "Call men to the way of the Lord with goodness and fair exhortation and have arguments with them in the best manner" (16:125). This verse, in turn, is commonly connected to the equally familiar verse: "Let there be no compulsion in religion" (2:256). Finally, there is an eschatological dimension of *da'wa*. At the end of time, the archangel Jibril (Gabriel) will call humans from their graves: "Then when He calls you by a single call from the earth, behold you come forth at once" (30:25).

All in all, the Qur'anic conceptualizations of *da'wa* conjoin a number of fundamental principles of Islamic theology. First of all, *da'wa* animates Islamic doctrine into an effective vocation, by interconnecting and urging humans to recognize the two core principles of the creed, as rendered in the *shahada*: "There is no god but God, and Muhammad is the messenger of God." Acknowledging and responding to God's *daʿwa* further means recognizing the sacredness of the *umma* and implementing *shariʿa*. Last but not least, *daʿwa* refers to the invitation of humankind to afterlife. It is, thus, hardly surprising that *daʿwa* sometimes is presented as interchangeable with the concept of Islam itself.

## Historical Development

After the death of Muhammad (632 C.E.), the leadership of the Muslim community became a controversial issue. A group called Shiʿat ʿAli, later to be known as Shiʿa, argued that ʿAli, Muhammad's cousin and son-in-law, and his descendants were the rightful caliphs, that is, vicegerents of the Prophet. ʿAli was eventually appointed caliph, and he is included as the fourth among the first four caliphs who Sunnites generally celebrated as righteous. In 661 he was killed, however, and the Umayyad dynasty, based in Damascus, established a hereditary rule. During the eighth century, the legitimacy of the Umayyads was increasingly put into question. Based in Baghdad, the Abbasids were accusing them for claiming kingship, *mulk*, thus vesting human leadership with an attribute and power that only God possesses. The lavish customs of the Damascus court underscored the anti-Umayyad *daʿwa*.

In this sense, *daʿwa* came to inherit a religio-political dimension, being the call to accept the rightful leadership of a certain individual or family. *Daʿwa* in the religio-political sense aimed at establishing or restoring the ideal theocratic state, based on monotheism. Here *daʿwa* can be understood as political propaganda inflated by Qurʾanic terminology. In spite of variations in the use of the term throughout history, this has been a recurring tendency.

*Daʿwa* thus became mainly an internal Muslim matter. However, the external aspect of *daʿwa*, "calling mankind," acquired increasing juridical importance in connection with the military expansion of Islam. According to the classical theory of jihad of the early Muslim conquests, warfare against non-Muslims could not be undertaken, nor could the protective tax of non-Muslims, *jizya*, be levied, had not a summons to Islam, *daʿwa*, been issued. During the late eighth century four *madhahib* (*madhhab*), schools of Sunni law (*fiqh*), developed. Here *daʿwa* was formalized into a set of judicial principles and rules included in martial law.

An important example of the application of *daʿwa* in history is the case of the Shiʿite Fatimids. Between 969 and 1171 they ruled a vast empire, with Cairo as the capital. For the Fatimids, who belong to the Ismaʿili branch of Shiʿa, *daʿwa* meant the appeal to give allegiance to the seventh imam, Muhammad b. Ismaʿil. Initially, their propaganda was directed against followers of the main branch of Shiʿa, the Imamis or Twelvers. As their power grew, the Fatimid *daʿwa*

turned against the Abbasid Sunnites, challenging their caliphal authority.

The Fatimids amplified the concept of *daʿwa* in accordance with Shiʿite doctrines of permanent revelation through the imams. The *daʿwa* of the imam was held to complete the *daʿwa* of the prophet Muhammad. The Fatimid *daʿwa* differed from the Abbasid *daʿwa* in that it did not cease after the establishment of the dynasty. Rather, it became increasingly organized and extensive. *Daʿwa* was thus institutionalized, integrating political claims with theological elaboration, centered around several educational institutions, most notably the al-Azhar University of Cairo. In areas controlled by the Fatimids, their *daʿwa* propaganda was overt, while the message was transmitted more secretly in other regions.

In a functional perspective, the core of the Fatimid use of *daʿwa* was similar to that of the Sunnite Abbasids. The amplification of *daʿwa* among these competing groups involved an understanding of political propaganda and aspirations based on theological criticism against other rulers. In both cases, thus, the core concern was the leadership issue. The Qurʾanic term *daʿwa* was rendered relevant primarily in the context of claims to political power. The Fatimid idea that propagation and acceptance of Islam should not be regarded as a singular event, but as a continuous process, forebears central themes in modern uses of *daʿwa*.

From the time of the Fatimids to early modern times, that is the late eighteenth and early nineteenth centuries, there are surprisingly few references to the concept of *daʿwa*. Paradoxically, *daʿwa* discourses seem to have entered a phase of recession despite the significant expansion of Islam that occurred in both Asia and Africa. Two of the reasons for this recession may be the legal formalism and the development of Sufism. While the Abbasid and Fatimid regimes relied on an Islamic ambience in which *daʿwa* held a politically central and strategic importance, Sufis were able to spread their message without such an ambience. Authority was vested in their leaders or shaykhs, who were often victims of state-centered persecution. Such a model of authority facilitated the transplantation of Islam to new regions, where mass conversions could take place. It is true that, with the exception of the earliest period, when Sufis were largely individualistic and ascetic, Sufism has frequently been politically important. However, the logic of Sufi expansion has usually been essentially different from state-centered or establishment Islam and, as a consequence, not in need of conceptions of *daʿwa* in the religio-political sense.

Since *daʿwa* as early as in the eighth century was a formal concept included in martial law, it became part of the Islamic jurisprudence, *fiqh*. From the tenth century onward, Sunnite leaders held the apparatus of *fiqh* as finalized. Thus, the gates of *ijtihad*, (new interpretations based on the main sources of Islamic law), the Qurʾan, and the sunna, were regarded by many jurists as closed. Legal matters were henceforth to be guided by *taqlid*, imitation of previous rulings. With the rise of *taqlid*-oriented *fiqh*, the learned scholars, ulema and *fuqaha*, were installed as its lawful, if largely impotent, administrators. When the quest for authority through personal interpretation (*ijtihad*) and opinion (*fatwa*) was rendered impossible or at least heavily curtailed, there was little or no need for *da'wa* discourse. In this sense, the authority of institutional law appears to have contributed to circumventing the centrality of the concept of *da'wa*, which was primarily understood in terms of the connection between religious legitimacy and political power.

It should be noted, finally, that at least one example of *da'wa* activity since Fatimid times has been recorded by scholars, namely a correspondence between the rulers of the Ottoman and the Safavid Empires during the early sixteenth century. This controversy over religio-political authority carries many similarities with the struggle between Abbasids and Fatimids. There may well have been others too. Thus, one cannot rule out scholarly omission or lack of interest as partly responsible for the silence of *da'wa* after the early centuries of Islam.

## Modern Times

European colonialism and Christian mission brought Muslims into intense encounters with non-Muslim ideas and practices. The processes of modernity (secularization, individualism, social reorganization, etc.) increasingly transformed Muslim societies. Technological, educational, and infrastructural changes made a lasting impact, and deeply rooted Islamic ideas and ways of life were put into question. Facing such challenges, many Muslims felt a need to reconsider or defend Islam, as well as to inform non-Muslims about Islamic principles and creeds. In this context, partly novel conceptualizations of *da'wa* claimed a core position in the Islamic debates and practices.

A precursor for the modern use of *da'wa* was the Ottoman sultan 'Abd al-Hamid II, who ruled between 1876 and 1909. Claiming the title of caliph, he took on the responsibility for the *umma*. He included the concept of *da'wa* in his "imperial ideology" and intended to lead Muslims like the Pope leads the Catholics. Hence, this is an example of a modern use of *da'wa* discourse for the sake of religio-political authority.

Of more lasting impact with regard to the rethinking of *da'wa* was the Salafiyya movement, the leading figures of which were Jamal al-Din al-Afghani (d. 1897), Muhammad 'Abduh (d. 1905), and Rashid Rida (d. 1935). Inspired particularly by Ibn Taymiyya's (d. 1329) early critique of *taqlid* and legal formalism, they called for the reform of Islamic law by reopening the gates of *ijtihad*. The movement also took a decisively critical stance to the influence of secular and Christian ideas. Both al-Afghani and, later, Rida were connected to the pan-Islamic movement that aimed at uniting Muslim peoples under the Ottoman caliphate. Rida even

attempted to launch his small organization, Jami'yat al-Da'wah wal-Irshad, as a cornerstone of pan-Islamism, indicating the constancy of the political dimension of *da'wa* conceptions. Of more lasting impact, however, were the Salafiyya efforts to strengthen Islamic awareness and solidarity in face of modernity. Thus, *da'wa* increasingly was understood in terms of edification and, most prominently, education, *tarbiya*.

The disruptive period of Islamic reformism around the turn of the nineteenth century also saw the birth of the Ahmadiyya, founded in 1889 in India by Mirza Ghulam Ahmad (d. 1908). Due to its deviant doctrines (such as the claims of Ahmad to have received new revelations from God and to be, among other things, an incarnation of Krishna), most Muslims do not accept Ahmadiyya as a part of Islam. Nonetheless, the movement has persisted as a very active *da'wa* organization, concentrating particularly on publication.

During the twentieth century, the Salafiyya ideal of *tarbiya* made a lasting impact on the understandings of *da'wa*. As of the 1930s, however, the political as well as the educational and devotional aspects of *da'wa* were understood and used in partly novel ways. A preceding event of paradigmatic importance was the abolition of the caliphate in 1924. *Da'wa* increasingly became an endeavor to reform the individual, rather than the public, institutions of society. Thus, society was to be Islamized "from below." This vision can be ascribed mainly to Hassan al-Banna (d. 1949) and Abu l-A'la' Maududi (d. 1979), who were both of towering importance for the conception of *da'wa* among later generations of Islamists.

Founder in 1928 of the Muslim Brotherhood (*al-Ikhwan al-Muslimin*), al-Banna spoke of *da'wa* as the call to "true Islam." With an allegoric reference to *hijra*, Muhammad's emigration from Mecca to Medina, al-Banna urged Muslims to abandon the materialism and superficial pleasures of society. By living in accordance with Islamic rules, Muslims will restore an "Islamic Order" and, eventually, establish an Islamic state.

Maududi was more favorable to direct political action and mobilization. His organizational base, Jama'at-e Islami, was set up as a regular political party, although it has gained significance primarily as an informal network. Maududi agreed with al-Banna's *da'wa* strategy of internal reform from below. However, instead of envisioning an Islamic order, he launched the popular concept of the "Islamic movement," *al-Haraka al-Islamiyya*. Here *da'wa* is aimed at creating an Islamic state of mind and a matrix of life rather than an institutional order.

A different methodology of *da'wa* was suggested by Tablighi Jama'at, founded by Mawlana Muhammad Ilyas in 1927. This movement of Sufi background turns its back on political activity and concentrates on the devotional life. Yet, it emphasizes the centrality of *da'wa* in terms of a missionary duty.

The Sufi background is highlighted by the centrality of the form of prayer called *dhikr* (remembrance). By repeating prayers many times each day, an Islamization of daily life is envisioned. Ilyas himself distinctly deviated from the character of al-Banna and Maududi and did not stand out as a religious scholar, either as a speaker or writer. This he compensated by missionary zeal and novel strategies of organization and education. In fact, the theological simplicity of the Tablighi's *da'wa* appears as a key to popular success. The prerequisites for acting as a Tablighi *da'i* are based on familiarity with basic Islamic doctrines and traditions, the practice of *salat* and *dhikr*, respect of other Muslims, and sincerity in actions. *Da'wa* is to be performed as voluntary preaching of the message in small groups. Instead of, for instance, publishing books or arranging publicly visible events and campaigns at university campuses, *da'wa* is performed from door to door. The Tablighi communities, not least among Muslim minorities around the world, are built on close, personal relations and social support.

Some years after the Second World War, when the large-scale process of decolonization started, modern *da'wa* activities increased in an even more rapid speed. Gradually, *da'wa* developed into a key concept for cultural identity and political change. Jamal 'Abd al-Nasser, who ruled Egypt between 1952 and 1970, built up a *da'wa* network in the Middle East and Africa. He championed the cause of Islamic socialism and pan-Arabism, which influenced nationalist leaders in many predominantly Muslim countries, such as Algeria, Syria, and Iraq.

Other Muslim leaders challenged the socialist, nationalist, and secularist aspects of postcolonial development and took recourse to a more classic understanding of *da'wa*. Most notably, Saudi Arabia's King Faysal challenged, and eventually took over, Nasser's leading role, by stressing the ideal of a transnational, Muslim solidarity based on Islam, not Arabism. In 1962, Saudi Arabia founded the Muslim World League, Rabitat al-'alam al-Islami, for promoting international *da'wa* efforts. This was one year after the establishment of an Islamic university in Medina for the training of *da'wa* workers. The activities of the Muslim World League increased in the 1970s when several councils, such as the World Council of Mosques, were formed. The idea of promoting international Islamic cooperation through the Council of Mosques was partly inspired by the previous establishment of the World Council of Churches. The Muslim World League cooperated with the governments of certain countries, such as Egypt, after Nasser had been followed by Anwar Sadat. As a result, the World Assembly of Muslim Youth was founded in 1972. Due to the the oil boom of the 1970s, enormous oil revenues allowed countries like Saudi Arabia and Kuwait to lend most substantial support to the Islamic movement that worked for the (re)establishment of "true" Islam. Funds were used for, among other things, Islamic research projects,

charities, distribution of Islamic literature, international conferences, and festivals, not least in Europe. Notably, this support predominantly favored Islamist-oriented movements, such as the Deobandi-inspired communities of Britain.

Previously, Muslims had been largely opposed to relief-work and social-welfare concerns as part of *da'wa* endeavors, criticizing Christian missions for using such efforts in order to make proselytes. Increasingly, however, charity directed primarily to Muslims has become an integral part of much *da'wa* work. It may even be argued that the provision of social amenities is one of the main aspects of Islamism.

As a reaction to the Saudi influence on organizations like the Muslim World League, new *da'wa* instruments were formed in other countries. In Libya, for instance, Mu'ammar al-Qadhdhafi established the Islamic Call Society, Jam'iyat al-Da'wah al-Islamiyya, in 1972, concentrating on *da'wa* efforts in sub-Saharan Africa. A decisive blow on Saudi Arabian hegemony was the Iranian revolution of 1979. The *da'wa* efforts of the Iranian Islamic Information Organization once again highlighted the question of political legitimacy. During the war against Iraq in the 1980s, Iran increasingly emphasized its Shi'ite foundation, thus loosening the slack on Saudi Arabia. The tensions between Saudi Arabia and the increasingly independent *da'wa* organizations have increased since the Persian Gulf War in the early 1990s, when Saudi Arabia supported the military coalition led by the United States. Saudi Arabia was heavily criticized by Muslim organizations all over the world, and some lost the Saudi support of petrodollars.

In the late twentieth century, new *da'wa* organizations cropped up all over the Muslim world, including in Europe and North America. Moreover, many governments set up *da'wa* departments for education and propaganda, particularly in the universities. In Pakistan, for example, the University of Islamabad in 1985 created a Da'wah Academy for training *da'wa* workers, producing and distributing literature in several languages as well as organizing conferences, special courses, and other events. The academy has an extensive international network of cooperating *da'wa* organizations, including the Muslim World League. Another important *da'wa* organization, whose primary objective is to propagate Islam through missionary activities, is the Islamic Propagation Centre International (IPCI), which was started in 1982 by Ahmed Deedat in Durban. It was preceded by the Islamic Propagation Centre, founded in 1957. Particularly significant in Europe and North America, the IPCI has concentrated on polemics against Christianity. The increasing interest in social welfare as a part of *da'wa* work was reflected, for instance, in the formation in 1988 by the Muslim World League of the World Muslim Committee for Da'wah and Relief. Education and health care is on the program of many *da'wa* organizations, like the Indonesian Diwan Dawat al-Islam and the West African Ansar al-Islam.

Among Muslim intellectuals, not least in Europe and North America, da'wa to a significant degree has been associated with interfaith dialogue. Thus, Qur'anic injunctions such as "Invite all to the Way of thy Lord" (16: 125) have been reinterpreted in an ecumenical sense. Proponents of interfaith dialogue such as Mahmoud Ayoub, Hasan 'Askari, Khurshid Ahmad, Mohammad Talbi, Isma'il al-Faruqi, and Seyyed Hossein Nasr agree on the need for ijtihad and the contextualization of shari'a, and they have excluded proselytism from the conceptions of da'wa.

However, the visions of al-Banna and Maududi are continuously present, especially in European and North American organizations. Two examples are the International Institute of Islamic Thought (IIIT) in the United States, founded by al-Faruqi, and the Islamic Foundation in United Kingdom, an offshoot of the Jama'at-e Islami, headed for many years by Maududi's disciple, Khurram Murad. The conception of da'wa among such organizations combines ecumenical efforts with insistence on edification and mobilization among Muslims, predominantly by book publishing and, increasingly, by engagement in the political and educational systems of the Western societies.

See also **Conversion; Expansion; Jama'at-e Islami; Shari'a.**

## BIBLIOGRAPHY

Arnold, Thomas W. *The Preaching of Islam: A History of the Propagation of the Muslim Faith*, 3d ed. London: Luzac, 1935.

Baldick, Julian. *Mystical Islam: An Introduction to Sufism.* London: Tauris, 2000.

Canard, Marius. "Da'wa." In Vol. 2, *Encyclopedia of Islam.* Leiden: Brill, 1965.

Eickelman, Dale, and Piscatori, James. *Muslim Politics.* Princeton, N.J.: Princeton University Press, 1996.

Faruqi, Ismail R al-. "On the Nature of Islamic Da'wah." In *Islam and Other Faiths.* Leicester: The Islamic Foundation, 1998.

Halm, Heinz. *Shi'ism.* Edinburgh: Edinburgh University Press, 1991.

Janson, Torsten. "Da'wa: Islamic Missiology in Discourse and History." *Swedish Missiological Themes* 89, no. 3 (2001): 355–415.

Köse, Ali. *Conversion to Islam: A Study of Native British Converts.* Padstow: Kegan Paul International, 1996.

Otayek, René, ed. *Le radicalisme islamique au sud du Sahara: Da'wa, arabisation et critiques de l'Occident.* Paris: Karthala, 1993.

Popovic, Alexandre, and Veinstein, Gilles, eds. *Les voies d'Allah: Les ordres mystiques dans l'islam des origines à aujourd'hui.* Paris: Fayard, 1996.

Poston, Larry. *Islamic Da'wah in the West: Muslim Missionary Activity and the Dynamics of Conversion to Islam.* Oxford: Oxford University Press, 1992.

Rahnema, Ali, ed. *Pioneers of Islamic Revival.* London: Zed Books, 1994.

Schimmel, Annemarie. *Sufismus: Eine Einführung in die islamische Mystik.* Munich: Beck, 2000.

Sharon, Moshe. *Black Banners from the East.* Jerusalem: Magners, 1983

Siddiqui, Ataullah. *Christian-Muslim Dialogue in the Twentieth Century.* London: Macmillan, 1997.

*Christer Hedin*
*Torsten Janson*
*David Westerlund*

# DAWLA

The Arabic word dawla is derived from the root D-W-L, meaning "to turn, alternate, or come around in a cyclical fashion." The Qur'an (59:7), for example, speaks of the Prophet's distribution of the spoils of war to those in need, "so that it may not [merely] make the circuit (dulatan) among the wealthy of you." Another Qur'anic reference (3:140) speaks of the cyclical nature of human vicissitudes, so that triumph one day is replaced by defeat another day. This sense of alternating periods of fortune and misfortune led Arab writers to use the word dawla when speaking of dynastic succession, particularly in the period after the rise of Abbasid power. The Abbasid "turn" in power had come, just as earlier the Umayyads had had their turn before being overthrown.

As the Abbasid house became entrenched in power, however, the dynastic sense of dawla became conflated with notions of the empire or state that this family ruled. Premodern Muslim writers, like their Western contemporaries, did not generally speak in the abstract of the state apart from those who actually wielded power at any given time. For example, Ibn Khaldun's use of dawla signifies, as Franz Rosenthal notes, that "a state exists only insofar as it is held together and ruled by individuals and the group which they constitute, that is, the dynasty. When the dynasty disappears, the state, being identical with it, also comes to an end." (Ibn Khaldun, *Muqaddimah*).

With the advent of Turkish and Kurdish governors under the nominal authority of the later Abbasid caliphs, titles composed of the word al-dawla combined with an honorific adjective became commonplace. Such titles as nasir al-dawla or sayf al-dawla could be rendered equally as "helper" and "sword," respectively, of the state, the body politic, the government, or the dynasty, all of which were identified (albeit theoretically) as a common entity.

In the nineteenth century, as Western distinctions between the state and the government began to filter into Muslim countries, dawla became increasingly disentangled from its more personalistic connotations and began to be used almost exclusively in the sense of "state." Thus, the 1861 Tunisian constitution, the first promulgated in a Muslim country, was known as *qanun al-dawla*. Framed under European pressure, the constitution consciously sought to differentiate the traditional powers of the bey, the ruler of Tunisia, from the new constitutional regime of the state under which even the bey was theoretically subordinate. To differentiate it from the state, which was relatively unchanging, the idea of the government and its personnel, which came and went, was connoted now by the term *hukuma*.

*Dawla* in contemporary Arabic (*devlet* in Turkish) is used in the sense of the nation-state, and encompasses the full range of meanings associated with that term in English, including a community of citizens residing within a given set of territorial boundaries as well as the political authority under which they live. The League of Arab States is thus rendered as *Jami'at al-Duwal al-'Arabiyya* (*duwal* being the plural of *dawla*) and anything "international" is rendered as *dawli* or *duwali*.

One also finds in contemporary Islamist writings the neologism *dawla Islamiyya*, or "Islamic state." This concept is invariably not well defined, but it reflects the holistic approach to religion and state that is at the core of the fundamentalist project. The Islamic state, unlike secular national states, is one in which *shari'a*, or divine law, is fully applied as the only legal code in the state. Beyond this general aspiration, the specifics of what constitutes *shari'a*, how *shari'a* principles are to be discerned or interpreted, and how non-Muslims are to be accommodated within the Islamic state are all highly contested issues.

*See also* **Hukuma al-islamiyya, al- (Islamic Government); Ibn Khaldun; Political Organization; Shari'a.**

### BIBLIOGRAPHY

Ayalon, Ami. *Language and Change in the Arab Middle East: The Evolution of Modern Arabic Political Discourse.* New York: Oxford University Press, 1987.

Enayat, Hamid. *Modern Islamic Political Thought.* Austin: University of Texas Press, 1982.

Ibn Khaldun. *Muqaddimah.* Translated by Franz Rosenthal. Princeton, N.J.: Princeton University Press, 1967.

Lewis, Bernard. *The Political Language of Islam.* Chicago: University of Chicago Press, 1988.

*Sohail H. Hashmi*

# DEATH

The end of human life is a central concern of Muslim thought and occasions a variety of ritual practices connected to the dying process, burial, and mourning. The most widely held view is that death is the fate prescribed by God for all living things, and that the event itself marks a transition or journey of the soul from worldly existence in the body to bodily resurrection and immortal life in either paradise (*janna*) or hell (*nar* and *jahannam*). In Islamic eschatology, as in rabbinic Judaism, God delegated the power of death to an angel of awesome appearance who separates the soul from the body.

Death (*maut*) is a dominant theme in the Qur'an, where it is closely linked with the understanding of life (*haya*) and belief in God. Thus, "God has possession of the heavens and the earth, he gives life and death" (9:116). Death is an eventuality that all living souls shall "taste" (3:185, 21:35), and precipitates their inevitable return to God (10:56). The Qur'an even speaks of human existence as being defined by two deaths and two births: nonexistence and entry into worldly life, then death and resurrection in the hereafter (2:28, 22:66). The return to God leads to the final reckoning and immortality for the blessed in paradise and for the damned in hell. Moreover, a special reward is promised those killed on God's "path," who are also said to be alive with God, not dead (3:157, 3:169, 22:58). In Qur'anic narratives of sacred history, death is depicted as affliction suffered by prophets at the hands of unbelievers (2:61, 3:21), and as a punishment meted out by God to unbelievers (25:35–40). Ethical and juridical passages place a high value on human life (4:29, 5:32, 6:151, 17:31), but call for death as a punishment for those who war against God and Muhammad (5:33). The schools of Muslim jurisprudence later delineated with more precision the kinds of offenses that required capital punishment, as well as mitigating factors (*hudud*).

Burial and mourning are rites of passage that are codified in *fiqh* literature. They involve declaration of the *shahada* by or on behalf of the dying person, and a cleansing of the body (*ghusl*), followed by enshrouding. Within a few hours of the death, a party of men transport the body to the cemetery, where it is buried facing toward Mecca. Funerary prayers may be performed at the grave site itself, or at a mosque on the way to the cemetery. Jurists prohibit women from participating in funerals, even if the deceased is female. Burial at sea is permitted if landfall is not possible. If the body of the deceased is not recoverable, funerary prayers are still required. Martyrs' bodies remain unwashed and are interred in their bloodstained garments without prescribed prayers, reflecting conditions of combat and a belief that they will immediately gain paradise. In all cases, the bereaved are urged to mourn in dignity for up to three days only, for excessive grieving is an affront to God, the giver of life and death. Grieving may also enhance the suffering of the soul of the deceased. Nonetheless, participation in funerals and visiting cemeteries are endorsed as occasions for cultivating piety and remembering the fate awaiting all creatures.

Ulema and indigenous cultural traditions in the Middle East, Asia, Africa, and recently Europe and the Americas have shaped Muslim beliefs and practices pertaining to death and immortality. A rich and diverse body of eschatological literature developed in medieval Islam that included narratives about the exemplary deaths of prophets and saints, visionary accounts of the torments of the grave, the death angels, and the intermediate condition of the soul between death and resurrection (*barzakh*), as well as detailed descriptions of the pleasures of paradise and punishments of hell. The major *kalam* schools defended Islamic doctrines about resurrection and final judgment against the influence of various Christian, Jewish, sectarian, mystical, and philosophical teachings. The deaths of the imams, particularly Husayn, came to hold a dominant place in Twelver Shi'ite doctrine and ritual practice. Sufis taught that death obliges seekers to engage in greater self-scrutiny, as the qualities of life after death reflect those of their worldly existence. Other mystics understood pain and death both as the experience of separation from God the Beloved and as metaphors for ecstatic annihilation (*fana'*) of the self in him, as exemplified by al-Hallaj (d. 922). To achieve "death before dying," was to attain spiritual union with the divine. A few mystics and philosophers, contrary to orthodox belief, advocated belief in metempsychosis (*tanasukh*) and denied the reality of personal death, resurrection, judgment, and heaven and hell.

In many Muslim communities, death has been seen as a contagious threat to domestic prosperity caused by the evil eye and malevolent spirits rather than a direct result of God's will. Mourning practices vary widely, but they routinely entail expressions of profound grief, especially by women, and include prayer gatherings and meals for up to a year after the loss of a loved one. Moreover, most Muslims recount visions of the dead in their dreams and believe that the saintly dead, especially the prophet Muhammad and his descendants, have the power to intercede on their behalf both in this world and in the hereafter. Saints' tombs, found in most Muslim communities, have consequently evolved into important pilgrimage and cultural centers. Since the nineteenth century, some Muslim writers have adapted European spiritualism to traditional Islamic understandings of death and the afterlife, while Islamists have revived discourses about the tortures of the grave, the corporal punishments of hell, and the bodily pleasures of paradise to advance their radical political and moral agendas.

*See also* '**Ibadat; Jahannam; Janna; Pilgrimage: Ziyara.**

## BIBLIOGRAPHY

Campo, Juan Eduardo. *The Other Sides of Paradise: Explorations into the Religious Meanings of Domestic Space in Islam.* Columbia: University of South Carolina Press, 1991.

Ghazali, Abu Hamid al-. *The Remembrance of Death and the Afterlife* (Kitab dhikr al-mawt wa-ma ba'dahu): Book XL of the Revival of the Religious Sciences (Ihya' 'ulum al-din). Translated by T. J. Winter. Cambridge: Islamic Texts Society, 1995.

O'Shaughnessy, Thomas. *Muhammad's Thoughts on Death.* Leiden: E. J. Brill, 1969.

Smith, Jane Idleman, and Haddad, Yvonne Yazbeck. *The Islamic Understanding of Death and Resurrection.* Albany: State University of New York Press, 1981.

*Juan Eduardo Campo*

# DEOBAND

Deoband, a country town ninety miles northeast of Delhi, has given its name to ulema associated with the Indo-Pakistani reformist movement centered in the seminary founded there in 1867. A striking dimension of Islamic religious life in colonial India was the emergence of several apolitical, inward-looking movements, among them not only the Deobandis but the so-called "Barelwis," the much smaller Ahl-e Hadis/Ahl-i Hadith, and the controversial Ahmadiyya. The Deobandi, Barelwi, and Ahl-e Hadis ulema not only responded to Hindu and Christian proselytizing, but engaged in public debate, polemical writings, and exchanges of *fatawa* among themselves. Each fostered devotion to the prophet Muhammad as well as fidelity to his practice; each thought itself the correct interpreter of hadith, the guide to that practice. All depended on means of communication, above all print, as well as on institutional changes that came with British colonial rule.

The *Dar al-'Ulum* at Deoband utilized the organizational model of British colonial schools. Its goal was to hold Muslims to a standard of correct individual practice in a time of considerable social change, and, to that end, to create a class of formally trained and popularly supported ulema to serve as imams, guardians, and trustees of mosques and tombs, preachers, muftis, spiritual guides, writers, and publishers of religious works. At the end of its first centenary in 1967, Deoband counted almost ten thousand graduates, including several hundred from foreign countries. Hundreds of Deobandi schools, moreover, have been founded across the Indian subcontinent and now in the West as well.

The Deobandis followed Shah Wali Allah Dihlawi (1702–1763) in their shift from emphasis on the "rational sciences" to an emphasis on the "revealed sciences" of the Qur'an and, above all, hadith. Unlike him, however, they have been staunch Hanafis in jurisprudence. They have also been Sufi guides, bound together by shared spiritual networks, especially Chishti Sabiri. Among the most influential writers was Maulana Ashraf 'Ali Thanawi (1864–1943), who published scholarly works on Qur'an, hadith, and Sufism. He also wrote an encyclopedic guide for Muslim women, *Bihishti Zewar*, disseminating correct practice, reform of custom, and practical knowledge.

After about 1910, individual Deobandis began to be involved in politics in opposition to British rule in India and also to British intervention in the Ottoman lands. Many Deobandis supported the Khilafat movement after World War I in support of the Ottoman ruler as *khalifa* of all Muslims, and were also strong supporters of the Jam'iyat 'Ulama-e Hind who was allied with the Indian National Congress and opposed to the creation of Pakistan. The apolitical strand within the school's teaching has taken shape for many in the widespread, now transnational, pietist movement known since the 1920s as Tablighi Jama'at. The popular writings of Maulana Muhammad Zakariyya Kandhalavi (1897–1982), associated with the second major Deobandi school in India, the Mazahir-e 'Ulum in Saharanpur, are utilized extensively in the movement. In Pakistan, the Jam'iyat 'Ulama-e Islam party represents Deobandi ulema. In striking contrast, the Taliban movement, which emerged in Afghanistan in the 1990s, had its origins among refugees in Deobandi schools in Pakistan and also identifies itself as Deobandi.

*See also* **Education; Jam'iyat 'Ulama-e Islam; Law; South Asia, Islam in; Tablighi Jama'at.**

## BIBLIOGRAPHY

Metcalf, Barbara Daly. *Islamic Revival in British India: Deoband 1860–1900.* Princeton, N.J.: Princeton University Press, 1982.

Thanawi, Maulana Ashraf 'Ali. *Perfecting Women: Maulana Ashraf 'Ali Thanawi's Bihishti Zewar.* Berkeley: University of California Press, 1990.

*Barbara D. Metcalf*

# DEVOTIONAL LIFE

The meaning and analytical value of the phrase "devotional life" needs clarification in the case of Islam. "Devotional" is derived from the Latin term *devotio*, which was originally the name of a ritual in Roman religion, and became predominantly a Christian term, which in the Middle Ages and in modern speech means the obedient submission to God. The theologian John Renard defines devotion as "the elements of personal investment"—energy, feeling, time, substance—that characterize a Muslim communal and individual response to the experience of God's ways of dealing with them. The Islamic-Arabic term closest to *devotio* may be *ikhlas* (cf. S. 4:146, speaking about those who "*akhlasu dinahum lillah*," that is, are sincere in their obedience to God), but this term is not used in religious studies in the same way as it is used in Constance Padwick's classic *Muslim Devotions*. Even though the devotional practices as described below include the "canonical" rituals (*'ibadat*) as well, one assumes that in quantitative terms a great part of devotional life takes place outside the prescribed rituals even though it remains closely connected and intertwined with them. As in other religious traditions, many aspects of devotional life seem to fulfill a

need for the "sacramental" aspect: to touch or be near and close to the object of veneration, believed to have healing or intercessional powers.

The term *devotion* can therefore only be used for the widest variety of forms of engaged, affectionate worship: from the *'ibadat* to the veneration of the prophet Muhammad (for example, in the celebration of his birthday, Ar. *mawlid),* saints (*awliya'*), or intermediary beings such as the *jinn* and *zar* spirits, taking place within a wide variety of institutional settings, and under the guidance of a particular leadership. Hence, devotional life refers here in the first place to a broad range of personal, popular behaviors and beliefs that stand in a dialectical relationship with scriptural orthodoxies of various kinds and varieties. The reasons for this tension may vary: Many practices are without precedent in the time of the Prophet (*bida's*), and there may be forms of reprehensible moral behavior such as joint gatherings of men and women, and particular forms of trance. However, it is the alleged veneration of mortal and created human beings instead of God, the Creator, which is condemned as *shirk.*

Devotional life in Islam has yet to be mapped and its history is still to be written. So far, most studies have focused on written sources (such as Padwick, *Muslim Devotions*; Ayoub, *Redemptive Suffering*): small books and booklets, pamphlets, and manuscripts (amulets) that can be purchased in small bookshops, in the streets, and at religious institutions. Among them are many prayer manuals and devotional texts, often originating in the ritual practices of one of the mystical traditions, the subject of Padwick's classic study. The pamphlets may be written by classical authors, most often mystics, such as the famous 'Abd al-Qadir al-Jilani (d. 1166), but there are also many modern authors.

Devotion to the Prophet is a dominant element in many Sufi movements. A very popular text is the *Dala'il al-khayrat* (Guide to happiness) by the Moroccan mystic al-Jazuli (d. 1465). In it, the 201 names of the Prophet occupy an important place, as well as the *tasliya*, or prayer on the Prophet, which reads in translation: "O God, send your blessing [*salli*] on our Lord Muhammad and on the family of our Lord Muhammad and greet them with peace!" The family of the Prophet is sometimes taken very broadly and may include all people of belief. In Shi'ite books it also includes all the 'Alids.

In popular pamphlets older texts such as the *Qasidat al-burda* by al-Busiri may be found together with modern texts, forming handbooks of devotion for individual and communal life. Padwick lists different types of ritual forms in addition to the term *salat*, which may indicate the obligatory *salat*, the voluntary (*nafila*) *salat*s, and *salat*s for special occasions, as well as the prayer on the Prophet. These include *'ibada*, which refers to the outward aspects, and *wazifa* or *ratib*, the daily individual devotional office. In addition to forms Padwick mentions different types of texts: *munajat*, or conversations between God and Prophets or other saintly persons; *du'a*, a

This muezzin in Istanbul calls faithful Muslims to pray in an important Islamic daily ritual. Written instruction on Islamic devotion is available in prayer manuals and devotional texts in bookstores and on the street in the Muslim world. © David Rubinger/Corbis

very important term indicating invocations and prayers that can also be said during the *salat*, particularly the *sujud;* or prosternation. In this regard, it is important to observe that whereas it is obligatory to recite the Qur'an (undoubtedly the most important devotional text) during the *salat* in Arabic, *du'a*s can also be said in the vernacular. There is a connection between prayers in the vernacular and the emergence of popular literature in such Islamic vernaculars as Persian, Turkish, and other languages. *Dhikr* literally means "remembrance," namely of God and the ninety-nine beautiful names (memorization of which, tradition holds, almost assures a person entrance into Paradise), and may refer both to a type of text (especially in the plural, *adhkar*) and the ritual of reciting them. A *wird* is a litany often accompanied by a name and associated with the devotional life of a particular Sufi order. Other texts are referred to as *hizb*, litany, a term which also refers to an allotted part, namely of the Qur'an, or of a text such as the *Dala'il* (divided into eight *ahzab*). Al-Shadili (d. 1258) composed the famous *Hizb al-bahr* aboard a vessel on his way to Mecca. *Ahzab* have a strong connotation of offering protection against hostile natural or human forces. The same holds true for the *Hirz*, which literally means "stronghold." All such types of texts are recited at different ritual occasions. In addition, many popular pamphlets deal with other devotional subjects such as magic (Ar. *sihr*), evil powers, for example, those of the *jinn* and the evil eye (*al-hasad, al-'ayn*) and how to avert or control them, and with the afterlife and eschatological subjects (for example, "life" in the

grave). Devotional life should also be approached through music and literary works of prose and poetry. For example, in his autobiographical work *Ein Leben mit dem Islam* (A Life with Islam; 1999), Nasr Abu Zaid reminds us that recitation of the Qur'an had spiritual as well as aesthetic and physical aspects. Another interesting autobiography, and an important source for devotional life of a woman in the Islamist movement, is that of Zaynab al-Ghazali.

Studies into devotional life based on field work exist, but do not abound and is only rarely the subject of a monograph. One may think of the accounts by Edward Lane (*Manners and Customs of the Modern Egyptians*; 1846), Snouck Hurgronje of life in Mecca, Edward Westermarck's *Ritual and Religion in Morocco*, Usha Sanyal on Barelwi devotions (although it focuses on *fatwa*s rather than on field work), Abdul Hamid El Zein's study of saint veneration in Lamu, John Bowen's *Muslims Through Discourse* (a study in the Gayo highland), or Ian Netton's book on Sufi ritual in the United Kingdom.

Images, pictures, and paintings form an important source for the study of devotional life. In this respect, a promising new contribution can also be expected of visual anthropology (e.g., films such as those by Fadwa El Guindi, *El Sebou'*, on life-cycle rituals in Egypt). Finally, the Internet, in particular the World Wide Web, has emerged as a medium for the spread of devotional life. Quite a few Sufi orders are active in cyberspace, and noteworthy developments take place there with regard to publications as well. A great lacuna remains, however, the lack of empirical analysis on a micro level in which textual (and musicological and iconographical) study is combined with (participant) observation.

*See also* **Adhan; Dhikhj; Du'a; 'Ibadat; Tasawwuf.**

## BIBLIOGRAPHY

Ayoub, Mahmoud. *Redemptive Suffering in Islam. A Study of the Devotional Aspects in Twelver Shiism.* The Hague: Mouton, 1978.

Biegman, N. H., and Hunt, S. V. *Egypt. Moulids, Saints and Sufis.* The Hague: Gary Schwartz/SDU, 1990.

Bowen, John R. *Muslims through Discourse. Religion and Ritual in Gayo Society.* Princeton, N.J.: Princeton University Press, 1993.

Kriss, Rudolf von, and Kris-Heinrich, Hubert. *Volksglaube im Bereich des Islam.* Wiesbaden: O. Harrassowitz, 1960–62.

Netton, Ian Richard. *Sûfi ritual. The Parallel Universe.* Richmond, U.K.: Curzon Press, 2000.

Padwick, Constance. *Muslim Devotions. A Study of Prayer-Manuals in Common Use* (1961). Reprint. Oxford, U.K.: Oneworld, 1996.

Parker, A., and Neal, A. *Hajj Painting. Folk Art of the Great Pilgrimage.* Washington, D.C.: Smithsonian Institution Press, 1995.

In Bandar Seri Begawan, Brunei, a young boy watches the men in their noon prayer at the 'Omar 'Ali Saifuddin Mosque. © MICHAEL S. YAMASHITA/CORBIS

Renard, John. *Seven Doors to Islam: Spirituality and the Religious Life of Muslims.* Berkeley: University of California Press, 1996.

Sanyal, Usha. *Devotional Islam and Politics in British India: Ahmad Riza Khan Barelwi and his Movement, 1870–1920.* Delhi: Oxford University Press, 1999.

Schimmel, Annemarie. *And Muhammad Is His Messenger: The Veneration of the Prophet in Islamic Piety.* Chapel Hill: University of North Carolina Press, 1985.

Schnubel, Vernon James. *Religious Performances in Contemporary Islam. Shii Devotional Rituals in South Asia.* Columbia: University of South Carolina Press, 1993.

Westermarck, Edward. *Ritual and Belief in Morocco* (1926). Reprint. London: Macmillan, 1960.

Zein, Abdul Hamid el-. *The Sacred Meadows. A Structural Analysis of Religious Symbolism in an East African Town.* Evanston, Ill.: Northwestern University, 1974.

*Gerard Wiegers*

# DHIKR

*Dhikr* is a complex word variously translated as "remembrance" or "recollection." The word *dhikr* was developed initially in the Qur'an to reflect a special kind of piety toward God, then extended in the hadith to reflect the multiplicity of ideas associated with the Prophet's own pious practices, and ultimately adapted by the ascetic and mystic traditions as an institutional meditational ritual.

The word *dhikr* and its cognates form a dense structure in the Qur'an, which insists that the prophets were all linked together by virtue of the message they collectively brought: They were all members of one brotherhood (23:51–52) and all brought the same *din* (religion). The Qur'an identifies them all as *mudhakkirat*, a word derived from the root "to remember" or "to recollect"; thus, they are all rememberers. Their message is *tadhkira*, reminder. Humans, however, are in a state of forgetfulness, and they need to be reminded by believers; it is the believer's chore to constantly witness (*dhakir*), both because of the human propensity to forgetfulness, but also because God has allowed Satan to entice humans away (17:62–64).

The remembrance of Allah as a rite has a special place in Islam. The Qur'an says, "Those who believe, and whose hearts find satisfaction in the remembrance of Allah; for without doubt, in the remembrance of Allah do hearts find satisfaction" (13:28). The remembrance of Allah is understood to embrace both acts of service and kindliness, and failure to do so curbs spiritual growth (83:9). At the same time, the Qur'an envisions *dhikr* of wider significance than the formal requirement of prayer, including devotions such as silent meditation and personal contemplation (24:37). Remembrance is also linked directly to accepting Allah's guidance, a key initiative of God in human salvation, and failure to remember leads to the withdrawal of God's grace (72:17). In short, "Remembrance of Allah is the greatest thing in life, without doubt" (29:45).

### *Dhikr* in Mystical Islam or Sufism

Sufis adhere to the Qur'an's words to "remember God" and they do so in rituals both rich and variegated. Some Sufis regard *dhikr* as the mystical equivalent of canonical prayer, and wherever *dhikr* as liturgical remembrance has been practiced, it has generally been held to encompass the same pious goals as prayer and to reflect the same ritual effectiveness. The *dhikr* tradition, then, is a means of meditation on past verities and on the transcendent being of God, a base upon which Sufism built a structure for probing higher consciousness, engaging with spiritual forces, and ultimately coming into a personal encounter with God.

*Dhikr* developed into a pious ritual very early in the growth of ascetic practices, and, with the establishment of the orders, became specifically designed for brotherhood meditations. It became the means to develop internal cohesion within the order, and for the head of the order to maintain control over the adepts. *Dhikr* thus evolved into part of the discipline imposed by Sufism's institutional structure. While its practice was open to those "on the Way," each order required *dhikr* to be approved and carried out in the presence of the shaykh or the order's other officials.

Such teachings embraced the following notions: *Dhikr* could be either silent or spoken, reflecting the domains of practice, that is, remembrance of the heart (*dhikr khafi,* or *dhikr al-qalbi)* or remembrance of the tongue. Spoken *dhikr* is ultimately overcome by silent *dhikr,* since words fail before the grandeur of God, or they inevitably maintain the self separate from the source of all life. By the sixteenth century, *dhikr* would encompass seven different levels of meaning, according to some practitioners.

Finally, *dhikr,* spoken by saintly people or their representatives, is widely regarded as having spiritual potency, and the vehicle of memory suggests that *dhikr*'s inspiration can be carried beyond the atmosphere of the order into Muslim society itself, where it can effect change in unpredictable but significant ways.

*See also* **Devotional Life; 'Ibadat; Tasawwuf.**

### BIBLIOGRAPHY

Burke, Michael. *Among the Dervishes.* London: Octagon Press, 1973.

Hisham, Ibn. *The Life of Muhammad: A Translation of Ibn Ishaq's Kitab Sirat Rasul Allah.* Translated by A. Guillaume. Karachi, Pakistan, and New York: Oxford University Press, 2001.

Hodgson, Marshall G. S. *The Venture of Islam.* Chicago: University of Chicago Press, 1974.

Hoffman, Valerie. *Sufism, Saints, and Mysticism in Modern Egypt.* Columbia: University of South Carolina Press, 1995.

Schimmel, Annemarie. *Mystical Dimensions of Islam.* Chapel Hill: University of North Carolina, 1975.

Schubel, Vernon. "The Muharram Majlis: The Role of a Ritual in the Preservation of Shi'a Identity." In *Muslim Families in North America.* Edited by Earle H. Waugh, Sharon M. Abu-Laban, and Regula B. Qureshi. Edmonton, Alberta, Canada: University of Alberta Press, 1991.

Waugh, Earle H. *The Munshidin of Egypt: Their World and Their Song.* Columbia: University of South Carolina Press, 1989.

*Earle Waugh*

# DIETARY LAWS

Islam's dietary laws are based on scripture, juridical opinions, and local custom; the latter, in turn, reflects the religious milieu of pre-Islamic Arabia. Foods are designated as lawful (*halal*), unlawful (*haram*), and reprehensible (*makruh*). Generally, all things, including foods, remain lawful unless proven otherwise. The Qur'an rules that the flesh of swine is unlawful, as is carrion, blood, animals that have been strangulated, beaten to death, killed by a fall, gored to death, or savaged by other animals. Apostolic traditions render unlawful carnivorous animals, birds of prey, and most reptiles. The schools of law differ with regard to some foods: For the Hanafites, crustaceans such as lobster, shrimp, crab, and the like are reprehensible, for the Malikites even reptiles are lawful, and for the Shafiites meat products not consumed by the early Arab community are unlawful.

The name of God must be invoked on all animals before slaughter, although some jurists waive this rule where the slaughterer is Muslim. The trachea, and at least one carotid artery, must be severed with a sharp instrument to minimize pain and suffering. Game hunters need not follow these rules if the name of God was invoked when their properly trained hunting animals were set loose. Also lawful is an animal killed by weapons such as arrows, lances, and so on that when launched—in the name of God—tear through flesh and cause bleeding. Because no bleeding occurs when live ammunition is used, some jurists render the consumption of such animals as unlawful.

Animals slaughtered by people of the book, that is, Jews and Christians, are lawful, although some jurists insist that they too invoke only the name of God, and not that of Jesus, or any other deity. More recently, and as a consequence of migrations to the West, a further distinction, particularly evident among Muslims in the United States, is made between animals slaughtered by people of the book, termed *halal*, and those slaughtered by Muslims themselves, termed *dhabiha*.

Intoxicants are unlawful, even in small quantities, and so too are profits, salaries, or rentals obtained through commercial ventures involving intoxicants. Fresh grape and date juice cannot be consumed if left overnight in summer and after three days in winter. By analogy, chemical substances that impair the senses are also unlawful.

Meals must be consumed with the right hand, preferably while sitting, and God's name must be invoked before and after meals. Using utensils of gold and silver is reprehensible, as is eating garlic or onion before prayer, and filling the belly more than two-thirds with food and drink. Some large fast-food chains now cater to Islamic dietary requirements, and use a crescent in some places to indicate that *halal* meals are served.

*See also* **Fatwa; Ijtihad; Madhhab; Mufti; Shari'a.**

## BIBLIOGRAPHY

Cook, Michael. *Commanding Right and Forbidding Wrong in Islamic Thought*. Cambridge, U.K., and New York: Cambridge University Press, 2000.

Qaradawi, Yusuf. *The Lawful and the Unlawful in Islam*. Indianapolis: American Trust Publications, 1994.

*Muneer Goolam Fareed*

# DISPUTATION

Disputation is the ritual practice of dialectical argument among schools of thought. In early and medieval Islamic societies, disputation is especially important in regard to the elaboration of competing religious doctrines. Two Arabic terms, *jadal* (and its more intensive form *mujadala*) and *munazara* designate dialectics or disputation with an opponent. A culture of disputation was well established in the Middle East prior to the rise of Islam, between and within the Jewish and Christian communities and among philosophical schools, such as the Peripatetics (Aristotelians), Stoics, Neoplatonists, Skeptics, Materialists, and others. Emblematic of this dialectical form of scholarship in the Middle Eastern environment of nascent Islam are the writings of the Church Father, John of Damascus (d. 749). In a tractate "Against the Saracens," written under Umayyad Islamic rule, John instructs Christians in the methods and the limits of disputing with Muslims on matters of belief.

Engaging the opponent through argument is also well attested in the Qur'an. Humans are referred to "as the most disputatious (*jadal*) of things" (18:54). The verbal noun *mujadala* and its active verb form, meaning disputing with an enemy, occur twenty-seven times, in such phrases as "the Satans

inspire their friends to dispute with you" (6:121) and "dispute not with the People of the Book" (29:46). Qur'an 16:125 associates disputing with proselytism or inviting unbelievers to become Muslim: "Invite (humankind) to the way of your Lord with wisdom and kind words and dispute with them (*jadilhum*) in (a manner) which is less offensive."

By the ninth century, in Baghdad, Basra, and other centers of learning, disputation was recognized as a skill and an art that enhanced one's scholarly status. The biographical dictionaries mention accomplishment in the "science of disputation" ('*ilm al-jadal*) or the rules of conduct in debate (*adab al-jadal*), alongside knowledge of law, theology, the Qur'an, hadith, and the grammar and lexicon of the Arabic language. Although the earliest manuals of instruction in the art of disputation no longer exist, the existence of such works as early as the ninth century is attested by references that appear in the tenth-century catalogue of Arabic works by Ibn al-Nadim (*Kitab al-fihrist*).

Arabic theological texts from the ninth to eleventh centuries give evidence of the oral environment of debate and argument in which claims were made, scripture was interpreted, rulings were established, and ideas were advanced and criticized. Typical of these texts is the following pattern. An incipit formulation of a problem is stated, for example, the Mu'tazilite theological school's claim that the Qur'an, like all material things in the world, is created and not eternal—a view that orthodox Muslims rejected. Next, the claim or doctrine is broken down into constituent subsections of the argument. Often the contending positions of other schools of thought are stated. The text then proceeds to advance the details of counterargument, followed by the teacher's reply to that argument. A typical text reads: "If the interlocutor (*al-qa'il*) should ask such and such, then the following should be said to him. . . ." The textual forms of these disputes are in reality school texts that were dictated by a shaykh or teacher in his home, at a *madrasa*, or in the corner or outer halls of a mosque, often to quite large gatherings of students. That the same problems were disputed over and over by succeeding generations of students and teachers, as was, for example, the claim that the Qur'an was created, or that the Qur'an was a miracle that proved Muhammad's prophethood, indicates a dynamic conception of religious truth that always had to be tested and defended with strengthened arguments.

This very method of teaching invited disputes in the lecture halls, and both teachers and pupils often became practitioners. At the simplest level, students would often be given a problem to dispute in practice session. Medieval annalistic historians like Abu Mansur ibn Tahrir al-Baghdadi (d. 1037) describe how on many occasions the more advanced students of a shaykh would go or be sent to the sessions of a rival teacher to challenge the latter with counterarguments. Other medieval observers of this form of teaching through public debate commented upon how loud and contentious they would often become, even late at night, disturbing neighbors who were trying to sleep. The theologians Abu ʿUthman ʿAmr ibn al-Jahiz (d. 869) and Abu Hamid al-Ghazali (d. 1111) argued that common people who were not trained in the rules and discipline of disputation should not be allowed to debate religion and theology in public, because their lack of knowledge and skill often led to public disorder and raucousness.

The advanced cultural context for highly developed disputational skills were the evenings sponsored by local rulers and other patrons, in many cases bringing together Sunni and Shiʿite religious spokesmen as well as representatives of the Orthodox, Nestorian, and Monoiphysite Christian communities, Rabbanite Jews, philosophers, poets, and other intellectuals to debate whatever important issue of the day interested the patron. In many cases, religious truth was framed as the problem and debated across confessional lines. In many cases, too, disputation over religious truth was conducted across disciplines. In one celebrated debate in the year 932 in Baghdad, for instance, the grammarian Abu Saʿid al-Sirafi debated the logician Abu Bishr Matta. The logician held that truth is determined in formal logic, not in natural language (which is the medium of the Qurʾan). Al-Sirafi successfully argued that meaning is embedded in the language of the text itself, thus preserving the importance of the text of scripture, which in Islamic religious thought is more than propositional truth.

Not every scholar appreciated or participated in public disputations, especially across confessional lines. The literary historian Abu ʿAbdallah al-Humaydi (d. 1095) tells of a certain Hanbali religious scholar who reported having attended one such public disputation in eleventh-century Baghdad. He complained that nonbelievers (kuffar) were allowed to stand up and say that Muslims would not be allowed to argue using their Book (the Qurʾan), but rather that all disputants would be restricted to rational argument. When all present, including the other Muslims, agreed to the terms of the dispute, the Hanbali reported that he left and never went back.

In modern literary and anthropological terms it is possible to see the phenomenon of jadal and munazara as a form of poetics and social ritual. Taking the form of verbal conflict, such practices occurred in the highly charged atmosphere of competing religious communities living under Islamic rule in the central Islamic lands of the Middle East, especially during the Abbasid Age (750–1258). Potentially dangerous and volatile conflicts were defined and framed, then regulated and controlled by rules of conduct. A measure of how effective these cultural forms were is the fact that often those who refused to dispute according to the rules took their concerns to the streets of Baghdad in more physical and even violent forms of conflict. Violence, however, was often outweighed by the more civil forms of conflict. In no small measure it was

the cultural practice of agreeing to disagree in disputation among contending religious communities that made civil society possible in the Islamic Middle Ages.

See also **Christianity and Islam; Kalam.**

## BIBLIOGRAPHY

Mahdi, Muhsin. "Language and Logic in Classical Islam." In *Logic in Classical Islamic Culture*, edited by G. E. Grunebaum. Wiesbaden: Harrassowitz, 1970.

Miller, Lawrence. "The Development of Islamic Dialectics." *American Research Center in Egypt Newsletter* 34 (1986): 24–27.

Moreen, V. B. "Shiʿi–Jewish 'Debate' (*munazara*) in the Eighteenth Century." *Journal of the American Oriental Society* 119, no. 4 (1999): 570–89.

*Richard C. Martin*

## DISSIMULATION See Taqiyya

## DIVORCE

In Islamic law, the husband has the exclusive right to *talaq*, termination of marriage. *Talaq* is defined as a unilateral act, which takes legal effect by the husband's declaration. Neither grounds for divorce nor the wife's presence or consent are necessary, but the husband must pay his wife's *mahr*—translated in English as "dower," this is the gift the bridegroom offers the bride upon marriage—if he has not done so at the time of marriage, and maintenance (*nafaqa*) during the ʿidda period (three menses after the declaration).

The wife, however, cannot be released from marriage without her husband's consent, although she can buy her release by offering him compensation. This is referred to as "divorce by mutual consent" and can take two forms: In *khulʿ*, the wife claims separation because of her extreme dislike (*ikrah*) of her husband, and there is no ceiling on the amount of compensation that she pays; in *mubarat* the dislike is mutual and the amount of compensation should not exceed the value of the *mahr* itself.

If the wife fails to secure her husband's consent, her only recourse is the intervention of a judge who has the power either to compel the husband to pronounce *talaq* or to pronounce it on his behalf. Known as *faskh* (recission), *tafriq* (separation), or *tatliq* (compulsory issue of divorce), this outlet has become the common juristic basis on which a woman can obtain a court divorce in contemporary Muslim world. The facility with which a woman can obtain such a divorce and the grounds on which she can do so vary in the different schools of Islamic law and in different countries. The Maliki school is the most liberal and grants the widest grounds upon which a woman can initiate divorce proceedings. Among Muslim states where Islamic law is the basis of family law, women in Tunisia enjoy easiest access to divorce.

*See also* **Gender; Law; Marriage.**

### BIBLIOGRAPHY

Carroll, Lucy, and Kapoor, Harsh, eds. *Talaq-i-Tafwid: The Muslim Woman's Contractual Access to Divorce.* Grabels, WLUML (Women Living Under Muslim Laws), 1996.

Esposito, John L., and Delong-Bas, Natana J. *Women in Muslim Family Law.* 2d ed. Syracuse, N.Y.: Syracuse University Press, 2001.

*Ziba Mir-Hosseini*

# DOME OF THE ROCK

The Dome of the Rock (Ar. *Qubbat al-Sakhra*), a large octagonal building in Jerusalem commissioned by the Umayyad caliph 'Abd al-Malik in 692 C.E., is the earliest major monument of Islamic architecture to survive. Muslims today consider it the third holiest shrine in Islam, after the Kaaba in Mecca and the Mosque of the Prophet in Medina. Its age and its sanctity, along with its visibility and extraordinary decoration, make it a major monument of world architecture and one of the most important sites in Islam.

The Dome of the Rock is set over a rocky outcrop near the center of the large esplanade known in Arabic as *al-Haram al-Sharif* (the Noble Sanctuary), which was once the site of the Jewish Temple, the traditional religious center of Jerusalem. The building is a large low octagon divided internally by an arcade into two octagonal ambulatories encircling a tall cylindrical space measuring approximately 20 meters (65 feet) in diameter. A high wooden dome, whose metal roof is plated with gold, spans the central space and covers the rock.

The glory of the building is its decoration. Above a high dado of quartered marble, the exterior and interior walls were once entirely covered in a mosaic of small cubes of colored and gold glass and semiprecious stones. In the sixteenth century the mosaics on the exterior were replaced with glazed tiles, themselves replaced in the twentieth century, but the mosaics on the interior stand much as they did when they were put up in the late seventh century. They depict a vast program of fantastic trees, plants, fruits, jewels, chalices, vases, and crowns. A long (about 250 meters, or 820 feet) band of Arabic writing in gold on a blue ground runs along the top of both sides of the inner octagon. The text is largely Qur'anic phrases and contains the earliest evidence for the

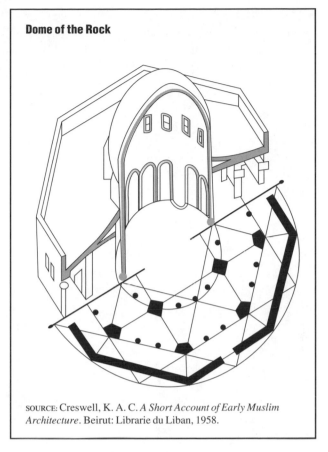

**Dome of the Rock**

SOURCE: Creswell, K. A. C. *A Short Account of Early Muslim Architecture.* Beirut: Librarie du Liban, 1958.

Cross-section Dome of the Rock diagram.

writing down of the Qur'an. It ended with the name of the patron, the Umayyad caliph 'Abd al-Malik (replaced in the ninth century by that of the Abbasid caliph al-Ma'mun), and the date of construction.

In form, materials, and decoration, the Dome of the Rock belongs to the tradition of late Antique and Byzantine architecture that flourished in the region before the coming of Islam. The domed, centrally planned building was a typical form for a martyrium, and the Dome of the Rock is similar in plan and size of dome to the nearby Holy Sepulcher, the building (also raised over a rock) that the emperor Constantine had erected in the fourth century to mark the site of Christ's burial on Golgotha. Other Christian buildings erected in the area in the eighth century, notably the Church of the Nativity in Bethelem, show a similar use of marble and mosaics, perhaps executed by the same team of mosaicists.

Despite its antecedents and even its workmen, the Dome of the Rock is clearly a Muslim building, commissioned by a Muslim patron for Muslim purposes. Its mosaic decoration, notably its inscriptions in Arabic and its lack of figural representation, immediately distinguishes it from contemporary Christian buildings in the area. It was not intended as a place for communal prayer; that function was fulfilled by the

Women praying in front of the Dome of the Rock, the third holiest shrine in Islam. The Dome of the Rock was built on the site where the Jewish Temple, Jerusalem's traditional Jewish center, stood before it was destroyed. Although it was built for Muslims, the decoration and architecture of the Dome of the Rock reflect Antique and Byzantine traditions that predate the arrival of Islam. AP/WIDE WORLD PHOTOS

nearby Aqsa Mosque. Rather its domed octagonal form suggests a commemorative function, though its exact purpose is unclear.

Already in the ninth century several alternative explanations for its construction were proposed. One author suggested that 'Abd al-Malik had commissioned the Dome of the Rock to replace the Ka'ba, which had fallen into enemy hands. This explanation, however, is simplistic and undermines one of the five central tenets of Islam, though the building could have functioned (and does today) as a secondary site of pilgrimage. Another explanation, also current from the ninth century, associates the building with the site of Muhammad's *mi'raj*, his miraculous night-journey from Mecca to Jerusalem and back. However, the Qur'anic inscriptions around the interior of the Dome of the Rock, the only contemporary source for explaining the building's purpose, mention neither of these subjects. Rather, they deal with the nature of Islam and refute the tenets of Christianity. The inscriptions suggest that the building was intended to advertise the presence of Islam. Together with the traditional identification of the rock as the place of Adam's burial and Abraham's intended sacrifice of his son and of the esplanade

as the site of Solomon's Temple, the inscriptions suggest that the Dome of the Rock was meant to symbolize Islam as the worthy successor to both Judaism and Christianity.

The Dome of the Rock continued to play an important role long after it was built. The Abbasids, who succeeded the Umayyads, restored it several times, and the Fatimids restored it in the eleventh century after the dome collapsed in the earthquake of 1016. The Crusaders considered it Solomon's Temple itself and rechristened the building Templum Domini. Saladin, the Ayyubid prince who recaptured Jerusalem for the Muslims in 1187, had the building rededicated as part of his campaign to enhance the city's sanctity and political importance. The Mamluks, rulers of Egypt and Syria from 1250 to 1517, had the wooden ceilings of the ambulatory and the central dome restored. The Ottoman sultan Suleyman (r. 1520–1566), whose name is the Turkish form of Solomon, ordered the building redecorated as part of his program of embellishing the holy cities of Islam. It was restored six more times in the twentieth century and has become a popular icon of Islam, decorating watches and tea towels and replicated in miniature models made of mother-of-pearl and plastic. The first great monument of Islamic architecture, it has taken on a new life as the symbol of Palestinian resistance to Israeli occupation.

*See also* **Architecture; Holy Cities.**

## BIBLIOGRAPHY

Creswell, K. A. C. *A Short Account of Early Muslim Architecture.* Beirut: Librarie du Liban, 1958.

Creswell, K. A. C. *Early Muslim Architecture.* 2d. ed. Oxford, U.K.: Clarendon Press, 1969.

Grabar, Oleg. *The Shape of the Holy: Early Islamic Jerusalem.* Princeton, N.J.: Princeton University Press, 1996.

Johns, Jeremy, ed. *Bayt al-Maqdis. Part II: Jerusalem and Early Islam.* Oxford, U.K.: Oxford University Press, 2000.

Nuseibeh, Said, and Grabar, Oleg. *The Dome of the Rock.* New York: Rizzoli, 1997.

*Sheila S. Blair*
*Jonathan M. Bloom*


# DREAMS

Muslims throughout history have attached great importance to dreams. Portions of the Qur'an were believed to have been revealed to Muhammad in dreams. Muhammad was also thought to have received numerous prophetic dreams. Moreover, dreams were considered the primary means by which God would communicate with Muslims following the death of Muhammad and the cessation of Qur'anic revelation. Indeed, according to tradition, on the day before his death Muhammad declared, "When I am gone, there shall remain naught of the glad-tidings of prophecy, except for true dreams."

Medieval Muslims cultivated numerous forms of literature on dreams. Accounts of dreams were collected to establish the sanctity of those who saw the dreams, a practice especially common among Sufis. Accounts of dreams were also collected to resolve points of controversy, to determine the proper reading and interpretation of the Qur'an, for instance, or to resolve legal or theological debates. Especially important, in this regard, were dreams in which the prophet Muhammad appeared, because, according to tradition, Muhammad himself had declared, "Whoever sees me in a dream has seen me in truth, for Satan cannot imitate me in a dream." Also of great importance was the dream manual, a work that taught its readers how to interpret their dreams. Many Muslim dream manuals were associated with Ibn Sirin (d. 728), the eponymous founder of the genre. While there is little reason to think that Ibn Sirin was in fact the author of a dream manual, it is certain that he was responsible for putting into oral circulation much dream lore.

Famous early dream manuals were written by the litterateur Ibn Qutaybah (d. 889), the historian al-Tabari (d. 923), and the philosopher Ibn Sina (d. 1037). Prominent later dream manuals include works written by al-Salimi (d. 1397), Ibn Shahin (d. 1468), and al-Nabulsi (d. 1730). Many Muslim dream manuals made heavy use of the Greco-Roman tradition of dream interpretation, to which access was had through the dream manual of Artemidorus, a Greek work composed in Asia Minor in the second century C.E. and translated into Arabic by the Christian physician Hunayn b. Ishaq (d. 877). It would be hard to overemphasize the importance of dream interpretation to medieval Muslims. Hundreds of dream manuals have been preserved, some in Arabic, others in Persian and Turkish.

Modern Muslims have been, not surprisingly, divided in their reception of dream interpretation. Some have cast it aside as superstitious nonsense, while others have sought to appropriate it through reinterpretation, suggesting that it foreshadows the discoveries of Sigmund Freud and Carl Jung. Yet others, especially Sufis and traditionalists, have shown little hesitation in proclaiming the continuing validity of this ancient tradition.

## BIBLIOGRAPHY

Fahd, Toufic. *La Divination arabe.* Leiden: E. J. Brill, 1966.

Katz, Jonathan G. *Dreams, Sufism and Sainthood.* Leiden, E. J. Brill, 1996.

Lamoreaux, John C. *The Early Muslim Tradition of Dream Interpretation.* Albany: State University of New York Press, 2002.

Schimmel, Annemarie. *Die Träume des Kalifen.* Munich: C. H. Beck, 1998.

*John C. Lamoreaux*


# DU'A

In contrast to the prescribed rituals of Islam, such as the daily prayers, the *du'a* is generally a spontaneous, unstructured, conversation with God. There are, however, prescribed supplications or *du'a ma'thur* that are considered particularly propitious because of their scriptural origins.

Whereas form is essential for the performance of the prescribed rituals, consciousness is central to *du'a*. And whereas every *du'a* is a form of prayer, only a prayer performed conscientiously becomes a *du'a*. The *du'a* is the very essence of worship because it venerates God, celebrates His sublime attributes, and puts trust in Him. Specific requests, however, are frowned upon: A *du'a* is considered most auspicious when framed broadly to seek protection from evil, solicit the good of this world, and salvation in the afterlife.

For the believer, supplications are always answered, but not in the form of a wish list. Human beings, it is said, lack the capacity to distinguish good from evil, and often solicit, and are denied, that which is essentially harmful to them.

A *du'a* also serves as an incantation to ward off evil, or secure grace. A traveler, for instance, is encouraged to read: "In God's name let its run be, and let its stopping be!"

*See also* **Devotional Life; 'Ibadat.**

**BIBLIOGRAPHY**

Ghazali, Muhammad al-. *Remembrance and Prayer: The Way of the Prophet Muhammad.* Translated by Y. T. DeLorenzo. Beltsville, Md.: Amana Publications, 1996.

Nakamura, Kojiro. *Invocations and Supplications: Book IX of the Revival of the Religious Sciences.* Cambridge, U.K.: Islamic Texts Society, 1990.

*Muneer Goolam Fareed*

# E

## EAST ASIA, ISLAM IN

Islam has spread to all parts of East Asia, a region that features some of the world's major centers of Islamic influence.

### China

With a Muslim population conservatively estimated at twenty million, China today has a larger Muslim population than most of the Arab countries of the Middle East, and yet few scholars have concentrated on this unique community located at the far reaches of the Muslim world. Of China's fifty-five officially recognized minority peoples (China's majority ethnic group is known as Han Chinese), ten are primarily Muslim: the Hui, Uighur, Kazak, Dongxiang, Kirghiz, Salar, Tajik, Uzbek, Bonan, and Tatar. The largest group, the Hui, are spread throughout the entire country, while the other nine live primarily in the northwest.

As a result of the extensive sea trade networks between China and Southwest Asia dating back to Roman times, there have been Muslims in China since shortly after the advent of Islam. Small communities of Muslim traders and merchants survived for centuries in cities along China's southeast coast, the most famous settlements being Canton and Quanzhou (Zaitun in the Arabic sources). During the first several centuries there was limited intermixing between the Muslim traders and the local Chinese population. It was not until the thirteenth century with the establishment of the Mongolian Yuan dynasty (1278–1368) that thousands of Muslims from Central and Western Asia were both forcibly moved to China by the Mongols as well as recruited by them to assist in their governance of their newly acquired territories. Although some of the higher-ranking Muslim officials may have been able to arrange marriages with women from their places of origin, it is generally assumed that most of the soldiers, officials, craftsmen, and farmers who settled in China during this early period married local women. Despite centuries of intermarriage, the Muslims who arrived at this time were able

to establish communities that have survived with many of their cultural and religious traditions intact down to this day.

During the early part of the Ming period (1368–1644), the emperor Yongle ordered Zheng He, a Muslim eunuch from Yunnan in southwest China, to lead a series of massive naval expeditions to explore the known world. In all, between 1405 and 1432, seven major expeditions were launched involving hundred of Chinese vessels and thousands of tons of goods and valuables to be traded throughout the southeast Asian archipelago, the Indian Ocean, and as far as the east coast of Africa. The success of these trading expeditions was no doubt in part due to Zheng He's religion and his ability to interact with many of the Muslim rulers and merchants encountered along the way. However, shortly after the death of the Yongle emperor, China's cosmopolitan and international initiatives gave way to a period of conservatism and the redirection of imperial resources toward domestic issues and projects. During this period numerous laws were passed requiring "foreigners" to dress like Chinese, adopt Chinese surnames, speak Chinese, and essentially in appearance become Chinese.

Despite these restrictions and requirements, the Muslims of China continued to actively practice their faith and pass it on to their descendants. By the end of the Ming dynasty there were enough Chinese Muslim intellectuals thoroughly educated in the classical Confucian tradition that several scholars developed a new Islamic literary genre: religious works on Islam written in Chinese that incorporated the vocabulary of Confucian, Buddhist, and Daoist thought. These texts, known as the *Han Kitab*, were not apologist treatises written to explain Islam to a non-Muslim Chinese audience, but were rather a reflection of the degree to which the Muslims of China had become completely conversant in intellectual traditions of the society in which they lived. Moreover, as more and more Chinese Muslims lost their fluency in Arabic and Persian, it became clear that in order to insure that future generations of Muslims were able to have a sophisticated

Small groups of merchant and artisan Muslims were present in China just after the rise of Islam. This mosque in Linxia, Gansu Province, is topped with a pagoda-shaped minaret, an elegant example of how Chinese Muslims have combined two cultures. © BOHEMIAN NOMAD PICTUREMAKERS/CORBIS

understanding of their faith, religious texts had to be written in Chinese.

The linguistic challenges of transliterating Arabic and Persian religious terms and proper names into Chinese also facilitated the blending of Chinese and Islamic principles as Chinese Muslim authors sought to create new Chinese terms to replace Arabic and Persian ones. Several of these terms are striking in their ability to use traditional Chinese characters to reflect fundamental Islamic concepts: God is translated as *zhen zhu*, or "the true lord"; Islam is *qingzhen jiao*, or "the pure and true religion"; the five pillars of Islam become the five constants, *wu chang*; and the prophet Muhammad is known as *zhi sheng*, or "utmost sage."

In 1644, the Qing dynasty was established, marking the beginning of a period of unparalleled growth and expansion, both in terms of territory and population. Travel restrictions were lifted, and the Muslims of China were once again allowed to make the pilgrimage to Mecca and study in the major centers of learning in the Islamic world. During this period several Hui scholars studied abroad and upon their return they started a movement to revitalize Islamic studies by translating the most important Islamic texts into Chinese and thus making them more accessible.

Despite the opportunities for travel and study that arose during this period, the Qing dynasty also represented a period of unparalleled violence against the Muslims of China. As reform movements led by Muslims who had studied overseas spread, conflicts arose between different communities. In several instances the government intervened, supporting one group against another, leading to an exacerbation of the conflict, outbreaks of mass violence and the eventual slaughter of hundreds of thousands of Muslims, and several rebellions.

In southwest China, it was the growing number of Han Chinese migrants moving into areas where Muslims had lived for centuries that led to violent conflicts. During the seventeenth and eighteenth centuries, China experienced a massive population explosion resulting in millions of Han Chinese moving into the frontier regions. As more immigrants moved into Yunnan province along the southwest frontier, there were increasing clashes with the Hui who had settled there in the thirteenth century and whose population is estimated to have been one million. In a series of disputes between newly arrived Han migrants and Hui who had lived there for centuries, local Han Chinese officials (who themselves were not local residents), repeatedly decided to support their fellow Han Chinese against the local residents. Fighting escalated and eventually a Chinese Muslim leader led a rebellion and in 1856 established an independent Islamic state centered in Dali, in northwest Yunnan. The state survived for almost sixteen years, and the Muslims worked closely together with other indigenous peoples. Eventually, however, the Chinese emperor ordered his troops to concentrate their efforts on destroying it. The massacres that ensued wiped out the majority of Muslims in Yunnan. Some fled to nearby Thailand, and their descendants still live there, while others fled to Burma or neighboring provinces. Estimates of those killed range from 60 to 85 percent, and more than a century later, their population has still not recovered its original number. Another consequence of the rebellion was a series of government regulations severely restricting the lives of Muslims.

In the aftermath of the rebellions, the first priority of the survivors was to pool their resources, rebuild their mosques, and open Islamic schools. Having lost most of their material possessions, they were clearly determined not to lose their religious legacy. This period saw renewed contact with other centers of learning in the Muslim world and the establishment of schools that concentrated equally on secular and religious education.

The collapse of the Qing dynasty in 1911 was followed by a period of unrest and warlordism. After the rise of the Guomindang and the Chinese Communist Party, a civil war ensued, in which both parties sought the support of the nation's largest minority groups with promises of religious freedom and limited self-government. Many of the Muslims chose to support the Communists, and in the initial period of the People's Republic of China, the Muslim minority peoples enjoyed a period of religious freedom. However, during subsequent political campaigns, culminating with the Cultural Revolution (1966–1976), the Muslims of China found their religion outlawed; their religious leaders persecuted, imprisoned, and even killed; and their mosques defiled, if not destroyed. During this period all worship and religious education were forbidden, and even simple common utterances such as *insha' allah* (God willing), or *al-hamdulillah* (thanks be to God) could cause Muslims to be punished. Despite the danger, Muslims in many parts of China continued their religious studies in secret.

In the years immediately following the Cultural Revolution, the Muslims of China lost no time in rebuilding their devastated communities. Throughout China, Muslims began slowly to restore their religious institutions and revive their religious activities. Their first priority was to rebuild their damaged mosques thereby allowing communities to create a space in which they could once again pray together, but also so that the mosques could reassert their role as centers of Islamic learning. Over the next two decades mosques throughout most of the country organized classes for not only children and young adults, but also for older people who had not had the opportunity to study their religion. Beginning in the late 1980s and continuing to the 1990s Islamic colleges have also been established throughout most of China.

Within China, when asked how to explain the recent resurgence in Islamic education, community members cite two main reasons: a desire to rebuild that which was taken from them, and the hope that a strong religious faith would help protect Muslim communities from the myriad of social problems presently besetting China in this day and age of rapid economic development. Chinese Muslims studying overseas reiterate the need to equip themselves and their communities for their future in a state that seems to be ideologically adrift.

## Korea

In some respects, the history of Islam in Korea mirrors that of China, but more as a faint reflection than as a comparable historical phenomenon. Little archaeological evidence has survived but it is commonly believed that some of the Muslim sea traders who regularly traveled to the southeast coast of China also made it as far as Korea. Arabic geographers note the existence of al-Sila, a country beyond China, and it is believed that this name is derived from the Korean dynasty Silla (668–935). Although there is some archaeological evidence of goods from Western and Central Asia being found in ancient tombs in Korea, it is not known if they were brought there directly or acquired by Korean traders in China, which had much more extensive sea and land trading routes with the rest of Asia.

During the Mongol Yuan dynasty (1278–1368), Korea also fell under the control of the Mongol empire. As they had a policy of recruiting tens of thousands of men from Central and Western Asia to help them in administering their newly acquired territory, it is probable that some of these Muslims ended up serving in Korea, and that many of them settled there. However, it appears that over the centuries those who settled completely assimilated to Korean society and culture. It was not until the modern period that Muslims returned to Korea. Beginning in the 1920s, thousands of Muslims escaping the Bolshevik Revolution in Russia fled overland through Korea, and many settled there before being forced to leave in the 1940s. The next group of Muslims who arrived were Turkish soldiers sent under United Nations auspices during the Korean War. Several soldiers settled in Korea, establishing the first mosques in Seoul, Pusan, and Taegu. Today the fledging community of Muslims living in Korea is made up of some converts, but primarily recent Muslim immigrants from South Asia.

## Japan

Although Muslim traders had sailed the seas off the coast of Japan for centuries, there is no known evidence of any Muslim communities settling in Japan until the early part of the twentieth century, when of the thousands of Muslims who fled Russia in the aftermath of the Bolshevik Revolution, several hundred were granted asylum in Japan. Many were settled in Kobe and Tokyo, which became the sites of Japan's first two mosques, built in 1935 and 1938. In the years leading up to the Second World War, the Japanese military government became increasingly interested in encouraging scholarship on Islam as part of its policy to portray itself as a protector of Islam to the Muslim communities of China and southeast Asia. As Japan invaded neighboring countries under its "Greater East Asia Coprosperity Sphere" campaign, it justified its actions in part as a plan to safeguard all of Asia from Western imperialism, but also to protect Islam.

At present there are an estimated 100,000 Muslims living in Japan, the overwhelming majority of which are immigrants from South Asia and Iran; only a few thousand are Japanese who have converted. Scholarly research on the Middle East and Islam has developed tremendously since the early 1980s, with several research centers at major universities around the country.

*See also* **East Asian Culture and Islam; South Asia, Islam in; Southeast Asia, Islam in.**

## BIBLIOGRAPHY

Armijo, Jaqueline. "Narratives Engendering Survival: How the Muslims of Southwest China Remember the Massacres of 1873." *Traces: An International Journal of Comparative Cultural Theory* 1, no. 2 (2001): 293–329.

During the Muslim holy month, Ramadan, a Chinese Muslim prays at Nijue Mosque in Beijing, which was built in 996. ANAT GIVON/AP/WIDE WORLD PHOTOS

Fletcher, Joseph. *Studies on Chinese and Islamic Inner Asia*. Aldershot, U.K.: Variorum, 1995.

Gladney, Dru. *Muslim Chinese: Ethnic Nationalism in the People's Republic of China*. Cambridge, Mass.: Harvard University Press, 1991.

Jaschok, Maria, and Jingjun, Shui. *A History of Women's Mosques in Chinese Islam: A Mosque of their Own*. Richmond, Surrey, U.K.: Curzon Press, 2000.

Leslie, Donald Daniel. *Islam in Traditional China: A Short History to 1800*. Canberra, Australia: Canberra College of Advanced Education, 1986.

Lipman, Jonathan. *Familiar Strangers: A History of the Muslims in Northwest China*. Seattle: University of Washington Press, 1997.

Miyazi Kazuo. "Middle East Studies in Japan." *Middle East Studies Association Bulletin* 34, no. 1 (summer 2000): 23–37.

Murata, Sachiko. *Chinese Gleams of Sufi Light: Wang Tai-yü's Great Learning of the Pure and Real and Liu Chih's Displaying the Concealment of the Real Realm*. Albany: State University of New York Press, 2000.

Wang, Jianping. *Concord and Conflict: The Hui Communities of Yunnan Society*. Stockholm: Almqvist & Wiksell International, 1996.

*Jacqueline M. Armijo*

# EAST ASIAN CULTURE AND ISLAM

Within the field of Islam in East Asia, the major developments and most lasting influences between Islam and the indigenous peoples have taken place in China, where Muslims traders first settled in the early decades of the *hijra*. This early interest in China as a destiny for Muslim travelers is reflected in the famous hadith, "seek knowledge, even unto China." Despite centuries of relative isolation from the rest of the Islamic world, the Muslims in most regions of China have managed to sustain a continuous knowledge of the Islamic sciences, Arabic, and Persian. Given extended periods of persecution combined with periods of intense government efforts to legislate adoption of Chinese cultural practices and norms, that Islam should have survived, let alone flourished, is an extraordinary historical phenomenon. Although some scholars have attributed the survival of Muslim communities in China to their ability to adopt Chinese cultural traditions, when asked themselves, Chinese Muslims usually attribute their survival to their strong faith and God's protection.

In the aftermath of the Cultural Revolution (1966–1976), a period of extreme political violence and chaos when Muslims together with other minority groups were persecuted, Muslim communities throughout China actively sought to reclaim their religious identity and revive Islamic education. In addition to repairing and rebuilding mosques returned to them after the revolution, Muslim communities have also pooled their resources to build new mosques and Islamic schools. These schools are filled with students of all ages, including the elderly, who after decades of government control are anxious to study Islam and Arabic. More recently a growing number of Chinese Muslims are pursing advanced Islamic studies at international Islamic centers of learning.

Although there are now Muslims present in virtually every region of China, there have undoubtedly been many communities that were either completely destroyed during government military campaigns, or that simply assimilated to the point of dissolution. One interesting example of a community that came to the brink of complete assimilation, only to be revived for political reasons, was documented by an anthropologist in the early 1980s. In Quanzhou (known as Zaytun in the Arabic sources), a city located along China's southeast coast, a large clan existed whose members had so assimilated to local customs as to be completely indistinguishable from the local Han Chinese. They took part in the full range of traditional religious practices, many of which had to do with honoring one's ancestors. They knew nothing of Islam, ate pork, and drank alcohol. There was one slight difference though: During the annual sacrifices made to one's ancestors, when preparing food to offer ceremoniously to their ancestors, they would not include pork or alcohol. This tenuous connection to their ancestors (Muslim traders and officials who had first settled in this region in the early years of the *hijra*) was called upon in 1981 when this extended family sought government recognition as one of the officially recognized minority groups. As they had the genealogical records to prove their descent from Muslims, they were able to change their status from Han Chinese to Hui (Chinese Muslim).

## Mosques and Calligraphy

Mosques and the calligraphy within them have also served as an interesting barometer of the waxing and waning of traditional Chinese influences on the development of indigenous Chinese Islamic traditions.

Although no mosques dating back to the pre-Mongol period have survived, it is assumed that mosques during this period reflected the architecture of the immigrant Muslims who built them, as they were required to live in special districts separate from the general population. By the Ming period in the fourteenth to the seventeenth centuries, however, there was significant pressure for Muslims to outwardly conform to Chinese traditions. The Huajue mosque in Xian, which dates back to the Ming period and has survived down to the present, is an exquisite example of how Chinese Muslims were able to incorporate traditional Chinese motifs, decorative arts, and temple architectural styles into the structure and decoration of mosques. In this mosque, as in most others in China, Arabic calligraphy is interspersed with carvings and paintings of traditional Chinese images of flowers, fruit, mythical animals, and Chinese calligraphy. The rooftops are protected by small animal figures along the ridges of roof tiles, and the minarets take the form of pagodas. In addition, the Arabic calligraphy is a highly stylized form that differs from region to region and reflects local calligraphic traditions that have evolved in relative isolation over centuries.

However, in recent years, in part as a result from pressure from outside funding sources and the growing number of Chinese Muslims going overseas for the hajj and to study, many communities have torn down these traditional mosques and replaced them with ones believed to be more "authentic." Over the past twenty years untold numbers of mosques dating back centuries have been destroyed. Nevertheless, in some parts of China in recent years, there has been a growing movement among Chinese Muslims to protect their unique architectural traditions.

## Local Celebrations

As there are Muslims communities in every part of China with their own histories and local traditions it would be difficult to generalize about the ways in which Islamic practices have been influenced by other local Chinese traditions. However, by looking at local celebrations of 'Id al-Fitr and the *Maulid* (birthday of the prophet Muhammad) one can gain some sense of the variety of ways in which these interactions have developed. For example, in Yunnan province in southwest China, Muslim communities spread throughout the region. Many are direct descendants of Sayyid 'Ajall Shams al-Din, a Muslim from Bukhara, who served as an official under the Mongol Yuan dynasty and settled in Yunnan at the end of the thirteenth century. Seven centuries later, during the annual celebrations of 'Id al-Fitr, after communal prayers at the mosque, Muslims from different areas travel to the site of Sayyid 'Ajall's grave where special prayers are held. First there are readings from the Qur'an, then the tomb is swept and cleaned (reminiscent of the traditional Chinese Qingming festival held once a year when Chinese go to the graves of their ancestors, sweep and clean the area and then make food offerings), and then the accomplishments of Sayyid 'Ajall are retold. In conclusion, a special service is held to honor the hundreds of thousands of Muslims killed during the Qing dynasty, and the hundreds killed more recently in this area during the Cultural Revolution.

In another region of Yunnan, a group of Muslim villages spread out over a vast plain have developed there a way of celebrating the birthday of the Prophet, which allows them to reassert their ties to one another. Every year the Mawlid is celebrated in the fall over a period of two months beginning with the end of the major harvests. Each village is assigned a weekend when it will host all the other villages in a Mawlid celebration. Although the dates clearly are not connected

In southwest China, Muslim women generally take part in communal prayer in mosques. The women's section is to one side, and demarcated by a half-length curtain. In central China there is a centuries-old tradition of women having their own separate mosques; while in northwest China, women do not usually take part in communal prayers in the mosques. JACQUELINE M. ARMIJO

with the Islamic calendar, their tradition allows them to share their bounty with their neighboring Muslim communities and strengthen their networks.

Meanwhile, in northwest China, the decision of when to celebrate the Prophet's birthday is influenced not by seasonal harvests, but rather by the desire to offer younger Muslims an alternative activity during the widely and elaborately celebrated Chinese New Year. In recent years local Muslim religious leaders in Xian have considered scheduling celebrations of the Prophet's birthday to coincide with the festivities surrounding the Chinese New Year.

### The Role of Women

Another example of how local histories and traditions within the diverse communities of Muslims in China have evolved over the centuries can be seen in the roles of women in different communities. In central China there is a long tradition of active involvement by women in both Islamic education and religious leadership. Not only is there a long history of women imams in this region, there is also a tradition of separate women's mosques. In northwest China, however, women have tended not to play an active leadership role within Muslim communities, and usually they do not

pray in the mosques with the men. According to Muslims in other parts of China, these attitudes in the northwest toward women are the result of the Muslims adopting local Chinese views, which are considered quite chauvinistic. In southwest China, however, women play an active role within Muslim communities and are also widely credited with insuring the survival of the Muslim population in the aftermath of a brutal massacre that took place in the 1870s. In most mosques men and women pray side by side with a half curtain dividing the prayer hall. Although over the centuries many Chinese Muslim women adopted the custom of footbinding, historically and down to the present, the Muslim community has not adopted the widespread practice of female infanticide.

In conclusion, although maintaining their religious beliefs and practices over the centuries has been a continual challenge, Muslims in China have always been confident of their identities as both Muslims and Chinese. Although some Western scholars have presumed that these identities were somehow inherently antagonistic if not mutually exclusive, the survival of Islam in China belies these assumptions. Islamic and Chinese values have both proven to be sufficiently complementary and dynamic to allow for the flourishing of Islam in China.

In southwest China the tradition of education for Muslim girls dates back to the mid-nineteenth century. These girls are taking part in after school Arabic and Islamic studies classes in a village in central Yannan province. JACQUELINE M. ARMIJO

*See also* **East Asia, Islam in.**

## BIBLIOGRAPHY

Armijo, Jacqueline. "Narratives Engendering Survival: How the Muslims of Southwest China Remember the Massacres of 1873." *Traces: An International Journal of Comparative Cultural Theory* 1, no. 2 (2001): 293–329.

Fletcher, Joseph. *Studies on Chinese and Islamic Inner Asia.* Aldershot, U.K.: Variorum, 1995.

Gladney, Dru. *Muslim Chinese: Ethnic Nationalism in the People's Republic of China.* Cambridge, Mass.: Harvard University Press, 1991.

Jaschok, Maria, and Jingjun, Shui. *A History of Women's Mosques in Chinese Islam: A Mosque of their Own.* Richmond, U.K.: Curzon Press, 2000.

Leslie, Donald Daniel. *Islam in Traditional China: A Short History to 1800.* Belconnen, Australia: Canberra College of Advanced Education, 1986.

Murata, Sachiko. *Chinese Gleams of Sufi Light: Wang Tai-yü's Great Learning of the Pure and Real and Liu Chih's Displaying the Concealment of the Real Realm.* Albany: State University of New York Press, 2000.

*Jacqueline M. Armijo*

# ECONOMY AND ECONOMIC INSTITUTIONS

The Islamic world and its development have often been examined through its economic development and its relationship with Christian Europe. This has been particularly true of analyses that dealt with the earlier period of Islamic history. The Belgian medievalist, Henri Pirenne, proffered a provocative theory about the end of the Rome Empire in the West and the beginning of the Middle Ages. He asserted that the Middle Ages did not begin in 325, as his contemporaries would have it, but rather that they began after the Arab conquest broke through the perimeter of the Mediterranean, in the seventh and eighth centuries. The Arab incursion destroyed the unity of the Roman Empire, fracturing its political, economic, and cultural cohesiveness. Pirenne hypothesized that this situation, along with the isolationism of much of Europe, eventually led to feudalism in Europe and the rise of Islamic civilization.

## Agriculture in the Early Islamic World

Whether or not one agrees with Pirenne's views of the effect of Arab conquest on European society, it is undisputed that the expansion of the Islamic world had a profound impact on Muslim society. Most notable is its effect on agriculture, where new crops and techniques to enhance production were rapidly introduced from places as far east as Southeast Asia and Malaysia. Some of the new crops introduced during the early Islamic period included rice, sorghum, hard wheat, sugar cane, cotton, watermelons, eggplants, spinach, artichokes, sour oranges, lemons, limes, bananas, plantains, mangoes, and coconut palms. These crops, as well as changes in agricultural techniques, were not only significant in their impact on food production, but also in the role they played in fostering the development of industry, cities, and monetary authorities within the Muslim world.

It is believed that after the rise and spread of Islam, many of the new crops were obtained from the fallen Sassanian Empire and the Indian subcontinent, where the new province of the Sind, conquered in 711, gave early Muslims a foothold in a part of India. The crops from India first came to Iraq and Persia, then diffused into the westerly parts of the Islamic world. By the tenth and eleventh century, the western part of the Islamic world had taken on major crop changes that had been introduced from territories to the east.

In time, the new crops were also introduced into Europe by way of Spain, Sicily, and Cyprus. Unlike the Islamic world, where these new crops were quickly adapted to local culture and tastes, they were not rapidly developed in Europe. In a 1981 article on the "Medieval Green Revolution," Andrew M. Watson cites spinach as an example of this differential development. He states that spinach was one of the earliest crops to be received into Europe, but although it was quickly adopted throughout the Islamic world, it spread much more slowly in Europe, along with sorghum, sour oranges, and lemons. One reason given for this slowness to adopt new crops was the European peasantry's lack of skill and technical knowledge about agriculture.

In contrast, the Islamic world saw extensive changes in agricultural techniques. One area of great importance was irrigation. Since many of the new crops came from regions of heavy rainfall, it is significant that they could be grown successfully in the much drier environment of the Middle East. In Persia and the Nile Valley, long underground canals

This etching depicts medieval European merchants doing business with Arabs. © BETTMAN/CORBIS

known as *qanat* were used. These canals connected catchments of ground water to surface canals, but they were inadequate to meet the needs of the new crops. A new and more sophisticated system of irrigation was introduced during the early Islamic period that relied on ground water from wells, aquifers, and springs, augmenting older irrigation systems. Dams and cisterns were also used to store water for later use. Taken together, these systems allowed for the irrigation of land that had never before been used agriculturally, or extended the time that other lands could be kept under cultivation each year.

These changes in agriculture gave rise to other changes in the Islamic world. The increase in food production led to increases in population growth, fostering urbanization and industrialization. These developments fed on each other, for as the population grew new importance was put on agricultural improvements in productivity. As towns increased in size there was continued pressure to expand the cultivation of new lands. As villages grew, they often gave rise to new cities.

## Industrialization, Trade, and Coinage

Industrialization, too, was an outgrowth of agricultural surplus in many parts of the Islamic world. The cities became the place where much of the processing of the new crops occurred. This refining of agricultural goods involved drying, cooking, pickling, and milling of many crops. Watson states that this refining often led to further processing, as in the case of sugar, which gave rise to the confectionery industry, and cotton, from which the textiles industry evolved. The cities also became the marketplace, where people from the rural areas would come to trade crops for processed goods. It has thus even been argued that agricultural change was at the heart of local and, eventually, long distance trade. As the Islamic world spread, the demand for its raw materials as well as finished goods increased. Consequently, trade between the Islamic world and many parts of Europe grew. As ports and waterways became more important for transporting goods, the cities that lay along waterways grew. There was also the birth of a new class of urban intermediaries—merchants, transporters, financiers, and warehouse owners.

This expansion in trade and commerce also led to a more sophisticated monetary system. At the onset of the rise of Islam, the use of various coins in different parts of the Islamic world was not uncommon. In fact, the Muslims inherited the circulation of metallic money from the Byzantines and Sassanids who preceded them. The Byzantine state had used gold coinage, which constituted an imperial monopoly, whereas the Sassanid empire used silver coinage. As the Islamic world continued to expand, the need to secure an adequate supply of coinage grew more pressing. Initially, the Byzantine and Sassanid coins were used, but eventually a new, Islamic, coinage was introduced. There were two new coins: silver (*dirham*) and gold (*dinar*). The introduction of these coins is referred to as the monetary reform of ʿAbd al-Malik.

Professor of Islamic history Andrew S. Ehrenkreutz has stated that the monetary reforms of the early Muslim world go beyond these new coins. The caliphate assumed responsibility for the supply of currency, taking upon itself the problems of finding precious metals for minting and the distribution of coinage. Muslim coins have been found as far away as Scandinavia and Russia, suggesting that at least some parts of the West had a favorable balance of trade with the Muslims. A number of scholars believe that the Varangians (Vikings) were the middlemen, moving goods from the Muslim world to Scandinavia and Russia. This theory is supported by evidence that, beginning sometime between the late seventh or early eighth century C.E., the Varangians migrated from Scandinavia south to the Black Sea, establishing many trading towns and stations along the way.

### Growth of Cities and Guilds

As this system of commerce expanded, the Islamic city grew in importance as well. These cities were multiethnic, and their citizens practiced a variety of religions. Different ethnic or religious groups resided in separate, usually exclusive, quarters of the cities, and these residential divisions were associated with occupational specialization as well. Z.Y. Hershlag points out that ethnic Turks were officials and soldiers, the Greeks as well as the Jews were engaged in trade and finance, and the Armenians were artisans. There were certain cities where the main activities of the town were associated with their dominant ethnic or religious groups.

Even the marketplace was organized along ethnic and religious lines, as various kinds of goods and services were associated with particular groups and were made available in separate parts of the bazaar.

In addition, most residents of cities were organized into corporations, termed *asnaf*, *naqabat*, or *tawaʾif* in Arabic. These corporations were mainly professional guilds, but while their social functions were on the whole broader than those of the European guilds, their economic power and their control over their professions were less absolute than in their Western counterparts, nor did the Muslim guilds encompass all urban craftsmen or merchants. The case of the Damascus guilds offers insights into how these institutions worked. The Damascus guilds were rigidly organized and exclusive. They had a hierarchy of officers, the head of which was the shaykh, who either inherited his position or was elected. In other Middle Eastern countries, however, the autonomy of the shaykh was not the case. For example, in Egypt guilds were an important mechanism for the government to collect taxes, and the shaykhs became accountable to the government for the actions of guild members as well as for their members' payment of taxes. In Turkey, guilds were very restrictive and mandated that the number of people participating in a given trade be kept at a certain number.

There has been much debate by scholars as to the significance of guilds as well as their links to Islamic syndicates and trade unions; however, there is little evidence that the craftsmen's guilds had any influence on these later organizations. Furthermore, there has been much speculation as to why the guilds dissolved. Some writers assert that the decline of the guilds had to do with the rigid structure of the organizations. However, evidence seems to indicate that the dissolution of the guilds is more likely tied to the introduction of European finished goods into the Muslim markets, which disrupted the local handicrafts industry as a whole.

### Agriculture and Trade in the Modern Era

Like the earlier period of Islamic history, the modern economic history of the Middle East has been shaped by its relationship and interaction with Europe and Western civilization. Most economic historians of the region trace the origin of this new relationship to the early 1800s and the expansion by many European countries into other regions of the world in search of natural resources and markets for their finished goods. In spite of its earlier economic advances, the Middle East eventually lagged behind Western society in terms of modernization.

As the Europeans expanded their control into other parts of the world, the Middle East itself was galvanized into the formation of a broad network of international trade and finance. The region had witnessed much social upheaval throughout the Middle Ages, much of it attributable to an unstable food supply that had been devastated by famine, plagues, and wars. To safeguard their local populations from disruptions in the food supply, governments of the region, in particular the Ottoman Empire, turned to the importation of European consumer goods. This approach to trade fit well with the mercantilist mentality of the Europeans, who were looking for export markets but did not care to reciprocate the trade with equal imports. In fact, this lack of trade reciprocity gave rise to the belief, in many parts of the Middle East and North Africa, that exports impoverished a country and that sales to foreigners should be discouraged. Nonetheless, the Middle East became one of the lowest-duty (import tariff) areas in the world, ultimately providing a large market for European goods. It should be mentioned, however, that during both the First and Second World Wars, the Middle East became a net exporter to Europe, as supply chains were disrupted and Europe needed to provision its troops in the region.

The exception to this trade arrangement was found in Egypt. Under Muhammad 'Ali (r. 1805–1849), Egypt used foreign trade to raise revenue, while taking steps to allocate local resources and protect its domestic industries. In fact, Egypt in the early 1800s was careful not only to minimize imports but also to maximize exports, thus protecting domestic industries from being supplanted by foreign-made products. Muhammad 'Ali's most successful venture was the development of the cotton trade. Egypt was able to produce a much higher quality cotton crop than Europeans. Consequently, beginning in 1821, Egyptian cotton exports rose from 100,000 to 50 million pounds by 1850. Cotton exports continued to surge into the 1860s, as the American Civil War significantly halted production in the United States.

The focus on cotton in Egypt should not be surprising, as agricultural production has played an important role throughout the Middle East. Yet, most of the land in the region is less than well suited to agricultural development. There is a lack of rain throughout the region and the few existing waterways are heavily drawn upon, a scarcity that continues to be a source of great tension throughout the area. Consequently, the crops that have dominated agricultural production have been those that are less irrigation intensive, such as cereals, with the limited introduction of silk production in the late nineteenth century in Lebanon, coffee production in Yemen, and cash crops such as dates, nuts, and fruits in the better-watered parts of Arabia and North Africa.

Turkey under the Ottoman Empire began producing tobacco in the seventeenth century. As with cotton, the American Civil War was a factor in the growth of the Turkish tobacco industry, as the plantations of the American South ceased production and demand for the commodity from other sources increased significantly. Turkey's tobacco production rose from an estimated 10,000–13,000 tons in the 1870s to 31,000 tons in 1900, and 64,000 tons in 1911. Tobacco remains an important export for Turkey today.

## Land Ownership and Reform

In addition to the problems of attempting to cultivate marginal land for agricultural use, many scholars have cited land tenure as a major deterrent to productive agricultural development in the Middle East. Land is normally classified into three types in the Middle East: *raqaba*, which means ownership by the state or ruler; *milk*, which refers to private ownership; or *waqf*, which is land whose revenues are intended for religious or charitable purposes. Of course, there was a complex system of land-holding arrangements in the region, but in general, during the period prior to the nineteenth century, much of the land was held by the state. The land was often worked by peasants who were heavily taxed. Later, as agricultural production became more profitable, much of the land was transferred to private ownership, held in large estates and, again, worked by peasant farmers.

It wasn't until after the Second World War that major land reforms took place that favored small farmers. The Egyptian Land Reform Law of 1952 served as a model for the region. The act redistributed land held by absentee landlords, transferring ownership to those who actually worked it. The large estates were broken up into small plots and parceled out to farmers who belonged to cooperatives. Although in most cases land reform was hailed as a needed change, it has proven over time to have been less than successful, for it established a system of small and inefficient farms that has hampered productivity and hindered the use of mechanization in the modern period.

## Industrialization

Industrialization also experienced a number of ups and downs in the region. Before the late nineteenth century, the Middle East boasted of a thriving handicraft industry. However, the production of local handicrafts declined with the introduction of European and Indian goods on the Middle Eastern market. There was also a perception, particularly among the middle and upper classes, that local goods were inferior to European goods, and this attitude helped seal the fate of handicrafts in the region. Meanwhile, the development of industrialization in the region was slowed by unfavorable commercial treaties, which did not support export markets. There was also a lack of capital for industrial development, as well as governments that lacked the foresight to foster local entrepreneurs.

Yet, again, the First World War was important for setting the stage for industrialization. The rise of nationalism, coupled with the realization that European instability could interfere with its ability to provide necessary imports for export to the Middle East, led to widespread industrialization projects. With the abolition of trade agreements that favored Europe, a further incentive for industrialization was created. Industrialization continued to be important through the Second World War, for now the countries of the Middle East not only had to provide for themselves, but some of them also had taken on commitments to supply the Allies.

Because of Egypt's ambitious development initiatives in the 1800s, foreign investment came to play a significant role. The first half of the nineteenth century saw the dissolution of the old trading companies and the emergence of private traders, and the second half saw the emergence of private and incorporated banks. Along with these banks came large accumulation of debt by many governments in the region. Moreover, much of the money that was borrowed was poorly invested, and thus did not create much economic growth. In the cases of Egypt, Tunisia, Morocco, and Turkey, this debt eventually led to foreign occupation. By 1914, the countries of the Middle East had a total debt of about $2 billion, or nearly one-twentieth of the total world debt, of which a little over half was public and the rest private. North Africa had a public debt of about $250 million and a much larger amount of foreign investment in the private sector. Although foreign occupation ultimately led to much political turmoil in the region, it has been attributed initially to better debt management and investment strategies.

### The First World War through the Cold War

The two world wars were important events in terms of their impact on the Middle East. The First World War destroyed the old colonial trading system and allowed the region to regain both political and economic independence. This took the form of new trade treaties that were aimed at creating fairer and more appropriate commercial arrangements. The special agreements that had given foreigners extraterritorial rights and sheltered them from local laws and taxation were abolished. Subsequently, the period between the two world wars found the Europeans preoccupied with domestic problems and postwar reconstruction, minimizing their influence and interference in the region. The Second World War was even more significant, for it enabled the creation of a new agenda for the Middle East as political and economic power continued to move from the hands of foreigners to the hands of the endogenous class.

As foreign nationals lost economic and political control in many of the countries of the Middle East, a massive exodus of Europeans took place. This exodus created a vacuum in the upper tiers of the labor market as many of the foreigners had positioned themselves not only in roles as traders and financiers, but as entrepreneurs and managers as well. This vacuum caused the endogenous governments of these states to take on increasingly active roles within their own economies. In spite of the fact that many of these states began espousing socialism, the period of the 1950s was really marked as the period of state capitalism, in which the various governments began to take on the economic roles that are normally associated with the private sector. While the Soviet Union and the West, led by the United States, attempted to win allies in the region through the distribution of foreign aid and loans, governments within the region began experimenting with many alternative economic paradigms.

The cold war policies of the West concentrated on modernizing the Third World through economic development. In Europe, the Marshall Plan provided the capital it needed to rapidly rebuild and develop; consequently, it was believed that an equally big push, in the form of capital infusion, would be similarly effective if applied to the Third World. Foreign aid with an emphasis on industrialization began to pour into the region. Egypt under Jamal 'Abd al-Nasser (1918–1970, president from 1954 to 1970) was very successful at playing the United States and its allies off against the Soviet Union, winning capital and investment from both sources.

In 1952, Jamal 'Abd al-Nasser had led a military coup, seizing power of Egypt. Under his leadership, monopolistic capitalism came to the forefront as the institutional structure of the economy. He nationalized a number of industries, including the Suez Canal Company, and carried out radical land reforms. Much of the logic for restructuring the economy was not only to create an equitable distribution of resources within Egypt, but also to offset the damage done by decades of colonial policies, which left Egypt with little to no indigenous business community. Moreover, Nasser saw the need to generate resources to fuel his hopes of economic expansion. Such resources were unavailable in the private sector, but the government was receiving much foreign aid during the 1950s and 1960s. Nasser adopted a foreign policy of nonalignment, courting both the United States and Soviet Union without offering full allegiance to either.

The dilemma for many of the countries in the Middle East, however, was that they were essentially rural, agrarian societies, ill equipped in terms of human capital to absorb the foreign aid that was being given to them. This situation led to economic policies that favored the development of urban centers at the expense of the countryside. This phenomenon, known in development literature as "urban bias," led to much migration of laborers from rural areas to the urban centers, and this influx of prospective workers often outpaced industrialization. Consequently, many countries in the region saw the rapid growth of urban poverty, as the cities attracted vast numbers of underemployed or unemployed citizens for whom no jobs could be found.

### Oil and Labor

Although the region boasted some of the world's largest known oil reserves even during the middle of the twentieth century, it wasn't until the 1970s that the governments of the Middle Eastern states came to appreciate the power of this resource. In fact, oil was relatively insignificant to the foreign aid and development policies of the region throughout the 1950s and 1960s. When the 1973 Arab-Israeli War broke out, however, Arab petroleum-producing countries took measures to pressure Western powers in favor of the Arab cause.

First they introduced restrictions on the sale of oil to certain states that supported Israel. Second, they cut back on oil production. By the end of December 1973, they had reduced the production of oil by 25 percent of its earlier levels. The price of oil increased as a result. On 16 October 1973, the ministerial committee representing the six Gulf countries, which are members of the Organization of Petroleum Exporting Countries (OPEC), decided to further increase the price of oil by 70 percent. Coupled with the oil embargo, the price was later pushed up to $11.56 per barrel. These events, although politically motivated, substantially fueled the economies of the states in the Gulf region.

The initiation and implementation of development plans in the Gulf States required large numbers of migrant workers of many nationalities. Much of Saudi Arabia's initial needs were in construction, where high levels of unskilled and semiskilled workers were needed. Many of its neighbor states had large numbers of unskilled or semiskilled workers in need of jobs. They constituted a large available labor force with easy access to the Saudi Arabian labor markets, and they flooded into the country.

This situation, coupled with higher wage rates in Saudi Arabia relative to labor–rich states, led to a massive labor migration from Egypt, Yemen, and Jordan (mainly Palestinians) to Saudi Arabia and other, similarly well-off Gulf States. This migration would climax and then halt abruptly with the Gulf War of 1990. It has been estimated that, in 1975, the Gulf region had a labor requirement of 9,728,000. Saudi Arabia alone had a labor requirement of 1,968,000 in 1975, but its national work force numbered only 1,300,000. Although it is difficult to know how reliable these figures are, they do illustrate the great need for laborers in the Gulf region.

Middle Eastern oil reserves and the revenues they generate have divided the region into two groups of countries: oil rich/labor scarce and oil poor/labor abundant. Although these countries have not integrated into one system, they have benefited greatly from their proximity to each other. The oil-rich countries have relied heavily since the early 1970s on the labor from the labor abundant states. The labor-abundant states have used capital inflows from migrant remittances, along with financial aid from the Gulf and the world's superpowers, to build growth economies through state-owned enterprises. From 1960 to 1985, the Middle East outperformed all other regions of the world except East Asia in income growth.

The Middle East witnessed much change in the 1980s and 1990s. Political instability, coupled with too much government control and regulation, caused much of the international financial and business community to shun this region and to invest their capital in the emerging superstars of Southeast Asia. Fund managers estimated that out of a total of $65 billion of capital that floated into emerging markets in

the peak year of 1993, only 0.3 percent trickled to Arab markets. Yet, this region continues to be rich in both human and natural resources. It is the home of 6 percent of the world's population, with a wealth of highly-skilled workers and a GDP of over $600 billion.

The late 1980s, however, was a sobering period for the Middle East. An increase in the world supply of oil caused prices to plummet at the same time as financial aid from the Gulf and abroad came to a halt. Since 1986, real per-capita incomes have fallen by 2 percent per year. The oil producers were hit even harder with the per-capita fall in oil output of 4 percent per year between 1980 and 1991. These events caused the Arab world to rethink its stance on two major fronts: the structure of their economies and the state of war with Israel. These have not been mutually exclusive acts. It can be argued that much of the government control and lack of liberalization in the region was in response to the continuous uncertainty caused by the state of war.

## Arab–Israel Conflict

The end of violence between Arabs and Israelis has been seen as paramount to the economic stability and liberalization of the region, beginning in the 1990s. This confrontation had first erupted with the proclamation of the State of Israel on 14 May 1948 on land that had hitherto been occupied by Palestinians. The ensuing hostilities between Arab states and Israel have cost the region much in terms of human and capital resources. In the late 1980s and early 1990s, however, there appeared to be a consensus in the Arab world that Israel was there to stay and that stagnating economies and poverty in the region were more pressing concerns. For the Israelis, the need for security was tempered with the realization that the threat of hostilities could only be diminished by compromising with its neighbors. The Arabs, on the other hand, sought justice from an unjust colonial legacy, which is how they perceived the creation of a state for the Jews on land already occupied by Palestinians. What these aspirations initially translated into was a land-for-peace settlement.

In March of 1979, Israel and Egypt signed a peace agreement that included the return of the Sinai to Egypt. On 13 September 1993, Israel and the Palestine Liberation Organization signed a Declaration of Principles. It set the ground rules for the transfer of authority of the Gaza Strip and West Bank Palestinian areas to a Palestinian authority. On 26 October 1994, Jordan and Israel also signed a peace accord.

During the mid 1990s there was much discussion of what was to be the peace dividend: the reallocation of resources away from military expenditures and toward other sectors of the region's economies. Peace was also associated with an opening of political and economic systems that had been overcontrolled by governments, a situation that initially had been due to the lack of an endogenous entrepreneurial class and then later continued in response to the region's chronic

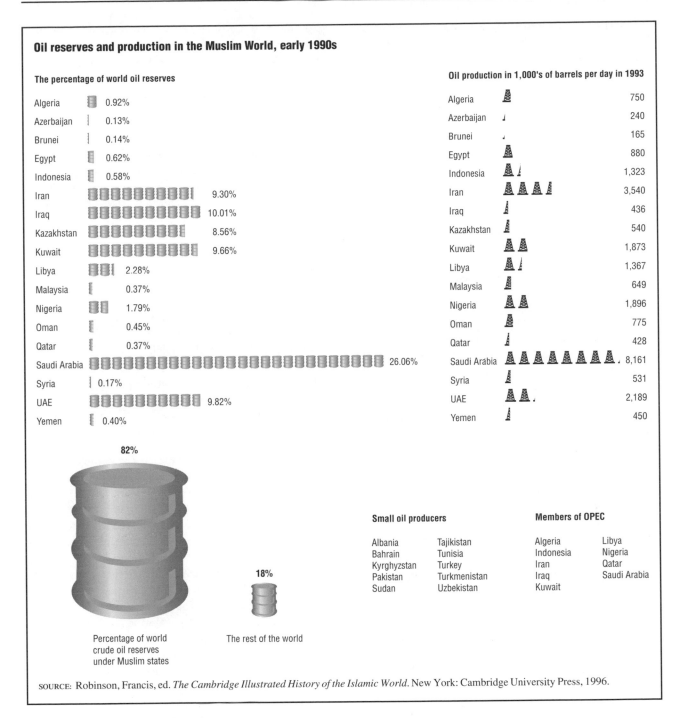

**Oil reserves and production in the Muslim World, early 1990s**

The percentage of world oil reserves

| | |
|---|---|
| Algeria | 0.92% |
| Azerbaijan | 0.13% |
| Brunei | 0.14% |
| Egypt | 0.62% |
| Indonesia | 0.58% |
| Iran | 9.30% |
| Iraq | 10.01% |
| Kazakhstan | 8.56% |
| Kuwait | 9.66% |
| Libya | 2.28% |
| Malaysia | 0.37% |
| Nigeria | 1.79% |
| Oman | 0.45% |
| Qatar | 0.37% |
| Saudi Arabia | 26.06% |
| Syria | 0.17% |
| UAE | 9.82% |
| Yemen | 0.40% |

Oil production in 1,000's of barrels per day in 1993

| | |
|---|---|
| Algeria | 750 |
| Azerbaijan | 240 |
| Brunei | 165 |
| Egypt | 880 |
| Indonesia | 1,323 |
| Iran | 3,540 |
| Iraq | 436 |
| Kazakhstan | 540 |
| Kuwait | 1,873 |
| Libya | 1,367 |
| Malaysia | 649 |
| Nigeria | 1,896 |
| Oman | 775 |
| Qatar | 428 |
| Saudi Arabia | 8,161 |
| Syria | 531 |
| UAE | 2,189 |
| Yemen | 450 |

82%

18%

Percentage of world crude oil reserves under Muslim states

The rest of the world

Small oil producers

| | |
|---|---|
| Albania | Tajikistan |
| Bahrain | Tunisia |
| Kyrghyzstan | Turkey |
| Pakistan | Turkmenistan |
| Sudan | Uzbekistan |

Members of OPEC

| | |
|---|---|
| Algeria | Libya |
| Indonesia | Nigeria |
| Iran | Qatar |
| Iraq | Saudi Arabia |
| Kuwait | |

SOURCE: Robinson, Francis, ed. *The Cambridge Illustrated History of the Islamic World.* New York: Cambridge University Press, 1996.

Oil reserves and production in the early 1990s.

state of war. There was also a realization that small states such as Jordan, Lebanon, Israel, and the Palestinian territories had much to gain from regional coordination.

**Emerging Markets**

As the mid-1990s ushered in an era of tremendous economic growth in the West, many investors were looking to the Middle East as an emerging financial market for investments. The first important variable for identifying an emerging high-growth market is a government that is willing to change financial and economic policies to suit the needs of the international market. The opening of stock exchanges in the region, coupled with the rapid pace in which legislation for privatization and liberalization were being passed in the Middle East, augured well for this first factor of emergence.

Israel, Egypt, Morocco, Tunisia, Bahrain, and Jordan were developing active stock exchanges. Lebanon's stock exchange reopened in September 1995 after having been closed during its civil war. However, even during the war years, the lack of a stock exchange had not kept Lebanon from issuing foreign currency debt as a means of tapping international markets. Moreover, the drive to encourage foreign investment had led many Middle East nations to seek independent credit ratings by recognized agencies. Moody's Investors Service set up an office in Cyprus in March of 1995 to keep an eye on this region, and the European rating agency IBCA was involved in a joint venture to set up a rating agency in the Arab world.

Privatization in the form of government assets being sold to other actors, such as individuals or corporations, was also taking place throughout the region. Economic policies were liberalized in order to expand the economic freedom of the private sector as well as encourage foreign investment. For most of these countries, and particularly Egypt and Jordan, the International Monetary Fund (IMF) and World Bank were active in assisting them to meet their goals.

The second factor for determining whether a regional or national economy is about to take off is the local willingness to remove the maladaptive conditions that had caused that country or region to be uncompetitive in the past. The political instability caused by the state of war with Israel since the 1950s has been the principal inhibiting factor for economic development for this region. The confrontational relationship that the Arab world has had with Israel since the latter's creation not only cost much human capital, but also much time and resources that could have been used to build their economies. Consequently, peace with Israel was seen as a step in allowing a very well endowed region to start operating more efficiently.

**Privatazation and liberalization policies.** Most of the North African and Levantine countries now embarked on ambitious economic reforms. Egyptian president Hosni Mubarak (b. 1928) delivered a May Day 1990 speech calling for economic privatization and liberalization. He also signed a standby credit agreement with the International Monetary Fund in 1991. These events were intended to signal to Egyptians as well as the international business community that Egypt was serious about reforming and restructuring its economy. There are many groups that have vested interests in the reform process in Egypt, including local labor unions, business groups, nongovernmental organizations, international donors, and government officials.

The countries of North Africa, particularly Morocco and Tunisia, also embarked on ambitious privatization and liberalization schemes. Much of the reform in Egypt as well as in other countries in the region centered around trimming the public sector by cutting price subsidies on energy, food, and transportation, along with ending government control of certain sectors of the economy as a means of encouraging private investment. The IMF had been the primary force in calling for reforms in most of these countries. In May 1987, a standby agreement was reached between the IMF and the government of Egypt. The IMF provided $342 million. Egypt was then able to reschedule its debt payments with the Paris Club (a group of creditor countries that treat in a coordinated way the debt due to them by developing countries). This IMF agreement, however, was never fully implemented, due to concerns about the slow pace with which the Egyptians were conducting reforms.

**Reducing deficits.** Many of these countries were also taking steps to reduce their budget deficits. Egypt, Jordan, Morocco, and Tunisia were all seen as initial success stories in reducing their deficits. Most of the reduction was achieved by eliminating food subsidies, raising energy prices to market rates, instituting sales taxes, financing the deficit through Treasury bill auctions, and reducing the ranks of government workers. One of the biggest problems Egypt and its neighbors faced was undoing the excessive level of bureaucratic control over the economy that had been put in place during past regimes. Although they had begun to liberalize many of the investment laws, change was slow. They were also slow selling off government enterprises. The public sector represented 70 percent of industrial production in the early 1990s in Egypt. In 1993, the 314 public sector enterprises were organized into seventeen holding companies, which are permitted to sell, lease, or liquidate company assets and sell government-owned shares.

**Jordan.** Jordan has been one of the most promising emerging markets in the Middle East. It vigorously implemented a structural adjustment plan in the late 1980s, even in spite of a geographical location that has made it very vulnerable to regional political instability. Jordan is estimated to have a population of 4.2 million, of which an estimated 60 percent is Palestinian. The Palestinians first came to Jordan in 1948, when the creation of Israel triggered their subsequent exodus from Palestine. Each time the Israelis and Arabs had a military confrontation, Jordan experienced an echo effect from Palestine, the most notable of which occurred in 1967. Jordan also served as the gateway for hundreds of thousands of refugees fleeing Iraq and Kuwait during the Gulf crisis of 1990. In fact, it is estimated that as many as 300,000 returnees from Kuwait emerged on the Jordanian labor market in 1990. All these events have taken their toll on the Jordanian economy.

Unlike Egypt, Jordan has always been viewed as being a free market economy. Yet, it has a substantial public sector, with the government actively controlling 62 percent of the economy and being the largest employer. This is mainly because Jordan has long been a *rentier* economy, one that collects rents rather than generating its income from domestic production. The rents that Jordan has survived on have been in the form of foreign aid and remittances from Jordanians/Palestinians working abroad. Much of this revenue was generated in the oil-producing countries of the Middle East. In fact, Jordan has been termed an oil economy without oil. This situation was acceptable during the 1970s and early 1980s, when the oil industry was booming. However, as oil prices plummeted so did the Jordanian economy. This situation has led to a restructuring of the Jordanian economy and a peace settlement with Israel.

**Syria.** Syrian economic policies since the late 1980s represent an attempt to liberalize and privatize the economy while still maintaining government control. In 1988, Syria began deregulating its economy and coming to terms with the fact that its diversified economy was faltering as a result of excessive government control. A currency that had been ridiculously overvalued was devalued by 70 percent. Land that had been held by the ministry of agriculture was now freed up for private sector use. A group of twelve Syrian entrepreneurs formed an agricultural investment company to work 5,000 hectares of farmland in the Euphrates valley. There were also changes in the law to promote private sector growth; however, the state has continued to play a significant role in overseeing and conducting much of what are supposed to be private sector initiatives.

Syria's economy has improved since 1990. From 1990 to 1993, its GDP grew at 8 percent annually. Much of this has been due to the quadrupling of oil production, record harvests for the agricultural sector, and significant foreign aid from the Gulf as a reward for Syrian support and participation in the Gulf war coalition. This aid has been used largely to rebuild and repair Syria's infrastructure. The private sector is also expanding in an environment of liberal investment laws, particularly in the area of agriculture and industry. Yet, there has been a general reluctance by many foreign investors to get involved in Syria, for the government is still in control of many of the major sectors such as oil, electricity, and banking. Consequently, most business opportunities in Syria presently are for exporting to the private sector in areas such as agricultural equipment and inputs as well as capital goods for industrial projects, food processing, and textiles.

Privatization and liberalization have been slow in Syria for a number of reasons. First, this is a regime that has long had a socialist orientation and favors central control. Second, the labor movement is very powerful in Syria and opposes privatization. Although the regime realizes that it must restructure its economy if it wants to survive in an era of globalization, there is a general reluctance to disturb the present balance of power.

## Oil Dependency

Despite the wealth accumulated by the Gulf States, the oil dependency of the region's economies and exports had become alarming by the late 1980s, when the fluctuation of oil prices made for a very unpredictable revenue base. Of course, the 1970s and 1980s saw some improvements, as all the Gulf States built modern infrastructures, increased their standards of living, and enhanced their regional and world power during these decades. With the collapse of oil prices in the 1980s, however, the Gulf Cooperation Council (GCC) states

fell on comparatively hard times. Several of the countries, notably Saudi Arabia, had ratcheted up government spending and import purchases so that, when oil revenues fell sharply, the country began running chronic balance-of-payments deficits. Government budgets also began to run into the red. These events have caused many of these states to attempt to diversify their economies, with Bahrain endeavoring to become the financial capital of the Middle East. However, these states remain driven by oil markets, and there is little evidence that their attempts to diversify have been successful.

By the late 1990s and early part of the twenty-first century, the Middle East again entered into a new era. The economic pragmatism of the 1990s has given way to politics. The lack of real changes in the underlying factors affecting economic development has bred despair. Many of the countries that were liberalizing and privatizing their economies have fallen victim to a world financial bubble that rose and then burst. Financial markets around the world suffered; however, those in less stable regions such as the Middle East, are hardest pressed. The peace dividend with Israel, too, did not materialize. Meanwhile, foreign aid in the post–cold war era has not been forthcoming.

Although oil prices have risen, the Gulf countries are more cynical about sharing with their neighbors in the post–Gulf War era. As many of these countries reach out to the World Bank and the IMF for financing, the economic austerity measures demanded by these institutions seem unbearable, given the rise of poverty throughout the region. The lack of stability, coupled with a post–11 September 2001 realization by the West of the impact that radical Islamic groups can have has left the citizens and economies of these regions feeling abandoned. Consequently, the economies of this region remain heavily guided by the state, with a private sector attempting to operate in a state of uncertainty.

*See also* **Capitalism; Coinage; Riba; Waqf.**

## BIBLIOGRAPHY

Abed, George T. *The Palestinian Economy.* London: Routledge, 1988.

Berberoglu, Berch, ed. *Power and Stability in the Middle East.* Atlantic Highlands, N.J.: Zed Books, 1989.

Colton, Nora. "The Maghribi Economies as Emerging Markets?" In *North Africa in Transition: Socio-Economic and Political Change in the Post-Cold War Era.* Edited by Yahia H. Zoubir. Gainesville: University of Florida Press, 1999.

Cook, M. A. *Studies in the Economic History of the Middle East.* Oxford, U.K.: Oxford University Press, 1978.

Cuno, Kenneth M. *The Pasha's Peasants.* Cambridge, U.K.: Cambridge University Press, 1992.

Ehrenkreutz, Andrew S. *Monetary Change and Economic History in the Medieval Muslim World.* Edited by Jere L. Bacharach. Brookfield, Vt.: Ashgate Publishing, 1992.

Fischer, Stanley; Rodrik, Dani; and Tuma, Elias. *The Economics of Middle East Peace.* Boston: MIT Press, 1993.

Gerner, Deborah J., ed. *Understanding the Contemporary Middle East.* Boulder, Colo.: Rienner, 2000.

Halliday, Fred. *Arabia Without Sultans.* Middlesex, N.Y.: Penguin Books, 1974.

Hershlag, Z.Y. *Introduction to the Modern Economic History of the Middle East.* Leiden: Brill, 1980.

Issawi, Charles. *The Economic History of the Middle East 1800–1914.* Chicago: University of Chicago Press, 1966.

Issawi, Charles. *An Economic History of the Middle East and North Africa.* New York: Columbia University Press, 1982.

Mehmet, Ozay. *Westernizing the Third World.* London: Routledge, 1995.

Pirenne, Henri. *Economic and Social History of Medieval Europe.* New York: Harcourt, 1937.

Pridham, B. R. *The Arab Gulf and the Arab World.* Exeter, U.K.: University of Exeter, 1988.

Oweiss, Ibrahim. *The Political Economy of Contemporary Egypt.* Washington, D.C.: Georgetown University, Center for Contemporary Arab Studies, 1990.

Owen, E. R. J. *The Middle East in the World Economy, 1800–1914.* London: Methuen, 1981.

Richards, Alan, and Waterbury, John. *A Political Economy of the Middle East.* Boulder, Colo.: Westview Press, 1990.

Saqqaf, Abdulaziz. *The Middle East City.* New York: Paragon, 1987.

Serageldin, I., et al. *Manpower and International Labor Migration in the Middle East and North Africa.* London: Oxford University Press, 1983.

Shami, Seteney. *Population Displacement and Resettlement, Development and Conflict in the Middle East.* New York: Center for Migration Studies, 1994.

Udovitch, A. L., ed. *The Islamic Middle East, 700–1900: Studies in Economic and Social History.* Princeton, N.J.: The Darwin Press, 1981.

Watson, Andrew M. "A Medieval Green Revolution: New Crops and Farming Techniques in the Early Islamic World." In *The Islamic Middle East 700–1900: Studies in Economic and Social History,* Edited by A. L. Udovitch. Princeton, N.J.: The Darwin Press, 1981.

*Nora Ann Colton*

# EDUCATION

Islam, like Christianity and Judaism, is a "religion of the book"—a religion, that is, which derives its authority from a revealed scripture. The Qur'an does not stand alone, however; it is supplemented by a wide array of other texts of a religious nature, such as collections of hadith (stories about the words and deeds of the prophet Muhammad and his companions), commentaries on the Qur'an and hadith, and books from a variety of different fields of intellectual endeavor. The Islamic tradition is thus very much a textual one. That fact has helped to make learning and education a central pillar of the religion, in virtually all times and places.

## Islamic Education in the Premodern Period

Like most things in the Islamic tradition, the centrality of learning finds expression in sayings (ahadith, sing. hadith) attributed to Muhammad, such as one that quotes him as instructing his followers: "Seek knowledge, even in China." That injunction applies with special force, of course, to scholars, but it is directed in a more general way at all Muslims, who need at least rudimentary instruction in those demands which the shari'a, Islamic law, placed upon their lives. Moreover, Muslims typically viewed the process of transmitting knowledge and texts—or at least knowledge and texts of a religious nature—as itself a form of worship. And so, for example, one was not supposed to commence reading the Qur'an, or participating in a class on a religious topic, without performing ritual ablutions similar to those which are to precede prayer.

It is hardly surprising, therefore, that an important thirteenth-century treatise on instruction and study by Burhan al-Din al-Zarnuji would stress the importance of education to a pious Muslim life, and conclude that "learning is prescribed for us all." It is of course impossible to estimate with any degree of certainty the number of individuals in premodern Islamic societies who were educated or literate, and it may even be difficult to be precise about what it meant to be "educated" or "literate." Nonetheless, it is almost certain that premodern Islamic societies achieved (at least in comparison to premodern European societies) relatively high levels of literacy and of familiarity with the texts in which knowledge was embedded. Inevitably education was largely a concern of men, but the biographical sources available for the reconstruction of the social history of many premodern Islamic societies demonstrate that girls often received some level of education and religious training, and that many became recognized scholars in their own right.

The "knowledge" that Muslims are to seek is known in Arabic as 'ilm (pl. 'ulum). The word can mean knowledge of almost any sort. In more traditional contexts, however, it refers specifically to knowledge acquired through some course of study, and especially in fields of intellectual endeavor that we would now label "religious." In this narrower sense, it constitutes the foundation of the authority of the group known by the etymologically related term ulema (sing. 'alim), literally "those who know." The ulema are those scholars who are involved in the transmission of the religious sciences. In premodern Islamic societies, they included men who functioned in those positions for which training in the religious sciences was required—the judge (qadi) who ruled according to Islamic law, the professor (mudarris) who transmitted religious learning to a rising generation of scholars, the preacher (*khatib*) who delivered sermons in mosques, and so on.

The ulema were not, however, a clergy (a group of people set aside by an act of consecration). Consequently, their social origins and status varied widely. Virtually anyone could be considered one of the ulema if he or she had acquired sufficient learning and the social respect that came with it. Collectively, however, they constituted perhaps the most important indigenous group in most traditional Islamic societies, and so were sometimes identified as the "heirs of the prophets"—that is, as the inheritors (in the absence of the Prophet) of religious authority, the arbiters of the religious tradition. Virtually all premodern Islamic societies have left a record of the respect in which the ulema were held. So, for example, a jurist named Ibn al-Hajj who lived in fourteenth-century Cairo commented that, when a true scholar died, the whole of creation would mourn his passing, even the birds of the air and the fish of the sea.

In many respects the distinction between that which is "secular" and that which is "sacred" is meaningless in the Islamic tradition. Nonetheless, Muslims came to distinguish broadly between those subjects and disciplines that they inherited from pre-Islamic civilizations, such as philosophy, astronomy, medicine, and the like, and those which were more immediately connected with the Qur'anic revelation and the religious tradition that stemmed from it. The former were referred to as the "sciences of the ancients" (*al-ʿulum al-awaʾil*) or the "rational sciences" (*al-ʿulum al-ʿaqliyya*). For many centuries, these sciences flourished in the Islamic world: names such as that of the great physician and philosopher Ibn Sina (d. 1037), known to the West as Avicenna, and the Spanish philosopher, theologian, and natural scientist Ibn Rushd (d. 1198), known as Averroes, are sufficient to demonstrate that. Clearly the processes by which the knowledge they had mastered was transmitted to subsequent generations formed a part of the educational world of classical and medieval Islam. In some cases, education in these sciences was supported by institutions, the most famous of which was the Bayt al-Hikma, or "House of Wisdom," established by the caliph al-Maʾmun in Baghdad in the ninth century, and devoted to the translation and transmission of Greek scientific and philosophical works, and a similar institution established by the Fatimid caliph al-Hakim in Cairo over a century later. More often, they were transmitted informally, directly from teacher to pupil.

It was subjects and disciplines more closely related to the religious experience, however, that formed the core of what Muslims recognized as *ʿilm*. The circumstances under which they were transmitted were somewhat different than for the rational sciences.

Education would begin at a young age, with instruction in Arabic and the Qur'an. This instruction might take place in the home, or alternatively in a primary school known as a *maktab* or *kuttab*, often attached to a mosque. The emphasis at this level was on the rote memorization of the Qur'an, the foundation without which more advanced education was impossible. *Kuttab*s developed within the first century or so of Islamic history, and have in many places continued to function down into modern times, sometimes in competition with schools offering a more modern curriculum.

Once the Qur'an was memorized, some students would proceed to more advanced training in various subjects. Those subjects included the study of hadith, *tafsir* (Qur'anic exegesis), and especially *fiqh* (jurisprudence), although the boundaries between them were not always sharp. In many ways, jurisprudence was the most important of the religious sciences, because of the centrality of Islamic law in guiding not only the worship but the social and political behavior of Muslims. Here, too, memorization was important, and the medieval sources are full of accounts of scholars who had committed to memory thousands of hadiths and other texts. But education in the advanced forms of the religious sciences involved much more. Two things in particular stand out. First, higher education trained the student to participate, as reader and as writer, in an interlocking nexus of texts and commentaries on those texts—in essence, it trained the student to engage in a "conversation" or "discourse" that constituted the essence of intellectual life for the ulema. This "conversation" was quite vigorous, and the ulema of the early and medieval periods of Islamic history have left a significant textual record of it. Second, higher education involved a process of socialization, in which the student gradually acquired status in the eyes of other scholars. In the absence of any consecrated priesthood or formal degree system, this element of the educational process was especially important. So a student might attach himself to one or more teachers, developing close personal as well as intellectual relations with them.

For the first several centuries of Islamic history, the transmission of the religious sciences at an advanced level took place in an entirely informal fashion. Scholars would offer classes in mosques, or in private homes. Such informal settings never ceased to be important to the transmission of *ʿilm*. Beginning in the eleventh and twelfth centuries, however, rulers and other leading figures in the Muslim societies of the Near East began to establish institutions known as madrasas that were devoted specifically to advanced instruction in the religious sciences, and especially jurisprudence. As an institutional type, madrasas may have originated in Khurasan, in eastern Iran. They soon spread throughout the Near East, and became common in the cities and towns of Egypt, Syria, Iran, and later the Anatolian and Balkan provinces of the Ottoman Empire. Particularly important cities, such as Cairo, might boast dozens of madrasas of varying sizes. Each madrasa would typically consist of a building providing space for lessons as well as accommodations for one or more teachers and a certain number of pupils. The institution and its activities would be supported by an endowment (*waqf*) provided by the individual who had founded the madrasa in the first place. As a result, madrasas might vary considerably in terms of their size and the value of the endowments supporting them: Some might employ several professors and provide stipends for hundreds of students, while others might support only a few.

Several aspects of the madrasa and of the educational system it supported deserve comment. In the first place, the spread of these institutions was closely linked to political structures in the medieval Islamic world. In general, political power in the medieval Near East was fairly localized. Much of the central Islamic lands were ruled by military elites of an alien, often Turkish or Mongol, and sometimes only recently and superficially Islamized nature. The rulers' decisions to establish and endow institutions for the transmission of the Islamic sciences constituted one strategy for securing the support, or at least the acquiescence, of the ulema who commanded considerable respect among the local Muslim population. So, for example, especially in the cities of Egypt and Syria, madrasas would often be associated with elaborate tombs constructed for the benefit of the schools' patrons, a linkage that had both spiritual and political advantages.

Second, for all the importance of madrasas, the system of transmitting religious knowledge and of training the next generation of ulema remained persistently informal, at least through the end of the Middle Ages. The medieval sources tell us at great length with whom an individual studied, and with which professors a student developed close relationships, but very little about where those studies took place. There was no system of institutional degrees; rather, certification of the character and quality of an individual's education was found in the *ijaza*. The *ijaza* could take different forms: It could be a formal attestation of a scholar that some individual had, in some fashion, studied a particular text with him, or it could be his statement that the student had mastered an entire field of learning. In any case, it was a personal document, which confirmed the relationship of the student to his teacher, and through him to his teacher's own instructors. Through it, the student took his place in a genealogy of authorities that constituted the only recognized hierarchy of the educational system. Under the Ottoman Empire, this loose and personalized system gave way to a more carefully defined and delineated structure. At least in the capital of Istanbul, madrasas were graded according to a hierarchy that was in turn tied closely to the career paths of the students who passed through them. In other parts of the Muslim world, however, Islamic education continued to follow informal patterns. In Indonesia, for example, education in the Islamic sciences (including Qur'anic exegesis, jurisprudence, etc.) took place in institutions known as *pesantren*. On the whole the *pesantren* were less formal institutions than Near Eastern madrasas: They might be supported by fees and alms provided by local Muslims as well as endowments, and often were established by particular scholars themselves (and might not survive their founder's death).

Third, the spread of madrasas in the Middle Ages had important social consequences, in particular a tendency to bind an increasingly diverse society together in a united cultural project. This tendency can be seen on a number of different levels. The texts and methods of instruction of Islamic legal and religious education were remarkably uniform across the Sunni Muslim world, and a student or scholar from Iran who found himself in, say, Damascus or Cairo would often be able to find a position in a madrasa there. Since these institutions provided stipends for students as well as salaries for teachers, they may have helped to broaden the social base of those able to devote themselves to the long process of becoming a recognized scholar. They also helped to spread Islamic teachings beyond the urban centers in which most of the ulema concentrated, as young men from the countryside might study for a time in a madrasa in the city, and then return home to supervise and instruct the religious lives of peasants and others in the villages.

## Islamic Education in the Modern Period
In the modern period, the field of education, along with that of the family and of the social and political status of women, has been one of the principal targets of reformers, and thus also one of the major battlegrounds over the character and direction of Islamic societies. Given the traditional status and social role of the ulema, this is hardly surprising. Developments in the field of education can be grouped into three distinct areas: the establishment by Muslim governments of modern schools that have competed with traditional Islamic schools; the establishment in some places of schools sponsored by foreign groups, many of them by missionaries; and the reform of traditional schools themselves.

The establishment of a new network of schools has been one of the principal tasks of various groups of political and social reformers in the modern Muslim world. At the end of the eighteenth and beginning of the nineteenth centuries, for example, the Ottoman government established a series of schools designed to train students in mathematics, medicine, and various other subjects. Those efforts picked up speed during the period of aggressive reforms known as the Tanzimat, from 1839 to 1876. The Ottoman viceroys of Egypt, Muhammad 'Ali and his successors, undertook a similar program over the course of the nineteenth century. In both these cases, educational reform was connected with a campaign to reform and improve the effectiveness of the military: The students, that is, were originally drawn from the ranks of army officers. In both cases, also, the social effects were profound. Very often the instructors in these schools were European, and the textbooks written in European languages. Accordingly, instruction in those languages, especially French, formed a core component of the new schools' curricula, and so they became

**Cartography and Geography**
The Mediterranean Sea as depicted in an eleventh-century Arabic geographical manuscript (*Kitab al-masalik wa al-mamalik*) of al-Istakhri. By the thirteenth century, copies of maps proliferated and circulated all over the Islamic world. *The Art Archive/National Library Cairo/Dagli Orti*

**Bukhara, Khanate and Emirate of**
The arched entrance to the Miri-Arab Madrasa, built circa 1536, in Bukhara, Uzbekistan. This structure is decorated with intricate tile mosaic set in floral and calligraphic designs. *© Diego Lezama Orezzoli/Corbis*

J. G. S Sauveur Del    Mixelle j Sculp.

*Homme & Femme de Mylasa en Carie*

**Clothing**
Turkish man and woman wearing traditional attire from the Milas region of Turkey, as shown in this 1801 French print. The Turkish mode of dress for both men and women usually involved loose trousers and a shirt topped with various jackets, vests, and long coats: layering was an important element of the aesthetic. *Collection of Charlotte Jirousek*

**Clothing**
A Palestinian woman in traditional Arab dress, the thawb, which is based on the tunic, a common garment in the region since the Roman era. It is suitable for desert heat as it provides protection from the sun as well as ventilation. *Cornell Costume and Textile Collection*

**Conflict and Violence**
A mosque destroyed in the Bosnian war (1992–1995), in the central Bosnian village of Ahmici. In January 2000, after sixteen months of testimony from 158 witnesses, U.N. judges in the Hague, Netherlands, convicted five Bosnian Croat militiamen for participating in a killing spree in Ahmici which left more than one hundred Muslim men, women, and children dead, and every Muslim home burnt to the ground. *AP/Wide World Photos*

**Empires: Mongol and Il-Khanid**
A page from Rashid al-Din's (d. 1318, wazir to Ghazan Khan) *Compendium of Chronicles* manuscript depicts Mongol leader Genghis Khan and his sons. Although the Mongols battled Islam in the early years of their rise to power, Mongol conquests ultimately spread Islam throughout Central Asia. *© Art Resource, NY*

**Empires: Safavid and Qajar**
A seventeenth-century painting of Shah Tahmasp, a long time leader of the Safavid Empire, receiving the Mogul Emperor Humayun. Shah Tahmasp's court prioritized culture; illuminated manuscripts produced during his reign are of the highest quality known. © *SEF/Art Resource, NY*

**European Culture and Islam**
Aristotle depicted with students of physical science in the manuscript *The Best Maxims and Most Precious Dictums* by al-Mubashshir, who composed it through 1048 and 1049. The manuscript was translated into Spanish in 1250, although al-Mubashshir's name was dropped, and from there into Latin, French, Provencal, and English. Until the sixteenth century, Europe was only familiar with the Greek philosophical tradition through the extensive Arabic descriptions, translations, commentaries, and analyses of these works. *The Art Archive/Topkapi Museum Istanbul/Dagli Orti*

**Falsafa**

This detail from a fresco by Filipino Lippi (1457–1504) depicts Ibn Sina (980–1037), a Persian mathematician. A major figure in Islamic thought, Ibn Sina was heavily influenced by Aristotle, and in turn influenced the Catholic thinker St. Thomas Aquinas, who in his own work mentioned Ibn Sina over five hundred times. © *Scala/Art Resource, NY*

**Ibn Battuta**

Ibn Battuta (1304–1368/69) of Tangier, Morocco, traveled an estimated eighty thousand miles across three continents. It was the longest known overland journey until the steam engine came into existence. *XNR Productions/Gale*

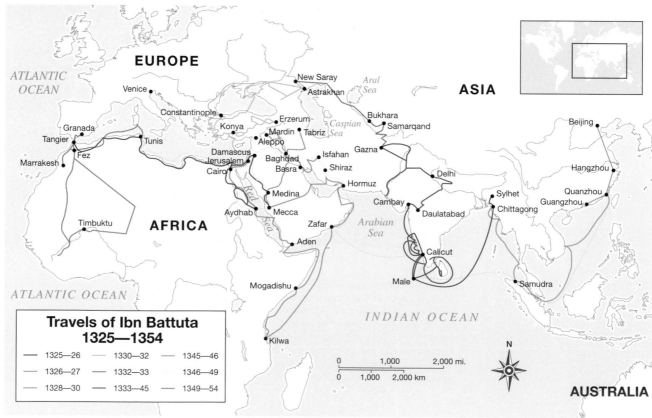

a channel for the importation into the Muslim world, not simply of scientific knowledge in fields such as chemistry or engineering, but also of new political ideas values and new ways of thinking about social organization. There was some opposition to these new educational institutions from the ulema, many of whom looked askance at innovations, particularly those adopted in an explicitly Westernizing form, and who resented the challenge that the new schools posed to their former monopoly on education. In the long run, however, the principal consequence of the new schools was the development of a new social elite, trained in a more-or-less European fashion and attuned to the political and social values of modern Europe, a new elite that did not replace the older elite represented by the ulema, but deprived it of much of its social recognition and authority.

Over the twentieth century, a full system of government-sponsored schools developed in most parts of the Muslim world. In many places, this task of educational reform has been linked in one fashion or another to Westernizing elites and to a conscious program of modernization. In Egypt, for example, after the military coup of 1952, the government expanded the network of primary and secondary schools as well as universities, in the process broadening considerably the social base of those with access to a modern education. A similar process took place in Turkey, where the first university was founded in the late Ottoman period, with others established after the emergence of the republic following the First World War. In Turkey, however, the process went further than in many places, because of the pronounced laicism of Mustafa Kemal "Ataturk" and his republican regime. In the aftermath of the Kemalist victory, many of the madrasas were closed, along with other religious institutions. (After Ataturk's death, restrictions on religious education were loosened: A faculty of theology was established at Ankara university in 1949, for example, and instruction in religious matters was returned to the curriculum of the elementary schools.) In Iran, too, the regime of Reza Shah and his son, Muhammad Reza Shah, undertook a vigorous program to secularize and modernize the educational system; there, however, the traditional network of madrasas training Shi'ite religious scholars remained more or less intact, though it shrank in size and lost its appeal to middle-class students. The result was considerable tension between a secularizing government and the traditional ulema, a factor of enormous significance in the Islamic revolution of 1978 and 1979. Saudi Arabia, by contrast, has followed a different model, in which the traditional madrasa system has been largely replaced by state-supported schools and universities, but traditional religious subjects have remained an important part of the curriculum of the government institutions.

In many parts of the Muslim world, such as Egypt, Syria, and India, educational institutions established by Europeans (or Americans) have also played an important role during the last two centuries. Many of those responsible for establishing these schools represented religious communities or organizations. Some, such as the institutions established by the Alliance Israelite Universelle, saw their mission as the education, and often the Westernization, of students from particular communities of religious minorities. Others, however, tried to attract a more ecumenical student body, although the success of those efforts varied from place to place. Among the more notable such institutions were Robert College in Istanbul and the Syrian Protestant College (later the American University in Beirut), both founded by American Protestant missionaries. The latter in particular has had a distinguished place in the modern history of the region, as it was associated with a rebirth of Arabic literature and culture in the nineteenth and twentieth centuries and so contributed to the development of a modern Arab national movement. The fate of these institutions in the post-colonial world has been mixed: Robert College, for example, has been effectively integrated into the larger Turkish educational system, whereas A.U.B. and the American University in Cairo have remained independent, and have continued to offer a distinctive and distinctively Western education.

Finally, there is the question of what became of the traditional network of schools, kuttabs, madrasas, and so on in the wake of the emergence of the state-supported educational system. In most parts of the Muslim world, where kuttabs and traditional systems of education have survived, they have done so at the expense of coming to constitute a separate, "religious" educational sphere. From the perspective of the classical and medieval Islamic periods, this in itself is an odd development. Moreover, the conditions that made the ulema so important in previous historical eras have disappeared or been eroded. The religious scholars can no longer rely on the patronage of rulers or an extensive network of waqfs (religious endowments) to provide financial support. Since they have had to compete with more modern, state-supported schools, those who trained and taught in them, the ulema, have often found their social status and power significantly reduced. With a variety of educational and professional options now available, traditional schools and religious subjects have held less appeal for bright and ambitious students. In contemporary Egypt, for example, where subjects such as medicine and engineering attract the most successful pupils, those studying the religious sciences typically rank at the bottom of the academic ladder.

There have been efforts to reform the traditional schools themselves. In Egypt, for example, the organization of the ancient mosque of al-Azhar and its educational program have evolved considerably in the last century. It has expanded its mission and become a full-fledged university, adding new faculties (in medicine, engineering, etc.), instruction in a number of disciplines (English, the social sciences, etc.) which previously had no place in traditional religious education, as well as a separate college for women. At the same

At the Mohabat Khan mosque in Peshawar, Pakistan, a student receives instruction in the Qur'an. In ancient traditions of Islamic education, students were required to memorize the Qur'an before pursuing additional learning, and this early emphasis on rote memorization remains today in many religious schools. GETTY IMAGES, GETTY IMAGES NORTH AMERICA

time, al-Azhar has come much more decisively under government supervision, with the result that its officials are sometimes perceived as lacking that independence which lent authority to the medieval ulema. The Muslim community in India under British rule also produced several distinct movements of educational reform. Chief among them was that associated with the Dar al-'Ulum ("House of Sciences") at Deoband, a school founded in the nineteenth century to provide a traditional religious education with methods and in an institutional environment of a more modern nature, and which has inspired the establishment of similar institutions throughout the subcontinent. More recently, newly established institutions known as madrasas have flourished in Pakistan and elsewhere in connection with the rise of political Islam.

*See also* **Azhar, al-; Deoband; Knowledge; Madrasa; Modernization, Political: Administrative, Military, and Judicial Reform; Science, Islam and.**

## BIBLIOGRAPHY

Berkey, Jonathan P. *The Transmission of Knowledge in Medieval Cairo: A Social History of Islamic Education.* Princeton, N.J.: Princeton University Press, 1992.

Eickelman, Dale. *Knowledge and Power in Morocco: The Education of a Twentieth-Century Notable.* Princeton, N.J.: Princeton University Press, 1985.

Makdisi, George. *The Rise of Colleges: Institutions of Learning in Islam and the West.* Edinburgh: Edinburgh University Press, 1981.

Rosenthal, A. L. *Knowledge Triumphant: The Concept of Knowledge in Medieval Islam.* Leiden: Brill, 1970.

Starrett, Gregory. *Putting Islam to Work: Education, Politics, and Religious Transformation in Egypt.* Berkeley: University of California Press, 1998.

Tibawi, A. L. *Islamic Education: Its Traditions and Modernization into the Arab National Systems.* London: Luzac, 1972.

*Jonathan Berkey*

# EMPIRES

## ABBASID

The early Islamic empire fell to Abbasid control with the overthrow and decimation of the Umayyad house in 750 C.E. The "Abbasid revolution" followed an extended period of clandestine organization centered in the eastern province of Khurasan. Modern scholarship has devoted considerable attention to the formation and execution of the anti-Umayyad movement. Opposition to Umayyad rule appears easier to explain, however, than the movement itself. Factors contributing to the collapse of the Umayyads included the deleterious effects of several rounds of civil war; divisions within the Syrian-based armed forces; persistent problems of legitimacy fueled by charges of fiscal corruption and impious conduct on the part of the caliphs and their kin; serious military setbacks along the frontiers of North Africa, Armenia, and Central Asia; and a fierce ideological challenge posed by leading 'Alids and their Shi'ite partisans that gave rise to repeated uprisings, particularly late in the Umayyad period.

Abbasid success against the Umayyads was due in part to support emanating from Shi'ite quarters as well as, it appears, the broader populace of *mawali* (non-Arab Muslim "clients"). The leadership of Abbasid partisans, key among them Abu Muslim (d. 775), and the strength of the Khurasan-based forces under his command, tipped the balance in favor of the Abbasid movement. As Elton Daniel has made clear, alongside other historians, modern scholarship remains divided on at least two questions.

The first question concerns the point at which the Abbasid family assumed leadership of the anti-Umayyad movement. Evidence indicates that the movement remained clandestine until a very late point and that its propaganda was kept deliberately vague. In an attempt to appeal to 'Alid sympathies, the slogans of the movement spoke only of restoring "a chosen one" (from the Prophet's family) rather than a member of the Abbasid house specifically. The Abbasids only showed their hand at a very late point; assuming control of the caliphate, the dynasty alienated the 'Alids and their Shi'ite backers. The second question relates to the composition of the movement itself. One view is that the movement, however broad-based it later became, only succeeded because of the participation of Arab tribesmen that had settled in Khurasan during the early Islamic conquest period. In response to the "Arabist," and hence largely ethnic, argument, other scholars have sought an explanation based variously in the socioeconomic conditions of eighth-century Khurasan and the religiopolitical appeal of Shi'ite ideals for Arab and non-Arab Muslims alike.

The reigns of the first two Abbasid caliphs, Abu 'l-Abbas al-Saffah (r. 750–754) and al-Mansur (r. 754–775), began with a period of consolidation that led to the elimination of Abu Muslim among other leaders of the revolutionary movement. A period of sustained prosperity, if continued political unrest, ensued. Al-Mansur established Baghdad in the 760s and is properly viewed as the real founder of the dynasty. At its height, under al-Mansur's immediate successors, al-Mahdi (r. 775–785), al-Hadi (r. 785–786) and, most significantly, Harun al-Rashid (r. 786–809), the Abbasid empire stretched from the central Maghrib across the Middle East and southern Anatolia into Transoxiana. Sustained civil war, initially a conflict between the sons of al-Rashid, Muhammad al-Amin (r. 809–813) and 'Abdallah al-Ma'mun (r. 813–833), followed by the effort at consolidation by al-Ma'mun over Baghdad and its hinterland, initiated the gradual dissolution of the empire. Despite the skilled leadership of later caliphs, by the end of the ninth century, local dynasties and semiautonomous governing families had come to the fore in Egypt, Khurasan, Spain, and the Maghrib.

Fragmentation of the imperial domain and a dissolution of dynastic legitimacy set in by the first quarter of the tenth century with an eclipse of Abbasid authority at the hands of bureaucratic families and condottiere. By the 940s, Syria, Iraq, Fars, and western Iran were divided into principalities under Hamdanid or Buyid (Buwayhid) control; members of both families had served in the Abbasid military before asserting control over regions of the empire. Egypt, by the 970s, fell to the control of the Fatimids, an Isma'ili Shi'ite dynasty created in the central Maghrib earlier in the tenth century; the dynasty controlled Egypt, and, for extended periods, Syria and the Hijaz, into the second half of the twelfth century. Buyid rule gave way in the mid-eleventh century to a Sunni Turkish dynasty, the Seljuks, whose reign was largely defined by rivalry with the Fatimids, conflict against the Crusader states, and the onset of an extended period of Turkish domination of Near Eastern political life. From the Buyid period on, the Abbasids themselves usually wielded little more than the trappings of authority; in Iraq, Abbasid history came to an end with the Mongol invasion in 1258. A branch of the family retained a wholly symbolic role under the Mamluks in Egypt until the Ottoman invasion of 1517 that brought an end to Abbasid claims upon the caliphate.

## Politics and Administration

Taking their lead from the Umayyads, the early Abbasids worked quickly to fashion a highly centralized state. Like their predecessors, the Abbasids drew inspiration from Sassanian, Byzantine, and more deeply rooted patterns of Near Eastern imperial statecraft. For example, the caliphs relied upon elaborate systems of monarchical ritual and symbolism, such as the use of screens used to shield them during open sessions of the court. More dramatic still was the plan of Baghdad: The city, known as the Round City, was originally built around a massive circular core containing the caliphal residence, mosque, treasuries, and barracks. Historians understand the plan in terms of the assertion, through symbolic means, of the coming of a new imperial age. No less than earlier dynasties, the first Abbasids thus devoted themselves to massive building programs. In Baghdad, Samarra, and elsewhere, extensive palace complexes emerged alongside congregational mosques, extensive markets, and an impressive infrastructure of roads, canals, way-stations, and the like.

It appears as well that the early Abbasids sought to imbue their office with religious as well as political meaning. Commitment to holy war (*jihad*), a presiding role in the hajj, patronage of religious scholars: All were efforts to perpetuate the caliph's moral leadership. The claim found little sustained support within the religious community. For the ulema, the traditions of theocratic monarchy contradicted the model of leadership crafted by the prophet Muhammad and the first generation of caliphs. The problem of delineating lines of authority was gradually resolved by the middle Abbasid period as the scholars asserted a near-monopoly over legal and social authority. No less significant a source of challenge to Abbasid legitimation were the sectarian movements of the Kharijites and the various Shi'ite tendencies, all of whom viewed Abbasid authority as illegitimate. Early Kharijite rebellions under the first Abbasid caliphs were suppressed at a moderate expense to the state. Far more costly, in ideological and political terms, was the challenge of their Shi'ite detractors. If the emergent Twelver Shi'ite tendency in Iraq and elsewhere remained relatively quiescent, by the early tenth century, a prominent Isma'ili movement had won support from local forces in the central Maghrib (modern-day Tunisia) and laid the foundation for the Fatimid state.

The considerable wealth of the early Abbasid empire drew predictably on agricultural production and commerce. Al-Mansur's decision to build a new capital beside the two major Iraqi rivers and in the midst of the extensively farmed areas of central and southern Iraq, had much to do with assuring control over both sources of income. To assure a reliable flow of money and goods, the early Abbasids continued late Umayyad efforts to systematize tax collection. These efforts, initially successful, ultimately came up short as the health of the Abbasid economy fell victim to the civil war that followed the death of al-Rashid in the early ninth century and, some decades later, the turmoil sparked by the assassination of al-Mutawakkil (r. 847–861). By the early tenth century, the Iraqi agrarian system was in sharp decline. Commercial activity flourished in the early to mid-Abbasid periods, fueled by rapid urbanization in the Near East and the related rise in investment opportunities, urban surplus wealth, and the spread of new products, chief among them paper, cotton, and sugar. Merchant networks would play a key part in the dissemination of Islam into Central Asia, the Pacific Basin, and Saharan Africa from the ninth century on.

To administer their empire, the Abbasids relied on skilled bureaucrats, many of Persian or Christian origins. These officials (*kuttab*) oversaw a growth in the Abbasid bureaucracy to a size and complexity unknown under the Umayyads. The offices (*diwans*) of the Abbasid administration included the chancery, treasury, police, and intelligence-gathering services, and a special court of appeals (*mazalim*) presided over by the caliph. Control of the treasury and access to the imperial family allowed key families to build extensive networks of influence as exemplified by the eastern Iranian (and originally Buddhist) Barmakid family under al-Rashid. In 803, al-Rashid, having long tolerated Barmakid authority, finally turned against the family. By the first half of the tenth century, however, his successors, such as al-Muqtadir (r. 908–932), proved incapable of resisting pressures exerted by their top bureaucrats. High-level bureaucrats retained no less crucial a role under the Buyids and Seljuks; prominent civilian officials played a similar part in Egypt, particularly late in the Fatimid period.

To defend its borders and assure political calm, the Abbasids, like the Umayyads, relied upon a semiprofessional army largely supplied and paid by the state. The mainstay of the earliest Abbasid armies were the Khurasani troops that had fought to bring the dynasty to power. A number of these regiments were settled in Baghdad by al-Mansur and his successors, and naturally viewed themselves as integral to the fortunes of the new state. The civil war that brought al-Ma'mun to power in the early ninth century witnessed the defeat of these regiments at the hands of a new generation of eastern troops recruited by the new caliph bolstered by a new-style regiment of Turkish slave troops led by his brother, and successor, Abu Ishaq al-Mu'tasim (r. 833–842). In good part to house these new forces, al-Mu'tasim founded a garrison center in Samarra, north of Baghdad; his successors would administer the empire from Samarra for the next half-century. The practice of using slave regiments, many of which were drawn from Turkic peoples of Central Asia, would be emulated by later Near Eastern dynasties. The

The Al-Kazimayn mosque in Baghdad. Early in its reign, the Abbasid empire possessed substantial wealth from agriculture and commerce, enabling ambitious building projects that included palaces, mosques, and markets. THE ART ARCHIVE/DAGLI ORTI

heads of the Samarran Turkish regiments, however, would rely on their troops, and close ties to the caliphate, to interfere in caliphal decision-making; the result was a period of violence and instability in Samarra that sapped the resources of the caliphate and set the stage for the humiliations of the tenth century.

## Culture and Society

A revival of Near Eastern urban culture, rooted in Umayyad history, was a hallmark of the Abbasid period. The early Arab garrison centers, among them Basra, Kufa, Fustat, and Qayrawan, were now functioning towns while, under Umayyad and then Abbasid rule, Damascus and other pre-Islamic centers witnessed rapid population growth and cultural development. Constructed expressly as an imperial center, and occupied probably by the late 760s, Baghdad quickly emerged, however, as the nexus of early Islamic culture and scholarship.

(Samarra, the imperial administrative seat for much of the ninth century, never replaced Baghdad in this sense.) Much of this activity was directly tied to the patronage of the imperial state and networks of elite urban families. Historians are divided, however, over the question of whether to credit the support of the caliphs and elite urban society with the complex translation movement that rendered, in Arabic, nearly the entire corpus of Greek scientific and philosophical work over a period of roughly two hundred years beginning under al-Mansur in the later eighth century. Equally significant was urban literary production. The list of writers, poets, musicians, and cognoscenti that flourished in the Iraqi urban milieu included such luminaries as the grammarian Sibawayh (d. 793); the poet Abu Nuwas (d. 810); the essayist, linguist, and theologian al-Jahiz (d. 868); and the tenth-century polymath Abu Hayyan al-Tawhidi (d. 1023).

Urban patronage and the demands created by steady conversion to Islam throughout the empire explain the formation of a community of sophisticated and increasingly self-confident religious scholars (ulema). Their efforts yielded seminal contributions to Qur'anic exegesis, hadith scholarship, and Islamic law. In the Sunni regions, four major schools of legal interpretation emerged: the Hanafi, Maliki, Shafi'i, and Hanbali. The work of the great exegete and historian Abu Ja'far al-Tabari (d. 923) exemplifies both the remarkable scholarly achievements of the ulema and their ambivalent stance vis-à-vis the caliphal state. Ulema served the empire in their capacity as judges, market inspectors, and the like; their role in imperial administration was crucial. As noted earlier, however, they were loath to provide yet further backing to the caliphate. The trajectory to socioreligious prominence of the scholars occurred as the fortunes of the Abbasid state sharply declined.

*See also* **Empires: Byzantine; Empires: Umayyad; Mahdi, Sadiq al-; Rashid, Harun al-.**

## BIBLIOGRAPHY

Ashtiany, Julia, et al., eds. *'Abbasid Belles-Lettres.* Cambridge, U.K.: Cambridge University Press, 1990.

Crone, Patricia. *Slaves on Horses: the Evolution of the Islamic Polity.* Cambridge, U.K.: Cambridge University Press, 1980.

Daniel, Elton. "The 'Ahl al-Taqadum' and the Problem of the Constituency of the Abbasid Revolution in the Merv Oasis." *Journal of Islamic Studies* 7, no.2 (1996): 150–179.

Gutas, Dimitri. *Greek Thought, Arabic Culture. The Graeco-Arabic Translation Movement in Baghdad and Early 'Abbasid Society (2nd–4th/8th–10th centuries).* New York: Routledge, 1998.

Kennedy, Hugh. *The Prophet and the Age of the Caliphates: The Islamic Near East from the Sixth to the Eleventh Century.* New York: Longman Group Limited, 1986.

Kennedy, Hugh. *The Armies of the Caliphs: Military and Society in the Early Islamic State.* London: Routledge, 2001.

Lassner, Jacob. *The Shaping of 'Abbasid Rule.* Princeton, N.J.: Princeton University Press, 1980.

Young, M. J. L., et al., eds. *Religion, Learning and Science in the 'Abbasid Period.* Cambridge, U.K.: Cambridge University Press, 1990.

*Matthew Gordon*

## BYZANTINE

The Byzantine Empire, which spans the period from 330 to 1453, grew gradually from the old Roman Empire. The first reference to the Byzantines in the Islamic sources occurs in the Qur'an (*surat al-Rum*) in conjunction with the Byzantine-Persian wars that exhausted the Byzantine Empire and allowed for the conquest of its richest and most prosperous areas by the nascent Islamic community. The Byzantine Empire was, nevertheless, to remain a main political and ideological rival to the Islamic empire. In Arabic-Islamic writings, the Byzantine Empire became the only real "House of War" and the war against it the very model and prototype of jihad.

The first period marked the greatest Byzantine influence on the developing Islamic civilization. The Arabs borrowed abundantly from Byzantine institutions. Byzantine influence was reflected in the retention of the Byzantine civil service; the use of Byzantine administrative, legal, and numismatic traditions; and language. Another striking legacy of the imperial heritage is furnished by the Umayyad policy of erecting imperial religious monuments. Indeed, it was the presence of imposing Christian monuments in Greater Syria that encouraged them to construct the Dome of the Rock in Jerusalem and the Umayyad mosque in Damascus. Umayyad caliphs are said to have requested Byzantine help in the decoration of the mosques in Medina and Damascus.

The ambition of the first-century caliphs seems to have been directed toward the establishment of their power in Constantinople. The repeated failed attempts to conquer Constantinople, together with the transfer of the capital to Iraq after 750, distanced the center of the Islamic empire from the Byzantine frontiers and made the idea of the conquest of Constantinople a distant dream rather than a goal toward which forces and efforts were directed in a continuous and organized fashion. Predictions of a future conquest waned and were replaced by apocalyptic expectation.

Arab-Byzantine warfare settled now into episodic warfare and raiding. In the course of the eighth century, Islam reached its limits and gradually recognized a pause in the expansion of the Muslim state and faith. The practice of making two or three expeditions a year against Byzantine territory became so established in the ninth century that officials soon laid down a schedule for these operations. Under the late Umayyads and the early Abbasids, the frontier line between Arabs and Byzantines was formed by the great ranges of the Taurus and Anti-Taurus (the northeast extension of the range across the Seyhan River). Here, a line of fortresses, called *al-thugur*, marked and guarded the frontier. Behind this line was a second-line district containing the strongholds known as *al-'awasim*, fortresses where the warriors would seek refuge. Economically, these invasions resulted in a diminution in agricultural, commercial, and industrial activity for the Byzantine Empire. Demographic changes took place as a result of the massive displacement of population. The chronicles paint a picture of devastation and abandonment of the more exposed settlements in favor of the less accessible sites. Life in these areas, which were regularly plundered, meant yearly raids, constant insecurity, and frequent flights. A certain symbiosis, nevertheless, took place along the frontier region. The result of the interpenetration between the two populations was not only the diffusion of military techniques, material goods, and methods of economic production but also the diffusion of political ideas and general cultural aspects. This period, thus, witnessed the transmittal of classical and Hellenistic scholarship, via the Byzantines, to the Arab Muslim world.

Indeed, the relationship between the Muslim and Byzantine empires was interspersed with diplomatic, cultural, and commercial relations. While no permanent diplomatic posts were maintained in either capital, embassies were frequent on both sides, either to congratulate a new ruler, or to conclude a treaty, or to negotiate an exchange of prisoners. Commercial relations and cultural exchanges are attested in an almost continuous fashion throughout the history of the Byzantine Empire.

Whereas in the eighth and ninth centuries the Byzantines had been on the defensive, the tenth century witnessed a Byzantine military revival. Increasing Byzantine consolidation was paralleled with Muslim weakness and division. The Byzantine Empire's successes in the tenth century have to be seen against this background of Muslim disunity and collapse. The rivalries between the Abbasid state, the Umayyad state of al-Andalus, and the newly founded Fatimid state in North Africa colored to a considerable extent the bilateral relations these competing states had with Byzantium.

The whole period of the Macedonian dynasty between 867 and 1025 was a brilliant time in the political existence of the Byzantine Empire. It was now the turn of the Muslim lands to suffer repeated incursions accompanied by looting and devastation. The Hamdanid principality of Aleppo rose to the occasion but the victories of its prince Sayf al-Dawlah were short-lived and soon the emirate of Aleppo and other parts of the Islamic caliphate were to feel the weight of Byzantine invasions. The main events of these wars found an echo in the poems of one of the greatest poets of the Arabic language, al-Mutanabbi.

The late eleventh century contrasted with the early part of the century when Byzantium had been powerful and wealthy. Internal difficulties in addition to the appearance of the Turks in the Near East accelerated the decline of the Byzantine state, leading to the crushing Byzantine defeat at Manzikert in 1071. This marked the collapse of Byzantium as a great political power and the beginning of the Turkification of Asia Minor. The appearance of the Crusaders and the establishment of Crusader states in the Near East revolutionized relations between the Byzantines and their Muslim neighbors. Following the conquest of Constantinople by the Latins in 1204, relations between the Byzantines and the Mamluk sultans of Egypt steadily improved in the late thirteenth century. The existence of threats common to both states, including the Mongol threat, led to the establishment of privileged relations between them. In the fourteenth century, the Byzantine empire systematically lost ground to the Ottoman Turks. In 1453 the Ottoman sultan, Mehmed II, conquered Constantinople, thus spelling the end of the Byzantine Empire.

*See also* **Christianity and Islam; Expansion.**

## BIBLIOGRAPHY

Bosworth, C. E. "Byzantium and the Arabs: War and Peace between Two World Civilizations." *Journal of Oriental and African Studies* 3–4 (1991–1992): 1–23.

El Cheikh, Nadia Maria. "Surat al-Rum: A Study of the Exegetical Literature." *Journal of the American Oriental Society* 118 (1998): 356–364.

Gibb, H. A. R. "Arab Byzantine Relations under the Umayyad Caliphate." *Dumbarton Oaks Papers* 12 (1958): 219–233.

Kennedy, Hugh. "Byzantine-Arab Diplomacy in the Near East from the Islamic Conquests to the Mid-Eleventh Century." In *Byzantine Diplomacy*. Edited by Jonathan Shepard and Simon Franklin. Aldershot, Hampshire, U.K.: Variorum, 1992.

Vryonis, Speros. *The Decline of Medieval Hellenism in Asia Minor and the Process of Islamization from the Eleventh Century Through the Fifteenth*. Los Angeles: University of California Press, 1971.

*Nadia Maria El Cheikh*

## MONGOL AND IL-KHANID

The Mongol empire, which at its peak stretched from Java to Lithuania, was the creation of Genghis Khan (c. 1167–1227) and his descendants. They exercised direct rule for over a century in Iran and Transoxania, southern Russia, and China, and in the less accessible heartland of these regions, particularly in parts of Central Asia, where Mongol khans were recognized as the legitimate rulers until well into the seventeenth century.

The father of Temujin, the future Genghis Khan, was murdered by a rival tribe of Tatars when Temujin was still a small boy. Abandoned by most of his father's followers, he spent a hard childhood, first simply surviving and then working for revenge. By 1206 he had succeeded in unifying most of the tribes in Mongolia and eliminating the Tatars and other powerful groups, incorporating the survivors into his own forces. He was enthroned as ruler of the Mongols and adopted the title Genghis Khan.

There followed a sustained attack, first on the neighboring powers such as the Tanguts (Hsi Hsia) and then on north China, ruled by the Jurchen (Chin) dynasty (1115–1234). Peking fell in 1215, but it took many more campaigns for the Chin to be crushed. The scale and determination of their resistance was one of the factors that helped to transform the Mongol assaults from raids on the traditional nomadic model into more permanent wars of conquest and occupation, for there is little to suggest that the annexation of north China was part of Genghis Khan's original intentions.

As the Mongol war machine gathered momentum, its belligerence necessarily attracted further acts of defiance and inevitable punishment. Their attention drawn ever westward by the flight of their vanquished foes, the Mongols came up against the Khwarazmian empire, based on the cities of the Jaxartes and Oxus rivers. The massacre of a Mongol-sponsored merchant caravan in Otrar in 1218 provided the pretext for the invasions of the Transoxania and eastern Iran, where the Khwaramshah's tenuous control was quickly destroyed in a devastating series of sieges. Pursuing the Khwaramshah across northern Iran, the Mongol generals Subetei and Jebe then turned north across the Caucasus and defeated a Russian force at the Kalka river in 1223, before returning to Mongolia.

By Genghis Khan's death in 1227, these widespread and crushing victories opened up huge new territories to the Mongols. It was the work of his descendants to consolidate them into an empire. His son and successor, Ögedei (1229–1241), continued the conquest of North China and further expansion west, where the Mongols won great victories in Poland and Hungary before consolidating their rule over southern Russia based on the steppes north of the Caspian Sea. These territories, of the so-called Golden Horde, were held by the descendants of Genghis Khan's oldest son, Jochi. They maintained their dominance over the disunited Russian princes until the early sixteenth century, by keeping separate from them and retaining the essence of their nomadic lifestyle. Nevertheless, their capital at Sarai on the Volga became a great cosmopolitan trading center. As early as the 1260s, but definitively by the 1330s, the khans of the Golden Horde had converted to Islam.

By contrast, in Iran, an ancient sedentary civilization (like China), a transformation in outlook was required if the nomadic Mongols were to rule effectively. The original conquests were consolidated by Genghis Khan's grandson, Hulegu, who captured Baghdad in 1258 and took the title Il-Khan or subject Khan (to the Great Khan in Mongolia, and later in China). Hulegu's dynasty, the Il-khanids (1258–1335), relied heavily on the Persian bureaucratic families to operate their oppressive financial administration, but there remained a fundamental reluctance to abandon Mongol precedents. The unwritten Mongol code of law, the *Yasa*, continued to be honored, even after the accelerated Islamization that followed the conversion of Ghazan Khan in 1294. Ultimately, the Il-khanate ran out of heirs, the dynasty suffering from an endemic instability in the succession to the throne that had first caused the fragmentation of the empire into four main regional states and then the weakening of the states themselves.

In the last of these states, the Chaghatay Khanate, which embraced Transoxania, Turkestan, and Sinkiang, the Mongols retained rule longer than elsewhere, owing partly to the terrain and the preponderance of desert and steppe over the isolated oases along the celebrated "silk route." Even more than in the case of the Golden Horde, the Mongols could prey on their subjects from a distance, while the largely Turkicized subjects were more like the Mongols themselves: not Russians, Persians, or Chinese, with their alien traditions and norms. These regions were initially part of the inheritance of Ögedei and his elder brother Chaghatay, but the descendants of Ögedei were almost eliminated when they lost the succession to the Great Khanate in 1251 as the result of a coup by the Toluids (descendants of Genghis Khan's youngest son, Tolui). While the Western Chaghatay leaders began to embrace Islam in the early fourteenth century, pagan ways prevailed in the east up to the sixteenth century.

Controlling a vast area of Asia, the four contiguous Mongol empires opened up territories to new movements of people, fueling a process of cultural exchange, artistic patronage, and commercial relations, which did much to counteract the initial savagery of their conquests. Despite their first assault on Islam, ultimately the Mongols were responsible for spreading Islam among the Turkic peoples and tribes who were brought into Central Asia as a result of the Mongol conquests.

*An illustrated manuscript of Genghis Khan and his sons appears in the volume one color insert.*

*See also* **Political Organization.**

## BIBLIOGRAPHY

Allsen, Thomas T. *Culture as Conquest in Mongol Eurasia.* Cambridge, U.K.: Cambridge University Press, 2001.

Morgan, David. *The Mongols.* Oxford, U.K.: B. Blackwell, 1986.

Spuler, Bertold. *A History of the Muslim World.* Princeton, N.J.: M. Wiener Publishers, 1994.

*Charles Melville*

## MOGUL

The Mogul empire of India was established by Zahir al-Din Muhammad Babur (d.1530), a descendant of Emir Timur (d.1405). On his mother's side, Babur was related to the Chaghtai khans of Kashghar. Expelled from his ancestral principality of Farghana (modern Kokand) because of internecine feuds of the Timurid princes and the rise of Uzbek power under Shaibani Khan, Babur eventually established himself at Kabul in 1505, and in 1526, defeating Sultan Ibrahim Lodi in the Battle of Panipat, founded the Mogul dynasty in India. The name "Mogul" was given to it by popular usage in India; the later Central Asian designation for it, equally loose, was Chaghatai. The family continued (with the exception of the Sur interlude, 1540–1555) to exercise imperial hegemony over much of the Indian subcontinent until 1739 when defeat at the hands of Nadir Shah of Iran signaled the empire's rapid disintegration.

Babur brought with him a tradition in which respect for Mongol customs was quite strong, though modified by the conventional attachment to Sunni orthodoxy. The further fact that the Timurids were highly urbanized and cultured drew them irresistibly to Iranian culture, despite the fact that in the sixteenth century it assumed a radical Shi'ite color. All these factors demonstrated an eclectic attitude that made the Moguls particularly suited to govern a country of varied cultural traditions like India.

Babur is credited with recruiting a large number of Afghans and Indian Muslims into his nobility. The recruitment of many Persians by Humayun (1540–1556) was a further important development. But the decisive transformation in this respect came under Humayun's son Akbar (1556–1605). Having recruited a large number of Rajput chiefs, Akbar rendered the Mogul nobility a truly composite group, a characteristic that persisted until 1739.

Akbar, however, was not simply motivated by eclecticism. He came to have strong views on reason and religion. He evoked Ibn al-'Arabi's philosophy to justify a policy of universal tolerance under the principle of *Sulh-e Kul* (Absolute Peace) and became a sturdy defender of reason and critic of old social customs. He, and his major spokesman, Abu'l Fazl, sought to give to sovereignty a nonsectarian character; the sovereign was held to be a direct representative of God and claimed almost limitless authority, as necessary for carrying out the sovereign's abundant responsibilities.

It is arguable that Akbar's claims to absolute sovereign powers derived from his own practical success in achieving not only a series of conquests that brought most of India under his control but also from achieving an immense degree of administrative systematization and centralization. The latter was reflected in the introduction of *mansab* or number-rank (1574) for rigorously setting the pay and size of military contingents of the nobles, and the division of the empire into provinces (*suba*s) (1580) where the administration of one province was like that of any other. The practice of linking *mansab* obligation to expected income (*jama'*) from revenue assignment (*jagir*) gave new impetus to financial unification.

The political authority and control on resources in the Mogul empire tended to be concentrated in the hands of high nobles. They, along with hereditary chiefs allied closely with the empire, formed the ruling class, whose unity and cohesion, according to Irfan Habib in *The Agrarian System of Mughal India*, "found its practical expression in the absolute powers of the emperor" (p. 366). Detailed regulations governed the extraction of agrarian surplus by the revenue collection machine of the empire, which tended to the method of assessment by measurement and collection of revenue in money rather than in kind.

The urban-based educated Muslims (*ashraf*) claiming noble descents along with favored non-Muslim scholar priests were marked out for state patronage. Some of the *ashraf* manned the offices in the Department of Ecclesiastical Affairs (*Sadarat*) including those of judges (*qazis*) who enforced

Muslim as well as customary law and even imperial regulations. The criminal (*faujdari*) cases were generally decided by local military commanders (*shiqdar*s, *faujdar*s, and the like) in accordance with regulations (*zawabit*) laid down from time to time by the emperor.

The bulk of the Mogul army was represented by mounted archers and spearmen employed by the *mansabdar*s out of the income of their revenue assignments. An imperial functionary (*bakhshi*) maintained a descriptive roll of these troopers who were brought to muster. To check fraud, branding (*dagh*) of horses was practiced. A special corps of cavalry (*ahadi*s), a park of artillery (*top-khana*), and a large number of musketeers employed by the emperor supplemented the armed might of the empire significantly. The matchlock muskets introduced in India by Babur seem to have contributed significantly to the centralizing process in the Mogul empire.

Under Akbar's successors Jahangir (1605–1627), Shahjahan (1628–1658), and Aurangzeb (1659–1707), the empire continued to expand, though Kandahar was finally lost to Iran (1648). Practically the entire peninsula (excluding Kerala) came under Mogul control, especially with the annexations of the kingdoms of Bijapur (1686) and Golkunda (1687).

Broadly, the administrative institutions of the empire as established by Akbar were maintained by his three successors, with certain changes of a relatively minor character. The religious policy of Jahangir followed mainly that of Akbar, while under Shahjahan and Aurangzeb, it tended to incline toward Muslim orthodoxy. In 1679 Aurangzeb imposed the *jizya* or poll-tax on non-Muslims, which Akbar had abolished in 1564.

The Mogul emperors were great patrons of art and architecture. In both it was Akbar again under whom the great achievements began. He gave to Mogul painting its particular humanistic touch and realism; and immense innovativeness to architecture as in Fatehpur Sikri and Sikandra. Under Jahangir, painting reached its highest technical perfection, and under Shahjahan, the Taj Mahal stands as testimony to the greatness reached by Mogul architecture.

Under the Mogul emperors several Sanskrit works were translated into Persian. Akbar had had the *Mahabharata* translated; and Dara Shukoh (d.1659), the Mogul prince, translated the Upanisads. There was also the growth of a lively literature in Persian, leading in the eighteenth century to the development of the literary Urdu language, a real legacy of Indo-Mogul culture.

The Maratha uprising under Shivaji (d.1680) greatly weakened the Mogul empire, and the decline of the empire began with the repeated struggles for succession during 1707–1719. After a little recovery of stability in the early years of Muhammad Shah (1719–1748), the Mogul empire began to cede territory after territory to the Marathas. The coup de grace

This c. 1590 Mogul painting depicts nobles entertained in a garden by musicians and dancers. THE ART ARCHIVE/DAGLI ORTI

was delivered by Nadir Shah in 1739–1740, with the Persian conqueror's great victory at the Battle of Karnal, near Delhi. The Mogul empire rapidly lost control over provinces. Delhi itself passed under the control of Marathas (1772–1803) and finally the English in 1803. Henceforth, the emperor's writ was confined to the Red Fort in Delhi. The Rebels in 1857 attempted to restore the last emperor, Bahadur Shah II Zafar (1775–1862), to power, but the English deposed him on recapturing Delhi and so terminated the dynasty.

*See also* **Political Organization.**

## BIBLIOGRAPHY

Habib, Irfan. *The Agrarian System of Mughal India, 1556–1707.* Rev. ed. New Delhi: Oxford University Press, 1999.

Khan, Iqtidar Alam. "State in Mughal India: Re-examining the Myths of a Counter-vision." *Social Scientist* 29, Nos.1–2 (January–February 2001): 16–45.

Richards, John F. "The Mughal Empire." In Vol. 1.5, *The New Cambridge History of India* (1922). Reprint. Edited by Gordon Jonson. New Delhi: Foundation Books, 1993.

*Iqtidar Alam Khan*

## OTTOMAN

Ottoman state builders (c. 1300–1922) erected and maintained one of the more durable and successful examples of empire-building in world history. Born during medieval times in the northwest corner of then Byzantine-Asia Minor, the Ottoman state achieved world-empire status in 1453, with its conquest of Constantinople. For a century before and two centuries after that epochal event, the Ottoman Empire was among the most powerful political entities in the Mediterranean-European world. Indeed, but for the Ming state in China, the Ottoman Empire in about 1500 was likely the most formidable political system on the planet.

The rapid expansion of the Ottoman state from border principality to world empire was due partly to geography and the proximity of weak enemies; but it owed more to Ottoman policies and achievements. After the migrations of Turkish peoples from Central Asia broke the border defenses of the Byzantine Empire back in the eleventh century, many small states and principalities vied for supremacy. The Ottoman dynasty emerged on the Byzantine borderlands not far from Constantinople, and its supporters employed pragmatic statecraft and methods of conquest and rewarded the human material at hand—whether Greek, Bulgarian, Serb, Turkish, Christian, or Muslim—for good service. These pragmatic policies, coupled with an exceptional openness to innovation, including military technology, go far in explaining why this particular minor state ultimately attained world-power status.

Due to developments elsewhere in the world, notably the rise of capitalism and industrialism in Europe and then elsewhere, and the New World wealth that poured into Europe, the Ottoman Empire lost its preeminent position, and by about 1800 it had declined to the status of a second-class economic, military, and political power. Internally, after its initial rapid expansion, innovation diminished as entrenched bureaucrats and statesmen acted to preserve positions for their children and closed entry to newcomers with fresh ideas. Internationally, the state encountered increasingly powerful European states on its western and northern fronts, and some of these new states had been enriched by New World wealth. Warfare became more expensive and more difficult, and expansion finally ground to a halt in the late seventeenth century.

The empire's grand defeat before the gates of Vienna in 1683 was followed by some victories, but mainly it experienced defeats during the subsequent one hundred years. During the nineteenth century, a successful series of programs measurably strengthened both the state and its military. The state grew vastly in size and in the scope of its

A sixteenth-century Venetian portrait of Ottoman sultan Suleyman I. Between the fourteenth and seventeenth centuries, the Ottoman Empire was among the most powerful in the world. © ALI MEYER/CORBIS

activities. Whereas the early modern state primarily collected taxes and maintained order, the more modern state took responsibility for the health, education, and welfare of its subjects. Despite an impressive record of reform, however, the empire was defeated in the First World War, and was partitioned by the Great Powers, notably Great Britain and France. Ottoman successor states today include Albania, Bosnia, Bulgaria, Egypt, Greece, Iraq, Israel, Lebanon, Montenegro, Rumania, Saudi Arabia, Serbia, Syria, Turkey, and other states in the Balkans, the Arab world, North Africa, and along the north shore of the Black Sea.

## Military, Fiscal, and Political Organization

In its domestic politics, the Ottoman state underwent continuous change. The Ottoman ruler, the sultan, began as one among equals in the early days of the state. Between about 1453 and the later sixteenth century, however, sultans ruled as true autocrats. Subsequently, others in the imperial family and other members of the palace elites—often in collaboration with provincial elites—maintained real control of the state until the early nineteenth century. Thereafter, bureaucrats and sultans vied for domination. In sum, the sultan nominally presided over the imperial system for all of Ottoman history but actually, personally, ruled only for portions of the fifteenth, sixteenth, and nineteenth centuries. It seems important to stress that the principle of sultanic rule by the

Ottoman family was hardly ever challenged through the long centuries of the empire's existence. While this rule was a constant, change otherwise was the norm in domestic politics.

Political power almost always rested in the imperial center and, depending on the particular period, extended into the provinces either through direct military and political instruments or, indirectly, through fiscal means. The state exerted its military, fiscal, and political authority through a number of mechanisms that evolved continuously. One cannot speak of a single, invariant Ottoman system or method of rule, except to say that it was based on policies of flexibility and adaptiveness. Military, fiscal, and political instruments changed constantly, hardly a surprising situation in an empire that existed from the medieval to the modern age. Moreover, much of what historians thought they knew about Ottoman institutions has been challenged and rewritten. Take, for example, the cliché that the janissaries' prowess as soldiers declined when they ceased living together in bachelor barracks and served as married men. It turns out that already in the fifteenth century, when the janissaries were the most feared military unit in the Mediterranean world, at least some were married with families.

The Ottoman state at first depended on the so-called *timar* system to compensate much of its military, which was dominated by cavalrymen fighting with bows and arrows. Under this system, the cavalryman was granted revenues from a piece of land sufficient to maintain himself and his horse. He did not actually control the land, but only the taxes deriving from it. Peasants worked the land and the taxes they paid supported the *timar* cavalryman while he was on campaign as well as when he was not fighting. In reality, the *timar* was at the center of Ottoman affairs for the earlier era of Ottoman history, perhaps only during the fourteenth, fifteenth, and part of the sixteenth centuries. Hardly had the state developed the *timar* system when the regime began to discard it, and the cavalry it was meant to support. Increasingly, the empire turned to infantrymen bearing firearms. As it did, the janissaries ceased to be a small, praetorian elite and evolved into a firearmed infantry of massive size. To support these full-time soldiers required vast amounts of cash, and so tax-farming replaced the *timar* system as the central fiscal instrument. (*Timar* holders owed service in exchange for the *timar* revenues, whereas tax farmers paid a sum at the tax farm auction for the right to collect the taxes, and they incurred no service obligation.) By 1700, lifetime tax-farms—seen as better cash cows—began to become commonplace. Varying combinations of cavalry and firearmed infantry, along with massive uses of artillery worked quite well for a time, but lost out in the arms race to central and eastern European foes by the end of the seventeenth century. The Ottoman military continued to evolve and, in the eighteenth century, firearmed troops of provincial notables and the forces of the Crimean Khanate largely replaced both the janissary infantry and the

A nineteenth-century watercolor depiction of Ottoman sultan Mehmet IV (1642–1692). Early in the Ottoman Empire, the role of the sultan was less autocratic than it became in the later fifteenth and sixteenth centuries. THE ART ARCHIVE/TURKISH AND ISLAMIC ART MUSEUM ISTANBUL/DAGLI ORTI

*timar* cavalry. During the nineteenth century, universal male conscription controlled by the central state slowly developed, and this was perhaps the most radical transformation of all. Lifetime tax-farms were abandoned but tax-farming continued, often in the hands of local notables in partnerships with the Istanbul regime.

## Judicial Organization

Both religious and secular law regulated the lives of Ottoman subjects. The Ottoman state determined who administered the laws, members drawn from the Muslim, Christian, or Jewish communities, or other officials of the imperial state. That is, the sultan or his agents determined the judges in the respective communities, either directly or by appointing officials who, in turn, named the judges. In principle, the religious laws of the respective communities prevailed, be that community Muslim, Jewish, or Christian. In practice, however, the Muslim courts were commonly used by subjects of all religions. This was due in part to the quality of the justice which the judge (*kadi*) administered, and in part because it was understood that rulings from such courts might well have greater weight than those from Christian or Jewish sources. In addition to this religious law, the state routinely passed its own, secular ordinances (*kanun*), while

always paying lip-service to its adherence to Islamic principles. In the nineteenth century, when a flood of ordinances and regulations marked the presence of an expanding bureaucratic state, even this lip-service frequently fell away, replaced by claims to scientific management.

## Economic Organization

Throughout most of its history, the Ottoman economy remained agrarian, although again the specifics underwent considerable changes over time. During the various periods of the empire's existence, most Ottoman subjects raised a wide variety of different crops for subsistence and for sale. The particular mix of crops changed over time, but cereals remained dominant throughout, supplemented by a changing array of other crops. During the seventeenth century, for example, tobacco imports from the New World ceased as tobacco became commonly cultivated in the Balkan, Anatolian, and Arab provinces of the empire. In the nineteenth century tobacco became a major export commodity.

In theory, the vast majority of land was owned by the sultan and merely used by others to grow crops and raise animals. In practice, however, these land users generally enjoyed security of tenure. Sharecropping was widespread and was the major vehicle by which goods were brought to market. Most cultivators were small landholders; large estates were comparatively unusual. Slave labor was common for domestic work but very rare in agriculture. Commercialization of agriculture enjoyed considerable development in the eighteenth and nineteenth century in order to meet mounting foreign demand and, in the latter period, the increasing number of Ottoman urban residents. The increasing amount produced for sale derived from committing increasing acreage to cultivation, not from more intensive exploitation.

Ottoman manufacturing, for its part, was and remained largely the domain of small-scale hand producers, although there was some mechanization in the late period. During the seventeenth and eighteenth centuries, foreign markets for Ottoman manufactures fell away, but producers continued to enjoy a vast domestic market for their wares. During the nineteenth century, moreover, several new export industries emerged, notably rug making and silk spinning, staffed largely with female labor working outside the home. In transportation and communication there were important technological breakthroughs during the second half of the nineteenth century. Steam replaced sail on the sea, while a relatively thin network of railroads emerged; telegraph lines, for their part, were built to connect most towns and cities.

## Religious and National Identity

There is considerable debate about the nature and quality of Ottoman intercommunal relations, and there are many popular stereotypes around the "terrible Turk" who slaughtered Ottoman Christians. For nearly all of Ottoman history, this stereotype is not true. From the fourteenth century until the 1870s, the majority of Ottoman subjects professed one or another version of Christianity as their religion. Yet, throughout this period, the state's official religion was Islam. The key to Ottoman success and a major reason for its longevity lay in the tolerant governmental treatment of those who did not share its professed religion. The Ottoman state, for nearly all of its history, was a multinational, multireligious entity that did not seek to impose Islam on its subjects. This fact has often been forgotten in the confusion surrounding the emergence of the Ottoman successor states, but it remains nonetheless true that much of the credit for the durability of the empire lay in the flexibility of Ottoman rule and the lightness of the Ottoman hand on the subject masses.

The Ottoman system recognized difference and protected those differences so long as its subjects paid their taxes and rendered obedience. Until the eighteenth century, the era of the Enlightenment, minorities in the Ottoman world likely were treated better than in Europe. During some years of the final Ottoman era, however, there admittedly were atrocities. These should be understood in the context of the generally admirable record of intercommunal relations over the 600-year lifespan of the Ottoman Empire.

*See also* **Balkans, Islam in the; Christianity and Islam; Europe, Islam in; Expansion; Judaism and Islam; Kemal, Namek; Nur Movement; Nursi, Said; Young Ottomans.**

## BIBLIOGRAPHY

Brown, Leon Carl, ed. *Imperial Legacy: The Ottoman Imprint on the Balkans and the Middle East.* New York: Columbia University Press, 1996.

Goffman, Daniel. *The Ottoman Empire and Early Modern Europe.* Cambridge, U.K.: Cambridge University Press, 2002.

Imber, Colin. *The Ottoman Empire, 1300–1650.* The Structure of Power. New York: Palgrave Macmillan, 2002.

Inalcik, Halil. *An Economic and Social History of the Ottoman Empire, 1300–1914.* Cambridge, U.K.: Cambridge University Press, 1994.

Kafadar, Cemal. *Between Two Worlds: The Construction of the Ottoman State.* Berkeley: University of California Press, 1995.

Lowry, Heath. *The Nature of the Early Ottoman State.* Albany: State University of New York Press, 2003.

Quataert, Donald. *The Ottoman Empire, 1700–1922.* Cambridge, U.K.: Cambridge University Press, 2000.

Todorova, Maria. *Imagining the Balkans.* Oxford, U.K.: Oxford University Press, 1997.

*Donald Quataert*

## SAFAVID AND QAJAR

The Safavid period (1501–1722) continued many Mongol and Timurid practices, but may also be seen as the beginning of modern Iranian history. The Safavids unified much of Iran under single political control. Under them a political system emerged in which political and religious boundaries overlapped. The Safavid concept of kingship, combining territorial control with religious legitimacy, would endure, with modifications, until the late twentieth century. Many administrative institutions established by them survived well into the Qajar era. The Safavid era, finally, saw the beginning of frequent and sustained diplomatic and commercial relations with Europe.

The Safavids, who were of Kurdish ancestry, began in about 1300 as a mystical order centered in the northwestern Iranian town of Ardabil, the burial place of the order's founder, Shaykh Safi al-Din. The nature of their original beliefs remains unclear but in time they turned to a extremist form of Shi'ism that included the veneration of a leader seen as an incarnation of god. Though the Safavid leaders were spiritual leaders rather than tribal chiefs, they built their state with the military assistance of tribal groups. Known as Qizilbash, redheads, in reference to their red headgear, these Turkmen migrants from Syria and Anatolia were to become the mainstay of the Safavid army.

Under Shah Isma'il (r. 1501–1524) the Safavids evolved from a messianic movement to a political dynasty. Upon seizing power, Isma'il proclaimed Tabriz his capital and Shi'ism the faith of his realm, thus endowing his new state with a strong ideological basis. In time, Isma'il extended his territory as far as Iraq and the Persian Gulf. His expansionism brought him into conflict with the Uzbeks in the east and the Ottomans in the west, both Sunni powers that felt threatened by the formation of a militant Shi'ite state on their borders. Equipped with firearms, the Ottomans in 1514 routed the Safavid army in the battle of Chaldiran and briefly occupied Tabriz.

Aside from waging war, Isma'il concentrated on state building. In 1508 he took a series of measures that increased the power of Iranian administrators at the expense of that of the Qizilbash. Henceforth a functional division emerged between ethnic Iranians, who in majority staffed the bureaucracy, and ethnic Turks, who dominated the army. Under Isma'il the first example of the influence of court women is also seen, a legacy of the Central Asian element in Safavid statecraft. Tajlu Khanum, one of his wives and the mother of the future Shah Tahmasp, was as powerful as the shah himself in Isma'il's later reign.

Shah Isma'il was succeeded by his ten-year-old son, Tahmasp (r. 1524–1576). The first decade of his long reign was marked by a civil war among the Qizilbash that nearly overwhelmed the shah. Once he emerged from this conflict, Tahmasp adopted a policy designed to curtail the unruly Qizilbash. He continued to appoint Tajik officials to key positions traditionally reserved for Turks, and began the trend of giving administrative posts to Georgians and

Armenians, so-called *ghulam*s, who were captured during expeditions into the Caucasus. (The women became employed in the royal harem.) Until 1555, when he concluded a peace accord with them, Shah Tahmasp also fought three wars against the Ottomans, and in the process moved his capital from Tabriz to Qazvin, a city located further in the interior.

Shah Tahmasp presided over a court that fostered culture. The quality of the illuminated manuscripts produced during his reign would never be surpassed. His religious policy focused on the further implantation of Shi'ism and saw attempts to standardize religious practice around a scriptural, urban-based version of the faith as opposed to the folk beliefs of the Turkmen. To disseminate the creed, the shah also invited Shi'ite scholars from Arab lands, most notably from Lebanon, to migrate to Iran.

These trends continued and culminated under Shah 'Abbas (r. 1587–1629), the strongest and most visionary of the Safavid rulers, who came to power in 1576, following the interregnum of the cruel Shah Isma'il II and the nearly blind Mohammad Khodabandeh. Shah 'Abbas was above all a brilliant strategist, keen to regain the territories that had been lost to internal sedition and outside enemies during the turmoil preceding his reign. Well aware that he could not fight on two fronts at once, he made a humiliating peace with the Ottomans so as to be able to take on the Uzbeks and attend to domestic matters. This done, he resumed war with the Ottomans and reconquered large parts of Azerbaijan, Armenia, and Georgia. In later years, 'Abbas recaptured Qandahar (lost again in 1638), established control over the Persian Gulf littoral by ousting the Portuguese from Hormuz, and seized part of Mesopotamia, including Baghdad (lost again in 1639).

In his domestic agenda Shah 'Abbas pursued centralized, personalized power and the maximization of cash revenue. He liquidated a number of powerful Qizilbash leaders, including the ones who had helped him come to power, and suppressed any religious group that challenged his authority. He also resettled tribes to far-off regions with the aim of strengthening frontiers and breaking up loyalties. In the 1590s the shah transferred his capital from Qazvin to Isfahan, a move that gave Iran an administrative center closer to its geographical center, aside from completing the shift from a Turkish to a Persian cultural focus. Most importantly, Shah 'Abbas set out to break the power of the Qizilbash. He removed a great deal of the state land that they controlled as fiefs by turning it into crown domain administered directly by a wazir appointed by the shah, so that revenue would flow into the royal treasury. *Ghulam*s were appointed as governors of these newly formed crown provinces. Shah 'Abbas's reforms mark an important phase in the evolution of Safavid Iran from a steppe formation to a bureaucratic state.

Shah 'Abbas is especially famous for encouraging trade. He reestablished road security and had numerous caravanseries constructed throughout his realm. Under him, Isfahan, endowed with a newly built administrative and commercial center, became a thriving city of some 500,000 inhabitants. His special focus on the Persian Gulf trade and his efforts to stimulate the export of silk combined a need for revenue and a desire to open up an alternative outlet to the land-based routes via Ottoman territory. He allowed Western merchants to settle in the newly founded port of Bandar 'Abbas, offering them commercial privileges in return for royal profit and the promise of naval assistance. His overtures to the West, expressed in countless embassies to European courts, were mostly aimed at finding allies in his anti-Ottoman struggle.

Under Shah 'Abbas's direct successors, Safi (r. 1629–1642) and 'Abbas II (1642–1666), Iran offered the outward appearance of stability. Baghdad was lost to the Ottomans, but Shah 'Abbas II managed to recapture Qandahar from the Mughals. Though competent rulers, both lacked the vision and determination of their predecessor. Under them, economic problems became apparent and state control weakened. Some of these problems were perhaps inevitable given Iran's inherent weaknesses—much arid, unproductive land, an unevenly spread and heavily nomadic population, a dependence on the outside world for precious metal. Others stemmed from the very same measures taken by 'Abbas I. Good examples of those are the conversion to crown land and his practice of isolating the heir to be in the royal harem for fear that he might present a premature challenge to royal power. The first led to extortion of the peasants by supervisors who only leased the land for a limited time and thus saw no reason for long-term investment. The second produced inept rulers and empowered those who inhabited the royal quarters, eunuchs and women. The army, already weakened by the continuing antagonism between the Qizilbash and the *ghulam*s, became largely neglected following the conclusion of a definitive peace accord with the Ottomans in 1639.

It was under the last two Safavid shahs, Solayman (r. 1666–1694) and Sultan Hosayn (r. 1694–1722), that order and stability began to unravel. Whereas their predecessors had been roving warriors, forever vigilant in patrolling their realm to pacify unruly tribes and repel border raids, they reigned as stationary monarchs who, aside from occasional hunting parties, preferred to live immured in the palace, hidden from the public eye. Disconnected and hardly interested in administrative affairs, they relied on their grand wazirs for the daily running of the state. Though able administrators who successfully tapped new sources of revenue to fill the royal coffers, these chief ministers were unable to combat the increasingly abusive practices of provincial governors and to reverse the crippling corruption and factionalism in court circles. The results were seen in a deteriorating currency, a fall in agricultural output, and growing numbers of bankruptcies among merchants. Equally serious was the pressure that began to be put on non-Muslims, a function of the growing influence of the Shi'ite clergy, especially under the pious and impressionable Shah Sultan Hosayn, who ruled under the spell of his maternal grandmother, Miryam Begum; the court eunuchs; and Muhammad Baqir Majlisi, a conservative cleric who advocated a literal interpretation of the faith. The Armenians of New Julfa near Isfahan, a group with a disproportionately large role in the economy, lost their tax advantages and by the late seventeenth century many wealthy merchants began to migrate to Europe, India, and Russia.

As of 1710 disintegration set in. While the shah built pleasure gardens, the cost of which was extorted from peasants and merchants, the country faced internal rebellion and outside attack. The final blow came from the east, with Baluchi and Afghan tribesmen occupying Kerman and Mashad. In 1722 a small contingent of Afghan Ghilzai warriors penetrated the interior, defeated a hastily assembled Safavid army, and proceeded to besiege Isfahan. The city fell six months later, brought to its knees by starvation, and Sultan Hosayn was forced to confer the title of shah on Mahmud, the Afghan leader. Meanwhile, Russia and the Ottoman Empire took advantage of the turmoil by occupying Iran's northwestern regions.

Artwork original to the period appears in the volume one color insert.

*See also* **'Abbas I, Shah; Isma'il I, Shah; Majlisi, Muhammad Baqir; Political Organization; Tahmasp I, Shah.**

## BIBLIOGRAPHY

Matthee, Rudolph P. *The Politics of Trade in Safavid Iran: Silk for Silver 1600–1730*. Cambridge, U.K.: Cambridge University Press, 1999.

Savory, Roger. *Iran under the Safavids*. Cambridge, U.K.: Cambridge University Press, 1980.

*Rudi Matthee*

## SASSANIAN

With the Arab victory over the Iranian forces at Nihavand in 641–642 C.E., referred to by the Arabs as the "Victory of Victories," the fall of the Sassanian Empire was final. The Sassanians had been a formidable power that had endured for four centuries, but in the end the corruption and greed of the ruling and priestly classes had left the imperial coffers depleted and, perhaps more importantly, eroded support among the empire's numerous heterodox subjects. Such internal problems hampered efforts to efficiently muster and deploy the impressive Iranian defenses. The ponderous Sassanian cavalry ultimately succumbed to the speedy attack and retreat tactics of the lightly armed Arab troops.

Fifteen years after Nihavand, most of the erstwhile Sassanian lands had come under Muslim control. Nevertheless, many of the fallen Iranian cities revolted and had to be reconquered several times. Even after the murder of the last Sassanian monarch, Yazdgard III, ended his flight from province to province from 651 to 652 C.E., parts of the population in various provinces continued to break their treaties of surrender to the Arabs and returned to their old religious practices and traditions. Particularly, changes of local governorship and the deaths of caliphs presented occasions for revolt, as was the case after the murders of 'Umar, 'Uthman, and 'Ali.

In spite of this ongoing resistance and the polemics that were directed against the Arab conquerors—who were at times portrayed as devils and associates of Ahriman (the evil spirit in Zoroastrian belief)—a new landholding class eventually emerged, whose strength gradually increased through intermarriage with the indigenous residents.

The arrival of the new Arab overlords in Iran also brought with it a new religion. But the conversion of Iran to Islam was neither swift nor of a piece. Certain groups converted to Islam on a collective basis, but this was the exception rather than the rule. Some sections of the population opted for the *jizya* (tax levied on non-Muslims) and the *kharaj* (land tax), accepting the *dhimmi* status (a second-class-citizen status granting non-Muslims protection and limited religious freedom under Muslim rule) in order to hold on to their old ways. The privileges that came with conversion were, however, a decisive argument for many, especially those who had been disadvantaged by Zoroastrian religious organization and its rules. Artisans and craftsmen had been specifically affected in this way, as the Zoroastrian taboos regarding the pollution of the elements of fire, water, and earth clashed with many aspects of their professions, branding them unclean by association.

Ultimately, greater parts of the populace recognized some of the fundamental similarities between Islamic and Zoroastrian faith, which share the belief in one good god, one evil spirit or devil, a final judgment, and the notions of Paradise and Hell. Acceptance of the Islamic faith became more and more widespread. But even for those that held to the Zoroastrian faith, the restrictions imposed by the *dhimmi* status were less severe, and the privileges greater, than had been the case for Christians and Jews under Zoroastrian rule. During the Umayyad period, however, there was a marked increase in contempt and intolerance of Muslims toward Zoroastrian subjects, prompting a group of them to eventually emigrate to Gujarat, where their descendants, known as Parsees, practice their belief to this day.

It is noteworthy that adherents of non-Zoroastrian religions, or of groups that had been considered heretics by the Zoroastrian establishment in Sassanian times, enjoyed a distinctly greater amount of religious freedom under Muslim

This relief depicts the Sassanid king Shapur on horseback. After a four-century rule, the Sassanian Empire fell to Arab control in 641–642 C.E. THE ART ARCHIVE/DAGLI ORTI

rule. The Sassanians had suppressed the heterodox groups existing in their empire, and to them the Islamic practice of giving *dhimmi* status to the "people of the Book" was tantamount to liberation.

The decline of Zoroastrianism in the face of the advent of Islam was by no means a rapid nor an altogether peaceful process. Interfaith strife and competition over local authority and resources persisted into Buyid times, and as late as the end of the tenth century an unsuccessful uprising of Zoroastrians took place in Shiraz. Although urban Zoroastrianism had declined at the close of the tenth century, attacks on Muslims on their way to worship were apparently still quite frequent in some provinces, and religious riots occurred constantly. The Muslims—Arabs as well as Iranian converts—usually emerged victorious from such confrontations due to their increasing numbers, bolstered both by conversion of Iranians as well as immigration of Arabs into Iran.

The rivalry between Zoroastrians and Muslims found expression not solely in riots and skirmishes. The two segments of the population also competed over economic assets, specifically the trade between China and Iran via Central Asia. On the other hand, some Arab immigrants joined existing trade networks, a cooperation that resulted in an increase of overland trade.

The degree of either cooperation or enmity between the two communities depended to a large extent on the way the conquest of each particular area or province had unfolded. The provinces in Iraq, Khuzistan, Azerbaijan, and Sistan, for example, had surrendered to the Arab invaders after comparatively few battles. In the absence of memories of prolonged and bloody conflict, amicable relations were more readily forged. In these areas, where Arabs and Iranians even stood together against outside aggressors like Turks and Mongols, the Muslim colonizers encountered a more fertile climate for their efforts toward religious conversion, which subsequently took place in a comparatively peaceful manner.

Urban strongholds central to Zoroastrian power, in which had to be conquered in protracted battles under immense bloodshed, were far less welcoming to the invaders, who in turn employed draconian measures to ensure their dominance. The resulting atmosphere in such locales was consequently characterized by mutual resentment, distrust, and general tension, a state of affairs that was ameliorated only with great hesitation. Finally, there were areas where hostility and active conflict persisted long after Arab settlements had been established. In the Transoxanian and Caspian regions, constant military confrontations between Iranian lords and Arab generals precluded coexistence, cooperation, and peaceful conversion longer than anywhere else in Iran. But ultimately, all efforts to oust the Arabs failed. The late Sassanian Empire had not fostered a society that stood united behind its ruling and priestly classes. After its fall, Zoroastrian leaders attempting to rally military opposition against the Arab conquest could summon neither the trust nor the support of the masses required for such undertakings.

See also **Islam and Other Religions; Minorities: Dhimmis.**

## BIBLIOGRAPHY

Boyce, Mary. *Zoroastrians: Their Religious Beliefs and Practices.* London and Boston: Routledge & Kegan Paul, 1979.

Choksy, Jamsheed K. *Conflict and Cooperation: Zoroastrian Subalterns and Muslim Elites in Medieval Iranian Society.* New York: Columbia University Press, 1997.

Frye, Richard Nelson, ed. *The Cambridge History of Iran*, Vol. 4: *The Period from the Arab Invasion to the Saljuqs.* Cambridge, U.K.: Cambridge University Press, 1975.

Tabari, Abu Jaʾfar Muhammad b. Jarir al-. *The History of al-Tabari (Taʾrikh al-rusul waʾl-muluk)*, Vol. 14: *The Conquest of Iran.* Translated by G. Rex Smith. Albany: State University of New York Press, 1994.

*Henning L. Bauer*

## TIMURID

The Timurid Empire was a powerful, conquest-driven empire that devolved into disunited dynasties more noted for artistic than political endeavors. Tamerlane (Timur Lang) (1336–1405) was not a Mongol but emerged out of the chaos of post-Mongol Turkistan. He was born on 8 April 1336 at Khwarju Ilghar, just south of Samarkand near Shahr-e Sabz. Although his people (Turks), the various lineages of the Barlas, lived a pastoral life and became nomads, they existed in close proximity to sedentary people and sedentary culture, even while antagonistic to it. Thus, like Genghis Khan (r. 1206–1227), Tamerlane was the product of a mixed environment and was not a man of the deep steppe. The political system that he later employed to rule his empire was also mixed. It continued the Chaghatay *ulus* tradition of a strict separation between sedentary and nomadic sectors, with the sedentary world (the tax base) protected from destructive nomadic incursions to the greatest degree possible and ruled, not by tribal chieftains, who were simultaneously commanders of tribally based military forces, but by local administrators, bureaucrats appointed for set periods of time.

Their methods were primarily rooted in Iranian techniques, including largely Iranian and not Mongolian methods of taxation. By the fourteenth century, to be sure, the two sides of the former Chaghatay domains had begun to interpenetrate, Tamerlane was himself a reflection of the type of changes going on, and much of the formerly nomadic aristocracy had moved into the cities that they ruled, even if indirectly. Nonetheless, they remained culturally and physically quite distinctive and a class apart from their subjects, even the assimilated Turkic ones. One major way in which the nomadic side of Timurid domains differed from the sedentary was in the nomadic tradition that treated land as a collective possession, belonging to an entire tribe, and not to individuals, institutions, or the state, as was the case in sedentary areas. This made groups, and not territory, the key organizational element for the nomadic sector, as had been the case under the Mongols.

Tamerlane's early life and career is obscure and surrounded by legend, but it is clear that he showed military talents at an early stage of his life and the kind of charisma necessary to acquire a following. He gained power first within his own Barlas people and then, in a manner typical of the steppe-based societies of the era, carefully began to make allies outside it. The most important of these allies was Amir Husayn of the Qaraʾunas, descendants of a nomadic garrison, or *tanma*, placed by the Mongols in Afghanistan during the early thirteenth century. Unlike Tamerlane, or Amir Temür, as he was then known, Amir Husayn was an important part of the Chaghatay political establishment of the area, offering a legitimacy much sought by Tamerlane.

Ultimately, Tamerlane and Amir Husayn, after back and forth relationships, had a falling out. Husayn was killed by Tamerlane, who now became the effective ruler of Chaghatay domains, although not its actual ruler since Tamerlane maintained the fiction of a ruling khan (*qan*) of the line of Genghis Khan to the end. As Tamerlane was only associated with it by marriage, as a *guregen*, or imperial son-in-law, he did not qualify for this office. Tamerlane received a formal coronation at Balkh on 9 April 1360.

Tamerlane spent the remainder of his life warring against his enemies, conquering and reconquering territories, all the while building up and beautifying his capital of Samarkand. The major campaigns were into Khwarazm in 1371, into the Semiryechye and beyond from 1375–1377, into Iran and Afghanistan from 1381–1384, and into the Caucasus and Iran from 1386–1388. He undertook two campaigns into the Golden Horde, first from 1391–1392, again from 1392–1396. Next, he brought war against Delhi between 1398 and 1399, and into Anatolia and Syria between 1399 and 1404. At the time of his death, Tamerlane was preparing to attack China. His military strategy was based on the use of steppe archers to the maximum extent, except that by this time these were no longer the lightly armed force of the Mongolian empire, and siege trains and other special forces were a regular part of his armies which, nonetheless, remained highly mobile.

Like Genghis Khan and other Mongol rulers, Tamerlane used terror as a weapon, systematically massacring his enemies in hideous ways, and in terms of numbers of victims he outdid the Mongols. His most enduring military accomplishments were his utter defeat of Golden Horde forces under Toqtamysh (r. 1377–1395) on the Terek River on 14 April 1395, from which the Golden Horde never recovered, and his defeat of the powerful Ottoman sultan Bayezid I (r. 1389–1402) in the Battle of Ankara on 28 July 1402, an event which considerably slowed development of the Ottoman empire. It was not during these campaigns but during his youthful fights for survival that Tamerlane sustained the wound that provided him the Persian nickname, Temur-e lang, "lame Temur," from which our own name for him originated.

After his death, Tamerlane's empire fell apart quickly and his primary successors, Shahrukh (r. 1404–1447) and Khalil-Sultan (r. 1404–1409), controlled no more than a small portion of its original territory. Later this shrinking realm was subdivided even further. Nonetheless, despite the growing political impotence of the Timurids, whose rule was finally extinguished in the early sixteenth century, Herat and other centers of Timurid power in Transoxiana witnessed an unparalleled cultural development. This was the era of some of the finest books ever produced in the Islamic world, and during this time the already substantial architectural achievements of Tamerlane's own reign (his mausoleum in Samarkand and the classic shrine of Ahmad Yasavi in Turkistan City) were further enhanced with such marvels as the Registan in Samarkand. This is a planned complex, one of the earliest of its kind in the Islamic world. It focuses on a central square and

was once comprised of a mosque, a caravansary, and a *khanaqa* (Sufi convent), in addition to the madrasa of Ulugh Beg ibn Shahrukh (1394–1449), grandson of Tamerlane, who was responsible for the other buildings, too. With Tamerlane's mausoleum, Gur-e Amir, the complex celebrates not only the power and glory of the Timurid ruler, but also the artistic fusion achieved under Chaghatay and other Mongol rulers. The colored tiles that are characteristic of the architecture of the time are directly derived from Chinese blue-and-white porcelain that itself represented a response to the tastes of the Mongol world conquerors.

The late Timurid period was also the time of the great wazir, 'Ali-Sher Nawa'i (1441–1501), who single-handedly turned Chaghatay Turkic into a literary language. A minor Timurid prince, Babur (r. 1483–1530), conquered India, and his descendants, the moguls of India, carried on the Timurid tradition, including the Caghatay language, which persisted in India until the 1920s, and Central Asian cuisine, which still survives.

*See also* **Political Organization; Sultanates: Delhi;**

## BIBLIOGRAPHY

Buell, Paul D. *An Historical Dictionary of the Mongol World Empire*. Lanham, Md., and London: The Scarecrow Press, 2003.

Carswell, John. *Blue & White, Chinese Porcelain Around the World*. Chicago: Art Media Resources, 2002.

Jackson, Peter, and Lockhart, Laurence. *The Cambridge History of Iran*, Vol. 6, *The Timurid and Safavid Periods*. Cambridge, U.K.: Cambridge University Press, 1986.

Lentz, Thomas W., and Lowry, Glenn D., eds. *Timur and the Princely Vision: Persian Art and Culture in the Fifteenth Century*. Los Angeles: Los Angeles County Museum of Art, Arthur M. Sackler Gallery, 1989.

Manz, Beatrice Forbes. *The Rise and Rule of Tamerlane*. Cambridge, U.K.: Cambridge University Press, 1989.

*Paul D. Buell*

## UMAYYAD

The Umayyad dynasty ruled the early Muslim community from 661 to 750 C.E. The Umayyad Empire had its capital in Damascus and was supported through the military strength of Syrian troops. It was characterized by a continuous effort at territorial expansion of the Islamic empire, reaching its apogee in the early eighth century. The territorial growth of the empire set into motion processes of Arabization and Islamization that would shape the culture of the region. Umayyad overexertion of military forces in the continuation of expansionist efforts, together with an unequal treatment of Arab and non-Arab Muslims, and problems of religious and political legitimacy contributed to the weakening of the Umayyad dynasty and its eventual downfall.

Muslim historiographical sources generally portray the Umayyads in a negative light, accusing not only the Umayyad caliphs, but also their ancestors and relatives, of all kinds of moral failings and un-Islamic behaviors. Much of this criticism needs to be sifted carefully for anti-Umayyad biases, as most of the available Muslim sources have been penned in late Umayyad and early Abbasid times, when anti-Umayyad sentiments were extensive, particularly among the emerging religious class that left its imprint on many of the literary sources at our disposal.

Mu'awiya b. Abu Sufyan, whose caliphate marks the beginning of the Umayyad dynasty, was appointed the governor of Syria under caliph 'Umar b. al-Khattab (r. 634–644 C.E.). During the first Civil War (656–661 C.E.) the third caliph, 'Uthman b. al-'Affan (r. 644–656) had been assassinated by discontented elements in the growing Muslim empire. Mu'awiya, his relative, challenged the authority of 'Uthman's successor, 'Ali b. Abi Talib (r. 656–661) purportedly because the latter did not prosecute the murders of 'Uthman. While Mu'awiya's direct challenge to 'Ali at the battle of Siffin (657) ended in a stalemate, 'Ali's assassination by a Kharijite (separatist) in 661 effectively put Mu'awiya in power. During Mu'awiya's long reign, from 661 to 680, a relative calm returned to the Muslim empire, as Mu'awiya successfully kept discontented elements in check. The relative stability of the empire allowed Mu'awiya to reinvigorate the expansionist warfare of the earlier caliphs. Yet the issues that had led to the First Civil War, namely a different understanding of legitimate leadership of the Muslim community, continued to plague the Muslim community. Upon Mu'awiya's death in 680 C.E., his son Yazid, designated heir apparent, faced revolts by Husayn b. 'Ali b. Abi Talib, grandson of the prophet Muhammad, and 'Abdallah b. al-Zubayr, son of a prominent companion of Muhammad. Disorganization and woefully inadequate military support for Husayn brought about his quick defeat and death at the Battle of Karbala in 680 C.E. Yet while Yazid's military success against Husayn was swift, the ideological repercussions of the Battle of Karbala would come to haunt Umayyad ambitions for political legitimacy for centuries. Husayn's martyrdom at Karbala became a powerful symbol for Shi'ite aspirations.

With the death of Mu'awiya b. Yazid in 683 C.E., Umayyad control of the empire suffered a nearly total collapse during the Second Civil War (683–692), until Marwan b. al-Hakam assumed the caliphate, inaugurating the Marwanid lineage. Marwan, and later his son 'Abd al-Malik, gradually restored Umayyad control of the empire, defeating a number of opponents in different parts of the empire. 'Abd al-Malik reestablished full Umayyad control in 692 C.E., when he defeated counter-caliph 'Abdallah b. al Zubayr after a siege on Mecca that had led to a fire, destroying part of the Ka'ba. The siege itself and the damage done to the Ka'ba reinforced criticism against the Umayyads as irreligious usurpers of

**Umayyad Caliphs**

**SUFYANIDS**

| | |
|---|---|
| Mu'awiya b. Abu Sufyan | 661–680 C.E. |
| Yazid b. Mu'awiyah | 680–683 C.E. |
| Mu'awiyah b. Yazid | 683 C.E. |

**MARWANIDS**

| | |
|---|---|
| Marwan b. al-Hakam | 684-685 C.E. |
| 'Abd al-Malik b. Marwan | 685–705 C.E. |
| al-Walid b. 'Abd al-Malik | 705–715 C.E. |
| Sulayman b. 'Abd al-Malik | 715–717 C.E. |
| 'Umar b. 'Abd al'Aziz | 717–720 C.E. |
| Yazid b. 'Abd al-Malik | 720–724 C.E. |
| Hisham b. 'Abd al-Malik | 724–743 C.E. |
| al-Walid b. Yazid | 743–744 C.E. |
| Yazid b. al-Walid | 744 C.E. |
| Ibrahim b. al-Walid | 744 C.E. |
| Marwan b. Muhammad | 744–750 C.E |

An illustration of the two caliphate families of the Umayyad dynasty.

power. 'Abd al-Malik also began the process of making Arabic the lingua franca of the empire, and he built the Dome of the Rock in Jerusalem.

After the Second Civil War between the Umayyad forces and the nascent Shi'a, a new phase of imperial extension was inaugurated. Of particular importance were annual raids against the Byzantine Empire, including further attempts to conquer its capital, Constantinople (716–717). Additionally, successes in North Africa led to a defeat of the last remaining Byzantine outposts. With the conversion of Berber tribes of North Africa, the conquest forces were reinvigorated, leading to the crossing of the straits of Gibraltar in 711 and a vanquishing of the Visigothic kingdom of the Iberian peninsula. After the overthrow of the Umayyad dynasty in the Muslim heartlands by the Abbasids in 750, a descendant of the Umayyads would find refuge in Muslim Spain where an Umayyad kingdom and later caliphate was founded, lasting until 1031. The eastward expansion of the empire in the early eighth century included successful conquests into Transoxania and Sind.

Yet the increase of military failures on the frontiers in the second quarter of the eighth century, coupled with growing tensions among different tribal factions in the Syrian army (which had provided the main support for Umayyad power), and growing unrest among different groups of "piety-minded" opponents led to a weakening of Umayyad strength and its final demise. A carefully organized underground movement, coordinated by the Abbasid agitator Abu Muslim in the eastern province of Khurasan garnered support among various groups in opposition to the Umayyads. The Abbasids's initial claim to rally troops against the Umayyads in favor of the family of Muhammad particularly appealed to Shi'a. Only after the Umayyads had been decisively defeated did the

Abbasids reveal their claim to the caliphate, centering its claims to legitimacy on descent from Muhammad's paternal uncle al-'Abbas.

The geographical spread of the Islamic empire did not directly correlate with the spread of Islam as a religion among the inhabitants of conquered territories. Indeed, during much of the Umayyad caliphate Islam as a religious tradition was in a state of flux and only gradually assumed more identifiable contours. Forced conversion of local populations was rare; conquered peoples usually continued to practice their religious traditions, and Islamization of these territories spanned several centuries. In addition to a gradual spread of Islam among the conquered peoples, Muslim traders and pious preachers spread Islam as a religion beyond the borders of the conquered territories. Likewise, Arabization in the newly conquered territories was a slow process; Arabic as the official language of Umayyad administration seems not to have been prevalent before 700, and specifically Muslim coinage does not seem to have been in use before the end of the seventh century.

The major contribution of the Umayyads to Islamdom consists not only in their military successes, its Islamization and Arabization, but also in its support for the development of Islam as a religious tradition. In spite of the negative attitude in which later sources portray the Umayyads, the first collections of sayings of Muhammad and of early Muslim historiography were undertaken with some support of the Umayyads; likewise, Umayyad patronage in religious buildings produced a first, identifiable Islamic architecture in buildings like the Dome of the Rock in Jerusalem and the Umayyad mosque of Damascus.

*See also* **Arabic Language; Arabic Literature; Dome of the Rock; Empires: Abbasid; Empires: Byzantine; Husayn; Islam and Islamic; Karbala; Kharijites, Khawarij; Marwan; Mu'awiya; 'Umar.**

## BIBLIOGRAPHY

Blankinship, Khalid Yahya. *The End of the Jihad State. The Reign of Hisham Ibn 'Abd al-Malik and the Collapse of the Umayyads.* Albany: State University of New York Press, 1994.

Hawting, G. R. *The First Dynasty of Islam. The Umayyad Caliphate AD 661–750.* London and New York: Routledge, 2000.

Hodgson, Marshall G. S. *The Venture of Islam*, Vol. 1: *The Classical Age.* Chicago: The University of Chicago Press, 1977.

Wellhausen, Julius. *The Arab Kingdom and Its Fall.* 1927. Translated by Margaret Graham Weir. Edited by A. H. Harley. Reprint, London: Curzon Press, 1973.

*Alfons H. Teipen*

# ERBAKAN, NECMEDDIN (1926–)

Necmeddin Erbakan served as Turkey's prime minister (1996–1997) and was the founder of the Welfare Party (Refah Partisi). A mechanical engineer, university professor, diesel factory founder, and Union of Chambers of Commerce and Industry president, he was elected to Parliament in 1969 as a spokesman for small business.

Erbakan started the National Order Party (Milli Nizam Partisi) in 1970, which was banned after the 1971 military coup. As founder of the National Salvation Party (Milli Selâmet Partisi, 1972) he became deputy premier. After the 1980 coup this party also was banned and Erbakan ousted from politics. Erbakan's third party, the Welfare Party (formed in 1983), which opposed corruption and demanded a pro-Islamic, anti-Western foreign policy, received 21 percent of the vote in 1996. Erbakan headed a coalition government with Tansu Çiller of the True Path Party.

As prime minister Erbakan became more moderate, improving Turkey's Mideast relations while maintaining its Western alliances. Domestically, he raised civil service salaries and cleaned up the cities. He could not halt corruption, however; coalition partners as well as opponents were involved.

Pressure from the military, alarmed by Islamism, forced Erbakan's resignation (1997) and the party's closure (1998). He was imprisoned for a year for "inciting hatred," though supporters considered him a fighter for religious freedom. After his ouster, Erbakan unofficially backed a successor party, Virtue (Fazilet), which disavowed radical Islamism.

*See also* **Modernization, Political: Participation, Political Movements, and Parties; Political Islam.**

## BIBLIOGRAPHY

Howe, Marvine. *Turkey Today: A Nation Divided over Islam's Revival.* Boulder, Colo.: Westview Press, 2000.

Zurcher, Erik J. *Turkey: A Modern History.* London and New York: I. B. Tauris, 1993.

*Linda T. Darling*

# ETHICS AND SOCIAL ISSUES

It is important to distinguish how the term ethics was used in premodern Islam compared to its usage in the modern period. In the premodern period, ethics was chiefly concerned about the formation and disciplining of the self through the cultivation of practices that were deemed "good conduct." Such conduct was naturalized through education, ritual, and disciplinary practices that were intended to help the devout Muslim internalize the values that underlay an ethical life.

In the modern Muslim context, by contrast, matters such as education, ritual, and disciplinary practices have themselves undergone a significant, if not radical, change from previous eras. The modern period is governed by the logic of systems, bureaucratic processes, and the logic of abstraction. Education in particular, but ritual, and other social practices too, have felt the influences of bureaucratic modernity. Now ethics is conceived of as a set of abstract values, derived from sources that do not always completely resonate with the historical self, given the massive global transformations of cultures and values. Although the earlier understandings of and approaches to ethics are only partly adhered to, Muslim communities are forging new ethical identities in the maelstrom of paradigmatic transitions in knowledge, culture, and history.

## Terms and Historical Developments

Ethics in premodern Muslim thought finds its expression around concepts such as character (*khuluq*) and in the literary genre of civility or etiquette (*adab*). Historically, Muslim ethics draws from several cultural sources: the pre-Islamic ethical traditions of Arabia and the Arab-Islamic tradition followed by cross-pollination with the practices of neighboring cultures, such as Persianate, Greek, and Indian philosophical and ethical traditions, in addition to mystical (sufi) sources all of which no doubt left their marks on the face of Muslim ethics.

Within the first three centuries of several Islamicate cultures of the Near East, several ethical traditions arose. The two principal genres of early ethical writing were pietist (or mystical) and philosophical. The earliest texts are primarily concerned with the ethics of the self, especially with the disciplining of the body and soul. The literary genre of *'ilm al-akhlaq*, literally meaning "the science of innate dispositions" and the emergence of the discourses of civility, urbanity, or *humanitas*, called *adab* are among the most prominent contexts in which ethical debates were set forth. In fact, materials in the form of prophetic reports (hadith) make up the bulk of what we consider to be the "science of innate dispositions."

Normative discourses about morality can be found in both the hadith literature and in the Qur'an. There is a famous report in which 'A'isha describes her husband, the prophet Muhammad, as the embodiment of Islamic values, saying that his character mirrors the Qur'an. In this pithy statement, the linkage between the Qur'an and ethical values cannot be ignored. In short, the expression suggests that the prophet Muhammad had internalized the virtues proposed in the Scripture. In fact, the Qur'an, addressing the prophet Muhammad, says: "Indeed you [Muhammad] have been endowed with a noble character." (68:4) Here the word *khuluq* (character) assumes extraordinary emphasis.

Innumerable reports attributed to the Prophet place special value and emphasis on the need to cultivate good character, *husn al-khulq*. The phrase also has an aesthetic quality of beauty (*husn*) to it. In other words, character is related to an inner magnificence. In fact, numerous hadith stress that the perfection of character is equal to the perfection of faith. In some hadith, good character is described as half of faith. Similarly, good character was viewed as the most effective antidote to the human predisposition to commit sins. In early Islam, as today, moral education is the primary responsibility of parents and teachers, who should not only transmit moral knowledge, but also supervise its application through practice, discipline, and training.

## The Pietists and the Philosophers

The early Muslim ethicists differentiated between the etiquette of the self (*adab al-nafs*) and the etiquette of pedagogy (*adab al-dars*). 'Abd al-Nabi al-Ahmadnagri (d. 1769), the Indian encyclopedist, describes the etiquette of the self as being designed to protect the limbs as well as religious symbols from harm: Implicitly this invokes the obligation not to inflict harm intentionally (the ethical principle of nonmaleficence). Ideally, through regular practice, this etiquette should become internalized by the practitioner, becoming a part of his or her very disposition, or personality. The ethics of learning, on the other hand, relate to the production of knowledge, especially to questions of language and epistemology. Here the concern is to figure how knowledge is constituted and the manner in which its authority is implemented. Knowledge is deemed to be highly beneficial and almost intrinsically to contribute to the welfare of the self and others, and invokes the active ethical principle of beneficence. Almost all the early Muslim sources discuss prescriptive norms that relate in some way to aspects of nonmaleficence and the promotion of beneficence, among other principles.

A more formal discipline of the "science of ethics" took shape under the influence of philosophical writers like Miskawayh (d. 1030), Abu Hayyan al-Tawhidi (d. 1023), and Abu 'l-Hassan al-Amiri (d. 992), among others. These writers expanded the sphere of ethics, developing new meanings within a primarily Persianate environment but in conversation with other regional intellectual traditions. Many of these teachings were intended as moral pedagogy for the young, for bureaucrats, and also for the ruler's entourage and his *aides de camp*. In time, more specialized forms of political ethics were developed as part of the *nasiha* or advice-genre, offered in the form of "mirrors for princes." The philosophical writers also contributed to a marked growth in moral pedagogy, in the form of the *adab* genre.

Even among the early Muslim pietists the cultivation of character and the disciplining of the self is a preeminent concern. Through pious acts and obedience to the norms were said to be derived from revelation (*shari'a*) the individual was thought to be able to develop an inner disposition that compares favorably to a notion of conscience. Figures like Harith al-Muhasibi (d. 857), Raghib al-Isfahani (d. ca. 1108), and Abu Hamid al-Ghazali (d. 1111) produced extensive and detailed treatises and manuals dealing with topics that address intentionality, the cultivation of virtuous habits, good character, and how to perfect practices that lead to salvation. Each of these texts specified how a novice in the path of piety could attain sanctity for ethical ends by giving attention to practices. Readers were taught how to undertake a moral self-evaluation in order to identify character flaws, and were also taught how to remedy such ills.

Often the remedial path advocated a conscientious approach to rituals and practices prescribed by legal discourses, both those of the *shari'a* and those embodied in the legal regulations called *fiqh*. The fulcrum of Muslim ethics is ideally expressed in the practical applications of the law at the most public level.

Nonetheless, the ethics practiced by both the mystics and philosophers is highly specialized, with its own rarified vocabulary that was aimed at serving a certain elite and educated strata of Muslim societies. No less an authority than the intellectual historian 'Abd al-Rahman Ibn Khaldun (d. 1406) noted the difference in the perspectives on the *shari'a* held by jurists (*fuqaha*) and juriconsults (*ahl-futya*) on the one hand, and the mystics and ascetics on the other. While the former advocated the general rules for devotional practices, social transactions, and customs, the latter provided the etiquette of practice, relying on intuitive cognition or aesthetic sensibility (*dhawq*) informed by ascetic practices (*mujahada*) and self-examination (*muhasaba*).

### The Influence of al-Ghazali

In the twelfth century, Abu Hamid al-Ghazali combined the methods of both the jurists and the mystics. He grew dissatisfied with the popular understanding of law, *fiqh*, and with what he believed to be the ultimate perversion of the law: reductionism, hairsplitting, specialization, and arcane debates. Al-Ghazali admonished that legal debates about marriage, divorce, the manumission of slaves, or the execution of sales and contracts do not result in reverential fear and awe of the divine; in fact they result in the opposite. He argued for the need to retrieve the meaning of *fiqh* from its earliest usage, when it meant "the path of salvation in the afterlife."

In order to restore *fiqh* to its former meaning, Al-Ghazali believed that a deep knowledge of the tribulations of the soul and what constitutes morally detrimental acts was required, rather than a familiarity with the minutiae of the law. He called for *fiqh al-nafs* (discernment of the soul), a form of inner enlightenment. He believed that a proper understanding of *fiqh* should inspire awe of the divine within the heart and soul of the practitioner. Ghazali explicitly stated that *fiqh* primarily signifies the requisites of faith, and least of all was concerned with the dictates of jurisprudence (*fatwa*, pl. *fatawa*).

Later on, the martyred jurist-mystic, Ayn al-Qudat al-Hamadhani (d. 1131) considered the necessity of relying on the dictates of the heart, *fatwa al-qalb*. For him there was no doubt that the heart was the seat of conscience, basing his position on a report attributed to the Prophet, which says: "Solicit a response (*fatwa*) from your heart, even though the jurisconsult (*mufti*) had issued a response (*fatwa*)." This caution places the ultimate ethical responsibility on the individual, and detracts from the expert knowledge of the legal specialist. In short, for al-Hamadhani, *fiqh* was the medieval homology for what today is called applied ethics.

### The Changing Concept of *Fiqh*

In seeking to identify broad historical trends in Muslim thought on the subject of ethics, Ibn Khaldun provides a valuable starting point. He argued that *fiqh*, as practiced within its original Arabic linguistic habitat, was an embodied disposition and aptitude (*jibilla wa malaka*). The idea of *malaka* can be understood as something akin to a sociobiological disposition or aptitude, rather than a purely biological or psychological one. In this sense it has a strong resemblance to what Marcell Mauss calls a *habitus*. Ibn Khaldun argued that the concept of *malaka* was subject to cultural erosion as Islam expanded into other cultural and linguistic traditions. In these new contexts, the need arose to theorize about and develop rules and principles of the Arabic language, law and legal theory, and other disciplines. With this development, concepts such as *malaka* underwent alteration. This altered state of cultural and ethical subjectivities led to the development of what Ghazali would denounce as the soulless formalism of *fiqh*, deprived of its ethical and moral purposes.

Despite the efforts of people like al-Ghazali, the bulk of Muslim jurisprudence developed along very formalistic lines, and the ethical stress within law (*fiqh*) in the end gave way to legalism. By the twelfth century, the line was clearly drawn between those who held that *fiqh* was part of the development of the self and those who saw it as part of a a formal legal edifice. If formal jurisprudence during this period retained certain ethical concerns, these are most likely traces of previous understandings of ethics, rather than the product of a lively contemporaneous ethics in conversation with the immediate society in which the law is practiced.

To be fair, some jurists, other than the mystics, did attempt to engage *fiqh* in a dialog with moral and ethical objectives. In order to highlight the ethical strains implicit in the law, some jurists began to emphasize the role of public interest (*maslaha*) by elaborating its ethical purposes (*maqasid*), such as in the protection and advancement of religion, life, reason, wealth, and paternity or family. This method, popularized by the work of scholars like al-Ghazali, Najm al-Din al-Tufi (d. 1316), 'Izz al-Din Ibn 'Abd al-Salam al-Sulami (d. 1262), Abu Ishaq al-Shatibi (d.1388), and Ibn Qayyim al-Jawziyya (d. 1350), enjoyed only limited success. It is no coincidence that several of these jurists also adhered to certain mystical traditions.

In fact, in order to reinvigorate the law with an ethical component, many modern-day Muslim jurists have also taken recourse to the doctrines of public interest and the objectives of the law. In fact, much of contemporary jurisprudence and ethics is indebted to this method, but it has met with mixed outcomes. A brief recapitulation of some of these efforts as applied to major issues of the day may shed light on the developments in modern Muslim ethics and the way they relate to the inherited tradition.

## The Ethos of Killing

The unlawful killing of a human being is categorically forbidden in Islamic law and ethics, and deemed as a major sin. Both the Qur'an and hadith sources, as interpreted by the jurists, view life as sacrosanct. The preservation of life is one of the moral objectives of the law and intrinsic to human dignity. Life can only be taken as part of a just recompense for the crime of murder and for defensive purposes such as war and restoring order during chaos. The noted hadith scholar, Muhammad b. Ahmad al-Dhahabi (d. 1348), however, made an interesting point about the legitimate amount of force that is allowed to be used in self-defense. In self-defense against seditious rebels, he argued, the goal is not to kill them, unless of course one's life is endangered. To kill without need is to revert to a state of spiritual infidelity, according to a hadith attributed to the Prophet. Whoever kills without a just cause carries the burden of killing all of humanity; and whoever saves a life, it is as if the whole of humanity had been rescued, according to the Qur'an (5:32).

Some classical jurists, motivated by an exclusivist and triumphalist ethos, have interpreted these and other Qur'anic teachings to forbid the compensatory execution of a Muslim for killing a non-Muslim or a slave. More egalitarian countervailing viewpoints have discredited this view. Nonetheless, the abolition of the death penalty is not widely advocated in contemporary Muslim societies. Even though the modern state now implements secular criminal codes, in classical Islamic law the right to seek redress in cases of murder belongs to the family of the deceased. The family of the deceased has the right to choose from several options: they might seek material compensation for their loss, they may call for the execution of the offender, or they may even pardon the offender. In other words, the death penalty is not a mandatory requirement in terms of Islamic law. However, some theologians of the classical period viewed the mere desire to be an abolitionist as a doctrinal offense.

## The Question of Abortion

Abortion remains a vexing issue in Muslim societies. Most classical Muslim jurists consider a fetus in the first 120 days after conception to be nonviable. However, there is no denial that as the fetus incrementally develops, so too does the complexity of fetal life. This point of view is informed by the theological doctrine that the spirit (ruh) enters the fetus around 120 days (four months) after conception. Those who take a strict position argue that, once the sperm enters the womb, it is destined to produce life, and thus abortion is proscribed. Given the 120-day rule, however, many jurists find it less morally onerous to sanction a justifiable abortion within this period.

The classic precedent for permitting abortion within the first 120 days is the case where a nursing mother falls pregnant. The new pregnancy would stop her from lactating, and the husband may be unable to afford to pay a wet-nurse to breastfeed the infant. When facing two competing harms, it is proposed that one choose the lesser nonmaleficence. In a similar vein, there is almost universal unanimity that if a pregnant woman faces a life-threatening risk, it is permissible to terminate the pregnancy, irrespective of the stage. Preserving the life of the mother takes precedence over the rights of the unborn child.

Muslim ethicists disagree as to what reasons justify termination and, more importantly, how such a determination is to be made. For most jurists, a medical diagnosis that detects a fetus to be severely deformed or defective, carrying a life-threatening hereditary or untreatable disease, or afflicted with a serious handicap is not sufficient grounds for termination. Only the official Egyptian fatwa-body sanctions terminations prior to 120 days in the above-mentioned instances. However, if pregnancy has advanced beyond this period, then termination of such fetuses is not permitted even there. A fetal abnormality that would result in blindness or deafness, for example, is not to be terminated, because the handicap is viewed as tolerable. The Deoband seminary in India only sanctions termination if there is an actual threat to the life of the mother, not on the grounds of a presumed or calculated risk; and fetal defect is not a valid reason to terminate at any stage of pregnancy. Many Muslim jurists are increasingly retreating from the 120-day rule as advances in medical technology provide more visible and definitive evidence of early fetal life.

Abortion for the purpose of family planning or to terminate pregnancies caused by rape or conceived outside wedlock is a controversial topic. Some contemporary jurists permit abortion for family planning purposes within the 120-day period. Ayatullah Fadl Allah of Lebanon is one of the few authorities who permits termination within 120 days, on the grounds that the pregnancy and its consequences will cause an intolerable social hardship for the mother and her family. On the other hand, the mere deformity of a fetus does not constitute grounds for termination, even within the 120-day period. Other scholars counter by arguing that the birth of offspring is predestined and cannot be limited on the grounds of material considerations.

Muslim women in the waiting room of a birth control clinic in Cairo. Abortion is a contentious topic in the Muslim world. © PETER TURNLEY/CORBIS

Mufti Nizam al-Din Azami of the Deoband seminary does not consider pregnancy outside wedlock or one caused by rape to be a valid reason for termination. For him, the sanctity of the new life takes precedence over the autonomy of the pregnant woman and the negative social consequences arising from her added responsibilities. A minority of Egyptian jurists at al-Azhar University also shares this view. However, the highly respected Indian jurist, 'Abd al-Hayy al-Laknawi (d. 1886), argued that it is permissible to terminate a pregnancy conceived outside wedlock, even if there are visible signs of fetal formation, in other words even if the pregnancy has advanced beyond 120 days. He gives greater consideration to the mother's autonomy and the need to liberate a single woman from social stigma and the accompanying reduced life-chances she would encounter if she carried such a pregnancy to term in very unfavorable cultural conditions. A minority of jurists in contemporary India draw on the rationale of al-Laknawi to permit termination for pregnancies caused by rape and sex outside of wedlock.

## Other Reproductive Issues

Ayatollah Fadl Allah has issued several rulings related to modern reproductive technologies, as has the Islamic Fiqh Committee of the Organization of the Islamic Conference (OIC). Artificial insemination from a husband is deemed permissible, while that from any other donor is impermissible. Islamic law insists on legitimate paternity being an essential requirement for reproduction, thus outlawing donor insemination, since the donor and donee are not married. Ayatollah Fadl Allah expresses some concern that a woman seeking artificial insemination, even legitimately, might be guilty of indecent exposure of her body to a male physician during the course of the medical procedure. Such an indecent exposure is legally prohibited, unless an emergency necessitates it. However, it is acceptable for a female physician to look at the body of another female. Mufti Nizam al-Din of India outrightly prohibits artificial insemination, declaring these procedures are contrary to religion and natural law and increase the prospect of dehumanization.

With regard to sperm banks, Ayatollah Fadl Allah discourages the use of a husband's stored sperm after his death, since the marital tie ends with death. However, he states that any child posthumously conceived legitimately belongs to the wife and is to be attributed to the deceased husband, cautiously avoiding the implication that the child may be illegitimate. However, such a child would not be able to inherit from the father's estate, since the fetus was produced after his death. In Egypt the permissibility of such a practice has also been a subject of serious contention.

Ayatollah Fadl Allah permits a female to store her eggs in order to be fertilized later. Fertilized embryos can be used for experimental purposes, he argues, reasoning that such organisms cannot be equated to be a living person, which only occurs at ensoulment around 120 days after conception. He also permits the sale of unfertilized female gametes for experimental purposes, provided that the financial compensation involved covers only the use rights of the gametes; there can not be a monetary value placed on these or any other body parts, per se. He also permits surrogacy, under limited circumstances. Surrogacy is only permissible if the surrogate mother at least temporarily becomes a wife to the man whose sperm fertilized the egg she is carrying to term. Technically, however, the child is attributed to the female whose egg was fertilized, and not to the female who delivers the child. The Ayatollah finds several objections to an argument that allows a mother to act as a surrogate if her daughter is incapable of carrying a pregnancy to term.

### Adoption and Fosterage

A limited form of adoption is permissible in Muslim ethics. This form prevents the adopted child from taking on the fictional identity and paternity of his or her adoptive parents. Forging a fictional identity between persons not related biologically is prohibited according to Muslim ethics. As long as the adopted child knows that he or she has biological parents other than the ones in whose household he or she is being reared, then there can be no ethical reservation to deny such children from enjoying all the care and security of family life within the adoptive family. For Muslim ethicists the concern is that creating identity based on nonbiological grounds increases the risk of biologically related offspring unknowingly marrying each other and violating the incest taboo.

In Islamic law, fosterage is when an infant is nursed by someone other than his or her mother (a wet-nurse). This practice creates the same ethical boundaries between child and nurse that exist between children, their biological parents, and their siblings, particularly as they apply to the incest taboo. If an adopted infant is nursed by an adoptive mother, these same bonds and boundaries are also created. The effect is to prevent biological and adopted siblings from unwittingly marrying each other, since they either share the same person as wet-nurse or biological mother. The permissibility of fosterage has also led to the permissibility of milk-banks, where infants get milk from anonymous donor wet-nurses. Mufti Nizam al-Din also supports the idea of milk-banks, and does not raise concerns about how they may affect the relations among siblings who share a wet-nurse.

### Contraception

Birth control is deemed permissible, provided that the means of contraception are temporary and not irreversible. The most popular premodern means of contraception was by way of coitus interruptus and other forms of prophylactics. Al-Ghazali held that it was permissible for a wife to practice coitus interruptus if she wished to protect her body aesthetically and avoid the changes to her body that accompany pregnancy and child birth. Birth control can also be pursued in order to avoid the burden of material difficulties of providing for a large family. There is almost unanimity that vasectomy and hysterectomy, unless recommended for sound medical reasons, are not permissible, because they result in irreversible change to the body.

Birth control as part of a national family planning programs whereby governments place an upper limit on the permissible size of a family, has often been controversial and bitter in the Muslim world. Some suspect that the Western-controlled transnational institutions wish to use family planning to limit Muslim populations. Another concern is that that birth control measures such as the pill and condoms may increase promiscuity. The controversy remains unresolved. In Egypt, for instance, former al-Azhar shaykh opposed the use of the pill, while another senior official, the state mufti, encouraged its use. With the spread of the HIV/AIDS virus, the opposition to birth control measures has lessened.

### Organ Transplantation and Cloning

Indian and Pakistani authorities have been opposed to organ transplantation from its very inception. Several *fatwa*s, including one issued by Mufti Nizam al-Din, allow organ transplantation only under conditions of emergency. Blood transfusion, too, is only permissible under extreme conditions of necessity. For many traditionalist Muslim ethicists from the Indo-Pak subcontinent, transplantation surgery is an affront to human dignity and to the sanctity of life. However, in recent years there have been attempts to reverse the almost four-decade-old consensus on organ transplantation on the Indian subcontinent. Some scholars in this region have been cautious and have agreed to permit cornea transplantations only.

In the Middle East the ethical committees of several institutions permit both organ transplantation and organ donation. The OIC's Islamic Fiqh Academy recognizes irreversible brain-stem damage as legal death, and permits doctors to harvest organs from victims of such injury for purposes of transplantation. Scholars supporting transplantation believe that this form of medical care advances human dignity, and argue that such measures are taken precisely to promote the sanctity of life.

There is perhaps greater uniformity among the diverse ethics committees in their approach to the subject of reproductive and therapeutic cloning; all express great caution and apprehension. Fears stem from the idea that biogenetic technology can radically transform human identity, undermining if not perverting current moral and ethical practices. For this reason the Islamic Fiqh Academy prohibits all cloning practices that allow a third party to be associated in genetic reproduction between two married persons, whether it is by means of another womb, the provision of third-party gametes, or through the manipulation of animal or human cells. For now all forms of human cloning are banned, but the future may bring exceptions on a case-by-case basis, as knowledge and experience in genetics advance. Although the Academy permits research in animal and plant cloning, it encourages governments to adopt legislative measures to close all the avenues for direct and indirect experimentation in human cloning until substantive knowledge makes it safe. Similarly the Academy has declared a moratorium on genetic engineering and the human genome project until greater clarity is achieved and its ethics committee is in a better position to offer meaningful and practical guidelines.

## Euthanasia

Indian Muslim scholars rule out both active and passive forms of euthanasia. Active forms of euthanasia are a major moral sin and an unthinkable act within Muslim ethics. Mufti Nizam al-Din argues that for terminally ill individuals, suffering has a redemptive quality that should be borne with patience by both the patient and his or her caregivers. Seeking to hasten the death of the terminally ill is tantamount to the abdication of a caregiver's responsibility, and would be deemed both a criminal offense and a major sin. Passive euthanasia on the part of a caregiver would amount to gross negligence, and such deplorable ethical conduct is deserving of disciplinary consequences. For this school of thought there remains an irreconcilable gap between ethical and medical standards of assessing life and death. The Indian ethicists do not accept any standard of death to be conclusive, save for the cardiopulmonary standard (cessation of all heart and lung activity). For medical practitioners, other measurements of ascertaining death, such as brain-stem death, are acceptable.

Some of the scholars of the Islamic Fiqh Academy concur with this cautious view, and oppose such acts of passive euthanasia as taking a patient off life-support or withholding treatment. However, the official resolution of the Islamic Fiqh Academy permits withholding treatment and the removal of life-support machines from patients whose doctors affirm that they have suffered irreversible brain-stem damage.

## Ethics and Sexuality

Homosexuality is strictly forbidden in Muslim ethics, on the grounds that it is an unnatural act. Some jurists suggest severe penalties for homosexuality, ranging from death to flogging, whereas others disagree. The latter group holds that no punishment can serve as an effective purgative for this act, and therefore that its immorality precludes an earthly penalty. Some jurists are so morally offended by homosexuality that even to raise the question of its permissibility is enough to lead to calls for excommunication and anathematizing. However, Muslim ethicists have yet to reach consensus as to whether homosexuality is a socially constructed practice or part of a biological, genetic predisposition. Such an inquiry may prompt a deeper ethical investigation into whether or not persons can be held accountable for responding to their natural proclivities, even if those proclivities may be deemed unnatural by heterosexual standards.

## Ethical Trends for the Future

Over the centuries, Muslim ethics have undergone tremendous change, even though little attention has been paid. In the modern period, new scientific discoveries and technologies have severely challenged the ethical heritage of early Islam. Yet, Muslim ethics remain deeply embedded in the premodern legacy, and little of modern scientific thinking has seeped into ethical discourses in any meaningful way. The cultural, political, and economic encounter with the West continues to elicit great caution from Muslims, especially those within the traditional religious sector, who view the premodern Muslim ethical legacy as a bulwark against external ethical and moral encroachment. Clearly there is very little consensus between various and diverse Muslim religious groups that adhere to diametrically opposed views on ethics. However, the above survey of current ethical issues demonstrates that there are pragmatic approaches to Muslim ethics that seek accommodation with the ethics of modernity. At the same time, there are approaches to ethics that seek to preserve distinctive Muslim subjectivities and identities, finding their best models for such preservation in the historical legacy of ethics in Islam.

*See also* **Fatwa; Futuwwa; Ghazali, al-; Homosexuality; Ibn Khaldun; Law; Shari'a.**

## BIBLIOGRAPHY

Brockopp, Jonathan E., ed. *Islamic Ethics of Life: Abortion, War, and Euthanasia*. Columbia: University of South Carolina Press, 2002.

Hourani, George F. *Reason and Tradition in Islamic Ethics*. Cambridge, U.K.: Cambridge University Press, 1985.

Musallam, B. *Sex and Society in Islam*. Cambridge, U.K.: Cambridge University Press, 1983.

Rispler-Chaim, Vardit. *Islamic Medical Ethics in the Twentieth Century*. Leiden: E. J. Brill, 1993.

Skovgaard-Petersen, Jakob. *Defining Islam for the Egyptian State*. Leiden: E. J. Brill, 1997.

Tahanawi, Muhammad 'Ali. *Mawsu'a-t Kashshaf Istilahat al-Funun*. Edited by Rafiq al-'Ajam, et al. Beirut, Lebanon: Makataba Lubnan, 1996.

Yacoub, Ahmed Abdel Aziz. *The Fiqh of Medicine*. London: Taha Publishers, 2001.

*Ebrahim Moosa*

# ETHIOPIA

Ethiopia was the third political entity to embrace Christianity after the Roman Empire and the Kingdom of Armenia, in 334 C.E. It remained a Christian state, never separating the church from the crown, up to the 1974 revolution. Her long, multifaceted relations with Islam and Muslims can generally be analyzed along two themes. One is the concept of Christian Ethiopia as it has been conceived throughout the ages by Muslim scholars and politicians of the "land of Islam." The other is the role played by Islamic minorities in Ethiopian history. The two aspects, naturally, have developed with dialectical mutuality.

In a way, Ethiopia was the state most affected by Islamic foreign relations. Muhammad's sending of the *sahaba* (Companions) in 615 and 616 to seek asylum with the Christian king of Ethiopia, *al-Najashi* Ashama, was also known as the first *hijra*. The *sahaba* were saved from Meccan persecutors by the Ethiopian king, and this gesture gave birth to a legacy of eternal gratitude. This history was reflected in the hadith whose essential message was "leave the Ethiopians alone as long as they leave you alone." Most orthodox Muslim jurists, scholars, and moderate politicians interpreted this admonition as a declaration that Christian Ethiopia would be a land of neutrality, *dar al-hiyyad*. On the other hand, the same *sahaba-najashi* episode was said to have ended with the *najashi* (king), in 628 C.E., embracing Islam. This assumption of Ethiopian neutrality in religious matters was interpreted differently by more radical Muslims—pointing to Christian Ethiopia's illegitimacy. This principal argument among Muslims over the legitimacy of historical Ethiopia resurfaced whenever Ethiopia became a subject of the radical Muslim agenda, and it remains an active issue today.

Islamic thought concerning Ethiopia was shaped by dynamic cultural, economic, and strategic relations between the Middle East and the Horn of Africa. It has been also influenced by the presence of Islamic communities within Ethiopia. Muslims lived in Ethiopia from the very beginning of Islam, and tradition has it that members of the *sahaba* established the first community there, which was tolerated by the Christians. In time Muslims speaking the Semitic Ethiopian languages (Amharic, Tigrinya, etc.) and living in the core regions were called Jabarties. As Ethiopian Christians looked down upon traders and Muslims were often deprived of landowning, there developed a functional economic coexistence, mixed with some cultural segregation, in the country's central areas. Most Muslims during Ethiopia's history were members of various ethnic-linguistic groups surrounding the Ethiopian core. Peoples like the Oromo, Afar, Sidama, Somali, the various tribal groups of today's Eritrea, and various other groups adopted elements of Islamic culture partly due to the long processes of their confrontations with Ethiopia. In medieval times fourteen Islamic emirates, notably Ifat and Adal, centered on the town of Harar, emerged in what is today southern Ethiopia. Their Islamic history culminated in 1529 when, under the leadership of the imam Ahmad ibn Ibrahim (nicknamed Gran), they united and conquered Christian Ethiopia for a short period lasting to 1543.

Ahmad Gran's short-lived Islamic unification was inspired by the rise of the Ottomans in the Red Sea area and by simultaneous Islamic scholarly revival in the Arab peninsula. Ulema from Arabia helped the process of Islamic unification by spreading Arabic and the teaching of Islamic law. However, after the demise of Gran the various Islamic groups of the whole region failed to reunite. They remain to this day divided along linguistic, ethnic, and regional criteria. Centers of Islamic learning remained in Harar and in some other towns, but most communities followed popular versions of Sufism and adopted just the basic elements of religious education and law. In the eighteenth and nineteenth centuries Islam flourished again when the Oromo clans began abandoning their sociopolitical system to develop a chain of emirates, and when Egypt captured the Sudan and the Red Sea coast and sent learned men to spread Islam from Harar to its surrounding Oromo-inhabited areas and from the Sudan to western Eritrea. However, during the last quarter of the nineteenth century the Christian Ethiopian empire expanded and conquered nearly all Ethiopian territories and the people who lived there. The process of assimilation into the Ethiopian state and society in modern times has been multidimensional. Coercive measures and forced Christianization were applied, for example, by Emperor Yohannes IV (1872–1889). In general, however, Muslims, who numbered about one half of the population during this period, remained free to pursue their ways as long as they accepted Christian political hegemony. Where Islam was politicized, or when Muslims adopted Arab identity—like in Eritrea of the 1960s—the Ethiopian leadership, recalling the history of Ahmad Gran, mobilized to stem it. Under Emperor Haile Selasse (1930–1974) only a few Muslims could be counted among the country's political elite. Yet most Muslims, especially the elite, were integrated into Ethiopian life and culture, used the Amharic Ethiopian language, and went on dominating trade in both the periphery and the center.

In the last quarter of the twentieth century Islam seemed to be experiencing a resurgence in Ethiopia. First, the 1974 revolution and Mangistu Haile-Mariam's communist-inspired regime separated the church from the state. By eroding Christianity, and by recognizing major Islamic holidays as national ones, the new regime helped to grant the two religions more equal national recognition. Then the 1991 revolution reshaped Ethiopia along a decentralized cultural and administrative line, meanwhile fostering a free market economy. The end result was a visible strengthening of Islam in practically all aspects. As more Muslims make their way to the core of Ethiopian life, the new phenomenon underlines an old question—is their advent a contribution to cultural pluralization and economic progress, and is it therefore a major aspect of Ethiopia's modernization? Or, is Islamic revival turning political, gradually reviving those old radical ideas about the need to Islamize Ethiopia?

*See also* **Africa, Islam in; Ahmad Ibn Ibrahim al-Ghazi; Empires: Ottoman.**

## BIBLIOGRAPHY

Ahmed, Hussein. "The Historiography of Islam in Ethiopia." *Journal of Islamic Studies* 3, no. 1 (1992): 15–46.

Erlich, Haggai. *Ethiopia and the Middle East.* Boulder, Colo.: Lynne Rienner Publishers, 1994.

Spencer, J. Trimingham. *Islam in Ethiopia.* Oxford: Oxford University Press, 1952.

*Haggai Erlich*

# ETHNICITY

The Middle East is distinguished by its ethnic and cultural diversity. This diversity, often referred to as a "human mosaic," is the product of long historical processes of which the people themselves are acutely aware. Almost every country in the region has local communities and groups that are distinct from the larger society as a whole and are recognized as such both by themselves and by others. In fact, the recognition and acceptance of communal or ethnic differences has been a basic component of social and political organization in the Middle East. This is best exemplified by the Ottoman *millet* system whereby the ruling Sunni Muslim Ottomans formally recognized the authority of the religious and communal leaders of the different sectarian communities in their empire. By the nineteenth century, the Ottoman list consisted of about seventeen millets, which included Jews, Druze, Alavis, Armenians, and a number of Christian sects. Ethnicity basically refers to a social or group identity that individuals ascribe to themselves and that is accepted by others; ethnic identities are most commonly based on shared religious affiliation, language or dialect, tribal membership, and regional or local customs.

Ethnic identity, which tends to be perceived as immutable and ascribed at birth, is most commonly a cultural construction that, in practice, is both malleable and contextual. Individuals may choose to stress their ethnic identity in one context and mute it in another; thus an individual may claim to be a Kurd, a Muslim, or an Iranian depending on the particular social or political context. In the Middle East, the primary significance of ethnic identity is its role in the social and political structure of the society. Until the mid-1950s, for example, particular ethnic groups tended to be associated with specific occupational niches: the Jews of the Iranian city of Isfahan specialized in fine metal work and trading in gold and silver, Assyrian Christians of Iraq dominated the hotel and restaurant business, Azeri Turks in Iran were car mechanics and long-distance truck drivers, and most of the cooks in Egypt were Nubians. Today this pattern is changing; mass education, social mobility, and the emergence of new occupations have all but eroded the traditional ethnic divisions of labor in the region.

What are the basic sources of ethnic differentiation in the Middle East? The single most important source of individual and group identity and, by extension, social cleavages, is religious affiliation. Coreligionists perceive themselves as having rights and obligations to each other and interfaith marriage is generally discouraged if not strictly prohibited by all the communities. On a larger scale sectarian divisions have important implications for political action. Secular nationalistic movements within any one country or those like pan-Arabism that seek to transcend national frontiers are usually undermined by sectarianism. Likewise, pan-Islamist movements that presume to encompass all Muslims tend to fracture along Muslim sectarian divisions of Sunnis, Shi'a, and Alawis, among others. And while non-Muslim communities like the Jews (until the mid-fifties) and the various Christian sects have, on the whole, accommodated themselves to the dominant Muslim rule throughout the Middle East, questions of what constitutes nationality and full citizenship have yet to be resolved in most of the states in the area. This includes the modern Jewish state of Israel as well as that of the Muslim Wahhabi kingdom of Saudi Arabia.

Ethnicity in the Middle East is also structured along linguistic differences which, in general, set the largest cultural boundaries between groups. There are three major language families in the region: Semitic, Indo-European, and Altaic or Turkic. Arabic and Hebrew are Semitic languages. Hebrew is spoken exclusively in Israel while Arabic, with its many dialects, is the national language of the countries of North Africa, Egypt, Lebanon, Syria, Jordan, Iraq, Saudi Arabia, Yemen, and the Gulf states. Modern Persian and Kurdish are Indo-European languages; Turkish and Azeri belong to the Altaic family of languages. The Berbers of North Africa who, like the Arabs, are Muslims, speak different dialects of Berber, an Afro-Asiatic language and generally refer to themselves as Imazighin (or Imazighen). In countries where large linguistically differentiated populations exist, such as the Kurds of Turkey, Iraq, and Iran and the Berbers of Morocco and Algeria, language assumes a political dimension. National governments tend to strongly promote one national language and may even at times seek to suppress minority languages, as happened in Turkey with Kurdish. To educate their children and to participate fully in the national economy and culture, members of minority ethnic groups must adopt the national language and, to a certain extent, dissociate themselves from their mother tongue.

Of all the elements that may be used to define groups or social categories, phenotypic race or biological variation is the least important in the Middle East, where the vast majority of the people from the west in Morocco to the east in Afghanistan tend to fall within the same racial category often referred to as "Mediterranean." Where a markedly differentiated population exists such as the 'abid or blacks in Saudi Arabia and the Gulf region, the Nubians in Egypt, or the Turkmen of Iran (with their pronounced Mongolian features); such phenotypic differences are locally recognized but are not necessarily associated with an ethnic identity as such. Islam has no racial ideology based on color and, while slavery was practiced throughout the Islamic world, it was not exclusively associated with Africans or any other particular population. The Ottomans recruited slaves from both eastern Europe and the Caucasus and their descendants today do not form either racially or ethnically distinct groups. Outside of a few towns in southern Arabia, slavery in the Middle East was not a primary means of organizing menial labor; as a consequence, the association of class and race or ethnicity and race is not well developed and has no significant implication or social and political organization in the region.

See also **Pluralism: Legal and Ethno-Religious; Tribe.**

### BIBLIOGRAPHY

Banuazizi, Ali, and Weiner, Myron, eds. *The State, Religion, and Ethnic Politics: Afghanistan, Iran, and Pakistan.* Syracuse, N.Y.: Syracuse University Press, 1986.

Bates, Daniel G., and Rassam, Amal. *Peoples and Cultures of the Middle East.* Upper Saddle River, N.J.: Prentice-Hall, Inc., 2001.

Gross, Jo-Ann, ed. *Muslims in Central Asia: Expressions of Identity And Change.* Durham, N.C.: Duke University Press, 1992.

Weekes, Richard V., ed. *Muslim Peoples: A World of Ethnographic Survey.* 2d edition. Westport, Conn.: Greenwood Press, 1984.

*Amal Rassam*

# EUNUCHS

In the Near East, the use of eunuchs to guard rulers' and their families' private quarters dates at least to Achaemenid times. They were certainly employed by the Byzantine and Sassanian empires, which were the early Islamic state's chief models for court culture. Eunuchs were regarded as the most loyal slaves because they were not only separated from their families and territories of origin but robbed of reproductive capability. Hence, their sole loyalty was ostensibly to the ruler who enslaved them, and they had an enormous stake in the continuation of the system in which they were employed.

The earliest mention of eunuchs in Islamic empires dates to the Abbasid era (750–1258 C.E.). In his ninth-century description of Baghdad, al-Ya'qubi notes quarters for African eunuchs in the central square of the original round city. No doubt the most famous eunuch of the Abbasid era is Kefir, the African eunuch who became de facto ruler of Egypt following the death of the last autonomous Ikshidid governor, just before the Fatimid invasion of Egypt in 969. The Fatimids employed eunuchs not only in their palaces but in their armed forces as well. In one confrontation between the Fatimid and Byzantine fleets, the admirals on both sides were eunuchs.

Eunuchs played a number of important roles under the Mamluk sultanate, which ruled Egypt, Syria, and the western Arabian peninsula from 1250 to 1517. The Mamluks imported large numbers of eunuchs from the Caucasus and from India, as well as from Africa. They evidently pioneered the practice of employing eunuchs to guard sultans' tombs in Cairo and, ultimately, to guard the prophet Muhammad's tomb in Medina.

The greatest fund of information about eunuchs under Islamic regimes comes from the Ottoman Empire (1299–1923), which employed eunuchs from the Caucasus and eastern Africa. Because Islamic law forbids enslaving and castrating subjects of a Muslim ruler, castration was typically performed by Christian physicians: Armenians in the Caucasus, Copts in Upper Egypt. Yet evidence exists of castration being performed in the Ottoman palace itself, so the prohibition must at times have been ignored. During the sixteenth and seventeenth centuries, a number of Caucasian eunuchs rose to be grand wazirs or provincial governors. At the same time, both black and white eunuchs served at Topkapi Palace. By 1592, the corps of African eunuchs had acquired a monopoly over the post of chief eunuch of the imperial harem (Darussaade Agasi or Kizlar Agasi), who guarded the residence of the palace women. White eunuchs guarded the "Gate of Felicity" (Babussaade) separating the outer court from the sultan's throne room. The chief black eunuch also supervised the pious foundations (*waqf*, Turk. *vakaf*) endowed to provide services to the poor and to pilgrims to the Holy Cities. Beginning in 1644, the chief black eunuch, on his deposition, was routinely exiled to Egypt, where he cultivated ties of patronage with the provincial grandees.

The last surviving eunuchs under Islamic rule were guards of the Prophet's tomb in Medina, who were pensioned off by the Saudi government in the 1920s.

*See also* **Gender; Harem.**

### BIBLIOGRAPHY

Ayalon, David. *Eunuchs, Caliphs, and Sultans: A Study of Power Relationships.* Jerusalem: Magnes Press, Hebrew University, 1999.

Marmon, Shaun E. *Eunuchs and Sacred Boundaries in Islamic Society.* New York and Oxford, U.K.: Oxford University Press, 1995.

Penzer, Norman M. *The Harem: An Account of the Institution as It Existed in the Palace of the Turkish Sultans, with a History of the Grand Seraglio from Its Foundations to the Present Time* (1936). Reprint. New York: AMS Press, 1974.

*Jane Hathaway*

# EUROPEAN CULTURE AND ISLAM

Since the rise of Islam in the seventh century there has been continuous interaction between Europe and the Islamic world, often with profound implications on either side. Deepest and with greatest effect has been the interaction between Europe and Islam in the Middle East and North Africa, that is, Arab Islam. The new Arab-Islamic state, established in the 640s and 650s, included major areas that had been conquered from the East Roman (Byzantine) empire. Many aspects of Byzantine culture and custom were absorbed into the nascent Islamic culture, including administrative and legal practices. Over a longer term, the Hellenistic philosophical heritage played a major role in the development of Islamic philosophy, and its gnostic tradition in Islamic mysticism. Through both official and unofficial translation projects, major Greek works of philosophy and science became available in Arabic, laying the foundation of a flourishing of the sciences, including mathematics, astronomy, and medicine, in Arabic.

Arab-Islamic civilization in turn made a major contribution to the development of European Christian civilization a few centuries later. The main routes for this transfer were Sicily and Spain. The influence of Islamic art and architecture on the early Renaissance is often quite explicit, as in many of the well-known churches and palaces of Florence and other Italian cities. Likewise, the impact of the Spanish Islamic philosophers, above all Ibn Rushd (Averroes), on Thomas Aquinas, is widely acknowledged. It is also the case that much of the Greek philosophical tradition, in particular that of Aristotle, was for a long time known primarily through the Arabic versions of the texts. It has been suggested that the influence goes much deeper. Especially via the Norman connections, from Sicily to northern France and England, and through Italian networks, the patterns and structures of learning, of the organization of institutions, and of professional development were transmitted from the Mediterranean Islamic world into western Christendom. So it is suggested

that the earliest universities in Europe, such as Bologna, Paris, and Oxford, were founded on Islamic models. Similarly, many of the financial instruments and techniques of long-distance trade, which became so important in the early development of European capitalism, were borrowed from Middle Eastern models. The Crusades, by contrast, appear to have brought into Europe primarily certain military techniques.

Over the following centuries, cultural exchange both ways was diminished. The Ottomans very quickly adopted some of the new military technologies of Europe, especially artillery, while Europe during the eighteenth century developed a fascination with things "oriental" in the arts and crafts. The globalization of European trade combined with the industrial revolution firmly moved the initiative into European hands. At the same time the encounter between Europe and Islam spread beyond the Mediterranean into South and South-East Asia and into sub-Saharan Africa. The imperial expansion was the context for the adoption of "curious" elements of Islamic culture into European culture, but Islamic cultures came under an all-pervading European impact. Initially, this impact was mainly economic. As the industrial revolution gathered pace, so European industrial exports began to replace the products of local craftsmen, and the colonized economies became suppliers of raw materials. Egypt was a good example of this process as it switched its agriculture from producing food to producing raw cotton during the first few decades of the nineteenth century. When Egypt took control of Syria in the 1830s and cut import duties, the finished cotton goods produced in the mills of England from Egyptian cotton replaced the locally produced crafts of the Syrian cities.

But European ideas also started attracting the urban intellectual and professional classes of the Islamic world. Initially the attraction was limited to individuals, but as states began to restructure on European patterns, either because they came under European rule, as in India, Indonesia, or Algeria, or because they sought to meet the European political challenge, as in the Ottoman empire, Egypt, and Persia, they also built up new education systems to produce the kind of manpower they needed. By the end of the nineteenth century there were a number of European-style universities and many more secondary schools. The early attractions of the social and political ideas of the French revolution were supplemented by the end of the nineteenth century by many of the nationalist philosophical ideas that had been developed in Germany. These ideas were being circulated ever more widely among a growing urban middle-class and literate population through newspapers, a new literature of poetry, histories, essays, and political pamphlets.

The early precursors of national movements can be found throughout the Islamic world by the beginning of the twentieth century. Their ideas often combined elements of European ideas with Islamic ones, and many times used Islamic

The Selimiye Camii Mosque sits on a hill in the center of Edirne, Turkey, and dominates the city's skyline. It was completed in 1575 after six years of construction. © Archivo Iconografico, S.A./Corbis

against modernity or withdrawing from participation in it, providing some of the Islamist political movements much of their support. On the other hand, many younger people have started using their newly gained educational resources to challenge the traditions of the older generation. They seek to separate local custom from the core of Islamic expectations and principles, placing themselves on a collision course with many of their parents' generation. A number of Islamic intellectuals have recognized this and have become prominent participants in a rethinking of Islamic law and theology that has a large audience both in Europe and the Islamic world.

*A Seljuk manuscript of Aristotle and students appears in the volume one color insert.*

*See also* **Andalus, al-; Balkans, Islam in the; Europe, Islam in.**

## BIBLIOGRAPHY

Daniel, Norman. *Islam and the West: The Making of an Image.* Oxford, U.K.: One World, 1993.

Haddad, Yvonne Y., ed. *Muslims in the West: From Sojourners to Citizens.* New York: Oxford University Press, 2002.

Makdisi, George. *The Rise of Humanism in Classical Islam and the Christian West.* Edinburgh: Edinburgh University Press, 1990.

Waardenburg, Jacques, ed. *Muslim Perceptions of Other Religions: A Historical Survey.* New York: Oxford University Press, 1999.

*Jorgen S. Nielsen*

terms to express European ideas. During the 1930s, a growing sense of disillusion with European models could be discerned. The European ideas of liberty and democracy were not being extended to the colonies, so many intellectuals began to look for their ideas in Islamic traditions, the most radical formulating explicit and complete rejections of anything European. This trend was strengthened in response to the establishment of Israel in 1948, perceived as an imposed foreign body, and even more so after the Israeli victory in 1967, after which the Islamic trends gradually moved center-stage.

However, throughout the twentieth century the continuing impact of a globalizing economy appeared irresistible. Declining agriculture and the growth of industry and services led to a massive movement of populations from the countryside to the large cities. A small proportion of that movement took the form of migration to European cities. The impact on Islam of this urbanization—and with it the growth of education and literacy—is difficult to underestimate, and the impact is similar whether in Islamic cities or in European cities. The traditional synthesis of Islamic practices and local customs finds it very difficult to function in the modern urban environment. Many have responded to this by rebelling

# EUROPE, ISLAM IN

The main concentrations of Muslim population in Europe today are to be found in Russia (25–30 million), France (4–5 million), Germany (2.5–3 million), Britain (c. 2 million), former Yugoslavia (2–3 million), Albania (3 million), and Bulgaria (c. 1 million). Many of the smaller countries of western Europe are home to several hundred thousand Muslims each.

## History

Almost from the beginning of the history of Islam, there has been a Muslim presence in Europe, first in the form of envoys and traders to the Byzantine empire and soon, as Arab Islam spread across North Africa, into the main trading centers of Mediterranean Europe. The first major arrival of Islam in Europe was a result of the conquest of the Iberian peninsula, which started in 711 C.E. Through settlement and conversion, large Muslim communities became part of the indigenous population of the peninsula. Spanish Muslim intellectuals became significant participants in Arabic and Islamic culture, including most famously Ibn Rushd (Averroes) and Ibn Khaldun. As the Christian kingdoms, led by Castille and Aragon, gradually pushed the borders of Islam southward, so the Muslim population also was pushed south. When the Muslim kingdom of Granada finally fell in 1492, substantial Muslim populations left for North Africa. But many, under the general term Moriscos, remained throughout the region for several generations. For a shorter period Sicily had also fallen under Muslim rule. The conquest was slow, lasting from 827–878, and Muslim control lasted until the Normans conquered the island later in the eleventh century.

While Muslim populations thus disappeared from the European side of the western Mediterranean, the establishment of a continuous Muslim presence in the east had started. In the early thirteenth century the Mongols had spread their power far into Russia. While Genghis Khan's empire did not last long, it left behind a number of Mongol-Tatar successor states that had adopted Islam. The Tatar state of Kazan survived until the 1550s when it was conquered by Russia, while the Crimean Tatars had fallen under Ottoman rule already in 1475. The Muslim populations of these regions stayed and later spread around the Russian empire as soldiers, craftsmen, and traders settling at various times in regions ranging from the Ukraine and Poland to Finland. Here they remained more or less undisturbed until the great forced migration of the Stalinist period of the 1930s and 1940s, when a large proportion, in particular the Crimean Tatars, were transported to Soviet Central Asia.

Founded at the beginning of the fourteenth century in western Anatolia, the Ottoman empire gained its first foothold in the Balkans in 1354 and within ten years had restricted the Byzantine empire to the region around Constantinople (which finally fell to the Ottomans in 1453). The Ottoman armies then proceeded to spread Ottoman rule westward and northward, reaching the gates of Vienna in a failed siege in 1529. Substantial permanent Muslim communities established themselves in the Balkans as a result. In some cases such communities were Turkish immigrants from the east, some arriving voluntarily, others as part of a deliberate Ottoman policy of settlement. Significant numbers of indigenous people of Slavic culture also converted to Islam. The majority of Albanians became Muslim at this time. As the Ottoman empire was gradually pushed out of the Balkans during the nineteenth century, many Muslims also left. The Ottoman defeat in the First World War led to major population exchanges between Greece and Turkey. But the major communities in Bosnia, the Albanians and the Bulgarian Muslims, often called Pomaks, remained as did large numbers of Turks in Bulgaria, smaller numbers in Greek Thrace, and parts of the former Yugoslavia.

## Immigration

On this background the most recent arrival of Muslim communities in Europe is a new departure, since it arises not from Muslim expansion but from European expansion. Today's Muslim communities in western Europe are a consequence primarily of empire. This is most evident in Britain and France. The first major growth came about as a result of the opening of the Suez Canal in 1869, when British shipping from India began taking on Yemeni and Somali labor in Aden. Over the following decades many of these people settled in and around Cardiff, Liverpool, Newcastle, and London. The first mosques in the country were established in Liverpool and the London suburb of Woking already around 1890. Between the two world wars, the London-based elite sought to lay the foundations for a London central mosque. It was only when a plot of land was granted by the king during the Second World War that the project began to move forward, leading to the opening in 1977 of the Islamic mosque and center in Regent's Park.

In France, there was an elite immigration during the nineteenth century, including exiles such as Muhammad 'Abduh and Jamal al-Din al-Afghani. But labor migration also started then, recruiting mainly into the olive oil industry of the south and mining and heavy industry in the northeast. During the First World War large numbers of North Africans were requisitioned into industry and infrastructure works. Recognizing their contribution during the First World War the government sponsored the establishment of a mosque in Paris, opened in 1926. Numbers of migrant workers fell during the recession of the 1930s and reached a low at the end of the Second World War. But migration soon rose again and, despite their active involvement in the Algerian war of independence, the number of Algerians working in France continued to rise.

The other main country of Muslim immigration in Europe during the twentieth century was the Federal Republic of Germany. Its historical proximity to the Ottoman empire meant that there had been for a long time a cosmopolitan Muslim population in the main trading cities and, after the rise of Prussian power, in Berlin. The numbers grew especially after the two empires started drawing closer to each other toward the end of the nineteenth century. The economic ties between them were such that by the outbreak of the First World War they might be termed at least pseudo-colonial. The defeat of both empires in 1918 left only a small Muslim community in Berlin but it did manage to establish a mosque. During the Third Reich, the German armed forces established several units of Muslim troops that had defected from the Soviet army. While some were handed back at the end of the war, many remained in Germany permanently. It also must not be forgotten that in German-speaking Europe, Vienna had for long been the capital of an empire that included significant Muslim populations. In 1878 the Austro-Hungarian empire had occupied the Ottoman regions of Bosnia-Herzegovina. Vienna soon had a resident mufti. In 1909 the state extended official recognition to Islam. During

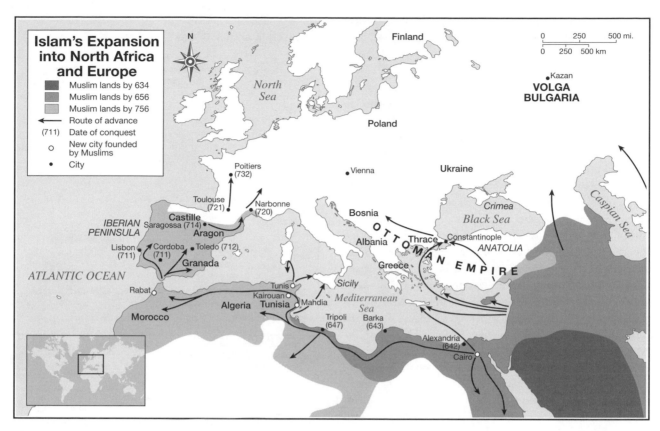

Islam's Expansion into North Africa and Europe. XNR Productions, Inc./Gale

much of this period the Austrian courts were administering Islamic family law for those Muslim populations.

These historical precedents have tended to be forgotten under the overwhelming impact of immigration post-1945. Initially, once the reviving West European economies had absorbed their returning armies, the search for additional labor had extended first into the domestic countryside and then into the countries of southern Europe, which resumed their traditional patterns of sending labor abroad. It was Britain and France that first looked outside Europe. In the latter case, the recruitment from Algeria grew and was supplemented from the 1960s by immigrants from Tunisia and Morocco, then from sub-Saharan West Africa, especially Senegal, and finally, from the 1970s, by Turks as a result of a treaty signed between the two countries. Britain first found its additional labor needs satisfied from the Caribbean, with immigration starting already in the late 1940s. During the 1950s, migration from India came on stream, and in the early 1960s immigration from Pakistan (East and West) took off. By this time other industrial countries of northern Europe also began to need additional labor. Having for some time recruited from Yugoslavia, Italy, and Greece, the Federal Republic of Germany signed a labor agreement with Turkey in 1962. The smaller countries followed the lead of their larger neighbors. During the 1960s the Netherlands signed agreements with Turkey, then Morocco, Yugoslavia, and

Tunisia, while Belgium started finding labor in Turkey and Morocco. Labor immigration into the Scandinavian countries during this period was smaller but was also more varied in its sources, including Turkey, North Africa, and Pakistan.

Just as immigration from Muslim sources into mainland Europe was taking off, so Britain reached a turning point. After almost two years of debate, the doors of labor immigration were closed by the 1962 Commonwealth Immigration Act. However, family reunion remained possible. The length of the debate was a major reason for the sudden influx of men from Pakistan, arriving to beat the expected ban. More significantly in the long run, the establishment of family life brought with it a much greater awareness of Muslim self-identity. The closing of the gates of labor immigration and the consequent immigration of women and children led directly to a marked increase in organized Muslim activity and the establishment of mosques and other places of worship.

## Organization

A decade after Britain closed its doors, the rest of continental Europe followed in response to the economic downturn sparked by the rise in oil prices during 1972 through 1974. The effects were similar: a marked rise in the opening of Muslim places of worship and in Muslim organizational activity. The process of organization followed a similar pattern across the various countries. Often the initiative came from a small group of local leaders who were concerned simply with finding a place where the required prayers could be conducted, and where children could be taught the rudiments of Islamic knowledge, how to conduct the core rituals and how to recite the Qur'an. Soon, however, the initiative passed to specific movements. These had usually existed in the country of origin and were now following the émigrés to the country of settlement. They had the resources and the organizational experience to meet community needs and, often, to provide support to local initiatives. In West Germany a leading organization of this kind during the 1970s was the *Verband islamischer Kulturzentren* acting as the German branch of the Suleimançi movement. Since the 1980s the Milli Gorus, closely associated with the National Salvation Party of Necmeddin Erbakan, has gained prominence. Similar roles have been played in Britain by extensions of the Deobandi and Brelwi networks, and by a network of organizations related to the Jam'iyat-e Islami, and in France during the 1980s by *Foi et pratique*, a movement arising out of the Tablighi Jam'iyat, which subsequently forged links with the Islamic Salvation Front (FIS) in Algeria. Many of these movements had found themselves at odds with the regimes in the countries of origin; some of them, indeed, had experienced repression. To counter their influence, governments sought to establish their own organizations to meet the needs of their émigrés. The *Amicales* of Moroccan workers was thus a means for the monarchy to maintain close ties to the émigrés, and after the Turkish coup of September 1980, the new government aggressively promoted the role of the official Diyanet among Turks in Germany.

## Legal Status

A complicating element has been the very different legal statuses available to immigrants across the continent. For a long time some of the West German states adopted a policy of rotation, whereby no residence extension was given after a certain period, so "guest workers" were regularly replaced. In other German states, longer-term residence was the norm. Germany generally made it very difficult for foreigners to acquire citizenship, as did several other countries, most notably Switzerland. Both Britain and France had comparatively easy access to permanent residence and citizenship, and children born in those two countries had virtually automatic right to citizenship. The Scandinavian and Benelux countries allowed comparatively easy access to citizenship and soon also gave local voting rights to foreigners. These very different stances were reflected in work permit policies. Since the late 1980s immigration for work has been a minor dimension of Muslim immigration, replaced by a growing number of entrants as refugees and asylum seekers, an issue that came to dominate public debate at the end of the twentieth century.

As a result, the situation in each locality in Europe often differed significantly depending on the various patterns of organized presence. A further dimension of such differences

**Muslims in western Europe**

| Country | Number of Muslims (x 1,000) | Muslim % of total population |
|---|---|---|
| Austria | 200 | 2.6 |
| Belgium | 370 | 3.8 |
| Denmark | 150 | 2.8 |
| Finland | 20 | 0.4 |
| France | 4,000–4,500 | 7 |
| Germany | 3.040 | 3 |
| Greece | 370 | 3.7 |
| Ireland | 7 | 0.2 |
| Italy | 600 | 1 |
| Luxembourg | 5 | 0.8 |
| Netherlands | 696 | 4.6 |
| Norway | 23 | 0.5 |
| Portugal | 30–38 | 0.3 |
| Spain | 300 | 0.7 |
| Sweden | 300 | 1.2 |
| United Kingdom | 1,400 | 2.5 |

SOURCE: Felice, Dassetto; Maréchal, Brigitte; and Nielsen, Jorgen, eds. *Convergences musulmanes: Aspects contemporains de l'islam dans l'Europe élargie.* Paris: Academia Bruylant, 2001.

Muslim population in western Europe.

was that each European country had its own practices regarding establishment and registration of voluntary organizations, as well as often very different traditions of relations between religion and state. At one extreme, France had inherited an almost complete separation of church and state, which for a long time excluded Muslim groups from any participation in public life. At the same time it was not until a change in the law took place in 1982 that it was possible for foreign citizens to set up their own organizations. At the other extreme were states in which there was a status of officially recognized religions. Under this heading Islam gained official recognition in Belgium in 1974, in Austria in 1979, and in Spain in 1992. One of the main issues of public contention in Germany has been the continued refusal by the state to admit the Muslim community to the recognized status enjoyed by the main churches and the Jewish community.

## Public Participation

Over the 1990s Muslim participation in public life has become marked. In many countries Muslim immigrants have become citizens and have started taking part in political life through political parties. In most countries there are now Muslims elected onto local councils, national parliaments, and the elected bodies of European institutions. This is an indication also of the change of generation. The 1989 protests against Salman Rushdie's *The Satanic Verses* in Britain, and against the banning of girls' head scarves in certain French schools served to mobilize a new generation into political life, as their immigrant parents began to retire from organizational leadership. Responses to the events of 11 September 2001 have further highlighted some of the tensions which have been arising since a younger, more active generation of Muslims has reached adulthood. In various European countries, demands for faith-based schools have grown and have met mixed reactions. In Denmark, where there has been a strong tradition of community-led "free schools," the political swing to the right has been accompanied by challenges to Muslim schools, while in Britain the government has been actively encouraging the expansion of this sector. Everywhere, the media have been attacked by Muslims for "Islamophobia," often with a degree of justification. In some countries, such as Sweden, Spain, the Netherlands, and Britain, both the media and government have sought to balance their reporting and presentation, although it remains difficult to separate domestic and international priorities in news evaluation.

*See also* **European Culture and Islam.**

## BIBLIOGRAPHY

Dassetto, Felice. *La construction de l'islam européen.* Paris: L'Harmattan, 1996.

Felice, Dassetto; Maréchal, Brigitte; and Nielsen, Jorgen, eds. *Convergences musulmanes: Aspects contemporains de l'islam dans l'Europe élargie.* Paris: Academia Bruylant, 2001.

Ferrari, Silvio, and Bradney, Anthony, eds. *Islam and European Legal Systems.* Aldershot, U.K.: Ashgate, 2000.

Foblets, Marie-Claire, ed. *Familles–Islam–Europe. Le droit confronté au changement.* Paris: Karthala, 1996.

Martin Muñoz Gema, ed. *Islam, Modernism and the West.* London: I. B.Tauris, 1996.

Metcalf, Barbara, ed. *Making Muslim Space in North America and Europe.* Berkeley: University of California Press, 1996.

Nielsen, Jorgen. *Muslims in Western Europe,* 2d ed. Edinburgh: Edinburgh University Press, 1995.

Nonneman, Gerd, Niblock, Tim, and Szajkowski, Bogdan, eds. *Muslim Communities in the New Europe.* Reading, U.K.: Ithaca Press, 1996.

Poulton, Hugh, and Taji-Farouki, Suha, eds. *Muslim Identity and the Balkan State.* London: L Hurst, 1997.

Shadid, Wasit A. R., and van Koningsveld, P. Sjoerd, eds. *Religious Freedom and the Position of Islam in Western Europe.* Kampen, Netherlands: Kok Pharos, 1995.

Vertovec, Steven, and Peach, Ceri, eds. *Islam in Europe: The Politics of Religion and Community.* Basingstoke, U.K.: Macmillan, 1997.

*Jorgen S. Nielsen*

# EXPANSION

The expansion of Islam historically embraces two phenomena. The first is the expansion of Islamic states—that is, states whose ruling elite consisted of Muslims and which consciously aimed to extend Islamic rule to new regions. The second phenomenon is the spread of Islam as a religion or faith—that is, the actual process (often called "conversion") by which individuals and groups came to identify themselves as Muslims, both inwardly and publicly.

These two processes are not unrelated but are far from identical and must be carefully distinguished from one another. On the one hand, Islam historically first came to some (but not all) regions of the world through the expansion into those regions of states whose leading cadres were Muslims and which espoused a self-consciously Islamic view of the world. State expansion was justified by the doctrine of jihad, "striving" or "exerting oneself" (i.e., in God's service). Jihad embraced a variety of practices, including the moral struggle against sin (even within oneself), peaceful proselytization of others, the use of violence by believers in defense of their way of life when attacked, or aggressive warfare against nonbelievers (nonmonotheists) to force them to recognize God's oneness and to submit to Islam. All these interpretations of the sense of jihad are rooted in Qur'anic verses (for example, 25:48–52 on proselytization; 22:39–41 on self-defense; 9:29 on aggressive warfare). It was the last understanding of the meaning of jihad that was most germane to the process of Islamic state-expansion.

The most important instance of this process was the spread of the first Islamic state in the early years of the Islamic era (seventh to ninth centuries C.E.), but it also is visible in numerous later historical episodes, such as the expansion of the Ottoman Empire into the Christian Balkans in the fourteenth through eighteenth centuries, the Ghaznavid and Ghurid conquest of Sind and adjacent parts of South Asia in the eleventh and twelfth centuries, the conquests of the Delhi sultans in India during the thirteenth and fourteenth centuries, the expansion of jihad states in the western Sudan in the eighteenth and nineteenth centuries, and so on. In almost all such cases, the objective of these Muslim rulers or states was not immediate conversion of the local population to Islam, but rather the more mundane concerns of seizing booty or securing the tax revenues of the conquered lands, or gaining control of strategically important areas. In many instances, however, the conquerors were responding not only to these mundane incentives, but also (or, sometimes, exclusively) to a general desire to establish in the newly conquered territories an Islamic public order—that is, a social order in accord with Islamic law (*shariʿa*). This they wished to do both in order to extend the glory of the faith they espoused, and in order to ensure that Muslims living in such areas could meet their religious obligations to God under Islamic law: open confession of their faith, regular public prayer, fasting during Ramadan, giving of alms, and performance of the pilgrimage to Mecca if that was within their means. In most cases, however, the establishment of an Islamic order in new areas was not accompanied by forced conversions to Islam or by official pressure on non-Muslims to convert; the image of Muslim warriors coming to an area and offering the conquered the stark choice between "Islam or the sword" is mostly a myth propounded by Western anti-Islamic polemicists.

The establishment of an Islamic public order in a hitherto non-Muslim area, however, particularly if sustained over the span of several generations, generally created the conditions under which many non-Muslims gradually embraced Islam. This is why it is said that the processes of state-expansion and of individual and group conversion, while distinct, are intimately related. Still, even under the aegis of an Islamic state, the converts' actual decisions to join the Islamic community openly (to "convert") seem to have been shaped primarily by individual factors that were also operative outside the realm of control of any Islamic state. These included social, economic, and other practical incentives, as well as the intrinsic appeal of Islam as a faith-system in its own right.

These historical processes can only be sketched here in the broadest outlines; their reconstruction by the historian is moreover bound to be somewhat uneven because of the nature of the sources, which are for many parts of this story seriously deficient or even nonexistent. In general, however, one can say that the process of state expansion is much better documented than is the process of Islam's adoption by new "converts," whether within or outside of Islamic states, for whose individual decisions, and the factors contributing to them, there is often no trace whatsoever.

The remainder of this article will examine first the general factors that have contributed historically to people's decision to embrace Islam, followed by a brief overview of the spread of Islam in various regions of the world, during which the relative importance of state-expansion and other factors will be noted.

## Causes and Agents of Islamization

As with most complex social processes, the Islamization of a population that hitherto did not identify itself as Muslim normally involved a multitude of causes or factors. These factors impinged in differing degrees on various individuals in the population depending on their cultural, social, economic, and political situations and their personal temperament. It is therefore impossible to generalize from one person's conversion narrative what the relative importance of various factors in conversion was for his society as a whole, just as it is impossible to work back from the aggregate factors operative in a certain historical situation to deduce just which ones would have been most influential on a particular individual who chose to embrace Islam; the selection of factors that were most important to a given person can only be known if that person leaves some written record of his own reasons for embracing the new faith—something that happens only in a tiny minority of cases.

First and foremost, we must acknowledge that Islam, as a faith system, has significant intrinsic appeal to the intellect.

The relative simplicity and transparency of its basic doctrines (monotheism, prophecy, last judgment, etc.) makes them easy to grasp and to defend in philosophical or theological discourse against religious systems with more convoluted doctrines (e.g., the Christian doctrine of the Trinity). The fact that Muslims developed over the first two centuries of their existence a strong tool for legitimizing some of these doctrines in the form of an elaborate origins narrative helped bolster the intellectual cogency of Islam's doctrines. Islam's emphasis on justice (frequently stressed in the Qur'an) and on the brotherhood of all believers—the latter made especially manifest in the daily communal prayers and in major ritual observances such as collective fasting during Ramadan—were also capable of exercising a strong intellectual attraction on many individuals (aside from their obvious possible social attractiveness).

As noted above, the establishment of states with Muslim rulers and an Islamic public order usually created the conditions under which many people came to embrace Islam. Many converted in response to the working of economic or social or other factors that the existence of an Islamic public order made possible. Some, however, embraced Islam for explicitly political reasons. Besides those who wished to enter government service (or who were already in it, and believed that openly confessing Islam would enhance their career chances), many others were doubtless attracted to the faith that was now "official," publicly proclaimed, and so increasingly prominent, and associated with success and victory. On the other hand, the use of political pressure or force by Muslim authorities to coerce people to embrace Islam, while not unknown in Islamic history, was very seldom practiced, even when politically dominant Muslims absorbed populations of nonmonotheists or "pagans."

At various times individuals or communities may have responded to economic incentives to embrace Islam. The structure of taxation under an Islamic regime—according to which non-Muslims paid a special tax, the *jizya* or poll-tax, to the Muslim authorities—sometimes seems to have encouraged individuals to embrace Islam. Generally, however, the tax inequities seem to have been minimal (Muslims, after all, were liable according to the *shari'a* to some taxes not levied on non-Muslims, such as the *zakat* or alms-tax) and not sufficient to generate waves of conversions to Islam. After all, the non-Muslim communities of the Near East embraced Islam only very slowly—a process taking hundreds of years. Far more important, probably, was the force of general economic (and social) dislocation caused by the policies of various Muslim states, which caused great flux in all communities under their rule—Muslim as well as non-Muslim—resulting in a shattering of the communal solidarity of some non-Muslim communities, in the aftermath of which the uprooted individuals may well have embraced Islam in order to find a secure place for themselves in some community. The agrarian distress of the middle Umayyad period in Egypt, for example, which led to widespread abandonment of lands by their peasant cultivators, many of whom fled to the (predominantly Muslim) towns, weakened or destroyed rural non-Muslim communities and doubtless led many such refugees to embrace Islam more or less out of desperation, as their only economic foothold became one dominated by Muslims among whom they now lived and worked.

Many social factors also contributed to the acceptance of Islam by individuals or groups. Non-Muslims from highly stratified societies who lived in contact with Muslims could not fail to observe the relative egalitarianism of Islam (reflected, for example, in the fact that all believers, from the wealthy merchant to the poorest laborer, prayed side-by-side in the mosque); this may have had an impact in societies with caste-like social restrictions, such as were found in Hindu society in South Asia or among Iran's Zoroastrians. More generally, the highly visible collective rituals of Islam, particularly communal prayer and fasting during Ramadan, created an obvious sense of solidarity among believers that could exercise a strong attraction on those non-Muslims who yearned for the security of a strong social matrix. These rituals also provided apparent popular affirmation for the cogency of Islam's doctrines. For some men, particularly of the wealthier classes, the relative ease of divorce and the toleration of polygamy may have been attractive features of Islam's social system. Perhaps most important of all, however, was the simple desire among some non-Muslims to attain fuller social integration (including intermarriage) with Muslims among whom they lived and worked, and with whom they had other business or social ties. (Since apostasy from Islam was punishable by death, according to Islamic law, Muslims rarely converted to other religions, even when they lived outside an Islamic state.) The fact that Muslim men could, according to Islamic law, marry non-Muslim women meant that a non-Muslim who converted to Islam did not even necessarily cut himself off from the possibility of marrying a woman of his former religious community.

Cultural factors at times also played an important role in the spread of Islam among new populations. During the first several centuries of the Islamic era (roughly eighth through twelfth centuries C.E.), the urban-based Arabic-Islamic civilization that developed in the Middle East was by far the most sophisticated cultural tradition of western Eurasia. As such it exercised a powerful attraction on many people, who both embraced Islam and adopted the Arabic language. (The adoption of Arabic and Arabo-Islamic cultural patterns by numerous people in Andalusia who remained Christian, on the other hand, reveals that the processes of Arabization and Islamization were not always congruent.)

Another cultural development of importance to the spread of Islam was the rise of Islamic literary traditions in languages other than Arabic; this helped to make the faith more accessible and familiar to speakers of those languages, once Islam had begun to spread beyond the Arabic-speaking lands of its beginnings. Usually, the language in which an Islamic discourse was newly developing adopted the Arabic script as an outward marker of its Islamic character, to distinguish such writings from earlier, non-Islamic writings in the same base language. The first appearance of Islamic writings in Persian but using a modified form of the Arabic script, for example, which began in the tenth century C.E., contributed significantly to the consolidation of Islam in the Iranian cultural zone over the next several centuries, against its local rivals, especially Zoroastrianism, which continued to write in a form of Persian using the older Pahlavi script. Similar processes accompanied the rise of Islamic literary traditions in various dialects of Turkish, among Indic languages for which Urdu became the vehicle of Islamic literary culture and identity, and in Indonesian-Malay; the rise of each of these contributed significantly to the consolidation of Islam in areas where these languages were spoken.

It is important to note that the spread of Islam often has followed a pattern of initial superficial Islamization followed after a generation or more by a "reform" movement. The initial Islamization may be little more than nominal and marked by much syncretism and the survival of older, non-Islamic beliefs and practices; the "reform" along the lines of a more rigorous variant of Islam is sometimes carried out by indigenous Muslims (not infrequently led by returning pilgrims), sometimes by revivalist preachers from outside the area. Examples of this can be seen in historical contexts as disparate as the Maghrib in the eleventh through thirteenth centuries (Almoravid and Almohad movements), Anatolia during the twelfth through fifteenth centuries, the puritanical Wahhabi movement in the Arabian peninsula beginning in the sixteenth century, the revitalization of Islamic practice in nineteenth-century Indonesia at the hands of returning pilgrims, and the transformation of the Black Muslim movement in the United States into a form of orthodox Sunni Islam during the second half of the twentieth century. Islamic reformers naturally decry the laxity and heterodox character of the superficially Islamized communities they strive to reform, but it must be recognized that these communities' loose initial affiliations with Islam, however unorthodox in practice and belief, nonetheless represent a decisive turn on the part of these people toward identification with the broader Islamic community. This early identification with Islam may be an easier step for individuals to take precisely because it is still tentative, tolerant of some cherished pre-Islamic practices of the local community, or associated with political or other programs that are not those of Islam in general (for example, black separatism in the case of the Black Muslim movement); yet it results in a fundamental reorientation of the individual's identity toward Islam, and so offers the base on which later reformers can subsequently build.

The agents of Islamization are of course almost infinite in variety, as in principle people of any kind can, under appropriate conditions, proselytize others or serve as positive models that attract nonbelievers to the faith. Historically, however, three groups of people in Islamic society have been especially important to the spread of the faith: merchants, popular preachers, and mendicant Sufis (mystics). Muslim merchants, who often established themselves as self-contained colonies in non-Muslim areas, historically were the first to bring awareness of Islam to many new areas. Because of the nature of their work, they usually established close personal ties with the non-Muslims among whom they lived, which gave them many opportunities to engage in patient proselytization among their associates. Moreover, their prosperity, general reputation for honest dealing and upright behavior, and powerful sense of collective identity as Muslims made them strong positive examples of the Islamic way of life that quietly drew many converts.

In some situations, popular preachers also were important to the spread of Islam. Motivated solely by personal piety, these individuals were especially effective in situations where Islam was already known but not yet embraced by many people. The impact of mendicant Sufis was not dissimilar to that of preachers, although the form of Islam they popularized was in some cases less rigorous than that espoused by the preachers; as such it appealed to people who were unwilling to give up all aspects of their former belief-system, and initiated that kind of superficial Islamization that, as has been seen, was often an important first step down the road to full immersion in the faith.

## The Expansion of Islam in Various World Regions

Islam began in western Arabia with the preaching of the prophet Muhammad (ca. 570–632 C.E.). Under the caliphs, or successors to Muhammad as temporal leaders of the Muslims, the community he had founded in Medina and Mecca expanded quickly to control all of the Arabian peninsula, Iraq, Syria-Palestine, Iran, and Egypt; most of these areas were seized through military action from the two great powers of the day, the Byzantine and Sassanian Persian empires. While the early Islamic conquests remain difficult to explain in full as a historical phenomenon, they are probably best seen as an example of state-formation followed by rapid state expansion. Once firmly established, the Islamic state, led by the Umayyad caliphs (660–750 C.E.), established major garrison towns in newly conquered areas (Kufa and Basra in Iraq; Hims in Syria; Fustat in Egypt; Qayrawan in Tunisia; Qom, Marv, and others in Iran). These became important urban centers where Islamic literary culture developed, particularly under the Abbasid caliphs (750–1258 C.E.). From these garrison towns the caliphs launched further campaigns of conquest that brought ever-wider areas under their sway. North Africa was conquered in a series of campaigns sent from Egypt in the middle and later decades of the seventh century, and Muslim armies crossed the Straits of Gibraltar in 711 C.E. and quickly seized most of the Iberian peninsula, followed in subsequent decades by raids deep into Gaul and occupation of significant areas of what is now southern France. All these areas have ever since remained part of the Islamic world, with the exception of southern France and Iberia, from which Muslims were expelled in 1492 by a resurgent Spanish monarchy, and some islands in the Mediterranean, notably Sicily, where Muslims established themselves during the ninth and tenth centuries C.E. In the east, Muslim forces defeated the last armies of the Sassanian Great Kings in western Iran already in the middle of the sixth century, and within several more decades Muslim forces had seized areas far to the east, particularly Khurasan, although some areas of Iran (Sistan, Gilan) resisted Muslim encroachment stubbornly for many more years. From Khurasan, the caliphs dispatched armies into other parts of eastern Iran, Afghanistan, and areas beyond the Oxus River in Central Asia.

The caliphs not only organized and maintained the conquering armies that carried out this remarkable expansion of the first Islamic state, they also benefited from the conquests in the form of a share of booty and captives and subsequently in the form of regular taxes imposed on the conquered areas. But it is important to note that for at least two centuries, Muslims constituted a minority (at first, indeed, a very small minority) of the population of the vast area controlled by the early Islamic empire between Spain and Afghanistan; it is estimated that the population of the caliphal domains only became 50 percent Muslim around the middle or end of the ninth century. The conversion of the population of the Middle East, then, even in lands like Syria, Egypt, and Iran, was clearly something that happened very gradually.

It was also during the early Islamic centuries that certain peoples living adjacent to the caliphal empire, but outside its borders, embraced Islam. The Bulgars, who lived along the Volga, had embraced Islam by the ninth century, probably under the influence of Muslim merchants coming from the south. The pastoral nomadic Turkish peoples of the Central Asian steppes were also increasingly converted to Islam during the ninth and tenth centuries; some may have embraced Islam on the advice of itinerant preachers or Muslim merchants to avoid being preyed upon by slave-raiders coming from the fringes of the caliphal empire in Khurasan. Their conversion was to prove of great importance, for in the eleventh century the Turks began their epic migration westward through northern Iran and into Azerbaijan, the Caucasus region, and Anatolia; this folk migration, which their political leaders the Seljuks partly orchestrated and partly followed, brought both the Turkish language and Islam for the first time to many parts of Anatolia. Under the aegis of various rival Turkish-Islamic states, much of the formerly Christian population of what we today call Turkey gradually embraced Islam between the eleventh and the fifteenth centuries C.E.—in this case, a process in which both merchants and syncretistic Sufi fraternities played a significant part.

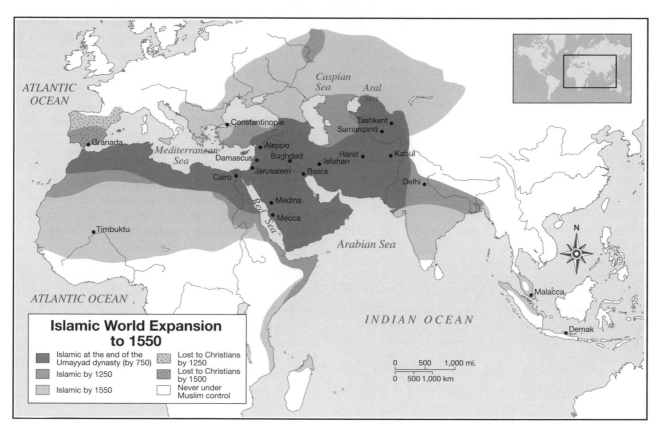

## Islamic World Expansion to 1550

**Islamic at the end of the Umayyad dynasty (by 750)**

**Islamic by 1250**

**Islamic by 1550**

**Lost to Christians by 1250**

**Lost to Christians by 1500**

**Never under Muslim control**

0    500    1,000 mi.

0    500  1,000 km

Islamic World Expansion to 1500. XNR Productions, Inc./Gale

Eventually, this Turkish-Islamic matrix gave rise to the Ottoman state, which in the fifteenth, sixteenth, and seventeenth centuries conquered vast new territories for Islam in the Balkans and created the conditions under which the faith spread there, particularly in Albania and Bosnia.

The first Muslim presence in South Asia was established already in the early eighth century C.E. in the Indus river valley (Sind and Punjab) by the conquest of key towns in the region, but although this community survived for many centuries little is known about it. The real beginning of the extensive spread of Islam in South Asia came in the late tenth and the eleventh centuries C.E., when the Ghaznavid dynasty began to launch raids from its main base in Afghanistan into the Indus valley and beyond, in order to secure the rich plunder the area offered. Eventually, some of these raids resulted in the establishment of permanent Ghaznavid outposts in Sind, especially as the Ghaznavids's control of their original base in Afghanistan was challenged and then taken away by others; their Indian possessions thus became a refuge for the Ghaznavids. The Ghaznavids were succeeded by the Ghurids, who in the later twelfth century held not only Sind and Punjab but also came to control most of northern India as far east as western Bengal. With the fall of the Ghurids in Afghanistan in the thirteenth century under pressure of the Khwarizmshahs and Mongols, some Ghurid commanders in India established the first Delhi Sultanate, which engaged in

constant campaigning to spread its control against local Hindu and rival Muslim princes. By the fourteenth century, the Delhi sultans had brought an intermittent patchwork of areas under their control, extending all the way to south India and to Orissa in the southeast, and continued battling other Muslim and Hindu principalities. The degree of Islamization resulting from this political control varied, however, from region to region in South Asia; in general, Islamization was (and remains) much more extensive in the regions of Sind, Punjab, Bengal, and, by the fourteenth century, Kashmir in the north and Deccan in the south, than it was in other areas of India, including the Ganges plain.

Although military expansion was important to the spread of Islam in India, however, it was far from the only factor. Perhaps equally important was the establishment, no later than the twelfth century, of numerous trading colonies of Muslim merchants, usually of Arab or Persian origin, particularly along the west coast of India. These merchant colonies brought to the rulers (usually Hindu) in whose territories they established themselves not only important economic benefits, but also an exposure to some aspects of Islamic high culture, and a reputation for honesty and fair dealing. The Muslim merchant colonies were therefore important catalysts for the conversion to Islam of many people in India, even before a Muslim prince or the Delhi sultans brought their area under the domination of an officially Muslim state. Also important to the spread of Islam in South Asia were members of various orders of Sufis (mystics), such as the Chishtiyya. Some Sufi saints were closely associated with a Muslim ruler, while others avoided such ties and operated independently; whatever the case, their egalitarianism, emphasis on the spiritual life, and eagerness to welcome new adepts made them powerful magnets for the faith.

In China, Muslims have always been a minority. Already by the ninth century C.E. there was a large colony of Muslim (presumably Arab and Persian) merchants in Canton; it was largely massacred or expelled by the Chinese in 878, though some Muslims remained. The largest communities of Muslims in China were established in Xinjiang in the west during the thirteenth and following centuries, during the period of Mongol rule of China (the Yuan dynasty), when the Mongols, who cared little about religion, allowed Muslim merchants free access to the country. The Mongol Golden Horde conquered parts of central Asia and southern Russia, destroying the Muslim Bulghar kingdom, but by 1290 the khans of the Horde had themselves embraced Islam.

The first Muslims in Southeast Asia seem to have been Arab merchants who established a colony in Palembang in the trading state of Shrivijaya in eastern Sumatra in the seventh century C.E. In the subsequent centuries, colonies of Arab, Persian, and Indian Muslim merchants established themselves along the coasts of the Malay peninsula and Sumatra, some fleeing the Chinese destruction of the large Muslim trading colony at Canton in 878. As in coastal India and East Africa, Muslim merchants established a foothold in most of the trading ports of Malaysia and Indonesia. The important colony of Aceh on the northern tip of Sumatra is mentioned already in the thirteenth century by Marco Polo as having a Muslim ruler. The trading entrepot of Malacca, which controlled the crucial shipping lane through the narrow strait separating Malaya and Sumatra, seems to have had a Muslim ruler by the early fifteenth century. In both cases, the wealth and commercially based assertiveness of these trading entrepots resulted in the spread of Islam to neighboring areas. The sultans of Malacca extended their control over nearby areas of the Malay peninsula, bringing to Islam local populations that had not already been attracted to Islam by the glittering prosperity of Malacca's rulers; but after Malacca's conquest by the Portuguese in 1511, its commerce declined sharply, particularly because Muslim merchants preferred to take their commerce to Muslim Aceh. The sultans of Aceh eventually expanded their influence and control southward in Sumatra and in adjacent areas at the expense of other local chieftains, particularly in the seventeenth century C.E.; they continued to ply their traditional occupations of commerce and piracy, and the sultanate ended only in the late nineteenth century during the war against Dutch colonial occupation. The spread of Islam to other parts of Southeast Asia—in particular Java, Borneo, and the Moluccas—was carried out through a combination of peaceful commerce, proselytization,

and warfare launched against their neighbors by local Muslim princes. In Java, Islam became influential at the court of Majapahit around the mid-fifteenth century, and subsequently spread widely through the island. Similar patterns can be traced in Borneo, Sulawesi, the Moluccas, and Luzon during the fifteenth and sixteenth centuries. Rivalry between Muslim preachers and Christian missionaries (Portuguese and later Dutch) in the fifteenth through seventeenth centuries sharpened the effort of Muslim proselytizers, who presented their cause increasingly as one of jihad against Christian aggression. In the nineteenth century, Muslim pilgrims returning to Indonesia from extended stays in Arabia were instrumental in fueling a revivalist or purification movement that did much to deepen the local commitment to Islam.

Islam came to North Africa, as we have seen, as part of the rapid expansion of the first caliphal state in the seventh century C.E. South of the Sahara, Islam spread more slowly, arriving by several different routes: up the Nile, across the Sahara to the Niger region of West Africa, and by sea to the East African coast. From Egypt, caliphal control, and with it Islam, spread already in the seventh and eighth centuries southward up the Nile into Nubia and from there into the northern parts of the modern state of Sudan and to the fringes of Ethiopia. Farther west, Muslim merchants from North Africa were by 1000 C.E. crossing the Sahara in caravans via key oasis towns such as Sijilmasa, Tadmekka, and Awdaghast, and had established merchant colonies near the great bend of the Niger River, particularly at the trading center of Timbuktu. The revivalist Almoravid movement established a Muslim state in Mauretania in the eleventh century, and began attacking the Soninke kingdom of Ghana before expanding rapidly northward again. By the thirteenth century, these initial seeds of Islamization had grown into several powerful Muslim kingdoms in the western Sudan: Mali and Gao in the Niger valley, and Kanam, in the vicinity of Lake Chad. These kingdoms and other smaller ones periodically waged jihad against neighboring non-Muslims, and also encouraged commerce, which drew local tribal peoples into closer contact with Muslim merchants and their cosmopolitan vision of the world.

The spread of Islam in East Africa, along the Indian Ocean littoral, resembled in some ways Islam's penetration of Southeast Asia. The first agents of Islamization were Muslim merchants from Arabia, Iran, and India, who came with the monsoon and founded or established colonies in the major coastal trading ports from Somalia southward, particularly in Zanzibar, where sectarian (Khariji) Muslims from Oman established ties that endured in political form until the mid-twentieth century. Other Muslim colonies remained subject to local rulers, but retained close communal and family ties to their coreligionists in Arabia or India. From the coastal trading ports, Islam gradually penetrated some distance into the hinterlands from which came the goods exchanged at the ports of trade.

Muslim communities became prominent in Western Europe and North America only during the middle and latter decades of the twentieth century. In Western Europe, Muslim communities became established in some cases as an unforeseen by-product of a European country's possession of Asian or African colonies or protectorates with large Muslim populations. Whether in search of work, education, or (after the colony's independence) sanctuary from oppression, migrants from these colonial or ex-colonial possessions sometimes found a way to move to the metropolitan country, whose language and sometimes culture they had often learned. Salient examples are the large communities of Muslims of North or West African origin in France, those of South Asian origin in Great Britain, and those of Southeast Asian origin in the Netherlands. Other Muslim migrants to Europe came to countries with no colonial connections to the Islamic world, mainly for economic reasons, such as the many Turkish guest workers in Germany, or for political reasons (Iranians after the overthrow of the shah in 1979, Bosnians during the collapse of Yugoslavia in the 1990s). Whatever the cause, many of these Muslim migrants to Europe settled there permanently, so that the large and growing Muslim communities of Western Europe are now in their third and fourth generations.

In North America, large numbers of immigrants from majority-Muslim lands in Asia and Africa came to pursue economic opportunities or education, or to escape political oppression or economic deprivation (such as the large influx of Iranians of middle- or upper-class backgrounds who came after 1979). The Islamic community in the United States, however, also includes a sizable number of indigenous African-Americans. Beginning in the 1930s, some African-Americans joined Elijah Muhammad's Nation of Islam, originally a black separatist movement. The Nation of Islam espoused many ideas that were not part of traditional Islam and most of them identified only weakly with mainstream Muslim communities around the world. During the 1950s and 1960s, however, this movement underwent an internal transformation (led by such figures as Malcolm X) that led increasing numbers of its members to adopt mainstream Islamic values and to abandon the movement's black separatist origins. The American Muslim Movement that emerged from the Nation of Islam after Elijah Muhammad's death in 1975 is thoroughly orthodox in its doctrines.

*See also* **Conversion; Da'wa; Jihad; Tasawwuf.**

## BIBLIOGRAPHY

Arnold, Thomas. *The Preaching of Islam. A History of the Propagation of the Muslim Faith.* (1896). Reprint, Lahore: Sh. Muhammad Ashraf, 1961.

Bulliet, Richard. *Conversion to Islam in the Medieval Period: An Essay in Quantative History.* Cambridge, Mass.: Harvard University Press, 1979.

Chaudhuri, K. N. *Asia Before Europe: Economy and Civilisation of the Indian Ocean from the Rise of Islam to 1750.* Cambridge, U.K.: Cambridge University Press, 1990.

Donner, Fred M. *The Early Islamic Conquests.* Princeton, N.J.: Princeton University Press, 1981.

Hodgson, Marshall G. S. *The Venture of Islam.* Chicago: University of Chicago Press, 1974.

Holt, P. M.; Lambton, Ann K. S.; and Lewis, Bernard, eds. *The Cambridge History of Islam.* Vol. 2: Indian Sub-continent, South-East Asia, and Africa. Cambridge, U.K.: Cambridge University Press, 1970.

Levtzion, Nehemia, ed. *Conversion to Islam.* New York: Holmes and Meier Publishers, 1979.

McCloud, Aminah Beverly. *African American Islam.* New York: Routledge, 1995.

Qureshi, Ishtiaq Husein. *The Muslim Community of the Indo-Pakistan Subcontinent, 610–1947: A Brief Historical Analysis.* Karachi: Ma'aref, 1977.

Richards, D. S., ed. *Islam and the Trade of Asia.* Oxford, U.K.: Bruno Cassirer, 1970.

Risso, Patricia. *Merchants and Faith: Muslim Commerce and Culture in the Indian Ocean.* Boulder, Colo.: Westview Press, 1995.

Schimmel, Annemarie. *Islam in the Indian Subcontinent.* Leiden: E. J. Brill, 1980.

Smith, Jane I. *Islam in America.* New York: Columbia University Press, 1999.

Trimingham, J. Spencer. *A History of Islam in West Africa.* Oxford, U.K.: Oxford University Press, 1962.

Trimingham, J. Spencer. *Islam in East Africa.* Oxford, U.K.: Clarendon Press, 1964.

Trimingham, J. Spencer. *The Sufi Orders in Islam.* Oxford, U.K.: Clarendon Press, 1971.

*Fred M. Donner*

# F

## FADLALLAH, MUHAMMAD HUSAYN (1935– )

Muhammad Husayn Fadlallah, spiritual leader of the Shi'a of Lebanon, was born in Najaf, Iraq, in 1935 to a religious family from Southern Lebanon. Known in the West as the spiritual leader of Hizbullah, unlike most Shi'a ulema, he traces his genealogy to Imam Hassan rather than Imam Hossein. He studied with Ayatollah Khu'i in Najaf, following which Fadlallah settled in eastern Beirut and became Khu'i's representative. He lived and worked as a Shi'a among Sunnis and Christians during the civil war in Lebanon. At the onset of the war he wrote about the relationship between political power and ideology and became an active community organizer. In his relationship with the Islamic Republic of Iran, he has both continued his contacts with Tehran as well as maintained a distance from the Iranian leadership.

Fadlallah's career is marked by differences from other Shi'a ulema. These differences include his focus on social and charitable organizations, women's participation in public life, and a rather decentered view of leadership. He believes that *marja'iyya*, religious leadership, should be distinguished from *wilayat al-faqih*, or political leadership. There should be many *waly* (political leaders), whereas only one person should hold the title of *marja'*. This means that there are many *waly* who are the interpreters of religion and politics in society. On the other hand, *marja'* is a symbolic and religious leadership and jurisdiction goes beyond the political and national boundaries. Fadlallah believes that *marja'* should be unified under one authority. Regarding jurisprudence, he argues that the Qur'an takes precedence over the *sunna*, and that jurists need to interpret meaning directly from the Qur'an. Fadlallah's religious and political status increased, especially among radicals, after Ayatollah Khomeini gave him *ijaza* (religious permission) to collect *khums* (religious tax) from his followers in 1982.

*See also* **Political Islam.**

**BIBLIOGRAPHY**

Aziz, Talib. "Fadlallah and the Remaking of the Marja'iya." In *The Most Learned of the Shi'a: The Institution of the Marja' Taqlid.* Edited by Linda S. Walbridge. Oxford, U.K.: Oxford University Press, 2001.

*Mazyar Lotfalian*

## FALSAFA

Philosophical speculation in Islamic culture has triple roots in theology (*kalam*), philosophy proper (*falsafa*), and mysticism (*tasawwuf*).

### Theological Beginnings

The genesis of Muslim philosophical theology is manifested in the marriage of Greek logic and monotheistic apologetics in the school of Mu'tazilah initiated by Wasil ibn 'Ata (d. 748) and developed by Abu al-Hudhayl al-'Allaf (d. 849/850), his nephew al-Nazzam (d. c. 435/445), and the jurist 'Abd al-Jabbar (d. 1204/1205). They inquired into such questions as the compatibility of free will for creatures and Divine omnipotence. Can a person act against the will or knowledge of God? If persons have no free will, how can a just God punish them for predetermined actions? If rewards and punishments are arbitrary, why does God send prophets and reveal sacred scriptures to guide His creatures? Wrestling with such key issues in theodicy, the prevalent adherents of the Mu'tazilah position support the legitimacy of the doctrine of punishment and rewards by proffering their view that persons are free and that God is just. Their position criticized subjectivism in ethics and upheld a rationalist ethic that persons can reason about ethics and thus are responsible for moral actions. Against this family of doctrines arose the school of Ash'arites (founded by Abu 'l-Hasan al-Ash'ari, d. 935), which advocated the so-called theory of occasionalism. Popularized later in Europe by Nicolas Malebranche (d. 1715), occasionalists

247

confronted the thorny problem of causality as follows. Among created occasions in the world, there is no causation (neither agent-patient nor an event-type of causation). Specifically, minds/mental events or bodies/physical actions are subject only to an ultimate cause, namely God. Belonging to the Sunni school of theology, this school questioned the meaningfulness of the notion of free will; by contrast, it advocated that God ordained a total resignation to the cosmos, which it claimed. This position does not imply any negative states for humanity; in this tenor, persons (including someone in the position of Job) should envision nature and themselves as mere gifts of the Divine grace; faith commands creatures to passively witness the glory of creation as an icon of the Creator. Other key issues included the controversy as to whether or not the Qur'an is co-eternal with the Divine; this controversy is based on a reading of the *Timaeus* where Plato postulates a co-eternity among the ideas/forms/universals and the creator-artist-demiurge. Finally they have constantly debated the place of reason versus revelation and the place of philosophy in an Islamic society. A number of Sunni theologians like Abu Hamid al-Ghazali (d. 1111) and Ahmid ibn Taymiyya (d. 1327) criticized what they considered to be untenable attempts of philosophers to intrude into theology. In contrast, Shi'a writers like Nasir Khusraw, Nasir ad-Din Tusi (d. 1274), and Sadr ad-Din Shirazi (known as Mulla Sadra), all of whom were philosophers in the school of Isfahan in the following three centuries, and even as recent as Ruhollah Khomeini (d. 1989), all view theology and philosophy as interdependent disciplines. The most philosophical group of Muslim sects consists of the so-called Isma'ilis, among them Khosrow, Hamid al-Din Kirmani, and Nasir al-Din Tusi.

## Classical Philosophy (Ninth to Thirteenth Century)

The classical age of Islamic philosophy is marked by the following features: (a) an increasing awareness of the importance of Greek philosophy, especially of Aristotelian delineation and division of philosophical studies such as ontology, epistemology, normative types of inquiry, analytical disciplines such as logic and mathematics, natural sciences, and theology; (b) the production of commentaries on the Greek texts, and the development of new and creative solutions to the traditional controversies such as the nature of imaginations and the problem of universals; and (c) the pursuit of philosophical investigations independent of religious concerns. A majority of recent and some contemporary investigators in Islamic philosophy focus on the so-called Greek into Arabic, or/and Arabic into Latin/Hebrew. There is no doubt that this historical-reductive approach is a legitimate field as illustrated in the case of the Persian-born philosopher and scientist Ibn Sina (known to the West by his Latin name, Avicenna). He claimed that he had read Aristotle's *Metaphysics* about forty times, and both peripatetic and Neoplatonic influences are imprinted over his several encyclopedic collections. In turn, Ibn Sina was mentioned over five hundred times by the most important Catholic thinker, St. Thomas Aquinas (d. 1274), who grounded much of his metaphysics in

Ibn Sina's concepts, such as the essence-existence distinctions. In this light Islamic texts may be useful both in tracing the development of Greek thought as well as in revealing the genesis of some Latin and Hebrew philosophical writings.

**Major Muslim thinkers of the classical period.** A key figure is Abu Ya'qub Al-Kindi (d. 873), who proffered a search for truth over reliance on authority. Moreover, he supported the theory of creation by arguing that the eternity of the world would imply the existence of an actual infinite, which was proven to be impossible by Aristotle. Abu Nasr Al-Farabi (d. 950), is known as "the second teacher," an original thinker and a logician. His numerous contributions include: (a) construing a Muslim version of the theory of emanation adopted by a majority of subsequent Muslim philosophers; (b) holding a Platonic position that philosophizing takes place in context of a polity and its societal ethics; and finally (c) having insights in analytical ontology on topics such as the relation between language and ontology. He demonstrated that in the spite of the fact that Semitic languages like Arabic do not contain the copula, they are nevertheless as capable as any Indo-European language like Greek or Persian to express primary ontic concepts designated by terms such as *being*, *existence*, *existent*, and *substance*. Abu 'Ali ibn Sina (d. 1037), who is perhaps the most original and systematic Muslim thinker, as is illustrated by the following ideas.

With respect to the logical structure of metaphysics, Ibn Sina modified the ontology of the peripatetic substance-event language ontology (where the first division of *being* was into the categories of substances and accidents) to a primary encounter with *being* and the threefold modalities of necessity, contingency, and impossibility. A concatenation of *being* with *necessity* leads to *necessary being*, which, in the second version of the ontological arguments, leads to the notion of The Necessary Existent, the cause of the actualization of all contingent beings.

With respect to the epistemic meditative experience, he postulated a four-phase hermeneutic phenomenological encounter as follows: (i) *being*, (ii) *the field of experiencing* the world as the immediate phenomenon, (iii) a search from a contingency of the agent to *the inner essence of the agent*, which is the necessary existent, and (iii) finally an aim toward dealienation through a unity of existents. Ibn Sina's system may be used to reread the ontological argument of both St. Augustine (d. 430) and René Descartes (d. 1650). In this light the most celebrated argument for the existence of God is not a static, empty logical argument based on definition, but a phase of transformation due to a search from being, to the self-field of experience, to God and finally a desperate attempt to form a dealienating unity among all existents.

In the field of mysticism, Ibn Sina's account of meta-mysticism and his distinctions between *mystical*, *religious*, and *ascetic*, as well as his description of states and stations of mystics, paved the way for subsequent scholarships on mysticism.

His original system integrated various aspects of Aristotelian and Neoplatonic Greek theories with the Islamic intellectual tradition. Subsequent philosophers had to take account of Ibn Sina's system, criticizing him, in the case of al-Ghazali, Fakhr al-Din Razi (b. 1149), and Ibn Taymiyya, following him (as with Tusi), or including in their philosophy some of his visions, like Ibn Rushd (d. 1198), Shihab ad-Din Suhrawardi (d. 1191), Aquinas, and Sadr ad-Din Shirazi (known as Mulla Sadra). In sum, a comprehensive Islamic philosophical system emerged through Ibn Sina's encyclopedic works.

A parallel vibrant tradition of original philosophy, mysticism, and scholarly commentaries developed in Islamic Spain. Mention has already been made of Ibn Rushd—known to the West by his Latin name, Averroes—who also wrote a number of commentaries on Aristotle's work as well as on Plato's *Republic*. He is known in Christian medieval circles as the originator of the so-called double-truth theory, which renders religious and philosophical languages to be isomorphically compatible, although scholars today question this interpretation of his theory of truth. Noteworthy among the list of other philosophers is Ibn Tufayl (d. 1185), who presents in a Robinson Crusoe–like tale, an allegorical account of various phases of the development of persons in light of which issues are portrayed such as the acquisition of language, communication with nature and human being, and finally with God.

### The Post–Ibn Sina Developments of Metaphysics and Epistemology

Ibn Sina's original insights culminated in a number of the following ideas in later Islamic philosophy.

**The world depicted as a process analogous to a flowing river or a shining sun.** To begin with, for Aristotle, the ultimate constituent of the world consists of what he called first substances, which are primarily individual, concrete particulars like the stars, living persons, animals, trees, and rocks. Consequently, other features of the world like quantity, quality, place, time, relations, and alike are accidental and are actual only because of the characterization of a subspace. Against Plato, he argued that the entity, "being green," does not exist in or by itself; it is realized if it endures as a color of a specific tree or the color of a person's eyes. The key issue is his accidental depiction of time, which postulates that the primary account of the world is in the language of substances, for example, rocks or trees, and events such as their locomotion, damnation, and growth, and the alteration of their character. By contrast, in the post–Ibn Sinan philosophy, temporal dimensions of phenomena such as experiences of persons were depicted as an essential aspect of their reality, for which Mulla Sadra coined the expression "substantial motion." In Sadra's ontology the universe was depicted as a continuum of realms of existents, from the pure absolute existent, identified as God, to series of layers of entities.

Consequently, reality was depicted as a process; analysis was compared to waves in the ocean or wind in motion. Now there are two sides to such a process: an external one, like drops of water coming from a river that in turn came from an ocean; thus a drop of water going back to the ocean, or a person dying as an individual and then becoming part of the world, both of which depict the unity of being as entities returning to their archetypal mother, or to the source of their generation. The other side, an internal, an intentional one in light of which a person is transformed from one state of mind to another, is depicted either in celebrated cases like the conversion of St. Paul or in typical cases like becoming a parent, falling in love, and the like. Muslim philosophers needed this Neoplatonic framework of process language as they dealt with the key issue of the paradox of mystical union, which aimed to bring an ultimate intimacy between persons and their source of genesis, like a child seeking to return to the mother. In Aristotle's vocabulary no two substances could have become identical with one another, as the only substantial changes were generation and corruption; for example, a cat cannot become a dog. But in process language, two waves can merge and become a single wave, or a drop of water can return to the sea or a fire of love to its source, the heavenly sun. In authentic personal experiences, the birth of their child represents the visible fruit of the merged love of two lovers. Medieval Muslim philosophers use the method of allegorical theology by appeals to motifs such as "drowning" or "light"; in such a framework "mystical union" can be clarified by a symbolic or an allegorical theology. Moreover, unlike Aristotle's system, such processes in the world that were external to persons' bodies had also a personal and an intentional side. It should be noted that Aristotle's system is not a static metaphysics, as the ultimate model is an organic depiction of nature, where the highest state consists in imitating the prime movers' theoretical structure of the cosmos.

**The rise of philosophical analysis.** An aspect of recent postidealism in the West has been the rise of philosophical analysis, characterized by features such as clarification of key primitive terms and the reconstruction of a clear syntactical meta-linguistic framework. This feature was developed in the philosophy of logical positivism at the turn of the twentieth century and culminated in Rudolph Carnap's (d. 1970) doctrine of reconstructionalism. Similar themes are depicted in the following three theses of Islamic philosophy.

The first case lies in Ibn Sina's tripartite solution to the so-called theory of universals, which questioned the ontic status of universals (indicated by notions such as "being a number," or "goodness"). Ibn Sina held the position that the meanings of single philosophical terms are to be found in the context of their applications as follows: Syntactical universals (such as "evenness") as well as a syntactical analysis of universals are significantly independent of our mental state or the actual world; conceptual universals, such as intentions, are mid-dependent; and finally in the realm of empirical sciences, essences and universals follow our encounter with facts that are existents and particulars. An awareness of the linguistic import of philosophical issues can also be found in the clever solution of Nasir Khusraw (d. 1077) to the question of "Which comes first? The chicken or the egg?" He pointed out the similarity of this paradox with the inquiry about the "initiation of the beginning segment in a circle." He replied that a chicken means an actualized egg, while an egg means a potential chicken. Thus, a comprehensive language addresses the question's need to place both of them in the same object language level of terms (in the same way *space* and *time* are placed as primitive notions in contemporary physics). Finally let us consider Tusi's analysis of infinity. As a rational philosopher, he had to agree with Aristotle that there is no actual infinite, but as a mathematician, he sought to take "infinite number" as a significant notion. Thus, he made a meta-linguistic distinction between several senses of infinity, syntactical and ontic, accepting the first sense and rejecting the second. These three examples well illustrate that Islamic philosophy contains an awareness of philosophical analysis, meta-mathematics, and logic.

### Depiction of the self as a ground of experience.

The concept of a person is a cardinal issue in the philosophical system due to the observation made by Ludwig Wittgenstein (d. 1951) that we can never see our eyes directly, or that the self is not in the world, but that it is implied in the ground of being-in-the-world. Also, he pointed out that the notion of language is like a game, a societal entity; consequently, a substantial notion of the self may prevent the possibility of language and thus of knowledge all together. It is for this reason that a number of western philosophers have rejected the Cartesian depiction of the self as a substance. For example, David Hume (d. 1776) depicts the self in terms of a bundle of impressions, while Kant attempts to clarify the phenomenal self in the search for what he calls a transcendental unity of perception. Finally, Martin Heidegger's depiction of self as *Dasein*, meaning "being-in-the-world" is one of the most celebrated philosophical formulations of the twentieth century. Long before these European thinkers, a number of Muslim philosophers focused on a depiction of the notion of a person in ways to avoid the standard paradoxes such as "private language fallacy." Ibn Sina, for instance, states that if a person abstracts his sensations one by one, he can never presuppose that the subject of this experience is empty. In a similar manner, al-Ghazali points out that both God and the self are without any quality or quantity —they belong to the ground of experience and not to objects of experience (like Hume's point that there is no impression of the self). In a Sufi depiction of the self, persons are construed in a process which is a continuum of the development of states (*ahwal*) and stations (*maqamat*); eventually the finite limited ephemeral self is annihilated (*fana*) and is merged into its ultimate source; in such a state, a person merging into its essence persists (*baqa*) eternity in this blessed state of union. Here a person is not depicted as a substantial soul but in the context

of what William James (d. 1910) stipulated as "stream of consciousness"; thus the focus is not on persons as things-substances but on the temporal nature of experiencing the world. In this light, both Ibn Sina and Mulla Sadra construe a phenomenological metaphysics in which the mind directly encounters being rather than itself as a substance. In sum, a major contribution of Islamic philosophy lies in its depiction of "persons" in the context of the field of experience.

### Key epistemological concepts depicted in light of both value and experience.

Traditionally epistemic models followed theoretical frameworks of Platonic writings, where knowledge was identified with the abstraction of concepts. Later knowledge was limited either to concepts received by the intellect or sense data experienced by the senses. Analogous to many recent epistemologies such as American pragmatism, Muslim philosophies examined layers of consciousness/awareness in varieties of knowing, as well as the relation between knowledge and morality. Let us consider some examples from everyday life.

In teaching a trade, the apprentice learns "how to" perform a task, for example, learning how to ride a bicycle, or learning to dance. In these examples, one learns "how to do an activity," instead of learning and conceiving a clarification of an analytical fact like an axiom of geometry or empirical data, like the distance between the sun and earth; one can also become a better perceiver of danger or have a richer experience of music, or sport. With respect to morality and ethics, one may follow Plato's equation of knowledge with virtue and vice with ignorance. Accordingly, learning from the world makes one also a better human being. The primary sources of these practical and holistic epistemologies are the works of Plato and Plotinus. Specifically, Plato uses the allegory of a blindfolded prisoner who, through a continuum of epistemic ascents, finally confronts the source of all sight, which is the sun; he also depicts love as a ladder through which a lover encounters the true form of absolute beauty, which is another icon for the highest good. Plotinus also discusses the ascent of the soul as it seeks to be united with the One, analogous to a daughter, who, recognizing her true love for the father, seeks "no otherness" from the One. Muslim philosophers developed their epistemologies in ways that resemble Ibn Sina's theory of pragmatic imagination. Ibn Sina postulates the epistemology of internal senses, translated here as "prehensive imagination," as illustrated in the case of sheep running away at the sight of a wolf. In such a response, it is not necessary for an agent to be conscious in order to act prudently. Similar cases are found in Muslim theories of learning through the mystical apprenticeship with a Sufic master, as the Disciples of Christ learned from Jesus' acts or one learns from parables in the sacred texts. Recent development in the West in "fuzzy logic," Gestalt psychology, the epistemologies of Marxists, American pragmatists, the views of a number of philosophers such as Henry Bergson (d. 1941), Alfred North Whitehead

(d. 1947), and Wittgenstein—all these question the legitimacy of the notion of a conscious state independent of life activity. Al-Ghazali ironically wrote against philosopher's mistakes, but in fact was instrumental in strengthening philosophy among subsequent Muslim scholars. For him the major feature of God and persons is intentional volition. In the case of the Divine, there is the will to create the cosmos. In the case of persons, we have intentional epistemic virtues of the soul's urge in seeking salvation. The most outstanding features of humanity are found in immediate existential feeling tones of exuberance (*dhawq*), urgency (*shawq*), and authentic states of intimacy (*uns*). Al-Ghazali's system integrates a number of insights from various traditions, such as the supremacy of the power of good will in the Zoroastrian tradition and in Friedrich Nietzsche, in Wittgenstein's earlier doctrine as well as in St. Augustine's account of the similarity between persons and the world, of the soul and God. Al-Ghazali's writings were instrumental in integrating the philosophical dimensions with extensive mystical (Sufi) writings in enriching Islamic epistemology and ethics.

**Facets of the ethics of self-realization.** A major issue in Islamic moral philosophy is various epistemic and normative facets of the ethics of self-realization. The essence of the self is presupposed to be the divine-God-nature; accordingly, the ultimate self-knowledge lies in the archetypal theme of the return to the origin of cosmogony, expressed as dealienation.

As is to be expected, there are varieties of Islamic ethics, such as treatises on pragmatics of politics for princes, and ethical issues in legalistic theology, as well as standard philosophical ethics such as utilitarianism and the Kantian type of morality emphasizing a sense of duty. The most original and complex Muslim contribution to ethics is the Sufi prescription of the good life. Amazingly, this type of ethics may be described in the context of the problem of alienation—estrangement—taken by Marxists, existentialists, phenomenologists, and psychoanalysts to be the most important problem in modern times. The Islamic mystics, known as the Sufis, take a theme common to both Neoplatonism and the Qur'an that all entities seek to return to their source. Because persons are finite and the ultimate being, such as the God of monotheists or the One of the mystics is without a limit, there is a need for a Christ-like sage, a mediator figure who is half-human and half-divine, who can link the two realms. Usually this union assumes the absorption of persons into the ultimate being, as a river returns to the sea. Here is an example. Suppose a male realizes that his beloved resembles his mother, the first instance of the feminine archetype for the male child. If so, then naturally his "new love" integrates his urge to return to the blessed state of an infant cared by his mother. The love of the specific mother induces the unconscious love of the feminine archetype that results in his discovery of the actualization of an instance of the feminine archetype in his future spouse. Thus, love in a sense signifies a return to the

original desire. The Muslim mystic's vision of the ethics of unity is much stronger than the simple case stated above. The mystical return is, in fact, an integration of the last phase of the ethics of self-realization, which constitutes the perfection (*kamal*) of persons. The Isma'ili philosopher Nasir Khusraw presents the following Neoplatonic version of this theme of unity through emanation and return. To begin with, neither temporality nor existence may be applied to the term *God*. What can be talked about is the cosmogony of the emanation of the world from the first intelligence, having been begotten from the One who emanates the universal soul; the latter emanates the individual souls. Now the problem is what to do with these individual souls, as they need to be differentiated from one another in the spiritual realm. In this context, Khusrau proffers the view that the souls are temporarily embodied in order to partake of morally significant experiences, and in life's struggle, they have an opportunity to become purified. The theme is a repetition of Plotinus's view that a body is like the useful instrument of a musician who sets it aside after the dance of earthly life. This example clearly signifies that the Islamic ethos is not an ascetic one, as Muslim philosophers, such as Ibn Sina, clearly distinguish between ascetics, religious devotee, and mystics. In this tenor, it should be mentioned that the prophet Muhammad's personal life is embodied as a prophet statement, as well as in an Islamic religious law (*shari'a*), which is concerned with the practical dimension of life on this earth as well as in the afterlife. The Qur'an itself has a number of references to practical issues such as the economics of gender relations, and to God as a provider of blessings available in this life to His creatures.

**A global vision of politics.** As exemplified in the works of the greatest Muslim social philosopher, 'Abd ar-Rahman ibn Khaldun (d. 1379), Muslim political philosophy, in contrast to the individualism of John Locke (d. 1704) and John Stuart Mill (d. 1836), focuses on the Unitarian view of persons, viewing these not as independent individuals, but rather as members of a society or even a global village. The essence of an individual is being a member of a polity. Official Muslim theology is tolerant of Zoroastrians, Christians, and Jews, for these "people of the [sacred, monotheistic] book." Accordingly, Muslim rulers have a moral obligation to protect temples and churches, assuring a societal condition wherein monotheistic believers can practice their own kind of worship. In a so-called imaginary jihad, it is conceivable that Jewish and Christian armies can assist Muslims in converting heathens to monotheism. Names of Jewish prophets taken by Muslims and numerous references to parables from the *Torah*, in the literature of Muslims, show that Muslims regard Jews as the chosen people of the Lord. In the same tenor Jesus, who is taken to be human but a prophet of God, born of a virgin, is often depicted as the mediator figure in Islamic mysticism. In light of these affinities, one may ask in what sense Islamic political philosophy may be unique.

Muslims envision themselves not as being opposed to the earliest monotheistic approaches to society and the *poleitia*, but as a recipient of the later revelation of God to humanity. The Hebrews received the gift of monotheism, calling Elohim/Yahweh the only God of the universe, a source of divine justice prescribing both rewards and punishment. Christians preached the message of a loving God, who sacrificed His Son, God incarnate, for humanity. The salient feature of Islamic political philosophy is its vision of a unity applied to the global politics of achieving a political unity under a theocratic order. A further delineation of this political philosophy has two implications. First is the rejection of the legitimacy of separating the state and religion, similar to Plato's vision expressed in the *Republic* that morally useful "myths" should be embedded in the praxis of the state. Among the Shi'a, a minority of Islamic creed, this theocracy takes a stronger turn.

The salient philosophical framework of Islam, unlike Judaism and Christianity, points to a theocratic political philosophy of globalism—that moved individual alliances away from nationalistic conflicts to a single world community of faithful global citizens. Consequently, several modern Muslim thinkers have offered a number of theories about the encounter between Islam and Western cultures. A partial list of these social philosophers includes Jamal al-Din Asadabadi (also known as al-Afghani, d. 1897), Muhammad Iqbal (d. 1938), Muhammad Husayn Tabataba'i (d. 1989), and Ruhollah Khomeini. Afghani appealed to special Islamic virtues, such as a combination of rationalism and pragmatics of the religious life, such as modesty, honesty, and truthfulness. He suggested that by adopting these archetypal virtues and joining pan-Islamic movements, Islamic culture would be able to encounter positively the power of Western culture. Iqbal was of the opinion that the essence of Islamic culture lies in its transformation of Greek abstract philosophy into an empirical mode of knowledge that takes account of concrete scientific facts; he also saw the active expression of mystical virtues compatible with an Islamic political agenda. Both he and Afghani objected to passive mysticism and attempted to integrate personal intuition and reflections with societal praxis. Tabataba'i integrated the Shi'a notion of the imam as an essential mediator figure in a person's search for his essence, which leads to knowledge of God. A number of followers of Tabataba'i became part of the group of ayatollahs who initiated and carried out the later Islamic revolutions in the Islamic Republic of Iran, led by the Ayatollah Khomeini. The praxis of his political vision culminated in a division of government into branches (legislative, executive, and judicial) under the supreme leadership of a jurist who has the ultimate power in the state. The new doctrine known as *valayat-e faqih* has important political implications. In fact it establishes the supreme ayatollah jurist as the guardian of the state, since he holds the ultimate political power in the government. This interpretation of Islamic theology views the supreme jurist not as a mere interpreter of archetypal meta-theories for making particular laws but as a direct power that intervenes in national and international politics of the nation and is backed by the military branch of the government.

Islamic themes have been integrated in the social thoughts of a number of recent African political thinkers. For example 'Ali A. Mazrui (b. 1933) proffers Islam as the first Protestant type of reformation of Christianity; also Islam is viewed as the last revealed universal religion. Moreover, he questions the Eurocentric approach of alienating Africa from the Middle East and advocates a rewriting of the social map of the area under the concept of "Afrabia." Mazrui's Islamic themes envision the Afrocentric agenda as a phase of a dialectical encounter to the Eurocentric perspective of the earlier centuries. Following the Islamic principle of unity (*tawhid*), he proposes a synthesis found in Islamic political philosophy, namely a vision of global harmony based on justice such as praxes of Black reparation—a vision suited for the global village of the present millennium.

**Symbolic/allegorical theology.** An outstanding feature of the Islamic intellectual tradition lies in its symbolic expression, which is embedded in allegory and extensive metaphysical poetry. These texts should not be treated as "soft minded" philosophy. A number of philosophers, such as Ibn Sina, Tusi, and Mulla Sadra, who could and did write technical philosophy, such as logic treatises, also chose to write mystical works. Unlike the descriptive dimensions of physical science, and the analytical and deductive dimensions of syntactical studies like logic and mathematics, mysticism neither explains the world, nor analyzes concepts. It is the primary aim of mysticism to transform the intentional phenomenon of the authentic experiences of persons from an alienating one to one marked by harmony—a harmony in which even the death of one's body is integrated in one's life experience. Another reason for the use of the symbolic method is that the subject matter of discourse is neither empirically observable, sensible, nor an analytically conceivable specific concept. In contrast, it is concerned with topics such as a Gestalt vision of the unity of being, which places the individual and his experience into a harmonious, unified, connected cosmos, where death and birth, knowledge, and ignorance, good and evil are connected. Let us illustrate this point in the pragmatics of the light motif. As Plato uses light symbolism for the sun in the allegory of the cave, Aristotle's depicts the active intelligence as light, and with Plotinus's use of the Sun as an image of the One, it becomes evident that the Sun depicts the Divine in its emanating light. The culmination of the "light motif" is found in the system of the post–Ibn Sina school of philosophy of illumination, founded by Suhrawardi (d. 1119). According to this system, reality may be depicted as a continuum of light; the primordial emanatory called the Light of Lights (depicting the Divine), is part of an eschatological order; last entities are particular bodies, which are also lights. The illumination type of metaphysics overcomes some problems of dualistic ontologies. For example, a mind-body dualism is avoided by depicting mental experiences as enlightenment, and physical entities as particles; thus a single notion, namely that of light, can be used in an ontology without breaking reality into two incompatible primary terms. Also knowledge as illumination can be used in the context of the incarnation (hull) theory of mystical union. For instance, the mystic poet Rumi calls his own master Shams-e Tabrizi, literally "the Sun of [the City] of/from Tabriz". The Sufi circular dance with one hand to the center of the circle, the other extended to the sky, depicts an act of imitating the sun and the process of its radiation. In the same tenor, faith is symbolized by warmth in the heart of the believer, fire as love of the Divine, and finally the mirror as the prescribed state in which the creature is open to be a witness of the world, which is a creation. The theme of the cycle of descent and ascent is also found in other common sets of icons, such as drowning in the sea, a flight of the bird to the heavens, and the like. In sum, Islamic epistemologies include but are not limited to the standard views of sense perception, conception by analysis and deduction. The dominance of symbolism in the pragmatic theories of knowledge is due to the emphasis of the Islamic intellectual tradition on mysticism, its ethics of self-realization, and its refined delineation of topics like prophecy and various intentional senses of memory, imagination, and communication.

## Conclusion

Philosophical speculations comprise an essential dimension of the Islamic intellectual tradition not only in its technical philosophical corpus, but also in its religious, mystical, and literary traditions. It is true that its major framework lies in Greek philosophical sources, especially in Aristotle and Plotinus, and that its content derives from Islamic sources (the Qur'an, the tradition or hadith, as well as early theologians). However, a number of Muslim philosophers reformulated the earlier Greek views with novel elements that resemble a number of new trends in Western philosophy. Among noteworthy views are a metaphysics of intentional processes, the depiction of persons in the language of fields of experience, a unified global vision of political philosophy, the integration of ethics and metaphysics to form a mystical process of dealienation, and the application of philosophical analyses to both ethics and metaphysics. The salient features of Islamic philosophy are not only special features that differentiate it from other traditions, but they are themes that constitute paradigmatic refinement of philosophical thinking.

See also **Ibn Rushd; Ibn Sina; Kalam; Law; Tasawwuf; Wajib al-Wujud.**

## BIBLIOGRAPHY

El-Bizri, Nader. *The Quest for Being: Avicenna and Heidegger.* Binghamton, N.Y.: Global Publications, 2000.

Fakhry, Majid. *A History of Islamic Philosophy,* 2d ed. New York: Columbia University Press, 1983.

Ibn Sina. *The Metaphysica of Avicenna (Ibn Sina).* Translated by Parviz Morewedge. New York and London: Columbia University Press and Routledge Kegan Paul, 1972.

Morewedge, Parviz. "Theology." In *The Oxford Encyclopedia of Islamic World.* Edited by John Esposito. New York and Oxford, U.K.: Oxford University Press, 1995.

Morewedge, Parviz. *The Mystical Philosophy of Ibn Sina.* Binghamton, N.Y.: Global Publications, 2001.

Leahman, Oliver, and Morewedge, Parviz. "Islamic Philosophy, Modern." In *Routledge Enyclopdia of Philosophy.* Edited by Edward Craig. London and New York: Routledge, 1998.

Sharif, M. Muhammad. *A History of Muslim Philosophy.* Wiesbaden: Otto Harrassowitz, 1963–1966.

*Parviz Morewedge*

# FARRAKHAN, LOUIS (1933– )

Louis Farrakhan was born Louis Eugene Walcott on 11 May 1933 in the Bronx, New York. He attended Winston-Salem Teachers College in North Carolina from 1951 to 1953, where he majored in English. He joined the Nation of Islam in 1955.

The Nation of Islam is a community of African Americans formed in the 1930s. The community's spiritual identity is Islam, and its political identity is black nationalism. Louis Farrakhan joined the Nation of Islam because of the message of community and the coherence of faith offered by the community in the face of white American racism and violence against blacks in the Jim Crow era. After the death in 1975 of Elijah Muhammad, the community's founder and leader for over forty years, his son Warithudeen Muhammad changed the philosophical base from black nationalism to the global philosophy of Islam. He also enhanced the spiritual identity in Islam. This move into orthodox Islam caused a breach in the leadership in the Nation of Islam and its collapse. In 1977 Louis Farrakhan reestablished the Nation of Islam with black nationalism as its philosophy and Islam as its spiritual identity.

Between 1953 and 1956 Farrakhan worked as a club singer and musician. He is married to Khadijah (née Betsy Ross), with whom he has had nine children. In 1979 Farrakhan established the newspaper *The Final Call* (whose name is derived from the message in the Qur'an 74:38), and in 1981 he held the first national convention of the Resurrected Nation (a name used briefly to describe the Nation of Islam). On Savior's Day, 26 February 1989, the community that Farrakhan founded inaugurated the National Center, named Mosque Maryam in honor of black womanhood, in Chicago. During the 1990s Minister Farrakhan was embroiled in a number of controversies: with the American Jewish community over alleged anti-Semitism, with other Muslims over the ideology of the Nation of Islam, and with many others over the black nationalist stance of the Nation of Islam.

During the 1990s Minister Farrakhan embarked on a steady program to reestablish the Nation of Islam as an African American Sunni Muslim community. This process continues today, and the Nation of Islam is recognized as a member of the world community of Islam.

*See also* **American Culture and Islam; Malcolm X; Muhammad, Elijah; Nation of Islam; United States, Islam in the.**

## BIBLIOGRAPHY

Farrakhan, Louis. *A Torchlight for America*. Chicago: FCN Publishing, 1993.

Muhammad, Elijah. *Message to the Blackman in America*. Chicago: Muhammad Mosque of Islam No. 2, 1965.

*Aminah Beverly McCloud*

## FASI, MUHAMMAD 'ALLAL AL- (1910–1974)

'Allal al-Fasi was a leading figure in the Moroccan independence movement. From the launching of the new nation, in 1956, al-Fasi was also known as president of the influential Istiqlal (independence) party. Born to an elite family of Islamic scholars (ulema) in Fez, the religious capital of Morocco, al-Fasi studied at the prestigious Islamic university of al-Qarawiyyin, and later joined the protest movement against the French and Spanish colonial presence on Moroccan soil. He quickly became one of the most visible national leaders in the pro-independence struggle, and was exiled for nine years by the French to Gabon and Congo-Brazzaville. Shortly after his return to Morocco, he chose to leave again, spending another nine years in Cairo, where he and his party thought he could best advance the nationalist cause.

Author of some twenty books, al-Fasi's writings fall into four categories. The first consists of his reformist, or *salafi*, works, which focus on the renewal of Islamic law. These include *al-Naqd al-dhati* (1952, Self-criticism), and *Maqasid al-shari'a al-islamiyya wa-makarimuha* (1964, The objectives and ethics of Islamic law). The second category is made up of his political essays on the Islamic socialist positions of the Istiqlal party and its support for Morocco's claim to Mauritania and the Spanish Sahara, and includes *Manhaj al-istiqlaliyya* (The method of self-reliance). A third category comprises his writings on the modern history of North Africa, especially Morocco, and the fourth consists of his contributions to the genre of nationalist poetry.

*See also* **Reform: Arab Middle East and North Africa; Salafiyya.**

## BIBLIOGRAPHY

Cohen, Amnon. "'Allal al-Fasi: His Contribution Towards Morocco's Independence." *Asian and African Studies* 3 (1967): 121–164.

*David L. Johnston*

## FATIMA (C. 605–633)

Fatima (d. 633) was the daughter of the prophet Muhammad and Khadija, spouse of Muhammad's cousin and companion 'Ali b. Abi Talib, and mother of al-Hasan and al-Husayn, the Prophet's only male descendants. 'Ali headed the line of the Shi'ite imams. Fatima's genealogical position reveals the significance attributed to her throughout the Muslim world and explains the veneration she enjoys.

Fatima is said to be the source of blessing (*baraka*), and is a saint, particularly the patron saint of fertility, and is appealed to as a mediator between God and humans. Her blessing hand is commonly used to protect against the evil eye.

Little is known about the actual figure hidden behind a blooming legend that combines the historical with fictional and mystical elements. Early Islamic literature such as the Prophet's biography, historiography, hadith collections, and exegetical literature do not provide a comprehensive biography of Fatima. However, they present some genealogical and biographical cornerstones and occasional events of her life. The date of her birth remains uncertain as well as the date of her marriage to 'Ali b. Abi Talib (622 or 623). Her son Hasan was born in 624 and Husayn in 626. She also gave birth to two daughters, Umm Kulthum and Zaynab. The authors agree with regard to the year in which she died, although there is no clear reference to the month, that is, the exact period of time after her father's death. Furthermore, we find contradictory indications concerning the circumstances of her last hours, her burial at night, and the location of her tomb. Only few records deal with historical events she was involved in.

The legend woven about Fatima provides further insights as to her importance as a spiritual personality, both for Sunni and Shi'ite Muslims. Hagiographical literature is manifold and portrays the Prophet's daughter as a multifaceted personality, appearing in Shi'ite texts as early as the tenth century.

The Fatima of the legend is given numerous epithets as al-Zahra' (the Shining one), the Resplendent, or the supreme Mary; they all indicate that she represents the female ideal of Islam.

Sunni hagiography emphasized the "orthodox" virtues, such as her piety and her rank as the Prophet's daughter, whereas Shi'ite sources created a figure of cosmic importance, the final avenger on the one hand and a luminous, celestial being working miracles on the other. Her closeness to the Prophet and the imams is expressed by her belonging to the people of the Prophet's house, to the five people of the mantle, to the immaculates, and to the people of the ordeal.

Fatima's first biographers were two European scholars, Henri Lammens and Louis Massignon. Their portraits of the Prophet's daughter stood in striking contradiction to each other. Whereas Lammens's Fatima is unattractive, of mediocre intelligence, and lacking in significance, Massignon depicts an almost mystical and sublime personality with a religious significance akin to that of the Virgin Mary. Laura Veccia Valieri's comprehensive study tries to emphasize the fact that historical reality ranges between the two portraits. Since historical sources are few and sometimes even contradictory, the conflict in historical apprehension continues. Hagiographical models in the earlier Islamic literature show—even in historical literature— that making a clear distinction between the real person and the legend can be quite difficult.

In the course of the Islamic revolution of Iran the legend of Fatima enjoyed a considerable renaissance and actualization as the female role model. She symbolized the committed fighter, engaged for the Muslim community and thus became the model in opposition to the Western woman pursuing only her individual emancipation.

*See also* **Abu Bakr; ʿAli; Biography and Hagiography; Hasan; Husayn; Shiʿa: Early; Succession.**

## BIBLIOGRAPHY

Hermansen, Marcia K. "Fatimeh as a Role Model in the Works of Ali Shariʿati." In *Women and Revolution in Iran.* Edited by Guity Nashat. Boulder, Colo.: Westview Press, 1983.

Klemm, Verena. "Die frühe islamische Erzählung von Fatima bint Muhammad: Vom habar zur Legende." *Der Islam* 79 (2002): 47–86.

Shariʿati, ʿAli. *Fatima ist Fatima.* Bonn: Embassy of the Islamic Republic Iran, 1981.

Veccia Valieri, Laura. "Fatima." In *Encyclopaedia of Islam.* Edited by B. Lewis, C. Pellat, and J. Schacht. Leiden: Brill, 1954.

*Ursula Günther*

## FATWA

A *fatwa* (pl. *fatawa*) is an advisory opinion issued by a recognized authority on law and tradition in answer to a specific question. *Fatawa* can range from single-word responses (e.g., "Yes," "No," or "Permitted") to book-length treatises. Although typically focused on legal matters, *fatawa* also treat more general religious issues, including theology, philosophy, creeds, and ʿ*ibadat* (religious obligations or acts of worship). Traditionally, despite numerous exceptions (particularly since the eleventh century), the issuer of *fatawa*, termed a mufti—whose authority derives from his knowledge of law and tradition—has functioned independently of the judicial system, indeed often privately.

While court rulings rely on the sifting of evidence and conflicting testimonies, muftis assume the facts presented by their questioners, which, obviously, can bias the answer. Moreover, a *fatwa* differs from a court judgment, or *qadaʾ*, not only in its wider potential scope—for instance, although ʿ*ibadat* are essential parts of Islamic law, they transcend the jurisdiction of the courts—but also because the *qadaʾ* is binding and enforceable, "performative," while the *fatwa* is not. Instead, it is "informational," and, while decisions of *shariʿa* courts usually pertain only to the specific cases they adjudicate, thus setting no legal precedents, *fatawa* are very often collected, published, and cited in subsequent cases.

*See also* **Law; Mufti; Religious Institutions.**

## BIBLIOGRAPHY

Schacht, Joseph. *Origins of Muhammadan Jurisprudence.* Oxford, U.K., and New York: Clarendon Press, 1979.

Weiss, Bernard G. *The Spirit of Islamic Law.* Athens: University of Georgia Press, 1998.

*Daniel C. Peterson*

## FEDAʾIYAN-E ISLAM

Fedaʾiyan-e Islam was a Shiʿite fundamentalist group that was founded in Iran in 1945 by Sayyed Mujtaba Mir Lauhi (known as Navvab-e Safavi), a man then in his early twenties, with little or no formal Islamic education. Unsettled by the writings of the controversial essayist and historian Ahmad Kasravi, Safavi masterminded his assassination in March 1946. This was followed by the assassination in November 1949 of ʿAbd al-Husayn Hazhir, the influential minister of court, and in March 1951 of prime minister Hajji ʿAli Razmara, who opposed the nationalization of the British-owned oil industry. The Fedaʾiyan had enlisted the support of the activist ayatollah Abu 'l-Qasem Kashani, but failed to win over the highest-ranking religious authority in the country, Grand Ayatollah Borujerdi.

The Fedaʾiyan's relations with Kashani became strained due to the latter's support for prime minister Mohammad Mosaddeq, who assumed power in late April 1951. Refusing to give in to the Fedaʾiyan's demands for the establishment of *shariʿa* regulations, Mosaddeq detained Safavi in June 1951. In February 1952, the Fedaʾiyan's attempted assassination of

Mosaddeq's key colleague, Husayn Fatimi, left Fatimi severely injured. By mid-1952 the Feda'iyan had resumed its ties with Kashani, who had begun to oppose Mosaddeq. In the months preceding the coup of August 1953, which toppled Mosaddeq, the Feda'iyan's antigovernment position led the American and British secret services to count on the group to help oust Mosaddeq. In November 1954 the group's failed attempt on the life of prime minister Husayn 'Ala resulted in the execution of Safavi and three of his colleagues. Despite this crippling blow, affiliates of the group were able to assassinate another prime minister, Hasan 'Ali Mansur, in January 1965.

Based mainly in Tehran, the Feda'iyan largely consisted of young men of limited education, lower class origins, and traditional occupations. The group appealed to the resentments of the lower and underclass urban elements; this, together with its challenge to the ruling elite, enabled it to acquire a significance disproportionate to its size. Ideologically resembling the al-Ikhwan al-Muslimun (Muslim Brotherhood) in Egypt, the Feda'iyan espoused a literal reading of Islamic writings and laws; they abhorred what they considered to be decadence resulting from irreligion; they feared modernity, secularism, communism, and civic-nationalism, and were bent on eliminating those whom they regarded as obstacles in their path or stooges of foreigners. Their primary goal was to establish the *shari'a*, giving a crucial sociopolitical role to clerics. Following the revolution of 1978 and 1979, many of the beliefs that had animated the Feda'iyan became part of the ruling ideology but gradually came to be identified with the proclivities of the Iranian regime's traditionalist and right-wing factions.

*See also* **Fundamentalism; Political Islam.**

## BIBLIOGRAPHY

Kazemi, Farhad. "The Fada'iyan-e Islam: Fanaticism, Politics and Terror." In *From Nationalism to Revolutionary Islam*. Edited by Said Amir Arjomand. Albany: State University of New York Press, 1984.

*Fakhreddin Azimi*

# FEMINISM

There is a struggle within Islamic societies over the definition of Islam and the role of women within it. This struggle has accompanied Muslims throughout their history.

The term "feminism" is controversial. It may conceal a Western attempt at cultural hegemony or it may be labeled as that by those who oppose women's rights but would not admit to it. Many Muslim women who may support women's rights may not choose to identify themselves as feminists. For many women there may be a perceived psychological, social, and physical danger even in expressing the desire for equal rights.

Whereas one cannot avoid making general comments about Muslim women, it ought to be kept in mind that Muslim communities are widespread and diverse, consisting of a complex set of interwoven subcultures. For example, the issues and realities of Saudi Arabian Muslim life, where women must cover their bodies and hair in public, are very different from those of Indonesian Muslim women, where there is currently a female Muslim head of state.

A common claim is that pre-Islamic Arabia oppressed women and Islam liberated them. There is a similar claim made today by Islamist movements that Western societies or women in non-Muslim cultures in general are oppressed and traditional Islam liberates them. One should remember that spiritual or emotional liberation through Islam is individual and personal and cannot be judged from the outside. But economic, social, and political rights can be gauged by intersubjective criteria and Muslim women lag far behind Muslim men in all these areas, especially in Muslim majority countries. Whether this is due to or despite Islam is open to debate.

At the other end of the spectrum from the Islamists, there is a stream of feminist thought that considers Islamic tradition as irredeemably misogynist and patriarchal. These sentiments are an echo of those voiced by the women of al-Ta'if in the seventh century who wailed and protested when the temple dedicated to the Goddess was destroyed at the instruction of prophet Muhammad. Between these two extremes lie a variety of approaches and convictions, both defined and undefined, regarding the issue of women and Islam. Whereas the Islamists may desire to discredit feminism as a Western ploy, one may posit that neither Islam, nor feminism as a movement for the full dignity and equality of women in society, are either Western or Eastern. Feminism represents a deep human aspiration for a sense of community with the world, and Islam, at its core, represents the same aspiration for a sense of community both with the human race and the realm of the Unseen.

Most of the literature produced by Muslims in the previous centuries is still in manuscript form waiting to be discovered or published. The extent to which women participated in the production of the Muslim cultures that they inhabited cannot be determined without access to information that may not have been recorded or that may not have been adequately preserved even if initially recorded. One of the tasks for feminists today is to use the available sources to construct a more accurate picture of women in early Islam, from which they can deduce early Islam's implications for modern women. This study may entail a wider use of noncanonical texts and sources, as theological canons generally reflect the biases of the male elites.

Egyptian feminist Nawal Saadawi in her Cairo home in July, 2001, a day before an Egyptian court would decide whether to take legal action against her for calling Islam a pagan religion. The case arose because a group of male Islamist lawyers accused Saadawi of being an apostate for this statement; if convicted, she would no longer be able to call herself a Muslim and would face compulsory divorce from her Muslim husband. The case was finally thrown out of court, but not before alarming human rights groups worldwide. © REUTERS NEWMEDIA INC./CORBIS

In the recent past there has been an urgent attempt to understand the definitive political defeat and colonization of Muslims at the hands of the Christian West, as this shattered the imperial Muslim self-image. Modernist male Muslims forced to study and understand their subjugation, and thus feminization, began to name its causes. Some identified the malaise of the *umma* (community of believers) as intellectual backwardness and lack of dynamism, whereas others identified it in falling away from the path of the earliest generations of Muslims whose political success was seen to stem from their adherence to a certain static conception of Islam. The former stream of thought endeavored to study and emulate the West whereas the latter warned of its moral decadence and sought only to appropriate its material technologies of power to regain Muslims' freedom, dignity, and even supremacy.

It was from among the reformist modernist male thinkers that the first proponents for the education and rights of Muslim women arose. Women raised in reformist homes became the first Muslim feminists. As anticolonial nationalist movements took over the Muslim world women participated in them along with men. However, the disillusionment of the postcolonial era with its dire economic problems, political instabilities, corruption, and military or dynastic dictatorships, as well as covert and overt interference from the superpowers, militated against civil liberties and human rights in Muslim countries. Under such conditions Islamist movements gained ascendancy in many of the Muslim countries causing women to lose many of the rights that they had gained in earlier decades. The loss of women's human rights where religious fundamentalism gained in power is merely an indication of the lack of human rights for all in such societies. Such a situation has given rise to a spectrum of Muslim feminist responses.

Among Muslim women who had the benefit of higher education are feminists who consider Islam to be a matter of personal choice that ought not to be "used or abused" for political purposes. There are also women feminist scholars who are socialist, agnostic, atheist, or Marxist in their orientation. There are scholars who see Islam as a rich and viable culture in need of a thorough and yet sympathetic feminist critique. There are liberal Muslim theologians writing in the politically free Western environment who nonetheless remain apologetic, staying within the prescribed traditional approach to the Qur'an and the sunna.

Finally, in the Muslim countries where one sees a mismatched marriage between feminism and Islamism it is not clear whether the Islamist Muslim women leaders/preachers are contributing toward the relative subjugation or relative liberation of their large female following. The ideological or intellectual differences among Muslim feminist scholars are paralleled in the various forms of feminist activism in various parts of the Muslim world. In certain areas one finds highly visible feminist movements, in others only guarded private conversations.

In general, the area that takes up the attention of most feminists, whether they work within a traditional Islamic framework or not, is the implementation of various Islamic laws. Until recently the area of *shari'a* (Islamic law) that was discussed and implemented in most of the Muslim world was the Muslim family law covering issues of marriage, divorce, child custody, and inheritance. In all of these women do not have equal status with men. For example, Muslim family laws and the social consciousness associated with them circumscribe and constrain women's lives, and so-called honor killings that dishonor the lives of innocent women and the indiscriminate application of *hudud* (Islamic criminal) laws directly threaten their lives.

Dishonor killings (an integral feature of all patriarchal societies) as well as female infanticide (a preemptive dishonor killing practiced in pre-Islamic Arabia) were outlawed by the prophet Muhammad as evidenced both by texts in the Qur'an and the sunna. However, the taking of innocent female life in the name of male honor continues to exist in many Muslim countries with the tacit approval of law enforcement agencies and clerics, instilling a deep-seated fear of their male family members in the hearts of women.

More recently, the enforcement of some of the most severe *hudud* punishments has alarmed a majority of Muslims, human rights activists, and feminists internationally. Pseudo-liberal Muslims, who in principle do not disagree with an informed application of *hudud* laws, question its implementation in the absence of social welfare and economic justice, as is the case in some of the areas attempting to implement *shari'a* laws. But these Muslims fail to recognize or address the significant lack of political, social, and religious freedom for individuals in such areas to carry out an expression of religion that is harsh and lacking in compassion.

In the twentieth century, progressive Muslim scholars have come to look at the hadith corpus as a record of the concerns and understandings of earliest Muslim male communities rather than an authoritative divine guide to all the details of one's life. Yet they have continued to adhere to an understanding of the Qur'an as the literal word of God. This, however, is giving way to a more complex and self-reflective reading of the Qur'an as a vehicle engendering a "theo-ethics" and aesthetics of mercy and justice as well as a record of the Prophetic struggle, both within his own person and with the community of Muslims. The Qur'an, the primary symbol of Muslim identity, for the most part has become an idol that petrifies the community's understanding of the compassionate will of God in their lives. In an intellectually and spiritually mature and honest Muslim community the Qu'ran and its readings would be seen as progressive records both of an individual's and a community's encounter with, as well as projection unto, the Unseen. Such a Muslim community that understands the good example of the Prophet not in terms of any particulars of his life, apparel, and so on, but in terms of the ethical values that he struggled to embody at his best, shall provide the context within which women and other groups targeted for discrimination (simply due to a difference in their religion or sexual orientation) will find dignity and equitable treatment.

*See also* **Gender.**

## BIBLIOGRAPHY

Abou El Fadl, Khaled. *Speaking in God's Name: Islamic Law, Authority and Women.* Oxford, U.K.: Oneworld, 2001.

Abu-Lughod, Lila, ed. *Remaking Women. Feminism and Modernity in the Middle East.* Princeton, N.J.: Princeton University Press, 1998.

Afkhami, Mahnaz, and Friedl, Erika, eds. *Muslim Women and the Politics of Participation. Implementing the Beijing Platform.* Syracuse, N.Y.: Syracuse University Press, 1997.

Ahmed, Leila. *Women and Gender in Islam: Historical Roots of a Modern Debate.* New Haven, Conn.: Yale University Press, 1992.

Barlas, Asma. *"Believing Women" in Islam. Unreading Patriarchal Interpretations of the Qur'an.* Austin: University of Texas Press, 2002.

Cooke, Miriam. *Women Claim Islam. Creating Islamic Feminism Through Literature.* New York: Routledge, 2001.

Esposito, John. *Women in Muslim Family Law.* Syracuse, N.Y.: Syracuse University Press, 1982.

Mernissi, Fatima. *Beyond the Veil. Male-Female Dynamics in Muslim Society* (1975). Rev. ed., Syracuse, New York: Al Saqi Books, 1985.

Spellburg, Denise. *Politics, Gender and the Islamic Past: The Legacy of A'isha bint Abi Bakr.* N. Y.: Columbia University Press, 1999.

Wadud, Amina. *Qur'an and Women. Rereading the Sacred Text from a Woman's Perspective.* New York: Oxford University Press, 1999.

*Ghazala Anwar*

# FEZ

The oldest of Morocco's four imperial cities, Fez (Ar., Fas) is situated just above the Sefrou valley, at a natural intersection of the commercial routes connecting the Atlantic and Mediterranean coasts with the Atlas mountains and the Sahara. Fez's location and water-rich surrounding helped the city become an important political, religious, and commercial center of the medieval Islamic world.

Founded on the east bank of the Wadi Fez in 789 C.E. by Mulay Idris b. 'Abdallah, a descendent of the Prophet who had fled from Mecca to Morocco to avoid Abassid persecution, Fez was expanded onto the west bank by his son, Idris b. Idris, in 809. Fez grew under the Idrisi dynasty when waves of immigrants from southern Spain (Andalusia, or Ar., Al-Andalus) and northern Africa quickly inhabited both sides of the city. With the foundation of the Qarawiyyin mosque and university in 859 (believed to have been established by a wealthy woman from the Tunisian city of Kairouan) and the Andalusian mosque in 862, Fez became an Islamic capital of learning that rivaled Al-Azhar University in Cairo.

Alternating Fatimid and Umayyad influence over Fez nourished bitter rivalry between the two parts of the city, which ensued until they were united by the Almoravid dynasty at the end of the eleventh century. Under the Almoravids and the Almohads (who ruled the city from 1145 to 1175) Fez also became an essential military base and was surrounded by a defensive wall pierced by eight huge gates, which are still functioning today. Fez reached the peak of its political and cultural prosperity under the Marinid dynasty, which conquered the city in 1248 and made it the capital of Morocco for almost three centuries. This period saw the construction of numerous prestigious religious colleges in rich Hispano-Moorish style, the finest examples of which are the Al-Saffarin and the Al-ʿAttarin *madrasas* (Islamic colleges). The city became home to the famous Arab traveler Ibn Battuta, who composed the memoirs of his journeys across Asia while living in Fez, where he remained until his death in 1369. Although Fez's political importance waned in the sixteenth century when Marrakesh was preferred as a capital by the Saʾadi dynasty (1517–1666), it has retained a religious primacy throughout the centuries. The treaty of Fez, which established the French protectorate in Morocco, was signed on 30 March 1912.

In the twentieth century Fez, whose urban population exceeds 510,000 (1994 census), expanded into four distinct areas:

1. The old city (locally referred to as Fez al-Bali), which was declared a world heritage site by the UNESCO in 1981, is characterized by rich al-Andalus architecture, narrow dark alleys crossing at irregular patterns, high-walled houses, and traditional markets. It treasures the Qarawiyyin mosque and university, whose present dimensions date back to the 1135 Almoravid enlargement.

2. The thirteenth-century Fez al-Jedid (New Fez in Arabic), lying west of the old medina, served as the Marinid administrative center and consists of the Royal Palace with its adjoining Great Mosque, a Muslim neighborhood, and a formerly vibrant Jewish quarter (the Mellah).

3. The Ville Nouvelle (the New City in French), built by the French administration in 1916 to accommodate modern colonial lifestyle, lies on the southwest plateau and is largely a residential and industrial area.

4. A new town, which has sprung up since Morocco's independence, lies to the northwest.

Fez, which gave its name to the brimless, red felt hat and was its sole producer until the nineteenth century, remains today a center of religious learning, traditional crafts, and tourism.

*See also* **Africa, Islam in; Sultanates: Modern.**

## BIBLIOGRAPHY

Burckhardt, Titus. *Fez, City of Islam*. Cambridge, U.K.: Islamic Texts Society, 1992.

Mezzine, Mohamed, ed. *Fès médiévale, entre légende et histoire, un carrefour de l'Orient à l'apogée d'un rêve*. Paris: Edition Autrement, 1992.

Le Tourneau, Roger. *Fez in the Age of the Marinides*. Norman: Oklahoma University Press, 1961.

*Claudia Gazzini*

# FITNA

The word *fitna* (pl. *fitan*) is used in the Qurʾan to mean both "a temptation that tests the believer's religious commitments" and "a punishment by trial." In classical Arabic historical texts, it is used primarily to mean "civil war," "rebellion that leads to schism," or "violent factional strife," but even in historical texts, it bears connotations of "communal test, affliction" and "the temptation to turn upon one's fellow Muslims." In the hadith literature, *fitna* signifies both "strife between Muslims," and "a trial by which God tests and purifies the believer." Especially when combined in the hadith literature with the words *malahim* (great battles) or *ashrat al-saʿa* (signs of the [Last] Hour), *fitan* specifically indicate apocalyptic schisms and battles predicted to break out within the Muslim community before the Last Hour. The apocalyptic connotation that the word *fitan* acquired during the first two centuries of Islamic history likely arose partly out of perceptions that the early civil wars that were cleaving the fledging Islamic community asunder were signs that the world was ending, and partly from the propagandistic use of apocalyptic hadiths during those wars.

Early Islamic history saw a series of *fitan*, or civil wars, unfold in relatively rapid succession. Interspersed between many smaller uprisings and rebellions, the first three major *fitan* dominated the historical memory of the early community. The first *fitna* broke out in 656 c.e.—within twenty-five years of the Prophet's death—and lasted until 661 c.e. The long second *fitna* erupted nearly a generation later, in 680 c.e., and because various rebellions continued to erupt in different places, it was a dozen years before Umayyad dynasts again consolidated power, in 692 c.e. The third *fitna*, the Abbasid revolution (747–750 c.e.), successfully overturned the Umayyads, bringing to power the new Abbasid dynasty. A fratricidal fourth *fitna* (which will not be treated here) erupted in 810 c.e. between two sons of the Abbasid ruler Harun al-Rashid, the brothers al-Amin and al-Maʾmun, and lasted until the complete victory of al-Maʾmun in 814.

Armed strife between Muslims began with complaints about oppressive or unjust practices of the third caliph, ʿUthman, and led to that caliph's assassination by a party of Muslims in 656 c.e. Many Muslims then supported the leadership of ʿAli, the son-in-law and cousin of the Prophet, who was chosen to succeed ʿUthman. But troubling questions about the assassination of ʿUthman harried the caliphate of ʿAli. Was the assassination of ʿUthman justified, or should the assassins have been promptly punished? Different religio-political parties formed in response to these questions and engaged in battles against each other over the correct response (although this was by no means the only issue involved). One group supported the leadership of ʿAli, with his apparent decision not to punish those who had killed ʿUthman. Another group, led by the Prophet's wife ʿAʾisha and two of his most important companions, Talha and al-Zubayr, opposed the leadership of ʿAli and called for the punishment of the assassins of ʿUthman. The forces of these two parties met at the Battle of the Camel (656 C.E.) during which ʿAli's forces routed their opponents, Talha and al-Zubayr were killed, and ʿAʾisha was sent home chastened.

ʿAli's troubles did not cease with this victory, since a new opponent arose: Muʿawiya, a relative of the slain caliph ʿUthman, and a seasoned governor of the province of Syria. Muʿawiya sent his Syrian forces against ʿAli and his supporters, and the two sides engaged in battle at a village called Siffin. The battle of Siffin ended with an agreement to engage in arbitration. One group of ʿAli's supporters rejected this agreement, and eventually turned against ʿAli, demanding that Muslims adhere to "God's judgment" alone (manifested on the battlefield and in Qurʾanic injunctions) rather than fallible human judgments exercised in arbitration. This group (the Kharijites) was defeated by ʿAli's forces but lived on to challenge both the Umayyad and the early Abbasid dynasties in later rebellions and depredations.

It was not only the Kharijites who threatened ʿAli's rule, however. Since the arbitration agreed to at Siffin did not resolve the conflict, the Islamic community became fractured for a time into three competing groups: the supporters of ʿAli, the supporters of Muʿawiya, and the Kharijites. After a Kharijite assassin killed ʿAli in 661 C.E., Muʿawiya was eventually recognized as caliph by all but the Kharijites, whose rebellions during Muʿawiya's firm rule were promptly put down. Thus, although the first *fitna* came to an end in 661 C.E., the issues of the first *fitna* did not disappear. They would erupt again in the second and third civil wars, to haunt and eventually undermine the Umayyad dynasty established by Muʿawiya.

The sons of several of the leaders involved in the first *fitna* became embroiled in the second *fitna* in 680 C.E.: Al-Husayn, the son of ʿAli and the grandson of the Prophet, rejected the caliphate of Muʿawiya's son Yazid, and set off for the Iraqi city of Kufa to gather support for his own bid for the caliphate. He and a small band of supporters were intercepted en route from Mecca and cut down by Umayyad forces at Karbala. Al-Husayn was rapidly transformed into a martyr-figure among those Muslims who looked to the family of the Prophet to provide just religious and political leadership, namely, the early Shiʿites. The dramatic story of how al-Husayn and his supporters were killed has long loomed large in Shiʿite historical memory, and their deaths are still annually mourned in Shiʿite ritual.

Several other important Muslims rejected Umayyad rule in the years immediately following the death of al-Husayn, including al-Mukhtar, who claimed to represent another son of ʿAli, Ibn al-Hanafiyya, and Ibn al-Zubayr, who represented a pious alternative to certain oppressive Umayyad policies. Although this *fitna* ended in 692 C.E. with the Umayyads having regained control, the ideological seeds of the third *fitna* had already been planted. The early Abbasid movement that eventually successfully overturned the Umayyads called for rule by a member of the Prophet's family, and the earliest Abbasids claimed to have inherited their legitimacy from a descendant of the same man whom al-Mukhtar had earlier claimed to represent, Ibn al-Hanafiya. In terms of political ideology, all of the first three major civil wars were thus linked, and all involved competing notions of who should rule.

Later Sunni historical works betray some reworking of historical accounts aimed at dealing with the vexing question of how the Companions of the Prophet and their immediate successors, venerated and idealized by Sunnis, could have engaged in such violent conflict with each other. The memory of these wars and the fracturing of the religious community were particularly problematic for Sunnis, because the Qurʾanic verse, "You are the best community that has been raised up for mankind" (3: 110) was widely interpreted as referring to the Prophet's Companions. This presented difficulties, since the Sunnis eventually developed the concept that all of the Companions, including ʿAli and several of the Companions who fought against him, were to be considered righteous.

This series of civil wars—along with many other smaller rebellions—brought up not only issues related to Islamic leadership, but other theological issues as well, in part because these conflicts over leadership of the community were not understood as mere contests over temporal power, but rather as struggles to establish righteous Islamic governance. The early Shiʿites deemed ʿAli and his descendants (or, more broadly, "the family of the Prophet") to have had exclusive rights to legitimate leadership based on their relationship to the Prophet, their designation by the Prophet as his successors, and their superior knowledge and religious insight. The Kharijites, on the other hand, argued that genealogy played no role in the leadership of the community, which instead should be based on pious righteousness and rigorous observance of the religious law alone. The Sunni position, as it eventually developed, included a requirement that the leader be from the Prophet's tribe, but not necessarily of his family, and strongly promoted obedience to constituted authorities, no matter how unjust, so as to prevent the chaos, violence, and schism engendered by *fitna*. Issues that arose out of the competing claims made by these groups included, among other issues, the legitimacy of rebellion against unjust or invalid rulers, predestination and free will, and the question of whether or not those who committed grave sins should continue to be considered Muslims.

The impact that the early *fitan* had on the Sunni hadith literature is manifested in several ways. There are a variety of hadiths that reflect arguments about the relative virtues of ʿAli on the one hand and the earlier caliphs, Abu Bakr, ʿUmar, and ʿUthman on the other. These arguments were linked to competing conceptions of history. In addition, the early civil wars bequeathed to Islamic eschatology a number of formative apocalyptic hadiths. Certain hadiths about the figure of the Mahdi, the rightly-guided restorer predicted to usher in a reign of justice before the End Times, can be traced, as Wilferd Madelung and others have argued, to the second *fitna*. The Sufyani, a mythical heroic figure associated with the End Times, emerged as part of Umayyad propaganda during that conflict. Finally, the earliest portrayals of the figure of the Dajjal ("the Deceiver"), akin to the Christian Anti-Christ, predicted to battle the Mahdi in the End Times in apocalyptic hadiths, may have been modeled in part upon another of the participants in the second *fitna*, al-Mukhtar. The Dajjal and the Mahdi are still prominent in Islamic eschatological ideas. The third *fitna*, too, produced numerous hadiths extolling the Abbasids, often in the form of apocalyptic hadiths aimed at motivating men to fight for the Abbasid cause.

More broadly, the impact of the confusing profusion of battles and competing groups associated with the first two *fitan* in particular can be seen in the positive value placed in Sunni sources on neutrality or quietism, usually called *quʿud*. The apocalyptic hadiths found in the canonical sources, as well as in early collections such as those of Nuʿaym b. Hammad, give a clear sense of the despair engendered by *fitna* that in part led to this Sunni emphasis on *quʿud*. One such hadith, cited by Nuʿaym b. Hammad, predicts that "there will come a time when men will come to graves and roll on them, as animals roll in the dust, wishing that they could be in the graves in place of their occupants—not out of a desire to meet God, but because of the *fitan* they witness." This aversion to internecine conflict found expression in numerous quietist hadiths attributed to the Prophet, such as one cited by al-Bukhari: "Whoever dislikes something that his leader has done, let him be forbearing, for whoever departs even a hand's span from authority will die the death of a pagan."

While this quietist position, expressed in credal statements as well as in hadith, was obviously congenial to the political elites, one cannot understand these condemnations of *fitna* only as tools of domination. Rather, they should be understood as Sunni responses to some of the claims of the Shiʿites and Kharijites, and to the bloodshed, schism, and

destruction wrought by intra-communal conflicts in general. Although the injunction to obey authorities even when unjust and corrupt was strongly expressed in the hadith literature, some Sunni exegetes and jurists, as Khaled Abou El-Fadl has shown, allowed for activist responses to tyranny and oppression (which also served to justify the actions of ʿAli and others in the past.) The Shiʿites, too, developed quietist tendencies as a result of their successive defeats in their early struggles for leadership of the community, eventually relegating the duty to "fill the world with justice as it is now filled with injustice" to a descendant of ʿAli who would appear at the End of Time. Despite the claims of the early Kharijites that Muslims must be held responsible by other Muslims for their actions (rather than by God alone), and that rebellion against unjust and impious rulers was religiously incumbent upon true Muslims, later moderate Kharijite groups also developed quietist doctrines. Thus, the early civil wars and the religious schisms that they engendered led to sectarian divisions and doctrinal developments that continued to be influential throughout Islamic history until today.

*Sandra S. Campbell*

## FOLKLORE, FOLK ISLAM *See* Vernacular Islam

## FUNDAMENTALISM

The term fundamentalism generally describes a religious attitude or organized movement that adheres to most or all of the following characteristics: a holistic approach to religion, one that sees religion as a complete moral or legal code, providing answers for all life's questions; a tendency toward literal understanding of scriptures; a belief in a foundational golden age, when the principles of the faith were perfectly applied, and a desire to recreate such a period today; suspicion and sometimes renunciation of not only people of other faiths, but also supposedly hypocritical adherents of the same faith; and discomfort with or rejection of many aspects of modern, secular societies. The term was coined in the early twentieth century to refer to a Protestant movement in the United States that reasserted a literal reading of the Bible in opposition to the new biblical criticism and to such scientific theories as evolution, which had gained currency at the time. Because of its Christian origins, many scholars and religious activists reject its use in other religious contexts. The term is particularly controversial in the Islamic context, where, it is argued, "Islamic fundamentalism" is used indiscriminately to describe all Islamic activists, whether they are radicals or moderates, and because it is generally laden with pejorative meanings, such as obscurantism, dogmatism, sexism, and violence. Many alternatives have been suggested, including "Islamic revivalism," "political Islam," or simply "Islamism." These terms, however, have the drawback of not allowing comparative treatment of a phenomenon common to many religious traditions. Namely, from the 1970s to the present there has been an increased social mobilization and political activism on the basis of religion. Moreover, by equating fundamentalism with political Islam, the alternatives discount another ideological strand that has played an important role in Islamic revivalism, namely, Islamic modernism. So, for the lack of a satisfactory alternative, "Islamic fundamentalism" has been widely adopted in both scholarly and general parlance.

Islamic fundamentalism is found today, in varying degrees of strength and popular support, in every Muslim-majority country and in many countries with large Muslim minorities. Although they do not form a monolithic movement, fundamentalists do share certain common features in both their ideology and their organization. The similarities derive from the fact that most contemporary Islamic fundamentalist groups trace their origins to two organizations, the Muslim Brotherhood in the Arab countries and the Jama'at-e Islami in the Indian subcontinent. Both emerged during the 1930s and 1940s as responses to the problems confronting Muslims under British imperialism and to the perceived conformism of secular or modernist Muslim elites to European ideas and institutions. Thus, twentieth-century Islamic fundamentalism is in many ways a modern phenomenon, a product of both foreign and indigenous influences. Yet, it is also the latest manifestation of a long tradition of reform and revival movements within Islamic culture. Fundamentalist ideologues often quote the Hanbali jurist Ibn Taymiyya (d. 1328) to provide a classical sanction for their ideas. Similarly, Hanbali influences are evident in the Wahhabi fundamentalist movement of the late eighteenth and early nineteenth century, which had a profound, conservative impact, not only in the Middle East but also in India and Africa. A more direct forerunner of contemporary fundamentalism was the Salafiyya movement led by Jamal al-Din Afghani, Muhammad 'Abduh, and Rashid Rida in the late nineteenth and early twentieth century. The more liberal spirit of Afghani and 'Abduh animated Islamic modernism, while the more conservative approach of Rida hints at the conservative backlash against modernism that moved Hasan al-Banna' to found the Muslim Brotherhood and Abu l-A'la' Maududi to create the Jama'at-e Islami.

Both the Brotherhood and the Jama'at were organized by local chapters, into which members were initiated only after they had been tested for their conviction, piety, and obedience. The local cells answered to a central coordinating committee. The head of the organization was the *murshid* (guide) or *emir* (leader), who was assisted by the *majlis al-shura*, an advisory council of senior members. Thus, the organization putatively mirrored the structure of the early Prophetic community in Medina, but it also resembled the Sufi orders whose quietism the fundamentalists rejected.

The ideology of the Jama'at was elaborated primarily through the prolific writings of Maududi. Al-Banna's writings are more limited because of his early death. Sayyid Qutb would become the chief ideologue of the Brotherhood and because of Maududi's influence upon him, the main conduit for propagating Maududi's ideas in the Arab world.

The fundamentalist worldview is premised on the idea that most societies, including nominally Muslim societies, are in a state of *jahiliyya*, or "ignorance," akin to the *jahiliyya* that prevailed in Arabia before the advent of the prophet Muhammad's mission. Only a small, committed vanguard of true Muslims discern the corrupted state of Muslim affairs and the proper means to remedy it. Their initial mission is to withdraw mentally and even physically, if need be, from the *jahiliyya* in order to inculcate truly Islamic values within themselves and their organization. This *hijra*, or "flight," is the first type of jihad that they must wage. On the instructions of the leader, the Muslim vanguard must transform their inner jihad into an outer jihad aimed at overthrowing the un-Islamic order and correcting societal ills. The details of an authentic Islamic political system are left vaguely defined in most fundamentalist writings. The basic principle of such an order, however, is declared to be *hakimiyyat Allah*, or the "sovereignty of God." This requires the application of divine law, or *shari'a*, in all its dimensions. The fundamentalists generally do not feel bound to any one school or to the entire corpus of classical jurisprudence that defined *shari'a*. They feel empowered to perform *ijtihad*, that is, to derive law themselves through their own reading of the Qur'an and sunna. Compared to the modernists, who also claim the right to *ijtihad*, the fundamentalist reading of scriptural sources is far more literal and conservative.

Both Qutb and Maududi castigated those Muslims who renounced forceful means in the jihad to establish an Islamic order. Qutb was executed for his views and the Muslim Brotherhood after his death officially renounced revolutionary violence against the Egyptian state. The Jama'at under Maududi was always a loyal opposition party within Pakistani politics. During the late 1970s, inspired in part by the Islamic revolution in Iran, splinter groups consisting of a younger generation of activists broke off from the two older parties to form new, much more violent groups. One of these groups, Islamic Jihad, assassinated Anwar Sadat in October 1981. Other spin-offs are at the forefront of violent struggles in such diverse parts of the Muslim world as Algeria, Palestine, Afghanistan, Kashmir, and Indonesia. It should be noted, though, that one of the most widespread and important fundamentalist organizations, the Tablighi Jama'at, is not only nonviolent in its tactics, it generally eschews politics altogether.

Shi'ite fundamentalism differs from Sunni fundamentalism in a few particulars, mainly in the greater millenarian emphasis that results from Shi'ite expectations of the return of the Hidden Imam, the greater emphasis upon *shahada*, or "martyrdom" in jihad, and the theory of the direct rule of the Shi'ite religious scholars as enunciated by Ruhollah Khomeini in the doctrine of *velayat-e faqih*. Yet, in most other ideological aspects and in organization, Shi'ite fundamentalist groups can hardly be distinguished from Sunni groups. Greater interaction and mutual influences are evident, for example, in the upsurge in suicide attacks by Sunni groups, a tactic pioneered by the Shi'ite Hizb Allah in Lebanon.

*See also* **'Abduh, Muhammad; Afghani, Jamal al-Din; Banna, Hasan al-; Ghazali, Muhammad al-; Ghazali, Zaynab al-; Ibn Taymiyya; Ikhwan al-Muslimin; Jama'at-e Islami; Khomeini, Ruhollah; Maududi, Abu l-A'la'; Political Islam; Qutb, Sayyid; Rida, Rashid; Salafiyya; Tablighi Jama'at; Velayat-e Faqih; Wahhabiyya.**

## BIBLIOGRAPHY

Choueiri, Youssef M. *Islamic Fundamentalism.* Boston: Twayne, 1990.

Euben, Roxanne L. *Enemy in the Mirror: Islamic Fundamentalism and the Limits of Modern Rationalism.* Princeton, N.J.: Princeton University Press, 1999.

Marty, Martin E., and Appleby, R. Scott, eds. *Fundamentalism Project.* Chicago: University of Chicago Press, 1991.

Roy, Olivier. *The Failure of Political Islam.* Translated by Carol Volk. Cambridge, Mass.: Harvard University Press, 1994.

Sivan, Emmanuel. *Radical Islam.* New Haven, Conn.: Yale University Press, 1985.

*Sohail H. Hashmi*

# FUTUWWA

The term *futuwwa* refers to organized groups of youth adhering to a code of honor who devoted themselves to manly, noble virtues. By the twelfth century, *futuwwa* organizations appeared throughout the Fertile Crescent and Iran as organized entities with elaborate rituals and initiation rites.

Derived from the Arabic word for youth (*fata*, pl. *fityan*), *futuwwa* groups are mentioned in texts related to Sufi orders; they existed in Transoxiana and Khorasan and as *akhi*s (brotherhoods) in Turkic areas, where they sometimes appeared as paramilitary fighters and had connections with artisan guilds. During the eighth through tenth centuries, individuals were referred to, such as Nuh al-'Ayyar, a *fata* of

Nishapur who adhered to an ascetic way of life, as groups of well-to-do *fityan* who lived apart from society and enjoyed each other's company. Some, when traveling to a new town, looked to men's organizations for musical entertainment, drinking, and self-indulgence.

Generally, however, during the periods of intermittent anarchy and competition for political power that characterized the Fertile Crescent from the ninth through the twelfth centuries, these societies were active in the cities, some forming paramilitary groups in Baghdad. Some of these groups included *fityan* and '*ayyarun*, often defined as vagabonds, who, at times, fought with the political regime, at other times defended local autonomy against the military invader, and frequently terrorized, plundered, harassed, and extorted the wealthy. In Syria, similar groups called *ahdath* formed urban militias and were used by important notable families for political purposes: as hired toughs to fight against each other or the regime in power.

Historians have disagreed about the origins and nature of these groups. Some see their antecedents in earlier versions of men's groups that existed in the Middle East such as Byzantine circus factions that originated in the Roman Empire or the Sassanid Persian fraternities (*javanmardi*), whose wrestling devotees met at the "House of Strength" (*zurkhaneh*) in a master-novitiate relationship. Others look to their relation to Sufi orders or guilds of artisans.

By the twelfth century, chroniclers tell of the existence of *futuwwa* organizations in the Fertile Crescent that were distinctly men's clubs. Some were paramilitary organizations or youth gangs. Some were clubs devoted to sports such as crossbow shooting, wrestling, and training homing pigeons while some were mutual aid organizations. Members could include Muslims and non-Muslims. There were artisans and workers, but also the lower class or the marginalized—eunuchs and slaves. Women, tax collectors, wine merchants, fortune-tellers, magicians, diviners, astrologers, astronomers, and perpetrators and accomplices of any serious crime were excluded. There were members who practiced celibacy while some married; often groups lived together in *futuwwa* clubhouses or ate in a common mess hall.

Taking different forms in various locations, they nevertheless had common characteristics that set them apart from the rest of Muslim society. They wore special clothing and were invested with their *futuwwa* trousers and belt of honor (*libas al-futuwwa*) during an initiation ceremony when they drank the *futuwwa* drink, a cup of salted water. The members were supposed to adhere to the *futuwwa* code of honor: generosity, solidarity, courage, and hospitality toward those in their group, the last a virtue not necessarily applicable toward society at large.

*Futuwwa* groups were urban, consisting of groups of youth probably not large in number who formed associations. Some lived apart in special clubhouses, with novices under the supervision of and discipline of superiors. Each clubhouse (*bayt*) was distinguished from the others by a particular belief or opinion and there was often animosity between groups. Houses were subdivided into parties (*hizb, pl. azhab*), each under the supervision of an elder (*kabir*) with whom the members had a mutual bond. Members or companions (sing. *rafiq*) drank to the honor of the *kabir* who supervised their behavior and adjudicated disputes. If companions disagreed with the *kabir*, they could move to another house but not change elders within the same club to avoid dissension in the *bayt*.

In this evolving, mobile world, *futuwwa* orders provided a niche for men without social status or genealogical prestige. With their emphasis on personal qualities as a standard for nobility instead of Arab tribal kinship, religious lineage, or military prestige, *futuwwa* organizations provided marginal men with social links that crossed class and religious boundaries.

As part of his program to revitalize the Abbasid caliphate, in the face of military threats and competition for leadership, Caliph al-Nasir li-Din Allah (1181–1223) used the *futuwwa* as a mechanism to instill loyalty to the caliph. He became a member of a *futuwwa* group in Baghdad and in 1207 declared himself head of all *futuwwa* organizations in Baghdad and throughout the Islamic world. Creating an elitist, courtly version of *futuwwa* with privilege, he forbade pigeon raising and crossbow shooting except under his auspices, and issued decrees setting proper behavior for members. As the head of *futuwwa*, al-Nasir used the society and its codes of behavior to reduce endemic conflict in Baghdad; and, after initiating neighboring rulers into the order, to create diplomatic bonds between local dynasties and himself.

The new regulations bound by tradition were legitimized by 'Umar al-Suhrawardi (1145–1234), al-Nasir's confidant and founder of pragmatic Sufi orders, and by Ibn al-Mi'mar (d. 1248) whose *Kitab al-Futuwwa* was written to provide all those interested with information about *futuwwa*, noting that *futuwwa* was incorporated in the *shari'a*, and that only a true believer can be a *fata*. *Futuwwa* advocates linked *futuwwa* ideals with pre-Islamic poetry, the Qur'an, and the hadith. Often cited, these refer to the generosity of Hatim al-Ta'i; the trust in God by the young men in the cave and Ibrahim's rejection of idolatry (Qur'an 18:10 and 21:60); and a tradition about 'Ali as the heroic *fata* exemplar: "There is no sword but Dhu al-Fiqar ['Ali's sword] and no *fata* but 'Ali."

By the late medieval period, *futuwwa* groups, guilds, and Sufi orders had become interwoven through institutionalization, membership, and adaptation of geneology, rites, and ritual. In modern times, *futuwwa* has denoted such organizations as the Iraqi paramilitary youth organization of the late 1930s and protectors of Cairo neighborhoods. The *javanmardi* of Iran maintain the religious and social connections closest to the medieval prototype.

*See also* **Youth Movements.**

## BIBLIOGRAPHY

Arnakis, G. G. "Futuwwa Traditions in the Ottoman Empire: Akhis, Bektashi Dervishes and Craftsmen." *Journal of Near Eastern Studies* (1970): 28–50.

Cahen, Claude, and Taeschner, F. "Futuwwa." In Vol. 2, *Encyclopedia of Islam.* Edited by B. Lewis, Ch. Pellat, and J. Schacht. Leiden: Brill, 1965.

Floor, Willem. "Guilds and *Futuvvat* in Iran." *Deutsche morgenlandischen Gesellschaft Zeitschrift* 134 (1984): 107–114.

*Reeva Spector Simon*

# G

## GASPRINSKII, ISMA'IL BAY (1851–1914)

Isma'il Gasprinskii (Gaspirali), a leading intellectual in the Turkic world, was born in Bahcesaray, Crimea, on 8 March 1851 and died in the same city on 11 September 1914. He received his early education in his hometown and later attended the Gymnasium in Akmescit (Simferopol). After graduating from the Military Academy in Moscow in 1867, he briefly served in the Ottoman army, and then subsequently taught at various Muslim schools in Russia. It was the latter experience that made him realize the necessity of educational reforms for Russian Muslims to achieve social and economic progress.

From 1883 on, when he established the newspaper *Tercuman* (Interpreter), Gasprinskii advocated reforms in curriculum and teaching methods, with an emphasis on advancing the abilities of students in reading, writing, and arithmetic. In his view, religion was to be taught as culture and for spiritual revival. He believed that many of the ills of Muslim societies could be cured by an improved new educational system (Usul-i Cedid).

At the First and Second Congresses of the Union of Russian Muslims in 1905 and 1906, held in Nizhni Novgorod and St. Petersburg, respectively, Isma'il Gasprinskii's ideas on educational reforms and politics received close attention. In 1907 he helped found Ittifak-i Muslumanlar (Union of Muslims) urging not political but linguistic and cultural unity among the Muslim Turkic peoples of Russia. During the following decade, voicing his motto of "Unity in language, thought and action," he traveled to Istanbul, Cairo, and India urging educational and social reforms in the Islamic world. Despite opposition from existing traditional Muslim educators, by the time of Gasprinskii's death, around five thousand Usul-i Cedid schools had been established.

Isma'il Gasprinskii also championed women's rights and the importance of education for Muslim women. In one of his important journals, *Alem-i Nisvan* (Women's world), which he began publishing with his daughter Sefika Hanim in 1906, he consistently argued that society could only reach a high level of civilization if women were also educated.

*See also* **Education; Feminism.**

### BIBLIOGRAPHY

Bennigsen, Alexandre A. *Ismail Bey Gasprinski (Gaspiraly) and Origins of the Jadid Movement in Russia*. Oxford, U.K.: The Society of Central Asian Studies, 1985.

*A. Uner Turgay*

## GENDER

To speak of gender is necessarily to make a distinction between sex and gender. While sex is the biologically defined capacity of the human body, gender connotes the social significance attached to members of a particular sex. Gender is, therefore, a human construction that nevertheless draws upon divinely inspired texts, social and cultural conventions, and biological capacities to define its role in public and private life and societal institutions.

### Gender-Related Verses in the Qur'an

In the Qur'an, which is regarded as divine revelation by Muslims, female life is considered intrinsically valuable (Q. 81:9). The creation of the female is attributed, along with that of the male, to a single soul (4:1) from which the other is created as its mate (4:1). Another verse declares: "Allah created you from dust, then from a little fluid, then He made you pairs" (35: 11). These verses have been interpreted as granting both sexes equality from the perspective of origin and spiritual status. Although the Qur'anic texts do not specify which sex is the primary creation, some argue that the feminine form of the noun "soul" (*nafs*) in Qur'an 4:1 could be read to suggest that the female was created first. Unlike the account found in the second book of Genesis, the Qur'an does not make the creation of the female derivative from the male or for the purpose of the male. However, such a view enters the Islamic interpretive framework through various sources, chiefly through the writings of the very earliest commentators on the Qur'an, as detailed in Barbara Stowasser's excellent study.

With respect to morality and spirituality, men and women are equally accountable to God for their actions and for their religious beliefs and responsibilities (33:35), and in this regard, the Qur'an holds an egalitarian vision, as has been pointed out by Leila Ahmed. In the social sphere, women are entitled to inherit (4:7) half the portions received by men (4:11), two women's testimonies count in weight to that of a single male's (2:282), and men are placed in charge of women because they excel over them and are financially responsible for them (4:34). Women must remain monogamous, although nowhere is this specified in the Qur'an but rather is implied in the injunction that "all married women" are forbidden to men (4:24). Men are permitted as many as four wives on the condition that each wife be treated equally, with the additional caveat that if a man cannot provide for four he should marry only one. He may also possess as many concubines as he can afford ("their right hand may possess") (4:3). Verse 3:129 further declares that "You will not be able to deal equally between [your] wives, however much you wish [to do so]," suggesting to some Muslims that the Qur'an preferred monogamy as the marital state, but in keeping with the customs of the time allowed polygamy. Men may marry any of the women of the *ahl al-kitab* ("people of the Book") (5:5) whereas women may marry only Muslim men (this being a traditional stipulation rather than a Qur'anic injunction). Marriage to idolatresses is forbidden (2:221), as is marriage to one's father's wives (4:22), one's mother, daughters, sisters, father's sisters, mother's sisters, brother's daughters, sister's daughters, foster-mothers, foster-sisters, mothers-in-law, stepdaughters born of women with whom one has had conjugal relations, the wives of blood-sons, and two sisters from the same family (4:23) as well as all married women except slaves already owned (4:24). Marriage with former wives of adopted sons is permitted (33:37). Women with whom marriages have not yet been consummated may be divorced, and should a marriage portion have been promised, half of that must be paid unless the woman—who is encouraged to do so as a pious act—is willing to give it up (235–237).

Conjugal relations are forbidden with menstruating women (2:222); otherwise, conjugal relations are permitted at will (2:223). Disobedient wives are subject to a graduated set of measures ranging from admonishment to beating, depending on how the term *darraba* (admonish, strike) is interpreted (4:34). Should a conflict arise between a married couple, then an arbiter from each one's kinsfolk should be appointed to attempt a reconciliation (4:35). According to the Qur'an, a man who forswears his wife must wait four months (2:226) during which time he may change his mind; however, if divorce is determined as a course of action, then the woman must wait a term of three menses to ensure that she is not impregnated; if the wife is found to be pregnant it is recommended that the husband take her back as his wife (2:227). Should divorce proceed in such an instance, the wife is entitled to support from the husband until she gives birth (65:4), and, if mutually agreeable, while she nurses (65:6). A woman may be divorced no more than twice by the same husband in order to be retained; after the third time, she may not be taken back unless she has married another man in the meantime. In cases where a man chooses to divorce a pregnant wife, the Qur'an urges the man to release her with honor only after the birth of the child. Additionally, the husband must not obstruct her remarriage if there has been a mutual agreement based on kindness. Furthermore, upon divorce, nothing that has been given to the woman can be taken back (2:229–232). Widows may choose their own course of action regarding remarriage after a waiting period of four months and ten days (2:234). A married man who is about to die should make provisions for his wife or wives for a period of one year, including a provision for housing, unless the wife or wives choose to leave of their own accord prior to his death (2:240).

Women should suckle their children for two years unless both parents mutually agree to wean the child earlier, and the father is charged with the duty of feeding and clothing the nursing mother appropriately. The child may also be given out to a wet nurse, provided the nurse is adequately compensated (2:233).

In matters of dress and comportment, both men and women are enjoined "to lower their gaze and be modest" (24:30–31); however, in addition women are asked to draw their veils (*khumur*) over their bosoms, and only reveal of their adornment (*'awra*, lit. pudendum) that which is manifest, and reveal their adornment only to a specified list of close relatives with whom marriage is disallowed (*mahram*), eunuchs, and children not yet conscious of women's nakedness. Similarly, women should not stamp their feet in such a manner that might reveal their adornments by drawing attention to their bodies (24:31). Testimony against women accused of lewdness must be brought by four witnesses, and if the charge is proved, the woman must be confined to her house until her death or until God provides new legislation (4:15). Those accused of adultery, including the adulterer and the adulteress, are subject to a punishment consisting of one hundred lashes (24:2).

Special sanctions are placed upon the wives of the Prophet: the punishment for lewdness is doubled compared to other women (33:30), as is the reward for surrendering to God and

In Jakarta, Indonesia, Muslim women use fountain waters to make their ablutions before praying. The role of women in Muslim countries varies tremendously: Indonesia has a woman president as of 2003, yet in some countries women are required to cover their hair. © AFP/CORBIS

the Prophet and engaging in righteousness (33:31); they are declared not to be "like any other women" and cautioned to keep their speech customary, not soft, lest it causes another's desire (33:32). They are commanded to stay in their houses (33:33) and abstain from ornamentation, as was the case in the days before Islam. The Prophet's wives should pray regularly, engage in charity, and obey God and his messenger (33:33), keeping in mind the revelations of God and wisdom (33:34). Conversation with the wives of the Prophet is to be conducted from behind a curtain (*hijab*) and visits to the Prophet's household are to occur upon invitation, with the guests departing after the meal is ended. The Prophet's wives may not remarry after his death (33:53). They may converse freely only with a stipulated set of males: fathers, sons, brothers, nephews, the sons of their female slaves, or their male slaves (33:55).

Further, the wives of the Prophet, his daughters, and the women of the believers are enjoined to "draw their cloaks" (*jilbab*) close around them while going out in order that they

may be recognized as Muslims and not be harassed (33:59). Women past childbearing age with no hope of marriage may discard such outer clothing, provided they do not reveal their adornments, though it is better for them to retain such coverings (24: 60).

The Qur'an views women as human beings who are creations of God and are vouchsafed full ontological equality with men. With regard to their moral agency, women are not subordinate to men and, like men, they are called upon to surrender to God and the Prophet and embark upon a path of righteousness for which they will be justly rewarded.

In the social sphere, the Qur'an protects and safeguards women's right to life, inheritance, legal recognition, dowry, upkeep, child support after divorce, protection from male voyeurism, and safety while in public. These considerations are laudable given the seventh-century context into which the Qur'an was revealed. As previously stated, restrictions are, however, placed on the portion women may inherit (4:11) and on the weight of their legal testimony. The Qur'an's least egalitarian verse is to be found in 4:34, which declares: "Men are in charge of women, because Allah hath made the one of them to excel the other, and because they spend of their property [for the support of women]. So good women are the obedient." Traditionally, this verse has been interpreted as granting to men authority over women, as well as advocating a social division of labor, suggesting that it is men's responsibility to support women (and hence, that women need not work but rather should tend the affairs of the hearth). Many Muslims, women included, believe that the Qur'an's objective with regard women is to vouchsafe their rights as they apply to the economic and legal spheres, especially during childbearing and child-rearing years. With regard to dress codes, there do not appear to be any specific Qur'anic guidelines for male dress, although both men and women are called to observe modesty, a term that could include dress as well as behavior. Qur'an 34:59 asks the Prophet to "Tell thy wives and thy daughters and women of the believers to draw their cloaks (*jilbab*) close around them [when they go out]. That will be better, that they may be recognized and not annoyed." The Qur'an's concern here clearly is to protect women from the male gaze, especially harassment from the "hypocrites" or religious backsliders (*munafiqun*), thereby tacitly suggesting that women are vulnerable to impropriety on the part of males and that males posed a significant threat to women's safety in that era. In all of these stipulations, the Qur'an's spirit of affording protections and rights to women illustrates that it is a sacred document in support of women.

## Sources for Gender Construction

Should the Qur'an be construed as a patriarchal text? Later Muslim theology developed the notion that the Qur'an, as a body of revelation, is eternal and a copy of a heavenly prototype, that is, it is eternally valid in all its aspects. The Egyptian shaykh Muhammad 'Abduh (d. 1905) argued that while all Qur'anic injunctions pertaining to 'ibadat (worship or ritual acts) were eternally valid and binding on Muslims, other Qur'anic injunctions, such as those pertaining to maslaha or societal well-being, were valid within the context in which they were revealed. Hence, Muslims must assume responsibility for following the intention, and not necessarily the letter, of the Qur'an in matters pertaining to societal well-being. Some modern scholars, such as Amina Wadud-Muhsin, have also argued that the social aspects of the Qur'an should be viewed in a historical and cultural context. From this perspective, pronouncements that were received and intelligible to the patriarchal milieu of an earlier period must be reviewed in light of present-day social arrangements and thus reinterpreted.

Historians such as Leila Ahmed have convincingly shown that Islam did not invent patriarchy; rather, it was a form of social organization well established in the Mesopotamian, Greek, Iranian, and Byzantine spheres of influence that Muslims encountered during the first century of Islam. Thus, the key discourses generated in the classical period of Islamic civilization (from the seventh century to 1250 C.E.) took place within a patriarchal frame of reference. Indeed, Eleanor Doumato has argued that much of the legislation derived from the Qur'an and other sources was consistent with the contemporary Jewish and Christian legal praxis.

There are several strands of literature during the first three centuries of Islamic self-definition that are critical to the formation and articulation of gender constructs. These include the qisas al-anbiya'; the asbab al-nuzul; the hadith; the tafsir; and the fiqh. The qisas al-anbiya', literally the "stories of the prophets," was one of the pathways through which Biblical lore entered the Islamic realm of discourse, through which Muslims in general—bearing in mind that many Muslims were converts from Judaism or Christianity—gained an intimate familiarity with Biblical figures and stories. The asbab al-nuzul, literally the "context of the revelation," was a genre imbedded within many tafasir (commentaries) on the Qur'an, seeking to explain the reasons for a particular revelation, reasons that were orally transmitted until such time as the Qur'anic commentators sought to incorporate them within their commentaries. The hadith (tradition literature), which recalled narratives of the Prophet's thoughts and deeds, was also orally transmitted through succeeding generations until hadith collectors such as al-Bukhari (d. 869 C.E.) and others sought them out, collated them, checked them for accuracy using various methods, and combined them to form canonical collections in the ninth and tenth centuries. Finally, the fiqh (jurisprudence) drew upon various sources, including primarily the Qur'an, the hadith, 'urf or local custom, and juridical reasoning (variously ra'y, qiyas, ijtihad, ijma'), to formulate the legal regimes adopted by Muslim rulers. It is in these bodies of literature that extra-Qur'anic features of the social construction of gender are largely located. For instance, the interpretive lens through which the Qur'an was

understood and utilized as a basis for social organization adopted the essentialized notions pertaining to the female gender that were well established as part of the patriarchal norms of the conquered societies. Further, key social institutions such as the legal regimes that would govern Muslim societies were inscribed with gendered markings consonant with the cultural practices of the conquered societies comprising the Muslim empire. To illustrate, while nowhere in the Qur'an is Adam's partner named or identified as having proceeded from the male, for the purpose or in service of the male, biblical antecedents of the derivative and service-oriented origin of the female from the rib of the male enter the Islamic interpretive frame through biblical lore, most likely through the qisas al-anbiya' literature, thereby ensuring for the Muslim female a subordinate role in society. To be sure, the Muslim interpreters granted greater weight to the subordinate account found in Genesis 2:21 than to the more equitable account found in Genesis 1:27, but they did so in a social and intellectual context in which such a view was favored within their subject peoples. The subordinate role, with respect to the essential nature of the female, however, was firmly lodged through the Muslim appropriation of the biblical notion that the female, unnamed in the Qur'an but named Hawwa by Muslim tradition, was ultimately responsible for the fall of the male, Adam, from the paradisiacal garden as a consequence of her seduction by Iblis, the Arabic equivalent of the devil, or Satan. Such moral frailty on the part of the female is attributed by Muslim commentators variously to her weak intelligence, her willful disobedience, or to her sexually heightened powers of seduction, and punishments similar to those meted to the biblical female sex are attached to the Muslim female. All this despite the many occasions in the Qur'an where either both the primordial couple together or Adam explicitly are named as responsible for the act of disobedience, and where no punishment save expulsion from the beatific state enjoyed in the garden is visited upon the couple; indeed the primordial couple is assured of God's guidance, with the pledge that "whoever follows My guidance shall have no fear, nor shall they grieve" (2:38).

Having appropriated and elaborated upon the Biblical Eve in order to establish women's essential nature as morally frail, seductively powerful in order to create moral and social chaos, and eternally punishable, the Qur'anic commentators continued their implicit project of gender construction through their interpretations of the female figures mentioned in the Qur'an, whether Biblical, pre-Islamic, or Muslim (such as the wives of the Prophet). In this project, they were aided by the bodies of discourse also being produced at that time and by the social and institutional arrangements already in place in Arabia and in the conquered territories. Included in these discourses are the asbab al-nuzul literature that "remembered" the context in which a verse was revealed; the qisas al-anbiya literature that glorified the lives and acts of prior biblical figures; and the isra'illiyat literature that comprised the narratives deemed biblical lore. These discourses served both to illuminate and reinforce the contemporaneous understanding of the role of God's prophets and their concomitant social arrangements as divinely ordained rather than as an ever-dynamic result of historical factors, and played a significant role in directing the attitude toward the female gender in the construction of the emerging legal regimes between the first century after the Prophet's passing and the third century (eighth to tenth centuries of the common era).

Stowasser suggests that the Qur'anic commentators interpreted the references to biblical figures mentioned in the Qur'an as paradigmatic for women's behavior. Thus, the story of Joseph and Zulaykha was seen to be reflective of the social chaos (*fitna*) engendered by a woman, and the story of Moses's future brides was considered paradigmatic for female conduct in the presence of males (work only if there is no other male to do so; walk behind the male, remain bashful and shy in his presence). Ironically, the cumulative effect of such discourse was to define the male in relation to and by contrast to the female, and thus, as argued by Abu-Odin, was far more relevant to the construction of male gender than, as might ostensibly appear, to the construction of female gender. To be sure, the picture was never entirely a simple one: The prophetic status of Mary, the mother of Jesus, was debated, and the wives of some of the prophets were depicted as moral agents in their own right, able freely to choose the path of righteousness or disobedience. However, the notion that a woman might be a moral agent in her own right was not pursued except insofar as how that freedom might be contained given woman's essential nature.

Similarly, in the hadith literature, an ambiguous picture of women emerges again: on the one hand, women are accorded authority by implication through the relatively large number of hadith narrations attributed to women, such as the Prophet's wife 'A'isha; On the other hand, as Mernissi has pointed out, perhaps the adjudicators of the hadith literature's veracity were less vigilant when it came to retaining hadith from sources that reflected unfavorably on women from less than trustworthy sources, as, for example, the hadith stating the prophetic remark, "Those who trust their affairs to a woman will never know prosperity" (Mernissi, quoting a hadith cited in Bukhari). Such a hadith inculcated in many Muslims a mistrust of the innate capacity and ability of women to hold political office. In a similar vein, commentators on the Qur'an gave relatively short shrift to the account and interpretation of the female political leader, Bilqis (the Queen of Sheba), mentioned in the Qur'an. Despite the later historical record in which women successfully negotiated their way through political institutions to attain leadership roles (as, for instance, the medieval Yemeni Sulayhid queen Sayyida Hurra) and the modern record in which there have been more female heads of state in Muslim nations than in North America, the force of the hadith continues to be cited by opponents as an impediment when Muslim women agitate for inclusion in the political process or in political leadership.

The legal regimes developed over the course of this formative period, from the eighth to the tenth centuries, again reflect a patriarchally informed lens that led to a greater weighting of the socially restrictive verses in the Qur'an over the morally equitable verses also found in the Qur'an. Thus, for instance, the legal formulators found it far more important to lay down the rules under which polygamy was to be practiced than heeding the Qur'anic suggestion that God was aware that men would not be able to deal justly with more than one wife. The discrepancies with respect to gender issues between the various Sunni legal schools, and between the Sunni and the Shi'ite legal schools, suggest, at the very least, that jurists exercised their discretionary interpretive skills in addressing issues of gender, thereby belying the notion that the legal regime is divinely ordained, eternally valid, and therefore immutable. The jurists also saw fit to inscribe legal codes with concurrent views of gender, thus, for instance, although the Qur'an says nothing about the validity of ritual prayer as predicated on proximity to women, a legal code invalidates all prayers performed by men if not distanced from women by a space of at least two arms' length, perhaps in keeping with the segregation of men and women in Jewish and possibly Christian ritual prayer contexts. The essentialist views pertaining to women's weakness that enter the Islamic commentarial discourses through biblical lore may explain why the statement found in 4:34 ("Men are in charge over/superior to women") resulted in the legal arrogation of guardianship rights to the male, extending to women's buying and selling property, their commercial activity, and their ability to contract their own mates and so forth, again, none of which rights are accorded to men in the Qur'an explicitly. Rather, these rights are given over to the male through the explicit statement found in 4.34, and the creative interpretation of a Qur'anic verse that required guardians to handle the legal affairs of orphans and children (4:6) and those of inferior intellect (4:5).

The present observations regarding the legal regimes produced in the three centuries following the Prophet's death are not meant to suggest that males willfully and misogynistically curbed women's legal agency and comportment. Nevertheless, the claim that authoritative discourses in the Islamic world are divinely decreed or generated needs to be more carefully examined and analyzed, as it does not take into account the historical and social factors and processes through which *shari'a* law came to be constructed, defined, and implemented, a process that took at least a couple of centuries. Further, the claim imputes to the divine being legal and social discrimination against women, who are creatures considered in the Qur'an to be equally worthy of life as men, created from the same soul, equally morally accountable, and as much moral agents as men. Such a claim does not stand up to theological reason. Rather, the historically and sociologically constructed nature of many of the authoritative discourses in the Islamic world must be acknowledged, namely, that the hadith collectors, the Qur'anic commentators, and the jurists were doing the best they could to contribute to and illumine a self-understanding of what it meant to be Muslim in their day, in social frameworks intelligible to and consistent with the cultural modes of the time in the diverse geographical locales of the Muslim empire(s). Studies in legal praxis, such as those of Mir-Hosseini and Tucker, indicate that jurists treated the *shari'a* as a fluid set of directives that allowed them some limited scope in taking context into account and in treating each case on its own merit, something that one sees in practice in Iran today.

## The Challenges of Gender Reform

Several developments at various points in history left in their wake significations of gender that are almost impossible to dislodge, and render gender legal reform difficult in the contemporary world. A brief examination of three such developments is merited. In the first, the influential theologian and jurist al-Ghazali (d. 1111) who, in a move reminiscent of St. Augustine, linked piety to *shari'a* observance. He suggested, thereby, that a Muslim, by definition, was one who adhered to the *shari'a*, in contrast to the more loosely articulated view that defined a Muslim as one who ascertained the *shahadah* (lit. testimony, namely, "There is no God but Allah, and Muhammad is His messenger," to which Shi'a add: "and Allah is the Master of the believers"). In addition to according the *shari'a* quasi-divine status, such a move on al-Ghazali's part ensured the difficulty of ameliorating the *shari'a* in any manner as to do so would be to suggest that it was a humanly crafted instrument for the governance of society, albeit one taking its cue from a divinely ordained text, the Qur'an. The implications of this theological development for gender are immense: Does any attempt to introduce gender-equitable treatment under the *shari'a* then suggest that one is tampering with what it means to be a Muslim? It is no surprise that the Hudood Ordinances introduced by President Zia ul-Haq in Pakistan in 1978 under the advisement of the *shari'a* bench have proven to be one of the greatest obstacles in assuring Muslim women in Pakistan equal consideration under the law. Indeed, the infamous *zina'* (adultery) laws have provoked international debate with respect to the setback rather than the protection, let alone reparation, they provide raped women who, as a consequence of these laws, are punishable for the rape. Muslim women academics and activists, such as Asifa Qureshi, have proposed different ways in which the issue of rape might be conceived within an Islamic framework.

The second development was the caliphal prerogative, rendered justifiable by his titular mandate as "Defender of the Faithful," to set up institutions whereby his office could govern society in manners he saw fit. Thus, for instance, in Abbasid and Ottoman times, the caliph could and did set up institutions through which criminal, property, and foreign policy law was handled by his appointees, while laws pertaining to worship and to the family were rendered under the jurisdiction of the religious specialists, thereby further linking worship with laws pertaining to gender issues and making it even more difficult to modernize or otherwise ameliorate the latter without implicating the former. Legal institutions under the direct control of the caliph, on the other hand, were more amenable to context-driven adjustments, as reflected in the work of the Ottoman administrator Ahmad Cevdet Pasha (d. 1895), a member of the ulema, who took his inspiration from Roman and French legal systems, while remaining within the fold of Islamic principles in working out the Ottoman code in order to take into account early modern legal challenges and approaches.

The third development concerned the colonial, especially British, practice of relegating personal and family law issues to the control of religiously defined communities, thereby undermining traditional or customary practices developed over time and resurrecting and perpetuating legal regimes developed by religious institutions that were, in the Muslim case, formulated several centuries ago. Such a practice further reinforced the connection of family law with religious identity and perpetuated gender equities inscribed in the religiously formulated legal system. The colonial attitude of pointing to the "backwardness" of Islamic societies by holding up, for example, the segregation of women from public spaces, has ironically created, as observed by Leila Ahmed, the very signifiers through which Muslims now assert their identity as different from the West and their former colonial masters. In other words, the bodies of women are the sites on which the postcolonial struggles to define and delineate the authenticity, integrity, and marks of an Islamic identity are to be fought. Such a resignification of women's bodies, comportment, and legal status has been no more vociferously and proudly proclaimed than by resurgent Muslim groups. Such groups, often armed with a political agenda that includes taking control of the institutions of governance—assisted by all the tools of modern technology, including print, Internet, and educational media—and attempting to convince Muslim youth disenchanted with global Western political and economic hegemony, as well as with the ineptitude of local government and economic instability, that wearing one's Islamic identity on one's head and a public expression of Muslim piety establish one's identity as a site of resistance to the West. There is no doubt that modern Muslims face significant challenges, both internal and external, to building viable and healthy postcolonial societies; however, the use of religion for political ends has resulted in the creation of organizations calling themselves Muslim who serve to whip minorities, governments, secularists and non-Muslims into pious (thereby unquestionable) submission to a specific political aim in the name of God by offering the indisputable promise: (their form of) Islam is the solution. Their goals and methods run contrary to the Qur'anic call to humans to believe, to act righteously and with social justice (76:5–9; 90:13–17), and to impose no compulsion in matters of religion.

In contemporary times, Muslim women are caught in the nexus of Islamic resurgence, state agendas, feudal social structures, and the economic forces of globalization with its sometimes devastating impact on developing societies. State agendas include the desire to deliver education, training, health, and legal parity in order to facilitate social development that can harness the productive capacity of women in order to build viable societies. However, the need for states at times to buy into the legitimating power of Islamic parties has meant a nimble bartering away of women's rights, or simply a stalling of reforms in exchange for political power. Islamist parties have often reinforced feudal social structures that reinforce a gendered division of labor, thus dovetailing nicely with the Islamist perception of gender roles and laws. The effects of globalization have resulted in an increasing number of women finding it essential to join the paid workforce, a labor migration in search of work, often separating families or creating a subclass of domestic worker or sex-worker slavery, and a movement away from the rural areas into urban outskirts in search of work, leading both to urban congestion and rural impoverishment, thereby providing increasing fodder for Islamist movements. Globalization paradoxically supports both the state agenda for its female population and the Islamist resistance to western economic hegemony, leaving the often already weak state machinery further vulnerable to negotiations with the political threat posed by Islamist parties. Any attempt at discussion of gender issues in many parts of the Muslim world has been silenced through tactics that have attempted to delegitimize the discussant; such tactics include accusing the discussant of being brainwashed by the West, being a western feminist, blaspheming, and so forth.

Muslim gender activists, mostly but not exclusively women, have explored various routes toward addressing issues of gender equity in Muslim societies. In Iran, for instance, women's magazines have taken on the challenge of reexamining patriarchal interpretations of the Qur'an, arguing that the verse supporting male privilege could be understood differently if greater attention were paid to the language of the Qur'an, as in the spirit of the work of the Moroccan feminist sociologist Fatima Mernissi and the American Muslim activist Amina Wadud. Iranian Islamist women, as elsewhere, have also sought to create a parallel universe for women that would enable women to participate in activities not normally possible in a gender-segregated society, as for instance in the Iranian Women's Games. Islamist women in various parts of the world have argued that nowhere do sacred texts prevent women from acquiring an education or participating in the political and the legal spheres. Many Islamist women hold the position that the broad display of headwear and piety has earned them the right to have a say in public affairs, and here the example of the Egyptian Zaynab al-Ghazali comes to mind. Islamist women also argue that the application of Islamic law has ameliorated women's rights over and against feudal or tribal or customary practices. Characteristic of all these approaches is the underlying assumption that Islam as a social and legal system offers gender equality, often drawing upon the oxymoronic adage "equal but different" that bears the semblance of erasing hierarchy but reinscribes it in making the woman the upholder of the shariʿa vision of respectability as the "difference" inevitably reintroduces differential equations of power. In the current climate of Islamic resurgence, it is likely that the Islamist form of gender activism, which entails a form of reinscription of Islamic legal frameworks, is likely to prevail and will continue to do so until such a time as Muslim societies can work out forms of governance that keep Islam out of politics and enable a fresh approach to juridical principles that emphasize women's agency, control over their bodies and destinies, and full humanity. Such a prospect requires fresh thinking on how it might be possible to remain a Muslim spiritually while allowing for clear thinking on what an egalitarian and just society might look like without being fettered by social and legal norms developed historically under very different circumstances. In this regard, issues of health, poverty, and universal access to education, work, and childcare should be addressed, and regimes seeking populist affirmation through Islamization policies need to be examined closely.

Another approach has been to argue that a Muslim cannot be Islamized, since a person who is already a Muslim should not be made subject to punitive laws in the name of Islam or be subject to an interpretation of Islam that does not accord well with its principles of fairness and social justice. Further, one does not need to be an Islamist, that is, one who believes that public and state institutions must adhere to shariʿa prescriptions, developed under different circumstances several centuries ago, in order to work for the benefit of society, especially with respect to gender. Thus, for instance, Maha Azzam has argued that the challenges facing Muslim women ought to be articulated and addressed "with the use of analytical frameworks that, for example, draw on the sociology of religion and on the political and economic dynamics of nationalism and dependency" (quoted in Esposito and Haddad, p. 49) and not conducted within a religious framework that dispenses what the correct comportment of a Muslim woman should or should not be from a seventh-century social perspective. Others, such as the sisters Asma Jahangir and Hina Jilani Jahangir in Pakistan, have sought to address gender equity issues under the rubric of the law and state enforceability, while activist lawyers, academics, and other intellectuals such as Asifa Quraishi, Amira Sonbol, Riffat Hasan, and Amina Wadud in North America have sought to address issues as widely divergent as rape laws in Pakistan, gender issues in legal regimes in parts of the Muslim world, honor killings, and rereading sacred texts, to name a few. A significant form of activism is the consciousness raising evident in the production of literary and analytical works by Muslim women throughout the world, which, if read by Muslims and non-Muslims alike, may result in transnational feminist activism that may finally unmask and address the endless varieties in which Islam, as all world faiths, is used for patriarchal purposes.

*See also* **Divorce; Feminism; Ghazali, Zaynab al-; Marriage; Masculinities.**

## BIBLIOGRAPHY

Afkhami, Mahnaz, and Friedl, Erika, eds. *Muslim Women and the Politics of Participation: Implementing the Beijing Platform.* Syracuse, N.Y.: Syracuse University Press, 1997.

Afkhami, Mahnaz. *Faith and Freedom: Women's Human Rights in the Muslim World.* Syracuse, N.Y.: Syracuse University Press, 1995.

Afshar, Haleh. *Islam and Feminisms: An Iranian Case-Study.* New York: St. Martin's Press, 1998.

Ahmed, Leila. *Women and Gender in Islam.* New Haven and London: Yale University Press, 1992.

Coulson, N. J. *A History of Islamic Law.* Islamic Surveys 2. Edinburgh: Edinburgh University Press, 1964.

Daftary, Farhad. "Sayyida Hurra: The Isma'ili Sulayhid Queen of Yemen." In *Women in the Medieval Islamic World.* Edited by Gavin R. G. Hambly. New York: St. Martin's Press, 1998.

Haddad, Yvonne Yazbeck, and Esposito, John L., eds. *Islam, Gender and Social Change.* New York: Oxford University Press, 1998.

Hassan, Riffat. "On Human Rights and the Qur'anic Perspective." *Journal of Ecumenical Studies* XIX, no. 3 (Summer 1982): 51–65.

Mernissi, Fatima. *The Veil and the Male Elite: A Feminist Interpretation of Women's Rights in Islam.* Translated by Mary Jo Lakeland. Reading, Mass.: Addison-Wesley Publishing Co., 1991.

Moghadam, Valentine. *Modernizing Women: Gender and Social Change in the Middle East.* Boulder, Colo.: Lynne Rienner, 1993.

Moghissi, Haideh. *Feminism and Islamic Fundamentalism: The Limits of Postmodern Analysis.* London and New York: Zed Books, 1999.

Poya, Maryam. *Women, Work and Islamism: Ideology and Resistance in Iran.* London and New York: Zed Books, 1999.

Stowasser, Barbara Freyer. *Women in the Qur'an, Traditions, and Interpretation.* New York: Oxford University Press, 1994.

Tucker, Judith E. *In the House of the Law: Gender and Islamic Law in Ottoman Syria and Palestine.* Berkeley and Los Angeles: University of California Press, 1998.

Voll, John Obert. *Islam: Continuity and Change in the Modern World.* 2d ed. Syracuse, N.Y.: Syracuse University Press, 1994.

Wadud-Muhsin, Amina. *Qur'an and Woman: Rereading the Sacred Text from a Woman's Perspective.* 2d ed. New York: Oxford University Press, 1999.

Webb, Gisela, ed. *Windows of Faith: Muslim Women Scholar-Activists in North America.* Syracuse, N.Y.: Syracuse University Press, 2000.

*Zayn R. Kassam*

# GENEALOGY

Genealogy plays an important role in Islamic civilizations, often drawing on local pre-Islamic traditions, common to most oral cultures, of preserving memory and history through recitation of long chains of ancestors. The pre-Islamic Arabian tribes, such as Quraysh, the tribe of Muhammad, traced their lineage back to a common ancestor who was the eponym of the group, which was further subdivided into smaller clans, each sharing a common line of descent. Islamic concepts of genealogy derive from pre-Islamic Arabian identification with tribal lineages, honor, and prestige, participation in early Muslim history, and relationship to the Prophet and his Companions.

With the triumph of the Islamic vision, tribal loyalties were to be superceded by common Muslim brotherhood. Traces of the tribal genealogical precedence and concept of nobility persisted, however, augmented by specifically Islamic associations. One genre of Arabic historical recordings was the citation of lineages (*ansab*), and this was incorporated in the compilation of early Islamic biographical compendia such as the *Tabaqat* of Ibn Sa'd. The importance of lineage was based conceptually on the idea of noble ancestry as shaping character through lineage (*nasl*) or origin (*asl*). Priority in accepting Islam also had pragmatic benefits in early Islamic history as the caliph Umar established a system known as the *diwan*, recording precedence in conversion and apportioning payments to families based on this ranking.

As the Muslims expanded into new territories, they initially garrisoned Arab troops separately from local populations, who needed to form client relationships with Arabs and establish quasi-genealogical links to them as they Islamicized. Gradually these populations converted and assimilated, the dates of this process having been traced by historian Richard Bulliet through genealogical material and especially nomenclature preserved in the early biographical compendia. This tracing of conversion dates is possible because the period of the family's conversion to Islam is visible in the name of the final ancestor to preserve a local pre-Islamic first name.

Arabic names include various components. The *kunya* (patronymic) tends to be in the form "son of" (*ibn*), "daughter of" (*bint*), father (*abu*), or "mother of" (*umm*), and additional long strings of a person's ancestors (*nasab*) are recorded in more formal documents or histories. Names may further contain what is called a *nisba* or relational suffix that may indicate city of origin or principal residence, tribal or ancestral relationships, and a further *laqab* or descriptive epithet based on physical characteristics or profession.

Descendants of the Prophet are often designated by the title *sayyid* and given special respect in certain Muslim societies. For example, in Iran, *sayyid* males wear a black turban in ritual settings, in Morocco they are known as the *shurafa*, and in India and Pakistan they are the highest "caste" of Indian Muslims, followed, respectively, by those claiming Arab, Mogul, or Pathan ancestors. These groups are the nobles (*ashraf*) or descendants of migrants to India rather than the descendants of indigenous converts (*ajlaf*). This honoring may thus be seen to emerge from religious sentiment of respect for and charisma of the Prophet's household and Companions, and also of the cultural precedence accorded to Arab Muslims in non-Arab contexts. A modern example of this respect based on genealogy is the designation of Jordan as "the Hashemite kingdom," Banu Hashim being the clan of the Prophet, as a factor legitimizing the ruling dynasty, who claim descent from the Prophet's lineage.

A further element of genealogical understanding in Islamic cultures is the concept of spiritual or intellectual lineages in Sufi or scholarly traditions. Here chains of succession are established to previous masters and authorities, often ascending to the prophet Muhammad himself. This concept is known as the *shajara* (tree) of descent and diagrams tracing such trees form a component of hagiographic and other biographical genres and may be ritually recited as part of Sufi ritual.

*See also* **Biography and Hagiography; Historical Writing; Tariqa.**

### BIBLIOGRAPHY

Bulliet, Richard W. *Conversion to Islam in the Medieval Period: An Essay in Quantitative History.* Cambridge, Mass.: Harvard University Press, 1979.

Rosenthal, Franz. "Nasab." In Vol. 7., *Encyclopedia of Islam.* 2d ed. Leiden: E. J. Brill, 1993.

*Marcia Hermansen*

## GEOGRAPHY *See* **Cartography and Geography**

## GHANNOUSHI, RASHID AL- (1941– )

Rashid al-Ghannoushi is a prominent Islamic thinker and political activist. Born in 1941 into a religious family in rural Tunisia, Ghannoushi received a bachelor's degree in philosophy from Damascus University in 1968. After a year in Paris, he returned to Tunisia to teach philosophy at a secondary school. A former member of the Tablighi Jama'at and a Qur'anic study group, he founded the Islamic Tendency Movement (*harakat al-ittijah al-islami*) in 1981, which later formed the Renaissance Party (*hizb al-nahda*, or Ennahda). Ghannoushi was first arrested in 1981, released in 1984, rearrested and sentenced for life in 1987, but amnestied in 1988. Shortly thereafter he left for exile in London. While his role in the Islamic opposition movement within Tunisia remains controversial, his stature as an eminent representative of modern Sunni Arab Islamic thought is largely undisputed. In a series of books, articles, lectures, and interviews he presented his aim to make Islam relevant for modern society, notably for the young, by integrating key concepts of modern sociopolitical thought such as good governance, human rights, social justice, freedom, pluralism, and equality into an Islamic framework, insisting on general norms and values rather than conventional understandings of Islamic law and theology, which he considered to be largely irrelevant to present realities.

*See also* **Political Islam.**

### BIBLIOGRAPHY

Hermassi, Abdelbaki. "The Rise and Fall of the Islamist Movement in Tunisia." In *The Islamist Dilemma. The Political Role of Islamist Movements in the Contemporary Arab World.* Edited by Laura Guazzone. Reading, N.Y.: Ithaca Press, 1995.

Tamimi, Azzam. *Rachid Ghannouchi: A Democrat Within Islamism.* Oxford, U.K.: Oxford University Press, 2001

*Gudrun Krämer*

## GHAYBA(T)

*Al-Ghayba* (Persian *ghaybat*), literally "the hiding," is sometimes translated as "the Occultation." While a number of early Shi'ite theological groupings proposed that their imam had gone into "hiding," it was the Twelver Shi'a, the only such group to survive into the classical period in any significant numbers, who fully developed the doctrine. Proclaiming that one's imam had gone into hiding had a number of advantages for persecuted Shi'ite groups. First, it reduced their explicit challenge to the established political order. A hidden imam is (potentially) less disruptive than a manifest imam, thereby reducing political tension with the ruling Sunni authorities. Second, if this imam is predicted to return at some point, the community can be charged with merely waiting (*intizar*) for his return, rather than actively agitating against the governing political powers. Third, while the Shi'a had divided into various groups, based around the charisma of particular would-be imams, a hidden imam could act as a unifying factor, as personality conflicts between imams were avoided.

The majority of Shi'a settled upon both an individual and a point in time when the imam went into hiding. The individual was Muhammad, son of Hasan al-'Askari (a descendent of Imam 'Ali and proclaimed as the eleventh imam), and the time was 868 C.E. According to Shi'ite reports, Hasan died when Muhammad was only six. Muhammad, also referred to as the Mahdi, went into hiding in order to avoid persecution from the Abbasid rulers. At first, he continued to communicate with his Shi'a through intermediaries. These four intermediaries (known as "gates" or "ambassadors") passed on the orders of the hidden imam. After sixty-nine years (in 941), when the fourth agent was close to death, the imam announced that from that point on there were no further agents. While the imam was not leaving the world, he would remain in hiding until God decreed an appropriate time for his return. This ended the lesser occultation (al-ghayba al-sughra), and the greater occultation (al-ghayba al-kubra) began. The Shi'a are still awaiting the return of the imam, known as the Mahdi.

This doctrine appears to have taken some time to reach its final formulation, and later it was subjected to extensive theological justification. For example, in the eleventh century Muhammad b. al-Hasan al-Tusi, in his Kitab al-Ghayba, outlined both textual and rational justifications that later became common in Shi'ite texts of theology. He argued that God would not leave his community without a guide—for to do so would entail his neglect of the Shi'a and hence his injustice. There must, then, be an imam present in the world who acts as God's guide, and this imam must be sinless. Because there is no manifest imam who is both sinless and recognizable as the emissary of God, the imam must, therefore, be in hiding.

The doctrine of the ghayba also has a number of legal consequences. For example, the zakat and khums taxes, collected by the imam, become problematic. Eventually, Shi'ite jurists avoided these duties being lapsed by proposing the doctrine of niyaba (deputyship) of the scholars to carry out these functions.

See also **Imamate; Shi'a: Imami (Twelver).**

## BIBLIOGRAPHY

Arjomand, Said Amir. "The Consolation of Theology: The Shi'ite Doctrine of Occultation and the Transition from Chiliasm to Law." *Journal of Religion* 76, no. 4 (1996): 548–571.

Kohlberg, Etan. "From Imamiyya to Ithna-'Ashariyya." In *Belief and Law in Imami Shi'ism*. Edited by E. Kohlberg. Hampshire, U.K.: Variorum, 1991.

Sachedina, Abdulaziz. *Islamic Messianism: The Idea of the Mahdi in Twelver Shi'ism*. New York: State University of New York Press, 1981.

*Robert Gleave*

# GHAZALI, AL- (C. 1059–1111)

Abu Hamid Muhammad bin Muhammad al-Ghazali (or al-Ghazzali) (1058/9–1111) was born some seven years before the Battle of Hastings, the Norman conquest that transformed England. As an intellectual and thinker, Ghazali's legacy is not only rich, but his imprint on the Muslim tradition is both diverse and complex. For this reason the enigma of his legacy makes him both a highly esteemed as well as a controversial figure. Generations of scholars have debated Ghazali's role, studying the range of texts he had written in order to get a better picture of the man and his oeuvre. For some people Ghazali is the great "Defender of Islam" (*Hujjat al-Islam*, *hujjat* literally meaning "proof"). Others blame him for damaging the rational edifice of Islamic thought in his sharp critique of Muslim philosophers such as Ibn Sina and al-Farabi. However, Ghazali's ideas can best be described as a work in progress and not easily abridged. Therefore, reducing his work to such polarities is to grossly oversimplify the achievements of a very complex life and mind.

Ghazali's childhood was marked by a frugal and impoverished existence, partly caused by the untimely death of his father. His early years were spent in his birthplace in Tus, near what is today the city of Mashhad in modern Iran. After his elementary education with his tutor Ahmad al-Radhkani, he traveled to the city of Jurjan near the Caspian Sea for higher studies with a leading scholar, Isma'il b Mis'ada al-Isma'ili (d. 1084). We learn of the apocryphal story of his encounter with brigands during his return journey from Jurjan. After the brigands had robbed all the travelers in the caravan, Ghazali pleaded with the brigands' leader to return only his precious dissertation (*ta'liqa*), offering him the rest of his possessions in return. The brigand leader ridiculed Ghazali's claim to knowledge and mocked him by showing that a thief could so easily take it away. Struck by this insight, Ghazali later commented: "He [the leader of the brigands] was an oracle (*mustantaq*) whom God made to speak, in order that He could guide me through him." After that episode Ghazali committed all his notes to memory.

But the major transformation in Ghazali's intellectual life took place when he attended the Nizamiyya College in Nishapur. There he impressed the leading scholar of the day, Abu 'l-Ma'ali al-Juwayni (d. 1085), renowned for his expertise in dialectical theology (*'ilm al-kalam*) and Shafi'i law. Juwayni's influence on Ghazali effectively brought him into a full engagement with the rational sciences, especially law, theology, logic, and later philosophy. Thus in Nishapur one begins to see the first signs of Ghazali's extraordinary strength in law and dialectical theology. In law he followed the Shafi'i school while also studying Ash'ari theology without being a slavish adherent to this orientation. These intellectual gifts would serve him well in his rise to intellectual celebrity. At Nishapur, Ghazali learned Islamic mysticism (*tasawwuf*) from Abu 'Ali al-Farmadhi (d. 1084/5). It is not clear what Ghazali did for roughly seven years after completing his formal studies in Nishapur. Most historians believe that he remained in Nishapur but regularly joined the retinue of scholars cultivated by the indomitable Seljuk wazir (Ar. *wazir*) Nizam al-Mulk.

In 1091 Nizam al-Mulk appointed Ghazali professor of Shafi'i law at the Nizamiyya College in Baghdad. It is in Baghdad that Ghazali's intellectual reputation culminated in the honorific "Defender of Islam." It also marked one of the most productive periods in his life. He wrote several books on logic and law. It was also during this period that he wrote his famous refutation of the controversial doctrinal beliefs held by Muslim philosophers about the eternity of the world, their rejection of corporeal resurrection and that God only knew universals, *The incoherence of the philosophers* (*Tahafut al-falasifa*), followed by a vitriolic exposure of the doctrines of the Isma'ili Shi'a called *The obscenities of the esoterists* (*Fada'ih al-batiniyya*). But his meteoric rise came to an abrupt and dramatic end when he experienced a debilitating spiritual crisis, which he described in some detail in his spiritual testimony, *Deliverance from error* (*al-Munqidh min al-dalal*). He decided to abandon his public life of teaching and embarked on a life of contemplative reflection and asceticism. Explanations abound for this dramatic turn in Ghazali's life. Some argue that he suffered intellectual self-doubt in his engagement with philosophy. Others link his anxieties to the series of Ismail'ili assassinations targeting political and religious figures, which gave Ghazali cause to fear for his own life. There is also a view that he found his political alliances with the Seljuk rulers and his ties to the Abbasid caliphal palace to be a source of moral suffocation. Perhaps cumulatively all these pressures had a deleterious impact on his mind and soul.

Under the pretext of making the pilgrimage to Mecca, Ghazali left his family in the province of Khurasan and sought the anonymity of Jerusalem and Damascus, where he spent time meditating at the Dome of the Rock and the Umayyad mosque. After an absence of nearly five years (1095–1099) Ghazali returned to his native Tus. During this period, as a novice on the mystical path, he engaged in reflection and disciplinary practices of the self as taught by master mystics such as Junayd of Baghdad, Harith al-Muhasibi, and others. It is also in this period of his life that he undertook the writing of his magnum opus for which he is best known in the world of scholarship, *The revivification of the sciences of religion* (*Ihya* '

*ulum al-din*). This is now a classic in Muslim religious writing and is widely used to this day. In it Ghazali explores the ethical purposes of religious practices but more importantly provides a road map as to how this can lead to a transformation of the self. As a body of writing, *Revivification* represents Ghazali's personal journey, in which he writes his ailing soul to health. Given his broad intellectual repertoire, Ghazali was able to explore a variety of themes in a complex and convincing manner, drawing on a variety of sources and ideas that he combines into an almost seamless narrative. The *Revivification* consists of four books, each addressing an overall theme: starting with rituals (*'ibadat*), customs and practices (*'adat*), practices that lead to peril (*muhlikat*), and salvific practices (*munjiyat*).

*See also* **Ash'arites, Ash'aira; Falsafa; Kalam; Law; Tasawwuf.**

### BIBLIOGRAPHY

Ghazali, al-. *Freedom and Fulfillment: An Annotated Translation of al-Munqidh min al-Dalal and Other Relevant Works of al-Ghazali.* Translated by Richard J. McCarthy, S. J. Boston: Twayne Publishers, 1980.

Watt, W. Montgomery. *Muslim Intellectual: A Study of al-Ghazali.* Edinburgh: Edinburgh University Press, 1963.

Zarrinkub, Abd al-Husayn. *al-Firar min al-Madrasa: Dirasa fi Hayat wa Fikr Abi Hamid al-Ghazali.* Beirut: Dar al-Rawda, 1992.

*Ebrahim Moosa*

## GHAZALI, MUHAMMAD AL- (1917–2001)

Born in 1917, al-Ghazali was an Egyptian Islamic thinker who was educated as a jurist at Al-Azhar University, Cairo, and held prominent positions with the Ministry of Awqaf and the Mosques Department. During his early career he sided with the Muslim Brotherhood party until he separated himself from the organization in the 1950s. Al-Ghazali wrote over forty books that are considered to be very important in the field of modern legal studies and modern theology. In *Islam and Political Despotism* and *Prejudice and Tolerance in Christianity and Islam*, he advocated the variety of ways in which religion could be a source of social justice and promote peace in the modern world.

As a scholar, al-Ghazali was known for an independent, well-balanced approach to jurisprudence, and he cited Islamic texts in favor of gender equality, greater political participation, environmental awareness, and human rights.

He was critical of modern Muslim scholars who focus too much on pedantic details of adhering to rituals and not enough on governance, finance, ethics, and moral philosophy. Al-Ghazali was critical of radical and neoconservative scholars who failed to understand the comprehensive nature of religion and he refused to recognize their myopic views of faith. He felt that they were poorly trained scholars who purposely select esoteric hadiths and sunna accounts to argue their point and further their political agendas. Al-Ghazali's contribution to modern Islamic thought was to treat faith as integrally linked with the political, economic, and social order.

See also **Political Islam.**

*Qamar-ul Huda*

## GHAZALI, ZAYNAB AL- (1917– )

Zaynab al-Ghazali al-Jabili (b. 1917) is Egypt's prominent female Islamist, a leading figure as a lecturer, teacher, and propagator of Islam who describes herself as the "mother" of the Muslim Brotherhood. After a short interlude in Huda Sha'rawi's Egyptian Feminist Union, she resigned and founded the Muslim Women's Association (1936–1964). Her Islamic upbringing molded her conviction that a secular and Western-oriented movement for women's liberation was not adequate for Muslim society. Moreover, she emphasizes that the rights of Muslim women were entirely guaranteed by Islam as long as they fulfill their duties as mothers and spouses.

Until 1945 she refused Hasan al-Banna's offer to incorporate her organization into the Muslim Brotherhood, but she asserted her readiness for cooperation. This refusal safeguarded her independence and leadership position, taking into consideration the patriarchal patterns and hierarchies within the Muslim Brotherhood. After the ban of the Brotherhood she gave al-Banna her oath of allegiance and formally joined the organization in 1948, becoming the driving force behind its secret reestablishment.

Her own organization was banned in 1964. In the course of the arrests of Brotherhood members she was imprisoned and tortured. Six years later, in 1971, she was released. Her memoirs from prison made her famous, even beyond Egypt's borders.

The fact that Zaynab al-Ghazali's own life as a religious activist appears to contradict women's primary duties (as mothers and spouses) should in no way diminish her significance.

See also **Banna, Hasan al-; Ikhwan al-Muslimin; Political Islam.**

BIBLIOGRAPHY

Cooke, Miriam. "Zaynab al-Ghazali: Saint or Subversive?" *Die Welt des Islams* 34, no. 1 (1994): 1–20.

Ghazali, Zainab al-. *Return of the Pharaoh. Memoirs in Nasir's Prison.* Translated by Mokran Guezzou. Broushton Gifford, Wiltshire, U.K.: Cromwell Press, 1994.

Hoffman, Valerie J."An Islamist Activist: Zaynab al-Ghazali." In *Women and the Family in the Middle East.* Edited by Elisabeth Warnock Fernea. Austin: University of Texas Press, 1985.

*Ursula Günther*

## GHAZI, AHMAD B. IBRAHIM AL-

*See* **Ahmad Ibn Ibrahim al-Ghazi**

## GLOBALIZATION

The term *globalization* is used in various related senses to refer to the intensified integration of the world economy, declining autonomy and separation of the nation-states, the growth of international and transnational forms of governance, and the rapidly expanding communication networks across national, regional, and religious boundaries, especially with the advent of the Internet. With the exception of Indonesia, Malaysia, and Turkey, the impact of economic and financial globalization on the Muslim world has been smaller than in other parts of the world. The integration of Middle Eastern and North African countries into the global economy has been particularly slow, except for the case of Turkey, and the attempts at the privatization of the economy have been largely unsuccessful in the region.

By contrast, the Internet and e-mail have created rapid forms of communication linking different parts of the Muslim world, from Morocco to Indonesia, to each other and to the rest of the world, even though the spread of these electronic media has been slower than in many other parts of the world. This has sometimes been called "globalization from below," to distinguish it from economic globalization through multinational corporations and international financial institutions. The globalization of communication through the Internet, as well as somewhat older media, such as telecommunications and broadcasting, has had a significant and ongoing impact on Islam as a religion. There has also been unprecedented migration, both from the Muslim world into North America and Western Europe, and within the Muslim world into the Gulf countries. Last but not least, transnational political trends and international organization have also had a notable impact on the Islamic world.

## The Push toward Universalism

The missionary expansion of the world religions among nations and across the frontiers of empires can itself be considered the prototype of the process of globalization. These religions have a tendency toward missionary expansion because they are in principle universalistic, which gives them a built-in tendency to overcome many forms of particularism and to expand their influence beyond familial, ethnic, and national boundaries. In practice, the ideal commitment to universalism is tempered by all sorts of compromises with the forces of particularism. As a result of globalization, however, these very compromises transform the character and terms of reference of particularism from local to what sociologists have called "glocal" (from the combination of "global" and "local"). Furthermore, globalization is an important factor in the contemporary resurgence of Islam and the growth of Islamic fundamentalism.

The Internet and satellite communication have weakened the very tight control of the states over national radio and television networks that had once compartmentalized the Muslim world into differently oriented nation-states, and have stimulated the growth of a new, transnational Muslim public space within the global context. These effects of globalization on Islam are interpreted very differently by different observers. Some see the combined effect of globalization as it impacts upon the world's one billion Muslims. They point to the growth of education and vigorous discussion of Islam in books and in public debates in the press, the audio-visual, and the electronic media as contributing to an Islamic Reformation. In this view, the current Islamicization of social life has been both far-reaching and dispersed, lacking any focus or single thrust. Whether or not one concurs with the value-judgment that it constitutes Reformation, it is undeniable that there is an unmistakable dispersion of the current trends in Islamization. The opposite view holds that globalization has put Islam on the front lines of a "Jihad versus McWorld" confrontation, creating a sharply focused and vehement anti-Western as well as anti-universalist struggle. This latter view tends to obliterate the distinction between Islam and Islamic fundamentalism.

The negative view on Islam and globalization, though widely shared by journalists and commentators, seems essentially mistaken. Not only is there variety in Islamic fundamentalism, but Islamic fundamentalism is by no means identical with all the contemporary manifestations of Islam as a universalist religion. Urbanization, development of roads and transportation, the printing revolution, and other contemporary processes of social change, including globalization, simply reinforce trends toward expansion and intensive penetration of society that are typical of Islam as a universalist religion.

These trends remain distinct and are not swamped by fundamentalism.

The twentieth century also gave rise to a combination of internal subglobalization processes typical of the early modern period and externally stimulated globalization. On the one hand, the continuous improvement and declining cost of transportation since the Second World War has greatly increased the number of pilgrims to Mecca, and of missionaries from Africa and Asia to the main centers of Islamic learning in the Middle East. It should be noted that this aspect of globalization reinforces Islam's old universalism, which was institutionalized around the hajj. On the other hand, the postcolonial era has also witnessed the massive immigration of Muslims into Western Europe and North America, where sizable Muslim communities have formed. Meanwhile, there has been unprecedented global integration of Muslims through the mass and electronic media.

The international repercussions of the Salman Rushdie case are the best illustration of the impact of the media on a globally integrated Muslim world. The protests and burning of his *Satanic Verses* by indignant Muslims began in Bradford, England. Images of these protests were broadcast throughout the world, and stimulated more violent protests in Pakistan and India. In a particularly low point of Iranian post-revolutionary politics, after the book had been banned in India, South Africa, Bangladesh, Sudan, Sri Lanka, and Pakistan, Ayatollah Ruhollah Khomeini broadcast his famous *fatwa* condemning Rushdie, a non-Iranian writer who lived in England, to death for apostasy on 14 February 1989.

## Particularism within Globalization

An interesting feature of globalization is the unfolding of antiglobal sentiments in particularistic, variety-producing movements, which seek local legitimacy but, nevertheless, have a global frame of self-reference. The flexibility of signing international conventions with reservations has allowed a large number of Muslim states to confirm their membership in the international communities by signing such agreements while retaining their own particularity of identity and interests. For instance, Muslim nations could sign onto the United Nations' human rights instruments, such as the 1989 UN Convention on the Rights of the Child, but insist upon significant reservations that affirmed the priority of the *shari'a* rules.

More typically, however, global integration induces many Muslims to emphasize their unique identity within the frame of reference of their own culture, which can be said to be at once universal and local or subglobal. There can be no doubt that global integration has made many Muslims seek to appropriate universalist institutions by what might be called Islamic cloning. We thus hear more and more about "Islamic science," "Islamic Human Rights," an "Islamic international

In a shop in downtown Cairo, an Egyptian woman drinks Coca-Cola. In February 1999, a Muslim Internet site started a rumor that the Coca-Cola logo, looked at upside down or reflected in a mirror, read "No Mohammed, no Mecca." Mufti Nasr Farid Wasel, Egypt's highest religious authority, concluded after a study of the logo that the allegation was false and that "there was no defamation to the religion of Islam from near or far." Enric Marti/ AP/Wide World Photos

system" and a variety of organizations modeled after the United Nations and its offshoots, most notably the Organization of the Islamic Conference, which was founded in 1969 and has fifty-seven countries as its members.

The cloning here is unmistakable. Not only is the charter of the Organization of the Islamic Conference derived from the UN charter, but it has an Islamic Development Bank (modeled after the World Bank), a Commission of the International Crescent (corresponding to the Red Cross), and an Islamic Educational, Scientific, and Cultural Organization (corresponding to the UNESCO). In 1980, the OIC voted to establish an International Islamic Law Commission to secure representation of the Islamic viewpoint before the International Court of Justice. The OIC has also set up the International Islamic University of Malaysia as a modern university

for the study of Islamic subjects in accordance with global standards. This phenomenon is a direct result of globalization, not an outcrop of fundamentalism. It is a reactive tendency, however, and can be viewed as a form of defensive counter-universalism. This defensive counter-universalism diverges from the old universalism of Islam as a world religion in its reactive character and "glocal" self-consciousness.

Despite its intent, however, the assimilative character of defensive counter-universalism is quite pronounced. It has already resulted in the assimilation of universal organizational forms, and albeit restrictively, of universal ideas such as human rights and the rights of women. It is difficult to escape the conclusion that, despite its intent, defensive counter-universalism is inevitably a step toward the modernization of the Islamic tradition.

## A Changing Islam in the Global Context

The increasing integration of the Middle Eastern states into the international system has exposed them to the global wave of democratization and the promotion of the rule of law. This exposure has introduced a new element of legal pluralism and generated ambivalent reactions throughout the Middle East. The impact of the human rights revolution on the legal culture of Middle Eastern societies has been significant, and constitutional and supreme courts of a few Muslim countries, such as Egypt and Malaysia, have insinuated international rights provisions into their national legal systems.

Among the human rights, the ones with the strongest social backing that results from structural and occupational changes in contemporary Middle Eastern societies are those concerned with women's rights. Women's rights are represented by official organs of the states, and by a growing number of nongovernmental organizations (NGOs) that are increasingly linked with international NGOs and the United Nations agencies. According to some reports, the women's NGOs stole the show from the state delegates at the International Conference on Population and Development in Cairo (1994), and delegates from the Muslim countries were conspicuous in the Fourth World Conference on the Status of Women in Beijing (1995). In Iran, women constituted the largest group of President Mohammad Khatami's supporters, and the reformists in the *Majles* include a few prominent women. The Iranian women's movement has made significant gains since 1997, and is acting as a channel for the slow but continuous influence of international conventions on women's rights on Iran's administrative and civil law.

In contrast, the transnational Islamic resurgence has caused the rejection of the assertion of the universality of human rights, and has generated an official "Islamic alternative." This Islamic alternative is embodied in the 1990 Cairo Declaration on Human Rights in Islam. As is to be expected in an imitative document, much of the legal terminology of the international human rights conventions is swallowed, even as quite a number of rights are in substance nullified. For instance, the Cairo Declaration offers no guarantee of religious freedom. It prohibits the use of any form of compulsion or exploitation of poverty and ignorance to convert anyone to atheism or a religion other than Islam (Article 10). Article 22 of the Declaration bars "the exploitation or misuse of information in such a way as may violate sanctities and the dignity of Prophets, undermine moral and ethical values, or disintegrate, corrupt, or harm society or weaken its faith." It is interesting to note that, in flat contradiction to the historical experience and the public law of virtually all the signatory countries, Article 19 of the Cairo Declaration provides that "There shall be no crime or punishment except as provided for in the Shari'ah." Article 25 further declares the *shari'a* the only source for the explanation and clarification of the articles of the Declaration. While endorsing the Cairo Declaration, the Islamic Conference of Foreign Ministers in April 1993 also confirmed "the existence of different constitutional and legal systems among [the] Member States and various international or regional human rights instruments to which they are parties." This amounts to a very significant qualification of the categorical recognition of the *shari'a* in the Cairo Declaration, as most Middle Eastern countries are signatories to several such international instruments. Iran, for instance, is among the signatories to the International Covenant on Civil and Political Rights. The acknowledgment, therefore, leaves open the kind of insinuation of the international law on human rights into national laws of the kind undertaken by the Supreme Constitutional Court of Egypt.

An increasing number of Muslim intellectuals are defending the right to the freedom of expression by insisting that religious liberty and freedom of conscience are clearly deducible from the text of the Qur'an. A number of Qur'anic verses strongly imply a form of "natural religion" among mankind, which entails religious liberty, and make explicit the concepts of freedom of conscience and religion, most notably, "there is no compulsion in religion" (2:256). Proliferation of the communications media beyond government control has made the freedom of interpretation of Islam itself a prominent feature of the emerging Muslim public sphere. In Iran, 'Abd al-Karim Sorush has gone so far as putting all the world religions on an equal footing in the 1998 essay, *Saratha-ye mostaqim* (Straight paths), the very title being a sacrilegious pluralization of a fundamental Qur'anic concept. In Syria, Muhammad Shahruhr has offered a similarly radically modernist interpretation of Islam.

*See also* **Internet; Networks, Muslim.**

## BIBLIOGRAPHY

Arjomand, Saïd Amir "Islam." In *Global Religions: An Introduction*. Edited by M. Juergensmeyer. Oxford, U.K.: Oxford University Press, 2003.

Eickelman, Dale F., and Anderson, Jon W., eds. *New Media in the Muslim World. The Emerging Public Sphere.* Bloomington: Indiana University Press, 1999.

Therborn, G. "Globalizations: Dimensions, Historical Waves, Regional Effects, Normative Governance." *International Sociology* 15, no. 2 (2000): 151–179.

*Saïd Amir Arjomand*

## GOVERNMENT, ISLAMIC *See* Hukuma al-Islamiyya, al- (Islamic Government)

## GRAMMAR AND LEXICOGRAPHY

In the period before Islam the Bedouin tribes in the Arabian peninsula held poets (sing. *sha'ir*) as well as soothsayers (sing. *kahin*) in the highest esteem. Both delivered their message in a fixed form of meter or rhyming prose and they occupied an important position in their own tribe, while they were feared and respected by other tribes. This shows how much power was assigned to language and the spoken word in Bedouin society. When the prophet Muhammad brought the message that had been revealed to him, it was therefore only fitting that this message emphasized its sacred force by referring to the linguistic and rhetorical qualities of the revealed book: The Qur'an was delivered in a clear, eloquent language (*qur'anan mubinan*), which was the language of the Arabs. At the same time, the message emphasized the difference between the revelation and other literary productions: the Prophet was not a poet and the fact that he had never learned to read or write demonstrated the miraculous nature of the revelation.

Right from the start, the believers were concerned with the preservation of the revealed book. According to Muslim tradition, during the life of the Prophet parts of the message were written down on scraps of writing material, and the Prophet himself sometimes employed scribes to whom he dictated the revelations. It was not until the third caliph 'Uthman (r. 644–656) that a codified text of the Qur'an was made, the so-called *mushaf*. Although this codex became the canonical text for all later generations, the presence of a large number of variant readings forced the believers to concentrate not only on the contents of the text, but also on its form.

After the death of the Prophet, the Islamic conquests led to a drastic transformation, not only of pre-Islamic values and customs, but also of the language of the Arabs. The inhabitants of the conquered territories had to acquire the new language in a short period of time, and their mistakes affected Arabic to such a degree that a new type of Arabic arose, which eventually became the basis for the modern dialects. As a result of this process, which was regarded by the Arabs themselves as a process of corruption of speech (*fasad al-lugha*), the text of the Qur'an became difficult to understand.

Because of the central place of the Qur'an in Islamic society it is not surprising that specialists came forward in the community to help the common believers understand the text. The name most often cited in this connection is that of Ibn 'Abbas (d. 687), but we may be sure that each city in the empire had its own experts. The earliest commentaries all shared a semantic approach, since they focused on the implications of the text for religious, legal, and ritual purposes. Yet, the existence of variant readings and the discrepancies between the language of the text and everyday vernacular speech also led to an interest in formal elements in the text as well. For instance, signaling the presence of foreign loanwords in the Qur'an and discussing the tribal provenance of some of the lexical items were not essential for the understanding of the text, but nevertheless most of the commentaries provide such information.

Some of the earliest commentators, such as Mujahid (d. 722) and Muqatil (d. 767), used conventional terms in discussing, for instance, the various text types that are found in the Qur'an or the vowel-endings of words. The terms for the vowel-endings, which were probably derived from the Syriac grammatical tradition, provided a starting point for later grammarians and may therefore be regarded as the beginnings of the discipline of grammar in Islam.

### From Text to Language

The preoccupation with the formal properties of the text of the Qur'an inevitably led to an interest in the structure of the language in which the revelation was couched. The sources have preserved the names of some scholars in the second century of Islam, who dealt with the Arabic language on a professional basis, not only in order to study the revealed book, but also to understand the structure of the language, to find out the *qiyas al-'arabiyya* "the rules of Arabic." Since what is known about these grammarians comes only from later sources (chiefly the quotations in the first complete grammar of Arabic, *Kitab Sibawayhi*), it is difficult to say with any certainty what their opinions were, but so much seems to be certain that they did not hesitate to correct the text of the Qur'an whenever they thought it was contradicted by the linguistic usage of the Bedouin.

This attitude toward the text and the language of the Qur'an was to change with Sibawayhi (d. c. 793), a Persian, who became the first grammarian to compile a book encompassing the entire structure of the language. For Sibawayhi the text of the Qur'an had been established once and for all by the 'Uthmanic codex, compiled by order of the third caliph, and he did not feel the need to concern himself with the text itself. Instead, he turned to the structure of the language of the Arab Bedouin, which was assumed to be identical both with the language of the revelation and with that of the pre-Islamic poems. In his *Kitab*, Sibawayhi set himself a task that went beyond the explanation of the text and aimed at a much larger scope: the explanation of grammar. He dealt with all possible constructions in the language and accounted for their structural differences in terms of the different case endings found in them.

Sibawayhi introduced a framework that was truly innovative, the system of declension (*i'rab*) that became one of the central notions of Arabic grammar. Nouns, and to some extent imperfect verbs, were assumed to have a series of endings whose function differed from that of the permanent end vowels of other words such as the perfect verbs or the particles. The declensional vowels were the result of the action of an *'amil*, an operator governing the case endings. This function could be performed either by a verb (e.g., in the sentence *daraba zaydun 'amran* "Zayd hit 'Amr" the verb is the operator of the nominative in the agent, *zaydun*, and the accusative in the object, *'amran*), or a particle (e.g., the particle *fi* is the operator of the genitive in *fi l-bayti* "in the house").

Since it is not always possible to explain the structure of the actually spoken sentence, it is sometimes necessary to have recourse to an underlying level of speech (*taqdir*). Thus, for instance, in the sentence *an-najdata!* "help!" the grammarian posits an underlying verb *ad'u* "I call for, I ask" in order to explain the accusative in the noun. With the help of the notion of *taqdir* grammarians built a large explanatory framework that was neither intended as normative (after all, the Bedouin were native speakers and did not need correction), nor as a simple description, but as an explanation of the rules of grammar. Exceptions were not allowed in this analysis, since language was regarded as part of God's creation, of which even the minutest detail must find an explanation.

Even though after Sibawayhi competing schools arose in Basra, Kufa, and Baghdad, the theoretical framework remained the same for all grammarians. Both the grammarians in Basra, such as al-Mubarrad (d. 898), and those in Kufa, such as al-Farra' (d. 822) and Tha'lab (d. 904), used the principle of *'amal* to account for the case endings in the language, and although they differed as to the scope of the examples they allowed as a basis for their *qiyas*, essentially they may be regarded as belonging to one linguistic paradigm.

The science that worked with this paradigm is called in Arabic *nahw* (which also means "syntax"). Almost right from the beginning a strict distinction was made between this science and that of lexicography (*'ilm al-lugha*). The earliest beginnings of lexicography are found in the commentaries of the Qur'an, some of which concentrated on the lexical meaning of words that had become archaic by that time. These early attempts at compiling word lists of the Qur'an or the hadith culminated in the *Kitab al-'ayn*, initiated and perhaps partly based on the notes of al-Khalil ibn Ahmad (d. 791),

Sibawayhi's teacher in grammar. Like the *Kitab Sibawayhi*, this dictionary no longer concentrated on the Qur'an but on the language itself, as is evident from the fact that poetic quotations are far more frequent in it than quotations from the Qur'an. The *Kitab al-ʿayn* set the trend for a long line of ever larger dictionaries that attempted to encapsulate the lexicon of the entire language, culminating in Ibn Manzur's (d. 1311) famous lexicon, *Lisan al-ʿArab*.

### From Language to Language Use

A new development in Arab linguistics was initiated by the introduction of Greek logic and philosophy in the Islamic world. The translation of Greek texts that had already started under the Umayyad caliphs, usually through Syriac, started in earnest under the Abbasid caliph al-Maʾmun (d. 833), who personally supported this development by founding the *Bayt al-Hikma* (an academy of translators in Baghdad). The influx of new ideas in Arabic had a profound influence on Islamic thinking, especially in the theological system of the Muʿtazilites, who for some time enjoyed official recognition of their ideas.

Thanks to the Muʿtazilites rationalist logic became the cornerstone for theological thought. Because of their emphasis on the unity of God, they refused to accept an eternal status for the revealed book, which they regarded as created (*khalq al-Qurʾan*). Through the discussions on this topic the Muʿtazilites became interested in questions about the status of God's speech, the relationship between word and meaning, and the intricate question of the origin of speech. This last issue had always been connected with the revelation of the Qur'an, but was discussed now as a logico-philosophical problem.

Although grammarians in general avoided any contact with the "Greek sciences," they could not avoid some of the topics that had become popular in general debate, such as the relationship between words and the things they referred to or the logical correlates of grammatical categories, as in Zajjaji's (d. 949) *Kitab al-idah*. Greek influence also manifested itself in the debate about the status of grammar vis-à-vis logic and about the competence of logicians and grammarians. Significantly, many grammarians in this period adhered to Muʿtazilite ideas. Apart from its influence on the public debate Greek logic also insinuated itself in the general format of grammatical treatises. Contrary to the earlier tradition, it became customary to define grammatical notions and to devote special attention to the division of their treatises into separate topics. Likewise, grammarians started to write introductory treatises, such as Zajjaji's *Kitab al-jumal* or Farisi's (d. 989) *Kitab al-idah*.

In the third/fourth centuries of Islam, grammar had become a technical discipline with its own terminology and apparatus. Although grammarians such as Ibn Jinni (d. 1002) showed a vivid interest in all matters pertaining to language in his linguistic encyclopedia *al-Khasaʾis*, most grammatical treatises in this period were concerned with repeating and refining the contents of Sibawayhi's *Kitab* rather than innovating the discipline.

This situation started to change with grammarians such as Jurjani (d. 1078) who combined their interests in rhetoric and grammar and criticized their predecessors for not having taken into account the semantic aspect of speech by focusing exclusively on the syntactic parameters. This new interest in a comprehensive science of language, including style and poetics, may be yet another example of Muʿtazilite thinking in linguistics. Their influence is certainly evident in the field of the *ʿilm usul al-fiqh*, in which the epistemological value of linguistic utterances was studied for its relevance to legal reasoning. These new developments meant effectively a separation between grammar in the strict sense and other language-related sciences.

*See also* **Arabic Language; Arabic Literature; Qur'an.**

### BIBLIOGRAPHY

Bohas, Georges; Guillaume, Jean-Patrick; and Carter, Michael G. *Arab Linguistics: An Introductory Classical Text with Translation and Notes.* Amsterdam: J. Benjamins, 1981.

Gully, Adrian. *Grammar and Semantics in Medieval Arabic: A study of Ibn-Hisham's Mughni l-Labib.* Richmond, Surrey, U.K.: Curzon Press, 1995.

Kouloughli, Djamel Eddine. *The Arabic Linguistic Tradition.* New York and London: Routledge, 1990.

Larkin, Margaret. *The Theology of Meaning: ʿAbd al-Qahir al-Jurjani's Theory of Discourse.* New Haven, Conn.: American Oriental Society, 1995.

Owens, Jonathan. *The Foundations of Grammar: An Introduction to Medieval Arabic Grammar.* Amsterdam: J. Benjamins, 1988.

Owens, Jonathan. *Early Arabic Grammatical Theory: Heterogeneity and Standardization.* Amsterdam and Philadelphia: J. Benjamins, 1990.

Talmon, Rafael. *Arabic Grammar in Its Formative Age: Kitab al-ʿAyn and its Attribution to Halil b. Ahmad.* Leiden: E. J. Brill, 1997.

Versteegh, Kees. *Qurʾanic Exegesis and Arabic Grammar in Early Islam.* Leiden: E. J. Brill, 1993.

Versteegh, Kees. *The Arabic Linguistic Tradition.* London and New York: Routledge, 1997.

Versteegh, Kees. *The Arabic Language.* 2nd ed. Edinburgh: Edinburgh University Press, 2001.

*Kees Versteegh*

## GREEK CIVILIZATION

The rapid expansion of the Islamic empire led to its speedy contact with a cultural world heavily marked by Greek thought. Greek civilization had spread throughout the urban areas of the Middle East, North Africa, and the Iberian peninsula, and it was reflected in the relatively high standards of living and education, for at least a portion of the citizens. When the Arabs came to confront this culture, they might have rejected it totally and sought to destroy it. After all, it was a culture that rested on unbelief, from an Islamic perspective, and whose practitioners were ethnically quite distinct from the Arabs themselves. In the early Middle Ages, however, there was an attempt to understand and learn from the Greek-influenced cultures, and to use that knowledge to improve the delivery of the Islamic message itself. Several theories could explain this. It could be because the new rulers were intent on obeying those parts of the Qur'an that recommend toleration of divergent points of view, at least when held by other people of the book; it could have been because Islam was not at this stage confident enough to alienate those under its recent control; or it could be that the Muslims were impressed by the level of wealth and culture that they observed and sought to emulate it by coming to grips with its basis in Greek culture.

A very practical issue that soon faced the Muslims was the need to argue with their new subjects, since the issue of conversion was a live one. Yet the non-Muslims were often far better at disputation than the Muslims, given their long practice of rhetoric and logic. The ancient Greeks had developed the art of disputation to a very high degree, and this continued to be studied and practiced by their successors in the Middle East. Perhaps even more significantly, the Greeks had developed a sophisticated scientific system, not only one that was theoretically rich in its understanding of how the universe might operate, but also a system that was capable of making a very substantial practical contribution to everything from how to design cities to how to cure (or at least alleviate symptoms of) a variety of diseases. Clearly any rational ruler was going to avail himself of this intellectual largesse if he could, and the Muslims certainly took advantage of what they found in their new territories.

The first step that needed to be taken was to rapidly translate Greek texts, often via Syriac (a Semitic language like Arabic). It was an expensive and time-consuming process carried out largely by Christian translators. The Abbasid caliph al-Ma'mun founded in 832 C.E. the House of Wisdom (an institution where translators and collectors of Greek and Syriac manuscripts could cooperate; *bayt al-hikma*), and its scale is an indication of the importance with which the rulers of the time regarded Greek thought. The availability of Greek texts in Arabic formed the basis of what came to be a very rich tradition of Islamic philosophy, which continued in the Arabic world until the twelfth century as philosophy, and that was to enjoy an even longer life in the Persian world, where philosophy continued to be studied and written for far longer. The problems that philosophy met in the Arabic-speaking world owed much to its Greek, and hence non-Muslim, origins. There was a prolonged campaign by many

thinkers to oppose the use of Greek-inspired thought, from Abu Sa'id al-Sirafi (893–979) to al-Ghazali (1058–1111) and Ibn Taymiyya (d. 1328). Interestingly, the arguments against Greek thought often employed Greek mechanisms and so could be representative of Greek civilization's ultimate success in the Islamic world.

In some parts of the Islamic world such as al-Andalus (the Iberian peninsula) there was a particularly happy combination of Greek thought and Islam, resulting in a great outburst of science and culture generally. There is much evidence that the intellectual wealth thus produced had as a side-effect considerable material wealth, and certainly during this period the Islamic world was far more advanced than Christian Europe. It may be significant that Christian Europe during the early Middle Ages had only a limited supply of Greek texts, and indeed only acquired any significant degree of these when they were translated out of Arabic into Latin (often via Hebrew).

It is sometimes argued that the Islamic world was not able to make creative use of Greek thought, merely being transmitters of Greek civilization. This is plainly false, as a great number of original and innovative theories came out of the Islamic world, and the Greeks were not the only group to make a contribution to the culture of the Islamic world, since the role of the Indians within Islamic life deserves careful consideration.

In a whole range of disciplines such as mathematics, astronomy, chemistry—and, of course, philosophy—Greek-inspired thought was the catalyst for a creative outburst. In what are today not regarded as respectable sciences, alchemy and astrology, Greek thought played an even more important role. Greek thought affected the paradigmatically Islamic sciences of theology and law that came to acquire many of the techniques and principles used in Greek thought. Finally, the Islamic *adab* tradition of literature was also influenced by the Greeks. There were many editions of books that contained "wisdom" literature of the Greeks, chiefly consisting of aphorisms often incorrectly attributed to thinkers like Socrates. Despite the questionable sources the wisdom literature was probably widely read and certainly had an effect on the notion of what constituted style in literature. Abu Sulayman al-Sijistani's collections of wisdom literature were particularly widely distributed from the tenth century onward. In short, it is difficult to find an aspect of Islamic civilization that was not affected by the Greeks.

Another area of thought where Greek civilization played a notable part was the development of political thought. The idea of a ruler who combines the roles of legislator, thinker, and religious authority was constructed by adding Islam to Plato, as it were, proving to be a very fruitful way of analyzing the state and the nature of political authority. The description of the state as organic in Plato's *Republic* fit in nicely with the Islamic notion of the state being necessarily structured in terms of a religious doctrine, where every individual has a role that satisfies higher purposes than merely providing him with particular benefits and duties. It was not difficult to add to the characteristics of the ruler the status of prophecy, or intermediary between the community and the Prophet, and this enables the state to claim a higher purpose than merely assuring the material welfare of its members. Even long after the direct influence of Greek thought disappeared from the Islamic world, this theme in political thought continued and flourished.

*See also* **Africa, Islam in; Americas, Islam in the; Falsafa; Islam and Other Religions; South Asia, Islam in; Southeast Asia, Islam in.**

## BIBLIOGRAPHY

Abed, Shukri. *Aristotelian Logic and the Arabic Language in Alfarabi.* Albany: State University of New York Press, 1991.

Gutas, Dimitri. *Avicenna and the Aristotelian Tradition: Introduction to the Reading of Avicenna's Works.* Leiden: E. J. Brill, 1988.

Leaman, Oliver. "Philosophical and Scientific Achievements in Islamic History." In *Intellectual Traditions in Islam.* Edited by Farhad Daftary. London: I. B. Tauris, 2000.

Leaman, Oliver. *Introduction to Classical Islamic Philosophy.* Cambridge, U.K.: Cambridge University Press, 2002.

Nasr, Seyyed Hossein, and Leaman, Oliver, eds. *History of Islamic Philosophy.* New York: Routledge, 1996.

Peters, Francis E. *Aristotle and the Arabs: The Aristotelian Tradition in Islam.* New York: New York University Press, 1968.

Walzer, Richard. *Greek into Arabic: Essays on Islamic Philosophy.* Oxford, U.K.: Bruno Cassirer, 1962.

*Oliver Leaman*

## GUMI, ABU BAKR *See* **Abu Bakr Gumi**

# H

## HADITH

Hadith is a genre of Muslim literature that originated in the early period of Islamic history. It is found in the earliest preserved compilations of legal and historical material ascribed to authors of the eighth century. Since then and continuing until the present time, a huge number of hadith collections have been brought to light.

The term hadith (often capitalized by Western scholars) denotes both the genre of literature and an individual text of this genre. Originally the term meant story, communication, or report but as a scholarly term hadith means tradition. Muslim scholarship tends to limit the term hadith to the accounts of the prophet Muhammad. Many Western scholars use hadith more broadly to include the traditions of the Prophet's Companions and even later generations. In this broader meaning, however, it was also used by early and a few later Muslim hadith scholars.

In the early and classical sources, that is, those dated until the eleventh century, one mostly encounters the hadiths in a typical form. Every single tradition begins with a chain of transmitters, called *isnad* (support, foundation). The first transmitter in the *isnad* is often the collector (sometimes even his pupil) in whose compilation the hadith in question is found, then the collector's informant is mentioned, then the latter's informant, and so on until the chain arrives at the original reporter of the text. The text, which is called *matn* in Arabic, could be either a short sentence or a long story. Here is an example of a hadith:

> Yahya related to me from Malik from Ibn Shihab from 'Ata' b. Yazid al-Laythi from Abu Sa'id al-Khudri that the Messenger of God, may God bless him and grant him peace, said (= *isnad*): "When you hear the call to prayer (*adhan*), repeat what the muezzin (*mu'adhdhin*) says" (= *matn*).

In this tradition the *isnad* informs us that Abu Sa'id al-Khudri, a Companion of the Prophet, reported this saying of the Prophet, and that his report has been transmitted via 'Ata', Ibn Shihab, Malik, and his pupil Yahya to the editor of the collection in which the hadith is found.

### Role in Muslim Culture

The hadiths, embodying the tradition on the origins of Islam, are for Muslims an important source of guidance next to the Qur'an. The "way" (sunna) of their Prophet and of the first generations of Muslims is taken as a model of how Muslims should live in this world in order to lead a happy eternal life in the hereafter. This is most obvious in that this sunna, particularly that of the Prophet, became after the Qur'an the second fundamental source of the *shari'a*, the Law of God. According to Muslim scholars this status of the sunna is advocated both in the Qur'an and in hadiths of the Prophet and was already acknowledged by his Companions. In contrast, Western scholars usually think that the sunna acquired its status as second source of the Law only gradually during the eighth century and that in Sunnite law the hadiths of the Prophet gained the absolute superiority over other expressions of the sunna only in the first half of the ninth century. In Imami Shi'ite law the traditions of the Prophet did not acquire such a superiority but are considered equal in value with that of the imams.

The important role that the hadiths came to play in Muslim scholarship in general, and for the establishment of the *shari'a* in particular, induced Muslim scholars to scrutinize the tradition material critically and to define rules as to which hadiths could be accepted and which must be rejected. The traditional Muslim hadith criticism focused on the chains of transmitters (*isnad*s), which accompany a hadith, but also checked whether its content (*matn*) is compatible with other recognized traditions and with the Qur'an. This led among the Sunnites to a classification of hadiths in four classes: (1) *sahih* (sound); (2) *hasan* (fair); (3) *da'if* (weak), with some subcategories of this class; and (4) *mawdu'* (spurious).

Additionally, special classification systems were developed for the evaluation of *isnad*s and *matn*s. The critical evaluation of the hadiths found its expression in special compilations in which their authors collected the hadiths, that they considered reliable or accepted. The "six books" (see the section "Collections" below), which among the Sunnites acquired an almost canonical status, belong to this type of collection. Nevertheless, the evaluation of particular hadiths, even of those contained in the most revered collections, remained disputed in Muslim scholarship. In Imami Shi'ism hadith criticism was less sophisticated and appeared late because the *isnad*s consisted in large part of the (infallible) imams.

In modern times the Muslim debate about the reliability of the hadiths got a new impetus. Reform-minded scholars and intellectuals tried to revise the issue of which hadiths are essential and binding for a Muslim and which are not. Names like Sayyid Ahmad Khan (d. 1898), Muhammad 'Abduh (d. 1905), Rashid Rida (d. 1935), Mahmud Abu Rayya, and Ghulam Ahmad Parwez are connected with the critique of the traditional hadith scholarship. Scholars advocating Islamic revivalism, such as Abu l-A'la' Maududi (d. 1979), Muhammad al-Ghazali, or Yusuf al-Qaradawi, also called for a reassessment of the classical hadith literature in light of the Qur'an and modernity. They argued for a more sophisticated criticism of the content (*matn*) of the hadiths. A few others like Fazlur Rahman (d. 1988) and Mohammed Arkoun advocated a new understanding of the development of the hadiths.

## Collections

The earliest preserved hadith collections confine themselves to certain types of traditions. For example, the *Sira* of Ibn Ishaq (d. 767) in the recension preserved from Ibn Hisham (d. 828 or 833) contains mainly historical traditions on Muhammad and his time. The *Muwatta'* of Malik b. Anas (d. 795) as transmitted by Yahya b. Yahya (d. 848) is a collection of legal hadiths, as is the Zaydi Shi'ite *Majmu' al-fiqh* ascribed to Zayd b. 'Ali (d. 740), but probably compiled only by Ibrahim b. Zibriqan (d. 799). By contrast, the *Tafsir* of 'Abd al-Razzaq al-San'ani (d. 827) contains exegetical traditions.

This manner of collecting traditions continued and there are many later examples of compilations confined to a certain type of tradition or to traditions on certain topics. From the ninth century onward more comprehensive collections became available. There are two main types. In most of the comprehensive collections the traditions are put together in chapters and paragraphs according to the content of the traditions. Thus we find chapters on prayer, marriage, commercial transactions, Qur'anic exegesis, *maghazi* (campaigns of the Prophet), and so forth in which traditions on the particular topics are combined. This type of ordering of the subject matter is called *musannaf* (classified). The oldest comprehensive collections preserved, such as the *Musannaf* of 'Abd al-Razzaq (d. 827), the *Musannaf* of Ibn Abi Shayba (d.

849), the *Sunan* of Sa'id b. Mansur (d. 841), or the *Sunan* of al-Darimi (d. 868), belong to this type, as do the six hadith collections of al-Bukhari (d. 870), Muslim (d. 874), Ibn Maja (d. 886), Abu Dawud (d. 888), al-Tirmidhi (d. 892), and al-Nasa'i (d. 915), which over time were recognized by Sunnite scholars as the most reliable ones. The collections of al-Bukhari and Muslim were even called the "sound" (*sahih*). The canonical hadith collections of the Imami Shi'ites compiled by al-Kulini (d. 939), al-Babuya al-Qummi (d. 991), and al-Tusi (d. 1067) also belong to the *musannaf* type.

Several comprehensive collections compiled from the ninth century onward show another method of ordering the hadiths. All traditions whose *isnad*s go back to the same original reporter are put together; for example, the hadiths transmitted from the above-mentioned Abu Sa'id al-Khudri. The entries are arranged alphabetically according to the name of the original reporters. Such a type of collection is called *musnad*. Generally it confines itself to hadiths of the Prophet. The most famous compilation of this type is the huge *Musnad* of Ahmad b. Hanbal (d. 855), but there are earlier ones, such as the *Musnad* of al-Humaydi (d. 834) and the *Musnad* of al-Tayalisi (d. 813)—the latter probably compiled by one of his pupils—and many later ones, like the *Tahdhib al-athar* of al-Tabari (d. 923), which is incomplete; the *Musnad* of Abu Ya'la (d. 919); or *al-Mu'jam al-kabir* of al-Tabarani (d. 970).

Muslim scholars did not always use the terms *musannaf* and *musnad* consistently in the titles of the collections, and they classify hadith collections also according to several other criteria.

## History

Hadiths are available in collections dating from the ninth to the eleventh centuries or even later. The hadiths themselves, through their *isnad*s, claim to have been transmitted from earlier times. There are four sources that allow us to know more about the history of these hadiths: (1) the *isnad*s of the traditions; (2) their texts (*matn*s); (3) biographical traditions about the transmitters found in the *isnad*s; and (4) the later norm and practice of transmitting traditions (known from different types of sources).

Most Sunnite Muslim scholars are convinced that it is possible to reconstruct the history of the hadiths on the basis of the four sources, which they consider on the whole as being reliable. They usually sketch the origin and development of the hadiths as follows: The Prophet taught his "way" (sunna) to his Companions orally, by writing or by practical demonstration. He encouraged his Companions to diffuse his teachings and sent teachers and preachers to newly converted tribes. His Companions were very eager to learn as much as they could from their Prophet. They learned his sunna, that is, his practice, by doing it with him, they memorized it, or—if they could write—wrote it down. After the death of the

Prophet, his Companions continued their efforts to memorize the hadiths and to write them down, and instructed others whenever they felt that this was needed, and some Companions even attracted circles of students whom they taught regularly.

In this way the hadiths were also transmitted to the following generations. The students of the Companions, the older Successors, became teachers themselves and the circles of students committed to the study of the Qur'an and to the preservation of traditions grew steadily. There were only few Successors who had collected hadiths from different sources, but their students, who flourished in the first half of the eighth century, devoted themselves to the task of collecting traditions more systematically. They also began to arrange them thematically and transmitted their written collections to wider circles of students. This is the material out of which the early substantial collections of traditions were compiled, such as Ibn Ishaq's *Sira* or Malik's *Muwatta'*, which are preserved through recensions of their pupils.

This scenario, which has a certain attraction by appearing natural or even inevitable, at least as far as the Prophet and his Companions are concerned, is almost completely based on information taken from traditions that go back, according to their *isnad*s, to eyewitnesses of the time of the Prophet, the Companions, and the Successors. It is rejected outright by a Western school of thought that argues that the precise history of the hadiths available in the collections of the ninth century and later cannot be reconstructed anymore. Scholars belonging to this school of thought doubt, first of all, the historical value of the *isnad*s, which they consider as generally fabricated and as arbitrarily attached to the traditions. They furthermore argue that the biographical traditions about the transmitters who appear in the *isnad*s are not an independent historical source, because the information contained in the biographical traditions may be invented to support the *isnad*s. If these two sources, *isnad*s and biographical traditions, are unreliable, then we are left with the texts alone. On the basis of their content and style, only a very global reconstruction of their history is possible. As models for such a reconstruction, the developments of the Jewish and Christian religious literature can be used. The result is "salvation history," the reconstruction of how the Muslim community at the turn of the eighth century reflects through its traditions on its own origins. This school of thought derives its inspiration from the studies of J. Wansbrough (1977, 1978). According to this approach the hadiths are generally inauthentic in the sense that they do not reflect the factual history of the first two Islamic centuries. This skepticism of the traditions has its roots in the studies of I. Goldziher (1890) and J. Schacht (1950).

Not all Western scholars hold to the extreme skepticism that doubts the historical reliability of the Muslim traditions altogether. Many Western scholars of Islam assume that there may be both unreliable and reliable traditions and that

it might be possible to discern between them. They differ, however, widely as to the methods through which this could be achieved. In this respect more or less skeptical and sophisticated approaches can be distinguished. Some scholars (like M. W. Watt) rely in their methods mainly on the texts of the hadiths, while others (like Juynboll) focus on the *isnad*s, and yet others (like J. van Ess, H. Motzki, or G. Schoeler) use a combination of *matn* and *isnad* analysis. The latter method starts from collections in which the traditions are available and tries to detect indications in the *isnad*s and the texts as to whether the traditions in question were really transmitted or fabricated. The investigation can be focused either on a single tradition, of which variants are available in different collections, or on the traditions contained in one and the same collection. In the first case the aim is to find out whether it is possible to reconstruct the transmission history of a particular hadith. In the second case the issue is scrutinized to determine whether the history of a whole collection can be reconstructed, whether the collector may have invented the hadiths or the *isnad*s or both, or whether he has received them from the informants he names.

This source-critical approach produces another scenario of the history of the hadiths. In contrast to the pictures drafted by Muslim scholars and extreme skepticists, the conclusions of the source-critical scholars are general but confined to the collections and traditions studied. Their scenario is therefore fragmentary and provisional.

According to the source-critical approach there are collections, such as 'Abd al-Razzaq's *Musannaf* or Ibn Hisham's *Sira*, which can be shown to have been compiled from earlier sources. That means that the names to which the collectors ascribe their materials are, at least partially, their real informants. This does not yet say anything about the quality of their textual transmission. These informants or sources of the collectors, like Ibn Jurayj or Ibn Ishaq, lived in the first half of the eighth century. It is also obvious that the huge amounts of traditions that were transmitted by these informants were mostly not invented by them or falsely ascribed to some other informants, but were really received from the persons named. This is suggested by the great variation between the *isnad*s and the *matn*s, which are said to derive from the different informants and by formal peculiarities that suggest a real transmission. In this manner the materials going back, for example, to 'Ata' b. Rabah (d. 733) or 'Amr b. Dinar (d. 744), some of the key informants of Ibn Jurayj (d. 767), or the material going back to al-Zuhri (d. 742), a key informant of both Ibn Jurayj and Ibn Ishaq (d. 767), can be recovered. The quality of the material transmitted from these informants—flourishing in the first quarter of the eighth century and belonging to the Successors, the generation following that of the Prophet's Companions—can be evaluated on internal grounds and by comparing their traditions with variants of them found in other reliable sources and transmitted by compilers other than Ibn Jurayj and Ibn Ishaq. In this way suspicious transmitters can be detected as well. The procedure can, at least in some cases, also be applied to the material deriving from the Successors. That means that through this method it is possible to date large amounts of traditions step by step back until, at least in some cases, the time of the Companions.

The materials reconstructed as being earlier sources allow for conclusions about the way hadiths were transmitted from generation to generation until they were incorporated in the collection in question, for example 'Abd al-Razzaq's *Musannaf*. It could be established, for example, that the transmission of traditions in Mecca and Medina from the middle of the seventh until the middle of the eighth century occurred orally but was accompanied by written notes. This indicates that the transmission focused on the content of the traditions, not on the exact wording. In the succeeding generations transmission occurred orally in combination with verbatim copying. The use and quality of *isnad*s differed among the early scholars. It seems that incomplete *isnad*s coexisted with complete ones from the time of the Successors onward until the end of the eighth century.

It can also be said that in early Meccan scholarship transmission of traditions played a minor role compared to that of Medina, but the situation changed in Mecca in the course of the first half of the eighth century. These differences notwithstanding, there can be no doubt that there are traditions about the Companions and the Prophet that were known and transmitted in both centers of learning already in the second half of the seventh century. It is improbable, however, that the source-critical approach can lead to an earlier period, aside from exceptional cases. One of the limitations of this method is that it cannot generalize. That means that as long as a single hadith or a group of traditions has not yet been or cannot be scrutinized by this method, their dating remains obscure. A judgment about their historical reliability must be postponed or cannot be made.

*See also* **Succession.**

## BIBLIOGRAPHY

Abbott, Nabia. "Hadith Literature—II: Collection and Transmission of Hadith." *The Cambridge History of Arabic Literature*. Vol. 1, *Arabic Literature to the End of the Umayyad Period*. Edited by A. F. L. Beeston, et al. Cambridge, U.K.: Cambridge University Press, 1983.

Abdul Rauf, Muhammad. "Hadith Literature—I: The Development of the Science of Hadith." *The Cambridge History of Arabic Literature*. Vol. 1, *Arabic Literature to the End of the Umayyad Period*. Edited by A. F. L. Beeston, et al. Cambridge, U.K.: Cambridge University Press, 1983.

Berg, Herbert. *The Development of Exegesis in Early Islam. The Authenticity of Muslim Literature From The Formative Period*. Richmond, Surrey, U.K.: Curzon Press, 2000.

Brown, Daniel W. *Rethinking Tradition in Modern Islamic Thought*. Cambridge, U.K.: Cambridge University Press, 1996.

Burton, John. *An Introduction to the Hadith*. Edinburgh: Edinburgh University Press, 1994.

Cook, Michael. "The Dating of Traditions." In *Early Muslim Dogma: A Source-Critical Study*. Cambridge, U.K.: Cambridge University Press, 1981.

Donner, Fred M. *Narratives of Islamic Origins. The Beginnings of Islamic Historical Writing*. Princeton, N.J.: The Darwin Press, 1998.

Ess, Joseph van. *Zwischen Hadith und Theologie. Studien zum Entstehen prädestinatianischer Überlieferung*. Berlin and New York: Walter de Gruyter, 1975.

Goldziher, Ignaz. *Muslim Studies*. Edited by S. M. Stern. Translated by C. R. Barber, and S. M. Stern. London: George Allen & Unwin Ltd., 1971.

Juynboll, G. H. A. *Muslim Tradition. Studies in Chronology, Provenance and Authorship of Early Hadith*. Cambridge, U.K.: Cambridge University Press, 1983.

Juynboll, G. H. A. *Studies on the Origins and Uses of Islamic Hadith*. Aldershot, U.K.: Variorum Collected Studies Series, 1996.

Kohlberg, Etan. "Shi'i Hadith." *The Cambridge History of Arabic Literature*. Vol. 1, *Arabic Literature to the End of the Umayyad Period*. Edited by A. F. L. Beeston, et al. Cambridge, U.K.: Cambridge University Press, 1983.

Motzki, Harald. "The Prophet and the Cat: On Dating Malik's *Muwatta*' and Legal Traditions." *Jerusalem Studies in Arabic and Islam* 22 (1998): 18–83.

Motzki, Harald. "The Murder of Ibn Abi l-Huqayq: On the Origin and Reliability of Some *Maghazi*-Reports." In *The Biography of Muhammad: the Issue of the Sources*. Edited by Harald Motzki. Leiden: Brill, 2000.

Motzki, Harald. *The Origins of Islamic Jurisprudence. Meccan Fiqh before the Classical Schools*. Translated by M. H. Katz. Leiden: Brill, 2002.

Schacht, Joseph. *The Origins of Muhammadan Jurisprudence*. Oxford, U.K.: Oxford University Press, 1950.

Schoeler, Gregor. *Charakter und Authentie der muslimischen Überlieferung über das Leben Mohammeds*. Berlin and New York: Walter de Gruyter, 1996.

Siddiqi, Muhammad Z. *Hadith Literature: Its Origin, Development & Special Features*. Edited and revised by Abdal Hakim Murad. Reprint. Cambridge, U.K.: The Islamic Texts Society, 1993.

Wansbrough, John. *The Sectarian Milieu. Content and Composition of Islamic Salvation History*. Oxford, U.K.: Oxford University Press, 1978.

Watt, W. Montgomery. "The Reliability of Ibn Ishaq's Sources." *La Vie du prophète Mahomet*. Paris: Presses Universitaires de France, 1983.

*Harald Motzki*

**HAJJ** *See* **Pilgrimage: Hajj**

## HAJJ SALIM SUWARI, AL- (C. 1300)

Al-Hajj Salim Suwari is a name that appears in a number of scholarly lineages in West Africa. He is credited with transmitting a significant Maliki teaching tradition to a region stretching from Ghana and Burkina Faso to Senegal and Gambia in West Africa. This tradition included jurisprudence, exegesis, and the biography of the Prophet. Historians are divided between his provenance in the twelfth and thirteenth centuries and the early fifteenth century. Those who support the latter believe that he played a leading role in the cultivation of extensive trade in gold between West African kingdoms and North Africa. According to them, al-Hajj Salim Suwari laid the foundation for a Maliki tradition that fostered trade and accepted the authority of non-Muslim rulers. It is this tradition that played a leading role in relations between Muslims and other religious groups until the Fulani Jihad states emerged in the eighteenth and nineteenth centuries. But it is also a tradition that continues today in countries like Senegal and other regions in West Africa.

Following the local hagiographies more closely, S. O. Sanneh believes that al-Hajj Salim Suwari should be situated in the twelfth century. Al-Hajj Salim Suwari performed the pilgrimage seven times, and on returning from the last one, he began a migration from Diakhe-Masina on the Niger River to Diakhe-Bambukhu further southwest on the Senegal River. There he founded a city-state with his many followers, and established the scholarly tradition that flourished for the next several generations. Sanneh also believes that al-Hajj Salim Suwari and his followers, the Jakhanke, were not directly engaged in the gold trade. Rather, they were engaged in agriculture (through the extensive use of slaves) and were devoted to travel and study. The Diakhe-Babukhu of al-Hajj Salim Suwari became a model for many similar city-states in the long history of Islam in West Africa.

*See also* **Africa, Islam in; Islam and Other Religions; Networks, Muslim.**

### BIBLIOGRAPHY

Levtzion, N. "Patterns of Islamization in Black Africa." In *Conversion to Islam.* Edited by N. Levtzion. New York: London: Holmes and Meier Publishers, 1979.

Sanneh, S. O. *The Jakhanke: The History of an Islamic Clerical People of the Senegambia.* London: International African Institute, 1979.

Wilks, I. *Wa and the Wala: Islam and Polity in Northwestern Ghana.* Cambridge, U.K.: Cambridge University Press, 1989.

Wilks, I. "The Juula and the Expansion of Islam into the Forest." In *The History of Islam in Africa.* Edited by N. Levtzion and R. L. Pouwels. Athens: Ohio University Press, 2000.

*Abdulkader Tayob*

## HAJ ʿUMAR AL-TAL, AL- (1797–1864)

The last revolutionary in the *jihad* tradition of Western Sudan, Shaykh ʿUmar al-Tal was born in Futa Toto, in the Senegambia region, where he received his religious training. While in Mecca for pilgrimage in 1826 he was appointed the caliph of the Tijaniya brotherhood in the Western Sudan. He lived in Mecca and Cairo, and eventually settled at the court of the Sokoto Caliphate. After almost a decade away from home he decided, in the late 1830s, to return to the Senegambia region. He settled first in Dingirai, a town on the frontiers of the Futa Jalon imamate. There he began to preach and build his own following. For the next decade, his focused primarily on writing and teaching. He used his authority to challenge the leaders of the locally powerful Qadiriya Sufi order.

In his efforts to forge a large Muslim state, ʿUmar declared a jihad around 1852 or 1853, when he began to widen his military operations north toward the upper Senegal River through non-Muslim, Malinke-dominated areas. By then he had acquired firearms and was proving to be a formidable force in the region. By the mid-1850s he had established the Tukolor Muslim empire, with his capital at Nioro. His activities in the Senegambia eventually led to a confrontation with the French, who were seeking to establish absolute control over the region. ʿUmar's military operations further east in the Muslim state of Massina were largely successful, until he was killed in 1864 during a counterattack. His successors divided up the empire and continued to challenge the French over the next couple of decades.

*See also* **Africa, Islam in; Caliphate; ʿIbadat.**

### BIBLIOGRAPHY

Robinson, David. *The Holy War of Umar Tal: The Western Sudan in the Mid-Nineteenth Century.* Oxford, U.K.: Clarendon Press, 1985.

*Abdin Chande*

## HALLAJ, AL- (858–922)

The mystic and martyr Husayn ibn Mansur al-Hallaj was born in 858 in Bayda, Persia. An Arabized Iranian whose grandfather was a Zorastrian, al-Hallaj's father, a cotton-wool carder (*hallaj*) by trade, converted to Islam. The family had emigrated through textile centers in Iran, settling in Sunni (Hanbali) Wasit, Iraq, where the young Hallaj was educated in grammar, the Qur'an, and exegesis. He returned in 873 to Tustar and placed himself in the service of the noted Sufi shaykh Sahl. In 857 in Basra he received the Sufi habit (*khirqa*) and came under the influence of such noted shayks as Muhasibi and 'Amr Makki, both of whom were associated with al-Junayd, head of the Baghdad school of Sufism.

In the period between 877 and 883 he married and had a daughter and three sons. The third son, Hamd, left an eyewitness account of his father's last days in prison and his public execution. He became involved in the black slave (Zanj) revolt centered around Basra, which was driven ideologically by Shi'ite opponents of the Sunni 'Abbasid Caliphate. Though Sunni, he moved in Shi'ite circles and was later accused of having been influenced by Mahdism. He made the first of this three yearlong retreats to Mecca, and uttered his famous statement "I am the Truth" (*Ana al-Haqq*), which his opponents interpreted as blasphemy but which later supporters interpreted as "God has emptied me of everything but Himself." This was the most extreme expression of mystical union with God in the history of Islamic mysticism.

After his family settled in Baghdad, Hallaj departed on two long missionary journeys to Khurasan and India between 887 and 901, preaching especially to Turkish nomads and Manichean Uyghur Turks. During this period he composed his first books and was given the sobriquet "the reader of hearts" (*al-Hallaj al qulub*). Between journeys he made his second pilgrimage to Mecca and met two noted shaykhs, the aging Nuri and the young Shibli. In 904 he visited Jerusalem, praying in the Holy Sepulcher of Jesus, who in an earlier period he had proclaimed the Mahdi. At this time he also preached the idea of fulfilling the pilgrimage obligation outside Mecca by creating miniature Ka'bas in homes, which was raised against him as a transgression of sacred law at his trial. He preached openly against the tax scandals and political corruption linked to the weakened Caliphate, which finally resulted in his arrest, in the name of public order, and long imprisonment (913–922). In 922 in Baghdad he was charged with heresy, flogged, gibbeted, and his body was burned.

Masked as a legal trial for heresy, the death of Hallaj has remained a controversial subject throughout subsequent Islamic history, and has become a dramatic theme of many modern plays in Arabic, Persian, Turkish, and English.

Among his principal mystical ideas were total union with God and the Essence of Desire (*'ishq dhati*), speech with God (*shath*), the existence of substitute saints (*abdal*) for the whole community, the present witness (*shahid ani*) of the Eternal, fraternal union of two souls (*ittihad an-nafsayn*), and the outcry for justice (*sayha bi'l-haqq*).

*See also* **Heresiography; Kharijites, Khawarij; Mahdi; Muhasibi, al-; Tasawwuf.**

## BIBLIOGRAPHY

Massignon, Louis. *La Passion d'al-Hallaj* (1922). Reprint. Princeton, N.J: Princeton University Press, 1982.

Mason, Herbert. *al-Hallaj*. Richmond, Surrey, U.K.: Curzon Press, 1995.

*Herbert W. Mason*

# HAMAS

HAMAS is an acronym drawn from the Arabic initials of the Islamic Resistance Movement (*harakat al-muqawamat al-Islamiyyah*), but which also bears a literal meaning of "zeal." An offshoot of the Muslim Brotherhood, HAMAS was established in 1987, during the first Palestinian intifada (uprising). The context for the creation of HAMAS was the continued failure of efforts such as the Camp David Accords to achieve the goal of Palestinian statehood.

In November of 1987, the Arab League met in Amman, Jordan, and issued a statement identifying the export of Islamic revolution from Iran as the greatest threat to stability in the region. This was the first time the Arab League had not identified Israel's occupation of Palestinian territory as the major threat to regional stability. Feeling betrayed by the international community and abandoned by fellow Arabs, some members of the Palestinian branch of the Muslim Brotherhood lost faith in the approach to the problem of Palestinian statelessness taken by that organization during the past few decades. The immediate cause of the intifada was the death of some Palestinian workers hit by an Israeli driver. A group of Islamist Palestinians came together at a meeting called to discuss the incident, and the result was the formation of HAMAS. While the Palestinian Brotherhood's parent organization, the Jordanian Muslim Brotherhood, continued to follow a quietist approach to achieving Palestinian goals, HAMAS leaders were persuaded that militarism would be required to achieve security for Palestinians.

In addition to distinguishing itself from its parent, the Muslim Brotherhood, by insisting on the need for armed resistance, HAMAS distinguishes itself from the PLO (Palestine Liberation Organization) in rejecting the right of the Zionist entity (as it calls Israel) to exist because Israel denies Palestinians the rights of freedom and independence. Further distinguishing itself from the PLO, HAMAS demands that an Islamic state be established in place of Israel or a secular Palestinian state. The basis of this position is the claim that Jerusalem and, by extension, all of Palestine, are *waqf*, that is, properties entrusted to Muslims to administer in perpetuity, for the benefit of society. HAMAS ideologues believe that an

Islamic state is necessary to ensure the rights of all citizens, Jews and Christians as well as Muslims, since Islamic law protects the rights of religious minorities. Thus, the HAMAS charter proclaims, "God is the goal, the Prophet is the model, the Qur'an is the constitution, jihad is the path, and death on God's path is our most sublime aspiration."

The spiritual leader of HAMAS, Shaykh Ahmad Yasin (b. 1936), was leader of the Muslim Brotherhood in Gaza and founder of Gaza's Islamic Center. He sought to establish HAMAS as an alternative to the PLO. HAMAS, therefore, devotes the majority of its budget to an array of social services. These include support for the families of slain, jailed, or exiled activists; health centers; kindergartens and other schools; mosques; and mediation services (a common form of civil conflict resolution in Arab societies). Its military activities, which it considers legitimate resistance to Israel's military occupation which is in violation of UN Security Council Resolutions 242 and 338, are conducted by an armed wing called 'Izz al-Din al-Qassam Brigades, named after a Palestinian hero killed by the British during its "Mandate" occupation of Palestine in 1936.

The ability of HAMAS to provide its services depends upon its funding, which is both local and international. Internal funding comes from the Islamic charity offering, *zakat*. Support also comes from Muslim governments, such as those of Saudi Arabia and Iran, from Islamic organizations throughout the world, as well as remittances from Muslims living abroad.

Organizationally, HAMAS is linked to the Muslim Brotherhood. According to the HAMAS charter of August 1988, it is a wing of the Muslim Brotherhood Society in Palestine. Its activities are coordinated by liaisons between Gaza, the West Bank, Jordan, and HAMAS leaders living abroad. Its leadership structure is informal, with several founders and ideologues. Shaykh Yasin remains the acknowledged spiritual leader, but specific decisions are taken by a consultative council (*majlis al-shura*) with a flexible membership. This structure is in accordance with the traditional Sunni Islamic model, and is effective in allowing the organization to survive the incarceration and exile of its leaders from time to time.

HAMAS is most notorious for its use of suicide bombings in its armed struggle against Israel, targeting both military personnel and civilians. Both suicide and the targeting of civilians are forbidden by Islamic law. Both have been condemned by major Islamic scholars since the attacks against America on 11 September 2001. However, many religious scholars make an exception to the prohibition of suicide in the case of the Palestinian struggle against Israeli occupation, provided the victims of the attacks are military personnel.

The HAMAS charter describes the organization as the resistance wing of the Muslim Brotherhood, and therefore a part of an international movement. At the same time, Shaykh

Yasin describes the movement as essentially political, in that its goal is to secure the rights of Palestinians in their homeland. Like other political movements, the significance of HAMAS is based not so much on the number of its official members as on the popularity of its political agenda. The popularity of HAMAS among Palestinians is impossible to measure precisely without general elections. However, elections among students in Palestinian universities indicate that by the mid-1990s, HAMAS had the second-largest following, after FATAH (*harakat al-tahrir al-watani al-filastini*, the largest organization in the PLO). While the popularity of militant Islamic groups in general was declining slightly by the end of the 1990s, that trend was reversed following Israel's withdrawal from southern Lebanon in 2000. Without clear benefits to the majority of Palestinians from the 1993 Oslo Accords, and in the context of stalled negotiations between Israel and the PLO, the claim that militant Islam had defeated Israel in Lebanon and could do so in Palestinian territories as well became believable to some.

Because of its military activities and political positions, HAMAS is banned in Israel. Many of its members have been arrested or deported, and a number of its leaders have been assassinated. HAMAS was designated a terrorist organization by the United States in 1995, and contributing to it was prohibited by the Anti-Terrorism and Effective Death Penalty Act (Pub. Law 104–132) of April 1996.

*See also* **Arab League; Fundamentalism; Intifada; Lebanon; Majlis; Martyrdom; Terrorism.**

## BIBLIOGRAPHY

Abu Amr, Ziad. *Islamic Fundamentalism in the West Bank and Gaza: Muslim Brotherhood and Islamic Jihad.* Bloomington: Indiana University Press, 1994.

*Mithaq harakat al-muqawama al-Islamiyya (Hamas) [Covenant of the Islamic Resistance Movement (Hamas)],* n.p., 18 August 1988.

Rashad, Ahmad. *Hamas: Palestinian Politics with an Islamic Hue.* Anandale, Va.: United Association for Studies and Research, 1993.

Schiff, Ze'ev and Ehud Ya'ari. *Intifada: The Palestinian Uprising—Israel's Third Front.* New York: Simon and Schuster, 1989.

*Tamara Sonn*

# HAREM

The practice of the harem (Ar., *harim*), or the seclusion of women, dates back to the pre-Islamic period. The root *h-r-m* also refers to *al-haram al-sharif*, the sanctuary of Mecca as the reserved space for Muslims. The form *harem* connotes a sacred and inviolable space, which is forbidden to any men, other than the members of the immediate family. Its institution and derivate forms have been common in the Middle Eastern and Mediterranean cultures as an integral part of royal and upper-class families.

Culturally, the Mesopotamian, Greek antiquity, and Persian societies shared in common the practice of the harem. While women were confined to their quarters, men enjoyed the privilege of engaging in the public sphere. This segregation also marked a labor division based on sexual difference; females were responsible for the management of the household, whereas males served as head of the family and were responsible for public affairs. As the women's role was limited to managing the house, their presence in the public sphere was also regulated through a manner of dress that rendered them invisible from public gaze. Historically, followers of Judaism and Christianity also secluded women. For example, in the early Jewish family, where gender relations varied, women were nonetheless confined to a private sphere in which they performed household duties for the family as well as religious rites. In the early Christian era, women were often secluded within their own residence, guarded by eunuchs, and required to be veiled when they left the home. These practices found their way into the caliphate as the Abbasids conquered the lands inhabited by the dominant Christian and Jewish cultures, and so the elite female members of the Abbasid caliphate were secluded within their own quarters called "harem." The institution of harem flourished in Muslim societies during the successive invasions and conquests of the Mediterranean and Middle Eastern regions, Africa, and India. The conquest of Persia during the Sassanian times led to the assimilation of Persian culture, especially in the garrison towns. This conquest and the subsequent expansion of the Muslim territory provided Muslim dynasties with the opportunity to own, inherit, and capture prisoners of wars, including eunuchs, slaves, and minors, as well as the wives of royal families. For example, the Abbasid nobles and leaders adopted the Persian custom of the ownership of hundreds and thousands of concubines and slaves. Muslim dynasties and the notables maintained a harem as a part of their palaces.

The inclusion of the harem fit well with the societal structure adopted from the Irano-Semitic culture in its Islamic form, called the *a'yan-amir* system. In this form of administration, the "notables" (*a'yan*) of the towns and villages and the *umara'* (leaders or commanders) of local or regional garrison courts shared power and authority. Within this web of social relationships, individual social status depended on the male's ability to settle formal quarrels among the tribes or factions and to invite sexual jealousy. The patterns of feuding and sex relations with numerous concubines marked masculine honor and worthiness in society. These masculine traits belonged exclusively to the notables (the *a'yan*) and the commanders/leaders (the *umara*). As the masculine honor within the *a'yan* system depended heavily on the honor of wives, concubines, and female slaves, the total control and the

subservience of these females became necessary. For this reason, it was in the best interest of the masters to institute a severe seclusion and rigid privacy for the females.

For outsiders, the "imagined harem" came to represent the abased and subjugated treatment of women in Islamic civilization. This harem discourse emerged in the seventeenth century after the Europeans discovered harems filled with women. The explicit connection between the "imagined harem" and the status of women in Muslim society and Islam was generally produced and reproduced by the European Orientalists in the two centuries following the colonization of the Muslim lands. This harem element shifted the medieval discourse on Muslim women, which previously portrayed them as victimized, yet powerful in charm and deceit.

Stimulated by the translation from the Arabic of the folk story *The Thousand and One Nights*, the "imagined harem" produced narratives of Muslim women whose sexual desire was strong, yet subordinated, oppressed, veiled, and secluded. These harem narratives circulated in the eighteenth and nineteenth centuries, functioning not only to feed the Orientalist imaginary of the harem, but also to serve the superiority of imperialist power over the Muslim world.

The harem as a social institution for women in the Muslim world, especially in the Middle East, Africa, and South Asia, finally came to an end in the early twentieth century. It ended not because Muslims discovered that it was incompatible with Islam, but because they lost control over their land and politics.

*See also* **Gender; Marriage; Purdah.**

## BIBLIOGRAPHY

Ahmed, Leila. *Women and Gender in Islam: Historical Roots of a Modern Debate.* New Haven, Conn.: Yale University Press, 1992.

Mernissi, Fatima. *Dreams of Trespass: Tales of A Harem Girlhood.* New York: Addison-Wesley Publishing Company, 1994.

*Etin Anwar*

# HARON, ABDULLAH (1924–1969)

Abdullah Haron was an imam in Cape Town, South Africa, and a symbol of Muslim involvement in the antiapartheid struggle. Born in Cape Town in 1924 he lived all his life in that city and died there in 1969, a victim of apartheid's security police. He attended a Muslim school in the city and as a youth spent two years as a devotee of a shaykh in Mecca.

On his return to South Africa he studied under respected local scholars. In 1955 he was appointed to the position of imam at a mosque in a Cape Town suburb. He was a keen sportsman and played rugby and cricket even after he became imam. He concentrated on social issues and established an organization devoted to making Islam meaningful to youth in South Africa. He was the first editor of *Muslim News*, an influential weekly among the country's Muslims.

As apartheid rule intensified the imam was among a small group of Muslims that explored ways to challenge the state from an Islamic basis. But Abdullah Haron also believed in a united front of the oppressed against racial domination. He grew close to members of the then proscribed Pan-African Congress. On his travels to the Middle East he met exiled South Africans and spoke out against apartheid to Arab audiences and leaders, including King Faysal of Saudi Arabia. In September 1969 he was reported dead in detention, the eighteenth political detainee to die in police custody in the 1960s. During the 1980s, in the last wave of rebellion and resistance to the apartheid state, his memory and image were revived as a symbol of Islam's stand against injustice. He became better known and more revered as a martyr than when he was alive.

*See also* **Africa, Islam in; Modern Thought.**

## BIBLIOGRAPHY

Desai, Barney, and Marney, Cardiff. *The Killing of the Imam.* London: Quartet Books, 1978.

Donaldson, Dwight M. *The Shiʿite Religion.* New York: AMS Press, 1984.

Haron, Muhammed. "Imam ʿAbdullah Haron: Life, Ideas and Impact." Master's thesis, University of Cape Town, 1986.

Momen, Moojan. *An Introduction to Shiʿi Islam: The History and Doctrines of Twelver Shiʿism.* Oxford, U.K.: George Ronald, 1985.

*Shamil Jeppie*

# HASAN (624–670)

Hasan ibn ʿAli ibn Abi Talib was the grandson of the prophet Muhammad and the second Shiʿite imam. Born in Medina in 624, three years after the *hijra*, he died at age forty-six in Medina in 670. In Shiʿite parables he and his brother Husayn, the third imam, are figured as two alternative political strategies against injustice in the world and in politics. Hasan embodies the path of patience, which allows the enemy slowly to demonstrate unworthiness and lose any claim to legitimacy. Husayn embodies the path of armed revolt.

After the death of his father, ʿAli bin Talib, the first imam, Muʿawiya became caliph. According to the Shiʿite account, Hasan should have succeeded his father. Hasan was an important *rawi* (reciter) and interpreter of the hadith and sunna (sayings and practices) of the Prophet and his Companions, reflecting the role of the imams in having access also to the divine meanings of revelation. But Hasan was too weak politically to challenge Muʿawiya for the leadership of the community. After Muʿawiya attempted to have him assassinated, and many of his followers abandoned him, Hasan came to an understanding with Muʿawiya, wherein Hasan was sent to live in Medina, while Muʿawiya promised that leadership would revert to the family of the Prophet upon his death. But Muʿawiya broke his promise by appointing his son Yazid to succeed him, and convinced Jaʿda, Hasan's wife, to poison the imam. In addition to paying Jaʿda, Muʿawiyya also promised to marry her to his son and heir, Yazid. The giving of poisoned water is the inverse of the denial of water to Husayn on the battlefield of Karbala, where the third imam was martyred by the forces of Yazid. Imam Husayn's revolt subsequently disgraced Yazid, and created in him the archetypal figure of evil in Shiʿite stories of injustice.

This parable structure is also encoded in a hadith quoted by Mohammad Baqer Majlesi, the preeminent *mujtahed* of the seventeenth century. On Id al-Fitr, according to the hadith, Gabriel descended with a gift of new white clothes for each of the Prophet's grandsons. The Prophet said that the grandsons were used to colored clothes. So Gabriel asked each boy what color he wanted. Hasan chose green, Husayn red. While the clothes were being dyed, Gabriel wept. He explained: Hasan's choice of green meant that he would be martyred by poisoning, and his body would turn green, and Husayn's choice of red meant he would be martyred and his blood would turn the ground red.

Hasan is buried in Medina with a green banner on his mausoleum. Husayn is buried in Karbala with a red banner, the sign of a martyr whose revenge is yet to come.

Sunni accounts of early Islamic history deny that Hasan was poisoned, claiming he died of consumption. Sunni accounts also stress the temporary shift of power to Damascus under Muʿawiya and Yazid, but since revenues came mainly from Iraq, power eventually shifted to Baghdad.

For Shiʿa, Hasan's story is a precursor to Husayn's martyrdom, which is the overarching cosmic and paradigmatic story of existential tragedy, of injustice in this world triumphing often by force over justice, and of the duty of a true Muslim to sacrifice himself, to witness for truth and justice.

*See also* **Ahl al-Bayt; Imamate; Shiʿa: Early; Succession.**

*Michael M. J. Fischer*

# HASHEMI-RAFSANJANI, 'ALI-AKBAR (1934–)

'Ali-Akbar Hashemi-Rafsanjani was born in Rafsanjan, Kerman province, Iran, in 1934 and was educated in Qom Seminary as one of Ruhollah Khomeini's students. (The Ayatollayh Khomeini became the revolutionary leader of Iran in 1979.) Rafsanjani was one of the exiled Khomeini's chief agents, opposed to the rule of Mohammad Reza Shah Pahlavi, and was arrested on several occasions. He spent three years in prison (1975–1977). Upon the overthrow of the shah in 1979, Rafsanjani was appointed to the Revolutionary Council. His loyalty to Khomeini, combined with political skills, resulted in his elevation to the leadership of the Iranian parliament.

Rafsanjani orchestrated the arms-for-hostages deal with members of the administration of the U.S. president Ronald Reagan, an action that later set into motion the Iran-Contra scandal in the United States. After the death of Khomeini in 1989, Rafsanjani emerged as the pragmatist president of Iran (1989–1997) and declared a plan of economic reform, known as an "adjustment program," that included unifying exchange rates, privatizing the economy, and canceling subsidies. Rafsanjani kept Iran from direct involvement in hostilities during the Persian Gulf War in 1991. After the war he continued to carve out a middle ground between his more conservative religious colleagues' calls for Iranian insularity and his own inclination toward oligarchic modernization. He also worked to renew close ties with Middle Eastern neighbors and the countries of Europe. Rafsanjani was accused by a federal court in Germany of ordering the murders of certain opponents who were gunned down in a Berlin restaurant. Rafsanjani was reelected to the presidency in 1993 but stepped down in 1997 and became the leader of the Expediency Council after completing his second term as president.

*See also* **Iran, Islamic Republic of; Revolution: Revolution in Iran.**

*Majid Mohammadi*

# HEALING

It is a hazardous task to attempt to offer a summary of Islamic medicine and healing and to map the contribution of the Islamic empire to human civilization. The Islamic empire covered a wide territory stretching from the western shores of Europe to the Indian subcontinent to the former Soviet states in Asia. The Islamic empire maintained unchallenged authority in medicine for over six centuries. This entry offers brief synopses of this history.

Islamic scholars have referred to the medicine that existed within the bounds of the Islamic empire as "Islamic." The term refers to a heritage consisting of two distinctive categories of medicine. First, there was what might be termed Islamic folk medicine, which existed among the populace throughout the Muslim world. Folk medicine did not enjoy the blessings of the ruling elite and is still very often dismissed as sheer quackery. Second, there was what might be termed Islamic state-sanctioned medicine. This category was the pride of the Islamic empire and enjoyed lucrative support from the Muslim ruling elite, particularly during the golden age of the Islamic empire (seventh to thirteenth centuries).

## Islamic Folk Medicine

Islamic folk medicine derives its legitimacy from its claim to have been based on the teachings of Islam. This claim is corroborated by frequent use of Qur'anic verses, prophetic prescriptions, and the wisdom of saints and imams. It should be noted here that exceptionally few passages in the Qur'an can be related directly to healing and medication. Prophet Muhammad made no claim to be an authority in medicine and most of his relevant speeches correspond with what was practiced within his culture. The hadith collection of *Sahih al-Bukhari*, one of the most authoritative works on prophetic narratives, stands as testimony to this, that is, to this continuity with pre-Islamic practices. Al-Bukhari's voluminous work contains less than one hundred entries that are of relevance to medicine. Most of these entries are no more than different versions of the same narratives. Other less authoritative collections exist, such as *al-Tibb al-Nabawi* (Prophetic medicine). There is a consensus among scholars that collections under the term *prophetic medicine*—a genre of medical writings intended as alternatives to the exclusively Greek-based system derived from Galen—do not stand up to any scholarly or theological scrutiny. The Arab philosopher Ibn Khaldun described this class of medicine as essentially a Bedouin craft that has no divine revelation and thus cannot be obligatory under religious laws.

Barely literate practitioners dominate Islamic folk medicine, serving primarily illiterate masses. Far from being a weakness, this made it more flexible and hence accommodating to the diverse cultures of the Islamic empire. The result is a craft that varies with cultures while retaining some degree of harmony within each. Many of these diverse cultures did no more than adapt their new medical creed to their original etiology and treatment of disease.

Four categories are identified in Islamic folk medicine as major causes of disease: sorcery, the evil eye, jinn, and adverse routine conditions (e.g., adverse weather, food problems, accidents, etc.). Holy power represents a primary source of medicine for all categories of disease except the last. Holy power is often manifested in combinations of Qur'anic verses and magical formulas in various forms: Qur'anic verses that are worn on the body or drunk; direct recitation from a holy person; an object from a holy site and saintly tombs; and so on.

## Islamic Medicine

In general, the contribution of the Islamic empire to modern medicine is often underrated in the West. More often than not, Western scholars have overlooked Islam's true contribution to human civilization. A Eurocentric outlook affects even the most authoritative scholars in the field. However, more recent scholarship shows that medieval Muslim physicians made many contributions to the medical knowledge from Greece, Persia, and India that passed through their hands. In reviewing medieval Islamic medicine, one should be wary of creating false impressions. The Islamic empire was more welcoming for non-Muslims than is popularly imagined in the West. In fact, many of its famous doctors were Jews (Musa ibn Maimun Maimonides, 1135–1204 C.E.), Christians (Hunayn ibn Ishaq, 809–873 C.E.), and non-Arabs, mostly Persians (al-Razi / Rhazes, 841–925 C.E.; ibn Sina /Avicenna, 980–1037 C.E.). Moreover, the term "Islamic medicine" disguises a fundamental aspect of this class of medicine. Namely, that it was not based on Islamic teachings. Instead, it simply existed, and prospered within that cultural space that the empire afforded.

In its technological advancement, and to its credit, the Islamic empire did not attempt to reinvent the wheel. Starting from where others stopped is now a central tenet of modern science. The empire was fortunate that the wealth of Greek philosophy was already at its doorstep. Up to the sixth century, Alexandria and Athens stood as rival centers of medical learning. Persia was the new flourishing abode for scientists following the expulsion of the "heathen philosophers" from Athens and Alexandria (527–565 C.E.). Khalid ibn Yazid (655–704 C.E.) was unquestionably the first emir who laid the foundation for the translation of Greek works into Arabic. Following its fall under Muslim rule in 641, Alexandria proved to be a rich repository of Greek manuscripts. A century later, caliph al-Mansur reinvigorated Baghdad as a center of knowledge enshrined in the famous Institute of Wisdom (Bayt al-Hikma). Scholars were enticed to convert foreign manuscripts appropriated from the city of Junde-Shappur (in Persia) into Arabic. This city provided a vast wealth of Latin manuscripts in addition to equal numbers of other documents of Indian and Chinese origin. The Christian medical scholar Abu Zakariya ibn Masawayh (died 857 C.E.), who was a personal physician for four caliphs, was in charge of this establishment. Other no less famous centers of knowledge and translation followed and were abundant across the Islamic empire from the Persian Gulf to the European Atlantic borders.

Early scholarship tended to portray the contribution of the Islamic empire to world medicine as no more than that of a diligent storekeeper. In other words, that no original contribution was made during the vibrant era of the Islamic empire (seventh to thirteenth century) when the Christian world was dormant. Nothing could be further from the truth—and it would be futile to even attempt to map out this vast contribution.

Almost every field of modern medicine has a founding figure in the early Muslim world. Avicenna, often called the "prince of physicians," left behind more than a million words in medical documents. His contribution to science in general, but medicine in particular, can also be found in his methodology, which insisted on the use of reason alone to solve all medical problems.

Ibn Haytham (965–1039 C.E.) made great strides in optics, earning the nickname "father of optics." He also made a broad paradigmatic shift in the pursuit of science, which he centered around the use of inductive reasoning in the search for knowledge. Experimentation—the backbone of modern science—is what he preached in his approach to medicine.

Sinan ibn Thabit (died 946 C.E.) earned a good reputation in both the Arab world and later in the West. He contributed significantly to the art of presenting medical teaching books. Moreover, he was instrumental in establishing a regulatory system of medical control, examination, and registration of doctors and formulating ethical rules to govern medical practice.

Another figure who made an immense contribution to the art of medical writing is ʿAli ibn al-ʿAbbas al-Majusi (died between 982 and 995 C.E.). He was distinguished by his influential style of presenting medical facts with clarity, lucidity, and freedom from both magical and astrological ideas of the past. Al-Majusi had a a wealth of knowledge that spanned several branches of medicine, but is legendary for his illustrated thesis on the movement of the blood in the human body.

The Islamic empire inherited a medical system in which surgery was regarded as an inferior branch of medicine, if it was ever a part of it at all. Abu 'l-Qasim al-Zahrawi (936–1013 C.E.) elevated surgery to a primary position in medicine. Ample literature attests to his successful clinical treatment of bone fractures, bladder lithotomies, hemorrhoids, hernia, wounds to the abdomen, tonsillectomies, and many other ailments that required surgery.

The contribution of Islamic medicine was also impressive in chemistry and preparation of medicinal drugs, distillation, and sublimation. Many drugs now in use in modern medicine are of Muslim origin.

It has often been argued that Islamic medicine was crippled by Islam's attitudes toward dissection. These attitudes are said to have been derived from the Islamic prohibition of human body mutilation. It is true that Prophet Muhammad instructed his followers to respect the dead, foes and friends alike, and to avoid mutilation. He also instructed his followers to hasten the burial of their dead, a practice that is favored to this day in the Muslim world. It is conceivable that following such commands would have made dissection or indeed autopsy a compromising practice. One must realize that such prohibition was issued in tandem with other prescriptions accompanying jihad wars and was designed to oppose excessive revenge and humiliation of slain enemies. While few theologians might have opted to extend this prohibition to the practice of medicine, the ban has never been a central issue in debating the advancement of medicine. The Muslim philosopher and theologian al-Ghazali (d. 1111 c.e.) did exactly the opposite when he hailed anatomy as an important branch of medicine, stating "whoever does not know astronomy and anatomy is deficient in the knowledge of God." Indeed many of the prime pillars of Islamic medicine have left writings and narratives as evidence of their practice in the field of *tashrih* (dissection or anatomy). To name but a few, the list includes Rhazes, Masawayh, al-Zahrawi, and Avicenna. It is important to note that not every religious prohibition was zealously observed, particularly by the powerful. After all, the prohibition against alcohol was flouted even in the palaces of the emirs. The biggest obstacle against dissection was possibly the Arabian weather. In the absence of modern methods of refrigeration, it would take much more determination to handle a cadaver hours if not days after death. It has often been argued that Islamic medicine was no more than a theoretical exercise that was not translated into practice. Nothing could be further from the truth as most major Islamic cities had their medical establishments, which were similar to modern teaching hospitals that combine healing with training. D. L. Wright narrates that hospitals were established in the Arab world as early as the seventh century; that in the thirteenth century, al-Mansuri's hospital in Cairo had four large quadrangles complete with fountains. The same hospital had wards for male and female patients, a library, a lecture hall, and a mosque. Such a hospital could indeed be the envy of modern hospitals in the modern Muslim world. In 1160 c.e., Baghdad city had some sixty dispensaries and infirmaries.

### Early Islamic and Modern World Medicine

The eleventh century saw Europe just beginning to awake from its long period of oblivion. It was Europe that was behind the Arabs in every field. The march to regain supremacy in medicine began with the rebuilding of knowledge, most of which was available only in Arabic scripts. In 1085, Toledo of Spain was won back from the Arabs and was soon to house the School of Translation founded by Domenicus Gundissalinus (1020–1087). Other scholars were also commissioned, most notably Gerard of Lombardy (joined 1150), who translated hundreds of Arabic works, including the masterpieces of Rhazes and Avicenna.

Italy, too, had its center (Salerno), which far exceeded Toledo's establishment. It was the Tunisian-born scholar Constantinus Africanus (1020–1087) who helped to realize the European dream of ascending to supremacy in medical knowledge. Salerno's medical establishment was reputed to be the first organized medical school in Europe. In his visit to Italy as merchant, Constantinus was appalled by the poverty of medical knowledge in Italy. He decided to go back to Tunisia for three years to study medicine and bring worthwhile knowledge to his new abode. That he did with spectacular success and he was later to rank among the most diligent translators of his time. These medical centers proved valuable sources of information and were replicated in other European cities. For many years to come, the same sources of knowledge were used in the other European schools, which mushroomed in Seville, Montpellier, Paris, Padua, Bologna, and elsewhere. While many texts of Arab origin continued in use in these European medical schools throughout the Middle Ages, names of their Arab authors continued to be filtered out through translation or otherwise.

*See also* **Medicine; Miracles; South Asian Culture and Islam; Southeast Asian Culture and Islam.**

## BIBLIOGRAPHY

El-Tom, Abdullahi Osman. "Drinking the Koran: The Meaning of Koranic Verses in Berti Erasure." *Africa* 55, no. 4 (1985): 414–431.

Savage-Smith, Emilie. "Attitudes Toward Dissection in Medieval Islam." *Journal of History of Medicine* 50 (1995): 67–110.

Ullman, Manfred. *Islamic Surveys II: Islamic Medicine.* Edinburgh: Edinburgh University Press, 1978.

Wright, D. L. "Medicine in the Golden Ages of Islam—The Islamic Legacy." *The Journal of Kuwait Medical Association* 20, no. 1 (1994): 98–103.

*Abdullahi Osman El-Tom*

## HERESIES *See* Heresiography; Kharijites, Khawarij

## HERESIOGRAPHY

Heresiography is, literally, the writing of and about heresies. It is, however, an extremely relative term as one group's heresy is ultimately another's religion. Those who write about heresies, known as heresiographers, are for the most part engaged in the documentation of the errors and incorrect beliefs of other groups, which are often pejoratively referred to as "sects." However, as Jonathan Z. Smith argues, "a 'theory of the other' is but another way of phrasing a 'theory of the self'" (p. 47). Heresiography, then, functions in two primary ways. First, it lists the perceived heretical doctrines or ideas of others, showing how they have either gone or been led astray; secondly, and most importantly, it allows the group doing the writing to present what it is not, thereby providing the contours of social, ideological, religious and political self-definition.

## Definition and Origin

The closest Arabic term for heresiography in Islam is *al-milal wa al-nihal*, literally meaning "religions and sects." The origin of this phrase is unclear and both words, despite occurring separately in the Qur'an, do not seem to appear together as a technical term before the tenth century. Shahrastani (d. 1153), one of the most famous medieval heresiographers, argues that *milal* (sing., *milla*) refer primarily to the parameters of a shared social or communal set of beliefs, whereas its synonym *din* more closely approximates what we would today call "religion." Other sources, however, do not make such a sharp differentiation between these two terms. In one of its earliest usages, that by Abu Bakr al-Khwarizmi (d. c. 977), it is employed to denote religions other than those of *ahl al-kitab* (i.e., "the people of the Book," meaning followers of Islam, Judaism, and Christianity). The first time the phrase is employed in a title is in the *Kitab al-milal wa al-nihal* of al-Baghdadi (d. 1037). Other Arabic terms used in Islamic heresiographical literature to designate heretics include *zandaqa* ("free-thought," or "atheism") and *ilhad* ("heresy," or "heterodoxy").

The Muslims were extremely interested in documenting the religious beliefs and doctrines of other groups. They did so, however, not as dispassionate scientists or academics, but often as legal scholars, whose main job was to delineate and establish the beliefs, and thus legal status, of other religious groups in order to determine both their taxation rates and rights under Islamic law (*shari'a*). The basis for all their categories of comparison, then, was not necessarily meant to be scholarly or anthropological in its own right, but rather it was grounded in the traditional sources of Islam (e.g., Qur'an, hadith). Yet, both the breadth and depth of the taxonomies that the Muslim heresiographers created were impressive. According to Gustave von Grunebaum, "in their books on sects, or comparative religion, the research acumen of the Muslims shows at its best." Precisely because so much of the *milal wa al-nihal* literature deals with the collection and subsequent listing of the beliefs of others, many modern scholars frequently refer to this genre as a genealogical precursor to the modern history of religions.

Steven Wasserstrom locates the origins of this technical genre of literature in the eighth and ninth centuries, when Muslims increasingly encountered other, rival, monotheisms in a highly "disputational, polemic, apologetic, and sectarian milieu." Despite the ambiguity surrounding the origins of *milal wa al-nihal* as a technical term, the literature associated with it seems to be predicated on the following hadith, in which the Prophet proclaims: "The Jews are divided into seventy-one sects, the Christians into seventy-two; my community will be divided into seventy-three sects." This tradition seems to be the proof text for all subsequent attempts to document and delineate the various heretical groups.

## Judaism and Heresy

In the background of much Islamic heresiographical writings is the monolithic category of "the Jews." Wasserstrom claims, for instance, that Muslim heresies can often be traced back to a Jewish origin. According to Islamic history, the Jews are the archetypal community that has gone astray. As such they are constantly held up as an example of what must not happen to the Muslim community. Yet because Islam and Judaism had been in contact with one another since the advent of Islam in the seventh century, they were phenomenologically very similar. As a result, much time is spent differentiating Islam and Muslim teaching and dogma from that of the Jews. Moreover, when the Muslim heresiographers look for internal divisions within Islam they tend to blame it on a Jew or a Jewish convert to Islam. In many ways all heresies within Islam begin with the fact that Muhammad produced no male heirs, something that was generally blamed on Jewish magicians. Moreover, it was Jews that were said to be responsible for the following "heresies": the Christian decision to worship Jesus, the *ghulat* (Shi'ite extremists), the Shi'ites, the Isma'ilis, the Fatimid dynasty, and one of the most divisive theological issues in early Islam, that of the created Qur'an.

A common feature used in the literature associated with heresiography is the list of sects and where they have gone wrong. Such lists are, according to John Wansbrough, "schematic and based on a variety of propositions: (1) numerical (to make up the celebrated total of 'seventy-three sects'); (2) *ad hominem* ('schools' generated from the names of individuals by means of the *nisba* suffix [denoting origin or descent]); and (3) doctrinal (divergent attitudes to specific problems)." Furthermore, despite the fact that Islam is generally considered to be an orthoprax ("correct practice") religion as opposed to an orthodox ("correct belief") one, heresiography is primarily concerned with documenting the incorrect or heretical beliefs, as opposed to actions, of others. The goal is to show how such beliefs are to be differentiated from what is considered to be "normative," which of course differs according to those doing the writing. Every Muslim group, then, is interested in showing how its belief system is "normative" and how that of its rivals is heretical. A common feature is that heretical belief is always something that deviates from, and is thus subsequent to, an original or pure teaching. For this reason heresy in Islam is often synonymous with the charge of innovations (*bid'a*).

## Muslim Heresiographers

One of the most famous of Muslim heresiographers is the Andalusian Ibn Hazm (994–1064), an important though idiosyncratic legalist, philosopher, exegete, and polemicist. His *al-Fisal fi al-milal wa al-ahwa wa al-nihal* (The book of opinions on religions, heresies, and sects) offers an elaborate account of all the religious groups that had ever come into contact with Islam from the seventh century to his own day. In addition to his extremely thorough historiographical method, Ibn Hazm was also a zealous theologian who employed a literalist (*zahiri*) reading of the Qur'an and Islamic doctrine. His *Fisal* examines both the histories of various groups, their offshoots, and their present status, thereby showing how they have changed or stayed the same over time. For example, his treatment of the Jews is severe, accusing the rabbis who produced the Talmud of heresy and of intellectual skepticism. Interestingly, he accuses the rabbis of the same heretical doctrine as the materialists of early Islamic theology. This reveals a common theme in Islamic heresiography: Often one loosely labels a number of one's opponents with the same heretical doctrine.

Ibn Hazm's goal, then, was not necessarily historical or theological accuracy. He did not simply study religions for their own sake; on the contrary, he attempts to demolish the errors of others and, in the process, set Islam up as the most perfect of all religions. As such, he is less interested in understanding other religions than in reducing them to certain dogmas or problems that allow him to compare them with, often artificially, Islam. In short, Ibn Hazm knew what his conclusions were before he ever set out to establish the premises of comparison.

Another famous heresiographer was the aforementioned Shahrastani, who wrote the *Kitab al-milal wa al-nihal*, which, in his own words, proposed to present "the doctrinal opinions of all the world's people." Like the work of Ibn Hazm, Shahrastani is interested not only in documenting the various religious groups both in his day and before, but also in examining the various doctrines of the philosophers. Shahrastani divides his book into two parts, with the first dealing with revealed religions that base their obedience on a book (e.g., Jews, Christians, Zoroastrians), and the second examining the doctrines that are of purely human origins (e.g., the Sabians, philosophers, and the pre-Islamic Arabians).

## Function of Heresiography

Heresiography was, and still continues to be, used as a means of legitimating the ideology—whether political, religious, legal, or other—of the group defining what constitutes the "real Islam." In recent years this has coincided with the increased use of the *fatwa*, a legal ruling that is given by a legal expert. Such legal experts need not occupy official positions, but they are generally recognized for their legal learning and acumen. More recently, *fatwa*s have become a convenient vehicle employed by various groups, many of whom are marginal, as a way of condemning the beliefs and practices of groups, Islamic or not, with differing opinions. For example,

certain Islamist groups have issued blanket *fatwa*s condemning all Jews and Christians as enemies of Islam; yet other groups have employed *fatwa*s to condemn the rulers of Arab countries as infidels. It should be noted, however, that many who issue such controversial *fatwa*s are often accused by those in the mainstream of having insufficient credentials to do so.

In recent times, heresiography has taken on even greater political and ideological dimensions, as it is used now as a means of silencing one's perceived enemies. In many Islamic countries this is as easy as employing the concept of *takfir*, or accusing someone, often one's political opponent, of *kufr* ("unbelief"). A famous example of this in the 1990s was the case of a University of Cairo professor by the name of Nasr Hamid Abu Zayd. An Islamic moderate, he called for an understanding of the Qur'an and other early Islamic literature according to literary, contextual, and historical principles. In particular, he asked the question: What does the Qur'an as a document, and not necessarily as the sacred scripture of Muslims, say about a given subject (e.g., human rights)? When Egyptian Islamists got wind of his academic work they accused him of heresy and began legal proceedings against him. An Egyptian high court, to the great surprise of many, agreed and declared him an apostate. As a result Abu Zayd was ordered to divorce his wife and was effectively forced out of Egypt. To this day he is a professor in the Netherlands. This case is so interesting and problematic because it raises the nature of the tenuous relationship between what is considered heretical, the religious establishment, and, at least in theory, the autonomous nature of the court system in Egypt.

Heresiography is, thus, instrumental in defining not only the parameters of what is considered to be normative for a religion, but is also employed by the various groups that constitute that religion. Heresiography has been used, in one way or another, since the advent of Islam in seventh-century Arabia. At that time, it helped to differentiate Islam from rival monotheisms in the area of the Hijaz. Gradually, however, it was employed as a genre to help establish "normative Islam" by showing how various "sects" had gone astray in terms of their beliefs. So although one uses heresiography as a way of showing who is "inside" and who is "outside" one's group, as a genre it often tells us more about the "in" group than it does about anyone else.

*See also* **Bid'a; Hadith; Hallaj, al-; Historical Writing; Islam and Other Religions; Kalam; Qur'an; Shari'a.**

## BIBLIOGRAPHY

Brann, Ross. *Power in the Portrayal: Representations of Jews and Muslims in Eleventh- and Twelfth-Century Islamic Spain.* Princeton, N.J.: Princeton University Press, 2002.

Grunebaum, Gustave E., von. *Medieval Islam.* Chicago: University of Chicago Press, 1969.

Laoust, Henri. "L'hérésiographie musulmane sous les Abbassides." *Cahiers de civilisation medievale* 10 (1967): 157–178.

Shahrastani, Muhammad b. Abd al-Karim, al. *Muslim Sects and Divisions.* Translated by A. K. Kazi and J. G. Flynn. London: Kegan Paul, 1984.

Smith, Jonathan Z. "What a Difference a Difference Makes." In *"To See Ourselves as Others See Us": Christians, Jews, and "Others" in Late Antiquity.* Edited by Jacob Neusner and Ernest S. Frerichs. Chico, Calif.: Scholars Press, 1985.

Wansbrough, John. *The Sectarian Milieu: Content and Composition of Islamic Salvation History.* Oxford, U.K.: Oxford University Press, 1978.

Wasserstrom, Steven M. *Between Muslim and Jew: The Problem of Symbiosis under Early Islam.* Princeton, N.J.: Princeton University Press, 1995.

*Aaron Hughes*

# HIJAB *See* Veiling

# HIJRA

In 622 C.E. the Meccan prophet Muhammad immigrated to Yathrib, later known as Medina (*al-nabi*), on the invitation of a group of Arabs from that town. This event is termed *hijra.* Having sent his adherents ahead, Muhammad secretly followed with Abu Bakr b. Quhafa, leaving 'Ali b. 'Abi Talib in his (Muhammad's) bed, to deceive the Meccans who sought to kill him. On the way they stopped at a cave on Mount Thaur, where a spider's web, spun across the entrance, fooled the Meccans into not looking within (Q. 9:40). Here, according to Sufi tradition, the Prophet taught Abu Bakr the secrets of silent remembrance, *dhikr-e khafi,* which earned Abu Bakr the title *Yar-e ghar,* friend of the cave.

*Hijra* has also been interpreted to mean "the breaking of old ties," cutting off the era of knowledge from the previous era of ignorance (*jahiliyya*). The caliph 'Umar b. al-Khattab, establishing an Islamic calendar, chose this event as its starting point. Muhammad reached Medina in September 622. The calendar opens wih the first month of the Arabic lunar year in June 622 and proceeds without intercalation for a 354-day year in keeping with the lunar months.

*Hijra* is based on the root h-j-r, the root of the name Hagar, the concubine of Abraham; the term Mahagraye was used by Christian sources to describe the Arab-Muslims, the descendants of Hagar. *Muhajirun* is the Arabic term given to those who emigrated from Mecca with the Prophet.

*See also* **Astronomy; Muhammad.**

## BIBLIOGRAPHY

Crone, P., and Cook, Michael. *Hagarism: The Making of the Islamic World.* Cambridge, Mass.: Cambridge University Press, 1977.

Guillaume, A. *Islam.* Middlesex, U.K.: Penguin Books, 1973.

Schimmel, Annemarie. *And Muhammad is His Messenger.* Chapel Hill: University of North Carolina Press, 1985.

*Rizwi Faizer*

# HIJRI CALENDAR

There is no reference in the Qur'an to the pre-Islamic system of *anwa* in which the year is divided into precise periods on the basis of the rising and setting of certain stars. According to tradition, this system was considered anathema in Islam. The most relevant Qur'anic allusion to calendar-related computation is to the stations of the moon (*manazil al-qamar*, 10:5, 36:39). There are twenty-eight such stations defined on the basis of a combination of the pre-Islamic system of *anwa* with the lunar stations system.

The official Islamic calendar is lunar, with year one coinciding with the year 622 C.E., the date of Muhammad's migration (*hijra*) from Mecca to Medina. This calendar was adopted during the reign of the second caliph 'Umar. The *Hijri* lunar calendar is used as the basis for computing the official months (*ahilla*, new moons), and for determining the dates for important religious activities such as fasting and pilgrimage. The lunar months alternate between twenty-nine and thirty days, and the lunar month retrogrades yearly by about eleven days. Although the beginning of the lunar month is determined by sighting the new moon, numerous methods were developed to compute the exact length of the lunar months, to determine the days of the lunar year in relation to the solar year, and to perform calendar conversions between different eras.

Initially, folk astronomy and nonscientific traditions provided handy methods for solving problems related to the regulation of the lunar calendar and the determination of the times of prayer. Folk astronomical methods, such as the observation of the lunar crescent and the use of simple arithmetical shadow schemes, were used even after the introduction and dissemination of sophisticated scientific methods. A more mathematical approach to timekeeping developed as Muslims acquired and developed skills in mathematical astronomy. Although the computations of astronomers may have initially been appreciated only by a small group of

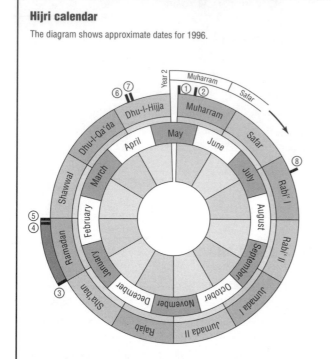

**Hijri calendar**

The diagram shows approximate dates for 1996.

**Key**

1 Muharram
2 Festival of ʿAshura
3 Beginning of Ramadan
4 Lailat al-Qadr

5 ʿId al-Fitr
6 8–13 Dhu-l-Hijja
7 ʿId al-Adha
8 Mawlid al-Nabi

**SOLAR CALENDAR DATES FOR 2003**

- ʿId al-Adha (Festival of Sacrifice), 12–15 February 2003
- Al-Hijra (New Year's Day), 4 March 2003
- ʿAshura, 13 March 2003
- The prophet Muhammad's Birthday (20 August 570 CE), 14 May 2003
- Lailat al-Israʾ Wal Miʿraj (The Prophet's Night Journey to Jerusalem & Ascension), 21 September 2003
- Lailat al-Baraʾh (Night of Forgiveness), 14 October 2003
- Ramadan (month of fasting) 27 October–25 November 2003
- Lailat al-Qadr (Night of Power), 23 November 2003
- ʿId al-Fitr, 25 November 2003

SOURCE: Breuilly, Elizabeth; O'Brien, Joanne; and Palmer, Martin. *Religions of the World*. New York: Facts on File, Inc., 1997.

The Hijri calender is normally 344 days, making it eleven days shorter than the Solar calender.

scientists, their methods eventually supplanted the simple methods of folk astronomy. The establishment of the office of a mosque timekeeper (*muwaqqit*) illustrates the official recognition, by the religious institution, of the authority of the exact-scientific methods of astronomers in the fields of calendar computation and the determination of times of prayer.

With the rise of the office of the timekeeper in the thirteenth century, the technical knowledge of the astronomers became more accessible because the compilation of extensive tables made the results of the exact-mathematical methods more readily usable. The science of timekeeping (*ʿilm al-miqat*) was thus an area of investigation where religion and science intersected.

Timekeeping tables, first compiled in Baghdad in the ninth and tenth centuries, were later expanded by timekeepers employed at the major mosques of Syria and Egypt to include hundreds of thousands of entries. In contrast to earlier Greek sources, Islamic astronomical handbooks often started with discussions of calendar computations and conversions between different eras (for example, Persian, Coptic, Syriac, Chinese-Ughur, Jewish, and Hindu calendars). In addition to the basic computational techniques, numerous works also provide additional information covering calendar-related subjects such as the length of day and night; patterns of weather and wind; dates and descriptions of Christian, Jewish, and Indian festivals; and agricultural practices at

various times of the year. Another problem of timekeeping that was addressed in various astronomical treatises is the problem of crescent visibility. The lunar month starts right after sunset with the sighting of the crescent. The visibility of this crescent, however, is itself a function of several variables, including the celestial coordinates of the sun and the moon, the latitude of the place where the crescent is sighted, and the brightness of the sky. Various methods were devised to determine the conditions under which the crescent would be visible.

*See also* **Astronomy.**

## BIBLIOGRAPHY

Breuilly, Elizabeth; O'Brien, Joanne; and Palmer, Martin. *Religions of the World*. New York: Facts on File, Inc., 1997.

Kennedy, E. S., Colleagues and Former Students. *Studies in the Islamic Exact Sciences*. Edited by David A. King and Mary Hellen Kennedy. Beirut: American University of Beirut, 1983.

King, David. *Astronomy in the Service of Islam*. Aldershot, Hampshire, U.K.: Variorum, 1993.

King, David. *Islamic Mathematical Astronomy*. Aldershot, Hampshire, U.K.: Variorum, 1993.

*Ahmad S. Dallal*

## HIKMA, BAYT AL- *See* **Education**

## HILLI, ʿALLAMA AL- (1250–1325)

ʿAllama al-Hilli was a Twelver Shiʿite jurist and theologian based in Hilla in southern Iraq. Hasan b. Yusuf al-Hilli is credited with establishing a set of Twelver theological and legal ideas that dominated subsequent Shiʿite learning. Biographical sources list around five hundred works attributed to him, though some of these are undoubtedly chapters within works or short treatises. Those that have survived form an impressive oeuvre encompassing theology, jurisprudence, and biography (*rijal*). In his theological works and creed commentaries, he argued, primarily from logic and reason, for all the main Twelver doctrines. This extensive use of reason rather than traditional textual sources was to be the dominant mode of theological discourse in Twelver Shiʿism from ʿAllama onward. His legal works were the subject of much commentary and in legal theory (*usul al-fiqh*), he showed extensive originality by incorporating the previously disparaged term *ijtihad* into Shiʿite jurisprudence. His biographical work is a comprehensive dictionary of early Shiʿite transmitters of the imam's doctrines. He soon outshone his teachers, who included such luminaries as Nasir al-Din al-Tusi (d.1274) and al-Muhaqqiq al-Hilli (d.1277). Hilli also had some relations with political powers, and is credited with the conversion of the Ilkhanid sultan Khudabanda of Iran to Twelver Shiʿism.

*See also* **Hilli, Muhaqqiq al-; Law; Shiʿa: Imami (Twelver).**

### BIBLIOGRAPHY
Arjomand, Saïd Amir, ed. "ʿAllama al-Hilli on the Imamate and Ijtihad." In *Authority and Political Culture in Shiʿism.* Edited by S. A. Arjomand. Albany: State University of New York Press, 1988.

Calder, Norman. "Doubt and Prerogative: The Emergence of an Imami Shiʿi Theory of *Ijtihad.*" *Studia Islamica* 70 (1989): 57–78.

Stewart, Devin. *Islamic Legal Orthodoxy: The Twelver Shiʿite Responses to the Sunni Legal System.* Salt Lake City: University of Utah Press, 1998.

*Robert Gleave*

## HILLI, MUHAQQIQ AL- (1205–1277)

Muhaqqiq al-Hilli Jaʿfar b. al-Hasan was a Twelver Shiʿite jurist based in Hilla, southern Iraq. Al-Muhaqqiq's *Sharaʾiʿ al-Islam* (Paths of Islam) is probably the most popular work of Shiʿite law among later commentators, and represents Muhaqqiq's most lasting influence on subsequent Shiʿite tradition. It belongs to the type of work known as abridged (*mukhtasar*), in which an author presents his interpretation of the *shariʿa* in a highly abbreviated form. This style made the work an excellent basis for later discussions of the law, even though subsequent jurists did not always agree with his conclusions. His other *mukhtasar*, an even more abbreviated legal compendium entitled *al-Nafiʿ* (The useful), was also the subject of commentaries by later generations of scholars. He also wrote an influential work of the principles of jurisprudence (*Maʿarij al-ahkam*), which one also finds regularly cited in later works. In particular, Jaʿfar al-Muhaqqiq introduced the idea that the rules and regulation of the *shariʿa* were not all known with absolute certainty, for the texts are not always clear and the reports from the Prophet and the imams are not always reliable. Such doctrinal advances paved the way for the full elaboration of these concepts by his nephew and pupil, al-ʿAllama al-Hilli (d. 1325). Other famous pupils include various members of the influential Ibn Tawus family.

*See also* **Hilli, ʿAllama al-; Law; Shiʿa: Imami (Twelver).**

### BIBLIOGRAPHY
Calder, Norman. "Doubt and Prerogative: The Emergence of an Imami Shiʿi Theory of *Ijtihad.*" *Studia Islamica* 70 (1989) 57–78.

Stewart, Devin. *Islamic Legal Orthodoxy: The Twelver Shiite Responses to the Sunni Legal System.* Salt Lake City: University of Utah Press, 1998.

*Robert Gleave*

## HINDUISM AND ISLAM

The relationship between these two great religious traditions in South Asia is often characterized as one of civilizational or cultural clashes, confrontations, and discontinuities. Popular accounts of South Asia's religious history often juxtapose Hinduism's tolerance of diversity, innate spirituality, and rootedness in the Indian soil with Islam's doctrinal rigidity, innate militancy, and foreignness. Such essentializations, which gained ascendancy during the era of British imperialism, fail to recognize that, as complex social and cultural phenomena, religions undergo historical change. A critical assessment of the relationships between Hinduism and Islam accounts for multiple histories involving subtle encounters, exchanges, and conversions, as well as overt confrontation and conflict. A more accurate and multifaceted range of perspectives emerges, reflecting the ways in which Hinduism and Islam interact with each other, and with other social, cultural, and political formations in South Asia through time.

## A Demographic Overview

Today there are an estimated 1.2 billion Muslims, one-third of whom live in South Asia—mainly in India, Pakistan, Bangladesh, and Sri Lanka. Indeed, there are as many Muslims in South Asia as there are in the Middle East and North Africa combined. The majority of South Asian Muslims come from indigenous ethnic populations. Muslims constitute clear majorities in Pakistan (96%) and Bangladesh (87%), while in India and Sri Lanka they are sizable minorities (12% and 7.6%, respectively). Prior to the 1947 partition an estimated 24 percent of greater India's population was Muslim, the remainder being predominantly Hindu. Today, there are more than 800 million Hindus in South Asia.

The extent of Islam's indigenization in the region is reflected in the languages spoken by its adherents: Numerous Arabic and Persian loanwords are found in local languages, especially those of the Indus and Ganges basins. Furthermore, the primary language of most Muslims is the same as that spoken by local non-Muslim populations, such as Punjabi or Bengali in the North and Malayalam or Tamil in the South.

Just as Hindu religious ideas and practices are constituted in a variety of traditions and movements, ranging from the brahmanic to the devotional, mystical, intellectual, and reformist, so too Indian Islam finds expression in diverse ways. Sunni Islam, primarily of the Hanafi legal tradition, has been the official religion for most urban Muslims and landholders. Less than one-fifth of South Asian Muslims adhere to one of two main divisions of Shi'ism, the Ithna'shariyya (Twelvers) or the Isma'iliyya (Isma'ilis). Most South Asian Muslims have been formally and informally affiliated with Sufi shrines and *tariqa*s (brotherhoods). Indeed, it is widely held that Islam was established in South Asia through Sufism, though there is little evidence of an organized, deliberate Sufi strategy of conversion. Nonetheless, Sufism has participated in the creation of local expressions of Islam, which embody the greatest degree of assimilation of Hindu religious ideas and practices. Since the sixteenth century, several Islamic reform and revival movements have emerged, directed in part against unorthodox practices among Sufis and the Shi'a, and also against Hindu influence on Muslim belief and practice. Thus, assimilation and differentiation are the two alternating processes governing relations between Hindus and Muslims through more than one thousand years of shared history.

## Medieval Hindu-Muslim Encounters

The first contacts between Hindus and Muslims occurred through trade and conquest. Arab Muslim colonies involved in the Indian Ocean spice trade appeared on the Malabar Coast of southern India as early as the ninth century, continuing a long history of commerce and migration between India and the Near East. Local Hindu rulers granted Muslims permission to build mosques and intermarry with their subjects. Though these early immigrants were merchants, Muslim legends remember them as holy men and pilgrims, and

*Jahangir Preferring a Sufi Sheik to Kings.* In this painting, Mogul emperor Jahanagir (1569–1627) makes King James I of England, the Sultan of Turkey, and a Hindu courtier wait while he converses with a Muslim mystic. Muslim Arab colonies emerged in southern India by the ninth century, arising from a history of commerce between the subcontinent and the Near-East. In the north, however, Islamic rule was established by invading armies under Turkish rule in the twelfth century. Relations between Hindus and Muslims in India have been frequently difficult and violent, and were exacerbated by colonial rule. Due to shared communities, intermarriage, and conversion, however, in many areas the two groups share strikingly similar cultures. FREER GALLERY OF ART

even claim that at least one Hindu prince converted to Islam and went to Mecca on the hajj. Muslim trading colonies also flourished in Sri Lanka and on the Coromandel Coast in what is now Tamil Nadu. By the time the Portuguese arrived in 1498, Islam was firmly implanted in the region, and intertwined with its Hindu cultures.

Islamization in northern India followed a different course. Arab Muslim expeditions reached the banks of the Indus by 711, but systematic raids into the heartland did not commence until the tenth century. Armies under the command of the Turkish rulers based in Afghanistan, most notably Mahmoud of Ghazni (r. 998–1030 C.E.), repeatedly plundered towns in the Punjab and Sind. Muslim rule in the Indian heartland was established when Turkish, Persian, and Afghan warriors crossed the northwest frontier, defeated Indian

Rajput forces in 1192, and established their capital at Delhi in the Indo-Gangetic plain. The Delhi Sultanate (1211–1526), bolstered by Muslim immigrants fleeing Mongol armies in the west, extended Muslim control across northern India to Bengal and southward into the Deccan, rendering the region a *dar al-islam*. However, the Delhi Sultans often yielded to local Muslim and Hindu rivals when they were unable to absorb them into the imperial order, as did the Mughal dynasty that succeeded it (1526–1857).

In retrospect, Muslim historians recalled the conquests as heroic wars against pagan infidels (*kafirs*), and they lauded conversions along with the destruction of Hindu temples. These accounts obscure the fact that where Muslim attacks were made on Hindu temples, they were aimed at enriching Muslim elites (temples were repositories of gold, jewelry, and cash), and undermining the power of local rulers, the traditional temple patrons. Mosques and shrines were erected in their stead. However, most rulers treated subjugated Hindus as "protected" peoples (*dhimmis*), leaving temples untouched, authorizing and often patronizing new shrines. Nonetheless, there were occasions when they followed the advice of men like Diya' al-Din Barani (1285–1357), a court historian, who, in counseling rulers to maintain the purity of the "true religion," urged them to "use their efforts to insult and humiliate and to cause grief to and bring ridicule and shame upon the polytheistic and idolatrous Hindus" (Mujeeb, p. 68). Brahmanic Hindus, for their part, regarded Muslim invaders as impure *mlecchas* (aliens), or as Turks, Tajiks, and even Greeks, which suggests that they defined Muslims more by their foreign ethnicity than by their religious identity.

Muslim elites sought to comprehend the religions of their subjects intellectually. Al-Biruni (973–c. 1050) gives the earliest and most detailed Muslim account of Indian religion, writing in detail about brahmanic concepts of divinity, cosmology, reincarnation, ritual practices, and yoga. He approached these topics comparatively, drawing parallels with Sufism and Greek philosophy. The Mogul emperor Akbar (r. 1556–1605), famous for his interest in comparative religions, sponsored Persian translations of Hindu epics, the Bhagavad Gita, and books on Vedanta philosophy. His great-grandson, Dara Shukoh (1615–1659), befriended Hindu holy men, translated the Upanishads and, inspired by Ibn 'Arabi's pantheistic ideas, attempted a synthesis of Sufism with Hindu Vedanta. He was executed for heresy by his brother and rival to the throne, Aurangzeb (r. 1658–1707). As a zealous promoter of Sunni revivalism, Aurangzeb reimposed taxes on Hindu subjects and razed temples in major Hindu religious centers. As Akbar and Dara Shukoh became emblematic of Hindu-Muslim conviviality, Mahmoud of Ghazni and Aurangzeb are today remembered as symbols of Muslim militancy and intolerance.

### Conversions and Convergences

Most South Asian Muslims are descended from indigenous peoples who converted to Islam. As a rule, conversion was not an all-or-nothing break with Hindu belief and practice, nor did it usually occur at the end of a sword. Rather, it was a process that occurred in different degrees, and it involved a variety of social, cultural, political, and economic factors. Indeed, one of the most striking aspects of the history of Islam in South Asia is that it gained the most converts in areas situated beyond the traditional centers of political power and brahmanical religious authority. Today, the largest proportions of Muslims are to be found in the northwest (now Pakistan and Kashmir) and northeast (now Bangladesh); even Kerala (1991: 23.3%) in the south has a higher percentage of Muslims than does Uttar Pradesh (1991: 17.3%), where Delhi and Agra are located.

The chief agents for Islamization on the local level were wandering Muslim saints, teachers, and warriors. Isma'ili missionaries in Sind and Rajasthan adopted Nath yogi guise and formulated their Islamic message in terms of Hindu concepts of divinity and cosmology. In Bengal, communities grew up around saint shrines and mosques built where lands had been newly converted to wet-rice agriculture during the Mughal era. Through local Sufi centers Islam was often introduced and integrated into the socioreligious landscape, establishing points of exchange between the Muslim rulers and the populace, thus integrating people and property into the infrastructure of the kingdom. Across India shrines are patronized and even managed commonly by Muslims, Hindus, Sikhs, Buddhists, Jains, and Christians, and some have evolved into major pilgrimage centers, such as that of Mu'in al-Din Chishti in Ajmer. Such places are identified with supermundane beings who offer their devotees power, healing, fertility, and occasions to participate in ecstatic rites. Muslim warrior saints have been incorporated as guardian deities into the cults of Hindu hero gods and goddesses, where Muslims as well as Hindus worship them. This is exemplified by Vavar, the battle companion of the popular south Indian deity Ayyappa, and by Muttal Ravutan, guardian of Draupadi shrines in Tamil Nadu.

The interpenetration of Hinduism and Islam is further evident in folk epics and religious poetry. Thus, regional oral epics contain elements from the classical Hindu epics of the *Mahabharata* and the *Ramayana* that have been reshaped as a result of interaction with Muslims. At assemblies of poets throughout India, Hindus, Muslims, and others recite the compositions of poet saints such as Kabir (died c. 1448), known as the "apostle of Hindu-Muslim unity." The compositions of vernacular poets like Baba Farid Shakarganj, Sultan Bahu, and Bulleh Shah are on the lips of every Punjabi, regardless of creed. The Sikh religion founded by the North Indian holy man Guru Nanak (d. 1539) is often characterized as a fusion of Islamic monotheism and Hindu devotionalism. Across north India and Pakistan, people sing romantic ballads, or *qissa*, such as *Hir-Ranjha*, *Sassi-Punnu*, *Mirza-Sahiban*, and *Layla-Majnun*. These are inevitably tragic tales of romantic heroes and heroines destined to remain apart and doomed to die because of differences in caste, class, and religion. Nonetheless, the songs in which these boundaries are crossed are sung and beloved by people from all walks of life. Through richly symbolic language and imagery *qissa* are also mystical allegories of the human soul seeking union with God.

Hindustani music is another excellent example of the interplay between Hindu and Muslim culture. One of the greatest innovators of Hindustani classical music is often identified as Tansen (d. 1589), the Great Mogul Emperor Akbar's court musician. The musical modes and the code of conduct within the musical lineages, or *gharanas*, draw on Indian and Perso-Arabic styles. The initiation ceremony of the student into the master's school closely mirrors that of the Hindu *guru-sishya* initiation. Furthermore, although many of these lineages are principally Muslim in terms of personnel, worship of Hindu deities, especially the goddess Saraswati, and the lighting of lamps and garlanding of musicians are all common practices associated with Hinduism. The popularity of explicitly Islamic devotional styles such as *kafi*, *ghazal*, and *qawwal*, and of Muslim singers such as Nusrat Fateh Ali Khan and Abida Parveen among all audiences indicates a shared aesthetic culture.

Finally, in many areas conversion, intermarriage, and shared community life have led to common cultural practices. Often customs and observations of lifecycle events, such as births, marriages, and death, are regionally extremely similar. The offering of a child's first haircutting or pilgrimage to bless a marriage is performed by all religious communities at local shrines. Dress and eating habits are frequently shared. Muslim social status usually reflects caste distinctions found among the wider society; and in Malabar, Muslim traders intermarried with Hindu locals to such an extent that they adopted their matrilineal social organization.

## Hindu-Muslim Encounters after 1857

The Mogul Empire's territory reached its apogee under Aurangzeb, encompassing the Deccan plateau and parts of the South Indian coast. After his death in 1707, Mogul power rapidly unraveled, paving the way for the British East India Company to transform its commercial power bases into political centers. In 1757 at the Battle of Plassy, the British forces took effective control of much of North India, placing it under the Raj. Though nominal authority still lay in Mogul hands, this ended following the British defeat of a large-scale rebellion of Hindu and Muslim troops in 1857. After this power shift, religious movements arose to address the new sociopolitical milieu, which rewarded modernism, secularism, and progressive scientific thought over traditional values.

Reaction to the impact of foreign rule was channeled in many cases through religious movements. Revivalist and reformist groups emerged representing the full range of responses to the new power structures. Some sought to incorporate and integrate Western values, others focused

Muhammed 'Ali Jinnah, left, an advocate for a separate Muslim state, and Mahatma Gandhi, in Bombay in 1944, outside of Jinnah's home, where the two met to discuss the Hindu-Muslim conflict. Tensions between Indian Muslims and Hindus worsened during the struggle for independence from British rule. Despite Ghandi's efforts to support Muslim endeavors, violence worsened between the two groups and over 500,000 people died when the British left in 1947. AP/WIDE WORLD PHOTOS

on internal revitalization, and still others mobilized to oppose British rule. Hindu revivalist groups such as the Brahmo Samaj, Arya Samaj, Hindu Mahasabha, and Rashtriya Swayamsevak Sangh (RSS) advocated different means of promoting Hinduism in modern society. Whereas the Mahasabha, RSS, and Arya Samaj strove to purify Hinduism and reestablish an inherently Hindu national identity, the Brahmo Samaj emphasized social reform and education more in line with modern Western concepts. Similarly, Muslim organizations addressed the educational, social, and political interests of the Muslim population. The Dar al-'Ulum Deoband was founded in 1867 to generate a new Indian body of ulema. In 1875, Sir Sayyid Ahmad Khan established Aligarh Muslim University with a westernized secular curriculum, to educate Muslims capable of reviving Islam and addressing the exigencies of modernity. The Jama'at-e Islami, founded by Abu l-A'la' Maududi in 1928, advocated religious renewal and political independence. Grassroots movements, like Tablighi Jama'at (founded 1926), arose to teach basic Islamic principles and practices and to eradicate "Hindu" accretions, such as pilgrimage to saints's tombs, music, elaborate weddings, and mourning and death rites. The Muslim League formed in 1906 as a political group working to protect minority Muslim interests in an independent India.

Throughout the independence struggle relations between Hindus and Muslims worsened. Many factors contributed to this: British divide-and-conquer policies, Muslim underdevelopment, the Hinduization of the nationalist movement, and Hindu and Muslim prejudices and fears. Following the Indian National Congress's (INC) formation (1892), Muslim participation decreased steadily. However, there were moments of cooperation, such as Gandhi's support for the Khilafat movement to reestablish the Ottoman caliphate. Gandhi viewed this as a kindred freedom struggle and a means of garnering Muslim support. Nevertheless, as the independence movement progressed, the Congress leadership consistently failed to address Muslim fears of a Hindu majority nation without safeguards for their sizable (24%) minority. The INC rejected power-sharing schemes proposed by the British in the Communal Award (1932) and during the final Cabinet Mission negotiations (1946). After the Muslim League in 1940 publicly called for the creation of a separate state for Muslims, many Hindus no longer trusted Muslim ambitions for a free and unified India. Hindus sought a strong center and Muslims wanted strong regional governments and electoral reservations. Unable to find a compromise, the rapid departure of the British in 1947 resulted in horrific violence—an estimated 500,000 to 1 million died as 8 million Hindus and Sikhs shifted to India and 7 million Muslims departed for East and West Pakistan.

Since Partition, India's non-Hindu population has steadily increased, whereas Pakistan's non-Muslim population has declined—currently below 5 percent. The secular mandate of India's constitution nominally protects equal rights, and several controversial government schemes—particularly reservation of seats for various minority groups in the civil service, elected bodies, and universities—ensure at least some Muslim presence in India's civic life. Nonetheless, divisive politics persist. Three issues in particular frustrate understanding between Hindus and Muslims: Muslim personal law, Ayodhya, and Kashmir.

Currently there is a separate personal law for Muslims regarding marriage, divorce, and inheritance. Hindu nationalists and many women's advocacy groups champion a uniform civil code, which would apply the same legal regulations to every Indian citizen. Many Muslims cling to their separate legal code as a small realm of autonomy and the only available institutional means of maintaining their cultural identity.

In the early twentieth century Hindu radicals identified the Babri Masjid, a sixteenth mosque in Ayodhya, Uttar Pradesh, as the god Rama's birthplace and began agitation for its "liberation." In the absence of decisive action by the state

and central governments and the Supreme Court, the situation remains unresolved. In 1992 Hindu radicals tore down the mosque and placed Rama's image at the site. The riots subsequent to this demolition claimed thousands of lives, and the tension is periodically reactivated with similarly tragic results. In 2002 a move by Hindu organizations to begin construction of a temple resulted in another round of disturbances, destabilizing interreligious relations.

Finally, at Partition, Muslim-majority Kashmir gained "special status," or semiautonomy, under Article 370 of the Indian Constitution. India has promised a referendum on statehood or independence, but three wars with Pakistan, continual border skirmishes, Pakistani support to militants and freedom advocates, severe government repression of Muslim movements, and Hindu agitation over Article 370 keep tensions high. This situation is more alarming now that both nations are nuclear powers.

Real fissures do exist between Hindu and Muslim communities testifying to continued Hindu resentment of temple desecration by Muslims (real or alleged) and persistent Muslim fears (both reasonable and baseless) of assimilation or annihilation in Hindu-majority India. This mutual suspicion and hostility threaten constantly to overshadow the enormously rich and diverse shared traditions of the subcontinent. Yet the constitutional secularism of the largest democracy in the world, the persistence of shared places such as the shrine of Vavar in Kerala, and the continuing popularity of common cultural traditions such as music, literature, and art forms, indicate that there is a sound and strong common ground.

*See also* **Akbar; South Asia, Islam in; South Asian Culture and Islam.**

## BIBLIOGRAPHY

Ahmad, Aziz. *Studies in Islamic Culture in the Indian Environment.* 1964. Reprint, Delhi: Oxford University Press, 1999.

Bayly, Susan. *Saints, Goddesses and Kings: Muslims and Christians in South Indian Society 1700–1900.* Cambridge, Mass.: Cambridge University Press, 1989.

Eaton, Richard M. *Essays on Islam and Indian History.* Oxford, U.K.: Oxford University Press, 2000.

Gilmartin, David, and Lawrence, Bruce, eds. *Beyond Turk and Hindu: Rethinking Religious Identities in Islamicate South Asia.* Gainesville: University Press of Florida, 2000.

Hiltebeitel, Alf. *Rethinking India's Oral and Classical Epics: Draupadi among Rajputs, Muslims and Dalits.* Chicago: University of Chicago Press, 1999.

Khan, Dominique-Sila. *Conversions and Shifting Identities: Ramdev Pir and the Ismailis in Rajasthan.* New Delhi: Manohar, 1997.

Metcalf, Barbara, ed. *Moral Conduct and Authority: The Place of Adab in South Asian Islam.* Berkeley: University of California Press, 1984.

Mujeeb, Mohammad. *The Indian Muslims.* London: Allen & Unwin, 1967.

Robinson, Francis. *Islam and Muslim History in South Asia.* New Delhi: Oxford University Press, 2000.

Wink, Andre. *Al-Hind: The Making of the Indo-Islamic World.* Leiden: E. J. Brill, 1990.

*Anna Bigelow*
*Juan Eduardo Campo*

## HISBA

The Arabic term *hisba* (or in later works *ihtisab*) is associated with the idea of "reckoning" or "accounting" and has, in works of Islamic law, come to refer to the activities of state-appointed individuals (usually termed *muhtasib*) who enforce the law of Islam (the *shariʿa*) in both the public and private spheres. The function is normally conceived of as more preventative than remedial: the *muhtasib*'s task is to prevent transgressions of the law, and thereby avoid the need for court proceedings. However, he does have the power to bring individuals before a judge (*qadi*) if they fail to take heed of the *hisba* regulations. Most works of law from the twelfth century onward contain some discussion of the role of the *muhtasib*, often in the section dealing with the role and functions of the *qadi*. While enforcing *hisba* ("bringing people to account") is conceived of in these works as the role of an appointed person, it is recognized that this person is merely performing the general duty (to which all Muslims are bound) of "promoting good and prohibiting evil" (*al-amr bil-maʿruf wal-nahy ʿan al-munkar*). This is a Qurʾanic phrase (e.g., 3:104 and 9:61), and linking it with the doctrine of *hisba* (which is not explicitly mentioned in the Qurʾan) gives *hisba* (and its institutional manifestations) a firm grounding in the Qurʾan.

Works that describe the function of *hisba* in Muslim society are often highly theoretical, and depict what might be termed an "ideal" law-enforcement system for an Islamic community. The works open with a discussion of the various meanings of *hisba* and *ihtisab*, followed by discrete chapters on various activities that a *muhtasib* is supposed to prevent, and finally a description of the powers of a *muhtasib* and his relationship with the judicial system. The list of activities considered forbidden, and therefore coming under the *muhtasib*'s power, are often an interesting indicator of local religious life in the area where the work was written. The *muhtasib* is recommended to restrict the playing of chess or backgammon in various works, and in the Indian sub-continent works, Muslims visiting the temples of Hindus is specifically mentioned as a reprehensible practice. Works written in the western parts of the Muslim world, such as *al-Hisba fil-Islam* by Ibn Taymiyya (d. 1328), mention the visitation of Muslims to tombs of the *shaykhs* in search of intercession, as a practice needing to be restricted by the *muhtasib*. Works of *hisba*, then, despite their appearance as theoretical, also provide an insight into medieval Muslim practices (many of which have been left unrecorded elsewhere) since the more literate scholars demanded that such practices be restricted.

The theory was translated into practice by the appointment of local *muhtasib*s in various parts of the Abbasid empire. After the Mongol invasions and the reemergence of Muslim dynasties in Turkey, Iran, and India, the position of *muhtasib* and the enforcement of *hisba* also reappeared. Local *muhstasib*s were charged with enforcing *hisba* in towns and cities across the Muslim world. One particular emphasis was the role of the *muhtasib* in ensuring that market law was obeyed, and official documents regularly refer to such a figure. In some parts of the Muslim world, the *muhtasib* was responsible solely for ensuring that traders used the correct weights and measures. In this role of restricting unscrupulous merchants, some *muhtasib*s gained a reputation as protectors of the poor. The institution only died out with the introduction of more organized police forces and administrative ministries in the nineteenth century.

*See also* **Ethics and Social Issues; Law; Political Organization.**

### BIBLIOGRAPHY

Amedroz, H. F. "The Hisba Jurisdiction in the Ahkam Sultaniyya of Mawardi." *Journal of the Royal Asiatic Society* (1916): 290–301.

Sergeant, R. B. "A Zaidi Manual of Hisbah from the 3rd Century (H)." In *Studies in Arabic History and Civilisation.* Edited by R. B. Sergeant. London: Variorum Reprints, 1981.

*Robert Gleave*

## HISTORICAL WRITING

The term *taʾrikh* is presently used in languages such as Arabic, Turkish, and Persian for "history." Similar to the connotations of the term in the major European languages it refers, on the one hand, to the past itself and, on the other hand, to the writing of history. Narrative texts (chronicles, biographical dictionaries, etc.), written with the explicit purpose to be preserved, have been of particular importance for studying the history of the Islamic lands. Even more than in the European and the Chinese contexts, substantial documentary and archival evidence of history for regions such as the Arabic-speaking lands is practically nonexistent for the period prior to the fourteenth century. Hence, most of our knowledge of the regions' past depends on its representation in Islamic historiography.

In contrast to the modern study of historical writing for other regions such as the European lands, the study of Islamic historical writing is to a large degree still characterized by predominantly philological concerns. It is only since the 1990s that an interest into the wider societal context of the production of historical knowledge has taken a significant place in works such as Tarif Khalidi's *Arabic Historical Thought in the Classical Period* (1994). Approaches taking up the challenges and possibilities arising out of the linguistic turn in the second half of the twentieth century are rare except isolated examples such as Aziz al-Azmeh's *Histoire et Narration* (1986).

Historiography, in the sense of reflecting on the writing of history itself, was restricted to short references in the introduction of historical works in the Islamic lands until the fourteenth century. The Persian religious philosopher al-ʿIji (d. after 1381/82) composed in Arabic the first reflection on the technique and methodology of writing history, the *Gift of the Poor Man*. This and similar treatises of the following century were partly translated by Franz Rosenthal in *A History of Muslim Historiography* (1968). The famous North African scholar and official Ibn Khaldun (d. 1406) developed in his *Introduction* a theoretical pattern to classify events of the past, well beyond mundane considerations of technique and methodology.

Similarly, history gained only over time an independent place in the Muslim canon of disciplines. Philosophical classifications of sciences such as those by al-Farabi (d. 950) did not refer to history as an independent field of knowledge, emulating the tradition of the Hellenistic classifications. However, educational classifications included it as a discipline in its own right from the tenth century onward, although it was rarely taught as such in *madrasas*. At the same time, introductions to chronicles show that the authors considered themselves, among others, as historians (*muʾarrikh*)—a term also often encountered in medieval biographical entries.

## Historical Writing in the Central Islamic Lands—Premodern Period

Islamic historiography, in the sense of recording history, started with texts written in Arabic, but its early development is still largely unknown. The Greek and Persian literary traditions of the newly conquered lands were not adopted as direct models to build upon. It was rather the oral pre-Islamic Arabic tradition that shaped early Islamic historiography to a certain degree. The focus on genealogy and the authentication of reports by means of chains of transmitters were remnants of this heritage. However, the concrete forms of this historiography developed very much within the dynamics of early Islamic history, that is, through the interplay between the different Near Eastern cultural traditions

Early Islamic historical writing was intimately linked to immediate theological concerns. The first writings, which might be labeled as being historical, treated the life of the prophet Muhammad and his Companions. These writings were recorded mainly as hadiths, that is, as reports on the deeds and sayings of the Prophet. For later historiography

this beginning was of importance: The outwardly isolated character of each single report (*khabar*) proved to be influential in shaping longer narratives. This early material has engendered a major ongoing debate in present-day scholarship about its authenticity as its dating has posed manifold problems. One of the earliest reliable examples is the *sira* by the hadith scholar Muhammad Ibn Ishaq (d. 761), a biography of the Prophet.

In the following centuries historiography found two main forms of expression: chronicles and biographical dictionaries. The religious scholar al-Tabari (d. 923) composed in Baghdad the typical example of the former category: the universal chronicle *History of Prophets and Kings*, which dealt with events from the creation of the world until his time. "Universal" referred here obviously to Islamic history and what was perceived to be its predecessor(s). At the same time, chronicles were produced with a more limited geographical focus on towns (e.g., Damascus) and regions (e.g., Syria). The writing of history in the form of chronicles is similar to the writings produced in Latin Europe or Early and Middle Imperial China.

On the contrary, the second major form of historical writing, biographical dictionary, was in its importance and elaboration unique to Islamic historiography. Reflecting pre-Islamic genealogical interests and Islamic concerns of tracing the reliability of transmitters, the genre experienced an important development from early times onward. An early example of this genre, Ibn Saʿd's (d. 845) *Grand Book of the Generations*, reflects its exclusive theological concern by focusing on transmitters of hadith. This focus changed over the centuries, and in the thirteenth century the jurist Ibn Khallikan (d. 1282), for example, included in his dictionary individuals from more varied backgrounds. More specialized works started to be limited to specific towns or specific professions, such as the *Generations of Physicians* by Ibn Abi Usaybiʿa (d. 1270).

This development was an expression of the gradual change in the social identities of authors of historical works. From the eleventh century onward important parts of the ulema started to interact more closely with court circles and rulers. Typical examples in this regard are Saladin's biographer Ibn Shaddad (d. 1234), who was the ruler's judge of the army, and Ibn al-ʿAdim (d. 1262), the author of a local chronicle of Aleppo, who served the ruler of the town as a secretary, judge, and *wazir*. Nevertheless, authors of historical works continued to belong almost exclusively to the elusive group of the ulema. Authors, being part of the military elite, continued to be rare, while authors belonging to the commoners remained nonexistent.

Toward the end of the tenth century Arabic lost its position as the exclusive literary language in the Islamic lands. The regionalization of political power also found its expression in the rise of Persian historiography. This development was not only of linguistic nature. Persian historiography gained specific characteristics, such as stronger efforts to offer an explicit unified narrative, a more limited focus on events linked to courts and, initially, a near-absence of biographical works. Rashid al-Din (d. 1318) produced with his *Collection of Chronicles* a Persian universal history unmatched in its breadth. This chronicle was written for the Mongol ruler and was outstanding as it included the history of all known people, instead of only those of the Islamic lands.

## Historical Writing Beyond the Central Islamic Lands— Premodern Period

Persian historiography spread subsequently also to newly Islamized regions like South Asia. There, Muslim historiography was from its outset in the thirteenth century almost exclusively written in Persian. Early Indo-Persian historical writings reflected closely the outlook of its Persian models, such as its intimate links with court life. It is only during the Mogul period (sixteenth to eighteenth centuries) that Muslim South Asian historiography developed distinct characteristics, like the genre of memoirs written by members of the royal family or private persons.

The life of Nur al-Din Raniri (d. 1658), a South Asian scholar with a partly Arab genealogy, might serve as an example for the close links between the historiographical traditions of the different predominantly Muslim regions. After moving to the sultanate of Aceh (Northern Sumatra) he composed a Malay chronicle striving to mirror the classical historiographical style (e.g., al-Tabari) and drawing simultaneously heavily on the *Malay Annals*. The *Malay Annals* are one of the early examples of Southeast Asian Muslim historiography, written around 1500. Here, an anonymous author writing in Malay had cautiously aimed at harmonizing indigenous traditions and Islam, that is, Raniri's text reflected a bundle of different regional historiographical traditions. This interaction within the Muslim world via members of its literary elites might not be sufficient to legitimize the use of the single term "Muslim historiography" for such diverse traditions. Nevertheless, it shows at least that texts shifted easily from one region to the other and were reworked during this process.

Central Asia and sub-Saharan Africa are further examples of how texts and genres were transferred and adopted. Muslim troops conquered the western lands of Central Asia during the early eighth century. Therefore, the region's historiography was part of the Arabic and later Persian and Turkic traditions as well. However, in regions beyond these initial conquests, the development of a Muslim historiography was more complex. Here, the interplay between local oral traditions and written Muslim works was more accentuated. For example, the earliest surviving history for the Volga-Ural area, the Turkic *Collection of Chronicles*, completed in 1602 by 'Ali Jalayiri, derived not only from Rashid al-Din's fourteenth-century work with the same name but also to a large degree from oral folklore sources circulating among the Muslim nomads.

The interplay between oral and written historical traditions was also a salient feature in sub-Saharan Africa. While historiography written by indigenous authors came into existence around 1500, these narratives continued to circulate simultaneously in a context of oral culture. The first written texts appeared in those regions that had previously been strongly Islamized and Arabized: the Sudan Belt and the East African Swahili coast. Consequently, chronicles such as the East African *Kilwa Chronicle*, written around 1530, or the West African *Ta'rikh al-Sudan*, written by the Timbuktu historian al-Sa'di in the seventeenth century, were generally composed in Arabic. West African Muslim historiography developed also the genre of biographical dictionaries, such as Ahmad Baba's (d. 1627) work on the learned men of the Western Sudan. During the nineteenth century, authors switched increasingly to indigenous languages such as Hausa and Fulfulde written first in Arabic and subsequently in Latin script. In combination with the developing dominance of European languages, Arabic ceased to be the literary elite's prime means of expression.

## Historical Writing in the Central Islamic Lands: Ottoman and Modern Periods

During the fifteenth century Ottoman Turkish emerged as a major literary language in Anatolia and in parts of the Arabic-speaking Middle East. Ottoman historiography started in the fourteenth century with rather short appendixes to existing chronicles. It was only in the fifteenth century that independent historical works in Ottoman Turkish were composed. These works were mainly chronicles written by individuals close to court circles. Other genres (e.g. biographical dictionaries) did not play a significant role in Ottoman historiography. *History of Events*, a work by the officially appointed imperial historian Mustafa Na'ima (d. 1716), enjoyed considerable popularity. His recourse to Ibn Khaldun's patterns in order to describe the perceived decline of the empire was typical for this period's historiography. With the Ottoman period the importance of narrative historiography for modern day scholarship decreases. The large amounts of surviving archival and documentary material for the central Islamic lands allow more varied venues to the history of this and the following periods.

Persian, Ottoman, and Arabic historiographies witnessed significant changes during the late nineteenth century. This process culminated for the Arabic context in works such as the *History of Islamic Civilization* by the Syrian Christian Jurji Zaydan (d. 1914), published in Egypt between 1902 and 1906. Here a distinct shift in form and content becomes visible, especially as he drew heavily on European works dealing with Arab or Islamic history. Nevertheless, these "modern" works were still to a large degree embedded in traditional historiography, visible in a similar use of poetry. Contrary to traditional assumptions, which refer the nineteenth century developments exclusively to the modernizing impact of the West, recent scholarship such as Crecelius

(2001) has stressed the vivacity of Arabic historiography also in the "declining" eighteenth century.

The changes led in the late nineteenth century to a reorientation of historiography toward narratives of Ottoman and Arabic national origins. In the early twentieth century the Ottoman narrative was Turkified and with the rise of Arab national states the Arabic version started slowly to be supplemented and ultimately replaced respectively by national narratives. This universal trend toward national identities was also visible in other Muslim regions. The politician and writer Muhammad Yamin (d. 1962), for example, integrated the *Malay Annals* into his narrative of an Indonesian national history dating many millennia back.

The dominant second trend during the twentieth century was the professionalization of the writing of history. The general expansion of higher education in the Middle East, especially after World War II, led also to a significant rise in the number of university history departments. This has changed the general pattern of the first half of the century when Middle Eastern historians generally took their degree from Western universities. However, historical research remains a difficult task because of limited material resources and the variant political conditions, which are not always favorable for dealing with certain topics.

*See also* **Arabic Literature; Biography and Hagiography; Heresiography; Ibn Khaldun; Tabari, al-.**

## BIBLIOGRAPHY

Azmeh, Aziz al-. "Histoire et Narration dans l'Historiographie Arabe." *Annales ESC* 41 (1986):411–431.

Choueiri, Youssef M. *Arab History and the Nation State. A Study in Modern Arab Historiography 1820–1980.* London and New York: Routledge, 1989.

Crecelius, Daniel. "al-Jabarti's *'aja'ib al-athar fi 'l-tarajim wa-l-akhbar* and the Arabic Histories of Ottoman Egypt in the Eighteenth Century." In *The Historiography of Islamic Egypt (C. 950–1800).* Edited by Hugh Kennedy. Leiden and Boston: Brill, 2001.

Frank, Allen J. *Islamic Historiography and 'Bulghar' Identity Among the Tatars and Bashkirs of Russia.* Leiden, Boston: Brill, 1998.

Freitag, Ulrike. "Writing Arab History: The Search for the Nation." *British Journal of Middle Eastern Studies* 21 (1994):19–37.

Hall, D. G. E. *Historians of South East Asia.* London: Oxford University Press, 1961.

Humphreys, R. Stephen. *Islamic History. A Framework for Inquiry.* 2d ed. London and New York: I. B. Tauris, 1995.

Khalidi, Tarif. *Arabic Historical Thought in the Classical Period.* Cambridge, U.K.: Cambridge University Press, 1994.

Lewis, Bernard, and Holt, Peter M., eds. *Historians of the Middle East.* London: Oxford University Press, 1962.

Meisami, Julie. *Persian Historiography to the End of the Twelfth Century.* Edinburgh: Edinburgh University Press, 1999.

Rosenthal, Franz. *A History of Muslim Historiography.* 2d ed. Leiden: Brill, 1968.

*Konrad Hirschler*

## HISTORY *See* **Historical Writing; Timelines and Genealogies in backmatter**

## HIZB ALLAH

Hizb Allah (Hezbollah, Hizbullah) from the Arabic *hizb allah*, or "party of God," became a popular name for political Islamist groups in the late twentieth century, after Ayatollah Ruhollah Khomeini of Iran began to use the Qur'anic phrase (5:56–59; 58:19–22) to distinguish the righteous from the oppressors.

Focusing on the perennial conflict between the forces of good and evil, and the Qur'an's apocalyptic vision in which the "party of God" will be "victorious" and will go to heaven, whereas the "party of Satan" will ultimately "be the losers," was effective in consciousness-raising and forging solidarity in the postcolonial context of sociopolitical strife. This general usage of "Hizb Allah" dominated in Iran in the late 1970s, when it was used by those who supported Ayatollah Khomeini in his opposition to the shah, "the West," and Israel, and in his advocacy of government based on Islam as interpreted by religiously trained (Shi'ite) legal scholars. Somewhat earlier, a group of Sunni political Islamists in Yemen called themselves Hizb Allah, and later another small Sunni Hizb Allah appeared in Egypt, reputedly under the leadership of Yahya Hashim. A faction that broke away from Islamic Jihad in Palestine during the 1980s, led by Ahmad Muhanna, also called itself Hizb Allah. The Palestinian Hizb Allah, like its parent Islamic Jihad, is military in nature, rejects compromise with Israel, and believes the question of Palestine is fundamentally religious in nature. That is, returning Palestine and, in particular, Jerusalem, to Islamic sovereignty is considered a religious duty.

However, the term Hizb Allah (Hezbollah/Hizbullah) is most frequently associated with the Lebanese Shi'ite group founded in 1982, following the Israeli invasion of Lebanon. Shi'ite leader Sayyid Muhammad Husayn Fadlallah, who had studied with Khomeini in Najaf during the latter's exile in Iraq, became an outspoken opponent of Israel, and of "the West" in general. At that time, Iran's Islamic government sent a contingent of Revolutionary Guards to Lebanon to assist in the resistance to Israel, becoming the core of Shi'ite militancy in Lebanon. The movement is led by a secretary general (most recently Hojjat al-Islam Hassan Nasrallah) and advised by a council (Jihad Council), including Lebanese Shi'ite scholars and military advisors. Since its inception, however, Fadlallah has been the movement's spiritual leader and spokesperson.

With support from Iran, Syria, and private donations, Hizb Allah expanded its activities to include assistance to families of those who have died in war or are imprisoned, medical facilities (hospitals, pharmacies, rehabilitation centers), factories, education (scholarships), social services (including scouting and sports activities), communications (radio and newspapers), as well as infrastructure (including rebuilding sites destroyed in war). Since 1992 it has operated as a political party as well, competing successfully for the Shi'ite vote in parliamentary elections. Nevertheless, Hizb Allah is most widely known for attacks carried out by its militia for covert operations, the Organization of the Islamic Jihad. These attacks have been waged against foreigners in Lebanon, both individuals (assassinations and kidnappings) and groups (such as the bombings of U.S. diplomatic and military installations in 1983 and 1984), as well as Israeli occupation forces in southern Lebanon.

In Iran, the popularity of Hezbollahi rhetoric has waned with the rise in popularity of Mohammed Khatami, who was elected president by a wide margin in 1997 on a campaign stressing the need for reform within Iran rather than opposition to the West. Israel's withdrawal from southern Lebanon in 2000 after eighteen years of warfare led by Hizb Allah forces, by contrast, greatly enhanced Hizb Allah's standing in Lebanon and the Arab Middle East.

*See also* **Political Islam.**

## BIBLIOGRAPHY

Jaber, Hala. *Hezbollah: Born with a Vengeance.* New York: Columbia University Press, 1997.

Kramer, Martin S. *Hezbollah's Vision of the West.* Washington, D.C.: Washington Institute for Near East Policy, 1989.

Saad-Ghorayeb, Amal. *Hizbu'llah: Politics and Religion.* London: Pluto Press, 2002.

*Tamara Sonn*

## HOJJAT AL-ISLAM

*Hojjat al-Islam* literally means "Proof of Islam." *Hojjat al-Islam* began as an honorific title given to high-ranking scholars (ulema) in both Sunni and Shi'ite Islam. Hence al-Ghazali (d. 1111) was given the title *Hojjat al-Islam*, to signify his skill in arguing for the truths of Islam. It appears to have remained a general term of respect for a scholar. In the nineteenth century, the title began to reflect the more hierarchical

structure of the Shi'ite seminary system. At first, scholars like Muhammad Baqir al-Shafti (d.1844) were given the titles *mujtahid, Ayatollah,* and *Hojjat al-Islam.* Later usage of the term *Hojjat al-Islam* was restricted to scholars of a rank lower than *Ayatollah.* A *Hojjat al-Islam,* since the Islamic revolution in Iran, is an "aspiring *Ayatollah*" who has completed his *bahth-e kharij* (the highest level of formal instruction) and is teaching, but has not yet gained sufficient prestige to be regarded as *Ayatollah.* While both *Ayatollah* and *Hojjat al-Islam* were titles of distinction in the late nineteenth and early twentieth centuries, the titles have become relatively common in recent years, and this may reflect either a lowering of the qualification threshold, or an improvement in educational techniques in the Shi'ite seminaries of Mashhad, Qum, and the Atabat.

*See also* **Ayatollah (Ar. Ayatullah); Shi'a: Imami (Twelver).**

## BIBLIOGRAPHY

Mottahedeh, Roy P. *The Mantle of the Prophet: Religion and Politics in Iran* New York: Simon and Schuster, 1985.

*Robert Gleave*

## HOJJATIYYA SOCIETY

The Hojjatiyya (Hojjatieh) Society is an anti-Baha'i group that was established in 1957 by Mahmood-e Halabi, one of the well-known preachers and publicists of Mashad, the religious center of Khorasan province in Iran. (Bahaism is a religious movement that originated in Iran in the nineteenth century.) After the resignation of Reza Shah (1941), who opposed political activity by clerics, Halabi began to criticize the history and doctrine of Bahaism. When Halabi moved to Tehran, after Mohammad Reza Shah's coup d'etat against the national government of Mohammad Mosaddegh at 1953, he found significant support from the conservative clergy, and the leading ulema approved of the Hojjatiyya Society's activities. Hojjatiyya opposed any radical or revolutionary activity, and consequently there were no prohibitions on its social and cultural approach.

After Iran's Islamic revolution in 1978–1979, the Ayatollah Ruhollah Khomeini, who opposed Hojjatiyya's thesis as criticizing and crushing Bahaism as the main agenda of the Islamic Revolution, put some limitation on the activity of this group. Nevertheless Hojjatiyya was successful in closing the Baha'i's public meetings and preventing the dissemination of the movement's ideas. In 1983, Halabi stopped the educational activities of the Hojjatiyya Society, following Khomeini's request that he do so. Hojjatiyya members have since been active in Iran's judiciary, security system, and in offices responsible for staffing Iran's governmental institutions.

*See also* **Baha'i Faith; Revolution: Islamic Revolution in Iran.**

## BIBLIOGRAPHY

Baghi, Emad al-din. *Hizb-e-Qaedin Zaman.* Tehran: Ettela'at Publisher, 1984.

*Majid Mohammadi*

## HOLY CITIES

The Prophet of Islam is reported to have said that a Muslim should not embark on a pilgrimage or pious visit to any mosque other than the Holy Sanctuary of Mecca, the Prophet's Mosque in Medina, and the al-Aqsa Mosque in Jerusalem. This statement in a sense maps out the sacred geography of the Islamic landscape. Muslims revere the cities of Mecca, Medina, and Jerusalem primarily because of the powerful spiritual symbolism associated with these sanctuaries.

Different religious traditions define sacred space according to different criteria, alluding to the multiplicity of ways in which holiness is conceptualized. Some traditions hold that sacred space is discovered through the manifestation of the divine, while others argue that holiness is created through a process of cultural labor. In the Islamic tradition, the origins and the performance of rituals of worship play an integral part in the sanctification of space. As such, the concept of the holy is more closely linked to the process of cultural labor, whereby space is sanctified due to its function in divine communion and not because of the perceived manifestation of the divine in a certain place. Therefore, the cities of Mecca, Medina, and Jerusalem are embraced as holy and regarded as sacred centers because of their intimate association with fundamental Islamic ritual practices.

In order to grasp the significance of these holy cities to the Muslim imagination their religious symbolism needs to be emphasized alongside their histories. Foremost among the three centers is Mecca, followed by Medina, and finally Jerusalem.

### Mecca

The city of Mecca has been venerated as a holy center since time immemorial. In the pre-Islamic period it served as a center of pilgrimage for the pagan Arabs and was home to their most important idol deities. Muslims, however, view Mecca as the center of monotheism and the city where the Ka'ba, the first house for the exclusive worship of the one true God—Allah—was established. The prophet Abraham is reported to have built the Ka'ba in this barren valley by divine command. Abraham had long before left his son, Isma'il, with his mother, Hagar, in this place, also by divine command. Returning many years later, Abraham and his son undertook the construction of the Ka'ba. The Arabs, who are the

At the end of the annual hajj in Mecca in March of 2000, tens of thousands of pilgrims at a time surround the Ka'ba in the Haram al-Sharif or "Noble Sanctuary." Because of the Ka'ba and this annual journey by millions of Muslims commemorating Abraham, Hagar, and Isma'il, Mecca is the holiest city in Islam. © AFP/CORBIS

progeny of Isma'il, flourished in the region but deviated from the pure monotheism of their noble ancestors, and at the time of the birth of the prophet Muhammad, Mecca was a center of idol-worship.

When Muhammad began preaching his message he was severely persecuted by his fellow Meccans and was forced to seek asylum in the nearby city of Medina. With the rise of Islam, the Prophet was finally able to conquer Mecca. He entered the city in 630 C.E., purging it of all its idols and reestablishing the Ka'ba as a symbol of pure monotheism once again. Mecca thus became a center of Muslim pilgrimage (hajj). Even today, Muslims from all over the world congregate in the city annually to perform the hajj, which is one of the five fundamental pillars of Islam.

The Prophet did not choose to remain in Mecca, and settled in Medina instead. Thus, Mecca never became a city of any political significance, and the seat of governance in the Muslim world was always located elsewhere. The only time the city was of political importance was during the brief period after the death of the caliph Mu'awiya. He was succeeded by his son Yazid in 680 C.E., but his rule was contested by 'Abdallah ibn Zubayr, who was proclaimed caliph in Mecca. Ibn Zubayr managed to gain ascendancy over most of Arabia and certain parts of Iraq, but was finally crushed and killed by the Ummayad general al-Hajjaj in 692 C.E.

When the Abbasids ousted their Ummayad cousins, they chose to continue ruling from Baghdad. Mecca was well patronized by the Abbasid caliphs, and they distributed vast sums of money to its inhabitants during their visits on pilgrimage. The appearance of the Qarmitiyya, a militant sect opposed to the Abbasids, made some impact on the history of Mecca in this era. Over a fifty-year period, the sect made constant raids on pilgrim caravans, and in 930 C.E. they raided Mecca, massacring its inhabitants. They even carried away the Black Stone, the cornerstone that marks the beginning of the ritual of circumambulation around the Kaʿba. It was, however, returned some twenty years later, and a relatively calm state of affairs ensued thereafter, with pilgrimage taking precedence over politics in Mecca once again.

The city's recent history also bears witness to some dramatic political events. In 1979 a group of Saudi militants stormed the sacred sanctuary that houses the Kaʿba and occupied it for sixteen days, killing many civilians and soldiers in the process. Apart from these infrequent events, however, Mecca has always been of preeminent importance to Muslims because of the Kaʿba and the hajj. It is solely because of the rituals of hajj performed in the city and its environs that Mecca is haloed in sanctity.

When viewed in terms of sacred geography, the city can best be conceived of as a patchwork of sacred spaces. At the very center is the Kaʿba, which is for Muslims a veritable gateway opening into the realm of the transcendent. Muslims the world over face in the direction of the Kaʿba during the performance of the five daily prayers, and the Kaʿba is undoubtedly the most potent symbol of Islamic identity, due to its intimate association with the obligatory act of prayer. The history of the Kaʿba is even detailed in the Qurʾan, and it is described as the first house established for the sole purpose of worshipping God (3:96). Although the Qurʾan describes Mecca as being "full of blessing" (3:96) and as an "asylum of security" (5:97), it goes on to emphasize the functional characteristic of the Kaʿba far more cogently. It was built for no other purpose but the establishment of prayer (14:37).

The immediate vicinity of the Kaʿba was also regarded as a sanctuary, and as such the Kaʿba and its surroundings make up the holy Mosque of Mecca, which is commonly known as *al-Haram al-Sharif* (the Noble Sanctuary). Two very important rituals of hajj are performed in this Mosque. The first is the circumambulation of the Kaʿba. This ritual is associated with Abraham and Ismaʿil's building of the house. As they laid the foundations, the two prophets supplicated Allah, imploring for mercy and asking that their sacrifice be accepted. In similar vein, the pilgrim reenacts the process and supplicates Allah as he or she completes the cycles known as *tawwaf*.

The second ritual performed in the Mosque is the *saiʿ*, which literally means to strive. The pilgrim reenacts the frantic search for water undertaken by Hagar, an African freed slave, who ran between the two hills of Saffa and Marwa. Abraham had left her there, alone with her son, without any provisions. She ran between the two hills until God finally rewarded her quest with the blessed well of Zamzam, which suddenly gushed forth from the ground. The pilgrim therefore recalls the anguish of this noble woman, and is also reminded of the mercy of Allah.

Another sacred space linked to the pilgrimage is found on the outskirts of Mecca, not too far from the holy Mosque. This is the campsite of Mina. Not only do the pilgrims spend most of the five days of pilgrimage camped at Mina, but they also perform the ritual pelting of Satan there. This ritual is associated with Satan's attempt to dissuade Abraham from obeying Allah's command, and Abraham is reported to have chased the Evil One away by pelting him with pebbles on three occasions. The pilgrim therefore reenacts this event through the ritual pelting, thereby striving to fight his or her own spiritual weakness rejecting temptation. Mina only comes to life once a year, during the pilgrimage, and is virtually uninhabited for the remainder of the year.

Moving on from Mina, the pilgrim follows the path to the plains of Arafat, about 9 kilometers away from central Mecca. Arafat also only comes to life during the pilgrimage, and is the site where the prophet Muhammad delivered the famous last sermon. Standing on the plains of Arafat and supplicating Allah is the pinnacle of the hajj. The pilgrim who does not manage to make his way to Arafat on the specified time and day invalidates his or her pilgrimage and has to perform it over again. This ritual, unlike most of the others, is not related to Abraham and is more directly associated with the prophet Muhammad, who is reported to have said that the essence of pilgrimage is the supplication at Arafat.

Between Mina and Arafat is Muzdallifa, an area intimately linked to the pilgrimage rituals as well. The pilgrim must pass through Muzdallifa on the way back to Mina after completing the supplication at Arafat and perform the obligatory prayers there, as was instructed by the prophet Muhammad.

Like any world capital, Mecca is continuously being transformed and upgraded. The pilgrimage sites have been developed to facilitate the millions that visit there, and the city itself will surely grow and expand in the future. However, Mecca will always retain its aura primarily because of the pilgrimage.

## Medina

Unlike Mecca, a visit to Medina is not an obligatory part of the pilgrimage, but the Prophet had personally sanctioned journeying to his mosque in Medina for the purpose of *ziyara*, or pious visit. During the early Islamic era, Medina, called

The second holiest city in Islam is Medina, where the Prophet's Mosque, shown here, is located. Though he was born in Mecca, Muhammad failed to convince people there of his beliefs and was severely persecuted before he resettled in nearby Medina, where he gained more followers. AP/WIDE WORLD PHOTOS

Yathrib in pre-Islamic times, had been the political capital of the nascent Islamic empire. Mecca was and still is by far the more important in terms of sacred geography, however. The oasis town of Yathrib, which lies about 500 kilometers away from Mecca, was renamed in honour of the Prophet, and is more properly referred to as *al-Madina al-Munawwarra*, or the Illuminated City.

The Prophet had migrated to Medina in 622 C.E., after failing to convince the Meccans of his mission. The city was far more diverse than Mecca, with a population comprised of Jews, Muslims, and idolaters. The Prophet attempted to unite the various factions into a single polity and his efforts were recorded in a pact known as *Sahifa al-Madina*, or the constitution of Medina. In the interim, the conflict between the nascent Muslim community of Medina and the Meccan pagans continued. The Prophet undertook over seventy expeditions against the Meccans from his new power base in Medina before finally conquering Mecca. The Prophet did not return to Mecca, however, as Medina was now his home. It was from here that he turned his attention to spreading the message of Islam to frontiers beyond the Arabian Peninsula. By the time of his death in 632 C.E., Islam stood poised to conquer the Byzantine Romans and the Persians that threatened its northern frontiers.

Medina remained the political capital of the Islamic Empire during the reign of the four caliphs who succeeded the Prophet. With the outbreak of civil war during the reign of 'Ali (the last of the four caliphs) the city slowly began to lose political importance. 'Ali left Medina in October 656 C.E. to quell insurrections in Iraq and never returned. The city of Kufa was for a brief period the center of events, but with the ascendancy of Mu'awiya as caliph in 661 C.E., Damascus became the political capital of the Muslim world. Apart from isolated instances of upheaval, not much else occurred in Medina that was of major political significance from here on.

While Medina may have become completely marginalized in the political sphere, it gained considerable fame as a center of Islamic intellectual life. The scholars of Medina played an important role in the early development of Islamic jurisprudence and in the collection of hadith (prophetic traditions). In this important formative period, the legal school of Medina was made famous through the work of one of its most outstanding scholars, Malik ibn Anas, who died in 795 C.E.

However, it is neither the intellectual nor the early political status of Medina that is ultimately of primary importance to the Muslim community. Medina is venerated because it is the city of the Prophet of Islam and the first Islamic polity. It is in Medina that Islam took root and was strengthened. The city is also the site of a few important mosques that are intimately associated with the history of the ritual prayers. This is perhaps the main reason why the Prophet encouraged Muslims to visit Medina. Its sacred sites not only capture the early history of the prayer ritual, but also strengthen the believer's resolve and commitment to these very practices.

The first mosque built in Medina was the mosque of Quba. This mosque lies on what was then the outskirts of the city, and it is where the Prophet paused for a few days before entering the city. Here he laid the foundations of the Quba Mosque. The mosque at Quba remained dear to the Prophet, and long after he had settled in Medina he would still make his way there on Saturdays to spend time in prayer and reflection. Muslims visiting Medina today still emulate this practice, and follow the path to the mosque of Quba in the early hours on Saturday mornings, where they remain until noon, as was the habit of the Prophet.

Nonetheless, the most important mosque in Medina is still the Prophet's Mosque, also referred to as the *Haram al-Madina* (the Sanctuary of Medina). The Prophet's own living quarters were attached to the mosque, and when he died he was buried in one of his apartments. The Prophet's gravesite is thus attached to his mosque even today. While orthodox Islamic doctrine frowns upon the veneration of gravesites, Muslims the world over come to the mosque to visit the grave. This practice is tolerated as long as it is done under the pretext of visiting the mosque, for the Prophet is reported to have said that prayer in his mosque is rewarded more greatly than prayer elsewhere, except for prayer in the *haram* of Mecca, which carries the highest reward. In Medina, as in Mecca, it is once again the act of prayer that lends sanctity to this important space.

The final mosque that enjoys special status is the Qiblatyn Mosque, which literally means the mosque of two directions. Unlike the first two, this mosque is more of historical than ritual significance. There is no special reward mentioned for praying in it, nor did the Prophet set a precedent of visiting it on a regular basis. However, it is important because of the momentous event that occurred in it. For a period of sixteen months after the Prophet's migration to Medina, the obligatory prayers were performed facing in the direction of Jerusalem. While praying in the Qiblatyn Mosque, the Prophet was ordered by divine directive to change orientation and face the Ka'ba in Mecca while praying (2:142). Even today, Muslims the world over pray facing Mecca, and in memory of God's command to the Prophet, Muslims still frequent this mosque when visiting Medina.

Religious literature on Medina is replete with accounts that outline the virtues of the city, but many of these are apocryphal and therefore not worthy of mention. Such accounts do, however, lend an added aura and appeal to the holy status of the city, even if they are not really of great importance.

## Jerusalem

Although Jerusalem's status as the third holy city of Islam is extremely well established in the primary Islamic sources, Muslims do not claim exclusive spiritual rights to the holy city. Jerusalem is dear to all three of the Abrahamic faiths, and has been severely battled over by Muslims, Christians, and Jews through the centuries.

The Jews have always venerated the city as the site of the holy temple, but the pagan Romans had already obliterated all remaining vestiges of Jewish life in Jerusalem about five centuries before the city came under Muslim rule, in 638 C.E. When the Roman emperor Constantine embraced Christianity, the city was covered in Christian monuments. Although there was no chance of the Jews rebuilding their temple, Constantine did allow them into the city once a year, on payment of a fee, so that they could mourn the destruction of the temple.

In 614 C.E. the Persians captured Jerusalem, massacring thousands of Christians in the process. Fourteen years later, the Roman emperor Heraclius was able to drive the invaders out and recover the land and the city. He, in turn, wreaked a terrible vengeance upon the Jews, who were accused of colluding with the Persian invaders. At the dawn of Islam, therefore, the Jewish presence in Jerusalem had once again been viciously purged by the Christians.

The Islamic Empire underwent massive expansion after the demise of the Prophet. In the reign of the third caliph, 'Umar ibn al-Khattab, the Byzantines conceded Jerusalem to Islam. In 638 C.E., the caliph himself accepted the capitulation of the city from its Christian patriarch, Sophronius. In an unprecedented display of tolerance, 'Umar granted the Christians protection of their religious sites and vouched for their safety. He even refused the patriarch's offer to perform the midday prayer in a Christian shrine, recognizing the significance of the prayer in the appropriation and sanctification of space. He explained his reasons for refusing, saying that he did not want to create a pretense for future generations that may seek justification for the confiscation of this Christian shrine and turn it into a place of Islamic worship.

'Umar immediately set about identifying the sites that were of religious significance to Muslims. Jerusalem is mentioned in the Qur'an as the city to which the Prophet had traveled in a night journey and in which he had assembled with all the previous prophets, leading them in prayer. 'Umar therefore sought out this area and marked it out as a sanctuary. It was here that the al-Aqsa mosque was built. The

Al Aqsa Mosque and Temple Mount in Jerusalem. After he conquered Jerusalem in 638, the third caliph, 'Umar ibn al-Khattab, built Al Aqsa. The caliph chose a site the Qu'ran describes the Prophet Muhammad having traveled to in a night journey in order to gather all the previous prophets and lead them in prayer. © DAVE G. HOUSER/CORBIS

Prophet is then reported to have ascended to the heavens, where the five daily prayers were obligated upon him and his followers by Allah. His ascension was from a large rock, which was discovered under a dung heap, indicating that the area of the sanctuary was of no significance to the other religious communities at that time. 'Umar ordered the area to be cleaned and performed the prayers there. Building of the structure known as the Dome of the Rock commenced round about 688 C.E. on the order of 'Abd al-Malik ibn al-Marwan, the fifth caliph after Mu'awwiya.

Jerusalem became known to Muslims as Bayt al-Maqdis or simply *al-Quds* (the Holy City). It was thereafter patronized and maintained as a sacred site by all the Muslim caliphs from the Abbasids right through to the Ottomans, who finally lost the city to British mandate in the early twentieth century. The city remained under Muslim rule for thirteen centuries, with the exception of the brief interruption effected by the Crusades. In this long period, the greatest calamity to have befallen Islam was the loss of Jerusalem to the Crusaders in 1099 C.E. The city was finally reconquered by Salah al-Din al-Ayyubi (Saladin) ninety years later, in 1187 C.E. In the interim, thousands of Muslims and Jews were slaughtered in the name of Christ. Saladin displayed remarkable tolerance not only to the Jews, but to the Christians as well, and under his

rule the Jewish community once again thrived in the city, finding safe asylum from persecution there.

It is important to note that no Jewish place of worship is made mention of from the time of the Arab conquest in Jerusalem. Mention of the Wailing Wall as a place where pious Jews came to lament the loss of the temple only appeared around the time of Saladin's reconquest. This wall was identified as the Western wall of the Al-Aqsa compound, and Jews from thereon frequented the place to pray.

This act of devotion was tolerated by the Muslim rulers of Jerusalem, with the gravest of consequences in recent times, after the establishment of the Jewish State of Israel in occupied Palestine. What was initially a gesture of tolerance came to be held by some faithful Jews as an absolute right, not merely of access but ultimately of possession. Today the strife between Jews and Muslims over the site of the al-Aqsa complex rages fiercely.

United Nations attempts to accord the city of Jerusalem international status, with equal access for all three faith-groups, has up until now been unsuccessful. What Jerusalem needs today is the tolerance and foresight of a modern-day 'Umar or Saladin; a leader with the temperament to show equal respect to all three faiths and uphold the sanctity of Jerusalem to the benefit of all.

Holy cities or sites are inextricably linked with the transcendent and will always dominate the religious imagination, in spite of the tremendous toll sometimes exacted through conflict and contestation. It is only in these sacred spaces that human mortality is ultimately transcended, enabling the believer to stand in the presence of the divine. As long as Muslim practice and faith prevail, there will always be people who lay claim to the sanctity of the three spiritual capitals of the Islamic world: Mecca, Medina, and Jerusalem.

*See also* **Caliphate; Dome of the Rock; 'Ibadat; Mi'raj; Muhammad.**

## BIBLIOGRAPHY

Armstrong, Karen. *A History of Jerusalem.* London: HarperCollins, 1996.

Chidester, David. "The Poetics and Politics of Sacred Space: Towards a Critical Phenomenology of Religion." In *From the Sacred to the Divine: A New Phenomenological Approach.* Edited by Anna-Teresa Tymieniecka. Boston: Kluwer Academic Publishers, (1994): 211–231.

Eliade, Mircea. *The Sacred and the Profane.* Translated by W. R. Tusk. New York: Harcourt, Brace & World, 1959.

Farouk-Alli, Aslam. "A Qur'anic Perspective and Analysis of the Concept of Sacred Space in Islam." In *Journal for the Study of Religion,* 15, no. 1 (2002): 63–78.

Goitein, S. D. "The Historical Background of the Erection of the Dome of the Rock." In *Journal of the American Oriental Society (JAOS),* 70 (1950): 104–108.

Goitein, S. D. *Studies in Islamic History and Institutions.* Leiden: E. J. Brill, 1966.

Hilali, T., and Khan, M., tr. *Interpretation of the Meanings of the Noble Qur'an in the English Language.* Riyadh: Dar-us-Salam, 1995.

Peters, F. E. *Hajj: The Muslim Pilgrimage to Mecca and the Holy Places.* Princeton: Princeton University Press, 1994.

Peters, F. E. *Mecca and the Hijaz: A Literary History of the Muslim Holy Land.* Princeton, N.J.: Princeton University Press, 1994.

Shariati, Ali. *Hajj: Reflection on its Rituals.* Translated by Laleh Bakhtiar. Chicago: Kazi Publications, 1993.

Tibawi, A. L. "Jerusalem: Its Place in Islam and Arab History." In *The Islamic Quarterly* XII, no. 4 (1968): 185–218.

Watt, W. M. and Winder, R. B. "Al Madina." In *The Encyclopaedia of Islam.* Edited by E. Van Donzel, B. Lewis, and C. Pellat. Leiden: E. J. Brill, 1978.

Watt. W. M., et al. "Makka." In *The Encyclopaedia of Islam.* Edited by E. Van Donzel, B. Lewis, and C. Pellat. Leiden: E. J. Brill, 1978.

*Aslam Farouk-Alli*

# HOMOSEXUALITY

Both erotic attraction and sexual behavior between members of the same sex have always been recognized phenomena in Islamic societies, but attitudes toward them have been complex, severe religious and legal sanctions against the latter coexisting with accommodating and at times indeed celebratory expressions of the former.

Religious discourse has mostly focused on sexual acts, which are unambiguously condemned. The Qur'an refers explicitly to male-male sexual relations only in the context of the story of Lot, but labels the Sodomites's actions (universally understood in the later tradition as anal intercourse) an "abomination." (Female-female relations are not addressed.) Reported pronouncements by the prophet Muhammad (hadith) reinforce the interdiction on male-male sodomy, although there are no reports of his ever adjudicating an actual case of such an offense; he is also quoted as condemning cross-gender behavior for both sexes, but it is unclear to what extent this is to be understood as involving sexual relations. Several early caliphs, confronted with cases of sodomy between males, are said to have had both partners executed, by a variety of means. While taking such precedents into account, medieval jurists were unable to achieve a consensus on this issue; some legal schools prescribed capital punishment for sodomy, but others opted only for a relatively mild discretionary punishment. There was general agreement, however, that other homosexual acts (including any between females) were lesser offenses, subject only to discretionary punishment.

Whatever the legal strictures on sexual activity, the positive expression of male homoerotic sentiment in literature was accepted, and assiduously cultivated, from the late eighth century until modern times. First in Arabic, but later also in Persian, Turkish, and Urdu, love poetry (by men) about boys more than competed with that about women, it overwhelmed it. Anecdotal literature reinforces this impression of general societal acceptance of the public celebration of male-male love (which hostile Western caricatures of Islamic societies in medieval and early modern times simply exaggerate). As in other premodern societies, such love was generally understood as an asymmetrical relationship, between an adult male (the lover) and an adolescent boy (the beloved), clearly paralleling the power differential between men and women in heterosexual relationships; rather than a single category of "homosexuals," there were two, or rather three: "active" male-male lovers, "passive" adolescent beloveds, and a third, pathological and despised, category of adult males who sought out the passive role. Female-female relationships (never a subject for literary celebration) were less role-dominated, at least in earlier times; by the late Middle Ages a "butch-femme" paradigm seems to have asserted itself for them as well.

With the impact of Western colonialism in the late nineteenth century, these patterns (specifically, accepted "active" homoeroticism, subject to the same strictures on behavior as obtained with regard to extramarital heterosexual relations) began to change in most Islamic societies. The Western construction of the "homosexual"—often, however, misinterpreted as representing only the traditional pathological adult "passive"—has imposed itself with increasing force. Legal sanctions on homosexuality in various Islamic countries today vary considerably, as does their degree of dependence on traditional pronouncements of Islamic law. Societal attitudes have become more negative, and increasingly dominated by the new, imported paradigm of what "homosexuality" is (for both males and females); but recent liberalizing shifts in attitude in the West are also having their effect, and the entire subject is currently a nexus of considerable conflict.

*See also* **Eunuchs; Gender.**

## BIBLIOGRAPHY

Murray, Stephen O., and Roscoe, Will, eds. *Islamic Homosexualities: Culture, History, and Literature.* New York: New York University Press, 1997.

Rowson, Everett K. "The Categorization of Gender and Sexual Irregularity in Medieval Arabic Vice Lists." In *Body Guards: The Cultural Politics of Gender Ambiguity.* Edited by Julia Epstein and Kristina Straub. New York and London: Routledge, 1991.

Schmitt, Arno, and Sofer, Jehoeda, eds. *Sexuality and Eroticism among Males in Moslem Societies.* New York: Harrington Park Press, 1992.

*Everett K. Rowson*

## HOSAYNIYYA

*Hosayniyya* is a rather recent name for public buildings in Iran, Iraq and Lebanon that are used by the Shi'a for mourning ceremonies, especially during the months of Muharam and Safar (the first two months in the Muslim calender) wherein the martyrdom of Imam Husayn b. 'Ali, grandson of the Prophet, is mourned. Their counterparts in India and Pakistan are called *imambara* or *'azakhana*, and in some places, *'ashurkhana, dargah,* and *'alawi.* Although mourning ceremonies have been common since the Buwayhid era, no definite date can be set for the emergence of the name *hosayniyya* before the last part of eighteenth century. Until that time these ceremonies were held in royal palatial halls, spacious houses, in streets, and open spaces. Apparently, from the second half of the Safavid era the *tekkeyyeh* and *khaneqa* (also *khanakha*), buildings that originally served as establishments of the dervishes, were gradually transformed into *hosayniyyas*, often assuming this name from the latter part of the Zand and

early Qajar periods onward. Starting in the mid-1950s, buildings serving similar religious purposes have been named after other imams and Shi'ite saints. For instance, in 1996 there were 1358 *hosayniyya,* 148 *tekkiyeh,* 34 *fatimiyya,* 32 *mahdiyya,* and 57 *zainabiyya* in the Khorasan province. Scores of such buildings built during the last few decades of the twentieth century in the city of Mashhad bear such names as *sajjadiyya, baqiriyya, sadiqiyya, kazimiyya, radawiyya, jawwadiyya, naqawiyya, 'askariyya, mahdiyya, fatimiyya, nargisiyya,* and *zaynabiyya.*

Apparently, the religious influence of the Safavid era (1501–1736) led to the building of the *ashurkhana*s of the Deccan during the reign of the Shi'ite Qutb-shahi dynasty, and Mir Muhammad Mu'min Astarabadi (d. 1625), an eminent religious and political figure, is known to have built several of them in and around the city of Hyderabad, establishing a tradition that later spread to the north and other parts of India. The magnificent *imambara* of Asaf ad-Dawlah at Lucknow is perhaps the most impressive of this kind of structures ever built.

*See also* **Rawza-Khani; Ta'ziya (Ta'ziye).**

*Rasool Ja'fariyan*

## HOSPITALITY AND ISLAM

Generous hospitality extended to family, friends, and strangers is one of the best-known feature of Muslim societies, whether pastoral, rural, or urban. This tradition of hospitality goes back to ancient times in the Middle East, an arid region where trade early became more important than in other regions and where the need for travelers to rely on the kindness of strangers was correspondingly greater. In Arabia, the pre-Islamic chieftain Hatim al-Ta'i represents the ideal generous host, and has remained a symbol of exuberant hospitality to this day.

For Muslims, the ideal of hospitality derives first from the Qur'an itself, which requires that hospitality or charity be offered to travelers: "It is righteous to believe in God; [and] to spend of your substance, out of love for Him. For your kin, for the needy, for the wayfarer, for those who ask," (2:177; 2:215; 4:36; 8:41; 9:60; 17:26; 30:38; 59:7) and to the poor (5:89; 22:28, 36; 58:4; 74:44; 76:8–9; 90:14–18, 93:10; 107:3). The Qur'an also mentions rules relating to the hospitality of relatives and friends (24:61), and portrays the Prophet Abraham as offering hospitality to the visiting angels by slaughtering a calf (11:69–70; 51:24–27). Refusing to offer hospitality is reproved (18:77), as is treating guests insultingly or threatening them (11:77; 15:68). Indeed, such behavior is considered a great shame.

The prophet Muhammad's own well-attested hospitality included reluctance to ask guests who had stayed too long to leave, even though he was the head of state at Medina (33:53), and he let multitudes of envoys, guests, and the poor there enjoy hospitality in the mosque, which was also the courtyard of his house. More directly, in many extra-Qur'anic traditions the Prophet insisted that generosity be shown to guests, travelers, and strangers. As a result, Muslim law recognized offering guests three days' hospitality as the Prophet's way (sunna).

*Khalid Yahya Blankinship*

# HUKUMA AL-ISLAMIYYA, AL- (ISLAMIC GOVERNMENT)

While continuing to refer to classical doctrines of the caliphate, contemporary Sunni concepts of the Islamic state, or Islamic order (*al-nizam al-islami*), have moved well beyond classical precedents to include elements of what is today considered to constitute "good governance": the rule of law, participation, accountability, and the independence of the judiciary, without abandoning certain specifically Islamic notions such as "Sovereignty lies with God, who has defined the fundamental moral and legal code regulating all human activity" (*shari'a*). Government and society derive their legitimacy from "applying" the *shari'a*. In their capacity as God's representatives or trustees on earth (sing. *khalifa*), men and women are equal (though within specific domains, their rights and duties are not identical). The ruler (caliph, imam, or president) derives his authority from the community of believers, who elect him and are bound to obey him as long as he stays within the limits of God's law. Consultation (*shura*) in all public affairs is obligatory, albeit not necessarily binding on the ruler. He is accountable before God and the community (though the instruments of sanction, including his removal from office, remain ill defined). Some authors further include universal suffrage, majority rule, and the separation of powers as basic elements of Islamic government in the modern age.

*See also* **Political Islam.**

## BIBLIOGRAPHY

Krämer, Gudrun. "Visions of an Islamic Republic. Good Governance According to the Islamists." In *The Islamic World and the West.* Edited by Kai Hafez. Leiden: Brill, 2000.

*Gudrun Krämer*

# HUMAN RIGHTS

Contemporary discourses concerning human rights (*huquq al-insan*) and Islam, or rather their compatibility or incompatibility, are manifold and controversial, both in the Near and Middle East and in the West. In the nineteenth century, concepts such as political rights, public liberties, constitutionalism and related issues, found their way into the Muslim world through thinkers such as the Egyptian scholar Rifa'a Rafi' al-Tahtawi (1807–1871) and the Persian diplomat Miza Malkom Khan (1833–1908). In the Ottoman Empire, significant reforms were initiated with the *hatt-i serif* (1839; noble rescript of Sultan 'Abdulmejid) and the *hatt-i humayun* (1856; imperial rescript, reaffirming the *hatt-i serif*) guaranteeing security of life, honor, and property, and a fair and public trial for individuals, and civil equality for all Ottoman subjects.

The United Nation's Charter of Human Rights of 10 December 1948 was signed by the Muslim countries. In 1990 the Organization of the Islamic Conference (OIC, founded in 1973), which is composed of all the Muslim countries, submitted the Cairo Declaration of Human Rights in Islam, in an attempt to identify specific Islamic features of human rights in combination with elements of international law. The Cairo Declaration has not been ratified; nevertheless it is referred to as a meaningful contribution to the discourse on human rights and Islam. Although the signatories emphasized in the OIC preamble their "commitment to the UN Charter and fundamental human rights," the document of 1990 reveals differences and even conflicts with international human rights theory, since the latter does not accept that religious concepts are of overriding importance.

Article 24 of the Cairo Declaration subordinates all rights and freedoms to *shari'a* (Islamic law), without clarifying the limits or questioning the area of conflict between civil and political rights, enacted in the constitution and international conventions on human rights, and the obligations that arise according to *shari'a*. The sensitive points lay in the area of equality, particularly gender equality, as well as in the fields of art and science. Some examples may illustrate the dilemma: Under *shari'a*, all human beings, men and women, Muslims and non-Muslims, are equal in terms of dignity, but not in terms of rights. For instance, Muslim women and non-Muslims are not equal with Muslim men regarding family law and the law of inheritance. Although non-Muslim citizens enjoy the same rights and obligations as Muslim citizens, they are excluded from certain positions. Freedom of expression has to comply with the principles of *shari'a*, that is, it must conform to the prevailing interpretation of Islam. Furthermore, the right of religious freedom is extremely limited for Muslims, since apostasy entails numerous civil law sanctions— such as the loss of the entitlement to inherit or the loss of the right to remain married to a Muslim partner—and even carries the possibility of a death sentence. It should be mentioned that numerous human rights organizations and activists in the Muslim world (for example, in Tunisia, Morocco and Algeria) have called for a revision of the Cairo Declaration in order to bring it into line with the fundamental principles of the UN Declaration.

The actual situation in Muslim countries reflects the complex social and political balance of power, inclusive of the monopoly of definition and interpretation, rather than the relation between Islam and human rights. This explains the existing gap between ideals and practice. Still, contemporary interpretations and applications of the *shariʿa*, especially under prevailing culturally or socially rooted inequalities and under authoritarian regimes, serve as a "legal" basis for violations of human rights. In these cases Islam is used to legitimize undemocratic measures. Pakistan provides one of the most striking examples because tribal (also patriarchal) traditions and customs, a gradual Islamization of the legal system, and a lack of adequate state protection there have resulted in the violation of several fundamental principles of human rights, such as freedom of religion, protection of minorities, and women's rights or gender equality. Muslim Shiʿite communities and members of the Ahmadiyya, who are considered to be heretical, and non-Muslim (Christians) minorities suffer severe persecutions and violence. Discriminatory practices against women, including honor killings, abuse, rape, institutionalized gender bias, among others, are widespread and rarely prosecuted.

The case of the Egyptian scholar Abu Zayd provides but one example of how the limits set by the principles of *shariʿa* are defended by orthodoxy. Abu Zayd was accused of apostasy in 1993 because of his writings. After having taken his case to Egypt's final court of appeal, he was condemned to divorce in 1996. Further, despite concepts in legal thought providing for the protection of minorities in Muslim societies, the actual situation contrasts sharply with existing theoretical ideals. Non-Muslim critics and intellectuals focus on the apparent contradiction between the United Nation's Declaration of Human Rights and the principles of *shariʿa*. On the one hand, civil and political rights are accorded to any citizen in Muslim countries by the constitution and the UN Charter but, on the other hand, the necessity of conformity with the norms and prescriptions of *shariʿa* are religiously legitimized. However, this discourse rarely includes the intense and diverse debates that are going on simultaneously within the Muslim world regarding the limits and possibilities of the adoption of human rights within the Islamic context.

The contemporary voices are complex and diverse, but an inquiry into two positions should be ample to give an idea of the wide range of interpretations and readings with regard to human rights within the Muslim world. Secular positions, such as that of the Egyptian scholar ʿAli ʿAbd al-Raziq (1888–1966), argue that the Qurʾan does not prescribe any particular form of government, and therefore a system wherein religion and politics are separated is not necessarily un-Islamic. Many scholars and intellectuals are in favor of ʿAbd al-Raziq's model, for example, the Egyptian jurist Muhammad Saʿid al-ʿAshmawi and the Syrian sociologist Burhan Ghaliyun. Proponents of this position state that Islam implies

individual responsibility before God, and in this sense provides a moral and ethical basis for a society, but this does not imply any specific form of political system.

Some modernists even go further in arguing the secularists' thesis. Like the secularists, they hold that Islam does not impose political or legal prescriptions, and add that Islam does not resolve the problems concerning the few and definitive legal regulations specified in the Qurʾan and in the tradition. For Islam to do so, they argue, would call into question the Qurʾan's authenticity as the eternally valid word of God. In order to avoid this, modernists such as the Syrian Muhammad Shahrur argue that although the Qurʾan is the last revelation and thus the last truth, this does not mean that there is only one interpretation. To the contrary, the Qurʾan is open for different approaches and readings. Shahrur's ideas elicit a great many positive responses within the Arab world. He is but one example of a scholar who pleads for an interpretation of Islam supportive of human rights. He, and scholars like him, challenge the prevailing Western perspective on Islam, while revealing that it is not Islam as such that is (or is not) compatible with human rights, but rather that certain interpretations of Islam are at the root of the issue.

*See also* **Ethics and Social Issues; Gender; Law; Organization of the Islamic Conference; Secularism, Islamic; Shariʿa.**

## BIBLIOGRAPHY

An-Naiʿim, Abdullahi Ahmed. *Toward an Islamic Reformation: Civil, Human Rights, and International Law.* Syracuse, N.Y.: Syracuse University Press, 1990.

ʿAshmawi, Muhammad Saʿid al-. "Shariʿa: The Codification of Islamic Law." In *Liberal Islam. A Sourcebook.* Edited by Charles Kurzman. New York and Oxford, U.K.: Oxford University Press, 1998.

Mayer, Ann. *Islam and Human Rights: Traditions and Politics.* Boulder, Colo.: Westview Press, 1991.

*Ursula Günther*

# HUMOR

There is no classical Muslim definition of humor, but professor Franz Rosenthal offers one that attempts to be universally inclusive. In his *Humor in Early Islam*, Rosenthal suggests that the hallmark of humor is a "certain freedom from conventional motions" that, in ordinary circumstances, constrain us all. Thus any "deviation" from what is expected may cause laughter even if it happens to be partially tragic.

### Humor in Early Islam

Humor is a modality for releasing tension. Muslims, like all other peoples, have their share of jokes, anecdotes, and other "deviations from ordinary reality," to use one of Rosenthal's phrases. While in early Islam there was a tendency to lean toward seriousness because of the need to maintain *hilm* (dignified and civil behavior, propriety), there was considerable divergence from this austere stance. In the first century of Islam, for example, there were several schools of humorists, storytellers, and professional entertainers. These schools trained individuals in the art of devising as well as relating humorous anecdotes (*nawadir*, sing. *nadira*), along with teaching the skills of vocal and instrumental music. While there was religious objection to these arts, the justification for humor in early Islam was also based on religious arguments. The Qur'an does not forbid laughter as it is God "who grants laughter and tears" (53:43). In fact, there are many instances of humor in Muslim scripture, providing testimony to Islam's "lighter side."

Second only to the Qur'an are the traditions of the prophet Muhammad, who is said to have made frequent use of humor. There are numerous reports, found in authentic hadith collections, of the Prophet either smiling or laughing, or causing others to laugh. 'A'isha, the wife of Muhammad, reportedly said that the Prophet often smiled. She noted, however, that he never laughed in a loud manner or exposed his uvula. The following anecdote, found in *Sunan Abu Dawud*, illustrates the Prophet's humor:

> A man broke his fast during Ramadan. The Messenger of God commanded him to emancipate a slave or fast for two months, or feed sixty poor men. He said: "I cannot provide." The Apostle said: "Sit down." Thereafter, a huge basket of dates was brought to the Messenger of God. He said: "Take this and give it as *sadaqa* [charity]." He said: "O Messenger of God, there is no one poorer than I." The Messenger of God thereupon laughed so that his canine teeth became visible and said: "Eat it yourself."(Hasan 1984., hadith 2386)

The eleventh-century Muslim author al-Husri refers to the prophet Muhammad's liking of humor, saying he possessed a rather pleasant personality and was not averse to a decent joke. He even reports that the Prophet played practical jokes. For instance, he reports that the Prophet told an elderly woman that old women will not enter Paradise, causing her great distress. The Prophet then cited the Qur'an, which promises that she will enter Paradise as a young woman. Other companions of the Prophet are also reported to have approved of humor. For example, Ibn al-Jawzi refers to Imam 'Ali as having said: "Whoever possesses a humorous element is cured of vanity and self-pride."

### Classical Attitudes Toward Humor
In traditional Muslim religious discourse, one finds a general reproach for laughter and joking (*al-hazl*) within a religious context. A widely circulated hadith in support of this stance is taken from *Sahih al-Bukhari*, which quotes the Prophet as saying: "By God, if you knew what I know you would weep much and laugh little." At the same time numerous scholars in early Islam and continuing on into the Middle Ages found laughter and joking to be of extreme importance to their literary enterprise. The most notable reference work listing collections of humor stories comes from Ibn Nadim's *Kitab al-fihrist*, a bibliographic work from the tenth century.

Among the works of notable Muslim scholars and mystics, who have either mentioned amusing anecdotes in their otherwise serious scholarly (*adab*) works, or have devoted entire works to the subject of humor, al-Jahiz's (d. 868) *Kitab al-bukhala'* (Book of misers) stands out. There are many others, including *'Uyun al-akhbar* by Ibn Qutaybah (d. 889), *al-'Iqd al-farid* by Ibn 'Abd Rabbih (860–940), *al-Basa'ir wa'l-dhakha'ir* by al-Tawhidi (d. 1010). In al-Jahiz's style of writing, serious subjects are presented together with jokes and amusing stories, and he quotes the Qur'an in associating laughter with life, stating that while laughter is not prohibited, it must be carried out in moderation.

Other scholars, such as al-Husri al-Qayrawani (d. 1022) in his *Jam' al-Jawahir fi al-Mulah wal-Nawadir*, followed al-Jahiz in inserting amusing stories in their *adab* works. Similarly, many Shi'ite scholars, such as Baha al-Din al-'Amili (d. 1621) and Ni'mat Allah al-Jaza'iri (d. 1701), argued for and made use of anecdotal humor in their writings, often citing hadith examples specific to Shi'ism.

There is ample evidence that numerous collections of such anecdotes (*nawadir*) existed in early centuries of Islam. Some collections have survived, but many disappeared during the Middle Ages due to criticism of witticism from orthodox circles. It is therefore to be noted that jocularity and laughter was not just a literary issue but also a moral and a religious one for many Muslim authors. Despite religious stiffness, however, a rich heritage of Arab and Islamic humor exists today by way of folklore. Contemporary Islamic and Sufi studies have also helped revive the humorous in conjunction with learning.

### Humor Characters in Islamic Literature
In his 1927 essay on humor in Arabic literature, Margoliouth reports that in early Islam there were not only the professional entertainers and court-jesters (sing. *maskhara*) whose job was to keep the ruler entertained, but even some cities had their known jesters and entertainers. One such personage was Ghadiri of Medina, who earned his living by telling amusing stories to his rich patrons and who was later taken over by Ash'ab. The figure of Ash'ab, called "the greedy," was clearly known for his comic poetry and humorous remarks in a variety of circumstances, and his jokes remained popular well into the Abbasid period. In one of the many Ash'ab anecdotes, the greedy one is told:

> "If you would transmit traditions [*ahadith*, sayings of the Prophet] and give up your jokes, it would be more becoming of you." Ash'ab replied: "Indeed, I have

heard traditions and transmitted them." Asked to tell a tradition, he said: "I was told by Nafiʿ on the authority of Ibn ʿUmar that the Messenger of God said: 'A man in whom there are found two qualities belongs to God's chosen friends.'" When asked what the two qualities were, Ashʿab replied: "Nafiʿ had forgotten one, and I have forgotten the other." (Rosenthal 1956, p. 117)

Another personage who came to be famous in many Islamic societies and who has survived till the present is Juha, also variously called Joha, Hoca, Zha, and many other names. Juha is seen as a strange character who combines wit and simplicity in his actions. He appears to be foolish and yet his foolishness contains a deeper wisdom. Juha has a reputation for escaping trouble, and his silly actions are a sign of foresight. For instance, when Juha was appointed governor by Timur, the emperor, he wrote his accounts to be submitted to the emperor on thin pieces of bread. This seemingly foolish act is, in fact, quite wise, because he knew that Timur, when angered by his previous governor, had forced that unfortunate man to eat his account books. There were other characters, such as Abu Nuwas and Bahlul, who had similar reputations.

By the eleventh century Juha was accepted as a historical entity, but his precise name and lineage were still a matter of much confusion. In the late Middle Ages, Juha appears in Turkish writings as Nasreddin Hoca (in Arabic, Nasr al-Din Khwaja, the name signifies "a learned man"). The name of Hoca seems to have replaced Juha in popular folklore, and in later Islamic writings they are seen as the same person with two different names. Among Persian speaking peoples, he became known as Mulla Nasr al-Din (or Nasrudin). In the seventeenth century, Turkish folklore absorbed vast number of anecdotes from earlier centuries in the name of Hoca, even though these stories existed in some form before the development of the latter figure.

This jester is still known by various names. As Nasrudin or Nasreddin, he has over twelve hundred stories attached to his name. In Egypt they know him as Juha, in Turkey and Persian-speaking countries he is widely known as either Hoca or Nasreddin; in other regions, including Indonesia, his jokes are told in the name of Abu Nuwas. He thus represents a vast number of characters that have been developed over the centuries by professional humorists and other religious and *adab* writers, and can be found in some form in every Muslim culture. He has gained considerable popularity in many non-Muslim countries.

Humor and wit are also found in poetry, which is a developed art form in Islamic civilization and finds expression in Arabic, Persian, and other Islamic languages, such as Urdu. The poetic humorists especially flourished during the Abbasid period. They were called *shuʿaraʾ al-mujjan*, and included court poets such as Abu Dulama, who used to entertain by

way of bringing insults on himself. A description of Abu Dulama's style of entertainment is found in al-Husri's *Jamʿ al-jawahir*:

Let it be known to you, Abu Dulama

You neither belong to a noble people,

nor do you have any nobility in you.

When you put on the turban, you appear like a monkey,

And when you put off the turban, you look like a swine.

You have combined in yourself both ugliness and meanness,

And meanness is always followed by ugliness.

If you happen to have obtained the worldly pleasure,

Don't shout, for the Day of Judgement is quite near at hand.

(Ali, 1998, p. 57)

## Contemporary Humor

Although modern humorous literature may properly be shelved under folklore, contemporary Sufi writers have argued that the use of humor has always been essential in conveying the spiritual wisdom of the sages. Idries Shah, for example, has related many stories featuring the character of Mulla Nasrudin. In his work on the Sufi use of humor, *Special Illumination*, Shah argues that humor endures because it has the power to teach while it amuses:

Jokes are structures, and in their Sufic usage they may fulfill many different functions. Just as we may get the humor nutrient out of a joke, we can also get several dimensions out of it on various occasions: there is no standard meaning of a joke. Different people will see different contents of it; and pointing out some of its possible usages will not, if we are used to this method, rob it of its efficacy. . . .The joke, like the non-humorous teaching-story, thus presents us with a choice instrument of illustration and action. (Shah 1977, p. 11)

Humor is also a medium for expressing social and political criticism. Often it can present a subject which is otherwise prohibited by political or religious authorities. In her article "Humor: The Two-Edged Sword," Afaf Lutfi al-Sayyid Marsot offers one example of political humor from Egypt.

When Nasser died, the question of where to bury him arose during a cabinet meeting. One minister said, "Let us bury him in the tomb of the Unknown Soldier." Another objected, saying, "You can't bury a colonel with a common soldier." A third suggested that he be buried in one of the tombs of the Mamluk sultans. "No! No!" was the objection. "You can't bury the Rais with a slave." Finally running out of burial sites, someone suggested Jerusalem. Whereupon, the rest of the cabinet rose in horror and said, "Never! The last time they buried someone there, he came back after three days!" (p. 263)

During the Gulf War in the early 1990s, many Palestinians came up with their own jokes to escape the otherwise horrible experiences of the war and its aftermath. One such joke is related by Sharif Kanaana in his article "Palestinian Humor during the Gulf War":

Shortly after the Iraqi occupation of Kuwait, Saddam's little daughter had a birthday. Saddam asked her, "What would you like me to get you for your birthday?" She replied, "Get me Qatar." (Kanaana 1995, p. 70)

## BIBLIOGRAPHY

Ali, Abdul. "Humour Literature: An Arab-Islamic Legacy." *Hamdard Islamicus* 21 (1998): 47–59.

Hasan, Ahmed, trans. *Sunan Abu Dawud*. Lahore: Sh. M. Ashraf, 1984.

Kanaana, Sharif. "Palestinian Humor During the Gulf War." *Journal of Folklore Research* 32, no. 1 (1995): 65–75.

Margoliouth, D. S. "Wit and Humour in Arabic Literature." In *Arabic Literature and Thought*. Edited by Mohamed Taher. New Delhi: Anmol Publications, 1997.

Marsot, Afaf Lutfi al-Sayyid. "Humor: The Two-Edged Sword." In *Everyday Life in the Muslim Middle East*. Edited by Donna Lee Bowen and Evelyn A. Early. Bloomington and Indianapolis: Indiana University Press, 1993.

Marzolph, Ulrich. "Timur's Humorous Antagonist, Nasreddin Hoca." *Oriente Moderno* 15, no. 76 (1996–1997): 485–498.

Pellat, Ch. "Seriousness and Humour in Early Islam." Islamic Studies 2 (1963): 353–362.

Rosenthal, Franz. *Humor in Early Islam*. Leiden: E. J. Brill, 1956.

Shah, Idries. *Special Illumination: The Sufi Use of Humour*. London: The Octagon Press, 1977.

*Irfan A. Omar*

# HUSAYN (603–661)

Husayn ibn 'Ali ibn Abi Talib, grandson of the prophet Muhammad, the third Shi'ite imam, was born according to Sunnis on 6 Ramadan, according to Shi'a, on 3 Sha'ban. He was martyred at Karbala at noon on Friday the tenth ('Ashura') of Muharram at the age of fifty-eight in the year 680 C.E. For Shi'a, Husayn's martyrdom is the paradigmatic story of

existential tragedy, of injustice in this world triumphing over justice, of the duty a true Muslim has to sacrifice oneself, to witness for truth and justice as Husayn did, and to shock others into returning to the cause of Islamic social justice, a theme that has come again to political importance in the rhetoric of Iran's Islamic Revolution of 1977 through 1979, but also in Iraq in the aftermath of the overthrow of Saddam Husayn in 2003.

## The Importance of the Difference between Sunni and Shi'a Interpretations

What is at issue in the different understandings of Sunni and Shi'a is not mere history, but the abstractions from history that compose the mythos or symbolic structure of religious belief. The account of early Islam by Western historians, as well as the Sunni account, is a story of alliances among Bedouin tribes that controlled the trade between the three great agrarian empires of Byzantium, the Sassanians, and Abyssinia. The second caliph, 'Umar, was the architect of expanding the polity that Muhammad had initiated. He nominated Abu Bakr to succeed Muhammad, then 'Umar became the second caliph. Conquest proceeded quickly across the Fertile Crescent, Egypt, and Iran. The state was based on the separation of the Arab military garrisons from the conquered populations. 'Umar's governor in Syria, Mu'awiya, commanded from Damascus, but elsewhere garrison towns were established: Kufa near Ctesiphon, Basra on the Gulf, Fustat at the head of the Nile delta. A register of Muslims was established so that these garrisons could be paid from the booty of war and revenue from lands conquered. As expansion slowed, this system caused problems under the third caliph, 'Uthman, who reacted by relying increasingly on his own clansmen, the Umayyads. This provoked further complaints. In an attempt at symbolic unity, 'Uthman imposed a standardized Qur'an; this also led to resentment. 'Ali became a center of opposition to these policies. 'Uthman was assassinated in 656, and 'Ali was proclaimed the fourth caliph in an attempt to stabilize the state by using his religious position as imam to strengthen the secular position of amir al-mu'minin. But it did not work: he was assassinated, Mu'awiya became caliph, and he appointed his son, Yazid, to succeed. The Hejaz refused to recognize Yazid, and Kufa invited Husayn to lead a revolt. It failed, ending with Husayn's death at Karbala.

This history can be followed in the Shi'ite version but with quite different nuances, emphases, and meanings: Leadership should have passed from Muhammad to 'Ali, his cousin and son-in-law, whom the Prophet had adopted as a boy even before Muhammad's first marriage. According to Sunnis succession was elective, and Abu Bakr, the father-in-law of Muhammad's youngest wife, was legitimately elected. But according to Shi'a this was an usurpation, not just of Muhammad's designation but of the special access to the infallible interpretation of the Qur'an that passes via the lineage of the twelve imams from 'Ali to Hasan and Husayn. 'Ali withdrew into quiet teaching, and also compiled an authoritative edition of the Qurʾan (having been one of the recorders of Muhammad's recitations of revelation), allowing the first three caliphs to show by their actions and legal decisions how imperfect and unfit they were to lead. The story of ʿAli's martyrdom while praying in Kufa on the 19 Ramadan 661 C.E. provides Shiʿa with a prologue to the central maryrdom of Husayn: ʿAli's foreknowledge of his death, his generosity toward his assassin, his courage in battle, his knowledge of Islamic law, his humility as an officeholder, and his wisdom as a judge. These are celebrated by Shiʿa. Hasan, ʿAli's eldest son, who was too weak to wrest the leadership from Muʾawiya, was poisoned, and Muʾawiya declared his own son, Yazid, his successor.

### Husayn's Martydom at Karbala

Husayn, ʿAli's second son, refused to swear allegience. It is alleged by Shiʿa that Yazid sent assassins to mingle with pilgrims at the hajj. To avoid bloodshed during the hajj, Husayn cut short his pilgrimage. Foreseeing his martyrdom, he released his followers from any obligation to follow, and with his family and seventy-two men, he went toward Kufa. Yazid had co-opted the Kufans. Husayn's forces, who were trapped in the desert at Karbala, were denied access to water (to the Euphrates), and on the tenth of Muharram all but two of Husayn's men were slain, his body was desecrated, and the women were taken prisoner. According to a Shiʿite legend Husayn's head was taken to Damascus, where the caliph Yazid beat it with sticks in a vain attempt to keep it from reciting the Qurʾan. The details of the battle of Karbala form the key imagery of passion plays (taʿziyeh, shabih) and preachments (rawzehs).

The details heighten the significance of Yazid's tyranny and desecration of the sacred and proper order of life and Islam. Not only had Yazid usurped the caliphate and was using that office tyrannically, but he had attempted to desecrate the hajj, had desecrated the time of communal prayer (Friday noon), and had destroyed one by one the elements of civilized life symbolized most powerfully by the denial of water. Three sons of Husayn were slain: the infant ʿAli Asghar, the five-year-old Jaʾfar, and the twenty-five-year-old ʿAli Akbar. Destruction of family, community, government, and humanity are all themes of the Karbala story, retold and relived in rawzehs (a form of preaching that uses the Karbala story to frame the topic of the sermon), taziyehs or shabihs (passion plays), dasteh or matam (lines of men chanting, beating their chests, and flagellating their foreheads and backs with knives), and the carrying in processions of naqls (large wooden structures representing Husayn's bier that requires scores of men to carry; called taʿziyehs in India and Trinidad, there in the shape of the Taj Mahal).

### The Karbala Paradigm

For Sunnis, the tenth of Muharram is merely a day of voluntary fasting that has to do, not with Husayn, but with Muhammad. Sunnis focus their symbolic structure on Muhammad, while Shiʿa, also honoring the details of Muhammad's life, focus attention on ʿAli, Husayn, the Five Pure Souls of the Family of the Prophet, and the twelve imams. Key calendrical events differ: For Shiʿa, Husayn's birthday is not the 6 Ramadan, nor ʿAli's 22 Ramadan, as they are for Sunnis, and all such happy events are in other months the better to focus on the martyrdom of ʿAli during Ramadan. Sunnis deny that Hasan was poisoned: He died of consumption; Sunnis say that Abu Bakr, not ʿAli, was the first man (after Muhammad's wife Khadija) to accept the call to Islam.

Such systematic differences help signal the Shiʿite drama of faith: Believers are witnesses (shuhada) through their acts of worship (ʿibada) to the metaphysical reality that is hidden (ghaʾib). Shuhada means both martyrs and witnesses. Husayn, knowing he would die, went to Karbala to witness the truth, knowing that his death would make him an enduring, immortal witness, whose example would be a guide for others. Ghaʿib refers to a series of inner truths: a God who is not visible, a twelfth imam who is in occultation, a personal inner faith, and the special light (nur) that created Muhammad, ʿAli, Fatima, Hasan, and Husayn, the Five Pure Souls of the Family of the Prophet (33:33), and whose direct connection with the divine passes down through the line of the imams. The nur doctrine parallels the divine royal farr of Persian epic tradition. There is a story that Bibi Shahbanu, the daughter of the last Sassanian king, married Husayn so there is a connection between Persian royalty and the imams. The nur doctrine says that all 124,000 prophets as well as the imams were created from a ray of divine light, often making for a divine birth, as was the case with Husayn. Fatima emerged from a stream pregnant, the pregnancy lasted only six months, and her womb glowed with incandescent light.

There are thus three parts to the notion of the Karbala paradigm as encoding for the Shiʿa story of Husayn: (1) a story expandable to be all-inclusive of history, cosmology, and life's problems; (2) a background contrast (of Sunni conceptions, but also other religions) against which the story is given heightened perceptual value; and (3) ritual or physical drama to embody the story and maintain high levels of emotional investment: rawzeh, shabih, taʿziyeh, data, and matam.

Husayn is an intercessor at Judgment Day, and with various interpretive sophistication, one is induced by the pietistic and didactic exercise of the rawzeh to weep for Husayn in an act of repentance so that he may intercede and judge one's sins more lightly and with compassion. Some rawzeh-khwans (preachers) elicit tears for the injustice of the world and the misfortunes that befell Husayn and Shiʿa; others stress Husayn as an example of bravery and courage in the fight for freedom rather than as a victim. Ayatollah Ruhollah Khomeini at the time of the Iranian revolution stressed that one should not cry for Husayn, but one should march with the same determination that he showed to fight

Muharram is a Muslim festival commemorating the death of the martyr Imam Husayn, Muhammad's grandson and the third Shi'ite imam (pictured here with Nawab of Nurshidabad in prayer). Sunni and Shi'ite Muslims conflict in their versions of Husayn's story. THE ART ARCHIVE/ BRITISH LIBRARY

for justice against all odds. Since martyrs are said to go to heaven, one need not mourn their deaths as one does the deaths of ordinary people. During the Iranian revolution young men wore white shrouds to symbolize their willingness to die, and wall graffiti proclaimed that those who died did the work of Husayn, those who fought did the work of Zaynab (she kept the survivors of Karbala together and maintained the message of Husayn until the fourth imam had recovered and could assume leadership), and those who did not fight did the work of Yazid.

The dramatic performances of the events of the first ten days of Muharram at Karbala (the passion plays, *shabih*, *ta'ziyeh*, and *rawzeh*s) are occasions when the story can be expanded to stories of the earlier prophets who had fore-knowledge of the martyrdom of Husayn and were told that their own sufferings were minor in comparison. Thus, Adam, when first put on Earth, wandered across the future site of the battle of Karbala and cut his toe, a prefiguration, God told him, of the more serious blood that would be shed there by Husayn. The infant Isma'il suffered thirst but found water;

Husayn and his children suffered a greater thirst and were denied water. God substituted a ram for Isma'il, but Husayn was in fact slain.

In politically charged times—as in the years before the 1977–1979 Islamic revolution in Iran—the Karbala paradigm could be a vehicle for political mobilization. The shah was identified with the caliph Yazid (who sent his army to defeat Husayn) and injustice, while Ayatollah Ruhollah Khomeini, who would lead the revolution, was identified with Husayn and with the forces of justice. Preachers could speak against Yazid and be understood to be attacking the shah. In the Persian Gulf and the Subcontinent (Lucknow, Karachi), the processions of 'Ashura', the tenth of Muharram—when the bier of Husayn (*ta'ziyeh*s in India, *nagl*s in Iran) is carried through the streets along with chanting ("Husayn! Husayn!") and breast-beating groups of men (*dasteh*) sometimes also beating their backs with chains and slashing their foreheads with knives—in the nineteenth and twentieth centuries often caused riots between Sunnis and Shi'a. Under Khomeini, conflict with Saudi Arabia was stirred up by invoking the hajj in the Husayn story, and using the hajj as a site for organizing and spreading the message of the revolution; in the war with Iraq, Iran utilized slogans about Karbala and a series of military operations were code-named Karbala.

In less politically charged times, as well, the emotional work of the passion plays, processions, and *rawzehs* is one of instilling stoicism and determination to fight for justice even against the overwhelming odds of a corrupt world. After the ousting of Saddam Husayn from power in Iraq in 2003, on the fortieth day after the tenth ('Asura') of Muharram, hundreds of thousands of Shi'a joyfully joined processions to Karbala (a practice forbidden under Saddam Husayn) with many *dastehs* of chanting men, head slashing and flagellation with chains.

*See also* **Imamate; Martyrdom; Shi'a: Early; Shi'a: Imami (Twelver); Succession.**

## BIBLIOGRAPHY

Fischer, Michael M. J. "Shi'ite Islam: The Karbala Paradigm and the Family of the Prophet." In *Iran: From Religious Dispute to Revolution*, 2d ed. Madison: University of Wisconsin Press, 2003.

Lassy, Ivar. *The Muharram Mysteries Among the Azarbeijan Turks of Caucasia.* Hesingfors, Finland: Lilius and Hertzberg, 1916.

Shaban, M. *The Abbasid Revolution.* Cambridge, Mass.: Cambridge University Press, 1970.

Strothman, R. "Shi'a." In *Shorter Encyclopedia of Islam.* Edited by H. A. R. Gibb and J. H. Kramers. Ithaca, N.Y.: Cornell University Press.

*Michael M. J. Fischer*

## HUSAYNI, HAJJ AMIN AL- (1895–1974)

Amin al-Husayni was both the religious and preeminent political leader of the Palestinians during British rule in Palestine (1917–1948). Born in Jerusalem to a patrician family, he studied briefly at al-Azhar University.

The British appointed him mufti (jurist who gives legal decisions, or *fatawa*) of Jerusalem in 1921, and President of the Supreme Muslim Council in 1922. Fearing Zionism's consequence on his people, he helped galvanize the Palestinians and the Arab and Islamic world against the Zionist program in Palestine. To emphasize the centrality of Jerusalem to Muslims, he renovated in the 1920s the Dome of the Rock, with Muslim funds, and organized two Islamic conferences in Jerusalem in 1928 and 1931.

The 1929 disturbance (Western [Wailing] Wall riots) catapulted him to political power. He cooperated with the British and attempted to change their pro-Zionist policy. But his attempts failed and he joined the Arab Revolt in 1936. When the British tried to arrest him, he fled to Baghdad, where he participated in an unsuccessful anti-British revolt. Al-Husayni fled to Germany and cooperated with the Nazis until 1945. He rejected the 1947 UN partition resolution, and the Palestinians, despite Arab military help, were unable to stop the establishment of Israel. Some 726,000 Palestinians fled or were expelled by Israel during the 1948 war. The Mufti spent the rest of his life as a religious leader in the Islamic world, where he had been popular since the 1930s.

## BIBLIOGRAPHY

Husayni, Amin al-. *Haq'iq 'An Qadiyyat Filastin.* 2d ed. Cairo: Dar al-Kitab al-'Arabi bi-Masr, 1957.

Mattar, Philip. *The Mufti of Jerusalem: al-Hajj Amin al-Husayni and the Palestinian National Movement.* Rev. ed. New York: Columbia University Press, 1992.

*Philip Mattar*

## HUSAYN, SADDAM *See* Ba'th Party; Modernization, Political: Administrative, Military and Judicial Reform; Nationalism: Arab; Pan-Arabism

## HUSAYN, TAHA (1889–1973)

Taha Husayn was a prominent Egyptian writer and educational reformer. Born in a village in upper Egypt, Husayn was left blind after an illness at age two. In 1902, he began studies at al-Azhar in Cairo and was quickly at odds with its traditional curriculum and teaching methods. Switching to the newly opened Cairo University, he became the first student to receive a doctorate there in 1914. He completed a second doctorate at the Sorbonne (Paris, France) in 1919. As a professor of Arabic literature at Cairo University, he quickly emerged as one of the most prolific and controversial literary figures in the Arab world. His book *Fi'l-shi'r al-jahili* (On pre-Islamic poetry), published in 1926, incurred the condemnation of religious conservatives for casting doubt on the authenticity of pre-Islamic poetry and, by extension, possibly of the Qur'an and other early religious texts. His most systematic work of social commentary is *Mustaqbal al-thaqafa fi Misr* (The future of culture in Egypt), in which he argues that Egypt was historically an integral part of the Mediterranean culture that gave birth to Western civilization. Modern Egyptians should therefore see themselves, and be seen by others, as part of Europe. Essential to this new identity is the secularizing of national life in Egypt. His three-volume autobiography, begun in 1929 as *al-Ayyam* (The days), is considered a milestone in modern Arab literature.

*See also* **Arabic Literature; Modern Thought.**

## BIBLIOGRAPHY

Husayn, Taha. *Al-Ayyam*, Vol. 1: *An Egyptian Childhood.* Translated by E. H. Paxton. London: Routledge, 1932; Vol. 2, *The Stream of Days.* Translated by Hilary Wayment. London and New York: Longmans, Green, 1948; Vol. 3, *A Passage to France.* Translated by Kenneth Cragg. Leiden: E. J. Brill, 1976.

Malti-Douglas, Fedwa. *Blindness and Autobiography: Al-Ayyam of Taha Husayn.* Princeton, N.J.: Princeton University Press, 1988.

*Sohail H. Hashmi*

# I

## ʿIBADAT

The sacred law of Islam (the *shariʿa*) distinguishes two kinds of practices: *ʿibadat* (practices concerning the relations between God and human beings, or devotional practices) and *muʿamalat* (social ethics, i.e., the part of the law that guides the relations between humans). The *ʿibadat* include the *salat* (prayer), *zakat* (alms giving), *sawm Ramadan* (fasting during the holy month of Ramadan), and the hajj (the pilgrimage to Mecca and the holy places near to this holy city, namely ʿArafat, Muzdalifa, and Mina).

Some aspects of the *ʿibadat* can be qualified as ritual and other aspects fit less easily in this category. For example, *zakat* regulations pertain to goods or wealth that are to be handed over to certain categories of persons who are entitled to it (in particular, the needy). This takes place in a nonritual context on the one hand, and a ritualized context, that of giving *zakat* (*zakat al-fitr*) on the Day of the Breaking of the Fast, on the other.

According to the *shariʿa*, the *ʿibadat* are all the individual duties that each mentally competent, mature, and healthy Muslim (male and female) is obligated to perform. The formulation of the *niyya*, the intention to perform these rituals before performing them, is of crucial importance for their validity, or, as the Prophetic tradition has it: "The works are (only) rendered valid by their intentions."

In the *fiqh* (jurisprudence), actions are qualified as follows. *Fard* or *wajib* indicates that an act is obligatory in such a way that omission will be punished and the performance will be rewarded. The qualification sunna or *mustahabb* indicates that an act is recommended but that omission will not be punished. *Mubah* or *jaʾiz* means that it is indifferent, and *makruh*, reprehensible, that is, omission will be rewarded. Finally, forbidden (*haram*) indicates that omission will be rewarded and performance will be punished. These qualifications may vary among the law schools with regard to their precise connotation.

Together with the testimony of faith (*shahada*), the *ʿibadat* constitute the five pillars of Islam (*arkan al-Islam*) According to Islam, humans have been created to serve God. Both the individual and the community are under the obligation to follow the stipulations of the revealed law. According to the scholars, the religious duties are clearly set out in the two sources of the revelation: the *ayat al-shariʿa* in the Qurʾan and in the sunna, the Prophetic tradition. There is no difference of opinion among scholars with regard to the obligatory and clear (*bayan*) nature of these duties. This status explains why someone who denies them their obligatory character places him- or herself outside religion. That person expresses *kufr*, unbelief.

### Status

According to religious views, the *ʿibadat* are constant and do not allow for varying interpretations based on spatial and temporal circumstances. In reality, however, some changes in the way the *ʿibadat* have been performed and interpreted by the believers have taken place. There can be no doubt that its religious status explains why the *ʿibadat* changed far less than the *muʿamalat*. They are the "symbolic capital" (the term was coined by Pierre Bourdieu) of the ulema, who have been able to retain their position until the present day. Nowadays that position is being challenged by emerging religious authorities, such as liberal intellectuals like Mohamed Arkoun, and also Islamist leaders who enjoined no traditional religious education, such as the late Sayyid Qutb.

New media and political situations also allow further possibilities to acquire authority. For example, "Cyber muftis," who give *fatwa*s via the Internet, and often have unclear backgrounds, draw new audiences. In 1960 Tunisian president Habib Bourguiba argued in various addresses to his

After Friday prayers during the fasting month of Ramadan in Kuala Lumpur, Malaysia, Muslims descend a staircase underneath five clocks showing the daily prayer times at the National Mosque. © AFP/CORBIS

population that under the circumstances in which the nation found itself, namely that of the recently recovered freedom from French colonial rule, it should be permitted not to fast during Ramadan. According to him, Tunisia could be considered to be in an economic jihad, with regard to its struggle for a better economic position. Fasting, he stated, would bring about too considerable a loss of productivity. It soon appeared, however, that the most important Tunisian ulema did not endorse the proposal and that the population did not give up the fast.

The aforesaid high status of ritual obligations does not always correlate with a high rate of performance. Empirical research by Bruno Etienne and Mohamed Tozy showed that only 10 percent of the men in the Moroccan city of Casablanca attended the obligatory Friday prayer and that only one out of every thousand persons performed the daily *salat*s in a mosque.

Although often discussed as if they are isolated phenomena, the *'ibadat* are in practice embedded in and closely interwoven with a complex system of informal and formal religious behaviors. These behaviors are not only guided by

the rules of the *fiqh*, but also by cultural and political traditions, local circumstances, the norms and values of the believer's own community and other religious communities, politics, and society at large. A discussion about whispering or reading aloud particular recitations during the *salat* among the Gayo (Indonesia) had a background in local debate between traditionalists and reformists about conceptions of community and faithfulness to the normative example of the prophet Muhammad. This shows that the opposition between universal versus local meaning, or great and little traditions, does not hold in the case of the *salat*. Other researchers made it clear that connected oppositions, namely between orthodox (male) versus heterodox (female), did not hold in the case of gender roles, either.

### Ritual in Pre-Islamic Arabia

The rituals that became the *'ibadat* as we know them today were not unknown in sixth-century Arabia. Rituals such as fasting were known (see Q. 19: 26–27). Certain fasting practices and purity regulations were also observed by Meccan monotheists. Hence, the religious scholars make a distinction between the meaning of a term such as *sawm* (fasting) in daily use and its meaning in the *shari'a*. In daily use, *sawm* means abstention, for example, from food or drink. In the terminology of the *shari'a* it has received the (revealed) meaning of refraining from food and drink from dawn to sunset.

The hajj was also practiced in the pre-Islamic period ("time of ignorance"), but in a form different from the Islamic hajj. Unlike today, pilgrims performed different hajj rituals. For example, the tribal alliance called the Hums, to which the Prophet belonged, refrained from performing the standing at 'Arafat and the running between the hills al-Safa and al-Marwa for religiopolitical reasons. Instead, the importance of the Ka'ba as a central sanctuary was enhanced. It is also known that tribes had different *talbiya*s, and *ihram* practices.

In pre-Islamic times, the rituals were embedded in a cycle that was determined both by the solar and lunar calendars. The *'umra* was a spring ritual in the month of Rajab in which animals were sacrificed, the hajj fell in the autumn, celebrating the harvest. The eleven days separating the lunar from the solar year were compensated for by the so-called intercalation, the *nasi'*. The *nasi'* was abolished by the Prophet after the conquest of Mecca, as is attested in the Qur'an (9:37). From that moment onward calendrical feasts and rituals were no longer tied to the seasons.

Other ritual changes introduced by the Prophet aimed at dissociating rituals from sunset and sundown, for example, the running of the pilgrims between 'Arafat and Muzdalifa and prayer during sunrise. Ritual restrictions observed by the Hums were also abolished in order to symbolize the unity of mankind in Islam. Hence the Qur'an states that there is no sin (2:158) in performing the *sa'y* (pacing back and forth seven times) between Safa and Marwa, something that the Hums had refrained from doing. Through the example of the Prophet during the farewell-pilgrimage, the *'umra* was joined to the hajj and so both rituals became united. They can still be performed separately, however. Moreover, the rituals of running around the Ka'ba and running between the Safa and Marwa were united with the rituals in 'Arafat, particularly one of the hajj's central rituals of "standing." This ritual takes long hours where, ideally, the pilgrims stand in prayer. A preferred place for this ritual is near or on the Hill of Mercy.

Thus, prayer, giving *zakat* (2:215, 9:6), fasting (2:179), and the hajj (3:91) became individual Islamic duties. Friday afternoon became the day of communal prayer, accompanied by a sermon (*khutba*). This day and time were chosen since a market was held in Medina in the morning and many people gathered there. After the death of the Prophet in 632 c.e. the rituals further developed both with regard to actual practice and the norms and values held by the community. In this process the religious identity of Islam as a separate religion played a great part.

## Religious Identity

Traditions recommended that believers distinguish themselves from the followers of other religions and not assimilate with regard to dress and prayer rituals (for example, whether or not to pray while wearing shoes). These traditions were an expression of the desire to establish an Islamic religious identity, and they have continued to influence Muslim attitudes and behavior until today and are the cause of numerous discussions. For example, the present-day custom among Dutch Muslims of Surinamese origin to make a ball of flour out of the child's hair and throw it in the river should be shunned, for it was said to have been taken over from the Hindus. Another example is the question of whether Muslims are allowed to attend Christmas celebrations, a matter that is hotly debated in many places.

But not only did such behavior serve to mark off Islam from other religions, it also functioned inside the Islamic community. For example, in medieval times there was a great ritual divide between Sunni and Shi'ite Islam about the acceptability of the purification ritual of passing the hand over the boots, which even found its way to medieval creeds. The issue here was whether it was permissible to wipe the boots instead of the feet themselves when travelling. Shi'ites did not allow this, while Sunni Muslims did.

## Emerging Rituals

New customs were not always looked upon favorably by the ulema. In many cases they were qualified as innovations (*bid'a*s). The celebrations of the birthday of the Prophet (the *mawlid al-nabi*) and of the middle night of Sha'ban are two famous cases in point. Complete inventories of such *bid'a*s came into existence in the Middle Ages. Many ulema applied the same sort of rules to these *bid'a*s as to other actions, hence they might vary from laudable to forbidden. Rispler Chaim argues that the purpose of such inventories was not to prohibit such new ritual forms, but rather to bring them under control and steer them in such a way that their performance would not infringe on morality and good manners (for example, by mixing men and women).

Muslim are exhorted not to devote themselves to rituals to the detriment of the body. Hence, women may abstain from fasting, and the ill and sick do not have to perform the *salat* or fast. Islam advises believers to take care of the body and soul in a harmonious way. Islam incorporated and transformed existing rules of purity in its religious system. The overall term for these rules is *tahara*, which means purity. A well-known tradition says "Purity is half the faith." All *'ibadat* are in one way or the other related to notions of purity. For example, giving alms is associated with purifying goods as well as oneself (see 9:103, "Take alms from their wealth, wherewith thou mayst purify them and mayst make them grow, and pray for them"). The *salat* should also be performed in a ritually clean state (5:6.).

**Prayer (Salat)**

The following passages from the Qur'an form the foundation of the five daily prayer times.

So give glory to God when you reach evening and when you rise in the morning. Yes, to Him is praise in the heavens and on earth and in the afternoon and when the day begins to decline. (30:17–18)…celebrate the praises of your Lord before the rising sun, and before its setting. Yes, celebrate them for part of the night and at the sides of the day, so that you may have spiritual joy. (20:130)

The five prayers should take place in the following order:
*   Fajr: break of day
*   Zuhr: midday
*   Asr: during the afternoon
*   Maghrib: evening
*   'Isha: night

These are a few of the words and positions of prayer, which is always said in Arabic. Movements one through five constitute one *rak'ah*. Each of the prayer times consists of two to four *rak'ahs*. Movements six and seven complete the prayer.

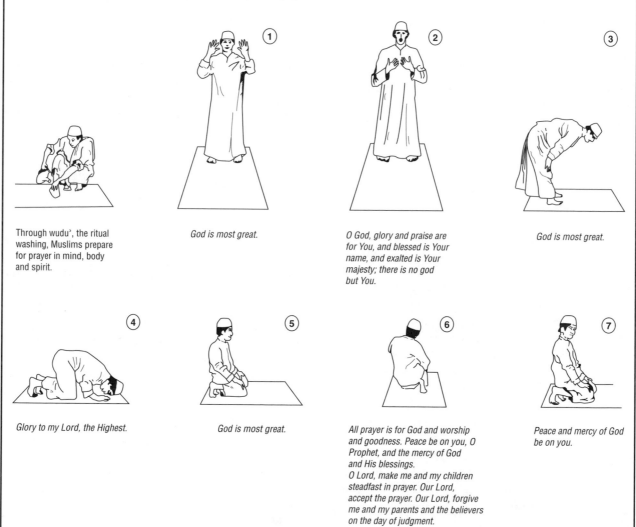

Through wudu', the ritual washing, Muslims prepare for prayer in mind, body and spirit.

① God is most great.

② O God, glory and praise are for You, and blessed is Your name, and exalted is Your majesty; there is no god but You.

③ God is most great.

④ Glory to my Lord, the Highest.

⑤ God is most great.

⑥ All prayer is for God and worship and goodness. Peace be on you, O Prophet, and the mercy of God and His blessings.
O Lord, make me and my children steadfast in prayer. Our Lord, accept the prayer. Our Lord, forgive me and my parents and the believers on the day of judgment.

⑦ Peace and mercy of God be on you.

SOURCE: Breuilly, Elizabeth; O'Brien, Joanne; and Palmer, Martin. *Religions of the World*. New York: Facts on File, Inc., 1997.

The prayer order and traditions, diagrammed.

For this reason books on *fiqh* usually begin with a discussion of purity rules. A key term in this respect is that of the *fitra*, a concept that can be rendered as the natural disposition of humankind created by God. The state of *fitra* includes circumcision (*khitan*), the clipping of the nails, trimming the mustache, removing the hair from armpits and pubis. All these acts refer to bodily practices with a connotation of purity. According to many Muslim scholars, the *salat* performed by an uncircumcised man is void, nor can he serve as an imam during prayer. However, that purity is not of a

Sudanese Muslims in ceremonial clothing on the first day of Ramadan, a thirty-day period that requires Muslims to fast during daylight hours. Ramadan is an important part of 'ibadat, Islamic devotional practices. © Hulton-Deutsch Collection/Corbis

medical-material nature, but has a religious symbolic side, it appears, from the possibility of using sand or dust instead of water for the ablution when the latter cannot be found (*tayammum*, mentioned in 5:6). The ground on which the *salat* is performed (hence the use of prayer rugs) should also be pure. Dress should be modest. Private parts should be covered. In addition to the body, Islamic devotional life structures time (rites of passage, feasts, festivals, pilgrimages) and place and space (the home, mosque, *masjid*). These aspects will be discussed below.

**The Ritual Calendar**

The ritual cycle is connected to the lunar year, which opens with the feast of 'Ashura on 10 Muharram. For Shi'ite Muslims this marks the day on which the martyrdom of the grandson of the Prophet, al-Husayn, at Karbala in 680 C.E., is commemorated by emotional and at times violent mourning rituals. According to Sunni *fiqh* 'Ashura had been a fasting day before the prescription of the Ramadan fast, and it has remained a voluntary fasting day until the present. In Morocco it is a festival on which the dead are honored, and during which the participants give alms, eat dried fruit, and buy toys for their children. It is accompanied by reverie and carnival-like rituals such as masquerades, processions, and theater.

On 12 Rabi' I, the third month, the birthday of the Prophet is celebrated. This festival grew out of the Fatimid Shi'ite ritual practice (eleventh century C.E.), commemorating the birthdays of the members of the the Prophet's immediate family, the Prophet, and the reigning Fatimid imam. It was gradually introduced in Sunni circles in successive parts of the Middle East and the Muslim West. Nowadays, celebrated nearly everywhere (although exceptions, such as Saudi Arabia, exist), its status as a feast has nevertheless remained controversial. It is considered to be a *bid'a* (see

above) and is rejected by movements that consider it to be veneration of a human being, something that should be reserved exclusively for God and hence as *shirk* (the act of associating with God).

The first Friday night in Rajab, which is especially celebrated in Turkish Islam, is a holy night, called *laylat salat al-ragha'ib*. On 27 Rajab, the Laylat al-Mi'raj, or night of ascension, is celebrated. The ascension of the Prophet via Jerusalem (*al-isra'wal-mi'raj*) is one of the great symbols of Islam in which the believer ascends toward God. It is at this occasion that the number of daily *salat*s was fixed at five. Elements of the ritual celebration may include recitation of *surat al-isra'* (17), followed by commentaries, singing, and the recitation of religious poems of sorts.

The celebration of the fifteenth middle night of Sha'ban, also called *laylat al-bara'a*, is another *bid'a*. Its popularity can be explained by its age-old associations with the divine decision of who will die the next year, which is believed to be made on that night .

The month of Ramadan is marked by the fast, and on the 21, 23, 25, 27, and 29 of that month *Laylat al-qadr* (97) is celebrated. Ramadan is the holy month par excellence. Even those who otherwise hardly practice Islam participate in the Ramadan fasting. According to popular beliefs, the devils (*shayatin*) and jinn are powerless, while in contrast God is nearer than during other months. This increased religious awareness culminates in *laylat al-qadr*, when, as some people believe, the gates of heaven are opened. On 1 Shawwal, the Day of the Breaking of the Fast ('*id al-fitr*) is celebrated. After the *salat al-'id*, people pay visits to relatives, which often includes visits to the graves (*ziyarat al-qubur*).

On 10 Dhu-l-Hijja, the twelfth month of the Islamic year, 'id al-adha is celebrated. This ritual marks the end of the year, but in fact it does not represent the end of the ritual cycle, since there is a clear connection between the 'id and the 'Ashura rituals.

## Rites of Passage

Other elements of the 'ibadat fit in the life-cycle rituals or rites of passage. This holds true for birth rituals, circumcision, and death rituals. Birth rituals include the custom of whispering the adhan and iqama in the newborn's ear. This includes the recitation of the shahada or Confession of Faith, as discussed below. This ritual is recommended according to the Shafi'ite madhhab. The 'aqiqa, the sacrifice of a sheep or goat, takes place on the seventh day, through which joy and thanks for the child are expressed. It is usually accompanied by a naming ceremony (tasmiya) during which the child receives its name, and shaving the hair of the child as a sacrifice. The meat of the sacrifice and the weight of the hair in silver are sometimes given away as alms. Circumcision (Ar. khitan, tahara) is a fixed sunna (strongly recommended) according to most schools. The Shafi'ites are of the opinion that it is obligatory. In actual life, virtually all male Muslims are circumcised.

The deceased is purified by a ritual bath (ghusl), and the corpse is dressed in a kafan, which resembles in many ways the clothing of the pilgrim, the hajji. The salat al-janaza is performed. The deceased is buried with the face in the direction of the qibla. Marriage, another life cycle ritual, is not reckoned among the 'ibadat, but among the mu'amalat, and will therefore not be considered here.

## Daily Rituals

The days of the believers are marked by the rhythm of five obligatory salats: the morning salat (salat al-subh or fajr) consisting of two rak'as, to be performed between first dawn to sunrise; the noon prayer (zuhr) to be performed after the sun has reached its highest point until the mid-afternoon, consisting of four rak'as; the 'asr (from mid-afternoon to sunset) consisting of four rak'as; the prayer after sunset (maghrib) consisting of three rak'as; and the 'isha' (after complete darkness). It is sunna to perform the call to prayer (adhan). In places where Muslims live as minorities (about 30%) the public performance of the call to prayer has always been a very important symbol call to prayer has always been a very important symbol for the public presence of Islam. In Western Europe, the adhan is especially publicly performed before the salat al-jum'a (see above). The formula of the adhan is the following: "God is great [4 times, only the Malikites pronounce it twice], I testify that there is no god but God [2 times], I testify that Muhammad is the messenger of God [2 times]. Come to Prayer, Come to salvation, God is most Great, there is no God besides God." This formula is the same for all schools of law; although they differ with regard to repetition of some lines. In the adhan before the salat al-subh

the phrase "prayer is better than sleep" is inserted. Shi'ites insert between the fifth and the sixth line the words: "Come to the best work."

Many believers at times perform voluntary (nafila) salats, for example, during Ramadan, when the salat al-tarawih is performed in the mosques. In addition to the salat, there exist numerous invocations (du'as), to be said at different times of the day, and for different reasons. There are also many motives why Muslims may fast outside Ramadan. The fiqh books detail these different types of fasting.

## Place and Space

Prayers and other rituals can and may be performed at any place, in agreement with the injunction that it is laudable to pray together with others. The Friday prayers (salat al-jum'a) are obligatory for men and must be performed in the mosque. Moreover, a hierarchy of sacred places exists. Such places may be buildings such as mosques, graves (the visiting of the graves or ziyarat al-qubur), zawiyas—but also geographical areas; mountains, rivers, wells, and cities. Often the relative merits of these places, for example, in the works on the fada'il, or merits, express political notions as well.

The hajj has Mecca (the Ka'ba and the Safa and Marwa, nowadays all part of the complex of the Masjid al-Haram) and the holy places near to it (Muzdalifa, Mina, 'Arafat) as its direct objects. Mecca, whose haram was founded, according to Muslim tradition, by the prophet Ibrahim, and Medina, the haram of which was founded by the Prophet himself, became the most holy cities in Islam. On the haram where the Masjid al-Aqsa was built, Caliph 'Abd al-Malik erected the Dome of the Rock at the end of the seventh century.

Rituals, among which a is a tawaf, performed in the opposite direction as the tawaf in Mecca, were instituted in order to divert the pilgrims from Mecca, which at the time was in the hands of an opponent, 'Abdallah b. al-Zubayr (624–692 C.E.). It was in this period that Jerusalem became an established object of pilgrimage. Many other places throughout would follow. Nowadays, ziyaras, visits to the tombs of the male and female saints (Ar. wali, pl. awliya; 10:63), and to sacred places, are quite common in many parts of the world both in Sunni and Shi'ite Islam.

Also very important is the birthday festival ('urs or mawsim) of the saint, when huge celebrations may take place. The veneration of saints serves the psychological needs of many believers to be close to their objects of veneration, from which they hope to receive baraka (blessing), cure from illnesses, help in misfortune, intercession with God, and so on. The connection with notions of kinship and descent from the Prophet is symbolized in the notion of nobility (sharaf). Because of large-scale globalization and diasporic processes, one nowadays witnesses the creation of many new "Muslim spaces."

*See also* **Devotional Life; Law; Shariʿa.**

## BIBLIOGRAPHY

Abu Zahra, Nadia. *The Pure and the Powerful: Studies in Contemporary Muslim Society.* Reading, U.K.: Ithaca Press, 1997.

Antoun, Richard T. "The Social Significance of Ramadân in an Arab Village." *The Muslim World* 58 (1968): 36–42, 95–104.

Bashear, Suleyman. "On the Origins and Development of the Meaning of Zakat in Early Islam." *Arabica* 40, no. 1 (1993): 84–113.

Buitelaar, Marjo. *Fasting and Feasting in Morocco: Women's Participation in Ramadan.* Oxford, U.K.: Berg, 1993.

Denny, Frederick M. "Islamic Ritual: Perspectives and Theories." In *Approaches to Islamic Studies.* Edited by Richard C. Martin. Oxford, U.K.: Oneworld, 2001.

Elad, Amikam. *Medieval Jerusalem and Islamic Worship: Holy Places, Ceremonies, Pilgrimage.* Leiden: Brill, 1995.

Goitein, Shlomo Dov. "The Origin and Nature of Muslim Friday Worship." In *Studies in Islamic History and Institutions.* Edited by Shlomo Dov Goitein. Leiden: Brill, 1966.

Grunebaum, Gustave von. *Muhammadan Festivals* (1956). Reprint. London: Curzon, 1992.

Etienne, Bruno, and Tozy, Mohamed. "Le glissement des obligations islamiques vers le phénomène associatif à Casablanca." *Annuaire de l'Afrique du Nord* 18 (1979–1980): 235–259.

Haarmann, Ulrich. "Islamic Duties in History." *The Muslim World* 68 (1978): 1–24.

Kister, M. J. "'Rajab is the month of God. . .' A Study in the Persistence of an Early Tradition." *Israel Oriental Studies* 1 (1971): 191–223.

Peters, Francis E. *The Hajj. The Muslim Pilgrimage to Mecca and the Holy Places.* Princeton, N.J.: Princeton University Press, 1994.

Rispler-Chaim, Vardit. "Medical Aspects of Islamic Worship." In his *Islamic Medical Ethics in the Twentieth Century.* Leiden: Brill 1993.

Stillman, Yedida. "Costume as Cultural Statement: The Esthetics, Economics and Politics of Islamic Dress." In *The Jews of Medieval Islam.* Edited by Daniel Frank. Leiden: Brill, 1995.

Tayob, Abdulkader. *Islam: A Short Introduction. Signs, Symbols and Values.* Oxford, U.K.: Oneworld, 1999.

*Gerard Wiegers*

# IBN AL-ʿARABI (1165–1240)

Ibn al-ʿArabi was a prolific, influential, and controversial scholar whose writings, based on close readings of the Qurʾan, combined the perspectives of jurisprudence, philosophy, *kalam*, and Sufism. His more complete name is Muhammad ibn ʿAli ibn Muhammad ibn al-ʿArabi al-Taʾi al-Hatimi.

He was born in the Moorish kingdom of Murcia, where his father was a government official. After his family moved to Seville, a visionary experience shook him out of adolescent concerns. He famously recounts how his father took him, his beard not yet sprouted, to visit the great philosopher Averroes, who was awed by the God-given understanding he saw in the boy. He studied hadith and the other religious sciences with many teachers in Andalus. In 1200, a vision instructed him to go to the East. In 1202 he made the pilgrimage to Mecca, then traveled widely through the Arab countries and Anatolia, and in 1223 settled down in Damascus, where he taught and wrote until his death. He is the author of over four hundred highly sophisticated and technical treatises, including the encyclopedic *al-Futuhat al-makkiyya* (The Meccan openings), the celebrated *Fusus al-hikam* (The ringstones of wisdom), and a few collections of poetry. His teachings became controversial with Ibn Taymiyya (d. 1328).

In the later literature Ibn al-ʿArabi's name is closely associated with the notion of *wahdat al-wujud* ("oneness of being"), though it is difficult to explain why this should be so simply on the basis of his writings. Few of his works have been studied with care by modern scholars, but it is safe to say that they circle around a number of themes. Chief among these is the depiction of the various paths to perfection represented mythically by the 124,000 prophets sent by God, though he focuses on Abraham, Moses, Jesus, and Muhammad. He is commonly labeled a "Sufi," but not by himself; he would have much preferred the term *muhaqqiq*, "realizer" or "verifier," the active participle of the word *tahqiq*. Derived from the word *haqq*—truth, reality, worthiness—*tahqiq* means to see all things in relation to the unity (*tawhid*) of *al-haqq*, the absolute truth and reality that is God, and then to act appropriately. To achieve *tahqiq*, one must open the two eyes of the heart (*qalb*), which are reason (*ʿaql*) and imagination (*khayal*). With the eye of reason, the heart verifies that the absolute *haqq* is transcendent and incomparable with any created thing. With the eye of imagination, it verifies that this same infinite *haqq* is immanent and present in every created thing. The indispensable guidelines for achieving *tahqiq* are provided by the Qurʾan and the sunna.

The *Fusus al-hikam*, object of well over one hundred commentaries before modern times, offers an epitome of Ibn al-ʿArabi's methodology and goals. In twenty-seven chapters it discusses twenty-seven wisdoms, each designated by one of the fundamental attributes of reality, such as holiness, realness, light, unity, and mercy. Each wisdom is embodied in a divine word (*kalima*) that takes human form, the first of which is Adam and the last Muhammad. Adam incarnates the wisdom of the name Allah, which comprehends the meaning of all the divine names. It was Allah—not the Creator or the Compassionate—who created Adam in his own image, and it was Allah who "taught him all the names" (Q. 2:30). Human perfection is then to realize every divine attribute as one's own, in keeping with the prophetic saying, "Assume the character traits of God." The children of Adam represent the infinitely diverse synthetic images of God that arise because of the differing proportions in which the divine names become manifest in each individual. The twenty-six perfect human beings to whom the remaining chapters are devoted realized the full divine image while simultaneously displaying the characteristics of one specific divine attribute. Each chapter builds on references in the Qur'an and the hadith to illustrate the applicability of the revealed passages to the prophet in question and to human beings in general.

The *Fusus* has attracted much attention partly because its often obscure contents allowed scholars to demonstrate their mastery of the science of *tawhid*. Its sometimes provocative interpretations of Qur'anic verses, rare in Ibn 'Arabi's other writings, aroused the ire of a great number of critics and produced an extensive secondary literature of attack and defense.

*See also* **Falsafa; Kalam; Tasawwuf; Wahdat al-Wujud.**

## BIBLIOGRAPHY

Addas, Claude. *Quest for the Red Sulphur: The Life of Ibn 'Arabî.* Cambridge, U.K.: The Islamic Texts Society, 1993.

Chittick, William C. *The Self-Disclosure of God: Principles of Ibn al-'Arabî's Cosmology.* Albany: State University of New York Press, 1998.

Chodkiewicz, Michel. *An Ocean Without Shore: Ibn Arabi, the Book, and the Law.* Albany: State University of New York Press, 1993.

*William C. Chittick*

## IBN BATTUTA (1304–1368)

Ibn Battuta (sometimes Batuta or Battutah), whose full name was Abu 'Abdallah Muhammad ibn 'Abdallah ibn Muhammad ibn Ibrahim Shams al-Din al-Lawati al-Tanji, was a Moorish traveller who was born 25 February 1304. He died in Morocco in 1368 or 1369.

Although some details of Ibn Battuta's itinerary are lost or uncertain, it is known that he left Tangier on 13 June 1325, and traveled across North Africa to Egypt and Syria to Mecca. He toured the Middle East and the Near East, sailed along the East African coast, returned to Mecca, and then traveled through Asia Minor, stopping in Constantinople, capital of the Byzantine Empire. Ibn Battuta journeyed through the territories of The Golden Horde (the steppes of Central Asia) and across the Himalayas to India, where he stayed for eight years. Afterward he traveled to the Maldives, Sri Lanka, Bengal, Assam, Sumatra, sailing all the way to China. He returned to North Africa through India and the Middle East during the time of the Black Death. He arrived back in Morroco in November 1349. After a short stay he visited Moorish Spain and later traveled to Mali. He ended his travels in December 1353.

After completing his long journey Ibn Battuta spent two years dictating the story of his travels to his secretary, Ibn Juzayy, who was appointed to him by the sultan of Morocco. The result was a masterly contribution to the genre known as *rihla*, and Ibn Battuta gave this kind of travel narrative a new dimension. Less than a century earlier Marco Polo had made a journey to Asia with a resulting narrative of lesser scope and detail.

Ibn Battuta's account of his journeys is a narrative of travels through three continents, 120,000 kilometers (80,000 miles) of known and unknown cultures, and included, among other observations, ceremonies at the courts of sultans, the burning of widows in India, and African cannibals. Ibn Battuta's travels represent the longest journey overland before the invention of the steam engine.

*See also* **Cartography and Geography; Travel and Travelers.**

## BIBLIOGRAPHY

Dunn, Ross E. *The Adventures of Ibn Battuta.* Berkeley: University of California Press, 1989.

*Thyge C. Bro*

## IBN HANBAL (780–855)

Ahmad b. Muhammad Ibn Hanbal was a renowned traditionist, theologian, and jurist who was born in Baghdad where he spent most of his life studying and teaching. As a young man, he traveled widely in connection with his studies, most especially in the cities of Kufa and Basra in Iraq and Mecca and Medina in Arabia. He made the pilgrimage to Mecca five times. Ibn Hanbal had inherited a modest estate and was able to spend most of his time in study. He was not, in any formal sense, a teacher or part of a school, but as his reputation for knowledge grew, he was widely consulted as an expert on all matters of law and religion. As a scholar, Ibn Hanbal was one of the foremost members of a group called the traditionists, or *ahl al-hadith*. The traditionists believed that as a source of religious knowledge, the sunna, or practice of the Prophet and the early community of Muslims, was second only to the Qur'an and that the sunna could be ascertained through a study of traditions, or hadith.

After the death of the Prophet, the members of the early community transmitted knowledge of the sunna orally and in anecdotal form, but as time went on, and the first few generations of Muslims died off, remembering and recording the sunna became an important scholarly task. Hadith collections provide the documentation of the sunna. Each hadith consists of a text (*matn*) preceded by a chain of its oral transmitters (*isnad*), beginning with the most recent. The earliest transmitter is usually a relative of the Prophet, one of his close associates, his Companions, or someone who knew one or more of his Companions. Ibn Hanbal's collection, his *Musnad*, is among the most esteemed of the Sunni hadith collections.

By Ibn Hanbal's day, there were thousands of hadiths in circulation, some patently false, others less obviously so. The traditionists separated the genuine from the false, and then compiled and presented the genuine traditions in an orderly fashion. This required knowledge about the reliability of the people included in *isnad*s, as well as about the subject matter of each *matn*. Ibn Hanbal's knowledge of traditions was prodigious, and traditionists traveled to Baghdad from other parts of the Muslim world specifically to study with him. His *Musnad* contains between twenty-seven and twenty-eight thousand traditions, whereas the standard collections of Sunni hadith, the "Six Books" contain fewer than half that number. Further, unlike these somewhat later collections, the *Musnad* is arranged according to the name of the initial transmitter rather than according to subject matter.

Ibn Hanbal's activity was not limited to teaching and answering questions about hadith. In theology, the traditionists were ranged against the "rationalists," and here, too, Ibn Hanbal was preeminent among the traditionists. They avoided rational speculation and held that belief in the divine nature of the text of the Qur'an and obedience to its tenets as practiced by the Prophet were the goals of the true believer. The rationalists speculated about the nature of God, His qualities, and His relationship to the created world. The group of rationalists who engaged in this kind of speculative theology during Ibn Hanbal's lifetime were the Mu'tazilites. A particular point of disagreement between the traditionists and the Mu'tazilites was on the nature of the Qur'an. The Mu'tazilites held that God had created it in time; the traditionists held that it was the uncreated word of God. In 833, shortly before his death, the caliph Ma'mun adopted a policy of demanding that prominent religious figures publicly embrace the doctrine of the created Qur'an. Ibn Hanbal refused to do this, and was imprisoned and tortured. Although the next two caliphs continued Ma'mun's policy, Ibn Hanbal was released from prison after two years. However, he did not resume teaching publicly until 847 when a new caliph finally abandoned the Mu'tazilite doctrine and reinstated traditionist Sunnism.

In jurisprudence too, the traditionists—again with Ibn Hanbal preeminent among them—were ranged against the rationalists. The traditionists wished all juridical problems to be solved by reference to the sunna as expressed through traditions. The rationalists, on the other hand, preferred to base their decisions on thinking through a problem rather than finding a solution in a tradition. The rationalists quoted the opinions of their teachers and colleagues as authoritative; the traditionists thought they thereby placed human reasoning above the divine guidance found in the Qur'an and the sunna. Although the practical results of the rationalist jurists were not very different from those of the traditionist jurists, the methodological differences between the two groups were fiercely debated.

At his death, Ibn Hanbal was widely mourned. His erudition, personal piety, and moral fortitude had made him a revered and famous scholar, and his tomb in Baghdad was much visited until it was destroyed by flood in the fourteenth century. His disciples carried on his teaching. A number of them, including his sons Salih (d. 879/880) and 'Abdallah (d. 903), compiled collections of his *masa'il*, the responses he gave to questions of ritual, law, and dogma put to him by colleagues and students. Ibn Hanbal's responses are important both for their specific content and for the traditionist method they illustrate. The Hanbalite legal school (or rite) of Sunni Islam evolved on the basis of the interpretation of these responses by successive generations of Hanbalite scholars. His son 'Abdallah was also responsible for collecting, editing, and commenting upon his father's *Musnad*. The *Musnad* is Ibn Hanbal's best-known work. Most of his other works have not survived intact although they are often quoted by later scholars, and very little if anything by him is available in English. For a translation of a creedal statement attributed to Ibn Hanbal, see Cragg and Speight; for several versions of his responses on topics related to marriage and divorce, see Spectorsky.

*See also* **Ahl al-Hadith; Hadith; Kalam; Law; Mu'tazilites, Mu'tazila.**

### BIBLIOGRAPHY

Cragg, Kenneth, and Speight, Marston, eds. *Islam from Within. Anthology of a Religion.* Belmont, Calif.: Wadsworth Publishing Company, 1980.

Melchert, Christopher. *The Formation of the Sunni Schools of Law, 9th–10th Centuries C.E.* Leiden: E. J. Brill, 1997.

Spectorsky, Susan A. *Chapters on Marriage and Divorce: Responses of Ibn Hanbal and Ibn Rahwayh.* Austin: University of Texas Press, 1993.

*Susan A. Spectorsky*

## IBN KHALDUN (1332–1406)

'Abd al-Rahman b. Muhammad b. Muhammad b. Abu Bakr Muhammad b. al-Hasan, better known as Ibn Khaldun, was born in the North African region of Ifriqiyah (Tunis) in 1332. Well known and controversial in his time, his *Muqaddima*

(Introduction), has become one of the best-known and important works on medieval historiography for modern scholars. Ibn Khaldun was also actively involved in the politics of the period and traveled extensively across Spain, North Africa, and the Middle East. He died in Cairo on 16 March 1406.

Ibn Khaldun came from an influential family that had originally settled in Andalusia at the beginning of the Muslim conquest of the Iberian Peninsula. Shortly before the beginning of the Reconquista his ancestors migrated to Tunis, where they became important administrators in local governments. His father, however, worked primarily as a jurist and a scholar. Because of his father's position as a legal scholar, Ibn Khaldun was able to attain an education from some of the most famous North African scholars of the age. In the mid-fourteenth century the western Berber Marinid tribe invaded Tunis and established a short-lived dynasty. The Marinids imported a large number of legal scholars and theologians into Tunis and for a short period Ibn Khaldun, at this time in his mid-teens, was able to learn from a wide array of scholars in a variety of fields. The Marinid occupation of Tunis was, however, short and by the time Ibn Khaldun was seventeen most of the great scholars had already left Tunis for Fez, Morocco.

The Marinid occupation of Tunis left its mark on the young scholar. He came to see the period as a model for the historical development and decline of Islamic societies. He argued that Islamic societies followed a specific path of development and decline whereby desert tribes invade a given society and infuse it with a sense of vitality and what he called *asabiyya* (group solidarity). *Asabiyya* becomes the foundation for all social relations and provides the fundamental motives for cultural, intellectual, and economic development. Over time, however, the sense of group solidarity breaks down, followed by a slow period of decline until a new group asserts itself into society and brings with it a new sense of *asabiyya*.

The withdrawal of the Marinids back into Morocco left an intellectual and political vacuum in Tunis, and by 1353 Ibn Khaldun decided to migrate west to Fez. In Fez, Ibn Khaldun rose quickly into the inner circle of the Marinid sultan Ibn Abi 'Amr. By 1357 he fell out of favor with the sultan and was thrown in prison until Ibn Abi 'Amr's death in 1358. Ibn Khaldun appears to have attempted to remain involved in the changing political situation, but by 1359 he decided to retire from politics and accepted a position as a judge. By 1362 his position became so untenable that he was forced to flee to Granada.

Over the next twelve years Ibn Khaldun continued to involve himself in the politics of Spain and North Africa. By his late forties, however, he had tired of politics and decided to return to scholarship once again. He wrote a number of works during this period and appears to have begun developing many of his ideas on history and sociology. He wrote his *Muqaddima* to his world history (*Kitab al-'Ibar*) between 1375 and 1379, as well as a number of other important works. By 1378, Ibn Khaldun returned to Tunis to work as a scholar and teacher. His ideas, however, were considered threatening by several of his peers and he was forced to flee to Cairo in 1382.

In Cairo, Ibn Khaldun continued to teach and write, and by 1399 was appointed judge. In 1400 he accompanied the Mamluk sultan al-Nasir to Syria during the invasion of Timur and was involved in negotiations with the Mongol leader for the surrender of Damascus. As had previously been the case, Ibn Khaldun frequently ran afoul of political powers and was dismissed from his judgeship upon his return. Over the remaining six years of his life he was appointed and dismissed from the judiciary five more times.

Ibn Khaldun remained a controversial figure even after his death. His *Muqaddima*, and to a lesser extent his other writings, were both respected and reviled by later scholars. In the *Muqaddima*, Ibn Khaldun sets forth a clear exposition of his theory of social and historical development and decline. He describes the various Islamic sciences, their development, and the process of professionalization that scholars had to endure to become certified by their contemporaries as qualified academics. This process of professional certification, according to Ibn Khaldun, which had become so extensive by the medieval period that it prevented scholars of in-depth knowledge in any one field, was one of the factors that led Muslim societies to decline. His theories about the decline of Muslim society would influence late-nineteenth and twentieth-century Muslim scholars who embraced Ibn Khaldun's theories as evidence of the need for renewal of Islamic culture and thought.

*See also* 'Asabiyya; Falsafa.

## BIBLIOGRAPHY

Baali, Fuad. *Social Institutions: Ibn Khaldun's Social Thought.* Lanham, Md.: University Press of America, 1992.

Brett, Michael. *Ibn Khaldun and the Medieval Maghrib.* Brookfield, Vt.: Ashgate Variorium, 1999.

Rosenthal, Franz, trans. *The Muqaddimah: An Introduction to History.* Princeton, N.J.: Princeton University Press, 1969.

*R. Kevin Jaques*

## IBN MAJA (824–887)

Ibn Maja, Abu 'Abdallah Muhammad b. Yazid, was from Qazwin in Persia and lived from circa 824 until 887 C.E. He is the compiler of the last of the "Six Books" of authoritative (*sahih*) Sunni hadith collections. Ibn Maja's *Kitab al-Sunan* contains 4,341 reports that he collected during his peregrinations through the Hejaz, Syria, Iraq, and Egypt, conducted in search of hadiths. About three thousand of these hadiths are contained in the other five standard collections. Initially Ibn Maja's collection was criticized for containing a number of weak (sc. defective) (*da'if*) and discredited reports, which prevented it from being accepted by the large majority of scholars as a reliable compilation. Although Abu Da'ud and al-Tirmidhi, editors of two other authoritative hadith compilations, also recorded weak hadiths, they identified them as such, whereas Ibn Maja did not. For these reasons, some of the traditionists preferred the *Sunan* work of al-Darimi (d. 869), another well-known hadith scholar, over that of Ibn Maja. However, by about the early twelfth century C.E., Ibn Maja's standing as a traditionist (*muhaddith*) had improved considerably and his *Sunan* ultimately became recognized as one of the Six Books, although it is still regarded as the weakest one.

*See also* **Hadith.**

## BIBLIOGRAPHY

Rauf, Muhammad Abdul. "Hadith Literature: The Development of the Science of *Hadith.*" In *The Cambridge History of Arabic Literature.* Vol. 1: *Arabic Literature to the End of the Umayyad Period.* Edited by A. F. L. Beeston, et al. Cambridge, U.K.: Cambridge University Press, 1983.

*Asma Afsaruddin*

## IBN RUSHD (1126–1198)

Ibn Rushd, whose Latin name was Averroes, was the most outstanding philosopher in the Islamic world working within the Peripatetic (Greek) tradition. He was particularly interested in the work of Aristotle and wrote a large number of commentaries of differing length on his works. Ibn Rushd was not only a philosopher but also a judge, legal thinker, physician, and politician, like so many of the other philosophers in the Islamic world. His work is marked by its commitment to what he took to be pure Aristotelianism and his relative antipathy to Neoplatonism. He defended the acceptability of philosophy in the Islamic world, arguing that it does not contradict religion but complements it. Ibn Rushd held that philosophy represents the system of demonstrative or rational argumentation, while religion presents the conclusions of philosophy to a wider audience in a form that enables the latter to understand how to act.

This thesis came to be characterized as the "double-truth" thesis, which held that philosophy and religion are both true despite contradicting each other. Nevertheless, Ibn Rushd did not hold such a thesis, whatever views were attributed to him outside of the Islamic world after his death. During his lifetime, Ibn Rushd suffered at the hands of rulers who were occasionally unsympathetic to philosophy, and after his death his style of philosophy soon fell out of fashion in the Arabic-speaking Islamic world. It is the commentaries that led to his

continuing influence in Jewish and Christian Europe long after he was forgotten in the Islamic world.

*See also* **Falsafa; Law.**

## BIBLIOGRAPHY

Leaman, Oliver. *Averroes and his Philosophy.* Richmond, U.K.: Curzon, 1997.

Nasr, Seyyed, and Leaman, Oliver, eds. *History of Islamic Philosophy.* London: Routledge, 1996.

*Oliver Leaman*

## IBN SINA (980–1037)

Ibn Sina (Avicenna), was a poet, music theorist, astronomer, and politician, but he was best known as a philosopher and as a medical doctor.

From his autobiography we learn that he was born in an Isma'ili family in Afshana, in the Persian region of Bukhara. By the age of ten, he had completed the study of language and literature and memorized the Qur'an. He studied Greek logic and mathematics under his father's friend al-Natili, a teacher and a prominent advocate of Isma'ili Shi'ism. However, he soon felt that his education and skills exceeded his teacher's and he no longer needed him. By the age of sixteen, he had covered the various sciences and became a teacher and practitioner of medicine. Because of his fame as a doctor, he was called upon to treat the prince Nuh Ibn Mansur, who then gave him access to the princely library, which was rich in rare books. By eighteen, he was confident that he had mastered the sciences except for metaphysics. He read Aristotle's metaphysics many times without understanding it until he came across al-Farabi's interpretation of it. He spent his last years writing and practicing medicine in Isfahan, but owing to constant travel, insufficient sleep, and hard work, he fell sick and died. He was buried in Hamadhan.

Ibn Sina wrote over 250 works, including books, odes, and essays. The most important of his philosophical books are *Healing* and *Remarks and Admonitions.* Each has four parts, the first three being logic, physics, and metaphysics. The first work closes with a part on mathematics, the second with one on Sufism. His most important medical work is the *Canon of Medicine,* which served as a significant reference in Europe from the eleventh to the seventeenth century.

Ibn Sina's philosophy centers primarily on the divine and human natures and their relationship to each other and the rest of the universe. The human soul individuates its body and gives it motion and life. Thus the body is dependent for its survival on its soul, but the soul's existence is independent of the body. In life the soul uses its body for gaining sensory knowledge. This knowledge, when abstracted, becomes pure universals that can be imprinted on the theoretical intellect, the highest and noblest part of the rational soul—the latter being the highest part of the human soul and the only part that survives death. Such imprinting actualizes the theoretical intellect, rendering it eternal, because these universals are eternal and because known and the knower are one. With eternity, the soul attains its highest pleasure or happiness.

Ibn Sina was an intellectual giant whose philosophy combined Greek and Islamic thought but was unique in many respects. His ideas left a strong impact on future Eastern and Western thought.

See also **Falsafa; Wajib al-Wujud.**

## BIBLIOGRAPHY

Avicenna. *Healing: Metaphysics X.* In *Medieval Political Philosophy: A Sourcebook.* Edited by Ralph Lerner and Mhusin Mahdi. Translated by Michael E. Marmura. New York: Free Press, 1963.

Gohlman, William E., ed., trans. *The Life of Ibn Sina: A Critical Edition and Annotated Translation.* Albany: State University of New York Press, 1974.

Shams, Inati. *Ibn Sina and Mysticism: Remarks and Admonitions, Part Four.* London: Kegan Paul, 1996.

*Shams C. Inati*

## IBN TAYMIYYA (1263–1328)

Taqi al-Din Ahmad ibn Taymiyya was born in Harran in northern Syria in 1263 C.E. and died at the age of sixty-five in Damascus in 1328. A prolific writer on all subjects related to the Qur'an, hadith, sunna, theology, law, and mysticism, he was a dynamic and controversial figure during his lifetime, and he remains to this day an influential figure in Islamic thought and practice. A loyal associate of the Hanbali theological and legal school of thought, he put his beliefs into practice as a religious, political, and social reformer. Responding to various crises of the late thirteenth and early fourteenth centuries in the Middle East, such as the Mongol invasions, the destruction of the Abbasid caliphate, and the eventual rise of the Mamluk dynasty of Egypt and Syria, Ibn Taymiyya sought the revival of Islamic society based on a model of what he believed was the pristine community of Muslims at the time of the Prophet and his companions at Medina. But his efforts to revive Islamic society were not only aimed at political and social reform, he sought also to achieve the revival of the inner or spiritual components of Islam. In fact, he believed the inner reform had to occur first before any outward reform would be possible. This perspective on his part brought him into conflict with many speculative theologians (*mutakallimun*), philosophers, and Sufi mystics, whom

Ibn Taymiyya accused of deviating from the pure Islam of Muhammad and the Qur'an by adopting non-Islamic systems of belief, in particular the logic and philosophy of the ancient Greeks.

Ibn Taymiyya's life can be divided into three distinct periods, each representing a significant phase in his development as a thinker and reformer. The first phase goes from his birth until 1304, during which time he received his training as a scholar and was involved in defending Damascus from incursions by the Mongol Ilkhans of Persia. The second period lasts from 1304 until 1312, during which time he was in Egypt. This period is marked by his growing controversy with Sufi mysticism as well as his involvement with the political turmoil related to Sultan al-Nasir Muhammad b. al-Qalawun's consolidation of power. Ibn Taymiyya spent many years on trial and in prison during this time, stemming from his religious pronouncements and his support for al-Nasir Muhammad. The third phase begins with his return to Damascus in 1312 and lasts until his death in 1328. This is the period of the maturing of his ideas and the time of his most prolific and significant writings. Although these years were relatively free of controversy, toward the end of his life he came into conflict with religious and state authorities over doctrinal and legal issues. Ibn Taymiyya died in prison in Damascus shortly after being denied contact with all but his closest family members and being forbidden to write any more letters, essays, or legal rulings.

The core of Ibn Taymiyya's thought revolves around a set of principles from which he develops an elaborate worldview. These principles can be summarized as follows: an absolute distinction between the creator and the creation, revelation as a complete and self-sufficient system, and a necessity to constantly return to and understand the Qur'an and the sunna in light of the traditional teachings of the earliest generations of Muslims (*al-salaf al-salih*).

Ibn Taymiyya has been described as a "dogmatic historian," for he developed a theology based on the concept of a necessarily preserved true religion. This religion as embodied in the Qur'an and the sunna of prophet Muhammad was transmitted intact by the *salaf al-salih*. The canonical collections of authenticated hadiths contain this transmitted wisdom, and thus, for Ibn Taymiyya, forms the basis for all interpretation and practice in Islam. His methodological approach is premised on the correct use of five sources for gaining knowledge of the beliefs and practices that are pleasing to Allah. These are (1) the Qur'an, (2) the sunna of the Prophet, (3) the statements and actions of the companions of the Prophet (*al-sahaba*), (4) the opinions of the followers (*al-tabi'un*) of the companions, and (5) the Arabic language, which for him is the only divinely ordained religious language. These sources make up what Ibn Taymiyya believes is a comprehensive notion of revelation. Any methodology or belief system outside revelation is not deemed to be an acceptable means of attaining truth.

In relation to jurisprudence and the schools of law (*madhahib*), Ibn Taymiyya maintains that theoretically the four imams of the recognized Sunni schools of law agreed on the principles (*usul*) of Islam, but pragmatically they differed concerning particular rulings (*furu*). Thus he upholds the legitimacy of the four schools yet argues that scholars must continue exerting independent judgment (*ijtihad*) in an effort to come ever closer to the theoretically pure Islam. He argued that blind following (*taqlid*) of one scholar or school of thought was tolerated for the layperson, but scholars were under an obligation to seek out and follow the truth even if it is found to lie outside their particular affiliation to a school of thought. This stance brought him into conflicts with other jurists, even with his fellow Hanbalis.

But more than his political and legal opinions, Ibn Taymiyya's theology remains the most salient feature of his religious thought. Devoted to a defense of a monotheism that does not compromise the nature and attributes of Allah as derived from the Qur'an and the sunna, he set himself against the great traditions of speculative theology (*kalam*), philosophy, and mysticism that had evolved in Islamic civilization. Following closely the creeds established by Ahmad Ibn Hanbal and other hadith scholars of the ninth century, Ibn Taymiyya developed a very sophisticated and subtle theology that he promoted quite vigorously. His theology begins with the notion of God as the eternal, omniscient, and omnipotent creator who brought the universe into existence out of nothingness (*ex nihilo*) as a willful act. He rejects any form of pantheistic thought that compromises this belief. Thus he devotes much of his writings to refutations of mystical philosophies, such as that of Ibn al-'Arabi (d. 1242). However, he does not want to compromise the idea of a personal God with whom a believer can establish an intimate spiritual relation. Therefore, he also rejects the sterile descriptions of Allah put forth by philosophers and speculative theologians, who stripped him of many of his essential names and attributes. His main targets of refutation are the Mu'tazilites, the Ash'arites, and philosophers such as Ibn Sina (d. 1043). These theological debates often brought the charge of anthropomorphism against Ibn Taymiyya because he insisted on affirming attributes to Allah such as that he has a hand and a face, that he loves and hates, and that he ascends and descends while remaining risen above the throne over the heavens. Ibn Taymiyya's defense is that these descriptions appear in the Qur'an and authentic hadiths and have been maintained by the companions of the Prophet. He also argues that these attributes cannot be comprehended by human intellect but must be accepted as a matter of faith without questioning (*bi la kayf*) the manner in which these attributes exist in Allah.

*See also* **Fundamentalism; Law; Reform: Arab Middle East and North Africa; Traditionalism.**

## BIBLIOGRAPHY

Hallaq, Wael B. *Ibn Taymiyya against the Greek Logicians.* New York: Oxford University Press, 1993.

Makari, Victor. *Ibn Taymiyyah's Ethics: The Social Factor.* Chico, Calif.: The Scholar's Press, 1983.

Memon, Muhammad Umar. *Ibn Taymiyya's Struggle against Popular Religion: With an Annotated Translation of his* Kitab iqtida' as-sirat al-mustaqim mukhalafat ashab al-jahim. The Hague and Paris: Mouton, 1976.

Michel, Thomas. *A Muslim Theologian's Response to Christianity.* Delmar, N.Y.: Caravan Books, 1984.

*James Pavlin*

# IDENTITY, MUSLIM

In Islamic societies, religion, rather than language and ethnicity, has typically defined political, social, and personal identity. Obviously, Muslims have always been aware of linguistic, ethnic, and territorial divisions, but, through much of Islamic history, these have seemed relatively unimportant to them. Their formative past and spiritual ancestry were to be found in the line of prophets and believers chronicled in the Qur'an, prominently including the prophet Muhammad and his companions, rather than, depending upon where they lived, among the related but spiritually foreign peoples of, say, pharaonic Egypt, or polytheistic Babylonia.

Although the situation has become more complex during the past two centuries, Muslims have traditionally been integrated by their common identity as followers of Muhammad and the Qur'an, and, secondarily, by their allegiance to dynastic rulers (caliphs and sultans). At least in theory (but very often in fact), Muslims of entirely distinct tongues and genealogies have recognized one another as brothers, yet reject as aliens compatriots who, while sharing both dialect and ancestry, differ in religious affiliation. In recent years, certain unfortunate consequences of these attitudes—generally reciprocated with at least equal fervor by the non-Muslims involved—have been strikingly illustrated in the Balkans and elsewhere.

Before residents of the region adopted such nineteenth- and early twentieth-century terms as *Middle East* and *Near East*, no equivalent vocabulary, and, hence, no unifying concept of shared geographical identity, seems to have existed in the area. Until modern times, the Turkish language had no word for *Turkey*; the word used today to designate the nation-state originated in Europe. Arabic still lacks a word for *Arabia*. On the other hand, such distinctions as that between the *dar al-islam* (the "abode of Islam" or "of submission [to God]") and the counterpoised *dar al-harb* ("the abode of strife" or "of war") were readily available and far more salient.

It must be understood that religion in the areas dominated by Islam has commonly included rather more than a mere system of belief and worship, distinct from and possibly subordinated to national and political allegiances. Those of Muslim background often retain a shared communal identity even in instances where Islamic faith and practice have been abandoned.

Initially, the fact that the Qur'an had been revealed in Arabic, while obviously useful to its first hearers, was not enough to forge a unique identity. After all, its entire original audience, both believers and unbelievers, were Arabic-speakers. With the spread of Islam westward to Iberia and eastward to India, however, the Qur'an's Arabic character (emphasized in the book itself at 12:2; 13:37; 16:103; 20:113; 26:195; 39:28; 41:3; 42:7; 43:3; 46:12) marked the Arabs as a favored nation whose ethnic identity was intimately connected with the identity most of them shared as Muslims. Arabic came to be the principal language of a vast civilization that, although it included considerable numbers of non-Muslims who enjoyed the status of protected *dhimmi*s, had been formed and shaped by Arab-Islamic sensibilities. In this were sown the seeds of later Arabic nationalism.

From the start, there also existed a sense of distinct Islamic peoplehood that went beyond ethnicity. It was compounded of both genuine reality and idealistic aspiration. "Let there be from among you," says the Qur'an, "an *umma* summoning to good and forbidding evil" (3:104; compare 3:110, also 2:143). The term *umma* is used several times in the Qur'an to refer to ordinary ethnic groupings, both past and present. In certain passages, however, it plainly characterizes the body of Muslim believers as a new kind of supertribe, transcending family, clan, and ethnic affiliation. "This your *umma* is one *umma*," says the Qur'an (21:92).

Even in the days of the Prophet and his immediate successors, however, old tribal and other affiliations proved resilient, as appears in early tensions between the *muhajirun*—the "emigrants" who, like Muhammad himself, had sought refuge in Medina—and the *ansar* or "helpers" who took them in. Long-standing tribal rivalries continued to be a factor in the early days of the Arab conquests. And even as Arabian tribal divisions decreased in importance, other ethnic rivalries—such as those between Arabs and non-Arabs (particularly Persians)—came to the fore in such movements as the so-called *shu'ubiyya*. Moreover, the question of precisely what constituted a believer, and what caused one to forfeit that status, was a matter of significant controversy in the first period of Islamic thought.

The survival and even flourishing of non-Muslims within areas of Islamic rule also helped adherents of Islam to refine and sharpen their own sense of identity. Central to this was the Qur'anic Arabic term *milla* (Turkish *millet*). In the Qur'an, the word *milla* is essentially equivalent to religion, and it came, with the passage of time, to signify a religious community, especially the Islamic community. Opposed to the community of Muslims, according to a popular tradition rather dubiously ascribed to the prophet Muhammad, was the community of unbelievers—undifferentiated because their differences, like those among believers, were unimportant: "Unbelief is one *milla*," the Prophet is reported to have said. Nonetheless, by the time of the Ottomans in the fourteenth century, the term *millet* also signified non-Muslim communities, legally recognized to be plural and varied.

From at least the fifteenth century, Muslim rulers (particularly among the Ottomans) managed religious diversity in their domains through a system based on the *millet*s. A quite complex structure of semiautonomous communities whose religious leaders had formal relations with their Muslim overlords promoted peaceful coexistence and minority representation at court. In the nineteenth century, however, under the influence of European nationalism and with grave implications for traditional arrangements, *millet* came to mean "nation" as well as "religious community."

## The Ottoman Empire and Its Immediate Aftermath

In its classic Ottoman form, the *millet* system dates from the reign of Mehmed II (r. 1451–1481), and endured until the nineteenth century. By the end of Mehmed's reign, Orthodox Christian, Armenian Christian, Jewish, and Muslim *millet*s had been organized. Each was headed by its own highest-ranking religious dignitary (respectively, the Orthodox patriarch, the chief rabbi, the Armenian patriarch, and, for Muslims, the Shaykh al-Islam). Once chosen by their respective communities, these officials were confirmed into office (or, occasionally, rejected) by the Ottoman government. *Millet*s decided on issues related to religious doctrine and practice and questions of personal status (e.g., marriage, divorce, and inheritance).

However, Ottoman sultans understood themselves, first and foremost, as Muslim emperors ruling an Islamic empire. Subsequent Ottoman monarchs accordingly sought to transcend their dynasty's origin as a line of successful war lords and border skirmishers—so frankly expressed in the title *sultan* itself, which is derived from the Arabic word *sulta*, meaning "power"—and to claim religious sanction for their rule. This is evident in the treaty of Kucuk-Kaynarca (1774), in which, for the first time, the sultanate asserted extraterritorial religious jurisdiction over non-Ottoman Muslims. A few years later, the story appeared that the last Abassid caliph had transferred the caliphate—the right to universal Islamic rule as legal heir of the prophet Muhammad—to Selim I upon the Ottoman conquest of Egypt in 1517. While the claim had relatively little practical impact beyond the effective borders of Ottoman political power, it reinforced the sultan's claim to authority based on the religious identity and self-understanding of the majority of his subjects.

Vocal claims to Islamic authority, however, carried no weight with the sultan's non-Muslim subjects, and, indeed, probably tended to alienate them. Thus, as the empire weakened and Western influences (including legal and commercial privileges granted to European powers) increased in Ottoman lands, nationalist sentiments arose among the empire's Christian minorities, who had a natural kinship to the Christian West and were understandably more susceptible to its influence. These new nationalist ideas were introduced to populations lacking any prior experience of secularism, or of a separation between religion and politics. Minority nationalisms therefore came to be expressed religiously, within the context of the already existing *millet* system.

In partial reaction, the Ottoman government attempted to establish "Ottomanism" as the legal basis of the empire as reflected, for example, in the law of nationality and citizenship promulgated in 1869 and the Constitution of 1876. The related concept of *hubb al-vatan*, "love of country" or patriotism, had already appeared in Turkish by 1841. Thinkers connected with the Young Ottoman movement (formed in 1865) were promoting the "fatherland" (*vatan*; Arabic *watan*) and the Ottoman "nation." Ottomanism, however, was somewhat ambivalent with regard to the weight to be placed upon Islamic faith as component in individual, societal, and political identity. The new constitution also included a formal declaration that the "high Islamic caliphate" belonged to the Ottoman ruling house, thus staking a claim to universal Muslim authority. And the writings of Namik Kemal, the Young Ottomans's intellectual leader, show interest neither in the history of Anatolia prior to the arrival of the Muslim Turks nor in the history of the Turks before their conversion. In fact, he seldom uses the word *Turk* at all. Instead, he emphasizes the term *Ottoman*, which, although it sometimes designates all of the sultan's subjects, of whatever religion, often denotes only the sultan's Muslim subjects.

Ottomanism was, in fact, incoherent, torn between particularistic loyalty to the multiethnic, multi-faith empire as it was and a dream of Muslim unity similar to that which motivated the famous pan-Islamic activist, Jamal al-Din Afghani (d. 1897). Of course, despite his own public piety, Afghani himself seems to have been a natural-law deist and rationalist, and to have valued Islam primarily as a civilization rather than as a religious faith. Clearly indicating that he recognized its power as a political force, however, he insisted on orthodox Islam for the masses.

Ottomanist ambivalence did not escape the non-Muslim minorities. Understanding that they were not, and could not be, incorporated into the empire as full equals, sharing a common culture, they realized that they could not truly be Ottoman patriots in the same sense that English, Spanish, or French patriots were loyal to a country and a unified nation-state. In contrast, the separatist ethnic nationalism that had already arisen in the polyglot empires and small principalities

of eastern and central Europe was fully available to them. Thus, when in 1875 the Ottoman treasury declared insolvency, nationalist revolts broke out among the Christians of the Balkans, leading to bloody ethnic and religious confrontations. Responding, the European powers pressured Ottoman leadership to grant autonomy to Christians. And, in fact, the short-lived legislative assembly established by the Constitution of 1876 included deputies from all the peoples of the empire.

A disastrous war with Russia nearly ended the Ottoman state in 1877, and the difficult negotiations that ensued continued until 1882. Ultimately, the Ottomans surrendered large territories to Russia, the Balkan states, and other powers. These territorial losses, which cost the sultan many of his Christian subjects and precipitated a substantial migration of Muslims from Russia and the Balkans into the remaining Ottoman lands, left the empire overwhelmingly Muslim. Seen by many Muslims as an episode in the battle between the *dar al-islam* and the *dar al-harb*, the crisis inflamed religious sentiments and, by the century's end, inspired a yet more insistent Muslim nationalism—before which the ambivalent and never very popular "Ottomanism" quickly gave way.

Attempting to cope, ʿAbd al-Hamid II (r. 1876–1909) concentrated government investments and reforms in the predominantly Muslim parts of the empire. He emphasized Islam as a basis of internal social and political stability and solidarity, further stressing his authority not merely as sultan but also as caliph in a bid to simultaneously neutralize opposition from the varied Muslim ethnicities within his dominions and to mobilize support, when needed, among Muslims beyond his borders. Although he affirmed the principle of legal equality for minority religions, he felt that Muslims were the only truly loyal Ottoman subjects. For this reason, pan-Islamists like Afghani regarded ʿAbdulhamid as a symbol of Islamic solidarity and cohesion.

By the opening of the twentieth century, however, nationalistic movements in and about the Ottoman empire had destroyed more than the idea of political unity among Muslims, Christians, and others. With the imperial regime in Istanbul looking increasingly helpless both domestically and in foreign affairs, separate nationalist movements arose even among Muslims—which severely undermined ʿAbdulhamid II's appeal to Islamic solidarity. As various non-Turkic peoples sought to dissolve their ties to the sultanate and to forge their own destiny, Ottoman intellectuals became aware of the pre-Islamic history of the Turks. Partially on that basis, they created a distinctively Turkish nationalism. At the same time, centralizing, industrialized European nation-states—foreign to the reality in which they found themselves—became the ideal among the Ottoman elite. Consequently, when the Young Turk revolution occurred in 1908, it was strongly pro-Turkic, devoted to a centralizing and secularizing vision.

Mustafa Kemal Ataturk's famous and more lastingly significant political involvement began in terms of Ottomanism, and, early on, he tended to speak in pan-Islamic terms. His conversion to Turkish nationalism was accelerated by the disastrous 1912–1913 Balkan War, but, although he is associated with secularism, there is no evidence that he ever sought to attack Islam. Ataturk's notable successes garnered immense prestige for the secular nationalism he came to espouse, which has assured its dominant role in Turkey into the twenty-first century.

## Among the Arabs

The Young Ottoman thinker Namik Kemal argued that separatist movements would not arise among the empire's diverse ethnic groups because they were too intermingled to be able to form viable states. The only possible exception to this, he felt, was the Arab community. However, he reasoned, Arabs were bound to the Ottoman state not only by their loyalty to the sultan but by their sense of Islamic brotherhood with the empire. And, in fact, Afghani's great Egyptian disciple, Muhammad 'Abduh (d. 1905) opposed local patriotism or nationalism as a threat to Islamic unity. Race and nation, in his view, were unimportant accidents, irrelevant to one's fundamental identity as a member of the Islamic *umma*.

Kemal was wrong. Arab nationalism—the idea that Arabic speakers form a single nation with legitimate aspirations to separate statehood—seems to have been born among the Christian Arab elite of Lebanon, perhaps under the influence of their European fellow believers. They, of course, felt no religious loyalty to the sultan, but deeply prized the language and culture they shared with their Muslim fellow-Arabs. In 1860, the Christian journalist Butrus al-Bustani founded "The Patriotic School" (*al-madrasa al-wataniyya*); by 1870, the motto "love of country is part of the faith" appeared on the masthead of the magazine he edited. The *watan* of which he spoke, however, was not the Ottoman empire. His "country" was Syria, an Arabic-speaking land.

Graduates of newly founded schools in Syria and Iraq were likewise infected with nationalism and political consciousness, but their pride, too, was in Arabic language and Arabic history. They called first for decentralization, then independence. The Arab revolt of 1916 resulted in the eventual creation of at least nominally independent states in Syria, Iraq, Lebanon, and Jordan after the interwar British and French mandates ended. These were constructed essentially on the European model that had been invoked previously by the Young Turks.

Local patriotism did appear in Egypt, somewhat later than in Turkey, largely under the influence of Shaykh Rifaʿa Rafiʿ al-Tahtawi (d. 1873). In numerous odes and poems, al-Tahtawi, also fond of the formula "love of country is part of the faith," praised Egypt, the Egyptian army and its soldiers, and the then-ruling dynasty of the Khedives. While his works evince little or no interest in other Muslims or Arab speakers beyond Egypt, the history and legacy of the pharaohs clearly fascinated him. They also served the complexly pan-Islamic purposes of Afghani, who praised the glories of pagan Egypt (as well as the ancient polytheistic Hindus) in polemics composed, unlike those of Kemal and the Young Ottomans, in Arabic.

For their part, the khedives encouraged and even sponsored this new patriotism, since the cultivation of a distinctive Egyptian identity and personality so obviously furthered their own separatist ambitions, and the "National" or "Patriotic Party" (*al-hizb al-watani*) was founded in 1879. It cannot be maintained that the new Egyptian patriotism was wholly secular—for most of its advocates, Islam was an essential part of Egyptian identity—but it grounded a movement that even non-Muslim Egyptians felt they could join. Thus, even prior to British occupation in 1882, the Christian journalist Selim Naqqash coined the slogan "Egypt for the Egyptians," which was then popularized by the Jewish pamphleteer Abu Naddara and put into practical action by the Muslim soldier 'Urabi Pasha. But the Syrian intellectuals and others who had taken refuge in the relatively open society of Egypt were often marginalized as "intruders" (*dukhala*) by prominent Egyptian patriots.

Significantly, it was chiefly Syrian immigrants who brought the idea of political Arabism to Khedivial Egypt. Prominent among these were 'Abd al-Rahman al-Kawakibi (d. 1902), who was perhaps the first to demand an Arab state headed by an Arab caliph independent of Ottoman Turkish rule, and Muhammad Rashid Rida (d. 1935). On the whole, however, Egypt proved resistant to pan-Arabism, although that ideology played a substantial role during the presidency of Jamal 'Abd al-Nasser (under whom, for a time during and after his abortive merger with Syria, the venerable name *Egypt* was officially sacrificed in order to build a "United Arab Republic").

'Abd al-Hamid II's imperial pan-Islamism thus proved entirely unsuccessful. And, eventually, with the abolition of the sultanate in 1922 and of the caliphate in 1924, the last effective, legitimate political symbol of collective pan-Islamic identity disappeared. Former Ottoman Muslims found themselves residing in a disunited variety of nation-states, much as their descendants do today.

## The Mogul Empire

Founded in 1526 and lasting until the mid-eighteenth century, the Mogul empire ultimately dominated the entire Indian subcontinent excepting the south. Yet the existence of a vast, subjugated population of Hindus had always posed a problem for India's Muslim rulers, and continued to do so under the Moguls.

Acutely aware of the problem, Akbar (r. 1556–1605), arguably the greatest of the Mogul emperors, chose a radical method of dealing with it. He integrated Hindus into all levels of imperial administration, married Rajput princesses, and abolished the *jizya* tax on non-Muslims. Worse, in the eyes of many devout Muslims, he began to experiment with an eclectic blend of Islamic and Hindu concepts. Akbar's actions, in their view, represented a serious threat not only to the Islamic identity of Muslim India but to Islam itself.

The most significant opposition to Akbar's syncretistic liberalism emerged out of the Naqshbandi Sufi brotherhood. This helped to foster a religious revival among Indian Muslims in the face not only of the emperor's heresies and the resurgence of local Hinduism, but, as time passed, in opposition to Portuguese, Dutch, English, and French incursions into India. Ahmad Sirhindi (d. 1624), an Indian Sufi who powerfully influenced the development of the Naqshbandi order, is often considered by Muslim admirers to have saved Indian Islam.

Certainly Sirhindi represented a challenge to Mogul authority. Accordingly, a subsequent emperor, Awrangzib (r. 1658–1707), banned portions of his writing. But as Naqshbandi-inspired Islamic opposition grew, and amid spreading Hindu and Sikh restiveness that many Muslims attributed to Mogul laxity, Awrangzib also found himself obliged to dismiss non-Muslims from government service and to replace them with Muslims. Furthermore, under pressure from the orthodox ulema, he ordered the restoration of the *jizya* tax and reimposed *shari'a* (Islamic law).

But Naqshbandi revivalism was by no means limited to the Indian subcontinent. As early as 1603, Naqshbandi emissaries had entered the Arabic lands, and, soon thereafter, texts of the order were being translated from Persian into Arabic. The important Naqshbandi figure Shah Waliullah of Delhi (d. 1765), in fact, sometimes composed his works in Arabic, probably in an effort to address a much wider Islamic public.

Mogul power had virtually disappeared by the mid-eighteenth century, and the British deposed the last emperor in 1858. Many Muslims, however, feared that their loss of political power would also result in Islamic cultural and religious losses. Accordingly, figures such as Sir Sayyid Ahmad Khan, while still maintaining loyalty to British rule and admiration for English culture, insisted on a separate political identity for Indian Muslims. Similarly, educational movements such as the Deobandis sought to cultivate and preserve Muslim traditions. More dramatically, Sayyid Ahmad Barelwi emerged from circles close to the family of Shah Waliullah to lead a jihad in northwestern India, seeking to restore Muslim political rule in that region. His followers persisted in the attempt for roughly thirty years after his death in battle in 1831.

The concept of a sovereign Islamic political domain was kept alive by various figures over the intervening years. In 1906, the All-India Muslim League was established as a counterweight to the Hindu-dominated Indian National Congress. Eventually, Muhammad 'Ali Jinnah (d. 1948), arguing that both Islam and Hinduism were comprehensive social orders that could not be merged into a single nationality, concluded that the religious, political, and cultural interests of Muslims could be safeguarded fully only in a separate Muslim state. Interestingly, the Deobandi ulema overwhelmingly opposed Jinnah and his proposed separate state, presumably because his vision for Pakistan—and that of the poet-philosopher Muhammad Iqbal (d. 1938)—was insufficiently grounded in strict observance of the *shari'a*. Nonetheless, Pakistan came into existence on 14 August 1947, following the independence and partition of British India, and is now the world's second most populous Muslim nation. Uniquely among Islamic countries, it was expressly established in the name of Islam. More than a hundred million adherents of Islam continue to live in India, however, making it roughly equal to Pakistan (and thus one of the largest of all nations) in terms of Muslim population.

### Iran

Iran, the ancient Persia, resembled Egypt in possessing a long and distinguished history and relatively clearly demarked borders. Its people spoke a distinct language that was deeply rooted in antiquity. Perhaps most importantly, it was distinguished from the Sunni Ottomans to the west and the Sunni Uzbeks and Moguls to the east by the Shi'ite form of Islam that it had adopted after the founding of the Safavid dynasty in 1501. When the Shi'ite Safavids assumed power, Iran was mostly Sunni, but descendants of 'Ali enjoyed prestige and privileged status among ordinary people. The Safavids themselves were originally Turkic speaking, possibly even of Kurdish extraction, so Persian nationalism as such was not acceptable to them as a basis for fostering unity within their domain and between themselves and their subjects. A national transition from Sunni to Shi'ism suggested itself to them, therefore, as both desirable and reasonably easy, and, thus, within the first century of Safavid rule, an orthodox form of Twelver Shi'ism was established as the state religion.

In the sixteenth century Iran was already far along the path to becoming what we would today recognize as a national state. There has been relatively little tension between Iranian patriotism and Islamism as foci of national identity, since the two are so closely related. Despite strong interest in Persia's ancient past (as reflected, for example, in Firdawsi's epic tale, *Shahnameh*) and with some fluctuations of emphasis, Islam has maintained its primacy in Iranian self-identification. The constitutional revolution of 1906 gave a considerable boost to the Iranian national identity and to patriotism, and the modernization of the state under the Pahlevis (r. 1921–1979) went hand in hand with the enhancement of Iranian national identity in modern schools. The late shah, like his father before him, launched a campaign to glorify pre-Islamic Iran. Leaders of the Islamic Revolution denounced the effort as a return to paganism and even spoke of destroying the ruins of Persepolis (as, more recently, the Afghan Taliban obliterated the Buddhas of Bamiyan). But an unmistakably Iranian patriotism thrives even amid the explicitly religious rhetoric favored by leaders of the Islamic Republic.

### The Persistence of Islamic Identity

Through the ideological turbulence of the past two centuries, the fundamental self-understanding of Muslims as Muslims remained intact, though sometimes tacit. The first Arab rebellion against Ottoman Turkish rule came with the rise of Wahhabiyya in the eighteenth and early nineteenth centuries, and its attempt to repair, Islamically, what it perceived as serious defects in Muslim society. Although that irruption was contained and reversed, Wahhabiyya again came to power, this time more lastingly, with the Saudi conquest of the holy cities of Mecca and Medina in 1925. The discovery of Arabian petroleum in the 1930s has made advocates of this brand of militantly Islamic self-identification both wealthy and influential.

Resistance to European imperialism has been most effectively captained, in many instances, not by political or military officials but by popular religious figures. For example, Ahmad Brelwi, who was both an initiate of the Naqshbandi order and a Wahhabi, led armed resistance between 1826 and 1831 both to perceived encroachments of the Sikhs and to the rising menace of British power in northern India. Slightly later, from 1830 to 1859, Shamil of Daghistan, another Naqshbandi, led similar resistance against the infidel Russians, and, between 1832 and 1847, ʿAbd al-Qadir, a chief of the Qadiriyya dervish order, fought the infidel French in North Africa. Likewise, the struggle of the Sanusi order in Libya against the Ottomans and, later, the Italians, and the revolt of the Sudanese Mahdi, were explicitly conducted in the name of Islam, not local patriotism.

The Young Turk revolution faced a short-lived mutiny in 1909, when members of a pan-Islamic group calling itself the "Muhammadan Union" joined with the First Army Corps to demand imposition of the *shariʿa*. Later, the Young Turks themselves flirted with pan-Islamism (at least for propaganda purposes) with Enver Pasha's 1918 launch of the "Army of Islam," designed to liberate the Muslims of Russia. The previous year, the grand wazir Mehmed Said Halim Pasha had delivered a classic statement of pan-Islamic belief, declaring that "the fatherland of a Muslim is wherever the *shariʿa* prevails." Even the communists, jockeying for power in the months after the fall of the Ottoman empire, found themselves constrained to invoke Islamic solidarity rather than class struggle.

The Muslim masses have continued to see the chief threat to them not in foreigners but in infidels. (That the two were often identical obscures but does not remove the distinction.) When, for example, on 2 November 1945, Egypt's political leaders invited protests to mark the anniversary of the Balfour Declaration, resulting demonstrations turned into anti-Jewish riots and then into attacks on Catholic, Armenian, and Greek Orthodox churches. In January 1952, anti-British demonstrators in Suez, angry at the British, killed several Coptic Christians—arguably Egypt's most Egyptian residents—and looted and burned a Coptic church. Meanwhile, many hundreds of miles away, the Algerian response to the French slogan of "*Algérie française*" was neither "*Algérie arabe*" nor "*Algérie algérienne*," but "*Algérie musulmane*" ("Muslim Algeria"). During the Lebanese civil war, when civil government lost effective authority over the country, residents reverted to their essential identities as Maronite Christians, Druze, and Sunni and Shiʿite Muslims.

*See also* **ʿAbd al-Qadir, Amir; ʿAbduh, Muhammad; Afghani, Jamal al-Din; Ataturk, Mustafa Kemal; Balkans, Islam in the; Dar al-Harb; Dar al-Islam; Ethnicity; Kemal, Namik; Pan-Islam; Secularization; Shaykh al-Islam; Umma; Wahhabiyya; Young Ottomans; Young Turks.**

### BIBLIOGRAPHY

Dawn, C. Ernest. *From Ottomanism to Arabism: Essays on the Origins of Arab Nationalism.* Urbana: University of Illinois Press, 1973.

Hourani, Albert. *Arabic Thought in the Liberal Age, 1798–1939.* London and New York: Oxford University Press, 1970.

Keddie, Nikki R. *An Islamic Response to Imperialism: Political and Religious Writings of Sayyid Jamal ad-Din "al-Afghani."* Berkeley: University of California Press, 1983.

Lewis, Bernard. *The Shaping of the Modern Middle East.* New York: Oxford University Press, 1994.

Lewis, Bernard. *The Emergence of Modern Turkey.* 3d ed. New York: Oxford University Press, 2002.

Schimmel, Annemarie. *Islam in the Indian Subcontinent.* Leiden: E. J. Brill, 1980.

Shaw, Stanford J., and Shaw, Ezel Kural. *The History of the Ottoman Empire and Modern Turkey,* Vol. 2: *Reform, Revolution, and Republic: The Rise of Modern Turkey, 1808–1975.* Cambridge and New York: Cambridge University Press, 1977.

*Daniel C. Peterson*

# IJTIHAD

In early Islam *ijtihad*, along with terms such as *al-raʾy*, *qiyas*, and *zann* referred to sound and balanced personal reasoning. By the third century of Islam, however, prophetic traditions replaced these terms as the primary indicators of the law after the Qurʾan. The term *qiyas* remained operative but was severely curtailed by jurists of all schools. *Ijtihad*, however, was universally embraced by all jurists and theologians, including those who, in all other matters, held strongly opposing views. This was perhaps due to *ijtihad*'s authority residing in a prophetic tradition, but more likely it was because the actual definition of the term varied from jurist to jurist. Al-Shafi'i, for instance, when asked, replied that *ijtihad* and *qiyas* are two names for the same process. Ibn Hazm, in contrast, denounced *qiyas* but not *ijtihad*: The former, he maintained, referred to baseless speculation, and the latter, to the individual's attempts at unraveling the truth by textual corroboration. All nonetheless used *ijtihad* to refer to no more than the search for the legal norm (*hukm*) in Islam's *corpus sancta* without much regard for context.

In contrast, postcolonial Islamic thinkers used *ijtihad* as shorthand for intellectual and social reform, and as a break from *taqlid* or blind imitation of past legal rulings. The Indian poet/philosopher, Muhammad Iqbal, for instance, saw *ijtihad* as the catalyst for Islam's intellectual resurgence, whereas the grand mufti of Egypt, Muhammad 'Abduh, considered it a break from traditional scholarship, and Maududi as the key to establishing an Islamic political order. The relationship between *taqlid* and *ijtihad* during this period became less juridical and more symbolic: The former now referred to the general deterioration of everything Islamic and the latter to its reformation. In general, *ijtihad* served to validate the reformist's efforts to subordinate the sacred texts to the exigencies of a modern context.

While *ijtihad* was warmly received, no methodology for reasoning by *ijtihad* was established, as was the case with *qiyas*, for instance. Jurists spoke of the four essential constituents of *qiyas*, and its various forms, but in the case of *ijtihad*, spoke only of the qualifications of the *mujtahid*s who do *ijtihad*, and of their rankings within particular schools of law. More importantly, they spoke of the closing of the doors of *ijtihad*. The Crusades, the rise of regional dynasties subsequent to the collapse of the Abbasid empire, and the Mongol invasions were seen as threats to Islamic intellectualism in general. Coupled with this, attacks by rationalists and philosophers on Muslim orthodox thinking convinced jurists that any further *ijtihad* posed a great danger to orthodoxy itself. The doors of *ijtihad* were thus closed in the fourth Islamic century, and a long period of *taqlid* followed. Recent scholarship has challenged this view based on evidence that *mujtahid*s existed well into the sixteenth century, and that several prominent premodern scholars denied the closure of the doors of *ijtihad*.

*See also* **Law; Madhhab; Reform: Arab Middle East and North Africa; Shari'a.**

### BIBLIOGRAPHY

Fareed, Muneer. *Legal Reform in the Muslim World.* San Francisco, 1996.

Hallaq, Wael. *Law and Legal Theory in Classical and Medieval Islam.* Brookfield, Vt.: Variorum 1995.

*Muneer Goolam Fareed*

# IKHWAN AL-MUSLIMIN

The first modern Islamic mass movement, the Society of the Muslim Brothers (*Jam'iyyat al-ikhwan al-Muslimin*), was born in Ismailia, Egypt, in 1928. Its founder, Hasan al-Banna (1906–1949), was from a pious Muslim home and inherited his father's Salafiyya (reformist) orientation. He was strongly affected by both the rigor and devotion of Sufism and the nationalist spirit of the 1919 anti-British uprising. Upon graduating in 1927, he was appointed to teach primary school in the Suez Canal town of Ismailia, where he called people to fervently practice Islam (*da'wa*).

There al-Banna founded a society which, in its first four years, built a mosque, a boys school, and a girls school. The society's branches multiplied around the country, founding numerous Qur'an schools, clinics, and hospitals, and establishing a system of cooperative insurance for its poorer members. In the 1930s it rapidly developed its own distinctive characteristics, enabling it to endure and continue to play a key religious and sociopolitical role in many Muslim countries until today.

### Features of the *Ikhwan*

The Society of the Muslim Brothers aims to bring complete spiritual revival (*nahda*) to society under Islam—a vision encompassing the moral reformation of youth through physical training, sports, religious and ideological indoctrination, social welfare, national pride, resistance against foreign domination, and the establishment of a state run by Islamic norms. Its members share an activist ethos, critical of traditional Islam, as well as a certain pragmatism that sanctions the use of Western ideas and technology as a tool to advance Islam. Its founder's unique talents and sense of divine call was evidenced by his celibacy and his tireless self-sacrifice in visiting the society's branches all over Egypt, as well as a commitment to writing, speaking, and organizing.

The society enjoyed phenomenal growth right from the start. Although it could boast only 5 branches in 1930, that number had jumped to 2,000 in 1949; by 1941 the society had become so influential that the British had the Egyptian prime minister arrest al-Banna and his lieutenant, Ahmad al-Sukkari, but he soon released them without British permission, fearing that their continued imprisonment would touch off a revolt that would topple his government.

The society was organized in a tight, hierarchical structure. Executive power was vested in the General Guide (*al-murshid al-'amm*), who was supported by a General Guidance Bureau (*Maktab al-irshad al-'amm*) whose members numbered fifteen in 1934 and who were handpicked by the General Guide. During the 1930s, most administrative tasks were carried out by a Central Consultative Council (the *Majlis al-shura al-markazi*)—a structure which required centralization—at the district level (*al-dawa'ir*), of which there were eighty-nine in 1937. The society possessed an efficient system for recruiting, training, and multiplying cadres and, over time, several levels of commitment were developed. For instance, the Rover scouting movement (*jawwala*) emphasized teaching (*ta'rif*) with summer camps, athletic training, prayers, Qur'anic study, and charitable work. The Battalions (*al-Kata'ib*, meaning "formation") were added in 1937 and were composed of one to four subgroups of ten members, each subgroup being headed by a deputy (*mandub*), to whom the local members pledged an oath of strict obedience, discipline, and secrecy. Later, al-Banna replaced the Battalions with the "cooperative family" (*usra*).

A third level of commitment (*tanfidh*, "execution") materialized around 1940, when al-Banna founded the Special Apparatus, which served as the secret military branch of the organization. Current research suggests, however, that pressure from his more militant members led al-Banna to allow the formation of the Special Apparatus earlier than he might have personally chosen, and that he worked hard to maintain its low profile during the period of the Second World War.

The society's core belief was that, just as the Prophet ruled in Medina, there could be no Islamic society without an Islamic state. But in the 1930s and 1940s, al-Banna explicitly sought to reform society though education and to foster Islamic principles within the existing government. Although he condemned the multiparty system, he sought to increase the *Ikhwan*'s political influence within the Palace and the *Wafd* parties. The Brotherhood's clear ideological stance of social justice and championing the rights of the educated lower classes, peasants, and urban poor presented a strong challenge to ruling elites.

### Ikhwan Milestones

The evolution of the *Ikhwan* reveals unresolved inner tensions between the moderate and pragmatic option chosen by al-Banna and more militant options that would seek immediate military overthrow of the state. In 1939 dissenters broke off from the Brotherhood to form the more militant Muhammad's Youth. In 1947 and 1948 al-Banna collaborated with the Arab League to send arms, money, and some of his trained units as volunteers for the Palestinian resistance. Further, in 1948, in a climate of great unrest, the *Ikhwan*'s organization (including its publications arm) was shut down, and al-Banna was placed under house arrest. In response, in December of that year, the Egyptian prime minister was assassinated by some *Ikhwan* brothers. Al-Banna publicly condemned this action, but was himself assassinated in February 1949 by government agents.

The *Ikhwan* reached the zenith of its influence in 1952, after the "Free Officers" revolution, but consequently drew the ire of Jamal 'Abd al-Nasser. Legally dissolved in January 1954, the Brotherhood was decimated: Six of its top leaders were hanged publicly, and thousands of members were imprisoned. Since then the organization has remained mostly underground, yet its activities nonetheless have exerted a powerful influence at the grassroots.

Sayyid Qutb (1906–1966), after a three-year assignment in the United States for the Ministry of Education, returned in 1951 as a convert to the *Ikhwan*'s version of Islam and became the Brotherhood's chief ideologue. Arrested and tortured with others in the movement in 1954, he spent most of the rest of his life in prison. This is where he wrote two of his most influential works, a voluminous Qur'anic commentary, *Fi zilal al-Qur'an* (1952–1965, In the shade of the Qur'an), and *Ma'alim fi al-tariq* (1964, Signposts along the way), which inspired an entire generation of more radical Islamist groups. Central to his writings were his identification of Nasser with Pharaoh, and the bulk of Muslims with the "ignorant" people who preceded Islam in Arabia (*al-jahiliyya*). Under these conditions, he wrote, only through violent jihad could a truly Islamic state be instituted.

Four milestones can be discerned since the 1980s, with the mainstream of the *Ikhwan* increasingly turning toward peaceful, progressive methods of implementing Islamic law (*shari'a*). Between 1974 and 1981 there appeared several militant groups, including al-Jihad, which was responsible for Anwar al-Sadat's assassination in 1981. Between 1981 and 1988 the Brotherhood founded a number of Islamic investment companies and joined with other political parties in order to have its people elected to parliament. In 1984, the Brotherhood claimed twelve parliamentary seats, and in 1987 that number rose to thirty-eight seats. The Mubarak government (1981 to the present) has cracked down on Islamic businesses and, with a failing economy, Egypt has witnessed greater violence on the part of Islamists targeting police and tourists. At the same time, the influence of the Brotherhood has been felt in all strata of society, especially within professional syndicates. Since 1998, the violence has lessened, and a new party has broken off from the Brotherhood. This is the *Wasat* ("middle ground"), which includes both Christians and women. Some analysts view this as possibly the dawning of a "post-Islamist" era in Egypt.

### The Ikhwan in Syria and Jordan

The *Ikhwan* spread their message into Syria in the mid 1930s, chiefly through students returning home from Egypt. In addition, Hasan al-Banna visited Syria in 1946, after which the movement officially entered Syrian politics as the Islamic Brotherhood Party. Its first General Secretary (*al-muraqib al-'amm*) was Mustafa al-Siba'i, an al-Azhar graduate.

When the Syrian *Ikhwan* entered the fray of democratic politics, some Brotherhood members entered parliament, while others accepted ministerial portfolios. This stopped, however, after the Ba'thist coup of 1963. The general secretary, 'Issam al-'Attar, chose self-exile in Europe, and the rest kept to a more traditional Brotherhood role. In their place, new Islamist groups rose up, with militant names and agendas.

Mathematics and deductive subjects, including, interestingly enough, music

Physical and natural sciences, including the study of biology of living things and culture

Psychology and intellectual inquiry

Religious science and knowledge, including ethics and governance

The hermeneutical approach of the *Ikhwan*, and their blending of knowledge traditions, reflects the growth and diversity of learning in the Muslim world of the ninth and tenth centuries. In particular, the translation of the ancient heritage of Greece and the Mediterranean world had made available to Muslims tools from philosophy and science that could serve to underpin an interpretation and explanation of Qur'anic principles. The Ikhwan like other Muslim philosophers or rationalist groups, such as the Mu'tazila, were committed to building such an intellectual framework, but in the process they wished to affirm a commitment to core notions such as *tawhid*, the unity of God, the necessity of religious faith, law, and salvation, which they perceived, quoting the Qur'an (89:26), as the return of the contented soul to the God of Unity.

Just as the symbolic significance of numbers and mathematical values reflected their methodological approach to science, so with regards to the Qur'an, whose verses they considered as having an interior, symbolic meaning (*batin*) that required a rational interpretation and a hermeneutical approach.

The *Rasa'il* also contains many references to Christian and Jewish scriptures and traditions, acknowledging respect and recognition of the commonalities the Abrahamic traditions share and the affirmation that an ecumenical spirit is a prelude to knowledge and appreciation of the other. In addition, the Ikhwan draw from the literature of ancient Iran, India, and Buddhism. They used well-known stories and parables, such as the legend of Bilawhar and the Debate of the Animals, which suggest the diverse milieu of the time, but are also indicative of the *Ikhwan*'s efforts to broaden and deepen Muslim discourse by engaging it with the intellectual strands of the time. Their approach thus reflects the ethos of the period—a time of debate, intellectual ferment, and synthesis in many fields of Muslim thought, including philosophy, theology, law, and politics.

By and large their work was read by and influenced many later Muslim thinkers. The *Rasa'il* were translated into many languages and transmitted all over the Muslim world. Their writings have also attracted the attention of Muslim and other scholars in modern times, and their approach and commitment to education as the most constructive vehicle for change appears to have stood the test of time

*See also* **Falsafa; Shi'a: Isma'ili.**

## BIBLIOGRAPHY

Nanji, Azim. "On the Acquisition of Knowledge in the Ras'il Ikhwan al-Safa." *Muslim World* 66 (1976): 262–271.

Nasr, Sayyed Hossein. *Islamic Cosmological Doctrines.* London: Thames and Hudson, 1978.

Netton, Ian. *Muslim Neoplatonists: An Introduction to the Thought of the Brethren of Purity.* London: George Allen and Unwin, 1982.

Poonawala, Ismail. K. "Ikhwan al Safa." In Vol. 7, *The Encyclopedia of Religion.* Edited by Mircea Eliade, et al. New York: Macmillan Publishing Company, 1987.

*Azim Nanji*

# IMAM

The word "imam" is an Arabic term signifying a leader, a model, an authority, or an exemplar. The term occurs in the Qur'an, for example at 2:124, with reference to God's promise to make Abraham an "imam for the people," and at 11:17 and 46:12, where the "Book of Moses" is characterized as an "imam." In early theological and juristic literature, the Qur'an and the sunna are sometimes referred to as imam, although the Qur'an does not describe itself as such. The leader of the congregational prayers is typically designated as an imam, and from the ninth century onwards the term was also used for leading Sunni religious scholars. Most commonly, however, the term refers to the caliph in the Sunni juristic literature and, in Shi'ism, to the infallible guide of the community.

Debates on the question of who was best qualified to be the imam and whether a sinful leader might be removed from his position as the head of the community played an important role in the development of Sunni religious and political thought. Medieval Sunni jurists held the position of the imam to be deducible from revelation rather than reason, and considered this position to be essential for the defense of Islam and the implementation of the sacred law, the *shari'a*. In general, they required that the caliph/imam be a member of Muhammad's tribe of Quraysh, be duly elected by the people or nominated by his predecessor, and possess moral probity, religious knowledge, and the physical faculties necessary for the discharge of his duties. With the decline of the caliphate and the rise to power of the military warlords, however, the jurists came to recognize that any ruler—and not necessarily the caliph—who wielded effective political power was the legitimate imam, as long as his actions did not flagrantly contravene the *shari'a*.

To the Shi'ites, the term imam has a different signification altogether. It refers to a member of the family of the Prophet (*ahl al-bayt*), and usually to a member of "the family" as descended from Muhammad's daughter Fatima (d. 633) and her husband 'Ali ibn Abi Talib (d. 661). The history of Shi'ism is marked by numerous disagreements on the precise identity and number of the imams, as well as on how to define the imam's authority and functions; and many of these disagreements have continued to the present, as have distinct Shi'ite communities. The Imamis, who came to be the most numerous group among the Shi'ites, believe in twelve imams, hence their common designation as "Ithna 'asharis" or "Twelvers."

The Twelver imams are believed to be sinless, the repository of authoritative knowledge, and indispensable for the guidance and salvation of the community. The last of these imams is believed to have gone into hiding in 874. While leading Twelver-Shi'ite jurists (mujtahids) have continued the imam's function of providing religious guidance and leadership to the community (even as they have long debated the scope of their own authority in his absence), belief in his eventual return is a cardinal feature of the Twelver religious system.

## BIBLIOGRAPHY

Amir-Moezzi, M. A. *The Divine Guide in Early Shi'ism.* Translated by David Streight. Albany: State University of New York Press, 1994.

Calder, Norman. "The Significance of the Term Imam in Early Islamic Jurisprudence." *Zeitschrift fur Geschichte der arabisch-islamischen Wissenschaften.* Edited by F. Sezgin. Frankfurt: Institut fur Geschichte der arabisch-islamischen Wissenschaften, 1984.

Madelung, Wilferd. "Imama." In *The Encyclopaedia of Islam,* 2d ed. Leiden: E. J. Brill, 1960.

Sachedina, A. A. *Islamic Messianism: The Idea of Mahdi in Twelver Shi'ism.* Albany: State University of New York Press, 1981.

*Muhammad Qasim Zaman*

## IMAMATE

Imamate is the English word used to describe the office of the imam. In works of Muslim jurisprudence, both Shi'a and Sunni, the leader of the Muslim state is referred to as the imam. The term *imam* is also used in other religious contexts (such as a prayer-leader). This entry will concentrate on the former usage.

The imam, in Sunni political theory, was the head of the Muslim state, whose responsibility it was to ensure that the state operated in the correct Islamic manner. It was to the imam that the Muslims should pay their alms (*zakat*) and land tax (*kharaj*). It was with the imam that minority communities (such as Christians or Jews, normally termed "the protected people" or *ahl al-dhimma*) would make their agreement of protection, and when necessary, it was the imam who would lead the state in war with the enemies of Islam. This theoretical presentation was rarely realized, and the gap between theory and practice was recognized by other terms for the actual holders of political power (*khalifa, sultan, amir,* and even *shaykh*) that were rarely used to describe leaders in the theoretical works of jurisprudence, but were the standard appellations in works of history and biography, and in the increasingly popular mirror works, containing advice for kings and governors. The compromise evident in the interface between the theory and the historical development of the Muslim community is neatly exemplified by the debate among Sunni thinkers concerning the imamate of one who, though not the most pious of the community, has the appropriate political skills.

It is perhaps in the Shi'ite tradition that the term imam has been subject to the most discussion. For all the Shi'a, the imam was the descendant of 'Ali (the cousin and son-in-law of the prophet Muhammad), who held both religious and political authority (irrespective of the extent of his own personal power). The imam was commonly held to have inherited these roles from the prophet Muhammad. In this sense, an imam was like a prophet. However, in other ways the imam was distinguished from a prophet. In particular, the imam was not the recipient of a divine revelation (*wahy*), but was "inspired" to lead the community. This was often attributed to an unusually close relationship with God, through which God guides the imam, and the imam in turn guides the people. The divisions between the various contemporary Shi'ite groupings (Twelvers, Zaydis, and Isma'ilis) are, primarily, over questions of the imamate (What authority does he have? What power can he exert? Who, precisely, is the imam at the present time, and how is the imam selected or elected from among the Prophet's descendants?). The Zaydi Shi'a (so called because of their belief in the imamate of Zayd b. 'Ali, a son of the great-grandson of the prophet Muhammad) have determined the imam to be a learned and pious descendant who comes forward to claim the office of the imam. For Zaydis, there may be periods when the world is devoid of an imam, and for some Zaydis, there may be times when there are two Imams. The major Zaydi community is based in Yemen, and the political leaders of Yemen were usually considered imams. However, in 1962, the last Zaydi imam (Imam Ahmad Hamid al-Din) died, leading to a revolution in Yemen and the end of the Zaydi imamate there. There has been no universally recognized imam for Zaydi Shi'ite since then, though there is no theoretical bar to one emerging in the future. The Isma'ili Shi'a have consistently argued that the imam is the current oldest male in a long line of descendants of the Prophet descended from Isma'il, the son of Ja'far (the great-great-great grandson of the Prophet). Isma'il fathered Muhammad, and the Isma'ili imams are all, supposedly, descended from him. The Isma'ilis have splintered into various groups over the past one thousand years. Some believe the line of imams to have disappeared and been replaced with a line of "propogators" (*du'at*); many others have recognized a line of imams, right up to the present day. The current holder of the imamate (according to these Isma'ilis), is Karim Khan Agha Khan, who became imam in 1971.

A most extensive discussion of the Shi'ite theory of the imamate is that found within the Twelver Shi'ite tradition. Twelver Shi'a (or *Ithna' 'ashari*) are so named because of their belief in twelve imams ('Ali, followed by eleven descendants), the last of whom has gone into hiding on a semipermanent basis (*ghayba*), to return at some point in the future to judge humankind. The Twelver Shi'ite writers shared with some Isma'ili theologians a rational argument for the existence of an imam: God would not leave the world without some sort of "guidance" (*huda*) for humanity, for to do so would make him both uncaring (in terms of neglect for his creation) and unjust (in that people would be punished in the afterlife for sins committed due to a lack of guidance from God). The imam, then, becomes a necessary condition of humankind's continuation of religious life in the world. In Twelver philosophical works (such as those of the Twelver Mulla Sadra [d. 1637]), the imam's role is expanded, from a mere guarantor of religious life to a creational conduit, through whom the world was created, and by whom the world is maintained in existence. In addition to these rational deliberations on the nature of the imam, there were exegetical efforts, whereby the imams were identified with certain expressions within the Qur'an. Qur'an 7:181, for instance, mentions people created by God to "guide [human beings] to the truth." This for Twelver Shi'ite writers like the great Qur'anic exegete al-Tabarsi (d. 1158) is a clear reference to the imams. The Twelver Shi'ite theologian al-Shaykh al-Tusi (d. 1067), for example, outlines the qualities of an imam, which include designation (*nass*—by a previous imam), omniscience, being the most excellent (*afdal*) of the people, and (most crucially) being infallible (*ma'sum*).

While the strictly political functions of the imam in Shi'ite thought do not differ significantly from those outlined in Sunni writings, the notion (particularly evident in Isma'ili and Twelver writings) of the imam's infallibility (*'isma*), both in terms of interpretation and in terms of behavior, makes the Shi'ite conception distinctive. The imam, therefore, holds a more central role in Shi'ite community life than the imam of Sunni political theory. He is both perfect political leader and unchallenged religious authority.

*See also* **Ghayba(t); Mahdi; Shi'a: Imami (Twelver); Shi'a: Zaydi (Fiver).**

### BIBLIOGRAPHY

Abrahamov, Binyamin. "al-Kasim Ibn Ibrahim's Theory of the Imamate." *Arabica* 34 (1987): 80–105.

'Allama al-Hilli. "'Allama al-Hilli on the Imamate." In *Authority and Political Culture in Shi'ism.* Edited by S. A. Arjomand. Albany: State University of New York Press, 1988.

Momen, Moojan. *Introduction to Shi'ite Islam.* New Haven, Conn.: Yale University Press, 1985.

*Robert Gleave*

# IMAMZADAH

*Imamzadah*, literally "one borne of an imam," refers to a descendant of a Shi'ite imam and, by extension, to a shrine where such a descendant is buried. *Imamzadah*s exist throughout the Shi'ite world; their relative importance is determined by the perceived legitimacy of their genealogy. The major tombs of Zaynab, daughter of the first imam, 'Ali b. Abi Talib, and Ruqayyah, daughter of the third imam, Husayn, are located in Damascus, Syria. Prominent *imamzadah*s in Iran include the tomb in Qum of Fatimah, also known as Ma'sumah, sister of the ninth imam, Riza, and the tomb of Ahmad b. Musa, popularly known as Shah Cheragh (King Light) in Shiraz. *Imamzadah*s of less-certain provenance are venerated in cities, towns, and the countryside. Although formally educated Shi'ites often disdain less well known *imamzadah*s and view fervent devotion of them as tantamount to idolatry, those who visit *imamzadah*s approach the shrines with sincere faith and affection. *Imamzadah*s are regarded as accessible local representatives of divinity, and are appealed to as intercessors.

Pilgrimage to an *imamzadah* is known as *ziyarat*, a formal personal visit. The amount of time spent visiting an *imamzadah* is proportional to the saint's importance. For example, three days are considered appropriate for a visit to Hazrat-e Ma'sumeh; one day suffices for *ziyarat* to Shah Cheragh. Cursory visits are paid to small neighborhood shrines. Pilgrims visit the shrines in much the same spirit as they would visit senior relatives.

*Imamzadah*s have distinct characters, and are often regarded as having specialties related to the character and personal history of the individual to whom they are dedicated. For example, the Seyyed 'Ala al-din Husayn shrine in Shiraz, burial place of an *imamzadah* who died at thirteen years of age, is renowned as a site where children may be cured. Other shrines cure particular diseases or provide special kinds of assistance. Female *imamzadah*s are particularly responsive to women's and girls' concerns, such as the desire to find a suitable husband or have an easy childbirth.

Visits to small local *imamzadah*s are popular among many women. Men are more numerous at formal religious sites, which are generally less comfortable places for women to spend time. Locations of *imamzadah*s are suggested by dreams or the discovery of old tombstones, and confirmed by the occurrence of miracles. Graves of popular *imamzadah*s are marked by *zarihs*, often elaborate barred enclosures that surround the tombs and protect them from visitors anxious to carry away some of the shrine's blessing, or *barakat*. Letters of petition addressed to the saints as well as money and gifts may be placed inside the *zarih* to signal vows made or answered. Shrines that attract many visitors may be divided into separate men's and women's sections, each on one side of the *zarih*.

Political figures eager to demonstrate their piety may pay well-publicized visits to prominent shrines or assure that the shrines are refurbished with government funds. Since the advent of the Islamic Republic in 1979 in Iran, *imamzadah*s in that country have received a great deal of official attention and investment. Shrines are maintained by support from donations given to the *imamzadah*s or, lacking these, from the government endowments (*awqaf*) office. Popular *imamzadah*s are frequently located near bazaars, which benefit from the flow of pilgrims. As sacred space, shrines can provide sanctuary and often serve as focal points for Shi'ite rituals, such as 'Ashura observances.

*See also* **Devotional Life; Dreams; Imam; Pilgrimage: Ziyara; Religious Beliefs; Religious Institutions.**

## BIBLIOGRAPHY

Ayoub, Mahmoud. *Redemptive Suffering in Islam: A Study of the Devotional Aspects of 'Ashura in Twelver Shi'ism.* The Hague: Mouton, 1978.

Betteridge, Anne H. "Muslim Women and Shrines in Shiraz." In *Everyday Life in the Muslim Middle East,* 2d ed. Edited by Donna Lee Bowen and Evelyn A. Early. Bloomington: Indiana University Press, 2002.

Chelkowski, Peter. "Imamzadah." In *The Oxford Encyclopedia of the Modern Islamic World.* New York: Oxford University Press, 1995.

Friedl, Erika. "Islam and Tribal Women in a Village in Iran." In *Unspoken Worlds: Women's Religious Lives.* 3d edition. Edited by Nancy Auer Falk and Rita M. Gross. Belmont, Calif.: Wadsworth/Thomson Learning, 2001.

Momen, Moojan. *An Introduction to Shi'ite Islam.* New Haven: Yale University Press, 1985.

*Anne H. Betteridge*

# INTERNET

The Islamic presence in cyberspace relates to both religious authority and the accessibility of authoritative texts, scriptural and juridical, reflecting a spectrum of views internal to the diverse Muslim community. Digital Islam projects Muslim values yet is also bound by them. It is further influenced by the American origins of the World Wide Web: Afro-Asian Muslim students who came to the United States to be trained as engineers were also the first to create specifically Islamic websites (especially through Muslim Student Associations, or

MSAs). Their concerns remain the concerns of Muslims worldwide: to foster cyber Islamic environments that reinforce Muslim values no matter what the dominant culture or the vocational demands that individual Muslims face.

## The Boundaries of Digital Islam

One of the most fertile and recurrent metaphors from Muslim imagery is the Straight Path. It is first introduced in the opening chapter of the Qur'an. "Guide us on the Straight Path," each Muslim asks of Allah each day and each time that he or she engages in canonical prayer (*salat*). The Straight Path, and only the Straight Path, leads to peace, to truth, to certainty, in this world and also in the next.

The boundaries of digital Islam reflect the scriptural, creedal, and historical boundaries of Islamic thinking before the Information Age. There can be no Islam without limits or without guideposts. One cannot have a Straight Path unless what is beyond or outside or against the Straight Path is known. Cyberspace, like social space, must be monitored to be effectively Muslim. As Gary Bunt has noted, "much is done by Muslims in the name of Islam that is dismissed as inappropriate, or worse, by other Muslims. Not every surfer (Muslim or non-Muslim) is able to make appropriate judgments, or possess the knowledge to determine 'the truth.'"

Yet the horizontal, open-ended nature of the Internet makes the boundaries of digital Islam more porous and more subject to change than those of its predecessors. There are still the same guideposts: the scripture (the Qur'an), the person (the Last Prophet) and the law (with the ulema or religious specialists as its custodians). Each has to be defined or redefined in cyberspace in order to reflect the staggering diversity within the worldwide Muslim community (*umma*). The cyber-*umma* remains a subset of, not a substitute for, the actual *umma*.

The most profound diversity is the global distribution of Muslims themselves. Muslims comprise between one-quarter and one-third of the world's population. More Muslims are Asian than African, more are African than Arab, and many Muslims now live outside their countries of origin, whether in Europe or North America. It is Euro-American Muslim immigrants who form the leading edge for change in the Muslim world as a whole. Children of the information technology revolution, they have a heightened sense of diversity, at the same time that they use expanded human and material resources to link themselves with other, like-minded groups.

There is a debate about whether or not the Internet encourages democracy in the Muslim world. Some cybernauts have assumed that the expansive technology of the World Wide Web makes it as democratic in access as it is global in scope. But others claim that the Internet further shores up traditional authority, since only certain groups of Asian (or Arab or Iranian) Muslim immigrants get their views projected on web pages in cyberspace. The South Asian cultural critic

Ziauddin Sardar (1996), for instance, lambasts cyberspace as "social engineering of the worst kind. . . . The supposed democracy of cyberspace only hands control more effectively back to a centralized elite, the ideology of the free citizen making everyone oblivious to the more enduring structures of control."

## The Internet and the Information Age

For those Muslims who do have access to cyberspace, two key terms frame their experience of the Internet. Both terms, Muslim networks and the Information Age, come together in digital Islam. Muslim networks precede and inform the Information Age. Manuel Castells accents the difference inaugurated by the information technology revolution. This revolution did not erase prior networks, but it did enhance the way they function. The information technology revolution has made the internal diversity and historical networking of Muslims more apparent. The Internet, in particular, opens up access to communities that were closed or inaccessible, thus facilitating an investigation of the ways in which diverse peoples encounter their diversity and interpret their experiences. It provides options for new forms of collective interaction.

During the 1990s, the Internet became part of daily life in many parts of the world. While access in Africa and Asia remains limited for economic and political reasons, grassroots organizations are learning how to exploit the democratizing potential of e-connectivity and to circumvent attempts to centralize control. In Malaysia, for example, networks opposed to the government have established a tiered system of distribution. Elites with computer access download materials as hard copies, which are then widely distributed into rural areas, where they can be read aloud to groups of illiterate people. Virtual communities are becoming the norm, even as technophiles debate with neo-Luddites about whether they are the harbingers of a brave new world or the end of fully human life.

While the information revolution emerges out of technological developments and organizational patterns long in place throughout the world, it can be marked as a revolution because of its difference from these same antecedent patterns. What is different are the speed, scope, and directness of communication, nowhere more evident than in the concept of telepresence.

## Telepresence and Resistance

Telepresence is a new form of association, and, as such, it compels a reconsideration of the meaning of community: What is community when participants do not share place but can communicate as if they did? If shared place is not a necessary condition, is the notion of community as embodied contact a romantic projection of an idealized past? Sociologists since the nineteenth century have been worrying about the impact of technology on community, as though it possessed a solid, immutable core. But a century later, communities survive, albeit in less solid but no less real forms. While it

is too early to predict how transformative the Internet will be, its impact on individual, communal, and national identity is growing.

The challenge for Muslim cybernauts is the same as for other "netizens" (a neologism meaning "internet citizens"): How to define place and community in new ways that do not oppose virtual and real but rather see them as complementary? Can social networking in the flows of the information superhighway provide an alternate context within which to build communities as small as a kinship group, or as large as a nation?

The cybernetic revolution provides unprecedented opportunities for local and transnational community formation. Whether Muslims aggregate in virtual associations, such as cyber-Muslim chat groups, or actual networks, such as Women Living Under Muslim Laws (<http://www.wluml.org>), they project a common pattern of fragmentation, dispersal, and reaggregation. In this era of mass migration, when violence and economic necessity have forced many to travel, diasporic Muslims are split from their birth communities. They are compelled to negotiate multiple speaking positions as they imagine and project national identities. Nationalism today, though geographically fragmented, is socially networked through language and systems of meaning that allow participants to share cultural practices and experiences. People are able to diversify their participation in various communities to reflect shared interests rather than shared place or shared ancestry. They may also form contingent virtual communities to respond to emergencies at the collective and individual levels, as well as to provide companionship, social support, and a sense of belonging.

The Internet seems to empower individuals who would not otherwise have a public voice to express and present their opinions to strangers. However divergent from the norm, an individual can insist on his or her unorthodox position. A debate that could be closed in real space by the assertion of dominance by a majority remains open in virtual space. Consider the fierce debate concerning women's rights as human rights and Muslim women as fully the equal of Muslim men. Often this debate centers on one hadith of the prophet Muhammad, to wit, that "a nation which places its affairs in the hands of a woman shall never prosper." Traditionalists have used it to deny women any role in affairs of state or the public domain, but a contemporary Nigerian jurist, Sanusi Lamido Sanusi, has demonstrated through an essay circulated on the Internet (at <www.gamji.cm/sanusi. htm>) the extent to which rival interpretations of this hadith render it suspect as the eternal norm governing Muslim women's access to professional employment and political power.

Heteroglossia and contestation do not automatically replace the ideological closure of other forms of telecommunication such as newspapers, television, radio, and even telephone.

Still, dissension that might have been quashed previously in an environment where hegemonic discourse held sway might today persist beyond presumed endings. To the extent that the necessarily horizontal nature of relationships on the Net challenges traditional hierarchies, the democratizing potential of the Net holds out hope for people living under authoritarian rule in many postcolonial Muslim states.

## Consequences of the Information Technology Revolution

The Information Age is an age defined by media, whether print (newspapers), auditory (the radio and telephone), audiovisual (television and movies), or print-auditory-visual-tactile (the World Wide Web). There could be no World Wide Web without antecedent technological breakthroughs, yet it represents the culmination of a process the further consequences of which no one yet knows. While Muslims did not create the World Wide Web, they have been among its beneficiaries, at least in those nodes of the global capitalist community where Muslims work, live, and pray either in their own cosmopolitan centers or as part of the demographic pluralism of Western Europe, North America and South/Southeast Asia.

What will be the consequence of the information technology revolution for Islam during the next two decades? Castells has argued that it will augur the biggest revolution experienced by humankind since the invention of the Greek alphabet in 700 B.C.E. It is too early to confirm Castells' grand vision, but even if one acknowledges its long-term potential, its immediate impact has to be qualified on two major points. First, the boundaries of religious knowledge are not so easily or so swiftly changed. The major web site for Muslims in the Euro-American diaspora today is IslamiCity in Cyberspace, located at <www.islam.org>, <www.islamic.org>, and <www.islamicity.org>.

It has been embraced by Muslim Student Associations throughout North America, at the same time that it has benefited from the early endeavors of student-based webmasters to create Cyber Islamic environments. Because IslamiCity in Cyberspace claims 120 million hits since January 2001, it would seem that it fulfills its mission, namely, to service the global Muslim ecommunity.

But does IslamiCity actually represent all Muslims, in geographic space as well as in cyberspace? IslamiCity in Cyberspace is itself an offshoot of HADI, the acronym for a Saudi overseas holding company based in California: Human Assistance and Development International. In Arabic, *hadi* means guide or leader. *Hadi* is also one of the "99 Most Beautiful Names of God," and it echoes the phrase from the Qur'an cited above: "Guide us on the Straight Path." In this case, however, the Straight Path guides the Muslim cybernaut towards norms and values that reflect the Saudi sponsors of HADI. It reflects the effort of the Saudi government to project itself as the bastion of Islamic orthodoxy, at once the

conduit and the center for the one billion strong *umma*. Yet the HADI-sponsored websites have little relationship to other cyber-Muslim voices with a variant notion of Islamic loyalty and ritual practice.

Among the numerous alternative Muslim websites, two kinds contrast sharply with Islamicity in Cyberspace. One is the principal Twelver Shi'ite website at <www.al-islam.org>. This site, like HADI, originates from North America, in this case from Canada, but instead of the dominant Sunni stress on scripture and Prophetic practice, it projects a personal loyalty to 'Ali, the cousin/son-in-law of the Prophet and an individual whom Shi'ite Muslims esteem as one of the Infallibles, or perfect beings who guide others to Allah. Also reflecting a personal loyalty, but to other semidivine mediators, are numerous Sufi sites, among them those dedicated to the Chishti-affiliated Sufi Order of the West and its founder, Hazrat Inayat Khan. For example, <www.cheraglibrary.org/library.htm> is the home page of a Chishti devotee from New Mexico, and it offers a broad appeal to numerous, non-Muslim spiritual paths, all under the canopy of a universal perspective of Sufism.

The huge conceptual gap between the IslamiCity sites and their Shi'ite or Sufi counterparts illustrates the second major demurral from a cyber-utopia of the sort that Castells projects. Differences in virtual space will be as multiple and myriad as ground-level disparities within the *umma*. Not only will there be a limited number of Muslims who have access to the World Wide Web, but those who do become Muslim netizens will find many competing notions of Islamic loyalty and options for ritual practice. It will also continue to matter where one resides. In Malaysia or Turkey the government is less prone to monitor or to filter websites than in Saudi Arabia or Syria, and, while hacking can take place as easily within a cyber-Islamic environment as elsewhere, it will occur more often in border zones of actual conflict, such as Palestine and Kashmir. Because information technologies, like religious traditions, are inherently conservative, they tend to reinforce global structures and asymmetries rather than to bode a new era for civil society and transformative justice. The information technology revolution will continue to benefit diasporic Muslims more than their homeland co-religionists. The disparity between north and south, between rich and poor will be as evident, alas, among Muslims as it is among non-Muslims, at least for the foreseeable future.

*See also* **Globalization; Networks, Muslim.**

## BIBLIOGRAPHY

Bunt, Gary R. *Virtually Islamic: Computer-Mediated Communication and Cyber Islamic Environments.* Lampeter: University of Wales Press. 2000.

Castells, Manuel. *The Information Age: Economy, Society, and Culture.* Oxford, U.K.: Blackwell, 1997.

Eickelman, Dale F., and Anderson, Jon W., eds. *New Media in the Muslim World: The Emerging Public Sphere*. Bloomington and Indianapolis: Indiana University Press, 1999.

Mandaville, Peter. "Digital Islam: Information Technology and the Changing Boundaries of Religious Knowledge." *International Institute for the Study of Islam in the Modern World Newsletter*, no. 2 (March 1999): 21–24.

Sardar, Ziauddin. *Cyberfutures: Culture and Politics on the Information Superhighway*. New York: New York University Press, 1996.

*Bruce B. Lawrence*
*Miriam Cooke*

# INTIFADA

*Intifada* ("shaking off") is the name given to two Palestinian uprisings against the Israeli occupation of the West Bank and Gaza Strip. The first began in December of 1987 as a popular uprising, its hallmark being the image of Palestinian youths throwing rocks at Israeli soldiers and settlers in the occupied territories. This Intifada was triggered by an incident in Gaza that turned violent and subsequently spread rapidly to the West Bank territories. Over the next several years, the Intifada escalated, involving demonstrations, strikes, riots, and violence against Israelis. The Intifada lasted until 1993 when, in response to the uprising, the Oslo Accords were drawn up between Israeli and Palestinian negotiators.

Al-Aqsa Intifada began after Ariel Sharon, a leader of the Israeli right-wing LIKUD Party, visited al-Haram al-Sharif (Temple Mount), in Jerusalem, on 28 September 2000. Al-Haram, which contains al-Aqsa Mosque, is the third holiest shrine of Islam. The visit was provocative to Palestinians, especially because Sharon was accompanied by one thousand riot police, but what triggered the Intifada the following day was the Israeli police use of live ammunition and rubber bullets against unarmed, rock-throwing Palestinian demonstrators, killing six and injuring 220.

The fundamental cause of al-Aqsa Intifada was the breakdown, in July 2000, of the Israeli-Palestinian peace process that had begun with the Oslo Accords of 1993. Palestinians expected that the Palestine Liberation Organization's (PLO) recognition of Israel, which was a part of that agreement, would lead to an end of the thirty-three-year Israeli occupation of the West Bank and Gaza, and to the establishment of a Palestine state. However, the number of Israeli settlers in the West Bank and Gaza doubled to 187,000 and increased to 170,000 in East Jerusalem in the 1990s, and Israel confiscated more Palestinian land for the settlements and their access roads. Israel extended its policy of restricting the movement of Palestinians, and of establishing checkpoints where Palestinians experienced humiliation. Israel also continued to demolish homes and to uproot and burn olive and fruit trees,

as a form of collective punishment and for security reasons. In short, Israeli repression and unmet Palestinian expectations of freedom and independence contributed to years of pent-up frustration, despair, and rage.

Like the first Intifada, Palestinians in October 2000 began by using nonviolent methods. After 144 Palestinians had been killed, however, Islamist groups, such as HAMAS and Islamic Jihad, began a campaign of suicide bombings against mostly civilians in the occupied territories and Israel, while groups associated with Fatah organization, such as al-Aqsa Martyr's Brigade, focused on resistance against Israeli army incursions and conducted attacks on settlers in the West Bank and Gaza. Starting in January 2002, al-Aqsa Brigade also began conducting suicide bombings against mostly Israeli civilians, a practice condemned by the international community. Yasir 'Arafat, head of Fatah and the PLO, and president of the Palestinian Authority (PA) since 1996, did not initiate the Intifada, but he reportedly gave tacit approval to armed resistance and terrorism, despite his promise made in the Oslo Accords in 1993 to Prime Minister Yitzhak Rabin to renounce "the use of terrorism and other acts of violence."

Sharon became Israel's Prime Minister on 6 February 2001. A proponent of Greater Israel, an architect of the settlements, and an opponent of the Oslo process, he proceeded, with broad public support, to use harsh measures against the Palestinians in the West Bank and Gaza. In response to Palestinian violence, he initiated a policy of assassinations, euphemistically called "targeted killings," of suspected terrorists leaders, but which included activists and innocent bystanders. He reoccupied major Palestinian cities, using helicopter gunships, war planes and tanks. Some of Sharon's methods were condemned by both human rights groups and the United States.

The Intifada was costly to the Palestinians, Israel, and the United States during the first thirty months. Some strategists, including Palestinian analysts, considered the militarization of the Intifada to be a blunder. The Oslo process was destroyed, 'Arafat sidelined, the Palestinian economy damaged, and the PA areas occupied, while settlement construction continued apace. Sharon's harsh measures cost the lives of over 2,000 Palestinians, of whom most were civilians, including about 275 children. In addition, the Palestinians lost much popular, moral, and diplomatic support around the world. The Intifada also cost the lives of over 700 Israelis, most of whom were civilians, brought insecurity to their lives, and resulted in the loss of faith in the Palestinians as peace partners.

*See also* **Conflict and Violence; HAMAS; Human Rights.**

## BIBLIOGRAPHY

Lockman, Zachary, and Beinin, Joel. *Intifada: The Palestinian Uprising Against Israeli Occupation*. Boston: South End Press, 1989.

O'Ballance, Edgar. *The Palestinian Intifada*. New York: Macmillan, 1998.

*Philip Mattar*

# IQBAL, MUHAMMAD (C. 1877–1938)

Muhammad Iqbal, South Asian poet and ideological innovator, wrote poetry in Urdu and Persian and discursive prose, primarily in English, of particular significance in the formulation of a national ethos for Pakistan. A popular lyric and patriotic poet in his youth, he later shifted to more philosophical themes that sought to discover in the heritage of Islam a spirit of individual and social activism that would inspire an alternative path to modernity and demonstrate the universal relevance of Islam for the modern world. An opponent of nationalism, particularly the Indian nationalist movement, he promoted a renewed aspiration for a worldwide Muslim *umma*. Nevertheless, his advocacy of Muslim social self-sufficiency and his occasionally more specific political statements were later construed in Pakistan as the guiding principles for the country's separation from India.

Born in Sialkot, Punjab, of Kashmiri background and modest economic circumstances—his father had a small tailoring and embroidery shop—Iqbal received an early education in Arabic and Persian and a British colonial education that earned him a masters degree in philosophy at Government College, Lahore, where he also established his reputation as a poet. His academic brilliance won him a scholarship to continue his studies at Cambridge University in 1905, while also qualifying him as a barrister. He then earned a Ph.D. in philosophy from Munich in 1908 with a dissertation, *The Development of Metaphysics in Persia*, which was published that year. His three years in Europe, during which he was immersed in philosophical idealism, also inspired a powerful concern with the historical circumstances of Muslims throughout the world in the face of the technological and political domination of the West. His Urdu poem *Shikwa* (Complaint), in 1911, asked why God had allowed Muslims to fall from their position as leaders of humanity.

To reach a wider Muslim audience and establish a deeper historical connection with the cosmopolitan civilization of Islam, Iqbal chose to write most of his later and more philosophically ambitious poetry in Persian. *Asrar-e khudi* (Secrets of the self, 1915), his first major poem in Persian, was a sharp rejection of the mystical goal of absorption into undifferentiated being, which Iqbal associated with passivity on the part of individuals and communities. For Iqbal, the assertion of *khudi*, individuality, allows for the possibility of love and creativity in the unfinished creation of the world.

Although calling for practical action in the world, Iqbal's poetry remained steeped in erudite, abstract, and metaphorical language and in the metrical conventions of the Persian tradition. At the same time he mixed in allusions to European literature and contemporary events. His most ambitious work, the *Javid Nama* (1932), a kind of *Divina Commedia*, recounts the poet's journey through the solar system, guided by the great Sufi poet Jalaluddin Rumi (1207–1273 C.E.), encountering a wide range of mythic and historical figures. *The Reconstruction of Religious Thought in Islam* (1930) sets forth his social and religious philosophy, which seeks to construct a concept of a dynamic, democratic society inspired by the Qur'an and the life of the prophet Muhammad. Rejecting the goals of secular nationalism associated with Europe as a false division of matter and spirit, Iqbal's ventures into politics as president of the Muslim League in 1930, participation in the London Round Table Conferences in 1931 and 1932, and occasional commentary, set forth a positive vision of a modern Muslim social and political order.

*See also* **Liberalism, Islamic; Persian Language and Literature; South Asia, Islam in; Urdu Language, Literature, and Poetry.**

## BIBLIOGRAPHY

Iqbal, Muhammad. *The Secrets of the Self (Asrar-i-Khudi): A Philosophical Poem*. Translated by Reynold A. Nicholson. Lahore, Pakistan: Sh. Muhammad Ashraf, 1940.

Iqbal, Muhammad. *Javid-Nama*. Translated by A. J. Arberry. London: George Allen and Unwin, 1966.

Iqbal, Muhammad. *The Reconstruction of Religious Thought in Islam*. 1951. Reprint, Lahore, Pakistan: Sh. Muhammad Ashraf, 1971.

Iqbal, Muhammad. *Iqbal: a Selection of the Urdu Verse*. Translated by D. J. Matthews. London: School of Oriental and African Studies, University of London, 1993.

Schimmel, Annemarie. *Gabriel's Wing: A Study of the Religious Ideas of Sir Muhammad Iqbal*. Leiden: E. J. Brill, 1963.

*David Lelyveld*

# IRAN, ISLAMIC REPUBLIC OF

Founded in 1979 in the wake of a violent and dramatic revolution, the Islamic Republic of Iran walked a delicate tightrope between modernity and theocracy. For millions of Muslims throughout the world, the Islamic Republic inspired hope that Muslim law could be applied to a modern nation state, while for others who were opposed to its agenda, the country stood out as a repressive, fearful regime.

The Islamic Revolution of 1978 and 1979 destroyed the monarchy of the Pahlavis, who had pursued a secularization policy at the expense of the majority public opinion and allowed foreign investment to control large sectors of the national economy. Millions of Iranians of varying political persuasions—leftists, merchants, and ulema—were particularly troubled by the predominant influence of the American government on Iranian foreign policy and economic decision-making. Despite some gains for the population during the White Revolution (1967–1963) most Iranians lived in poverty, totally alienated from the luxury of the Pahlavi regime, and repressed by its security forces.

The revolution forced Muhammad Reza Shah (1919–1980) to abandon the country by January 1979, ushering the return of the exiled Ayatollah Ruhollah Khomeini (1902–1989). Although Khomeini had been in exile since 1964, his anti-Western and anti-secularization messages had been distributed widely throughout the country, in both print and cassette form. In the wake of the shah's exile, Khomeini returned to Iran in February 1979, becoming the spiritual figurehead of what was now an Islamic Revolution. On 1 April 1979, Iranians voted overwhelmingly to found an Islamic Republic. Their action was inspiring to some, and frightening to others.

From 1979 until 1982, Iran existed in a revolutionary crisis mode. The entire apparatus of government had collapsed, along with the economy. The military and police forces were in disarray, and battles between hard-line clerics and more moderate politicians raged in an effort to determine who would control the new society. The extreme anti-Western, and particularly anti-American, tone of the revolution cut Iran off from the West, compounding its economic problems, yet giving strength to its revolutionary credibility among struggling nations. Although there were many factions against him, Khomeini was able to come to the forefront of the government with the backing of the Revolutionary Guards, formed in 1979 to suppress opponents of the Islamic Republic, and a series of revolutionary tribunals, which meted out harsh justice to collaborators of the Pahlavi regime. For the next few years, those shaping the new Islamic government would completely crush their opposition in a bid to consolidate their power over Iran.

By the end of 1979, Iran had a new constitution, officially declaring the nation an Islamic Republic. The government was structured with an elected president, a prime minister chosen by the president, and an elected parliament, the *Majlis*, and a twelve-member Council of Guardians, dominated by six religious jurists with veto power over all legislation passed by the elected parliament. Finally, the most powerful position in the government lay in the institution of *velayat-e faqih*, which established the office of supreme jurist, one who would rule on all workings of government on behalf of the Hidden Imam of Twelver Shi'ism. This jurist would be Khomeini, effectively making him the supreme leader of the Islamic Republic.

In 1980, the new republic faced serious new crises. In November of 1979, students took control of the United

Iranian clergymen wait to vote in Iranian parliamentary elections in February, 2000, in the courtyard of the Masoumeh holy shrine in Qum, Iran. Though Muhammad Khatemi, elected as president in 1997 and reelected in 2001, is seen as a liberal reformer interested in opening ties with the West, his stances are balanced by a conservative Islamic legislature heavily influenced by the ulema. AP/WIDE WORLD PHOTOS

States Embassy in Tehran, holding fifty-seven hostages for 444 days. This inflamed Western hatred of the revolution, fueling its radicals further. Moreover, in September 1980, Iraq invaded Iran, hoping to take advantage of its fragility to seize control of its large oil fields, as well as to prevent the spread of the revolution across its borders. While anti-Western sentiment was fueling the purge of the military establishment, Iran was now forced to mount a military defense.

In the midst of these international problems, the Islamic Republic's first president, the secular leftist Abu 'l-Hasan Bani-Sadr (b. 1933), attempted to rein in the power of the ulema at home by consolidating the power of local revolutionary tribunals under the watch of the central government and by promoting secular reforms. However, the ulema resented his attempts to assert secular authority, as well as his botched efforts to resolve the hostage crisis with the Americans and the escalating war with Iraq. By 1981 Bani-Sadr was impeached and forced into exile in France, the same place he had been exiled during the shah's regime. Now the road was paved for Khomeini and his Islamic Republic Party (established in 1979) to take full control of Iran.

In the first years of the Republic, a radical program of Islamization purged all secularists and leftists from education, civil service, the military, and other aspects of public life. Universities were particularly altered, with new curricula and libraries privileging Islamic values over all others, and all students with leftist backgrounds barred from attendance. Strict sex-segregation in public was enforced, and women were required to wear the traditional *hijab* while in public. The Islamic Republic's strict moral codes were enforced by the Revolutionary Guards, who maintained a vigilant watch over society on behalf of the clerical ruling class. All secular law was replaced by Islamic interpretations, and those who rebelled against Islamization were subject to imprisonment.

Meanwhile, the war between Iran and Iraq continued. For eight years these neighboring nations battled in a brutal war of attrition, ultimately resulting in 262,000 Iranian casualties and 105,000 Iraqi deaths. Iran stunned the world by repelling the Iraqis and maintaining its borders, but it was not without cost. Iraqi bombing left 1.6 million Iranians homeless, and the nation was forced to dip deep into its already unstable financial reserves to accommodate widowed families and rebuild its damaged infrastructure. However, the Islamic Republic was not toppled by Iraq; indeed, its ability to maintain its sovereignty boosted public morale, despite the terrible human and economic costs.

In 1988 the war with Iraq ended, and Iranians now faced a hard question: Should they continue to reject all Western overtures or was it possible to engage economically with Western nations and still remain Islamic in government? In the next decade, Iran restored diplomatic relations with many European countries. However, it did not restore ties with the United States, which continued to be its primary adversary on the world stage. Even as late as 2002, the United States considered Iran part of an "axis of evil" in the world, while Iran continued regular anti-American protests in response.

With the death of Khomeini in 1989, grief struck the Islamic Republic, and the ruling establishment had to find a replacement for the society's preeminent religious guide. The new supreme jurist, Sayyed 'Ali Khamane'i (b. 1939), had been president since 1981 and had assumed the position, knowing full well that Iran faced tremendous difficulties. Normalizing the nation after years of revolution and war, and stabilizing an economy facing a shocking demographic shift would be difficult. In the early 1980s, the new regime had banned birth control and abortion, and the government promoted the notion that all families should have as many children as they could provide for. This gave Iran a birthrate of 3.9 percent by 1983, and the population nearly doubled to over sixty million people by 1990. That year the government, overloaded with trying to provide for such a massive increase, changed its policy, allowing contraception once again. In

1992 it went a step further and revoked government assistance from any family with more than three children; and it made abortion legal up to 120 days after conception.

Such reforms made Khamane'i and Iran's third president, 'Ali-Akbar Hashemi-Rafsanjani (b. 1934), popular with moderates in the country, but the republic continued throughout the 1990s and beyond to vacillate between periods of liberalization and moments of hard-line crackdown. Under Rafsanjani, Iran's markets became more open to Western goods, but the clerical ruling class continued to exercise dramatic influence over all aspects of public life, particularly in the realm of gender segregation and speaking out against Islam. Meanwhile, sales from Iran's vast oil reserves could not stabilize its economy, and people struggled to maintain their families in the wake of increased prices.

At the end of Rafsanjani's second term, in 1997, spiraling inflation and public dissatisfaction with censorship ushered in the presidency of Mohammad Khatami (b. 1943), a man many saw as a reformer interested in opening up debate in Iranian political life and building social and political bridges with the Western nations. Although he was reelected in 2001, Khatami's liberal positions were balanced by the clerical elite, who continue to exert their influence over a conservative legislature. Opening up Iran's public culture to the influences of Western consumerism, secular government and non-Islamic culture is still a sensitive issue in the Islamic Republic, more than two decades after the beginning of its dramatic revolution. Despite landslide victories in two presidential elections (1997 and 2001), in the elections for municipal and village councils in 1999, and in the parliamentary elections in 2000, Khatami and the reformists have made little progress in the power struggle against the clerical ruling elite.

The creation of the Islamic Republic of Iran was one of the most dramatic events of the twentieth century. For millions of Muslims throughout the world, its foundation was a symbol of the continued validity of their religion for the modern world. For those weary of theocracy, however, it stood as a symbol to be feared. For many Iranians and others, the Islamic Republic continues to represent, in the words of its founder Khomeini, a "third way, neither East nor West."

*See also* **Abu 'l-Hasan Bani-Sadr; Hashemi-Rafsanjani, 'Ali-Akbar; Khomeini, Ruhollah; Muhammad Reza Shah Pahlevi; Revolution: Islamic Revolution in Iran.**

## BIBLIOGRAPHY

Keddie, N. R. *Modern Iran: Roots and Results of Revolution.* New Haven, Conn.: Yale University Press, 2003.

Mackey, Sandra. *The Iranians: Persia, Islam and the Soul of a Nation.* New York: Dutton, 1996.

*Nancy L. Stockdale*

**IRHAB** *See* **Terrorism**

## ISHRAQI SCHOOL

The term *ishraq*, from the Arabic root *sh-r-q*, meaning both illumination and orient, has been used in a general sense in several contexts in Islam, including in reference to certain currents of Sufism. More specifically, however, the term *ishraqi* refers to the school of philosophy/theosophy founded by Shaykh Shihab al-Din Suhrawardi in the twelfth century c.e. The most important source of this school of thought is the major opus of Suhrawardi, *Hikmat al-ishraq* ("Theosophy of the Orient of Light" also known as *The Philosophy of Illumination*), which is also the name of this school in traditional Islamic languages. Certain other works of Suhrawardi, especially his *Hayakil al-nur* (Temples of light), are also of much importance for the later *ishraqi* tradition.

After Suhrawardi was killed by the political authorities in Aleppo in 1191, followers of his teachings went underground for a generation. But in the middle thirteenth century two major commentaries on *Hikmat al-ishraq* appeared, the first by Shams al-Din Shahrazuri and the second by Qutb al-Din Shirazi, the next two major figures of the *ishraqi* school. From that time on, the teachings of this school became widespread, especially in Persia itself from which Suhrawardi had hailed. Such figures as 'Allama al-Hilli and Jalal al-Din Dawani wrote commentaries on Suhrawardi in the thirteenth and fourteenth centuries. The founder of the School of Isfahan, Mir Damad, who lived in the Safavid period that began in Persia in 1499 and lasted until the eighteenth century, was influenced by Suhrawardi and used the name Ishraq for his pen name. Mulla Sadra, his student, wrote one of the major works of the *ishraqi* school, his annotations on the *Hikmat al-ishraq*. Later Persian philosophers such as Sabziwari were also deeply interested in *ishraqi* teachings, and a figure such as the nineteenth-century philosopher Shihab al-Din Kumijani was a purely *ishraqi* figure.

The school of *ishraq* also spread into India and had many followers there, including Fathallah Shirazi and Muhammad Sharif Hirawi. Suhrawardi's teachings became in fact a part of the program of traditional Islamic *madrasa*s, a program that came to be known as the Nizami curriculum. The *ishraqi* school attracted even the attention of Hindus and the Parsis of India.

Likewise, the teachings of the *ishraqi* school spread widely in the Ottoman Empire, especially in Anatolia, and produced some notable figures such as Isma'il Anqarawi, who lived in the seventeenth century. The complete history of this school in the Islamic world, especially in India and the Ottoman Empire, has not been fully studied. As for the West, Suhrawardi was not translated into Latin but there are indications that some of his ideas were known in the Latin West perhaps through Hebrew sources and a number of Jewish philosophers who were *ishraqi* in their perspective.

The *ishraqi* school holds that the origin of philosophy is divine revelation and that this wisdom was handed down in ancient times to the Persians and the Greeks, creating two traditions that met again in Suhrawardi, who spoke explicitly of eternal wisdom or the perennial philosophy. This school believes that authentic philosophy must combine the training of the mind with the purification of the heart and that all authentic knowledge is ultimately an illumination. The *ishraqis* always emphasized the unbreakable link between philosophy and spirituality and the salvific power of illuminative knowledge. They considered God to be the Light of lights and all degree of cosmic reality to be levels and grades of light. They rejected the sensualist epistemology of Aristotle and were critical of not only Aristotelian cosmology but also of his logic and epistemology.

During the twentieth century the teachings of Suhrawardi were introduced to the West by Henry Corbin and have attracted many European philosophers. In Persia and certain other Islamic countries there is also a major revival of interest in Suhrawardi and the *ishraqi* school.

*See also* **Falsafa; Ibn al-'Arabi; Mulla Sadra; Tasawwuf; Wahdat al-wujud.**

### BIBLIOGRAPHY

Aminrazavi, M. *Suhrawardi and the School of Illumination.* London: Curzon, 1997.

Corbin, Henry. *History of Islamic Philosophy.* Translated by L. Sherrard. London: Kegan Paul International, 1993.

Nasr, Seyyed Hossein. *The Islamic Intellectual Tradition in Persia.* London: Curzon, 1996.

Ziai, H. *Knowledge and Illumination. A Study of Suhrawardi's Hikmat al-ishraq.* Atlanta, Ga.: Scholars Press, 1990.

*Seyyed Hossein Nasr*

## ISLAM AND ISLAMIC

The word *islam* is a verbal noun (Ar., *masdar*) in Arabic for the action of submission or total commitment, usually referring to acceptance of and submission to the will of God. It is the name identifying the faith tradition and community of those who believe that there is one God and that the prophet Muhammad was God's messenger, and the person who submits is a "Muslim." In the Qur'an, *islam* appears eight times. It is associated with the concept of *din*, which is translated in modern times as "religion" but has a broader sense of including creed, normative standards, and the whole range of standard behavior. The Qur'an affirms that "With God, the *din* is *al-islam*" (3:19), which can be translated more generally as stating "With God, the true way is submission" or more specifically, "With God, true religion is Islam."

In the historical development of the faith tradition and community of Muslims, the term "Islam" is important in at least two different frameworks. In religious thought, one important issue was defining the relationship between Islam, identified as submission to God expressed in observance of ritual requirements and social behavior, and *iman* or the inner faith of the believer. In this issue, the concept of *islam* was a component part of the broader structure and vocabulary of theology.

A second significant framework is that "Islam" was used as the term denoting the whole body of the faith tradition and the peoples and regions where Islam was practiced. Within this context, the identification of someone as a "Muslim" gave emphasis to being a member of the community of those who recognize the Qur'an as the record of God's revelation and Muhammad as the messenger of God, with less emphasis on the particular practices and behavior of the individual Muslim.

This usage facilitated the transition to modern usage in which "Islam" is identified in the scholarly study of this religion as one of the major religions of the world. This reification of "Islam" was similar to the processes of Western scholarly classification of other "world religions," as in what came to be called "Hinduism" or "Confucianism." Initially, other objectionable and historically inaccurate terms like "Mohammedanism" were used but they have gradually been displaced in common usage by "Islam."

By the late twentieth century, in the context of the Islamic resurgence, some made a distinction between "Muslim" used as an adjective and "Islamic." The term Muslim is increasingly identified with the existing community and the practices of people self-identified as Muslim. The term "Islamic" has sometimes been reserved for those instances where there is a conscious effort to reflect the fundamental principles and ideals of Islam interpreted in a relatively restrictive way. In this usage, for example, a "Muslim state" is a state where the majority of the people are Muslim, while an "Islamic state" would be one in which there is a formal program of implementation of the regulations and ideals of Islam. "Islam" remains the identification of the religion underlying both usages.

*See also* **Islamicate Society.**

## BIBLIOGRAPHY

Arkoun, Mohammed. *Rethinking Islam: Common Questions, Uncommon Answers.* Translated by Robert D. Lee. Boulder, Colo.: Westview, 1994.

Asad, Talal. *Genealogies of Religion.* Baltimore, Md.: The Johns Hopkins University Press, 1993.

Smith, Wilfred Cantwell. *The Meaning and End of Religion.* New York: Macmillan Company, 1963.

*John O. Voll*

## ISLAM AND OTHER RELIGIONS

Understanding the relations between Muslims and a variety of religious "Others," including Jews, Christians, Zoroastrians, Hindus, Buddhists, as well as Africans, Chinese, Mongols, Turks, and Westerners, depends on how one defines *religion* and *religious.* In addition, there is a diversity of Muslim identities that shapes the various perceptions of and relations to religious Others, just as there are many identities other than religious ones that intersect with the Muslim-Others duality, such as tribal, ethnic, linguistic, national, and the like.

As with any categorization of identities and concepts, the boundaries between Islam and Others remain fluid, and exceptions can often be found. The most striking example of this fluidity is the term *umma,* which came to mean, from the first centuries of Islam until today, the community of all Muslims in contradistinction to all Others, whether religious or not. Yet, initially, *umma* included Muslims as well as non-Muslims, and it especially included Jews, as indicated in the so-called Constitution of Medina negotiated by the prophet Muhammad as a basis for the migration of his nascent Islamic community from Mecca to Medina in 622 C.E. The *umma* referred to then was inclusive of all the peoples living in Medina under the leadership of the prophet Muhammad.

It is nevertheless possible to generalize and say that the history of Muslim-Other relations has been interpreted by Muslims through the lenses of a tripartite theological division of the human world: Muslims, who submit to the will of God as revealed in the Qur'an; People of the Book, who believe in the same God although their knowledge comes from a distorted version of the original divine revelation; and Unbelievers, who either associate idols to God or deny God's existence. This categorization emerged out of the unique historical context of the lifetime of the prophet Muhammad, (ca. 570–632 C.E.) in central Arabia, and evolved over time, becoming increasingly complex as Islam grew in numbers and in geographical spread.

### The Lifetime of the Prophet Muhammad

The first period of Muslim-Other relations corresponds to the lifetime of the prophet Muhammad. The best sources on these first relations between Muslims and religious Others include pre-Islamic poems, the Qur'an, early hadith, and biographies. While the reliability of these sources for historical reconstruction has been highly debated in recent years, it remains possible to infer that prior to 610 C.E., when the prophet Muhammad is believed to have received the first

Qur'anic revelation, his encounters with religious Others primarily included Christians and Jews that he may have met in some Arabian oasis as well as during his northern caravan trips into greater Syria. With subsequent revelations, which he continued to receive until his death in 632 C.E., the prophet Muhammad gradually distanced himself from the various tribal practices of his fellow Quraysh tribesmen while developing a new Islamic identity, thereby turning most Meccans of his own clan and tribe into religious Others too. Together with the earliest converts, the prophet Muhammad experienced a series of encounters with religious Others that included an increasingly hostile Meccan resistance as well as *hunafa* (sg. *hanif*: monotheistic ascetics), Jews, and Christians of mostly unknown theological leanings, except for the small number of early Muslim converts who sought refuge with Ethiopian Christians in the Abyssinian kingdom in 615 C.E.

A greater formative influence came from 622 C.E. onward, after the prophet Muhammad had negotiated the Constitution of Medina, which allowed the Muslim community to migrate there from Mecca. This agreement not only provided an escape for the nascent Muslim community increasingly threatened in Mecca, but it also propelled the prophet Muhammad to the status of both arbitrator and religiopolitical leader of this oasis. Its two largest, formerly animist tribes, the Aws and Khazraj, had been fighting each other for many years before they settled on the prophet Muhammad as their arbitrator. The Constitution stipulated the conditions for the Prophet's intervention as leader, as were the respective rights and responsibilities of the immigrant Muslims and Ansars (the newly converted Medinan Muslims of the the Aws and Khazraj), as well as those of the three small Jewish tribes (Banu Qaynuqaʿ, Banu Nadir and Banu Qurayza).

Within the Constitution, Jews were included in the definition of the one community or *umma*. This marked the beginning of a short period of cooperation between Muslims and Jews that has left permanent traces in Muslims' self-understanding as monotheists, such as the incorporation into Islamic beliefs of the long genealogy of Jewish prophets. In addition, early Muslims recognized Jesus as another Jewish prophet, albeit with some unique Christian characteristics, such as the virgin birth and the special role he played in being the messenger of the *injil* (Gospel). Other influences included the brief use of Jerusalem as the direction for daily prayers, the development of fasting during the month of Ramadhan in opposition to and part imitation of the day of atonement (*yom kippur*), and the emphasis on orality within a sacred textuality, later developing into the unique religious legalism that makes Islam so similar to Judaism. However, in 624, due to attacks from the Meccans and accusations of treasons, the Jewish tribe of Banu Qaynuqaʿ was expelled from Medina. A year later, after another defeat, the Banu Nadir suffered the same fate. Finally, in 627, after a long siege of Medina itself, the barely victorious Muslims exterminated the last Jewish tribe, the Banu Qurayza, under recurring accusations of treason.

The short history of Muslim-Jewish relations in Medina that had started well with the Constitution of Medina ended up tragically with the disappearance of the Jewish tribes from the oasis. These various historical events are reflected in the many, and at times contradictory, Qur'anic passages regarding the Jews in general and Muslim-Jewish relations in particular.

This brief history holds the hermeneutical keys to the subsequent treatment of Jews and other minorities on the basis of analogy. The hermeneutical concept of abrogation (which holds that later revelations supercede earlier ones) has been used at different times in Islamic history, but especially in the later part of the twentieth century, to claim more intolerant and exclusivist positions regarding Jews, but others favor a return to the ideal of the constitution of Medina because it implies that a more tolerant and inclusivist approach was willed initially by the prophet Muhammad. In reconstructing these historical encounters, contemporary Muslims and non-Muslims alike have uncovered a dual historical process: The historical events of the pristine community become paradigmatic models that shape future relations. With newer historical events, new interpretations emerge, but always within the conceptual framework of what the paradigm initially set forth. This process can be exemplified today in how the constitution of Medina serves as a rich historical and theological document to guide contemporary reinterpretations of how Muslims ought to relate to religious Others, especially within contemporary nation-states in which Muslims comprise the majority population.

### The Early Muslim Conquests: 632–750 C.E.

The second period in Muslim-Other relations begins after the death of the prophet Muhammad, in 632 C.E. With the sudden departure of their religiopolitical leader, Muslims developed additional and, at times, overlapping categorizations and concepts to manage their relations with religious Others, whether within the nascent Islamic polity or outside of it. The dual categorization of the house of Islam (*dar al-islam*) versus the house of war (*dar al-harb*) emerged to describe the relations between Muslims in Muslim-controlled areas and Others in non-Muslim controlled areas.

Within Muslim-controlled areas, the concept of the protected people (*ahl al-dhimmi*) arose to regulate Muslim-Other relations. The *dhimmi*s, organized collectively by religion, had to pay a head tax (*jizya*) and a land tax (*kharaj*) in exchange for military protection by Muslim armies. They included Jews, Christians, and Sabians, as noted in the Qur'an, but soon also included Zoroastrians, who constituted the majority population of the Sassanian Empire, which was taken over by Muslims within a decade of the Prophet's death. There were a few exceptions to this general practice, such as the Armenians contributing men to the Umayyad army to fight against the Byzantine Empire, thereby briefly avoiding the *jizya* tax. Yet, on the whole, these new categorizations and concepts remained central to Islam for over a thousand years. They continue to this day to be used in their traditional meanings by many Muslims, while a few others reinterpret them in light of new modern political realities. The silent majority probably dismisses these traditional categorizations and meanings as no longer relevant.

### The Consolidation of Power: 750–1258 C.E.

The centralization and consolidation of Muslim political power was exemplified respectively by the first and second halves of the Abbasid Empire (749–1258 C.E.). This long period witnessed a slow conversion process that led to the gradual emergence of majority Muslim societies in what came to be known as central Islamic lands from Spain (al-Andalus) to central Asia. Internally, most religious Others within Muslim polities were Islamized over generations. In part because Islamic worldviews and practices became normative in these regions, exerting social pressure to convert, and in part because *dhimmi* laws came to be perceived as discriminatory and no longer as relevant in a period of *pax islamica*. Externally, in addition to the People of the Book, Muslims in South and Central Asia came into contact with increasing numbers of Hindus, Buddhists, and a variety of Turkic and Chinese Others, which often rendered the boundary between religion and culture harder to delineate.

The greatest experiment in coexistence and mutual respect between Muslims on the one hand and Jews and Christians on the other is undoubtedly the case of Muslim Spain, al-Andalus, during its own Umayyad dynasty (756–1031 C.E.). The degree of symbiosis that emerged, especially during the respective but not sequential reigns of the three 'Abd al-Rahmans (styled I, II, and III), is exemplary of its popular name, the Golden Age of Spain.

By the end of the weakened Abbasid Empire, the destruction brought about in the mid-thirteenth century by the Mongol invasions from the east to what had been the center of Islamic power surprisingly resulted in the Islamic conversion of this new enemy. The changes brought about by this rapid influx of new cultural traditions from peripheral nomadic cultures were therefore not as dramatic, but they did bring about a certain cleansing that resulted in a greater homogeneity in those parts of the Muslim world. A similar phenomenon had already happened earlier at the extreme west of the Islamic world, with the sequential waves of the al-Murabitun (Almoravids 1056–1147) and the al-Muwahhidun (Almohads 1130–1269), sweeping from the Sahara into what is now Morocco and Spain. They were reacting in part to the Christian Reconquista that was gradually taking over Muslim-controlled areas in the Iberian Peninsula.

The long Abbasid period was marked by the consolidation of Islamic laws that became normative and remain so up to this day. They consolidated many practices regarding non-Muslims through the integration of earlier key concepts such as People of the Book and *ahl al-dhimma*, together with customary practices (*'ada*) in various parts of the expanding Muslim world. This flexibility in the Islamic legal system to accommodate many local cultural practices that did not directly infringe on central Islamic tenets greatly enabled the long term consolidation of Islam wherever it spread. Muslim-Other relations thus often proved to be a two-way bridge with mutual influences.

An important incursion into the heart of Islamic lands occurred when the Crusaders captured Jerusalem, in 1099. Their arrival was marked by massacres of both Muslims and Jews. They were considered barbarians by the mostly Muslim local population. Salah al-Din recovered Jerusalem in 1187 without any bloodshed. The Crusaders slowly lost control of their principalities until their last defeat, in 1302. The memory of the Crusades remains alive to this day, having caused great distrust between Muslims and Christians in particular. Today, many Arab Muslims use this historical vignette as a trope for interpreting mid- to late-twentieth and early twenty-first-century politics associated with the creation of the State of Israel.

### The Continued Expansion of Islam: 1258–1798 C.E.

After consolidation, Islam continued to spread through a slow process of land migrations and conversions in Southeastern Europe; sub-Saharan Africa; and South, Southeast and East Asia, up to and into the colonial period. This was a vast and mostly peaceful expansion on the peripheries of central Islamic lands, with two exceptions: the Ottoman Empire (1300–1918), centered in what is today called Turkey, and the Mughal Empire (1483–1858) of South Asia. Between the two, the smaller and short-lived Safavid Empire (1501–1722) exemplified the internal Islamic conversion from Sunni to Twelver Shi'ite Islam, bringing few changes to the interpretation of religious Others. The continued presence, albeit dwindling, of Zoroastrians, Assyrian Christians, and Jews proved the long-term resilience of the traditional Islamic system of *ahl al-dhimma*, traces of which are found today in the fixed Jewish, Christian, and Zoroastrian seats in the democratically elected parliament of the Islamic Republic of Iran.

At the height of its power in the sixteenth and seventeenth centuries, the Ottoman Empire expanded dramatically into Southeastern Europe and besieged Vienna twice (1529 and 1683). The Ottomans refined the *millet* system, an administrative elaboration on the *ahl al-dhimma* concept that accommodated religious diversity and often provided each religious community (*milla*) with a large degree of autonomy. However, the Ottomans also developed the practice of *devshirme*: the forcible conscription and conversion to Islam of young Christian boys, especially in the Balkans, in order to build an elite military corps, the Janissaries. Since much benefit could have come from a link to central power through one's son, at times, Christian elite families, even some Muslim families, offered up their sons to the Ottomans voluntarily.

At the same time, in South Asia, the Mughal Empire reached its apogee. The difference was that the majority of the population under its control, mostly Hindus, never converted to Islam. The Mughal emperors used radically different approaches in their relations to their subjects. While the initial and later Muslim military and political presence in South Asia witnessed much intolerance and destruction, the most powerful of its emperors, Akbar (1542–1605) and his nephew Dara Shukoh (1615–1659), tried to have Hindus recognized as People of the Book. Emperor Akbar even developed his own religion, *din ilahi*, that combined Islamic and Hindu worldviews and practices. While his efforts were ultimately unsuccessful, a similar but more popular effort led to the development of Sikhism in the Punjab.

## The Colonial Period: 1798–1945 C.E.

The period of Western European colonization of most majority Muslim lands radically changed the nature of power dynamics in Muslim-Other relations. In 1798, Napoleon invaded Egypt for a brief period of three years. This event is often referred to as the symbolic beginning of a major shift in power between Muslims and non-Muslim Others, whether religious or not. While earlier political events such as the Crusades, the Reconquista, as well as the Mongol and Turkic (Tamerlane 1336–1405) invasions directly impinged on majority Muslim areas, the first was relatively brief, the second took place over centuries, and the third and fourth resulted in the conversion to Islam of the new Mongol and Turkic rulers, the last two being more inconspicuous in the collective memory despite their even more violent histories than that of the Crusades. In contrast, the military and political Western European takeover of most of the world between 1492 and 1945 took place together with an economic, cultural, and ideological penetration that overwhelmed majority Muslim societies. For the first time in their history they lost control over the balance of power that they had collectively held since their earliest memories. Only Turkey, Saudi Arabia, and to a lesser degree, Iran, retained some measure of independence.

Parallel to this colonial enterprise was the introduction of new scientific discourses that have sought, ever since the Enlightenment period, objective truth about the world, both material and human. The part of science which has dealt with discovering the truth about Islam has been known as Orientalism. This influential school of thought helped consolidate power in the hands of the colonial masters by means of arguments that often, though not always, supported the logic of empire: The West would civilize the backward Islamic world (as part of the 'Orient'). Yet, despite its politically pro-Western bias, Orientalist scholarship also brought about new standards of interpretation and preservation of much Islamic heritage, resulting in greater mutual understanding. Nonetheless, much of the Muslim-Other relations during this period were reduced to Muslim-Westerner relations, due to the unavoidable colonial power of the West.

## The Post-Colonial Period: 1945 to the Present

The post-colonial period has seen a continuation of many established trends, despite the emergence of independent nation-states. New technologies, however, brought about radical changes in migration patterns: Muslim workers were brought into Western Europe in the 1950s and 1960s, others migrated to Australia and the Americas, especially to North America. In the United States, important African-American conversions to Islam started a local Islamization process that is currently unfolding rapidly, despite the backlash in American perceptions of Muslims.

Scientism was imported initially through colonialism and later strengthened by programs of national education supported by the westernized Muslim elites of newly independent majority Muslim nation-states. With this, much Orientalist thinking was integrated into popular modern Islamic self-understanding. This influence is clearly at work in the rise of militant Islam, which is a phenomenon similar to Christian fundamentalism in the West in that they both essentialize their understanding of religion in political discourses. The result is a growing reciprocal popular intolerance between the West and Islam, further fueled by the 11 September 2001 events in the United States and their subsequent impact on world politics.

The encounter with modernity through colonialism has taken a toll on the possibility of seeing positively the values of democracy, the rule of law (Western style), and human rights, because such discourses come from political oppressors. With the continuation of this control through the more subtle forces of neo-liberal discourse and globalization, the West has become an overarching Other among many Muslims worldwide. The cost of this has been the development of a major malaise for many westernized Muslims, and especially for Muslims living in the West itself. Yet, the Muslim world is no different from many other religiocultural worlds that have fought to distinguish between modernization, which they want to participate in for its obvious material benefits, and westernization, which often imposes Western values and models for democracy upon societies that have their own cultural heritage and blueprints for collective decision-making.

The interaction between Muslims and Others in general remains a two-way bridge of potential mutual benefits, if only reciprocal fears did not prevent many of both sides from traveling across it. The advent of interreligious dialogue in the later part of the twentieth century has encouraged this movement, however. Many contemporary Muslims are thinking anew not only their relationship to sacred Islamic texts and their various traditions of interpretation in light of historicocritical and dialogical methods of inquiry, but are also reconsidering the very nature of their interdependence with religious Others, whether by opposition or attraction. With the advent of Western European colonialism and the emergence of postcolonial nation-states, as well as the expansion of Muslims worldwide in modern times, the balance of power has recently undergone radical change. Many of the older Islamic categorizations and concepts that have served Muslim-Other relations relatively well in the past have now either faded or been judged as obsolete by well-thinking but often paternalistic modernists, or else are in the process of being reinterpreted for a better integration of past and present, as well as internal and external aspects of Islam.

### The New Expansion of Islam in Cyberspace: 1995 to the Present

The advent of the Internet is radically changing the nature of communication worldwide, creating transnational communities of all kinds into virtual entities that are both global and local at once. This transformation brings in its wake new rules of communication and the potential for new forms of grassroots politics, as well as a paradoxical understanding of what constitutes private and public spaces, thereby affecting both traditional Islamic self-understanding as well as Muslim-Other relations. The potential impact of this new period of expansion is as yet unknown for the future of Islam and Muslim-Other relations. This cyberspace expansion helps at once to sustain greater cultural and religious continuities globally, despite large migration movements, and yet threatens the fabric of traditional Islam by its very intrusion into the private spaces of those who can afford being wired into this new space to be explored, shared, disputed, but never truly conquered.

### Complex, Ongoing History

Throughout their long history, Muslims have continued to develop and expand worldwide, bringing them into contact with a variety of religious and nonreligious Others. The legacy of those encounters is rich and complex, with moments of great tolerance and cross-fertilization as well as episodes of intolerance and mutual violence. External and internal influences from religious Others have been felt at all times and continue to this day. What has changed the equation from tolerance to intolerance at different times in history, including very recently, is the degree to which threats and insecurities are perceived by a Muslim community that has internalized the ideal of political control as an implicit measure of its collective identity and success, from the inherited reading of its own history from the time of the prophet Muhammad until today.

The history of Muslim-Other relations is, therefore, a complex and ongoing set of both tolerant and intolerant attitudes and episodes. Both sets are diverse in kind at any one time, even sometimes contradictory to one another; they are shaped by socio-political, theological, and ideological realities that change over time, albeit at different rhythms. Internal dynamics within Muslim societies have always been interdependent with external ones. The history of Muslim-Other relations is, therefore, an integral part of any search to understand Islam. The converse for any religious Others who have come in contact with Muslims throughout their history is equally true.

*See also* **Andalus, al-; Central Asia, Islam in; Christianity and Islam; Dar al-Harb; Dar al-Islam; East Asia, Islam in; European Culture and Islam; Expansion; Hinduism and Islam; Hospitality and Islam; Internet; Judaism and Islam; Modernism; Networks, Muslim; Orientalism; Science, Islam and; South Asia, Islam in; Theology; Umma; Vernacular Islam.**

### BIBLIOGRAPHY

Bamyeh, Mohammed A. *The Social Origins of Islam: Mind, Economy, Discourse.* Minneapolis: University of Minnesota Press, 1999.

Daniel, Norman. *Islam and the West: The Making of an Image.* Oxford, U.K.: Oneworld, 1993.

Esack, Farid. *Qur'an, Liberation, and Pluralism: An Islamic Perspective of Interreligious Solidarity Against Oppression.* Oxford, U.K.: Oneworld, 1997.

Hillenbrand, C. *The Crusades: Islamic Perspectives.* Edinburgh: Edinburgh University Press, 1999.

Laiou, Angeliki E., and Mottahedeh, Roy Parviz, eds. *The Crusades from the Perspective of Byzantium and the Muslim World.* Washington, D.C.: Dumbarton Oaks Research Library and Collection, c. 2001.

Madigan, Daniel A. *The Qur'an's Self-Image: Writing and Authority in Islam's Scripture.* Princeton, N.J.: Princeton University Press, 2001.

Runciman, S. *A History of the Crusades.* Cambridge, U.K.: Cambridge University Press, 1951.

Waardenburg, Jacques, ed. *Muslim Perceptions of Other Religions: A Historical Survey.* Oxford, U.K.: Oxford University Press, 1999.

Ye'or, Bat. *Islam and Dhimmitude: Where Civilizations Collide.* Teaneck, N.J.: Fairleigh Dickinson University Press, 2002.

*Patrice C. Brodeur*

## ISLAMICATE SOCIETY

The term *Islamicate culture* was coined by Marshall Hodgson (d. 1968) in the first volume of his *The Venture of Islam* (1974). Hodgson invented the term in response to the confusion surrounding such terms as "Islamic," "Islam," and "Muslim" when they are used to describe aspects of society and culture that are found throughout the Muslim world. Hodgson used the term to describe cultural manifestations arising out of an Arabic and Persian literate tradition, which does not refer directly to the Islamic religion but to the "social and cultural complex historically associated with Islam and the Muslims, both among Muslims themselves and even when found among non-Muslims" (p. 59). For example, Hodgson argued that there are a variety of artistic, architectural, and literary styles indicative of Islamicate culture. No matter where these aesthetic styles are found, they are identifiable as deriving from Islamicate cultural complexes. Thus, if one finds the use of arabesques, calligraphy, or arched doorways anywhere in the world, these forms are identifiable as Islamicate in origin. In constrast, Hodgson argued that those elements of Islamic society that are not shared by non-Muslims are not indicative of Islamicate culture (for instance, mosque architecture). Due to the overriding influence of Islam on non-Muslims living within Muslim realms, however, Hodgson used the term to demonstrate the importance of Islam as a cultural force that influenced non-Muslim forms of art, literature, and custom.

*See also* **Islam and Islamic.**

## BIBLIOGRAPHY

Hodgson, Marshall G. S. *The Venture of Islam: Conscience and History in a World Civilization.* Chicago: University of Chicago Press, 1974.

Martin, Richard C. *Islamic Studies: A History of Religions Approach.* Upper Saddle River, N.J.: Prentice Hall, 1996.

*R. Kevin Jaques*

# ISLAMIC JIHAD

Two groups have the name Islamic Jihad (sometimes called the Organization of the Islamic Jihad), one Egyptian, the other Palestinian. These two movements contend that armed struggle is the Islamically ordained form of striving against a corrupt authoritarian regime in Egypt and military occupation in Palestine. Both were influenced by the teachings of the Muslim Brothers, but grew more critical of its reformist approach.

A small group of students founded the Egyptian *Tanzim al-Jihad* (Jihad organization) in Alexandria in 1977. The Jihad concentrated its activities in Cairo, while its rival *al-Gama'a al-Islamiyya* (The Islamic Group) dominated Upper Egypt. Despite similarities in dogma and membership—and an attempt at unification in 1981—Jihad has not formed a grassroots movement. The main theorist of the Jihad is Muhammad 'Abd al-Salam Faraj, who wrote a tract entitled *al-Farida al-gha'iba* (The forgotten obligation). The forgotten obligation among Muslims today is jihad, or the struggle to uproot Muslim leaders perceived by the group as infidels, and replace them with a comprehensive "Islamic state." The main path to its goal is by penetrating the military. The closest the group came to attaining its goal was when members of Jihad assassinated President Anwar Sadat on 6 October 1981, but failed to complete the takeover of the state. Conspirators were executed and hundreds of other members arrested. Arrested members were young, educated, and lower to middle class. It was not until the late 1990s that the Egyptian government

succeeded in eliminating the security threat of the Jihad, at a high cost of repression and violation of the basic human right of nonviolent opposition. Some Jihad members escaped into Afghanistan and joined Usama bin Ladin in forming al-Qa'ida. The most prominent of them is Ayman Zawahiri, second to Bin Laden and linked to the terrorist attacks of 11 September 2001.

The Palestinian *Harakat al-jihad al-Islami* (Islamic Jihad Movement) was founded by Fathi al-Shiqaqi and 'Abd al-'Aziz 'Auda in 1981. Both studied in Egypt and were influenced by the teachings of Egyptian radical Islamists. Another inspiration was the Iranian Revolution. The main goal of this organization is the liberation of Palestine, as the central issue for Muslims, and the establishment of an Islamic state. At least two other groups embrace the same name, but the Shiqaqi faction remains the largest. The group carried out several violent attacks against Israelis prior to the first intifada (1987–1993), in which it was active. Israel retaliated by expelling its two founders, and arresting and even assassinating some of its activists, including Shiqaqi, who was murdered by the Mossad (the Israeli secret service) in Malta in October 1995. Ramadan Shalah succeeded Shiqaqi as the organization's Secretary General. Since the establishment of Hamas in 1988, the Islamic Jihad has lost some of its appeal. Despite hostility in the late 1980s between the two groups, both have closed ranks in their opposition to the Oslo agreement and the Palestinian Authority, and after 1994, were joined in this effort by leftist Palestinian groups. Since the outbreak of the second intifada in September 2000, the Jihad has taken active part in fighting occupation forces and assailing Israeli civilians.

*See also* **Ikhwan al-Muslimin; Political Islam; Qa'ida, al-.**

## BIBLIOGRAPHY

Faraj, Mohamed 'Abd al-Salam. *Al-Jihad: al-farida al-gha'iba* (Jihad: The forgotten obligation). Jerusalem: Maktabet 'Iz al-Din al-Qassam, 1982.

Ghadbian, Najib. "Political Islam and Violence." *New Political Science* 22 (2000): 77–88.

Shiqaqi, Fathi al-. *Al-Mashrou 'al-islami al-mu 'asir fi filastin* (The contemporary Islamic project in Palestine). n.p., 1995.

*Najib Ghadbian*

# ISLAMIC SALVATION FRONT

Even for Algerians, the founding of the Islamist party, the Islamic Salvation Front (FIS, *Front Islamique du Salut,* or *al-Jabha al-Islamiyya li-l-inqadh*), in February 1989, and its sweeping electoral victories in the 1990 municipal elections, and then in the first round of legislative elections in December 1991, were events as unforeseeable as they were phenomenal. Islamic symbols and discourse had been used repeatedly to oppose the alliance between the army and the sole legal political party, the National Liberation Front (FLN, or *Front de Libération Nationale*), since Algeria's birth as a nation in 1962. Nonetheless, the meteoric rise of the FIS can mostly be attributed to the growing economic gap between the elites and the masses, which worsened in the 1980s and pushed people over the edge of frustration and despair.

In October 1988 young people took to the streets to protest the state's inability to satisfy their basic needs, and in five days the army had killed over five hundred protesters. President Chadli Benjedid, sensing the gravity of the situation, boldly proposed a constitution to pave the way for multiparty elections. Yet it was not the handful of secular-leaning parties who gained from the riots, but rather those who saw in Islam the salvation for the nation's woes—Algeria's homegrown Islamism.

Islam had already played a key role in Algeria's struggle against French colonialism. The reformist Salafiyya movement was launched by Shaykh 'Abd al-Hamid Ibn Badis when, in 1931, he founded of the Association of Algerian Ulema. The FIS's two founding leaders claimed to wear Ibn Badis's mantle, yet only 'Abbasi Madani (b. 1931) could realistically do so. Indeed, he grew up in ulema circles, joined the FLN, and spent several years in French prisons. He later obtained a doctorate in philosophy in England. As a professor he and other Islamic leaders cultivated the growing Islamist student movement of the 1980s. By contrast, the second leader, 'Ali Belhadj, born in 1956, was a school teacher, and knew no French. His rise began as a young, fiery, eloquent imam who successfully organized a massive peaceful rally at the end of the bloody 1988 riots. From the start, Madani led the more moderate, reformist wing of the FIS, and Belhadj its more radical wing.

The army arrested Madani and Belhadj in June 1991 and, after the December first-round elections, which portended an Islamist majority in parliament, deposed Benjedid and banned the FIS. With all of its leaders either imprisoned or exiled, the uneasy populist coalition fell apart. A more moderate leadership took over the party under 'Abdelkader Hachani, and the radicals broke off to found the GIA (*Groupe Islamique Armé*). In the bloody civil war that ensued (over 120,000 killed, mostly civilians, in ten years), two rays of hope appeared in the 1990s. First, eight opposition parties, including the FIS, signed the Rome Platform in 1995, condemning violence and calling for the reestablishment of democracy. Second, single presidential candidates were successively elected by majority vote, Liamine Zeroual (1995) and 'Abd al-'Aziz Bouteflika (1998). In the early 2000s the army retained its strong grip on power, but in spite of the continued ban on the FIS and the competition of two other legal Islamist parties (HAMAS and al-Nahda), most Algerians believe that without the reinstatement of the FIS, Algeria will not likely see the return of democracy and national reconciliation.

*See also* 'Abd al-Hamid Ibn Badis; Madani, 'Abbasi.

## BIBLIOGRAPHY

Shahin, Emad Eldin. *Political Ascent: Contemporary Islamic Movements in North Africa*. Boulder, Colo.: Westview Press, 1997.

Shah-Kazemi, Reza, ed. *Algeria: Revolution Revisited*. London: Islamic World Report, 1997.

*David L. Johnston*

# ISLAMIC SOCIETY OF NORTH AMERICA

The Islamic Society of North America (ISNA) was founded in 1982 and is currently based in Plainfield, Indiana. ISNA grew out of the Muslim Students Association (MSA), which was founded in the 1960s by predominately South Asian Muslim students who, upon graduation, sought to organize professional Muslim associations under one administrative apparatus. The ideology of the organization is influenced by the writings of Abu l-'Ala' Maududi (d. 1979).

Maududi argued that Islam had become corrupted because of a general Muslim ignorance of Islamic history and piety. Only through an active movement of community organization and education could Islam return to the position of power and authority that Maududi understood the classical Muslim world to possess. ISNA has sought to educate American Muslims through a variety of programs and by funding workshops and conventions to teach people how to develop strong Muslim communities in a North American cultural context. Since the mid-1990s, and especially after the 11 September 2001 terrorist attacks on Washington, D.C. and New York, the centerpiece of ISNA activities has been its Community Development Department, which organizes a variety of conferences and workshops dealing with such issues as community development, domestic violence prevention, conflict resolution, and media relations.

In contrast to other Muslim organizations, ISNA has tended to stay out of electoral politics, preferring to educate Muslims about the American political system and allowing local communities to choose candidates based on local needs. In addition, ISNA also publishes a bimonthly magazine, *Islamic Horizons*, which discusses issues relating to Muslim life in North America, and includes information on conventions and workshops as well as a matrimonial section. ISNA does not currently publish membership statistics. As of the year 2003, however, *Islamic Horizons* reported a circulation of approximately 60,000. Since many, if not most members receive the magazine as a part of their membership, this figure most likely reflects membership totals.

## BIBLIOGRAPHY

Haddad, Yvonne. *The Muslims of America.* New York: Oxford University Press, 1991.

Mawdudi, Abul A'laa. *Towards Understanding Islam.* n.p.: Islamic Circle of North America, 1986.

Smith, Jane I. *Islam in America.* New York: Columbia University Press, 1993.

*R. Kevin Jaques*

# ISMA'IL I, SHAH (1487–1524)

Shah Isma'il (r. 1501–1524) was founder and first king of the Safavid dynasty, which ruled Iran until 1722. Isma'il lived during a turbulent time in Iran's history, in a period of political fragmentation and decentralization. When Isma'il's brother Sultan 'Ali was killed in battle by the ruling house of Aq Qoyunlu in 1494, Isma'il went into hiding in northern Iran. In 1499, he and his Qizilbash followers, Turkoman tribesmen, attempted to seize power, and defeated the last Aq Qoyunlu ruler. He was crowned king in the northern Iranian city of Tabriz in 1501.

Before becoming king, Isma'il's religiosity reflected Shi'ite "exaggerated" beliefs such as anthropomorphism with respect to God, transmigration of souls, and occultation and return. In his poetry, he claims divinity for himself, and proclaims to be the Hidden Imam. His followers were said to have followed him into battle without wearing armor, believing him to be invincible.

In 1501, however, Isma'il established not *ghuluww* Shi'ism, but orthodox Twelver Shi'ism as the official state religion, imposing this sect upon a predominantly Sunni Iran. He spent the next ten years of his career consolidating and expanding his rule inside Iran and beyond. He was defeated in Azerbaijan by the Ottomans at the battle of Chaldiran in 1514. This led to a ceasing of military campaigns. Isma'il died ten years later, in 1524.

*See also* **Empires: Safavid and Qajar.**

## BIBLIOGRAPHY

Savory, Roger. *Iran under the Safavids.* Cambridge, U.K.: Cambridge University Press, 1980.

*Sholeh A. Quinn*

# J

## JA'FAR AL-SADIQ (C. 701–765)

Born sometime between 700 and 702, Ja'far al-Sadiq died in 765 C.E. An erudite jurist of Medina, al-Sadiq was associated with a wide range of scholars. Abu Hanifa, and Malik b. Anas, among other prominent figures, are alleged to have heard hadith from him. Regarded as a reliable traditionalist in Sunni circles, he is cited in several *isnad*s (chains of transmissions). Al-Sadiq is credited with the construction of a legal system called Ja'fari school of law, which Shi'ites follow. He is also seen as an eminent ascetic and is revered in Sufi circles. Many mystical ideas are narrated from him. According to the alchemist Jabir al-Hayyan, al-Sadiq was also a teacher in alchemy.

Sunni sources maintain that Shi'ites, such as Hisham b. al-Hakam, formulated distinctive doctrines like that of the imamate and ascribed it to al-Sadiq. In Shi'ite sources, al-Sadiq is considered as the sixth Imam and the author of thousands of traditions that were recorded by his disciples and documented in the writings of al-Kulini and Ibn Babuya, among other, later, scholars. These sources also indicate that al-Sadiq was responsible for the formulation and crystallization of the Shi'ite doctrine of the imamate. This stipulated that the imam be designated by God through the Prophet or another imam. The imam was also believed to be infallible, hence he was empowered to provide authoritative interpretations of Islamic revelation. Designation and infallibility were complemented by the imam's possession of special knowledge that was either transmitted from the Prophet or derived from inherited scrolls. The imams reportedly had access to esoteric knowledge and were able to foretell future events.

Al-Sadiq's political stance became the cornerstone of Shi'ite political theory, which taught coexistence with rather than opposition to tyrannical rulers. The removal of the imamate from a political role was compounded by al-Sadiq's teaching of dissimulation, which meant the imam did not have to publicly proclaim his leadership.

Al-Sadiq attracted an intellectual and cohesive following. He is reported to have trained thousands of disciples in diverse fields such as theology, jurisprudence, and Arabic grammar. Speculative Shi'ite theologians and jurists like Hisham b. al-Hakam, Zurara b. A'yan, and Muhammad b. Muslim were associated with him. Some of his prominent disciples are reported to have differed with him on major points of law and theology, for which they were condemned or excommunicated. Al-Sadiq claimed that they had misrepresented his teachings.

Al-Sadiq was at the center of much extremist speculation. Abu 'l-Khattab (d. 755–756) claimed that al-Sadiq had designated him to be his deputy and had entrusted him with esoteric knowledge and the greatest name of God, thus empowering him to comprehend occult sciences. He also attributed divinity to al-Sadiq. Along with other extremist groups, Abu 'l-Khattab was repudiated by al-Sadiq.

After his death, al-Sadiq's followers differed on his successor. The Isma'ilis claimed al-Sadiq had designated his eldest son, Isma'il, to succeed him. Most of al-Sadiq's followers initially accepted 'Abdallah, the eldest surviving son. When 'Abdallah died without a son, the majority accepted al-Sadiq's next son, Musa. They formed the basis of the Twelver Shi'ites. The Nawusiyya asserted that al-Sadiq was in occultation (hiding), and would reappear as the eschatological Messiah (*mahdi*).

*See also* **Imamate; Law; Succession.**

### BIBLIOGRAPHY

Hodgson, Marshall G. "How did the Early Shi'a Become Sectarian?" *Journal of the American Oriental Society* 75 (1955): 1–13.

Jafri, Syed H. *The Origins and Development of Shi'a Islam.* London: Longman, 1979.

Sachedina, Abdulaziz A. *The Just Ruler in Shi'ite Islam: The Comprehensive Authority of the Jurist in Imamite Jurisprudence.* New York: Oxford, 1988.

*Liyakatali Takim*

# JAHANNAM

Jahannam is a designation for hell and is related to the cognate Hebrew word *gehinnom* ("Hinnom Valley"), originally a site near ancient Jerusalem where children were immolated as sacrificial offerings, which subsequently became a garbage dump. In early Jewish and Christian eschatology, Gehenna was believed to be where wrongdoers would be punished by fire in the hereafter. This is the meaning Jahannam carries in the Qur'an (where it is mentioned seventy-seven times), the hadith, and later Islamic eschatological discourses. It is often used synonymously with "the Fire" ("*nar*"), and in juxtaposition to "the Garden" ("*janna*"), the Islamic paradise of the blessed.

The Qur'an depicts Jahannam as an infernal dwelling or refuge with seven gates (counterparts for the seven heavens) awaiting unbelievers, hypocrites, and other sorts of offenders (4:140; 15:43–44). It will be the fiery abode of jinns and satans, as well as humans (11:119; 19:68), including polytheists and "people of the book" (98:6). Indeed, according to one verse, all will go to Jahannam, but God will save the pious and abandon wrongdoers there on their knees (19:72). Polytheists and their idols will become fuel for its fire (21:98). The authoritative hadith collections, such as those of al-Bukhari (d. 870), Muslim (d. 875), and Ibn Hanbal (d. 855), expand upon these Qur'anic discourses, detailing its horrific features and inhabitants. Hadiths describe it as a pit of fire seventy times hotter than earthly fire, guarded by the angel Malik, into which plunge the damned who fail to cross a narrow test bridge (*al-sirat*) that traverses it. They enumerate the kinds of sinners punished there, among whom are the Jahannamites—Muslims who have committed major transgressions, but who will eventually win entry to paradise.

The most elaborate descriptions were formulated in the tenth century C.E., and later commentaries and eschatological texts are those of al-Tabari (d. 922), al-Samarqandi (d. c. 983), al-Ghazali (d. 1111), al-Qurtubi (d. 1273), Ibn Kathir (d. 1373), Ibn Qayyim al-Jawziyya (1350), and al-Suyuti (d. 1505). In these books, Jahannam is said to consist of seven hierarchical levels, the highest for Muslims and the lower levels for Jews, Christians, Zoroastrians, polytheists, and hypocrites. Commentators furnished it with geographic features such as blazing mountains, valleys, rivers, and seas, as well as houses, prisons, bridges, wells, and ovens. They also provided it with venomous scorpions and snakes to torment its inhabitants. In modern times, Jahannam remains a popular sermon topic.

*See also* **Calligraphy; Janna; Law; Muhammad; Qur'an; Tafsir.**

## BIBLIOGRAPHY

Achtemeier, Paul J., ed. "Gehenna." In *Harper's Bible Dictionary.* San Francisco: Harper & Row, 1985.

Jeffrey, Arthur, ed. *A Reader on Islam: Passages from Standard Arabic Writings Illustrative of the Beliefs and Practices of Muslims.* The Hague: Mouton & Co., 1962.

*Juan Eduardo Campo*

# JAHILIYYA

The word *jahiliyya*, rendered as ignorance or barbarism, occurs several times in the Qur'an (3:148; 5:55; 33:33; 48:26). Used pejoratively to describe pre-Islamic Arabia, it means the period in which Arabia had no dispensation, no inspired prophet, and no revealed book.

The seven *Mu'allaqat*, written down in Umayyad times, are believed to be a collection of prize-winning pre-Islamic poems on the courage and endurance of its warriors, recited in contests at the annual fair at 'Ukaz. Fragments of similar poems are also found in the *Kitab al-aghani* of al-Isbahani (d. 967). The ideal Arab virtues referred to in this literature are *muru'a* (courage, loyalty, and generosity). and *'ird* (honor). Courage was reflected in the number of raids undertaken, and generosity in the readiness with which one sacrificed one's camel for a guest. Killing was discouraged. Murder resulted in blood feuds and vendetta. Three months of the year (Rajab, Dhu-l-Qa'da, and Dhu-l-Hajj) were pronounced sacred, however, when no fighting or raiding were permitted.

Trade had brought wealth to some, but the poverty of many was disregarded, and there was no strategy to care for them. Females were regarded as a burden and many were killed at birth. Muhammad viewed this attitude as ungodly. The religion of the pre-Islamic Bedouin was primarily animistic, while urban populations, such as the Meccans, worshiped a supreme God, al-Ilah, and its three daughters, al-'Uzza, al-Lat, and Manat. Hubal was the chief deity of the Ka'ba. Women were required to circumambulate the Ka'ba in the nude. Various tribes in different regions identified with different gods to whom they turned for immediate favors. There was no belief in an afterlife or a day of judgment. Muhammad, who preached the existence of one, invisible God, taught that man would be judged for his actions, and rewarded accordingly. He fought to establish Islam in Arabia, and had the pre-Islamic idols systematically destroyed. Thus, he claimed, Islam brought an end to *jahiliyya*. Nevertheless, several pre-Islamic observances have been incorporated into Islamic ritual, such as the circumambulation of the Ka'ba, and the running between Saffa and Marwa, with new significance attributed to them.

In the twentieth century, *jahiliyya* took on a new meaning. Writing from Pakistan, Abu l-A'la' Maududi (d. 1979) had considered aspects of modern life reflecting Muslim imitation of the West, as comparable to *jahiliyya*. On the same lines, the Egyptian Sayyid Qutb (1906–1966) asserted that the world consisted of but two cultures, Islam and *jahiliyya*, which included both the West and the atheistic communist world. The polytheistic societies of Asia, and Christian and Jewish societies, were now considered "ignorant" or *jahili* because of their movement away from God, as were the Muslims who accepted Western elements into the Islamic system. For Qutb the only antidote to *jahiliyya* was *hakimiyya*, that is, the adherence to the belief that governance, legislation, and sovereignty belong only to God.

*See also* **Arabia, Pre-Islam; Modern Thought; Political Islam; Qutb, Sayyid.**

## BIBLIOGRAPHY

Boullata, Issa. *Trends and Issues in Contemporary Arab Thought.* New York: SUNY Press, 1990.

Guillaume, Alfred. *Islam.* Middlesex, U.K.: Penguin Books Ltd., 1956.

Hodgson, Marshall G. S. *The Venture of Islam.* Vol. 1. Chicago: University of Chicago Press, 1974.

*Rizwi Faizer*

# JAMA'AT-E ISLAMI

Jama'at-e Islami (JI) is one of the most influential religiopolitical parties in the Muslim world, particularly in South Asia. It was founded in 1941 in Lahore, the creation of Abu l-A'la' Maududi, who was working for the Islamization of Pakistan. The party's goal was to contest the Congress (representing the Hindu majority) and the Jam'iyat-e 'Ulama-e Hind (JUH; aiming for composite nationalism) as well as the Muslim League (with territorial nationalism as its platform). In contrast to these other parties, the Jama'at-e Islami party echoed the ideas of Maududi, who favored the creation of an Islamic state. Maududi was supported by a number of young, activist religious scholars, among them some Deobandis and Nadwis. Maududi was the first emir (commander) of the Jama'at-e Islami, a post he held until 1972. As can be seen from the shifting areas of popularity, the history of the JI cannot be separated from the emirs's lives—Maududi (1941–1972), a muhajir settled in Punjab; Miyan Tufail Muhammad (1972–1987), a muhajir-converted Punjabi; and Qazi Husain Ahmad (since 1987) from the frontier province—a fact also reflected in its seats in provincial assemblies.

To start with, the Jama'at-e Islami needed to consolidate its base, which would strengthen its internal bonds and permit the development of a sense of *umma*, a term that means "the imagined community." From its founding days in the city of Pathankot, the party grew through a strong campaign that disseminated its ideals through a variety of channels of communication, including political conventions and the use of the mass media.

The Jama'at-e Islami is strictly and hierarchically organized, under the leadership of its emirs. Party affiliation can be broken down into two categories, fully-fledged members (*arkan*) on the one hand, and sympathizers and workers (*karkun*) on the other. In the first year of the party's existence, 1941, there were 75 members. A decade later, in 1951, membership had grown to 659, with 2,913 sympathizers. By 1989, membership had swelled to 5,723, with some 305,792 nonregistered but active sympathizers. In 2003, membership reached 16,033, and the number of sympathizers to the party's goals had reached 4.5 million. The party is guided by an emir who is obliged to consult an assembly called the *shura*. This authoritarian, pyramidlike structure is complemented by other sub-organizations, such as women's wings and student organizations, all working toward the common goal of establishing an ideological Islamic society, particularly through educational and social work. Jama'at-e Islami's organizational structure is replicated throughout the world, wherever it has taken root.

The Jama'at-e Islami is based on social action in a variety of fields, and encourages Muslims to set up a better society here and now through constantly contesting the political establishment. In Pakistan, most of its members come from the educated lower-middle class, including immigrants from India, called the *muhajirun*. The party never did appeal to the upper-class clientele that favored most of Pakistan's other parties, such as the Pakistan People Party and the Muslim League, who frequently based their platforms upon traditional landowning loyalties. The Jama'at-e Islami also failed to attract the poorer classes, who lacked the literacy that would permit them to comprehend the Jama'at's rhetorics.

Anchored firmly in the rather ambitious middle class, with a following drawn from the newly rising elites, the Jama'at-e Islami increasingly finds itself in confrontation with the power assertions of the postcolonial political establishment, which is characterized by the party as westernized and corrupt. The discontent that motivates the collective membership of the Jama'at-e Islami derives from the difficulty people face in gaining access to political power and cultural privilege. The party has enlisted the help of a small religious elite that is itself struggling for political survival and controls a mass base, and which provides a common language and symbolism with which to express and generalize the social discontent that Jama'at-e Islami seeks to redress. In the terms of this language

Qazi Husayn Ahmed, head of the Pakistani religious party Jamaʿat-e-Islami (Party of Islam) in Peshawar, Pakistan, speaking to religious students in a mosque, where he condemned the introduction of new laws by the Musharraf government designed to bring the *madrasa* system under greater government control, as well as American presence in Pakistan. Jamaʿat-e-Islami was founded in 1941 by al-Maududi in Lahore to advocate an Islamic state. AP/WIDE WORLD PHOTOS

and symbolism, only the spread of Sunni Islam throughout the world can make possible the revival of an ideal, if mythical, original community. The Jamaʿat-e Islami relies heavily upon the concept of purification. Not being bound by history, the party is free to distinguish itself from secular politicians, sometimes radically, and see itself as the avant-garde.

Jamaʿat-e Islami's fundamentalist critique centers on issues of moral decline, particularly on sexual morality, and sets itself up in opposition to European culture and values and the concept of modernity. The social pathologies resulting from modernization are often cited as evidence of a Machiavellian strategy employed by the West with the goal of seizing power. The purpose of such rhetoric is to produce a normative consensus, to increase cultural self-confidence, and to mobilize the party's membership and sympathizers. In its dealings with the broader society, the party's spokespersons generally employ ideological arguments, keeping references to purely Islamic symbols to a minimum. But when addressing traditionalist groups, the party employs a more overtly theological approach, supporting public worship and participating in debates on religious issues.

When Maududi first became politically active in post-partition India and Pakistan, it was through the party that he articulated his political visions and ideas. Only a few years after the creation of Pakistan, the Jamaʿat-e Islami was forced to face the issue of the role of religion in politics. Maududi

consistently confronted the Pakistani government on this issue, questioning the state's legitimacy, ultimately forcing the politicians to include provisions regarding Islam in the national constitution. The ongoing struggle between Jamaʿat-e Islami and the government led to the party being outlawed several times. The anti-Ahmadiyya movement in 1953–1954, however, was the party's ticket into the mainstream of Pakistani politics because by heresizing the Ahmadiyya movement, thereby questioning the Islamicity of state functionaries, the JI also opened up to other schools of thought.

During the Ayub era (1958–1969), the Jamaʿat-e Islami was forced into the background for a while, until 1965, when it entered into new political alliances against the Ayub regime and, at last, became a proper political party. Its participation in the anti-Bhutto coalition intensified the politization of the Jamaʿat-e Islami, for it could now call the government un-Islamic. Eventually the party was able to mobilize a large enough portion of the society to topple the Bhutto regime. It supported Zia ul-Haq's coup d'etat in 1977, and earned leading positions within the government. But the party was unable to widen its social basis, and found itself being used by the government to further its own ends, instead. Hence, in the elections that followed, the JI was not able to secure enough seats to gain an effective political voice.

Since the 1980s, the party has started to diversify its membership, spreading out from Karachi into other areas of the country. It has accomplished this through its welfare program, especially in the field of university higher education, and by establishing *madrasa*s (religious training centers), as well as by working hand in hand with the relief agencies in the Afghan refugee camps after 1979.

In spite of its limited electoral success prior to 1988, the Jama'at-e Islami has become a powerful political and cultural force in Pakistani politics. In the late twentieth and early twenty-first centuries, the party has been increasingly successful in recruiting members and sympathizers, and thus has been able to establish links with future leaders drawn from a wide spectrum of society, including the bureaucracy and the civil service. In 1997 the party publicly called for the adoption of a more populist approach, and was rewarded with a swelling of its ranks to 2.2 million registered members by mid-August of that year. In the 2002 elections, the Jama'at-e Islami could claim sixty-eight members in the National Assembly, gaining for itself the ability to play "kingmaker" within Pakistani politics. The party's success in Pakistan has not been mirrored by equal success for its counterpart in India. Since the Pakistani-Indian partition in 1947, the Indian branch of the party has taken a much more docile and secular approach toward politics and religion. As one of the few national Islamic parties in India, it has attracted a following through its activities in missionary work, social services, publications, and conventions.

*See also* **Maududi, Abu l-A'la'; Pakistan, Islamic Republic of.**

### BIBLIOGRAPHY

Ahmad, Mumtaz. "Islamic Fundamentalism in South Asia: The Jamaat-i-Islami and the Tablighi Jamaat of South Asia." In *Fundamentalism Observed*. Edited by Martin E. Marty and Scott R. Appleby. Chicago: Chicago University Press, 1991.

Nasr, Seyyed Vali Reza. *The Vanguard of Islamic Revolution: The Jama'at-i Islami of Pakistan*, London: I. B. Tauris, 1994.

*Jamal Malik*

## JAMI'

The *jami'*, like the *masjid* and the *musalla*, is where the Islamic community performs the daily prayer. And while both the *masjid* and the *jami'* are also used for teaching and preaching, only a *masjid* specially dedicated to the Friday prayer is designated a *jami'*. Whereas previously local mosques were managed by area residents and the *jami'* by the state, nowadays many states, under the pretext of law and order, strictly control even the *musalla*s. Apart from Medina and Jerusalem, some of Islam's greatest Friday mosques are located in Kuala Lumpur, Delhi, Lahore, Cairo, and more recently, in London, Paris, and Washington, D.C.

*See also* **'Ibadat; Masjid; Religious Institutions.**

### BIBLIOGRAPHY

Campo, Juan Eduardo. *The Other Side of Paradise: Explorations into the Religious Meanings of Domestic Space in Islam*. Columbia, S.C.: University of South Carolina, 1991.

*Muneer Goolam Fareed*

## JAMIL AL-AMIN, IMAM (1943– )

A gifted rhetorician and civil rights activist, the American Muslim leader Jamil al-Amin (formerly H. Rap Brown, born in 1943) came to national prominence in the 1960s as an outspoken advocate of black power. In 1967, Brown succeeded Stokely Carmichael as leader of the Student Non-Violent Coordinating Committee (SNCC), a prominent African-American civil rights organization. Brown also became known for his advocacy of black self-defense and his saying that "violence is as American as cherry pie." In 1969, he published his most famous work, *Die Nigger Die*, a blistering critique of American racism. Because of Brown's radical rhetoric, he became a target of the FBI's Counter Intelligence Program (COINTELPRO), which harassed many black leaders during this period. In 1972, Brown was apprehended on federal weapons charges, tried, convicted, and sentenced to four years in prison. During his prison term, he converted to Islam under the auspices of Darul Islam, a predominately African-American Islamic group organized in the 1960s. He also adopted a new name, Jamil Abdullah al-Amin. Paroled in 1976, al-Amin moved to Atlanta, Georgia, where he became the owner of a community store and an imam (leader) at a local mosque. Over the next two decades, he emerged as a Sunni Muslim leader with followers throughout the United States. Over thirty mosques recognized Imam Jamil as leader of a group called the National Islamic Community. Focusing on economic and social, as well as religious, empowerment, he also became known for his role in attempting to revitalize the West End of Atlanta. In March 2000, Imam al-Jamil was accused of murder in connection with the death of a police officer. But many American Muslims of diverse racial and ethnic backgrounds defended Imam al-Jamil's innocence and offered him financial and moral support as he prepared for his trial. In March, 2002, he was convicted of murder and was sentenced to life in prison without parole.

*See also* **American Culture and Islam; Americas, Islam in the; Nation of Islam.**

### BIBLIOGRAPHY

McCloud, Aminah Beverly. *African American Islam*. New York: Routledge, 1995.

Van Deburg, William. *A New Day in Babylon: The Black Power Movement and American Culture, 1965–1975.* Chicago: University of Chicago Press, 1992.

*Edward E. Curtis IV*

Friedmann, Yohanan. "Jam'yatul 'Ulama'-I Hind." In *The Oxford Encyclopedia of the Modern Islamic World.* Edited by J. L. Esposito, et al. New York and Oxford, UK: Oxford University Press, 1995. Vol. 2, pp. 362–363.

*Jamal Malik*

## JAM'IYAT-E 'ULAMA-E HIND

Muslim politics saw the era of institutionalization in two new religiopolitical bodies that formed in 1919: All-India Khilafat Committee and Jam'iyat-e 'Ulama-e Hind (The Association of Scholars of India, or JUH). The JUH was the first political solidarity foundation of Indian ulema, who saw themselves as religious guides, even in political matters, at the peak of the Indian Muslim agitation for the Ottoman Caliphate. By using the potential of the religious infrastructure, along with new political structures, ulema were mobilized and unified to defend the caliphate. The first meeting in November 1919 in New Delhi demanded that Muslims abide by Islamic tenets, strengthen their relationship with the Islamic world, and foster Muslim-Hindu amity. The holy places of Islam were to be defended, separate *shari'a* courts and *zakat* system were to be established, and the Indian Congress supported. This solidarity traditionalism found its climax in a *fatwa* for noncooperation and civil disobedience in 1920. Use was made of Islamic repertory—proselytization and forcible conversion were rejected. JUH stood for an independent, multireligious India in which Muslims and Hindus would have their separate institutional structures.

The major contribution of the JUH was the idea of composite nationalism (*muttahida qaumiyat*), in contrast to the two-nation theory proclaimed by the Muslim League in 1940. This concept of territorial nationalism was unique in Islamic thought, and was put into practice by a nationalist campaign against the creation of Pakistan.

Shortly before the partition of India in 1945, a dissident group was formed, the Jam'iyat-e 'Ulama-e Islam (JUI).

After 1947, JUH pursued noncommunalism, stood for social and religious reforms, and supported the secular constitution of the Republic of India. However, it still holds rigid positions concerning Muslim personal law, but the ambivalent image created through the tussle between political pragmatism and religious dogmatism has been improved through its social activities.

*See also* **Jam'iyat-e 'Ulama-e Islam; South Asia, Islam in.**

### BIBLIOGRAPHY

Agwani, M.S. *Islamic Fundamentalism in India.* Chandigarh, India: Twenty-First India Society, 1986

## JAM'IYAT-E 'ULAMA-E ISLAM

Jam'iyat-e 'Ulama-e Islam (JUI) broke off from the Jam'iyat-e 'Ulama-e Hind (JUH), which stood for Indian nationalism and opposed the demand for an independent Pakistan. In contrast to its mother organization, the JUI, established in 1945 under the leadership of Shabbir Ahmad 'Uthmani, supported the Muslim League's demand for Pakistan. However, after independence in 1947 it had to struggle for a long period before being accepted by the Pakistani elites. The JUI remained a religious organization until the late 1960s, when general elections were announced after the collapse of the Ayub Khan regime. The JUI then entered the Pakistan political arena, where it demonstrated a remarkable career. It soon split into a a politically quiet faction, led by the Karachi-based Ihtisham al-Haqq Thanawi, and a more activist group centered around Mufti Mahmud and Ghauth Hazarawi, primarily in the Northwest Frontier Province (NWFP). During the elections of 1970 Mufti Mahmud's faction of the JUI became quite popular by making use of Islamic symbolism, postulating the establishment of *shari'a* in Pakistan, and advocating the implementation of Islamic economic and social reforms. The party benefitted from the use of traditional infrastructure, such as *madaris* (Islamic schools) and *waqf* (pious foundations), and established an umbrella organization of religious schools. In this way it won quite a number of seats and eventually entered into a coalition with the National Awami Party (NAP) and thus managed to form provincial governments in NWFP and Baluchistan. Mufti Mahmud became chief minister of the NWFP from 1971 to 1973. The Islamization of this region under his tenure influenced the following political scenario.

Under the leadership of Fazl al-Rahman, the son of Mufti Mahmud, the JUI became increasingly orthodox and also anti-Shi'ite, as can be witnessed in the activities of the Punjab-based communal Anjuman-e Sipahan-e Sahaba, a militant splinter group of the JUI established in 1985. In the same year JUI senators Sami' al-Haqq—who runs the largest religious school in Pakistan, the Dar al-'Ulum Haqqaniya—and Qadi 'Abd al-Latif introduced the Shariat Bill to the National Assembly.

Although the JUI has not been very successful in gaining political influence at the national level, it is one of the most powerful political and social forces in Pakistan, particularly in the NWFP and Baluchistan. It controls a large number of religious schools throughout the country that have been recruitment centers not only for thousands of young religious scholars but also for the Afghan *mujahidin* who fought against the Soviets in Afghanistan. Since the mid-1990s the *madaris* also have been very actively supporting the Taliban. The talibanization of Pakistan goes to the extent that after the Afghani Taliban takeover of Kabul in 1996, the JUI openly declared abjuring the electoral politics of Pakistan. The JUI is also believed to have a wide international jihadi connections, such as in Tajikistan, Chechnya and Kashmir.

*See also* **Deoband; Jam'iyat-e 'Ulama-e Hind; South Asia, Islam in; Taliban.**

### BIBLIOGRAPHY

Malik, Jamal. *Colonialization of Islam: Dissolution of Traditional Institutions in Pakistan*, 2d ed. New Delhi: Manohar Publications, 1998.

Nasr, Seyyed Vali Reza. "Jamiat-e Ulama-e Islam." In *The Oxford Encyclopedia of the Modern Islamic World*, J. L. Esposito, ed.Vols. 1–4. New York and Oxford, UK: Oxford University Press, 1995.

Waseem, Mohammad. *Pakistan under Martial Law, 1977–1985*. Lahore: Vanguard Books, 1987.

*Jamal Malik*

## JAM'IYAT-E 'ULAMA-E PAKISTAN

The Jam'iyat-e 'Ulama-e Pakistan (JUP) is a Barelwi-dominated religious party established in 1947 under the leadership of Abu al-Hasanat (1896–1961) and 'Abd al-Hamid Badayuni (1898–1970). The JUP attempted to give legitimacy to the cause of Pakistan and the Muslim League, contrary to the Jam'iyat-e 'Ulama-e Hind (JUH), and also in some contrast to the Jam'iyat-e 'Ulama-e Islam (JUI). The JUP proclaims Ahmad Reza Khan, the founder of the Barelwi movement, as the first to advocate the two-nation theory, which led to the partition of Pakistan and India. Engaged in social activities—mainly the settlement of refugees in Sindh and rural Punjab—the JUP remained politically insignificant for more than two decades. It established, however, a Sufi organization in 1948 and a student wing in 1968, when its leader Shah Ahmad Nurani (born 1926) started propagating Islamization. In 1973, Nurani was nominated for the position of prime minister by the member parties of the United Democratic Front against the Pakistan People's Party (PPP). When in 1977 the JUP stood for the establishment of the Muhammadan System, it united the Islamic parties in the Pakistan National Alliance (PNA) against Zulfiker Ali Bhutto's PPP. After 1977, JUP changed sides several times—sympathizing at times even with its main adversaries, the JI (Jama'at-e Islami) and JUI. Its integrity thus suffered and therefore it split into two major factions (Nurani faction and 'Abd al-Sattar faction). Its success lies in its reliance on oral tradition, its drawing its constituency from the followers of Sufi *pirs*—preferably Qadiris—observance of ritual traditions associated with saint worship, and usage of millenarian postulates and symbols mediated in a multimedial staging. Like the JUI, the JUP runs an umbrella organization of *madaris* (Islamic schools), and has been actively defending the nationalization of pious foundations.

*See also* **Deoband; Jam'iyat-e 'Ulama-e Hind; Jam'iyat-e 'Ulama-e Islam; South Asia, Islam in.**

### BIBLIOGRAPHY

Ahmad, Mujeeb. *Jam'iyyat 'Ulama-i-Pakistan 1948–1979*, Islamabad: National Institute of Historical and Cultural Research, 1993.

Malik, Jamal. "The Luminous Nurani: Charisma and Political Mobilisation among the Barelwis in Pakistan." Pnina Werbner (ed.): *Person, Myth and Society in South Asian Islam*, Adelaide 1990.

*Jamal Malik*

## JANNA

*Janna* (Ar. "garden," pl. *jannat*; Persian *firdaws* "paradise," "enclosure," "orchard") is the designation for the primordial paradise of Adam and Eve and for the paradisal garden (or gardens) in the hereafter, where the blessed will dwell for eternity after passing the trial of the last judgment. This dual significance of the garden in Islamic cosmography is rooted in ancient Near Eastern myths and afterlife visions that were subsequently adapted to biblical narratives about the origin and destiny of the human being, and were further elaborated within the communities of rabbinic Judaism and early Christianity. In Islamic discourse, *janna* is usually juxtaposed to *nar* ("fire"), the hellish abode of wrongdoers (*nar* and *jahannam*).

Muslims usually conceive of *janna* as a real place where humans experience contact with supramundane beings, as well as pleasurable bodily existence. This understanding of paradise was canonized in the Qur'an and elaborated further in the hadith, theological tracts, and visionary literature. Thus, Adam and Eve enjoyed communion with God and the angels, and consumed the fruits of the garden until they ate of the forbidden tree (2:35–36, 20:117–123), which caused their fall into the abode of mortal life. God then promised their return to immortality in the hereafter. In contrast to the Bible, extensive passages of the Qur'an deal with the subjects of resurrection and the afterlife, beginning with chapters traditionally consigned by scholars to the Meccan phase of Muhammad's career (c. 615–622 C.E.). In the Qur'anic afterlife world, paradise is a domesticated arboreal garden or park perfumed by musk, camphor, and ginger, through which rivers of milk, honey, and wine flow (47:15). It is populated by families of immortal believers who dress in elegant garments and who dwell in heavenly mansions furnished with couches, carpets, and precious household vessels (9:72, 15:47, 36:55–58, 88:10–16). Angels greet them (13:23–24), and handsome youths and beautiful *houri*s (black-eyed maidens) offer food and drink (43:71, 52:19–24, 76:15–22). The Qur'an also intimates that the blessed will enjoy the vision of God there (10:26, 39:75, 75:22–23), a doctrine that was later subject to much debate among theologians and Qur'an interpreters. The hadith mention that paradise has eight gates, each named for a virtue through which the blessed possessing that virtue will enter. They also speak of the existence of eight paradises rather than a single one, each deriving its name from a Qur'anic term or phrase, such as *dar al-salam* (House of peace), *jannat al-khuld* (Garden of eternity), and *jannat 'Aden* (Garden of Eden). In number, therefore, paradise surpasses hell, which is said to have only seven levels or gates (*jahannam*). It is also speculated that God's throne (*kursi*) stood above paradise. Sufis acknowledged the lower levels of paradise, but stressed the ecstasy of communion with God in the heart, or in the highest level of paradise—that of the elect.

Ideas of paradise so captured the Muslim imagination that they inspired caliphs and sultans, artists and architects, learned scholars—even ordinary people—to invest the cultural landscape with heavenly significance. According to the hadith, the Ka'ba and the Black Stone in Mecca originated in paradise, and the span between the Prophet's grave and the *minbar* in his Medina mosque is one of the gardens of paradise. Representations of heavenly gardens occur on the Umayyad Grand Mosque in Damascus (seventh century C.E.), in the Alhambra of Granada (fourteenth century C.E.), on Persian royal pavilions (seventeenth century), and in illuminated Turkish and Persian manuscripts of the Muhammad's Night Journey and Ascension (fifteenth to eighteenth centuries). The city and palaces of Baghdad, the imperial capital of the Abbasids (r. 750–1258), were named and described as earthly paradises. In India, the enclosed park within which the Taj Mahal, the grand mausoleum of Shah Jahan (r. 1628–1657) and his queen Mumtaz Mahal (d. 1631), was constructed was an adaptation of the "four garden" (*chahar bagh*) design of royal Persian gardens, a microcosmic image of paradise with its four rivers. The magnificent building itself may well represent God's throne in heaven, believed to be located above paradise. Elsewhere, inscriptions and murals in mansions and ordinary Muslim homes created metaphorical relations between the domestic spaces of the living and the abodes of the blessed in the hereafter.

*See also* **Calligaphy; Jahannam; Law; Muhammad; Qur'an; Tafsir.**

## BIBILIOGRAPHY

Blair, Sheila, and Bloom, Jonathan M., eds. *Images of Paradise in Islamic Art.* Hanover, N.H.: Hood Museum of Art, Dartmouth College, 1991.

Campo, Juan Eduardo. *The Other Sides of Paradise: Explorations into the Religious Meanings of Domestic Space in Islam.* Columbia, S.C.: University of South Carolina Press, 1991.

Ghazali, Abu Hamid al-. *The Remembrance of Death and the Afterlife* (Kitab dhikr al-mawt wa-ma ba'dahu): Book XL of the Revival of the Religious Sciences (Ihya' 'ulum al-din). Translated by T. J. Winter. Cambridge, U.K.: Islamic Texts Society.

*Juan Eduardo Campo*

## JERUSALEM *See* Holy Cities

## JEVDET PASHA (1822–1895)

Ahmet Jevdet Pasha was an Ottoman historian, administrator, and educational and judicial reformer. Born in Bulgaria, he pursued a religious education; dissatisfaction with traditional methods led him to study secular mathematics, law, and history. He wrote the first Ottoman grammar primer in Turkish, *Kavaid-i Osmaniye.*

Jevdet's unique combination of religious and secular education made him useful as an advisor to the Tanzimat reformer, Mustafa Resit Pasha. He worked on educational reforms, wrote a religious text for schoolchildren, and began his history of the later Ottoman Empire, *Tarih-i Jevdet*, based on state papers and personal observation. He became a judge and member of the government, writing judicial and cadastral regulations. After a series of administrative positions in the reformist government of the Tanzimat, he became minister of justice, established a secular court system, and drew up a modernized Islamic law code, the *Mejelle* (1869–1876), based not on French law but on Islamic Hanafi law.

Jevdet opposed the constitution of 1876 and the deposition of Sultan 'Abdulaziz. He served the absolutist Sultan 'Abd al-Hamid II in various ministerial posts and prosecuted the reformer Midhat Pasha for the murder of 'Abdulaziz (1881). He retired in 1882 and continued work on his history and his memoirs, *Tezakir*, but returned to government service from 1886 until his death in 1895.

*See also* **Modernization, Political: Administrative, Military, and Judicial Reform.**

## BIBLIOGRAPHY

Chambers, Richard L. "The Education of a Nineteenth Century Ottoman *Alim*, Ahmed Cevdet Pasa." *International Journal of Middle East Studies* 4 (1973): 440–464.

Lewis, Bernard. *The Emergence of Modern Turkey.* Oxford, U.K.: Oxford University Press, 1961.

*Linda T. Darling*

# JIHAD

The word jihad is derived from the Arabic root *jahada*, meaning "to strive" or "to exert oneself" toward some goal. In this general sense, jihad could mean striving to achieve something with no particular moral value, or even a negative value. The Qur'an itself twice uses the verb when describing the efforts of pagan parents to induce their Muslim-convert children to return to polytheism (29:8, 31:15). Other occurrences of this verbal form and its derivatives, however, are limited to the struggle of the Muslims to attain and maintain their faith. Thus, jihad has come to mean in the Islamic context only a virtuous struggle, toward some praiseworthy end, as defined by religion. It is therefore often linked with the phrase *fi sabil Allah*, meaning "struggle in the path of God."

The term jihad occurs infrequently in what are believed to be the Meccan revelations of the Qur'an. During this first part of the Prophet's mission, lasting some twelve years, jihad is used in the sense of cultivating personal piety, perseverance in the preaching of Islam, and forbearance and patient suffering in the face of persecution by the Muslims' enemies. Qur'an 25:52, for example, advises Muslims to "listen not to the unbelievers, but strive against them with it [the Qur'an] with the utmost effort." There is no recorded instance during the Meccan period in which the Prophet ordered or allowed his followers to use violence against their enemies. Jihad during this period meant exclusively nonviolent resistance.

Following the Prophet's migration to Medina (the Hijra), occurrences of jihad increase in the Qur'an. While some of these verses may be understood as still referring to nonviolent struggle, the majority clearly refer to physical force or fighting (*qital*). Qur'an 22:39 is believed by many scholars to be the first verse on this topic. It permits the Muslims to retaliate with force against those who continue to attack and persecute them. A subsequent series of verses (2:190–191) converts the permission of self-defense into an obligation, with the argument that "oppression is worse than killing." Then, after eight years of warfare between the Muslims and their polytheist enemies, the Jewish tribes of Medina, and the Christian empire of the Byzantines, the Qur'an seems to enjoin a war of conversion against all remaining polytheist Arabs (9:5) and a war of subjugation against Christians and Jews (9:29).

## The Classical Theory
Following the Prophet's death, Muslim scholars produced a large body of literature analyzing Qur'anic terms and collecting traditions of the Prophet as part of their effort to codify divine law (*shari'a*). Defining and understanding jihad, a concept with complex religious and moral significance, naturally occupied a great deal of their attention. The scholars outlined a number of different types of jihad, all of which may be grouped into two basic categories, the spiritual jihad and the physical jihad. The objects of the first type included one's own soul (*nafs*), whose evil inclinations had to be overcome, or Satan (*Shaitan*), whose attempts to sow doubt and confusion and to lead the believer astray had to be perpetually fought. The physical jihad was aimed at unbelievers outside the Muslim community, as well as hypocrites and troublemakers within the Muslim ranks. Its goal was to establish the supremacy of divine law and thereby to promote justice and social welfare according to Islamic values. In this sense, jihad was closely related to the Qur'anic injunction that Muslims "command the right and forbid the wrong" (*amr bi'l-ma'ruf wa nahy 'an al-munkar*).

The classical scholars also listed various means by which both the spiritual and the physical jihad could be conducted, including by the heart, tongue, pen, hand, and sword. Some traditions ascribed to Muhammad profess the merits of jihad conducted by the tongue, as in one hadith in which the Prophet said, "The greatest jihad is a word of truth spoken to a tyrant." Other traditions describe the jihad of the pen, that is, of scholars, as more meritorious than the jihad of the sword. One of the most famous such hadiths declares the spiritual jihad to be the greater jihad (*jihad al-akbar*) as compared to the physical jihad, which is the lesser jihad (*jihad al-asghar*).

But the most widespread use of the term *jihad* in classical Islamic thought was in the sense of a divinely sanctioned struggle, through war if necessary, to establish Islamic sovereignty and thereby to propagate the Islamic faith to unbelievers. In classical jurisprudence (*fiqh*), the dominant strand of intellectual activity in these early centuries, the chapters on jihad in legal treatises contained rules for the declaration, conduct, and conclusion of such religiopolitical wars.

At the heart of the classical theory was the division of the world into two basic spheres, *dar al-islam* (land of Islam), a unitary state comprising the community of Muslims, living by the *shari'a*, and led by the just ruler (imam); and *dar al-harb* (land of war), where Islamic law did not prevail, leading presumably to anarchy and moral corruption. It was commonly understood that Muslims had an individual obligation (*fard 'ayn*) to defend *dar al-islam* whenever it was threatened by aggression from *dar al-harb*. This type of war received little attention in the chapters on jihad.

The jurists' attention was focused on what may be called the expansionist jihad. The imam was obliged to undertake a jihad whenever the conditions of the Islamic state permitted him to reduce *dar al-harb* and bring its lands and peoples into *dar al-islam*. This was a collective duty of the Muslim community (*fard kifaya*), one that required participation only from

During an Islamic Jihad rally at Hebron University in 1997, some two thousand students rallied and chanted against Israel and America as a round of Palestinian and Israeli peace talks began in Washington D.C. This protester's headband reads "Allahu Akbar" (God is Great). Though the idea of jihad has been used by some terrorist groups to advocate killing civilians, mainstream Muslim scholars condemn such supposedly Qu'ranic justifications. AP/WIDE WORLD PHOTOS

those financially and physically capable of undertaking it. One school of Sunni jurisprudence, the Shafi'i, interposed a third category between the other two, *dar al-sulh* (land of truce), comprising peoples with which the Muslims had a treaty of truce, which suspended, but did not end, the jihad obligation. The maximum duration of such a truce, according to most scholars, was ten years, although nothing prevented the imam from renewing the truce if he deemed it in the Muslims' interest.

The jihad in *dar al-harb*, in the view of the scholars, was aimed at bringing Islam's higher civilization to those unaware of it, not territorial conquest or plunder. Thus, they elaborated rules on what Muslim armies may or may not do in *dar al-harb*. The basis for such moral injunctions was the Qur'an's general command, "Do not transgress limits, for God loves not transgressors" (2:190), which was given greater specificity by the practice of the Prophet and his first four successors.

Before the start of any attack, the enemy was to be offered the choice of accepting Islam, in which case no further action against them was permissible. If they refused, they were to be offered *dhimmi* (protected) status as an autonomous community within *dar al-islam*. This option, deriving from Qur'an 9:29, initially pertained to Jews and Christians, but was steadily expanded to include Zoroastrians, Hindus, and Buddhists as the Islamic frontiers expanded. Only the polytheist Arabs who had fought so bitterly against Muhammad and the early Muslim community were excluded from the *dhimmi* option and forced to convert according to Qur'an 9:5.

In fighting the enemy, Muslim soldiers were to avoid directly targeting women and children. Some jurists included old men, peasants, hermits, merchants, the insane, and other males who do not ordinarily take part in fighting on the list of prohibited targets. According to most scholars, all able-bodied adult males could be killed at the discretion of the imam, whether they were fighting or had been taken prisoner. The scholars permitted the use of all types of weapons or military tactics that were necessary to overcome the enemy, including laying siege to fortresses, firing incendiary devices, cutting off the water supply, or flooding. The exceptions were certain practices that were categorically prohibited by the Prophet, such as killing by mutilation or torture, burning individuals alive, and violating oaths or grants of security to soldiers or envoys.

The difference in Shi'ite views on jihad was that only the righteous imam, a descendant of 'Ali, could lead the expansionist jihad. Because the line of imams ended with the disappearance of the twelfth imam in the ninth century, according to the dominant strand of Shi'ism, only a defensive jihad to repulse enemy aggression is theoretically possible.

The classical theory was already outdated as it was being formulated in the eighth, ninth, and tenth centuries. With the launching of the Reconquista in Spain and the Crusades in Syria and Palestine, the expansionist jihad gave way to a defensive struggle. In the nineteenth century, as European imperialism advanced throughout much of the Muslim world, the defensive aspects of jihad assumed paramount importance.

## Modern Interpretations

The Christian missionary activity that accompanied British rule in India led some Indian Muslims to undertake major revisions of classical notions of jihad. The literature produced by these writers is unmistakably apologetic in tone, straining to answer the charge of Christian writers that Islam was spread by the sword. According to the apologists, the wars of early Islam were purely defensive in nature, and jihad in modern times should be largely divested of its military connotations and reduced mainly to its spiritual aspects.

Such writings inevitably created a backlash among other Muslim interpreters. Two broad reactions may be identified, the modernist and the fundamentalist. The modernists' goal is not so much to respond to criticisms of early Islamic history and dogma, but to reinterpret jihad in ways that make it compatible with the principles of modern international law. Thus, they challenge the classical theory's conception of a *dar al-islam* in opposition to a *dar al-harb*, pointing out that such categories are nowhere to be found in the Qur'an or hadith. If these two basic sources for Islamic law and ethics are properly analyzed, they claim, jihad cannot be properly understood as a war to spread Islam or subjugate unbelievers. It is waged only in self-defense, in conformity with international law, when the lives, property, and honor of Muslims are at stake.

The fundamentalists also appeal to the Qur'an and hadith to challenge what they consider various false understandings of jihad. First, they refute the mystical strand of thought that emphasizes the superiority of the inner, spiritual jihad over the outer, physical jihad. By the end of the Qur'anic revelation, according to them, jihad meant a struggle, through

fighting if necessary, to establish the Islamic order over all unbelievers. The more tolerant and pacific texts relating to unbelievers were abrogated by the later, more belligerent verses. But the category of unbelievers in fundamentalist writings includes nominal Muslims as well as non-Muslims. The transformation of hypocritical Muslim societies into true Islamic communities, led by true Muslim leaders, is the immediate goal of most fundamentalist ideologies. Although some writers continue to speak of *dar al-Islam* and *dar al-harb*, the jihad to spread Islam beyond its current borders seems for most fundamentalists to be a secondary concern.

As for the proper conduct of war today, the vast majority of Muslim scholars agree that principles of international humanitarian law are compatible with Islamic teachings. These include the notion of noncombatant immunity and the prohibition against inhumane forms of killing. Muslim terrorist groups have, however, sought to justify the killing of civilians on Islamic grounds, but their arguments and tactics have been condemned by mainstream scholars.

Finally, many Muslims today are trying to reclaim the broad meaning of jihad as "effort" or "struggle" apart from war. Increasingly, we find references to such struggles as the "jihad for literacy" or the "jihad for economic development."

*See also* **Conflict and Violence; Terrorism.**

## BIBLIOGRAPHY

Hamidullah, Muhammad. *Muslim Conduct of State.* 7th ed. Lahore: Shaykh Muhammad Ashraf, 1961.

Johnson, James Turner, and Kelsay, John, eds. *Cross, Crescent, and Sword: The Justification and Limitation of War in Western and Islamic Tradition.* New York: Greenwood, 1990.

Kelsay, John, and Johnson, James Turner, eds. *Just War and Jihad: Historical and Theoretical Perspectives on War and Peace in Western and Islamic Tradition.* New York: Greenwood, 1991.

Khadduri, Majid. *War and Peace in the Law of Islam.* Baltimore: Johns Hopkins University Press, 1955.

Peters, Rudolph. *Islam and Colonialism: The Doctrine of Jihad in Modern History.* The Hague: Mouton, 1979.

Peters, Rudolph. *Jihad in Classical and Modern Islam.* Princeton: Markus Wiener, 1996.

*Sohail H. Hashmi*

# JINNAH, MUHAMMAD 'ALI (1876–1948)

Muhammad 'Ali Jinnah was born on 25 December 1876 in Karachi and became one of the most celebrated leaders of the independence movement. Later he became the founder of Pakistan. He died one year after independence on 11 September 1948.

People of Pakistan know him better by his title, Quaid-i Azam, meaning "the great leader." After earning his degree in law from London's famous Lincoln's Inn in 1896 and with a certificate to join the bar of any court in British India, he returned to his homeland. He settled in Bombay where he practiced law and soon rose to fame as the most distinguished attorney in the country. He split his time between the legal profession and politics. As a liberal nationalist trained in British constitutional and democratic tradition, he became a passionate advocate of Hindu-Muslim unity against British rule. For almost two decades, he devoted his energies to bringing the two communities together on one political platform by focusing on the idea of common political interests against British imperialism.

By the early 1920s, he began to feel disenchanted by the leaders of the Indian National Congress Party. He did not feel comfortable with their militant, confrontational style with the British. Rather, he advocated the course of moderation and dialogue to win freedom. His real disappointment came on the issue of minority rights, specifically those of the Muslims who comprised nearly 20 percent of the population, with concentration in the eastern and western parts of the British Indian Empire. Given their numbers, they were not a minority in a traditional sense, but a people with a heritage of more than one thousand years of Muslim rule and separate sense of identity. Jinnah favored a tripartite understanding on the constitutional guarantees for the rights of the Muslims once India became independent.

Muslim nationalism developed parallel to secular Indian nationalism in the later part of the nineteenth century. Muslims in the Indian subcontinent regarded themselves as a separate community with distinctive culture and civilization. But their political separatism was confined to the issue of minority rights that Muslim leaders like Jinnah strongly advocated in seeking representation in elected councils through separate electorates for Muslims. That ensured that Muslims would get adequate representation according to the size of their population. The dominant Hindu groups, including the Congress Party, were opposed to continuing any such arrangements once the British left.

By the late 1930s, Jinnah began to argue for a separate country for the Muslims in the eastern and western fringes of British India. With the passage of the Lahore Resolution in 1940 by a great assembly of Muslim leaders from all over India, Jinnah formally demanded the creation of a Muslim homeland. For the next seven years, he mobilized the Muslim masses on the basis of separate nationhood and convinced the British that that was the only option to prevent a communal war between Hindus and Muslims. Although Jinnah invoked Islamic symbols for political mobilization, he was a liberal, constitutionalist politician with a rational and progressive outlook.

Muhammed Ali Jinnah (1876–1948) was the leader of the Indian Muslim League and the driving force in the creation of Pakistan as an independent Muslim state in 1947. © HULTON ARCHIVE/ GETTY IMAGES

*See also* **Pakistan, Islamic Republic of.**

*Rasul Bakhsh Rais*

# JUDAISM AND ISLAM

Jewish-Muslim relations have been shaped by the interactions of the theological perspectives of both religions and the historical circumstances in which they are found. Both use sacred texts and history to form the basis of their perceptions of the other, with the result that there are often conflicting versions of the same events. This entry will show how historical circumstances, the place of Jews in Islamic religious text, and political ideology combine in varying degrees to shape Jewish-Muslim relations.

### Historical Perspective

In each historical period, the definition of who was a Muslim or a Jew has shifted. Often only a religious identification, more frequently it signifies a particular social, economic, or political group. Ethnic categories and religious identities have been conflated by both insiders and outsiders alike, thus complicating the task of analyzing intergroup and intercommunal relations. In the first two centuries of the Islamic era, for example, we have evidence that some Jews who had converted to Islam still retained Jewish home practices, not from hypocritical motives, but because the development of Islamic practices for the home were somewhat underdeveloped.

Another important tool for Jewish-Muslim intergroup analysis is the placement of behaviors and ideas in specific temporal and geographic contexts. Visions and ideas of the past have a strong influence on both religions. Many Muslims have as keen an awareness of the events around the time of the Prophet as they do their own time. The Qur'an and the sunna of the Prophet are guides for a Muslim's relations with Jews, as they are in all areas of behavior. A similar level of historical consciousness, albeit with different perspectives and details, helps shape Jewish attitudes toward Muslims. The historic interactions of Muslims and Jews have resulted in each being shaped and transformed by the other, and both by interactions with Christians, Zoroastrians, Hindus, and others. It is hard to imagine how each religion would be as it is without the presence of the others.

When the prophet Muhammad was born in 570 C.E., Arabia, a central trade and military location, was caught in the Byzantine-Sassanian rivalry. Arabs, including Jewish Arabic-speakers, were in the armies of both sides, providing horse and camel cavalries, and each empire maintained Arab client states as buffers and bases of operation. Only around fifty years earlier, the last Jewish kingdom in southern Arabia, allied with the Persians, had been defeated, replaced by a Byzantine-supported Christian army from Abyssinia. According to early Muslim historians, this army, led by a general named Abraha, is referred to in Surat al-Fal in the Qur'an.

The Hijaz had numerous Jewish settlements, most of long standing, dating to at least the time of the destruction of the Second Temple in 70 C.E.. According to some scholars, the earliest Jewish presence in the Hijaz was at the time of Nabonidus, circa 550 B.C.E. The Jews in these settlements were merchants, farmers, vintners, smiths, and, in the desert, members of Bedouin tribes. The most important Jewish dominated city was Yathrib, known later as Medina. The Jews of the Hijaz were semi-independent, but often allied with both Byzantium and the Persians. Some made the claim to be "kings" of the Hijaz, most probably meaning tax collectors for the Persians, and for a variety of reasons, more Jews were loyal to Persian interests against those of the Byzantine empire. Jews, as well as Christians, seem to have been engaged in attempting to convert the Arabian population to their religious and political views, often with some success. The loyalties of the Jews and Christians to one or the other of the two empires meant that choosing either Judaism or Christianity meant also choosing to ally with a superpower interested in dominating Arabia.

Arab sources report that at the time of Muhammad's birth, some Meccans had abandoned polytheism and had chosen monotheism (Ar. *hanif*), in a Jewish, Christian, or nonsectarian form. From Qur'anic and other evidence, it is clear that Meccans were conversant with the general principles of Judaism and Christianity and knew many details of worship, practice, and belief.

When Muhammad had his first revelation in 610 C.E., his wife, Khadija, tested the validity of his experience by seeking the advice of her cousin, Waraqa b. Nawfal, a *hanif* learned in Jewish and Christian scriptures. In declaring that Muhammad was a continuation of the prophetic traditions of Judaism and Christianity, he said that he had been foretold in Jewish and Christian scripture. A central doctrine of Islam places Muhammad at the end of a chain of prophets from God, starting with Adam and embracing all the prophetic figures of Judaism and Christianity, and holds that Muhammad's advent is announced in the Torah and Gospels. Denial of this central idea by Jews and Christians is said to be a result of the corruption of the sacred texts, either inadvertently or on purpose. This disparity of perspective underlies much of what Muslims believe about their Jewish and Christian forebears and conditions Islamic triumphalist views about the validity of Islam against the partial falsity of the other two traditions.

The Qur'an and the *Sira*, the traditional biography of Muhammad, present ambivalent attitudes toward Jews and Christians, reflecting the varied experience of Muhammad and the early community with Jews and Christians in Arabia. Christians are said to be nearest to Muslims in "love" in Qur'an 5:82, but Muslims are not to take Jews or Christians as *awlilya*, "close allies or leaders" in Qur'an 5:51. The Qur'an sometimes makes a distinction between the "Children of Israel," that is, Jews mentioned in the Bible, and "Jews," members of the Jewish tribes in Arabia during Muhammad's time. This distinction is also present in the *Sira* and other histories, and one sees some Jews as hostile to Muhammad and his mission, while others become allies with him. The so-called Constitution of Medina, which Muhammad negotiated with the Ansar, the Muhajirun, and the Jews of Medina, include Jews in the *umma*, allowing them freedom of association and religion in return for the payment of an annual tax, originally called the *kharaj*. This agreement and the subsequent treaties negotiated by Muhammad with the Jews of Khaybar, Tayma', and other cities in the Hijaz, establish the precedent of including "people of the book" (Ar. *ahl al-kitab*) in the *umma*. As the armies of conquest encountered communities of Jews, Christians, and Zoroastrians, the model of Muhammad's accommodating behavior extended the original notion to incorporate all these recipients of God's revelation as *ahl al-dhimma*, or *dhimmi*.

Moses Maimonides (1135–1204), a rabbi, philosopher, and physician, was born in Cordoba, Spain, where Christians and Jews participated in a lively intellectual community along with Muslims. When Maimonides was still young, however, Almohads from North Africa arrived in Cordoba and forbade Christians and Jews to worship openly, so his family left and eventually settled in Egypt. © Corbis-Bettmann

The death of Muhammad and the subsequent expansion of Islam out of Arabia brought about a break with the Jewish Arabian communities, so that subsequent relations are built on Jewish and Christian interactions with Muslims who knew the Prophet's actions only as idealized history. During the first Islamic century, the period of the most rapid expansion of Islam, social and religious structures were so fluid that it is hard to make generalizations. Jews and Christians were theoretically expelled from Arabia, or, at least, the Hijaz, but later evidence shows that Jews and Christians remained for centuries afterward. As late as the eighteenth century, for example, Jewish Bedouin roamed Northwestern Arabia, terrorizing pilgrims.

The era of the Umayyads was a time in which Muslims, Jews, and Christians negotiated the new power arrangements. The parameters of *dhimmi* status were developed, and both head and land taxes were paid to the Muslim rulers. Jews and Christians related to the Muslim caliphs through representatives and not individually. For the Jews, the Resh Geluta or exilarch was designated as a "prince" in the Muslim court, representing all the Jews. Because the exilarch was from the Rabbinic branch of Judaism, it became the dominant form,

generally displacing other groups. Also, because Muslims expanded to include most of the world's Jews in their polity, Rabbinic Judaism was able to develop its institutions within the context of the Islamic *umma*. For the newly forming Islamic state, the loyalty of the exilarch, and, by extension, the Jews, added legitimacy to Muslim claims to legitimate rule over its various non-Muslim populations. The interaction between Jews and Muslims thus produced profound effects on both Judaism and Islam. The occasional uprisings against Muslim rule—as the Jewish uprisings of the early eighth century—were local, over specific grievances, and not anti-Islamic as such. In fact, the Jewish revolt against the Umayyads, driven, it seems, by messianic visions, was sympathetic to early Shi'ite ideology while it unsuccessfully tried to overthrow the last Umayyad caliph.

The first two Islamic centuries were a time of translating Jewish and Christian scripture into Arabic, along with a vast body of commentary, particularly on biblical figures. Qur'anic *tafsir* became the repository of much Jewish tradition about such figures as Abraham, Moses, Solomon, and others. It was during this period that Rabbinic Judaism met a strong challenge from Karaite Judaism and ultimately triumphed as the dominant form of Judaism in the world.

The period from the tenth through the eighteenth centuries of the common era witnessed a rise of Western military, technological, and economic power, ultimately eclipsing the great agrarian-based Islamic empires that had formed in the wake of the collapse of the Abbasid caliphate. In the western Islamic lands of the Iberian peninsula and North Africa, Jews, Christians, and Muslims combined in a society that is often described by later historians with the adjective "golden." The areas of poetry, music, art, architecture, theology, exegesis, law, philosophy, medicine, pharmacology, and mysticism were shared among all the inhabitants of the Islamic courts and city-states at the same time that Muslim armies were locked in a losing struggle with the Christian armies of the Reconquista. In the eastern Mediterranean, similar symbiotic societies could be found. Within the intellectual circles of the Islamic world, Jews become Hellenized through contact with Muslim philosophers and theologians, just as Muslims had from contact with Christians earlier. In the areas of commerce, world trade was dominated by trading associations made up of Muslims, Jews, and Christians from Islamic lands.

## Political Ideology

The twin attacks on the Islamic world in the Middle Ages by the Crusaders from the West and the Mongols from the East transformed Muslim attitudes toward the *dhimmi*. In the resulting visions of society, the influence of Jews, Christians, and Shi'ites was circumscribed and made more rigid, but not eliminated. Muslim religious scholars used depictions of Jews and Christians found in the foundation texts as cautionary models for Muslims, but actual communities of Jews and Christians were treated with strict adherence to Islamic legal precedent. *Dhimmi*s had to wear distinctive clothing and badges to indicate their position in society, as did Muslims as part of a general "uniform" indicating rank and status. Certain occupations became common for Jews and Christians, such as tanning, which was regarded as imparting ritual impurity to Muslims, and it became less common in this period to find Jews and Christians in the highest ranks of advisors to the rulers. Jews and Christians usually lived in separate quarters of cities, and, while they were inferior to Muslims in public, barred from riding horses or blocking the public way with religious processions, they lived autonomously with respect to their communal affairs. This autonomy, while protective of the individuals, was to prove to have long-term consequences, however.

When Jews and Muslims were expelled from Spain in 1492, the majority of Jews chose to move to Islamic lands, the area of the Ottoman Empire in particular. The Iberian Jews were so numerous, well educated, and prosperous that Iberian Jewish culture often supplanted that of the older Jewish communities so that Sephardic became the general term for Jews living in Islamic lands. The trading and manufacturing skills and the capital of these immigrants to the Ottoman empire provided much of the wealth for Ottoman expansion. Under the Ottomans, Jewish and Christian communities achieved the greatest degree of autonomy. Through the *millet* system, each community was distinct and responsible directly to the sultan.

In the Ottoman Empire, the British and French found Jews and Christians to be attractive agents for their commercial activities, and the Ottomans, in turn, were pleased to employ the *dhimmi* for these purposes as well. Many Jews sought to secure the benefits of Western societies for themselves and their offspring by asking for and getting Western protection, passports, and, in some instances, citizenship. The increasing identification of Jews and Christians with non-Muslim powers served only to isolate these non-Muslims from the rest of Islamic society. By the end of the nineteenth century, most Muslims were under Western political and legal influence. The secular legal systems devised in the West supplanted Muslim customary and religious law, seriously challenging or eliminating the category of *dhimma* in those countries. The result was often a complete separation of Jews from a relationship in law with Muslims and an increasing identification of Jews as "European." This was particularly the case in Western Islamic lands, where a knowledge of the growth of European forms of Judaism was greatest.

The dissolution of the Ottoman Empire at the end of World War I resulting in the creation of a number of small nation-states brought about a further separation of non-Muslims from Muslims. The ideology of nationalism reduced religion to the status of only one of the components of a nation-state ideology. Education became Western, technological, and secular, further reducing religion to peripheral status. By the eve of World War II, most Islamic countries were prepared to overthrow colonialism and establish nation-states along Western secularist models. When this happened after World War II, constitutions were modeled after such countries as Switzerland, the United States, and France, usually guaranteeing freedom of religion, but providing no particular safeguards for religious expression. Other religious and ethnic groups also desired nation-states. Christian states were formed in the Balkans and the Jewish state of Israel was formed in the formerly British Mandate territory of Palestine. The creation of the state of Israel in 1948 became a central focal point for Jewish-Muslim relations that had steadily deteriorated since before World War I. The worsening conflicts in Palestine increased Jewish-Muslim conflict in the Arab states, where Jews were seen as both foreign and instruments of Western colonial designs. Within twenty years after the formation of the state of Israel, the majority of Jews living in Arab lands migrated to Israel, thus crystallizing the conflict in Palestine into a Jewish-Muslim conflict. Rulers in predominantly Muslim countries no longer had a constituent Jewish population. Jews became an abstract and hostile Other, and Judaism, increasingly identified with Zionism by Jews and non-Jews alike, was revalorized as the ever-present opposition to Muslims in Islamic history. This last notion, while having its roots in the foundation texts of Islam, was now abstracted in a way unlike any time in the past, and Jewish-Muslim relations took a new direction.

## Jews in Islamic History

A common thread among many Islamic intellectuals concerned with the role and direction of Muslims in the postcolonial world is the role of the Jews in Islamic history. As mentioned above, the historical circumstances of a strong Jewish presence in the Hijaz during Muhammad's time and the opposition of a few of the Jewish tribes to Muhammad's mission, embedded numerous seemingly anti-Jewish statements into the early literature. For a few, in a quest to use the Islamic historical past to explain the present, the negative accounts of Judaism and Christianity became abstracted so as to conflate the past with the present Arab-Israeli and East-West conflicts. Biblical descriptions of Jews rebelling against God's commands, Medinan Jewish opposition to the forming Muslim state, and Israeli actions against Palestinians were read together as an eternal Jewish character, a view sometimes informed by Western anti-Semitic literature. The article by Egyptian intellectual Sayyid Qutb, "Our Struggle with the Jews," is one example, as are the views expressed in America by leaders of the Nation of Islam.

Other Muslim intellectuals read the same foundation texts with an emphasis on the special relationship between God and people of the book. While deploring the problems in Palestine, they separate the Arab-Israeli conflict from discussions about Jews (and Christians). Some at Al-Azhar in Egypt cite Qur'an and sunna to support peace accords between Israel and the Palestinians, and Warith D. Muhammad, the son of Elijah Muhammad, has countered the anti-Jewish essentialist reading of the past with a Qur'anic-based message of mutual cooperation among Muslims, Jews, and Christians.

Discourse about Jewish-Muslim and Christian relations has been dominated in the last century by the problems of forming new group identities after the dissolution of colonialism. Muslim, Jewish, and Christian communities have all suffered from conflicts pitting one ethnic group against another. As with any conflict, this period has produced considerable polemic. It has also produced positive calls for mutual respect and cooperation. It remains to be seen if the positive richness of past Jewish-Muslim relations can overcome the current antipathies.

*See also* **Christianity and Islam; Islam and Other Religions; Minorities: Dhimmis.**

*Gordon D. Newby*

# K

## KALAM

*Kalam* is an Arabic term for speech, and has several other, related, technical connotations in Islamic religious thought. Used in the phrase *kalam allah* it means the word of God as revealed to humankind through prophets (2:75, 9:6, and 48:15). In this sense, *kalam* is analogous to the Greek term *logos*, as it is used in Jewish theology by Philo of Alexandria in about the first century C.E. In its second sense, *kalam* designates God's creative word. In the Qur'an, God's words, as commands, create reality. This can be seen in such Qur'anic quotations as: "Yet when We will a thing We only have to say 'Be' and it is" (16:40). In this context, the word of God, *kalam*, takes on a performative function—the utterance of the word accomplishes the creative act.

The third and the most primary usage is found in the phrase *'ilm al-kalam*, which connotes "the science of (dialectical) theology" that establishes and elaborates on the doctrinal teachings of the various schools (sing. *madhhab*) of theology, such as the Mu'tazilites, Ash'arites, and Maturidites. In Islamic intellectual traditions, the scholars of *kalam* gradually came to be delineated as dogmatic theologians (*mutakallimun*), as distinct from philosophers (*falasifa*) and mystics (Sufis).

The *mutakallimun* developed a dialectical method of framing and defending religious claims over rival teachers and schools. Some scholars believe that Greek and Hellenistic philosophy influenced the rise of *kalam* as a form of theology, while others point out that Islam, as a revealed, word-centered religion, was the primary factor in the emergence of the *kalam* method and schools of thought. The latter method, as it appears in literary form, strongly indicates the disputational context of early and medieval Islamic thought. A theological claim was made, then defended against critics in a series of conditional statements of the form: "if someone from such and such a school asks you so and so, then say to him . . . ."

The subject matter of *kalam* included such topics as God and his attributes, classification of and arguments against other religions, ethical responsibility and its eschatological consequences, and the doctrine of the imamate (political theology). *'Ilm al-kalam* became the lingua franca of most religious discourse among sects and groups in medieval Islamic society from the eighth century onward. Sunni and Shi'ite schools adopted the *kalam* method. So, too, did medieval Christian and Jewish communities living in Iraq and Iran and elsewhere in the central Islamic lands. After the eleventh century, Aristotelian philosophy and logic began to wax as the *kalam* methods and schools waned. Nowadays, *kalam* is studied historically but does not claim thriving schools or exponents. Nonetheless, in his widely read theological treatise on Islam and modernity, *Risalat al-tawhid* (Theology of unity), Shaykh Muhammad 'Abduh (d. 1905) preserved a modified version of the dialectical method of the medieval Mu'tazilite and Ash'arite schools.

*See also* **Ash'arites, Ash'aira; Disputation; Falsafa; Knowledge; Murji'ites, Murji'a; Qur'an.**

### BIBLIOGRAPHY

Wolfson, Harry A. *The Philosophy of the Kalam*. Cambridge, Mass.: Harvard University Press, 1976.

*Parviz Morewedge*

## KANO

Kano is the capital city of Kano State, in northern Nigeria. Its 1992 population (the last year for which census data is available) was estimated at 700,000 inhabitants. Kano State has an area of 16.630 square miles and an estimated population 5.6 million.

Archaeological evidence suggests that Kano was founded in the fifth century as a settlement at the foot of Dalla Hill.

The early inhabitants were animist, believing that a soul or spirit inhabited all things. The animist tradition is still followed by some peoples of northern Nigeria, but Kano's inhabitants were introduced to Islam possibly as early as the tenth century.

Kano was visited by strangers in the tenth century. These newcomers may have been early Muslims, but a firm Islamic presence was not established until the fourteenth century. By the late 1300s, Kano became an independent Islamic sultanate, with close links to other Islamic centers located across the Sahara to the north. With the creation of the sultanate, the people of Kano began to publicly observe Islamic festivals, and the appointment of eunuchs to office—a practice common in courts elsewhere in the Islamic world—was begun in Kano as well.

By the fifteenth century, Kano had assumed control of the trans-Sahara caravan trade, due in large part to its powerful army. Camels appeared in the city, acquired through trade, and slave raiding in the countryside to the south had become a profitable occupation of the Kano aristocracy. Later in the fifteenth century, Kano came in direct contact with European traders, and further expanded their trade repertoire by specializing in indigo-colored textiles and red "Morocco-leather."

During the period of European colonization, Kano developed as a center of Western-style education. The British colonial government set up a school to train teachers of Arabic and Islamic sciences in the methods of modern pedagogy. Nonetheless, the city remained an important center of Sufi activities as well. It became in the same period an emporium of the new groundnut trade, on which the economy of northern Nigeria today largely depends.

Kano is not remarkable for creative literary contributions. It relied on works that were imported from peripheral Islamic areas. The first Kano scholar in Islamic literature was Usuman, an imam from Miga, who lived in the middle of the eighteenth century. A century later Asim Degal contributed works on astrology. The Makarantan Ilmi schools of higher Islamic learning play an important part in the Islamic life of Kano City. There are at least twelve establishments of this kind in Kano, but the number is believed to be much higher.

In the eighteenth century Kano was besieged by the Fulani, a powerful West African people. After the Fulani came the Europeans. British troops took the city in 1903 and imposed indirect colonial government. The emir stayed in power, but a British colonial official was present at all times. Kano grew during the twentieth century. A railroad was built in 1912, an airport in 1937, and a system of roads and highways expanded over the years. Today the city preserves a mixture of the old and the new. Its walls still stand. Built in the fourteenth century of mud-brick, the walls are nearly 30 kilometers long, with 15 gates. Still standing, too, are traditional houses of mud-brick, finely decorated in Hausa style.

Other prominent buildings in Kano are the Amir's palace, the Grand Mosque, and the museum.

*See also* **Africa, Islam in; Marwa, Muhammad; 'Uthman Dan Fodio.**

## BIBLIOGRAPHY

Hogben, S. J., and Kirk-Green, A. H. M. *The Emirates of Northern Nigeria.* London: Oxford University Press, 1966.

Smith, M. G. *Government in Kano, 1350–1950.* Boulder, Colo.: Westview Press, 1997.

*Thyge C. Bro*

# KARAKI, SHAYKH 'ALI

Nur al-Din Abu 'l-Hasan 'Ali b. al-Husayn b. 'Abd al-'Ali al-Karaki, also known as al-Muhaqqiq al-Thani (d.1533), was an Arab Twelver Shi'ite jurist from Karak Nuh in present-day Lebanon, who acquired the scholastic tradition of Jabal 'Amil in Syria and stood in the intellectual line of descent from Muhammad b. Makki (d.1384), who was known as al-Shahid al-Awwal (the First Martyr). Al-Karaki was the first major Shi'ite scholar to emigrate from Jabal 'Amil to Najaf in Iraq during the sixteenth century and from there to Safavid Iran (1501–1736), where Shah Isma'il (r. 1501–1524) appointed him *shaykh al-Islam*. He implemented the Ja'fari (Twelver Shi'ite) legal rulings, observed the previously suspended Friday prayer, and tried to draw Shi'ism out of its scholastic puritanism to fit the Safavid state structure. In 1532, and as a visible sign of al-Karaki's eminence at the court, Shah Tahmasp (r. 1524–1576) issued a royal decree declaring him the deputy (*na'ib*) of the imam and the seal of jurisconsults (*khatam al-mujtahidin*), thus undermining the position of the Iranian *sadr*s, chiefs of the Safavid religious administration who adjudicated in criminal and religious matters. Shah Tahmasp also conferred on al-Karaki extensive land holdings as a hereditary *waqf* (religious endowment). Al-Karaki's ardent defense of the Shi'ite faith earned him the nickname "inventor of the Shi'ite religion." Among his descendants was the seventeenth-century Iranian jurist and philosopher Mir Damad.

*See also* **Empires: Safavid and Qajar; Isma'il I, Shah; Shaykh al-Islam; Shi'a: Imami (Twelver); Tahmasp I, Shah.**

## BIBLIOGRAPHY

Arjomand, S. A. "Two Decrees of Shah Tahmasp Concerning Statecraft and the Authority of Shaykh 'Ali al-Karaki," In *Authority and Political Culture in Shi'ism.* Albany: State University of New York Press, 1988.

Arjomand, S. A. "The *Mujtahid* of the Age and the *Mullabashi*: An Intermediate Stage in the Institutionalization of Religious Authority in Shi'ite Iran." In *Authority and Political*

*Culture in Shi'ism.* Albany: State University of New York Press, 1988.

*Rula Jurdi Abisaab*

## KARBALA

Karbala is the second largest town in Iraq, with over 350,000 inhabitants in the early twenty-first century. It is situated about sixty miles southwest of Baghdad, where the mausoleum of Muhammad's grandson Husayn (Mashhad Husayn) was erected and frequently destroyed and restored during the early centuries of Islam.

When the first Umayyad Sunni caliph, Mu'awiya, died in 680 C.E., his son Yazid came to power. The majority of Muslims saw the nomination of Yazid to the caliphate as an usurpation of the notion of consensus (*ijma'*), the legitimate means of choosing a caliph. When Husayn received confirmation of the loyalty of the Kufis from his cousin Muslim Ibn 'Aqil, he headed toward Kufa. On his way, Husayn learned that his cousin had died at the hands of Yazid's men and that the Kufis had shifted their allegiance to Yazid.

Husayn nevertheless continued in the direction of Kufa. Ibn Ziyad, the governor of Kufa, with one thousand soldiers at his command, told Husayn that he could neither go to Kufa nor return to Mecca, and was permitted only to go to Damascus, the capital. Instead, Husayn led his heavily outnumbered and underequipped followers to battle in Karbala, where they were slain mercilessly on the battlefield. This event played an important role in the development of Shi'ite theology and has been the source of dissension among Muslims. The battle of Karbala accentuated the split between the two major branches of Islam. The event forged in Shi'ite Muslims an identity as believers who are subjected to persecution for the sake of the true succession of Muhammad.

A cult of martyrdom is linked to the death and downfall of Husayn at Karbala. The *'Ashura* (date of Husayn's death) was elaborated upon and systematized in the articulation of Shi'ite theology. Every year during the first ten days of the month of hijra, the battle of Karbala is commemorated by Shi'ite Muslims during Muharram, and many go on pilgrimage to Karbala. Husayn's martyrdom has become a source of strength and endurance for Shi'ite Muslims in times of suffering, persecution, and oppression.

During its long history the tomb of Husayn was desecrated several times and had to be restored. In 850 and 851, the Sunni Abbasid caliph al-Mutawakkil destroyed the tomb of Husayn and prohibited pilgrimages to the sanctuary. Sulayman the Magnificent visited the tomb in 1534 and 1535 and participated in its restoration. At the end of the eighteenth century Agha Muhammad Khan, the founder of the Qajar dynasty, covered the dome in gold and the *manara* of the sanctuary. In April 1802, twelve thousand Wahhabis under Shaykh Sa'ud invaded Karbala, killed over three thousand inhabitants, and sacked the city.

*See also* **'Ali; Husayn; Qur'an; Shi'a: Early.**

### BIBLIOGRAPHY

Honigmann E.. "Karbalâ'." In Vol. IV, *The Encyclopaedia of Islam.* Leiden: E. J. Brill, 1978.

Jafri, S. H. M. *The Origins and Early Development of Shi'a Islam.* New York: Longman, 1981.

Momen, Moojan. *An Introduction to Shi'i Islam.* New Haven, Conn.:Yale University Press, 1985.

*Diana Steigerwald*

## KEMAL, NAMEK (1840–1888)

Namek Kemal, a writer and journalist belonging to the group of the Young Ottomans, attempted to introduce political liberalism into the bureaucratic despotism of the Tanzimat reform era. Kemal came from an aristocratic background, and after learning French he began his career in the Translation Office of the Ottoman government in Istanbul in 1857. He published a journal and wrote essays on reform in a simple but powerful Turkish style. In 1865 he helped found a secret political society and was dismissed from his government position when this became known. In exile in Europe (1867–1870), he discovered European civilization and French revolutionary thought, which he found compatible with certain Islamic political ideas. He popularized the concepts of fatherland and freedom, and started the newspaper *Hurriyet* (Freedom) to develop public opinion (1868). On returning from exile he became a journalist and political essayist, advocating liberal political rights founded on Islamic principles, constitutional separation of powers, and halting of European economic penetration. His controversial 1873 patriotic play, *Vatan* (Fatherland), resulted in renewed imprisonment and exile. In 1876 he returned to join state service under the constitutional regime. He criticized Ottoman modernization as insufficiently liberal, destroying old safeguards against absolutism, notably the *shari'a* and the Janissaries (elite corps of Turkish troops) without providing new ones. Suspected of plotting to depose Sultan Abdulhamit after the 1878 abrogation of the constitution, he was again exiled and his writings were banned. He died in exile, but his works, read secretly, fired the imagination of the Young Turks, who took up the cause of liberalism during the autocratic regime of 'Abdulhamit.

*See also* **Young Ottomans.**

**BIBLIOGRAPHY**

Mardin, Serif. *The Genesis of Young Ottoman Thought: A Study in the Modernization of Turkish Political Ideas.* 1962. Reprint, Syracuse, N.Y.: Syracuse University Press, 2000.

*Linda T. Darling*

## KHALID, KHALID MUHAMMAD (1920–1996)

Khalid Muhammad Khalid was a popular Egyptian writer on religious and political topics, and the author of more than thirty books and numerous newspaper and magazine articles. He received his theological degree from the faculty of *shariʿa* at al-Azhar University in 1947, and then gained a teaching certificate, also from al-Azhar. He taught Arabic language, and then worked in the Egyptian Ministry of Education and in the Ministry of Culture. He became a supervisor in the Department for the Publication of the Heritage.

His first book, *From Here We Begin* (*Min huna nabdaʾ*), published in 1950, was a forceful and controversial call for separation of religion from state, as well as for a democratic socialism, effective birth control, and furtherance of the rights of women. It was shortly translated into English, as was the Islamist response to it, *Our Beginning in Wisdom*, by his friend Muhammad al-Ghazali. These two books provide a good sample of the secularist-Islamist debate in Egypt at mid-century. Khalid expressed similar views in other passionately written books in the 1950s and early 1960s.

Later he wrote a number of books on Muhammad and other heroes of early Islam. In his book *al-Dawla fi al-Islam* (*The State in Islam*), published in 1981, he revised his earlier secularist position, stating that Islam does have civil principles that should be applied by the state, although it does not prescribe a "religious government." According to Khalid, parliamentary democracy is the contemporary application of the Islamic principle of *shura* (consultation).

*See also* **Ghazali, Muhammad al-.**

**BIBLIOGRAPHY**

Khalid, Muhammad Khalid. *From Here We Start.* Translated by Ismail R. al-Faruqi. Washington, D.C.: American Council of Learned Societies, 1953.

*William Shepard*

## KHAMANEʾI, SAYYED ʿALI (1939– )

Sayyed ʿAli Khamaneʾi, the leader of the Islamic Republic of Iran (r. 1989– ) was born in Mashad, Khorasan province, Iran, in 1939. Khamaneʾi finished his study in Qom Seminary in 1964. During the rule of Mohammad Reza Shah, Khamaneʾi was a student of Ruhollah Khomeini, the future leader of the Iranian Revolution. Khamaneʾi was arrested many times during the shah's rule, served a total of three years in prison between 1964 and 1978, and was exiled for a year between 1978 and 1979, spending his time in Kanshahr, Baluchistan province. In 1979, following the overthrow of the shah, he was selected as the representative of the Revolutionary Council in the army as well as Deputy for Revolutionary Affairs at the National Ministry of Defense. He was also chosen as the leader of the Friday prayer in Tehran.

In 1980 Khamaneʾi was elected to the Iranian Parliament. He was one of the founding members of the Islamic Republic Party. In June 1981 he became the target of an unsuccessful assassination attempt. In 1981, following the assassination of President Rajaʾe, he was elected as the third president of revolutionary Iran. He was reelected president in 1985 and served a second four-year term. On 4 June 1989, after the death of the ayatollah Ruhollah Khomeini, the Assembly of Experts chose Khamaneʾi as the *vali-ye faqih* or leader of the Islamic Republic of Iran. His main problem in leadership as a substitute for his predecessor, Khomeini, has been his lack of traditional and charismatic legitimacy.

After several attempts to make him the sole *marjaʿ al-taqlid* (Twelver Shiʿa leader) had failed, he was endorsed as one of seven *marajeʿ* by the conservative Qom clerics in December 1994. His political modus operandi includes conspiracy theory, religious authoritarianism, antipluralism, and anti-intellectualism. Khamaneʾi has been accused of killing about eighty political activists and intellectuals both within and outside Iran since the 1990s. He closed more than eighty newspapers and imprisoned sixty journalists, political activists, and intellectuals in 2000 and 2001.

*See also* **Iran, Islamic Republic of; Revolution: Islamic Revolution in Iran.**

*Majid Mohammadi*

## KHAN

The meaning of the word khan is dependent upon the context in which it is used. It is often used as a title, but can also refer to an office, a form of address, an attribute of rulership (following Genghis Khan's thirteenth-century Mongol unification), or as part of a place name. Its etymology is obscure, though probably Turkic. It continues to be used commonly in Central Asia, North India, Pakistan, Iran, and Turkey. It is seldom used in Arabic, except as a place name.

*G. R. Garthwaite*

# KHANQA (KHANAQA, KHANGA)

In twelfth century Sufism—a new strand of Islam based on the knowledge of God through personal experience of a spiritual nature—developed its own institutions, the most important of which were the *zawiya* and *khanqa*. *Zawiyas* were mostly associated with Tariqas (Sufi "orders"). They spread a type of popular Sufism, which appealed to the masses, and they were left free to develop from the control of the ruling elite. *Khanqas*, known for their spread of a type of "orthodox" Sufism, often had their fate closely linked to that of the ruling elite, whose patronage was crucial to their survival.

The *khanqa* institution made its first appearance in Persia from where it spread rapidly to the rest of the Muslim world. It was introduced to Egypt in the twelfth century by Saladin, who put the institution under the control of the state. Two centuries later, the *khanqa* had reached its full development thanks to patronage of the Mamluks.

According to the fifteenth century historian al-Maqrizi, the term *khanqa* (Arabic form, pl. Khawaniq) derives from the Persian. It is formed by two words: *khan*, which means sultan, and *kah*, which means people. In the Eastern lands of Islam, the term *khanqa* was used to refer to foundations reserved for Sufis. In these "monasteries" Sufis and their master could dedicate their lives to the practice of orthodox Sufism according to the rules set by their patrons. For medieval Egypt and Syria, the set of rules that regulated the communal life of Sufis are known from extant endowment deeds (*waqfiyyas*). Sufis and their master were generally appointed by the founder of the *khanqa* or his successors. They were housed in the foundation, and were given a salary, food, and clothing. Sufis living in a *khanqa* were to remain celibate; the ones married would spend the day there but would live outside it. All Sufis were required to attend the daily Sufi gatherings, perform the ritual of Dhikr (remembrance) and spend time in meditation. As the *khanqa* evolved, its function became associated with that of the *madrasa*. As a result, Sufis' activities also included attending classes in the various religious sciences.

*Khanqas* were mostly urban foundations to which the founders often attached their funerary domes. The plan for *khanqas* did not differ much from that of the *madrasa*. Most *khanqas* followed the four *iwan* (vaulted hall) plan with an open courtyard in their middle. In time the latter's size was reduced and it was covered by a roof. Fifteenth-century *khanqas* consisted of elaborate complexes that included a grain mill, a bakery, an oil press, and living quarters for the founder and his family.

The presence of a *khanqa* within an urban setting affected the life of the individuals living around it. Often the growth of the whole quarter depended on the *khanqa*'s survival, and sometimes the ruin of the *khanqa* meant the gradual disappearance of the quarter.

By the sixteenth century, *khanqas* began their steady decline as they had lost their patrons. Indeed, the Ottomans, new masters of the region, were rather interested in patronizing Sufi orders. Since *khanqas* did not follow any particular order, the Ottomans showed no interest in maintaining these institutions. Moreover, times had changed and the whole society had experienced a rise in popular Sufism sponsored by the masses. Although it had managed to maintain itself a little longer, soon the institution became defunct. Sufism survived in the *zawiyas*, which remain active today.

*See also* **Architecture; Tariqa; Tasawwuf.**

## BIBLIOGRAPHY

Fernandes, Leonor. "The Foundation of Baybars al-Jashankir in Cairo: Its Waqf, History and Architecture." *Muqarnas* 4 (1987): 21–42.

Mala, S. B. "The Sufi Convent and its Social Significance in the Medieval Period of Islam." *Islamic Culture* 51 (1977): 31–52.

Trimingham, John Spencer. *The Sufi Orders in Islam.* Oxford, U.K.: Clarendon Press, 1971.

*Leonor Fernandes*

# KHAN, REZA OF BAREILLY (1856–1921)

Ahmad Reza Khan Barelwi (Bareilly) was an influential scholar and Sufi whose followers emerged in the colonial period as one of two major groupings among South Asian Sunni Muslims—the other being the Deobandis. Ahmad Reza's voluminous writings include a translation of the Qur'an and many volumes of advisory opinions, or *fatawa*. Although often called "Barelwi" by outsiders, those associated with this religious style claim the name Ahl al-Sunna wa al-Jama'at, that is, the true Sunnis. They follow the Hanafi school of legal interpretation and primarily follow the Qadiri order in Sufi affiliation.

For the Barelwis, a good Muslim is defined as one faithful to the *shari'a* and personally devoted to the prophet Muhammad as continuous intercessor to Allah through the mediation of the Sufi master. Unlike other reformers, they participate in ceremonies like the *'urs* observances at Sufi shrines (the saint's "wedding" with the divine) and the *mawlid* celebration of the Prophet's birthday. Conflict with the Deobandis revolved around issues related to the Prophet's attributes: his ability to see into the future, to have knowledge of the unseen, and to be present in multiple places, all of which they accepted. Ahmad Reza charged those who differed with him as being "Wahhabi," a politically charged label in the colonial context because it linked opponents with the militant followers of the Arab Muhammad 'Abd al-Wahhab (1703–1787).

Ahmad Reza opposed participation in the Khilafat movement and, subsequently, his followers were aloof from the Jamʿiyat-e ʿUlama-e Hind. Mosques and *madrasa*s identifying themselves as Ahl al-Sunna wa al-Jamaʿa are currently found across South Asia and in places of Indo-Pakistani settlement like Britain and South Africa. The Jamʿiyat-e ʿUlama-e Pakistan political party represents these ulema in Pakistan. The apolitical Dawat al Islami movement engages in grassroots "Barelwi" proselytizing in both India and Pakistan.

*See also* **Jamʿiyat-e ʿUlama-e Pakistan; Khilafat Movement; South Asia, Islam in; Wahhabiyya.**

## BIBLIOGRAPHY

Metcalf, Barbara Daly. *Islamic Revival in British India: Deoband 1860–1900.* Princeton, N.J.: Princeton University Press, 1982.

Sanyal, Usha. *Devotional Islam and Politics in British India: Ahmad Riza Khan Barelwi and his Movement, 1870–1920.* Oxford, U.K.: Oxford University Press, 1996.

Zafaruddin Bihari. *Hayat-i Aʿla Hazrat.* Karachi, Pakistan: Maktaba Rezwiyya, 1938.

*Barbara D. Metcalf*

# KHARIJITES, KHAWARIJ

The Kharijites, or Khawarij, began as a group of ʿAli's supporters who "exited" (*kharaju*) after the battle of Siffin (657 C.E.), when ʿAli accepted arbitration (*tahkim*) with Muʿawiya (r. 661–680). The "exiters" (*khawarij*) opposed a human tribunal in place of a battle victory decided by God's judgment, hence their slogan, "Judgment belongs to God alone," echoing Qurʾan 6:57, 12:40, and 12:67. They subsequently identified themselves as "exchangers" (*shurat*) for God's pleasure, as in Qurʾanic verse 2:207. Both militant activists and quietists used the exchange concept in their rhetoric, including their highly esteemed poetry. In opposition to the dynastic nature of the Umayyads, they purported to choose leaders by religious merit rather than by heritage. Considering themselves true Muslims, they developed rigid standards for proving one's faith and for what is permissible in Islam, which led to a variety of practices and consequent divisions. Militant groups attacked towns, engaging Umayyad generals al-Hajjaj and al-Muhallab for decades. Major leaders included the activists Nafiʿ b. al-Azraq al-Hanafi, Qatari b. al-Fujaʾa, and Shabib b. Yazid al-Shaybani, and quietists Najda b. ʿAmir al-Hanafi, and ʿAbdallah b. Ibad al-Tamim. "Sufriyya" is a general term used for quietists. Many quietists took up arms after the Umayyad's brutal massacre of Abu Bilal Mirdas b. Hudayr b. Udayya and his men while praying, in 680. Women were involved militarily and culturally. The Khawarij/Shurat were found variously in Arabia, Iraq, and Iran until largely eradicated at the end of the Umayyad period (750). A branch of Kharijites known as the Ibadis persevered and are found today in Oman and North Africa.

*See also* **Law.**

## BIBLIOGRAPHY

Madelung, Wilfred. "Kharijism: The ʿAjarida and the Ibadiyya." In *Religious Trends in Early Islamic Iran.* Albany, N.Y.: Bibliotheca Persica, 1988.

Mubarrad, Abu l-ʿAbbas Muhammad b. Yazid. *Al-Kamil fi l-lugha wa-l-adab.* Edited by Muhammad Abu al-Fadl Ibrahm. 4 vols. Cairo: Dar al-Fikr al-ʾArabi, n.d.

Shahrastani, Abu al-Fath Muhammad b. ʿAbd al-Karim. *Al-Milal wa-l-nihal.* Edited by Muhammad Sayyid Kilani. (1396.) Reprint. Cairo: Maktabat wa-Matbaʿat Mustafa al-Babi al-Halabi, 1976.

*Annie C. Higgins*

# KHIDR, AL-

Al-Khidr ("the green" man) is the guide and mentor of Moses described in Sura Kahf (Q. 18.60–82) as "Our exceptional servant to whom We gave compassion from Ourselves and inner knowledge from Our presence." Exegetes interpret this as "God-given knowledge" (*ʿilm laduni*), which complements Moses's knowledge of *shariʿa*. The Qurʾan narrates that Moses vowed to his servant (identified in hadith as Joshua) to reach the place where the two seas meet. When Moses learns their fish has plunged into the water, he resolves to return and finds al-Khidr, God's exceptional servant filled with God's Compassion and Inner Knowledge. Moses asks to follow al-Khidr. Al-Khidr cautions that since Moses will neither be able to be patient with him nor understand, he must agree not to ask any questions until al-Khidr gives him permission. Moses protests when al-Khidr scuttles the boat in which they ride. Al-Khidr renews his warning about patience. When al-Khidr kills a child, Moses protests, and receives a similar reprimand. In a village where they are denied hospitality, al-Khidr rebuilds a wall. When Moses protests, al-Khidr announces their parting and explains the true meaning (*taʾwil*) of the events: The ferrymen were poor people whom al-Khidr wanted to prevent from having their boat seized by an approaching king; the child would have corrupted the faith of his believing parents and will be replaced; and the wall concealed an inheritance belonging to two orphan sons of a righteous man, a "treasure which is a mercy from your Lord," signifying the deep meaning, learned through patience, that behind apparent injustice lies mercy.

In al-Bukhari's collection of hadith, the prophet Muhammad is quoted as saying: "He was named al-Khidr because after he sat upon barren land, it became green with vegetation." Bukhari presents the story of Moses and Khidr as a model for seeking knowledge with diligence and humility.

The association of al-Khidr with Alexander the Great (356–323 B.C.E.) stems from the fact that the Khidr narrative in the Qur'an precedes that of Dhu l-Qarnayn (the man "of two horns"), who is often identified with Alexander, and from the motif in the narrative of the water of life reviving a cooked fish; al-Khidr, like Elijah, Jesus, and Idris, is considered immortal. Al-Khidr is a protector of travelers, a rescuer, and a saint. In the Levant, sacred places often have multiple dedications to Khidr, Elijah, and St. George. In India, Khwaja Khidr is depicted as resembling Vishnu's Matsya (fish) Avatar.

In Sufism, al-Khidr represents the saint and the spiritual master. For Sufi Qur'an commentators, al-Khidr represents spiritual guidance (suhba) as distinguished from instruction (ta'lim). In hagiographies, Khidr gives to humankind initiation, guidance, and liturgies. The famous Sufi Ibn al-'Arabi reported receiving al-Khidr's mantle of initiation (khirqa) twice, and the poet and mystic al-Rumi's relationship to Shams-e Tabrizi was described by Rumi's son, Sultan Veled, as being like that of Moses and Khidr.

See also **Prophets.**

## BIBLIOGRAPHY

Wheeler, Brandon. "Moses or Alexander? Early Islamic Exegesis of Qur'an 18.60–96." *Journal of Near Eastern Studies* 57, no. 3: 191–215.

*Hugh Talat Halman*

# KHILAFAT MOVEMENT

The Khilafat movement (1919–1924) was an agitation on the part of some Indian Muslims, allied with the Indian nationalist movement, during the years following World War I. Its purpose was to pressure the British government to preserve the authority of the Ottoman sultan as caliph of Islam. Integral to this was the Muslims' desire to influence the treaty-making process following the war in such a way as to restore the 1914 boundaries of the Ottoman empire. The British government treated the Indian Khilafat delegation of 1920, headed by Muhammad 'Ali, as quixotic pan-Islamists, and did not change its policy toward Turkey. The Indian Muslims' attempt to influence the treaty provisions failed, as the European powers went ahead with territorial adjustments, including the institution of mandates over formerly Ottoman Arab territories.

The significance of the Khilafat movement, however, lies less in its supposed pan-Islamism than in its impact upon the Indian nationalist movement. The leaders of the Khilafat movement forged the first political alliance among Western-educated Indian Muslims and ulema over the religious symbol of the *khilafat* (caliphate). This leadership included the 'Ali brothers—Muhammad 'Ali and Shaukat 'Ali—newspaper editors from Delhi, their spiritual guide Maulana Abdul Bari of Lucknow, the Calcutta journalist and Islamic scholar Maulana Abu'l Kalam Azad, and Maulana Mahmud al-Hasan, head of the Deoband madrasa. These publicist-politicians and ulema viewed European attacks upon the authority of the caliph as an attack upon Islam, and thus as a threat to the religious freedom of Muslims under British rule.

The Khilafat issue crystallized anti-British sentiments among Indian Muslims that had been increasing since the British declaration of war against the Ottomans in 1914. The Khilafat leaders, most of whom had been imprisoned during the war, were already politically active in the nationalist movement. Upon their release in 1919, the issue of the *khilafat* provided a means to achieve pan-Indian Muslim political solidarity in the anti-British cause and a source of communication between the leaders and their potential mass following. The Khilafat movement also benefited from Hindu-Muslim cooperation in the nationalist cause that had grown during the war, beginning with the Lucknow Pact of 1916 between the Indian National Congress and the Muslim League, and culminating in the protest against the Rowlatt anti-sedition bills in 1919. The Congress, now led by Mahatma Gandhi, called for nonviolent noncooperation against the British. Gandhi espoused the Khilafat cause, as he saw in it the opportunity to rally Muslim support for the Congress. The 'Ali brothers and their allies, in turn, provided the noncooperation movement with some of its most enthusiastic troops.

The combined Khilafat-noncooperation movement was the first all-India agitation against British rule. It saw an unprecedented degree of Hindu-Muslim cooperation and it established Gandhi and his technique of nonviolent protest (*satyagraha*) at the center of the Indian nationalist movement. Mass mobilization using religious symbols was remarkably successful, and the British Indian government was shaken. In late 1921 the government moved to suppress the movement. The 'Ali brothers were arrested for incitement to violence, tried, and imprisoned. Gandhi suspended the noncooperation movement in early 1922, following a riot in the village of Chauri Chaura that resulted in the deaths of the local police. He was arrested, tried, and imprisoned soon thereafter. The Turks dealt the final blow by abolishing the Ottoman sultanate in 1922 and the caliphate in 1924.

See also **South Asia, Islam in.**

## BIBLIOGRAPHY

Bamford, P. C. *Histories of the Non-Cooperation and Khilafat Movements* (1925). Reprint. Delhi: Deep Publications, 1974.

Hasan, Mushirul. *Nationalism and Communal Politics in India.* New Delhi: Manohar Publications, 1991.

Minault, Gail. *The Khilafat Movement: Religious Symbolism and Political Mobilization in India.* New York: Columbia University Press, 1982.

Qureshi, M. Naeem. *Pan-Islam in British Indian Politics: A Study of the Khilafat Movement.* Leiden: Brill, 1999.

Gail Minault

# KHIRQA

A *khirqa* is a wool cloak, often patched (*muraqqaʿa*). Sufis wore the *khirqa* as a sign of having embarked on the Sufi path from at least the eighth century. By the eleventh century Sufis had developed ways of transmitting spiritual knowledge and authority: Sufi authors describe the binding of a disciple to a master through an oath (the *akhdh al-ʿahd* or the *bayʿa*), becoming part of the master's spiritual chain of authority (*silsila*), the inculcation (*talqin*) of a method of prayer (*dhikr*), and the bestowal of the *khirqa* from a master to a disciple. Investiture with the *khirqa* had an initiatic aspect. A disciple could be given the *khirqa* at the beginning of his training with a shaykh, in which case the *khirqa* indicated that the disciple had been invested with the means necessary for progressing along the path. The bestowal of a *khirqa* could certify that the novice had been trained by a master who could attest to his spiritual fitness and preparedness. The *silsila* and the *khirqa* served the same purposes as the chain of authority (*isnad*) and the certificate of permission (*ijaza*) in ulema circles: They certified that the Sufi had studied and trained under an authoritative master, whose spiritual pedigree could be traced back to the Prophet, and they gave him the authority to transmit a particular spiritual way.

*See also* **Clothing; Khilafat Movement; Tasawwuf.**

## BIBLIOGRAPHY

Schimmel, Annemarie. *Mystical Dimensions of Islam.* Chapel Hill, N.C.: University of North Carolina Press, 1975.

Sells, Michael, trans., ed. *Early Islamic Mysticism: Sufi, Qurʾ, Miraj, Poetic and Theological Writings.* New York: Paulist Press, c. 1996.

Margaret Malamud

# KHIVA, KHANATE OF

The khanate of Khiva (Khwarazm) was established in 1511 on the eastern shore of the Caspian Sea, to the south of the Aral Sea and along the lower course of the Amu Darya River. The main ethnic groups living in the khanate were Uzbeks, Turkmen, Karakalpaks, Kazakhs, and Sarts, the latter being the original inhabitants of the region.

The first ruler of the khanate was Sultan Ilbars, who had a Shaybanid Uzbek connection. He founded the Yadigarids dynasty in Urgench, a city in the north of Khiva, today situated in Uzbekistan. In 1619, following a catastrophic drought, the capital of the khanate was moved to Khiva. By the late seventeenth century the effective reign of the Yadigarids began to decline, and their successive khans were left as protégès of influential Uzbek clans. During this period the unvarying assaults by Turkmen tribes, in addition to the endeavors at subjugation by Peter the Great of Russia in 1719, and by Nadir Shah of Persia in 1740, accelerated the process of disintegration of the khanate. In 1804, Inaq Iltuzer deposed the latest Yadigarid khan and established the Qungrats dynasty. Following their earlier unsuccessful attempts to conquer the khanate, the Russians eventually (1873) occupied Khiva and imposed a protectorate status on the khanate. The protectorate status lasted until 1920 when, with the aid of Red Army, the era of the khanate of Khiva came to an end and Khiva became the capital of the newborn Khwarezm People's Soviet Republic. In 1924 Khiva was incorporated into the Soviet Republic of Uzbekistan.

In the khanate of Khiva, the khan was the absolute supreme ruler in all affairs. During the early period of its formation, the khanate was divided between the male associates of the ruling dynasties, each enjoying the military support of various leading tribes. However, following the establishment of Qungrats dynasty, the administrative hierarchy was systematically developed. Below the khan was the *divan-begi* or prime minister, who was followed by the *kush-begi*, who was in charge of military affairs, and finally the *mehter*, who ran the civil administration of the khanate. Furthermore, the khanate was divided into a capital and twenty districts, known as *beglik*s; each *beglik* was governed by a *hakim* or local governor. The nomads' chieftains, usually bypassing the *hakim*s, were directly accountable to the khan.

The khanate's judiciary system was based on s*hariʿa* or Islamic jurisprudence and *adat* or customary values. The highest position belonged to the *qazi-kalan* or chief judge/prosecutor. Following *qazi-kalan*, there were *qazi*s and then the *qazi*'s agents or *reʾis* who were policing the civil as well as moral behavior of the population. The Khanate's tax-collectors, known for their corrupt behavior, were also subordinate to the *qazi*s.

On the eve of the twentieth century, the population of the khanate of Khiva was estimated at 700,000. A majority of the people worked in agriculture, either as tenant farmers, share-croppers, or slaves. Cotton, wheat, and fruits were the main agricultural products. Cattle breeding was common among the Turkmen. The Sarts chiefly engaged in foreign trade, which was mainly with Russia and Iran.

During the Soviet era, the city of Khiva, like the other old khanate capitals, lost its political importance.

*See also* **Central Asian Culture and Islam.**

## BIBLIOGRAPHY

Hambly, G. *Central Asia*. London: Weidenfeld and Nicolson, 1969.

Holdsworth, M. *Turkestan in the Nineteenth Century: A Brief History of the Khanates of Bukhara, Kokand and Khiva.* Oxford, U.K.: Central Asian Research Centre & St. Antony's College – Soviet Affairs Study Group, 1959.

Soucek, S. *A History of Inner Asia.* Cambridge, U.K.: Cambridge University Press, 2000.

*Touraj Atabaki*

# KHO'I, ABO 'L-QASEM (1898–1992)

Sayyed Abo 'l-Qasem Musavi, Grand Ayatollah, was born in Khoi, Azerbaijan. He was one of the well-known Shi'ite *maraje* (sources of emulation). His book *Ajvad al-Taqrirat* (The best interpretations) is one of the more important texts in Shi'ite seminaries. His other book, *Al-Bayan* (Explanation), is a comprehensive text on Qur'an commentaries. He taught at the highest level of seminaries in Najaf, Iraq. He also instituted the Al-Khu'i Foundation with many branches around the world, including London and New York.

Kho'i was apparently the undisputed *marja* of Iraq and gained ground among the Shi'ite people of Iran, Lebanon, India, and other parts of the Muslim world. Kho'i was a traditionalist of the old school and disagreed with the notion of clerical rule, or the Islamic state under the rule of the jurist (*velayat-e faqih*), as put forward by the Ayatollah Khomeini.

Kho'i had good relations with the shah of Iran and received the Iranian queen shortly before the Islamic revolution of 1979. After the invasion of Kuwait by Iraq, Kho'i, having observed absolute silence during the Iraq-Iran war (1980–1988), published an anti-Saudi *fatwa* prohibiting the "recourse to the non-believers against Muslims "and inviting the latter "to resist to the enemies of God, who seek to attack Islam." This was reportedly issued under great pressure from Iraqi president Saddam Hussein.

## BIBLIOGRAPHY

Razi, Mohammad Sharif. "Ganjine ye Daneshmandan." In *Encyclopedia of Shi'ite Mullahs.* Vols. 2 and 4. Tehran: Eslamieh, 1974.

*Majid Mohammadi*

# KHOJAS

Derived from the Persian *khwajah*, a term of honor, the word *Khoja* referred to those converted to Nizari Isma'ili Islam in the Indian subcontinent from about the thirteenth century onward. More particularly, it included certain groups, predominantly from Gujarat and Cutch, who retained strong Indian ethnic roots and caste customs while sustaining their Muslim religious identity under continual threats of persecution. In the nineteenth century, the Isma'ili imamat (office of the imam) became established in India and a program of consolidation and reorganization of the community and its institutions began. These changes led to differences of opinion among Khojas. While the majority of the Khojas remained Isma'ili, one group became Ithna' 'Ashari and a smaller number adopted Sunnism.

In the context of the overall policy of the Isma'ili imam of the time, Aga Khan III, of consolidating the Shi'a Isma'ili identity of his followers, the ethnic connotation of being "Khoja" became diluted over time and a wider sense of self-identification as Isma'ili Muslims began to emerge. With the increasing recognition of the diversity of the worldwide Isma'ili community itself and the positive value of the pluralist heritage represented within each of the traditions, the Khojas now regard themselves as an integral part of the larger community, to whose development they make a strong contribution.

The Khoja Ithna' 'Asharis, while seeking to develop relations with the larger Twelver Shi'a community, retain their own organizational framework.

The Khojas live today in East Africa, the Indian subcontinent, Europe, and North America and show a strong commitment to values of Muslim philanthropy in their entrepreneurship and contribution to societies in which they live.

*See also* **Aga Khan; Nizari; South Asia, Islam in.**

*Azim Nanji*

# KHOMEINI, RUHOLLAH (1902–1989)

Spiritual and political leader of the Islamic Revolution in Iran, Ruhollah Khomeini became one of the most influential theologians of the twentieth century. A prolific writer and charismatic speaker, Khomeini inspired millions of Iranians to rise up against the Pahlavi regime and establish Iran as a truly Islamic republic.

Khomeini was born in 1902 in Khumayn, into a family of Shi'ite clerics. As a child and young man, he learned Arabic and studied Islamic law, and by 1923 he was a student in the holy city of Qum. Here Khomeini dedicated nearly forty years to the study of traditional *shari'a*, as well as mysticism, gnosticism, ethics, and philosophy.

By 1944, Khomeini had grown increasingly angry at the secularization of Iranian life under Reza Shah Pahlavi. He continued to teach at Qum, but also began his prolific career of political writings. Over the next two decades he collected disciples, whom he taught to relate their study of the *shari'a* to all aspects of public and private life.

In 1963, Khomeini stepped into the national spotlight by leading anti-Pahlavi protests in Qum. Horrified by the violence of the government's response, he became the leading religious figure opposing the regime. Exiled for his outspoken views, he ultimately went to Iraq (1965), settling in the holiest of Shi'ite cities, Najaf. Through his writings, however, Khomeini's views were widely disseminated throughout Iran, denouncing the shah and his allies in the United States.

In 1978, a variety of anti-Pahlavi forces—leftists, merchants, and ulema—rose up in open revolt, inspired by Khomeini's vision of a new future for Iran that eliminated the corruption of the shah's regime. Finally, in January 1979, the shah fled Iran and Khomeini returned from exile to lead the revolution. In March 1979 a referendum established the Islamic Republic of Iran, and Khomeini became its spiritual leader.

In opposing the shah, Khomeini had taken the title of *imam*, legitimizing his leadership by associating himself with Holy Imams of Iranian Shi'ism. Surrounding himself by a coterie of former students, he created a revolutionary government dedicated to restoring Islam to the center of Iranian life. He created new national institutions predicated on the teachings of Islam and administered by clerics, using the confiscated property of the previous rulers to pay for his reforms. Although he called for an elected governing body, all political offices were reserved for clerics. In an attempt to shake off Western influences, he supported the 1979 occupation of the United States embassy, holding its staff hostage, and thereby touching off a world crisis.

In 1980, Iraq invaded Iran with United States support. The war, which lasted eight years, became increasingly unpopular, and Khomeini ultimately agreed to sign a cease-fire. In its aftermath, Khomeini continued his attempt to create a truly theocratic state, suppressing dissenters, including those who practiced minority variants of Islam.

As ruling jurist of the new, theocratic Iran, Khomeini grew increasingly vehement in putting down dissent, ordering mass executions of prisoners who had run afoul of his revolutionary courts. Isolated from the West by his anti-American rhetoric and from the Soviet Union for his insistence on the centrality of religion in his government, he further incensed outside observers when, in February 1989, he issued a *fatwa* (a judgement carrying the sentence of death)

against author Salman Rushdie for having written a novel that contained passages offensive to his view of Islam. Khomeini died in June 1989, still hugely popular among the people who looked to him as Iran's spiritual leader. His funeral was attended by over one million mourners.

*See also* **Iran, Islamic Republic of; Muhammad Reza Shah Pahlevi; Revolution: Islamic Revolution in Iran.**

## BIBLIOGRAPHY

Algar, Hamid. "Imam Khomeini: The Pre-Revolutionary Years." In *Islam, Politics, and Social Movements.* Edited by E. Burke III and I. M. Lapidus. Berkeley: University of California Press, 1988.

Arjomand, Said A. *The Turban for the Crown: The Islamic Revolution in Iran.* New York: Oxford University Press, 1988.

Brunner, Rainer, and Ende, Werner, eds. *The Twelver Shia in Modern Times: Religious, Cultural, and Political History.* Leiden: Brill, 2000.

Khomeini, Ruhollah. *Islam and Revolution.* Translated by Hamid Algar. Berkeley, Calif.: Mizan Press, 1981.

*Nancy L. Stockdale*

## KHUTBA

The sermon, or *khutba*, serves as the primary formal occasion for public preaching the Islamic tradition. Sermons occur regularly, as prescribed by the teachings of almost all legal schools, at the noon (*zuhr*) congregation prayer on Friday, the weekly day of assembly, which it is incumbent upon all free and able adult male Muslim residents to attend. In addition, similar sermons are called for on the two festival days, or in response to an eclipse or excessive drought, although these sermons are expected to contain features relevant to the celebrations or the natural phenomena at hand. For instance, on *'id al-fitr* the preacher is charged to instruct the faithful concerning *zakat*, or almsgiving, while on *'id al-adha* he is to include remarks specifying rules for the sacrifice.

Sermons or related types of religious oratory may be pronounced in a variety of settings and at various times, but the term *khutba*, abbreviating the more ample expression *khutba al-jum'a*, usually refers only to the address delivered in the mosque at these weekly and annual rituals. Other occasions of preaching may be described as a lesson (*dars*) or an admonition (*wa'z*), and their formats would differ accordingly.

The *khutba* is believed to have its origins in the practice of the prophet Muhammad, who used to speak words of exhortation, instruction, or command at gatherings for worship in the mosque, which consisted of the courtyard of his house in Medina. However, the word *khutba* with this technical meaning does not appear in the Qur'an. But one passage that explicitly alludes to the Friday noon prayer summons believers to "the remembrance of God" (*dhikr Allah*) [Q. 62:9], an expression that some commentators have regarded as denoting the sermon.

Building on this precedent, the *khutba* has been closely associated with authoritative discourse in several important ways. Initially, for example, the delivery of the Friday sermon was restricted to the caliph himself, or his official representatives such as provincial governors. Eventually, however, the task was delegated to others, chosen for their learning and eloquence, who then spoke in the ruler's name. From this relationship, the practice emerged that the preacher (*khatib*) was obliged to include within the sermon an explicit mention of the sovereign, normally in the form of a blessing upon him. This aspect of the sermon resulted in a political function for *khutba* as it became, notably in periods of great tension and instability, the moment for signaling a change of regime, a shift in loyalty, or a call for rebellion.

In modern times, the naming of a ruler in a Friday sermon has largely fallen into disuse, expect perhaps on patriotic occasions, although the established bond between the pulpit and political legitimacy has not disappeared. This deeply rooted relationship helps to account for the shape of controversies in many Islamic lands, where governments may variously, through financial subsidies or censorship, seek control over preachers, while some who contest this assertion in the name of reform or resistance may resort to sermons as effective vehicles for opinion formation and mobilization.

Another important way that sermons have expressed their authority derives from the physical context framing their presentation. Traditionally, as defined by classical legal treatises, Friday congregational prayers were restricted to urban centers and normally to one major mosque in each city. Such a site designated as a *masjid jami'*, that is, a "Friday Mosque" or a "cathedral mosque," would typically be distinguished by its central location, extraordinary dimensions, and monumental architecture. This facility would also contain a number of symbolic furnishings indicative of its exalted stature, the most demonstrative of which was a ritual pulpit or *minbar*.

It was from this platform, possibly several meters high and frequently impressively built and adorned, that the sermon was proclaimed, and only the preacher would occupy it. Likewise, a number of fixed rubrics were to accompany the *khutba*. These specified such details as the preacher's dress, his posture, a sequence of standing and sitting, and the directive that he speak while leaning on a bow, a sword, or a staff. In the contemporary Islamic world, many of these archaic specifications may no longer be observed, while other culturally appropriate elements have been adopted. Most notably, both in largely Islamic lands and elsewhere, Friday congregational prayers with sermons are no longer restricted to a few central locations, but are common in mosques of all sizes and conditions, as well as being dispensed through newspapers and broadcast on radio and television. Moreover, a formidable market of sermons circulated on cassette recordings has emerged in recent decades, providing an especially appealing medium for dissident preachers who are denied access to official channels.

Finally, the *khutba* has drawn traditional authority from its conformity to a classically defined structure and rhetorical style. Recommendations regarding preaching arise, for instance, in certain hadith, such as the well-known dictum: "Make your prayers (*salat*) long and your sermon (*khutba*) short." But the recognized legal sources also specify set features and formulas for the validity of a *khutba*'s performance. First, a Friday sermon must consist of two parts, sometimes referred to as two sermons, between which a pause occurs. Second, within the sermon, a preacher is obliged to pronounce the praise of God, blessings upon the Prophet, and prayers on behalf of the congregation. Third, he is to exhort his listeners to virtue, such as warning of judgment, and to recite from the Qur'an.

Sermons were also to be delivered in classical Arabic, a linguistic requirement that not only assumed substantial training on the part of preachers if their sermons were to consist of original compositions, but a notable degree of education on the part of listeners, especially non-Arab Muslims, if the sermons were to be fully intelligible. Not surprisingly, this expectation of the *khutba* contributed to the growth of a literary genre consisting of model sermons, such as those by the renowned ibn Nubata (d. 984), which were committed to memory by some preachers and then recited with little adaptation. However, preaching in colloquial languages, while often retaining certain Arabic expressions, has become increasingly common. This, in turn, has led to disputes between traditionalists, who prefer classical Arabic, and revivalists, who insist that the sermon should be delivered in a language understood by the audience.

Like many elements of Islamic learning and piety in modern times, the sermon has been the object of concerted efforts at reform and revitalization. These efforts have led to a renewed scholarly interest in the history of the *khutba* and a widening enthusiasm regarding its use.

*See also* **Arabic Language; 'Ibadat; Minbar (Mimbar); Masjid; Religious Institutions.**

## BIBLIOGRAPHY

Antoun, Richard T. *Muslim Preacher in the Modern World: A Jordanian Case Study in Comparative Perspective.* Princeton, N.J.: Princeton University Press, 1089.

Berkey, Jonathan P. *Popular Preaching and Religious Authority in the Medieval Islamic Near East.* Seattle: University of Washington Press, 2001.

A mullah delivers a sermon, or *khutba,* in Termez, Uzbekistan. The majority of religious schools require a weekly *khutba* on Fridays, the Muslim day of assembly. All able male adults are expected to attend. AP/WIDE WORLD PHOTOS

Gaffney, Patrick D. *The Prophet's Pulpit: Islamic Preaching in Contemporary Egypt.* Berkeley: University of California Press, 1994.

Wensinck, A. J. "Khutba." In *Encyclopaedia of Islam.* 2d ed. Leiden: E. J. Brill, 1960.

*Patrick D. Gaffney*

# KHWARAZM *See* **Khiva, Khanate of**

# KINDI, AL- (801–866)

Abu Yusuf Ya'qub Ibn Ishaq al-Sabbah al-Kindi, also known as "the philosopher of the Arabs," was born around 801 and died in Baghdad around 866. He belonged to the courts of the caliphs al-Ma'mun and al-Mu'tasim, but lost influence at the end of his life during the caliphate of al-Mutawakkil. Al-Kindi flourished during the period of both the Arabic translation movement of Greek philosophical and scientific texts, of which he played a limited role as a translator, and the Mu'tazilite controversy, of which al-Kindi appeared to have affinities with Mu'tazilism.

A significant contribution of al-Kindi is his assimilation and appropriation of Greek science and philosophy, writing nearly two hundred and fifty treatises on philosophy and science, of which less than forty are extant. Examples of this assimilation are his adoption of such Aristotelian concepts as the act/potency, form/matter, substance/accident relations, and the four causes. One also finds hints of Neoplatonism in his discussion of the "one" and the "many" in his On First Philosophy and his subsequent positing of the One True Being. Still al-Kindi did not blindly follow the Greeks, especially when Greek philosophy contradicted the Qur'an. Thus, notably, he rejected the eternity of the world, a doctrine held by most Greek philosophers and most other Islamic *falasifa* (e.g., al-Farabi, Ibn Sina, and Ibn Rushd).

Al-Kindi's scientific achievements included work in mathematics, optics, medicine, and music. Again, although Greek scientists such as Hippocrates, Euclid, and Ptolemy influenced him, his work shows originality, especially in optics and medicine.

*See also* **Falsafa; Mu'tazilites, Mu'tazila.**

## BIBLIOGRAPHY

Ivry, Alfred. *Al-Kindi's Metaphysics: A Translation of Ya'qub Ibn Ishaq al-Kindi's Treatise "On First Philosophy"*. Albany: State University of New York Press, 1974.

Jolivet, Jean, and Rashed, Roshdi. "Al-Kindi". Vol. 15, suppl. 1, *Dictionary of Scientific Biography*. New York: Scribner's, 1978.

*Jon McGinnis*

# KNOWLEDGE

The concept of knowledge in Islam is generally designated by two Arabic terms that have overlapping meanings but different connotations, *'ilm* and *ma'rifa*. *'Ilm* designates knowledge, the "science or study of" a field such as the Qur'an, prophetic traditions (hadith), grammar, dialectical theology (*kalam*), and astronomy. It also denotes the knowledge of God in particular. *Ma'rifa* acquired two different meanings, secular knowledge on the one hand and gnosticism (secret knowledge) on the other. This latter sense was particularly characteristic of the language of *tasawwuf* (Sufism). The mystical Islamic vision of knowledge expresses the celebrated Arabic proverb that "He who knows [has the gnosis of] his soul also knows [has the gnosis of] his God."

Other terms give the concept of knowledge in Islam an even richer complexity of breadth and depth. For example, *shi'r* also translates as knowledge, but usually in the special sense of learning or knowing something intuitively. One of the primary meanings of *shi'r* is "poetry." *Fiqh* means to understand or comprehend something, to have knowledge of something, particularly legal knowledge. The chief antonym or opposite of *'ilm* is *jahl*, which connotes ignorance, but also includes the concepts of boorishness and cultural crudeness. Islam teaches that the time before the revelation of the Qur'an was a dark age of ignorance of knowledge of God. This era is called the *Jahiliyya*.

## The Traditional Sense of Knowledge

The key sense of knowledge, in both Persian and Arabic, then, is the one attributed to *'ilm*. This term is related to the Persian *danish*, the Latin *scientia*, and the Greek *episteme*. In ordinary English, this term refers to the concept of scientific knowledge. By adopting this sense of knowledge for the sciences, the subsequent Jewish, Christian, and Muslim epistemologies formulated natural science as having two major constituents: (external) sense experience and analytic conception. According to this epistemology, external senses provide the knowledge of the surface of bodies. Both sense data and analytical (mathematical and logical) axioms are constituents of an axiomatic system, which provided the genesis of contemporary notion of a "model." Such a system uses scientific laws to both explain and predict nature.

The nonobservational dimension of scientific knowledge employs concepts in a syntax depicting logical and mathematical axioms of the model used in scientific theory. Here, knowledge is achieved primarily by carrying out an analysis of concepts and making deductions of conclusions from premises according to valid rules of logic, thus preserving a correspondence of truth that continues, unbroken, from the premises to conclusion. Muslims contributed to the development of logic through the discussion of temporal modalities, including the modalities of necessity, impossibility, and contingency. Within these discussions, these modalities, along with temporal indexes, were relevant in evaluating the truth value of statements.

A small number of Muslims, such as Abu Hamid Ghazali (d. 1111), as well as a minority of European thinkers, such as René Descartes, followed the views of ancient Greek skeptics, who held that neither perception nor analysis provides certainty. In spite of such occasional skepticism, philosophers subsequent to Aristotle, including Muslims as well as Jews and Christians, followed Aristotle's classification of scientific knowledge into three kinds: theoretical (in which the subject-matter of knowledge is not related to the inquirer), practical (where the inquirer is involved in the inquiry), and productive (which aims to produce useful entities).

Whereas, in Aristotelian philosophy, there are three categories of scientific knowledge, there are five kinds of theoretical inquiries, or sciences. First, are the dialectical religious sciences, such as *kalam* (speculative theology) and *fiqh* (disciplined interpretation of the sources of the sacred law). Next is philosophy, understood as a study of being and a study of causes. Here subjects of inquiry are unrelated to physical bodies (things) in definition or examples. The next type of speculative inquiry is analysis, to which belong the disciplines of mathematics, logic, and music. Here the subjects of inquiry are not related by definition, but are conceptually related to physical bodies. Finally there are the natural sciences, such as physics proper, physics of motion, astronomy, meteorology, zoology, botany, and psychology. Here, both definitions and examples are related to bodies. Finally, there are the practical sciences, which include public management (with religious laws and politics as subdisciplines), and household management. Subdisciplines of the latter include the science of the household, civics, which concerns one's duty as a citizen, the science of the self, which includes the various senses, and the science of the soul.

Among all of the aforementioned sciences, the subdiscipline of practical science known as the science of the soul is most relevant to epistemology. Like those of its Western counterparts, Islamic epistemologies follow Aristotle's tripartite doctrine of the classification of the souls into vegetative, animal, and rational types. Two kinds of intelligence, the passive and the active, mark the rational soul. The passive intellect

This painting from a thirteenth-century Seljuk Turkish manuscript in Arabic called "The best Maxims and Most Precious Dictums of Al-Mubashir" depicts a philosophical debate between master and students. THE ART ARCHIVE/TOPKAPI MUSEUM ISTANBUL/DAGLI ORTI

abstracts conceptual features from the sensible, such as the symmetry between two figures; whereas the active reason receives by intuition the first principles of science. Muslim philosophers and theologians, like other medieval monotheistic theologies, added a religious, spiritual dimension to the active intelligence.

*Al-ʿaql* (reason, intellect) has many functions in Islamic thought. In theology and law it is usually contrasted with tradition (*naql* or *samʿ*). While a majority of epistemologies of physical sciences follow the Aristotelian model, in the mystical as well as the post–Ibn Sina (Avicenna, b. 980, d. 1037) traditions, Muslims go beyond the peripatetic (that is to say, Aristotelian) model. For example, the Muslim instrumental theory of knowledge emphasizes the intentional, pragmatic, practical, and normative senses of knowledge. Moreover, it also encompasses an account of knowledge as wisdom, which includes but goes beyond discursive science by seeking norms, and thus partakes of the search for the secret of the good life. For the religious devotee, the best life is lived in imitation of the lives of the prophets, like Moses, Jesus, and Muhammad,

and expressed by service to humanity in imitation of Imam Husayn and ʿIsa (Jesus).

### Three Senses of "Imagination" and a Creative Vision of Knowledge

Traditional epistemology divides the senses into the five external senses (sight, touch, taste, smell, and hearing), and a set of "internal senses," such as memory. Muslims extend the Greek theories of internal sense, which included common sense and the notion of memory as "sense imagery," into refined accounts of "intentional" memory and three special senses of imagination. In this usage, a psychological notion is "intentional" if it fails the so-called rule of extensionality. This rule can be exemplified in the following way. Suppose "John thinks he loves Mary" and "Mary is a spy"; it does not follow that "John thinks that he loves a spy." A number of philosophers hold that intentional notions cannot be explained by a materialistic, reductionist psychology. Because Muslim philosophical psychology followed an experiential or a phenomenological method, it did not use materialistic causes to explain a number of psychological notions.

In this light, new Muslim theories of imagination extended beyond the passive, reproductive type to embrace creative and productive types of images experienced, in both waking and dream states, variously characterizing it as: (a) imagination providing cognitively significant icons, (b) imagination providing sacred and mystical insights, and finally (c) an intentional sense of imagination with pragmatic and prehensive significances (when the meaning of an event is different for every person, i.e., love).

The first sense of iconic imagination points to the creative role assigned to visions and dreams, and follows an earlier tradition, exemplified in the Hebrew Bible. It is the sense of Joseph's celebrated interpretation of the pharaoh's dream, where a specific dream has a social significance. The cognitive import of this interpretation points to an iconic imagery through a natural revelation. This medium (the dream) contains insights about future events, mediated by an agent, the pharaoh in this case, who is not a prophet; instead, he or she is a spokesperson who can be understood in the role of the religious archetype of the messenger. Consequently, in addition to its psychological and therapeutic significance, the iconography of mystical and religious symbolism and rituals contains cognitive information about the actual world.

The most celebrated of these kinds of symbolism is the light motif, employed by Plato, Aristotle, and Plotinus, all three of whom use light to symbolize self-realization and mystical progress. Plotinus takes this symbolism the furthest, using an allegorical or symbolic type of theology to express the emanation of the word from the One (which is suprabeing) in the language of illumination (he also uses the analogies of a fountain of water and the reflection in the mirror). In a similar vein, the Qur'an depicts God as the Light of the Heavens and the earth. Following from this, the illumination philosophy of Suhrawardi depicts the ultimate being (God) as the Light of Lights, with the rest of the world being its emanation. Other symbolism includes drowning in the water (recalling the fish as a symbol of Christ in Christian iconography), and the flight of the birds toward the heavens. In Islamic carpets, four-footed animals depict the body, the tree symbolizes the various phases of life-experience, and a bird depicts the soul. Other ways of symbolically depicting the mystical way of self-realization include parables that tell of awakening (attaining puberty) and stories of birds caught by hunters.

These examples illustrate various different dimensions of the Islamic notion of knowledge. To begin with, the primary sense of knowledge used in science is to explain experience and to predict the future, in order to produce a technology that will control nature for useful projects. In contrast, the aim of the present iconographically related experience transforms a person through dealienation—through the recognition that an individual participates in a larger social or spiritual context. Consider the case of a young person who

has fallen in love. This person begins to comprehend her or his transformation from a self-involved individual to an entity who is part of a union with a partner in the context of love, marriage, and family. To the members of such a couple, their child is a living testimony to their intended union through marriage.

In Islam, revelation and sacred insights are provided to a privileged few, such as the prophets, imams, mystics, and Ayatollah-jurists. These images imparted are not of particular objects, which are available through the senses, but of societal and meta-legal dictums, from the Qur'an and other sources, delineating religious social law (shariʿa) and formal jurisprudence. It is the third sense of imagination, as an intentional sense of imagination with pragmatic and prehensive significances, that signals a radical departure of Islamic epistemology from the confines of mainstream, realistic, discursive epistemology. A paradigmatic case of this type of epistemology is the notion of prehensive imagination (wahm), as illustrated by the example of a sheep running away from a wolf, providing a symbolic representation of apprehension (realization) of fear.

Muslim philosophers took the Aristotelian notion of active reason, extended it, and incorporated it into their mystical framework. They began with the assumption that the distinguishing faculties of the human soul are passive and active faculties of reason. Passive reason expresses the soul's ability to abstract non-sensible relations from experience, for example, in observing the topological symmetry between two figures. In such an operation, the mind does not create a new datum in the actual world, but has the ability to abstract relations of particulars observed by the senses. A majority of the Muslim philosophers who followed Aristotle did not share the Platonic view that interpreted mathematical and other forms as suprasensible realities independent of human minds. A few philosophers, such as Shihab ad-Din Suhrawardi (d. 1234) and Mir Damad (d. 1631) adopted the realist ontology in taking mathematics to be re-cognition of actual entities and not intellectual abstraction from particulars. Most Muslim philosophers postulated that, unlike passive intellect, active intelligence demonstrates an ability to intuit the first principles of science, such as the premises of Euclidean geometry. They held that, as these axioms are derived by deduction, we can derive knowledge of arithmetic, various types of geometries, and other analytical sciences, which provide the frameworks that are used in the empirical sciences.

### Theological Knowledge as an Activity

The celebrated theologian Abu Hamid Ghazali (1058–1111) proffered that philosophy should begin with an inquiry into how creatures should imitate the Divine will in the act of creation. This "vector" of will to life-reality is analogous to the theoretical axiom of the ancient Persian Zoroastrian religion, according to which believers, by positive living—for

This painting depicts Ibn al-Muqaffa' trapping birds in a net, from the fourteenth-century Persian manuscript of the Tale of Kalila and Dimna. The term *'ilm* is the primary type of knowledge in Persian and Arabic; its English translation refers to the concept of scientific knowledge, but in the Islamic tradition it also indicates knowledge of Allah. THE ART ARCHIVE/NATIONAL LIBRARY CAIRO/DAGLI ORTI

example, being engaged in farming, begetting children, developing cities, and creating social order—adopt a perspective that denies the evil force (*Ahriman*). Evil here is understood as the denial of life and the privation of all existence.

In this tenor, Ghazali outlined a list of mystical virtues, which are both epistemic and ethical. They include archetypal recall (memory), exuberance, intimacy, and a taste for life. Such a doctrine moves ontology from an investigation of substances to the pursuit of the good will. Ghazali posits that facts and values are interrelated. His thought also upholds an instrumental theory of knowledge, rejecting the so-called spectator theory, which places the mind of the agent outside of the object of knowledge. In contrast, Ghazali's instrumental theory of knowledge mixes ethics with a practical sense of knowledge.

Up to the last thirty years of the twentieth century, most investigators approached Islamic philosophy from the standpoint of Aristotlian thought. This approach imposed a limited rendering of Islamic epistemology in the peripatetic, static context of the discursive knowledge of external senses and axiomatic system. However, to take account of some of the refinements of Muslim epistemologies, it is necessary to use the frameworks of post-peripatetic Western philosophers. Recent Muslim investigators such as Nader El-Bizri use the conceptual frameworks of philosophers such as Gottfried von Leibniz (1646–1716), who held the nexus of metaphysics is monads as energy; Martin Heidegger (1889–1976), who began his metaphysics by the temporal concept of "being-in-the world"; Alfred North Whitehead (1861–1947), who proffered a process instead of a substance-event metaphysics); and Rudolf Carnap (1891–1970), who clarified the notion of "scientific model."

## Mystical Knowledge as an Authentic Hermeneutic Dealienation

It is revealing that Ibn Sina, who was one of the most significant Muslim philosophers, wrote an Arabic version of Plato's *Symposium*, wherein he shared with the Greek philosopher the vision that love is the salvation of the human soul. For Plato, the highest knowledge is a confrontation with the Absolute Good, a stance that is analogous to the notion of *Shahada* (being an authentic witness to God's gifts—unique existence, guidance, and creation) as presented in Islamic mystical theology. In addition, Ibn Sina's version shares with

Plotinus's vision a view of the mystical journey as a return to the origin and the ground of all existence.

For Ibn Sina, three main phases of this journey are alienation, love, and union. In the first phase, a person individuates his or her personality by building a castle, a wall of privacy, that protects and distinguishes the person from others. Soon, this castle or wall of protection imprisons the person and alienates him or her from the rest of humanity and nature. In the next phase, by falling in love, a person transcends his or her egocentric perspective to form a relation of intimacy, leading to the opening up of an authentic encounter with others. This is a phase that is often depicted through the archetypal role of the beloved, who acts as a mediator figure, a *logos*, or through the role of a prophet, who links the alienated self to its source. Finally the last phase is a mystical union between the person, symbolized as a river that flows toward Divine-nature, which is the origin, *arche*, as well as the completion of the person. This union is often depicted as a drop of water joining a river that returns it to an ocean.

The process of self-enlightenment in Sufism points to two distinct but interrelated dimensions of knowledge that can be illustrated in the common pedagogy used to teach a foreign language. The teacher instructs the pupil to perform externally imposed tasks, such as memorizing a set of words, using verb-conjugation flashcards, practicing writing exercises, and repeating sentences in conversation courses. The pupil obtains a certain level of knowledge in vocabulary and rules of grammar. Having reached this stage, the pupil can now recognize the content of a conversation and a written French communication. In a similar sense, the more persons in love share experiences, like cooking and traveling together, visiting each others' parents, and working on common tasks, the more they "prehend" each other's personality and are able to make crucial decisions such as marriage.

This notion of "prehension," as used in the philosophy of Alfed North Whitehead, signifies an epistemic, non-conscious state of immediate-intimacy and intuition, is also expressed by the Arabic-Persian term, *hal*, which refers to the role of the mystical master in directing his disciple. For example, a person believing himself to be pious is directed to walk into a bazaar carrying bloody pig meat on his shoulder, which makes people lose their respect for him. After such an experience, he loses his pride and is able to reflect authentically on the ground of his soul. Such tasks lead to self-knowledge as well as to self-strength, as the disciple learns that his happiness should not depend on gaining the approval of the common people. In the Sufic tradition, knowledge is thus associated with goodness, as in becoming a better person, and in learning to live in harmony with nature. It is a process of dealienation, enabling people to cope with responsibilities outside of parental protection as well as with problems, such as aging, and fates like death. In addition, knowledge is explainable in both theoretical terms and through practical experiences, as well as by its psychosomatic features, such as habits and unconscious behaviors.

## Philosophical Knowledge as an Immediate Encounter with "Being"

Ibn Sina and a number of his successors challenged the peripatetic model of knowledge by adopting the phenomenological method, in which ontology is not separated from epistemology. Here, philosophy begins with the world as it is revealed in experience. Accordingly, Ibn Sina, Nasir al-Din Tusi (d. 1274), Mulla Sadra (b.1571–1640), and others replaced the substance-event language of ontology with an intentional phenomenology of the mind's direct encounter with "being" (*wujud, hasti*). Subsequent, ontology proceeds by an application of "being" to three modalities (impossibility, contingency, and necessity), which then results in impossible entities (such as a round square), necessary entities (namely the Necessary Existent), and contingent entities (such as an entity of humanity, a unicorn, or a chair).

In the next phase, the mind encounters the subject of being-in the world—experience. This entity is not a Cartesian substance, but rather a field of experience. It is similar to the phenomenal self, or the notion of "a transcendental unity of apperception," as it is termed in the philosophy of Immanuel Kant (1724–1804). It is also analogous to Martin Heidegger's (1889–1976) notion of "*dasein*." Unlike Aristotle and, later, René Descartes, (1596–1650), Kant, David Hume (1711–1176), and Heidegger, as well as a number of other Western thinkers, reject the view that a human soul is a substance.

The third phase is an inquiry for the inner-essence (*dhat*) of the self. This notion differs from another sense of (common) essence (*mahiyya*) shared by other members of the same species. For example, it is common to say that an essence of a child's mother, like the essence of any human, is her possession of a rational soul; but for the child, there is another, existential sense of "essence" (expressed by the Arabic-Persian '*dhat*'), which concerns the peculiar dependence of a specific child to a particular mother. In Persian mystical poetry, God, or one's mother, is depicted as "the existence of my existence," or "the cause of the actualization of my life." The mystics seek a connection with this sense of essence. The nature mystics add a last phase to this process, namely a search for a dealienation or the unity of existence (*wahadt al-wujud*). Here we come back to the celebrated Arabic proverb, that "he who knows [gnosis] his self-soul, also knows [gnosis] his God."

In the primary sense of knowledge as "scientific inquiry," Muslims philosophers followed the Greek tradition as outlined by Aristotle. In addition to a few innovations in logic, such as temporal and modal types of logic, the Muslim contribution to epistemology is found in secondary senses of knowledge. These include a phenomenological intentionality, the development of the pragmatics of an instrumental theory of knowledge, creative theories of imagination, and iconography. The crown of Islamic epistemology, however, lies in a unique application of the notion of unity (*tawhid*), which integrates persons with God, or the ultimate being of philosophers. Similarly, Judaism and Christianity seek an authentic encounter with the Divine, but Islamic mysticism seeks an identity beyond any duality. It follows the theme that the soul seeks no "otherness" from the One.

*See also* **Ghazali, al-; Ibn Sina; Mulla Sadra; Tasawwuf; Theology; Tusi, Nasir al-Din.**

## BIBLIOGRAPHY

Corbin, Henry. *Creative Imagination in the Sufism of Ibn 'Arabi.* Translated by R. Manheim. London: Routledge and Kegan Paul, 1970.

Ha'iri, Mehdi. *The Principle of Epistemology in Islamic Philosophy: Knowledge by Presence.* Albany: State University of New York Press, 1992.

Morewedge, Parviz. *The Mystical Philosophy of Avicenna.* Annandale-on-Hudson, N.Y.: Institute of Advanced Theology of Bard College, 2002.

Rahman, Fazlur. *Prophecy in Islam: Philosophy and Orthodoxy.* Chicago: University of Chicago Press, 1979.

Rosenthal, Franz. *Knowledge Triumphant: The Concept of Knowledge in Medieval Islam.* Leiden: Brill, 1970.

*Parviz Morewedge*

## KOMITEH

The Komiteh-ha-ye Enghelab, or Revolutionary Committees, were created immediately after the victory of the Islamic Revolution in Iran in February 1979. The Komiteh substituted for some of the governmental institutions that no longer functioned after the shah was deposed, such as social services, security, and police. The Komiteh were more widespread and active in cities than rural areas and were located in captured police centers, in the houses of former government officials, and in some public places such as the parliament. Before the establishment of the Revolutionary Guard Corps (Sepah-e Pasdaran-e Enghelab) in 1979, these committees were responsible for eliminating counterrevolutionary elements within Iran. During the Iran-Iraq War, the revolutionary committees served on the front alongside Iran's Army, Besiege and Revolutionary Guard Corps. In cities, they fought against the narcotics trade and worked as agents of the judiciary and security systems. The members of these committees were mostly uneducated, undisciplined revolutionaries.

After the death of Ayatollah Khomeini and during the first period of 'Ali-Akbar Hashemi-Rafsanjani's presidency, Iran's police, gendarmerie, and revolutionary committees were merged, and a new organization, called the Disciplinary Force (Niru-ye entezami), was established. With this change, members of the the revolutionary committees received formal ranks in the police staff, based on their experience.

*See also* **Revolution: Islamic Revolution in Iran.**

*Majid Mohammadi*

## KUNTI, MUKHTAR AL- (1729–1811)

Al-Shaykh Sidi-Mukhtar al-Kabir al-Kunti was born in 1729 near Arawan north of Timbuktu. He was a descendant of a highly ramified Arabic-speaking tribe, the Kunta, that has become widely dispersed over the Southern Sahara, from Mauritania to the Adrar-n-Ifoghas in Eastern Mali and beyond. The Kunta tribe claims descent from noble origins, specifically from the celebrated Qurashite Muslim commander 'Uqba b. Nafi' al-Fihri, who was the stepbrother of 'Amr b. al-'As al-Sahmi, the first governor of Muslim Egypt.

According to the so-called *ta'rikh*, Kunta Sidi 'Ali, a descendant of 'Uqba b. Nafi', married the daughter of Muhammad b. Kunta b. Zazam, who was chief of the Ibdukal (also called Abdukal), a subgroup of the Lamtuna Berbers, allegedly in the early fifteenth century. Their son, Muhammad, married into another Lamtuna group, as did also his son, Ahmad al-Bakka'i. Ahmad al-Bakka'i then had three sons of his own, from whom all the later branches of the Kunta were derived.

After the death of Sidi Ahmad-al Bakka'i in the second half of the sixteenth century, a quarrel broke out between two of his sons, which is said to have caused the Kunta to split into two groups. The Western Kunta lived in and around the Hawd, today the southern part of Mauritania, and the Eastern Kunta lived in and around Azwad, the area of the Sahara immediately southwest of Tadmakkat.

While a young man, Sidi al-Mukhtar gained a wide reputation as greatly gifted, intellectually, and as an outstanding Muslim scholar. When only twenty-five years old he was given the title of Shaykh al-tariqa al-Qadiriyya, making him a spiritual leader within the Qadiri order of Sufis. In this position he attracted many students, who came to study in the *zawiya* he established at al-Hilla in Azwad. His camp at al-Hilla rapidly became not only the center of studying the Qadiriyya teachings, but also the center from which a new Qadiri suborder was spread throughout the Sahara regions. This new suborder bore the name of Sidi al-Mukhtar, and its followers came to be known as al-Mukhtariyya.

Al-Kunti achieved a high degree of social and political influence among the active political players in the Sahara arena. He succeeded in healing the rift between the eastern and western branches of the Kunta, and he did much to help conclude a peaceful settlement between the Tuareg chiefs and Arab warrior groups in the area. He also mediated between the leadership of the city of Timbuktu and the Tuaregs, who were known to harass that city on several occasions, most notably in 1770–1771, when a siege of the town was lifted only after his intervention.

Al-Kunti furthered the use of peaceful means in spreading the Islamic faith among infidel groups in the Sahara. He also adopted tender and graceful methods for preaching and for the propagation of the Qadiriyya order, but although he restricted himself to this moderate approach, he nonetheless expressed his approval of the militant jihad employed by 'Uthman dan Fodio in the first decade of the nineteenth century. Shaykh Sidi al-Mukhtar proclaimed himself a regenerator (*mujaddid*); in fact, he claimed to be the sole regenerator of the thirteenth century of the *hijra*.

Shaykh Sidi al-Mukhtar the Great died in 1811. His son, Sidi Muhammad (1765–1826), inherited his position as the Shaykh and leader of the Mukhtarriyya-Qadiriyya suborder. The *wird*, a phrase-patterned devotion used by the Mukhtarriyya order, became widely propagated in south Mauritania and in Hausaland in northern Nigeria, by the successive shaykhs of the Kunta tribe.

*See also* **Africa, Islam in; Tariqa; Tassawuf; Timbuktu.**

## BIBLIOGRAPHY

Batran, A. A. "The Kunta, Sidi al-Mukhtar al-Kunti and the Office of Shaykh al-Tariqa al-Qadiriyya." In Vol. 1, *Studies in West African Islamic History*, Edited by J. R. Willis. London: F. Cass, 1979.

Clarke, Peter B. *West Africa and Islam*. London: E. Arnold, 1984.

Hisklett, Marvin. *The Devolopment of Islam in West Africa*. London and New York: Longman, 1984.

Levtzion, Nehemiah. *Muslims and Chiefs in West Africa*. Oxford, U.K.: Clarendon, 1968.

Trimingham, J. Spencer. *A History of Islam in West Africa*. Oxford: Oxford University Press, 1970.

*Khalil Athamina*

# L

**LANGUAGE** *See* **Arabic Language; Persian Language and Literature; Urdu Language, Literature, and Poetry**

## LAW

The emergence of Islamic law originates in a definition of human deeds as understood from a specifically Islamic viewpoint. This could only be developed over time, as notions of good and bad evolved according to the interpretation of the Qur'anic verses, Prophetic sayings, and the Islamic legacy as a whole. The evaluation of the goodness or badness of deeds according to the Islamic point of view was called *fiqh* (understanding), and the person holding the qualities of knowledge and competence to produce opinions in this respect was called *faqih* (the knowledgeable who understands well). The consideration of human actions within an Islamic religious context was encouraged by sayings of the Prophet, such as "He whom God favors with good, God makes him the one who understands in religion (*faqih*)," (Bukhari, *Sahih*, I, 25) and "there may be some narrators who may narrate the words to some of the receivers who may be able to understand better (*afqah*) than the narrators themselves" (Tirmidhi, *Sunan*, V, 34). In the Prophetic era and years immediately following, *fiqh* was not specifically about practical human deeds, but covered a general range of issues that were of religious concern, such as general religious knowledge and the understanding of the sacred texts. However, the day-to-day practice of Islam at this early stage of development was still being worked out, and *fiqh* came to be employed for the creation of legal definitions and interpretations of proper behavior. Over time, the role of *fiqh* was gradually narrowed to the consideration of legally relevant matters, dealing with both personal and public concerns.

---

**Central concepts in law**

| | |
|---|---|
| *fiqh* | understanding, law |
| *usul al-fiqh* | sources of law: Qur'an, *hadith* (sayings of the Prophet); *ijma* (consensus of schools and community); *qiyas* (reasoning by analogy) |
| *'ilm* | knowledge, especially of law, the learning of the *'alim* (pl. *ulema*) |
| *taqlid* | imitation; following the established teachings |
| *ijtihad* | independent judgment of qualified legal scholar (*mujtahid*) |
| *shari'a* | the way, the total corpus of Muslim law and belief |
| *fatwa* | advisory opinion on a matter of law given by a *mufti* (jurisconsult) |
| *qada* | court judgment made by a *qadi* (judge) on the basis of *shari'a* |

SOURCE: Lapidus, Ira M. *A History of Islamic Societies*. New York: Cambridge University Press, 1988.

Key concepts of Islamic law.

In the second century of Islam, a theoretical foundation for juridical thought evolved, leading to a properly constituted legal system. At this point, *fiqh* came to concern itself with codifying this theoretical understanding, while still dealing with issues relating to the proper conduct of worship (*'ibadat*). To complement the now more narrow scope of *fiqh*, a broader legal context, embodied in the concept of religious law (*shari'a*), extended the formal Islamic legal order to all aspects of societal life.

Beginning with the initial concept of *fiqh*, Islamic law organizes the understanding and, thus, definition, of human deeds along a continuum. At one end are those behaviors deserving of the utmost prohibition, and at the other end are those deeds subject to the utmost imperative injunction. At the very center point of the continuum are found the behaviors deemed to be neutral, neither prohibited nor enjoined. Thus, the prohibited and the enjoined share the same quality of being mandatory, whereas acts falling between these two extremes become a matter of scholarly opinion and are therefore less binding.

In evaluating the potentially infinite range of human deeds, criteria of judgment (*dalils*) were needed. There are two sources of these: the Qur'an and the prophetic sunna. The Muslim community was explicitly referred to these by the Prophet himself, who said, "I have left for you two principles; should you stick to them you will never err" (Malik, *Muwatta*, II, 899). These two principles were by no means the sole criteria offered by the Prophet. They were supplemented by the practice of *shura*, for example, which held that authorities should seek the counsel of the wise when running the affairs of the community. In addition, judges were enjoined to employ reasoning in order to make proper decisions. Moreover, legal decision-making had to be carried out within the larger context of Islamic tradition. Finally, the evolution of Islamic law was influenced by politics, war, and other societal events, which variously endorsed, transformed, or replaced traditional practices. All these factors provided the framework within which the development of Islamic society and law occurred during the time of the Prophet and, later, the prominent Companions (the immediate successors of the Prophet).

This early, emerging structure of Islamic society prevailed in the first century of Hijra, which covers the age of the Prophet and largely that of the Companions. The significance of this era was twofold. On the one hand, the Companions were concerned with the preservation of the Qur'anic texts, and were therefore conservative in their application of the Prophet's sayings when substantial legal matters were at stake. On the other hand, the Companions' era was a time in which trends of legal thought and methodology were initiated for the forthcoming generation of Islam's leading thinkers. In the first century of Islam, Medina was the main center for the development of Islamic knowledge and practice, but these were complemented by the work of other competent figures who were appointed to fulfill juridical and administrative duties elsewhere. Among these were Ibn Mas'ud, who served in Iraq, and Mu'az Ibn Jabal and Abu Musa al-Ash'ari, both of whom served in Yemen. In the late decades of the first century, in addition to the ruling political authorities, there were others living throughout the expanding Muslim world who made substantial contributions to juristic thought. Among there were Sa'id Ibn al-Musayyab (d. 713), 'Urwa Ibn al-Zubayr (d. 716), 'Ubeydullah Ibn 'Utbah (d. 717), and Abu Bakr Ibn 'Abd al-Rahman (d. 713) in Medina; and 'Alqamah Ibn Qays (d. 682), Shurayh Ibn al-Harith (d. 679), Masruq Ibn al-Ajda (d. 683), and Ibrahim al-Nakha'i (d. 714) in Kufa.

By the turn of the first century of Islam, the political authorities had already pursued two main policies relating to the use of the textual sources of Islamic law. First, the standardization of Qur'an began under the reign of Abu Bakr and was later finalized under the reign of 'Uthman. Second, the Umayyad caliph, 'Umar Ibn 'Abd al-Aziz, encouraged the collection of the sayings of the Prophet. In the early decades of the second century, scholarship regarding Islamic law was expanded, giving rise to two schools of juridical thought, one centered in Medina, the other in Kufa. The scholars of Medina included Rabi'at al-Ra'y (d. 753) and al-Zuhri (d. 742), who were early proponents of the pro-hadith school (hadith refers to sayings of the Prophet). Leading scholars in Kufa included al-Nakha'i and his disciple Hammad Ibn Abu Sulayman (d. 738), followed by Abu Hanifa Nu'man Ibn al-Thabit (d. 757), who favored the reasoning approach. These legal trends are also known, respectively, as *ahl al-hadith* (the people of the hadith line) and *ahl al-ra'y* (the people of the pro-reasoning line). They were also called the schools of Hijaz and of Iraq, respectively, making reference to their geographical domains.

The line of distinction between these two early trends in legal thought was found in their perceptions of the hadith. For the school of Hijaz, hadith was the actual legacy of the Prophet, and was the ultimate source of both legitimacy and solutions to social problems. This approach was well suited for Medina, which provided a strong Islamic culture of practice starting from the exemplary Prophetic era. By contrast, Iraq was relatively new to Islam. In addition, Iraq was something of a gate for the eastward advancement of Islam, and thus was host to many travellers passing through, each with a competing understanding of the life of the Prophet. This gave rise to multiple hadith, leading to doubt about the accuracy of the narrations. To overcome such doubts, reasoning was applied. Thus, Abu Hanifa of Iraq understood hadith through applying his concept of *dhabt* (precise preservation). *Dhabt* was, in his view, the precise understanding of the juristic content of the hadith and its precise transmission. The narrator himself therefore needed to be *faqih* in order to understand the precise content of what he narrated. Here, the significance of reasoning prevails over the literal transmission of the texts.

Although Medina stood as the center of political power in Islam during the era of the Prophet and in the thirty years that followed, it was later transferred to Syria. There it remained for the entire duration of the Umayyad reign, and it was in Syria where the prominent and influential jurist 'Abd al-Rahman al-Awza'i (d. 764) built his legal career in association with the Hijazi trend of law. Al-Awza'i is famous for his work, called *al-Siyar*, but this text has been lost to later generations. Nonetheless, it is known that this lost work marked the beginning of a literature that developed later and that dealt with issues of war and peace. It also influenced the work of Abu Yusuf, one of the prime disciples of Abu Hanifa of Iraq. Abu Yusuf wrote *al-Radd 'ala siyar al-Awza'i* (The response to the Siyar of al-Awza'i), and from it one can glean not only Abu Yusuf's counterviews but also al-Awza'i's original theses.

Abu Yusuf's treatise provides insights into interregional activities and the flourishing state of legal thought. Medina, the birthplace of the Islamic society, had a special advantage for traditional Islam and remained a main center of gravity for

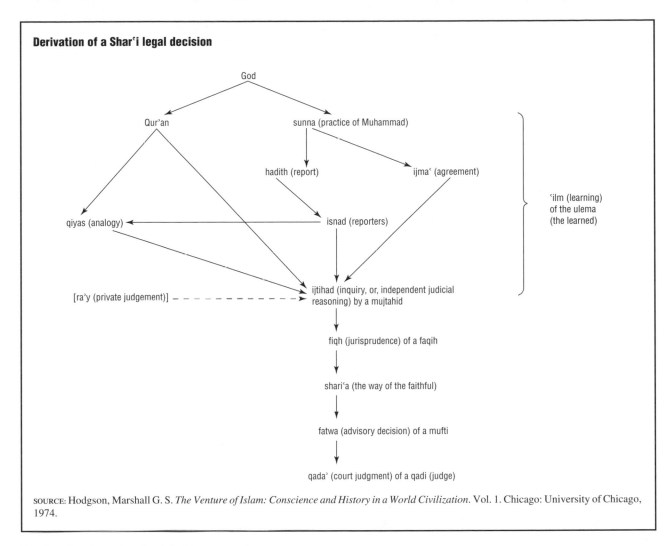

**Derivation of a Shar'i legal decision**

SOURCE: Hodgson, Marshall G. S. *The Venture of Islam: Conscience and History in a World Civilization.* Vol. 1. Chicago: University of Chicago, 1974.

Visual explanation of how legal decisions are made.

the Islamic legal scholarship. Medina's dominance in this field is expressed in the concept of *'amal ahl al-Medina* (the practice of the Medinese people), which served as an example of proper practice throughout the Islamic world. Jurists were thus enjoined to follow the Medina example when seeking a better understanding of Islamic laws. The vital role attributed to Medina attracted the scholarly attention of several important jurists, such as Shaybani (d. 804), and Shafi'i (d. 819), who eventually argued against it. Shaybani, who was a key jurist of the Iraqi school, studied the hadiths called *al-Muwatta'*, Malik's collection of mainly legal content. In his own work, Shaybani often mentioned the disagreements of the Iraqi jurists with the views presented by Malik. Furthermore, Shaybani compiled an independent work called *al-Hujjah 'ala ahl al-Medina* (The argument against the people of Medina).

Shafi'i, too, had studied the Medinese and the Iraqi notions of law. He took a position against both, arguing for the elimination of regional concepts and promoting instead

an overarching, ecumenical system of legal thought. In Shafi'i's point of view, the Iraqi concepts were inaccurate or inconsistent, while the Medina-based Hijazi school was too regionally specific. The diversities in legal thought that arose through these interregional argumentative dialogues gradually paved the way for the evolution of a supra-regional system of legal thought, an evolution inspired by Shafi'i's leadership.

In the first half of the second century, the Iraqi-led legal trend was mostly identified with Abu Hanifa and, thus, with a more free use of reason. He recognized three sources of Islamic law: the Qur'an undisputedly came first, followed by the hadith of the Prophet and then the *ijma'*, which is the consensus of the Companions. Abu Hanifa had a relatively cautious and restrictive attitude toward accepting hadiths, giving greater weight to the juristic contents of the sayings than to the literal understanding of the words themselves. He treated the diverse opinions of the Companions as various options that needed to be evaluated before choosing one from among them. He held that the methodological key to this

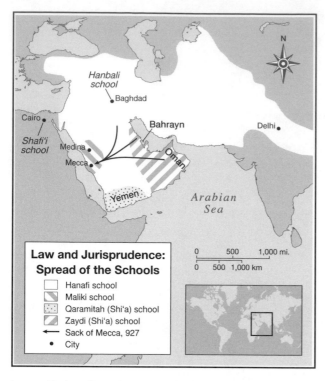

Law and jurisprudence 816–963. XNR Productions, Inc./Gale

Early schools of law.

evaluation was a methodology called *qiyas* (analogical reasoning), which required that a jurist look to previous cases for precedents when determining the outcome of a current case. Through this method of *qiyas*, the jurist could establish connections between the present and the past and thus produce systematic juristic opinions, but it sometimes failed, when similar cases could not be found, or their similarities were only superficial. At such times, Abu Hanifa would abandon *qiyas* and instead employ free reasoning, or *istihsan*. He described his approach to legal thought in the following terms.:

> What comes from the Companions [in disagreement] we do not abandon altogether. . . [we chose from among their varying opinions]; and what comes from the Successors we ignore them. (Ibn al-Qayyim, *I'Lam*, IV, 123)

This statement shows Abu Hanifa's lack of interest in the narrated opinions of the Successors of the Companions. It also demonstrates his confidence in the reasoning abilities of jurists of his own generation. This confidence in the reliability of free reasoning allowed Iraqi jurists to override textual or systematic limitations. Iraqi jurists also opposed the Umayyad political power based in Syria, which meant that they were not employed by the government and thus did not have to compromise their methodology to suit the practical limitations that such political affiliation might impose. However, this freedom from political constraint would not last for long.

In about 750 C.E., the Umayyads were overthrown by the Abbasid revolution, and the center of power in the Muslim world moved from Damascus to Baghdad. The new regime sought to bring a new order to Islamic society. This need for change was most felt by Ibn al-Muqaffa' (d. 757), the chief advisor to the Abbasid caliph Abu Ja'far al-Mansur, who diagnosed an intolerable state of disorder in the judiciary and decried the injustices that the people were suffering. Ibn al-Muqaffa' asked the caliph to take control of the matter by imposing consistency in judicial administration and a coherent system for the application of laws. He further urged the caliph to codify the law, making it possible to perpetuate the legal system. In addition, he advised the caliph on the selection of the team of jurists who should be assigned these tasks, making a strong case for the use of Iraqi scholars over those from other regions.

The Abbasid regime followed the recommendations of Ibn al Muqaffa', and in time managed to overcome the reluctance of famous jurists to serve the government that had long characterized the scholars of the Iraqi school. Abu Yusuf was appointed to the newly created post of *qadi al-qudat* (chief judge) and was granted discretionary power over the administration of the entire judiciary. First among his tasks was the grand project of codifying the laws and policies of the new judicial and fiscal order, thus demanding a degree of textual orientation never previously confronted by the Iraqi school of law. Abu Yusuf's thought on finance is contained in his *Kitab al-Kharaj* (The book of taxation), which was written during the reign of Caliph Harun al-Rashid. (Abu Yusuf's other main works are *Kitab al-Athar*, *Ikhtilaf Abu Hanifa wa Ibn Abi Laila*, and *al-Radd 'ala Siyar al-Awza'i*).

Muhammad al-Shaybani, another preeminent disciple of Abu Hanifa, was also employed by the new Abbasid regime, serving as judge and as a teacher of jurisprudence. Shaybani, though lower in rank than Abu Yusuf, was a more prolific writer, and thus achieved more real advances for the Hanafi

School of law. His main works, known collectively as *Zahir al-riwaya* (The reliable narrations), consist of the following titles: *al-Asl*, *al-Jami' al-kabir*, *al-Jami' al-saghir*, *al-Siyar al-kabir*, *al-Siyar al-saghir*, and *al-Ziyadat*. In general, these works cover a wide range of religious-legal issues, such as prayer, tax, marriage, divorce, commerce, and punishment, with the exception of *al-Siyar al-kabir* and *al-Siyar al-sighir*, which are thematic of laws of war and peace. Also, these works that represent early Hanafite legal thought were collected by al-Hakim al-Shahid al-Marwazi (d. 955) in the tenth century and presented under the title of *al-Kafi*. They were later reinterpreted and elaborated upon by Sarakhsi (d. 1090) under the title of *al-Mabsut*. Shaybani's work, as well as Sarakhsi's commentary, discloses the evolution of law in Iraq, starting with the free use of reason as championed by Abu Hanifa and his predecessors and moving toward greater textual orientation and structural regulation. This trend toward the institutionalization of juristic principles can be attributed to two factors: the accession of leading post-Abu Hanifa Iraqi jurists into the official power circles and, later, to the indelible impact of al-Shafi'i (d. 819).

Al-Shafi'i came to dominate the next phase of the evolution of Islamic legal theory. He limited the legitimate sources of juristic knowledge to four: the Qur'an, the sunna, *ijma'*, and *qiyas*. He utterly rejected the principle of *istihsan* that had been advanced by Abu Hanifa. Shafi'i's approach to each of the four approved sources emphasized the development of a centralized perception of Islamic law, and rejected the validity of regional variations that contradicted this unitary conception of the law. Moreover, in his work titled *al-Risala*, he argued that the only language suitable for Islamic scholarship was Arabic: "[T]he entire book of God came down in none but the Arabic language" (Shafi'i, *Risala* 40).

Shafi'i's emphasis on Arabic as the language of the Qur'an meant that translations of the Qur'an into other languages were not equivalent of the Qur'an. From this it follows that not only scripture and scholarship, but also the prayers of the faithful, must be in Arabic, for the language was held to be an essential element. This position was in outright contrast with that of Abu Hanifa, who approved of the recitation of the Qur'an in Persian in prayers. As Shafi'i's literalist approach gained ascendency, Abu Hanifa's disciples were forced to reinterpret their mentor's position (that prayer in Persian was permissible) as exclusive and temporary, applicable only in certain exceptional cases until people could learn the proper Arabic recitation of the Qur'anic verses.

Shafi'i's sunna of the Prophet was twofold. He considered the further sacralization of the Prophet, whose sayings were divinely inspired, and held that the authenticity of the sayings' transmission through narrators was directly dependent upon the literal faithfulness of their narrations. In other words, it was the letter of the narration, rather than the content, that was paramount in determining the legitimacy of the narrations and recitations of the sunna. This approach contradicted the Medinese perception of the sunna which was more concerned with Medina tradition and practice as it reflected the legacy of the Prophet, and it differed from previous Iraqi legal trends, which judged the authenticity of hadiths on their content as distinct from their sole letter. Shafi'i's literalist understanding had an enduring impact upon the Hafanite legal thought. For instance, Abu Bakr al-Jassas (d. 980) of the Hanafi School was forced to attempt to distinguish among the words of the Prophet, conceding that at least some of the Prophet's utterances were divinely revealed or inspired, whereas others reflected his "ordinary" or more humanly derived opinion.

Shafi'i's approach to the *ijma'* is perhaps the most polemic of all. In the Shafi'ite view, the *ijma'* should mean the consensus of the entire *umma* (community), and this is not possible unless it is with the participation of each and every Muslim individual. This perception of *ijma'* contrasts with the perception held by the Medinese jurists, who restricted their understanding of *ijma'* to the consensus of the scholars of Medina, as it was reflected in the practice of the Medinese people. It also contradicted earlier Iraqi perceptions of *ijma'*, which called for the consensus only of the jurists of the Iraqi legal trend. However, Shafi'i's arguments were more explicitly directed against the views of his nearer contemporaries, the Iraqi jurists of the post-Abu Hanifa period.

Shafi'i's argument boils down to the claim that true consensus of all Muslims or even merely of all jurists on a juristic personal opinion (*ijtihad*) cannot be reached. At best, it can only be apparent, because a verbalized consensus could easily mask silent disagreements. In his view, the only viable *ijma'* is to be found in the already existing acceptance, by each and every Muslim, of obligatory matters such as belief in the necessity of prayer. Obviously, this conception of *ijma'* is better suited to theological purposes governing elements of faith than to legal ones, which are more concerned with matters of behavior.

Shafi'i's refutation of the *ijma'* of all jurists may be valid on grounds of logic, but it renders the concept irrelevant for legal purposes. Nonetheless, both al-Jassas and al-Sarakhsi were forced to contend with its implications. They responded by dividing the *ijma'* into two main types. The first follows Shafi'i's formulation, including all Muslims, whereas the second refers specifically to consensus among the jurists alone.

Shafi'i's approach to the *qiyas* rests in his rejection of *istihsan*. The legitimacy of *qiyas* arises from the fact that it relates new cases to previous ones. In this retrospective process, the *qiyas* ultimately draws the jurist back to the prime sources of juristic knowledge: the Qur'an, the sunna of the Prophet, and the *ijma'*. On the other hand, the Shafi'ite school of legal thought considers *istihsan* as disconnection

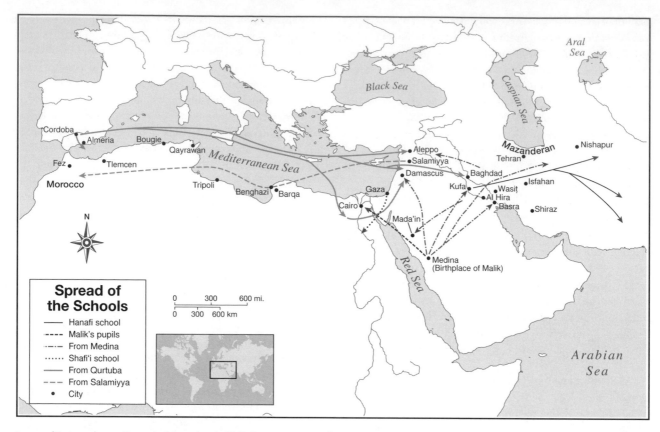

Law and jurisprudence: Spread of the schools. XNR Productions, Inc./Gale

from the letter of these three recognized sources of knowledge because, in contrast to *qiyas*, it involves the use of free reason without reference to the legitimate origins of law. Also, there can be no legitimacy accorded to the free use of reason when consensus is restricted to the scope of the *nusus* (the sacred texts), as in *Furud* and *Muharramat* (which are held to stem from a divine origin), the sunna of the Prophet (considered to be divinely inspired), and the Qurʾan. Yielding to the pressure from the Shafiʿite position regarding the use of *istihsan*, and the Hanafite School eventually replaced the term *istihsan* with the designation "hidden *qiyas*" to signify that *istihsan* was just another type of *qiyas*.

Shafiʿi rejected *istihsan* because it was the product of the human mind, rather than deriving from the *nusus*. This position attracted the attention and admiration of Dawud al-Isfehani (d. 883), because of the distinction it drew between divine and human decisions. Eventually, Dawud noticed that *qiyas*, too, involved human reasoning. Thus, he took a radical step further than the Shafiʿi, rejecting the *qiyas* in addition to the *istihsan*. This line of legal thought is known as the Zahiri (literalist) School of Law, because its theory strives to prove that legitimacy in religious law is confined to the literal scope and contents of the *nusus* and the *ijmaʿ* that are in agreement with the Qurʾan, and the hadiths, too, are held to be literal narratives of the acts and practice of the Prophet, devoid of interpretation. This line of thought is sharply opposed to the

use of *taʾlil* (reasoning) in *sharʾ* (legislation with religious overtones). The Zahiri School, zealously defended and systematized by Ibn Hazm, thus insists that human reason cannot be part of decision-making in religious law.

Ahmad Ibn Hanbal (d. 855), an admirer of Shafiʿi for his emphasis upon the hadith, became an inspiring source for a distinctly hadith-oriented trend of law called the Hanbali School. Ibn Hanbal is famous for his nonconformist position against the official pressure of the "rationalist" Abbasid regime (particularly of al-Maʿmun and al-Muʿtasim), which ordered him to speak in support of the theological belief that the Qurʾan was *makhluq* (created). Ibn Hanbal was a respected hadith scholar, but he was not particularly famous as a jurist. Indeed, the hadiths he presents in his main work, *al-Musnad*, are overwhelmed by the citations of the names of their narrators. However, his position, and his focus on hadith, helped inspire a certain pro-hadith line of legal thought.

The Hanbali School of Law in proper terms was systematized in the great work of Ibn Qudame (d. 1223), *al-Mughni*. Prominent scholars belonging to this legal school include such jurists as Ibn Taymiyya (d. 1328) and Ibn al-Qayyim al-Jawziyya (d. 1350). The Hanbali line of legal thought still holds enormous influence throughout most of Gulf region, and in Saudi Arabia, in particular.

Shafi'i's role in the development of Islamic legal theory was decisive in challenging the regional schools of law and their diverse methodologies, and in motivating them to evolve their concepts and terminology toward a centralized Islamic legal thought. In the formative period of Islamic law, the Medinese legal trend had been basically expressed by the Muwatta' of Malik and further substantiated by the voluminous work of Sahnun (d. 854), *al-Mudawwana*, which focused on the concept of Medinese practice. Meanwhile, the Iraqi legal trend evolved from being primarily rationalistic into being the gradually centralizing and relatively conservative Hanafi School of Law, in line with the prevalent Shafi'ite influence. The Hanbali School of Law was itself systematized long after the death of Ibn Hanbal, gaining a strong place in the history of Islamic law. The Zahiri legal trend, on the other hand, was denied legitimacy and was ultimately excluded from the Sunni arena of Islamic law, principally because of its rejection of *qiyas*. In today's Islamic law, the four "legitimate sources" of juristic knowledge, set forth by Shafi'i, provide the minimum of the compulsory criteria to be satisfied for any legal trend to take place within the context of Sunni legal theory.

## BIBLIOGRAPHY

Bukhari, Muhammad Ibn Isma'il. *Sahih al-Bukhari*. Istanbul: Cagri Yayinlari, 1981.

Hallaq, Wael B. "Was the Gate of *Ijtihad* Closed?" *International Journal of Middle East Studies* 16 (1984): 3–41.

Hallaq, Wael B. *A History of Islamic Legal Theories: An Introduction to Sunni Usul al-Fiqh*. Cambridge, U.K.: Cambridge University Press, 1997.

Ibn al-Muqaffa'. *Risala Ibn al-Muqaffa' fi al-Sahaba*. In *Rasail al Bulagha*. Edited by Muhammad Kurd Ali. Cairo, 1954.

Karaman, Hayreddin. *Islam Hukuk Tarihi*. Istanbul: Iz Yayincilik. 1999.

Malik, Ibn Anas. *al-Muwatta'*. Edited by Muhammad Fuad Abd al-Baqi. Istanbul: Cagri Yayinlari, 1981.

Sarakhsi, Muhammad Ibn Ahmad. *Sharh al-Siyar al-Kabir*. Edited by Salah al-Din al-Munajjid and 'Abd al-Aziz Ahmad. Cairo: Matba'at Shirkat al-I'lanat al-Sharqiyya, 1971–1972.

Sarakhsi, Muhammad Ibn Ahmad. *Islam Devletler Hukuku: Serhu's-Siyeri'l-Kebir*, Translated by Ibrahim Sarmis and M. Sait Simsek, edited by Ahmet Yaman, Konya: Egitas Yayinlari: 2001.

Shafi'i, Muhammad Ibn Idris. *al-Umm*, Beirut: Dar al-Ma'rifa, 1973.

Shafi'i, Muhammad Ibn Idris. *al-Risala*. Edited by Ahmad Muhammad Shakir. Cairo: Dar al-Turath, 1979.

Shaybani, Muhammad. *The Islamic Law of Nations: Shaybani's Siyar*. Translated by Majid Khadur. Baltimore: Johns Hopkins Press, 1966.

Shaybani, Muhammad. *al-Hujja 'ala Ahl al-Medina*. Edited by Mahdi Hasan al-Kaylani al-Qadiri. Beirut: Alam al-Kutub, 1983.

Tastan, Isman. *The Jurisprudence of Sarakhsi with Particular Reference to War and Peace: A Comparative Study in Islamic Law*. Unpublished Ph.D. thesis, the University of Exeter, 1993.

Tastan, Osman. "Islam Hukukunda Sahabi Otoritesinin Kaynagi ve Niteligi." *Islami Arastirmalar* 8, no. 2 (1995): 115–121.

Tastan, Osman. "Islam Hukukunda Literalizm: Anahatlariyla Mukayeseli Bir Analiz." *Islami Arastirmalar* 9, nos. 1–4 (1996): 144–156.

Tastan, Osman. "Merkezilesme Surecinde Islam Hukuku: Bolgesellige Veda veya Safi'i Faktoru." *Islamiyat* 1, no. 1 (1998): 25–34.

Tirmidhi, Muhammad Ibn Isa. *Sunan*. Edited by Ibrahim 'Atwah 'Iwad. Istanbul: Cagri Yayinlari, 1981.

*Osman Tastan*

# LEBANON

Like many other states in the Middle East, the state in Lebanon was established in the early 1920s, following the downfall of the Ottoman Empire in the First World War. Greater Lebanon, as the new state was initially called, was formed out of a territorial nucleus, the *Mutasarrifiya* of Mount Lebanon, established in 1861. A special political and legal arrangement devised after the 1860 civil strife and recognized by the six major European powers, the *Mutasarrifiya* gave Mount Lebanon a semiautonomous status within the Ottoman empire, and succeeded the *Imara* (1516–1842), the political system that prevailed in Mount Lebanon since the early sixteenth century, after a short interval. While confessionalism had its origins in the Ottoman *millet* system, the *Mutasarrifiya* formalized political representation along confessional lines in an elected twelve-member body, the Administrative Council, headed by an Ottoman governor (*Mutasarrif*) of the Catholic faith and representing Mount Lebanon's six major communities (four Maronites, three Druzes, two Greek Orthodox, one Greek Catholic, one Shi'a, one Sunni). Abolished by the Ottomans in 1914, the *Mutasarrifiya* gave Mount Lebanon over fifty years of political stability and orderly confessional relations.

Under the French mandate (1920–1943), Lebanon's 1926 constitution stipulated that representation in government office would be temporarily on a confessional basis. Confessionalism was institutionalized in post-1920 Lebanon, particularly in the personal status law of the seventeen recognized communities and in government office. The greatest beneficiary of the confessional system was the Shi'ite community whose Ja'fari jurisprudence was recognized by the state in 1926, a right that had been denied under Sunni Ottoman rule.

Although the 1932 census showed a slight Christian majority, the demographic structure in post-1920 Lebanon was radically transformed with the enlargement of the *Mutasarrifiya* to include territories with a Muslim majority. The Maronite community, for example, decreased from over 60 percent of Mount Lebanon's population to nearly 30 percent in post-1920 Lebanon, while the Sunni community increased from about 5 percent in Mount Lebanon to nearly 25 percent after 1920. Similarly, the Shi'ite community increased from about 5 percent in Mount Lebanon to nearly 20 percent after 1920. Beginning in 1937, the custom of the Maronite presidency and Sunni premiership was established while the Shi'ite speakership continued to be contested until 1947 between the Shi'a, the Greek Orthodox, and the Greek Catholic communities.

Independence was achieved in 1943 not only because Lebanese from different communities opposed French rule but also because leaders, particularly those of the two influential communities, the Maronites and the Sunnis, reached an understanding on the basis of the National Pact. An unwritten agreement, the National Pact confirmed the distribution of government office along confessional lines and sought to situate Lebanon's foreign policy on an equal distance between East, that is, the Arab world and particularly Syria, and West, particularly France.

Like other Arab countries shaken by the rise of Nasserism (pan-Arab populist movement led by Egyptian president Jamal 'Abd al-Nasser) in the mid-1950s during the height of cold war politics in the region, Lebanon witnessed a six-month armed conflict in 1958. Lebanon quickly recovered from the conflict and the decade 1958–1968 witnessed large-scale administrative reform, political stability, and economic prosperity, especially under President Fouad Chehab (1958–1964).

Once again, regional developments shaped the course of Lebanese politics: the Arab defeat in the 1967 Arab-Israeli war and the emergence of a militant Palestine Liberation Organization (PLO). From 1969, when Lebanon had to sign an agreement with the PLO (the Cairo Agreement) that allowed the PLO's military action against Israel from Lebanese territory, until the outbreak of war in 1975, political crises and armed conflict hinged on the PLO's armed presence. Confrontation between Lebanon's *raison d'état* and the PLO's *raison de révolution* was bound to occur, just as it did in Jordan in 1970–1971. But unlike Jordan's authoritarian state, Lebanon's openness, confessional democracy, and consensual politics did not enable the state to contain the PLO and to stop PLO-Israeli warfare in south Lebanon.

War broke out in April 1975 and ended in October 1990. It evolved in five phases; the most violent were the first and last two years of the war and the 1982 Israeli invasion of Lebanon. The war crippled government institutions, factionalized the army, and widened the sectarian divide.

Political parties-turned-militias exercised power in areas under their control along with several non-Lebanese parties directly involved in the war: the PLO until 1982–1983, Syria before and after that date, Israel in the south from 1978 to 2000, and the Islamic Republic of Iran since the early 1980s.

The fifteen-year war ended with another act of war, when Syrian forces joined units of the Lebanese army to oust an interim premier, General Michel 'Aoun, from office. Another development was the political settlement embodied in the Document of National Understanding, commonly called the Ta'if Agreement, which was signed on 22 October 1989 by Lebanese deputies in the Saudi city of Ta'if. One component of the Tai'f Agreement dealt with political reforms, the other with sovereignty. While the Ta'if Agreement preserved the custom of the Maronite presidency, the Sunni premiership, and the Shi'ite speakership, it greatly diminished the power of the president and enhanced that of the prime minister, the council of ministers, and the speaker. Ta'if also called for the abolition of political confessionalism according to a staged plan.

As for sovereignty, the Ta'if Agreement called for the redeployment of Syrian troops to specific areas two years after the incorporation of Ta'if's provisions into the constitution in September 1990, and for the withdrawal of Israeli forces from the south in accordance with the 1978 United Nations resolutions 425 and 426. Israel withdrew its forces in May 2000 but Syrian troops did not redeploy. Ta'if also introduced the notion of "privileged relations" with Syria. Beginning in May 1991, Lebanon and Syria signed a series of bilateral agreements that tied Lebanese affairs ever closer to Syria in the political, security, economic, cultural, and commercial arenas. Since 1990, the political decision-making process in Lebanon has been very much in Syrian hands. The Shi'ite community was greatly affected by the war and by regional developments that unfolded during the war years. It underwent drastic political change: from the control of traditional leaders prior to the war, to the reformist platform of Imam Musa al-Sadr, the founder of the Amal Movement in the mid-1970s, to the radical Islamist agenda of Hizb Allah since the mid-1980s. In a period of two decades, Shi'ite politics have been greatly radicalized. Backed by Syria, Iran, and the Lebanese government, Hizbollah—the only Lebanese party that was not disarmed after the war—led the war against Israel in south Lebanon in the 1990s and is today the most mobilized and active political-cum-military organization in the country.

The withdrawal of Israeli forces from the south has reactivated the debate on the presence of about twenty-five thousand Syrian troops in the country. Although the sectarian divide is deeper in postwar Lebanon than prior to the war, a politically significant Christian-Muslim consensus emerged in 2000–2001 on the need to implement properly the Ta'if Agreement and to establish balanced relations between

Lebanon and Syria. Consensus was confirmed by the formalization of the reconciliation between Christians and Druzes, following the historic visit of the Maronite patriarch, Cardinal Nasralla Sfeir, on 5 August 2001, to areas that were displaced during the war. The government's response to these positive developments was a massive crackdown on Christian activists in August 2001. But the casualty this time was not only the growing intersectarian opposition to the Syrian-backed Lebanese authorities but to the country as a whole: government institutions, the rule of law, and the economy with a public debt that rose from over $1 billion in 1990 to over $25 billion in 2001.

*See also* **Fadlallah, Muhammad Husayn; Hizb Allah; Sadr, Musa al-.**

### BIBLIOGRAPHY

Akarli, Engin. *The Long Peace: Ottoman Lebanon, 1861–1920.* Berkeley: University of California Press, 1993.

Binder, Leonard., ed. *Politics in Lebanon.* New York: John Wiley, 1966.

El Khazen, Farid. *The Breakdown of the State in Lebanon: 1967–1976.* Cambridge, Mass.: Harvard University Press, 2000.

Hanf, Theodor. *Coexistence in Wartime Lebanon: Decline of a State and Rise of a Nation.* London: The Center for Lebanese Studies and I. B.Tauris, 1993.

Harik, Iliya. *Politics and Change in a Traditional Society: Lebanon 1711–1845.* Princeton, N.J.: Princeton University Press, 1968.

Hudson, Michael, C. *The Precarious Republic: Political Modernization in Lebanon.* Boulder, Colo.: Westview Encore Edition, 1985.

Maila, Joseph. *The Document of National Understanding: A Commentary.* Oxford, U.K.: Center for Lebanese Studies, 1992.

Makdisi, Ussama. *The Culture of Sectarianism: Community, History, and Violence in Nineteenth-Century Ottoman Lebanon.* Berkeley: University of California Press, 2000.

Salibi, Kamal, S. *The Modern History of Lebanon.* New York: Praeger Publishers, 1965.

*Farid el Khazen*

## LEXICOGRAPHY (ARABIC) *See* **Grammar and Lexicography**

## LIBERALISM

Islamic liberalism may be defined as a movement to reconcile Islamic faith with liberal values such as democracy, rights, equality, and progress. Islamic liberalism forms one strand of Islamic modernism, which also encompasses modern values that are not associated with the liberal tradition, such as state-building and scientific authority.

Islamic liberalism emerged in the mid-nineteenth century as a response to the hypocrisy of European liberalism, which was introduced to the Islamic world by the highly illiberal means of imperial conquest. Since that time, conservatives have consistently accused Islamic liberalism of being overly enthralled with European traditions. Yet Islamic liberalism's self-understanding centers on Islamic traditions, including the sacred sources that require or allow liberal practices and the precedents in Islamic history for tolerance and peaceful coexistence. In the late twentieth century, a new form of Islamic liberalism added the argument that human interpretation of revelation is inherently fallible and pluralistic. In this view, the repression of Islamic liberalism is an illegitimate exercise in hubris, because no mortal can presume to know the meaning of divine revelation with any certainty. Islamic liberalism has generally been a minority position in the Islamic world. Its representatives have sometimes fared well when elections are free and fair, though more frequently liberalism has been stymied by hostile responses of traditionalists, revivalists, and secularists.

*See also* **Modern Thought.**

### BIBLIOGRAPHY

Binder, Leonard. *Islamic Liberalism.* Chicago: University of Chicago Press, 1988.

Kurzman, Charles, ed. *Liberal Islam: A Sourcebook.* New York: Oxford University Press, 1998.

*Charles Kurzman*

## LIBERATION MOVEMENT OF IRAN

The Liberation Movement of Iran (Nehzat-e azadi-ye Iran), or LMI (also called Iran Freedom Movement, or IFM), was established as a liberal Islamic opposition in May 1961. Its twelve founders, including Mehdi Bazargan, Ayatollah Mahmud Taleqani, and Yadollah Sahabi, presented it as Muslim, Iranian, constitutionalist, and Mosaddeqist; that is, they claimed the ideological legacy of Mohammad Mosaddeq's National Front. In 1963 the shah banned the LMI and imprisoned its leaders for a number of years.

LMI gained power during the Iranian revolution in 1978 and 1979. Its members formed the core of the postrevolutionary provisional government and on 5 February 1979, Mehdi Bazargan was appointed prime minister of the provisional government by Ayatollah Khomeini. He resigned in protest after the occupation of the American embassy in Tehran on 4 November.

Though formally banned by Khomeini in 1988, the LMI was generally tolerated, but not allowed to participate in elections. It openly criticized the doctrine of *velayat-e faqih* (i.e., the rule of the religious jurisprudent) as well as the executions, torture, and the ban of parties and free media. Although its members are mainly academic veterans of the opposition to the shah, since the 1990s LMI has also appealed to the young who admire Mosaddeq—the only democratically elected prime minister of Iran. The left wing of the LMI is represented by Ezzatollah Sahabi, who, in 1992 founded the magazine *Iran-e farda*.

After the death of Bazargan in 1995 and under its new chairman, Ebrahim Yazdi, the movement became more cautious. Nevertheless, in spring 2001, the revolutionary court ordered an end to all LMI activities. Although charged with conspiring against the Islamic system on 13 November 2001, Yazdi was not touched by the authorities. But more than thirty other members were sentenced to jail by the revolutionary court on 27 July 2002, among them Ezzatollah Sahabi. They were charged with a series of crimes, including seeking to topple the country's government. The trials were held behind closed doors.

*See also* **Bazargan, Mehdi; Iran, Islamic Republic of.**

## BIBLIOGRAPHY

Chehabi, Houchang E. *Iranian Politics and Religious Modernism. The Liberation Movement of Iran under the Shah and Khomeini.* London: Tauris, 1990.

*Claudia Stodte*

# LIBRARIES

Several factors contributed to the prevalence of libraries in the medieval Islamic world. First, manuscript books were relatively cheap. Papermaking technology arrived in the Islamic world in the eighth century, providing Muslims with a material cheaper than the papyrus used previously in the Middle East and far cheaper than the parchment and vellum made from animal hides used in medieval Europe. Moreover, the Arabic script with its cursive forms and many ligatures could be written much faster than the medieval versions of the Roman alphabet. Second, the medieval Islamic world was a literate culture. Men and even women of the upper and middle classes were almost always literate. Both religious and secular literatures were popular, and scholarly and literary attainments were respected. Islamic rulers, constantly hungry for legitimacy, collected books for the same reason they built

monuments and patronized scholars and poets—to acquire reputations as cultivated rulers. Libraries of elegant manuscripts and learned treatises were thus appropriate possessions for kings and those who imitated them, and it was not uncommon for Islamic rulers, military officers, and high officials to have well-earned reputations for literary taste and scholarship. Third, books were central to Islamic religious life. Despite a stress on oral learning in medieval Islam, books were necessary to record the masses of traditions of the Prophet, legal rulings, information concerning transmitters of religious lore, and linguistic lore that were the raw material of the Islamic sciences. Even the oral transmission of knowledge usually involved the production of a dictated book, so that studying a book involved producing a copy of it. Fourth, medieval Islamic bureaucrats were accustomed to use books: encyclopedias of useful information, literary manuals useful for producing elegant official documents, literature for amusement, and such things as manuals of occult sciences. Finally, the Islamic law of *waqf*, charitable endowments, allowed Muslim bibliophiles to donate their books to the libraries of mosques and *madrasas* with reasonable hope that their collections would be maintained intact.

The earliest Islamic libraries were the collections of Qur'ans that accumulated in mosques. Qur'an reading was an important Islamic devotional practice, and both copying Qur'ans and donating them to mosques were acts of piety. Larger mosques often acquired more diverse libraries, mostly through gifts. When a mosque was built or renovated, the donor often gave a collection of books as the basis of the library. Bibliophiles and scholars, particularly those who taught in a particular mosque, often willed their books to the mosque library. Books copied in class were often given to the mosque library. To this day, many of the most important collections of Islamic manuscripts are in mosque libraries—for example, al-Azhar in Cairo and Suleymaniyyeh in Istanbul.

There are records of royal libraries as early as Umayyad times, the earliest associated with the scholarly Umayyad prince Khalid b. Yazid. The zenith of Islamic royal libraries was in the Abbasid period. The Abbasid caliph al-Ma'mun (r. 813–833) founded the Bayt al-Hikma, the house of wisdom, which was the center for translation from Greek, Syriac, and Pahlavi and which was the basis of a caliphal library that survived for more than a century. The Umayyad royal library at Cordova, founded by al-Hakam II (r. 961–976), was supposed to have had 400,000 manuscripts. The greatest of the royal libraries was that of the Fatimids in Cairo, founded in 1004 by the caliph al-Hakim (r. 996–1021). It survived, despite some vicissitudes, until it was ordered closed by Saladin in the late twelfth century and its collections were dispersed and partly destroyed. The royal libraries sometimes had aggressive programs of commissioning both the copying and the composition of books. Both the Abbasid Bayt al-Hikma and the Mogul royal library in Delhi commissioned extensive translations, in the latter case often of Sanskrit Hindu literature of all sorts. Most of the great illustrated and illuminated Islamic books are the product of royal commissions.

There were also public libraries known as *dar al-ʿilm*, houses of knowledge. These were more or less public libraries, often established for sectarian purposes. These institutions played a role in the establishment of *madrasa*s, Islamic seminaries. With the rise of *madrasa*s in the eleventh century, their libraries became increasingly important.

### Size, Nature, and Organization of Premodern Islamic Libraries

Medieval accounts mention libraries containing hundreds of thousands or even millions of books, notably the royal libraries of Baghdad, Cairo, and Cordoba. Individual scholars are mentioned whose libraries consisted of some thousands of books. The higher numbers are scarcely credible. Istanbul, for example, has more than a hundred manuscript libraries or collections dating from Ottoman times, some four centuries old, yet in 1959 a careful survey indicated that there were only about 135,000 Islamic manuscripts in the city, the largest collection containing about ten thousand manuscripts. It certainly is credible, however, that the larger medieval Islamic libraries contained tens of thousands of manuscripts and that wealthy individual scholars and bibliophiles possessed libraries of several thousand volumes—collections dwarfing anything in Europe at the time.

At their finest, Islamic libraries were large, well-organized institutions with specially built facilities for book storage and reading, professional staff, regular budgets and endowments, catalogs, and even lodging and stipends for visiting scholars. Public access varied, depending on the nature of the libraries, but established scholars could generally gain access to most collections. Books were usually stored on shelves or in cabinets, stacked on their sides with a short title written on the upper and lower edge of the book to aid in finding it. (Traditional Islamic bookbindings do not usually contain the title or author.) Catalogs were either bound handlists, the *waqf* documents donating the books, or lists posted on the doors of the cabinet. Collections were organized by subject. Avicenna describes visiting the royal library in Bukhara, for example, where rooms were devoted to different subjects. Paper, pens, and ink were sometimes furnished for the use of patrons.

Smaller collections had less elaborate facilities. Most mosques and madrasas had libraries. Private libraries and individual books were often donated to such institutions as *waqf*, endowment, and the terms of the gift would be carefully recorded on the flyleaf. Donated collections were often kept as separate units. There were also family libraries. In a society where professions were often hereditary, some families produced scholars and clerics generation after generation for centuries. Not uncommonly a library would accumulate in the family home over many generations. Examples include the al-Husayni, al-Khalidi, and al-Budayri libraries in Jerusalem, each of which dates from the eighteenth century.

### Destruction and Dispersal of Libraries

Islamic chronicles mention the destruction of many libraries, either deliberately or, more commonly, accidentally. Apart from a few places and times, warfare was endemic in the Islamic world and took its toll. Few surviving libraries in the Islamic world predate the older Istanbul libraries. While the story that the Muslim invaders burned the library of Alexandria has long been known to be false—it had been destroyed in Roman times—the sack of cities did often result in the destruction of libraries. Most of the major libraries of Abbasid Iraq were destroyed during the Mongol invasion. The Islamic library in Tripoli was destroyed when the city was sacked by the Franks during the First Crusade, beginning in 1095. The American invasion of Iraq in 2003 apparently resulted in the destruction of much of the collection of the National Library in Baghdad.

Sometimes the destruction was ideologically motivated. Mahmud of Ghazna burned the heretical works in the library of the wazir Ismaʿil b. ʿAbbad and confiscated the rest. The books on philosophy and the natural sciences in the library of al-Hakam II in Cordoba were burned by the orthodox during his son's reign. The mass destruction of Arabic books was part of the Catholic kings' program to suppress Islam in Spain, including the burning of Arabic books in Granada at the order of Cardinal Cisneros. There also was a curious tradition of scholars destroying their own books at their death, either to suppress embarrassing or incomplete works or to avoid unauthorized transmission of hadith and other texts that ought to be transmitted orally.

Finally, lack of supervision led to the decay of many libraries, with books stolen by readers or dishonest librarians or lost to damp and insects, the latter a particular menace in South and Southeast Asia, where insecticide is still sometimes sprinkled between the pages of books.

The destruction of libraries in wartime was not always, or even usually, deliberate. Books were valuable, and thus were better stolen than destroyed. There is a report that when Constantinople fell to the Ottomans, the sultan ordered the surviving Greek manuscripts in the city collected for the palace library, and there can be no doubt that the size and quality of the manuscript collections in Istanbul are in good part the result of the imperial reach of the Ottoman armies. Likewise, many of the Islamic manuscript collections in Europe were, to some extent, the product of colonial wars. The great Islamic manuscript collections in Russia are the product of the Russian expansion into Central Asia in the eighteenth and nineteenth centuries. The treasures of the Mogul royal library were dispersed after the 1857–1858 mutiny, and many of the finest items ended up in London.

## Libraries in the Modern Islamic World

With some exceptions, the library situation in modern Islamic countries falls short of the glories of the medieval period. Some premodern libraries have survived and prospered. In Ottoman Turkey a stable bureaucratic tradition and internal stability meant that most of the old *waqf* libraries survived as functioning institutions until they were taken over by the modern Turkish state. Several of the larger Ottoman libraries in Istanbul are still functioning, and the collections of most of the smaller libraries have been gathered in a central library in the Suleymaniyyeh mosque. Al-Azhar University in Cairo has a library that has functioned for centuries in one form or another.

Most of the libraries of the Islamic world are of more recent date. These may be divided into two classes: libraries of traditional type founded in the nineteenth and twentieth centuries, and Western-style libraries founded by colonial administrations or modern independent Islamic states.

Even after the occupation of most of the Islamic world by European colonial powers and the establishment of modern nation states in the Islamic lands, libraries continued to be established that, despite occasional appurtenances of modern libraries and the prevalence of printed books, were indistinguishable in style and purposes from those established centuries earlier. The libraries of the Muslim rulers and nobility of princely states in British India were royal libraries of the old sort—for example, the Raza Library in Rampur, based on a collection started by the Rohilla Nawabs of Rampur in the eighteenth century, and the Salar Jung Museum Library in Hyderabad, Deccan. New mosques and madrasas had libraries indistinguishable from those of previous centuries, apart from the presence of printed books. A notable example is the Mar'ashi library in Qom, founded by a bibliophilic grand ayatollah in the mid-twentieth century, which emerged as a major library after the Iranian Revolution of 1979.

The colonial period marked a major change, with the introduction of European-style libraries intended to promote the diffusion of modern knowledge and to support the new systems of education and, to a lesser extent, to support modern industry. At the top of the pyramid are national libraries, supported by depository laws and national bibliographies. In some cases, such as Egypt and Iran, these libraries emerged from earlier royal libraries and are themselves important repositories of Islamic manuscripts. In other cases, such as Pakistan, they are new foundations rivaled or overshadowed by older university and traditional libraries. The introduction of modern educational systems led to the creation of school and university libraries. University libraries are well established across the Islamic world, though in general only a few of the older universities have really major libraries: Istanbul University, American University of Beirut, and Punjab University in Lahore, for example. Many newer universities have very limited library facilities. The high cost of foreign monographs and periodicals poses particular difficulties for academic libraries in the poorer Islamic countries, and the lack of such materials is one of the most difficult problems faced by academics in the Islamic world. The increasing importance of computers and electronic resources is an additional burden that few academic libraries in the Islamic world can afford.

Elementary and secondary school libraries are generally weak or nonexistent. Public library systems are also usually inadequate and rarely have much priority in competition for scarce public resources. Public libraries exist in major cities, but much less commonly in provincial cities or small towns. Translations of foreign works are relatively scarce. Cultural factors sometimes hinder progress. Where public libraries exist, there may be restrictions on circulation, subscription fees, or educational requirements that hinder free access, as is the case for the best public libraries in Pakistan. The Islamic world has not yet had its Andrew Carnegie, endowing mass self-education through free public libraries. As a result, foreign institutions such as the British Council still play a significant role in providing library facilities, despite their existing only in the largest cities. The new Alexandria Library being built in Egypt in emulation of the ancient library deserves mention, though it is far from clear that it will be able to achieve its goal to become a world-class research library.

There have also been challenges applying modern library techniques. The mixture of Arabic and Roman script books has posed problems for cataloging and computerization. The Dewey Decimal System has been widely adopted, despite the inadequacies of its treatment of Islamic and Middle Eastern topics.

*See also* **Education; Ma'mun.**

### BIBLIOGRAPHY

Atiyeh, George N. *The Book in the Islamic World: The Written Word and Communication in the Middle East.* Albany: State University of New York Press, 1995.

Nadim, al-. *The Fihrist of al-Nadim: A Tenth-Century Survey of Muslim Culture.* Edited and translated by Bayard Dodge. New York: Columbia University Press, 1970.

Pedersen, Johannes. *The Arabic Book.* Translated by Geoffrey French. Princeton, N.J.: Princeton University Press, 1984.

Rosenthal, Franz. *The Technique and Approach of Muslim Scholarship.* Rome: Pontificium Institutum Biblicum, 1947.

*John Walbridge*

---

**LITERATURE** *See* **Arabic Literature; Persian Language and Literature; Urdu Language, Literature, and Poetry**